DRAMA
CRITICISM

Guide to Gale Literary Criticism Series

For criticism on	Consult these Gale series
Authors now living or who died after December 31, 1999	*CONTEMPORARY LITERARY CRITICISM (CLC)*
Authors who died between 1900 and 1999	*TWENTIETH-CENTURY LITERARY CRITICISM (TCLC)*
Authors who died between 1800 and 1899	*NINETEENTH-CENTURY LITERATURE CRITICISM (NCLC)*
Authors who died between 1400 and 1799	*LITERATURE CRITICISM FROM 1400 TO 1800 (LC)* *SHAKESPEAREAN CRITICISM (SC)*
Authors who died before 1400	*CLASSICAL AND MEDIEVAL LITERATURE CRITICISM (CMLC)*
Authors of books for children and young adults	*CHILDREN'S LITERATURE REVIEW (CLR)*
Dramatists	*DRAMA CRITICISM (DC)*
Poets	*POETRY CRITICISM (PC)*
Short story writers	*SHORT STORY CRITICISM (SSC)*
Black writers of the past two hundred years	*BLACK LITERATURE CRITICISM (BLC)* *BLACK LITERATURE CRITICISM SUPPLEMENT (BLCS)*
Hispanic writers of the late nineteenth and twentieth centuries	*HISPANIC LITERATURE CRITICISM (HLC)* *HISPANIC LITERATURE CRITICISM SUPPLEMENT (HLCS)*
Native North American writers and orators of the eighteenth, nineteenth, and twentieth centuries	*NATIVE NORTH AMERICAN LITERATURE (NNAL)*
Major authors from the Renaissance to the present	*WORLD LITERATURE CRITICISM, 1500 TO THE PRESENT (WLC)* *WORLD LITERATURE CRITICISM SUPPLEMENT (WLCS)*

ISSN 1056-4349

DRAMA
CRITICISM

Criticism of the Most Significant and Widely Studied
Dramatic Works from all the World's Literatures

VOLUME 15

Rebecca Blanchard
Justin Karr
Editors

GALE GROUP
THOMSON LEARNING

Detroit • New York • San Diego • San Francisco
Boston • New Haven, Conn. • Waterville, Maine
London • Munich

STAFF

Library of Congress Catalog Card Number 92-648805
ISBN 0-7876-5219-9
ISSN 1056-4349
Printed in the United States of America

10 9 8 7 6 5 4 3 2 1

Contents

Preface vii

Acknowledgments xi

Preface

Drama Criticism (*DC*) is principally intended for beginning students of literature and theater as well as the average playgoer. The series is therefore designed to introduce readers to the most frequently studied playwrights of all time periods and nationalities and to present discerning commentary on dramatic works of enduring interest. Furthermore, *DC* seeks to acquaint the reader with the uses and functions of criticism itself. Selected from a diverse body of commentary, the essays in *DC* offer insights into the authors and their works but do not require that the reader possess a wide background in literary studies. Where appropriate, reviews of important productions of the plays discussed are also included to give students a heightened awareness of drama as a dynamic art form, one that many claim is fully realized only in performance.

DC was created in response to suggestions by the staffs of high school, college, and public libraries. These librarians observed a need for a series that assembles critical commentary on the world's most renowned dramatists in the same manner as Gale's *Short Story Criticism* (*SSC*) and *Poetry Criticism* (*PC*), which present material on writers of short fiction and poetry. Although playwrights are covered in such Gale literary criticism series as *Contemporary Literary Criticism* (*CLC*), *Twentieth-Century Literary Criticism* (*TCLC*), *Nineteenth-Century Literature Criticism* (*NCLC*), *Literature Criticism from 1400 to 1800* (*LC*), and *Classical and Medieval Literature Criticism* (*CMLC*), *DC* directs more concentrated attention on individual dramatists than is possible in the broader, survey-oriented entries in these Gale series. Commentary on the works of William Shakespeare may be found in *Shakespearean Criticism* (*SC*).

Scope of the Series

By collecting and organizing commentary on dramatists, *DC* assists students in their efforts to gain insight into literature, achieve better understanding of the texts, and formulate ideas for papers and assignments. A variety of interpretations and assessments is offered, allowing students to pursue their own interests and promoting awareness that literature is dynamic and responsive to many different opinions.

Approximately five to ten authors are included in each volume, and each entry presents a historical survey of the critical response to that playwright's work. The length of an entry is intended to reflect the amount of critical attention the author has received from critics writing in English and from foreign critics in translation. Every attempt has been made to identify and include the most significant essays on each author's work. In order to provide these important critical pieces, the editors sometimes reprint essays that have appeared elsewhere in Gale's literary criticism series. Such duplication, however, never exceeds twenty percent of a *DC* volume.

Organization of the Book

A *DC* entry consists of the following elements:

- The **Author Heading** consists of the playwright's most commonly used name, followed by birth and death dates. If an author consistently wrote under a pseudonym, the pseudonym is listed in the author heading and the real name given in parentheses on the first line of the introduction. Also located at the beginning of the introduction are any name variations under which the dramatist wrote, including transliterated forms of the names of authors whose languages use nonroman alphabets.

- The **Introduction** contains background information that introduces the reader to the author and the critical debates surrounding his or her work.

- A **Portrait of the Author** is included when available.

- The list of **Principal Works** is divided into two sections. The first section contains the author's dramatic pieces and is organized chronologically by date of first performance. If this has not been conclusively determined, the composition or publication date is used. The second section provides information on the author's major works in other genres.

- Essays offering **overviews and general studies of the dramatist's entire literary career** give the student broad perspectives on the writer's artistic development, themes, and concerns that recur in several of his or her works, the author's place in literary history, and other wide-ranging topics.

- **Criticism** of individual plays offers the reader in-depth discussions of a select number of the author's most important works. In some cases, the criticism is divided into two sections, each arranged chronologically. When a significant performance of a play can be identified (typically, the premier of a twentieth-century work), the first section of criticism will feature **production reviews** of this staging. Most entries include sections devoted to **critical commentary** that assesses the literary merit of the selected plays. When necessary, essays are carefully excerpted to focus on the work under consideration; often, however, essays and reviews are reprinted in their entirety. Footnotes are reprinted at the end of each essay or excerpt. In the case of excerpted criticism, only those footnotes that pertain to the excerpted texts are included.

- Critical essays are prefaced by brief **Annotations** explicating each piece.

- A complete **Bibliographic Citation,** designed to help the interested reader locate the original essay or book, precedes each piece of criticism.

- An annotated bibliography of **Further Reading** appears at the end of each entry and suggests resources for additional study. In some cases, significant essays for which the editors could not obtain reprint rights are included here. Boxed material following the further reading list provides references to other biographical and critical sources on the author in series published by Gale.

Cumulative Indexes

A **Cumulative Author Index** lists all of the authors that appear in a wide variety of reference sources published by the Gale Group, including *DC*. A complete list of these sources is found facing the first page of the Author Index. The index also includes birth and death dates and cross references between pseudonyms and actual names.

A **Cumulative Nationality Index** lists all authors featured in *DC* by nationality, followed by the number of the *DC* volume in which their entry appears.

A **Cumulative Title Index** lists in alphabetical order the individual plays discussed in the criticism contained in *DC*. Each title is followed by the author's last name and corresponding volume and page numbers where commentary on the work is located. English-language translations of original foreign-language titles are cross-referenced to the foreign titles so that all references to discussion of a work are combined in one listing.

Citing *Drama Criticism*

When writing papers, students who quote directly from any volume in *Drama Criticism* may use the following general formats to footnote reprinted criticism. The first example pertains to material drawn from periodicals, the second to materials reprinted from books.

Susan Sontag, "Going to the Theater, Etc.," *Partisan Review* XXXI, no. 3 (Summer 1964), 389-94; excerpted and reprinted in *Drama Criticism,* vol. 1, ed. Lawrence J. Trudeau (Detroit: Gale Research, 1991), 17-20.

Eugene M. Waith, *The Herculean Hero in Marlowe, Chapman, Shakespeare and Dryden* (Chatto & Windus, 1962); excerpted and reprinted in *Drama Criticism,* vol. 1, ed. Lawrence J. Trudeau (Detroit: Gale Research, 1991), 237-47.

Suggestions are Welcome

Readers who wish to suggest new features, topics, or authors to appear in future volumes, or who have other suggestions or comments are cordially invited to call, write, or fax the Managing Editor:

Managing Editor, Literary Criticism Series
27500 Drake Road
Farmington Hills, MI 48331-3535
1-800-347-4253 (GALE)
Fax: 248-699-8054

Acknowledgments

The editors wish to thank the copyright holders of the excerpted criticism included in this volume and the permissions managers of many book and magazine publishing companies for assisting us in securing reproduction rights. We are also grateful to the staffs of the Detroit Public Library, the Library of Congress, the University of Detroit Mercy Library, Wayne State University Purdy/Kresge Library Complex, and the University of Michigan Libraries for making their resources available to us. Following is a list of the copyright holders who have granted us permission to reproduce material in this volume of *DC*. Every effort has been made to trace copyright, but if omissions have been made, please let us know.

COPYRIGHTED EXCERPTS IN *DC*, VOLUME 15, WERE REPRODUCED FROM THE FOLLOWING PERIODICALS:

The American Scholar, v. 63, Summer, 1994. Reproduced by permission.—*Arizona Quarterly,* v. 26, Spring, 1970 for "'...Apart from the Known and the Unknown': The Unreconciled Worlds of Harold Pinter's Characters," by Francis Gillen. Reproduced by permission of the publisher and the author.—*The Catholic World,* v. 210, December, 1969. Reproduced by permission of America Press, Inc., 106 West 56th Street, New York, NY 10019 for the Literary Estate of Catharine Hughes.—*The Christian Science Monitor,* June 24, 1964. Reproduced by permission.—*Classical and Modern Literature,* v. 16, Spring, 1996 for "A Kind of Alaska: Pinter and Pygmalion," by Ronald Knowles. © 1996 CML, Inc. Reproduced by permission of the publisher and the author.—*Comparative Drama,* v. 26, Fall, 1992. Reproduced by permission.—*Contemporary Literature,* v. 11, Summer, 1970; v. 13, Winter, 1972. Both reproduced by permission.—*Critical Quarterly,* v. 20, Winter, 1978. Reproduced by permission of Blackwell Publishers.—*Drama Critique,* v. 2, 1968 for "Pinter and Menace," by Ray Orley. Reproduced by permission of the author.—*Drama Survey,* v. 4, Winter, 1965 for "The Fool-Hero of Michel de Ghelderode," by Helen Hellman. Reproduced by permission of the author/v. 5, Spring, 1966 for "Faust and Anti-Faust in Modern Drama," by Douglas Cole. Reproduced by permission of the author.—*English,* v. 22, Autumn, 1975 for "The Memory of All That: Pinter's Old Times," by Tony Aylwin. Reproduced by permission of the author.—*The English Record,* Winter, 1971 for "Perceiving Pinter," by Alfred E. Rickert. Reproduced by permission of the publisher and the author.—*English Studies,* v. 62, June, 1981. Reproduced by permission.—*Essays in Literature,* v. 18, Spring, 1991. Reproduced by permission.—*The French Review,* v. XXXXI, October, 1967; v. XLVIII, May, 1975. Both reproduced by permission.—*The Hudson Review,* v. 6, Summer, 1953 for "Beddoes: The Mask of Parody," by Louis O. Coxe. Reproduced by permission of the Literary Estate of Louis O. Coxe./v. 14, Spring, 1961; v. 14, Winter, 1961; v. 21, Autumn, 1968. All reproduced by permission.—*Kansas Quarterly,* v. 3, Spring, 1971 for "Harold Pinter—Past and Present," by Lois G. Gordon. Reproduced by permission of the publisher and the author.—*The Massachusetts Review,* v. 8, Autumn, 1967. Reproduced by permission.—*Massachusetts Studies in English,* v. 11, Summer, 1992. Reproduced by permission.—*Modern Drama,* v. 11, 1969; v. 16, 1973. Both reproduced by permission.—*The New Republic,* v. 162, April 25, 1970. Reproduced by permission.—*New Statesman,* v. 55, May 31, 1958; v. 59, January 30, 1960; v. 59, May 7, 1960; v. 69, June 11, 1965. All reproduced by permission.—*The New Yorker,* v. 38, December 8, 1962 for "Comedies of Terror" by Edith Oliver. © 1962 by The New Yorker Magazine, Inc. All rights reserved. Reproduced by permission of the Literary Estate of Edith Oliver.—*The Quarterly Journal of Speech,* v. 58, February, 1972 for "Non-Verbal Communication and the Overlooked Action in Pinter's The Caretaker," by Robert P. Murphy. Reproduced by permission of the publisher and the author./v. 55, December, 1969. Reproduced by permission of the publisher.—*Renascence,* v. 20, Autumn, 1967; v. 21, Autumn, 1968. Both reproduced by permission.—*Saturday Review,* v. 53, April 25, 1970. Reproduced by permission of *The Saturday Review,* © 1970, General Media International, Inc.—*The Southern Quarterly,* v. 12, April, 1974. Reproduced by permission.—*The Spectator,* London, June 11, 1965. Reproduced by permission.—*Stanford French Review,* v. 2, Winter, 1978 for "Michel de Ghelderode's Escurial: The Alchemist's Nigredo," by Bettina Knapp. Reproduced by permission of the publisher and the author.—*Studia Neophilologica,* v. 39, 1967; v. 63, 1991. Both reproduced by permission.—*Studies in English Literature, 1500-1900,* v. 29, Autumn, 1989. Reproduced by permission.—*Texas Quarterly,* v. 4, Autumn, 1961. Reproduced by permission.—*Theatre Studies,* v. 37, 1992. Reproduced by permission.—*The Tulane Drama Review,* v. 8, Fall, 1963; v. 11, Winter, 1966. Both reproduced by permission.—*University of Windsor Review,* v. 13, Spring, 1978. Reproduced by permission.—*Virginia Quarterly Review,* v. 68, Fall, 1992. Reproduced by permission.

COPYRIGHTED EXCERPTS IN *DC*, VOLUME 15, WERE REPRODUCED FROM THE FOLLOWING BOOKS:

Esslin, Martin. From "Harold Pinter's Theatre of Cruelty," in *Pinter at Sixty.* Edited by Katherine H. Burkman and John L. Kundert-Gibbs. Indiana University Press, 1993. © 1993 by Indiana University Press. All rights reserved. Reproduced by

Thomas Lovell Beddoes
1803-1849

English poet and dramatist.

INTRODUCTION

Called "The Last Elizabethan" by Lytton Strachey, Beddoes is chiefly remembered for his evocative poetic vision in such works as *Death's Jest Book or The Fool's Tragedy* (1850). Although his works are few, he was an important figure in the Elizabethan literary revival of the nineteenth century. His work skillfully combines macabre imagery, passages of haunting beauty, and elements of the supernatural.

BIOGRAPHICAL INFORMATION

Beddoes was born in Clifton, England, in 1803. His father was a celebrated physician of outstanding literary, as well as scientific, talent. Although he died when his son was young, he instilled in the young Beddoes an interest in literature and the sciences. Maria Edgeworth, Beddoes's aunt, was another important figure in his life and encouraged his writing. Beddoes was a brilliant child intellectually who won prizes for essays in Latin and Greek and published poetry in *The Morning Post* before entering college. However, he was also beset with emotional problems. His depression found expression not only in his personal life, but in the themes and characters of his works as well. In 1821 Beddoes attended Pembroke College, Oxford. After earning a B.A. and M.A., he traveled to Germany to attend medical school at Göttingen University. Beddoes was soon expelled from the university for drunken and disorderly behavior and for attempting suicide. He went on to Würzburg to earn a medical degree but was still dissatisfied with his achievements, and his outlook became increasingly morbid. In an effort to relieve his inner restlessness, Beddoes became involved with radical political activities. Beddoes traveled to Zürich, where he continued to work on *Death's Jest Book*, and wrote several short pieces, later collected in *Poems Posthumous and Collected of Thomas Lovell Beddoes* (1851). As the political climate in Europe became more intense, so did Beddoes's interest in revolutionary politics. In Germany, he delivered lectures for the liberal cause. Eventually, he was deported for his activities, and from that time on, wandered aimlessly throughout Europe, never settling in one place for long. Beddoes isolated himself from English society and his family, and in a state of complete despair, committed suicide in Basel on January 26, 1849.

MAJOR WORKS

In 1822 Beddoes wrote *The Brides' Tragedy,* a verse drama based on a college murder; this work established him as a writer of merit. The obsession with death and the grotesque imagery of the piece were to recur in much of his later verse. He began to compose *Death's Jest Book,* considered his major work, during his years in medical school. Although it contains brilliant passages and demonstrates definite lyrical talent, *Death's Jest Book* never satisfied Beddoes; he altered it repeatedly, and it was not published in his lifetime. A revenge drama set in thirteenth-century Ancona, Egypt, and Silesia, the play incorporates a mixture of verse and prose and is considered the ultimate manifestation of Beddoes's preoccupation with death.

CRITICAL RECEPTION

Although Beddoes had a remarkable capacity for lyrical, imaginative poetic drama, he was a poet of uneven gifts. Many commentators have urged increased critical attention to his plays; in fact, some important critical studies on Beddoes have been published in the past few decades. Several critics have debated his place within the English literary tradition, in particular whether his work should be classified as Elizabethan, German Romantic, Jacobean, or Gothic; scholars have also debated whether his works should be considered poetry or drama. Whatever his categorization, Beddoes is recognized by commentators as a compelling minor figure in English literature.

PRINCIPAL WORKS

Plays

The Brides' Tragedy 1822
The Last Man (fragment) 1823–25
Love's Arrow Poisoned (fragment) 1823–25
Torrismond (fragment) 1824
The Second Brother (fragment) 1824–25
Death's Jest Book or The Fool's Tragedy 1850
Thomas Beddoes: Plays and Poems (poetry and drama) 1950

Other Major Works

The Improvisatore, in Three Fyttes, with Other Poems (poems) 1821

Poems Posthumous and Collected of Thomas Lovell Beddoes (poetry) 1851

The Poetical Works of Thomas Beddoes 2 vols. (poetry) 1890

The Letters of Thomas Lovell Beddoes (letters) 1894

The Poems of Thomas Lovell Beddoes (poetry) 1907

The Works of Thomas Lovell Beddoes (collected works) 1935

Selected Poems (poetry) 1976

OVERVIEWS AND GENERAL STUDIES

Edinburgh Review (essay date 1823)

SOURCE: "English Tragedy," in *Edinburgh Review,* Vol. 38, No. LXXV, February, 1823, pp. 177-208.

[*In the following essay, the anonymous reviewer attempts to place Beddoes within the context of English drama and praises the poetic language of* The Brides' Tragedy.]

In the history of a nation, the progress and vicissitudes of its Literature are but too frequently disregarded. The crowning of kings, and the winning of battles, are recorded with chronological accuracy, and the resources of the country are laid open. The eye of the reader is dazzled with the splendour of courts, and the array of armies: The rise and fall of parties—the trial and condemnation of state criminals—the alternations of power and disgrace, are explained to very weariness. But of the quiet conquests of learning, there is small account. The philosopher must live in his own page, the poet in his verse; for the national chronicles are almost mute regarding them. The historian's bloody catalogue is not made up of units; but deals only with great assemblages of men—armies, fleets, and senates: The king is the only *'One'* included in the story; but of him, be he a cipher or a tyrant, we are told in a way to satisfy the most extravagant desires of loyalty.

There is in this, we think, an undue preponderance—a preference of show to substance—of might to right. There is at least as much importance to be attached to the acquisition of *Paradise Lost,* or *Lear,* as to the gaining of an ordinary victory. Accordingly, *we,* profiting by the historian's lapse, and in order to do those ingenious persons (the poets and philosophers) justice, assume the right of tracing, from time to time, *their* histories upon our pages, and of discussing, with something of historic candour, their good qualities and defects.

In contemplating the great scene of Literature, the Muses are, beyond doubt, one of the brightest groups; and, among them, those of the *Drama* stand out preeminent. To quit allegory—it comes more quickly home to the bosoms of men; it is linked more closely to their interests and desires, detailing matters of daily life, and treating, in almost colloquial phrase, of ordinary passions. It is as a double-sided mirror, wherein men see themselves reflected, with all their agreeable pomp and circumstance, but freed of that rough husk of vulgarity which might tempt them to quarrel with their likeness: while the sins of their fellows are stripped and made plain, and they themselves pourtrayed with unerring and tremendous fidelity.

Certainly dramatic poetry is more quick and decisive in its effects than poetry of any other kind; and this arises partly from its nature, and partly from the circumstances under which it is made public. In the imagination of a person visiting the theatre, there is a predisposition to receive strong impressions. The toil of the day is over, the spirits are exhilarated, and the nerves rendered susceptible by a consciousness of coming enjoyment. All the fences and guards that a man assumes in matters of business or controversy, are laid aside. Even the little caution with which he takes up a book (for we have now got a lurking notion that authors are not infallible) is forgotten: he casts off his care and his prudence, and sets both the past and future at defiance when he enters the limits of a theatre. It is impossible for a person unacquainted with dramatic representation, to understand the effect produced on a mixed mass of the people, when a striking sentiment is uttered by a popular actor. The conviction is instantaneous. Hundreds of stormy voices are awakened, the spirit of every individual is in arms, and a thousand faces are lighted up which a moment before seemed calm and powerless;—and this impression is not so transient as may be thought. It is carried home, and nursed till it ripens. It is a germ which blossoms out into patriotism, or runs up rank into prejudice or passion. It is intellectual property, honestly acquired; and yet debateable ground, on which disputes may arise, and battles are to be fought hereafter.

Men are often amused, and sometimes instructed, by books. But a tragedy is a great moral lesson, read to two senses at once; and the eye and the ear are both held in alliance to retain the impression which the actor has produced. A narrative poem is perhaps more tempting in its shape than a play, and may fix the attention more deeply in the closet; but it is addressed to a more limited class, and necessarily affects our sympathies less forcibly; for a Drama is an embodying of the present, while an Epic is only a shadow of the past. We listen, in one case, to a mere relation of facts; but, in the other, the ruin of centuries is swept away, and time annihilated, and we stand face to face with 'grey Antiquity.' We see and hear things which we thought had departed for ever; but they are (or seem to be) here again—in stature, in gesture, in habit, the same. We become as it were one of a crowd that has vanished; we mix with departed sages and heroes, and breathe the air of Athens, and Cressy, and Agincourt. Men who have been raised to the stars, and whom we have known but by the light of their renown, are made plain to our senses: they stand before us, flesh and blood like ourselves. We are apt to deny our sympathy to old events, when it is asked by the mere historian of the times; but, when the mimic scene is unfolded before us, we are hurried into the living tumult, without the power (or even wish) to resist.

Schlegel, in his acute and learned Lectures on 'Dramatic Art and Literature,' inquires, *'what is Dramatic?'* A definition is seldom an easy thing. Although we can understand what is called dramatic writing, it may nevertheless be difficult to define it correctly. It certainly does not consist merely in its shape of dialogue, because dialogue may be, and often is, essentially *un*dramatic. Speeches may be shaped, and separated, and allotted, and they may be raised or lowered in expression, as the king, or the merchant, or the beggar, is presented, yet the hue of the author's mind shall pervade them all. Such characters are *not* dramatic: they have no verisimilitude: they are like puppets worked with wires, the mechanism of the brain, but little more. They may startle our admiration, or tease our curiosity, by the ingenuity of the workmanship; but we have no faith in them, and they stimulate us to nothing. In Shakespeare (but he stands in this, as in every thing else, alone), we never see the prejudice of the author peeping out and interfering,—a mistake and an anachronism in the scene. He is the only one who ever had strength enough to cast off the slough of his egotism, and courage enough to lay his vanities aside, and array with the pure light of an independent intellect, the most airy creations of the brain. Like the prince in the Arabian fiction, he leaves one shape for another and another, animating each and all by turns; not carrying the complexion or tone, or diseases of the first, into the body of the second; and yet superior even to that ingenious metempsychosist, whose original love, if we remember aright, remained unaltered through all the changes that he underwent in story.

It is assuredly difficult,—and argues more than common disinterestedness, to set aside, of our own accord, our right to be heard, and to become the organ and mouthpiece of a variety of men. To invest ourselves for a time with the prejudices, and even with the very speech of statesmen and soldiers, kings and counsellors, knaves, idiots, friars and the like, seems like a gratuitous vexation of the intellect; and yet it must be done. We must give up our privilege to dictate, and lose the opportunity of saying infinitely better things than the parties concerned would utter, if we wish for eminent success in the drama. This is offensive to our self-love; and the truth is, that a vain man can never be a good dramatist. He must *forget himself* before he can do justice to others. We have heard it insisted, that this is neither possible nor desirable. But that it is possible, Shakespeare is a brilliant testimony. And that it is desirable, is equally certain, and, we apprehend, not very difficult of proof. A character (king or peasant) must speak like himself, or like another person, or like no person whomsoever:—which style is the best, we leave to the understanding of the reader. It is true that, without much of that particular faculty which we are inclined to call 'dramatic,' some authors have contrived to pourtray one or two characters with success; but these have been generally mere *beaux ideals*,—mere copies or modifica-

tions of themselves. Indeed, we have found, on a strict scrutiny, that their opinions might always be seen darkening one character, and their animal spirits gilding another; and that, whether didactic, or disputatious, or jocose, the fluctuation of their own spirit has been manifest through all the shiftings and disguises of their tale.

Schlegel, in reply to his own question of 'What is dramatic?' says—that it does not consist merely in dialogue, but that it is necessary that such dialogue should operate a change in the minds of the persons represented. If by this he means, that the character itself should be wrought upon and change, we think that this may be desirable; but the *nature* of the drama is a thing different from the result which it ought to arrive at. This assertion of Schlegel is therefore almost like saying, that argument is not sound (or rather that it is not argument at all) unless it shall produce conviction. In our own literature, at least, it is certain that we often find the personages at the end of the play in precisely the same state of mind as at the commencement. We make a play a succession and change of *events,* and not a change of sentiment. The sentiment of the hearer is indeed, if possible, to be wrought upon, but not necessarily that of any one character of the drama. The character, in fact, is frequently developed in the first scene, and we have nothing afterwards to learn except as to what accidents befall it. If the German critic means to say (for he is not very clear), that the tone of the several speeches in a play should be dependent on each other—that the first should give rise to the second, the second to the third, and so on, we entirely agree with him: For the bright spirit of dialogue can only be struck out by collision; and if the speech, the answer, and the replication, were mere independent and insulated sayings, each character would utter a series of monologues, and no more.

Shakespeare (as in the case of Macbeth and others) sometimes makes his tragedy an absolute piece of biography, and allows his characters to unfold themselves gradually, act by act: he does not, in truth, often bring forward a ready-made villain, whom we may know at a glance; but we have a map of the march and progress of crime or passion through the human heart: our sympathies are not assaulted or taken by surprise, but we move forward, step by step, with the hero of the story, until he perishes before our eyes. This is undoubtedly the perfection of the drama; but it exists in its weakness as well as in its strength; and even in Shakespeare, Iago is much the same person in the fifth act as he is in the first scene, and Richard undergoes little, if any, alteration.

If we were driven to a definition, we should say, that a good drama is—'A story told by action and dialogue, where the spirit and style of the speeches allotted to each character are well distinguished from the others, and are true to that particular character and to Nature.' It must involve a story (or event), or it will not have the strength and stature of a drama; for that is not a collection of scenes loosely hung together without object, but a gradual detail of one or more facts in a regular and natural way. It must have action, or it cannot be fit for representation; and dialogue, or it would be but narration. The speeches must possess character and distinction, without which, a play would be monotonous, and like the voice of a single instrument breathed through different tubes of one diameter: and that those speeches should be true to the characters to which they are assigned, and (as a consequence) to Nature, must be presumed, until we can show that Nature is wrong, or can find a brighter model to imitate.

The earliest dramatic amusements of modern times (they were common to Italy, and Spain, and England), were of a religious nature, and with us passed under the name of 'Mysteries.' In these, which were stories taken from the Bible and Testament, the characters were sustained by monks, or boys attached to ecclesiastical establishments; and, indeed, the literary part of the Mysteries (such as it is) must have sprung from the same source.

Much discussion has occurred among our industrious and inquisitive brethren in learning, as to whether our Drama is of foreign or English growth. Something plausible may no doubt be urged on each side of the question; but we must rest on circumstantial proof at last: And, after all, the discovery would scarcely compensate for the pains that must be bestowed on the inquiry; for the subject itself is not very important to the interests even of the Drama.

Some derive our dramatic literature at once from the tragedies of the ancient Greeks; some from the comparatively modern entertainments which the Jews and early Christians were accustomed to exhibit at Constantinople (Byzantium) and elsewhere: others say that it originated at fairs in the ingenuity of the itinerant dealers, who thus exerted their wits to draw people and purchasers together; while the rest (without referring to this origin) contend only that it is of pure English growth, and has no connexion with any that we have mentioned, nor even with the Mysteries of Italy or Spain. Schlegel himself is, if we remember correctly, of this last opinion.

Now, we can scarcely suppose that our earlier writers were indebted to the classic Grecian models; for the 'Mysteries' have been traced back as far as the twelfth century; and Chaucer, in the fourteenth century, speaks of 'plays of miracles;' at which time we are not aware that the Greek dramatists were known in England. But there is a better reason still against this supposed derivation, which is, that the early English performances bear no resemblance whatever to the tragedies of the Greeks. The latter are fine and polished entertainments, discussing matters of daily life, or immortalizing events in their own history; while the former are meagre didactic matters, taken solely from sacred history, and destitute of the chorus which forms so stirring a feature in the character of the Grecian plays. Had our forefathers imitated Sophocles, or Euripides, or Eschylus, it is but fair to suppose that they would have imitated them entirely; for the taste of the nation was not at the point to suggest *selections* from their style, nor to justify any deviation from their successful system. We

must therefore conclude, that the ancient Grecians had little to do (nothing directly) with the birth of our English Drama.

As to the opinion that it began in mimic and buffoonery at fairs, we cannot understand why, if this was the case, the subjects should be of so serious a cast. It is not reasonable to suppose, that the wandering merchants of the time would strive to attract purchasers, by laying before them some signal instance of God's vengeance. If they had mimicked any thing, it would have been the manners or the follies of the time, the gesture or the gait of individuals, or things that were in themselves obviously susceptible of mirth, and readily to be understood by the spectators. But we see nothing of this in the earliest specimens of the English dramatic writers; and without this we cannot well accede to the opinions of Warton or Schlegel, and think that our drama had no connexion with that of foreign countries. In the first place, our English Mysteries were essentially like those of Gregory Nanzianzen and the modern Italians. We had intercourse with Italy and Constantinople; and it is known that the stories of Boccaccio and his countrymen had been brought into England in the time of Chaucer.

If there had not been so decided a resemblance, in point of subject, between the 'Mysteries' of England and the sacred Dramas of Italy and modern Greece, we should have felt inclined to adopt the opinion of Schlegel. It is known that the same ingenious discoveries have been made in different parts of the world which had no acquaintance with each other; and it would have been but equitable to have given the English credit for a drama of their own invention. But, to say the truth, the earliest specimens of English plays do not look like inventions; they are at once too complete for originals, and too rude to be considered as copies from the polished Dramas of Sophocles and his cotemporaries. The first attempt at dramatic writing would naturally be in the form of a monodrame, or a simple colloquy, and not a drama with all its principal and subordinate parts illustrating a fact in history. It is said, indeed, that the Mysteries were composed by the monks, for the purpose of supplanting more vulgar entertainments of a similar nature; yet the fact of no such entertainments having come down to us, may well excite some scepticism; for the person capable of inventing a drama, would also, we should think, be able to record it. It is true, that the most ancient entertainment at Naples is Punch, who has descended, by tradition only, from father to son, and still keeps his place of popularity, in defiance both of improvement and innovation. But Punch was not the origin of the Italian Drama; nor would the fact of his having been so, or of his resemblance to our fair mimicry, alter the question as to the invention of the English 'Mysteries.' After all, however, the matter is not important, and scarcely worth the very small discussion which we have bestowed upon it.

The *'Moralities'* which followed, grew out of the old 'Mystery,' and were the natural offspring of such a parent.

They were mere embodyings of the vices and virtues; and though dressed up after a barbarous fashion, made some approach to the models of the ancient Greeks; at least in the titles of their *dramatis personæ.* 'Death,—Kindred,—Strength,—Discretion,' and others, for instance, which occur in the old Morality of *Everyman,* came nearer to the personages in the Prometheus of Æschylus than the nature of the 'Mysteries' would allow; and in the Morality of *Lusty Juventus,* the persons of 'Knowledge,—Good Councell,—Sathan the Devyll,' and others, explain at once the nature of their offices, and the entertainment they are likely to afford. These compositions (especially the Morality called *Hycke-Scorner*) possess occasional gleams of dramatic spirit; but, generally speaking, they have little of that quality beyond what is discoverable in the romances and narrative poems of the same period.

The first regular English comedy, *Gammer Gurton's Needle,* in every sense a very remarkable performance, is said to have been written in the year 1551; and if that statement be correct, the first English tragedy, *Ferrex and Porrex,* which was the joint composition of Sackville, Lord Buckhurst, and Thomas Norton, was written in the same year. Our business is not now with the comedy. With regard to the latter Drama, it is remarkable rather for its even style and negative merits, than for any one brilliant or sterling quality. It has none of the rudeness of the Dramas which preceded and followed it, but stands by itself, an elegant instance of mediocrity in writing. Without extravagance or flagrant error—without ribaldry, or any of the offensive trash that disgraced those days, it is nevertheless mournfully deficient in spirit and dramatic character. The hue of the authors' minds pervades the whole like a gloom. When Pope praised this tragedy for 'the propriety of sentiments, and gravity of style,' &c. 'so essential to tragedy,' and which, he says, 'Shakespeare himself perpetually neglected, or little understood,' he proves to us nothing but that he did not understand dramatic writing. Even Milton (and we say this very reluctantly) seems to have had an imperfect idea of true tragedy, when he calls the Greek writers 'unequalled,' and proposes them as models, in preference to our own great and incomparable poet. We have little to object to the 'propriety' of Lord Buchurst's sentiments, and nothing to the 'gravity' of his style. These things are very good, no doubt; but we have nothing else. There is no character—no variety, which is the soul of dramatic writing. What Lord Buckhurst says might as well be said in a narrative or didactic poem,—in a sermon, or an essay. But in a play, we want true and vivid portraits: we want the life and spirit of natural dialogue: we want 'gravity of style' occasionally, but we also want fancy, and even folly: we want passion in all its shapes, and madness in its many words, and virtue and valour,—not dressed up in allegory, nor tamed down to precept, but true and living examples of each, with all the varieties and inflections of human nature,—not too good for us to profit by, nor too bad for us to dread. Now, we have little of this in *Ferrex and Porrex.* The play is sterile in character, and, with all its good sense, is a dead and dull monotony. The following is one of the most favour-

able passages; but it will nevertheless afford a fair specimen of the style in which the whole is written. Hermon (a parasite) is addressing the King.

> —If the fear of Gods, and secret grudge
> Of Nature's law, repining at the fact,
> Withhold your courage from so great attempt,
> Know ye that lust of kingdoms hath no law,
> *The Gods do bear, and well allow in Kings*
> *The things that they abhor in rascal routes.*
> When kings on slender quarrels run to wars,
> And then, in cruel and unkindly wise,
> Commend thefts, rapes, murder of innocents,
> The spoil of towns, ruins of mighty realms,
> Think you such princes do suppose themselves
> Subject to laws of kind, and fear of Gods?
> Murders and violent thefts in private men
> Are heinous crimes, and full of foul reproach;
> Yet no offence, and deck'd with glorious name
> Of noble conquests in the hands of kings.
>
> > *Act 2. sc. 1.*

We have taken no liberty with this very edifying counsel, except that of altering the ancient spelling. The doctrine requires as little assistance.

After Lord Sacville followed *Edwards,* who, in 1571, wrote *The Comedy of Damon and Pythias.* It has, notwithstanding its title, some things of tragedy in it; but the serious parts are nearly worthless. The style is rude and bad enough, and the play is filled with anachronisms and inconsistencies; but there is an attempt at character in one or two of the persons of the drama, which serves in some small measure to redeem it. Aristippus is an instance of a philosopher turned courtier; and Carisophus is a specimen of the parasite plant, which we can easily suppose flourished and multiplied as readily at the foot of Etna, as on the banks of the Seine or the Thames, or on the shores of the sea of Archangel. About the same time with Edwards lived and wrote Thomas *Preston,* the author of *Cambises king of Percia.* This tragedy is remarkable only for its having been referred to, as is supposed, by Shakespeare in Henry the Fourth. The 'vein' of Cambises, however, is but a sorry vein; and is more dull than extravagant. It would probably long since have been forgotten, but for Falstaff's allusion. *Whetstone,* the author of *Promos and Cassandra,* is scarcely worth a mention, unless it be that Shakespeare has borrowed his subject of *Measure for Measure* from him;—neither is Kyd, who wrote *Soliman and Perseda,* and the Spanish Tragedy. We say this on the supposition that some other was the author of the scene in the latter play, where Hieronimo is discovered mad. There is in that scene, indeed, a wild and stern grief, painted with fearful strength, which we must not altogether pass over. The following short extract is powerful and fine.

> *The Painter enters.*
> 　*Paint.* God bless you, Sir.
> 　　*Hier.* Wherefore? why, thou scornful villain?
> How, where, or by what means should I be blest?
> 　*Isab.* What would'st thou have, good fellow?
> 　*Paint.* Justice, madam.

> *Hier.* Oh! ambitious beggar, would'st thou have
> that
> That lives not in the world?
> Why, all the undelved mines cannot buy
> An ounce of Justice, 'tis a jewel so inestimable.
> I tell thee, God hath engrossed all justice in his hands,
> And there is none but what comes from him.
> *Paint.* Oh! then I see that God must right me for
> My murdered son.
> *Hier.* How, was thy son murdered?
> *Paint.* Ay, Sir: no man did hold a son so dear.
> *Hier.* What! not as thine? that's a lic
> As massy as the earth: I had a son,
> Whose least unvalued hair did weigh
> A thousand of thy sons, and he was murdered.
> *Paint.* Alas! Sir, I had no more but he.
> *Hier.* Nor I, nor I: but this same one of mine
> Was worth a legion. But all is one; Pedro,
> Jaques, go in a doors, Isabella, go,
> And this good fellow here, and I
> Will range this hideous orchard up and down
> Like too she lions reaved of our young.

Besides these, there are some others who may be said to have flourished before the time of Shakespeare—*Wilmot,* who wrote *Tancred and Gismonde*—*Greene,* the author of *James the Fourth*—*Legge,* who is said to have written *Richard the Third*—the celebrated John *Lily* the Euphuist—George *Peele,* who wrote *David and Bethsabe* and *Mahomet and Hiron,* and some other dramas,—and last, but not least, Christopher Marlow. These authors, with the exception of Peele and Marlow (for Lily's plays can scarcely be considered within the limit of our subject) may be passed over without further mention. The lines of Peele are sweet and flowing, but they have little imagination and no strength; and he is without a notion of dialogue. He would have written pastorals perhaps smoothly and pleasantly, but the passions were altogether above him. One of his plays, *Mahomet and Hiron,* is probably the source from which ancient Pistol has derived a portion of his learning. David and Bethsabe reminds us of the Old Mysteries: its style, however, is different, and it has some lines that have undoubtedly great beauty. In Bethsabe's apostrophe to the air, she says—

> Deck thyself in loose robes,
> And on thy wings bring delicate perfumes—

which is delicacy itself; nor can the following lines in the same play (describing a fountain) be denied the merit of being extremely graceful.

> The brim let be embraced with golden curls
> Of moss that sleeps with sounds the waters make,
> With joy to feed the fount with their recourse:
> Let all the grass that beautifies her bower
> Bear manna every morn instead of dew;
> Or let the dew be sweeter far than that
> That hangs like chains of pearl on Hermon hill.

But *Marlow* was undoubtedly the greatest tragic writer that preceded Shakespeare. The spirit of extravagance seems to have dwelt in his brain, and to have imped him on to the most extraordinary feats: but his muse had a fiery wing, and bore him over the dark and unhallowed depths of his subject in a strong and untiring flight. This poet is less remarkable for his insight into human character, than for his rich and gloomy imagination, and his great powers of diction,—for whether stately, or terrible, or tender, he excels in all. His 'mighty line' was famous in his own time, and cannot be denied even now: Yet he could stoop from the heights of a lawless fancy, or the dignity of solemn declamation, to words of the softest witchery. He certainly loved to wander from the common track, and dash at once into peril and mystery; and this daring it was which led him naturally to his sublimity and extravagance. Unfortunately Marlow is never content with doing a little, nor even with doing enough; but he fills the cup of horror till it overflows. There is a striking instance of this in his tragedy of *Lust's Dominion,* which seems written from a desire to throw off a tormenting load of animal spirits. There is a perpetual spurning at restraints, a warring with reason and probability throughout the whole of the play. Eleazar, the Moor, is a mad savage who should have been shut up in a cage, and the queen, his paramour, with him; and the whole dialogue (though there are some strong well-sustained passages) is as unequal and turbulent as the characters.

Of all the plays of Marlow, *Faustus* is the finest, and *Edward the Second* perhaps the most equal. The *Jew of Malta* we cannot admire, (though there is in it certainly the first hint of Shylock); and *Tamburlaine,* generally speaking, is either fustian or frenzy. However, the poet's idea of the horses of the sun—

> 'That blow the morning from their nostrils,'
> is magnificent, and his description of Tamburlaine's
> person
> '(Such breadth of shoulders as might mainly bear
> Old Atlas' burden'—)

recals, not unpleasantly, to our mind the description of the great 'second spirit' of Milton. *Faustus* is the story of a learned man who sells himself to the devil, on condition of having unlimited power on earth for twenty-four years; and Mephostophilis (a spirit) is given to him as a slave. These two worthies pass from place to place, enjoying themselves in feastings, and love, and triumphs of various kinds; and, by the aid of Lucifer, they beat priests and abuse the pope to his face, and commit similar enormities in defiance of *'maledicats'* and other formidable weapons of church construction. There are many single lines and phrases in this play which might be selected as incontestable evidence that Marlow was in felicity of thought, and strength of expression, second only to Shakespeare himself. (As a dramatist, however, he is inferior to others.) Some of his turns of thought are even like those of our matchless poet; as when he speaks of

> —unwedded maids
> Shadowing more beauty in their airy brows
> Than have the white breasts of the queen of love;

or of a temple

    That *threats* the stars with her aspiring top;

and where he refers to a man who has an amiable soul,

    If sin by custom grow not into nature—

and many others. But Faustus's death is the most appalling thing in the play. It is difficult, however, to give the reader an idea of it by a brief extract—he must read it with its 'pomp and circumstance' about it. Faustus is to die at twelve, and the clock has already struck eleven. He groans forth his last speech, which begins thus—

> O Faustus!
> Now hast thou but one bare hour to live,
> And then thou must be damned perpetually.
> Stand still, you ever moving spheres of Heaven,
> That Time may cease, and Midnight never come!
> Fair Nature's eye, rise—rise again, and make
> Perpetual day; or let this hour be but
> A year—a month—a week—a natural day—
> That Faustus may repent, and save his soul, &c.

And now, to pass from the terrible to the gentle, nothing can be more soft than the lines which he addresses to the Vision of Helen, whom he requires to pass before him when he is in search of a mistress. He is smitten at once by her excelling beauty, and thus he speaks:

> Was this the face that launch'd a thousand ships,
> And burnt the topless towers of Ilium?—
> Sweet Helen, make me immortal with a kiss—
> Her lips suck forth my soul . . .
> Here will I dwell, for Heaven is in these lips,
> And all is dross that is not Helena.
> I will be Paris, and for love of thee
> Instead of Troy shall Wittenburg be sacked,
> And I will combat with weak Menelaus,
> And wear thy colours on my plumed crest.
> —Oh! thou art fairer than the evening air,
> Clad in the beauty of a thousand stars;
> Brighter art thou than flaming Jupiter,
> When he appear'd to hapless Semele,
> More lovely than the monarch of the sky
> In wanton Arethusa's azure arms,
> And none but thou shall be my paramour.—

Following Marlow, but far outshining him and all others in the vigour and variety of his mighty intellect, arose the first of all poets, whether in the East of West—Shakespeare. He had, it is true, many contemporaries, whose names have since become famous,—men who slept for a time in undeserved obscurity, and who are at last brought forward to illustrate the fashion of their time, and to give bright evidence of its just renown: Yet there is not one worthy of being raised to a comparison with Shakespeare himself. One had a lofty fancy, another a deep flow of melodious verse, another a profound reach of thought; a fourth caught well the mere manners of the age, while others would lash its vices or laud its proud deeds, in verse worthy of the acts which they recorded; but Shakespeare

surpassed them all. In the race of fame he was foremost, and alone. He was, beyond all doubt or competition, the first writer of his age or nation. He illuminated the land in which he lived, like a constellation. There were, as we have said, other bright aspects which cast a glory upon the world of letters; but *he alone* had that *radiating* intellect which extended all ways, and penetrated all things, scattering the darkness of ignorance that rested on his age, while it invigorated its spirit and bettered the heart. He was witty, and humorous, and tender, and lofty, and airy, and profound, beyond all men who have lived before or since. He had that particular and eminent faculty, which no other tragic writer perhaps ever possessed, of divesting his subject altogether of himself. He developed the characters of men, but never intruded himself amongst them. He fashioned figures of all colours and shapes and sizes, but he did not put the stamp of egotism upon them, nor breathe over each the sickly hue of his own opinion. They were fresh and strong, beautiful or grotesque, as occasion asked,—or they were blended and compounded of different metals, to suit the various uses of human life; and thus cast, he sent them forth amongst mankind to take their chance for immortality.

The contemporaries of Shakespeare were great and remarkable men. They had winged imaginations, and made lofty flights. They saw above, below, or around; but they had not the taste or discrimination which he possessed, nor the same extensive vision. They drew correctly and vividly for particular aspects, while he towered above his subject, and surveyed it on all sides, from 'top to toe.' If some saw farther than others, they were dazzled at the riches before them, and grasped hastily, and with little care. They were perplexed with that variety which he made subservient to the general effect. They painted a portrait—or two—or three only, as though afraid of confusion. He, on the other hand, managed and marshalled all. His characters lie, like strata of earth, one under another; or to use his own expression, 'matched in mouth like bells,—each under each.' We need only look at the plays of Falstaff, where there are wits and rogues and simpletons of a dozen shades,—Falstaff, Hal, Poins, Bardolph, Nym, Pistol, Hostess, Shallow, Silence, Slender,—to say nothing of those rich recruits, equal only to a civil war. Now, no one else has done this, and it must be presumed that none have been able to do it; Marlow, Marston, Webster, Decker, Johnson, Massinger, Beaumont and Fletcher—a strong phalanx, yet none have proved themselves competent to so difficult a task.

It has been well said, that it is not so much in one faculty that Shakespeare excelled his fellows, as in that wondrous combination of talent, which has made him, beyond controversy, eminent above all. He was as universal as the light, and had riches countless. The Greek dramatists are poor in the comparison. The gloom of Fate hung over their tragedies, and they spoke by the oracle. They have indeed too much of the monotony of their skies; but our poet, while he had the brightness of the summer months, was as various as the April season, and as fickle and fantastic as May.

It is idle to say that the characters of writers cannot be discovered from their works. There is sure to be some betrayal,—(Shakespeare is a wonderful and single exception in his dramatic works—but he has written others)—there is always some mark of vanity, or narrow bigotry, or intolerant pride, when either of these vices darken or contract the poet's heart: there is some moment when he who is querrulous will complain, and he who is misanthropic will pour out his hate; but—passing by the dramas, in which, however, there is no symptom of any personal failings—there is nothing to be found in all his lyrical writings, save only a little repining; and this the malice of his stars may well excuse. The poets and wits of modern times would, we suspect, spurn at the servitude which Shakespeare wore out with patience. But he, rich as he was in active faculty, possessed also the passive virtue of endurance—the Philosophy which enabled him to meet misfortune, and to bear up against the accidents of poverty and of the time. It is to the eternal honour of Lord Southampton, that he could distinguish in some measure the worth of our matchless poet, and that he had generosity enough to honour and reward it. So much has been written and said on Shakespeare, that we will not add further to the enormities of criticism. He breathes like a giant under the loads of rubbish which his pigmy critics and commentators have flung upon him. One good editor, with a reasonable knowledge of the manners and diction of the times, would do the world a service by casting aside nine-tenths of the barren dissertation that has been wasted on the subject, and which now remains, like a *caput mortuum*, weighing down the better text of our greatest poet.

After Shakespeare, *Beaumont and Fletcher* have altogether the highest claims to consideration. For, though Ben Jonson was more eminent in some respects, and Massinger better in others, they were, as serious dramatic poets, decidedly superior to both. It is difficult to separate Beaumont from Fletcher; especially as all the plays wherein the former had a share are not certainly known. Beaumont is said to have had the better judgment (to have 'brought the ballast of judgment,') and Fletcher the livelier and more prolific fancy; but as the latter was the sole author of *The Faithful Shepherdess, Valentinian, Rule a Wife and Have a Wife,* and *The Two Noble Kinsmen,* ['The Two Noble Kinsmen' is said to have been written by Fletcher and *Shakespeare*; and the early part of the play certainly betrays marks of the great master hand, or else an imitation so exquisite, as to cause our regret that it was not more frequently attempted.] besides being concerned jointly with Beaumont in some of the most serious plays which pass under their joint names, he is entitled on the whole to the greatest share of our admiration. An excellent critic has said of Fletcher, that he was 'mistrustful of nature.' We think rather that he was careless of her. He lets his Muse run riot too often. There is no symptom of timidity about him, (if that be meant:) he never stands on the verge of a deep thought, curbing his wit for propriety's sake. On the contrary, he seems often not to know where to stop. Hence it is that his style becomes dilated, and has sometimes an appearance of effeminacy.

If we may believe the portraits of Fletcher, there was something flushed and sanguine in his personal complexion. His eye had a fiery and eager look; his hair inclined to red; and his whole appearance is restless, and, without being heavy, is plethoric. And his verse is like himself. It is flushed and full of animal spirit. It has as much of this as Marlow's had; but there is not the same extravagance, and scarcely the same power which is to be found in the verse of the elder dramatist Fletcher, however, had a great deal of humour, and a great deal of sprightliness. There is a buoyancy in his language that is never perceptible in Massinger, nor even in the shrewder scenes of Ben Jonson;—but he had not a wit like Shakespeare, nor a tithe of his ethereal fancy. There is always something *worldly* in Fletcher, and the other poets of his time, which interferes with their airiest abstractions, and drags down the wings of their Muse. We see it in the *Witch* of Middleton, in the *Faithful Shepherdess* of Fletcher and others; whereas we do not feel it in *The Tempest,* nor in *Macbeth,* disturbing our delusion; and Oberon and Titania and her crew, even when they mix with the 'rude mechanicals,'

'Who work for bread upon Athenian stalls,'

remain to us a golden dream. They meet by moonlight upon the haunted shores of Athens, to make sport with human creatures, to discuss their tiny jealousies, to submit even to the thraldom of an earthly passion; but they still keep up their elfin state, from first to last, unsoiled by any touch of mortality.

Before we part with Fletcher, we will give the reader a passage from his tragedy of *Philaster,* that will illustrate, more than any thing we can say, both his merits and defects. Bellario (a girl in disguise) addresses the King of Sicily, on behalf of his daughter (Arethusa), who has just been married clandestinely to Philaster. The young couple come in as masquers; and thus the boy-girl intercedes:—

> Right royal Sir, I should
> Sing you an epithalamium of these lovers,
> But having lost my best airs with my fortunes,
> And wanting a celestial harp to strike
> This blessed union on, thus in glad story
> I give you all. These two fair cedar branches,
> The noblest of the mountain, where they grew
> Straitest and tallest, under whose still shades
> The worthier beasts have made their layers, and slept
> Free from the Sirian star, and the fell thunder-storke,
> Free from the clouds, when they were big with humour,
> And delivered
> In thousand spouts their issues to the earth;—
> Oh! there was none but silent Quiet there;
> Till never-pleased Fortune shot up shrubs,
> Base under-brambles to divorce these branches;
> And for a while they did so:—
> And now a gentle gale hath blown again,
> And made these branches meet and twine together,
> Never to be divided.—The God, that sings
> His holy numbers over marriage beds,
> Hath knit their noble hearts, and here they stand
> Your children, mighty king; and I have done.'

With regard to *Massinger,* there can be no doubt, we think, that he was decidedly inferior to Fletcher as a poet; but that he was a more equal writer is very possible, and he had perhaps as great a share of the mere dramatic faculty. His verse has been celebrated for its flow, we believe, by Dr Ferriar; but we cannot, we confess, perceive much beauty in it. It is not rugged and harsh, but it wants music nevertheless; it runs in a tolerably regular current, but it has seldom or never any felicitous modulations. Massinger himself has not much of the fluctuation of genius. We would not be understood to say that carelessness is the necessary concomitant of talent; but merely that Massinger rarely rises much beyond the level on which he sets out. He is less accessible to passion than Fletcher and others, and is not often either very elevated or very profound. His imagination does not soar, like Marlow's, nor penetrate like the dark subtle power of Webster. He has strength, however, and sometimes great majesty of diction. He builds up a character to a stately height, although he does not often endow it with the turns and vacillations of humanity. *Sforza* is the best which occurs to us at this moment, and is in some measure an exception to our opinion. We do not see any thing improbable in his conduct, more than is justified by the irregularities of human nature. His wild admiration and fierce injunctions are sufficiently consistent; and the way in which he rises upon us, from being the slave of a woman's beauty to the height of a hero and philosopher, has always attracted our deep regard. His return, and his remorse too, are all in character; and though Massinger's forte is by no means the pathetic, the death of Sforza is full of pathos.

> He sighs forth his breath thus—
> Yet I will not die raging; for, alas!
> My whole life was a frenzy.—
> Bury me with Marcelia,
> And let our epitaphs be—

[A]nd here death cuts short his saying; but the unfinished accents are more touching than the most elaborate and highly strained completion.

We think of *Ben Jonson,* almost as a matter of course, when we name Beaumont and Fletcher and Massinger. He was not equal to his companions in tragedy; but he was superior to them, and perhaps to almost all others, in his terse, shrewd, sterling, vigorous, comic scenes. He had a faculty between wit and humour (but more nearly allied to the latter), which has not been surpassed. His strokes were sometimes as subtle as Shakespeare's, but his arrowy wit was not feathered. His humour was scarcely so broad and obvious as Fletcher's, but it was more searching, and equally true. His tragedies were inferior to his comedies. He had a learned eye, and set down good things from the book; but he relies upon facts (if we may so speak) instead of Nature, and they do not provide for all the dilemmas to which his heroes are reduced.

Of *Middleton* it may be said, that he had a high imagination, and was an observer of manners and character; and that his verse was rich, being studded with figures and bright conceits. His play of the *Witch* is supposed by Stevens to have preceded Macbeth; and, if so, there can be no doubt but that Shakespeare made use of it. The relative merits of his witches, and those of Shakespeare, have already been decided by Mr Charles Lamb to our satisfaction. As a play, we prefer, on the whole, our author's *Women Beware of Women.* Leontio's speech, when he is returning home to his young wife, is a fine compliment to marriage.

Marston was more of a satirist than a dramatic writer. He was harsh in his style, and cynical and sceptical in his ideas of human nature. Nevertheless he was a deep and bold thinker; and he might have filled the office of a court jester, with all the privileges of a motley, for he could whip a folly well. He held up the mirror to vice, but seldom or never to virtue. He had little imagination, and less dilatation, but brings his ideas at once to a point. A fool or a braggart he could paint well, or a bitter wit; but he does little else; for his villains are smeared over, and his good people have no marks of distinction upon them. Yet there are a few touches of strange pathos in the midst of his satire; but they arise from the depth of the sentiment, rather than from the situation of things, or from any strength of passion in the speaker, either of love or pity or despair. Marston appears to us like a man who, having outlived the hopes of a turbulent youth, has learned nothing but that evil is a great principle of human nature, and mingles sparingly the tenderness of past recollections with the bitter consciousness of existing ill.

Decker had a better notion of character than most of his contemporaries; but he had not the poignancy of Marston, and scarcely the imagination of Middleton, and fell short of the extravagant power and towering style of Marlow. Perhaps, however, he had more of the qualities of a good dramatist than either. He understood the vacillations of the human mind. His men and women did not march to the end of the drama without turning to the right or to the left; but they gave themselves up to nature and their passions, and let us pleasantly into some of the secrets and inconsistencies of the actual world. His portraits of Mattheo and Bellafront (particularly the former), of Friscobaldo and Hypolito, are admirable. He is almost the only writer (even in his great time) who permits circumstances to have their full effect upon persons, and to turn them from the path on which they set out. He did not torture facts to suit a preconceived character; but varied the character according to events. He knew that to be inconsistent, and to change, was natural to man (and woman), and acted accordingly. As a specimen of the style of Decker, the reader may take the following extract. The Duke (of Milan) and his Doctor and servants are waiting for the revival of Infelicia, who has been thrown, by opiates, into a sleep.

> *Duke.* Uncurtain her.
> Softly, sweet doctor . . . You called
> For music, did you not? Oh, ho! it speaks,
> It speaks. Watch, sirs, her waking; note those sands,
> Doctor, sit down. A dukedom that should weigh

Mine own twice down, being put into one scale,
And that fond desperate boy Hypolito
Making the weight up, should not (at my hands)
Buy her i' the other, were her state more light
Than her's who makes a dowry up with alms.
Doctor,—I'll starve her on the Appenine,
Ere he shall marry her. I must confess
Hypolito is nobly born; a man,
Did not mine enemy's blood boil in his veins.
    Servant. She wakes, my lord.
    Duke. Look, Doctor Benedict.
I charge ye, on your lives, maintain for truth
Whate'er the Doctor or myself aver.
    Infel. Oh! God,—what fearful dreams!
    Servant. Lady!
    Infel. Ha!
    Duke. Girl!
Why, Infelicia!—how is't now? ha,—speak!
    Infel. I'm well. What makes this doctor here?—
I'm well.
    Duke. Thou wert not so, e'en now. Sickness'
pale hand
Laid hold on thee, e'en in the dead of feasting;
And when a cup, crowned with thy lover's health,
Had touched thy lips, a sensible cold dew
Stood on thy cheeks, as if that Death had wept
To see such beauty altered.

Chapman (the translator of Homer) was a grave and solid writer; but he did not possess much skill in tragedy, and, in his dramas at least, did not show the same poetic power as some of his rivals. Nevertheless he was a fine pedant, a stately builder of verse. In his best-known tragedy (*Bussy D'Ambois*), his hero will receive no human help, when dying; but says—

Prop me, true sword, as thou hast ever done.
The equal thought I bear of life and death,
Shall make me faint on no side: I am up
Here like a Roman statue: I will stand
Till Death hath made me marble. Oh! my fame,
Live, in despite of murder. Take thy wings,
And haste thee where the grey-eyed morn perfumes
Her rosy chariot with Sabæan spices.
Fly, where the Evening, from Iberian vales,
Takes on her swarthy shoulders Hecaté
Crown'd with a grove of oaks.
And tell them all that D'Ambois now is hasting
To the eternal dwellers.

Webster was altogether of a different stamp. He was an unequal writer; full of a gloomy power, but with touches of profound sentiment and the deepest pathos. His imagination rioted upon the grave, and frenzy and murder and 'loathed melancholy' were in his dreams. A common calamity was beneath him, and ordinary vengeance was too trivial for his Muse. His pen distilled blood; and he was familiar with the hospital and the charnel-house, and racked his brain to outvie the horrors of both. His visions were not of Heaven, nor of the air; but they came, dusky and earthy, from the tomb; and the madhouse emptied its cells to do justice to the closing of his fearful stories. There are few passages, except in Shakespeare, which have so deep a sentiment as the following. Ferdinand,

Duke of Calabria, has caused his sister (the Duchess of Malfy) to be murdered by Bosola, his creature. They are standing by the dead body.

    Bosol. Fix your eye here.
    Fer. Constantly.
    Bosol. Do you not weep?—
Other sins only speak: Murther cries out:
The element of water moistens the earth;
But blood flies upwards, and bedews the heavens.
    Fer. Cover her face: mine eyes dazzle. She died
young!
    Bosol. I think not so: her infelicity
Seemed to have years too many.
    Fer. She and I were twins:
And should I die this instant, I had lived
Her time to a minute.

We would not be supposed to assert that this writer was without his faults. On the contrary, he had several:—he had a too gloomy brain, a distempered taste; he was sometimes harsh, and sometimes dull; but he had great sentiment, and, not unfrequently, great vigour of expression. He was like Marlow, with this difference—that as Marlow's imagination was soaring, so, on the other hand, was his penetrating and profound. The one rose to the stars, the other plunged to the centre; equally distant from the bare commonplaces of the earth; they sought for thoughts and images in clouds and depths, and arrived, by different means, at the same great end. *Rowley* and *Field* are respectable names of this period; but, as they generally wrote in conjunction with others, we will not attempt to give them an independent reputation. We must not forget, however, that the former was the author of *The Witch of Edmonton,* and bore for some time the credit of *The Parliament of Love.*

Ford is sufficiently peculiar in his talent as well as his style, to call for a separate mention. His principal play, of *'Tis Pity She's a Whore,* betrays great powers of pathos, and much sweetness of versification; but they should not have been wasted on such a subject. We are not persons to put the Tragic Muse in fetters, nor to imprison her within very circumscribed limits; but there are subjects (be they fact or fiction) which are nauseous to all except distempered minds. There can be no good gained by running counter to the tastes and opinions of *all* society. There is no truth elicited, no moral enforced; and the boundaries of human knowledge can scarcely be said to be enlarged by anatomizing monstrous deformities, or expatiating upon the hideous anomalies of the species. Ford has not much strength or knowledge of character; nor has he much depth of sentiment, except in pourtraying the passion of love. In that, however, he excels almost all his contemporaries. He is remarkable, also, for his pathetic powers; yet scarcely for poetry, although his verse is generally sweet and tender. Some parts of *The Broken Heart* are as finely written as Fletcher, and Penthea herself (the true heroine, after all—a pale passion-flower) exquisitely drawn. The scene, however, in *'Tis Pity She's a Whore,* where Giovanni murders Annabella, is the finest thing that Ford has done; and there he will stand a comparison with any one, except

Shakespeare himself. *Tourneur* was the author of one or two tragedies of exceeding merit. He belonged to the age of Fletcher, and Jonson, and Decker, and was worthy of it: but his faculty, though excellent in itself, had not such a peculiar cast as to call for a separate mention. He deserved more, however, than the couplet with which one of his contemporaries has libelled his memory.

> His fame unto that pitch was only raised,
> As not to be despised, nor over-praised.

The *'Revenger's,'* and *'Atheist's Tragedies,'* should have saved him from this.

Shirley was a writer of about the same calibre as Ford, but with less pathos. And he was, moreover, the last of that bright line of poets whose glory has run thus far into the future, and must last as long as passion, and profound thought, and fancy, and imagination, and wit, shall continue to be honoured. There may be a change of fashions, and revolutions of power; but the empire of intellect will always remain the same. There is a lofty stability in genius, a splendour in a learned renown, which no clouds can obscure or extinguish. The politician and his victories may pass away, and the discoveries in science be eclipsed; but the search of the poet and the philosopher is for immutable TRUTH, and their fame will be, like their object, immortal.

We have now done with the ancients. We have endeavoured to trace, as well as we could, their individual likenesses: but they had also a general character which belonged to their age,—a pervading resemblance, in which their own peculiar distinctions were merged and lost. They were true English writers, unlatinized. They were not translators of French idioms, nor borrowers (without acknowledgment) of Roman thoughts. Their minds were not of exotic growth, nor their labours fashioned after a foreign model. Yet they were indebted to story and fable,—to science and art—and they had a tincture of learning; but it was mixed with the bloom of fresh inspiration, and subdued to the purposes of original poetry. It was not the staple, the commodity upon which these writers traded; but was blended, gracefully and usefully, with their own home-bred diction and original thought.

During the protectorate of Cromwell, the Drama lay in a state of torpidity. Whatever intellect the time possessed, was exhausted in tirades and discussions, religious and political, where cunning and violence, and narrow bigotry, alternately predominated. The gloom of an ignorant fanaticism lay heavy on the state, and oppressed it; and humour and fancy were put to flight, or sought shelter with the wandering cavaliers of the period. The spirit of the people was bent to arms. They fought for liberty or the crowned cause, as interest or opinion swayed them, while literature suffered in the contest. Milton, the greatest name of that age, was the grandest of the poets, but he had strictly no dramatic faculty. He himself speaks throughout the whole of *Samson Agonistes*,—throughout all *Paradise Lost*,—all

Comus. His own great spirit shone through the story, whatever it might be; and whatever the character, his own arguments and his own opinions were brought out and arranged in lucid order. His talent was essentially epic, not dramatic; and it was because the former prevailed, and not the latter, that we are indebted for the greatest poem that the world has ever seen.

After the restoration of the second Charles, the Drama raised its head, but evidently with little of its former character. It had lost its old inspiration, caught directly from the bright smile of Nature. It had none of that fine audacity which prompted the utterance of so many truths; none of that proud imagination which carried the poet's thoughts to so high a station. But it drew in a noisy, and meagre, and monotonous stream of verse, through artificial conduits and French strainers, which fevered and fretted for a time, but, in the end, impoverished and reduced the strength and stature of the English Drama.

Dryden is the principal name of this period, and he was foremost to overturn the system of his forefathers and substitute the French style in its stead. He vaunts, if we remember rightly, in one of his prefaces, of adding new words to our native tongue; and he certainly injured (as well as served) the cause of literature, by sanctioning by his example the prevalent taste of his time. The Restoration, perhaps, cherished and brought to life that bright phalanx of wits, Wycherley, and Congreve, and the rest; but it threw our graver dramatists into the shade. Comedy flourished, but Tragedy died; or, rather, it grew diseased, and bloated, and unnatural, and lost its strength and healthier look. It grew unwieldy, imitative, foreign. The French had studied and copied the Greek drama, and the English studied and copied the French. All fashions came at that time from Paris, and literature was not an exception. Corneille first, and afterwards Racine, who was cotemporary with Dryden, lent their help to put our native dramatists out of the play. In fact, our playwrights found it much easier to imitate the French authors successfully, than to rival their predecessors in England. To this, as well as to the force of fashion, which undoubtedly operated very strongly, may be ascribed the change in our dramatic literature. The declamatory plays of Dryden and the others do not contain a tithe of the original thought that was lavished upon many of the second-rate dramas of the Elizabethan age. The tone of tragedy itself became cold and bombastic, where it was once full of life and simplicity, and the sentiments degenerated with the style. They were heavy and commonplace, or else were pilfered from the elder writers without acknowledgment, and dressed up in gaudy and fantastic habits to suit the poor purposes of a play-mechanic. It is now well known that Rowe stole the entire plot and characters of his *Fair Penitent* from Massinger; but it is not so generally known that his production is contemptible in comparison with the original play.

Dryden was a striking and nervous writer. As a satirist, he has scarcely been equalled. As a dramatist, he had great command of language, and was full of high-sounding phrases; but these he showered indiscriminately upon all his characters, whatever their worth or occupation might be. The courtier, the tyrant, the victim, the slave, the cynic, were equally well provided with gorgeous words, and lavished them away alike upon all occasions. Dryden seems to have had a quick insight into one quarter of men's minds, and drew out their foibles and darker traits with the hand of a master; but he could not pourtray a whole character, the good and the ill, and those proper shades of the intellect, those turns and touches of passion, which have made Shakespeare immortal. On the contrary, he had an obliquity of understanding which led him to the discovery of error only. His intellectual *retina* seems to have been too small to receive the whole compass and sketch of man. If he praised, he praised in general, with little discrimination; and his writings have none of the nicer touches of affection or goodness. But, with the lash in his hand, and a knave or a fool to deal with, he was an exemplary person. No culprit could stand against him.

Of all the dramatic writers since the return of Charles, *Lee* may be considered as the first. It is true, that Otway has constructed the *best* drama, and the stage is most indebted to him; but Lee had assuredly more imagination and passion than his rival, although every play which he has written is disgraced by the most unaccountable fustian. There is great tenderness and beauty in *Theodosius*; and great power, mixed with extravagance, both in *The Rival Queens* and *The Massacre of Paris,* and others. This last-mentioned play, which is not, we apprehend, very generally known, shows a skill in character equal to Otway, to whom Lee is commonly decidedly inferior in that respect. As a specimen of the spirit of Lee's dialogue, the reader may take the following from *The Massacre of Paris.* The Duke of Guise and the Cardinal of Lorrain are speaking of Marguerite (de Valois), who has just left them in a transport of passion.

> *Car.* What have you done, my lord, to make her thus?
> *Guise.* Causes are endless for a woman's loving.
> Perhaps she has seen me break a lanc on horseback;
> Or, as my custom is, all over armed
> Plunge in the Seine or Loire; and, where 'tis swiftest,
> Plow to my point against the headlong stream.
> 'Tis certain, were my soul of that soft make
> Which some believe, she has charms, my heavenly uncle,' &c.

which he proceeds to discuss in a way to call down the rebuke of the Cardinal upon his amour,

> Not for the sin; that's as the conscience makes it,

as his Eminence says, but for the 'love.' To this Guise replies:

> *Guise.* I love, 'tis true, but most for my ambition:
> Therefore I thought to marry Marguerite.
> But, oh! that Cassiopeia in the Chair,
> The regent-mother, and that dog *Anjou,*
> Cross constellations! blast my plots ere born.

> The king, too, frowns upon me; for, last night,
> Hearing a ball was promised by the queen,
> I came to help the show; when, at the door,
> The king, who stood himself the sentry, stopped me,
> And asked me what I came for? I replied,
> To serve his majesty: he, sharp and short,
> Retorted thus—he did not need my service.
> *Car.* 'Tis plain, you must resolve to quit her;
> For I am charged to tell you, she's designed
> To be the wife of Henry of Navarre.
> 'Tis the main beam in all that mighty engine
> Which now begins to move—
> *Guise.* I have it, and methinks it looks like *D'Alva.*
> I see the very motion of his beard,
> His opening nostrils, and his dropping lids;
> I hear him croak, too, to the king and queen:
> "In Biscay's bay,—at Bayonne
> Fish for the great fish;—take no care for frogs;—
> Cut off the poppy heads;—lay the winds fast,
> And strait the waves (the people) will be still."

Otway, however, on the whole, seems to have shown in his great tragedy (*Venice Preserved*) more *dramatic* power than Lee; for although there is a good deal of commonplace in it, and more than enough of prose, that tragedy is certainly entitled to rank very high as a dramatic production. Otway's pretensions to mere poetry were very slight; and his lyrical pieces are entirely worthless. What he effected, he did by a strong contrast of character, by spirited dialogue, and by always keeping in view the main object of the play. He did not dally with his subject, nor waste his strength in figures and conceits, but went straight to the end, and kept expectation alive. It must be confessed, however, that Jaffier and Belvidera are sometimes sufficiently tedious: But Pierre is a bold and striking figure, who stands out, like a rock, from the sea of sorrow which is poured around him. He is in fact the hero of the play, and like a pleasant discord in music, saves it from the monotony which would otherwise oppress it.

Southern is less tumid than Lee and Dryden, and altogether more free from blemish, but he is a weaker writer than either. His *Isabella* possesses great pathos, and his dialogue is for the most part natural; but he has little else to boast of. *Congreve* was a wit of the first water, and the most sparkling comic writer perhaps in the circle of letters; and yet he wrote *The Mourning Bride.* We think that, with his wit, he could not have been insensible to its defects. Of *Rowe, Hughes, Hill, Howard, Murphey, Thomson, Cumberland,* &c. what can we say, but that they all wrote tragedies, which succeeded—we believe. *Addison's Cato* is as cold as a statue, and correct enough to satisfy the most fastidious of critics. We ourselves prefer his Sir Roger de Coverley: But these things are matters of taste. With regard to *Dr Johnson's Irene,* we must say that it would reflect little or no credit upon any writer whatever; and that it detracts from, rather than adds to, *his* deservedly great reputation, is, we apprehend, universally allowed. The author, we believe, once adventured an opinion, that nothing which had deserved to live was forgotten. We wonder whether, if he were alive, he would (in the present state of his play) retain his old way of thinking. These general maxims are dreadfully perilous to poets' reputations, and should not be proclaimed but with due deliberation.

Moore and *Lillo* were writers of *domestic* tragedy, and, with the exception perhaps of Heyword and Rowley, and we may add Southern, bear little resemblance to any of their predecessors. Their's was a muse born without wings, but nursed amidst sin and misfortune, and fed with tears. They neither attempted to soar, nor to penetrate below the surface, but contented themselves with common calamities, every-day sorrows. Their plays are, like the Newgate Calendar, or a Coroner's inquisition, true, but unpleasant. They give us an account of Mr Beverley, who poisoned himself but the other day, after his losses at hazard or rouge et noir; or they admit us into the condemned cell of a city apprentice, who has robbed his master. Their characters have all a London look; they frequent the city clubs, and breathe the air of traffic. These writers are as good as a newspaper—and no better. But Tragedy was surely meant for other and higher things than to bring the gallows (even with its moral) upon the stage, or to reduce to dialogue the Coroner's inquisition, or police reports. As in a picture, it is not always the truest imitator of nature who is the best painter; for an artist may make an unexceptionable map of the human face, and set down the features and furrows truly, and yet be unable to produce a grand work:—So is the minute detail of facts, however melancholy, insufficient in itself for the purposes of good tragedy. The Muse's object is not to shock and terrify, or to show what may be better seen at the scaffold or in the hospital; but it is to please as well as move us, to elevate as well as to instruct.

Of the Dramas of the present day, we have already spoken in a former Number; and we will not advert to them again: But will proceed, without more ado, to say a word on the merits of the two pieces which stand at the head of this article.

The authors of these plays may serve to illustrate the two qualities necessary to the construction of a good play. Mr Knowles, we apprehend, has the most *dramatic*—and Mr Beddoes (he is a *minor*, too, it seems!) the most *poetical* power. The poetry of the first seems to spring rather from passion, or to be struck out by the collision of events, than to be a positive and independent faculty. The language of Mr Beddoes, on the other hand, is essentially poetical. It is airy, fanciful, imaginative, and sometimes beautiful. His thoughts lie deeper, too, perhaps, than those scattered over Mr Knowles's verse; but his language is scarcely so real, and his scenes are less dexterously fashioned. In the **Brides' Tragedy,** there is a succession of delightful interviews; but in Mr Knowles's *Virginius,* there are groups; not merely dialogues between two persons, but family pictures, domestic stories, carrying a deep interest, the bustle of the forum, the lictor and his train, and the Roman father with his cluster of friends. The author, too, has contrived to excite the strong attention of the reader, and to keep it up to the end of Virginius's story. It is but

fair, however, to observe, that the intentions of one of our authors were directed principally to the stage; and the ambition of the other confined to the closet. Accordingly, in what they have aimed at, they have each, to a very considerable degree, succeeded. Indeed, the drama of Mr Beddoes betrays more promise (we ought to say, perhaps, more power) than that of almost any young poet, whose works have been before us for the first time. He does not graps his subject perhaps, nor subdue his scenes sufficiently to the end and purpose of his play; but he strews flowers in our path, and sets up bright images for our admiration, which may well serve to beguile us as we go, and to soften the austerities of criticism. Mr Knowles's play has, we are told, succeeded eminently on the stage, and with this he is probably satisfied. We may be allowed to say, that we think that it merited its success.

In order to give the reader a tolerable idea of Mr Knowles's style, we shall select a passage from one of his earlier scenes. It is the old story of the love of Icilius and Virginia, but it seems to us to be very delicately managed. Virginia is alone, having been left by her father and Dentatus, who have been talking upon the subject of her lover. The young persons, it is to be observed, are not yet acquainted with each other's regard.

> *Virginia.* I never told it yet;
> But take of me, thou gentle air, the secret—
> And ever after breather more balmy sweet.
> I love Icilius!—Yes, although to thee
> I fear to tell it, that hast neither eye
> To scan my looks, nor voice to echo me,
> Nor e'en an o'er apt ear to catch my words:
> Yet, sweet invisible confidant, my secret
> Once being thine,—I tell thee, and I tell thee
> Again—and yet again—I *love* Icilius!
> ICILIUS (*entering*).
>   *Icilius.* Virginia!—sweet Virginia!—Sure I heard
> My name pronounced. Was it by thee, Virginia?
> Thou dost not answer—then it was by thee—
> Oh! would'st thou tell me why thou named'st Icilius!
>   *Virginia.* My father is incensed with thee. Dentatus
> Has told him of the new Decemvirate,
> How they abuse their office. You, he knows,
> Have favoured their election, and he fears
> May have some understanding of their plans.
>   *Icilius.* He wrongs me then.
>   *Virginia.* I thank the Gods.
>   *Icilius.* For me?
> Virginia?—Do you thank the Gods for me?
> Your eye is moist—yet that may be for pity.
> Your hand doth tremble—that may be for fear.
> Your cheek is covered o'er with blushes. What—
> Oh! what can that be for?
>   *Virginia.* Icilius, leave me.
>   *Icilius.* Leave thee, Virginia? Oh! a word—a word
> Trembles upon my tongue, which, if it match
> The thought that moves thee now, and thou wilt let me
> Pronounce that word, to speak that thought for me,
> I'll breathe—
>   *Virginia.* Icilius, will you leave me?

Icilius. Love! love! Virginia. Love!—If I have
spoke
Thy thought aright, ne'er be it said again—
The heart requires more service than the tongue
Can, at its best, perform. Virginia!
Virginia, speak—(*Virginia covers her face with her
hands.*)
Oh! I have loved thee long:
So much the more ecstatic my delight,
To find thee mine at length.
　Virginia. My secret's yours.
Keep it, and honour it, Icilius.

pp. 19, 20.

Besides this, and besides the general good texture of the first four acts of the play, and the graceful scenes which it has, there are occasional specimens of very spirited dialogue; and the whole is as free from artifice as a play can well be. Here is an instance. It is, when Icilius, still 'harping on his daughter,' is checked by Virginius, who tells him that it is a time of war. The lover pleads, and the father softens.

Virginius. Well, well; I only meant to put it off:
We'll have the revel yet. The board shall smoke.
The cup shall sparkle, and the jest shall soar
And mock us from the roof. Will that content you?
Not'till the war be done, tho'—Yet, ere then,
Some tongue that now needs only wag, to make
The table ring, may have a tale to tell, &c.

This, once or twice, nearly degenerates, into the excess of the familiar. But Virginius's exclamation, in his insanity, when he is watching for the coming of his daughter—(she is dead)—is at once poetical and beautiful. He inquires, 'Will she not come?'—and adds,

—She will not dare—Oh! when
Did my Virginia dare—Virginia!
Is it a voice (or nothing) answers me?
I hear a sound so fine—*there's nothing lives
'Twixt it and silence.*

We have not troubled our readers with the particulars of Mr Knowles's tragedy. The story of Virginius saved (by death) from the lust and tyranny of Appius, is known to every one.

Mr Beddoes' play is founded on the fact of a manciple of one of the colleges havfing murdered a young girl whom he had privately married, in order to shield himself from the anger of his father, and to make way for a second marriage.

The following will show the way in which Mr Beddoes manages a subject that poets have almost reduced to commonplace. We thought all similes for the violet had been used up; but he gives us a new one, and one that is very delightful. Hesperus and Floribel (the young wedded lovers) are in a garden; and the husband speaks—

Hesperus.—See, here's a bower
Of eglantine with honeysuckles woven,

Where not a spark of prying light creeps in,
So closely do the sweets enfold each other.
'Tis Twilight's home; come in, my gentle love,
And talk to me. So! I've a rival here;
What's this that sleeps so sweetly on your neck?
　Floribel. Jealous so soon, my Hesperus? Look
then,
It is a bunch of flowers I pulled for you:
Here's the blue violet, like Pandora's eye,
When first it darkened with immortal life.
　Hesperus. Sweet as thy lips. Fie on those taper
fingers,
Have they been brushing the long grass aside
To drag the daisie from its hiding-place,
Where it shuns light, the Danäe of flowers,
With gold up-hoarded on its virgin-lap?
　Floribel. And here's a treasure that I found by
chance,
A lily of the valley; low it lay
Over a mossy mound, withered and weeping,
As on a fairy's grave.
　Hesperus. Of all the posy
Give me the rose, though there's a tale of blood
Soiling its name. In elfin annals old
'Tis writ, how Zephyr, envious of his love,
(The love he bare to Summer, who since then
Has weeping visited the world); once found
The baby Perfume cradled in a violet;
('Twas said the beauteous bantling was the child
Of a gay bee, that in his wantonness
Toyed with a peabud in a lady's garland);
The felon winds, confederate with him,
Bound the sweet slumberer with golden chains,
Pulled from the wreathed laburnum, and together
Deep cast him in the bosom of a rose,
And fed the fettered wretch with dew and air.

pp. 4, 5.

And there is an expression in the same scene, (where the author is speaking of sleepers' fancies, &c.)

While that wing'd song, the restless nightingale
Turns her sad heart to music—

which is perfectly beautiful.

The reader may now take a passage from the scene where Hesperus murders the girl Floribel. She is waiting for him in the Divinity path, alone, and is terrified. At last he comes; and she sighs out

—Speak! let me hear thy voice,
Tell me the joyful news!

and thus he answers—

Aye, I am come
In all my solemn pomp, Darkness and Fear,
And the great Tempest in his midnight car,
The sword of lightning girt across his thigh,
And the whole dæmon brood of night, blind Fog
And withering Blight, all these are my retainers;
How: not one smile for all this bravery?
What think you of my minstrels, the hoarse winds,
Thunder, and tuneful Discord? Hark, they play.

Well piped, methinks; somewhat too rough, perhaps.
  Flo. I know you practise on my silliness,
Else I might well be scared. But leave this mirth,
Or I must weep.
  Hes. 'Twill serve to fill the goblets
For our carousal, but we loiter here,
The bridesmaids are without; well-picked thou'lt say,
Wan ghosts of woe-begone, self slaughtered damsels
In their best winding-sheets; start not, I bid them wipe
Their gory bosoms; they'll look wondrous comely;
Our link-boy, Will o' the Wisp, is waiting too
To light us to our grave.'

          pp. 67, 68.

After some further speech she asks him what he means; and he replies—

  What mean I?   Death and murder,
Darkness and misery.   To thy prayers and shrift;
Earth gives thee back.   Thy God hath sent me for thee,
Repent and die.

She returns gentle answers to him; but in the end he kills her, and afterwards mourns thus over her body—

  Dead art thou, Florible; fair, painted earth,
And no warm breath shall ever more disport
Between those ruby lips: no, they have quaffed
Life to the dregs, and found death at the bottom,
The sugar of the draught. All cold and still;
Her very tresses stiffen in the air.
Look, what a face: had our first mother worn
But half such beauty, when the serpent came,
His heart, all malice, would have turned to love;
No hand but this, which I do think was once
Cain, the arch-murtherer's, could have acted it.
And I must hide these sweets, not in my bosom;
In the foul earth. She shudders at my grasp;
Just so she laid her head across my bosom
When first—oh villain! which way lies the grave?
  [*Exit.*

We had intended to have said something upon the occasionally bad structure of Mr Knowles's verse, and on the way in which Mr Beddoes loiters, when he should carry his readers onwards; as well as on both plays being defective towards the conclusion; but this article has already run to so great a length, that we must take an opportunity of acting upon our intentions hereafter.

Edmund Gosse (essay date 1890)

SOURCE: An introduction to *The Poetical Works of Thomas Lovell Beddoes,* J. M. Dent and Co., 1890, pp. xvii-xxxix.

[*In the following essay, Gosse provides a biographical and critical overview of Beddoes.*]

I

In a letter written to Kelsall in 1824, Beddoes makes the following remarks on the poetical situation of the moment:—

The disappearance of Shelley from the world seems, like the tropical setting of that luminary to which his poetical genius can alone be compared, with reference to the companions of his day, to have been followed by instant darkness and owl-season: whether the vociferous Darley is to be the comet, or tender full-faced L. E. L. the milk-and-watery moon of our darkness, are questions for the astrologers; if I were the literary weather-guesser for 1825 I would safely prognosticate fog, rain, blight in due succession for its dullard months.

When these words were written, the death of Byron four months previously had closed, for English readers, a romantic phase of our national verse. If Keats, Shelley, and Byron, however, were gone, it may be objected that all the other great poets of the age survived. This is true in a physical sense, but how many of them were still composing verse of any brilliant merit? Not Coleridge, long ago stricken dumb to verse; not Wordsworth, prosing on without the stimulus of inspiration; even Moore or Southey were vocal no longer; Campbell and Scott had practically taken farewell of the Muse. English poetry had been in blossom from 1795 to 1820, but the marvellous bloom was over, and the petals were scattered on the grass.

The subject of this memoir began to write at the very moment of complete exhaustion, when the age was dazzled with excess of genius, and when the nation was taking breath for a fresh burst of song. He had the misfortune to be a young man when Keats and Shelley were just dead, and when Tennyson and Browning were schoolboys. In the words which have just been quoted he has given a humorous view of the time, which shows that, at the age of twenty-one, he had grasped its characteristics. Among his exact contemporaries there was no one, except Praed, who was some months his senior, who inherited anything like genius. Beddoes was four years younger than Hood, two years older than Elizabeth Barrett. No other name has survived worthy of being even named beside his as a poet, except Macaulay, with whom he has nothing in common. He was early dissuaded from the practice of verse, and all that he has left, which is of any sterling value, was composed between 1821, when he published *The Improvisatore,* and 1826, when he practically finished **Death's Jest Book.** He belongs to those five years of exhaustion and mediocrity, and the effect of having to write at such a period, there can be no doubt, dwarfed, restrained, and finally quenched his poetical faculty. It is not saying much, yet it is mere justice to insist, that Beddoes was, during those five years, the most interesting talent engaged in writing English verse.

II

Thomas Lovell Beddoes was born in Rodney place, Clifton, on the 20th of July, 1803. He was the eldest son of a celebrated physician, Dr. Thomas Beddoes, who died in 1809, and left his son to the guardianship of Davies Giddy, afterwards known as Sir Davies Gilbert, P.R.S., who lived for thirty years longer. The boy's mother, Anna, was a sister of Maria Edgeworth, the novelist. He was educated at Bath Grammar School and at the Charterhouse, where, as early as 1817, he began to write verses. Of his character at school, where he showed signs at once of that eccentricity and independence of manners which were to distinguish him through life, a schoolfellow, Mr. C. D. Bevan, has preserved a very entertaining account, from which this short extract may be given:—

> He knew Shakespeare well when I first saw him, and during his stay at the Charterhouse made himself master of all the best English dramatists, from Shakespeare's time, or before it, to the plays of the day. He liked acting, and was a good judge of it, and used to give apt though burlesque imitations of the popular actors, particularly of Kean and Macready. Though his voice was harsh and his enunciation offensively conceited, he read with so much propriety of expression and manner that I was always glad to listen: even when I was pressed into the service as his accomplice, or his enemy, or his love, with a due accompaniment of curses, caresses, or kicks, as the course of his declamation required. One play in particular, Marlow's tragedy of *Dr. Faustus,* excited my admiration, and was fixed on my memory in this way.

At school he came under the influence of Fielding, and wrote a novel, entitled *Cynthio and Bugboo,* the loss of which we need scarcely deplore, as, according to the same authority, it was marked by "all the coarseness, little of the wit, and none of the truth of his original." The fragments of his schoolboy verse, in particular the rhapsody of "Alfarabi," display a very singular adroitness in the manufacture of easy blank verse, and precocious tendency to a species of mocking metaphysics, both equally unlike a child. In July, 1819, while still at Charterhouse, a sonnet of his was printed in the *Morning Post.* On the 1st of May, 1820, Beddoes proceeded to Oxford, and was entered a commoner at Pembroke, which had been his father's college.

Although he had been a forward boy at school, Beddoes passed through Oxford without any academic distinction. He was a freshman of eighteen when, in 1821, he published his first volume, *The Improvisatore,* of which he afterwards carefully tried to destroy every copy. In 1822 he published, as another thin pamphlet, *The Brides' Tragedy,* which has also become extremely rare. These two little books, the work of an undergraduate less than twenty years of age, are the only ones which Beddoes ever published. The remainder of his writings, whether lyrical or dramatic, were issued posthumously, not less than thirty years later. *The Brides' Tragedy* attracted some notice in literary circles; it secured for the young Oxford poet the friendship of a man much older than himself, but of kindred tastes, Bryan Waller Procter. The dramatic poems of "Barry Cornwall," of which "Mirandola" was then the latest, had been appearing in rapid succession, and their amiable author was a person of considerable influence. It was Procter who, in 1823, introduced Beddoes to Thomas Forbes Kelsall, a young lawyer practising at Southampton. It had been thought well that Beddoes, who was sadly behind-hand with his studies, should go down to this quiet

town to read for his bachelor's degree, and he remained at Southampton for some months, in great intimacy with Kelsall, and forming no other acquaintance.

While he was at Southampton, Beddoes wrote a great deal of desultory verse, almost all of a dramatic order; to this period belong *The Second Brother* and *Torrismond,* among other fragments. Already he was seized with that inability to finish, that lack of an organic principle of poetical composition, which were to prevent him from mounting to those heights of which his facility and brilliancy seem to promise him an easy ascent. The death of Shelley appears to have drawn his attention to the genius of that writer, by which he was instantly fascinated, and, as it were, absorbed. Outside the small circle of Shelley's personal friends, Beddoes was perhaps the first to appreciate the magnitude of his merit, as he was certainly the earliest to imitate Shelley's lyrical work. His letters to Procter and Kelsall are full of evidence of his overmastering passion for Shelley, and it was to Beddoes, in the first instance, that the publication of that writer's *Posthumous Poems* was due. In the winter of 1823 Beddoes started a subscription with his two friends, and corresponded with John Hunt on the subject. They promised to take 250 copies, but Hunt said that Mrs. Shelley ought to have some profit. This seemed hardly fair to Beddoes; "for the twinkling of this very distant chance we, three poor honest admirers of Shelley's poetry, are certainly to pay." At this time Beddoes was writing two romantic dramas, *Love's Arrow Poisoned* and *The Last Man,* both founded on the tragic model of Webster, Cyril Tourneur, and Middleton. Of these plays not very much was ever written, and still less is now in existence. Of *The Last Man* he writes, in February 1824: "There are now three first acts in my drawer. When I have got two more, I shall stitch them together, and stick the sign of a fellow tweedling a mask in his fingers, with 'good entertainment for man and ass' understood."

The year 1824 he spent in London, Oxford, and Bristol. Already his eccentric shyness had grown upon him. He writes to Kelsall from his lodgings in Devereux Court, Temple, March 29, 1824:—

> Being a little shy and not a little proud perhaps, I have held back and never made the first step towards discovering my residence or existence to any of my family friends [in London]. In consequence I have lived in a deserted state, which I could hardly bear much longer without sinking into that despondency on the brink of which I have sate so long. Your cheerful presence at times (could we not mess together occasionally?) would set me up a good deal, but perhaps you had better not draw my heavy company on your head. . . . I met an intelligent man who had lived at Hampstead, seen Keats, and was read in his and the poems of Shelley. On my mentioning the former by accident to him, he complimented me on my similarity of countenance; he did not think much of K.'s genius, and therefore did not say it insincerely or sycophantically. The same was said by Procter and Taylor before.

Mrs. Procter, who had known both poets, made the same remark about Beddoes to myself; but she added that she never saw in the latter the extraordinary look of inspiration which was ocasionally to be detected in the great eyes of Keats.

In the summer of 1824 Beddoes was hastily called to Florence by the illness of his mother, who was living there. She died before he could reach her, but he spent some weeks there, saw Walter Savage Landor, and then returned to Clifton in charge of his sisters. In October of the same year he began to study German, a language then but little known in this country. He attacked it languidly at first, then with ever-increasing eagerness and zest. But the Elizabethan drama was still his principal delight, and he studied it, even in its least illustrious forms, with extraordinary closeness and delight. Writing to Kelsall from Clifton (January 11, 1825), he remarks, apropos of revival of "The Fatal Dowry" of Massinger:—

> Say what you will, I am convinced the man who is to awaken the drama must be a bold trampling fellow—no creeper into worm-holes—no reviver even, however good. These reanimations are vampire-cold. Such ghosts as Marloe, Webster, etc., are better dramatists, better poets, I dare say, than any contempoary of ours, but they are ghosts—the worm is in their pages,—and we want to see something that our great-grandsires did not know. With the greatest reverence for all the antiquities of the drama, I still think that we had better beget than revive, attempt to give the literature of this age an idiosyncracy and spirit of its own, and only raise a ghost to gaze on, not to live with. Just now the drama is a haunted ruin. I am glad that you are awakening to a sense of Darley. He must have no little perseverance to have gone through so much of that play; it will perchance be the first star of a new day.

The result of so much meditation on the drama was the composition of more fragments. *The Second Brother, Torrismond,* and *The Last Man* occupied Beddoes during the winter and spring of 1824-5. But none of these approached completion. He then planned the publication of a volume of lyrics, to be entitled "Outidana, or Effusions, amorous, pathetic, and fantastical," which was to include most of the miscellaneous verses reprinted in this edition, and others which are now lost. On the 25th of May, 1825, he took an ordinary bachelor's degree at Oxford. He writes to Kelsall from Pembroke College, on the 8th of June, announcing for the first time the most celebrated of his writings:—

> Oxford is the most indolent place on earth. I have fairly done nothing in the world but read a play or two of Schiller, Æschylus and Euripides,—you I suppose read German now as fast as English. I do not finish that 2nd Brother you saw but am thinking of a very Gothic-styled tragedy for which I have a jewel of a name:—
>
> *Death's Jestbook—*
>
> of course no one will ever read it. Mr. Milman (our poetry professor) has made me quite unfashionable here by denouncing me as one of a 'villainous school.' I wish him another son.

He now suddenly determined to abandon literature, which had suggested itself to him as a profession, and take up the study of medicine. We find him, therefore, on the 19th of July, 1825, at Hamsburg, "sitting on a horse-hair sofa, looking over the Elbe, with his meerschaum at his side, full of Grave, and abundantly prosaic. Tomorrow, according to the prophecies of the diligence, he will set out for Hanover, and by the end of this week mein Herr Thomas will probably be a Doctor of the university of Göttingen." This, however, was rather premature. He did not become a doctor until much later. It is important to observe that the exodus to Germany thus casually and nonchalantly taken involved nothing less, as it proved, than a complete alteration in all his habits. Except for very few and brief visits, he did not return to England for the rest of his life, and he so completely adopted the language and thoughts of a German student as almost to cease to be an Englishman.

At Göttingen the celebrated man of science, Prof. Blumenbach, became the most intimate friend of Beddoes. The latter threw himself with the utmost ardour into the study of physiology and medicine. He did not, however, at first abandon his design of becoming an English dramatic poet. He writes to Kelsall (Dec. 4, 1825):—

> I am perhaps somewhat independent, and have a competence adequate to my philosophical desires. There are reasons why I should reject too much practice if it did intrude; really I am much more likely to remain a patientless physician. And now I will end this unnecessary subject, by telling you that *Death's Jestbook* goes on like the tortoise, slow and sure; I think it will be entertaining, very unamiable, and utterly unpopular. Very likely it may be finished in the spring or autumn.

His misanthropy, for it almost deserves so harsh a name, grew upon him. "I feel myself," he wrote, "in a measure alone in the world and likely to remain so, for, from the experiments I have made, I fear I am a non-conductor of friendship, a not-very-likeable person, so that I must make sure of my own respect, and occupy that part of the brain which should be employed in imaginative attachments in the pursuit of immaterial and unchanging good." In April, 1826, *Death's Jest Book* is still lying "like a snow-ball, and I give it a kick every now and then, out of mere scorn and ill-humour; the 4th act, and I may say the 5th are more than half done, so that at last it will be a perfect mouse, but such doggerell!" None the less did he anticipate that the poem would come "like an electric shock among the small critics." In October, 1826, it is "done and done for, its limbs being as scattered and unconnected as those of the old gentleman whom Medea minced and boiled young. I have tried 20 times at least to copy it fair." He intended at this time to send the MS. to Kelsall and Procter to be seen through the press, but he delayed until he could bring the poem himself to London.

His monotonous existence in Göttingen was broken in the spring of 1828 by a visit of a few days to England, where he took his degree of M.A. at Oxford, and hurried back to Germany. Meanwhile he had left *Death's Jest Book* with Procter and Kelsall for publication, but they decided that it must be "revised and improved." In his fifth year in Germany, "having already been at Göttingen the time which it is allowed for any student to remain there," he transferred his residence to Würzburg, in Bavaria; "a very clever professor of medicine and capital midwife brought me here, and a princely hospital." In 1831 there was again some abortive talk of publishing *Death's Jest Book.* About this time Beddoes became more and more affected by opinions of the extreme radical order; he subscribed towards "the support of candidates who were professed supporters of the Reform Bill," and he began to affect a warm personal interest in certain revolutionary Poles who had taken up their abode in Würzburg. He continued his medical studies with great thoroughness, and in the summer of 1832 he took his degree of doctor of medicine in the university, being now in his thirtieth year. He was more and more mixed up in political intrigue, and on the 25th of September, 1832, he somewhat obscurely says:—

> The absurdity of the King of Bavaria has cost me a good deal, as I was obliged to oppose every possible measure to the arbitrary illegality of his conduct, more for the sake of future objects of his petty royal malice than my own, of course in vain.

He was soon after obliged to fly, "banished by that ingenious Jackanapes of Bavaria," in common with several of his distinguished Würzburg friends. He took refuge, first in Strassburg, then in Zurich. He brought with him to Switzerland a considerable reputation as a physiologist, for Blumenbach, in a testimonial which exists, calls him the best pupil he ever had. It appears that he now assumed, what he afterwards dropped, the degree of M.D., and had some practice as a physician in the town of Zurich. In 1835 the surgeon Schoenlien proposed Beddoes to the medical faculty of the University as professor of Comparative Anatomy, and the latter unanimously seconded him. His election, however, was not ratified, according to one of his letters, for political reasons, according to another because he was found to be ineligible, from his having published nothing of a medical character. He spent several healthy and tolerably happy years in Zurich, "what," he says in March, 1837, "with a careless temper and the pleasant translunary moods I walk and row myself into upon the lakes and over the Alps of Switzerland"; and once more, as he quaintly put it, he began "to brew small ale out with the water of the fountain of the horse's foot," working again on the revision of *Death's Jest Book.* He also began to prepare for the press a collection of his narrative and lyrical poems, to be called *The Ivory Gate.* In 1838 he was engaged in translating Grainger's work on the Spinal Cord into German.

He had spent six years at Zurich, and was beginning to feel that city to have become his settled home, when, on the 8th of September, 1839, a political catastrophe destroyed his peace of mind. A mob of six thousand peasants, "half of them unarmed, and the other half armed with scythes, dung-forks and poles, led on by a mad fanatic and aided by some traitors in the cabinet, and many in the town," stormed Zurich, and upset the liberal government

of the canton. Beddoes observed the riot from a window, and witnessed the murder of the minister Hegetochweiber, who was one of his best friends. He wrote: "In consequence of this state of things, in which neither property nor person is secure, I shall find it necessary to give up my present residence entirely. Indeed, the dispersion of my friends and acquaintance, all of whom belonged to the liberal party, renders it nearly impossible for me to remain longer here." He loitered on, however, until March, 1840, when his life was threatened by the insurgents, and he was helped to fly from Zurich in secret by a former leader of the liberal party, whom he had befriended, a man of the name of Jasper.

It is probable that the seven years Beddoes spent at Zurich formed the happiest portion of his life. He was never to experience tranquillity again. The next few years were spent in what seems an aimless wandering through the length and breadth of Central Europe. Little is known of his history from this time forward. In 1841 he was in Berlin, where he formed an acquaintanceship with a young Dr. Frey, who remained his intimate friend to the last. In 1842 he made a brief visit to England. In 1843 he went to Baden in Aargau, where he seems to have stored his library, and, so far as Beddoes henceforth could be said to have a home, that home was in this little town of Northern Switzerland, not far from Zurich. He spent the winter of 1844 at Giessen, attracted thither by Liebig and his famous school of chemistry, after having lodged through the summer and autumn at Basel, Strassburg, Mannheim, Mainz, and Frankfurt in succession. At Giessen a little of the poetic fervour returned to him, and it was here that he wrote "The Swallow leaves her Nest" and "In Lover's Ear a wild Voice cried." But most of his verse now was written in German. He says (Nov. 13, 1844): "Sometimes to amuse myself I write a German lyric or epigram, right scurrilous, many of which have appeared in the Swiss and German papers, and some day or other I shall have them collected and printed for fun." It is needless to say that he never issued this collection, and the German poems, doubtless signed with a pseudonym or else anonymous, have never been traced.

In August, 1846, he came to England for a considerable stay. Intending to remain six weeks, he loitered on for ten months. His friends, few of whom had seen him for more than twenty years, found him altered beyond all recognition. He had become extremely rough and cynical in speech, and eccentric in manners. I am informed by a member of his family that he arrived at the residence of one of his relations, Cheney Longville, near Ludlow, astride the back of a donkey. He complained of neuralgia, and for six out of the ten months which he spent in England, he was shut up in a bedroom, reading and smoking, and admitting no visitor. In April, 1847, he went down to Fareham, to stay with Mr. Kelsall, and this greatly brightened him up. From Fareham he proceeded in May to London, and there he met with his old friends the Procters. From Mrs. Procter the present writer received a graphic account of his manners and appearance. She told me that his eccentricities were so marked that they almost gave the impression of insanity, but that closer observation showed them to be merely the result of a peculiar fancy, entirely unaccustomed to restraint, and of the occasional rebound of spirits after a period of depression. The Procters found Beddoes a most illusive companion. He would come to them uninvited, but never if he had been asked, or if he feared to meet a stranger. On one occasion, Mrs. Procter told me, they had asked Beddoes to dine with them, and proceed afterwards to Drury Lane Theatre. He did not come, and they dined alone. On approaching the theatre, they saw Beddoes in charge of the police, and on inquiry found that he had just been arrested for trying to put Drury Lane on fire. The incendiary, however, had used no more dangerous torch than a five-pound note, and Mr. Procter had little difficulty in persuading the police that this was much more likely to hurt the pocket of Mr. Beddoes than the rafters of the theatre.

In June, 1847, Beddoes returned to Frankfurt, where he lived until the spring of 1848 with a baker named Degen, who was then about nineteen years of age,—"a nice-looking young man dressed in a blue blouse, fine in expression, and of a natural dignity of manner," Miss Zoë King describes him. While Beddoes was in Frankfurt his blood became poisoned from the virus of a dead body entering a slight wound in his hand. This was overcome, but it greatly weakened and depressed him. For six months he would see no one but Degen. He complained of disgust of life, and declared that his republican friends in Germany had deserted him. He persuaded Degen to become an actor, and he occupied himself in teaching him English and other accomplishments, cutting himself off from all other company. At this time "he had let his beard grow, and looked like Shakespeare." In May, 1848, he left Frankfurt, inducing Degen to accompany him, and the two companions wandered together through Germany and Switzerland. In Zurich Beddoes chartered the theatre for one night, to give his friend an opportunity of appearing in the part of Hotspur. For about six weeks, so far as it is possible to discover, Beddoes was tolerably happy. But he was separated from Degen at Basel, where Beddoes took a room, in a condition of dejected apathy that was pitiful to witness, at the Cicogne Hôtel. Here very early nextmorning he inflicted a deep wound on his right leg, with a razor. "Il etait miserable,—il a voula se tuer," as the waiter who attended upon him said afterwards to Miss Zoë King. He was, however, removed with success to the Town Hospital, where his friends Dr. Frey and Dr. Ecklin waited upon him. He had a pleasant private room, looking into a large garden. He communicated with his English friends, being very anxious to allay all suspicion. He wrote to his sister: "In July I fell with a horse in a precipitous part of the neighbouring hills, and broke my left leg all to pieces." He begged no one in England to be anxious, and his version of the catastrophe was accepted without question. The leg, however, was obstinate in recovery, for the patient stealthily tore off the bandages, and eventually gangrene of the foot set in. On the 9th of September it became necessary to amputate the leg below the knee-joint; this

operation was very successfully performed by Dr. Ecklin. Beddoes seems to have been cheerful during the autumn months, and Degen came back to Basel, lodging near him in the town. The poet gave up all suicidal attempts, and it was considered that his mind on this matter was completely cured. His bed was covered with books, and he conversed and wrote freely about literature and science. He talked of going to Italy when he was convalescent, and in December he walked out of his room twice. The first time he went out into the town, however, on the 26th of January, 1849, he seems to have used his authority as a physician to procure the deadly poison called Kurara; in the course of the evening Dr. Ecklin was suddenly called to his bedside, and found the poet lying on his back insensible, with the following extraordinary note, written in pencil, folded on his bosom. It was addressed to one of the oldest of his English friends, Mr. R. Phillips:—

MY DEAR PHILLIPS,

I am food for what I am good for—worms. I have made a will here, which I desire to be respected; and add the donation of £20 to Dr. Ecklin my physician. Thanks for all kindnesses. Borrow the £200. You are a good and noble man, and your children must look sharp to be like you.

Yours, if my own, ever

T. L. B.

Love to Anna, Henry,—the Beddoes of Longvile and Zoë and Emmeline King. Also to Kelsall, whom I beg to look at my MSS. and print or not as *he* thinks fit. I ought to have been, [among a] variety of other things, a good poet. Life was too great a bore on one peg, and that a bad one. W. Beddoes must have a case (50 bottles) of Champagne Moet 1847 growth. Buy for Dr. Ecklin above mentioned Reade's best stomach-pump.

He died at 10 p.m. the same night, and was buried under a cypress in the cemetery of the hospital. The circumstances of his death, now for the first time published, were ascertained by Miss Zoë King, who visited Basel in 1857, and saw Degen, Frey, Ecklin, and the people at the Cicogne Hôtel. After some delay, the various MSS. of Beddoes were placed in Kelsall's hands, and that faithful and admirable friend published the version of **Death's Jest Book,** which seemed to him the most attractive, in 1850; and this he followed, in 1851, by the *Miscellaneous Poems,* with an unsigned Memoir. These two volumes form the only monument hitherto raised to the memory of the unfortunate poet. The reception which was given to them was respectful, and even sympathetic. It may be sufficient here to give one instance of it, which has never been made public. Miss Zoë King, in a letter to Kelsall, says: "I was at the Lakes with my uncle Edgeworth just after receiving the **Death's Jest Book,** and was very much pleased to lend it to Mr. Tennyson. He was just arrived (and at a distance from us) on his wedding tour, so that I merely *saw* him. He returned the book with a few lines . . . rating it highly."

III

It is not in the fragments that Beddoes has left behind him that we can look for the work of a full-orbed and serene poetical genius. It would be a narrow definition indeed of the word "poet" which should exclude him, but he belongs to the secondary order of makers. He is not one of those whose song flows unbidden from their lips, those born warblers whom neither poverty, nor want of training, nor ignorance, can restrain from tuneful utterance. He belongs to the tribe of scholar-poets, to the educated artists in verse. In every line that he wrote we can trace the influence of existing verse upon his mind. He is intellectual-rather than spontaneous. Nor, even within this lower range, does his work extend far on either hand. He cultivates a narrow field, and his impressions of life and feeling are curiously limited and monotonous. At the feast of the Muses he appears bearing little except one small savoury dish, some cold preparation, we may say, of olives and anchovies, the strangeness of which has to make up for its lack of importance. Not every palate enjoys this *hors d'œuvre,* and when that is the case, Beddoes retires; he has nothing else to give. He appeals to a few literary epicures, who, however, would deplore the absence of this oddly flavoured dish as much as that of any more important *pièce de resistance.*

As a poet, the great defect of Beddoes has already been alluded to,—his want of sustained invention, his powerlessness in evolution. He was poor just where, two hundred years earlier, almost every playwright in the street had been strong, namely, in the ability to conduct an interesting story to a thrilling and appropriate close. From this point of view his boyish play, **The Brides' Tragedy,** is his only success. In this case a story was developed with tolerable skill to a dramatic ending. But, with one exception, he never again could contrive to drag a play beyond a certain point; in the second or third act its wings would droop, and it would expire, do what its master would. These unfinished tragedies were like those children of Polynesian dynasties, anxiously trained, one after another, in the warm Pacific air, yet ever doomed to fall, on the borders of manhood, by the breath of the same mysterious disease. **Death's Jest Book** is but an apparent exception. This does indeed appear in the guise of a finished five-act play; but its completion was due to the violent determination of its author, and not to legitimate inspiration. For many years, in and out of season, Beddoes, who had pledged his whole soul to the finishing of this book, assailed it with all the instruments of his art, and at last produced a huge dramatic Frankenstein, which, by adroit editing, could be forced into the likeness of a tragedy. But no play in literature was less of a spontaneous creation, or was further from achieving the ideal of growing like a tree.

From what Beddoes was not, however, it is time to pass to what he was. In several respects, then, he was a poetical artist of consummate ability. Of all the myriad poets and poeticules who have tried to recover the lost magic of the tragic blank verse of the Elizabethans, Beddoes has come nearest to success. If it were less indifferent to human interests of every ordinary kind, the beauty of his dramatic verse would not fail to fascinate. To see how strong it is, how picturesque, how admirably fashioned, we have only to compare it with what others have done in the same style, with the tragic verse, for instance, of Barry Cornwall, of Talfourd, of Horne. But Beddoes is what he himself has called "a creeper into worm-holes." He attempts nothing personal; he follows the very tricks of Marston and Cyril Tourneur like a devoted disciple. The passions with which he invariably deals are remote and unfamiliar; we may go further, and say that they are positively obsolete. In another place I have compared Beddoes in poetry with the Helsche Breughel in painting. He dedicates himself to the service of Death, not with a brooding sense of the terror and shame of mortality, but from a love of the picturesque pageantry of it, the majesty and sombre beauty, the swift, theatrical transitions, the combined elegance and horror that wait upon the sudden decease of monarchs. His medical taste and training encouraged this tendency to dwell on the physical aspects of death, and gave him a sort of ghastly familiarity with images drawn from the bier and the charnel-house. His attitude, however, though cold and cynical, was always distinguished, and in his wildest flights of humour he escapes vulgarity. In this he shows himself a true poet. As we read his singular pages, we instinctively expect to encounter the touch of prose which, in Landor's phrase, will precipitate the whole, yet it never comes. Beddoes often lacks inspiration, but distinction he can never be said to lack.

As a lyrist he appears, on the whole, to rank higher than as a dramatist. Several of his songs, artificial as they are, must always live, and take a high place in the literature of artifice. As a writer of this class of poem his experience of the Elizabethans was further kindled and largely modified by the example of Shelley. Nevertheless his finest songs could never be taken for the work of Shelley, or, indeed, attributed to any hand but his own. Among them, the song in **Torrismond** is perhaps the sweetest and the most ingenious; "Dream-Pedlary" the most exquisite. The "Song of the Stygian Naiades" and "Old Adam, the Carrion Crow" are instances of fancy combined with grisly humour, of a class in which Beddoes has no English competitor. The Harpagus ballad in the fourth act of **Death's Jest Book,** and "Lord Alcohol," which is here for the first time printed, are less known, but no less vivid and extraordinary. Beddoes possesses great sense of verbal melody, a fastidious ear, and considerable, though far from faultless, skill in metrical architecture. His boyish volume, called *The Improvisatore,* which is here presented to the readers of Beddoes practically for the first time, shows, despite its crudity, that these gifts were early developed. To say more in this place is needless. Those readers who are able to take pleasure in poetry so grim, austere, and abnormal, may safely be left to discover its specific charms for themselves.

Barnette Miller (essay date 1903)

SOURCE: "Thomas Lovell Beddoes," in *Thomas Lovell Beddoes*, Vol. 11, No. 3, July, 1903, pp. 306-36.

[In the following essay, Miller discusses the defining characteristics of Beddoes's works, concluding that his "genius is undeniable, but it is limited in scope."]

Among minor English poets, there is no more striking figure than Thomas Lovell Beddoes, a man of unique personality and versatile talents. Between 1821-26, the five years of mediocrity which followed the deaths of Keats, Shelley, and Byron, and preceded the outburst of song in the Victorian Era, it is claimed by Mr. Edmund Gosse that "Beddoes was the most interesting talent engaged in writing English verse." It was during these years of exhaustion that he produced his best poems; in later life he ceased to write except as a pastime. Mr. Gosse points out, furthermore, that the effect of writing at such a period "dwarfed, restrained, and finaly quenched Beddoes's poetical faculty." He is a striking example of a poet who, at first glance, appears akin to his age in point of time only, and apparently utterly dissimilar in spirit and intellect, a curious instance of the effect of heredity, enhanced by circumstances and study. Beddoes was, moreover, heir to a sufficient patrimony to preclude the necessity of a systematic pursuit of one profession; it is the oft-repeated story of a man possessing very rare gifts, but so undisciplined by nature that he obeyed no law except his own whims. Had he followed his first inclination toward literature, or his later bent toward science, in either domain he might have gained a lasting name; but he was in turn littérateur, scientist, philosopher, politician; as he calls himself, "a moderate dabbler in many waters," squandering his mental gifts in order to satisfy an insatiable greed for knowledge of many things. Beddoes's poetical genius was not sufficient to impel spontaneous song, and the reason of his desultory efforts at verse-making is a small body of poems, narrow in range, but often exquisite in lyrical beauty and technical perfection.

Thomas Lovell Beddoes was born in Rodney Place, Clifton, on the 20th of July, 1803. He was the eldest son of Dr. Thomas Beddoes and Anna Edgeworth, the sister of Maria Edgeworth, the novelist. Dr. Beddoes was a man of vigorous intellect and talent, eminent both as a physician and as an author. His writings include several scientific treatises, a poem on "The Conquests of Alexander," a moral tale called "Isaac Jenkins," a work on Calculus, and a number of political brochures. The son inherited his father's creative faculty, his love of science, and his distaste for all established conventions. With strange fatality, he seems also to have inherited his father's lack of sustained effort in one direction. Beddoes realized this defect in his own nature; he writes from Hamburg in July, 1825: "What my intentions further may be I cannot say precisely, as I am not altogether endowed with the polar virtue of perseverance, and the needle with which I embroidered my cloth of life has not been rubbed with the magnet of steady determination."

At the time of Dr. Beddoes's death, in 1809, his son was intrusted to the guardianship of Sir Davies Gilbert, P.R.S. The young boy was first sent to Bath Grammar School, later to the Charterhouse. A minute description of Beddoes's personal appearance and characteristics at this period of his life, given by his schoolfellow and fag, Mr. C. D. Bevan, is quoted by Thomas Kelsall in the *Fortnightly* of July, 1872. He is described as "a youth with a shrewd, sarcastic face, of great humor, with propensity to mischief, and impatient of authority." In later life Beddoes is said to have looked like Keats. Among the various incidents of Beddoes's schooldays, related by Mr. Bevan, there is one that occurred when he was only fourteen, which shows both the precocity of the youth and the grim humor which so characterized his later life. A locksmith connected with the school had placed an inferior lock on Beddoes's bookcase, and had demanded an exorbitant price. In revenge, Beddoes wrote a burlesque, in which he represented the death of the locksmith, "disturbed by horror and remorse for his sins in the matter of the lock," and the funeral procession, interrupted by fiends who bore the soul of the transgressor to eternal torment. This farce was acted by Beddoes in the presence of the smith so realistically that the latter was overcome by terror. Mr. Bevan says that Beddoes was not a good student of the classics, but was at a very early age familiar with English literature, especially dramatic poetry. He was not popular among his schoolfellows, and yet he enjoyed a supremacy over them, due both to fear and to respect.

In 1820 Beddoes entered Pembroke College, Oxford, and in 1825 received the degree of A.B. He did not distinguish himself in college, but seemed quite content with mediocrity, submitting himself to no law or system of study. During his residence at Pembroke he formed a friendship with Thomas Kelsall, a lawyer, who remained his most constant friend throughout his life, and became his literary executor after his death. It is due to Mr. Kelsall primarily that the poet is known to the public.

After receiving the degree of A.B., Beddoes turned to the study of the German language and literature, "leaning to ultra-liberty and rationalism," with a hatred of old-time customs and institutions. This love of German thought and feeling led him, in 1825, to visit Germany. Here he spent the following four years, studying physics and philosophy, at the University of Göttingen. He writes from Göttingen that he was "never better employed, never so happy, never so well satisfied"—a great improvement on the melancholy mood to which he had been prey in the previous year. A letter from London, March 29, 1824, says: "The truth is, that being a little shy and not a little proud perhaps, I have held back and never made the first step toward discovering my residence or existence to any of my family friends; in consequence I have lived in a deserted state that I could hardly bear much longer without sinking into that despondency on the brink of which I have sate so long." It is almost certain that at a very early age Beddoes had been separated from his family, and from the beginning of his college course his letters show little trace of intercourse with his mother or sisters. The bibliography is so limited that it is impossible to judge with any degree of accuracy whether this estrangement grew from indifference on Beddoes's part, from a positive breach, or from his habitual dislike to companionship. His loneliness is shown in a letter dated Göttingen, Dec. 4th, 1825, to Mr. Kelsall: "I feel myself in a measure alone in the world and likely to remain so, for from the experiments I have made I fear I am a nonconductor of friendship, a not-very-likable person, so that I must make sure of my own respect and occupy that part of the brain which should be employed in imaginative attachments, in the pursuit of immaterial and unchanging good."

At the University of Göttingen Prof. Blumenbach, the first great German geologist, was one of his instructors, and in speaking of Beddoes said that "his talent exceeded that of any other student who received instruction from me during my professorship." Prof. Blumenbach's professorship covered a period of more than fifty years, so that these words indicate that Beddoes must have been an unusually promising student.

Beddoes returned to England in the spring of 1828, to receive his degree of A.M., remaining only a short time. Of this visit he writes, in a letter to Mr. Kelsall from Clifton, that he does not expect to spend more than two days in London, for "nothing can equal my impatience and weariness of this dull, idle, pampered isle." Already he had become infatuated with German thought and learning, and preferred the country of his adoption to his native land. In 1829 or 1830, he went to Würzburg, and there, in 1832, he received the degree of M.D. He was offered the professorship of Comparative Anatomy at the University of Zurich in 1835; but this offer was afterwards withdrawn, since he had published no scientific treatise. In a letter written about this time he states that he had no desire to write the required thesis. Beddoes seems to have toiled unceasingly in the pursuit of knowledge, not for professional distinction or financial gain, but for the personal satisfaction and pleasure which he derived from the mere acquisition. His innate scholarly instinct was fostered by German university life until his meditative faculty almost entirely absorbed his creative powers.

After his arrival in Würzburg, he began to sympathize with the revolutionary tendencies and democratic movement in Switzerland, aiding with his "pen and purse," until his residence there became endangered, and he was forced to flee. He took refuge in Strasburg in 1832, then in Zurich in 1833, where he remained seven years, probably the happiest of his life.

After 1825, Beddoes's intercourse with his friends in England almost ceased. His love of solitude and aversion for companionship increased to such an extent that he was misanthropic, and probably mildly insane. His complete adoption of Germany and Switzerland as his home had further estranged him in thought and feeling from England. In August, 1846, he spent ten months in England, and his friends scarcely recognized him. He was "rough and cynical in speech, and eccentric in manners." Six out of the ten months he refused to see any one. Mr. Gosse quotes Mrs. Proctor as having said that "his eccentricities at this time gave the appearance of insanity, but closer observation showed them to be the result of a peculiar fancy, unaccustomed to restraint." However, in an unsigned article published in the *Athenæum* of December 27, 1890, Mrs. Proctor is reported to have said that she considered Beddoes insane at this time.

In 1848 Beddoes writes that he has decided to return to England permanently, but he became poisoned by the virus from a dead body before he was able to carry out his intention, and the ensuing illness prevented his return. His long illness greatly depressed him. In July of the same year he attempted suicide by severing an artery in his leg with a razor. His purpose was defeated, but during his recovery he stealthily and systematically removed the bandages until it became necessary to amputate the leg. In December Beddoes was able to leave his room, and it was thought that he had given up all intention of suicide, but the first time he went into the town he obtained a poison called Kurara, and that evening was found unconscious. He died at ten o'clock the same night, January 26, 1849, and was buried at Basel. Beddoes left a memorandum, bequeathing his manuscripts to Mr. Kelsall, to be disposed of as Mr. Kelsall thought best, and he also left a most extraordinary note to a friend, in which he said, "Life was too great a bore on one peg and that a bad one." An attendant afterwards said: *"Il était miserable; il a voula [sic] se tuer."* These are the only reasons known for his suicide; there is no evidence of any disappointment or great sorrow. Probably it was the effect of monomania, due to long solitude. Death, over which he had brooded for years, with an irresistible, fascinating influence sucked him into its vortex, whose depth and mystery he had contemplated for so long a time.

During his lifetime, with the exception of a few poems which had appeared in current periodicals, Beddoes published only two volumes. One of these, *The Improvisatore* published at Oxford in 1821, was almost completely destroyed by him, so that only five or six copies are now in existence. The second volume was **The Brides' Tragedy,** published by the Rivingtons in 1822. At the time of his death, in 1849, the bulk of manuscript was still unpublished, and it was not until 1850, when Mr. Kelsall edited **Death's Jest Book,** that any of Beddoes's more mature work was given to the public. In 1850 Mr. Kelsall published some of the remaining poems and fragments, with a memoir of the poet, under the title, *Poems by the late Thomas L. Beddoes.* At Mr. Kelsall's death, in 1869 (?), he bequeathed the manuscript to Mr. Robert Browning, who admired Beddoes extravagantly. Mr. Browning had attempted to dissuade Mr. Kelsall from this intention, because of a superstitious fear he cherished toward the box containing the manuscript, but Mr. Kelsall persisted in his intention; Mr. Browning did not examine the manuscript for years, fearing that it would disclose some gruesome secret. When, after a lapse of years, he went through the papers with the assistance of Mr. Gosse, his presentiment was verified, for the fact of the suicide came to light, which hitherto had not been known.

In 1890, Mr. Gosse published, under the title *Poetical Works of Thomas Lovell Beddoes,* an excellent edition, in which he has made the best of the fragments. It was a matter of much surprise that no scientific works of any kind were found among Beddoes's manuscripts, for the trend of his mind from 1826 had been almost entirely in a scientific direction, and his letters make constant reference to scientific writings or translations then in progress. In April, 1827, he writes: "My next publication will probably be a dissertation on Organic Expansion." From Zurich, in 1838, he writes that he is employed in translating into German Mr. Graigner's work on the Spinal Cord. No trace of these two scientific works, or of the various publications which Beddoes is known to have made while in Germany, has ever been found.

It is when one takes up Beddoes's productions in detail that one marvels most at his originality and early signs of talent. His first attempt, written while at the Charterhouse, was a novel called *Cynthio and Bugboo,* now lost. Mr. Bevan says that it was modeled on a work of Fielding's, and had "all the coarseness, little of the wit, and none of the truth of the original."

Beddoes's second poem (as far as it has been possible to ascertain) was "Alfarabi," written about 1819, at all events before he went to Oxford. From every standpoint it is a most remarkable production for a boy of sixteen. Mr. Gosse says that this "rhapsody displays a very singular adroitness in the manufacture of easy blank verse, and precocious tendency to a species of mocking metaphysics." A few lines are of real beauty, and the poem as a whole shows an unusual appreciation of Nature and a rare discrimination in word shades:

> One snow-winged cloud,
> To wander slowly down the trembling blue;
> A wind that stops and pants along the grass,
> Trembles and flies again like thing pursued;
> And indescribable, delightful sounds,
> Which dart along the sky, we know not whence;
> Bees we have to hum, shrill-noted swallows
> With their small, lightning wings, to fly about
> And tilt against the waters.

The poem is a story of a man who seeks to know "the secret and the spell of life," and this motive is the beginning of the thread of thought which can be traced throughout all of Beddoes's writings and studies—the desire to solve the mystery of life and death. There is much doggerel in the poem, but as a whole it gives high promise of things to come. Curiously enough, it contains nearly all the traits of his later writings, wonderful imaginative faculty, delicate fancy, and a love of the ghastly picturesque. The last-named quality is easily recognized:

> As he who stalks by night,
> With the ghost's step, the shaggy murderer
> Leaves passed the dreamy city's sickly lamps.
> Then through the torrid twilight did they plunge
> The universe's suburb; dwelling dim
> Of all that sin and suffer; midnight shrieks
> Upon the water, when no help is near;
> The blood-choked curse of him who dies in bed
> By torchlight, with a dagger in his heart;
> The parricidal and incestuous laugh;
> And the last cries of those whom devils hale
> Quick into hell.

The most interesting fact in connection with this poem is the unmistakable influence of Milton, both in the choice of polysyllabic words and in the free use of the cæsura; a few lines (possibly sixty) have the full echo of the majestic swing and cadence of Milton's blank verse. Compare these lines with passages from the first book of Milton's *Paradise Lost:*

> It was within a space
> Upon the very boundary and brim
> Of the whole universe, the outer edge
> Which seemed almost to end the infinite zone;
> A chasm in the Almighty thoughts, forgotten
> By the Omnipotent, a place apart
> Like some great ruinous dream of broken worlds,
> Trembling through heaven, or Tartarus' panting jaws
> Open above the sun. Sky there was none,
> Nor earth, nor water; but confusion strange
> Of bursted worlds, and brazen pinions vast
> Of planets shipwrecked; many a wrinkled sun
> Ate to the core by worms, with lightnings crushed;
> And drossy bolts, melting like noonday snow.
> Old towers of heaven were there, and fragments bright
> Of the cerulean battlements o'erthrown
> When the gods struggled for the throne of light.

Beddoes's next production, *The Improvisatore,* published in 1821 at Oxford by J. Vincent, and in London by Whittaker, was written before Beddoes was eighteen. The poem is written in three fyttes, with an introduction to each. The introduction in each case furnishes the motive for the song which follows. While the verse is not without defect, it shows metrical skill and sense of melody. The tone of the whole poem is morbid. The descriptions of feminine beauty show remarkable powers of observation in one so young, as where in the first fytte he describes Emily:

> Those eyes were of a beauteous melting blue,
> Like a dark violet bathed in quivering dew;
> Her mouth seemed formed for signs of sportive guile
> And youthful kisses; and there played a smile
> About her lips, like an inconstant moth
> Around a flower, now settling, and now flown
> Into every passing breath, as through 'twere loth
> To stay and make the resting place its own.

Beddoes depicts Nature in her serener aspects with as much sane ease as he describes her in sterner moods; and with equal facility he describes dainty details of feminine beauty and flowers, or the horrible features of a charnel-house and great battlefield. Stanza xi. of the first fytte, and stanzas i., iv., v., vii. of the second fytte, illustrate this descriptive ability. The third fytte, "Leopold," surpasses both of these in repulsive, realistic details, and in the use of the supernatural element.

While Beddoes's scientific studies probably increased his tendency to dwell on gruesome subjects, and his natural tendency to gloom was aggravated by long association with Death, yet *The Improvisatore,* written before he began scientific investigation, proves beyond a doubt that these qualities were innate. Note the description of the battlefield in "Leopold":

> The dead are all reeking, a ghastly heap
> Slippery with gore, and with crushed bones steep;
> As if the flesh had been snowed on the hills,
> And dribbled away in blood-clammy rills,
> A swamp of distorted faces it lay
> And sweltered and throbbed in the broad day.
> There was one who had fainted in battle's crash;
> Now he struggled in vain with feeble splash
> Under his warm tomb of motionless dead;
> At last he dashed backward his bursting head,
> And gasped in his hideous agony,
> And ground his firm teeth, and darted his eyes;
> Then wriggled his lips in the last prayer of death,
> And mixed with the whirlwind his foamèd breath.

In marked contrast to such horrible pictures, the pastoral love scenes in "Albert and Emily," and the lyric songs in "Rudolph," are very refreshing. Beddoes strikes a reflective note in the poem, unusual with him:

> What is this life, that spins so strangely on
> That, ere we grasp and feel it, it is gone?
> Is it a vision? Are we sleeping now
> In the sweet sunshine of another world?

The last stanza of "Leopold," where doom is represented as advancing, is quite dramatic. "Leopold" might be interpreted as an allegory of sin and its growth, with its attendant evils. The poem, though crude and immature in many respects, gives great promise of things to come, a promise, unfortunately, never fulfilled.

The Brides' Tragedy was published by the Rivingtons in 1822, and, while rare in this edition, is not so scarce as *The Improvisatore* in the edition of 1821. A second edition was published in 1851, and it appeared for the third time in the Gosse edition of 1890. Beddoes began **The Brides' Tragedy** during his first year at Oxford, and completed it in his second year, before he was nineteen. It attracted much contemporary criticism, notably an article in *Blackwood's Magazine* in December, 1823, Vol. 14, p. 723, in which the play is dubbed "as silly as might be—trifling to a degree that is quite refreshing," but promising. The drama attracted the attention of Bryan Waller Procter, who gave the young poet great encouragement and became his lasting friend. In 1827 Beddoes writes: "I assure you that the approbation which you have pleased to bestow upon a very sad boyish affair, that **The Brides' Tragedy,** which I now would not even be condemned to read through for

any consideration, appears to me a remarkable solecism of your otherwise sound literary judgment."

Beddoes discovered his plot for the drama among the forgotten legends of Oxford. A student, having married in secret the daughter of a manciple of one of the colleges, becomes entangled during the following vacation in a betrothal *de convenance* arranged by his father. Eventually the student falls in love with his betrothed, and desires the death of his bride. He is weak, and the desire soon becomes a design to murder her. The unsuspecting wife is enticed to a lonely retreat, murdered, and buried in the Divinity Walk. In the legend, the crime remains undiscovered until the murderer confesses it on his deathbed, but Beddoes has altered this to suit his purpose, and Nemesis follows, swift and sure.

The drama is written in easy blank verse. The first act opens with a graceful love scene between Hesperus and his bride, Floribel, in striking contrast to the dark scenes of guilt and crime which follow. There are many passages, such as the following, marked with delicate, ethereal fancy and Elizabethan conceits:

> In Elfin annals old
> 'Tis writ how Zephyr, envious of his love
> (The love he bare to Summer, who, since then
> Has, weeping, visited the world), once found
> The baby Perfume, cradled in a violet;
> ('Twas said the beauteous bantling was the child
> Of a gay bee that in his wantonness
> Toyed with a pea bud in a lady's garland;)
> The felon winds, confederate with him,
> Bound the sweet slumberer with golden chains,
> Pulled from the wreathed laburnum, and together
> Deep cast him in the bosom of a rose,
> And fed the fettered wretch with dew and air.
> At length his soul, that was a lover's sigh,
> Issued from his body, and the guilty blossom
> His heart's blood stained. The twilight-haunting gnat
> His requiem whined, and harebells tolled his knell;
> And still the bee, in pied velvet dight,
> With melancholy song from flower to flower
> Goes seeking his lost offspring.

The long monologue of Floribel is marked with the same dainty imagery and delightful fancy. Act I., Scene 3, between Hesperus and his father, Lord Ernest, is the most powerful part of the tragedy, with the exception of the murder. The love scene between Hesperus and Olivia, his betrothed, is in a more serious vein than the scene between Hesperus and Floribel, and contains greater passion and strength. The first is all innocence, but the second is darkened by the shadow of guilt and crime. The speech of Olivia contains more power than any of Floribel's:

> But what's to be without my Hesperus?
> A life of dying. 'Tis to die each moment
> In every several sense. To look despair,
> Feel, taste, breathe, eat, be conscious of despair.
> No, I'll be nothing rather.

Hesperus is weak, evil, treacherous, yet sometimes moved by good impulses. His character stands out in bold relief to that of Floribel—gentle, affectionate, innocent, yet strong in her love. When Hesperus determines upon her death, he says:

> I would not have thee cross my path to-night.
> There is an indistinct, dread purpose forming,
> Something whose depth of wickedness appears
> Hideous, incalculable, but inevitable.
> Now it draws nearer, and I do not shudder.
> Avaunt! haunt me no more. I dread it not,
> But almost—hence! I must not be alone.

And again, of his shadow:

> I know thee now—
> 'Tis Malice's eldest imp, the heir of hell,
> Red-handed Murther. Slow it whispers me
> Coaxingly with its serpent voice. Well sung,
> Syren of Acheron.

It is interesting to compare the monologue of Hesperus before murdering Floribel with that of Macbeth before murdering Duncan. The personifications, epithets, and spirit of the two have a striking resemblance. When Hesperus tells Floribel that she must die, her reply is full of resignation and pathos:

> O, if thou will'st it, love,
> If thou but speak it in thy natural voice
> And smile upon me, I'll not think it pain,
> But cheerfully I'll seek me out a grave
> And sleep as sweetly as on Hesperus' breast.

Hesperus murders her, and, repenting almost instantly, he kisses her, and exclaims:

> What a shriek was that! It flew to heaven,
> And hymning angels took it for their own.

The murder scene, Act III., Scene 3, is very dramatic, as are the majority of the passages dealing with sin and crime. Beddoes strikes the chord of the darker passions with an almost master hand.

The plot of the drama is fit material for high tragedy, and Beddoes has handled it well. It is the only one of his dramas that has a central motive, and the only one possessing organic unity. Had Beddoes fulfilled with increasing years the promise that his play gave, he would have been a great dramatist, but instead he seems to have retrograded. *Death's Jest Book,* the work of his maturer years, is a more polished production, but it has far less dramatic power, and no unity.

The Brides' Tragedy, notwithstanding its vagueness of characterization and general haziness, has many good points. The horror of the tragedy and the superabundance of evil motives is relieved by scenes of tenderness and beauty, adorned with luxuriance of fancy. As the production of a youth of eighteen, one marvels at the excellencies and condones the defects. *Blackwood's Magazine* of December, 1823, says: "We sup full of horrors, but there

are gay and fantastic garnishings and adornments of the repast, disposed quite in the manner and spirit of the great old masters."

It has been impossible to ascertain the exact chronological order of all the poems; but it is quite certain that *The Second Brother* and *Torrismond* were written between 1823 and 1825, while Beddoes was on a visit to Mr. Kelsall at Southampton. During the winter of 1823, Beddoes also began *Love's Arrow Poisoned* and *The Last Man,* neither of which was ever completed, and are now so fragmentary as to leave little trace of plot. Mr. Gosse states that "already Beddoes was seized with that inability to finish, that lack of organic principle of poetical composition, which were to prevent him from mounting to those heights to which his facility and brilliancy promised him so easy an ascent." In a letter to Mr. Kelsall, August 25, 1824, Beddoes wrote: "I depend very little on my poetical faculty, but it is my intention to complete one more tragedy." In September of the same year he again writes: "I find literary wishes fading very fast;" and in April, 1826, says, "I never could have been the real thing as a writer." This doubting of himself probably increased his natural inability to develop a plot, to evolve a character successfully, or in fact to achieve any desired end.

The Second Brother is incomplete, consisting of only three acts and two scenes of the fourth act. It derives its name from the return of the second brother, Marcello, long thought dead, to claim his heritage from the third brother, Orazeo, who believes himself the rightful owner in the order of succession to the dukedom. Upon his return in disguise, Marcello's love for Orazeo and the indulgence that he might have shown to the usurper are turned to hate and revenge by the cruel treatment that he receives. The accession of Marcello to the dukedom after the overthrow of Orazeo is highly dramatic; but here all continuity ceases, for the character of Marcello is too poorly drawn to be able to foresee any satisfaction that he may derive from his revenge, or what the outcome of the whole will be. The characterization of Marcello is similar to the description of him by his servant, Ezriel:

> A fathomless and undiscovered man,
> Thinking above the eagle's highest wings
> And underneath the world.

Act I., Scene 2., between Orazeo and the wife whom he has deserted contains many fine passages and shows much human sympathy, a rather unusual element in Beddoes's writings. Orazeo's ruin is complete when the father of his deserted wife buys up all the mortgages on Orazeo's private estate, and drives him from his home. There is a marked resemblance between Valeria, Orazeo's wife, and Floribel, of *The Brides' Tragedy.* A splendid passage occurs in a dialogue between Valeria and an attendant:

> Do I love? I walk
> Within the brilliance of another's thought
> As in a glory. I was dark before
> As Venus' chapel in the black of night:

Then love came
Like the outbursting of a trodden star,
And what before was hueless and unseen
Now shows me a divinity, like that
Which raised to life out of the snowy rock,
Surpassed mankind's creation, and repaid
Heaven for Pandora.

Valeria appeals to Marcello for mercy:

I have a plea,
As dewy-piteous as the gentle ghost's,
That sits alone upon the forest grave,
Thinking of no revenge. I have a mandate
As magical and as potent as e'er ran
Silently through a battle's myriad veins,
Undid their fingers from the hanging steel,
And drew them up in prayer; I am a woman.

There is an obvious contradiction in the statement that Valeria's body is disfigured from drowning after a very few hours in the water. Here the manuscript stops abruptly, and it is impossible to anticipate the climax. The drama shows no advance over *The Brides' Tragedy,* is less promising in the evolution of a coherent plot, and has less lyrical beauty than the other dramas.

Torrismond belongs to the same period of production as *The Second Brother,* and is still less near completion, consisting of only one act, but that act contains a song which is one of the most famous of Beddoes's lyrical productions. In the fragment we have glimpses of a son indulged excessively, and in turn brooked with fierce restraint by his father. The drinking revel, Scene 2, is good, while the soliloquy of Torrismond, when he finds Veronica asleep, shows considerable descriptive powers. Like the Elizabethans, one phrase expands into another, until there are explanatory clauses within explanatory clauses. Some of the best passages are these:

This very night we both may die,
Or one at least; and it is very likely
We never meet, or if we meet, not thus;
But somehow kindred by the times, the place,
The persons. There are many chances else,
That, though no bigger than a sunny mote,
Coming between, may our whole future part—
. . . it may sever us
As utterly as if the world should split
Here, as we stand, and all eternity
Push through the earthquake's lips and rise between
    us.
Then let us know each other's constancy;
Thou in my mind, and I in thine shall be;
And so disseparable to the edge
Of thinnest lightning.

As a final pledge, Veronica answers:

As I believe thee steadfast and sincere;
And if it be not so, God pity me!
I love thee purely, dearly, heartily.
So witness heaven and our own silent spirits.

To which Torrismond replies:

And by my immortality, I swear
With the like honesty, the like to thee.

Gaudentio, interfering between the angry father and his son, says to the father:

There stands before you
The youth and golden top of your existence,
Another life of yours; for think your morning
Not lost, but given, passed from your hand to his.

And, speaking of the father to the son, he says:

Remember there's a kind of God in him,
And after him, the next of thy religion.

Gaudentio fails to reconcile them, and Torrismond says in his despair:

How many things, sir, do men live to do?
The mighty labor is to die; we'll do it,
But we'll drive in a chariot to our graves,
Wheeled with big thunder o'er the heads of men.

Of Act II. there is only one line, and the manuscript ends abruptly.

The Last Man, of which Beddoes, in February, 1824, wrote: "Proctor has the brass to tell me he likes that fool, *The Last Man.*" The play has no trace of a plot; but Mr. Gosse has pieced together scattered fragments which were evidently intended to form parts of a five-act tragedy. In another letter Beddoes says of *The Last Man*: "There are three first acts in my drama; when I have got two more, I shall stick them together, and stick the sign of a fellow tweedling a mask in his fingers, with 'good entertainment for man and ass' understood." These three acts were lost or destroyed, for no trace of them exists. In 1827 he writes from Göttingen that he expects to embody *The Last Man* in *Death's Jest Book.* The only characters mentioned are Dianeme, lamenting the death of her lover, Casimir, and an attendant. The fragment is not so rich in beautiful passages as some of the other dramas, but there are some worthy of note:

Is it not sweet to die? For what is death
But sighing that we ne'er may sigh again,
Getting at length beyond our tedious selves;
But trampling the last tear from poisonous sorrow,
Spilling our woes, crushing our frozen hopes,
And passing like an incense out of man?
Then, if the body felt, what were its sense,
Turning to daisies gently in the grave,
If not the soul's most delicate delight
When it does filtrate through the pores of thought
In love and the enameled flowers of song?

Again:

Yet men die suddenly;
One sits upon a strong and rocky life,

Watching a street of many opulent years,
And Hope's his mason. Well, to-day do this,
And so to-morrow; twenty hollow years
Are stuffed with action. Lo! upon his head
Drops a pin's point of time. Tick! quoth the clock,
And the grave snaps him.

From the dates given in his letters, it would seem that Beddoes had four unfinished plays in progress at one time—the last three discussed, and a fourth, *Love's Arrow Poisoned.* It is scarcely to be wondered at under these conditions that they were never finished. The fragments of *Love's Arrow Poisoned* show the unmistakable influence of Webster and Tourneur. The raving of Erminia against Nature, and her cruelty in particular, is much like Webster. The whole consists of only four scenes of the first act.

Death's Jest Book, or the Fool's Tragedy, the best known of Beddoes's writings, was begun at Oxford in 1825, and practically finished in 1826, although he continued to enlarge and alter it until 1844. On the 8th of July, 1825, he wrote Mr. Kelsall from Oxford: "I do not intend to finish that Second Brother that you saw, but am thinking of a very Gothic-styled tragedy, for which I have a jewel of a name—*Death's Jest Book.* Of course no one will ever read it." In December of the same year: "*Death's Jest Book* goes on like the tortoise, slow but sure; I think it will be entertaining, very unamiable, and utterly unpopular." April 1, 1826, he reported the fourth and fifth acts more than half done; "so that at last it will be a perfect mouse, but such doggerel," and added that if it is ever finished it will come "like an electric shock among the smaller critics." From Göttingen in 1826 he wrote that it is "done and done for." In 1844, from Giessen, in a letter to Mr. Kelsall, Beddoes quoted two songs that he had just finished, "The Swallow Leaves Her Nest" and "In Lover's Ear a Wild Voice Cried," and says that "he has stuck them into the endless J. B." This work, the link between his literary life at Oxford and his scientific studies on the Continent, is the one effort of his life to which he adhered with any perseverance. Although Beddoes with great effort completed it, the play is not the result of spontaneous inspiration, but the laborious work of many years, into which he interpolated stray thoughts, fragments of other dramas, and odd lyric songs. The effect is a conglomeration of the various ideas of a lifetime.

Beddoes thought of publishing *Death's Jest Book* in 1828, and again in 1831, but it did not appear until 1850, when Mr. Kelsall published it annonymously. Three texts were found among the manuscripts, the first called *Charonic Steps.* The second is that which Mr. Kelsall adhered to in the main; the third contained only one act. Mr. Gosse, in his edition of 1890, has used Mr. Kelsall's edition.

The contemporary criticism (in 1850) was very flattering. Walter Savage Landor wrote that "Nearly two centuries have elapsed since a work of the same wealth of genius has been given to the world," and John Forster said: "We must frankly say we are not acquainted with any living

DEATH'S JEST-BOOK

OR

THE FOOL'S TRAGEDY

ALDI DISCIP. ANGLVS

LONDON
WILLIAM PICKERING
1850

author who could have written *The Fool's Tragedy.*" Unfortunately for Beddoes's literary fame, posterity does not seem to have concurred in these flattering estimates, and *Death's Jest Book,* the one object to which he was constant, remains obscure. The drama was reviewed anonymously in the *Eclectic Magazine,* Vol. XXIV., p. 446 (the same article appeared in the *Living Age* of November 15, 1851), praising *Death's Jest Book* in the highest terms. Among other things, the writer says: "The merit of *Death's Jest Book* does not depend on philosophic delineations of the *dramatis personæ* (it is well that it does not, as there is practically no delineation of character) and nice gradations in their development, but the story is powerfully and graphically told." It is probable that Mr. Kelsall wrote the article, since it closely resembles a signed article by him in the *Fortnightly,* July, 1872; and if so, some allowance must be made for his personal feeling for the author, inasmuch as the story is not powerfully unfolded, there is no coherence of action, no continuity of plot, and, above all, no great motion or purpose around which all else centers and depends.

The drama is based on the disputed historical fact that Duke Boleslaus, of Münsterberg, in Silesia, was murdered by his court fool. The scene is Silesia and the time is the thirteenth century. The infant sons of the murdered man are sent into exile. Reaching manhood, they return and seek revenge. One of them, Wolfram, becomes greatly attached to his father's slayer, and discards the idea of revenge; the second, Isbrand, the more revengeful of the two, becomes the court fool. It is evident that Beddoes intended to duplicate the incident of the reigning duke, himself formerly a court fool, now a murderer and usurper, being in turn murdered by his own court fool, and that Isbrand should be the avenger of his father; but, "like an untrained terrier among members of a quarry," he was diverted hither and thither, and in the end evolved no one thought or plot to a climax. The usurper, Duke Melveric, is taken captive by the Moors, and Scene 1, of Act I., is the departure of Wolfram to rescue him. Isbrand upbraids his brother for his failure to avenge their father, and Isbrand is left to his solitary revenge. After the rescue of the Duke has been effected, he and Melveric become enamored of the same woman, Sibylla, and the ungrateful Duke slays his thrice-rescuer, Wolfram. The first act closes dramatically with the death of Wolfram and with the beautiful lyric:

> The swallow leaves her nest,
> The soul my weary breast;
> But therefore let the rain
>   On my grave
> Fall pure; for why complain,
> Since this will come again
>   O'er the wave?
>
> The wind, dead leaves, and snow
> Doth scurry to and fro;
> And, once, a day shall break
>   O'er the wave,
> When a storm of ghosts shall shake
> The dead until they wake
>   In the grave.

In meter and cadence this song suggests Shelley, but in etherealness and grace it is not equal to him. The Dirge, at the opening of Act II., Scene 1,

> If thou wilt ease thine heart
> Of love and all its smart,

also shows Shelley's influence upon Beddoes.

In Act I., which is the best part of *Death's Jest Book*, many passages show skill and power:

> What's this thought,
> Shapeless and shadowy, that keeps wheeling round,
> Like a dumb creature that sees coming danger
> And breaks its heart trying in vain to speak?
> I knew the moment; 'tis a dreadful one,
> Which in the life of every one comes once;
> When, for the frightened, hesitating soul,
> High heaven and luring sin with promises
> Bid and contend; oft the faltering spirit,
> O'ercome by the fair, fascinating fiend,
> Gives her eternal heritage of life
> For one caress, for one triumphant crime.

And again:

> Many the ways, the little home is one;
> Thither the course leads, thither the helm,
> And at one gate we meet when all is done.

The speech of Isbrand at the close of Scene 1, and of Ziba at the end of scene 2, of the same act, are very indicative of Beddoes's usual trend of thought.

From the beginning of Act II., we are confused by haziness of motive and characterization, by plots and counterplots, until it is impossible to follow the leading thought that Beddoes would define—each scene seems a part unto itself. The leading motif of Act I.—the Duke's passion for Sibylla, extinguished by remorse—has been abandoned, and a plot against Duke Melveric by Isbrand and the Duke's sons, Adalmar and Athulf, takes its place. This motif is in turn supplanted by Adalmar and Athulf's love for the same woman. The marriage of Adalmar to Amala follows, and Athulf slays Adalmar. The occult element is now introduced, and Zeba, an Arab, raises Wolfram from the dead. He consorts with the living most freely by day and by night without comment from them, and seems to be of substantial flesh. Beddoes manages this part by means of the introduction of a Hebrew legend, for which authority is found in rabbinical literature, that a bone exists in the body, "Aldabaron," called by the Hebrews "Luz," which "withstands dissolution after death," and out of which it is possible to raise the body, and by means of which God will re-create the body at the Resurrection. This bone, according to Mr. Gosse, was the os coccygis, a bone beneath the eighteenth vertebra.

The drama closes with only one thing clear—that Beddoes intended to make as clean sweep of the stage by means of the death of the *dramatis personæ* as Kyd does in his *Spanish Tragedy* and Death, to whom the drama is dedicated, reigns supreme. The proportions of the supernatural elements of lust for revenge and of Death, are used more than is palatable even in blood-and-thunder tragedy. Even when due allowance is made for the belief in the supernatural that prevailed in the thirteenth and fourteenth centuries, it is scarcely probable that this drama would have received credence at that time, and the effect on an audience of the present day might be psychologically interesting. Beddoes, in a letter dated February, 1829, says that it should be the typical aim of a dramatist to produce a drama to be *acted,* and that its fitness for this purpose is the most thorough test. It is scarcely to be credited that he thought *Death's Jest Book* practical for presentation on the stage, for his perception of his own shortcomings was ordinarily so keen, it is not likely that he was deceived in this instance. He must therefore have written *Death's Jest Book* solely for his own amusement.

The play as a whole presents a motley mixture; the Macaberesque influence of the thirteenth century is seen in the Dance of Death, Act V., Scene 4, where the figures in a painted representation of the Dance of Death in the cathedral cloister come out of the walls and dance. Beddoes probably borrowed this from some old German interpretation of the "Totentanz." The Rosicrucian influence of the fifteenth century is present in the use of the occult, where Wolfram is raised from the dead. Interspersed with these two incongruous elements, and further enhancing the strange effect, is the German metaphysics of the nineteenth century. *Death's Jest Book* seems but the overflow, the excrescence of unassimilated knowledge, and not the natural development of a genius. It is apparent that Beddoes did not improve or develop beyond *The Brides' Tragedy,* with the exception of greater perfection of meter and lyric grace. In dramatic power he had declined. Yet the drama is not without interest or merit; the originality, the startling conception, and the beauty of isolated passages make it worth the reading; as a unit, it is a deplorable failure. Mr. Browning said of it: "Now as to the extracts which might be made, why, you might pick out scenes, passages, lyrics, fine as might be; the power of the man is immense and irresistible." This opinion sums up all of its virtues and seems even a little extravagant in the light of its many defects, but it is certainly, from any view-point, a most remarkable production, on account of the originality of its subject-matter and the great beauty and power of many passages. Beddoes did not erect the "Gothic-styled tragedy," of which he wrote, stately in its grand outlines and convergence to a central plan or idea, but he produced instead a literary structure of loosely strung parts, some of exaggerated power and beauty, and some of diminutive dimension, the whole presenting an inharmonious effect. The beauty of some parts does not atone for the ugliness of others.

It is upon Beddoes's lyrics that his claim to fame rests; it is in these that he displays most gift for melody, harmony, and technical skill. But for the inevitable sinister note that mars the lyrical feeling, these lyrics could be called almost the consummate art of verse-making. What could be more sweet and exquisite than the love-song in *Torrismond*?

> How many times do I lose thee, dear?
>   Tell me how many thoughts there be
> In the atmosphere
> Of a new-fall'n year,
> Whose white and sable hours appear
> The latest flake of Eternity;
>   So many times do I love thee, dear.
>
> How many times do I love again?
>   Tell me how many beads there are
> In a silver chain
> Of evening rain
> Unraveled from the trembling main,
>   And threading the eye of a yellow star;
> So many times do I love again.

"A Dirge" is profound in its beauty and melancholy:

> To-day is a thought, a fear is to-morrow,
> And yesterday is our sin and sorrow;

> And life is a death,
>   Where the body's the tomb,
> And the pale, sweet breath
>   Is buried alive in its hideous gloom.
> Then waste no tear,
> For we are the dead; the living are here
> In the stealing earth, and the heavy bier.
> Death lives but an instant, and is but a sign,
> And his son is unnamed Immortality,
> Whose being is time. Dear ghost, so to die
> Is to live—and life is a worthless lie.
> Then we weep for ourselves, and wish thee good-by.

A second "Dirge" is very artistic:

> To her couch of evening rest,
> 'Neath the sun's divinest west,
> Bear we, in the silent car,
> This consumed incense star,
> This dear maid whose life is shed,
> And whose sweets are sweetly dead.

Mr. Gosse has called "Dream Pedlary" the most exquisite of Beddoes's lyrics. While it is very charming, it is not free from the sinister touch in which Beddoes so delights. The first three stanzas are the most beautiful:

> If there were dreams to sell,
>   What would you buy?
> Some cost a passing bell,
>   Some a light sigh,
> That shakes from Life's fresh crown
> Only a rose leaf down.
> If there were dreams to sell,
> Merry and sad to tell,
> And the crier rung the bell,
>   What would you buy?
>
> A cottage lone and still,
>   With bowers nigh,
> Shadowy my woes to still,
>   Until I die.
> Such pearl from Life's fresh crown
> Fain would I shake me down.
> Were dreams to have at will,
> This would best heal my ill,
>   This would I buy.
>
> But there were dreams to sell.
>   Ill didst thou buy;
> Life is a dream, they tell,
>   Waking, to die.
> Dreaming a dream to prize,
> Is wishing ghosts to rise;
> And, if I had the spell
> To call the buried well,
>   Which one would I?

In a letter written from Göttingen in 1836, Beddoes inclosed a poem, from which the following extract has been taken. It is one of the very few places where Beddoes strikes a high ethical note:

> Take thy example from the sunny lark,
> Throw off the mantle which conceals the soul,

The many-citied world, and seek thy goal
Straight as a star beam falls. Creep not nor climb
As they who plan their topmost of sublime
On some peak of this planet pitifully.
Dart eaglewise with open wings, and fly
Until you meet the gods. Thus counsel I.
The men who can, but tremble to be great—
Cursed be the fool who taught to hesitate,
And to regret; time lost most bitterly.

The "Ballad of Human Life," three stanzas representing the three stages of life, boy and girl, lad and lass, man and wife, is very human. There are a number of other lyrics, such as "The Swallow Leaves Her Nest," "If Thou Wilt Ease Thine Heart," "Love in Idleness," "Song by Sieg-fried," and "Aho, Aho, Love's Horn Doth Blow," especially the first two, that are excellent and deserve to be better known. While it must be acknowledged that there is a monotony about them, showing that as a lyrist Beddoes was of a high order, but not of wide range, yet the most prejudiced critic could not but conclude that the "Love Song" from *Torrismond,* "Dream Pedlary," and "The Swallow Leaves Her Nest" are exquisite, and rank among the best of their kind in the language.

In striking contrast to these poems, there is a second class which Mr. Gosse has classified as the poems of "Grisly Humour." "Song of the Stygian Naiades," "Lord Alcohol," "Adam, the Carrion Crow," "Song of Isbrand," from *Death's Jest Book,* "Harpagus' Ballad," and the "Dance of Death" are instances which vie with each other in grotesque and repulsive fancy.

"Song"

Old Adam, the carrion crow,
The old crow of Cairo;
He sat in the shower and let it flow
    Under his tail and over his crest;
        And through every feather
        Leaked the wet weather;
And the bough swung under his nest;
For his beak it was heavy with marrow.
Is that the wind dying? O, no;
It's only two devils that blow
Through a murderer's bones, to and fro,
    In the ghost's moonshine.

Ho! Eve, my gray carrion wife,
When we have supped on king's marrow,
Where shall we drink and make merry our life?
    Our nest it is Queen Cleopatra's skull,
        'Tis cloven and cracked,
        And battered and hacked,
But with tears of blue eyes it is full;
Let us drink then, my raven of Cairo.
Is that the wind dying? O, no;
It's only two devils that blow
Through a murderer's bones, to and fro,
    In the ghost's moonshine.

They are too gruesome for enjoyment, but are rather to be wondered at as objects in a museum, and to be preserved

for their variety of species rather than on account of their literary excellence.

"The Boding Dreams" and "From the German" show the effect of German mysticism and metaphysics. The "Romance of the Lily" and "The Ghost's Moonshine," belong to the same category, and, judging from their tone, were probably written after Beddoes went to Germany. They fairly repel one with their ghastliness and uncanniness of conception.

In addition to his gift as a lyrist, Beddoes shows great facility as a prose writer in his letters, which were collected and published by Mr. Gosse in 1894. Mr. Swinburne has said that Beddoes's "noble instinct for poetry was demonstrated in his letters more than in his poetry, and that his brilliant correspondence on poetical questions gives me a higher view of his fine and vigorous intelligence than any other section of his literary remains." The letters cover a period from 1824 to 1849, and are in the main written to Mr. Kelsall and Mr. Procter. They exhibit the reserve which always characterized Beddoes, and give little insight into his personality or the details of his life on the Continent, but they are replete with interesting literary criticisms and original ideas on various subjects. While it cannot be said that Beddoes was always correct in his literary criticisms—he attacked Goethe most unmercifully—yet as a usual thing he showed great discrimination. His estimate of Shelley's great genius, expressed in one of his letters written at the time of Shelley's death, was long before a general recognition came.

What would he not have done, if ten years more, that will be wasted upon the lives of unprofitable knaves and fools, had been given to him? Was it that more of the beautiful and good that Nature could spare to him was incarnate in him, and that it was necessary to resume it for distribution through the external and internal worlds? How many springs will blossom with his thoughts—how many fair and glorious creations be born of his extinction?

Beddoes esteemed Shelley and Keats most of all of his contemporaries, and his admiration for Shakespeare falls little short of worship. Of Shakespeare he says:

He was an incarnation of Nature; and you might just as well attempt to remodel the reasons and the laws of life and death as to alter "one jot or tittle" of his eternal strength. "A star," you call him. If he was a star, all the other stage scribblers can hardly be called a constellation of brass buttons. I say he was a universe, and all material existence, with its excellencies and its defects, was reflected in shadowy thought upon the crystal waters of his imagination, ever glorified as they were by the sleepless sun of his golden intellect. And this imaginary universe had its seasons and changes, its harmonies and its discords, as well as the dirty reality.

The letters contain many passages of this character, bits of gossip, much sarcastic humor, and many sallies of wit; all perfectly free from the melancholy and cynicism of his poetry. It would be difficult to find more racy, living expression of thought, with deep appreciation of all things beautiful in literature and art, than in these letters. The letter to Mr. Procter from Milan, June 8, 1824, is one of the best in the collection, and the description that it contains of the firefly is poetry in prose:

And what else have I seen? A beautiful and far-famed insect—do not mistake. I mean neither the emperor nor the king of Sardinia, but a much finer specimen—the firefly. Their bright light is evanescent and alternates with the darkness, as if the swift wheeling of the earth struck fire out of the black atmosphere; as if the winds were being set upon this planetary grindstone and gave out such momentary sparks from their edges. Their silence is more striking than their flashes, for sudden phenomena are almost invariably attended with some noise; but these little jewels dart along in the dark as softly as butterflies. For their light, it is not nearly so beautiful and poetical as our still companions of the dew—the glow worm and the drop of moonlight.

The volume contains many other passages of equal beauty and interest.

Beddoes had vast power of conception and mastery of rhythm, combined with "a delicate fancy and a strange choiceness of phrase," but he lacked universal sympathy and the power to express the vital emotions. *The Brides' Tragedy,* one of his earliest productions, shows more knowledge of human nature than any of his succeeding dramas, which, probably on account of his solitary life, have less and less sympathy with humanity. His writings were of the head and not the heart; he studied literature, not life.

Beddoes has been called a "belated Elizabethan, who strayed into the nineteenth century." He had little in common with his contemporaries, but belongs rather to the school that was founded by Kyd, sustained by Marlowe, perfected in Shakespeare's *Hamlet,* and illustrated in its decadence by Marston, Webster, and Tourneur. It was revived for only a last gasp by Beddoes. The influence of Shakespeare, Webster, and Tourneur is felt in his works, and, notwithstanding his strong originality of conception, there is little that does not show the direct influence of some one of the Elizabethans. Beddoes resembles Tourneur and Webster in style, but, while they reek with moral filth, Beddoes is always chaste and distinguished. A judgment expressed in the article in the ninth edition of the *Encyclopædia Britannica,* is interesting: "Beddoes borrowed nothing either from his Elizabethan precursors or the chief objects of his admiration among his contemporaries, Keats and Shelley." While Beddoes was in no sense a plagiarist, his debt to the writers must be acknowledged.

It is to the Romantic movement of the early nineteenth century that Beddoes is most closely allied. His affectation of the sinister and melancholy, his return to the mediæval, as in *Death's Jest Book,* his admiration for the Elizabethans, and particularly his employment of Gothic and supernatural machinery, are but the growth and outcome

against eighteenth century classicism. Beddoes represents the fusion of the English and the German revolt against conventionality; as a natural consequence the pendulum of Beddoes's genius swung to the other extreme of utter improbability. In this respect he may be classed with Horace Walpole and Mrs. Radcliffe, the chief exponents of Gothic romance. Moreover, there are curiously interesting resemblances between Beddoes and that group of eighteenth century poets known as the Graveyard School. The implements of verse used by this school, such as tomb, ravens, owls, skeletons, and ghosts, are found in Beddoes's verse, plus murders, suicides, grinning ghosts, carrion crows, charnel houses, prisons, and biers. Gray could not write of Eton boys, happy at play, without thinking

How all around them wait
For monsters of human fate
And black Misfortune's baleful train.

Beddoes, with even greater pessimism, sees Death everywhere:

Sleeping, or feigning sleep, well done of her; 'tis trying on a garb
Which she must wear, sooner or late, long: 'tis but a warmer, lighter death.

Both are amorous of misfortune, death, and the tomb.

Beddoes's genius is undeniable, but it is limited in scope. Had he developed naturally from the time of the writing of *The Brides' Tragedy,* he would have won a great literary fame; but his genius was stunted by his scientific studies and by the disuse of his own language. Browning once said of him: "If I were a professor of poetry, my first lecture at the university would be on 'Beddoes, a forgotten Oxford poet.'" Notwithstanding such generous praise, time has demonstrated that Beddoes belongs, not to the highways, but to the byways of literature, which are none the less original and exquisite in certain parts because of their remoteness, but trod only by lovers of the rare.

One is reminded by Mrs. Andrew Crosse of a striking coincidence in the lives of Coleridge and Beddoes; both poets were influenced by German thought, and the poetical genius of each was blunted by German metaphysics.

Beddoes was so dissatisfied with life that he was ever seeking to solve the impenetrable mystery of life and death; it may even be said that Death is the eternal note in his song. The 20th of April, 1827, he writes from Göttingen that "I am already so thoroughly convinced of the absurdity and unsatisfactory nature of human life that I search with avidity for every shadow of a proof or probability of an after existence, both in the material and immaterial nature of man, . . . for which Nature appears to have pointed one solution—Death." Mr. Gosse says that "Beddoes dedicates himself to the service of Death, not with a brooding sense of the terror and shame of mortality, but from a love of the picturesque pageantry of it, the majesty and somber beauty, the swift theatrical transitions, the combined elegance and horror that wait upon the sudden decease of monarchs."

Beddoes seems never to have contemplated death with spiritual hope. At times he views death with dread, with scorn, or with laughter; again with admiration of its power and malignity; but rarely with hope, and then it is the tolerant hope of the Stoic, never with the belief that death is the spiritual consummation of life.

> Lament! I'd have thee do it;
> The heaviest raining is the briefest shower.
> Death is the one condition of our life;
> To murmur were unjust; our buried sire
> Yielded their seats to us, and we shall give
> Our elbow-room of sunshine to our sons.
> From first to last the traffic must go on,
> Still birth for death. Shall we remonstrate then?
> Millions have died that we might breathe this day;
> The first of all might murmur, but not we.
> Grief is unmanly too.

Again and again he says that "Life is a dream, and death is the waking," but he never reasons beyond this point. The material seems ever to dominate the spiritual.

Despite a passion for energy and action, Beddoes's life shows the same defect seen in his schooldays. After becoming acquainted with a subject, he soon tired of it, and abandoned further effort in that direction before attaining perfection, ever following a will-o'-the-wisp which flitted from one object of learning to another. His conduct of life lacked sustained effort just as his dramas lacked sustained dramatic action and organic unity. There is no master motive in his life, as there is no master motive in his dramas, and the same haziness which surrounds his own purposes obscures the motions of his characters. This is the more deplorable, since Beddoes possessed unusual and strikingly original qualities of mind—gifts which should have made him a great poet instead of a minor nineteenth century lyrist.

Lytton Strachey (essay date 1907)

SOURCE: "The Last Elizabethan," in *Literary Essays*, Harcourt, Brace & World, 1907, pp. 171-94.

[*In the following essay, Strachey evaluates Beddoes's place in English literature and offers a stylistic analysis of his work.*]

The shrine of Poetry is a secret one; and it is fortunate that this should be the case; for it gives a sense of security. The cult is too mysterious and intimate to figure upon census papers; there are no turnstiles at the temple gates; and so, as all inquiries must be fruitless, the obvious plan is to take for granted a good attendance of worshippers, and to pass on. Yet, if Apollo were to come down (after the manner of deities) and put questions—must we suppose to the Laureate?—as to the number of the elect,

would we be quite sure of escaping wrath and destruction? Let us hope for the best; and perhaps, if we were bent upon finding out the truth, the simplest way would be to watch the sales of the new edition of the poems of Beddoes, which Messrs. Routledge have lately added to the 'Muses' Library.' How many among Apollo's pew-renters, one wonders, have ever read Beddoes, or, indeed, have ever heard of him? For some reason or another, this extraordinary poet has not only never received the recognition which is his due, but has failed almost entirely to receive any recognition whatever. If his name is known at all, it is known in virtue of the one or two of his lyrics which have crept into some of the current anthologies. But Beddoes' highest claim to distinction does not rest upon his lyrical achievements, consummate as those achievements are; it rests upon his extraordinary eminence as a master of dramatic blank verse. Perhaps his greatest misfortune was that he was born at the beginning of the nineteenth century, and not at the end of the sixteenth. His proper place was among that noble band of Elizabethans, whose strong and splendid spirit gave to England, in one miraculous generation, the most glorious heritage of drama that the world has known. If Charles Lamb had discovered his tragedies among the folios of the British Museum, and had given extracts from them in the *Specimens of Dramatic Poets*, Beddoes' name would doubtless be as familiar to us now as those of Marlowe and Webster, Fletcher and Ford. As it happened, however, he came as a strange and isolated phenomenon, a star which had wandered from its constellation, and was lost among alien lights. It is to very little purpose that Mr. Ramsay Colles, his latest editor, assures us that 'Beddoes is interesting as marking the transition from Shelley to Browning'; it is to still less purpose that he points out to us a passage in *Death's Jest Book* which anticipates the doctrines of *The Descent of Man*. For Beddoes cannot be hoisted into line with his contemporaries by such methods as these; nor is it in the light of such after-considerations that the value of his work must be judged. We must take him on his own merits, 'unmixed with seconds'; we must discover and appraise his peculiar quality for its own sake.

> He hath skill in language;
> And knowledge is in him, root, flower, and fruit,
> A palm with winged imagination in it,
> Whose roots stretch even underneath the grave;
> And on them hangs a lamp of magic science
> In his soul's deepest mine, where folded thoughts
> Lie sleeping on the tombs of magi dead.

If the neglect suffered by Beddoes' poetry may be accounted for in more ways than one, it is not so easy to understand why more curiosity has never been aroused by the circumstances of his life. For one reader who cares to concern himself with the intrinsic merit of a piece of writing there are a thousand who are ready to explore with eager sympathy the history of the writer; and all that we know both of the life and the character of Beddoes possesses those very qualities of peculiarity, mystery, and adventure, which are so dear to the hearts of subscribers to circulating libraries. Yet only one account of his career has ever been given to the public; and that account, fragmentary and incorrect as it is, has long been out of print. It was supplemented some years ago by Mr. Gosse, who was able to throw additional light upon one important circumstance, and who has also published a small collection of Beddoes' letters. The main biographical facts, gathered from these sources, have been put together by Mr. Ramsay Colles, in his introduction to the new edition; but he has added nothing fresh; and we are still in almost complete ignorance as to the details of the last twenty years of Beddoes' existence—full as those years certainly were of interest and even excitement. Nor has the veil been altogether withdrawn from that strange tragedy which, for the strange tragedian, was the last of all.

Readers of Miss Edgeworth's letters may remember that her youngest sister Anne, married a distinguished Clifton physician, Dr. Thomas Beddoes. Their eldest son, born in 1803, was named Thomas Lovell, after his father and grandfather, and grew up to be the author of *The Brides' Tragedy* and *Death's Jest Book.* Dr. Beddoes was a remarkable man, endowed with high and varied intellectual capacities and a rare independence of character. His scientific attainments were recognised by the University of Oxford, where he held the post of Lecturer in Chemistry, until the time of the French Revolution, when he was obliged to resign it, owing to the scandal caused by the unconcealed intensity of his liberal opinions. He then settled at Clifton as a physician, established a flourishing practice, and devoted his leisure to politics and scientific research. Sir Humphry Davy, who was his pupil, and whose merit he was the first to bring to light, declared that 'he had talents which would have exalted him to the pinnacle of philosophical eminence, if they had been applied with discretion.' The words are curiously suggestive of the history of his son; and indeed the poet affords a striking instance of the hereditary transmission of mental qualities. Not only did Beddoes inherit his father's talents and his father's inability to make the best use of them; he possessed in a no less remarkable degree his father's independence of mind. In both cases, this quality was coupled with a corresponding eccentricity of conduct, which occasionally, to puzzled onlookers, wore the appearance of something very near insanity. Many stories are related of the queer behaviour of Dr. Beddoes. One day he astonished the ladies of Clifton by appearing at a tea-party with a packet of sugar in his hand; he explained that it was East Indian sugar, and that nothing would induce him to eat the usual kind, which came from Jamaica and was made by slaves. More extraordinary were his medical prescriptions; for he was in the habit of ordering cows to be conveyed into his patients' bedrooms, in order, as he said, that they might 'inhale the animals' breath.' It is easy to imagine the delight which the singular spectacle of a cow climbing upstairs into an invalid's bedroom must have given to the future author of "Harpagus" and "The Oviparous Tailor." But 'little Tom,' as Miss Edgeworth calls him, was not destined to enjoy for long the benefit of parental example; for Dr. Beddoes died in the prime of life, when the child was not yet six years old.

The genius at school is usually a disappointing figure, for, as a rule, one must be commonplace to be a successful boy. In that preposterous world, to be remarkable is to be overlooked; and nothing less vivid than the white-hot blaze of a Shelley will bring with it even a distinguished martyrdom. But Beddoes was an exception, though he was not a martyr. On the contrary, he dominated his fellows as absolutely as if he had been a dullard and a dunce. He was at Charterhouse; and an entertaining account of his existence there has been preserved to us in a paper of school reminiscences, written by Mr. C. D. Bevan, who had been his fag. Though his place in the school was high, Beddoes' interests were devoted not so much to classical scholarship as to the literature of his own tongue. Cowley, he afterwards told a friend, had been the first poet he had understood; but no doubt he had begun to understand poetry many years before he went to Charterhouse; and, while he was there, the reading which he chiefly delighted in was the Elizabethan drama. 'He liked acting,' says Mr. Bevan, 'and was a good judge of it, and used to give apt though burlesque imitations of the popular actors, particularly Kean and Macready. Though his voice was harsh and his enunciation offensively conceited, he read with so much propriety of expression and manner, that I was always glad to listen: even when I was pressed into the service as his accomplice, his enemy, or his love, with a due accompaniment of curses, caresses, or kicks, as the course of his declamation required. One play in particular, Marlowe's *Tragedy of Dr. Faustus,* excited my admiration in this way; and a liking for the old English drama, which I still retain, was created and strengthened by such recitations.' But Beddoes' dramatic performances were not limited to the works of others; when the occasion arose he was able to supply the necessary material himself. A locksmith had incurred his displeasure by putting a bad lock on his bookcase; Beddoes vowed vengeance; and when next the man appeared he was received by a dramatic interlude, representing his last moments, his horror and remorse, his death, and the funeral procession, which was interrupted by fiends, who carried off body and soul to eternal torments. Such was the realistic vigour of the performance that the locksmith, according to Mr. Bevan, 'departed in a storm of wrath and execrations, and could not be persuaded, for some time, to resume his work.'

Besides the interlude of the wicked locksmith, Beddoes' school compositions included a novel in the style of Fielding (which has unfortunately disappeared), the beginnings of an Elizabethan tragedy, and much miscellaneous verse. In 1820 he left Charterhouse, and went to Pembroke College, Oxford, where, in the following year, while still a freshman, he published his first volume, *The Improvisatore,* a series of short narratives in verse. The book had been written in part while he was at school; and its immaturity is obvious. It contains no trace of the nervous vigour of his later style; the verse is weak, and the sentiment, to use his own expression, 'Moorish.' Indeed, the only interest of the little work lies in the evidence which it affords that the singular pre-occupation which eventually dominated Beddoes' mind had, even in these days, made its appearance. The book is full of death. The poems begin on battle-fields and end in charnel-houses; old men are slaughtered in cold blood, and lovers are struck by lightning into mouldering heaps of corruption. The boy, with his elaborate exhibitions of physical horror, was doing his best to make his readers' flesh creep. But the attempt was far too crude; and in after years, when Beddoes had become a past-master of that difficult art, he was very much ashamed of his first publication. So eager was he to destroy every trace of its existence, that he did not spare even the finely bound copies of his friends. The story goes that he amused himself by visiting their libraries with a penknife, so that, when next they took out the precious volume, they found the pages gone.

Beddoes, however, had no reason to be ashamed of his next publication, *The Brides' Tragedy,* which appeared in 1822. In a single bound, he had reached the threshold of poetry, and was knocking at the door. The line which divides the best and most accomplished verse from poetry itself—that subtle and momentous line which every one can draw, and no one can explain—Beddoes had not yet crossed. But he had gone as far as it was possible to go by the aid of mere skill in the art of writing, and he was still in his twentieth year. Many passages in *The Brides' Tragedy* seem only to be waiting for the breath of inspiration which will bring them into life; and indeed, here and there, the breath has come, the warm, the true, the vital breath of Apollo. No one, surely, whose lips had not tasted of the waters of Helicon, could have uttered such words as these:

> Here's the blue violet, like Pandora's eye,
> When first it darkened with immortal life

or a line of such intense imaginative force as this:

> I've huddled her into the wormy earth;

or this splendid description of a stormy sunrise:

> The day is in its shroud while yet an infant;
> And Night with giant strides stalks o'er the world,
> Like a swart Cyclops, on its hideous front
> One round, red, thunder-swollen eye ablaze.

The play was written on the Elizabethan model, and, as a play, it is disfigured by Beddoes' most characteristic faults: the construction is weak, the interest fluctuates from character to character, and the motives and actions of the characters themselves are for the most part curiously remote from the realities of life. Yet, though the merit of the tragedy depends almost entirely upon the verse, there are signs in it that, while Beddoes lacked the gift of construction, he nevertheless possessed one important dramatic faculty—the power of creating detached scenes of interest and beauty. The scene in which the half-crazed Leonora imagines to herself, beside the couch on which her dead daughter lies, that the child is really living after all, is dramatic in the highest sense of the word; the situation, with all its capabilities of pathetic irony, is conceived

and developed with consummate art and absolute restraint. Leonora's speech ends thus:

> . . . Speak, I pray thee,
> Floribel,
> Speak to thy mother; do but whisper 'aye';
> Well, well, I will not press her; I am sure
> She has the welcome news of some good fortune,
> And hoards the telling till her father comes;
> . . . Ah! She half laughed. I've guessed it then;
> Come tell me, I'll be secret. Nay, if you mock me,
> I must be very angry till you speak.
> Now this is silly; some of these young boys
> Have dressed the cushions with her clothes in sport.
> 'Tis very like her. I could make this image
> Act all her greetings; she shall bow her head:
> 'Good-morrow, mother'; and her smiling face
> Falls on my neck.—Oh, heaven, 'tis she indeed!
> I know it all—don't tell me.

The last seven words are a summary of anguish, horror, and despair, such as Webster himself might have been proud to write.

The Brides' Tragedy was well received by critics; and a laudatory notice of Beddoes in the *Edinburgh,* written by Bryan Waller Procter—better known then than now under his pseudonym of Barry Cornwall—led to a lasting friendship between the two poets. The connection had an important result, for it was through Procter that Beddoes became acquainted with the most intimate of all his friends—Thomas Forbes Kelsall, then a young lawyer at Southampton. In the summer of 1823 Beddoes stayed at Southampton for several months, and, while ostensibly studying for his Oxford degree, gave up most of his time to conversations with Kelsall and to dramatic composition. It was a culminating point in his life: one of those moments which come, even to the most fortunate, once and once only—when youth, and hope, and the high exuberance of genius combine with circumstance and opportunity to crown the marvellous hour. The spadework of *The Brides' Tragedy* had been accomplished; the seed had been sown; and now the harvest was beginning. Beddoes, 'with the delicious sense,' as Kelsall wrote long afterwards, 'of the laurel freshly twined around his head,' poured out, in these Southampton evenings, an eager stream of song. 'His poetic composition,' says his friend, 'was then exceedingly facile: more than once or twice has he taken home with him at night some unfinished act of a drama, in which the editor [Kelsall] had found much to admire, and, at the next meeting, has produced a new one, similar in design, but filled with other thoughts and fancies, which his teeming imagination had projected, in its sheer abundance, and not from any feeling, right or fastidious, of unworthiness in its predecessor. Of several of these very striking fragments, large and grand in their aspect as they each started into form,

> Like the red outline of beginning Adam,

. . . the only trace remaining is literally the impression thus deeply cut into their one observer's mind. The fine verse just quoted is the sole remnant, indelibly stamped on the editor's memory, of one of these extinct creations.' Fragments survive of at least four dramas, projected, and brought to various stages of completion, at about this time. Beddoes was impatient of the common restraints; he was dashing forward in the spirit of his own advice to another poet:

> Creep not nor climb,
> As they who place their topmost of sublime
> On some peak of this planet, pitifully.
> Dart eaglewise with open wings, and fly
> Until you meet the gods!

Eighteen months after his Southampton visit, Beddoes took his degree at Oxford, and, almost immediately, made up his mind to a course of action which had the profoundest effect upon his future life. He determined to take up the study of medicine; and with that end in view established himself, in 1825, at the University at Göttingen. It is very clear, however, that he had no intention of giving up his poetical work. He took with him to Germany the beginnings of a new play—'a very Gothic-style tragedy,' he calls it, 'for which I have a jewel of a name—***Death's Jest Book***; of course,' he adds, 'no one will ever read it'; and, during his four years at Göttingen, he devoted most of his leisure to the completion of this work. He was young; he was rich; he was interested in medical science; and no doubt it seemed to him that he could well afford to amuse himself for half-a-dozen years, before he settled down to the poetical work which was to be the serious occupation of his life. But, as time passed, he became more and more engrossed in the study of medicine, for which he gradually discovered he had not only a taste but a gift; so that at last he came to doubt whether it might not be his true vocation to be a physician, and not a poet after all. Engulfed among the students of Göttingen, England and English ways of life, and even English poetry, became dim to him; 'dir, dem Anbeter der seligen Gottheiten der Musen, u.s.w.,' he wrote to Kelsall, 'was Unterhaltendes kann der Liebhaber von Knochen, der fleissige Botaniker und Phisiolog mittheilen?' In 1830 he was still hesitating between the two alternatives. 'I sometimes wish,' he told the same friend, 'to devote myself exclusively to the study of anatomy and physiology in science, of languages, and dramatic poetry'; his pen had run away with him; and his 'exclusive' devotion turned out to be a double one, directed towards widely different ends. While he was still in this state of mind, a new interest took possession of him—an interest which worked havoc with his dreams of dramatic authorship and scientific research: he became involved in the revolutionary movement which was at that time beginning to agitate Europe. The details of his adventures are unhappily lost to us, for we know nothing more of them than can be learnt from a few scanty references in his rare letters to English friends; but it is certain that the part he played was an active, and even a dangerous one. He was turned out of Würzburg by 'that ingenious Jackanapes,' the King of Bavaria; he was an intimate friend of Hegetschweiler, one of the leaders of liberalism in Switzerland; and he was present in Zurich when a body of six thousand peasants, 'half unarmed, and the other half armed with scythes, dungforks and poles, entered the town and overturned the liberal government.' In the tumult Hegetschweiler was killed, and Beddoes was soon afterwards forced to fly the canton. During the following years we catch glimpses of him, flitting mysteriously over Germany and Switzerland, at Berlin, at Baden, at Giessen, a strange solitary figure, with tangled hair and meerschaum pipe, scribbling lampoons upon the King of Prussia, translating Grainger's *Spinal Cord* into German, and Schoenlein's *Diseases of Europeans* into English, exploring Pilatus and the Titlis, evolving now and then some ghostly lyric or some rabelaisian tale, or brooding over the scenes of his 'Gothic-styled tragedy,' wondering if it were worthless or inspired, and giving it—as had been his wont for the last twenty years—just one more touch before he sent it to the press. He appeared in England once or twice, and in 1846 made a stay of several months, visiting the Procters in London, and going down to Southampton to be with Kelsall once again. Eccentricity had grown on him; he would shut himself for days in his bedroom, smoking furiously; he would fall into fits of long and deep depression. He shocked some of his relatives by arriving at their country house astride a donkey; and he amazed the Procters by starting out one evening to set fire to Drury Lane Theatre with a lighted five-pound note. After this last visit to England, his history becomes even more obscure than before. It is known that in 1847 he was in Frankfort, where he lived for six months in close companionship with a young baker called Degen—'a nice-looking young man, nineteen years of age,' we are told, 'dressed in a blue blouse, fine in expression, and of a natural dignity of manner'; and that, in the spring of the following year, the two friends went off to Zurich, where Beddoes hired the theatre for a night in order that Degen might appear on the stage in the part of Hotspur. At Basel, however, for some unexplained reason, the friends parted, and Beddoes fell immediately into the profoundest gloom. 'Il a été misérable,' said the waiter at the Cigogne Hotel, where he was staying, 'il a voulu se tuer.' It was true. He inflicted a deep wound in his leg with a razor, in the hope, apparently, of bleeding to death. He was taken to the hospital, where he constantly tore off the bandages, until at last it was necessary to amputate the leg below the knee. The operation was successful, Beddoes began to recover, and, in the autumn, Degen came back to Basel. It seemed as if all were going well; for the poet, with his books around him, and the blue-bloused Degen by his bedside, talked happily of politics and literature, and of an Italian journey in the spring. He walked out twice; was he still happy? Who can tell? Was it happiness, or misery, or what strange impulse, that drove him, on his third walk, to go to a chemist's shop in the town, and to obtain there a phial of deadly poison? On the evening of that day—the 26th of January, 1849—Dr. Ecklin, his physician, was hastily summoned, to find Beddoes lying insensible upon the bed. He never recovered consciousness, and died that night. Upon his breast was found a pencil note, addressed to one of his English friends. 'My dear Philips,' it began, 'I am food for what I am good for—worms.' A few testamentary wishes followed. Kelsall was to have the manuscripts; and—'W. Beddoes must have a case (50 bottles) of Champagne Moet, 1847 growth, to drink my death in . . . I ought to have been, among other things,' the gruesome document concluded, 'a good poet. Life was too great a bore on one peg, and that a bad one. Buy for Dr. Ecklin one of Reade's best stomach-pumps.' It was the last of his additions to *Death's Jest Book,* and the most *macabre* of all.

Kelsall discharged his duties as literary executor with exemplary care. The manuscripts were fragmentary and confused. There were three distinct drafts of *Death's Jest Book,* each with variations of its own; and from these Kelsall compiled his first edition of the drama, which appeared in 1850. In the following year he brought out the two volumes of poetical works, which remained for forty years the only record of the full scope and power of Beddoes' genius. They contain reprints of *The Brides' Tragedy* and *Death's Jest Book,* together with two unfinished tragedies, and a great number of dramatic fragments and lyrics; and the poems are preceded by Kelsall's memoir of his friend. Of these rare and valuable volumes the Muses' Library edition is almost an exact reprint, except that it omits the memoir and revives "The Improvisatore." Only one other edition of Beddoes exists—the limited one brought out by Mr. Gosse in 1890, and based upon a fresh examination of the manuscripts. Mr. Gosse was able to add ten lyrics and one dramatic fragment to those already published by Kelsall; he made public for the first time the true story of Beddoes' suicide, which Kelsall had concealed; and, in 1893, he followed up his edition of the poems by a volume of Beddoes' letters. It is clear, therefore, that there is no one living to whom lovers of Beddoes owe so much as to Mr. Gosse. He has supplied most important materials for the elucidation of the poet's history: and, among the lyrics which he has printed for the first time, are to be found one of the most perfect specimens of Beddoes' command of unearthly pathos— "The Old Ghost"—and one of the most singular examples of his vein of grotesque and ominous humour—"The Oviparous Tailor." Yet it may be doubted whether even Mr. Gosse's edition is the final one. There are traces in Beddoes' letters of unpublished compositions which may still come to light. What has happened, one would like to know, to *The Ivory Gate,* that 'volume of prosaic poetry and poetical prose,' which Beddoes talked of publishing in 1837? Only a few fine stanzas from it have ever appeared. And, as Mr. Gosse himself tells us, the variations in *Death's Jest Book* alone would warrant the publication of a variorum edition of that work—'if,' he wisely adds, for the proviso contains the gist of the matter—'if the interest in Beddoes should continue to grow.'

'Say what you will, I am convinced the man who is to awaken the drama must be a bold, trampling fellow—no creeper into worm-holes—no reviver even—however good. These reanimations are vampire-cold.' The words occur in one of Beddoes' letters, and they are usually quoted by critics, on the rare occasions on which his poetry is discussed, as an instance of the curious incapacity of artists to practise what they preach. But the truth is that Beddoes was not a 'creeper into worm-holes,' he was not even a 'reviver'; he was a reincarnation. Everything that we know of him goes to show that the laborious and elaborate effort of literary reconstruction was quite alien to his spirit. We have Kelsall's evidence as to the ease and abundance of his composition; we have the character of the man, as it shines forth in his letters and in the history of his life—records of a 'bold, trampling fellow,' if ever there was one; and we have the evidence of his poetry itself. For the impress of a fresh and vital intelligence is stamped unmistakably upon all that is best in his work. His mature blank verse is perfect. It is not an artificial concoction galvanished into the semblance of life; it simply lives. And, with Beddoes, maturity was precocious, for he obtained complete mastery over the most difficult and dangerous of metres at a wonderfully early age. Blank verse is like the Djin in the *Arabian Nights*; it is either the most terrible of masters, or the most powerful of slaves. If you have not the magic secret, it will take your best thoughts, your bravest imaginations, and change them into toads and fishes; but, if the spell be yours, it will turn into a flying carpet and lift your simplest utterance into the highest heaven. Beddoes had mastered the 'Open, Sesame' at an age when most poets are still mouthing ineffectual wheats and barleys. In his twenty-second year, his thoughts filled and moved and animated his blank verse as easily and familiarly as a hand in a glove. He wishes to compare, for instance, the human mind, with its knowledge of the past, to a single eye receiving the light of the stars; and the object of the comparison is to lay stress upon the concentration on one point of a vast multiplicity of objects. There could be no better exercise for a young verse-writer than to attempt his own expression of this idea, and then to examine these lines by Beddoes—lines where simplicity and splendour have been woven together with the ease of accomplished art.

> How glorious to live! Even in one thought
> The wisdom of past times to fit together,
> And from the luminous minds of many men
> Catch a reflected truth; as, in one eye,
> Light, from unnumbered worlds and farthest planets
> Of the star-crowded universe, is gathered
> Into one ray.

The effect is, of course, partly produced by the diction; but the diction, fine as it is, would be useless without the phrasing—that art by which the two forces of the metre and the sense are made at once to combat, to combine with, and to heighten each other. It is, however, impossible to do more than touch upon this side—the technical side—of Beddoes' genius. But it may be noticed that in his mastery of phrasing—as in so much besides—he was a true Elizabethan. The great artists of that age knew that without phrasing dramatic verse was a dead thing; and it is only necessary to turn from their pages to those of an eighteenth-century dramatist—Addison, for instance—to understand how right they were.

Beddoes' power of creating scenes of intense dramatic force, which had already begun to show itself in *The*

Brides' Tragedy, reached its full development in his subsequent work. The opening act of *The Second Brother*—the most nearly complete of his unfinished tragedies—is a striking example of a powerful and original theme treated in such a way that, while the whole of it is steeped in imaginative poetry, yet not one ounce of its dramatic effectiveness is lost. The duke's next brother, the heir to the dukedom of Ferrara, returns to the city, after years of wandering, a miserable and sordid beggar—to find his younger brother, rich, beautiful, and reckless, leading a life of gay debauchery, with the assurance of succeeding to the dukedom when the duke dies. The situation presents possibilities for just those bold and extraordinary contrasts which were so dear to Beddoes' heart. While Marcello, the second brother, is meditating over his wretched fate, Orazio, the third, comes upon the stage, crowned and glorious, attended by a train of singing revellers, and with a courtesan upon either hand. 'Wine in a ruby!' he exclaims, gazing into his mistress's eyes:

> I'll solemnize their beauty in a draught
> Pressed from the summer of an hundred vines.

Meanwhile Marcello pushes himself forward, and attempts to salute his brother.

> *Orazio.* Insolent beggar!
> *Marcello.*   Prince! But we must shake hands.
>   Look you, the round earth's like a sleeping serpent,
>   Who drops her dusky tail upon her crown
>   Just here. Oh, we are like two mountain peaks
>   Of two close planets, catching in the air:
>   You, King Olympus, a great pile of summer,
>   Wearing a crown of gods; I, the vast top
>   Of the ghosts' deadly world, naked and dark,
>   With nothing reigning on my desolate head
>   But an old spirit of a murdered god,
>   Palaced within the corpse of Saturn's father.

They begin to dispute, and at last Marcello exclaims—

> Aye, Prince, you have a brother—
> *Orazio.* The Duke—he'll scourge you.
> *Marcello.*   Nay, *the second,* sir,
>   Who, like an envious river, flows between
>   Your footsteps and Ferrara's throne . . .
> *Orazio.*   Stood he before me there,
>   By you, in you, as like as you're unlike,
>   Straight as you're bowed, young as you are old,
>   And many years nearer than him to Death,
>   The falling brilliancy of whose white sword
>   Your ancient locks so silverly reflect,
>   I would deny, outswear, and overreach,
>   And pass him with contempt, as I do you.
>   Jove! How we waste the stars: set on, my friends.

And so the revelling band pass onward, singing still, as they vanish down the darkened street:

> Strike, you myrtle-crownèd boys,
> Ivied maidens, strike together! . . .

and Marcello is left alone:

> I went forth
> Joyfully, as the soul of one who closes
> His pillowed eyes beside an unseen murderer,
> And like its horrible return was mine,
> To find the heart, wherein I breathed and beat,
> Cold, gashed, and dead. Let me forget to love,
> And take a heart of venom: let me make
> A staircase of the frightened breasts of men,
> And climb into a lonely happiness!
> And thou, who only art alone as I,
> Great solitary god of that one sun,
> I charge thee, by the likeness of our state,
> Undo these human veins that tie me close
> To other men, and let your servant griefs
> Unmilk me of my mother, and pour in
> Salt scorn and steaming hate!

A moment later he learnt that the duke has suddenly died, and that the dukedom is his. The rest of the play affords an instance of Beddoes' inability to trace out a story, clearly and forcibly, to an appointed end. The succeeding acts are crowded with beautiful passages, with vivid situations, with surprising developments, but the central plot vanishes away into nothing, like a great river dissipating itself among a thousand streams. It is, indeed, clear enough that Beddoes was embarrassed with his riches, that his fertile mind conceived too easily, and that he could never resist the temptation of giving life to his imaginations, even at the cost of killing his play. His conception of Orazio, for instance, began by being that of a young Bacchus, as he appears in the opening scene. But Beddoes could not leave him there; he must have a romantic wife, whom he has deserted; and the wife, once brought into being, must have an interview with her husband. The interview is an exquisitely beautiful one, but it shatters Orazio's character, for, in the course of it, he falls desperately in love with his wife; and meanwhile the wife herself has become so important and interesting a figure that she must be given a father, who in his turn becomes the central character in more than one exciting scene. But, by this time, what has happened to the second brother? It is easy to believe that Beddoes was always ready to begin a new play rather than finish an old one. But it is not so certain that his method was quite as inexcusable as his critics assert. To the reader, doubtless, his faulty construction is glaring enough; but Beddoes wrote his plays to be acted, as a passage in one of his letters very clearly shows. 'You are, I think,' he writes to Kelsall, 'disinclined to the stage: now I confess that I think this is the highest aim of the dramatist, and should be very desirous to get on it. To look down on it is a piece of impertinence, as long as one chooses to write in the form of a play, and is generally the result of one's own inability to produce anything striking and affecting in that way.' And it is precisely upon the stage that such faults of construction as those which disfigure Beddoes' tragedies matter least. An audience, whose attention is held and delighted by a succession of striking incidents clothed in splendid speech, neither cares nor knows whether the effect of the whole, as a whole, is worthy of the separate parts. It would be foolish, in the present melancholy condition of the art of dramatic declamation, to wish for the public performance of **Death's Jest Book**; but it is impossible not to hope that the time may come when an adequate representation of that strange and great work may be something more than 'a possibility more thin than air.' Then, and then only, shall we be able to take the true measure of Beddoes' genius.

Perhaps, however, the ordinary reader finds Beddoes' lack of construction a less distasteful quality than his disregard of the common realities of existence. Not only is the subject-matter of the greater part of his poetry remote and dubious; his very characters themselves seem to be infected by their creator's delight in the mysterious, the strange, and the unreal. They have no healthy activity; or, if they have, they invariably lose it in the second act; in the end, they are all hypochondriac philosophers, puzzling over eternity and dissecting the attributes of Death. The central idea of **Death's Jest Book**—the resurrection of a ghost—fails to be truly effective, because it is difficult to see any clear distinction between the phantom and the rest of the characters. The duke, saved from death by the timely arrival of Wolfram, exclaims, 'Blest hour!' and then, in a moment, begins to ponder, and agonise, and dream:

> And yet how palely, with what faded lips
> Do we salute this unhoped change of fortune!
> Thou art so silent, lady; and I utter
> Shadows of words, like to an ancient ghost,
> Arisen out of hoary centuries
> Where none can speak his language.

Orazio, in his brilliant palace, is overcome with the same feelings:

> Methinks, these fellows, with their ready jests,
> Are like to tedious bells, that ring alike
> Marriage or death.

And his description of his own revels applies no less to the whole atmosphere of Beddoes' tragedies:

> Voices were heard, most loud, which no man owned:
> There were more shadows too than there were men;
> And all the air more dark and thick than night
> Was heavy, as 'twere made of something more
> Than living breaths.

It would be vain to look, among such spectral imaginings as these, for guidance in practical affairs, or for illuminating views on men and things, or for a philosophy, or, in short, for anything which may be called a 'criticism of life.' If a poet must be a critic of life, Beddoes was certainly no poet. He belongs to the class of writers of which, in English literature, Spenser, Keats, and Milton are the dominant figures—the writers who are great merely because of their art. Sir James Stephen was only telling the truth when he remarked that Milton might have put all that he had to say in *Paradise Lost* into a prose pamphlet of two or three pages. But who cares about what Milton had to say? It is his way of saying it that matters; it is his expression. Take away the expression from the *Satires* of

Pope, or from *The Excursion,* and, though you will destroy the poems, you will leave behind a great mass of thought. Take away the expression from *Hyperion,* and you will leave nothing at all. To ask which is the better of the two styles is like asking whether a peach is better than a rose, because, both being beautiful, you can eat the one and not the other. At any rate, Beddoes is among the roses: it is in his expression that his greatness lies. His verse is an instrument of many modulations, of exquisite delicacy, of strange suggestiveness, of amazing power. Playing on it, he can give utterance to the subtlest visions, such as this:

> Just now a beam of joy hung on his eyelash;
> But, as I looked, it sunk into his eye,
> Like a bruised worm writhing its form of rings
> Into a darkening hole.

Or to the most marvellous of vague and vast conceptions, such as this:

>   I begin to
>   hear
> Strange but sweet sounds, and the loud rocky dashing
> Of waves, where time into Eternity
> Falls over ruined worlds.

Or he can evoke sensations of pure loveliness, such as these:

> So fair a creature! of such charms compact
> As nature stints elsewhere: which you may find
> Under the tender eyelid of a serpent,
> Or in the gurge of a kiss-coloured rose,
> By drops and sparks: but when she moves, you see,
> Like water from a crystal overfilled,
> Fresh beauty tremble out of her and lave
> Her fair sides to the ground.

Or he can put into a single line all the long memories of adoration:

>   My love was much;
> My life but an inhabitant of his.

Or he can pass in a moment from tiny sweetness to colossal turmoil:

>   I should not say
> How thou art like the daisy in Noah's meadow,
> On which the foremost drop of rain fell warm
> And soft at evening: so the little flower
> Wrapped up its leaves, and shut the treacherous water
> Close to the golden welcome of its breast,
> Delighting in the touch of that which led
> The shower of oceans, in whose billowy drops
> Tritons and lions of the sea were warring,
> And sometimes ships on fire sunk in the blood,
> Of their own inmates; others were of ice,
> And some had islands rooted in their waves,
> Beasts on their rocks, and forest-powdering winds,
> And showers tumbling on their tumbling self,
> And every sea of every ruined star
> Was but a drop in the world-melting flood.

He can express alike the beautiful tenderness of love, and the hectic, dizzy, and appalling frenzy of extreme rage:—

. . . What shall I do? I speak all wrong,
And lose a soul-full of delicious thought
By talking. Hush! Let's drink each other up
By silent eyes. Who lives, but thou and I,
My heavenly wife? . . .
I'll watch thee thus, till I can tell a second
By thy cheek's change.

In that, one can almost feel the kisses; and, in this, one can almost hear the gnashing of the teeth. 'Never!' exclaims the duke to his son Torrismond:

> There lies no grain of sand between
> My loved and my detested! Wing thee hence,
> Or thou dost stand to-morrow on a cobweb
> Spun o'er the well of clotted Acheron,
> Whose hydrophobic entrails stream with fire!
> And may this intervening earth be snow,
> And my step burn like the mid coal of Ætna,
> Plunging me, through it all, into the core,
> Where in their graves the dead are shut like seeds,
> If I do not—O, but he is my son!

Is not that tremendous? But, to find Beddoes in his most characteristic mood, one must watch him weaving his mysterious imagination upon the woof of mortality. One must wander with him through the pages of ***Death's Jest Book,*** one must grow accustomed to the dissolution of reality, and the opening of the nettled lips of graves; one must learn that 'the dead are most and merriest,' one must ask—'Are the ghosts eaves-dropping?'—one must realise that 'murder is full of holes.' Among the ruins of his Gothic cathedral, on whose cloister walls the Dance of Death is painted, one may speculate at ease over the fragility of existence, and, within the sound of that dark ocean,

> Whose tumultuous waves
> Are heaped, contending ghosts,

one may understand how it is that

> Death is mightier, stronger, and more faithful
> To man than Life.

Lingering there, one may watch the Deaths come down from their cloister, and dance and sing amid the moonlight; one may laugh over the grotesque contortions of skeletons; one may crack jokes upon corruption; one may sit down with phantoms, and drink to the health of Death.

In private intercourse Beddoes was the least morbid of human beings. His mind was like one of those Gothic cathedrals of which he was so fond—mysterious within, and filled with a light at once richer and less real than the light of day; on the outside, firm, and towering, and immediately impressive; and embellished, both inside and out, with grinning gargoyles. His conversation, Kelsall tells us, was full of humour and vitality, and untouched by any trace of egoism or affectation. He loved discussion, plunging into it with fire, and carrying it onward with high dexterity and good-humoured force. His letters are excellent: simple, spirited, spicy, and as original as his verse;

flavoured with that vein of rattling open-air humour which had produced his school-boy novel in the style of Fielding. He was a man whom it would have been a rare delight to know. His character, so eminently English, compact of courage, of originality, of imagination, and with something coarse in it as well, puts one in mind of Hamlet: not the melodramatic sentimentalist of the stage; but the real Hamlet, Horatio's Hamlet, who called his father's ghost old truepenny, who forged his uncle's signature, who fought Laertes, and ranted in a grave, and lugged the guts into the neighbour room. His tragedy, like Hamlet's, was the tragedy of an overpowerful will—a will so strong as to recoil upon itself, and fall into indecision. It is easy for a weak man to be decided—there is so much to make him so; but a strong man, who can do anything, sometimes leaves everything undone. Fortunately Beddoes, though he did far less than he might have done, possessed so rich a genius that what he did, though small in quantity, is in quality beyond price. 'I might have been among other things, a good poet,' were his last words. 'Among other things'! Aye, there's the rub. But, in spite of his own 'might have been,' a good poet he was. Perhaps for him, after all, there was very little to regret; his life was full of high nobility; and what other way of death would have befitted the poet of death? There is a thought constantly recurring throughout his writings—in his childish as in his most mature work—the thought of the beauty and the supernal happiness of soft and quiet death. He had visions of 'rosily dying,' of 'turning to daisies gently in the grave,' of a 'pink reclining death,' of death coming like a summer cloud over the soul. 'Let her deathly life pass into death,' says one of his earliest characters, 'like music on the night wind.' And, in ***Death's Jest Book,*** Sibylla has the same thoughts:

> O Death! I am thy friend,
> I struggle not with thee, I love thy state:
> Thou canst be sweet and gentle, be so now;
> And let me pass praying away into thee,
> As twilight still does into starry night.

Did his mind, obsessed and overwhelmed by images of death, crave at last for the one thing stranger than all these—the experience of it? It is easy to believe so, and that, ill, wretched, and abandoned by Degen at the miserable Cigogne Hotel, he should seek relief in the gradual dissolution which attends upon loss of blood. And then, when he had recovered, when he was almost happy once again, the old thoughts, perhaps, came crowding back upon him—thoughts of the futility of life, and the supremacy of death and the mystical whirlpool of the unknown, and the long quietude of the grave. In the end, Death had grown to be something more than Death to him—it was, mysteriously and transcendentally, Love as well.

> Death's darts are sometimes Love's. So Nature tells,
> When laughing waters close o'er drowning men;
> When in flowers' honied corners poison dwells;
> When Beauty dies: and the unwearied ken

Of those who seek a cure for long despair
Will learn . . .

What learning was it that rewarded him? What ghostly
knowledge of eternal love?

> If there are ghosts to raise,
> What shall I call,
> Out of hell's murky haze,
> Heaven's blue pall?
>
> —Raise my loved long-lost boy
> To lead me to his joy.—
> There are no ghosts to raise;
> Out of death lead no ways;
> Vain is the call.
>
> —Know'st thou not ghosts to sue?
> No love thou hast.
> Else lie, as I will do,
> And breathe thy last.
> So out of Life's fresh crown
> Fall like a rose-leaf down.
> Thus are the ghosts to woo;
> Thus are all dreams made true,
> Ever to last!

Royall H. Snow (essay date 1928)

SOURCE: "*Death's Jest Book, or the Fool's Tragedy*," in
Thomas Lovell Beddoes, Covici & Friede, 1928, pp. 99-
128.

[*In the following essay, Snow deems* Death's Jest Book *a
unique but flawed drama, contending that the play's "brilliance is akin to that of a diamond crushed under a pile-
driver—scattered, chaotic, begrimed, but still there and
sparkling."*]

I

A STUDY IN INTENSITIES

It is in ***Death's Jest Book*** that Beddoes' spectacular and
morbid genius comes to its final flowering; and it is upon
this play, together with a handful of scattered lyrics, that
his fame must rest—that tentative fame a self-assured and
normal world concedes to an explorer of the uncharted
and a companion of spectres. For ***The Fool's Tragedy*** is
something that comes from the fringes, at least, of delirium
and despair. Skeletal figures, painted on the wall of a
ruined church, step down to feast and dance a gavotte; the
corrupted flesh of a dead knight grows firm again and rises
to haunt his murderer;—and such move on Beddoes' stage
with the assurance of the living. Skeletons pantomime life.
A lover, dying beneath his mistress's window, writhes to
the tune of her bridal serenade. A duke murders the
devoted friend who has saved him from captivity, and the
spectre of that friend returns to haunt him.

> . . . The days come
> When scarce a lover, for his maiden's hair,

Can pluck a stalk whose rose draws not its hue
Out of a hate-killed heart. Nature's polluted,
There's man in every secret corner of her,
Doing damned wicked deeds. Thou art old, world,
A hoary atheistic murderous star;
I wish that thou would'st die, or could'st be slain.[1]

And through all this Isbrand—a court fool whose one love
is hate—sings wild songs and shakes his cap and bells, the
music of which is in tune with the castanets of death and
the laughter of devils.

It is of such lurid stuff that ***Death's Jest Book*** is made.
And through it all there is an incandescence of fierce
language, and the daring metaphors blaze with the sparkle
of black stars before the bright glow of hell. In the orderly
sequence of the history of literature the play has no place;
it belongs to no school and no period. Written in the
nineteenth century its language has, by right divine and
not artifice, the fine unexpectedness of the days of
Elizabeth. Possessed of the verve of such robust and
healthy times, it is saturated with the grotesque and pessimistic diabolism of the Germany of E. T. A. Hoffman.
From its debris the disciples of Freud might quarry
unmentionable images. And, combining such elements, it
was written by an Englishman who died in the reign of
Victoria. It is unique.

But also, as a play, it has certain clearly marked limitations. Its brilliance is akin to that of a diamond crushed
under a pile-driver—scattered, chaotic, begrimed, but still
there and sparkling. Yet, despite all the diamond dust that
is in it, the play suffers from an excess of plain plaster. It
is patched and built, and the final edifice is a rickety one.
Tediums encroach upon intensities, a growth of rhetoric
chokes the poetic, the plot often eddies rather than flows;
beside men firm of intent are others merely gesticulatory,
and women who do nothing but simper. So that in the last
analysis, Beddoes, who in individual scenes may take rank
with Webster as a master of sombre intensities, has written
a play which is chaotic and ineffectual.

It is impossible to give any very coherent account of a
play whose action is so full of cross purposes. In the main
it centers about the plots of the vengeful jester, Isbrand,
against his duke. The duke, at the opening of the play, is a
fugitive in North Africa where he has been defeated—
Isbrand begins by trying to prevent the departure of a
rescue expedition. He fails, and the action shifts to Africa.
The duke is saved but he kills Wolfram, his rescuer, in a
quarrel over a woman. With the action shifted back to
Silesia, this murder furnishes Isbrand with a pattern for his
revenge—not only does he conspire for the political
overthrow of the duke, but also he goads the two sons of
the duke into quarrelling over a woman as the duke had
quarrelled with Wolfram—with the murder of one brother
by another as the conclusion. The action is further
complicated by the spectre of Wolfram, called back to
earth unqittingly by the very man who had killed him.

The action, however, is erratic and confused, and in the
end such greatness as the play may have rests mainly upon

two scenes and its wild fool. There have been plays enough of revenge and horror. Beddoes, however, brings into this alien atmosphere a tart cynicism and a dash of metaphysics, so that the conventional murder play keeps slanting off in unexpected directions. The result is vivid. To give one example: there is in the third act a conspiracy scene. The conspirators meet by moonlight under the ruins of a spacious gothic cathedral. Near them is the sepulchre of the dukes. This is impressive only in the usual melodramatic fashion. But Isbrand's imagination has deepened the significance of it, for he has rifled the tomb of Melveric's wife, and put in the place of her body, the body of the murdered Wolfram,—this that in due time:

> Melveric the dead shall dream of heaven
> Embracing his damnation. There's revenge.[2]

And revenge it is, of a more terrible sort than one expects to find amid such melodrama; and it is with a wry satisfaction Isbrand chooses to hold his meetings near.

So far the pattern is conventional enough, but, with their work done, the conspirators instead of slinking off, remain to carouse and jest. Jets of merriment flare out against the grim background. Isbrand, at once jubilant and ferocious, is at his best—his nerves stung to an intensity by the setting, and their purpose. In the end he contributes a song, a song that he had composed one night, "while picking poisons to make the rats a salad."

> Squats on a toad-stool under a tree
>   A bodiless child full of life in the gloom,
> Crying with frog voice, What shall I be?
> Poor unborn ghost, for my mother killed me
>   Scarcely alive in her wicked womb.
> What shall I be? shall I creep to the egg
>   That's cracking asunder yonder by Nile,
>   And with eighteen toes,
>   And a snuff-taking nose,
> Make an Egyptian crocodile?
> Sing, 'Catch a mummy by the leg
>   And crunch him with an upper jaw,
>   Wagging tail and clenching claw;
>   Take a bill-full from my craw,
>   Neighbor raven, caw O caw,
>   Grunt, my crocky, pretty maw!
>   And give a paw'.[3]

So opens the song. Bizarre, startling, perhaps revolting—in any case it is conduct most improper in a conspirator. And the scene is not yet ended. The duke, who has joined the conspirators in disguise, remains behind by the tomb of his wife. He tries by magic to recall her; there is a commotion in the tomb and out pops—Mandrake, a smart-aleck and rather crack-brained clown who, early in the play, had turned journeyman magician and set off to the Nile to learn wisdom.

> Excuse me: (remarks Mandrake, quite unabashed by the unusual situation) as you have thought proper to call me to the living, I shall take the liberty of remaining alive. If you want to speak to another ghost, of longer standing, look into the old lumber-room of a

vault again: someone seems to be putting himself together there. Goodnight, gentlemen, for I must travel to Egypt once more.[4]

It is only after this that the Spectre of Wolfram, grim and unhurried, emerges from the tomb of the wife.

Such is the flavour of Beddoes at his best, or worst. The power of the abnormal is there, and not an abnormal which is lurking and sly, but one which is robust and powerful, which occupies the foreground rather than lurks in the shadows of his mind. But there is also the sting of an astringent and cynical mind behind it. The familiar paraphernalia of death Beddoes uses, but in a fashion peculiar to himself. The trappings and terror of death, ruined churches, sepulchres, and ghosts have been often enough employed for the sake of the emotional pressure they put upon the living. It is only in Beddoes that the dead become the living, only in Beddoes that a scene of sombre association is used, not to depress, but to bring out the reckless and distorted gaiety of a principal character.

The second conspiracy scene, that of the fifth act, is similar in tone. This scene opens upon the churchyard empty. Upon the ruined walls of the church is painted a Dance of Death and the figures of it, made crazy by the midnight moon, step down from the walls to mimic life, dancing and feasting, while they sing that "Death's a droll fellow". As the conspirators enter, they slip back to their places, and the conspirators repeat their previous carousal. This time, however, it is the Spectre of Wolfram who contributes the most applauded drinking song. Full-throated he sings among the echoing tombstones:

> Old Adam, the carrion crow,
>   The old crow of Cairo;
> He sat in the shower, and let it flow
>   Under his tail and over his crest;
>   And through every feather
>   Leaked the wet weather;
>   And the bough swung under his nest;
> For his beak it was heavy with marrow.
>   Is that the wind dying? O no;
>   It's only two devils, that blow
>   Through a murderer's bones, to and fro,
>   In the ghosts' moonshine.
> Ho! Eve, my grey carrion wife,
>   When we have supped on kings' marrow,
> Where shall we drink and make merry our life?
>   Our nest it is Queen Cleopatra's skull,
>   'Tis cloven and cracked,
>   And battered and hacked,
>   But with tears of blue eyes it is full:
> Let us drink then, my raven of Cairo.
>   Is that the wind dying? O no;
>   It's only two devils, that blow
>   Through a murderer's bones, to and fro,
>   In the ghosts' moonshine.[5]

Such is the temper of the play. In the end Isbrand falls, stabbed and jesting still. But he has had his revenge. Both sons of the duke are dead, and the Spectre of Wolfram leads the unfortunate Melveric, still alive, back into that tomb from which the spectre had risen.

II

COMPOSITION OF THE PLAY

The play is a strange one, and unpredictable—melancholy in the diffusion and collapse of its power. And not the least strange thing about it is the history of its composition. In this history in fact, and in the changes which the nature of the poet underwent in the long period of its composition, perhaps lies the explanation of its structural weakness, its tendency to an overgrowth of rhetoric, and to wandering into bye-paths of action.

The tragedy, like so much of Beddoes' work, began with a burst of enthusiasm and the wreck of previous undertakings. There were the scattered bits of at least four unfinished dramas about him when, in June, 1825, he flung the best of them aside on behalf of "a very gothic-styled tragedy for which he had a jewel of name—*Death's Jest Book*".[6] And in Beddoes' career that phrase is like a sponge swept across a crowded slate. Facility had thus far been one of his most striking attributes. Kelsall has reported the speed and lavishness with which he wrote at Southampton, the overflow and abundance of his imagination. With the entrance of *Death's Jest Book* into his mind, and with the migration to Germany, all this tropical luxuriance of fancy vanishes. He began the play at twenty-two, a young man brilliant and fecund who had been hailed by *The London Magazine* as "a scion worthy of the stock from which Shakespeare and Marlowe sprang"; twenty-four years later when he died, desolate and an exile, the play was still being revised.

It was with assurance enough that Beddoes began, for in July, 1825, he wrote back from Germany, whither he had just gone, that he expected to return to England "with a rather quaint and unintelligible tragedy, which will set all critical pens nib upwards, à la fretful porcupine." That was the first intimation his friends had of the nature of the jewel-named tragedy he had embarked upon; their next news of it was in December when it had already begun to play its role of old man of the sea, for it was "a horrible waste of time, but one must now & then throw away the dregs of the day."[7] Yet the same letter makes no hint of giving over—it may be progressing tortoise-fashion but Beddoes is aware that it will be finished,—in the spring or summer he hopes. The spring finds it lying like a snowball which he gives "a kick every now & then out of mere scorn and ill-humour," but it has surely advanced, and will soon come like an "electric shock among the small critics."[8] October, 1826, just sixteen months after Beddoes struck upon his fantastically brilliant title, *Death's Jest Book* is complete, and he promises to send a copy of "my unhappy devil of a tragedy which is done and done for: it's [sic] limbs being as scattered and unconnected as those of the old gentleman whom Medea minced & boiled young."[9]

The small critics, however, were safe yet from the threatened electric shock, for Beddoes was too thoroughly in the toils of his own imagination to escape it so easily. *Death's Jest Book* was spokesman for a side of his nature—the artistic—he had been trying to suppress in the physician, it was spokesman, too, for his growing sense of disillusion and futility, and, as such, it was not to be lightly gotten rid of, not to be despatched out of his life with a postage stamp. Far from sending home a copy of his "unhappy devil of a tragedy" he was, precisely one year later, still at work on it, cementing into it various dramatic fragments, including portions of the earlier unfinished play, *The Last Man,* and it was not until February, 1829, that he at last forwarded to his friends in England a copy of the play he had been working on intermittently for over three and a half years.

At the moment his scheme seems to have been to seek the criticism of friends in England and, having revised accordingly, to publish. The manuscript of the play, to judge from Beddoes' end of the correspondence, called forth both enthusiasm and some drastic criticism. The good of the tragedy was too fine to be allowed to suffer from its obvious weaknesses. Bryan Waller Procter, in a letter whose friendly sanity deeply impressed Beddoes,[10] apparently called for nothing less than the rewriting of all the prose scenes and passages, almost all the first, and second, and a great part of the third act, not to mention a strengthening of the two principal scenes of the fourth and fifth act—"no trifle" as Beddoes commented in some dismay. The advice was good in the abstract—it was bad for one of Beddoes' unstable nature. He resolved to revise all summer and publish in the autumn, and of course did nothing of the sort.

The subsequent history of the manuscript is difficult to follow, as it must be based upon his correspondence with Kelsall, and this becomes more and more intermittent. The net result of his resolve to spend all the summer of 1829 upon revision was precisely nothing. A year later, [July, 1830] obviously in reply to proddings from across the channel, he retorted that everything about the play annoyed him and that he had utterly neglected it—a statement perhaps contradicted by his own account of having previously sent to another correspondent some alternative lyrics. Once again in a rather melancholy fashion, and with no appetite to the task, he promised to rewrite "this last unhappy play"—and six months later his mind is still upon it. Then there is a gap in his correspondence with Kelsall.

After six years of silence, broken only by brief notes to Revell Phillips, suddenly come two letters in March and May of 1837 to Kelsall. In contrast to the rather melancholy tone with which he had left off, these are letters of verve and good spirits—a fine lyric jostles a bouncing bit of rabelaisianism, his memory runs back to a comic incident of two years before and he is all agog—soon he will have ready for the press a volume of variegated prose and poetry. Also the "stillborn," *Death's Jest Book* is to be included, though it is of course to be again revised.

As suddenly, however, as the publishing project had flared up it vanished. But Beddoes was not yet done with *Death's Jest Book*: that "unhappy devil of a tragedy," "old," "endless," "stillborn," "wretched fool's Tragedy" as he variously called it. Begun in 1825, finished in the rough in 1826, cannibalistically absorbing *The Last Man* in 1827, completed again and sent to England in 1829, undergoing revision in 1831,[11] and preparing for the press in 1837, it would seem that it had claimed enough of Beddoes' energy, but when, after seven years of silence, he writes again to Kelsall in 1844 it is to enclose more lyrics for that "strange conglomerate."

So much of the history of the play is definite, and I think it belies the common assumption that *Death's Jest Book* belongs mainly to the Göttingen period. Not only does the play reappear persistently in his correspondence up to 1844 but also over the famous three texts there were alterations and additions "freely written"[12]—additions whose date we can only guess. And the texts themselves I am inclined to assign to a much later date than is usual, placing the third text not earlier than 1837, eight years after he had left Göttingen.[13] Everything points to the play's having been of much wider significance than if it had belonged to the early period alone. It apparently writes the history of Beddoes' emotional state over a period longer than twenty years, a state of mind indeed whose first clear symptoms appeared in the translation of Schiller's *Philosophical Letters* and which ended in an attempted suicide.

III

PERSONAL SIGNIFICANCE: THE TRAGEDY OF SCEPTICAL DESPAIR

Can one penetrate to any of the springs of his thought? Can one guess at the reasons for the fascination *Death's Jest Book* exercised upon his mind? For though he became progressively less and less occupied with poetry, and the torrential freshets of his springtime diminished to a mere trickle, they never altogether ceased. And if he never escaped from the poetry which was in him, which forced him to write, neither could he escape from *Death's Jest Book* which was the poetry he couldn't get out of him, couldn't complete. Beddoes, the brilliant young rationalist, had retreated to a monotonous German Elysium of golden brown pilsener, innumerable pipes, and painstaking anatomical studies. The history of his life thereupon becomes cloudy. It is difficult to trace the wonderings of his body, the countries in which his mind wandered may only be guessed at, and his letters reveal little—certainly they did not prepare his relatives for that man who reappeared out of obscurity riding upon a donkey, a gloomy philosopher subject to fits of terrible depression, and eccentric to the verge of madness. And it is in this long period of obscure transition that his play took shape.

The truth is that *Death's Jest Book* is the symbol of that emotional ferment and disillusion which was going on behind the placid tobacco smoke. The poetry in him was too strong to kill—medicine might bank but not extinguish the fire. And when it blazed he turned inevitably back to the one play which had been haunting him so long, simply because it was a symbolic account of the forces which were undermining his own intellect. The themes he abandoned had been picked up outside of himself—this was himself, and so in perpetual harmony with his mood. That Beddoes was mad in the ordinary dangerous sense of the word I do not believe. That his mind, under the pressure of isolation and certain other influences, made strange voyages, and came at last into that twilight country where the genius of mankind, as in Dürer's print of Melancholia, sits desolate among the symbols of human accomplishment, I do believe. And from this country his intellect returned contemptuous of, or rather, indifferent to conventionalities—hence his eccentricity. It also came back diseased with the despair which breeds in that pestilential twilight—hence the tone of his work.

Beddoes had brought to the cadavers and dissecting rooms of Germany a lonely and morbid mind. In his very early manhood his tendency toward despondency had frightened him. Now he found himself—at best a recluse and a "non-conductor of friendship"[14] in the perilous isolation of a stranger in a foreign country. But he had also at first a confident rationality, an engrossed absorption in meticulous studies. Very early (March, 1826) he writes back in a doggerel letter the first clear exposition of what he intends to do in *Death's Jest Book*—and it is the "uncypressing" of death he proposes. All the secrets of the dark monarch are to be exposed until he becomes the "fool o' the feast" and is sent back in the end "an unmasked braggart to his bankrupt den."

> For Death is more "a jest" than life: you see
> Contempt grows quick from familiarity.
> I owe this wisdom to Anatomy.[15]

That derisive familiarity Beddoes retained to the end in his play, but, as his own confident rationality began to go to pieces, death became powerfully transformed. In the end Beddoes is still mocking, but it is a wilder mockery as its object becomes more sinister. And death ends no braggart.

It was scarcely more than a year after this doggerel that Beddoes' rationalism began to fail him. The flaw of his character was his inability to harmonize the elements in his own nature. Incurable romantic and immaterialist that he was at heart, the neatly-jointed and mechanical world which his scientific brain presented to him left him starved and unsatisfied—he could add nothing to it simply because his precise mind would accept nothing but mathematical proof of that for which there exists only proof spiritual. By consequence his world collapsed about him. A conviction of the evil absurdity of human life pressed upon him heavily and yet more heavily. The dark wings of futility blackened the air about him.

Death's Jest Book is a mad play because behind it there is this despairing intellect. What is of consequence, of course, is the tone. That a dramatic character speaks for his creator, and that the young Shakespeare woos Ann Hathaway with Romeo, is an illusion so silly it scarcely deserves comment. But it is equally true that no writer can escape his own mind—he is guiltless of words and actions, but the mood, the prevailing impression left by a work of art, is the colour it takes from its creator and reflects him. Years of remaking and interpolation sprouted the growths which obscure the main lines of *Death's Jest Book* but reveal its author's mind. Years of brooding fashioned the intensity of certain scenes of entangled life and death. And Isbrand the jester, born of an intellect returned from the land of pestilential twilight, is a product of years. He is the recoil of an oppressed mind into angry laughter. He mocks. His creator despaired.[16]

Dramatically, Isbrand with his colossal hatred is the most potent force for coherence in this strange tragedy. There is much seething in his wild brain, but he knew beyond the possibility of self-deception what idea was his master.

> A sceptre is smooth handling, it is true,
> And one grows fat and jolly in a chair
> That has a kingdom crouching under it,
> With one's name on its collar, like a dog,
> To fetch and carry. But the heart I have
> Is a strange little snake. He drinks not wine,
> When he'd be drunk, but poison: he doth fatten
> On bitter hate.[17]

Isbrand's hatred is by implication, universal: there is no softening influence near and no affection in him. Liberty is but a word and a bait. This world is a "sepulchral planet", and his jests are made for their sting rather than their laughter. It is in this universal negative that Isbrand finds his kinship with his creator who had written of the "absurdity and unsatisfactory nature of human life." His hatred is an artistic, a positive accretion—what makes it possible that Beddoes' negative despondency should find poetic voice at all; for a pure negative has no dramatic possibilities. Universal hatred, again, is too diffuse for the action of a five act tragic plot; it exists in Isbrand but comes to a particular focus in his consuming animosity toward the duke he serves. And this hatred (the quite unconscious symbol of its creator's despair) is the strong central current which gives the play what unity it has, despite the eddyings and cross currents which combat it.

Beddoes himself conceived of the play as a tragedy of Nemesis. There is no mistaking the intent of the final speech of the Spectre to Duke Melveric with its

> The spirit of retribution called me hither.
> Thy sons have perished for like cause, as that
> For which thou did'st assassinate thy friend.[18]

But equally without mistake it is clear this intent was not carried out. Theoretically one might assume Wolfram, living or spectral, to be the central figure and Isbrand the tool of fate, but to make such an assumption is to make a serious mistake in emphasis. Melveric the duke, furthermore, is but a marionette attached to the strings of plot action:

he has several moments when he comes alive but he is a totally different man in each of these several moments, and there is no connection and no convincing transition. Isbrand on the other hand is always the one man in varying moods between anger and triumph. And his personality is so dynamic that he dominates the stage beyond challenge—the one consistently living figure among a group of gesticulating marionettes. To classify him then as a subsidiary—the tool of fate—in a tragedy revolving around Wolfram or Melveric would be grotesque.[19] And it is this conflict between the nemesis or Elizabethan revenge drama, and the play of the Wild Fool, with its obscure symbolic connection with Beddoes' own nature, which causes the dramatic action to waver.

Death's Jest Book does, indeed, have much in common with the old revenge play. The basic pattern is the same. But especially interesting because of the novelties he presents, is the Spectre of Wolfram as a representative of the ghost of the old Tragedy of Blood. The Elizabethan Ghost is a stock character—he has his manners and a cast of mind, and one knows about what to expect from him. Especially he can be counted upon to leave at cock-crow; and he is inclined to be morosely solitary. Wolfram, however, is preceded by a herald, the flimsy-witted Mandrake, so easily dislodged from death, who pops out of the tomb to herald Wolfram's coming; and he develops a taste for grim drinking songs. He becomes, moreover, a bona-fide resident of the earth, and sunrise and moonset are all one to him till the action has worked itself out.

But his persistence is the least striking of Wolfram's variations from his family type. Unlike the rest he takes little joy in this world.

> My soul, my soul! O that it wore not now
> The semblance of a garb it hath cast off;
> O that it was disrobed of these mock limbs[20]

is his comment, in marked contrast to King Hamlet's shudder at cock-crow. But Wolfram's testimony upon death is uncertain. He would be back among his kind, and yet he hesitates to plead for death. In one scene where, unrecognized, he talks to the girl he had loved, he is in reality the ambassador of the other world to her, and in an anguished aside he cries,

> Snake Death,
> Sweet as the cowslip's honey is thy whisper:
> O let this dove escape these! I'll not plead,
> I will not be thy suitor to this innocent.[21]

But that ghosts are of necessity evil, and a menace, he denies a moment later.

> I am a ghost. Tremble not; fear not me.
> The dead are ever good and innocent,
> And love the living. They are cheerful creatures.[22]

Such speeches mark the Spectre of Wolfram as a gentleman of originality. He is also something of a metaphysician, which is a departure from his dramatic forbears. To return to earth on an errand of revenge is, intellectually, simple enough, but one will look long among Wolfram's ancestors for any who might conceivably have asked,

> Are you alone,
> Men, as you're called, monopolists of life?
> Or is all being, living?[23]

That was the only possible attitude of course for a ghost, if he were going to remain one of those "cheerful creatures" he had spoken of, but Wolfram is unique in adopting it.

Interesting as are the parallels between **Death's Jest Book** and the tragedy of revenge, and even more interesting as are its variations, the play is no more than a melodrama when viewed from this angle. Much of the shape of the tragedy of blood is in it; its spirit is different. Structurally the weakness of the play lies in this conflict, and in the uncertain allegiance it leads Beddoes to pay towards what might be called the gospel of the straight line. A sense of steady and immutable progression is essential in great tragedy, and at least as old as Dryden is the statement that events are the province of the historian, emotions aroused by them the affair of the tragic poet. We may in true tragedy be curious about the action—it may be unexpected—but we are aware always that we are on the straight line.

When we stray; when uncertainty replaces curiosity, events *per se* usurp the attention, and we are instantly in the domain of melodrama. Here lies the structural weakness of **Death's Jest Book.** With two themes, intentional and subconscious, at war with one another it is impossible for Beddoes to keep his lines clear—only the ferocious energy of Isbrand is able to block one line vaguely through the tangle. But never certainly. And much of the best poetry in the play is but embroidery on a framework of melodrama.

IV

LOVE IN DRESDEN CHINA

The figures who posture and scurry about the striking Isbrand are almost always unconvincing. Particularly are the women inadequate. (And how important the truth-to-life of its women is to the greatness of a tragedy is a question worth pondering.) Sibylla is the immediate cause of a murder, but her creator, moving through his fool's chamber of horrors, seemed unable to escape the influence of his time and race in picturing her. She is the product of the violets-and-watered-milk conception of girlhood. At her appearance she is lurking with the duke in forests along the African coast, hoping for rescue, and under the impression she loves the duke. But, appropriate to her type, she is not quite certain even what love is, and asks questions about it; the Saxon knight who a year before had shared their prison had "strangely troubled" her, so she is touchingly confident her feeling for him was not placid enough to be love. The Saxon knight, however, reappears in the person of Wolfram. By the exercise of a commendable self-control, Sibylla at least waits until he addresses one speech to her before she hails him as "My lord, my love, my life." Her next positive action is to die opportunely, having plucked flowers for her own bier. There is, however, between these events the gap between the first act and the last—an interval Sibylla spends in being a pathetic and negligible figure.

Sibylla has however one potentially great scene left to her—that of her meeting with the Spectra of Wolfram, her dead lover, a scene which Beddoes recognized as "capable of being rendered perhaps the finest in a poetical point of view."[24] It is, as it stands, an extraordinary scene, rich with poetry and, to a degree, with sentiment; the conclusion also is very fine, with Sibylla answering the appeal of her spectral lover with her:

> O Death! I am thy friend,
> I struggle not with thee, I love thy state:
> Thou canst be sweet and gentle, be so now;
> And let me pass praying away into thee,
> As twilight still does into starry night.[25]

But Beddoes was rather embarrassed by Wolfram, once he got him back on earth, and he recoiled from the complications of a ghostly liaison. Wolfram appears to Sibylla in the guise of a monk, by no means a dramatically useful device; nor is it clear just how soon she recognizes him. A conversation between a lovelorn maiden and a strange monk had no point: the whole meaning of the scene was in her recognition of whom she had to deal with. It is doubtful whether another version where Wolfram, after Sibylla has been sung to sleep by her attendants, comes to her in his own person and speaks to her sleeping, might not have been truer in its sentiment. She wakes, presumably after Wolfram has gone, and then resigns herself to death.[26]

Despite its flaws, however, the scene is original in conception and poetically developed; and it is followed by another love scene equally original. One will look far to find in immediate succession two love scenes so powerful and strange in conception—and this, although love and women are but bye-paths in **The Fool's Tragedy.** The play, with figurines for heroines, ends by being almost entirely sexless—there is no pulsation of the blood in Dresden china. What we have of love is theatricalism rather than passion. Melveric and Wolfram in act one effervesce into heroics and come to murder over it, and Athulf and Adalmar contrive even after this a crescendo, in that scene which immediately follows Sibylla's interview with her spectre lover. Here it is the other woman of the play, Amala, who is the center of the disturbance. She, too, is a puppet introduced as cause for a quarrel between two men, in this case the Duke's sons.

It has been a quarrel long gathering. The warrior brother, Adalmar, "journeyman to Mars the glorious butcher", has been preferred by the lady to Athulf, rather a dandy and maker of verses. This brings Athulf onto the stage with an astounding burst of angry rhetoric and the vow to be "Hell's saint forevermore". Isbrand catches him in this mood, and goads him until the young man storms off the stage, a confusion of purposes whirling in his head. "Go," mutters Isbrand,

> Go where Pride and Madness carry thee;
> And let that feasted fatness pine and shrink,
> Till thy ghost's pinched in the tight love-lean body.
> I see his life, as in a map of rivers,
> Through shadows, over rocks, breaking its way,
> Until it meet his brother's, and with that
> Wrestle and tumble o'er a perilous rock
> Bare as Death's shoulder.[27]

The climax occurs in the garden outside the girl's window on her wedding evening. Athulf, torn by a conflict of feelings, takes poison and sinks down in a half-faint, hearing

> Strange but sweet sounds, and the loud rocky dashing
> Of waves, where time into Eternity
> Falls over ruined worlds.[28]

And he hears, too, the more cruel music of her bridal serenade as he lies prostrate, gnawed by regret drifting into smothered curses, and a hint of ribaldry.

> . . . I do deserve it. I lie here
> A thousand-fold fool, dying ridiculously
> Because I could not have the girl I fancied.
> Well, are they wedded; how long now will last
> Affection or content?[29]

And in his fierce mood he caps the bridal serenade with another which is also his own dirge:

> A cypress-bough and a rose-wreath sweet,
> A wedding-robe, and a winding-sheet . . .
>   Death and Hymen both are here;
>   So up with scythe and torch,
>   And to the old church porch,
>   While all the bells ring clear:
> And rosy, rosy the bed shall bloom,
> And earthy, earthy heap up the tomb.[30]

And it is all fruitless heroics: the poison is a trick put upon him, and really harmless. He staggers to his feet to stab his successful brother, and speaks from the garden dusk to his brother's bride.

V

ISBRAND THE VENGEFUL JESTER

This is powerful stuff, the raw material of blazing emotion. And its effect, enforced by the undoubted eloquence of Beddoes' rhetoric and the vigour of his metaphors, would be over-powering—if it rang true. But there is always a hint of the false. He is off his theme. A string tangles and for an instant his figures, caught in a tumult of emotion, are but mannequins on a tangled wire. Just for an instant, but just enough to break the illusion. And the bye-

path of love is revealed for what it is, a bye-path from the true tragedy of personal despair.

Isbrand himself, trapped in the necessities of the plot, is not always free of weakness, but so consistent is his character usually, and so powerfully stamped upon the attention, that it carries past the faulty touches. And the wild fool remains a great creation—the only dramatic figure created by Beddoes which does approach greatness. This is to take him, for a moment, not as the symbol of Beddoes' personal despair, but as a dramatic character. It is on the perfect harmony which Beddoes has brought out of a series of conflicting elements that the vividness of the figure rests. Isbrand is complex: there is the basis of his humanness. Now this, now that of the thousand facets of his mind catches the light, flashes, sinks subdued again into the general colour. But there is nothing inchoate about the figure—the flashes are all from one diamond: the hardest of stones and cut clean. The initial paradox of the jester whose one love is hate is but the most obvious one about him. He is a composite of paradoxes brought into harmony. He is cunning, with a cunning which suggests the weasel, the rat, and other creeping things. That species of guile belongs to the coward but about Isbrand there is not a hint of cowardice, rather, a reckless indifference. And he is cruel, so that the sound of certain bones upon the rack would have been music to him. Yet he never lets his hatred hurry him, blind his sense of values;

> . . . If you would wound your foe,
> Get swords that pierce the mind: a bodily slice
> Is cured by surgeon's butter: let true hate
> Leap the flesh wall.[31]

For this reason he slipped the corpse of a murdered man into the tomb of Melveric's wife, and goaded the duke's son into recommitting his father's crime—with the crime of Cain thrown in for good measure. All the confusion of **Death's Jest Book** never blurs Isbrand's clarity of purpose.

Prosecuting as we know he does such designs with such relentlessness, the manner of Isbrand's speech comes as a perpetual shock and stimulant. The years of quip-making and pranks at the feast tables of the great, punning, laughter, and contemptuous approval have fastened upon him the speech of the professional jester. His time has come in the play, and he is another man, but he cannot slough off his past. Not that everything or even many things that he says are laughable; but the jester's whimsy of words, his curious lore, his inability to say even the simplest thing without the trappings of metaphor, without the quick turn of phrase never leaves Isbrand. His metaphors become ferocious and his ambiguities sinister, but their genesis is in the wine cup and the jest book.

"Oh lion-heartedness right asinine," exclaims he of some heroics he thinks stupid; and, questioned concerning Mandrake when that gentleman in his first flesh is about to set out for Egypt, he showers conceits:

> Yesterday he was a fellow of my colour and served a
> quacksalver, but now he lusts after the mummy country,
> whither you are bound. 'Tis a servant of the rosy cross,

a correspondent of the stars; the dead are his boon companions, and the secrets of the moon his knowledge. But had I been cook to a chameleon, I could not sweeten the air to his praise enough. . . . We fools send him as our ambassador to Africa; take him with you, or be yourself our consul.[32]

The same staccato emphasis of the professional jester, trained to whip his points across with speed and unexpectedness, is with him when he speaks upon a very different topic. He stands beside the body of his brother.

> *Isbrand:* Dead and gone! a scurvy burthen to this ballad of life. There lies he, Siegfried; my brother, mark you; and I weep not, nor gnash the teeth, nor curse: And why not, Siegfried? Do you see this? So should every honest man be: cold, dead, and leaden-coffined. This was one who would be constant in friendship, and the pole wanders: one who would be immortal, and the light that shines upon his pale forehead now, through yonder gewgaw window, undulated from its star hundreds of years ago. That is constancy, that is life. O moral nature!
>
> *Siegfried:* 'Tis well that you are reconciled to his lot and your own.
>
> *Isbrand:* Reconciled! A word out of a love-tale, that's not in my language. No, no. I am patient and still and laborious, a good contented man; peaceable as an ass chewing a thistle; and my thistle is revenge. I do but whisper it now: but hereafter I will thunder the word, and I shall shoot up gigantic out of this pismire shape, and hurl the bolt of that revenge.[33]

Such is the language and temper of Isbrand.

To an extent, however, Isbrand is marred by the complexity of the intrigue. There is too much plot. It is only because his personality is so electric with vitality that he is able to dominate the plot. And this vitality is not the whole of him. Viciously scheming as he is, there is about him a species of perverse grandeur which springs from the largeness of his contempt for any and all supposedly great things.

The ability to do them is his, but he is, at bottom, unseduced by ambition. A dukedom falls to his lot but it was no real motive. He is Negation. The positive side of his nature goes into the prosecution of his local blood feud. Behind this is the wide horizon of contempt for all things mundane, and herein is the significance of the macabre church yard scenes and his wild songs, with their indifference to all normal standards. The extraordinary "squats on a toad-stool" song abhorred of "all persons of proper feeling," considering the circumstances which surround it, marks his position clearly. "If you say it is nonsense," is Beddoes' reply to criticism, "I and Isbrand reply that we meant it to be so."[34] Which is all very well—but nonsense on such a subject! Something was radically wrong with Isbrand's sense of values, and with those of Beddoes too. And in Isbrand's case the song must be coupled with his cynicism towards love, death, marriage, and liberty—to name only those general topics he touches upon explicitly.

Isband does not defy standards and make war upon them—such men are almost always beaten. He is their more terrible opponent in that he ignores them, perhaps is even unaware of them. And that of course is an attitude far-reaching in its implications; to quarrel over existing standards is to imply a reason and a sweetness in life; to remove them, substituting no others, reduces the world to a bit of congealed chaos.

VI

MEDITATION ON A THEME

Yet all this is a far cry from Dryden's dictum that the business of a tragic poet is with the human emotions aroused by a series of events. With a *dramatis personae* of eloquent mannequins, and a wild fool who devotes his energies to a vendetta that is only incidental to his real significance, it is hard to see how **Death's Jest Book** can be adjusted to the formula. It cannot. But critical dicta are important only in proportion as they are stimulants to thought—one to be all-inclusive would be so broad as to be meaningless, and neither Beddoes nor Dryden need be condemned for discrepancies. The action of **Death's Jest Book** is melodrama—it is the attitude which surrounds this melodrama and from which it springs that is important. The conflict of themes underlying it has been made clear, and from which of them it draws its blood and sinew. Viewed in this light **Death's Jest Book** becomes a Meditation on a theme, a long lyric dramatized, and the speeches of the mannequins—grotesque figures when we try to visualize them as human beings in a net of circumstance—take on point and richness. The duke is wondrously metamorphosed from the murderer of act one when he soliloquizes

> Methinks
> The look of the world's a lie, a face made up
> O'er graves and fiery depths; and nothing's true
> But what is horrible.[35]

And Sibylla, the little sawdust doll in silk, would be but posturing sentimentally when she comments

> I love flowers too; not for a young girl's reason,
> But because these brief visitors to us
> Rise yearly from the neighbourhood of the dead,
> To show us how far fairer and more lovely
> Their world is;[36]

except that her speech springs as much from the obsessing question in Beddoes' mind, as from her little part. It supplements the duke, and Beddoes was eyeing his problem of human significance despairingly from all angles. There is no solution to his meditation because the theme has none; and because of the insurgence of the melodramatic action, there is not even complete coherence—but there is more meaning to **Death's Jest Book** than there is to its melodrama.

Characteristically Isbrand points the whole moral in a passage of nervous prose that intrudes upon and has no place in the action.

I will now speak a word in earnest, and hereafter jest with you no more: for I lay down my profession of folly. Why should I wear bells to ring the changes of your follies on? Doth the besonneted moon wear bells, she that is the parasite and zany of the stars, and your queen, ye apes of madness? As I live I grow ashamed of the duality of my legs, for they and the apparel, forked or furbelowed, upon them constitute humanity; the brain no longer; and I wish I were an honest fellow of four shins when I look into the notebook of your absurdities. I will abdicate.

He proceeds to bequeath his emblems.

I will yield Death the crown of folly. He hath no hair, and in this weather might catch cold and die: besides he has killed the best knight I knew, Sir Wolfram, and deserves it. Let him wear the cap, let him toll the bells; he shall be our new court-fool: and, when the world is old and dead, the thin wit shall find the angel's record of man's works and deeds, and write with a lipless grin on the innocent first page for a title, 'Here begins **Death's Jest Book.**' There, you have my testament: henceforth speak solemnly to me, and I will give a measured answer, having relapsed into court-wisdom again.[37]

In this somewhat equivocal fashion, with the making of all the records of life but a jest-book for death, does Beddoes carry out his original intention, expressed so long before, of uncypressing death, and sending him back "an unmasked braggart to his bankrupt den."

Notes

1. Vol. II, p. 56. Act II, Sc. 2.

2. Vol. II, p. 60. Act II, Sc. 3.

3. Vol. II, p. 80. Act III, Sc. 3.

4. Vol. II, p. 91. Act III, Sc. 3.

5. Vol. II, p. 144. Act V, Sc. 4. The indentation of lines follows Kelsall's printing.

6. *Letters*, p. 68. June 8, 1825. How much more than the name Beddoes had in mind at the moment is debatable. I have not made any analysis of the possible sources of the play. Those interested will find his own statement of the nucleus idea in the *Letters*, p. 149 (October 21, 1827), and in his own notes to *Death's Jest Book* (Vol. II, p. 157) he gives the source of this disputed historical fact as Flögel's *Gesch. d. Hoffnarren Liegnitz v. Leipzig* 1789. 8, S. 297 u. folg.—a reference I have not verified and somewhat suspect, as the note on Luz which follows is a hoax. (See *Letters*, p. 160.) His general purpose is stated in the doggerel letter to Proctor of March 13, 1826 (*Letters*, pp. 91-6). Similarities with Schiller's *The Ghost-Seer* and Marston's *Antonio's Revenge* should also be taken into account in considering sources. Chapman also cannot be disregarded.

7. *Letters*, p. 79. December 4, 1825.

8. *Ibid.*, pp. 99-100. April 1, 1826.

9. *Ibid.*, p. 110. October 5, 1826.

10. See his reference to it many years later. *Letters*, p. 226. May 15, 1837.

11. And in 1832 also if we may supplement the *Letters* by Gosse's account of the texts. The first of the then extant texts he declares was prepared for publication in 1832 and bore the title: *Charonic Steps: A dramatic annual for 1833. Containing Death's Jest Book, a dithyrambic in the florid Gothic style. By Theobald Vesseldoom.* The pseudonym being changed to Wilfred Sword-bearer, and to Sir Theobald Grimbottle before being finally abandoned altogether. (Gosse's note, Vol. II, opposite Greek motto page.)

12. Kelsall, p. cxxi.

13. See Appendix B for an analysis of the date of the texts.

14. *Letters*, p. 83. December 4, 1825.

15. *Ibid.*, p. 95. March 13, 1926.

16. A recent article declares *apropos* of Beddoes' phrase on the "uncypressing" of death that,
    "Thus to tear down the trappings, the cloudy trophies and funereal plumes, is the work of one sick beyond patience with the comforting illusions of romance—for the conventions that add terror at the same time add grandeur to the unknown ordeal, and so are comfortable bolsters to self-respect, preferable to the realism that brings no cloak to horrid insignificance. His intention is, besides, a challenge to the stronghold of romance, for death, seeming always so far off, beyond experience and inaccessible to any but the rarest sympathy, is the last theatre for the posings of the romantic." (*Thomas Lovell Beddoes,* by Edgell Rickword, in *The London Mercury,* December, 1923.)

    Mr. Rickword is right, but he has gone only half way. Beddoes was weary of more than romance. Beddoes' own references to the play as a satire are explained by the swift reversals from the high-flown to the acidly grotesque—but he strips away illusions to leave only futility, and reveals the state of his own mind in doing so.

    Again, Mr. Rickword is one of the first to point out a connection between Isbrand and Beddoes. "It may be," he says, "permissible to see in the Court Fool certain elements of self-portraiture, of what Beddoes considered the 'essentially unpoetical' nature. He has given then to Isbrand the type of mind resembling his own—one not quick to the illusive reality of imagination, and altogether out of patience with the pretty, ingenious ascriptions of the less robust poets, but alert and keen, these limitations aside."

17. Vol. II, p. 58. Act II, Sc. 3.

18. Vol. II, p. 154. Act V, Sc. 4. Moreover the full title of text c according to Gosse is *Death's Jest Book; or the Day will Come,* a confirmation of the importance of the revenge motive.

19. Dr. Grete Moldauer in *Thomas Lovell Beddoes,* Vienna (Wilhelm Braumüller), 1924, a book to be highly recommended for its careful and stimulating analysis of the play and from which (p. 120) I have borrowed something of my comment on the novelty of Wolfram which shortly follows, does however maintain that *Death's Jest Book* is to be taken as a modern variant of the old revenge type. Dr. Moldauer's thesis is (p. 110) that in so far as a study of death enters, it is linked with Isbrand and enveloped in the pyrotechnics of wit which touch only superficially the phenomenon, the *fact*—not the *problem* of death. Feeling it is not the purpose of the play to put this at the center, Dr. Moldauer falls back on the revenge motive.

20. Vol. II, p. 105. Act IV, Sc. 2.

21. Vol. II, p. 103. Act IV, Sc. 2.

22. Vol. II, p. 105. Act IV, Sc. 2.

23. Vol. II, p. 148. Act V, Sc. 4.

24. *Letters,* p. 172. April 30, 1829.

25. Vol. II, p. 106. Act IV, Sc. 2.

26. The only record of this version is a short note apropos of Wolfram written on one of the manuscripts and reprinted by Kelsall in his *Memoir,* p. cxxii.

27. Vol. II, p. 64. Act II, Sc. 3.

28. Vol. II, p. iii. Act IV, Sc. 3.

29. Vol. II, p. 116. Act IV, Sc. 3.

30. Vol. II, p. 116. Act IV, Sc. 3.

31. Vol. II, p. 64. Act II, Sc. 3.

32. Vol. II, p. 8. Act I, Sc. I.

33. Vol. II, p. 41. Act II, Sc. I.

34. *Letters,* p. 174. April, 1829.

35. Vol. II, p. 95. Act IV, Sc. I.

36. Vol. II, p. 139. Act V, Sc. 3.

37. Vol. II, pp. 45-6. Act II, Sc. 2.

F. L. Lucas (essay date 1934)

SOURCE: "The Playboy of the Netherworld," in *Studies French and English,* Cassell and Company Ltd., 1934, pp. 217-41.

[*In the following essay, Lucas asserts that Beddoes's work was unique for his time and praises stylistic aspects of his poetic drama.*]

'Alors s'assit sur un monde en ruines une jeunesse soucieuse. . . . Et ils parlèrent tant et si longtemps, que toutes les illusions humaines, comme des arbres en automne, tombaient feuille à feuille autour d'eux, et que ceux qui les écoutaient passaient leur main sur leur front, comme des fiévreux qui s'éveillent.' This is not a picture of post-war Europe; at least, not of our post-war Europe. The words are all but a century old. Thus wrote Alfred de Musset, middle-aged already in his twenties, just as Byron had been 'a perfect Timon, not nineteen'. Even in his impudent little comedies, at moments, the same cry of anguish makes itself suddenly heard. 'Ce que tu dis là', exclaims Fantasio's friend, 'ferait rire bien des gens; moi, cela me fait frémir; c'est l'histoire du siècle entier. L'éternité est une grande aire, d'où tous les siècles, comme de jeunes aiglons, se sont envolés tour à tour pour traverser le ciel et disparaître; le nôtre est arrivé à son tour au bord du nid; mais on lui a coupé les ailes, et il attend la mort en regardant l'espace dans lequel il ne peut s'élancer.'

It was no mere affectation. No doubt youth is often affected; but youth is also often bitterly sincere. No doubt it was a mood. It passed as moods do. But it is curious to find that the last century, which we tend to picture as populated by brisk business men with a blind confidence in God, themselves, and Progress, could be in its early twenties, as well as in its nineties, thus *fin-de-siècle*. Yet can we wonder? There are dawns, indeed, when to be young is 'very heaven'; the morning after is apt to be less celestial. Then the young pass from excessive enthusiasm to excessive melancholy, feeling that they have been born out of due time and are making their first bow on a stage where all is over.

It was natural that the generation which came to birth with the nineteenth century should feel this disillusion. There seemed nothing but a puppet-show left in progress in the theatre of the world. It had been otherwise for their fathers. The Werthers had forgotten their own sorrows as they beheld the earth alight with Liberty, and the Rights of Man coming in glory on the clouds of Heaven. Like clouds, indeed, those Rights had vanished; in their place had risen in the same year, 1804, the pale and baleful stars of *René* and *Obermann*; but in their place also had ensued for twenty years, terrible and yet magnificently titanic, a Battle of the Gods. Disillusion was kept at bay. War still seemed intoxicatingly romantic then, however mistakenly; a field for genius, not merely for the muddling mediocrities that floundered through the slime of our last conflict. A Piedmontese private in the Grande Armée has told how, at the mere sight of that short grey-coated figure riding down the line before Moscow, he found himself breathing as hard as if he had been running, and bathed in sweat amid the cold of a Russian winter's day. It was not thus that the armies of 1917 felt about their generals. But after the romantic epic of Napoleon, there followed a poor farce of rejuvenated kings and reactionary governments. This was what the generation that had heard through boyhood the guns of Austerlitz and Jéna and Wagram sat down to contemplate, as they and the century together came of age.

And so there were other caged eaglets in these years besides the Duc de Reichstadt; other smouldering fire-brands, lit too late, besides the heroes of Stendhal. The enormous energy of a Balzac, a Dumas, a Hugo, might go trampling onward under that leaden sky after the lurid splendour of Byron had fallen from it like a final meteor; but others of the young, endowed with less vitality, felt weighed beneath a load of emotional, as well as political, reaction. Minor writers, like Maxime du Camp, bear out Musset's description; and though in England, so much less touched by the war and now at length victorious, we should not expect the same aftermath, it may be more than coincidence that so few writers are today remembered who were not either over twenty-five or under twelve—too old or too young to be vitally impressionable—when the year 1820 closed. In prose, between Carlyle (born in 1795) and Thackeray (born in 1811) the only names of any note are Macaulay (who would have been hard to damp in any age), Mill, Newman, and George Borrow. Similarly there is a gap in the lineage of English poets between the birth of Keats in 1795 and that of Tennyson in 1809. Such speculation about literary vintage-years must remain fanci-ful; yet there is one poet born between Keats and Tenny-son who was certainly cramped by a despondency like Musset's, due in part, no doubt, to his own temperament, but partly also, I believe, to his time. Thomas Lovell Bed-does came into the world in an evil hour for him, on a July day in 1803.

That the grandson of Richard Edgeworth and son of Dr. Beddoes should be eccentric, can surprise nobody, steady-ing as it might well seem to have Maria Edgeworth for an aunt; but between him and his elders there is one great difference. He lacked, not their energy—he could drudge like an emmet at anatomy, then throw down his pen to take a vigorous part in revolutions and conspiracies—but their unquestioning self-confidence. To Richard Edgeworth and Dr. Beddoes the world was on the whole a friendly sort of place, to be succeeded here and hereafter by another better still. They thought well of it; they thought well of themselves; they were all the more successful in conse-quence. Certainly they were much happier. 'Edgeworth', said a contemporary, 'must write, or he would burst.' Edge-worth did not burst. 'Her conversation', wrote Byron after meeting his daughter Maria, 'was as quiet as herself; no one would have guessed she could write her name. Whereas her father talked, not as if he could write nothing else, but as if he thought nothing else was worth writing.' The Richard Edgeworths, if not their hearers, are happy after their fashion. Similarly Dr. Beddoes had bounded about with tireless zest and an undivided soul from bleach-ing negroes to blackening Mr. Pitt. Like Browning he had been one that 'marched breast forward'. True, it is not easy to march in any other way—a point which Browning seems not to have quite considered; but at all events Dr. Beddoes marched; and discovered on the road many odd, and some useful, things. But when we turn to his son, the author of ***Death's Jest Book,*** the contrast is complete. In every apple of his Tree of Knowledge lay a little black wriggling worm of doubt. Outstanding as an anatomist,

dazzling as a poet, he yet perished by his own hand at forty-five, bequeathing to Dr. Ecklin a stomach-pump and to the world only a wild heap of poetic fragments, blood and sawdust mixed with diamonds.

Left fatherless in his sixth year, the boy was sent at fourteen to Charterhouse. Long afterwards, when Beddoes was dead, his friend Kelsall extracted strange tales of his doings there from a certain C. D. Bevan who had been his fag. Two of these details have been repeated by Sir Ed-mund Gosse and Lytton Strachey—the boy's habit of declaiming speeches from Elizabethan drama at the little Bevan (who was forcibly enlisted as accomplice, enemy, or mistress) with a rain of kicks or caresses as required; and his vengeance on a certain locksmith, whose bad work was repaid with a dramatic interlude composed and recited for his benefit, and depicting his death-bed or horror-stricken remorse, his funeral, and his consignment by a legion of devils to the Bottomless Pit. But there are other less-known anecdotes from the same source, too character-istic, I think, to be forgotten. The inborn oddity, the rebel-liousness, the eldritch humour, the Gothic grotesqueness, the love of Elizabethan poetry, the strange mastery of words—all these qualities of the poet we know, are already foreshadowed here at Charterhouse. Already he dominated his fellows. The nicknames he invented stuck like burs. His defiance, too, of authority had already begun. When the traditional liberty to play hockey in the cloisters was abolished, young Beddoes, who normally never played at all, appeared to lead one side in the now forbidden game, his head bedizened with feathers and his body adorned by a pasteboard shield where shone emblazoned a clenched fist, with the motto: *Manus haec inimica tyrannis.* This demonstration proved too much for the gravity of the authorities and the prohibition was dissolved in laughter. But if Beddoes could uphold the oppressed, he could also do his share of oppression. Readers of *The Newcomes* will recall how the old pensioners at Charterhouse were called 'Codds', and Colonel Newcome himself, 'Codd Colonel'. Three of these old brethren the young Beddoes particularly loved to torment—'Codd Curio', whom he called so because he collected curiosities; 'Codd Frolicsome', a Tra-falgar veteran who had St. Vitus's dance; and 'Codd Sine-breech', who was slightly crazed in the head. These old gentlemen, who were attended by the most Gampish of nurses, suffered such persecutions from their enemy that Codd Sine-breech was fain to hire a drummer of the Guards as reinforcement. Hostilities were not, however, continuous; every now and then both sides indulged in armistice feasts of oysters and lobsters, gin and porter, at which Beddoes would dance or give dramatic recitations. Another prank of his was to purloin all the fire-irons from the kitchen of the preacher's house, so that the infuriated cook went about cursing in a vain search for his pokers, tongs, and shovels; which were mysteriously restored to him at midnight, tied round the neck of Beddoes' fag, who was himself tied to the door-knocker with a resulting din, as the little boy struggled there, like a dozen coal-scuttles falling downstairs.

The same familiar imp of insubordination attended Beddoes to Pembroke College, Oxford, where he treated his fellows with cold aloofness and the college authorities, by Bevan's account, with 'a course of studied impertinence'. On one occasion, we are told, a lecturer, tired of seeing him sitting and glowering in complete inattention, exclaimed: 'I wish you would at least cut your book, Mr. Beddoes.' At once the young man rose, walked out, and returned with the largest butcher's cleaver money could buy, with which he proceeded to do as requested. The ensuing uproar brought the lecture to an untimely end. Few, again, will forget that deadly stab, that poisoned 'jewel five words long', in one of his Oxford letters: 'Mr. Milman (our poetry professor) has made me quite unfashionable here by denouncing me as "one of a villainous school." *I wish him another son.'*

Such things are trivial, no doubt. But only in such glimpses does Beddoes loom upon us, like a red-hot fogbound sun, out of the mists which have engulfed for ever the secrets of his inner life. We catch sight again of the young poet, with his strange physical resemblance to Keats, helping to print the posthumous verse of the still neglected Shelley, whose aery spirit held so strange an appeal for his own earthy one; or scribbling imitations of Elizabethan drama, with a power that seems to spring from him full-grown; or stealthily hacking the pages of his first published volume from the bindings of the copies on his friends' shelves. Then there appears for a moment the young law-student, working at Southampton under that most poetic of solicitors, Kelsall, who was to struggle with heroic resistance to keep alive the memory of Beddoes' work for a generation after its author's death and right up to the eve of his own; next, the young doctor, learning to prefer 'Apollo's pillbox to his lyre' and Germany to England; growing into a stoic, prosaic, grim anatomist, and yet still turning at instants from skull and scalpel to retouch the everlasting *Death's Jest Book*; and last of all the obscure revolutionary, hunted from Bavaria to Zürich, from Zürich back to Germany, then deported in turn from Hanover, from Prussia, and from Bavaria once more. He has by now almost forgotten his country. His rare visits only inflame his indifference into active irritation with 'this dull, idle, pampered isle'. He has become more and more bizarre. His talk shows a morbid preoccupation with death's-heads and skeletons. Sisters and cousins object to his habits of lying in bed all day, drinking perhaps (or, as he called it, 'having neuralgia'); and then prowling like a spectre about the house all night. He arrived at the residence of one relative at Cheney Longville in Shropshire mounted, it is said, upon an ass. Was he sane, this sombre recluse whom the Procters one evening found struggling with the attendants at Drury Lane Theatre, which he had been trying to set on fire by holding a lighted five-pound note under a chair? There must have been sighs of relief among the Beddoeses of Bristol and Birkenhead when their disreputable relative went back to cutting up dead Germans at Frankfurt. There he now lost his health, by pricking his hand during a dissection; and lost his heart in addition to a young baker called Degen, whom he was set on turning into an actor,

hiring the theatre at Zürich for him to play Hotspur. The rest is well known. The inhabitants of Zürich looked coldly on the heroics of Herr Degen; Degen in his turn grew cold towards Beddoes and went back to his dough in Frankfurt. The poet, bearded now and looking 'like Shakespeare', removed in deep despondency to Basel, where he tried to kill himself, first by stabbing his leg, then by tearing off the bandages in hospital, until the limb gangrened and had to be amputated. He recovered, in body, and seemingly in mind as well. Degen, too, had been persuaded to return to him. Yet as soon as he was well enough to go out, he took the opportunity to procure poison, came back to the hospital, and died unconscious the same night (26th January, 1849). In his bosom lay a pencilled bequest of a stomach-pump and a case of champagne: 'I am food for what I am good for—worms . . . I ought to have been among other things a good poet. Life was too great a bore on one peg and that a bad one.'

But though Death's Jester lay now quiet at last in the cypress-shade of the hospital-cemetery at Zürich, the jest was not ended. His works remained, to become in their turn the tennis-balls of chance. His family wanted them safely destroyed—all except those of an innocuous medical nature. Only Zoe King, the cousin who is said to have felt for him an attachment he could not return, and the faithful Kelsall resisted this proposal; and, through Kelsall, *Death's Jest Book* appeared in 1850, followed a year later by a volume of poems. But a new generation of writers had appeared by now; and the world of 1850, watching the birth in swift succession of works like *David Copperfield, Wuthering Heights,* and *In Memoriam,* had no eyes for this odd relic of the unknown dead. Only a few observers saw that something new had been added to English poetry; but among them were Tennyson and Browning. Years passed; Kelsall, devoted as ever, heard of Browning's admiration, met him (1867), begged him to write a preface for a new edition, sent him some of the manuscripts, offered to bequeath him all. Browning accepted; he contemplated, at a time when he seemed likely to be made Professor of Poetry at Oxford, giving his opening lecture on Beddoes. But nothing came of it, neither preface nor lecture; Browning had grown bored. And Kelsall, too, was growing old. In 1869 he made, with Zoe King, a pilgrimage to the scenes at Basel and Zürich where Beddoes' life had guttered out twenty years before; in July, 1872, he contributed an article on the dead poet to the *Fortnightly;* three months after this 'last stroke for Beddoes', as he called it, he too was dead.

The manuscripts duly passed to Browning, with a message from Mrs. Kelsall revealing to him what had been hitherto kept dark—that Beddoes had died by his own hand. This grim addition made the poet of optimism more disposed than ever to play ostrich and forget the whole affair. The box of yellowing papers acquired in his eyes a sinister horror. Another decade went by; then he talked of it to his young neighbour, Edmund Gosse; and finally, one day in 1883, led him to the locked box, pressed the key into his hand, and fled. However, once Bluebeard's Cupboard was open, Browning's repugnance weakened sufficiently for him to read over the manuscripts with Gosse; who in consequence produced a new edition of the *Works* in 1890, followed by a volume of the poet's *Letters* in 1894. But, half a century after his death, misfortune still dogged Beddoes. The edition was perfunctorily carried out; and the manuscripts, returned to Browning's son in Italy, disappeared in the confusion that followed his death. What became of them remains to this day obscure; there seems no basis for the story once told, that 'Pen' Browning's servants ransacked their dead master's house, and that no one knew what scented tresses of some dark Italian beauty, faded now in their turn, the papers of Beddoes might have perished at last to curl. Finally in 1928 Gosse produced a grandiose new edition of *The Letters and Poetical Works,* ornamented with decorations from Holbein's Dance of Death; but before its completion he too died; and with this new edition reappeared—alas!—the errors and corruptions and mutilations of the old. Beddoes might well have laughed in his grave.

Not that it is much easier to know what the poet was really like, than what he really did. The letters are eccentric, cold, impersonal—all the more impersonal for being filled with a great deal of bitter badinage. His jests serve him, one feels, for shield as well as sword. That sardonic smile makes his face more than ever of a mask. Poetry, Anatomy, Liberty—he pursued each in turn, to disillusion at the last. There is little trace in his life of affection, apart from the mysterious Degen: 'I fear I am a non-conductor of friendship, a not-very-likeable person, so that I must make sure of my own respect.' And yet this coldness has an air of being studied rather than natural. There is a Byronic pose in his saturnine description of his behaviour on a voyage to Hamburg—how he 'remained impenetrably proud and silent every wave of the way, dropping now and then a little venom into the mixture of conversation to make it effervesce'; and this impassivity is belied by passages in his poetry of a quivering tenderness:

> Your love was much,
> Your life but an inhabitant of his.

> Cyrano, Cyrano,
> I yearn, and thirst, and ache to be beloved,
> As I could love,—through my eternal soul,
> Immutably, immortally, intensely,
> Immeasurably. Oh! I am not at home
> In this December world, with men of ice,
> Cold sirs and madams. That I had a heart,
> By whose warm throbs of love to set my soul!
> I tell thee I have not begun to live,
> I'm not myself, till I've another self
> To lock my dearest, and most secret thoughts in;
> Change petty faults, and whispering pardons with;
> Sweetly to rule, and Oh! most sweetly serve.

Surely, if the writer of that lived withdrawn into his shell, it was precisely because he was too sensitive, and had suffered. It is as if part of him had perished young. His very portrait, as an undergraduate, has a mummy-like air. He resembles his own Wolfram, a dead thing in a living world,

gentle once but hardened now. Certainly his letters show him, if no lover, at all events a good hater. He reveals a particular dislike of British Philistinism, whether in individuals like 'Mr. Milman', or in the nation as a whole:

> Drink, Britannia! Britannia, drink your tea,
> For Britons, bores, and buttered toast, they all begin
>   with B.

> O flattering likeness on a copper-coin,
> Sit still upon your slave-raised cotton ball
> With upright toasting-fork and toothless cat!

But, for that matter, the whole world sickens him: 'I am now so thoroughly penetrated with the conviction of the absurdity and unsatisfactory nature of human life, that I search with avidity for every shadow of a proof or probability of an after-existence both in the material and immaterial nature of man.' One may wonder that a mind which found this life so tedious, should so sigh for eternity; but in such matters the human temperament is seldom very logical. Gnawed by the worm on earth, it speculates hopefully about the worm that never dies.

Still, if the letters throw but a glimmer on the poet's heart, they reveal very clearly those two qualities of his brain which go to make his poetry at times so astonishing—imagination and wit. Even as a child, his first favourite poet had been Cowley. And to read these letters brings home with fresh force how hardy a plant real originality is. Such a mind, read what it may, imitate whom it will, imposes as invincibly as a distorting mirror its own queer quality on all its reflections. It was a gift Sterne had. It belongs in our own day to Mr. E. M. Forster—who else but he would behold the United States, for example, with the most spontaneously innocent air in the world, as a brightly coloured apron tied chastely round the buxom waist of the American Continent? So with Beddoes. He too was born with this gift of seeing in every square a fifth corner; no doubt he cultivated his oddity, finding it succeed; but it always seems a natural part of him, as if he had had a mandrake for comforter in the cradle and made it his youthful hobby 'to chat with mummies in a pyramid, and breakfast on basilisk's eggs'. 'There is nothing of interest in town', he will write, 'except a pair of live crocodiles in St. Martin's Lane.' 'I will sacrifice my raven to you', is his answer when Kelsall recoils from the sinister menagerie of *Death's Jest Book,* 'but my crocky is really very dear to me.' This is, indeed, one of the few expressions of affection in his whole correspondence. Or again: 'Such verses as these and their brethren, will never be preserved to be pasted on the inside of the coffin of our planet.' Such excessive preoccupation with the macabre may seem affected; yet the reader who looks back at that cadaverous portrait, and forward to the last scene at Zürich, must surely admit that the affectation, if such it was, went deep. But his fancy does not always glimmer thus coldly like a glow-worm on a grave; its flames can dance gaily enough, though still perhaps with a slight breath of sulphur: 'Dear Kelsall. I have been in the native land of the unicorn about a week . . . I had no time to visit Procter

. . . but am told that he is appointed to a high office in the government in the kingdom of ye moon.' Such is Beddoes' way of conveying his own arrival in England and Procter's new Commissionership of Lunacy. Or he will write home of a castle at Göttingen: 'The date of the tower is said to be 963: if this be true, it may have earned a citizenship among the semi-eternal stony populace of the planet; at all events it will be older than some hills which pretend to be natural and carry trees and houses.' Just so might another metaphysical physician have brooded two centuries before; we should feel how characteristic was such an idea if we found it in a letter written home by Sir Thomas Browne to Norwich. But there is a more flashing fancy than Browne's at work when Beddoes turns to describe fireflies at Milan: 'as if the swift wheeling of the earth struck fire out of the black atmosphere; as if the winds were being set upon this planetary grindstone, and gave out such momentary sparks from their edges'. It might be a description of his own poetry. How many poets one might search from cover to cover without finding anything as brilliant as that round grindstone of a world!

Those, then, who know the poetry of Beddoes will have no difficulty in recognising the fainter shadow of his genius that lies across the pages of the letters; but there is one more disillusion here than even the poems show—disillusion about his poetry itself. He early expresses a sense of failure. He feels that he is trying to animate a corpse; that he is but the ghost of an Elizabethan dramatist, squeaking and gibbering in plays that are fit only for audiences long lapped in their winding-sheets. 'The man who is to awaken the drama', he writes of a *remaniement* of Massinger's *Fatal Dowry*, 'must be a bold trampling fellow—no creeper in worm-holes—no reviser even, however good. These reanimations are vampire-cold—we want to see something that our great grandsires did not know.' He must have felt the relevance of that judgement to himself. And if he is severe on his contemporaries, prophesying after Shelley's death 'nothing but fog, rain, blight in due succession', he is still harder on his own work: 'I am essentially unpoetical in character, habits, and ways of thinking: and nothing but the desperate hunger for distinction so common to young gentlemen at the University ever set me upon rhyming' (rather in the same way, it may be remembered, he denied himself a heart). *Death's Jest Book* he dismisses as 'unentertaining, unamiable, and utterly unpopular'. He finds himself wanting in the two indispensable qualities of a dramatist, 'power of drawing character, and humour'. Indeed at moments he feels 'doubt of my aptitude for any higher literary or commercial occupation'. He cannot even finish his plays: 'As usual I have begun a new tragedy'; 'a new tragic abortion of mine has absolutely extended its foetus to a quarter of the fourth act'; 'those three acts, which I cannot possibly show to any eye but that of Vulcan, are absolutely worthless'. What wonder if this hesitating Prince of Denmark begot no second *Hamlet,* but only dramatic fragments and brilliant incoherencies?

And yet I know no poet whose poetic moments are more rammed with poetry. How much one values this sort of spasmodic writer depends on temperament—whether one is 'classical' and asks for ordered beauty of form, or 'romantic' and prefers flashes of dazzling colour. But after all, why not love both? Beddoes can only give the second kind of pleasure; but he gives it so intensely, that I feel he is undervalued still. What he needs is a good selection of short passages, often of single lines. The anthologists have merely concentrated on a few of his lyrics, which have the sort of prettiness dear to their pussycat mentalities; just as they persist in representing, or misrepresenting, the author of *The City of Dreadful Night* by the cockney amenities of 'Sunday up the River'. As a lyric poet Beddoes can be lovely; but it is in his verse dialogue that he shows his strength, not only that power of phrase and image with which his letters vibrate, but something also that they could not reveal—his grip of that Proteus among metrical forms, so simple-seeming, so mockingly elusive in a hundred poets' hands—dramatic blank verse.

The strange thing is that his most living poetry is a pastiche of dead work. As a contemporary of Keats, writing in the manner of 1820, he is usually unreadable; it is as a contemporary of Webster, risen from the dust of two centuries, that he quickens into a quivering vitality. A far more practical surgeon than Crabbe, he had none of Crabbe's power as a poet of treating living subjects. His Muse is a Witch of Endor, her magic a necromantic gift of waking to utterance a tongue long buried. Yet this becomes a little less strange when we remember how Chatterton too, hopeless when he writes in the poetic style of 1770, found himself only by escaping back to an England older still than Beddoes ever revisited. Think, too, of the whole Renaissance with its aping of the Classics. There are poets who can write vitally of, and in the style of, their own age; there remain others for whom it is equally essential to escape from it. Generations of critics have lost their heads and tempers squabbling which is right. Surely both. Surely it is understandable that a poet may wish to break away to some magic islet of his own, where he can feel himself monarch of all he surveys, because he shares it only with the dead. For they do not cramp our style as the living can. We can learn from them without fearing to become too imitatively like them; and the older the dead, the easier they are to elbow aside when we turn to write ourselves, as if their ghosts wore thinner and more shadowy with the years. Distance can lend enchantment also to the voice.

At all events it is on borrowed plumes that Beddoes soars his highest, and when masquerading as a Jacobean that he seems most himself. No one since Dryden has so recaptured the splendour of blank verse as a medium for dialogue, freeing it from that marmoreal stiffness which Milton imposed. For it is, indeed, almost as if the author of *Paradise Lost* had turned the verse of *Hamlet* into stone; to be carved and built by him and others after him into shapes of monumental nobility, but never again to seem like living flesh and blood, as once in Elizabethan hands. Milton's 'organ-voice' has no *vox humana*; and musical as a Wordsworth or a Tennyson may be, Shakespeare's Cleopatra speaks what has since become a dead language.

Beddoes alone seems to me to have re-discovered the old secrets of varied stress and fingering, of feminine ending and resolved foot, in all their elasticity. His lines run rippling like wind along the corn: his Muse moves with the grace of his Valeria:

> She goes with her light feet, still as the sparrow
> Over the air, or through the grass its shade.

All the stranger is the contrast which combines with this perfect music such a grimness of ideas; until his verse recalls that tragic conception of the Greek—the Gorgon Medusa, 'the beautiful horror', the lovely lips twisted with eternal pain:

> I have seen the mottled tigress
> Sport with her cubs as tenderly and gay
> As Lady Venus with her kitten Cupids.

So, too, the Muse of Beddoes, dagger and poison-cup in hand, goes gliding on her way with the light feet and swaying grace of Herrick's loves in their wild civility:

> The snake that loves the twilight is come out,
> Beautiful, still, and deadly.

> But now some lamp awakes,
> And with the venom of a basilisk's wink
> Burns the dark winds.

> O that the twenty coming years were over!
> Then should I be at rest, where ruined arches
> Shut out the troublesome, unghostly day,
> And idlers might be sitting on my tomb,
> Telling how I did die.

> You're young and must be merry in the world,
> Have friends to envy, lovers to betray you,
> And feed young children with the blood of your heart,
> Till they have sucked up strength enough to break it.

> I will go search about for Comfort,
> Him that enrobed in mouldering cerements sits
> At the grey tombstone's head, beneath the yew;
> Men call him Death, but Comfort is his name.

The poison is given with a caress: the dagger tickles before it plunges home. It is interesting to compare the rhythm of Beddoes with the dramatic verse of a master of the metre in its statelier narrative form, Tennyson:

> I once was out with Henry in the days
> When Henry loved me, and we came upon
> A wild-fowl sitting on her nest, so still
> I reach'd my hand and touched; she did not stir;
> The snow had frozen round her, and she sat
> Stone-dead upon a heap of ice-cold eggs.
> Look how this love, this mother, runs through all
> The world God made—even the beast—the bird!

Any ear must notice the difference. Not only are the individual lines in Tennyson more regular and so more monotonous, and also slower through their avoidance of the feminine endings or extra syllables which lend speed to a verse like:

> And feed young children with the blood of your heart;

they also for the same reason refuse to coalesce with one another into a verse-paragraph, in spite of the author's deliberate effort to make them do so by ending his lines with words like 'upon'. Each decasyllable somehow persists in scanning itself separately, with a sort of conscious pride in its own virtuous avoidance of any undue licence. It is as if the passage were being written by a poetical typewriter, which very beautifully rang a little silver bell at the close of each line, and pulled itself elaborately back to begin each new one; whereas Beddoes has the sinuous onward gliding of a living adder through the grass. Open Webster:

> O men
> That lye upon your death-beds, and are haunted
> With howling wives, neere trust them, they'le re-marry
> Ere the worme pierce your winding sheete: ere the
>   Spider
> Make a thinne curtaine for your Epitaphes.

The kinship needs no stressing. Metrically, indeed, Beddoes may often seem even nearer to the slightly decadent softness of Fletcher or Shirley than to Webster's harsher rhythm; but in his style he shows the same swift and bitter strength:

> I have huddled her into the wormy earth.

> Let Heaven unscabbard each star-hilted lightning.

> If you would wound your foe,
> Get swords that pierce the mind; a bodily slice
> Is cured with *surgeon's butter.*

Of the two supreme excellences of Beddoes, then, as a poet, this power of rhythm and phrase seems to me one; the other is sheer imagination. He has ideas that are poetic in and by themselves, quite apart from their expression; like the silence of Ajax before Odysseus in Hades, like the symbols of Ibsen in his later plays. Indeed, the cry Beddoes wrings from the lips of one of his characters might well be his own:

> I'll go brood
> And strain my burning and distracted soul
> Against the naked spirit of the world
> Till some portent's begotten.

It is a typically 'metaphysical' conception. Yet he escapes that frigid ingenuity which has so often been fatal to poets of this kind, in the seventeenth century, and in the twentieth—clever persons, who have yet been so simple as to suppose that their creations could live and breathe without a heart. Thus Beddoes, thinking of Noah's Deluge, sees it, characteristically enough, through the eye of the daisy on which its first raindrop fell; but he feels also for the daisy itself with the tenderness of Burns.

I should not say
How thou art like the daisy in Noah's meadow
On which the foremost drop of rain fell warm
And soft at evening; so the little flower
Wrapped up its leaves, and shut the treacherous water
Close to the golden welcome of its breast.

Time itself may be twisted by his visionary hands into a thing of space, with all the tortured ingenuity of a Donne— and yet one does not really have a sense of torture, so much does his mind seem at home in its own strange labyrinths:

I have said that Time
Is a great river running to Eternity.
Methinks 'tis all one water, and the fragments
That crumble off our ever-dwindling life,
Dropping into it, first make the twelve-houred circle,
And that spreads outward to the great round Ever.

Or again:

I begin to hear
Strange but sweet sounds, and the loud rocky dashing
Of waves where Time into Eternity
Falls over ruined worlds.

It is this unusual power of at once thinking so abstractly and seeing so concretely, that makes him master of the macabre. For the macabre only too easily becomes a little vulgar. Poe can be frightful in quite another sense of the word than he intended. Cemeteries are no very healthy dancing-ground for the Muses, and not much real music has been got from bones. But Beddoes, though he has his lapses, has learnt that the hinted can be far more terrible than the explicit. In one of his scenes, for instance, a festive gathering is haunted by spectres:

There were more shadows there, than there were men.

Or again, before his vision a plague-infected air becomes

Transparent as the glass of poisoned water
Through which the drinker sees his murderer smiling.

What a concentrated brevity of horror—as if the picture were drawn on the thumbnail of the assassin! Or again, the earth's roundness—what is its cause? The answer of Beddoes is all his own:

Ay, to this end the earth is made a ball—
Else, crawling to the brink, despair would plunge
Into the infinite eternal air
And leave its sorrows and its sins behind.

Here is the old melancholy of Burton, with his speculations on the space Hell occupies in the globe's interior, fermenting in a more modern mind. Why, again, have ghosts and apparitions ceased? There is the same fantastic ingenuity in Beddoes' reply, the same wild eloquence:

To trust in story,
In the old times Death was a feverish sleep,

In which men walked. The other world was cold
And thinly peopled, so life's emigrants
Came back to mingle with the crowds of earth.
But, now great cities are transplanted thither,
Memphis and Babylon and either Thebes
And Priam's towery town with its one beech,
The dead are most and merriest: so be sure
There'll be no more haunting till their towns
Are full to the garret: then they'll shut their gates
To keep the living out.

Such concreteness of vision combined with passionate concentration of speech lends the hiss of an arrow to his single lines of scorn:

The shallow, tasteless skimmings of their love . . .
And scratched it on your leaden memories . . .
And lay thee, worm, where thou shalt multiply.

Indeed, nothing in him has so much the air of being written *con amore,* as these hot gusts from a furnace-mouth of hatred. It is as if he had taken to himself that cry of one of his characters:

Unmilk me of my mother, and pour in
Salt scorn and steaming hate.

The passions he deals in may be often poisoned, but they are at least passion; lack of that might easily have become the besetting weakness of a poet with so much sheer cleverness, as it is today with the young who set out to imitate Donne's ingenuity without his intensity, in a way that suggests Blake's Lamb trying to frisk itself into the likeness of Blake's Tiger. Cleverness, it seems to me, has its place in poetry, but only a second place, as the tiring-maid of passion or of beauty. The cleverness of Beddoes makes his loveliness not inferior, but a more complex, artificial thing than that of Wordsworth's Lucy or Tennyson's Mariana. Not for him

The silence that is in the starry sky,
The sleep that is among the lonely hills.

but

Crescented night and amethystine stars.

A violet is not for him a simple violet; it is like

Pandora's eye
When first it darkened with immortal life

(as if life, like death—even more than death, perhaps— threw a sad shadow when it came). A pine-tree across the moon turns into a river before his agile gaze:

One snowy cloud
Hangs like an avalanche of frozen light
Upon the peak of night's cerulean Alp,
And you still pine, a bleak anatomy,
Flows like a river on the planet's disk
With its black wandering arms.

(And yet there are persons who deny a visual imagination to be needed for enjoying poetry!) Even a moonlit water-drop holds for him within it the semblance of a whole world's unhappiness:

> For what is't to the moon that every drop
> Of flower-held rain reflects and gazes on her!
> Her destiny is in the starry heavens,
> Theirs here upon the ground, and she doth set
> Leaving her shadow no more to delight them,
> And cometh ne'er again till they are fled.

And even a lily of the valley becomes a jester with cap and bells, a symbol that motley is all men's wear. He follows beauty for ever through a maze, like some hidden Rosamond; he is himself

> the bird
> That can go up the labyrinthine winds
> Upon his pinions and pursues the summer.

He can to lucid grace the image of ambiguity itself:

> I know not whether
> I see your meaning; if I do, it lies
> Upon the wordy wavelets of your voice
> Dim as the evening shadow in a brook
> When the least moon has silver on't no larger
> Than the pure white of Hebe's pinkish nail.

There is nothing of which he cannot make music; even the streaks of rain seen in dark lines against the blue background of a showery sky become for his fingers the chords of a fantastic lyre. And yet with all his clever elaboration he can also be agonisingly simple:

> They are both dead, and God has suffered it;

or again:

> Now I shall see him
> No more. All Hell is made of those two words.

Still, Beddoes is seldom thus direct. He writes less of what he sees than of his thoughts in seeing it; what he describes is not so much like itself as like something else; and so a great part of both his strength and his sweetness will be found stored in his metaphors and similes. Like the Lady of Shalott, he watches the world remotely, in a strange mirror; like the Emperor Domitian, he walks, with terror about him, in a gallery of looking-glass.

Magic beauty and terror—as in his style and rhythm, so in his mind and soul, these two seem to me his essential qualities, moving inseparably side by side. It might have been of him that Victor Hugo wrote:

> A de certains moments toutes les jeunes flores
> Dans la forêt
> Ont peur, et sur le front des blanches métaphores
> L'ombre apparaît.
> C'est qu'Horace ou Virgile ont vu soudain le spectre
> Noir se dresser;

> C'est que là-bas, derrière Amaryllis, Électre
> Vient de passer.

Only with Beddoes such moments are continual. In his own pages there are more shadows than there are men. This dualism moulds all his writing,

> As out of the same lump of sunny Nile
> Rises a purple-wingèd butterfly
> Or a cursed serpent crawls.

His most characteristic work becomes like a duet between a raven and a nightingale upon a tree in Hell. Now they alternate; now they blend together, as in that lovely picture of a Love who is also Death—a thin, pale Cupid with ragged wings and, for his dart, a frozen Zephyr,

> Gilt with the influence of an adverse star.
> Such was his weapon, and he traced with it,
> Upon the waters of my thoughts, these words:
> 'I am the death of flowers and nightingales,
> Of small-lipped babes, that give their souls to summer
> To make a perfumed day with: I shall come,
> A death no larger than a sigh to thee,
> Upon a sunset hour.' And so he passed
> Into the place where faded rainbows are,
> Dying along the distance of my mind.

At times, again, this duet becomes a duel. Just as in real life 'he could be delightful if he chose' (said Mrs. Procter), 'but, oh, he chose so seldom', so in his letters the sardonic side of him will sneer at some pathetic passage just added to a play, and in his verse his raven will croak derision at his nightingale:

> I'll not be a fool like the nightingale
> Who sits up till midnight without any ale,
> Making noise with his nose.

At war within, he spared neither his country, nor his contemporaries, nor himself—poor dramatist devoid of dramatic gift! But he was too hard on his own work. It is difficult to read through. I have done so twice, and never shall again. But I return with ever fresh astonishment to his fragments. The unfinished traceries, the ruined aisles of this gaunt sham-Gothic cathedral that he left half-built and roofless to the scorn of Time, will outlast many a newer and more finished edifice; saved by the almost unearthly perfectness of here a carved line, there a sculptured monster; and by the strange owl-light of its atmosphere in which Death's Jester wandered to his early and disastrous end. There is often more quintessential poetry, I feel, in three lines of his than in as many pages of other poets not without repute. Only wreckage remains of him; but enough to sustain his memory in that sea of Eternity into which he heard Time's river falling, himself so soon to fall.

H. W. Donner (essay date 1935)

SOURCE: An introduction to *Works of Thomas Lovell Beddoes*, Oxford University Press, 1935, pp. xxivlv.

[*In the following essay, Donner traces Beddoes's literary history and discusses the difficulty in compiling a complete collection of the dramatist's work.*]

No task could appear more simple than that of editing the works of a poet whose publications did not reach beyond a single volume of poetry, one play, and a few poems and articles separately published; the bulk of whose manuscripts have unaccountably disappeared, while the majority of the rest are known to have perished either at his own hands or those of other people; whose works were edited by an executor, as conscientious as enthusiastic, in an edition to which little has been added later. But it was not always thus. The poet's devoted friend and literary executor, Thomas Forbes Kelsall, who first edited his works in 1851, had to grapple with insurmountable difficulties which prevented him from presenting to the public all of Beddoes and Beddoes entire. Some of these were external, and have been overcome by a long lapse of years; others were intrinsic to the task and must always remain. Of a poet of fragments, Kelsall presented the best; of an unfinished and unshapely work, Kelsall created a unity in an artificial whole. The Beddoes we know is Kelsall's Beddoes, as he was Kelsall's friend; and subsequent editors, reluctant to destroy, have been contented to complete. Where Kelsall had turned an inchoate tangle of alterations, corrections, forethoughts, and afterthoughts, into a finished work, who would split what had become whole, and undo the labour of love? Not even the present editor has had the heart entirely to rob Beddoes of one posthumous offspring, merely in order to hold an accurate inquest. No one more careless of the appearance of his manuscripts, no one a more careful reviser than Beddoes. If alternative readings were left by the dozen in his pages, they were only awaiting the final selection, which by a short-lived poet was consigned to the loving hand of his literary executor. There is something fragmentary in the very mind and genius of Beddoes, the traces of which even that hand could not wholly erase. Beddoes is a poet of fragments, and if exception be taken to the present edition on the ground that I have crowded the pages with variant readings and stray lines of promise unfulfilled, the answer is that such was Beddoes. The deleted lines or half-lines, or poems abandoned before they were hardly begun, may be as vital a part of the work as they are typical of their author. Again, it may be questioned whether it is right to burden the poet's fame with all that is insignificant or bad and which he himself would never have dreamt of forwarding to the press. The general public, certainly, can do without them, but to the scholar and the amateur alike they are indispensable. In the particular instance of Beddoes, moreover, their omission would fulfill no useful purpose (enough has been lost already, and the bad is inextricably mixed with the good); whereas their inclusion gives us that part of him from which he ever strove to free himself, but could not. In a work of such small compass, all that has survived innumerable vicissitudes is worth the saving. Only the complete work (complete as far as circumstances permit) can give us a just idea of the poet's rank and station.

The chronological arrangement within the categories of poems, plays, and prose-works I believe to be impregnable; not indeed in cases of doubtful chronology, the concealment of which I shall not attempt; but in the principle of the arrangement. Nothing could be more confusing to the reader and obstruct his understanding of the work before him more than the jumble made of late and early efforts presented and swallowed without discrimination. A glance at the present edition will convince the reader that the key to the poet's mind lies in the apprehension of his development, from the early prolific period of apparently desultory output; through years of determined seeking for something definite and yet elusive; arriving at the resignation of the will in the inevitable, although comparatively rare, creation of his mature period; previous to the breakdown of a mind beset by the miseries of life.

Of his earliest efforts we are on the whole well informed. The first of all his extant works is *Scaroni,* the manuscript of which is described in the Bibliography, and fragments of which were included in the edition prepared by the late Sir Edmund Gosse in 1928 (pp. 269-72: ['A Diabolical Assembly'] MS. F 4^r-4^v; ['A Death'] MS. F 6^r; and ['The Happy Ending'] MS. F 14^r-14^v). In editing this boyish composition I have been compelled to supplement the deficient punctuation. But while adding commas and semicolons I have attempted always to preserve Beddoes' period. Whoever dated the manuscript experienced some uncertainty regarding the exact time for its composition, and 1818 was substituted for 1816-17. There is nothing unlikely about the latest of these dates, and for all practical purposes it may be accepted. On the other hand, we cannot be certain that this was the only story written by Beddoes while still at school at the Charterhouse. It is possible that the main story of *Scaroni* had existed independently as the *Cynthio and Bugboo* mentioned by Bevan (Kelsall, p. cxxxii), but their identity cannot be taken for granted. Another manifestation of the precocious talent of Beddoes exists, however, in his appearance in print at the age of sixteen, when *The Comet* was published in *The Morning Post* on 6 July 1819. Of the plays, said to have been composed at school, nothing survives, and of the poems grouped under Juvenilia in the present edition, we cannot say for certain that any other than the Hymn from *Scaroni* was actually written before he left the Charterhouse. Be it sufficient that they belong to the first years of his authorship. 'Alfarabi', indeed, Kelsall states to be a boyish composition (p. 228), but the actual date is unknown. The two fragments of 'The New-born Star', on the other hand, may be of a later date. For the first of these Kelsall's transcript for the printer (described in the Bibliography) is the sole textual authority; the second, according to Dykes Campbell, was 'a very rough draft on a loose leaf', but for once he gives no indication of its place among the manuscripts, of the handwriting, or any other chronological criteria. It was Beddoes' habit in later years to jot down his compositions on loose scraps of paper, whereas his early poems were either written in note-books (like 'St. Dunstan' in **The Brides' Tragedy** Note-book, or 'Within a bower of Eglantine' and the *Song* from 'Eriphyle's Love' in the Bevan Note-book), or else they were collected, as I think, by Kelsall, and stuck into a large portfolio. The fragments of 'The New-born Star' were not among these, unless they had been copied into the collection of *Outidana,* the contents of which are unknown. On internal evidence, doubtful as it is, and in order to secure an attractive arrangement of the Poems, I have ventured to group them among the Juvenilia.

The text of these boyish effusions presents no difficulties. The deleted readings of 'Alfarabi' were noted by Dykes Campbell, who transcribed also 'St. Dunstan', the fragments 'Within a bower of Eglantine', and the *Song* from 'Eriphyle's Love'. The last mentioned gives an illustration of a habit which was to grow on Beddoes, namely to erase and alter his drafts until they became almost impossible to unravel. Typical of his stinginess with paper, so pronounced in later life, is the crowding of the second strophe into the margin of the first. But after the poem had been so drafted in the Bevan Note-book (the contents of which are described in Appendix A), he immediately proceeded to copy it out fair, and I have not even attempted to reproduce every change that the Song suffered in the course of its composition.

No manuscripts are known to exist of *The Improvisatore,* Beddoes' first published volume, Oxford, 1821, described in the Bibliography. *The Oxford University and City Herald* (the organ which counted Hartley Coleridge among its contributors) informs us of the exact date of publication, advertising as it does on 24 March 1821: 'This day was published, Price 5 s. / THE IMPROVISATORE in Three Fyttes.—/ with other poems. By THOS. LOVELL BEDDOES. / I have sung / With an unskilful, but a willing voice. / *Webster's Appius and Virginia.* / Oxford: printed for J. Vincent, near Brasennose Col-/lege; and G. and W. B. Whittaker, Ave-Maria-Lane, Lon-/don.' The present text in all respects follows that of the first edition, down to the quaint punctuation typical of the period. In one or two instances I have strengthened a comma into a semicolon, for the sake of clarity. For the rest I have been contented with the correction of printer's errors.

Of the note-books used by Beddoes about this time, two were written in repeatedly for several years, i.e. the Bevan and the Adye Note-books. Both were inscribed with the names of school-fellows (let us hope they were honestly come by). Charles Dacres Bevan, b. 1805, was Beddoes' fag at Charterhouse School, which he entered in 1818. He proceeded to Balliol in 1824; became a member of the Middle Temple, barrister of the Western Circuit, and Judge of County Court, Cornwall. Surviving Beddoes, he recorded his memories of the poet at the end of Kelsall's Memoir. Stephen Bawtree Adye, b. 1803, the son of Major R. W. Adye, R.A., entered Charterhouse School in 1816. He proceeded to Caius College, Cambridge, before joining the 98th Regiment, and was drowned when fording a river in Cape Colony, 1832 (*List of Carthusians, 1800-1879,* ed. W. D. Parish, Lewes, 1879). The Bevan Note-book was probably the one Beddoes used first of all, beginning at one end, where we find the first nine of his 'Early Dramatic Fragments', the juvenile poems already mentioned, and the Preface to 'Eriphyle's Love' immediately followed by the Song and monologue of which the fragment consists.

The first three of the 'Notes and Memoranda' were written in the same book, the order of the compositions being recorded in Appendix A. For the composition of *The Brides' Tragedy,* probably begun in summer 1821, after the publication of *The Improvisatore,* Beddoes resorted to another manuscript-book which Dykes Campbell has named the Brides' Tragedy Note-book, and the contents of which are recorded in chronological order in Appendix A. From this book are taken the 'Early Dramatic Fragments' XI-XXXI, the 'Notes and Memoranda' IV-VI, the observations on the *Caractacus* of Mason, the juvenile poem 'St. Dunstan'; and the fragment 'All night a wind of music', here printed in *Outidana.* The 'Early Dramatic Fragment' No. X, on the other hand, was copied by Kelsall in his manuscript for the printer as a dramatic fragment, but Dykes Campbell informs us that it was actually written on the same manuscript as 'Alfarabi', 'in the margin—lengthways . . . the result of an infinity of erasions & substitutions'.

The composition of *The Brides' Tragedy* seems to have been more facile, and only an insignificant part of the play actually took shape in the pages of the Brides' Tragedy Note-book. All the same, the publication of the play furnishes a *terminus ante quem* for the composition of the poems and fragments hitherto mentioned, as well as for such poems as Beddoes copied out fair at one end of the Adye Note-book under the title *Outidana.* The Oxford University and City Herald once more gives us an exact date, advertising on 30 November 1822: 'This day is published, in 8vo. price four shillings & sixpence, / THE BRIDE'S [*sic*] TRAGEDY. / By *THOMAS LOVELL BEDDOES,* of Pembroke / College, Oxford. / Printed for F. C. and J. Rivington, Waterloo-place, and / sold by J. Parker, Oxford.' As in the case of *The Improvisatore* I have in all respects followed the text of the first edition, correcting only the printer's errors, and preserving the punctuation of the original.

Of the poems now printed as *Outidana* but few belonged to the collection so called by their author. Yet I have thought it right to preserve that title, assigned to the collection he prepared after the publication of *The Brides' Tragedy.* Encouraged by the laudatory reviews of his play, Beddoes undertook to copy out fair 'what appear to be boyish verses', says Dykes Campbell. Among these were— the Song from *The Brides' Tragedy,* 'Poor old pilgrim Misery'; 'To Agrippina'; and the masque to which I have applied the title recorded on the manuscript of 'Alfarabi', 'The Masque in the Moon'. 'There are many more', says Dykes Campbell, of 'what appear to have been Beddoes' earliest verses . . .—but mostly very feeble, and quite without promise', and no one has taken the trouble as much as to record their titles. Edmund Gosse, after inspecting the contents of the Browning box, mentioned *Outidana,* together with scenes from *Love's Arrow Poisoned,* as the main portion of manuscripts still unpublished (*Athenæum,* 1883). While including the extant fragments of the Masque among the Dramas, I have added to *Outidana* the poems written in the blank leaves at the same end of the manuscript-book, composed later than the rest, but in all likelihood about the time of the publication of *The Brides' Tragedy.* These are the 'Drinking Song', and 'By the honeygolden gem'; to which I have added the fragment from *The Brides' Tragedy* Note-book, 'All night a wind of music'. The songs from *The Brides' Tragedy* naturally claim a place in this section, in which I have attempted to bring together all the poems written between 1822 and 1825. The arrangement within the group is not strictly chronological: 'The Romance of the Lily', by far the longest of the early poems in this section, precedes the short poems, actually written a little earlier; for 'The Romance of the Lily' was published in *The Album* in August 1823, whereas the 'Lines written in the Prometheus Unbound' were, on Kelsall's authority, written early in 1822 (*Athenæum,* 18 May 1833, p. 313). The 'Sonnet to Zoë King', which she transcribed for Kelsall from her Album, was dated 29 February 1824, and the Threnody, Dirges, Epitaph, and Songs from *Torrismond* and *The Second Brother,* were all written during that and the following year. 'Hushed be sighing', Dykes Campbell tells us, 'as printed, is a very clever compilation from a tangle of MS. really left quite inchoate by Beddoes'. What Kelsall printed as the ending of this Dirge was really an abandoned opening, and I have restored it to that place, while printing the end as copied by Dykes Campbell. A comparison with Kelsall's text can only serve to show with what delicacy of touch he strove to make the work of his friend presentable to the public. In the margin of the same manuscript was scribbled the Dirge, 'To her couch of evening rest', of which Dykes Campbell thought that it 'doubtless belongs to the same Dirge'. The drafts of the Epitaph, also, were written on the same page, but I am unable to say where the definitive version occurred, Kelsall being the sole textual authority; and it is possible that this poem did not receive its final form until two years later at Göttingen. The manuscript of the Threnody, written, it appears, on the same leaf as the 'Fragment of *The Last Man*' No. LVI, represented equal textual difficulties, the first draft being 'a wilderness of lines', but Beddoes had himself provided a comparatively 'fair' copy, which his patient transcriber Dykes Campbell noted. Whether these laments were actually written after his mother's death on 5 May 1824, or whether inspired by the knowledge of her extreme illness, there is no means of knowing. Certain is that the Dirge, 'To-day is a thought', was written in the following autumn, for it occupied the sheet on which *Torrismond* began. The Songs from *The Second Brother* were composed before the end of the year or early in 1825, while the Song from *Torrismond* is likely to have been written early in 1824 as the five middle lines of the second strophe occur in draft in the Adye Note-book preceding the poems inspired by the calamity of that year (see Appendix A). The 'Sonnet to Tartar' was found in the same note-book in a place which proves it to have been among the last poems Beddoes wrote before leaving England, and the 'Song of a Maid whose Love is Dead' followed 'Dianeme's Death-scene', written early in 1825. 'Pygmalion', which brings this section to a conclusion, was written at Oxford in the latter half of May in the same year, and was the poet's last great

effort before setting sail for Germany. The manuscript is described in the Bibliography.

Having finished *The Brides' Tragedy* Beddoes seems to have finished also with the note-book bearing its name, and now resumed his dramatic composition in the Bevan and the Adye Note-books alternately. In the first mentioned were written fragments destined for *Love's Arrow Poisoned,* while the Adye Note-book was reserved for *The Last Man* and other plays, perhaps, which occupied his thoughts during the summer spent with Kelsall at Southampton, 1823 (cf. Kelsall, p. xvii). But there is no consistency here, for all composition in the Bevan Note-book was soon interrupted. Many fragments composed in 1824 and 1825 were written on loose leaves, which Kelsall assembled in the large Portfolio described in Appendix A. A strictly chronological arrangement of all these fragments would not only be impracticable, but also destructive of their mutual interdependence. Of the 'Fragments of *The Last Man* and other projected plays' I-XXXIII are taken from the Adye Note-book in the order of composition, covering the period from 1823 till the early summer of 1824. Whether they were all intended for *The Last Man* it is impossible to know, but those which certainly were I have marked accordingly. No. XXXIV was written on the same sheet as the Lines written at Geneva in July 1824, and is in its sentiment connected with *Torrismond.* Nos. XXXV-XLIX are again from the Adye Note-book, and cover the period from the summer of 1824 to the spring of 1825, the first being intended for *Torrismond,* others seemingly connected with the theme of *The Last Man,* and the last few pointing forward to *Death's Jest Book.* Nos. L-LVII, finally, are from the large portfolio that contained the longer fragments, and recover the period from the late summer of 1824 to the spring of 1825. No. L was an independent manuscript stuck into the Portfolio, and the leaf containing LI-LV followed *Torrismond,* but the fragments must have been written earlier rather than later, since the last of these was incorporated in the play. No. LVI again was independent, and its place in the manuscripts uncertain; LVII was one of the last things written by Beddoes before he left for Germany, and almost certainly intended for *The Last Man.* The textual authority for the fragments, here printed for the first time, is Dykes Campbell's transcript, confirmed in the cases of LI, LIII-LIV, and LVI, by Kelsall's transcript for the printer.

The prose drafts of *Love's Arrow Poisoned,* wholly or in parts preserved in Dykes Campbell's transcript and the Memoranda printed by Kelsall (p. xx sq.) were written in the Bevan Note-book, from which the fragments of this play Nos. I-III and V are taken also. When Beddoes left Southampton in the autumn of 1823 this note-book seems to have remained with Kelsall (*The Browning Box; or the Life and Works of Thomas Lovell Beddoes, as reflected in Letters by his Friends and Admirers,* ed. H. W. Donner, letter CVI, now in press, cf. p. lv), and the fragments IV, VI-VII, and IX, were written in the Adye Note-book, the first three of these most likely in the late autumn of 1823, but the last only in the spring of 1825, when the subject of the play was revived once more. The fragments VIII and X-XI were copied from the large Portfolio, and it seems clear that the first of these was composed late in 1823, whereas the other two were among Beddoes' last compositions before his emigration. No. VIII was first printed by Gosse, but an independent transcript exists in Dykes Campbell's handwriting. The latter's copies are the authority for the fragments here published for the first time.

Having assigned the short fragments surrounding *Torrismond* in the manuscript portfolio to the 'Fragments of *The Last Man,* &c.', little need be said about this first act of a play, the whole of which is actually comprised within the narrow limits of this act. No doubt can be entertained as to this being the first act mentioned by Beddoes in his letter to Kelsall of 4 October 1824, and the text was collated and annotated by Dykes Campbell. Its composition was rapidly followed by that of *The Second Brother,* which no doubt was the play mentioned to Kelsall on 6 December following. At the end of March or beginning of April 1825 it was submitted to Kelsall for criticism, and soon afterwards abandoned altogether. The present text is once more based on Dykes Campbell's annotations to Kelsall's edition, which explain also an anomaly in Gosse's text. After the third act the composition seems to have been interrupted, and a new start made (Fragment No. IV) on the same leaf of manuscript, after which Act IV, scene i, followed immediately. The other fragments of this play are on a separate leaf, stuck into the Portfolio after the play, but covering, probably, the whole period of its composition. The textual authority is Dykes Campbell's transcripts, confirmed in the case of the first fragment by Kelsall's manuscript for the printer.

When leaving England about the middle of July 1825 Beddoes took with him the manuscripts of *The Last Man* and *Love's Arrow Poisoned* with the intention of utilizing them for a new play that was already taking shape, and we shall never know up to what point these dramas were ever finished. The Note-books and the contents of the Portfolio, however, so frequently referred to in these pages, remained at his lodgings in Devereux Court whither he meant shortly to return. In addition to the works so far enumerated the Bevan Note-book contained also the 'Fragment of a Preface'; and the Adye Note-book, the 'Notes and Memoranda' VII-XVII, whereas No. XVIII was to be found in the sheet following *The Second Brother* in the large Portfolio. The Note on the subject of *Love's Arrow Poisoned* was written at the end of the 'Lines written at Geneva', presumably pasted into the Portfolio, which contained also the review of St. John Dorset's tragedy *Montezuma*. The Notes on John Dee were no doubt among these papers, for they are clearly connected with the Note to the 'Romance of the Lily', composed 1823, but their place in the manuscripts was not indicated by Dykes Campbell. As for the translation of Schiller's *Philosophische Briefe,* no manuscript remains, and it is here reprinted from the *Oxford Quarterly Magazine* 1825, with no alterations save the correction of printer's errors. A glance at Appendix A will give a bird's-eye view of Bed-

does' production up to this date, recording as it does the manuscripts that were left behind and soon after consigned to the sole care of Kelsall, whose work of preservation started at this early stage in the career of a poet as regardless of the fate of his discarded fragments as he was aiming high in the new works that kept capturing his imagination.

Of his letters written during his youth, some of those addressed to his cousins of Cheney Longville have been destroyed, for only one survives, and after his visits there he must have written others which are not preserved. There is indeed one more in the possession of Miss Blandford to which I have not had access and even the date of which I do not know. Nor are his letters to his guardian preserved among the papers of Davies Gilbert, still in the possession of his descendants. Kelsall, however, took good care of every scrap of paper that originated from Beddoes, and his letters to this faithful admirer and friend are still preserved in the editions of Gosse and the transcripts of Dykes Campbell. The letters in verse I have ventured to group together in a small section by themselves, the first two being not far apart in their dates of composition, and the last elusive of all attempts at a definite dating. the first verse letter to Procter from Oxford was printed by Kelsall from a copy taken by himself (see *The Browning Box,* letter CXIV), and the original manuscript has not come to light. The verse letter from Göttingen, on the other hand, is still extant in the collection of Mr. C. H. Wilkinson, after Kelsall the devoted trustee of the Beddoes inheritance; and the manuscript is described in the Bibliography. In reproducing it among the poems I have taken the liberty to supplement the insufficient punctuation, but I have attempted to reproduce it among the letters exactly as it was written and dispatched by Beddoes. The jocular invitation to tea was copied by Zoë King for Kelsall, and has survived in Dykes Campbell's transcript, but we do not know except by conjecture even to whom it was addressed. (Cf. Notes.)

As far as medical studies permitted, the composition of *Death's Jest Book* occupied Beddoes during the whole course of his stay at Gottingen. The poems written during this period were generally included in the play or in some manner connected with it. A few were communicated by letter to Kelsall, and their dates of composition are thus approximately fixed. Internal evidence must decide the order of the rest. In the grouping of the poems within this section, however, I have been less concerned with the order of composition than with the internal connexion of emotional themes. The first two may be conjectured to have been written before the end of 1825 or early in 1826, while the poet's enthusiasm for his new mode of life and for the study of medicine was still fresh and buoyant. The grim Harpagus ballad with its variations is probably a little later, but almost certainly written before the autumn of 1826, when the work on the play came to a temporary close. The Songs sung by the Deaths, on the other hand, cannot have been written until 1827 or 1828, after Beddoes had become acquainted with the Romantic Irony of

Tieck which saved him from his long fit of depression. It is of little importance to know when the Drinking Song was written, but it is likely that it was about this time also. The first version of 'the ravens of Cairo' we know to have been written during the last days of October 1824, but no text survives, earlier than that in **Death's Jest Book.** The parody of Raupach was sent to Kelsall on 5 October 1826, and after it I have ventured to place a poem, equal to it in the bitterness of feeling, but somewhat of a mystery to the student of the text. There can be no doubt about this poem having been composed in Germany, after Beddoes' studies of German literature had come to include Bürger and the Terror School; yet it was written in the Adye Note-book which was then in the possession of Kelsall far away in Hampshire. Dykes Campbell, however, remarks that it was written in a very different handwriting from the earlier poems contained in the same note-book, and the only explanation I can offer is a conjecture that when Beddoes visited London in April 1828 Kelsall brought him his long-'forgotten' note-book (cf. *The Browning Box,* letter CVI) and asked him to leave in its pages some remembrance of his short visit to his native country. The deletions and alterations noted by Dykes Campbell are not numerous enough to disprove an hypothesis that Beddoes then reconstructed the poem from memory. The next two poems in this section were communicated to Kelsall by letter, and no uncertainty as to their dates need worry the student of chronology. After these I have placed the Song translated from Walther von der Vogelweide, although this was written nearly two years later. Of the songs supposedly sung after Amala's wedding, the first two are wholly insignificant and may belong to the year of exhaustion, 1827, after the severe crisis which had shaken Beddoes' inmost soul. The last of these wedding ditties is clearly connected with the poems that follow it and bring the section to a close. All, except the last, may be given to the year 1828; and these 'Dedicatory Stanzas', we may conjecture, were written when the labour of composition and transcription was brought to an end in the first months of 1829. 'These Stanzas are not to be found in any MS of DJB—but written on a detached sheet', says Dykes Campbell, 'evidently a fair copy'.

The composition of **Death's Jest Book** covered several years, and the finished play was very different from that which Beddoes had contemplated when he set out for Germany in the summer of 1825. All the drafts and composition copies have been destroyed, and what we know of the appearance of the play previous to the clean copy in MS. I is confined to the short extracts copied by Kelsall, perhaps in April 1828, and described in the Bibliography. The Duke's name was then Christian, and Isbrand's Wolfram; but the text is substantially that of the first complete version, a fact which seems to confirm the conjecture that the extracts were taken at a time not far removed from that of the first fair copy. What the play looked like in 1826, when 'finished in the rough', we do not know, except that 'its limbs' were all 'scattered and unconnected'. Only in 1828, it would seem, did Beddoes succeed in joining them together into the form of a play.

The Preface can hardly have been written earlier, for it was in that year he learned Dutch; and it was not so long before, that he became acquainted with the aesthetic doctrines of Tieck and A. W. Schlegel. Yet the Preface was copied out first in the manuscript-book called MS. I, and the date of this copy can thus hardly be earlier than the summer of 1828. Kelsall, who must have confused it with the composition copy, wrongly ascribed it to the year 1826. This is what I have described in the *apparatus criticus* as the α version. Our knowledge of it is due entirely to the transcripts of Dykes Campbell, although Kelsall's manuscript for the printer gives a word or a line from it here and there. The three different manuscripts of **Death's Jest Book** are described in Appendix A.

The second fair copy, or MS. II, must have been made immediately after the completion of the first, and not as Kelsall, who was by this time out of touch with Beddoes, thought, a year or two afterwards. MS. II is simply the transcript for the printer of the text previously copied into MS. I, with no more alterations than would naturally suggest themselves to the poet in the course of transcription. It cannot be credited with the name of a new version, but it is certainly a revised text of the play, and I have thus described it as β in the critical apparatus. Thanks to the industry of Dykes Campbell, we know the readings of this text also, and his detailed notes on the appearance of the manuscripts furnishes the proof of the correctness of my theory regarding these two texts. For whereas Beddoes wrote to Kelsall in July 1830 that the first act 'must end with the last words of Wolfram', MS. II in spite of this reproduces 'all the Ah!s and Ohs and Hells which follow'. They were never even crossed out in this copy, which would alone be sufficient evidence for the theory that this was the copy sent to England for publication. Apart from this, the many corrections and alterations in MS. I prove that this was the copy retained by Beddoes. It was here, also, that he altered the title-page for publication in 1833. MS. II was still in England in December 1829, and probably remained in this country for some time after (see *The Browning Box,* letter XXII). As far as the first act is concerned, the present text is that which Beddoes would have printed more than a hundred years ago, had his friends been satisfied with his performance. A parallel text, however, extending farther than the first act, would be sheer waste of space, and I have consequently been forced to print the last four acts with the revisions made in later years. In such cases the readings of the first version are consistently given in the critical apparatus, but without overloading it with the minutest variants of insignificant words, spelling, and punctuation. In one instance I have used the α reading in preference to β, where I believe the β version to be due to a scribal error by Beddoes himself (IV. iv. 37). We know that before leaving Göttingen Beddoes burned some of his manuscripts (see Letter to Phillips 18 Dec. 1833), and among these must have been all the drafts and composition copies of **Death's Jest Book,** the finished parts of **The Last Man** and **Love's Arrow Poisoned,** and we do not know how many poems more.

All that remains of the revision of 1829 is the fragments I and II, the second of these written on a loose scrap, the first on 'a ½ sheet of Bath-post', says Dykes Campbell, and headed by the title here reproduced. We cannot wonder if the poet tired of a task which had already occupied four years of his life. The despair into which he was thrown by the adverse criticism of his friends, and which so nearly cost him his life, produced, as I conjecture, that spirit of rebellion expressed in 'Doomsday,' the first of the poems in the next section. The rough draft of the Song which it contains was written in MS. I of *Death's Jest Book* on the flyleaf and the inside of the end-board, whereas the blank-verse part of the poem, as Dykes Campbell informs us, was written without any division of lines on a tiny scrap of paper, the first two strophes of the song on another scrap, and the rest on a half-sheet of post-paper. The text here printed is based on his transcript, confirmed as that is by Kelsall's manuscript for the printer. The next poem, 'The Old Ghost', presents no small difficulty. Gosse is here the sole textual authority, and it would not be impossible to extract his version from the rough draft of the song at the end of 'Doomsday.' But in July 1830 Beddoes told Kelsall that he had sent Bourne a Song 'about an old ghost', and it is not unlikely that a clean copy had found its way into the Browning box and was published by Gosse. Whether it had been removed later, or simply overlooked by Dykes Campbell, who is to say? The two songs placed after it exist in manuscript in the British Museum, but the text is not in every respect identical with that published by Kelsall. When sending the manuscript now in the British Museum to Robert Browning, Kelsall definitely stated that he had other manuscripts of them, and I do not think he was merely being polite. At least one of them was sent to Bourne at the same time as 'The Old Ghost,' and Kelsall is certain to have obtained copies of them. Dykes Campbell's investigation of the manuscripts was hurried, and he may have overlooked a few; neither is it certain that some manuscripts were not mislaid or lost in the course of several inventories. A careful comparison of 'Dream Pedlary' (in the British Museum MS.) and the letter to Kelsall of 19 July 1830 clearly shows that the poem was written only a very short time before, and another fixed date is thus provided in the uncertain chronology of Beddoes' poems. The text printed by Kelsall to which I have adhered incorporates some later variants.

How far the revision of *Death's Jest Book* proceeded at Würzburg it is impossible to say for certain. The alterations made in the Preface, the γ readings of the present edition, were most probably then made, for in later years Beddoes does not appear to have been in the least concerned with it. These passages were added in MS. I, where the paraphrase of Novalis and the Note on plagiarisms were introduced also. It is more than likely that these too were written at Würzburg, perhaps in 1831. As for passages added in the play itself, internal evidence alone can determine which were composed now, and which later. The fragment that Kelsall entitled 'Mourners Consoled' (the deleted reading of II. ii. 36-52), preceded by the first draft of the Dirge, 'No tears, no sighing, no despair', on a loose scrap of paper, is so closely related to other expressions of Beddoes' philosophy about this time that it is impossible not to assign them to the Würzburg period, and even definitely to the year 1831. It is more than likely that Beddoes destroyed many scraps with fragments once intended for his play, and we know that the revision cannot have proceeded very far, for after gaining his M.D. degree the poet became absorbed in the political turmoil in which Bavaria was then labouring, and we are fortunate enough to possess some traces of his political activity. The identification of the six articles reprinted from the *Bayerisches Volksblatt* is the result of the brilliant research of Dr. C. A. Weber of Göttingen, who has provided philological proof that the writer was an Englishman; and that this Englishman was Beddoes nobody will be able to doubt. In the notes I have provided English translations, such as they are, of these articles; and in the Bibliography, section Apocrypha, I have reprinted another two articles in which I am convinced that Beddoes had a share. His speech at the banquet given in honour of General Rybinsky was happily reported *in toto* in the newspaper to which he was himself a contributor, but in one place where I think the report must be mistaken I have for once ventured an emendation in the interest of common sense.

Stimulated by Beddoes' wish to establish contact with some English periodical, Kelsall in the meantime made determined efforts to get some of his friend's poems published in England. Already in 1828 Procter had sent one of Beddoes' letters to Leigh Hunt's *Companion,* and in 1832 the 'Song of a Maid whose Love is Dead' together with twenty lines from 'Dianeme's Death-Scene' appeared with an introductory note by Procter in the *Athenæum.* In the following year Kelsall himself succeeded in getting the 'Lines written in the Prometheus Unbound' published in the same periodical, but his efforts to make editors accept any longer compositions were all in vain (see *The Browning Box,* letters XXIV and XXVI-XXXI).

His pleasant and idle mode of life at Zürich was highly conducive to literary recreation, and Beddoes cannot have been there long before his poetical activities were resumed. On the back of a letter from his college friend Bourne, in the blank spaces each side of the address, Beddoes wrote early in 1833 the Fragment of *Death's Jest Book* IV, so closely connected with the two surrounding fragments that we cannot help attributing them all roughly to the same date. The manuscript of No. IV is still extant, whereas those of III and V, which were written on loose scraps, have disappeared. The strong feeling for nature awakened by an intimate communion is reflected in the discarded version of I. i. γ, 258-67, written in the margin of MS. II, at the end of the scene; in the Fragment VIII, written on the same scrap of paper as IX and the line I. ii. γ, 85, together with 'much prose in German'; and in the lines added in MS. I, II. ii. 36-42 and III. iii. 647-50. A fixed date is again provided by the manuscript of the Fragments XII-XIV, the last of which was written before the others on the back of a bill covering items from 1-30 September for 'Herrn M Dr T. L. Beddoes an Johann Waser', his landlord in Trittligasse, 1 October 1837, paid. These specimens help us to date other fragments that resemble them in style or sentiment. Nos. X and XI, written in the margin of MS. I; XV, on a loose sheet of post-paper; the abandoned opening of I. i. γ, on a loose scrap; the passage I. i. γ, 268-76, drafted with many alterations on a scrap of paper; the lines 281-5 of the same scene, written on another scrap of paper on which occurs also the Boat-Song (290-305); v. ii. 48-9, in the margin of MS. I; all these passages seem to belong to the years at Zürich. And thus *Death's Jest Book* slowly altered in the mind of its author, but few of these additions were actually incorporated in the text, and if Beddoes had never brought many of them together himself, they must have remained detached fragments, instead of constituting a new text the process of whose growth we are to some extent able to follow. The note on the subject of Wolfram's resurrection, on the first page of MS. II, is in accordance with Beddoes' views about this time; that on *The Last Man* was written on the same scrap as the 'Lament of Thanatos'.

Political circumstances again put an end to the work of revision, but before that time Beddoes had collected a number of lyrical poems which he intended to publish with some four or five prose tales and *Death's Jest Book,* under the title *The Ivory Gate.* Apart from a fragment published by Kelsall in *The Examiner,* 8 October 1864, only the shortest possible passages of the four tales actually finished have survived in Dykes Campbell's transcripts. No one undertook to copy the rest, and the manuscripts have disappeared without trace. The poems included in this volume were either sung by characters in the tales themselves, or marked for the 'Appendix of Songs'. To this category belong all the finished poems in this section, whereas I have included a certain number of drafts and fragments not so marked, because they were written during the same period, 1833-8. 'The Runaway' and 'Dial Thoughts' were written on the same sheet; 'And in that rosy rosy hour' was written in ink in the margin of 'The Father of the Deep', but occurred also pencilled on a loose scrap, 'barely legible'; the 'Dirge' 'Let dew the flowers fill' was on the same sheet as the 'Song of the Stygian Naiades'; 'The snake is come out' was composed on the same leaf as 'Silenus in Proteus'; the 'City of the Sea' on the same scrap as *The Flowery Alchemist*; and so on. 'The Lily of the Valley' was made up, as Dykes Campbell tells us, 'from a very imperfect scrap'. For one fragment, that of 'The Tree of Life,' Kelsall is the sole authority, and we know neither when it was written nor where the manuscript was to be found. Its familiarity with Scandinavian mythology establishes undeniable evidence that it was written after Beddoes had left England, and I have therefore grouped it with the 'Dial Thoughts' and the 'Epilogue to Human Woe' with both of which it is connected in theme and sentiment. It is regrettable that I have not been able to group the poems according to the Chapters of *The Ivory Gate,* but the precise places of so few poems are accurately known, that I have abandoned any such idea, and principally aimed at an attractive arrangement of the whole. By placing those of the first chapter last, I have

further provided a transition to the 'Last Poems'. 'The rosy hour' was transcribed by Kelsall, although not printed by him; for the other poems here published for the first time Dykes Campbell is the sole authority.

Beddoes himself tells us that 'The New Cecilia' was intended for the fifth chapter of *The Ivory Gate;* as a matter of fact it was included in the enlarged first act of *Death's Jest Book.* Indirectly this circumstance furnishes sufficient proof that even though the new version of the play may have existed in its entirety on loose scraps of paper and in marginal additions in MS. I, the text had not been copied out by this time. Otherwise Beddoes would have had no occasion to add the stage direction in MS. I: 'Peter sings Whoever has heard of St. Gingo.' A similar stage direction incorporates 'The Oviparous Tailor' into the play, and it is likely that it had been written about the same time as the other poem thus introduced. The fifth chapter of *The Ivory Gate* remained unfinished. One more poem, for the composition of which Beddoes' letters give a *terminus ante quem,* is the Song 'As sudden thunder' which was at first intended to bring the first act of *Death's Jest Book* to a conclusion, and which was copied into the margin of MS. I from a rough draft on the same leaf as the lines of dialogue I. iv. γ, 238-9. The title-page reproduced before the γ version confirms Beddoes' statement to Kelsall that he meant to publish his play at last, with such poems and prose tales as he had composed during five or six pleasant years at Zürich.

One of his German poems he published as a pamphlet signed with his own name (see Bibliography), the others are signed 'B', and their inclusion in this edition may seem to require some justification. The writer's native language was not German, and here and there he betrays his foreign birth. The prosody of *Der Weltvogel* (line 4) clearly proves that the writer was an Englishman, and the inversions remind us of Beddoes' grammar (e.g. the first sonnet of 1844, line 14). No countryman of his took any part in the political quarrels of Zürich at this time, and the poems occur in the very newspaper that showed a pronounced interest in Beddoes and gave a long report of his performance of Hotspur. The editor was a former medical student, and Beddoes cannot have helped being acquainted with him. The *Volksbote,* like the *Republikaner* where the first of the poems of this period appeared, was the organ of the radical party which counted among its numbers every one of Beddoes' friends. The signature 'B' cannot be identified as that of any other poet then active in the radical interest, and taken together all these circumstances seem to establish sufficient evidence for Beddoes' authorship. In the Notes I have attempted to give English translations of these poems, and in the Apocrypha I have included a hoaxing article from the *Volksbote* which was in all likelihood the result of a collaboration between Beddoes and Zottelmeyer, the editor. Nothing survives of the medical writings Beddoes undertook during these years. The physician who attended Beddoes during his last illness possessed a medical pamphlet written by him, but we do not know of what size or on what subject (*The Browning Box,* letter LXXXII).

After his flight from Zürich in April 1840 we know less than ever about Beddoes' activities, literary or political. His German poems of 1844 and 1845 are happily dated by their appearance in the *Republikaner*. Two of these, however, are unsigned and these are the sole exceptions to the rule I have set myself of including nothing but what bears the signature of B[eddoes]. There are many poems in the *Volksbote* of an excellent quality by unknown authors, and an editor of Beddoes has to resist the strongest temptation to include a larger number. The *Schweizerjüngling* also contains many a talented poem, but none, as I think, by Beddoes. What makes an attempt to identify their authors particularly difficult is the fact that the Swiss newspapers of that time are practically virgin soil, untouched by literary research, and their investigation is pioneer work. In the case of the two unsigned epigrams, however, there can be no doubt about the author's identity with the signature 'B', especially as they appear in company with a poem so signed, the last of them separated from it only by their appearance in succeeding numbers of the newspaper. There may of course be many more which have escaped my notice, and the non-preservation of some of the newspapers I would have liked to search hampered me to no small extent.

For Beddoes' last English poems, here divided in two separate groups in order to bring together those included in *Death's Jest Book*, the 'Lines written in Switzerland' provide one of the few dates approximately fixed. This poem must have been written after the death of Southey, or Beddoes could not have alluded to Wordsworth's appointment as Laureate (see R. H. Snow, *T. L. Beddoes: Eccentric and Poet*, New York, 1928, p. 218). The final version must thus belong to 1844, whereas the earlier rhymed version, here printed from Dykes Campbell's transcript, may easily have been written in the previous year. The stanzas were drafted on a loose scrap of paper, and Dykes Campbell tells us that there was 'yet another draft in rhyme on the subject—but it is grotesque, and very poor in its grotesquerie of rhyme', and he did not transcribe it. 'The Last Judgement', now but a fragment, had once been a fair copy on another scrap, 'but', says Dykes Campbell, 'pulled to pieces by a later pen—and left bleeding'. The 'Tiberius' fragments, on the other hand, were written on the same sheet as the 'Lines written in Switzerland,' and can thus be safely given to the year 1844. There is further an affinity in sentiment between these noble Lines and the first Sonnet that appeared in the *Republikaner* in that year. What I have termed an 'Epigram' is taken from the letters, and we need not assume that it ever occurred elsewhere. The 'Reflection' was written on a loose scrap, and copied by Dykes Campbell among the last of Beddoes' poems. There is at this period little difference between his poetic and dramatic fragments, all being equally reflective in their mood; and I have thus printed it among the Poems although it may just as well have been intended for *Death's Jest Book*.

The letter to Kelsall, begun in November 1844, but left unposted until the following January, helps us to determine what was in Beddoes' mind about that date. There is a long passage about Paracelsus, which suggests that the motto added 'in very pale ink' in MS. I and here placed before the γ version, was written somewhere about the time when Beddoes passed through Basle on his way to Germany. It is equally possible that the title-page I have placed after the fragments, the promised Comic Legend of which never got a leg to stand on, belongs to the same period. It was written on the 'outside page of MS. III' on which there was 'much pencilling', also, 'now illegible', but it has no connexion with the play. In the same letter were two poems taken from the enlarged first act of *Death's Jest Book*, 'The Boding Dreams' (first drafted on a loose scrap) and 'The swallow leaves her nest'. On the same leaf on which the latter poem was originally composed was on the other side the Threnody, 'Far away As we hear', which I have placed in the last section. The last strophe of the Threnody was made up by Kelsall from an unfinished draft, but since Kelsall did no more than select among the variants, I have left it as printed by him. In the letter to Kelsall, January 1845, there are further three and a half lines of poetry quoted from the enlarged first act of 'the never-ending Jest book'. We are thus led to assume that between 1838 and 1845 the text of the first act had been copied once more in its considerably enlarged form in the manuscript-book called MS. III. It may have been done at Berlin 1840-2, or during the long winter months at Baden in Aargau 1843; but it is much more likely that it was only at Zürich where creation was habitual to this taciturn poet, that the γ version of the first act was copied out fair during the year spent there from July 1843. Kelsall's theory that it was copied out before 1832 is untenable.

Most of it had been composed during the many years which lapsed between the first revision in 1830 and the date when it was copied into the new manuscript-book, and the composition copy of many a passage was to be found either on loose scraps or in the margins of MSS. I or II. The majority of corrections and alterations was made in MS. I, and this makes it sometimes difficult to distinguish between α and γ readings. Dykes Campbell is not clear on this point as, somehow, he had not realized that these alterations were later than MS. II. A proof that they are so is provided by the altered title-page in MS. I, which makes it clear that this was the copy Beddoes was working on in 1832. This title I have placed in front of the αβ version, as the work of revision had not proceeded far enough substantially to alter the text of the play. Although it involves some little repetition, I shall now enumerate the passages of the γ text added in ink or pencil in MSS. I and II and on loose scraps of paper. Dykes Campbell's indications of erasures and additions, be it mentioned, are clear beyond reproach or doubt, and a comparison between MSS. I and II generally solves the question of priority. The margins of MS. I thus contained the following passages of the γ text, later incorporated or discarded in MS. III, which comprises the first act alone: I. i, the deleted readings of lines 1 and 10 sq., the first two versions of the Song 61-70, 113-32 (previously drafted on a scrap), deleted reading of 268, lines 268-76 (previously drafted on scrap); 316 with the place for insertion marked with caret; I. ii, lines 129, 245, and 330-5; I. iii, indication of replacement of dialogue in favour of Songs; and I. iv, indication of insertion of 'The New Cecilia' and 'The Oviparous Tailor', as well as of entry of 'Fishermen'. In the margin of MS. II were: I, i, deleted reading of 258-67 (at end of scene); and I. iv, the deleted afterthought 193-4, and deleted version of 227: 'Ziba runs in', with the short ensuing dialogue. On loose scraps the following passages were composed: the list of Dramatis Personae; the alternative opening of I. i; the drafts of I. i. 113-32, 268-76, stage direction 280, and 281-5 (finishing: 'Then thou art wiser than thy father, Lie'—cf. motto to *The Ivory Gate,* Chapter IV—and with the 'Boat-Song' added to these passages; the last three items written on the same scrap), the 'Boat-Song' 290-305 together with the first version of 306-10 on another scrap; I. ii. 76-84; and 85 (on the same scrap as VIII and IX), and 166-70; I. iii. 119, the deleted reading of the stage direction, and Mandrake's speech (on two separate scraps); I. iv, draft of 122-35 with the draft of Song 136-47, and finally 238-9 on the same scrap as the Song 'As sudden thunder'.

But we have not finished yet with the enlarged first act and MS. III. Even after it had been copied fair Beddoes continued making alterations, and went on adding and deleting. This manuscript was written on one page of the leaf only, and in the blank pages opposite the passages that were to be altered Beddoes kept inserting alternative versions, while he deleted others without substituting anything. The MS. III thus contained all the minor alterations which I do not specifically note here, and in addition to these the following alterations: I. i, deleted reading of 3 and 20 crossed over here; 43-4 were added, 48, 56, 238, and 282 erased (the last but one after some friend's pencilling, probably Procter's); I. ii. 29 was the result of a pencilled suggestion 'by Bourne', says Dykes Campbell; the first draft of 31-4 and the final version of 31-45 occur in the blank page as an addition; similarly 76-83 (first drafted on a scrap), 192-4, 195-200 and the discarded reading of 367-77; the deleted reading of 375 is interpolated and crossed over; I. iii, the deleted reading of 159 was in the blank page; and I. iv, the alternative reading of 154-6 and line 180 were additions in the blank pages of MS. III. In addition to these passages the Fragment VII occupied one of these pages, but it is impossible to incorporate it in the text, as no clear indication of such a procedure was left by Beddoes. It was, moreover, run through with a pen; we may reasonably suppose, following on the failure to include it without substantial alteration. Finally some late alterations, among the latest of all, were made on loose scraps, after the completion of MS. III. They included: I. ii. 76-83 (together with the deleted afterthought for line 84 and the Fragment XVII, all on one scrap) and 192-4; I. iii, the deleted afterthought for 158, on the other side of which was the Fragment VI; and I. iv. 227, the second deleted afterthought: 'A voice, ye million cherubs,' &c.—It is a matter for profound regret on the part of the editor that it has been impracticable to

arrange the Fragments in chronological order, yet it seemed more satisfactory to connect them with the characters of the play in a resemblance of the sequence of its action.

As for the four remaining acts, I have adopted the γ readings wherever it was possible to do so. To exclude them from the main text would certainly have implied a complete accordance with Beddoes' intentions in 1829, but since Fate decreed against publication in that year, I have thought it right to present the play as it stood after the poet had done his best to improve on it. Nor can it be denied that the later additions include some of the best passages in the whole performance.—The revision of the last four acts proceeded in the same manner as that of the first, although they were never copied out fair into MS. III. It covers a period of many years from 1830 to a time shortly before the poet's death, and the alternative readings were introduced into the margins of the existing manuscripts or written on loose scraps of paper. Thus the margins of MS. I contained the following γ readings: II. iii. 310-32; II. iv, the abandoned alternatives to 87-8 and 87-91; indication of the necessity of rewriting the whole of III. i and ii; III. i. 40-9 γ; III. iii. 489-500 and 647-50; IV. i. 9-20 and 97; IV. iii. 364-7 and 376-8; IV. iv. 156-63; V. ii. 48-9; and V. iv. 251-3, 270, and 281-4. The scraps of paper suggesting alterations of these acts seem to have been few. The draft of II. ii. 34-52 was written on one, preceded by a few draft lines of the Dirge 'No tears, no sighing, no despair'. The final version of the same passage was written out on another loose scrap, whereas the Dirge occurs in its definitive form on the manuscript that contains the 'Song of the Stygian Naiades' and the Dirge 'Let dew the flowers fill'. It is easy to see that the Dirge, the substance of which was already incorporated in the dialogue, was only taken up, like several other poems, in the wish 'to be prodigal of lyrics'. But it is highly probable, also, that whereas the first draft of II. ii. 34-52 was composed at Würzburg in 1831 or 1832, the final version was only written at Zürich a couple of years later. The lines 83-7 of the same scene were drafted as well as copied fair on one scrap of paper, and 87-93 were composed on another. A most radical alteration of III. iii was suggested on a slip of paper containing the abandoned afterthought for lines 606-11. Evidently it was here the poet's intention to postpone the resurrection of Wolfram till the last scene, and the Duke is made to leave the stage before the appearance of the spectre. It is characteristic of Beddoes that the stage direction (line 610) is here written in German: 'Ab.' So long had he lived abroad that the foreign term suggested itself spontaneously, and not infrequently did he introduce a Gothic letter such as the Germans use, into the text of his English productions.—All the variant readings dispersed throughout the manuscripts, and faithfully copied by Dykes Campbell in the places where they occurred, I have brought together in the critical apparatus of *Death's Jest Book,* which also is now printed unabridged.

What I believe to be Beddoes' very last poems still remain to be accounted for. 'The Phantom Wooer' was composed in the Adye Note-book which since 1825 had been in

Kelsall's keeping, but Dykes Campbell tells us that it was 'written in the hand of the corrections of D. J. B., round and strong'. I do not think it is too bold to conjecture that Kelsall desired some slight memorial of Beddoes' final visit to Fareham in the early summer of 1847, and brought out the note-book in which his friend had been used to write of old. What Beddoes wrote, if my hypothesis is correct, was the first draft of this poem, for the final version of which Kelsall's edition is the sole authority. The little quatrain I have entitled 'On Himself' is dated by its occurrence in the second last letter to Kelsall; and the little scrap of manuscript containing the 'Last Fragments' may have been left behind at Fareham, or these may be the last traces of the workings of his mind in the solitude of Basle Hospital.

Many of the letters written from abroad were published by Kelsall, and the full text of Gosse's editions is supported by the independent transcripts of Dykes Campbell. The latter collated the letters to Procter also, of the present whereabouts of which I am ignorant. Mrs. Procter ordered her husband's papers to be destroyed (see letter from Bryan Charles Waller to Mrs. Kelsall, 2 Dec. 1894; manuscript in the possession of Miss Kelsall), and the originals of Beddoes' letters may have been among these. Soon after her husband's death Mrs. Bourne herself burned his papers, and doubtless the correspondence of Beddoes, intimate and uninterrupted for more than twenty years (*The Browning Box,* letter LVIII). His letters to Andrew Phillips were destroyed, as his son informs me, during the late war when the greed of the paper mills for waste paper was insatiable. What has happened to some sixty letters addressed to Revell Phillips I am unable to say, as every effort to trace them has been in vain. As it is, we know them only from the short extracts which Phillips sent to Kelsall to be used in his Memoir of the poet. A list containing the dates for the last of these letters is included in Appendix B. Of Beddoes' German correspondence I have found but two specimens, which are included in the present edition. His last letters to his sister were published by Gosse from the copies taken by Kelsall in 1849, but I am unable to say what has happened either to the originals of these or to the letters written to his brother. Happily some of his letters to his cousins of Cheney Longville have been preserved, and the family have courteously placed them at my disposal.

On his death-bed, a few hours before his death, Beddoes bequeathed his manuscripts to Kelsall to 'print or not as *he* thinks fit'. In a history of persistent bad fortune befalling the Beddoes papers this was the one fortunate circumstance. The poet's brother honourably delivered up the manuscripts, but he was not enthusiastic at the prospect of their publication (*The Browning Box,* letters L and LII), and while she would have welcomed scientific works by her late brother, his sister was definitely opposed to it (ibid., letter LI). So strong were her feelings on this point that Mrs. Andrew Crosse, who met her in later years, received the impression 'that had the MSS. come into their possession, they would most probably have been consigned to the fire' (*Temple Bar,* March 1894, vol. 101, p. 358).

Kelsall, however, whose admiration for the poet had not been diminished even by the many long years of his silence, tackled the job of literary executor immediately. His first concern was for **Death's Jest Book,** which he transcribed entirely in his own hand, selecting the readings he preferred and omitting weak passages, or such as might give offence. 'My office has been to collate, adapt, omit & transcribe—a labour of interest', he wrote to his sister Eleanor on 13 April 1850 (manuscript in the possession of Miss Kelsall). The arrangement for its publication by Pickering was by that time completed, Kelsall having received the estimates a few days previously. 'As there are but few purchasers of Poetry', the number of copies was limited to 500 to be sold at the price of 5*s.* fixed by Kelsall. The cost of 150 pages like the Aldine Poets was II*s.* 3*d.*, and that of the boards 6*d.* per volume, which Pickering recommended in preference to paper wrappers at 2*d.* The price charged to the trade would be 3*s.* 7*d.* A few advertisements were to be inserted in the Press, five copies allowed for libraries and twenty for the reviewers. (Letter from Pickering to Kelsall, 5 April 1850, transcribed by Dykes Campbell). The printed label, like that of the Aldine Poets, was chosen by Kelsall on Pickering's advice in preference to gilt. (Letter from Pickering to Kelsall, 10 June 1850, transcribed by Dykes Campbell.) The publication was anonymous, partly, I think, because Beddoes himself had intended it to be so, and largely out of consideration for the feelings of the family (*The Browning Box,* letter LII). 'The brother and sister both dislike it—& my object be[in]g to preserve the MSS. not to circulate the work, I shall avoid all the notoriety & expense I can', Kelsall wrote again to his sister on 29 April 1850 (manuscript in the possession of Miss Kelsall). Hence his omission to mention advertisements, the necessity of which was emphasized by Pickering in a letter of [18] June (manuscript in the possession of Miss Kelsall). The immediate cost to Kelsall, however, amounted to £30.

On 18 June Pickering was able to dispatch a copy to Captain Beddoes, which reached him at Cephalonia on 3 July 1850, and so gratified him that he gladly offered to pay the expenses of any further works by his late brother which Kelsall might think fit for publication (*The Browning Box,* letter LIV).—Kelsall was to receive his copies a few days later, when the work was also to be sent to the *Athenæum, Literary Gazette, Spectator, Examiner, Atlas, Critics,* [*Morning*] *Post,* and *Herald, Observer, Weekly News, New Monthly, Bentley's Miscellany,* and *Fraser's,* for reviewing. Whether to send it to the 'Church' magazines Pickering was uncertain, as he 'had not looked at a line' of it (manuscript in the possession of Miss Kelsall). Although the sales were not very large, the reviews were encouraging, and Kelsall proceeded to transcribe the Poems and Dramatic Fragments. It was then found desirable to include **The Brides' Tragedy,** and the consent of its publisher was readily obtained, 'as we have not more than a dozen copies of The Brides' Tragedy remaining' (letter from F. and J. Rivington to Kelsall, 7 March 1851, transcribed by Dykes Campbell). This provided a means to dispose of the remaining copies of

Death's Jest Book, of which no less than 250 were bound with *The Brides' Tragedy* as volume ii of *The Poems Posthumous and Collected of Thomas Lovell Beddoes,* Pickering, 1851. In a letter dated 23 May (postmarked 22 May 1851) Pickering was able to tell Kelsall that he had given the play to the printer. At Kelsall's express desire he had altered the 'Dramatis Personae' to 'Persons Represented', but against Kelsall's wish he had directed that the Preface be retained. 'I should keep it, as written by the Author.' Pickering had further made the best possible arrangement of pagination and signatures so as to make them follow *Death's Jest Book.* 'It will always take its place after D.J.B. when the *Works* are bound,—but temporarily will be done up in some copies of Vol. I' (manuscript in the possession of Miss Kelsall). It would appear that this was entirely Pickering's own idea, and actually half the 1851 edition, or 250 copies, appeared in one volume with a title-page of Pickering's own invention.

The edition appeared in September, and cost Kelsall another £30, acknowledged by Pickering on 31 October (transcript by Dykes Campbell). By that time 90 copies of the two-volume impression had been sent out, and 80 one-volume copies, including complimentary copies: 'upon the whole . . . a fair sale, considering that the season has been very dull', Pickering wrote to Kelsall. The absolute sale, however, was much less, and the figures quoted by Pickering on 30 January 1852 were 36 copies of the one-volume, and 124 of the two-volume impression, which, said Pickering, 'helps off Death's Jest Book, but I am disappointed at the small demand for the ii vol' (transcript by Dykes Campbell). At Pickering's death in 1854 it was found that owing to the failure of a friend for whom he had stood security, his liquid assets were insufficient to meet his liabilities, and it became necessary to realize his stock. Captain Beddoes then ordered 18 copies of the two-volume impression to be sent for him to Revell Phillips, and the remainder, 163 copies of the one-volume, and 47 of the two-volume impression, were sold by auction. The two volumes were then expected to fetch 5*s.* or 6*s.* per copy, and the one volume II*s.* 6*d.* or 2*s.*, as a transcript by Dykes Campbell of a letter to Kelsall from the office of E. W. Edwards informs us. It would seem, however, that they were not all sold, for in 1872 B. W. Pickering was willing to part with half a dozen of them to Dykes Campbell, who has transcribed his letter of 13 July, stating that he always had copies of Beddoes' works.

If, however, the public had been lukewarm in their support of Kelsall's enterprise, the reviewers had been on the whole most appreciative. Men of letters, such as Landor and Forster, and Sara Coleridge, were enthusiastic; and Tennyson and Browning full of admiration. Thus Kelsall did not lack the encouragement he needed after his long editorial labours. It is easy to criticize his edition, but an investigation of the facts proves it to have been not only a great achievement in itself, but also the very best that could be produced in the circumstances. Kelsall himself was always apologetic about his treatment of *Death's Jest Book* and anxious to obtain the opinion of others concern-

ing the suppression of the comic parts (*The Browning Box,* letter CVIII), but in his editorial work he had to consider the feelings of the family and exclude both from the play and from the letters everything that might strike them as coarse or vulgar. It was this manifest consideration that won for him the approval of the poet's brother. Some poems, such as 'The Oviparous Tailor' (which he actually copied in his transcript for the printer) and 'The New Cecilia', Kelsall himself considered 'unpublishable, to "ears polite"' (*The Browning Box,* letter CVI). Nor could he, even if he had wanted to, have published the play in its entirety. A variorum edition was out of the question when the play was printed for the first time, and to have published the first version alone would have implied a grave injustice to Beddoes as an artist. It would further have been impossible to print the first act from the last version, to be followed by the remaining acts revised to a much lesser extent. The only course that remained open to Kelsall was to select such readings as he preferred from the enlarged first act and adapt them to the contents of the earlier version. In the other acts the task was easier, and on the whole Kelsall adhered to the early version, reluctant to omit passages marked for deletion, while introducing at the same time reading from the added fragments. In this manner he was able to produce a text which will probably always remain more popular than the full version.

Excusable and even necessary as it may have been at the time, such treatment of the text would not be permissible in any other editor than the literary executor. In his wish to retain passages of beauty in fragments for which there was no room in his edition, Kelsall transferred lines from one composition to another. The Song 'As sudden thunder' in the enlarged first act was thus given a place at the end of IV. ii, where Beddoes had never dreamt of inserting it. Four and a half lines from Fragment XV were introduced into the scene which the fragment had at one time been intended to replace (IV. i. 35). The early fragment 'Leonigild's Apprehension' was made to serve Athulf in his moments of agony, in preference to the later version of the speech as written and revised in the pages of *Death's Jest Book.* Such instances of Kelsall's arrangement of the text are not included in the critical apparatus of the present edition, which comprises only the poet's own revisions and actual divergences of the textual authorities.

The repeatedly altered pagination and numbering of the Dramatic Fragments in the manuscript for the printer shows that Kelsall had originally intended to print them in chronological order, but for fear of giving an unfavourable first impression, I imagine, he rearranged them many a time before he hit upon one that satisfied his taste and sense of their respective importance. At the same time he provided them with titles after the model of Dodd's *Beauties of Shakespear* or Lamb's *Specimens* and the multitude of similar anthologies. A literary executor is no doubt permitted to deal somewhat freely with the works entrusted to him, and Kelsall was right to present that of his admired friend in the form most likely to appeal. Yet his system was to have consequences which he could not foresee, and it misled the late Sir Edmund Gosse to include one of Beddoes' very earliest pieces among the *Fragments of Death's Jest Book* (*A Countenance foreboding Evil,* 'Early Fragments' XIV). Beddoes had been sparing of punctuation, and his drafts could not have been published without some addition of commas and semicolons, yet it must be admitted that Kelsall was somewhat more addicted to excessive punctuation than even the contemporary taste for unnecessary commas warranted. Gosse to some extent relieved Beddoes' works of this obstructive load, and it has been the aim of the present editor to restore the original system of punctuation which, like Shakespeare's, was dramatic rather than syntactic, marking the pauses within the line and ignoring the need for punctuation both at the end of a line and where a strict application of grammar would have placed them as obstacles to the flow of the verse within the line. But in spite of the minor objections that might be raised from a scholarly point of view, Kelsall's text remains the sole authority for the bulk of Beddoes' work and the foundation for all subsequent editions. His services to English literature are inestimable and, as far as is permitted to human effort, everlasting. In his work of collating the texts he was assisted by Procter, who had taken copies of substantial portions of Beddoes' production, and this fact may explain why Dykes Campbell failed to find some of the manuscripts. (See *The Browning Box,* letter LVI.) As for his Memoir of Beddoes, prefixed to the Poems, it may be said without exaggeration that without it we would know next to nothing about him. With admirable restraint and objectivity he set forth the facts as far as they were known to him, allowing his friend's letters to speak for themselves wherever that was possible. His Memoir must in consequence form the basis of every future work on Beddoes, and a better and more sympathetic biographer has never been. The true circumstances of the poet's death were not known to Kelsall at the time he wrote, and although he became acquainted with them to his sorrow before his own death, it was a long time before they were disclosed to the public.

Kelsall's labours had preserved the work of Beddoes, but they had not secured a public to a poet himself so shy of publicity. Even the performance of the Dirge 'If thou wilt ease thine heart', set to music by H. B. Walmisley, and sung by the celebrated Miss Hayes on 21 June 1851, could not win for it a place in the nation's heart. Even the most superlative of the reviews failed to make Beddoes popular. The 'comet flaming through the orbit of Shelley and Keats' (*Critic,* 1 Nov. 1851) did not lure the minds of the public to follow its erratic course. He remained 'a man scarcely known to the public as an author, but reputed a true poet among poets', for in his poetry there was nothing of the self-representation for which the age was craving (*Critic,* 1 Jan. 1851). But if Kelsall had to be satisfied with a limited success, he never tired of the endeavour to win for Beddoes new admirers and post-humous friends. Nor were his efforts restricted to his personal acquaintance. In 1864 some simple verses in the *Cornhill Magazine* (Sept. 1864,

p. 281) struck him by their affinity to the sentiment of some of Beddoes' work:

I who had looked on Love had looked on Death.

So finished the insignificant poem signed W. S., and Kelsall promptly submitted to the editor the 'Tale of the Lover to his Mistress' from *The Ivory Gate,* but the answer (transcribed by Dykes Campbell) was disappointing: 'The Editor of the Cornhill Magazine presents his compliments to Mr. Kelsall and begs to thank him for the opportunity of reading Mr. Beddoes's striking apologue which however the editor must return. Sept. 28. 1864.' *The Examiner* then stood up for Beddoes, as it had done before, and 'Cupid, Death, and Psyche. An Apologue by the late Thomas Lovell Beddoes' appeared in its pages on 8 October.

Late in 1867 Bryan Waller Procter was instrumental in arranging a meeting between Kelsall and another enthusiastic admirer of Beddoes, Robert Browning; and their meeting inaugurated the interesting correspondence which led to the bequest of all the Beddoes papers to Browning (*The Browning Box,* section VII). After Kelsall's death they were accordingly sent by his widow early in 1873 in a large box, containing not only the manuscripts, but also all the biographical material about Beddoes which Kelsall had collected in the course of a lifetime. It had been Kelsall's dearest wish that Browning himself should undertake to edit Beddoes' works anew, but consideration for the relatives of his late friend made him direct that the truth about the poet's death should not be made public while his cousin Zoë King was still alive. The inquiries of Kelsall's young relative V. de S. Fowke in 1874 (cf. *The Browning Box,* letter CXXXIX) and of John Ingram in 1880 (*Letters of Robert Browning Collected by T. J. Wise,* 1933, p. 191) thus met with a negative answer. In the meantime, the interest in Beddoes had been growing, largely in consequence of Kelsall's admirable article in *The Fortnightly* (July 1872); and Landor and Forster, Sara Coleridge and Swinburne had paid generous tribute to his genius. Procter had recorded his memories of his friend and given him high praise. Browning still professed to have the matter 'really at heart'.

Zoë King died at Bristol on 28 September 1881, and with her another devoted friend of Beddoes'. No obstacle remained for the disclosure of all the facts relative to the poet, and Browning accordingly summoned the late Sir Edmund Gosse to aid him in the investigation. His letter written on Wednesday, 11 July 1883, inviting Gosse to visit him early on the following Sunday, has been printed among the Browning letters in Mr. Wise's collection. We are thus in a position to know that it was Browning's wish that Gosse should make the investigation and publish the material in the Box, with the sole exception of the papers relating to the suicide which Browning desired should be kept a secret. What exactly happened on that Sunday morning, 15 July 1883, it is difficult to make out owing to Gosse's contradictory accounts. The original version of the incident, given in the preface to the 1890 edition (p. xv) and repeated in 1928 (p. xxxiii), was that Gosse obeyed Browning's summons and the Box was then handed over to him for collation and transcription of the manuscripts. The other version, seemingly coloured by that element of imagination which takes the place of a fading memory of distant objects, is that 'without any preamble' Browning presented himself at Gosse's house 'on the 15th of July, 1883, with the box of Beddoes' MSS, gave me the key and told me to examine the contents. I begged him to stay with me while I did so, but he refused; he seemed to have an unaccountable horror of what would be discovered. However, a few hours later he overcame this scruple, and we examined the papers at leisure. He directed me to make public their contents.' (Gosse 1928, p. ix.) It is of course possible that Browning became impatient and himself went to Gosse instead of waiting for him—they were neighbours in Warwick Crescent—but that he did not do so 'without any preamble' is proved by the letter of 11 July. 'The unaccountable horror of what would be discovered' is disposed of by the same letter which proves that Browning had neither forgotten the true circumstances of Beddoes' death, communicated to him by Mrs. Kelsall in a letter of 6 February 1873 (*The Browning Box*, CXXXVII), nor the instructions with regard to this information, contained in Kelsall's last wishes and the bequest of the papers (*The Browning Box*, CXLI). A few days later Browning obtained for Gosse an interview with Mrs. Procter, who disclosed to him many facts of interest and importance. A first result of these investigations was Gosse's article on Beddoes in the *Dictionary of National Biography*, where, however, the full facts were not yet disclosed. Gosse's edition was delayed till after Browning's death.

The spell once broken, the Box could be delivered to other enthusiasts for inspection. The late James Dykes Campbell was so privileged. On 8 August 1886 Robert Browning answered his inquiries concerning Beddoes: 'at the end of September . . . you shall have the box and its contents at your own house, and examine the latter to heart's content' (*Letters of Robert Browning Collected by T. J. Wise*, p. 253). Dykes Campbell did not miss his chance. With unsparing labour he transcribed everything of importance that had been left unpublished by Kelsall: poems, fragments, letters, down to single lines that had been omitted, and all the important biographical and other material in the Browning box. Kelsall's emendations were all noted by him, and Beddoes' peculiarities of spelling and punctuation. He noted all the variant readings and described the manuscripts down to the paper, post-marks, and seal of all the letters now lost perhaps for ever. He produced copies *quasi facsimile* of all the drafts and composition copies of the poems, writing out the first version, crossing over what Beddoes had erased, substituting the afterthoughts, marking the places for the insertion of later additions; in short, everything that remained of what Beddoes had ever written or deleted was copied and deleted over again by Dykes Campbell going through the whole process of creation and revision as it had once happened in the poet's mind. In this manner he provided us with an opportunity, equalled

only by Mr. Geoffrey Keynes's edition of the *Writings of William Blake* (Nonesuch Press, 1925), of studying a poet at work, the growth and sifting of the material, and the gradual building up of the work of art round the nucleus of the first impulse. The disappearance of Beddoes' own manuscripts has made these transcripts the most important source for an edition of his writings. Not only does it contain a large number of pieces not to be found elsewhere, including the unabridged and variorum text of **Death's Jest Book,** but it corrects also the edition of Kelsall, on which the transcripts are based. It is thus the most authoritative text in existence, and invaluable to the editor of Beddoes. Following the indications of Dykes Campbell I have removed what can be proved to have been emendations by Kelsall, and restored the spelling and punctuation. As no one is infallible, and Dykes Campbell was pressed for time, it has naturally been necessary to check his text as far as possible by a careful collation with all other texts extant, and Kelsall's transcript for the printer has been of great importance. Where no other text exists an appeal to common sense has been sufficient to remove the blunders of the transcriber. Such mere slips of the pen are of course not noted in the critical apparatus. In some instances where it is impossible to check the actual text of Dykes Campbell, the remarks of Kelsall and Browning on the unpublished parts of Beddoes' work serve to prove that the contents were the same; and if Dykes Campbell's integrity were not beyond question, it would still be possible to prove that the new passages he gives us were actually written by Beddoes and not invented by a later pen.

It is a matter for profound regret that Dykes Campbell, who did all the spadework preparatory to a complete edition, should not have been permitted to edit the poet he so devoutly admired. But it was Browning's wish that Edmund Gosse should edit the Works of Beddoes, and Dykes Campbell's scribal activities remained obscure for wellnigh fifty years. Browning more than once expressed his desire to see **Death's Jest Book** printed as it had been written by its author unabridged (*The Browning Box*, letter CXI; and *Letters of Robert Browning Collected by T. J. Wise*, p. 191), but he seems to have failed to make this clear to Gosse, whose edition of the *Poetical Works* appeared in 1890, after Browning's death, As far as **Death's Jest Book** is concerned, it was no more than a reprint of Kelsall's text, although a line was added or restored here and there. In editing the poems and fragments Gosse followed the same principle, and his edition did not substantially alter the text of what Kelsall had already printed. To this, however, he added ten poems and a dramatic scene, never before printed, which were nearly all among Beddoes' later works and among his best. For this important contribution every lover of Beddoes must be deeply grateful. Yet the publication of the *Letters* four years later was even more important. This was the first time that a great number of them were printed at all, and that the rest were published unabridged, the additions to Kelsall's discreetly selective edition being of the greatest interest. Gosse's Memoir of the poet, also, which appeared prefixed to the poems in 1890, is a source of information not to be overlooked. For material he drew not only on the papers in the Browning box, which are happily still accessible in the transcripts of Dykes Campbell, but also on the oral communications of Mrs. Procter. As the facts so communicated are important as well as sensational, it may be useful to know from the witness of Procter's nephew, whose admiration for Beddoes knew no bounds, that Mrs. Procter 'cordially detested' Beddoes (letter from Bryan Charles Waller to Mrs. Kelsall, 2 Dec. 1894; manuscript in the possession of Miss Kelsall). While most of the facts which Gosse reported on her authority are possible to verify, they may have been involuntarily coloured by a deep-rooted antipathy in the recorder's mind. For these reasons Gosse's Memoir is inaccurate in detail and does not possess the biographical value that Kelsall's account still possesses. Yet its inclusion in *Critical Kit-Kats,* 1896, has done much to make Beddoes known to a wider circle than that of Walter Savage Landor, John Forster, Tennyson, and Browning.

A most important date in the history of Beddoes' texts is the edition of Ramsay Colles for 'The Muses' Library' series in 1907, which made a model text accessible to a large public. The editor did not have access to the manuscripts, but what could be done by a conscientious collation of the printed works was assuredly not left undone by this accurate scholar. Although his introduction, like all subsequent works, repeats the biographical distortions of the 1890 edition, it contains both good and appreciative criticism. Lytton Strachey's essay on 'The Last Elizabethan' appeared the same year in the *New Quarterly,* and has done much to make Beddoes known and admired. Nor should the late George Saintsbury be forgotten, who wrote about Beddoes in the *Cambridge History of English Literature,* 1896; and the late C. H. Herford's account in *The Age of Wordsworth,* 1911. But Professor Oliver Elton has seen more deeply and written with more understanding than any other critic of Beddoes.

Kelsall apart, no one has done more to spread the knowledge of Beddoes to an ever widening circle than the late Sir Edmund Gosse, and criticism may seem akin to ingratitude, but as it turned out his omission to publish in 1890 all that the Box contained was unfortunate. He failed to account for the evil fortune that has pursued Beddoes even after his death, and the manuscripts that he returned to Asolo in 1890 were nowhere to be found when 'Pen' Browning died on 8 July 1912. Their fate is a mystery. The hills above Treviso have kept their secret. It is an ironic epilogue to Browning's enthusiastic letters to Kelsall and his repeated assurances to provide for the safety of the manuscripts. The intention to bequeath them to Balliol, however (*Letters of Robert Browning Collected by T. J. Wise,* p. 191), did not materialize. It seems likely that the manuscripts still existed in 1890, when Gosse stated that they were then lent to him again by Robert Barrett Browning 'that I might revise my collation' (p. xv), and that a variorum edition was then possible (p. xii) which would certainly not have been possible without the manuscripts. In 1894 Gosse remarked somewhat oddly that Pen Brown-

ing had confirmed his father's wish 'that I should publish these papers, the originals of the remainder of which are now in his possession'. It is futile to speculate about what is hidden from our certain knowledge, but when a second edition of the *Works* was called for in 1928, all that the late Sir Edmund was able to add was one early letter (now in the collection of Mr. Wise) and three short extracts from the boyish tale of mystery and horror, *Scaroni.* The few reliques of Beddoes that are still extant are those which never came near the fatal Box and were thus saved from destruction. Most of these have been collected by Mr. C. H. Wilkinson, who has continued the work of preservation, begun more than a hundred years ago by the noble Kelsall.

Some of Beddoes' songs and dirges have found their way into most anthologies, and in recent years the interest in the poet has been increasing notably. In 1928 appeared not only the edition prepared before his death by Sir Edmund Gosse, but also Mr. Royall Snow's *Thomas Lovell Beddoes, Eccentric and Poet,* giving the American view of an English poet. German scholars, who had previously neglected the opportunity of elucidating his career in their country, have been doing valuable research, manifest in the *Würzburger Chronik* and in Dr. C. A. Weber's important contribution to the biography of Beddoes in *Literarisches Bristol.* The year 1930 brought essays on the subject both of the poet and of his father, the celebrated Dr. Beddoes, from the pens of Mr. John Sparrow and Mr. F. L. Lucas. The latter produced his selection of Beddoes' works in the 'Poets in Brief' series in 1932, and has reprinted his contributions on the subject in his *Studies French and English,* 1934. Reviewers apart, the Rev. Henry Card was the first to quote Beddoes in 1822; Mrs. Shelley followed suit in 1826; Swiss historians quoted him in 1840, 1845, and 1867; in 1864 Amelia Blandford Edwards introduced several quotations from *Death's Jest Book* into *Barbara's History;* and in 1932 Miss Dorothy Sayers chose the mottoes to every chapter of one of her popular detective stories from the poetry of Beddoes. In the last-mentioned year a competition was held under the auspices of *The Spectator* for a satisfactory completion of two of Beddoes' fragments (19 March 1932). We come across his name ever more frequently inbooks like Mr. V. F. Calverton's *Bankruptcy of Marriage,* and in articles in the *Times Literary Supplement* and the *Sunday Times* by Mr. Desmond MacCarthy and Mr. Edmund Blunden. There can be no doubt about the modern character of Beddoes' verse being conducive to a more intimate understanding of his genius and to the increased interest in his works culminating during the current year in Mr. W. Nugent Monck's production of *The Second Brother* at the Maddermarket, Norwich. In response to this growing demand the present editor has attempted to bring together as much of the contemporary evidence as has proved practicable, in *The Browning Box;*[1] and to assemble the biographical details and describe the career and development of the artist in *Thomas Lovell Beddoes;—the making of a poet.*[2] Professor Elton has already given Beddoes his permanent place as the heir of Shelley's lyrical genius, and M. Legouis in his *Short History of English Literature,* 1934, has pronounced him the most original of the poets who may be grouped with Shelley and Keats. Yet, though aesthetic appreciation has not been lacking, the establishment of the text has not been completed, and the present edition is an attempt to make up for that omission, as far as present circumstances permit. The Notes are designed to give such information as a reader of the Poems and Prose-works might desire.

Notes

1. Published simultaneously by the Oxford University Press.

2. To be published before the end of November by Basil Blackwell.

Horace Gregory (essay date 1935)

SOURCE: "The Survival of Thomas Lovell Beddoes," in *Spirit of Time and Place: Collected Essays of Horace Gregory,* W.W. Norton, 1957, pp. 42-51.

[*In the following essay, originally published in 1935, Gregory determines the influence of the Gothic imagination on Beddoes's work.*]

If the temptation exists to place Beddoes in biographical proximity to Byron, an even greater temptation to view him as a belated Elizabethan has not been resisted. If we could be content with a second glance at Beddoes's works in the huge, eight-hundred-page volume, so devotedly, almost devoutly edited by Dr. H. W. Donner,[1] we would agree with the reiterated opinions of Lytton Strachey, which were dutifully followed by F. L. Lucas, and George Saintsbury. All opinions chimed to the belated Elizabethan character of Beddoes's poetry—nor was the epithet entirely without foundation. Beddoes's literary indebtedness to Marlowe, Marston, Webster, and Tourneur was of no inconsiderable weight; he read them with the fascination and joy that Keats described at his discovering Chapman's *Homer.* In reading for ourselves the shadowed pages and the luminous passages of Beddoes's Gothic mystery play, *Death's Jest Book,* we are in little danger of forgetting the impress that Marlowe and Webster had left upon them— that is all too obvious, and to deny it would be as futile as denying Wordsworth's debt to Milton. Granting all this, the best of Beddoes's poetry merits a third reading, and in a final consideration a balance may be struck between a Victorian neglect of Beddoes's virtues and the excitement of their rediscovery in the twentieth century.

The story of Beddoes's extraordinary, brief, ineffectual, and obscure career has been told at length in H. W. Donner's biography.[2] Like many a patient, pure-minded labor of love, Donner's book has earned respect, if not reciprocal enthusiasm, and its sheets have not been imported to this side of the Atlantic. Beddoes's personality was formed by the same psychic disorder, maladjustment, and homo-

sexual pattern that shaped the behavior of Rimbaud in the nineteenth century and Hart Crane in the twentieth, yet the environment of his early youth was far more fortunate than theirs; he was the son of the prosperous and notoriously eccentric Dr. Thomas Beddoes and a nephew of the witty and famous Maria Edgeworth. At the age of nineteen and while still an undergraduate at Pembroke College, Oxford, the younger Thomas Beddoes achieved celebrity through the publication of his play in verse, **The Brides' Tragedy**—and in the second year after Keats's death in 1823, Beddoes received more spontaneous and authoritative praise than any young poet of his generation. Two years later, he had left Pembroke for the University of Göttingen, leaving England, and his "ambition to become poetically distinguished" behind him. Yet, as his friend Thomas Forbes Kelsall knew, Beddoes had already started work on the dramatic poem, **Death's Jest Book,** which was to become the true object of his ambitions and to haunt his imagination for the next twenty years. Kelsall, and another friend, James Dykes Campbell, saw how persistently the growth of **Death's Jest Book** broke through and was nourished by Beddoes's studies in medicine, and they were also in a position to know, through correspondence, the restless, guilt-haunted temper of Beddoes's intelligence, its release of energy in political oratory at Würzburg, its violence, its ardors, and the reaches of its last expression at its deathbed, "I am food for *what I am good for*—worms."

But even death itself and probable suicide in 1849 (which Donner establishes as a near certainty) did not check the pursuit of Nemesis which shadowed Beddoes's fame. Beddoes's misplaced confidence in the critical advice of Bryan Waller Procter ("Barry Cornwall"), which had smoothly glanced across the surfaces of fragmentary pieces from Beddoes's pen with an impartial lack of understanding, repeated its cycle in 1883 when Robert Browning, who had promised Kelsall that he would edit and publish Beddoes's manuscripts, called in the assistance of Sir Edmund Gosse. Both Sir Edmund and Browning were shocked at what they found within the box that Kelsall left them, and for the moment the incident served only to permit Dykes Campbell to make a transcript of everything the box contained.[3] We shall never be quite clear as to exactly what horrified the sensibilities of Gosse, but we do know that the box and its contents were handed over to the care of Browning's son, and were, thereafter, irrevocably lost. Gosse, with his adroit and habitual negligence, issued an edition of Beddoes's poetry in 1890, and in 1928 another edition appeared, prepared by Gosse and published in a manner that is usually reserved—including an evasive introduction and a garish typeface—for pornography. Aside from a few scraps of actual manuscript, and a pamphlet of verse in German, what we read today in Donner's excellent edition of *The Works of Thomas Lovell Beddoes* are the copies made of Beddoes's poems in Dykes Campbell's hand.

Because of the ill-luck which attended the posthumous publication of Beddoes's poetry, it would seem that we approach it with the utmost difficulty—and so we do. Sir Arthur Quiller-Couch's reprinting of a mutilated version of Beddoes's "Dream-Pedlary" in *The Oxford Book of English Verse* increased rather than diminished the general air of confusion which has so persuasively followed mention of Beddoes's name, and the question arises as to where and how the confusion originated. Were Procter, Browning, Gosse, and Sir Arthur wholly responsible for the obscurity of Beddoes's fame? It must be confessed that they materially aided its long career of darkness, but its true source lies in the uneasy relationship which existed between Beddoes and his work; self-knowledge was of slow and fatal growth within him, and when it came, it came too late. There was more of self-realization than of true humility or of pathos in Beddoes's last note to Revell Phillips: "I ought to have been among other things a good poet." It is not enough to say with Donner that Beddoes lacked self-confidence; the psychic split which marred his character and brought his private life within the area that we reserve for Rimbaud and Hart Crane, ran deeper than any loss of confidence in what he wrote. The attitude that he adopted toward his poetry swung between and often touched the two extremes of desiring an absolute perfection in its expression and the impulse to destroy it utterly, yet the ambition to write voluminously, to be heard, to speak aloud remained. His miscalculation in measuring the quality of Procter's literary friendship could almost be described as an act of literary suicide; it was his sin against the mark of his own genius, which had left its impress upon every brilliant passage that comes to light in the tortured progress of writing **Death's Jest Book.**

Beyond the sources of literary stimulation which Beddoes received from a reading of the lesser Elizabethan dramatists, was his greater effort to clothe and vitalize the spirit and temper of the Gothic myth, the genius that had created the gargoyles on the towers of Notre Dame, the giantchild Gargantua, the merry voyages of Pantagruel, the fiery journey of Mad Meg across Flanders, the Dance of Death itself (which actually enters a scene of **Death's Jest Book**), the very genius that had found its revival in Matthias Claudius's brief and exquisite lyric, *Der Tod und das Mädchen.* Beddoes's prose version of death and the maiden appears in semiclassical disguise in "The Tale of the Lover to his Mistress":

> After the fall of Jupiter came Love one night to Psyche: it was dark in her cottage and she began to strike a light. "Have done," said he, in a low whispering tone—in which the hinge of some dreadful dark truth out of another world seemed to turn. "Youth, power, and heaven have passed away from the gods: the curse of age has changed their shapes:—then seek not to look on me, Psyche; but if thou art faithful, kiss me, and we will then go into the darkness for ever."—"How art thou changed?" asked she; "methinks you do but try me, jestingly, for thou canst only have grown more beautiful. That thou art more powerful I hear, for the night air is full of rushing arrows, and many are struck and sigh. Hast thou lost thy wings that were so glorious?"—"Aye, but I am swifter than of old."—"Thy youth?"—"Aye, but I am stronger: all must fall before

me."—"Thy charms and wiles?"—"Aye, but he whom I have once stricken, is mine for ever and ever."—"Why should I not see thee then? Art thou Love no more?"—"Aye, but not fleeting, earthly; eternal, heavenly Love."—Just then the moon rose, and Psyche saw beside her a gaunt anatomy, through which the blue o' th' sky shone and the stars twinkled, gold promises beaming through Death, armed with arrows, bearing an hour-glass. He stepped with her to the seaside, and they sank where Venus rose.

The attraction that the Gothic imagination held for Beddoes may be sought for well outside the boundaries of his great admiration for Webster, Marston, and Marlowe, and the forces that drew him toward it were as strong as the impulse which Coleridge felt in the writing of "The Rime of the Ancient Mariner":

> Are those her *ribs* through which the Sun
> Did peer, as through a grate?
> And is that Woman all her crew?
> Is that a Death? and are there two?
> Is death that woman's mate?
>
> *Her* lips were red, *her* looks were free,
> Her locks were yellow as gold:
> Her skin was as white as leprosy,
> The Nightmare Life-in-Death was she,
> Who thicks man's blood with cold.

The genius toward which Beddoes moved was of an older heritage and of the same, yet deeper root than any reading of the Elizabethan dramatists would disclose; the power of attraction had its true origins behind the façades of Renaissance literature at their noontide; Beddoes's effort to recreate a truly Gothic metaphysic from the slowly increasing manuscript of **Death's Jest Book** was, if anything, kept alive and nurtured by his residence on central European soil, and the impulse which lay behind the creation of his incompleted masterpiece was as clear a symptom of his day as Coleridge's "Ancient Mariner" or Sir Walter Scott's translation of Goethe's remarkable "Erlkönig." Truly enough **Death's Jest Book** restrung and hinged together the common properties of Renaissance poetic drama, and among them the network of double plots and motives inspired by revenge, but what is important for us to rediscover is Beddoes's persistent stress upon those elements in Webster and in Marlowe in which the sources ran backward to the Middle Ages; and there it was that Beddoes had made his choice. Like Poe, Beddoes was a late arrival on the Romantic scene, and like the American poet, his lyricism expressed a last if fragmentary refinement of a first phase in Romantic emotion that had traced its conscious origins to the *Lyrical Ballads* of 1798. His fantastically late resurrection has blurred, almost beyond recognition, his true position within the literature of his day. No echoes of his voice were heard within it beyond the strains of that eminently precocious venture, **The Brides' Tragedy**; and Procter's friendly indifference had closed the door to those in England who might have heard him with a reawakened ear.

Since I have viewed at length the unfortunate aspects of Beddoes's career and its subsequent miscarriages of fame, one should modify that unequitable balance by saying that Donner's edition of *Works* appeared at a particularly happy moment for their twentieth-century revival. If Beddoes's relationship to his creative gifts and their fulfillment was, to put it mildly, sporadic and uncertain, their radical nature was remarkably consistent. In that respect alone, his life, his work, his political convictions, and the quality of his imagination resemble what we have read in the poems, the letters and notebooks of Gerard Manley Hopkins. Because of the singular likeness in radical temper, it can be said with certain obvious reservations that the discovery of Hopkins's poems immediately following the First World War prepared the critics for a favorable reception of Donner's edition of Beddoes's *Works*. In the mid-1930s and on both sides of the Atlantic, writers of conservative beliefs as well as left, sought out their origins of a radical heritage, and in this sense the revival of Beddoes's name carried with it associations of particular significance; and Beddoes's participation in revolutionary activity was of a nature that paralleled the activity of young British writers in the recent Spanish Civil War.

Beddoes's career in Germany and Switzerland had been punctuated by the writing of political satires, and the most successful of these were written in his adopted German, a language which he spoke with rapidly increasing facility. They were done as though the shift in language were a release from the demands of seeking the perfected line, the absolute phrase, the final word. Quite as **The Brides' Tragedy** had achieved distinction in the revival of Elizabethan dramatic verse, Beddoes's brilliantly turned political satires served a lively purpose in expressing the radical spirit of his time; among these, there are speeches and verses which were in effect a triple-edged attack on the forces that sanctioned the Holy Alliance, the Church itself, and reactionary Germany poetry. Quickened by Beddoes's wit and energy the German language was transformed into parody of itself, and what Beddoes had learned from reading Rabelais came to light in his pamphlet which contained verses *On the Enemies of David Friedrich Strauss,* his *Antistraussianischer Gruss.* To find their equal one must turn to John Skelton's satire *Why Come Ye Not to Court* or to certain passages of James Joyce's *Finnegans Wake*; and it is also of historical interest to remember that David Strauss and the incident which inspired the verses left an impression on the early education of Karl Marx. The pamphlet found an appreciative audience among Swiss and German revolutionaries, and its distribution warned educational authorities in central Europe of a certain medical student, Herr Beddoes, a little Englishman, who on one occasion at least had roused fellow students to revolt by reciting a mock tribute to the dying Wellington, "Prussia's one Field Marshal."

How deeply these activities affected the revised versions of **Death's Jest Book,** we shall never know, but in the play of plot and counter-plot of Beddoes's Gothic melodrama, the forces of established power, of revolution and of counterrevolution run their bloody courses, motivated by revenge. The two Fools in the play (and originally it was subtitled, *The Fool's Tragedy*) seem to speak in Beddoes's voice and certainly they recite a number of his finest lyrics, but what of Mario, a character who seeks a leader and who speaks with memorable eloquence?

> A Roman am I;
> A Roman in unroman times: I've slept
> At midnight in our Capitolian ruins,
> And breathed the ghost of our great ancient world,
> Which there doth walk: and among glorious visions,
> That the unquiet tomb sent forth to me,
> Learned I the love of Freedom. Scipio saw I
> Washing the stains of Carthage from his sword,
> And his freed poet, playing on his lyre
> A melody men's souls replied unto:
> Oak-bound and laurelled heads, each man a country;
> And in the midst, like a sun o'er the sea
> (Each helm in the crowd gilt by a ray from him),
> Bald Julius sitting lonely in his car,
> Within the circle of whose laurel wreath
> All spirits of the earth and sea were spell-bound.
> Down with him to the grave! Down with the god!
> Stab, Cassius; Brutus, through him; through him, all!
> Dead.—As he fell there was a tearing sigh:
> Earth stood on him; her roots were in his heart;
> They fell together. Caesar and his world
> Lie in the Capitol; and Jove lies there,
> With all the gods of Rome and of Olympus; . . .

Despite the weight of inversions in Mario's speech, despite the rhetorical extravagance of "Down with him to the grave! Down with the god!" which show the marks of Schiller's influence as well as the intonations of a distinctly unmodulated school of German acting, the speech reveals a clear and vivid strength of movement that distinguishes the best of Beddoes's poetry from the work of his better known contemporaries. The historical imagination which finds its voice within the speech displays an insight of remarkable force and energy, and is of that quality which we associate with the utterance of prophetic truth.

Perhaps **Death's Jest Book** by the very weight of its intentions was foredoomed to remain imperfect and unfinished; perhaps there is prophetic significance in the shift of its subtitle from *The Fool's Tragedy* to *The Day Will Come,* that is, the day of its completion placed forever in the future. Quite as D. H. Lawrence was never to complete the larger plan of "The Rainbow," or as Keats's "Hyperion" remains a fragment, or as Hart Crane's "The Bridge" could not attain the elaborated structure of its early inspiration, so **Death's Jest Book** falls short of its original design. The desire to create a work of all-embracing stature and dimensions is one of the deepest and most frequently noted pitfalls of the Romantic imagination; surely its shadows haunted Coleridge's "Kubla Khan" and his ode "Dejection," and from then onward the path went downward into the darkness of being unable to write poetry at all. The last days of Beddoes's life were spent in that same darkness, yet before his work can be dismissed as one who "had made failure his vocation," some attention must be given to two short poems, which are, to my knowledge, among the best examples of lyric verse written in Beddoes's generation.

Since the complete version of "Dream-Pedlary" still lacks the public it deserves, and since the quality of its imagination merits its rediscovery in all discussions of nineteenth-century poetry, I need not apologize for including an entire quotation of it here:

I

If there were dreams to sell,
    What would you buy?
Some cost a passing bell;
    Some a light sigh,
That shakes from Life's fresh crown
Only a roseleaf down.
If there were dreams to sell,
Merry and sad to tell,
And the crier rung the bell,
    What would you buy?

II

A cottage lone and still,
    With bowers nigh,
Shadowy, my woes to still,
    Until I die.
Such pearl from Life's fresh crown
Fain would I shake me down.
Were dreams to have at will,
This would best heal my ill,
This would I buy.

III

But there were dreams to sell,
    Ill didst thou buy;
Life is a dream, they tell,
    Waking, to die.
Dreaming a dream to prize,
Is wishing ghosts to rise;
    And, if I had the spell
    To call the buried, well,
Which one would I?

IV

If there are ghosts to raise,
    What shall I call,
Out of hell's murky haze,
    Heaven's blue hall?
Raise my loved longlost boy
To lead me to his joy.
There are no ghosts to raise;
Out of death lead no ways;
Vain is the call.

V

Know'st thou not ghosts to sue?
    No love thou hast.
Else lie, as I will do,
    And breathe thy last.
So out of Life's fresh crown
Fall like a roseleaf down.
    Thus are the ghosts to woo;

Thus are all dreams made true,
Ever to last!

Not even the sensitively gifted Tennyson of "The Lady of Shalott" or of the lyrical interludes in *Maud* quite equal the play of sound and echo, of sight and recall of image that weave and finally complete the garland so gracefully thrown across death's shoulders in "Dream-Pedlary." One would probably have a better chance of finding an equal among Hölderlin's lyrical remains, rather than in any selection of English poetry, but even there, only the like quality of spirit may be sought and not the melodic variations of Beddoes's lines. In contemporary literature, the nearest approach to Beddoes's lyric imagery may be found in the following lines from Walter de la Mare; the spirit has thinned and grown remote, but its shadow lingers:

Not toward Death, who, stranger, fairer,
Than any siren turns his head—
Than sea-couched siren, arched with rainbows,
Where knell the waves of her ocean bed.
Alas, that beauty hangs her flowers
For lure of his demoniac powers:
Alas, that from these eyes should dart
Such piercing summons to thy heart;
That mine in frenzy of longing beats,
Still lusting for these gross deceits.
    Not that way!

As one reads through the prose and verse fragments of *The Ivory Gate,* supposedly written by Beddoes between the years 1833 to 1838, the likeness of his verse and its imagery turns in the direction of his distant, and almost certainly unknown to him, American contemporary, Edgar Allan Poe; unfinished manuscripts bearing the title *The City of the Sea* appear, and the best (and apparently completed) union of prose and verse among the scattered papers is *Thanatos to Kenelm*:

"I have no feeling for the monuments of human labour," she would say, "the wood and the desert are more peopled with my household gods than the city or the cultivated country. Even with the living animals and the prevailing vegetation of the forest in this hemisphere, I have little sympathy. I know not the meaning of a daisy, nor what nature has symbolized by the light bird and the butterfly. But the sight of a palm with its lofty stem and tuft of long grassy leaves, high in the blue air, or even such a branch as this (breaking off a large fern leaf) awake in me a feeling, a sort of nostalgy and longing for ages long past. When my ancient sire used to sit with me under the old dragon tree of Dracaena, I was as happy as the ephemeral fly balanced on his wing in the sun, whose setting will be his death-warrant. But why do I speak to you so? You cannot understand me."—And then she would sing whisperingly to herself:

The mighty thoughts of an old world
Fan, like a dragon's wing unfurled,
    The surface of my yearnings deep;
And solemn shadows then awake,
Like the fish-lizard in the lake,
    Troubling a planet's morning sleep.

My waking is a Titan's dream,
Where a strange sun, long set, doth beam
    Through Montezuma's cypress bough:
Through the fern wilderness forlorn
Glisten the giant hart's great horn
    And serpents vast with helmed brow.

The measureless from caverns rise
With steps of earthquake, thunderous cries,
    And graze upon the lofty wood;
The palmy grove, through which doth gleam
Such antediluvian ocean's stream,
    Haunts shadowy my domestic mood.

It is highly probable that the speech and its song were originally spoken by Sibylla, one of the heroines of *Death's Jest Book,* that the song appeared in an early draft of the play's first act, and was later discarded from the revised versions. Like many passages within the play, the speech and the song circumscribe a completed unit of emotion and the forms which embody it, and as such it is one of the purest expressions of the Romantic genius in nineteenth-century literature. The first line of the song's last stanza recalls, of course, Coleridge's famous "caverns measureless to man," but on reading the entire passage, the impulse is to remark how Poesque it is, how gently it enters and then deeply penetrates the world that lives behind the conscious mind and eye; there it discloses as the song is sung the center of the world so persistently sought by the Romantic imagination, the heart of reality within the dream.

Beddoes's power to reawaken the images of Gothic heritage has its own force today; and in Poe's words, the death that looks gigantically down, stares with peculiar intensity upon the map of twentieth-century Europe. Now covered with the pall of rearmored warfare, one may perceive in the center of that map, the diminished figure of Beddoes's great Fool, Mandrake, and if one listens one may hear a few lines from a stanza of his song; the scene is lit only by flares dropped from the sky; death's triumph lingers there through broken streets and hallways, and human terror resumes its mask of Gothic irony:

Folly hath now turned out of door
Mankind and Fate, who were before
    Jove's Harlequin and Clown.
The world's no stage, no tavern more,
    Its sign, the Fool's ta'en down.

Notes

1. *The Works of Thomas Lovell Beddoes,* edited with an introduction by H. W. Donner. London: Oxford University Press, 1935.

2. *Thomas Lovell Beddoes: The Making of a Poet,* by H. W. Donner. Oxford: Basil Blackwell, 1935.

3. They probably found evidence of Beddoes's homosexuality.

Louis O. Coxe (essay date 1953)

SOURCE: "Beddoes: The Mask of Parody," in *Hudson Review,* Vol. 6, No. 2, Summer, 1953, pp. 252-65.

[*In the following essay, Coxe praises the singularity and fearlessness of* Death's Jest Book.]

The poetry of Thomas Lovell Beddoes should find in our time a place denied it in its own if only because we are today interested in deviation for its own sake. Beddoes' life, curious and expatriate, a life that shows him as radical, scientist, psychiatric case and necrophile, alone would attract our age. The poetry, however, is the subject here, and it is a poetry of a sort that seems to me to offer a way out for the modern writer while it exists in its own world as a strange, viable creation.

Beddoes wished to be a dramatist. His major work, *Death's Jest Book,* shows at once the limitations, potentialities and achieved merits of his dramatic verse. Its texture derives from morality and symbol, from poetic language, and these are the vehicles of the drama as exciting theater. A packed, metaphorical idiom, bristling with allusion and learning, a boisterous humor that moves deliberately into the grotesque, a sense of terror before the omnipresence of death: such is the element of the extraordinary play in the composition of which Beddoes spent the most productive years of his life.

"To have my way, in spite of your tongue and reason's teeth, tastes better than Hungary wine; and my heart beats in a honey-pot now I reject you and all sober sense." So speaks Mandrake, the disciple of Paracelsus, but it might well be Beddoes himself. Yet it was not in a "dérèglement de tous les sens" that he sought a freedom, but in an elusive grand synthesis in search of which he raided the culture, artistic and scientific, of the west. His poetry clearly reflects this search. From Hebrew lore to contemporary anatomy, from Pythagoras to Shelley, he roves back and forth through history, and the poetry is dense with references, literary and scientific, which reinforce and accentuate a genuine originality. *Death's Jest Book* may at times become pastiche on the one hand and chaos on the other. Brought up on a diet of the Elizabethan and Jacobean playwrights, Beddoes, like all his contemporaries who tried "dramaturgy", never got free of the influence. Yet in this instance it is a happy fault, for no other of the romantic playwrights caught the idiom they echoed as fully as he did, and none had the sense of drama in the very feel of the verse to anything like the extent notable in the best parts of *Death's Jest Book.*

The play's plot is, "God save us, a thing of naught", or rather, of a great deal too much, most of its confused. The satanic jester, Isbrand, usurps Melveric's dukedom—partly in vengeance for Melveric's murder of Isbrand's father and his brother Wolfram. As the plot to seize the duchy of Grussau culminates, Isbrand is betrayed and killed, Melveric drawn living into the grave, various other characters are variously slain. There is a sub-plot providing love interest, but plot is not the issue here.

To call such a congeries of implausibilities absurd is only proper; the action is eccentric; one cannot find a tragic hero or a single conflict. Beddoes alters his scheme and his intent more than once; the sub-plotting is at best irrelevant and at worst confusing as well as dull. The dramatic and poetic excitement resides in the by-play, and that for the most part concerns Isbrand, the demonic fool of Death, in whose actions and speeches we can find the essence of Beddoes' poetic gift and an adumbration at least of a form of tragedy.

Here excess is the key. Excess, calculated or at times merely chaotic, crowds into action, structure and metaphor. it is in this respect above all that Beddoes is a poet worthy of our attention, for he did not fear a risk, in particular that most dangerous of all risks: being caught out in a generalization or a cliché. And perhaps because he was remote from his contemporaries, because he was unafraid of traditional, stock situations, his best dramatic verse is exciting, in language, metaphor and movement. He had grasped what too few dramatists today believe, that the vehicle of a play is not character but language, a particular language that is theatrical in that it conveys the immediate action while it points ahead to impending tragedy. Consider this passage, in which Isbrand converses with one of his henchmen over the body of the treacherously slain Wolfram.

> ISBRAND: . . . This was one who would be constant in friendship and the pole wanders: one who would be immortal, and the light that shines upon his pale forehead now, through yonder gewgaw window, undulated from its star hundreds of years ago. that is constancy, that is life. O moral nature!
>
> SIEGFRIED: 'Tis well that you are reconciled to his lot and your own.
>
> ISBRAND: Reconciled! A word out of a love tale, that's not in my language. No, no. I am patient and still and laborious, a good contented man; peaceable as an ass chewing a thistle; and my thistle is revenge. I do but whisper it now: but hereafter I will thunder the word, and I shall shoot up gigantic out of this pismire shape, and hurl the bolt of that revenge.

The modern obsession with personality concerns Beddoes little. Somehow he knew that character as such is one thing in life and quite another in art, in the drama. In either case seeing a man as a mere agglomeration of motives or qualities is little help and no explanation. Since in a play what interests the spectator is the thing done; the way it is done, and its effect on people or on further action, the establishing of character is merely one way of making an action seem credible or interesting. In the romantic period, one that was curious about emotion, morality and ideas, "character" of an intricate sort had little function in drama, for there was more than enough character available in actual life. In our day, when symbol

and thing symbolized have split apart, "personality" has triumphed, with psychiatric quirks the stuff of drama and life alike. Beddoes, indifferent to this concern, instinctively returned to something like a doctrine of humors, of ruling passions, since his mind increasingly reached out for absolutes: the meaning of death, the vanity of human wishes, the nature of human freedom. What better convention, what more fascinating ritual, could he have chosen than the old revenge tragedy, with all its layers of association, its formal appeal to the spectators' powers of suspending disbelief, its open invitation to rhetoric and excess? We must not look to *Death's Jest Book* for originality of motive or plot; if there is a particular view of the action it would appear to be a double one. We are to see the events as deviations from a norm of moral behaviour and consequently to condemn them, but we are not to empathize automatically. One part of the mind must be reserved to participate in the poetic and dramatic processes, to judge of what allows one to be moved, and simultaneously to say: "That was a fine touch."

What is new about his? It is so old that a revival of the attitude in the theater today would create an effect of extreme novelty that no experiment with gadgetry could rival. Beddoes found in the Jacobean drama certain habits of mind that corresponded to his own:

> ISBRAND: . . . Isbrand, thou tragic fool,
> Cheer up. Art thou alone? Why so should be
> Creators and destroyers. I'll go brood,
> And strain my burning and distracted soul
> Against the naked spirit of the world
> Till some portent's begotten.

Beddoes, unlike his Isbrand, knows that man is less than angel, and indeed at the end of the play Isbrand has well earned his cap and bells. "For now indeed Death makes a fool of me," he says as he dies. And this was the same Isbrand who had earlier defied the universe:

> I have a bit of FIAT in my soul,
> And can myself create my little world.
> Had I been born a four-legged child, methinks
> I might have found the steps from dog to man,
> And crept into his nature. Are there not
> Those that fall down out of humanity,
> Into the story where the four-legged dwell?

The lesson we can learn from Beddoes may go something like this: it is all a risk, this writing poetry and plays. Yet if art is going to be different enough from life to be worth bothering about, then make that difference exciting, excessive, bold. Poetry must reassemble the bones of the language and recreate "the bloody, soul-possessèd weed called man", quickened out of sheer art, sheer creation.

But of course Beddoes is no playable dramatist. How stage the impossible slaughters, poisonings, tilts and apparitions? Perhaps there is no physical bar, but other more serious obstacles would confront the director. Beddoes had no stage craft, knew nothing at all about the theatre, his head full of Schiller and Goethe's *Goetz von Berlichingen*, of ideas about the stage that would make a modern producer shudder. And with reason. However promising the work of the inexperienced playwright may prove, it is only that. Beddoes had no chance to use a stage or to see his work performed; how could he have learned? Yet despite this, he had an attribute that is equally indispensable: he knew that language can be dramatic of itself and was able to make it so. No small measure of his success with dramatic language comes from his preoccupation with extremes, of subject and of expression. At times this becomes almost surrealist (if I understand the term), the driving to an extreme of fancy a conceit or an insight:

> ISBRAND: . . . One has said, that time
> Is a great river running to eternity.
> Methinks 'tis all one water, and the fragments,
> That crumble off our ever dwindling life,
> Dropping into't, first make the twelve-houred circle,
>   And that spreads outward to the great round Ever.
>
> THORWALD: You're fanciful.
>
> ISBRAND: A very ballad-maker . . .

There is often sarcasm or perhaps contempt in Isbrand's tone; he shares with the diabolic figures of much romantic verse a mocking attitude; like Goethe's Mephistopheles he has the "denying spirit", though it is certainly not as objectively expressed. Yet he also shares some of the qualities of the Shakespearean fool, since his wisdom continually clashes with the nonsense of Everyman. The vengeance Isbrand seeks, the power he would usurp, becomes under Beddoes' hand generalized, as though the Duke and his Grussau are mere surrogates for a contempt Isbrand (and Beddoes) feels for humanity: "As I live I grow ashamed of the duality of my legs, for they and the apparel, forked or furbelowed, upon them constitute humanity; the brain no longer; and I wish I were an honest fellow of four shins when I look into the notebook of your absurdities. I will abdicate." Isbrand is the intellectual who scorns the court, the world of mediocrity, yet maladjusted as he may be, there is no self-pity in him. "How I despise all such mere men of muscle," he says, and proceeds with his plan to seize the dukedom. If the world will not conform to his desire, he will force it, by the power of his intellect, to serve him. No irony here, save what eventuates in dramatic irony; Isbrand is deadly serious, committed to a program that entails convulsions in the state. This intellectual, this eccentric of many masks and desires, will get beyond human weakness if he die for it; and this is true of Beddoes' writing of the role. Isbrand, when in his more playful mood, resorts to the grotesque, to a species of surrealism as the lighter expression of a demonic will. He is conscious that he is at court, "and there it were a sin to call anything by its right name." Though he "abdicates", ceases formally to be a jester, yet the role of poet is ready for him, another mask that he may wear until the plot is ripe and he may put off disguises. We can often identify Beddoes with Isbrand if only because the surrealist tone of much of the poetry in **Death's Jest Book** derives from the dominant at-

titudes of Beddoes himself, from his recondite learning, his necrophilia, his passion for an all-containing synthesis. The grotesque element in the poetry is mask—the playful aspect, at times grim, behind which Beddoes hides his contempt for man as he is, his yearning for another form more suited to man's will to change and grow. Hence death is welcome, for it may mean ultimately rebirth, a new and more appropriate form. Poetry, then, should distort life and all normal views of it. That is what Isbrand does when he wears the mask of poet. It is Beddoes' mask too, and both their tragedies; to make man over is impossible, yet the unusual man must try. Tragedy comes from that trial. Poetry comes from expressing it. A poetic tragedy is an excessive showing of excess.

If Beddoes' idea of tragedy seems inadequate, too far removed from the possibility of alternatives, too personal, it is at least modern, one that should find sympathetic consideration today. Isbrand, as he is dying, understands that he "in a wicked masque would play the Devil" and that there can be ruin only for such a player. The diabolism strikes home. Isbrand further says: "But jealous Lucifer himself appeared / And bore him—whither? I shall know tomorrow." If there is to be real tragedy, a man must know in advance the risks he takes; both Beddoes and Isbrand see risks in the ways taken, but they do not know for sure the nature of the risks. They will "know tomorrow". In the faint of heart, such uncertainty leads to scepticism, to irony, to the disillusionment of the sophisticated child. In those strong enough to face the bitterness of wanhope, there is this resort: gesture, mask, and finally, parody. We can find a full expression of this in one of the play's songs, a curious piece of work that revolted Beddoes' friend "Barry Cornwall" and is of one temper with the unease conveyed to Browning, who would neither release nor reread the Beddoes manuscripts entrusted to him. This song shows us what Beddoes was after, shows us perhaps why no tragedy could ever contain it.

"What is the lobster's tune while he is boiling?" asks Isbrand, and begins his "Song". Whether one looks at the poem as a mere burlesque or as a whole genre by itself, there is still this question: how does critic or reader deal with such a work? For if we can call this irony, the word has finally lost any real meaning, and if we dismiss it as fanciful, grotesque, or Freudian we miss the point, a point we would do well to seize.

"Song by Isbrand"

> Squats on a toadstool under a tree
> A bodiless childfull of life in the gloom,
> Crying with frog voice, 'What shall I be?
> Poor unborn ghost, for my mother killed me
> Scarcely alive in her wicked womb.
> What shall I be? Shall I creep to the egg
> That's cracking asunder yonder by Nile,
>   And with eighteen toes
>   And a snuff-taking nose,
> Make an Egyptian crocodile?
> Sing, "Catch a mummy by the leg

And crunch him with an upper jaw,
Wagging tail and clenching claw;
Take a bill-full from my craw,
Neighbor raven, caw, o caw,
Grunt, my crocky, pretty maw!
   And give a paw."

'Swine, shall I be you? Thou art a dear dog;
But for a smile, and kiss, and pout,
I much prefer *your* black-lipped snout,
  Little, gruntless, fairy hog,
  Godson of the hawthorn hedge.
For, when Ringwood snuffs me out,
And 'gins my tender paunch to grapple,
Sing, "'Twixt your ancles visage wedge
  And roll up like an apple."

'Serpent Lucifer, how do you do?
Of your worms and your snakes I'd be one or two;
  For in this dear planet of wool and of
leather
'Tis pleasant to need neither shirt, sleeve, nor shoe,
  And have arm, leg, and belly together.
Then aches your head, or are you lazy?
Sing, "Round your neck your belly wrap,
  Tail atop, and make your cap
   Any bee and daisy."

'I'll not be a fool like the nightingale
Who sits up all midnight without any ale,
  Making a noise with his nose;
Nor a camel, although 'tis a beautiful back;
Nor a duck, notwithstanding the music of quack
  And the webby, mud-patting toes.
I'll be a new bird, with the head of an ass,
Two pigs' feet, two men's feet, and two of a hen;
Devil-winged; dragon-bellied; grave-jawed, because
 grass
Is a beard that's soon shaved, and grows seldom again
  Before it is summer, so cow all the rest;
   The new Dodo is finished. O! come to my
nest.'

Isbrand's song is parody, parody of a cosmology of a scientific generation that will commit any sin in the name of science. Autobiography apart, we can see parody, self-parody, in the Isbrand who sings this ballad and in him who later, on the eve of his own destruction, declares: "I have a bit of FIAT in my soul". One may play with ideas of evolution or metempsychosis if one chooses; certainly the Pythagorean theory was known to Beddoes. But it is the tone of mockery and excess that makes the poem wholly remarkable—unique in English verse. Poetry as play, serious and grim play but play none the less. One dares not label as nonsense a poem that explores with humor and learning the notion of man's free will, however idiosyncratically expressed. With his Mandrake, Beddoes might have said, "Thou knowest I hunger after wisdom as the Red Sea after ghosts", and it is not strange that of the masks he chose one of the most effective should be that of the alchemistic fool: "soul of a pickle-herring, body of a spagirical toss-pot, doublet of motley, and mantle of pilgrim." All of these personae were Beddoes, who had his bit of FIAT and died of it. If at times he doubted himself

and his gifts, he never doubted that one of the proper functions of art is to show men their own folly, smallness and mortality: "O world, world! The gods and fairies left thee for thou were too wise; and now, thou Socratic star, thy demon, the great Pan, Folly, is parting from thee." It is the logical paradox in Beddoes that his science should retain strong traces of alchemy, his poetry retain a firm grip on a tradition while it went far from the beaten path, his morality return to a kind of doctrine of humors while his own nature developed most involutely.

Isbrand says of his "noble hymn to the belly gods", that "'tis perhaps a little / Too sweet and tender, but that is the fashion; / Besides my failing is too much sentiment," but we must not consider this irony or mere sarcasm; it is one plane of the mask, this time a composite mask made up of every quality Beddoes found in the poet: fool, sage, demon, beast, and monster. What does his song show us if not the varied aspect of man's nature when he is most self-aware and creative? The "bodiless childfull of life" exerts will, a bit of FIAT, and selects at last no known form of life as its persona but the fabulous shape of the "new Dodo", a monstrous form of its own birthing, for the child owes no tie to the parent that aborted it. Beddoes' abortion is an "unborn ghost" inhabiting a limbo closer to the real world than we suspect; if it is to come to life it will do so through its own will and in no ordinary guise, for "the world's man-crammed; we want no more of them." The romantic agony of "anywhere, anywhere out of the world" was to Beddoes a real possibility, achievable through wisdom—science and art. These, energized by the will, could find the single secret of man's nature and force it to confess itself. That which much of *Death's Jest Book* states with seriousness and full conviction, Isbrand's song parodies—not for the sake of burlesque but as another aspect of the face of life, of man: the fool, the poet, the monstrous abortion who yet wills and selects his own mask: "I'll be a new bird with the head of an ass." Man has such a head whether he knows it or not; "thou great-eared mind," Isbrand calls Mandrake. "The world will see its ears in a glass no longer," Mandrake laments now that he, the fool, is departing. "Every man is his own fool" and in his song Isbrand tells how to make the fool as unlike his usual self as possible, though however altered he may be, he will have "the head of an ass".

We can consider this song as characteristic of Beddoes in his best vain of parody: excess, conceit, and surrealism. Here is the very "fool sublimate", the formal arrangement of a disgust with human life that never makes the mistake of becoming pettish. Man has no place in the world of this song, nor will Beddoes allow his "new Dodo" any of man's features save his feet—two out of six, on equal ground with a pig's and a hen's. For the rest of the creature's anatomy Beddoes raids a representative stock of lore, finding actual and fabled beasts, a whole bestiary of humors and passions. "In this dear planet of wool and of leather" he finds monsters and beasts better equipped than man to withstand the rigors of climate, and a barnyard duck has a pleasanter sound than the nightingale, the foolish bird that "sits up all midnight without any ale, / Making a noise with his nose." All normal and man-made standards shall be thrown down, all laws abandoned, all nature refashioned to suit the individual will. This has as much of the ethical as the artistic and intellectual; if not precisely "dérèglement de tous les sens", something rather closer to a genuine rebirth of the spirit through wilful metamorphosis. Beddoes was far too serious as poet and scientist to write these verses with action in mind; this is the area of the grotesque, that portion of the poetic map where actuality and imagination meet in a balance so perfect that each mocks the other. We mistake the purpose of grotesque if we look in it for what is morbid or ironic or merely fanciful; it is a kind of vision which takes nothing seriously except itself, which comes from anger rather than sympathy, and which requires a lively sense of ugliness. To these ends nothing serves so well as a close association of the homely and the exotic, the exotic made homely and the homely alien. Hence, the "unborn ghost", while debating the appropriateness of becoming "an Egyptian crocodile", turns that formidable beast into a harmless absurdity, though the real nature is below this surface still. Again, addressing "serpent Lucifer", the child talks of demon and reptile as if each were innocuous, though we realize that such natures are to be considered preferable to the human. In the final stanza, Beddoes gives his sardonic contempt free rein; all beasts, all monstrous forms, real and fabled, are to join in the forming of the "new Dodo", and that portion of the "unborn ghost" not yet made flesh shall be cow: "So cow all the rest; / The new Dodo is finished. O come to my nest." Contempt and anger, finely controlled, temper the tone, and the poem rises to a conclusion in which mingle colloquial gusto and a sinister "invitation au voyage". As the song progresses, the rhythms become more marked, more solemn, belying the apparent lightness of statement; pauses are heavy and a broken line begins again after the caesura to rush through another line and a half, where suddenly the movement checks violently. With abrupt decision the creature completes its form and issues its sardonic invitation.

The world the creature asks us to enter is one of familiar shapes in strange combinations and positions. Entrance into such a world tests our acumen, for certain kinds of good poetry are so close to bad that the reader needs skill and taste in order to discriminate. Some kinds of bad work are more satisfying than some kinds of good, and the vices of a particular way of writing usually form the conditions of that writing's existence; that is, without the vices, there could be no writing of that sort at all. Beddoes had to be very derivative, bombastic, and coy in much of his poetry before he could suddenly generate sufficient heat to light off his power. Yet after Beddoes has made proper obeisance to the formal love-story, he can suddenly surcharge banality with poetry, as in the scene between Sibylla and the ghost of her murdered lover, Wolfram:

> WOLFRAM: . . . Dar'st die?
> A grave-deep question. Answer it religiously.
>
> SIBYLLA: . . . With him I loved, I dared.

> WOLFRAM: . . . With me and for me.
> I am a ghost. Tremble not; fear not me.
> The dead are ever good and innocent,
> And love the living. They are cheerful creatures,
> And quiet as the sunbeams, and most like,
> In grace and patient love and spotless beauty,
> The new-born of mankind. . . .

Similarly, in the more blood-curdling passages, one must keep a sharp lookout lest one mistake some fine poetry for fustian; they are both there:

> ATHULF: Great and voluptuous Sin now seize upon
> me,
> Thou paramour of Hell's fire-crowned king,
> That showedst the tremulous fairness of thy bosom
> In heaven, and so didst ravish the best angels . . .

Surely bad enough. Yet Isbrand, a few lines later, tells Athulf:

> . . . Sire and mother
> And sister I had never, and so feel not
> Why sin 'gainst them should count so doubly wicked,
> This side o' th' sun. If you would wound your foe,
> Get swords that pierce the mind: a bodily slice
> Is cured by surgeon's butter . . .

If death is to a large extent the theme and subject of the play, Isbrand is death's jester, the fool of death who would turn the tables on his master only to become the more fool for his pains. At the last, Wolfram replaces on Isbrand's head the fool's cap; Sibylla's grave is decked with lilies of the valley, the plant that "bears bells":

> For even the plants, it seems, must have their fool,
> So universal is the spirit of folly;
> And whisper, to the nettles of her grave,
> 'King Death hath assess' ears'.

Isbrand in a sense becomes so closely identified with Death that it is with something of a shock that we finally discover him to be mortal—no supernatural creature, despite his "bit of FIAT", but a man and hence a fool. Early in the play he had tried to urge his laggard brother to join him in vengeance on the Duke; that was his greatest piece of folly, "for when he (his father's ghost) visits me in the night, screaming revenge, my heart forgets that my head wears a fool's cap . . ." If, as Mandrake says, "all days are foaled of one mother", no man can hope to escape his lot; then indeed Isbrand and Mandrake can never be other than they are: the jesters of the world. And in the final issue, of course, men who had been fools of life are finally capped in death, becoming jesters, mocking the living and mocked at by King Death, who wears asses' ears himself. "Human kind cannot bear very much reality," Beddoes would agree, and further shows that the result of man's overreaching himself can never be other than fatal:

> ISBRAND: . . . What shall we add to man,
> To bring him higher? I begin to think
> That's a discovery I soon shall make.

Thus, owing naught to books, but being read
In the odd nature of much fish and fowl,
And cabbages and beasts, I've raised myself,
By this comparative philosophy,
Above your shoulders, my sage gentlemen.
Have patience but a little, and keep still;
I'll find means bye and bye of flying higher.

Isbrand here forgets that he had earlier remarked to the apostate jester, Mandrake, "I mark by thy talk that thou commencest philosopher, and then thou art only a fellow servant out of livery": his own will, corrupted by power, has brought him to the point of believing he can transcend his humanity: "And man has tired of being merely human."

Much of *Death's Jest Book* is fragmentary and suggestive. Occasionally there are prolepses of other poets, as in the passage immediately above. Or sometimes a packed parenthesis will suddenly lift the tone of a passage or take the reader, by powerful suggestion, into another dimension:

ISBRAND: . . . Were I buried like him
There in the very garrets of death's town,
But six feet under earth, (that's the grave's sky)
I'd jump up into life . . .

ZIBA: For soon the floral necromant brought forth
A wheel of amber, (such may Clotho use
When she spins lives) . . .

When he is going about his business properly, Beddoes is an economical writer in that he depends on verbs and strong verbal forms to do the heavy work: "I laid the lips of their two graves together, / And poured my brother into hers; while she, / Being the lightest, floated and ran over." The macabre intent of Isbrand, the repulsive nature of the deed, strike us with the greater force because of connotation, here largely clustered about the verbs and arising from the image of liquor. At other moments he will give us poetic passages that are gently descriptive.

ZIBA: . . . For the drug, 'tis good:
There is a little hairy, green-eyed snake,
Of voice like to the woody nightingale.
And ever singing pitifully sweet,
That nestles in the barry bones of death,
And is his dearest pet and playfellow.
The honied froth about that serpent's tongue
Deserves not so his habitation's name
As does this liquor. That's the liquor for him.

or, direct and to the immediate point,

DUKE: . . . Nature's polluted,
There's man in every secret corner of her,
Doing damned wicked deeds. . . .

The thought of power can change Isbrand's expression "like sugar melting in a glass of poison". Again, "Never since Hell laughed at the church, blood-drunken / From rack and wheel, has there been joy so mad / As that which

stings my marrow now." Isbrand's hour of triumph "will be all eternal heaven distilled / Down to one thick rich minute." In such moments of the play, Beddoes does not need to conform to the exigencies of a character he has created, since that character is general, not a "personality". Beddoes has left out of *Death's Jest Book* much that modern readers want to find if they are to feel at home, for the play frankly explores other realities, taking risks of a sort we either do not approve or can not see.

Still, the failure (and it is a failure) of *Death's Jest Book* derives not from the incomplete application of a technique, nor from a lack of talent, but from a spiritual malaise which, if nothing else, we share with Beddoes. We have a thousand writers who would worship "heroes of culture" with whom a failing artist may identify himself. The weaknesses and the pathos of these "heroes" are known, but many writers would prefer to be committed to the sins rather than to the literature, to the personality rather than the talent, for these are public and they pay off in fame, success. Pastiche, rather than eclecticism, determines such lives and works; we are closer to romantic *mal du siècle* than we like to think, for Hart Crane's alcohol-and-jazz Muse is easy of invocation, the nostalgics of Fitzgerald are less difficult to contrive and sustain than are the torments and passion of Dickens or Tennyson, for all their "sentimentality". We somehow want genius to be less upsetting, tidier: the American writer is so accustomed to keeping his tongue in his cheek that he has trouble talking, and he who risks a direct high tone finds the shortest shrift. Yet it may be that we are ready for another kind of writing, another way of observing. R. P. Blackmur has shown us some of the uses of parody, has indicated how such a tactic may point a way out of the slough modern literature has foundered in. We could use another route. Whether we accept the way of parody or not, we ought to like Beddoes; he was a man for our time a century too soon, and his work defines certain excesses we may commit, certain risks we can take, if we would wrench out of the bog.

Anne Harrex (essay date 1967)

SOURCE: "*Death's Jest Book* and the German Contribution," in *Studia Neophilologica*, Vol. 39, No. 1, 1967, pp. 15-37.

[*In the following essay, Harrex assesses the influence of the German dramatic tradition on* Death's Jest Book.]

I

LITERARY AND PHILOSOPHICAL INFLUENCE IN DEATH'S JEST BOOK

Thomas Lovell Beddoes travelled to Germany in 1825 to study medicine, and although he had already begun to learn the language and read it a little before leaving England,[1] it was in Germany itself that he made his real discoveries in the literature, reading widely and critically among German writers to such an extent that by July 1830 he was able to express surprise at not having discovered sooner the work of Heinrich von Kleist, since, he writes to Kelsall, "I really believed I was acquainted with everything worth reading in German belles lettres, from the Niebelungenlied down to Tiecks last novel". References to German authors and their works abound in his letters; it would not be surprising, therefore, if some German influence should be perceptible in his original writing from 1825 onwards.

This original writing consists almost entirely of the monumental drama *Death's Jest Book,* completed in the first drafts by 1830 and added to and amended for at least another fourteen years. Beddoes' youthful and adolescent works had already shown in many aspects the influence of his reading of the Elizabethan and Jacobean dramatists and of the Gothic school of writers, and this predisposition to outside influence remained with him into his maturity. *Death's Jest Book* itself is full of echoes of English dramatists,[2] and though it was written in Germany the reminiscences of the German tradition absorbed from Beddoes' new reading are mainly of a different kind. Beddoes was no longer seeking a form, having discovered his affinity with the five act blank verse drama in the Elizabethan style, or phrases to express his content, but an approach to the fundamental problems of existence. *Death's Jest Book* is a play of ideas, the product of a speculative intellect which took to itself the elements of German thought to which it felt akin. This may, in fact, stand as a satisfactory definition of what constitutes influence. Beddoes' own preoccupation with questions of the relationship of life and death and his progressive exploration of these led him to take from the Germans exactly what he did and no more. *Death's Jest Book* is basically an English play, and not only by virtue of the language in which it is written; Beddoes was steeped in the English literary tradition, hence his conscious or unconscious reminiscences of Elizabethan and Jacobean playwrights. On the other hand, it is a play whose creator was domiciled in Germany, studying and assimilating German literature and thought, a fact which contributed to the finished play in various ways. As a play of ideas, *Death's Jest Book* contains tangible evidence of the influence of German literary theory, of philosophical thought, and of Beddoes' reading of German literature.

Death's Jest Book must ultimately face judgment as an English play, yet an examination of the German influences outlined above, in particular the first, provides an interesting study of the nature and extent to which Beddoes, a non-German who had already written prolifically, was prone to influence by a new cultural environment in the writing of a work whose main theme was already established before his arrival in Germany. No systematic analysis of this kind has yet been undertaken, and the present study attempts to illuminate a minor but nevertheless unjustifiably neglected aspect of the work of Beddoes.

However, it is necessary to be extremely careful in the tracing of this influence whose extent is not as great as might reasonably be expected from the range of his knowledge of German literature. The connections between the works of Schiller and *Death's Jest Book,* for example, are more honoured by tradition than by critical textual appraisal. Walter Schirmer, whose work on German influence in English literature excludes Beddoes for the good reason that he transmitted none, gives the single fact that *Death's Jest Book* contains "Anklänge an Schillers Geisterseher".[3] Royall H. Snow goes even further in claiming that the play has more than reminiscences: namely, two passages written under direct influence.[4] Donner disputes this claim,[5] and ultimately one must agree with him. There are a great number of resemblances between Schiller and Beddoes which can only be accidental, resulting from the use of the same traditional themes and a certain coincidence of interest, which is probably the very reason that Beddoes wrote to Bryan Waller Procter as early as 1826, "I have given up Schiller he's never very original".[6] An article which appeared in 1927, *Beddoes and the Continental Romanticists,* by Frederick E. Pierce deals in the main with the younger German Romantics,[7] and here the problems attendant upon the establishment of an influence proliferate. Pierce suggests a large number of tempting examples which on closer examination seem to prove no more than the very affinity of thought which caused English readers of Beddoes to dismiss apparent obscurities in his work as resulting from contact with "German metaphysics".[8] Beddoes' real and demonstrable debt to Tieck is entirely disregarded, while Pierce wishes one to believe that Beddoes gained inspiration from such secondary sources as the works or Arnim and Hoffman for themes which would be known to him from his general reading. In any case, Pierce's stated thesis is altogether too sweeping.[9] Such considerations tend to shed suspicion, perhaps a little unjustifiably, on the whole of Pierce's article, though it must be stated that by and large it is based on a series of false premises and faulty arguments.

We must, therefore, cut though the mass of conjecture and tradition and misunderstanding to discover exactly what Beddoes' work may be said with reasonable certainty to owe to individual German authors. His borrowings from literary works will be seen to fall into two categories, as the first two examples from Goethe will indicate; for the rest, he learnt from Tieck a different type of dramatic construction and applied it to the final extant version of Act I of the play, from Novalis the theory of Magic Idealism, and from Tieck and the Schlegel brothers the concept of Romantic Irony. His use of the last is the subject of the second part of the present article.

Prior to his departure from England, Beddoes is known to have translated some 120 lines of the *Nibelungenlied* and a section of Schiller's *Philosophische Briefe*; his reading comprised, according to his letters, various plays and poems of Goethe and Schiller. In the opening scene of *The Second Brother* the following lines are spoken by Orazio:

> Rosaura, this same night
> I will immortalise these lips of thine,
> That make a kiss so spicy. Touch the cup:

Ruby to ruby! Slave, let it be thrown
At midnight from a boat into mid sea.
Rosaura's kiss shall rest unravished there.

(15-20)

Rosaura is Orazio's mistress, and his fancy brings to mind what must have been its source: Goethe's lyric "Der König in Thule". The theme of the cup sanctified by its association with the mistress obviously caught Beddoes' imagination as a touch of dramatic embroidery he could add to the play then being composed just as, in the final scene of *The Brides' Tragedy,* he had taken the idea of death from poisoned flowers from Massinger. The value of each borrowing is exactly the same: each is a mere detail whose origin is immaterial, since dramatic effectiveness is the criterion.

The revised first act of *Death's Jest Book* concludes with the Song from the Waters, "The swallow leaves her nest", one of Beddoes' last poems.[10] It expresses a faith and resignation which came only to the poet in his mature years:

The swallow leaves her nest,
The soul my weary breast;
But therefore let the rain
    On my grave
Fall pure; for why complain?
Since both will come again
    O'er the wave.

The wind dead leaves and snow
Doth hurry to and fro;
And, once, a day will break
    O'er the wave,
When a storm of ghosts shall shake
The dead, until they wake
    In the grave.

These fourteen lines contain an extremely rich and condensed complex of ideas, perfect not only in the context but in themselves as a lyric. It is unmistakably Beddoes at his best, yet at the same time there is a remarkable resemblance to a lyric by Goethe, whom Beddoes appreciated as a lyricist rather than as the recognised colossus of German literature. Goethe's "Gesang der Geister über den Wassern"—note the similarity of the title—begins

Des Menschen Seele
Gleicht dem Wasser:
Vom Himmel kommt es,
Zum Himmel steigt es,
Und wieder nieder
Zur Erde muss es,
Ewig wechselnd.

In Goethe's poem it is soul and water that return, in Beddoes' soul and swallow, though water/wave are an integral part of his poetic statement: the rain on the grave stands outside the dynamic process, yet seems almost a symbol of it. Goethe proceeds by the use of simile, Beddoes by an accumulation of statements and implications which in their

relationship to one another assume the proportion of metaphor and ultimately fuse into a single symbol of resurrection in the cosmic order. The resemblances of the two lyrics are confirmed by their development. The second, third and fourth stanzas of Goethe's gradually weave soul and water into a single entity and achieve the same interpenetration of internal and external nature, or pathetic fallacy, as Beddoes' more concise statement. Detailed analysis of construction only tends to confirm the startling and consistent affinities in the development of the thought complex.

Nor is the second aspect of Beddoes' lyric missing from Goethe's:

Wind ist der Welle
Lieblicher Buhler . . .

Seele des Menschen,
Wie gleichst du dem Wasser!
Schicksal des Menschen,
Wie gleichst du dem Wind!

Wind and storm are the main symbols of Beddoes' second stanza: his wind/storm is exactly the wind/fate of Goethe; Beddoes' storm of ghosts is the force that resurrects the dead, the fate that achieves the return of the soul. Likewise the wind plays with the dead leaves and snow, which are surely a symbol of inner nature. In the matter of influence, one single reservation must be noted: Beddoes is concerned with a single resurrection, Goethe with a cyclic process. However, this does not controvert the fact that there are a number of marked similarities in the two lyrics of the sort that would arise from a more or less unconscious reminiscence on Beddoes' part of Goethe's poem. One must, of course, bear in mind the qualifications of Beddoes' own *One word on Plagiarisms,* and in fact Goethe's lyric poems of both *Sturm und Drang* and Classical periods express the same type of feeling for and attitude to nature in the cosmos as those of the English Romantics, Beddoes included.

Does it not seem as if, at certain periods of the world, some secret influence in nature was acting universally on the spirit of mankind, and predisposing it to the culture of certain sciences or arts, and leading it to the discovery even of certain special ideas and facts in these?

The words are Beddoes' own,[11] and the number and type of the examples he cites shows that he was conscious of the problems of the phenomenon. Yet while these considerations explain why "Dianeme's Death Scene" has the same feeling as Goethe's "Ganymed" when no "influence" may be suggested, they do not satisfactorily explain away the correspondences between the two Songs from the Waters. This instance, so far unnoticed by students of Beddoes' work, must therefore be recognised to have a viable claim as another passage influenced by a specific German work.

Both Pierce[12] and G. R. Potter[13] claim as an influence on *Death's Jest Book* the second part of Goethe's *Faust.* In doing so they make fundamental errors which a closer attention to publication dates alone might have obviated. The Auerbachs Keller scene from the first part of *Faust* may, however, find an echo in Act II scene i, set in the inn at Ancona. This also concerns a drinking situation, and both scenes occur as comic relief after a long exposition of the basic conflict of the play, which is all Beddoes' long first act amounts to, despite its self-contained action. Both contain an important measure of the occult, and though Mandrake is suffering from delusions, he is nevertheless a sorcerer figure, and like Mephistopheles in Goethe's play is physically attacked as a result of his pretensions. Though it may be argued that Beddoes' scene is necessary to the development of the Mandrake sub-plot and could scarcely have been inserted elsewhere, a certain parallel development in the two scenes undoubtedly exists and should be noted.

To Tieck Beddoes owes considerably more than the borrowing of the theory of Romantic Irony. One and possibly even as many as three episodes in *Death's Jest Book* evince the influence of his writing. Act II scene iii of Beddoes' play marks the transition of Isbrand from jester to power-seeker, from prose-speaker to verse-speaker. The public abdication is emphasised by more than the mere technical means; the relevant section of the scene was undeniably written under the influence of a portion of Scene i of Tieck's *Ritter Blaubart*. Tieck's example probably indicated to Beddoes the way to present the change more smoothly, yet it is from the contrasts rather than the likenesses in the treatment of a single idea that the significance of Beddoes' *Bearbeitung* can be guaged.

Tieck's incident, or scena, if the more precise operatic term may be used, occurs at the beginning of the play, thus its terms of reference cannot be extensive. In fact it hardly transcends its actual objective existence as a comic interlude. This of course is no criticism; Tieck's satire is projected through a comic, Beddoes' through a tragic vision; and comedy depends upon the lightness of touch, the avoidance of portentousness. Tieck's Claus is essentially an amiable fool and a minor character, while Beddoes' Isbrand is neither of these, as the reader is well aware by Act II. In the Tieck-inspired episode Beddoes reaches out through satire of the fool's insignia to the metaphysical and finally to a statement of one of the major themes of the play:

Yonder minister shall have my jacket; he needs many colours for his deeds. . . .

O cap and bells, ye eternal emblems, hieroglyphics of man's supreme right in nature . . . who shall be honoured with you?

I will yield Death the crown of folly . . . Let him wear the cap, let him toll the bells . . . and, when the world is old and dead, the thin wit shall find the angel's record of man's works and deeds, and write with a lipless grin on the innocent first page for a title, 'Here begins Death's Jest-book'.

(93-117)

Compare this with Claus's testament:

Aus meinem Narrenstock lässt sich ein herrlicher Kommandostab machen, man darf nur oben den Eselskopf herunterbrechen: den vermach' ich Euch!

Beddoes found the initial suggestion in Tieck, and this origin remains recognisable, but the differing demands of his subject condition the treatment.

Of greater interest is the fact that a second theme introduced by Claus recalls very strongly another section *Death's Jest Book,* and this too would seem to owe its existence to Tieck:

O über die lumpige Welt!—Wahrhaftig ich schäme mich jetzt, ich werde dafür bezahlt, um ein recht wahrer Narr zu sein, und nun bin ich ein Pfuscher gewesen, und war offenbar der verständigste von allen. Sie pfuschen dafür in mein Handwerk, und so ist kein Mensch mit seinem Stande zufrieden. Wollte nur Gott, ich könnte die Klugheit so wacker spielen, als sie sich in der Narrheit gut ausgenommen haben.

And of his wit, bequeathed to the counsellor, he says

So könnt Ihr immer noch Euren vernünftigen Rat damit flicken, denn ich glaube, dass Verstand kein besser Unterfutter finden kann, als Narrheit.

These two extracts have no parallel in Isbrand's abdication scene, but are exactly the two essentials of the vision expressed in the fragment "The Spirit of Folly", and incorporated into the c version of Act I.[14] There may not be direct influence, since, it must be stressed, though Beddoes borrowed constantly from works which shared some aspect of his attitude to the world, for the rest he was widely read and a poet in his own right. The fragment postdates the first versions *Death's Jest Book* and brings into prominence themes already implicit in the play; Tieck's contribution cannot be assessed, and if there is any, it indicates that Beddoes must have taken a second idea from the scene at a much later date. However, the basis of each situation is undoubtedly the same, and Tieck's lines must have remained in his mind. In "The Spirit of Folly" Mandrake introduces the subject of the confusion of folly and wisdom, and like Claus he is renouncing his fool's title to go off on affairs of "wisdom". Isbrand's response is of a piece with it. In both writers the suggestion is of a confused standard of values, of a changing world where no man knows his place. The difference is that this vision pervades Beddoes' entire play. A few lines of Tieck contain all the themes developed by Beddoes in parts of two scenes: the initial impulse is Claus's desire to make his will, and both he and Isbrand after him use the opportunity to indulge in satirical comment of differing tendency. Mandrake's dialogue with Isbrand develops one aspect of the satire. It is noteworthy that there is no actual point at which the bequests or the satiric comments correspond, and certainly no hint of a translation, yet Tieck's influence is undeniable.

One of Tieck's serious works, the chronicle play *Leben und Tod der heiligen Genoveva,* is mentioned for the first time by Beddoes in 1827, that is, some months after his statement that the play is finished in the rough.[15] In view of this, it may only be a coincidence that ***Death's Jest Book*** IV iii contains what seem like similarities to the scene in *Genoveva* in which Golo serenades the heroine from the garden. They are of a type which could result unconsciously from Beddoes' having composed his scene about the time of reading the other, which could easily have been the case. Similarities in the plot development are already there: Golo's situation in relation to Genoveva is very like that of Athulf vis à vis Amala; on the physical level, the man in each case is in the garden, the woman above in her apartment—Genoveva is actually on a balcony; it is night. Such correspondences could be explained by the conventional nature of the scenes, yet each also marks a turning point in the destiny of the man concerned. In addition, the two scenes follow the same pattern for the first thirty or so lines. Each opens with a soliloquy from the lover, upon which the woman's presence is perceived:

> *Athulf*: O beauty, beauty! Thou shed'st a moony night of quiet through me.

> *Golo*: Sie schimmert wie ein neuer Sternenhimmel, Ein neuer Mond ist sie emporgestiegen.

And in Tieck's scene, Genoveva's first words after Golo's soliloquy express the same pathetic fallacy as Athulf's lines:

> Wie sanft der Mondschein auf dem Grase spielt,
> Wie süss das Herz sich nun beruhigt fühlt.

There is nothing particularly original about the imagery but the sequence of the likenesses between the two passages leaves the impression that this cannot be entirely accidental, though both might well be independent Romantic versions of the most celebrated of all balcony scenes.

Here a reference should be made to two borrowings from another of the older German Romantics which, strictly speaking, are no more than that, since they are found in the two prefaces to ***Death's Jest Book*** and thus are not assimilated or restyled to serve the purpose of artistic creation as are the foregoing examples. The *Preface* of 1828 takes up A. W. Schlegel's analogy from the first of the *Vorlesungen über dramatische Literatur und Kunst* of the northern drama and Gothic architecture.[16] This Beddoes takes a stage further to suit the nature of his own play. Notably, he makes a point of the gargoyles, the medieval symbols of the grotesque, the evil and the dislocated in the moral world. "The Fragment of a New Preface"[17] is only a few lines long; it seems to be the opening of a restatement of the three classes of drama distinguished by Schlegel in his *Lectures*. The borrowings, in both cases acknowledged, are of little importance except in their implications.

The distinction made by Schlegel between these three classes, Classical Shakespearian and Spanish, was a real

one to the German Romantic critics. Beddoes himself was acquainted with all three, since he read Calderon shortly after taking up residence in Göttingen.[18] His own ***Fest-Book,*** like its predecessors, was conceived and executed in the "old English or Shakespearian" style, as he calls it: the one most suited to his purpose and talents. However, in the revisions of Act I, the c version of Donner's critical edition, the nature of the changes and expansions indicates the influence of another style which he had come to see as appropriate to and capable of expressing the diffuse and excursive nature of his thought.

This is none other than the technique of Calderon's dramas, adapted by Tieck in his own chronicle plays *Kaiser Oktavianus* and *Genoveva*; and it must be stated at the outset that as this style was largely absorbed from a German modification of the Spanish original it must count as German. An examination of Tieck's method in these chronicle dramas and of Beddoes' new treatment of material already set down in the ab version shows that Beddoes was consciously working on a new dramatic technique, by which increased length of both scene and play as a whole is offset by deliberately balanced contrasts of character and mood within a scene. Since in Beddoes' case the actual scene content and sequence was already fixed, there is no juxtaposition of scenes on the basis of mood contrasts as in Tieck, but the additional lyrics of the c version are all intended to emphasise the mood prevailing in their context. Contrast and mood: these are the salient structural principles of the technique Beddoes applied over the more rigid English form in the revisions of Act I by drawing out tendencies already present.

The prose opening of Act I scene i is not only extended but in some cases altered where this seems at first glance unnecessary. Thus "dear Mandrake" becomes "dainty Homunculus" (ab l. 15, c l. 18): the term evokes specifically the magic arts Mandrake intends to practice and of which he speaks in the altered passages of the opening, c lines 14 ff. and 25 ff., which now impress the fact. Thus the character is defined more precisely than before, and the "Spirit of Folly" extract sets Isbrand beside Mandrake the better to distinguish the two, since Isbrand adds the intellectual and satirical response to Mandrake's speech and song. The passage may have been inspired by Tieck as suggested above, but whatever its origin it emphasises early in the play and provides a focal point for the theme of folly that runs through the later acts. In making his revisions Beddoes had the advantage of knowing what he had written into later scenes and what he wished to develop.

Every bypath is also more fully explored in the revised scenes: in the first, for example, Mandrake's interruption of Wolfram (I. i. 103 ff., cf. ab 68 ff.) is extended into a passage resembling the folly dialogue in that Mandrake introduces the animal metaphor to which Isbrand adds an overtone of political satire. The loose epic form permits this type of expansion in which any motif may be developed in passing for its own sake. There is no subordination to structure as it is traditionally conceived. With the Isbrand-Wolfram exchange comes an outstanding illustration of the use of the "contrast" technique, since many lines are rewritten to point the difference between the two brothers which was less apparent in the ab text. Isbrand's affirmation of vengeance, I. i. 207f., has a new and more powerful climax; Wolfram is depicted more positively in his misdirected charity—compare ab 134-141 and c 225-233, ab 167-172 and c 258-267—and Isbrand is shown as almost beside himself with scorn for Wolfram, cynicism, and something akin to tragic desperation (I. i. 281 f.). The new Song from the Ship in conjunction with Isbrand's final speech serves to end the scene on a more dramatic note than previously.

The second scene has fewer additions, yet a comparison of the two texts shows that these are all designed to a specific end: to give greater depth and truth of feeling, particularly in the depiction of Sibylla's love for Wolfram both before and at his entrance, and in Melveric's growing awareness that the loss of Sibylla will destroy him. His vital speech, c. I. ii. 363f., compare ab 306f., is rewritten with more attention to psychological truth. The c version of scene iii has an entirely new opening section; the idyllic love scene of the ab text which glosses over the tension between Wolfram and Melveric is replaced by two lyrics and a short speech by Wolfram in which Beddoes makes telling use of dramatic irony to create atmosphere and define the discrepancy between reality and Wolfram's idea of it. By altering the opening Beddoes shows a surer sense of the dramatic necessities, for instead of allowing the tension of the climax of scene ii to dissipate as previously he focuses the impending tragedy more unequivocally still about the head of the unsuspecting Wolfram. The subsequent events are interrupted by Mandrake's entry, added in the c version, and a series of riddling puns. This interpolation serves no purpose at all, unless to juxtapose the comic and the serious as in life which may now be necessary in the growing melodrama of the situation. In a and b Mandrake and his boy only appear at the beginning of scene iv, and in c this passage too is amplified so that the imperilled Melveric is temporarily neglected for a farcical scene with two comic songs. Each such addition extends an already lengthy act, yet without creating the feeling that it is superfluous. This passage, for example, is a virtuoso bit of comedy and wit for which the play is all the better. In addition it offsets the mood of the rest of the scene, though its effect on the "serious" action seems deleterious. However, having led the plot away from the main aspect, Beddoes recreates the prevailing atmosphere in an exchange that bridges the two main sections of the scene, and does this far more tellingly than before. He presents the dialogue of the fishermen, "low-life" characters like Mandrake, and their song "As mad sexton's bell", as evocative as the song which opens scene iii.

The chronicle style develops the climax of the act with new skill. When he wrote in the Shakespearian manner of the ab version, Beddoes crowded his stage with characters, his plot with details and ornamentations that tended to obscure the main issue. His deliberate adoption of a looser form permitted each theme to be treated in a more leisurely fashion, so that such sections as the Isbrand-Mandrake dialogues and the scene between Mandrake and his boy seem no longer intrusions or baroque excrescences leading the attention outwards from the main centre, but integral parts of the text. Lines which formerly commanded only fleeting attention have been extended into the expression of some aspect of Beddoes' mind and thought, and for this reason deserve a response. In the c version, moreover, the lyrics are living and vital to the presentation of mood; nowhere more so than in the last hundred or so lines of the act, where they crystallise and reflect the drama more effectively than any dialogue, certainly more surely than the dialogue they replace. By comparison the lyrics of the four final acts are ornamental interludes, Wolfram's Dirge of II ii and Isbrand's Harpagus ballad of IV iv and V iv possibly excepted.

The c version of Act I shows Beddoes' grasp of the fundamentals of a new and perhaps more congenial dramatic style, one which turns diffuseness to good account. He undoubtedly met it too late, for the fact that he did not continue this large scale revision may indicate an inability to face the reshaping of the last four acts whose treatment is conditioned by the form: that is, the revenge plot may not have been adaptable to a less rigid structure. His vision, too, had undergone fundamental changes. Whatever the reason, one can only regret that the c version was not completed, for the new Act I shows Beddoes' ability to use effectively a technique unknown to him at the time of *Death's Jest Book*'s conception, a technique learnt from his contact with German literature.

Of the older German Romantics, only two were creative artists of any stature. Beddoes' debt to the more prolific of these, Tieck, has now been evaluated, and it remains to examine the precise relationship of the work of the other, Novalis, to *Death's Jest Book*. His central theory was that of Magic Idealism, and its possible connection with some otherwise difficult passages of Beddoes' play has never been defined. Like Romantic Irony, Magic Idealism was a development of philosophical theory by a writer who was not himself nominally a philosopher, and though both find a common origin in the doctrines of Fichte, they diverge radically from this point. Novalis's theory is not a simple one, and its essentials must therefore be discussed as a prerequisite to any examination of its possible influence upon Beddoes.

Belief in the supreme power of the mind and the spirit is inherent in the Romantic creed; Fichte himself was a Romantic in his valuation of the *Ich*, and his work laid the foundation for an even greater faith in its transcendental nature. If Fichte's theories begin where Kant's leave off, Novalis's theory of Magic Idealism is an extension of Fichtean doctrine; indeed, it is an autonomous whole whose tendency is a new and bold affirmation of the spirit which goes far beyond its Fichtean origin. Novalis began with the study of Fichte, searching for the essence of the

Fichtean *Ich.* His journals mark the moment of his actual discovery of "den eigentlichen Begriff vom Fichteschen Ich". The inner world is a microcosm of the divine; the essence of philosophy is morality; the moral world of the *Ich* corresponds to the moral outer world of nature—"Die Welt ist ein Universaltropus des Geistes, ein symbolisches Bild desselben", he later wrote—thus, as Novalis interprets and develops the concept, mastery of one's own *Ich* is mastery of the whole external world.

Novalis's *Ich* is no longer constituted, like Fichte's, of pure reason and reasonable will. It is an organ of perception which can and should be developed to a point of actual domination of external circumstances. The inner spirit is dynamic, and this dynamism, according to Novalis, realises itself through a kind of plurality. The *Ich* creates within itself a *Du,* and through the interaction of the two there occurs "ein höchst geistiger und sinnlicher Umgang, und die höchste Leidenschaft ist möglich". When this inner correspondence and self-development is achieved it may impose itself on external nature, so that "die Gedanken verwandeln sich in Gesetze, die Wünsche in Erfüllungen". This first stage of Magic Idealism presents an almost mystical conception of the *Ich,* yet there is an implicit practical side to Novalis's doctrine. He was more than an abstract philosopher: in typical late eighteenth and early nineteenth century manner he was creative writer, metaphysician, mathematician and man of science. His Magic Idealism is at once a philosophy of aesthetics[19] and the expression of a religious attitude:

> Wir sind gar nicht Ich, wir können und sollen aber Ich werden, wir sind Keime zum Ich-werden. Wir sollen alles in ein Du, in ein zweites Ich verwandeln; nur dadurch erheben wir uns selbst zum grossen Ich, das eins und alles zugleich ist.

From this point, where life and death become united within the spirit, and there is no barrier between Diesseits and Jenseits, spring the *Hymnen an die Nacht.*

In ***Death's Jest Book*** there is more than one passage expressing a philosophy which is either Magic Idealism or one of Beddoes' own indistinguishable from it. Its appearance is confined, as will be seen, to specific speeches in which it is appropriate. The terms of these leave little room for doubt that this is any other than Novalis's theory embodied in poetry. Beddoes was certainly acquainted with Kant and Fichte; he cannot have failed to read Novalis, for there is too much evidence of thinking along the lines of Novalis's in these two instances. The speech of Ziba, I. ii. 59-71, goes beyond the limits of Fichtean idealism in a manner which is completely consistent with Novalis. Ziba himself is a mysterious figure, privy to the secrets of nature, a figure from a past age of wandering the world; he is the child of Life and Death, though his symbolic stature in the play is never fully realised. And this is how he announces the sighting of Wolfram's rescue expedition to Melveric, who has asked in plain terms if Ziba has seen a Christian galley:

> I looked abroad upon the wide old world,
> And in the sky and sea, through the same clouds,

> The same stars I saw glistening, and nought else.
> And as my soul sighed unto the world's soul,
> Far in the north a wind blackened the waters,
> And after that creating breath was still,
> A dark speck sat on the sky's edge: as watching
> Upon the heaven-girt border of my mind
> The first faint thought of a great deed arise,
> With force and fascination I drew on
> The wished sight, and my hope seemed to stamp
> Its shape upon it. Not yet is it clear
> What, or from whom, the vessel.

The tenor of this speech is unique in its context, and is obviously designed to impart a sense of Ziba's occult powers. What it describes is no less than the creative force of Magic Idealism: the conjunction of world soul and inner soul of line 62, under circumstances where heaven and earth are in harmony, as the image of lines 60 and 61 indicates, creates the ship. This is the "wished sight"; the wish becomes fulfilment, in Novalis's terms. Ziba's mind is "heaven-girt", an epithet significantly transferred from the external world of his contemplation; the speck "watches", waiting for his spirit to create it in the shape he desires. The process of lines 63-4 is also very close to the transition of the *Hymnen an die Nacht*:

> da kam aus blauen Fernen—von den Höhen meiner alten Seligkeit ein Dämmerungsschauer . . .

> (Hymn 3)

These lines refer to a specific death-awareness in their context, but there is a valid point of comparison in that both concern the moment of attunement to the soul of the universe and the resulting breakdown of the traditional time/space barriers. The final line and a half of Ziba's speech are in keeping with the real tone of the scene, a fact that renders the rest of it all the more striking in its presentation of the ego-conditioned viewpoint that constitutes the metaphorical aspect of Magic Idealism.[20]

As stated above, Novalis's theory was not restricted to this more or less aesthetic function. As a scientist, he envisaged a practical application of this magic power of the self-developed communication of the moral will. While Beddoes looked as a pure scientist for dominion over life and death, Novalis began as a philosopher with a firm foundation of religious faith and from there expressed his belief that the mind, not rational scientific laws that Beddoes allowed sole validity, had actual power over the external physical world. "Mit der richtigen Bildung unseres Willens", he writes,

> geht auch die Bildung unseres Könnens und Wissens fort. In dem Augenblick, wo wir vollkommen moralisch sind, werden wir ein Wunder tun können, d. i., wo wir keine tun wollen, höchstens moralische.

The more moral the spirit, the greater the harmony with the divine. In actual fact, Novalis's theories on these lines received no more confirmation from the experience than did Beddoes', but his stated beliefs are extremely interesting. This is Haym's commentary:[21]

Wie die Sprache und Gebärde unserem Denken gehorche, so, meint [Novalis], müssen wir auch die inneren Organe unseres Körpers hemmen, vereinigen und vereinzeln lassen. Unser ganzer Körper sei schlechterdings fähig, vom Geist in beliebige Bewegung gesetzt zu werden. Dann werde jeder sein eigener Arzt sein, der Mensch werde vielleicht sogar imstande sein, verlorene Glieder zu restaurieren, sich bloss durch seinen Willen zu töten und dadurch erst recht wahre Aufschlüsse über Körper, Seele, Welt, Leben, Tod und Geisterwelt erlangen u.s.w.

In general outline, this theory is not unique to Novalis; however, its terms of reference are significant. The mind, properly trained, can achieve literally anything, even the penetration of the secrets of life and death, simply because it has become divine. Novalis's theory immediately calls to mind the poetic function of Wolfram; however, the possible influence of Novalis in the presentation of Wolfram and also Sibylla, and of Ziba, must be set aside temporarily while the most contentious passage of the entire play is examined in the light of Magic Idealism, a theory which seems to explain it more adequately than any other philosophical or scientific doctrine previously used as a key.

The passage in question is actually in two parts, apportioned to a single character and falling very close to one another. Isbrand is the speaker: Isbrand who has just become a duke, or as he expresses it, a king; and he is already dissatisfied:

O! it is nothing now to be a man . . .
    Now we're common,
And man is tired of being no more than human;
And I'll be something better:—not by tearing
This crysalis of psyche ere its hour,
Will I break through Elysium. There are sometimes,
Even here, the means of being more than men:
And I by wine, and women, and the sceptre,
Will be, my own way, heavenly in my clay.
O you small star-mob, had I been one of you,
I would have seized the sky some moonless night,
And made myself the sun . . .

(IV iv 182-98)

In the middle section he turns away from metaphysical possibilites to a pragmatism that recalls Melveric's view of kingly rank, IV ii 123-60. The essential thing is that quasi-divinity is to be attained on earth, if anywhere, and not in an intangible Beyond. The speech, however, is only a prelude to that which poses a riddle Isbrand cannot solve, though he grasps the means:

I have a bit of FIAT in my soul,
And can myself create my little world.
Had I been born a four-legged child, methinks
I might have found the steps from dog to man,
And crept into his nature . . .
    It was ever
My study to find out a way to godhead,
And on reflection soon I found that first
I was but half-created; that a power

Was wanting in my soul to be its soul,
And this was mine to make. Therefore I fashioned
A will above my will, that plays upon it,
As the first soul doth use in men and cattle.
There's lifeless matter; add the power of shaping,
And you've the crystal: add again the organs,
Wherewith to subdue sustenance to the form
And manner of oneself, and you've the plant:
Add power of motion, senses and so forth,
And you've all kinds of beasts; suppose a pig:
To pig add foresight, reason and such stuff,
And you have man. What shall we add to man,
To bring him higher? I begin to think
That's a discovery I soon shall make.
Thus I, owing nought to books, but being read
In the odd nature of much fish and fowl,
And cabbages and beasts, have I raised myself,
By this comparative philosophy,
Above your shoulders, my sage gentlemen.

(V i 38-69)

Those who interpret this speech in terms of an early theory of evolution neglect the philosophical implications of crucial lines; those who interpret it in terms of standard philosophy alone neglect its scientific aspect. Both clearly belong to the same complex of ideas. The evolution theory is Colles's;[22] his interpretation is convincingly refuted by Potter,[23] who does not offer any alternative. What Potter alone concedes is that Beddoes as a scientist was aware of the organisational hierarchy of nature and used it for poetic purposes. Nor does he refer to the earlier purveyor of an evolution theory, Lamarck, who posited the Will as performing the crucial function in the evolutionary process. This brings the question back to the philosophical science of the era without its offering a satisfactory solution to the real idea behind the speech. Donner refers it to the philosophies of Kant and Fichte, the "will" being the Absolute Will of Kant, and the fiat section referring to Fichte's *Ich,* setting its own limits and constantly striving beyond them.[24] The Kantian influence in this sense could in fact be absorbed by the Fichtean, since Fichte in his late writings came full circle and posited an absolute *Ich* which assimilates to itself both finite ego and its created world.

The confusion surrounding the speech and its actual basis thus resolves itself into two alternatives: is it the result of anatomical or of philosophical studies? Isbrand himself refers to his "comparative philosophy", and here, it would seem, is the key to the whole argument. The entire process of Isbrand's self-development depends on a single fact: he is "but half-created", and he strives to find the missing part of himself that precludes him from divinity. He has climbed the throne steps to find himself nearer his real goal, and turns inward for guidance. The development must be within his own mind, or soul, and if he uses the word "will", this should not be seized upon as indicating Kant or even Lamarck. "Therefore I fashioned / A will above my will, that plays upon it": the process described is that of Novalis; the ideal soul formed within the real soul elevates it towards the divine soul of the world, the "first soul" of line 54, through its own activity.

The description of the hierarchy of nature follows, but the actual detail is not the important part of it. Beddoes is a scientist, describing the order of things in the accepted, hence non-evolutionary, sense. While he has shown interest in the transmigration of souls in the song "Squats on a toadstool" of Act III scene iii, and in lines 40-42 of the present speech, the latter section does not return to a consideration of this; Isbrand is a man already, and looking upwards, not back. It is not the transitions from one form to another that concern him, for he seems to regard each as essentially separate, but rather the differences between them: "power of motion, senses and so forth" distinguish the lower animals from the plants; "reason and such stuff" distinguishes man from beast. He lists these in the attempt to discover the missing element, that which will "bring man higher". The soul he has named already, presumably regarding it as inherent in all forms of life, but the solution is implied in man's ability to project a non-soul. The "evolutionary" passage is more or less a process of elimination, a recapitulation of his "comparative philosophy" which has led him to the above conclusion. In fact, he has already propounded the essential difference between man and his vision of superman, but without the knowledge of how this power is to be used. And in fact Isbrand's early death, or his disharmony with the moral world which in any case leads to this, prevents him from pursuing the matter to any conclusion.

The speech seems to fall apart at line 55: Isbrand and Beddoes go back upon their reasoning when the conclusion has already been stated, hence the confusion in interpretation. The significance of the passage centres round the lines on the soul and the will; the conception of the second, it is obvious, contains more than Kant's. The philosophical influence is Novalis's Magic Idealism, which its originator regarded as the ultimate form of transcendental philosophy, the highest means of development of the divine essence of man.

The theory of Romantic Irony is a second important philosophical influence in **Death's Jest Book,** yet this is a mode of perception which conflicts in every way with that of Magic Idealism. Romantic Irony represents a negation of the autonomy of the creative spirit, while Magic Idealism is its highest affirmation. Therefore the two could hardly exist side by side in a single play without causing the gravest disharmony, or so it would seem. Yet they manage to remain within separate sections of the plot and thought content, and Romantic Irony emerges as the more central means to the expression of Beddoes' vision. So far the influence of Magic Idealism has been discussed in connection with two passages where it manifests itself in isolated speeches for a deliberately conceived purpose. In Isbrand's it is used less arbitrarily than in Ziba's, for Isbrand's speech depends for total effect and character revelation on a particular outlook which only this most radical transcendentalism can afford it. And since these passages are isolated, it does seem as if the influence of Magic Idealism did not go very deep. Unquestionably Beddoes lacked the deep religious faith behind Novalis's

conception, and this temperamental difference precludes any possibility of more integral influence. Beddoes' own turn of mind inclined him to the ironic outlook on life. This must be borne in mind in the interpretation of passages which seem to bear an ideological resemblance to Novalis's theory in both its more far-reaching and its poetic-metaphoric aspects.

One of these is the resurrection of Wolfram, which appears to be a perfect poetic illustration of Novalis's own way to penetrate the world of the dead and discover the true inter-relation of the worlds of life and death. The resemblance, one feels, is entirely fortuitous, though a case might possibly be made for it. If Beddoes had rewritten the play, as he suggested, with the resurrection postponed to Act V, and with Isbrand functioning as the instrument of earthly revenge, the concept of Romantic Irony might have been relegated to a lesser position, Mandrake reinstated as a purely comic figure, and the concept of Magic Idealism approximated to far more closely. Yet there would have been insurmountable difficulties in the equation of this with the satiric aim; the play would have required total reorientation of a kind which is not consistent with Beddoes' outlook. He is primarily an ironist with a satiric purpose—in his case the terms are not at variance, since irony is the form and satire the content—whatever philosophical bypaths he is led into by individual characters or situations.

One such may be found in the development, particularly in IV ii, of the Wolfram-Sibylla theme. The presence of death between the two lovers and the language employed by Sibylla at some points recall the situation and actual sections of the text of Novalis's *Hymnen an die Nacht.* For Sibylla the way to death is through love; though she does not know the mysterious monk is wolfram, his words woo her and seem to dissolve the boundaries between their two worlds:

> Speak as at first you did; there was in the words
> A mystery and music, which did thaw
> The hard old rocky world into a flood,
> Whereon a swan-drawn boat seemed at my feet
> Rocking on its blue billows . . .

> (47-51)

And the opening lines of the sixth Hymn, "Sehnsucht nach dem Tode", bear a resemblance to Wolfram's words of IV ii 30-36. Sibylla's dedication to a love-death recalls the origin and process of the *Hymnen an die Nacht;* her death becomes an act of Magic Idealism without the religious connotations of Novalis's. Her attitude at Wolfram's bier, II ii 45ff., expresses the same sentiments as Novalis's

> Nun weint an keinem Grabe,
> Für Schmerz, wer liebend glaubt.
> Der Liebe süsse Habe
> Wird keinem nicht geraubt . . .

> (Hymn 5)

Novalis's work and the Wolfram-Sibylla sections of **Death's Jest Book** constantly recall one another; several themes and motifs are present in both, though not the Christian faith that informs and transforms the *Hymnen.* Pierce[25] argues persuasively for an affinity with Novalis, if not an actual influence at work, in these scenes, yet his arguments do not shake one's conviction that Beddoes writes more from a personal standpoint, developing in his maturity, which resembles rather the German attitude to love and death than any English tradition. It appears in this case that to imply the influence of the best-known example in German, Novalis's *Hymnen,* falsifies the issue. The love-death theme in Beddoes' work predates his acquaintance with German, and it was a developing theme even then. *The Brides' Tragedy* has it; it is taken up in a fragment of *The Last Man* entitled "Dianeme's Death Scene". This is the metaphysical link with Sibylla's longing for death; elements present in it are developed in the later play to a degree approximating to Novalis's standpoing, with which Beddoes must have been familiar, though any influence could have been at most minimal. A common factor of the two Beddoes scenes is the image of flowers as death's emissaries, and the dying words of Dianeme, lines 50f., find a paler echo in such passages of *Death's Jest Book* as the deleted lines of Sibylla's speech at Wolfram's bier,[26] IV ii 125f., and V iii 52f. Dianeme's images and phrases, "infinity of azure", billowy music", "the world to turn / Within my blue embrace" and in particular the lines beginning, "All hail! I too am an eternity" seem to indicate that Beddoes was already more than capable of writing which shows a marked affinity to that of Novalis and the German Romantics. The obvious explanation can be found in Beddoes' own position as an English Romantic poet, and in his admiration for Shelley, to whose work his own bears a close resemblance at times. Thus any suggestion of actual influence of the *Hymnen an die Nacht* on passages of *Death's Jest Book* would have to be qualified to such an extent that one could only allow an affinity of temperament on a very superficial level, a similarity of treatment in certain portions: that Beddoes had come close enough in the treatment of a poetic theme in his work to show a resemblance to the metaphysical outlook of Novalis. On the other hand, there can be little doubt that the speeches of Isbrand and Ziba discussed above are influenced by Novalis's specific theory of Magic Idealism in its philosophical outline as distinct from its use in the *Hymnen,* the reason for this being that the mystic and transcendental nature of the theory supplied Beddoes with a means to create atmosphere and character at two points in his drama.

Thus far the German influence can be seen to be inconsistent in its effect, emerging in isolated scenes, in a lyric or two, and in a philosophical attitude which forms only a superficial part of Beddoes' vision. The number and nature of Beddoes' borrowings from literary sources cannot be established with any certainty; at one extreme it may be assumed, on his own evidence, that he read everything worth reading, and therefore anything even remotely resembling his own thought may have inspired him: this is Pierce's assumption, and it is patently nonsense. In these matters it is best to take the middle course and evaluate each case on its merits. The results seem to indicate an unsystematic borrowing of the right idea for a particular scene or situation, as would naturally be expected, and each is subordinated to the whole. The German influence does indeed seem to inform the play, particularly if the full realisation of the folly theme is to be attributed to German inspiration, and Beddoes' use of the concept of Romantic Irony, yet to be studied, cannot be underrated.

Notes

1. Letters to Thomas Forbes Kelsall of 4 October 1824, 25 March 1825 and others.

2. See H. W. Donner, *Thomas Lovell Beddoes, the Making of a Poet,* Oxford, 1935, Ch. viii, pp. 212f.

3. *Der Einfluss der deutschen Literatur auf die Englische im 19. Jahrhundert,* Halle/Saale, Niemeyer, 1927, p. 45n.

4. *Thomas Lovell Beddoes, Eccentric and Poet,* New York, Covici-Friede, 1928, pp. 167f.

5. Op. cit., p. 217 and note.

6. Prose appended to verse letter of March 7th.

7. *Philological Quarterly,* Iowa, VI, pp. 123-132.

8. The term is used by Barnette Miller, *Sewannee Review,* Vol. XI, July 1903, p. 331. Cf. also Beddoes' answer to Procter's criticism of the play, letter of April 19th 1829.

9. Op. cit., p. 126, "We are looking for characteristics . . . English models".

10. *The Works of Thomas Lovell Beddoes,* ed. H. W. Donner, Oxford, 1935, Introduction, p. xl.

11. Letter to Procter, April 19th 1829.

12. Op. cit., p. 130.

13. "Did T. L. Beddoes believe in the Origin of the Species", *Modern Philology,* Vol. XXI, 1923, pp. 89-100; p. 99.

14. I. i. 45-87. *Works,* pp. 329-31.

15. Letter to Kelsall [20 April]. Cf. letter of 18 October 1826, and also that of 1 April 1826 in which he states that he is working on Act IV.

16. See *Works,* ed. Donner, pp. 530f.

17. *Works,* p. 535.

18. See C. A. Weber, *Bristols Bedeutung für die deutsch-englische Beziehungen,* Halle/Saale, Niemeyer, 1935, Appendix E.

19. See Bruce Haywood, *Novalis: the Veil of Imagery,* The Hague, Mouton & Co., 1959, especially pp. 9-11 and chapter I. This interpretation restricts the function of Magic Idealism in a way its creator did not intend, but it does raise some interesting points.

20. Cf. Novalis's statement: Wenn ihr die gedanken nicht unmittelbar (und zufällig) vernehmbar machen könnt, so macht doch umgekehrt die äussern Dinge unmittelbar (und willkürlich) vernehmbar—welches ebensoviel ist als: wenn ihr die Gedanken nicht zu äussern Dinge machen könnt, so macht die äussern Dinge zu Gedanken. . . . Beide Operationen sind idealistisch. Wer sie beide vollkommen in seiner Gewalt hat, ist der magische Idealist.

21. Rudolf Haym, *Die Romantische Schule,* Berlin, Weidmannsche Buchhandlung, 1928, pp. 420-1.

22. Introduction to his edition of Beddoes' works, London, Muses Library, 1907.

23. Loc. cit.

24. *Thomas Lovell Beddoes,* p. 234.

25. Op. cit., pp. 127-8.

26. *Works,* p. 399 footnote.

James R. Thompson (essay date 1985)

SOURCE: *"The Brides' Tragedy* and Dramatic Fragments: Jacobean Romantic," in *Thomas Lovell Beddoes,* Twayne, 1985, pp. 24-50.

[*In the following essay, Thompson explores the major themes of* The Brides' Tragedy *as well as several of his incomplete dramas.*]

As we approach an examination of Beddoes's *The Brides' Tragedy* and other dramatic attempts, it will be useful to pause for a brief discussion of the significance of his choice of drama as a vehicle for self-expression, as well as our critical attitudes toward that choice.

"MENTAL THEATRE"

The earliest of Beddoes's reviewers and many critics since have treated *The Brides' Tragedy* and *Death's Jest Book* as drama, either in some abstract, almost Platonic sense or as an example of a neo-Elizabethan or Romantic version of the form. Such an approach is nearly impossible to avoid, despite the quite undramatic sprawl of *Death's Jest Book* and Beddoes's own assertion that *The Brides' Tragedy* was intended "exclusively for the closet" (172). In addition to his two published plays there are the host of dramatic fragments and false starts, his generally strong admiration for playwrights (especially those of the Renaissance), and his own keen observations on the stage.[1] His description of *The Brides' Tragedy* as a work designed to "court the reader in lieu of the spectator" (172), and his insistence in the preface that the glory of contemporary English drama exists in such productions, must be contrasted with his slightly scolding comments in a letter to Kelsall: "You are, I think, disinclined to the stage: now I confess that I think this is the highest aim of the dramatist, & I should be very desirous to get on it. To look down on it is a piece of impertinence as long as one chooses to write in the form of a play, and is generally the result of a consciousness of one's own inability to produce anything striking & affecting in that way" (640). This observation was made not in the first enthusiastic moments of playwriting but in 1829, seven years after *The Brides' Tragedy* had been published and at least one year after the completion of *Death's Jest Book.*

But unlike some Romantics, he actually makes slight distinction between closet drama and the stage; Beddoes would not agree with the American poet and critic Elder Olson in supposing that "everyone would agree that a universal and absolute condition of drama is the possibility of its being *enacted.*"[2] In fact, he would have agreed with Byron, who declared the wish to make a *"regular* English drama, no matter whether for the stage or not, which is not my object,—but a *mental* theatre."[3]

Beddoes and Byron are supported in this matter by modern theorists; Kenneth Burke, for example, calls genres "strategies for living." They are "fundamental ways of thinking about, organizing, and managing the vast, confusing swirl of life."[4] Northrop Frye sees genres as mythoi that shape rather than imitate life. Drama provides a specific "radical of presentation," the rhetorical structure of which in part predetermines significance, since in literature, as in language, form helps determine meaning. Hence if "a Romantic poet gives his poem a dramatic form, he may not expect or even want any stage representation; he may think entirely in terms of print and readers; he may even believe, like many Romantics, that the stage drama is an impure form because of the limitations it puts on individual expression. Yet the poem is still being referred back to some kind of theatre, however much of a castle in the air."[5]

Our realization of the significance of generic choice—even in the use of closet drama—is therefore an essential justification for considering Beddoes's work as drama, however unsuccessfully it may fulfill such obligations of that form as plot and characterization. Yet the problem of generic choice is for Beddoes, as for other Romantics, too complicated for the theory of genre alone to resolve. In the first place, the nature of generic determination does not, in itself, explain why the form was chosen. Equally important, the theory accounts for a general set of circumstances surrounding the work's significance; it must be made to take into account the relationship between the specific sensibility and the form.

We may start with the second issue as a means of returning to the first. Drama is, or traditionally was, a most objective form. The innumerable and unsuccessful attempts to get to the man behind Shakespeare's plays epitomize simultaneously the aesthetic distance found in drama and the common assumption that playwright and audience share values. Yet Romantic poets both wished to and were forced to explore the personal nature of truth, and the meditative lyric—that most private of public forms—was for them its chief expression. Terry Otten, in words especially relevant to Beddoes, puts one resulting difficulty perfectly: "Adopting Elizabethan dramaturgy to express modern subjective matter was too much like grafting an alien myth onto a new vision. The modern concern with the individual and the internal 'dialogue of the mind with itself' worked at odds with a communal drama directed to a homogeneous body of believers."[6]

Yet Beddoes, Shelley, and other Romantics (the significant exception was Byron) did attempt to embody in Elizabethan dramaturgy a truth the grounds of which were clearly subjective.

Much modern poetry, indeed much poetry generally, has been classified by Robert Langbaum[7] as "the poetry of experience"—that is, a poetry that does not assert propositional truth but rather explores it, does not prescribe reality but describes it. This is a poetry of process; it reflects the poet's mind in search of the significance of its own experience. Why then, in an age when such poetry emerged from the chaos of fragmented values and discredited mythologies, did Beddoes—and Byron, for that matter—elect the drama at all? The answer would appear to be found in the question; in many subtle personal ways as well as in broadly cultural ones, traditional drama had once reflected the very cosmic and cultural stability that was missing. In other words, the genre could suggest the very *shape* of value—a form historically associated with the testing of social norms or public myths, and with a celebration of their endurance. In this sense both tragedy and comedy had worked together to dramatize and endorse those values. Hence the more that modern culture disintegrated and writers like Beddoes imaginatively experienced that disintegration, the more nostalgia they felt for a form that seemed to receive its license from a permanently organized universe, a universe that reflected its organization in its cultural artifacts.

It is unlikely that Beddoes was aware of the ironical nature of his own commitment to the form; though he understood his failure in conventional terms he does not seem consciously to have recognized the retrospective longing in his choice. But this schizophrenia of personal experience and public form leads to the paradox of Beddoes's drama. The subjective material is forced into objective form, and whatever his self-awareness, the tension produced helps to account for the unusual energy and character of *Death's Jest Book*. Beddoes's contemporary George Darley, a poet and critic, was fully aware of the problem: "Subjective composition is however the natural tendency of our refined age, and on this postulate founds itself an argument I fear convincing against the probable regeneration of Acting Drama. Can we restrain that tendency? or *should* we, if we could? Though fatal to the drama, it may be vital to something else as desirable."[8] The poetry of experience was vital to Beddoes's self-expression; and though not fatal to the drama, it demands a special awareness on the part of the reader.

If Beddoes failed to understand the deeper implications of his choice, his judgment of the contemporary theater was nonetheless acute. Like other Romantics unable to escape the enormous pull of Shakespeare—"he was an incarnation of nature . . . he was an universe" (581)—Beddoes was all the same aware of the dangers of emulation. Only three years after *The Brides' Tragedy* was published and in the year he began *Death's Jest Book* (1825), Beddoes made a statement rare for its combination of good sense and overpowering self-irony:

> Say what you will—I am convinced the man who is to awaken the drama must be a bold trampling fellow—no creeper into worm-holes—no reviser even—however good. These reanimations are vampire-cold. Such ghosts as Marloe, Webster &c are better dramatists, better poets, I dare say, than any contemporary of ours—but they are ghosts—the worm is in their pages—& we want to see something that our great-grandsires did not know. With the greatest reverence for all the antiquities of the drama, I still think that we had better beget than revive—attempt to give the literature of this age an idiosyncrasy & spirit of its own; & only raise a ghost to gaze on, not to live with—just now the drama is a haunted ruin.

(595)

Byron, too, recognized the error in "following the old dramatists." For him, however, the danger results from the Elizabethan ignorance of classical regularity; he chastised Shelley for using "our old dramatists *as models*." He goes so far as to deny "that the English have hitherto had a drama at all."[9] Beddoes, for some curious reason, thought that *The Cenci* had been inspired by the Greeks and lamented that Shelley had not chosen Shakespeare "as his model" (578). It goes without saying that numerous critics and historians of the drama have seized upon Beddoes's "reanimation" argument as an example of Romantic myopia, which, of course, it is.[10] Yet Beddoes was compelled to the drama because he believed deeply that it "ought to be the most distinguished department of our poetic literature" (624), and drawn equally to the late Elizabethans because they provided an ambience perfectly suited to his own sense of a world become sick, evil, and decayed. It is obvious that for Beddoes the Elizabethans and Jacobeans were the drama.

Beddoes's relationship to the drama is important, then, more in its broad configuration than in its specific nature. A study of his plays on purely technical grounds will take us little beyond the long-since established indictment of Romantic failure in that genre. On the other hand, the assumption that the choice of closet drama was merely superficial ignores the deeper meaning in such a decision, as well as its significance for interpretation. Failures of plot construction and character development do not remove the importance to be found in the identification of genre with myth and vision; it is in this larger sense that we should view Beddoes as a playwright.

"A VERY SAD BOYISH AFFAIR"

As he did almost all his other work, Beddoes eventually repudiated *The Brides' Tragedy* (637). Written when he was nineteen, the play certainly has a "boyish" quality; yet despite its excesses, the work is much more than juvenilia. The play is to Beddoes what *Endymion* was to Keats—both a necessary act of apprenticeship designed to marshal and mature his poetic talent and the first real articulation of his personal vision. There are signs here of his own characteristic grotesque; during the vicious storm in which Hesperus murders Floribel the "Night with giant strides stalks o'er the world, / Like a swart Cyclops, on its hideous front / One round, red, thunderswollen eye ablaze" (204). And when the protagonist finds death in the bottom of his cup—"the sugar of the draught"—we catch the characteristic sound of the later Beddoes (208).

The plot, attacked by some critics for being too loose and by others for being too academic, is consciously designed with the actual stage in mind, yet unconsciously burdened with non-dramatic intentions. It was clearly planned to observe the dramatic unities, the events occurring in a severely limited period of time and an equally restricted area of action.

Act 1 opens with a private garden meeting of Hesperus, a young nobleman, and Floribel, his secretly married wife. Although theoretically it is a joyous occasion, an ominous tone of "fickleness, and woe, and mad despair" (177) creeps in with Floribel's reported dream and with the song "Poor old pilgrim Misery." Scene 2 reveals Orlando, another young nobleman, plotting to force Hesperus to marry his sister Olivia, so that he himself can marry the supposedly unwed Floribel. In order to "scare a rival and to gain a brother" (178) Orlando has had Hesperus's elderly and impoverished father arrested for debt; if Hesperus will agree to the wedding, Orlando will end this "show of cruelty" by freeing Lord Ernest and canceling his debt (178). In scene 3 Hesperus's father is discovered in prison, outwardly brave but ready to plead with Hesperus to comply. In the face of Lord Ernest's pathos Hesperus finds it impossible to explain his dilemma and agrees to the second marriage.

In Act 2, after an interval in scene 1 where we see Orlando with his page boy, the action shifts to the cottage of Mordred and Lenora, Floribel's high-born but impoverished parents. Floribel, ignorant of his problem, teases Hesperus. Faced with his lovely and much-loved bride, Hesperus mutters, "why let the old man die" (188), referring to Lord Ernest's prediction of his own destruction, should Hesperus fail to save him by marriage to Olivia. He leaves but returns to find Floribel giving Orlando's page an innocent kiss, having actually first torn up Orlando's letter of proposal. Hesperus, convinced she is unfaithful, repudiates her. Scene 3 finds him back in Orlando's palace, where he woos and wins Olivia, promising her true love only in the grave, however. Left alone by the troubled but acquiescent Olivia, Hesperus implies a threat to murder Floribel. Scenes 4 and 5, also located in the palace, show us first a tormented Hesperus waking from a terrible dream and fighting the desire to murder Floribel and then the troubled realization of Hesperus's deranged behavior by Lord

Ernest, Orlando, Olivia, and Claudio. The concluding scene in this act occurs at a suicide's grave; first Orlando and Claudio speculate on a "self-slaughtered" parricide and then, after their departure, Hesperus soliloquizes at this "shrine of blood' (198,199), pledging himself to evil.

The five scenes in act 3 take place in Orlando's palace, Mordred and Lenora's cottage, and a dark wood. While Hesperus sits in a deep trance in the palace, Floribel broods at home on his strange behavior and gives voice to her premonition. During a terrible storm in a wood, Hesperus meets Floribel and stabs her to death. Hunters see him burying something and, as he leaves to seek his "second bride," they linger on to discover his "hoard." In the palace we witness Olivia's sentimental farewell to her maids. This pleasant interlude is immediately followed by a grim scene in Mordred's cottage. Just when Lenora has informed Mordred that his last wish—for Floribel to marry well—has been fulfilled, the hunters enter with Floribel's body. The already feeble Mordred dies of grief and shock.

Act 4 opens with a deeply agitated Hesperus—now far gone in evil—vowing to kill a servant whom he suspects of knowing his secret. He has fixed on Olivia as his only salvation. In scene 2 Floribel's murder is reported to the duke, who, since Hesperus has left his easily recognized dagger in her grave, orders his immediate arrest. We next observe a banquet hall in Orlando's palace, where, before the mystery of Hesperus's strange behavior can be cleared up, officers come to arrest him. The act's final scene takes place in the street before the duke's palace; we first see guards, Floribel's body, and Lenora. When this group leaves, Hesperus, his father, and Orlando arrive. The act concludes with Hesperus hoping that Olivia might not also die, since "there are enough accusers in the tomb" (225).

Like acts 1 and 4, act 5 is short. The remaining four scenes in the play take place at Mordred's cottage (where Lenora, now also deranged, believes Floribel to be only asleep), at the ducal prison, at Orlando's palace, and at the place of Hesperus's intended execution. In prison we find Hesperus condemned to die for the murder, deeply confused about death and guilt. Lenora enters and begins to curse a Hesperus now beset by "Remorse and Conscience" (227). But because Floribel has loved him and he her, Lenora extends to him her disturbed sympathy. After Olivia prepares for death in scene 3, the play concludes in a scene set at the place of execution. Hesperus, now calm and contrite, is reconciled with his father. Just before he is executed, Lenora saves him from the ax with the perfume of poisoned flowers. He dies in an agonized vision of murder coming at him with "fiery fangs."

"DARK THOUGHTS"

One death from grief and another inevitable; two suicides; one murder—what are we to make of this body-strewn play written by a young man not yet twenty? Both Beddoes's peers and reviewers, as well as his early modern critics, thought that they had the answer. He was, in the best-known statement of this argument, "the last Elizabe-than." When Lytton Strachey[11] made this claim in 1907 it summarized a long-standing opinion; since then it has been frequently repeated. It is difficult to argue with several generations of critics.

Nor, up to a point, should we. Strachey, Donner, and D. W. Goode[12]—to name but three—have carefully studied and noted the parallels between Renaissance drama, especially later versions, and Beddoes's work; these critics differ mainly in their judgment of his success. Certainly a subject so thoroughly covered needs no detailed analysis here. Moreover, even the casual reader of Renaissance drama will recognize the characters, situations, and even language distinctive to that great period of English theater. Already as a schoolboy Beddoes had been immersed in the genre; like that of earlier Romantics his admiration for these playwrights was unbounded. Even his beloved Shelley, he thought, had too little followed Shakespeare "as his model" in *The Cenci*; close knowledge of Shakespeare and the Elizabethans was, he felt, essential for any dramatist (578).

But Beddoes's saturation in Elizabethan drama and the resulting evidence in his work should not cause us to substitute study of influence for study of specific plays. When Allardyce Nicoll in his history of the English stage dismisses *The Brides' Tragedy* as simply "dark thoughts culled from Jacobean drama,"[13] he misses the point completely. Beddoes's claim that "reanimations are vampire-cold" (595) is completely serious; the irony should not blind us to the two essential characteristics of Beddoes's work that develop in this period. First, he is no mere imitator as in "The Improvisatore," but rather feels a deep, imaginative affinity with these great predecessors in horror; in the Renaissance sense of the word he "possesses" these works. Second, *The Brides' Tragedy* illustrates how completely he has absorbed and modified the Romanticism of his age. The real significance of the play, despite its remarkable exploitation of Renaissance drama and its surprisingly successful blank verse, is its peculiar embodiment of late Romantic pessimism and preoccupation with death—in image, symbol, and theme.

There is, moreover, the question of source as opposed to influence. If influence accounts, at least superficially, for Beddoes's treatment of his source, the source itself is not Renaissance drama. In his preface Beddoes claims his play to be "founded upon facts" (172) and cites the ballad "Lucy" by Thomas Gillet, published in *The Midland Minstreal* (1822). This poem, and a slightly different prose version that Beddoes also employed, tell the supposedly true story, set in the early eighteenth century, of the secret marriage of a well-bred Oxford student to a college servant's daughter and his later murder of the girl when a better match presents itself.[14] As we will see, Beddoes alters the story significantly, not only by completely changing the context but, more importantly, by providing the murderer with a very different motive. Although Donner attributes these changes to a sort of Romantic reflex ac-

tion, Beddoes's alterations of the source of *The Brides' Tragedy* reflect—as does his special use of generic influences—the personal, if confused, nature of his theme.

And confused the play is, despite the relentless, even mechanical, logic of Hesperus's destruction of others and himself, suggested by the plot summary given earlier. Behind the bewildering though exciting mixture of melodrama, eloquence, and sentimentality, underneath the variety of motives for the murder, lies Beddoes's own ambivalence concerning death—one from which only death could free him. But since it is the theme of the play, not its action, that concerns him, and since that theme is connected with states of mind, the usual objections to the flawed dramaturgy or to a distorted reality produced by that dramaturgy have little significance. The action, in other words, is metaphorical, not sociohistorical. The work "dramatizes," in the largest sense, Beddoes's spiritual, and hence aesthetic, predicament; the choice of drama provides an occasion for poetic eloquence and a reassuring, traditionally significant container for a radically pessimistic vision, yet resolution is not possible. In other words, the form offered Beddoes what the ballad offered Coleridge in "The Ancient Mariner," a precious moment of closure so essential to the artist if he is to go on creating. However forced and tentative that closure was, he was never to achieve it again. For finally, the "dark thoughts" were Beddoes's own, not Jacobean, and the play looks as much toward the modern theater of the absurd as it recalls the Renaissance.

EROS AND THANATOS

The Brides' Tragedy is not a fully mature piece and we must not judge Beddoes by this work alone, even though it is his only technically complete play. However, both stylistically and thematically we have come much closer here to the view of life in Beddoes's major work. Although the deaths here may appear to be of the essentially Jacobean variety, Beddoes's peculiar obsession with all of its manifestations points ahead to *Death's Jest Book* and the late lyrics. But more specifically, the love story takes a characteristically ominous turn. Hesperus kills Floribel, his secret wife and first love; he then offers the alternate bride a consummation in death: "for when our souls are born then will we wed; / Our dust shall mix and grow into one stalk" (193). The metaphor of birth is neither ironic nor simply rhetorical. "Death's darts are sometimes Love's" (490), Beddoes will later argue; Thanatos and Eros join in all his major poetry and this identification becomes a central theme in *Death's Jest Book.* It is in the exploration of this theme that modern criticism most significantly alters and improves earlier studies of the poet.

The association of love and death can of course be found elsewhere in Romantic literature. Eric Bentley, commenting upon the Romantic element in Strindberg's plays, points out that the Romantic "rediscovered *eros* and *agape* precisely by rediscovering their ambivalence. It is the ambivalence of *eros* in Goethe's *Werther* that made the book at once a great scandal and a great event. Any eighteenth-century hack might have rhapsodized about passion; it was the closeness of passion and death, of creative love and its contrary, that Goethe put his finger on."[15]

The English Romantics also touched on this theme. A classic example is John Clare's "An Invite to Eternity." Here the woman is invited by her lover to pass through "night and dark obscurity" to the ideal world beyond: "Say maiden can thy life be led / To join the living with the dead / Then trace thy footsteps on with me / We'er wed to one eternity." In Shelley the apotheosis of love leads essentially to its destruction in the transcendent but static state. For Keats the woman can be the demon lover, as "La Belle Dame Sans Merci" suggests; in a similar way love is distorted or destroyed in Coleridge's "Christabel." Even in the satiric-comic mode of Byron's "Beppo" the lovers' gondola is likened to a coffin. More surprising yet are Wordsworth's "Lucy poems," each a testament to love and death. With Poe, of course, the identification is frequently dramatized, as for example in "The Fall of the House of Usher."

In Beddoes, who like Poe is a late Romantic, the theme is more central and more overt than in other English poets. In the source of *The Brides' Tragedy,* for example, the murder is purely social in origin. In the ballad "Lucy" the student is inspired by "ambition" (709) and in the *Oxford Herald* version, after meeting an aristocratic young woman, the student again returns to Lucy but now views her "only as a bar to his ambition" (711). In the original, therefore, the story is an early version of *An American Tragedy.* But Beddoes rejects that motive, overtly at least, for three others: Hersperus must escape his first marriage in order to save his father; he is jealous of Floribel after seeing her kiss a page; and he suffers periodic madness. One of the conventional dramatic weaknesses of the play is the confusion these three motives produce. But the murder is actually symbolic; its significance is not to be found in plot. Hence Beddoes's argument in the preface that the play dramatizes the "contest of duties and desires" (173) inherent in Hesperus's situation represents his conscious intention (and certainly dramatic tradition) but not the play's real conflict—the clash between conventional human norms and the deeply felt sense that only in death can love be realized.

While avoiding the intentional fallacy we can yet recognize the determined manner in which Beddoes's vision leads him from the middle-class, domestic tragedy of his source to a frightening study of the demon lover, a study that makes itself felt far more significantly on the symbolic rather than the narrative level. And nowhere is that determination more pronounced than in the play's first scene. Its dramatic logic is clear; at once we recognize the fragility of the relationship between Floribel and Hesperus. They love each other deeply, and have married for love, despite the threat of displeasure by Hesperus's "austere and old . . . sire" (176). But there is no hint of a

solution given; Hesperus lacks the will to devise their escape. And for all her love for Hesperus, Floribel cannot overcome the dismay she feels at her "sad and lonely fate / Thus to be wed to secrecy"; on her husband's face she sees only the "blank and ugly vizor of concealment" (175).

Moreover, the scene opens in growing darkness and takes place in a closed "bower of Eglantine" where "not a spark of prying light creeps in, / So closely do the sweets enfold each other" (174). This delightful privacy of love gives way to images of imprisonment, secrecy, and concealment, especially with the "tale of blood" (174) Hesperus chooses to tell Floribel. At first the story appears perfectly gratuitous, quite unnecessary to the dramatic action, and to be used simply as an excuse for Beddoes to indulge in "poesy" and Greek myth. The story tells how Zephyrus (ominously associated with the West) "once found / The baby Perfume cradled in a violet" and how after he had "bound the sweet slumberer with golden chains," he cast the "fettered wretch" into "the bosom of a rose." There the helpless child's "heart's blood stained" the flower, giving it its traditional color (175). Floribel, who in a lovely Keatsian passage has been previously associated with her gift to Hesperus, the "blue violet, like Pandora's eye, / When first it darkened with immortal life" (174), fails to see the story's meaning. But the reader—though probably not the theater audience—recognizes the tale for what it is, a rather Blakean parable of entrapment and death. Frye points out that Floribel, the "veiled Moon's . . . loveliest nymph" (174), is not a Diana as we might expect, but a Proserpine.[16]

Before the scene ends Floribel tells Hesperus of a waking dream she has had, a dream that starts in her world of passive, floral beauty and ends when one "who with wet downcast eyelids threw aside / The remnants of a broken heart" bid her be "'ware of love, / Of fickleness, and woe, and mad despair" (177). Hesperus's response is to sing her a song, "Poor old pilgrim Misery," and to promise—in words now inescapably ominous—that they would soon meet "to part never more" (178). The scene, at first glance appearing cluttered and unsure, has established far more than a vague sense of apprehension appropriate to the play's future action; it has presented and developed the tone and imagery of the Eros-Thanatos theme so central to the entire work.

"Now for My Second Bride"

By the end of the first act any possible solution is gone. Hesperus can murmur, "wed / Olivia; there's damnation in the thought" (181) but he cannot bring himself to tell his father why marriage is impossible. Lord Ernest, whom critics fail to recognize as well drawn, is lost in self-pity; he cannot see the terrible effect his plea has on Hesperus. The latter, an essentially passive character, from this point on can only react. His deep pessimism springs from the frustration of impotence and a profound sense of the world gone wrong:

Why are we tied unto this wheeling globe,
Still to be racked while traitorous Hope stands by,

And heals the wounds that they may gape again?
Aye to this end the earth is made a ball,
Else crawling to brink despair would plunge
Into the infinite eternal air,
And leave its sorrows and its sins behind.

(183)

This sentiment may seem exaggerated, given his predicament and its apparent solution. But Beddoes makes Hesperus flawed, if not already spiritually defeated, from the start; other characters hint at some strangeness always recognized in him (186, 188). Moreover, the play's first scene indicates that love, the single redemptive force the work offers, can succeed only when hidden outside life. In a scene effectively juxtaposed to the grim one that precedes it, the conventional Orlando can speculate that "the universe's soul . . . is Love" (185), but for Hesperus love means death. Hence his murder of Floribel is a kind of consummation, or would have been had he joined her. Instead, coerced by his father and Orlando, he lives to woo Olivia. The lovemaking is both extraordinary and sudden. Olivia, long in love with Hesperus, ignores the suddenness and, though troubled by his strange appeal, yields.

In some of the play's strangest lines, Hesperus defines the nature of their mutual realization:

Then thou shalt be mine own; but not till death.
We'll let this life burn out, no matter how;
For when our souls are born then will we wed;
Our dust shall mix and grow into one stalk,
Our breaths shall make one perfume in one bud,
Our blushes meet each other in a rose,
Our sweeter voices swell some sky-bird's throat
With the same warbling, dwell in some soft pipe,
Or bubble up along some sainted spring's
Musical course, and in the mountain trees
Slumber our deeper tones, by tempests waked:
We will be music, spring, and all fair things
The while our spirits make a sweeter union
Than melody and perfume in the air.
Wait then, if thou dost love me.

(192-93)

Something in this passage reminds us of John Donne—for instance the line "our dust shall mix." But we are actually much closer to Shelley; the "sweeter union," like other hints of consummation in the play, is sexless. Hesperus celebrates the briefest passage of time, for it will bring their union closer: "Joy, my love, / We're nearer to our bridal sheets of lead / Than when your brother left us here just now" (193). However, Beddoes gives no indication as to how death can be more than an escape into stasis. Olivia, essentially more spiritually healthy than Hesperus, knows that "it is not good / Thus to spurn life," but asks, "what's to live without my Hesperus? . . . I'll be nothing rather" (194). It is Hesperus himself who, despite his conviction of death's release, asks the obvious, though unanswerable, question:

And do those cherries ripen for the worms,
Those blue enchantments beam to light the tomb?

Was that articulate harmony, (Love uses
Because he seems both Love and Innocence
When he sings to it,) that summer of sweet breath
Created but to perish and so make
The deads' home loveliest?

(194)

But Beddoes has no answer.

The entire issue remains unclear. Floribel's mother, Lenora, recognizing the "loathed blessing of a cursed existence," asks "where thinkest our spirits go?" A minor character can answer only with pretty rumor:

Madam, I know not;
Some say they hang like music in the air,
Some that they lie ingirt by cloudy curtains;
Or 'mong the stars.

(222)

In a similar way Olivia's maid, facing the impending death of her mistress, hopes to persuade herself that this "intercourse / Of disembodied minds is no conjecture, / No fiction of romance" (231). Overwrought by Floribel's murder Lenora must "search about for Comfort," and though others may call him death, "Comfort is his name" (223).

In the play's final act Olivia can sincerely repudiate man's conventional fear and horror at the thought of dying:

Death! thou silly girl,
There's no such thing; 'tis but a goblin word,
Which bad men conjure from their reeking sins
To haunt their slumbers; 'tis a life indeed.

(230)

But exactly what kind of "life"? At first it appears to be vaguely Christian, and that is the sentiment Olivia no doubt wishes to convey:

These bodies are the vile and drossy seeds,
Whence, placed again within their kindred earth,
Springs Immortality, the glorious plant
Branching above the skies. What is there here
To shrink from?

(230)

However, death immediately becomes not a door to immortality but a welcome oblivion:

Though your idle legends tell
How cruelly he treats the prostrate world;
Yet, unto me this shadowy potentate
Comes soft and soothing as an infant's sleep,
And kisses out my being.

(230)

The "shadow potentate" who, in that marvelous clause "kisses out my being," is Eros-Thanatos—the gods of love and death become one. The imagery, and hence the implication, is even clearer in Floribel's speech in the third act:

> Come so to me, sweet death, and I will wreath thee
> An amorous chaplet for thy paly brows;
> And on an odoured bank of wan white buds
> In thy fair arms
> I'll lie, and taste thy cool delicious, breath,
> And sleep, and sleep, and sleep.
>
> (202)

Again the erotic becomes the static; love-as-death is not sexual passion, not ecstasy—only relief. At least in *The Brides' Tragedy,* love is not, as one critic has argued, "the force that keeps death from being the end."[17] Rather, the lover has, to use Keats's words, to its "high requiem become a sod."

Near the play's conclusion Hesperus, demon wooer of both women, admits that all he knows of death is "that 'twill come" (232). Perhaps "our minds share not corporeal sleep, / But go among the past and future," or possibly "inspire another [life] in some waking world" only to die yet again (233). But unlike other characters Hesperus is a murderer; beset by the "hounds of Lucifer" he feels "Remorse and Conscience too" (227). Although his final lines exhibit some of the spirit of Bryon's Manfred, who, though dying, can still repudiate external control, the ending more nearly reminds us of *Dr. Faustus.* Hesperus now associates death with punishment, although the play, only vaguely Christian, is ambiguous in this regard. Life may be our "ailment," as he earlier argues, but at least for Hesperus death is no cure. And if some cosmic law finally claims him, even a static consummation of love in death is impossible.

Eleanor Wilner, in her interesting analysis of Hesperus, extends the love-death theme considerably. Recognizing the extremely passive nature of Beddoes's women, she sees Hesperus's murder of Floribel as a perversely self-saving act; wishing to live himself he seduces others to death. "The killing of Floribel is the killing of tenderness in himself," a tenderness he "seems to equate with a passive and helpless femininity." For Wilner, death in Beddoes's world is a "purely male force."[18] Critics have long noted the passive nature of his female characters, it is true, and not only does Hesperus murder Floribel, he also brings about the deaths of her mother and, inevitably, Olivia. Yet Wilner's argument presumes a far more active Hesperus than the play offers us. He actually shares the female passivity; action is thrust upon him and he reacts in desperation to the ever-tightening trap that is his life. If, as Wilner implies, he defines life through death, then he does so with no sense of possible escape. As evidence for her view she cites his final words—"I'm not dead yet." But like his entire final speech, this line suggests a theatrical, rather than an actual, assertion of will.

But if we reject Wilner's contention that murder for Hesperus dramatizes a perverse version of Romantic individu-alism, we cannot so easily dismiss the opposite idea. The Romantic longing for fusion with the infinite may, as in the case of Shelley's "Adonais," take the form of a death wish. Certainly the death wish is frequently encountered in Beddoes's poetry, and we are reminded again and again that such a wish proved to be more than literary for him. But in Shelley death fractures life, which, "like a dome of many-colored glass / Stains the white radiance of Eternity." Therefore one does not merely "seek shelter in the shadow of the tomb"; rather one seeks to join with what Wordsworth calls the "active universe."[19] In *The Brides' Tragedy* death is simply the great void, and it brings nonbeing, not non-identity.

We have earlier discussed the generic considerations in Beddoes' work; a word must yet be said concerning its designation as tragedy. In his preface to the play Beddoes defines its theme as the "contest of duties and desires" (173). Nine years later in 1831 he defines the "pivot of all tragedy" as the "struggle between the will of man and the moral law of necessity, who awaits inevitably his past actions" (651), actually an elaboration of his earlier comment on the play.

Essentially, then, Beddoes articulates one version of the classic definition. But while it is possible that some Romantic dramas approach tragedy in this sense, it is clear that *The Brides' Tragedy* does not. The play fails to dramatize the conflict between free will and necessity; Hesperus is a passive, emotionally disoriented (although not insane, as other characters and some critics assume) spiritual bankrupt whose only solution is to negate life. Hence the play cannot validate human strength and dignity, as various kinds of Western tragedies do; rather, it forces us to recognize the already "dark and troubled" vision of its young author.[20] The Romantics, and Beddoes was no exception, often associated tragedy with pathos, melo-drama, or simply "serious" drama. But beneath the convention lurks Beddoes's deep, if as yet latent, pessimism.

DRAMATIC FRAGMENTS: "THIS ARABY OF WORDS"

During the three years following the publication of *The Brides' Tragedy* in 1822, Beddoes behaved like a developing dramatist, not like a future medical student and man of science. He produced numerous dramatic fragments, including major portions of two plays, and his letters frequently contain discussions of contemporary and Renaissance drama.[21] His letters (and the earliest extant come from this period) make numerous reference to "a hopeless confusion of new 'first acts,'" as one critic has complained.[22] The release and encouragement produced by the publication of *The Brides' Tragedy* made possible a rich creative period, especially when one considers his active role as a student, his trip to Italy, and his preparations for Germany. Concerning these dramatic projects he was characteristically self-effacing, but his enthusiasm is clear.[23]

Not surprisingly, these "plays" provide a kind of microcosm of Beddoes's career: they are largely fragmentary, they offer extrinsic interest as well as intrinsic value, and they vary widely in quality. Taken as a whole they show Beddoes groping inevitably—although at times almost blindly—toward the gigantic *Death's Jest Book.* In addition to some lyrics to which we will return in chapter 5, the group consists of four clusters of increasingly longer and more coherent works. *The Last Man* (1823-25) involves fragments only, tantalizing though some of them are. *Love's Arrow Poisoned* (1823-25), except for some fragments, exists in a short prose draft. *Torrismond* (1824) consists of one very full first act. Finally, *The Second Brother* (1824-25) is finished through three acts and part of a fourth; it also includes fragments.

As it exists, *Love's Arrow Poisoned* is only a collection of materials for a play: lines, speeches, and images. No plot can be discerned, but the work was apparently meant to include apparent incest, attempted regicide, the personal conflict of father and son, mistaken identity, revenge, and suicide. It would have involved "struggles of fear, remorse & ambition" (521), Beddoes tells us. Character types and names appear which will reappear in later fragments and in *Death's Jest Book,* especially the sinister Ziba, "born in an old ruined century / Three or four doors above the one we live in" (255). By the second fragment it is clear that, as in *The Brides' Tragedy,* love can be realized only in death, "for not externally this love can live, / But in the soul" since "the bower I spoke of is in Paradise" (254, 257). In both style and vision Beddoes has moved beyond *The Brides' Tragedy.* This globe has become a "fat, unwholesome star, / The bald fool-planet, that has men upon it, / And they nickname it 'world' . . . this humpy bastard of the sun" (261). The man who inhabits this star was created by the faultfinder, the satirist of the universe:

> Dost know
> That Momus picked a burnt-out comet up
> From Vulcan's floor, and stuck a man upon it;
> Then, having laught, he flung the wick away,
> And let the insect feed on planet oil:—
> What was't? Man and his ball.
>
> (261)

These lines spoken by Erminia generally represent the satiric tone of the work and specifically establish, in the final fragment, an attack on a nature—"hell-wombed witch"—the very antithesis of Wordsworth's (263).

In the one completed act of *Torrismond* a son is repudiated by his stern father, setting the son's mind on death and power. Torrismond, "whose veins are stretched by passion's hottest wine" and who "ranges and riots headlong through the world" (268), appears to his father as only a vicious wastrel. Yet like Prince Hal he loves his father, and riots only that he might quell his longing for some redeeming love. Far from being debauched, Torrismond is "not at home / In this December world, with men of ice, / Cold sirs and madams" (271). Like one of Byron's heroes he knows the "curse / Of being for a little world too great, / Demanding more than nature has to

give." In the central scene of the piece Torrismond meets Veronica in a secluded, moonlit garden, and discovers her deep and idealized love for him. Since he suddenly recognizes his own love in return, redemption should follow. But as in *The Brides' Tragedy,* love seems to thrive only in the "azure secrecy of night" (277), and at any rate Melchior, a courtier nursing some ambiguous wrong, poisons his father against him. All crises in Beddoes's work end in death; the break between father and son leaves Torrismond "cool as an ice-drop in a dead man's eye, / For winter is the season of the tomb, / And that's my country now" (282). The wish to be unborn—a frequent motif in all of Beddoes's major work—is Torrismond's response to his father's distorted view of his character:

> Tear all my life out of the universe,
> Take off my youth, unwrap me of my years,
> And hunt me up the dark and broken past
> Into my mother's womb; there unbeget me;
> For 'till I'm in thy veins and unbegun,
> Or to the food returned which made the blood
> That did make me, no possible lie can ever
> Unroot my feet to thee.
>
> (283)

If he could but "die to the root" he could deny all validity of life. For a spiritual exile like Torrismond, the "mighty labour is to die," but in dying "we'll drive in a chariot to our graves, / Wheel'd with big thunder, o'er the heads of men" (283). The act ends with Torrismond's negative will to power.

For Donner, *Torrismond* is essentially complete in one act; "as it stands, it conforms with the Aristotelian canon."[24] He also notes the major improvements in characterization, in dialogue, and in poetry: "phrasing, diction, and blank verse alike mark the formation of the mature style."[25] Indeed, he praises the work extravagantly, invoking Aeschylus and arguing that the garden scene has "all the grace and artifice of a tune by Mozart."[26] Unquestionably *Torrismond* is, even unfinished, an improvement in its particulars over *The Brides' Tragedy.* But it is not finished—only stopped—and there is no hint as to how the plot could be resolved.

The Second Brother, longest of these experiments, succeeds no better—despite the bulk. It grinds to a halt just as a grave-digging scene commences; even Shakespeare-as-muse cannot push the play beyond its wormy impasse. Here Torrismond has matured into Orazio, and the father-son conflict has become a conflict between brothers. The new situation retains the sense of tragic waste in familial struggles, and widens the political theme only latent in *Torrismond.* Orazio, the brother of the ruling Duke of Ferrara, is like Torrismond a pleasure-seeker, even a sybarite. And like the earlier protagonist, he is more than that. But he has put aside Valeria, his loving wife, and slipped into deep self-gratification; he is a failed Torrismond. He calls himself the "Lord of Love" (287), but he identifies even more strongly with Dionysus. We first see him coming through the street

Wrapt like Bacchus, in the hide
Of a specked panther, with his dancing nymphs,
And torches bright and many, as his slaves
Had gathered up the fragments of the sun
That fell just now. Hark! here his music comes.

(286)

The description is no accident:

From tower and hill, by trump and cannon's voice,
Have I proclaimed myself a deity's son:
Not Alexander's father, Ammon old,
But ivied Bacchus do I call my sire.
Hymn it once more.

(286)

His taste and behavior remind us of Byron's protagonist in *Sardanapalus*; like him he seems to hide much behind his apparently single-minded commitment to pleasure.

As the play begins Marcello, the long-absent second brother of the duke and his heir apparent, returns unrecognized to Ferrara. He thrusts himself in front of Orazio's procession; the meeting, as one critic has put it, "is in the tonality of death confronting life, the skeleton or death's head at the scene of festivity."[27] Marcello demands alms as the beggar he appears to be. Orazio, however, not only denies his appeal but—recoiling instinctively—utters a repudiation of the missing brother: "I would deny, outswear, and overreach, / And pass him with contempt, as I do you" (289). This gratuitous insult sets in motion the play's action. As Orazio banquets with his followers, his long-abandoned wife, Valeria (a married version of Torrismond's Veronica), enters and is reunited with her husband. At the very moment when his empty life is redeemed through the renewal of his love and the requital of hers, Valeria's father—and his creditor—comes to turn him out of his palace and rob him of his wife. He learns that his brother the duke has died and that Marcello, still in rags, has assumed the throne.

All of this happens in the first crowded act. The remaining two acts show the development of Marcello's revenge and his transformation into the tyrant who becomes death-as-sovereign. Orazio is imprisoned, Ferrara's other nobles are spurned, and the stage is set for some kind of gothic confrontation in the cathedral vault at midnight.

The macabre scene that was to have followed is only vaguely implied; it probably would have included murder and a faked resurrection of Valeria, who Orazio has been led to believe is dead. But it is difficult to see how Beddoes could have completed the play. Three acts have brought us only to the point at which the one act of *Torrismond* ended, essentially to Marcello's argument that "Death is the one condition of our life" (313). As projected, the vault scene could mean nothing to Beddoes; for though the pretended victory over death might fool Orazio, it could never fool the author. If imagination were to provide an answer to the eternal question of death, the answer had to be convincing.

There is a rather frenzied quality about the piece, suggesting Beddoes's lack of sureness about his materials and his theme. And while the power of language and poetry in *Torrismond* is extended, the dramatic "realism" of that work is starting to be displaced by Gothic distortion of situations and speech. This distortion is not simply the result of literary imitation (as it is in his juvenilia) but rather a sign of what is for him the breakdown of the barriers between life and death, a breakdown that will affect the character of *Death's Jest Book.* Something of that quality is embodied in Marcello's lines alluded to above:

Death is the one condition of our life:
To murmur were unjust; our buried sires
Yielded their seats to us, and we shall give
Our elbow-room of sunshine to our sons.
From first to last the traffic must go on;
Still birth for death. Shall we remonstrate then?
Millions have died that we might breathe this day:
The first of all might murmur, but not we.

(313)

However, Beddoes does murmur; more than that, he will make his major creative effort one huge "jest" against an absurd reality that in these lines Marcello accepts so calmly.

TOWARD *DEATH'S JEST BOOK*

"I do not intend to finish that 2nd Brother you saw but am thinking of a very Gothic-styled tragedy for w^h I have a jewel of a name—***Death's Jest Book***" (604). Thus in the failure of *The Second Brother* lies the origin of his great work; as he had so often done before, Beddoes will start over yet again.

Examination of *The Brides' Tragedy* and the dramatic fragments reveals, despite the *apparent* completeness of the published play, an author groping for a creative fulfillment that continues to be elusive. For Beddoes the drama remains compelling; each new start represents a recommitment to the dramatic shape of value and experience. He appears to think—or try to think—in acts. But the dramatic impulse is impeded by conventional theatrical assumptions and, more significantly, by his inability to define theme clearly—to realize his vision. In *The Brides' Tragedy* and in the fragments Beddoes swerves back and forth between concern for plot and his still largely undefined sense of the world.

But from the perspective of *Death's Jest Book* we can recognize the general direction, however confusedly, in which his imagination is moving in these works. On an obvious level, we see characters like Ziba in *Torrismond* and Melchior in *The Second Brother* emerge again in the major work. More important, however, is the way in which the dramatic impulse gradually comes to assume a "satiric" form. Ermina's impassioned speech in *Love's Arrow Poisoned,* to which we referred earlier, argues that man is the product of Momus, the god of ridicule. Gradually Beddoes assumes the perspective of the lonely cosmic outcast who—created by the god of jest—assumes the satiric function himself, almost in self-defense.

This is not to argue that **The Brides' Tragedy** or the fragments are satires. Nor is the satiric impulse like that found in Dryden, or even Blake, a poet with whom he has some affinity. Rather, the satiric element, if not the tone—latent here but powerful in **Death's Jest Book**—reminds us of the revolt against a world conceived as absurd, a conception found in Byron and in later nonsatiric writers. It is indicative of Beddoes's remarkable modernity that he should have come to recognize the inescapably problematic nature of human existence, and that his reaction would be, in Wilner's words, the "creation of an essentially absurdist world—grotesque, self-parodying, nihilistic."[28] If Wilner's last term seems an exaggeration, we need only recall the hopelessness in all these pieces: Hesperus, Floribel, and Olivia inhabit a world barren of spiritual growth; Torrismond, his father, and his lover can only be betrayed; Orazio must be destroyed by a man who returns, almost as from the dead, in a totally unreasonable distortion of probability. Moreover, even the best life can be no more than "a brief parenthesis in chaos" (248).

While there are some conventional aspects of satire here—in his letters and poetry Beddoes clearly scorns the "cold sirs and madams"—and while one also finds Manfred-like posturing, the vital element is a serious revolt against the absurdity of an existence hedged around by death. Marcello is, at moments, a spokesman for this view, a view formed by the realization of the tentative and constantly imperiled condition of life:

> Each minute of man's safety he does walk
> A bridge no thicker than his frozen breath
> O'er a precipitous and craggy danger
> Yawning to death.
>
> (310)

The result of such a realization is a growing desire to destroy death itself; for even while identifying death with love, Beddoes's imagination searches for a way to subvert it. And if one cannot "kill" death, one can be "mad and merry" at his "jovial feast among the worms" (206):

> But while you still are living,
> What say you to some frolic merriment?
> There are two grassy mounds beside the church,
> My husband and my daughter; let us go
> And sit beside them, and learn silence there;
> Even with such guests we'll hold our revelry
> O'er bitter recollections: there's no anguish,
> No fear, no sorrow, no calamity,
> In the deathful catalogue of human pains,
> But we will jest upon 't, and laugh and sing:
> Let pitiful wretches whine for consolation,
> Thank heaven we despair.
>
> (228)

The "frolic merriment," the "revelry," the ability to "jest upon 't"—all prepare us for his "very Gothic-styled" play, indeed his "fool's tragedy."

In the works discussed in this chapter we find that Beddoes's "Araby of words" ranges from the precious ("full of beeish truth"), through the crisp and trenchant ("I've given myself, like alms unto an idiot, / To be for nothing squandered"), to the rough and grotesque ("be his soporacles, and suck yellow truth / Out of the nipple of his jingling pouch").[29] But it is the latter tone that foreshadows **Death's Jest Book.** Here is Marcello as the spectator of death confronting Orazio, whom he likens to love:

> Let us shake hands; I tell thee, brother skeleton,
> We're but a pair of puddings for the dinner
> Of Lady worm; you served in silks and gems,
> I garnished with plain rags. Have I unlocked thee?
>
> (288)

It is not surprising to find this example in the last of the fragments; in **Death's Jest Book,** which he is now to begin, the grotesque and satirical will become the dominant tone.

When Beddoes left for Germany in July 1825 the personal isolation he would there assume was, in a sense, symbolic of the social and cosmic alienation he had already come to feel.[30] Whether or not his mother's death played any major role in his darkened vision is unclear; what is obvious is that at twenty-two years old he had none of the youthful optimism warranted by his age, success, and promise. More significantly, instead of the law, which it had apparently been his intention to pursue, he now chose not only his father's medical profession, but the life of the scientist in general. Such a choice reflects a deliberate and major shift; though he might dabble in poetry he would now trust reason over imagination, "prefer Anatomy &c to poetry" (618). While this new dedication partly reveals a lack of self-confidence—"I never cd have been the real thing as a writer" (618)—it chiefly reflects an increasingly desperate attempt to find an alternative avenue to truth.

His faith in the scalpel and microscope seems to have been real enough—at first. He felt, and tried unsuccessfully to explain in his letters, an important conjunction between anatomy and poetry. He chided Kelsall for "having anticipated a regular M.D. to arise" from his ashes after his "reduction in the crucible of German philosophy" (610-11). He now felt that the secret of life and death—the two were for him identical—could be found only by a thinker willing to try all the doors of Keats's "Chamber of Maiden Thought." He was, therefore, "determined never to listen to any metaphysician who is not both anatomist & physiologist of the first rank" (612). In the dissecting room and at his writing table the body—flesh, organs, and especially bones—obsesses his mind. And in Beddoes's Janus-faced search for the bone of Luz, **Death's Jest Book** is born.

Notes

1. In 1824 Beddoes had been "turning over old plays in the Brit: Museum" and was contemplating the editing of "another volume of specimens." *Works,* 592.

2. Elder Olson, *Tragedy and the Theory of Drama* (Detroit: Wayne State University Press, 1961), 9.

3. *Letters and Journals,* in *The Works of Lord Byron,* ed. Rowland E. Prothero (London: John Murray, 1898-1904), 5:347. For an interesting observation on "mental theatre" in contrast to the actual stage, see Thomas Hardy's preface to *The Dynasts.* He concludes by noting that "whether mental performance alone may not eventually be the fate of all drama other than that of contemporary or frivolous life, is a . . . question not without interest." *The Dynasts* (London: Macmillan, 1958), 1:x.

4. Kenneth Burke, *Attitudes Toward History* (Los Altos, Calif.: Hermes Publications, 1959), 39.

5. Northrop Frye, *Anatomy of Criticism* (Princeton: Princeton University Press, 1957), 247.

6. Terry Otten, *The Deserted Stage: The Search for Dramatic Form in Nineteenth-Century England* (Athens: Ohio University Press, 1972), 7-8. Otten is of course quoting a famous line in Matthew Arnold's preface to his 1853 "Poems," an essay designed as his opening attack on Romanticism.

7. Robert Langbaum, *The Poetry of Experience: The Dramatic Monologue in Modern Literary Tradition* (New York: Random House, 1957).

8. Quoted by Claude Colleer Abbott in *The Life and Letters of George Darley, Poet and Critic* (Oxford: Oxford University Press, 1967), 219.

9. *Letters and Journals,* 5:217, 268.

10. Donner points out that these observations were made while Beddoes was at work on *The Second Brother,* where he was, indeed, "trying to modernize traditional material," not simply imitate that material. See 167.

11. See note 4, Preface, above.

12. "Thomas Lovell Beddoes: A Critical Study of His Major Work," (Ph.D. diss., Ohio State University, 1968).

13. Allardyce Nicoll, *A History of English Drama 1660-1900* (Cambridge, 1955), 4:201.

14. For the full title and a detailed account see Donner, *Beddoes,* 84-86.

15. Eric Bentley, *The Playwright as Thinker* (New York: Meridian Books, 1957), 163.

16. Northrop Frye, *A Study of English Romanticism* (New York, 1968), 53. Flora was, interestingly enough, Zephyrus's wife.

17. Goode, "Beddoes," 45.

18. Eleanor Wilmer, *Gathering the Winds: Visionary Imagination and Radical Transformation of Self and Society* (Baltimore, 1975), 88, 81.

19. Percy B. Shelley, *Adonais,* ll. 462-63, 458; *The Prelude* (1850), 2, l. 254.

20. This apt expression is found in *Blackwood's Edinburgh Magazine,* December 1823, and is quoted by Snow, *Beddoes,* 45.

21. It was in 1825 that Beddoes made his trenchant observations on dramatic "reanimations."

22. Snow, *Beddoes,* 52.

23. See *Works,* 580, 586, 594, 601.

24. Donner, *Beddoes,* 145.

25. Ibid., 149.

26. Ibid., 152.

27. Frye, *English Romanticism,* 55.

28. Wilmer, *Gathering the Winds,* 74.

29. *Works,* 269, 274, 275, 267.

30. "I feel myself in a measure alone in the world & likely to remain so . . . I fear I am a non-conductor of friendship, a not-very-likeable person." *Works,* 610.

Daniel P. Watkins (essay date 1989)

SOURCE: "Thomas Lovell Beddoes's *The Brides' Tragedy* and the Situation of Romantic Drama," in *Studies in English Literature: 1500-1900,* Vol. 29, No. 4, Autumn, 1989, pp. 699-712.

[*In the following essay, Watkins situates* The Brides' Tragedy *within the tradition of Romantic literature.*]

Like Matthew Lewis and Mary Shelley before him, Thomas Lovell Beddoes published, before the age of twenty, a literary work of extreme horror that touches the dark underside of the Romantic imagination. Unlike *The Monk* and *Frankenstein,* however, **The Brides' Tragedy** has rarely been studied seriously, partly because it is a poetic drama (a genre out of favor with most scholars and critics of Romanticism), and partly because of numerous technical or expository weaknesses, especially in its handling of the motives for action and in its imbalance of dialogue and action. The few scholars who have admired and studied the drama systematically have not attempted to establish its place within Romanticism, explaining it, instead, either as a throwback to Jacobean tragedy or as an example of the death of the Romantic imagination, rather than as a work produced within, and shaped by, the Romantic situation itself.[1]

In the following pages I want to approach **The Brides' Tragedy** historically in an attempt to show that, despite its many obvious deficiencies and its perceived marginal status among the literature of the period, it powerfully registers the conditions under which it was produced. Not only does it capture the turmoil and anxiety of a once-stable social world on the verge of historical marginalization and extinction; it painfully articulates the loneliness, fear, and dread which haunt Romantic literature particularly after 1815, when both the apocalyptic hope for a utopian society and—at the other extreme—the nostalgic desire for a return to an aristocratic and feudal world had been irrevocably dashed.[2] To consider *The Brides' Tragedy* as both a product and expression of this historical predicament is to begin to understand its important place in the literature of Romanticism, and (in a larger sense) to glimpse what scholars are beginning to learn about the gothic works of Lewis and Mary Shelley, namely that the less privileged literary forms of the period—drama and gothic fiction[3]—often provide an indispensable means of understanding the crises of social forms and relations that both energize and limit the Romantic imagination.[4]

Situating *The Brides' Tragedy* historically requires at least a brief consideration of what happened to drama as a literary form during the Romantic period. Raymond Williams's work on the history of drama provides the most important basis for addressing this issue. According to Williams, the changes in the nature of drama and particularly the historical decline of drama as an aesthetic form in the eighteenth and early nineteenth centuries correspond directly to the crisis of social class, which involved the overthrow of the aristocracy by industrial capitalism and the emergence of a new social order governed by the middle class. This large sociocultural transformation, Williams argues, "broke up the old forms, which rested on meanings and interests that had decayed,"[5] weakening, or exhausting, the powerfully expressive voice that once had characterized drama in England. Since the Renaissance, drama had been one means of articulating the consciousness of an aristocratic worldview, but it could not be reformulated by artists to describe fully and effectively the new class consciousness coming to maturation in the eighteenth and nineteenth centuries.

This devastation of dramatic form, however, does not render Romantic drama insignificant. In fact it opens an aesthetic space within the drama of the period where certain important historical dimensions of culture and society become accessible. Marks of social crisis are seen in the fact that, at the level of plot, Romantic drama often portrays (as Renaissance drama had done) the actions of an aristocratic class, while, at another, deeper level, it betrays (to a much greater extent than Renaissance drama) a powerfully antagonistic bourgeois consciousness that denies aristocratic authority. This conflict between an aristocratic subject matter and a bourgeois sensibility reflects one of the key features of the Romantic historical moment, the difficult struggle of one social class to overthrow and replace another. While even in its closet form Romantic drama could not be made literarily suitable for articulating the triumph of a new social order, it nonetheless discloses the tensions, anxieties, and ideological struggles surrounding that triumph. Thus, while the conflict between a dying feudalism and an emergent industrial capitalism perhaps took its toll on drama, undoing its status as a premier aesthetic form in British literary

history, at the same time it made drama critical to our understanding of both social and literary history, because in this form the class struggle and many of the personal and public crises corresponding to this struggle play themselves out.[6]

The Brides' Tragedy offers an excellent example of Williams's general description of how Romantic drama attempts to formulate the conflict between aristocratic authority and a bourgeois political unconscious, capturing not only the painful transformations of social class, but also the connections between those transformations and relations of gender. In turning now to investigate the dimensions of this conflict, I bracket out, for the most part, questions of biography, psychology, and stage history (hence running the risk of duplicating the Romantic ideological tendency—seen most clearly in the critical writings of Lamb[7]—of reducing drama to literary text), not because these are unimportant, but because I want to focus on the network of social relations contained within the dramatic form, particularly on the way the drama portrays the decline of aristocracy, and the sense of loneliness, confusion, dread, and alienation accompanying that decline. The narrower concerns of biography and the larger concerns of stage history can and should be grafted on to the arguments offered here as part of the social history of drama.[8]

The extreme self-consciousness of *The Brides' Tragedy* about matters of social class places it squarely in the center of Romantic bourgeois drama. Despite its plot-level attention exclusively to the aristocracy, it never escapes entirely class anxiety and even class hysteria. While class struggle is never described or even implied as the cause of disruption and then of tragedy, its traces are everywhere in the action and in the network of social relations governing those actions. Changes in consciousness, crises in ordinary social institutions, and a generally increasing aristocratic vulnerability that promotes its own demise all point to turmoil larger than any individual character and larger even than the aristocracy itself.

The most immediate indicator of the class dimension of the drama is Hesperus's father, Lord Ernest, whose changing individual situation from beginning to end marks the larger social direction of change in the drama. The opening description of Lord Ernest establishes him as an aristocrat deeply in debt to another, greater, aristocrat, the deceased father of Orlando. This description is followed immediately by the incarceration of Lord Ernest by Orlando, who uses the imprisonment to persuade Hesperus (Lord Ernest's son) to give up his claim on Floribel, whom Orlando loves. When Orlando wins his purpose, Lord Ernest is released to become adopted into the Orlando estate, his outward integrity restored but his real power lost, as his position depends entirely on the mercy of Orlando. In the final scenes of the drama, after Hesperus spoils the compromise of the house of Lord Ernest and the house of Orlando by murdering Floribel, Lord Ernest reappears in peasant dress, telling his doomed son that

"Henceforth I'll live / Those bitter days that Providence decrees me / In toil and poverty" (V.iv.50-52).[9]

The decline of Lord Ernest's fortunes, and the difficulties accompanying that decline, may be seen as emblematic of the larger social and ideological deterioration of his world, of the ineluctable fragmentation and ultimate defeat of the aristocratic ruling class. All other actions and attitudes, though some are less explicitly class-bound than Lord Ernest's, are marked by class anxiety, by an attempt to preserve aristocratic hierarchy, order, and value, or by a desire to find some means of personal escape from certain class extinction—by the same needs and desires, that is, seen in the portrayal of Lord Ernest. The Duke's legal authority, Orlando's devious legal strategies, Hesperus's deranged behavior, Floribel's extreme sensitivity about money and social status: all of these, in ways that we shall see, develop within and against an exhausted feudal world that claims authority as its own even while it is unable to exercise that authority fully. Like Lord Ernest, the other characters in the drama can neither arrest nor avoid the fragmentation and death of their world, nor prevent the emergence of a new network of social beliefs, values, and relations.

To implicate all other characters—many of whom seem relatively autonomous through the course of the drama—in the same process of decline and defeat seen clearly in Lord Ernest's fortunes is not to argue that every individual character is more or less a passive carrier of invisible historical and social structures over which he or she has no control. It is simply to make the dialectical point that individual actions and choices are made within real social situations. Thus, for instance, while Lord Ernest cannot be said to cause the peculiar course of events in which he is caught, he is not entirely innocent of them, either, as his pathetic demands on his son to wed Olivia show. Nor, on the other hand, can Hesperus be viewed as the sole source of the drama's villainy (even though he certainly is not innocent), because his actions are motivated, at least in part, by the demands of his father's estate to marry Olivia. Lord Ernest and Hesperus, along with all other characters in the drama, are both agents and products; the larger social world is distilled in them even as it is partly created by them. On this view, the weight of Lord Ernest's individual history, like that of the other characters, is also the weight of social history, and it is played out both in terms of his individual needs and desires, and in terms of the sweeping network of relations undergirding his situation and that of the other characters.

Some additional plot-level matters help to establish the historical bind that the drama articulates, and particularly the class dimension of this historical bind. Most important among these is the fact that Floribel, whom Hesperus has secretly married, is extremely anxious about her "homely breeding" (I.i.78), and what this may mean for her relationship with her new husband. She desperately desires to have this anxiety laid to rest by public acknowledgment of her marriage and by the "blessing" (I.i.79) of Hesperus's father, acts which presumably would seal the love between Hesperus and Floribel by providing their marriage with social meaning. Much later in the drama, after Hesperus thinks he has caught her in an adulterous situation, Floribel maintains that her difficulties have less to do with her husband's character than with her own socially inferior position, and her confused effort to think through this social difficulty leads her to desire at once more wealth for her own family and less for Hesperus's family. As she tells her mother:

> *Floribel*: Dear mother, I will strive to be at ease,
>   If you desire; but melancholy thoughts
>   Are poor dissemblers. How I wish we owned
>   The wealth we've lost.
> *Lenora*:   Why girl, I never heard
>   One such regret escape your lips before;
>   Has not your Hesperus enough?
> *Floribel*:   Too much;
>   If he were even poorer than ourselves,
>   I'd almost love him better. For, methinks,
>   It seemed a covetous spirit urged me on,
>   Craving to be received his bride. I hope
>   He did not think so; if he does, I'll tell him
>   I will not share his wealth.
>
> (III.ii.28-39)

These and other comments by Floribel, though prompted and colored by intense personal anxiety, describe perfectly her understanding of the class and economic forces that both push her marriage into secrecy and drive her husband to unpredictability. And, as in the case of Lord Ernest, these forces generate (or throw into relief), without any ability to fulfill, Floribel's various personal needs and desires. The result is even further anxiety, confusion, and finally (for Floribel) death.

The class and economic realities to which Floribel's comments direct attention help to elucidate Hesperus's villainy, providing a social framework for understanding his madness. Hesperus's socially superior position demands that he secure that position by marrying upward rather than downward, and this prevents him from publicly acknowledging his relationship to Floribel. In hiding his marriage for reasons of social class and respectability, Hesperus becomes even more a victim of class demand, to the point where his personal identity is entangled in a life-or-death struggle with the class to which he belongs. And as his personal life becomes increasingly entangled in matters of estate—or, put differently, as matters of social class increasingly overwhelm personal life—he comes to see death as the only certain way of laying conflict to rest. Without denying his madness and villainy, and without attempting to justify or defend his actions, this perspective situates Hesperus in terms of the class conflict at the center of his world, insisting that personal motives are never only personal, that they are, on some level, a response to (or effect of) a social reality that encompasses and gives meaning to them.

Because the various elements and dimensions of class struggle presented in *The Brides' Tragedy* are, at the level of plot, connected directly to gender relations (such as the Hesperus-Floribel relationship and the Hesperus-Olivia relationship), they help to focus the structure and authority of patriarchy, and to illuminate some of the ways it is implicated in the social transformation from feudalism to capitalism. The connection between patriarchy and class in the drama can best be understood in terms of Eli Zaretsky's ideas on feminism and patriarchy in *Capitalism, the Family, and Personal Life.* Zaretsky's aim is to connect modes of personal life to particular modes of production, and to show specifically that the rise of the bourgeoisie entailed new ways of conceiving of personal life, the family, gender relations, and so on. Two components of his argument are particularly relevant here. First, following Engels, he argues that patriarchy is directly connected to the emergence of private property in history, a phenomenon which "spelled the downfall of women"[10] because it separated production within the home from production outside the home, relegating women to the former and giving men control of the latter, more rapidly developing forms of production. The household itself became converted into private property controlled by men, though the labor within it was by women. The rise of the state coincided with the emergence of private property, sealing women's subordinate role by safeguarding the relations of property.

While stressing the power of Engels's major thesis that "the oppression of women and the existence of the family [are tied together] with the economic organization of society,"[11] Zaretsky acknowledges that its weaknesses are its reductionism and a strong antihistorical dimension. He attempts to correct these deficiencies by developing a theory of personal life specific to the rise of the bourgeoisie, retaining Engels's theory of private property, but defining it more precisely in terms of commodity production. Because his explanation of bourgeois individualism is critical to understanding gender relations in *The Brides' Tragedy,* I want to quote it at length:

> In feudal society men and women occupied a fixed position with a stratified division of labor—they owed allegiance to a particular lord and worked on a particular plot of land instead of being free to sell their labor or property. Explicit and direct relations of authority defined people's sense of individual identity. Catholicism provided them with a common purpose outside themselves.
>
> Private property freed the early bourgeoisie from a fixed social role within the feudal order. On the basis of private property, the bourgeoisie has defined individual rights throughout history. . . . The bourgeoisie has consistently defended the right of individuals to rise and fall within the marketplace through their own efforts, rather than on the basis of birth; the bourgeoisie originated the idea of a necessary contradiction between the individual and society.[12]

With this new conception of the individual emerged a new conception of gender relations, one which involved the connection for the first time in history between marriage and sexual love, and at the same time a view of the family as a refuge from the conflict and sordidness of public life. Both of these features of bourgeois gender relations figure prominently in *The Brides' Tragedy,* and they conflict violently in the drama with the aristocratic world that they challenge. The complicated struggle of these new relations to find authority and shape in a world where feudal patriarchy is not yet dead is displayed powerfully in Hesperus's different relationships with Floribel and Olivia, the two women whom he marries.

Like Orlando, who also is young and wishes to marry, Hesperus sees the impoverished Floribel in idyllic terms, telling her, for instance, in the beginning of the drama that "the veiled Moon's mild eye / Has long been seeking for her loveliest nymph" (I.i.20-21). (Orlando's comment to Claudio in the following scene is almost identical, referring to Floribel as "my goddess, / The Dian of our forests," I.ii.18-19.) Floribel can take on this sort of pure value for the young aristocrats who desire her precisely because she does not belong to the aristocracy, which, as we have seen, is characterized by exhaustion and decay. In fact, her desirability as an object of love and as a repository of value for Hesperus increases in proportion to his ability to imagine her as independent not only of the aristocracy but of all social exchange. For him, she is, as Zaretsky says of the bourgeois family, a refuge from the threat facing his social class, a threat seen most emphatically in the infighting between his family and that of Orlando, for instance in the fact that Lord Ernest is deeply in debt to Orlando's father, and also in the fact that Orlando employs devious, legalistic strategies to win Floribel away from Hesperus. Whatever her real situation—which is made clear in her own anxieties about money and status—her constructed significance for Hesperus is that she inhabits and even constitutes a private and innocent realm more meaningful than the world of daily life that he inhabits.

The burden of innocence that Floribel is made to carry becomes evident not only in the scene where Hesperus catches her kissing Orlando's page but also in the description of his initial mad confusion over whether or not to murder her.[13] This brilliant scene takes place in an apartment of Orlando's palace, decorated with beautiful tapestries stitched with pictures out of feudal history. Produced by female labor ("she, whose needle limned so cunningly, / Sleeps and dreams not," II.iv.39-40), the tapestries tell stories of men whose hands have been gloriously dipped in human blood. These stories in cloth radically divide Hesperus from himself, promoting in him a desire to shed blood, which presumably would give him a place alongside the heroes whose stories are sewn into the tapestries, while at the same time making him even more committed to preserving the vision of purity and innocence that Floribel represents to him. As this fit of madness passes, and he suppresses his violent urges, he states emphatically to himself, "I tell thee Floribel / Shall never bleed" (II.iv.68-69). This comment, though on the surface level expressing an abhorrence of violence, carries within it the full weight of Hesperus's confusion, as well as the confusion of his world. The literal meaning here, that he will not for jealousy spill Floribel's blood, is bound up with larger cultural definitions of women as pure repositories for masculine desire, definitions which do not allow women the simple human functions of menstruating and consummating sexual relations. This contradiction between woman as ideal and woman as human being cannot be logically resolved, and it comes back repeatedly to haunt Hesperus, eventually overwhelming him to the point where he comes to believe that it can be laid to rest only by murder—by spilling blood despite his abhorrence of it.

The relationship between Olivia and Hesperus both duplicates and departs from the Floribel-Hesperus relationship, as it is defined first by the demands of aristocratic patriarchy, while at the same time it is pressured by, and ultimately responds to, the challenge of bourgeois gender relations. Unlike Floribel, Olivia is of the aristocracy, and thus faces personal life in quite a different way from her unknown rival. Her relationship with Hesperus is determined entirely by the demands of the estate rather than by love, and within this context she cannot represent a feminine ideal, as Floribel does, but rather appears as socially real: she serves the estate rather than subjective masculine desire. The question facing her and Hesperus in marriage is not whether they love one another in the beginning, but rather whether they can learn regard for one another while serving to unite two aristocratic houses, thus preserving the power and status of their families. What that regard entails is seen clearly when Orlando tells Hesperus, in an emphatic articulation of aristocratic patriarchal values: "School her [Olivia], sir, in the arts of compliment, / You'll find her an apt learner" (II.iii.17-18). While both Hesperus and Olivia accept the responsibility placed on them by their families, neither initiates the relationship, and neither is entirely comfortable with it: they do not seek out one another's company (as Hesperus and Floribel had done when they met secretly at great risk) but rather simply assume their positions within a prearranged social order.

If their marriage unites two houses of the aristocracy, it does not allay the tensions and anxieties pervading the aristocratic world, nor even assure survival of that world. In fact, the arranged marriage, even as it is being set in motion and socially authorized, is subject to disturbing and dismantling ideological and emotional processes that suggest the demise of the aristocracy, rather than its perpetuation. This is seen not only in the early stages of the courtship, when Hesperus's reflections on marriage and love (because of his secret relationship with Floribel) are overwhelmed by thoughts of death (II.ii.39-147), but more importantly in the fact that Hesperus, once forced into marriage to Olivia, attempts to recreate exactly the relationship that existed between him and Floribel by converting Olivia into a repository of emotional support apart from society. In lines that recall Keats's *Lamia,* he remarks: "Olivia / I'll tell thee how we'll 'scape these prying eyes; / We'll build a wall between us and the world" (IV.iii.65-67). While the immediate meaning of this com-

ment is doubtless determined by his guilt and confusion over Floribel, at the same time it carries much greater significance, expressing the emergence of a bourgeois individualist ideology within an aristocratic framework, an ideology that positions marriage against the public world and at the same time proclaims masculine authority to seek comfort in a privatized and idealized feminine world.

If Hesperus's comments display a bourgeois reconception of gender relations that marks the endurance of masculine authority in the passage of social power from the aristocracy to the bourgeoisie, the semilesbian exchanges between Olivia and her maidservants capture the dread, loneliness, and physical hardship that befall women as a result of that authority, and show, further, that, from a feminist perspective, there is relatively little difference between feudal patriarchy and bourgeois patriarchy. Shortly before the wedding, for instance, in describing her affection for Violet, Olivia remarks:

> Gentle maid,
> I'll not be sad; yet, little Violet,
> How long I've worn thy beauty next my heart,
> Aye, in my very thoughts, where thou hast shed
> Perpetual summer: how long shared thy being:
> Like two leaves of a bud, we've grown together,
> And needs must bleed at parting.
>
> (III.iv.14-20)

This mournful statement of separation is also a statement of submission to masculine power, and it acknowledges the sexual sacrifice that is made to that power, a sacrifice which destroys the sexual innocence that Olivia once had enjoyed in the company of other females. The blood which she knows must flow as she enters sexual union with a man is also the blood of her personal liberty. As she says to her nurse of her impending marriage:

> 'tis the funeral of that Olivia
> You nursed and knew; an hour and she's no more,
> No more the mistress of her own resolves,
> The free partaker of earth's airs and pleasures.
>
> (III.iv.33-36)

Following as they do immediately upon the scene of Floribel's murder—a scene which ironically had concluded with the sound of wedding bells (III.iii.194-97)—these exchanges disturbingly show the disempowerment of the feminine that is entailed in the sexual reality of marriage under patriarchy, whether patriarchy is feudal or bourgeois in construction.[14]

Another dimension of patriarchy that *The Brides' Tragedy* captures, one that is less explicitly centered on questions of sex and gender—though it includes them—involves the relations between fathers and sons, and the struggle between them for social authority. At the level of plot alone, the importance of fathers is suggested in the frequent references to the fact that Orlando's father is dead, in the portrayal of Hesperus's father as powerless, and in the portrayal of Floribel's father as near death through most of the drama, finally dying when he learns of his daughter's murder. These references focus the demise of a once-powerful social order—specifically of aristocratic, or feudal, patriarchy—and also describe the opening of an ideological space which allows the reconceptualization of personal life in individualist terms. With the death or disempowerment of all of the fathers in the drama, the sons and daughters seek new arrangements of power and gender relations, and these arrangements are consistently shaded by bourgeois power relations and ideological assumptions. For instance, Orlando engages in deceptive and legalistic strategies to secure the hand of Floribel, whom he describes and envisions in terms identical to Hesperus (see, for instance, I.ii.6-27), even at the very moment he would secure his public power by forcing Hesperus to wed Olivia. His plan denies the father-rights of Lord Ernest, while establishing his own personal authority. Hesperus, too, attempts to circumvent the authority of his father and Floribel's father by secretly marrying Floribel, thus asserting his own power against theirs. These actions of the sons are entangled both with love and private need, and, at the deepest levels, with the reality of money—Lord Ernest is indebted to Orlando's father, and Floribel's family is plagued by poverty, having lost the money it once had. Over against the demands of the estate, ruled by fathers, Hesperus and Orlando alike attempt to establish their individual authority, which at the same time would enable them to fulfill their personal desires.

It is clear that the transformations I am tracing here do not involve in any way the emergence of women as figures of social authority, or even as figures who enjoy real freedom. Nonetheless, Orlando and Hesperus do not represent the simple duplication of patriarchy in a new generation; rather, they represent the production and emergence of bourgeois patriarchy that displaces feudal patriarchy. This is seen not only in the characterization of their personal desires, noted above, but more importantly in the changing forms of social life charted through the drama. The feudal world of the fathers, for example, like the inchoate bourgeois world of the sons, recognizes public life as masculine and the private sphere as feminine, but in the world of the sons a political distinction is made between the public and private domains that is not made under feudalism. In the feudal world, women were simply property, and, at the level of aristocracy, their marriages were arranged for the purpose of securing or extending the estate; in this respect, there was no distinction between the home and the state. In the bourgeois world, however, the state and the family came to be conceptualized as distinctive categories, and women became part of what Zillah Eisenstein calls "a whole culture of privacy, intimacy, and individualism"[15] exemplified clearly, in *The Brides' Tragedy,* in the distinction between Hesperus's and Orlando's attitudes toward Floribel, on one hand, and the attitudes of Lord Ernest and Mordred toward marriage, on the other. In the world that Hesperus and Orlando would construct, in short, women are not liberated, but rather are oppressed in new and different ways.

In addition to class and patriarchy, other issues in *The Brides' Tragedy* could be sketched to elaborate the struggle of bourgeois social relations to be born. Further exploration of Orlando's use of the law, for instance, of Lenora's obsession with death, of Hesperus's madness, of the full significance and role of money: all of these, no less than the issues considered above, point toward a deep structure of bourgeois social life at the center of the drama that destabilizes and overwhelms the aristocratic and feudal relations reflected on its surface. The ideological and political struggles surrounding such matters, more than simply Beddoes's limitations as a dramatist, help to explain the formal and aesthetic shortcomings of the work, while at the same time pointing toward its larger significance for literary and social history.

Moreover, the essential structure of ideas and assumptions in *The Brides' Tragedy*—its expression of inchoate bourgeois needs and desires against a weakening aristocratic framework of authority—constitutes its particular Romantic significance and locates it among other dramas of the period, which, for all their differences, share an inability to escape the political unconscious of bourgeois social relations. Indeed, one of the defining features of Romantic drama, to which it has been the aim of this paper to call attention, is that it is a literary form that would look to a past world and ideology for its governing values, while in fact it is shaped and vitalized by a contradictory world and ideology. The various portrayals of this contradiction within Romantic drama are often aesthetically crippling (as they are in *The Brides' Tragedy*), and yet they give Romantic drama its particular and crucial importance. Romantic drama is a literary form in crisis, and investigation of the many dimensions of that crisis is necessary if we are to understand fully the processes whereby feudal aesthetic, political, and ideological authority were destroyed by bourgeois social relations.

Notes

1. For studies pursuing one or both lines of argument, see Northrop Frye, *A Study of English Romanticism* (New York: Random House, 1968), pp. 51-55; James R. Thompson, *Thomas Lovell Beddoes* (Boston: Twayne, 1985), pp. 24-41; Lytton Strachey, "The Last Elizabethan," in *Books and Characters, French & English* (New York: Harcourt, Brace, 1922), pp. 235-65; and Harold Bloom, *The Visionary Company: A Reading of English Romantic Poetry,* rev. edn. (New York: Cornell Univ. Press, 1971), pp. 428-34. While these conventional explanations may help to clarify certain isolated psychological or literary historical matters, at the same time they run the risk of distorting literary history in their attempt to find a suitable vocabulary for discussing the drama. To identify *The Brides' Tragedy* primarily in terms of Jacobean tragedy, for instance, is to forget that the central feature of most Jacobean tragedies is the destructive power of lust; in *The Brides' Tragedy* this is not the case. Hesperus's murder of Floribel is encouraged not at all by lust but rather by jealousy

in conjunction with the incarceration of Herperus's father and by the larger domestic and social situations flowing from these. Moreover, the argument that Beddoes's obsession with death in the drama represents the end of Romanticism is confusing when we consider that earlier Romantic works—for instance, *The Monk,* or even the *Rime of the Ancient Mariner,* both written in the 1790s—are as extreme in their portrayal of these matters as *The Brides' Tragedy,* and that works written in the later nineteenth century—for instance, Thomson's "City of Dreadful Night" (1874) and Hardy's *Jude the Obscure* (1898)—are equally given to physical violence and existential despair. If the work signals the demise of Romanticism, it is for reasons other than those most often cited.

2. For a discussion of this dark side of the Romantic imagination, from a psychological perspective, see Edward E. Bostetter's important work, *The Romantic Ventriloquists: Wordsworth, Coleridge, Keats, Shelley, Byron,* rev. edn. (Seattle and London: Univ. of Washington Press, 1975).

3. While he does not approach *The Brides' Tragedy* in the same terms used in the present study, Horace Gregory, in "The Gothic Imagination and the Survival of Thomas Lovell Beddoes," offers an excellent discussion of Beddoes and the Gothic. See *The Dying Gladiators and Other Essays* (New York: Greenwood Press, 1968), pp. 81-95.

4. For an excellent historical assessment of Beddoes along lines different from my own, see Eleanor Wilner, *Gathering the Winds: Visionary Imagination and Radical Transformation of Self and Society* (Baltimore: Johns Hopkins Univ. Press, 1975), pp. 73-106. For a general discussion of Romanticism in historical context that has been influential here, see Robert Sayre and Michael Lowy, "Figures of Romantic Anti-Capitalism," *NGC* 32 (1984):42-92.

5. Raymond Williams, *The Long Revolution* (New York: Columbia Univ. Press, 1961), p. 264.

6. As Raymond Williams states it: "This exceptional class consciousness, though leading in the short run to little significant drama . . . is a clear sign of a new social order." See Raymond Williams, *The Sociology of Culture* (New York: Schocken Books, 1982), p. 164.

7. Note for instance Lamb's remark on the plays of Shakespeare that they "are less calculated for performance on a stage, than those of almost any dramatist whatever . . . [T]he practice of stage representation reduces everything to a controversy of elocution." See "On the Tragedies of Shakespeare," in *The Complete Works and Letters of Charles Lamb* (New York: Modern Library, 1935) pp. 291-92.

8. For an excellent history of the stage during the Romantic period (without mention of Beddoes,

however) see the chapter entitled "Shakespeare and Tragedy: The View from Drury Lane," in John Kinnaird, *William Hazlitt: Critic of Power* (New York: Columbia Univ. Press, 1978) pp. 165-95.

9. All quotations from *The Brides' Tragedy* are taken from H.W. Donner, ed., *Plays and Poems of Thomas Lovell Beddoes* (London: Routledge and Kegan Paul, 1950). Act, scene, and line numbers are cited parenthetically in the text.

10. Eli Zaretsky, *Capitalism, the Family and Personal Life,* (1976; rev. edn., New York: Harper & Row, 1986), p. 70.

11. Zaretsky, p. 71.

12. Zaretsky, p. 40.

13. It should be noted that Hesperus's jealousy when he catches Floribel kissing Orlando's page is created as much by the patriarchal pressure from his father to wed Olivia as by his selfish and bourgeois desire to possess Floribel absolutely apart from the world.

14. This disempowerment, while enduring from feudalism to capitalism, gets redefined in ways that Olivia cannot here see. As suggested in the above descriptions of Hesperus, the isolation of the woman from female companionship involves at the same time her conversion into an ideal of pure value divorced from the world, a conversion which secures the individual subjectivity and power of men.

15. Zillah R. Eisenstein, *The Radical Future of Liberal Feminism* (Boston: Northeastern Univ. Press, 1981), p. 25. My general arguments here regarding the distinctions between feudal and bourgeois patriarchy draw very heavily on Eisenstein, especially pages 14-49. I wish to thank Professor Terence A. Hoagwood for his excellent and helpful critical reading of an earlier draft of this essay.

Christopher Moylan (essay date 1991)

SOURCE: "T. L. Beddoes, Romantic Medicine, and the Advent of Therapeutic Theater," in *Studia Neophilologica,* Vol. 63, No. 2, 1991, 181-88.

[In the following essay, Moylan investigates the relationship between Beddoes's career as a physician and his development as a writer and places his work within a medical context.]

Harold Bloom designated Thomas Lovell Beddoes (1803-1849) "a poet of death."[1] In ***Death's Jest Book,*** Beddoes' magnum opus, Gothic drama found a work worthy of the Elizabethan and Jacobean authors he studied so devotedly. His writings also show influences of an entirely different order. References in his plays and letters to psychology, medicine, and the life sciences point to his long fascination with the idea of reuniting the healing arts with poetry. The relationship between Beddoes' development as a physician and his development as a writer is critical to understanding his work. An anatomist, Beddoes was trained in the German states, where he remained from 1825 to his death. His career encompassed the entire history of German Romantic medicine, from its beginnings in Kantian "scientific medicine" to the advent of the materialist movement of the late 1840s. Without attempting an analysis of the drama itself, we will place his work in its medical context.

Beddoes' early life was co-extensive with the emergence and rapid decline of Romantic science in England. His father played a leading role in the scientific and political controversies of the Romantics. The elder Thomas Beddoes (1760-1808), who died when his son was five, divided his time among chemical research, social medicine, and writing, the latter consisting of poetry in the manner of his friend, Erasmus Darwin, and improving pamphlets in the manner of his father in law, T. L. Edgeworth. His outspoken, visionary belief in social medicine eventually led to trouble with the Home Office and to the decline of a career long plagued by allegations of eccentricity and charlatinism.[2] During the early 1790s, however, Dr. Beddoes was one of the most famous scientists in England an an important mediator of scientific research on the Continent. His translations and magazine reviews provided some of the earliest reports of German science and philosophy, including the work of Kant.[3] Coleridge, Southey, and Humphry Davy, among others, participated in his unsuccessful clinical experiments with nitrous oxide (laughing gas).

Several of these men showed the overreaching ambition and emotional fragility, the imaginative daring and analytic acuity that characterize many of the figures in Beddoes' plays. Certainly his father had more than his share of brilliant scientific apercus and abortive grand projects. After the failure of the pneumatic research, critics depicted the elder Dr. Beddoes as a fool, a bumbling alchemical charlatan, proffering his scientific wares in the service of an anarchic and leveling political vision. The author of the anonymous poem "The Golden Age" compared Dr. Beddoes to Paracelsus, the figure who was later to preside over ***Death's Jest Book*** as conqueror of death:

> Boast of proud Shropshire, Oxford's lasting shame,
> Whom none but Coxcombs scorn, but Fools defame,
> Eternal war with dulness born to wage,
> Thou Paracelsus of this wondrous age;
> BEDDOES, the philosophic Chymist's Guide,
> The bigot's Scourge, of Democrats the Pride,
> Accept this lay; and to thy Brother, Friend,
> Or name more dear, a Sans Culotte attend.[4]

When T. L. Beddoes was a middle-aged physician living in Switzerland as a political exile, he replied indirectly to his father's conservative critics. These lines, taken from a long fragment entitled "Lines Written in Switzerland (ca. 1844), answer the anonymous author of "The Golden Age":

> Well, Britain; let the fiery Frenchman boast
> That at the bidding of the charmer moves
> Their nation's heart, as ocean 'neath the moon
> Silvered and soothed. Be proud of Manchester,
> Pestiferous Liverpool, Ocean-Avernus,
> Where bullying blasphemy, like a slimy lie,
> Creeps to the highest church's pinnacle,
> And glistening infects the light of heaven.[5]

Although Beddoes' father does not enter the lines directly, we can hear the echo of his own causes, particularly of his epidemiological research in the conditions of England's industrial cities. For his son, the elder Dr. Beddoes was only the first representative of an embattled scientific left (as we would call it now) on both sides of the Channel.

The frustration which so distorted the elder Dr. Beddoes' career was not caused by politics alone. It was also a product of the backward state of medicine relative to other disciplines. At a time when experiential research was revolutionizing the physical sciences, medicine was only beginning to cast off the ineffectual and obfuscating techniques of earlier periods. Whatever the reasons for this lag between advances in physical research and their application in medicine, the physician was bound to feel tempted by research or theories which promised to close the gap. Theoretical work on the curative properties of oxygen attracted the elder Dr. Beddoes and brought him in contact with the speculative science being done in German states. Something of the sweeping enthusiasm of the *Naturphilosophen* seized hold of the elder Dr. Beddoes' imagination, though he expressed strong reservations concerning their assumptions and methodology which were not entirely believed during his lifetime.

It is not surprising that the younger Beddoes grew up a passionate devotee of the Romantic poet-scientists Goethe, Schiller, and Shelley.[6] The elder Beddoes' extensive contacts with German universities prepared the way for his son to study abroad, escaping to the Continent for a life of self-discovery in the manner of Byron and Shelley. However, by 1825, when T. L. Beddoes was ready to begin medical school, Romantic science and medicine were dying even in the German strongholds.[7] He came to Göttingen at the beginning of a twilight period in Romanticism.

In ***Death's Jest Book*** (1825-1849), which Beddoes began shortly before he arrived at Göttingen and continued to work on to some degree until his death, this cultural twilight found its apotheosis. Written during a critical period of medical history, when Romanticism in decline was yielding to the advent of scientific materialism, the play looked inward, anatomizing consciousness and science itself. In a letter to his friend Thomas Forbes Kelsall, Beddoes sketched an intriguing image of theater as a therapeutic exercise:

> I cannot help thinking that the study of anatomy, physiol-, psych-, and anthro-pology applied to and illustrated by history, biography and works of the imagination is that which is most likely to assist in producing correct and masterly delineations of the passions; great light would be thrown on Shakespeare by

the commentaries of one so educated. The studies of the dramatist and the physician are closely, almost inseparably allied; the application alone is different . . . The science of psychology, and of mental varieties, has long been used by physicians . . . for the investigation & removal of the immaterial causes of disease; it still remains for someone to exhibit the sum of his experience in mental pathology & therapeutics, not in a cold technical dead description, but a living semiotical display, a series of anthropological experiments, developed for the purpose of ascertaining some important psychical principle—i.e., a tragedy.[8]

This passage, appearing in the midst of a period of intense study and intellectual excitement, contains one of Beddoes' most extensive comments on drama. Beddoes envisions himself a technologist of the soul, a man whose knowledge of advances in the human sciences would make it possible to turn the stage into a form of clinical theater in which human suffering could be analyzed and diagnosed. A scientific stress on accuracy and exactitude has been assimilated into his critical terminology. The passions are to be "delineated" rather than expressed. This delineation is to be "correct and masterly," with the implication that drama now is to subject its insights to some objective process of verification.

Several terms in Beddoes' letter to Kelsall call our attention as having meanings peculiar to currents of thought in Germany: "semitiotical display," "anthropological experiments," and, as it relates to Romantic medicine, "psychical principle." As a group, these terms denote a Romantic "mental theatre" (to use Byron's phrase) designed to enact archetypal patterns of growth and turmoil in human consciousness.

The term "anthropological experiments" alludes to a holistic approach to psychiatry which "revolve[d] around the philosophical idea of man as a psycho-physical unity," as Gerlof Verwey writes in his book *Psychiatry in an Anthropological and Biomedical Context.*[9] Body and mind were one, and any illness had a psychological as well as a physical component. The anthropologists intuited several elements of psychoanalysis, including the unconscious, psychosexual conflict, mechanisms of repression and the death instinct. Such insights were divorced from any systematic approach to instinct or drive theory. Instead, they derived from a new receptivity to the significance of all forms of consciousness.[10] Beddoes' reading included proponents of animal magnetism, dream analysis, and study of fugue states. A representative example of his interests is Gotthilf Heinrich Von Schubert (1780-1860), a psychiatrist whose theories of the unconscious, dream symbolism and death instinct have been compared to those of Freud and Jung.[11]

The reference to semiotics ("semiotical display") in Beddoes' letter brings to the anthropological interest in the unconscious an emphasis on somatic depth and space. The OED defines "semiotics" as "the branch of medicine relating to the interpretation of symptoms." The first citation for the use of semeiotical is from Harvey (1588) and the

fourth and last from the remarks by Beddoes. We can only infer what Beddoes meant by the term. The clinical approach he studied at Göttingen was developed by Xavier Bichat.[12] To put it simply, this approach emphasized the importance of underlying processes of disease. Whereas before the development of clinical science the physician was once confined to interpreting the outward manifestations of pathology, such as skin discoloration or fever, he now used the stethoscope or other new diagnostic advances to infer the presence of pathology within the organic space of the body.[13] In dissection, the clinician cut and peeled away tissue to reach the specific sites of disease. Pathology, histology, anatomy and clinical diagnostics all shifted medicine to an understanding of disease processes in the depth of the body.

For Beddoes, the clinical method suggested the idea of drama as a general anatomizing of the human condition. The dramatist peeled away the tissue of social and personal life to reveal hidden sickness. Beddoes brought to this timeworn notion of the artist—we find the like in Donne and Burton, for example—an insistence that clinical anatomy is directly relevant to drama. Moreover, in the next letter to Kelsall (Jan. 11, 1826)[14] he extends the importance of anatomy, declaring his intention "never to listen to any metaphysician who is not both anatomist & physiologist of the first rank."[15]

What did this mean? We look for an answer to the metaphysicians (taking the term broadly) Beddoes himself listened to: Schelling, Novalis, Johann Christian Reil, Ritter, and later Johann Lucas Schoenlein. On a list of Beddoes' library borrowings at Göttingen, these are the only names one might associate with metaphysical thinking.[16] All conducted medical research with the hope of finding the vital principle or the essence of life itself. Their research was unabashedly imaginative and syncretic, drawing from poetry, religion, philosophy and even the occult. Beddoes, concluding his letter to Kelsall, described this approach as an attempt to reunite Apollo, god of healing and poetry:

> Shame on you for having anticipated a regular M. D. to arise out of my ashes after reduction in the crucible of German philosophy! Apollo has been barbarously separated by the moderns: I would endeavour to unite him.[17]

For the German Romantic scientists, the task of reuniting Apollo centered on determining the relation of mind and body. Theirs was the last systematic attempt to combine all the human sciences in a unified, comprehensive science of man. In medicine, the influence of the Jena group of scientists and writers—most notably Schelling, Novalis, and Ritter—led to the development of what has been called "Romantic Medicine." The movement was short-lived: it began in the German states in the early 1790s and was already in decline when Beddoes arrived at Göttingen. Its advocates were found as far as Russia in the east and the Nordic states in the west; France was impervious to its influence, and England was nearly so.[18] At no point did Romantic medicine comprise a cohesive school of philosophy, nor did it establish its own methodology in research.

Beddoes' vision of a unifying logos across the many disciplines reflected the Romantics' desire for a systematic groundwork upon which to proceed with research. The inspiration for the Romantic conception of such a groundwork came from Kant's epistemology.[19] We must look to this work, or rather the Romantic misinterpretation of it, to understand what Beddoes had in mind when he referred to metaphysics and medicine.

Since experimental work and naturalist observation required the scientist to contend with inexhaustible complexity and variety in natural phenomena, Kant argued that science should adopt a logical and systematic framework within which to order and arrange research findings.[20] This framework would be based on a formal analysis of human powers of understanding and observation, and would comprise a critique of science according to a priori concepts. That is, "science," as Kant understood it, was to be a purely philosophical undertaking, an analysis of fundamental and irreducible concepts.

For many German scientists the appeal of such a philosophic approach lay in what they perceived as its support for formulating intuitive explanations of natural processes: areas of inquiry which, in fact, Kant wished to avoid. The *Naturphilosophen* believed they were faithful to Kant's advocacy of speculation as "representing all connections as if they were ordinances of a supreme reason, of which our reason is but a faint copy."[21] Yet, what for Kant was a faint copy was for the *Naturphilosophen* a reflection of the absolute. Human reason now was associated with divinity, and if the relationship was a distant one, it might be strengthened and increased by deductive theorizing. Such productive and innovative scientists as the physicists Johann Wilhelm Ritter (1776-1810), and Hans Christian Oersted, the geologist Henrik Steffens (1773-1845), and the psychiatric theorist Gotthilf Heinrich Schubert (1780-1860), based their research on the mystical premises of *Naturphilosophie*: the organicity of nature and the notion of polarity in all natural processes.[22] This meta-biology traced all the principal aspects of life to primary forces in nature. The object was to reveal nature as a totality through its particular manifestations, to develop a universal consciousness in man.

The cultivation of this "inner sense" (*All-Sind*) sanctioned a heady period of intellectual adventurism among the Jena group of Romantics, most notably Schelling, Novalis, and Ritter. The period found its apotheosis in the encyclopedic projects of Novalis, where the sciences were to join in such odd marriages as "pathological logic" and "poetical psychology".[23] Romantic science would discover a "paradise of ideas"[24] through imaginative syntheses of various disciplines, according to Novalis, who envisioned his encyclopedic project as a "scientific bible".[25] Schelling spoke of the "holy revelations" in physics, and looked forward to the creation of a new mythology from the combination of science, ancient myths, and philosophy.

This stress on experimenting with mixed genres and modes of thought—Novalis' "scientific bible" and Schelling's

"poetic physics"[26]—gave precedent and artistic sanction for the vision of theater Beddoes proposed in his letter. In fact, such a program may have been very much in the air while he was at Göttingen, as Lundin writes:

> Goethe speaks closely enough along the same lines in the "Deutsches Theater" to suggest that his view of literature had a certain currency at the time: "*Des Tragischen Dichters Aufgabe und Thun ist nichts anderer als: einen psychisch sittliches Phänomen, in einem fasslichen Experiment dargestellt, in her Vergangenheit nachzuweisen.* ". . . The Göttingen *Verzeichniss der Vorlesungen* (Winter, 1825) shows that the study of "*Seelenkrankenheiten und ihre psychisch zu begrundende Heilung*" was an essential cognate of courses in anatomy, physiology and general therapy.[27]

Beddoes was a devoted reader of Goethe and no doubt knew the passage from "Deutches Theater." He also read widely in the works of all the major *Naturphilosophen*. His program for therapeutic theater, however, does not go as far as Novalis' "paradise of ideas." His syncretism was confined to those researches which are now associated with the term analysis: medical, psychological and self-analysis. In drama this was to be a composite of the various structures and spaces within which Beddoes' medical work arranged itself: the anatomical theater of diagnostic display and exposition of pathology and the analogous "therapeutic theater" developed during the early nineteenth century to display and expose mental pathology.

Above these, we find the Romantic notion of the macrocosm, the universe itself, as the ultimate field of scientific and artistic endeavour. Whatever the merits of various German Romantic exponents of this idea, Beddoes could not long conceal from himself the morbid character of his own interest. Even in an early draft note to the play, written when Beddoes was most enthusiastic about Romantic medicine, his discussion shows a strain in the exposition:

> Analytical chemistry which it may perhaps be more than a metaphor to call a sort of psychology of the macrocosm . . . teaches us that the combinations of inanimate matters are not innumerable, but confined to certain bounds and proportions—those on the other hand infinitely variable. If we consider that the inanimate creation lies nearer and more familiar to these binding powers which form, as it were, the active principle or spirit of our planet, we may perhaps, in some measure comprehend this fact and another in psychology (or [the] Analytical chemistry of the human/ microcosmical/spirit power) which seems to stand in contradiction with it.[28]

Qualifications, reconsiderations ("we may perhaps, in some measure"), and verbal pauses ("sort of," "that is to say," "as it were") abound, and the passage as a whole is halting and apologetic within its Promethean aspiration to comprehend the world soul. In itself, the idea of simplicity in the elemental composition of matter need not have caused Beddoes anxiety: the notion of a unified, systematic explanation of natural phenomena was dear to many scientists at the time, not all of them Romantics. For Beddoes, however, the desire for the absolute could not be disentangled from eccentric preoccupations with guilt, death, and the afterlife. The "psychology of the macrocosm" could only return him, with an inevitable and no doubt painful circularity, to the psychology of his own megalomania and self-destructiveness. More truly Paracelsian than his unjustly vilified father, Beddoes could neither extricate himself from his obsession with Romantic visions of divinity nor overcome his own melancholy sense of futility.

Through this melancholy, Beddoes came to the last and most important space for drama. This he termed his "private theater." The term appears as a title for a collection of his works. *Thanatos or the Private Theater,* which Beddoes planned for publication in 1838 and eventually abandoned, was to include works now lost as well as **Death's Jest Book.** No explanation of this enigmatic title has come down to us. However, his letters do discuss the private motivations of the poet, exemplified by Shakespeare. For Beddoes, the poet opens his soul to the public out of a profound loneliness, an emptiness to which he is compelled to bear witness:

> Dissatisfaction is the lot of the poet, if it be that of any being; & therefore the gushings of the spirit, these pourings out of their innermost on imaginary topics, because there was no altar in their home worthy of the libation.[29]

The public is a greedy voyeur demanding the poet fill the silence of hypocrisy and distrust by revealing his own longings and secrets. Shakespeare "built an ear for the tyrant vulgar where it might eavesdrop & overhear the secret communings of human souls" (May 27, 1827). "Communings" is a bleakly ironic term, as the poet introduces his voice into a communal void, a common silence inhabited, like an underworld of dim shades, by souls eager for these "gushings of the spirit." Writing becomes a form of sacrifice which, once undertaken, binds the writer to continue the "sacred" act of self-revelation:

> He had uncovered to profaner eyes some of the furthest sanctuaries of the heart, he had lent to vulgar tongues the sacred language of truth & divine passion, & it was this repentance & sorrow for the violation, which speaks so sorrowfully in that little poem, which deterred him from printing the compositions in which he had made his own soul a thoroughfare for the world.[30]

"Violation" of his privacy initiates Shakespeare into the "truth & sacredness of human feeling" as expressed in Sonnet 110.[31] The disappointment in Shakespeare's relationship with Pembroke opens to other disappointments, other wrongs. For Beddoes, poetry is a medium of loss, each work hearkening to an original anguish that the poet cannot remember or identify. "Methinks there's nothing in the world but names: / All things are dead," says Melveric in **Death's Jest Book** (III.iii.325-326). Names neither restore what has been lost nor expiate the crime— itself unnamable—which caused the loss. A compulsive murderer, Melveric suffers both unrelenting guilt and a

radical estrangement from the emotional well-springs of his actions. The poet, though not guilty of crimes, endures an analogous sense of moral or emotional bewilderment. Even Shakespeare's integrity and his "eternal nature" do not exempt him from the purgatorial labor of public confession; the "cold eyes" which his words "feed" are insatiable.

Publication brings the poet the solace of company— however unsympathetic or crude—and the relief of giving voice to private anguish. If the trouble or guilt is serious enough, however, this elemental form of therapy can itself contribute to the artist's torment. In a fragment entitled "The Murderer's Haunted Couch"[32] printing presses appear as infernal engines of torture, printing Melveric's crimes in "types of fire" each night, and vanishing by morning. Melveric will never confess, but suffer into old age reliving his crime. Worse, he will not despair, not lose himself in madness or oblivion. The slow extinction of all hope and happiness, the physical and emotional impoverishment without relief of madness or death, approaches Beckett's astringent absurdism. Melveric is unusual, and in a sense privileged, among Beddoes' characters in that he can trace his guilt and suffering to a crime he committed. Beddoes was similarly haunted—by what, one cannot say. Unwilling to publish, isolated from friends and colleagues in England, he spent his adult life living in Germany as a suicidal eccentric and political outcast.

In short, his attempt to provide a "psychology of the macrocosm" foundered on the limits of his individual psychology, his vision of a therapeutic theater was disrupted by his own emotional illness. Beddoes attempted a medical and philosophic interpretation of the most disturbing aspects of this illness, shaping them into a dramaturgical experiment that would stand on its own as a work of theater. **Death's Jest Book** was to be a form of therapeutic theater. Rather, the analogy Beddoes himself borrowed from A. W. Schlegel is more appropriate. Beddoes compared the play to a Gothic cathedral. "Intricate, vast and gloomy, both intimate the supernatural and are full of indistinct thoughts of immortality." But the true character of the play is in its constituent parts

> . . . each elaborately ornamented with the counterfeit of some agreeable image in nature, or figures that owe their being alone to a wild fancy, sometimes light and joyous, sometimes fearfully hideous—often satirical, grotesque or ludicrous.[33]

The **Jest Book,** "full of indistinct thoughts of immortality," was to draw Beddoes further and further into its "minor component parts" as the play's satirical and grotesque design allowed endless postponements, reconsiderations, and mock repetitions of its revelation: the raising of the dead. The "large masses" of a sublime over-arching structure are lost in labyrinthine turnings and grotesque humor. Exuberant, anguished, anachronistically Kafkaesque, the play does indeed lay bare the profound confusion of its author. Ironically, it is this satirical frame of reference, this anatomizing of the absurd, that has survived through the years and flourished.

Notes

1. Harold Bloom, *The Visionary Company* (London: Faber and Faber, 1961) 428.

2. Trevor Levere, "Dr. Thomas Beddoes (1750-1808): Science and Medicine in Politics and Society," *British Journal of the History of Medicine* 17 (1984): 191-203.

3. Trevor Levere, *Poetry Realized in Nature* (Cambridge: 1981) 16.

4. Levere, "Dr. Thomas Beddoes" 199.

5. Thomas Lovell Beddoes, *The Works of Thomas Lovell Beddoes,* ed. Henry Wolfgang Donner (London: Oxford, 1935) 156; ll. 23-30).

6. *Works* 599.

7. Nelly Tsouyopoulos, "German Philosophy and the Rise of Modern Clinical Medicine," *Theoretical Medicine* 5 (1984): 352.

8. *Works* 609.

9. Dordrecht: D. Reidel, (1985) 1.

10. Henri F. Ellenberger, *The Discovery of the Unconscious: The History and Evolution of Dynamic Psychology* (London: Basic Books, 1970) 209-211.

11. Ellenberger 205.

12. John T. Lundin, "T. L. Beddoes at Göttingen," *Studia Neophilologica* 43 (1971): 491.

13. Lester S. King, *Medical Thinking: A Historical Preface* (Princeton: Princeton UP, 1982) 77-80.

14. *Works* 611-13.

15. *Works* 612.

16. Lundin 491.

17. *Works* 610-611.

18. George Rosen, "Romantic Medicine: A Problem in Historical Periodization," *Bullentin of the History of Medicine* 25 (1951): 154.

19. Guenter B. Risse, "'Philosophical' Medicine in Nineteenth Century Germany: An Episode in the Relations between Philosophy and Medicine," *The Journal of Medicine and Philosophy* 1 (1976): 72-92.

20. L. Pearce Williams, "Kant, Naturphilosophie, and Scientific Method," in *Foundations of Scientific Method: The Nineteenth Century,* ed. by R. N. Giere and R. S. Westfall (Bloomington, Indiana UP, 1973) 13.

21. Williams 7.

22. See Walter D. Wetzels, "Aspects of Natural Science in German Romanticism," *Studies in Romanticism* 10 (1971): 44-50. Re Schubert, see Ellenberger 205-206.

23. Michael Hamburger, *Contraries: Studies in German Thought.* (New York: E. P. Dutton, 1970) 81.

24. Qtd. Wetzels 51.

25. Hamburger 80.

26. Hamburger 80.

27. Lundin 486.

28. *Works* 536.

29. *Works* 635.

30. *Works* 633.

31. Which begins:

    Alas, 'tis true I have gone here and there, And made myself a motley to the view, Gored mine own thoughts, sold cheap what is most dear, Made old offenses of affections new . . .

32. *Works* 494-497; the title is Kelsall's.

33. *Works* 533-534.

FURTHER READING

Biographies

Donner, H. W. *Thomas Lovell Beddoes: The Making of a Poet.* Oxford: B. Blackwell, 1935, 403 p.
    Biographical study of Beddoes.

Snow, Royall H. *Thomas Lovell Beddoes: Eccentric & Poet.* New York: Covici, 1928, 227 p.
    Biographical and critical overview.

Criticism

Thompson, James R. *Thomas Lovell Beddoes.* Boston: Twayne Publishers, 1985, 137 p.
    Full-length critical study of Beddoes.

Additional coverage of Beddoes's life and career is contained in the following source published by the Gale Group: *Dictionary of Literary Biography,* Vol. 96.

Michel de Ghelderode
1898-1962

(Born Adolphe-Adhémar-Louis-Michel Martens) Belgian dramatist, poet, and fiction writer.

INTRODUCTION

Ghelderode's plays have often been described as precursors to the New French theater of the 1950s and the theater of the absurd, but for the most part, his work defies easy categorization. Combining farce, tragedy, medieval morality plays, and imagery from Renaissance art, as well as such modern elements as film and expressionist set design, Ghelderode's plays—which were sometimes intended to be performed by marionettes—are often frenetic displays criticizing and lamenting the grotesqueries of the human condition.

BIOGRAPHICAL INFORMATION

Born in Ixelles, Belgium, in 1898, Ghelderode suffered from ill health as a child. He attended the Institut St-Louis from 1910 to 1914, but a serious illness that left him partially paralyzed forced him to abandon school and most of his favorite activities. Instead, he turned to literature as a source of amusement and creative inspiration. In 1916 he began to write his own works in French. *La mort regarde à la fenêtre* (*Death Looks In at the Window*) was produced in 1918, followed by *Le repas des fauves* in 1919. Ghelderode, however, became discouraged by the public's lukewarm response to his works; he left the theater scene for several years but continued to write. In 1921 and 1922 he was a professor at the Institut Dupuich but resigned because of ill health. The following year he worked as a bookseller. In 1923 Ghelderode earned the post of archives editor in the Communale de Schaerbeek, where he worked in a variety of capacities until 1945. In 1924 Ghelderode married Jeanne-Françoise Gérard. That year he also began contributing to such publications as *La Flandre littéraire* and *La Renaissance d'Occident* and wrote plays for the puppet theater Les Marionnettes de la Renaissance d'Occident. Ghelderode began staging plays again in 1925, working with the Dutch producer Johan de Meester; their collaboration lasted until 1930. Although published volumes of his plays made him well known in parts of Western Europe, Ghelderode completely gave up writing plays in 1939. Between 1946 and 1953 he wrote for *Le Journal de Bruges*. Despite his abandonment of the theater and a life in seclusion with his wife, Ghelderode was highly successful as a playwright. A 1949 production of *Fastes d'enfer* (*Chronicles of Hell*), originally written in 1929, caused a huge scandal on its opening night, an event that ensured his popularity. Until his death in 1962, Ghelderode received many honors and awards, and his plays were successfully produced on both the stage and the radio.

MAJOR WORKS

Ghelderode's plays have been described as visual interpretations of the tension between nightmare and reality. Strongly influenced by the art of the Renaissance in Europe, Ghelderode based many of his themes and much of his imagery on paintings by Hieronymous Bosch, El Greco, Goya, and Pieter Brueghel the elder, evoking the universal monstrosities of humankind as well as violence and alienation in the modern world. Ghelderode's plays are also known for being noisy and colorful spectacles, using various sound effects to punctuate the grotesque and cacophonous nature of nightmare and the vulgarity of waking life. Throughout his canon, Ghelderode held to several overriding themes: that the little virtue that exists in the world is almost always overcome by vice; that people are repeatedly and tragically seduced by illusions; and that cruelty directs most human actions. Ghelderode's first important play, *La mort du Docteur Faust* (*The Death of Doctor Faust*; 1928) is a twentieth-century interpretation of the Faust myth. Its subtitle, "A Music-Hall Tragedy," indicates Ghelderode's notion of life as an absurd carnival. In this version of the story, Faust leaves his sixteenth-century intellectual world to seek existential answers in a twentieth-century café. There his personality splits into two parts—actor and character—and the Devil, who has been watching the events as they unfold, declares in the end that neither is the true Faust; meanwhile, both Fausts are killed, and a servant dressed in Faust's clothing advances toward Faust's love Marguerite. *Christophe Colomb* (*Christopher Columbus*; 1929) is a farce satirizing the title character's search for a new and better world. *Escurial* (1929) is set in the early Renaissance. A king and his jester play a game that becomes increasingly bitter and sinister as it is revealed that the jester has been the queen's lover and that the king has poisoned her. In *Pantagleize* (1930), which has a modern setting, Ghelderode bitterly criticized capitalism. The title character, described as a "little man," becomes swept up in violent events when he inadvertently utters the password signaling the start of a revolution. *Fastes d'enfer* is a vehement attack on hypocrisy in religion and the barbarism in its followers. In *Magie rouge* (*Red Magic*; 1934), set in medieval Flanders, the avaricious main character withholds sex from his virgin wife because he doesn't want to waste his strength, while she plots against him with three thieves. The play ends in a violent and bloody betrayal. *La Balade du grand macabre* (*The Grand Macabre's Stroll*; 1953), a play that strongly resembles the paintings of Bosch, is a farce that features a character who claims to be Death incarnate. Announcing that the end of the world has come, he locks a pair of lovers in a tomb, insisting that they will have to repopulate the earth, and then goes on a drinking binge with friends. By the end of the day it becomes clear that the world will not end; the lovers are released, and everyone goes on as before, suggesting that even the threat of death is ultimately impotent and absurd.

CRITICAL RECEPTION

Although not widely embraced because of their pessimistic tone and absurdist plots, Ghelderode's plays have earned the admiration of many theater critics, professionals, and audiences around the world, who cite his poetic expression of esoteric themes as a major attraction to his work. Additionally, Ghelderode's use of influences ranging from paintings to folklore to Gothic literature lends a sense of romanticism to his otherwise grim subject matter. Despite the acclaim and awards he received in the last years of his life, Ghelderode himself insisted that his works were intended to attract popular, not critical, attention.

PRINCIPAL WORKS

Plays

La mort regarde à la fenêtre [*Death Looks in at the Window*] 1918
Le repas des fauves 1919
La farce de la Mort qui faillit trepasser [published in 1952] 1925
Oude Piet [published in 1925] 1925
Images de la vie de St François d' Assise [*Images of the Life of St. Francis of Assisi*; published in 1928] 1927
Barabbas [published in 1932] 1928
Don Juan, ou Les amants chimériques [*Don Juan, or The Chimerical Lovers*] 1928
La mort du Docteur Faust [*The Death of Doctor Faust*; published in 1925–26] 1928
Christophe Colomb [*Christopher Columbus*; published in 1927] 1929
Escurial [published in 1927–28] 1929
Pantagleize [published in 1929 and 1934] 1930
Trois acteurs, un drame [*Three Actors and Their Drama*] 1931
Le siège d'Ostende [*The Siege of Ostend*] 1933
Les femmes au tombeau [*The Women at the Tomb*] 1934
Mademoiselle Jaïre [*Miss Jairus*; published in 1942] 1934
Magie rouge [*Red Magic*; published in 1935] 1934
Le mystère de la passion de Notre Seigneur Jésus-Christ [*The Mystery of the Passion of Our Lord Jesus Christ*; published in 1925] 1934

Le cavalier bizarre [*The Strange Rider*] 1938
Hop, Signor! 1938
La pie sur le gibet [*The Magpie on the Gallows*] 1938
Sire Halewyn [*Lord Halewyn*; published 1943] 1938
D'un diable qui prêcha merveilles [*Of a Devil Who Preached Marvels*] 1942
La farce des ténébreux [*The Farce of the Dark Band*] 1942
L'école des bouffons [*The School for Buffoons*] 1942
Sortie de l'acteur [*The Actor Makes His Exit*] 1942
Le club de menteurs [*The Liars' Club*] 1943
Fastes d'enfer [*Chronicles of Hell*; *Splenders of Hell*; published in 1929] 1949
La folie d'Hugo van der Goes [*The Madness of Hugo van der Goes*] 1951
Le perroquet de Charles-Quint [*Charles the Fifth's Parrot*] 1951
Le soleil se couche [*The Sun Sets*; published 1942] 1951
Adrian et Jusemina 1952
Marie la misérable [*Marie the Miserable*; published in 1935] 1952
La balade du grand macabre [*The Grand Macabre's Stroll*; published in 1935] 1953
Les aveugles [*The Blind Men*; published in 1936] 1956

Collected Plays

Théâtre 1943
Théâtre complet. 2 vols. 1943
Théâtre. 5 vols. 1950-57
Michel de Ghelderode: Seven Plays, Volume 1 [translated and edited by G. Hauger; includes: *The Women at the Tomb, Barabbas, Three Actors and Their Drama, The Blind Men, Pantagleize, Chronicles of Hell*, and *Lord Halewyn*] (collected plays) 1960
Michel de Ghelderode: Seven Plays, Volume 2 [translated and edited by G. Hauger; includes: *Red Magic, Hop, Signor!, The Death of Doctor Faust, Christopher Columbus, A Night of Pity, Piet Bouteille*, and *Miss Jairus*] (collected plays) 1964
**The Strange Rider and Seven Other Plays* [translated by S. Draper; includes: *The Women at the Tomb, The Blind Men, Red Magic, Christopher Columbus, Evening Lament, The Old Men*, and *Pantagleize*] (collected plays) 1967

Other Major Works

La Corne d'abondance (poetry) 1925
Ixelles, mes amours . . . [under the pseudonym P. Costenoble] (poetry) 1928
Sortilèges (short stories) 1941
Théâtre d'écoutes (radio plays) 1951
Correspondance: Autour d'une amitié naissante [with Henri Vandeputte] (letters) 1964
Contes et dicts hors du temps (fiction) 1975
Autour d'Une Amitié littéraire: Correspondance 1932-1934 [with Henri Vandeputte; edited by Guy Descamps] (letters) 1984

*The dates listed for works preceded with an asterisk are publication dates; the first production dates for these works are not known. The dates listed for all other works are the date of the first production; publication dates appear in brackets.

**This work was published privately for the American Friends of Michel de Ghelderode.

AUTHOR COMMENTARY

Michel de Ghelderode with Samuel Draper (interview date 1963)

SOURCE: "An Interview with Michel de Ghelderode," in *Tulane Drama Review*, Vol. 8, No. 1, Fall 1963, pp. 39-50.

[*In the following interview, Draper and Ghelderode discuss the latter's career, influences, and artistic vision.*]

[*Samuel Draper*]: *Where can we begin? Anywhere you like. I am ready to listen.*

[Michel de Ghelderode]: Yes, yes. When I have a sensitive listener, I will talk well. Very well, indeed, in a French which most people find too elegant, too explicit, too regal if you will, in a French that has become superannuated. I went to high school at the Institut Saint Louis in Brussels. My education was extraordinary. Those priests, against whom I hold nothing, further inculcated in me a taste for funereal rites which I had difficulty in exorcising. Earlier my fascination with death had been a beautiful rather than morbid experience.

Before you go on, would you tell me how death came to be associated with beauty in your mind?

Yes. My preoccupation with death—my fascination and even my love of it—was nurtured by my mother, an intelligent and sensitive woman who was in tune with natural mysteries. She was a shy person who remained all her life close to nature—perhaps primitive is a better word. She understood supernatural events, even extra-sensory phenomena. She used to tell me many horror stories and magnificent fairy tales which fascinated me, but bored my two brothers and sister. They were more interested in automobiles and airplanes. Twentieth-century children, they. But not I.

My first encounter with Death was at five. On a sunny afternoon in early spring, I returned home from school to find a small bird asleep in our front yard. Picking it up carefully, I caressed it, was cautious not to wake it, and made it a bed in my coat pocket. Two days later a frightful odor permeated the house, and my mother searched in vain to localize the smell of decay. When questioned pointedly, neither I nor my brothers or my sister knew the cause of the acrid perfume. A few hours later, on finding the badly decomposed bird in the pocket of my coat hanging

in the hall closet, she was angry. Then she quietly listened to my explanation. I replied: "The bird was sleeping and had such a peaceful look that I didn't want to awaken him." "Crazy kid!" shouted my father, "don't you know *dead* things stink?" My brothers and sister jeered: "You don't know what being dead is, do you Michel?" . . . No, I didn't know what death was, and when I sought an explanation, my mother took me aside. "You are right, Michel; the little bird is asleep. He is living in a more beautiful world than ours. People say he is dead, but he is just asleep. Now he is flying over green fields, dipping his wings in a cool stream, perhaps soaring toward a rainbow or chasing a golden cloud. He is happier than all of us. He is unconcerned with our world. He has found his heaven. . . . To be dead is to be in a continuous dream of peace."

But you said while in high school your thoughts concerning death became morbid, particularly when in the hands of the priests.

Yes. That's true. But after I left school I analyzed these new terrors about death and got rid of them *forever* by writing them out in many of my plays.

How did you start writing plays?

I came into the theatre in a strange way. It was an accident—well, almost. A half-starved-looking bohemian approached me one day—toward the end of the First World War. He asked if I could give a lecture to a young group of avant-garde artists and writers. I applied affirmatively and made precise my subject: Edgar Allan Poe. "Bravo," he declared. "But a lecture is a little short. You should also present a play. Do you have any?" Presumptuous like all young writers, I replied: "Yes, a whole cupboard full. How many do you want?" "One will do." And it was thus that I came to write a play in the style of Poe.

Can you describe this work?

It was lugubrious beyond belief, a drama I called *Death Looks Through the Window.* The stage was plunged in darkness. Three candles were the only light. It was a frightening play in which all the characters were physically or morally defective, filled with blemishes. There was a senile and cynical old princess, a young girl with an enormous head, a deaf and hunch-backed chamberlain in the Pope's employ, an archdeacon who kept an inventory of his crimes, his rapings and kidnappings, and poisonings. Wouldn't you have said that all this took place in Rome during the Renaissance? The drama unfolded in a storm during which the church bells pealed forth, and wolves howled. Everything ended in hell and damnation. It was frightful, incoherent, macabre, and flamboyant. It was a smash hit, a howling success. I wondered if all the yelling and applause were for the play or for the lights which had finally come on. But whatever the reasons, the lesson was great for me. I had, without knowing it, applied all the theatrical ingredients.

But didn't you actually become a playwright with the Popular Flemish Theatre who commissioned you to write their plays?

Yes, but let's get one thing straight. I wrote my plays in French—nothing but French, although my blood for a thousand years has been Flemish. But I don't speak or write Flemish. My heart and mind are Flemish, but my tongue and my pen are French. My plays had to be translated into Flemish. The story is told the other way—that I wrote in Flemish and then had my plays translated in French. That is wrong. Yes, I wrote **St. Francis, Barabbas, The Strange Rider, The Old Men, The Passion of our Lord,** and many others for the Flemish Theatre.

How did you happen to get acquainted with the past and particularly with the sixteenth century?

I don't know exactly. It's a mystery. I've always had a strong attraction for the past which has consoled me. Because the present only brings me anxieties and uncertitude, I have turned to the past which gives me riches and peace. The present is a fugitive which constantly escapes me. The past is more alive for me than this very day. I can feel the presence of the dead and their lost age more keenly than I can feel their opposites. I have been attracted by some of the same grotesqueries like those performed by Eulenspiegel which Charles de Coster, my Belgian master, made famous. Legends of olden days, ancestral customs, the great centuries of violence like the sixteenth, the brutal life, and religious wars. I can see the massacres of those days and the terrible disease. I inhaled the fragrance of savory meats and of kegs of beer guzzled in hundreds of cafes, the wild carnivals, all the uproar of the centuries when Flanders staggered itself in war and danced in orgies of the flesh.

There are stories told about your methods of creativity. Have you let it be known that there was some mysterious force guiding you or even dictating to you?

The process of my writing is mysterious like so many things in my life. Once this cerebral machinery begins—this magic lantern—or whatever you want to call it, I am powerless to stop it. I must see the work through. That moment when I am seized with an idea for a play is always unexpected. But whenever the creative urge takes hold of me, I am like a man possessed. I am in a frenzy and work at a feverish pitch. That panic is felt in my drama. Such excessiveness is shown in my language and sometimes in the plots themselves. I've often been criticized for overdoing everything. But that is my way.

To which writers is your art closest?

The Elizabethans, of course. The conflicts and passions treated by Shakespeare were extreme, just as those I deal with are. But don't forget Ben Jonson and Marlowe who also influenced me. Then there is the Golden Age of Spain. Lope de Vega and Calderón played a large part in my development.

What modern authors have inspired you?

Maeterlinck's mysterious and supernatural drama gripped me. He taught me that dramatic art is not only physical

but metaphysical. In that way, my own plays have a double twist: they're both physical and metaphysical.

Didn't St. Teresa of Avila write this way? She believed that the visible was a manifestation of the invisible.

Yes, and I think she's right. When I was a young man I had an interview with Maeterlinck. He talked to me about what he called "The Deeper Life" and I've never forgotten what he said. Many of his ideas have become mine. We both believe that creation does not stop with man, that we are surrounded by invisible beings who are superior to us. That superiority consists in that they have communications whose nature we cannot possibly imagine. I have increased these communications—I've spent a lifetime doing just that. In the beginning I didn't have much of a spiritual personality. Our veritable birth dates from the day when we feel deeply within us that there is something unexpected or grave in life. When I was writing **Escurial** I shed many tears for the King who had poisoned the saintly Queen. He had never seen the light, the infinite, the beautiful, the unexpected in life. He had never seen the divine hand which I have beheld many times. One of Shakespeare's heroes says "John, before I loved thee as a brother, but now I do respect thee as my soul." If the evil king could have said that he would have been reborn. But Folial in his death opened the eyes of his soul to every ray of light. He had trained his soul, his heart, and made it too much alive . . . so that he longed for death.

Who else among the modern writers interests you?

Strindberg was my idol for quite a long time. Although my technique is not related to his, I do feel a fraternal bond with him. Perhaps our kinship is in the need both of us have to go to the center of the problem and see it through. Neither of us is afraid. The reason, above all, that I like him is that he was a suffering and sensitive soul.

Most people do know about your great physical and spiritual suffering.

Yes, without all the pain I've experienced, I'm certain that I wouldn't have written one line.

May I ask you about those so-called blasphemies in your plays? How do you justify them?

An artist doesn't have to justify anything. There are perhaps profane oaths in my plays and some vulgar language, but I don't believe you'll find any blasphemy.

Yes, but in the **Chronicles of Hell (Fastes d'enfer)** *the priests do poison the sacred host.*

Ah, but there you have a very moral play. Whatever may be said against it, I'm certain that I have created a deeply moral work of art. That is the point of view also of the great prelates of the Catholic Church who see things from an enlightened point of view. But of course the bourgeois sexton won't agree with them.

Please explain that a little more.

Chronicles of Hell is a play about an authentic Christian who is in a state of grace and who is opposed by shammers, fake believers, anti-Christians who are *so-called* priests. The true Christian dies in the end, but he dies fulfilled and appeased. There's nothing sacrilegious about the drama. No Catholic, in fact no Christian, should take offense. Some of the play's details are disturbing, and the form they take extreme. However, the moral tone of the play is quite high. This was proved by the aftermath of the scandal at the Theâtre Marigny in Paris in 1949. The conclusion of the disagreement was just that: **Chronicles of Hell** is a purely moral play. The difficulty is that the audience does have trouble in accustoming itself to seeing a group of ugly, grotesque, and hideous priests on stage. But the important thing to remember is that the good priests represent Truth and that Truth has been well dramatized. The audience can't help being struck by the end of the play when the true believer is heroic and sublime and the false Christians behave monstrously. Isn't that the same theme as Molière's *Tartuffe*?

Wouldn't you say that **Barabbas** *is a more traditional passion play than* **Chronicles of Hell?**

Some critics have called **Barabbas** a passion play. But I don't think it's a *religious* drama although it does deal with Christ's crucifixion. It's more a human tragedy than a Catholic play. No, **Barabbas** isn't dogmatic theatre which edifies and preaches. It concerns Barabbas, a physical giant, who wants to know the truth about Christ and his doctrine.

You've been accused of being both anti-clerical and anti-Semitic in **Barabbas** *because of your manner of treating the Jewish priests who hasten Christ's death.*

My intention was to make the priests impersonal symbols rather than members of any race or religion. They symbolize any organized priesthood and more specifically those Catholic priests in Europe who have played politics and betrayed the primitive religion of Jesus. Yes, I am anti-clerical, but I am a Christian and a mystic and always will be. That is one reason I write: I do believe. As for my being anti-Semitic, that's impossible. I'm against no race or religion.

What kind of writing have you done since 1938, when you finished your last play?

I returned to my first love of writing short stories. I also have been working for a number of years on my *Memoirs*, which will be published after my death. I quit writing for the theatre in 1938 because I felt I'd used up all the possibilities of my experience.[1]

Have you ever considered using the theatre as a means of spreading propaganda?

I've never written a *pièce à thèse* and I never will. The theatre is an art of instinct and not of reason. The playwright must live only by vision and divination, relegating reason to an auxiliary position. Any topical idea or fad is slavery. Look what happened to Scribe and to all the commercial playwrights whose work is forgotten. To write a doctrinaire play is to make a mistake. Such drama can only be transitory. Art cannot be subjugated to any system of ideas.

Hasn't the purpose of your art been to discover man?

Exactly. I hoped to express about man what had not been talked about before. Sometimes I liked to make fun of humanity. I've a certain predilection for caricature which I used to vilify man. Other times I have praised him. My characters are not just buffoons resembling the masks of my friend James Ensor. They are sentient beings capable of suffering and love. They are humanity—above all—not shells or objects of a still life. Some of them are cruel, some are evil, and some are good. I don't hesitate to show the Devil in my plays just as I show God, because the Devil is as real to me as a piece of beefsteak!

Some of your detractors call you an escapist because you live in solitude and are distrustful of our world.

Perhaps they're right. In that way I'm like my **Christopher Columbus**. Like him I sought freedom. He is a synthesis of all travelers, all the wandering gypsies, all the "seekers" of his time and of all time. Christopher Columbus was the man who escaped. *Escape!* What a magic word! But this problem of escaping seems to confront modern man as much as it did the Italian discoverer. Men have always tried to escape because life is hard. Columbus is related to Parsifal by his purity, and perhaps he's as mad as Don Quixote. And Columbus was misunderstood. Civilization rewarded my Columbus by putting him into prison and making him into a statue. But the innocent have been tortured since the beginning of the world.

Although you have violated the facts of history in your **Christopher Columbus,** *you have given us new insight into his psychology.*

That's what I intended. After all, when he's put in prison and is asked what he'll do, he replies "I'll travel, that's what!"

In spite of all the vituperation heaped upon you during your life, you remain essentially a moralist. The morality you create is not that of the hypocrites, bigots, or good-for-nothings, but the eternal morality that is the center of all man's thinking: those ultimate moral problems which eventually could bring the Devil over to the side of God.

If my work proves anything, it's that man's character has not improved with time.

Aren't you revolting against today's evils although you describe those evils in times past?

Yes, man is the same today as he was 2,000 years ago or 10,000 years ago!

And you're not afraid to say just that?

I am not afraid. . . . I don't fear anything or anyone—not the King, or the Pope, or any man, or institution . . . and not even God. *I am free.*

Do you know Brecht's work?

Yes, I know Brecht's work, the ideas in which I despise. He is a didactic playwright, a crusader for materialism. His plays teach me nothing because he is wrong. Yes, he is mistaken. Maybe his plays are those of the future; if so I'm relieved that I belong to the past—to Sophocles and Shakespeare. Divination and instinct are essential. Yes, Brecht is wrong . . . but he is a theatrical genius. But his ideas are banal.

GHELDERODE ON HIS PLAYS

The Old Men (1919)

Even as a young man—I was 17 when I first thought of the play—I hated hypocrisy. All those "believers" disgusted me, those who worshipped in name only, recited the appropriate prayers, and followed the outward forms of their religion without believing it or understanding it. **The Old Men** are like most people, unfortunately; they possess the secrets of life and death, but don't believe them, care about them, or practice them. And like most men they can be bribed—they are corrupt when it comes to money. But Barbara knows the truth as contained in The Lord's Prayer.

Evening Lament (1921)

My enemies wrote that I had copied Pirandello by writing **Evening Lament.** In 1921 no one in Belgium had heard of Pirandello, and I had not either. True I am interested in appearances and reality in my play but those ideas have been in the air since man began to think. Wasn't Shakespeare fascinated with them too? Pirandello, indeed. I hear he is great, but I don't read him. He is not one of my authors. Perhaps he copied me!

The Strange Rider (1922)

A Polish friend of mine, a poet, was an intimate of Boris Pasternak and visited him in his home outside Moscow. He and Pasternak discussed my dramas and the Russian writer expressed interest because he had seen **The Strange Rider** performed in Moscow in the late thirties with puppets. He made the Pole promise to send him more of my plays. At the time I didn't know Pasternak, although my friend called him a great poet. He quoted Pasternak about me in a letter which I didn't save, unfortunately. The gist was, however, that Pasternak liked what he saw. He liked Ghelderode! That praise means more to me than all the prizes, medals, citations in the world!

The Women At The Tomb (1928)

When I learned that the Broadway Chapel Players of New York City planned to perform **The Women At The Tomb** (March, 1959) in a small modern chapel I was pleased. We should have religious themes in plays on Broadway and good drama in our churches. All drama in the large sense is religious because not only is it rooted in and connected with the mimetic impulses of man but comes from man's religious or philosophic apprehension and comprehension of life. True for *Oedipus Rex* or *King Lear* and even for high comedy as we see it in Molière, who clarifies man's dimensions so he may realize where he fits in the universe. Originally, **The Women At The Tomb** was a longer play, but I cut it, synthesized it, worked it, and reworked it to its present form. Its shortness adds to its power, don't you think? There have always been a few limited souls who preferred "Sunday School Plays" to religious drama; of course, they believe the play to be off-beat and irreverent. On the contrary, the play is highly reverent, delivering unexpected and astonishing power in its closing moments. Each woman is a segment of human society, and above all they are sympathetic despite their foibles, foolishness, disbelief, and pride. Not a *humanist* interpretation of the crucifixion, the play's essence deals with the *humanity* of those different women who knew Christ, misunderstood him, loved him, believed him to be the Saviour, were puzzled by him, and even hated him.

Red Magic (1931)

Yes, I can laugh a wicked laugh. Laughter is not always good-natured. To laugh with scorn or sneeringly is my privilege—the privilege of my wicked side! Granted there are many ways of laughing. But a true laugh, profoundly motivated, is always satiric, always corrective. The laughs drawn by **Red Magic** will be satiric, and consequently moral whether anyone likes that or not. Molièrean laughs obey the same laws. Isn't he also a cruel author like me, this great Molière? No? I've often been accused of being like Hieronymous, which makes me laugh long and loud. Would I had dared attempt to buy the Trinity and Immortality!

Note

1. *Marie la Misérable* was written in 1952.

OVERVIEWS AND GENERAL STUDIES

Micheline Herz (essay date 1962)

SOURCE: "Tragedy, Poetry and the Burlesque in Ghelderode's Theatre," in *Yale French Studies*, No. 29, 1962, pp. 92-101.

[*In the following essay, Herz asserts that Ghelderode uses burlesque in his plays to emphasize the ambiguity of the human condition.*]

At every level, including the level of appearance, Michel de Ghelderode's theatre abounds in burlesque elements. There is nothing glorious about his men, nor about his women either. However upsetting some people may find this, it is clear that Ghelderode himself, as manifested in his plays, reveled in such an atmosphere. Monsters and misshapen beings accost us at every turn. Women, apart from a few saints and other privileged creatures, tend to be fiftyish, ample as to breast and buttock, with a gash by way of a mouth and peroxide hair: typical residents of a low-grade brothel. Their names are evocative: Salivaine, Visquosine, Crême, Chose, Boule, Olympia, Aurora, Venuska, and so forth. The more or less normal creatures in this feminine galaxy (Armande in *Sortie de l'acteur* or Emmanuèle in *La Farce des ténébreux*) remind one nevertheless of Baudelaire's "Woman is the opposite of the dandy." Even those very young girls, Purmelende d'Ostrelende in *Sire Halewyn* and the living corpse Mademoiselle Jaire, cannot entirely escape the grotesquerie of woman's condition. They are Woman, young or old as circumstances require, exemplars of their sex.

Men, though treated in less summary fashion, are etched in acidly. One recalls Hiéronymus in *Magie rouge*, Videbolle, Sire Goulave in *La Balade du grand macabre*, and a whole series, in *Hop Signor, Escurial, L'Ecole des bouffons* and elsewhere, of men blind or decrepit or otherwise infirm. In conjuring up all this ugliness and, at times, poking fun at it, Ghelderode is carrying out one of the missions of the theatre as he conceives it. His aim is to deflate a number of lying myths, and one of these is the delight man takes in his own beauty. So Ghelderode stresses man's physiological servitude and harps on his wretchedness. Like Sartre and like Céline, he dwells on the intestinal aspects of these miseries. His plays smell bad. Yet these odors—which, also, are man—engender comedy, however little it may appeal to the queasy. Are we not told that la Palatine, with the aid of her husband, a nincompoop in other domains of endeavor, used to organize crepitation contests—and this was France's great century! There is much talk of fecal matter in Ghelderode's plays, to underline the fact that man is not dust alone but also dung. He would prefer to see himself as a flower or a radiant body? So much the worse for him. Whereas, if he admits the restraints imposed by his bodily functions, he ceases to be civilizedly etiolated and enrols matter in his service. And matter, even fecal, is an inexhaustible source of comedy for the robust individuality imagined by Ghelderode.

Like man's lot, the plot in which he is caught up is frequently a burlesque one. The deceived husband of *Hop Signor* dies during the hoodwinking process because he played the aristocrat, with a sword, and airs and graces that did not befit his station. The miserly Hiéronymus (*Magie rouge*) harbors the horseman Armador, who has promised to manufacture gold. But Armador steals instead of providing, and with the help of the housewife Sybilla places responsibility for a murder on Hiéronymus, who has already gone mad. This husband, who shuts up his

wife with another man and marries off his doubloons so that they may multiply, is the central figure of a cruel farce in which avarice takes on hallucinatory dimensions.

Even in the more sober plays, the burlesque aspects are always present. While a father gives way to grotesque grief for his dying daughter (*Mademoiselle Jaïre*), the coffinmaker comes along to vaunt his merchandise: "For your soon-to-be-lamented daughter, I'll make a little masterpice of elegance, solidity and comfort." Or a bottle of Hollands gin consoles the three Mariekes, as they weep over the dead.

Death, in *Le Cavalier bizarre,* spares the terrified old men who await his coming and bears off a new-born child. The title character of *La Balade du grand macabre* himself dies and his victims outlive him. The author, in *Trois Acteurs, un drame,* commits suicide, and not the actor who had intended to do so. Examples could easily be multiplied.

The burlesque atmosphere allows the spectator to put up with a degree of tension that might well evaporate, if the author tried to maintain it too long. A further merit of the burlesque, in Ghelderode's eyes, is that it gives direct expression to the voice of the people, which in Greek tragedy is embodied in the chorus. He roundly declares this to be so, and refers to the Mariekes mentioned above and to the buffoons in all the plays where they appear. Even in *Barrabas* and *Marie la misérable,* his religious plays, these procedures are used. In the same strain are the "plays within a play," the processions, the lines of mourners and the speeches, to which Ghelderode sometimes turns too readily.

It is less easy to speak of a burlesque character or of burlesque psychology, since Ghelderode rejects all psychology. The dramatist, he maintains, must draw upon the wellsprings of vision or of instinct. The writer who accepts a system will sooner or later trap himself in a problem play. Jean-Jacques, the author who serves as spokesman for Ghelderode himself in *Sortie de l'acteur,* proclaims that "I have never wanted to reveal or demonstrate anything and, as long as men have been mumming, the theatre has never been known to reveal anything whatever."

The few characters who turn out well, in Michel de Ghelderode's plays, become human via their dehumanization. Like Jarry's personages, they are so untrue that they achieve a truth of their own. Nekrozotar and Videbolle, the former a divine executioner mounted on the drunkard Porprenaz, and the latter the philosopher of the kingdom and a henpecked husband, are related to Tyl Eulenspiegel. They act, like worthy representatives of legendary chronicles, in a totally unforeseeable fashion. And we accept the spectacle of Videbolle overwhelmed with blows that would kill any mortal, just as we accept the unbelievable malevolence of Videbolle's wife Salivaine, the kingdom's grey eminence. Ghelderode's more anthropomorphic heroes, among them Charles V and Barrabas, are not exempt from the hyperbole favored by this author. In that magnificent play *Le Soleil se couche* Charles V gives orders for his funeral mass, little suspecting that he is falling into the trap laid for him by his son Philip. The examination of conscience he makes, to the accompaniment of the objurgations of a talking parrot, shows him in turn as sincere and fraudulent, a believer and a skeptic, brave and cowardly, magnificent and pitiably deceived by Philip and the Holy Office.

The hero of *Barrabas* is a wild beast one cannot readily imagine associated with any kind of Christian communism. To say what Ghelderode's characters are, unavoidably one must relate what they are doing or have done. They enjoy their liberty in the midst of the incredible and the extraordinary, and this liberty appears to be gratuitous, for it is grafted much more firmly on a poetics than on any association of the characters with a world, a struggle or a passion, in which they would feel responsible for anything beyond themselves. With the sole exception of the cloistered Marie, the liberty of Ghelderode's characters revolves in a vacuum and may, in this sense, be classified as burlesque.

Ghelderode, in his *Entretiens d'Ostende,* asserts that his plays are neither clerical nor anti-clerical. "Why," he goes on to say, "don't they make me out to be a Catholic author, while they're at it, since after all I've put saints on the stage!" However that may be, his education at the hands of the "clerical gentlemen" awakened within him a sense of metaphysical anguish. At first this was stilled by the teachings of the Church, but later, as he himself expressed it, his faith "drifted" and he found himself obliged to find an answer for the problems of our human condition.

Whatever his religious feelings may have been at the time of his death, there can be no doubt that Ghelderode's guidelines are Christian. Ghelderodian man has a sense of sin. He knows that he is guilty. He is punished because he is guilty. He is capable of every "truculence," in the Latin sense of the word, and of every extravagance of behavior because, no matter what he does, he is certain to lose. His horizon is bounded by death. Thus the sense of the tragic, in Ghelderode's case, comes from the omnipresence of death. There is a lot of dying in his plays, he declares, because there is a lot of dying in life. Yet on several occasions he has let his characters protest against this bloody game. "There are three of us, and if only three of us die, it's because there's no one else."

It is, indeed, more economical to list the plays in which death has no part. They are *D'un diable qui prêcha merveilles, Le Club des menteurs, Les Vieillards, Adrian et Jusemina*—a total of four plays out of the thirty printed in the five volumes of the Gallimard edition! Death is often a medieval figure, with an eroded snubnose, who sees fit to wander among the living. In *Le Cavalier bizarre* he is described as "very taken with himself, with protruding jaw, hand on hip, scythe over shoulder, wearing white boots and wrapped in a torn cloak strewn with small silver crosses." In *Le Grand Macabre,* he resembles the disguise a student might dream up for the Beaux Arts ball. In *Escurial* the king imagines him "as a skeleton sauntering about, in monk's clothing." Death, in *Christophe Colomb,* appears as a "naval officer, ageless." He is featured in the train of the Ship of Fools, along with young men wearing shrouds aand women similarly attired. In *Masques Ostendais,* Death is dressed in a dirty garment covered with crosses, with a battered top hat.

In less incarnate fashion, death resolves the dilemmas confronting Doctor Faust and Sire Halewyn and Barrabas and Marie the wretched, for death alone confers peace. (The real drama for Ghelderode would be immortality, but not as Simone de Beauvoir has conceived it.) He tackles the related problem of resurrection in *Mademoiselle Jaïre* and in the religious plays. He looks on resurrection, it would seem, as a privilege reserved for the gods. Thus the attitude of Ghelderode toward death is ambivalent. He desires it because of its purity and fears it because it might funnel one into a beyond where the angels would bear a distressing similarity to cops.

He evolved, consequently, a kind of fetishism of death and brandished it, variously garbed, before the eyes of those eager to forget it. Western civilization, with its up-to-the-minute funeral rites and its painted and smiling corpses, has administered a tranquilizer to our feeling for death, and if ever Ghelderode set himself a mission, no doubt it was to remind men of how afraid they are—without overlooking the laugh that so often follows fear.

In his own way yet much as does Camus in *Caligula,* Ghelderode teaches his readers that men die and that they are not happy. But except in *Sortie de l'acteur* and *Pantagleize,* Ghelderode is on God's side—whether God exists or not. He sports death's colors no doubt because, having often been ill, he was able to become intimate with it, but also because he took great satisfaction in exorcizing it on his own account, while turning loose on other people his arsenal of Fates.

Death, finally, is also the order in which one can believe. He sometimes comes close to imagining that it's all some monstrous legpull that a jovial Creator has inflicted on us, and that serves to get the creation going again. The function of the devil, never far away from the figure of death in Ghelderode's theatre, is to restore the category of Evil and reinsert it in a cosmos beneath the blazing sun of Satan.

Love is the opium of the western world. Ghelderode goes further. Love, it is his conviction, is synonymous with lust, death's other companion on the portals of the churches. Thus eroticism is a source both of tragedy and of burlesquerie. It is tragic because it leads to nothingness, through the intermediary of sickness. Beauty, once possessed, is transmuted into a creature of the charnelhouse. But it is burlesque when baptized with the name of love and when the commentary is omitted that ". . . relates how the most azured and turtledovey amorous tale ends with the evocation of a bidet, of a bidet, Madame, were it made of gold and shaped like a heart." This is not to condemn the function that is sublimated under the name of love. The innocent Fernand d'Abcaude, in love with Azurine, is an object of ridicule until he does obeisance to the cult of Azurine, now unveiled and rebaptized Putrégina. Normal pleasure, however, cannot be found in these plays, unless perhaps in the past, when the exploits of some duke are evoked. The flesh, alas, is sad and putrescent.

The couples—Marguerite Harstein and Juréal, Hiéronymus and Sybilla—are sterile. Husbands appear to derive great pleasure from leaving their wives virgins, so that they can watch them suffer. Sexuality, or lust, imprisons man and more especially, perhaps, woman, who spices it with masochism when she is young and pretty and with ravenous unsatisfied instincts when she is older. In **Hop Signor,** which Ghelderode has characterized as the drama of impotence, Marguerite compares voluptuousness to a shortened form of torture and, finally, physical satisfaction coincides with the sleep of death. Love, with Ghelderode, has monstrous dimensions. Only in the brothel is it forgivable, and Putrégina is assuredly the least morbid of all these creatures.

Chastity is a virtue because love is a trap, leading to gestures by whose burlesque character Ghelderode is obsessed. In the kind of bacchanalian revel that permeates this theatre one may, perhaps, discern the ebullition of good health. Ghelderode has denied that he is "a pornographer-industrialist specializing in bourgeois orgasms." Perhaps he specializes in more literary orgies!

The validity of Ghelderode's theater resides in its poetry. This does not appear to be so at first glance, and it was never his aim to write poetic plays. In each work there can be discovered, after careful investigation, a particular rhythm that concords with Ghelderode's vision. The words are linked in a musical sequence of cadences and leitmotifs that reinforce the overall theme. Most of his plays could readily be adapted for ballet. With him, gesture is primary and speech is subordinate to it, forming a sort of ground bass that accompanies the actors' plastic expression.

When simplicity marks this poetry or these movements performed confronted by a veritable Chaplinade (to borrow the term created by ordinary folk as in **Pantagleize** or **Le Club des menteurs,** we are by Yvan Goll). The spectator, plunged in a world that precludes direct identification, has a poetic experience of or meets as in a dream protagonists endowed with a reality that to the spectator appears absurd. This moves him. He laughs. Ghelderode admired Chaplin. And an ironic satisfaction can be gleaned from the reflection that this figure of the poet as a gentle dreamer, innocent and pure, comic yet touching, links up beyond Chaplin with the scatterbrained characters of Yiddish folklore.

This poetry has a further strain of mystery, or of magic. The world contains things that are signs, and which may

awaken at any instant. Life swarms with hollow receptacles waiting to be filled and, sometimes kindly and sometimes maleficent, the forces that take them over plunge the individual if not in the religious sphere at least in the domain of the sacred. That is why puppets can represent the divine or, if one will, the essential element in human beings better than do actors of flesh and blood, whose gestures may lack the definitive or hieratic character that produces trance. And to that the spectator must be led, if the ceremony is to have its full effect.

The puppeteer, furthermore, at least in the rudimentary form of the spectacle, utilizes nothing but his own voice, dehumanized by means of a kind of whistle. There is only one mediator between author and public. The treason of language is, in this way, practically eliminated. We inhabit pure poetry, where the puppet master is God.

Clowns, puppets, buffoons and masks enrich this theatre with a poetry that is both fantastic and grotesque, realistic and allegorical, along with the "alienation" derived from a past left more or less vague. This is a specifically dramatic poetry, since the stage is needed, but in its elements it is mythical. Through allegory it can strike a didactic note, and embrace the burlesque and satirical. On a higher level, the use of puppet or clown and the availability of multiple identities, in Ghelderode's best plays, reveal a universe that transcends the one we inhabit but which we feel nevertheless belongs to us.

Thus Ghelderode's poetry, feeding on the supernatural, constitutes a kind of evocation, an incantatory art. **La Sortie de l'acteur** is concerned in part with the spell exercised by the author on his interpreter. He summons up half-extinct towns, bygone days, male and female saints. The pathetic thing about these voyages of discovery initiated by a lonely man is that they affect him too nearly. He does not always avoid psychodrama. The disharmonies that at times spoil or wreck the poetic beauty attained by Ghelderode are remarkably similar to those that sometimes irritate us in the films of Ingmar Bergman.

Michel de Ghelderode, despite his deliberately archaic and recherché vocabulary, neglected speech in favor of the visual. His world view is plastic. As a young man he haunted the art galleries, and philosophized as he looked at the canvases of the great masters of his own country: Bosch, Breughel, Teniers, Jordaens, James Ensor. "This Flemish nation in which I have my origins seems double to me. Matching its superb vitality and materialism is a preoccupation with metaphysical disquietude."

Among the friends of his maturity were the painters Jean Jacques Gailliard, Marcel Stobbaerts and others, who no doubt guided him in his scenic researches. He was, furthermore, passionately addicted to those spectacles in which speech as such plays little part, operas, ballets, and the puppets in the vaulted cellars of Brussels. Passionately he wandered through the churches, where he admired the statues of the Virgin, and in public gardens, where he admired whatever statues were to be seen. (His book, *Mes Statues,* has been published by the Editions du Carrefour.) As to everything else that was tangible, he reacted to the spectacle of everyday life, to funeral processions, festivals, passersby.

Born in 1898, Ghelderode was inevitably affected by all the distastes manifested by the literary leaders of the closing nineteenth and early twentieth centuries, before he came under the influence of surrealism or expressionism, those movements of his own generation.

He repudiated the rationalistic humanism of the eighteenth century and, in accord with the tendencies of his masters both of painterly thought and of thought unqualified, he turned back to the ideals of the Renaissance, that savage century so like our own, with the frightening perspectives it presented to men, its unknown horizons in space and thought, its intellectual and sensual frenzies, a century in which suffering rubbed shoulders with laughter or even engendered it.—Doubtless it was this last aspect that most keenly marked the sensibility of our author.

So he set out to acquire his own manner. Despite the inspiration he found in Charles de Coster's *Ulenspiegel* and Georges Eekhoud's *Siècle de Shakespeare,* his ancestry will turn out to be more French than could at first have been anticipated. Perceptible are Rabelais, Lesage and even Léon Daudet, whose *Le Voyage de Shakespeare* was cited by Ghelderode and whose countless novels, more richly expressive than they are descriptive, have been undeservedly neglected. For all his verbal ebullience, strange personages and startling, often grotesquely cruel scenes, Daudet remains nevertheless a pamphleteer, and we should not overstress the kinship.

Ghelderode's highly charged style is sufficiently motivated by the theatrical perspective and the passions he wished to convey. But here is a sample of the way he answered journalists whose indiscreet curiosity had angered him. "You mean the hypocrites, bigots, *cagots* and *matagots* forbidden by Gargantua to cross the threshold of his Abbey of Theleme? It's altogether too kind of you, my dear colleague, to concern yourself with this clerical scum! As for me, I sh . . . on them from the morning angelus to the evening angelus!"

The Word, here, is both sovereign and derelict. It is despised as a conveyor of certitudes but furbished anew with all its powers of suggestion, aristocratically, much as Louis-Ferdinand Céline did, in his own back-to-the-people vein. Pierre de Boisdeffre has actually maintained that Ghelderode wrote anti-plays! Well, yes, if the language of Céline's *Journey to the End of the Night* makes it an anti-novel. But it is no difficult matter to regard as essentially dramatic the whole weight of sensuality that is embodied and rendered visible in language. Such a utilization of language clearly engenders both poetic and burlesque elements requiring a sensitive direction that remains faithful to the author's intentions.

Michel de Ghelderode devalues the word as a bearer of meaning but reinstates it by loading it with poetry. This distrust of the word is also a distrust of the intelligence. Yet, to the extent that the burlesque expresses a certain delight in life's superabundance and that the poetic or comic elements spring from some encounter with the exaggerated and the ridiculous, in the end Ghelderode addresses himself to man's intelligence, not his sensibility.

With respect to sensibility and intelligence alike, this art has limits that the poetic afflatus cannot entirely make up for. Sometimes the mythical quality is lost, to be replaced by a symbolism of a rather shopworn kind. If modern drama is to provide a specific experience, it must present some passion involving the whole of man. Otherwise it vociferates oracularly and falls short of the universal. Confronted by man or by the created world, the dramatist must be touched by wonder, by love or its opposite. Quite certainly, in dealing with man, he must convey "something valid."

Ghelderode asserts that he loves men ". . . as they should be loved, from a certain distance, and I am just as indulgent and sympathetic toward their weaknesses as, professionally speaking, I am interested in their absurdities."

This statement seems to imply that Ghelderode himself is not always personally involved. He is fascinated by this world he has created but sometimes he remains "outside." This makes the demon of bad faith prick up his ears. Ghelderode's anti-Semitism may be explained, perhaps, as due to his preoccupation with magic. His characterizations of the children of Israel, for all that, could have found a fitting place in such publications as *Le Pilori.* In *Fastes d'enfer* Simon Laquedeem, the wandering Jew transformed into a suffragan bishop, invents a new version of ritual murder, and as the curtain descends on his scene of triumph "his visage expresses a demoniacal glee." In *Pantagleize,* Rachel Silberschatz sets out to avenge her persecuted people by persecuting others, and Pantagleize describes the projected revolution in terms already familiar to readers of *L'Action Française.* Of all the Jewish figures evoked by Ghelderode only the Judas of *Barrabas* is treated with some measure of sympathy, and in much the same way as did Léon Bloy, who recognized the metaphysical necessity of the betrayal.

The Negroes Bam-Boulas and Beni-Bouftout are blacks that have been carefully filtered through a white consciousness, and not a single cliché is missing. Might not Ghelderode's racism be one aspect of the profound attraction he feels for evil?

"Count Von Lauterbach"—that was the first literary pseudonym adopted by Adolphe Adhemar Martens. Vis-a-vis humanity his attitude was that of an aristocrat well equipped to practice the cult of the ego and with a marked predilection for magic. Far from clashing with this vaunted anarchism, a certain traditionalist outlook blended in very well with the rejection of the rational.

While all-out warfare against sentimental imbecilities may be thoroughly justified, there is a bookish quality about Ghelderode's notion of eroticism as a "seminal soup." The multiplicity of states of consciousness, and the unlimited transmutability of love and of the atmospheres it can conjure up—all that is absent from his work. For him, love is but the specter of a specter.

If love were as simple or as unabashedly sadistic as it appears in this witches' brew, its toxic properties would surely have been discovered some little while ago!

On the other hand, Michel de Ghelderode's dramatic œuvre is entirely modern in its insistence on the ambiguity of our human lot. The burlesque and the tragic remain in balance, and subsumed in a poetry whose unquestionable originality is due to a use of language devoid of all self-conscious "poetry." Yet man is man only because he is able to *declare* what he is. The modern theatre, and much of the avant-garde along with it, is perhaps all the weaker for its neglect of this basic truth. When, however, Michel de Ghelderode ventures an assertion, his thought has an undeniably reactionary ring, and leaves us dissatisfied.[1]

Note

1. Utilized in this study were the five volumes of Ghelderode's *Théâtre,* published by Gallimard, and his *Entretien de l'acteur,* published by L'Arche.

Samuel Draper (essay date 1963)

SOURCE: "Michel de Ghelderode: A Personal Statement," in *Tulane Drama Review,* Vol. 8, No. 1, Fall 1963, pp. 33-38.

[*In the following review, Draper presents a personal portrait of Ghelderode to gain greater understanding of his work.*]

The masks Ghelderode wore for the world were in many ways unfortunate because they alienated him from his contemporaries. His weird poses frightened many admirers away, denying them the happiness of knowing Ghelderode personally. That Ghelderode's art has a secure place in modern dramatic literature is almost universally agreed. That he was an affectionate, exemplary friend, a lovable man, that he possessed a droll sense of humor, incarnated hard work and literary discipline *à la* Voltaire and Balzac without being spoiled by worldly success, and that he was a pauper most of his life—all this is known only to a small group of friends. They include several Belgians, a few Frenchmen, one or two Englishmen, and a couple of Americans. I, one of the Americans, had the privilege of knowing Ghelderode during 1959 and 1960 when I spent a year in Brussels expressly to study his life and drama. After six months there, twenty-five interviews at his home, and dozens of letters exchanged in regard to our work, Ghelderode confirmed our friendship with a long, strong hand-clasp, a startling and incongruous gesture sharply contrasted to his ghostly emaciation, ephemeral countenance, and the legend of his "other-worldliness."

Ghelderode knew about friendship—what its responsibilities mean and what its joy engenders. "I ask only some measure of understanding from my friends," Ghelderode told me. "They can give me the one thing any human being can offer another: understanding. To the remark, 'That is not much,' I reply, 'It is everything.'"

Here are some of Ghelderode's thoughts about *l'amitié,* written to friends who range from an unknown French actor to a revered Queen: "Friendship is life's greatest treasure . . ." ". . . a mystical force lighted by a perpetual lamp held up before us by an invisible hand . . ." ". . . the golden chain of friendship cannot be broken, not even tarnished. It links us together forever . . ." ". . . your friendship is life's breath, a kind of last sacrament, a holy bell tolling outside the realm of my world of shadows . . ." ". . . your friendship is a beacon, a light which touches me, reassures me, tells me that our universe doesn't stop with the walls of my house."

Ghelderode's love of friends was boundless, ecstatic, and profound, even bewildering to those less ardent and responsive than he. His detractors mocked his written expressions of friendship as "romantic nonsense," but those he befriended found them elegant, sincere, and moving. Ghelderode scarcely concerned himself with his critics, with those he called "small men," "limited souls," for he was convinced that any mystic like himself could appeal only to the elect, to "*âmes bien nées*"—"souls well-born." Like his friend Maeterlinck, Ghelderode thought that at times the soul seemed to rise to the surface of humanity, revealing itself there in its full life and power.

To illustrate what he meant about the revelation of the soul, Ghelderode told me a story about his childhood. It concerned an old coal miner and a lost child on a cold winter's afternoon. Ghelderode was only five years old at the time. He had strayed a short distance from his home in Ixelles (a district of Brussels). He was lost, confused, and he began to cry. He sobbed loudly, but none of the well-dressed women passing by stopped to help. Suddenly, an aged coal miner stumbled across the street and took Michel in his arms, comforting him. Muttering Flemish, the old peasant could hardly make himself understood to the boy who was schooled only in French. But Ghelderode comprehended the tenderness, understanding, and sympathy in the old man's eyes. "That day I saw the essence of love in that man's face, although his appearance was coarse, his filthy clothes smelled foul, and his big boots and strange helmet frightened me. I wasn't deceived by the black soot which had permeated the hundreds of crevices in his wrinkled hands and which covered his face with a black mask. He treated me more tenderly, more protectively than my father ever had. I wasn't afraid—in fact I felt secure and warm as we walked back hand in hand to my neighborhood where he located my home.

Most children would have screamed with fright at the sight of that old bogey man, but I saw him differently. Even then I had an educated heart."

Another unknown side of Ghelderode was his aggressive sense of humor, which usually expressed itself in practical jokes. During the period when he was a civil servant at the town hall office of Saint-Josse-ten-Noode, in Brussels, Ghelderode was constantly the target of his co-workers' jibes. Performing few if any of his clerical duties, he preferred to—and did—write his plays. His colleagues, solid enough, but with little respect or understanding for the bizarre poet in their midst, took pride in upsetting Ghelderode's manuscripts after he had left the office. Each morning Ghelderode found his papers in disarray, some sheets folded into paper dolls, some ripped in two, others tied in toilet tissue. Finally, in retaliation, Ghelderode rubbed a few of the rough drafts with human excrement which stuck to the intruders' hands once they began their nightly jest. "After all," Ghelderode laughed, "they introduced the bathroom odor in their joke, so I gave them the real thing!"

When fame came suddenly in the late forties ("*la gloire,*" Ghelderode called it) bearing his name across Europe, he did not turn his head, nor could he substantially change his standard of living. (His fame never brought much money.) Too many years of obscurity, illness (incurable chronic asthma made him an invalid for more than twenty-five years[1]) and despair that his dramas might do harm rather than good ("I always hoped that my plays would elevate mankind, not the opposite") had gone by for him to change with his renown. Performances in Paris, Rome, Madrid, Copenhagen, Oslo, Krakow, and Cairo brought reputation and a little cash—but success, always spiritually dangerous for the artist, did not cause Ghelderode to put on airs. Worldly success meant little to him. "Fame and immortality are meaningless, empty words. I live to write and for the joy of being alive."

Many writers would have been tempted to come before their public playing a glamorous role, responding ceremoniously to the honors which had come so late. But Ghelderode only withdrew further into his own small universe, locking his huge sixteen-foot door to celebrity seekers, journalists, and the curious, refusing to appear on television or attend the theatre, fabricating those thousand stories which have emblazoned his all-too-infernal legend. He invented tales that he was the terror of his publishers, that he was a Don Juan who changed his women as often as he wrote a story, that he was rich but hoarded his money like Hieronymus in **Red Magic,** and most ironically of all, that he was indolent and wrote only occasionally when inspiration flashed across his brain.

But one of Ghelderode's editors at Gallimard in Paris admitted that the Belgian playwright was a gentleman, cooperative, responsible, and a pleasure to work with. Unlike the legend, Ghelderode told his confidants many times that he had lived in harmony with his wife Jeanne for over

forty years, a perfect soulmate of whom Ghelderode wrote he owed "everything." As his stories had it, he was lazy. Yet the strange recluse and grotesque visionary worked longer hours and harder than most modern executives or ambitious businessmen. Despite being a natural "dreamer"—that was Ghelderode's name for himself, wanting always to escape from work like his Christopher Columbus—the dramatist taught himself how to write long hours.

During the Second World War, he and his wife scarcely had enough to eat; but little bread, tattered clothing, and no coal did not stop Ghelderode from working. Then as before—since 1915—he wrote night after night, year after year, decade after decade—finally nearly a half century of filling thousands of sheets with that even, fine, curlicue handwriting reminiscent of times past. Indeed, Ghelderode possessed one of the most disciplined intelligences of our age. The effect of all Ghelderode's invented legend was that the world at large regarded him as an eccentric, not the genius his work shows him to be.

The scene of his industry was his small living room-museum filled with Ensor masks, theatrical posters, medieval wooden statues of saints, puppets, large marionette dolls, cheap department store mannequins, some nude, some dressed for various roles of the stage (Hamlet and Isolde side by side); a photo of a Venus, sumptuous in her nakedness next to a portrait of the Blessed Virgin, humble in her Gothic pose; sea shells, stuffed fish, and many unknown paintings as well as reproductions of Bosch, Breughel, El Greco, and Rouault. There, surrounded by his *objects* (of little intrinsic value)—"I am a *collectioneur* and each piece has special significance"—Ghelderode sat at an oval table, in an eighteenth century armchair covered with a scarlet chasuble. There he gave life to his colorful throng: an entire school of clowns, torturers, misers, lecherous and pious women, devils, angels, dwarfs, and midgets, characters who return from the dead, Christopher Columbus and Don Juan, Pantagleize, Barabbas and Folial—the possessed, the ecstatic, the bewildered, the frightened, the courageous—all full of the joy and juice of life.

At that table Ghelderode suffered his nights of pain, kept his hand to paper, and finally wrote himself to death.[2] Most of his work is difficult to classify: it is not exactly symbolist or poetic drama; neither is it romantic, naturalistic, epic, or "absurd" theatre. Ghelderode echoes ideas, perhaps, from many of these movements, but he has invented a unique school—his own. In a large sense, most of his work is religious because he saw good and evil first as metaphysical categories, and then in the second instance as moral ones. Do not many of his plays deal with God and the Devil and with the choices man must make between good or evil? These ultimate moral questions concerned Ghelderode. In a narrow sense, Ghelderode's work is also religious, that is, his writing is mystical, supernatural, and fantastic. "I believe in the mysteries of life and death," Ghelderode has written, "I am a poet just for that reason."

I never received a letter from Ghelderode in which he did not mention both God and death as well as describe the appropriate season of the Church calendar, whether Christmas time, Lent, or Advent. He referred to death as a "beautiful woman," "a faithful companion," as "red roses in the snow," "innocent violets in the eyes of Christ," "blue sunlight," as fulfillment, peace, destiny . . . as life itself. He called God and death by the same names. And now, after years of toil, suffering and pain, Ghelderode rests—if one believes him—"in the tender arms of God, comforted as well by my beautiful lady," whom he often crowned with flowers.

Notes

1. At the beginning of my interview of January 20, 1960, Mme. Ghelderode announced that Ghelderode would have to come into his bedroom for his medicine. He shuffled out. From the next room I heard wheezing, coughing, and throat-clearing. He breathed with great difficulty, heaving asthmatically. He looked particularly thin that day, old, worn, and frightened. His lips were blue, his skin a sickroom pale, fingernails bluer than his lips.

2. A careful inventory would show that Ghelderode's complete *oeuvre*—plays (over a hundred), short stories, poetry, letters, art criticism, and miscellaneous prose—would fill thirty or so substantial volumes.

Auréliu Weiss (essay date 1963)

SOURCE: "The Theatrical World of Michel de Ghelderode," in *Tulane Drama Review,* Vol. 8, No. 1, Fall 1963, pp. 51-61.

[*In the following essay, Weiss presents an overview of major themes in Ghelderode's plays.*]

The recent death of Ghelderode has awakened renewed interest in his drama. One of the most astounding figures in the contemporary theatre (a theatre full of astounding figures), his work is characterized by such bizarre aspects as fetishism, living dead men, leaps through time, devils, sorcerers, ghosts, grinning buffoons, legendary heroes stubbornly destroying their legend, historical characters denying the facts of their history, philosophical drunkards, and death as a character in farce.

Obsessed by a universe of dark forces in endless ferment, he saw evil and damnation everywhere. Plagued by them, it did not occur to him to attack them with righteous wrath, as did Calderón and Tirso de Molina, the priest-playwrights of the Golden Age of Spanish drama. In Ghelderode's works the devil is alive and active. Moreover, if one probes beneath his anxiety, one finds a certain satisfaction, a feeling of tenderness and amusement. Ghelderode's gift of anthropomorphic animism enables him to see the many incarnations of the forces of evil that fling themselves against man. Even inanimate matter, even objects made by man or machine, are able to hide mysterious powers capable of influencing human destiny.

In love with the late Middle Ages, Ghelderode cherished the revels of apocalyptic visions, the terrors of fanaticism. A latter-day romantic, Ghelderode sometimes slipped into melodrama instead of the mystery of the Middle Ages, as he believed. Thus, he juxtaposed noisy, uproarious, vividly drunken characters against heroes who were devoid of life, force, or human truth. Contemptuous of his own time, Ghelderode felt himself to be a contemporary of pre-Renaissance men; above all he loved what he believed to be their spirit, their way of life, their struggles and aspirations. He was ardently, jealously, and exclusively attached to them, and this attachment took possession of his creative powers, and even of his spare time. He believed these men to be freer and larger in their tumultuous passions than the men of our own day, weakened, frightened, and enslaved by material comfort.

No other modern dramatist has clung with such force and perseverance to a single period of history. And so that nothing foreign might disturb this plunge into the past, Ghelderode isolated himself from everything that could remind him of the pulse of contemporary life. "I work in a state of hypnosis; if someone speaks to me about what I'm doing, it's fouled up," he said in his picturesque language.

His is a vast world, created by a tortured imagination. At times he manages to captivate spectator and reader, evoking an unfamiliar *frisson*; at other times, he compensates for the darkness of his vision by comic contortions that are meant to arouse a vulgar, often trivial, belly-laugh which contrasts sharply with refined, complicated, cerebral art.

The plays he values most are characterized by verbal abundance, which has been chosen by abstract considerations. Only rigorous cutting and compression could save him from his tendency towards empty verbiage. Occasionally, Ghelderode has done just that. Paul Guth has reported that *Hop Signor* and *Chronicles of Hell* are "three-act plays concentrated into one act by dizzying compression. *Hop Signor* was reworked five times," and Ghelderode would have gained by applying this "dizzying compression" to all his dramatic works.

Psychoanalysis aroused his fury, and he condemned all of it, without distinguishing science from philosophy. Nevertheless, his plays: *The Death of Dr. Faust, Don Juan, The Actor Makes His Exit, Pantagleize, Christopher Columbus,* and even *Mademoiselle Jaïre* are philosophic attempts. His distaste for all knowledge that has contributed to progress is paralleled by the often surprising weakness of his thought. Deprived of all valid culture, his heroes suffer from the illusion that they are thinking profoundly, without suspecting how grotesque their ambitions are. From this illusion springs the politico-philosophical babbling of Ghelderode's Pantagleize or Christopher Columbus, their angelic naiveté, their astonishing frankness, their improbable tribulations. Most of Ghelderode's heroes are not alive; they are purely intellectual constructions; Don Juan, Faust, Columbus, Pantagleize, and the author Jean-Jacques from *The Actor Makes His Exit* speak abundantly and, endeavoring to reach far and wide, they proclaim their scorn for all the trivialities of the world.

Ghelderode's Don Juan is a poor hero who, during a carnival, disguises himself in the legendary masque and costume. "Pitiful, thin, pale, nervous" most of the time he thinks himself the real Don Juan, speaking and acting like a true hero. His Faust, hero of a "farcical play for the music-hall" is not a happier creation. The action of this "farcical play" takes place in Flanders in an "ancient and future" city, at once in the sixteenth and twentieth centuries. That is what has been called breaking the boundaries of time. The disciple of the "doctor" is no longer Wagner, but Cretinus. In this play, Margaret, "a young servant of seventeen," no longer plays at false virtue; and she proves it conclusively in a shabby hotel. Let us skip the details of this poor parody of the Faust legend; it would be too simple to show its deficiencies. Let us leave Faust to his Cretinus, to his devil (Diamotoruscant) and to his ineffable Margaret; Faust and Don Juan are twins, nourished from the same philosophic source.

If we leave the quicksand of legend to enter the domain of history, we meet Christopher Columbus. He too amuses himself by fusing different eras, crying "Long live Lindberg," and speaking of "gabardine." We see the fragility of the boundary of time; anything can violate it. But here the author has taken precautions; it is no longer a drama, but a "dramatic fairy-tale; it should be played quickly, without insistence, from the perspective of dreams." Curious dream! Ghelderode's one-act play *The Sun Sets,* has as protagonist Charles of Hapsburg, father of Philip II, and under this title (which implicitly denies the fact that the sun never sets on the immense Hapsburg empire) Ghelderode portrays the powerful monarch, after he abandoned his throne, when he had retired to the Monastery of Yuste, during the last phase of his life. Ghelderode has a curious conception of the greatness of his heroes. From an entire life that fills pages of history, Ghelderode retains the dubious legend of a man who witnesses his own funeral. In this sense some critics have found a greatness worthy of the most illustrious examples of heroic antiquity.

All the foregoing may seem severe, but it reflects my disillusion in re-reading most of Ghelderode's plays. This is an overall view, for it is true that each of the plays contains interesting details. Although the dialogue usually drags, it occasionally quickens, becoming incisive, tormented, rapid, poignant. The most banal ideas occasionally give way to quick striking phrases that reveal keen sensitivity. Painful trivialities follow close upon poetic expressions. Certain traits reveal a born painter.

His work is a curious mixture in which everything is piled up chaotically, so that one has to search for the precious

stone by digging in a bric-à-brac of capricious contrivances, caricatures, absurdities, agitated puppets, meditative platitudes, extravagances, esoteric obscurities, improbabilities, and naivetés. The whole recalls the strange décor of certain fantastic tales such as those of Hoffmann, to whom the Belgian writer felt closely drawn. All about him Hoffmann saw ghosts, dead men come to life, strange beings who fled from daylight to plunge into the shadows. There is certainly a striking parallel between the spirit of the German writer and that of the Belgian dramatist, not only in the proliferation of fantastic visions, but also in the need to react against the anguish that gripped them both.

Their mad hallucinations cover life and nature with a veil, upon which they embroider monstrosities and apocalyptic figures. In their works, artificial explosions replace natural light; curious costumes, strong colors, striking decorations, tortured thought replace natural scenes and movements, the free flow of the healthy imagination. A feverish agitation drives their grimacing world without respite; under the power of mysterious magic that world flings itself about frantically; but not a single noble feeling or inspired thought rises from all this uneasy throbbing, murky dreams, anxiety, fright. Reality, simplicity, idealism are absent. The vision of these two writers leads them to extremes, to excess in imagery and vocabulary, and with similar lack of moderation, their grotesque humor clashes with their terrifying revels. Their comic tone is as black as their darkest meditations or visions.

Ghelderode never succeeds in detaching himself from supernatural imagery in order to see things from a higher viewpoint. One might say that with each step he sinks deeper into the quicksand of fetishism. His voice always has a subterranean sound, even when he embarks on vast metaphysical considerations.

Is *Mademoiselle Jaïre* the expression of a subterranean spirit? Is this a mystery play which contains the secret of life and death, the intimate relationship between human life and the principle of universal life, the impenetrable enigmas of the esoteric world? Can this drama be subterranean, when it is not only a mystery, but also a miracle, in which death is only a passing event, a reflection, a preparatory step towards something so vast, so luminous, and so pure that words cannot express it? It is precisely here that the spirit is even more subterranean than in the other plays. The play deals with a resurrection, probably inspired by the Gospel of St. John, who speaks of the resurrection of Lazarus, a mystery that is widely known. However, the events of Ghelderode's play evoke other resonances, such as those of the plays of Tirso de Molina, of Calderón, and of Zorrilla's *Don Juan Tenorio.* One can trace this theme far back into the past, for *Mademoiselle Jaïre* deals again with the legend of the dead restored to life, which has haunted human imagination from earliest times.

Tirso de Molina's play, *The Man Damned for Lack of Faith,* presents a bandit, Paulo, who, having been hunted down and killed by the police, is buried in the forest where he fled. He revives for a few minutes before falling into an eternal sleep. Something similar happens in Calderón's *Devotion to the Cross.* Towards the end of this play, the bandit Eusebio dies, and the author says clearly: "he dies." Dying, he cries, "Alberto!" Three scenes later (the fifteenth scene of the last act) Alberto arrives in Rome, and hears the dead man still calling him: "I am Eusebio. Come, Alberto, come here where I am buried. Raise the branches. Fear nothing." Alberto approaches, finds the body of Eusebio who begs him to receive his confession before dying. "I should have died a while ago," he says. *"But although the terrible blow of early death has liberated my soul and made my body incapable of reclaiming it, death has not yet separated them."* He leads Alberto off stage to confess his sins, and, a little later, Alberto returns on stage to report the most astonishing miracle: "After having killed Eusebio, *heaven granted that his soul remain in its mortal envelope until he should confess his sins.* Such is God's grace to those who show devotion to the cross." Finally, in Zorrilla's drama, when Don Juan enters the tomb, after having challenged the statue of the Commander, he is completely changed: his legs barely support him, he has no weight. It seems that after a brawl, Captain Alvarez killed him at the door of his house, but Don Juan does not recall this fact. He is dead, but not completely. He walks like a ghost. The bells ring the death knell, and Don Juan asks, "For whom do the bells toll?" "For you." "And that funeral passing by?" "It is your own." Only then does he exclaim, "I am dead," and he asks for divine grace.

The resurrection of Lazarus and these three examples are enough to suggest where Ghelderode might have taken the idea of the resurrection of Blandine and her double death. But this was only the groundwork upon which the Belgian author built a more ambitious story. *Molina and Calderón simply gave expression to an idea that was widely circulated in their time.* In their works, the mystery is in the miracle, in divine will. The event that expresses it is clear, simple, precise, and as such, must have struck the popular imagination. Their explanation is temperate, short, concise; *there is no metaphysical debate, no verbal obscurity.* The resurrection and its heavenly overtones do not become the subject of dramatic commentary; he who believes, accepts, and on the stage the miracle is a *fact,* woven into the unraveling of the plot. In the Spanish works the resurrection is not the crux of the plot, but acts as a conclusion, giving the moral meaning of the drama; the human soul will leave for Heaven or Hell, depending upon whether it submits to or scorns the divine will.

Ghelderode builds his dramatic structure on the foundation of this supernatural event. It is no longer an episode but the very center of the action, the axis of his esoteric and metaphysical revels. The dream of Blandine Jaïre is heavy as a nightmare, although Ghelderode wished it to be light as a feather. This heroine is bound to the earth by innumerable superstitions, absurd naiveté, and the disconcerting intervention of characters created to break spells. And as if this were not enough, the dramatic development is blocked by ponderous metaphysics conveyed through esoteric dialogue whose meaning is deliberately obfuscated so as to appear profound.

Following the Romantics, Ghelderode seems to have wanted to seize upon the divine principle that governs the spiritual world. Unfortunately, his sense of the divine is so permeated with the monstrous visions of his esoteric universe, that he can no longer distinguish the divine from the monstrous, and it is the latter that rules supreme in his world. Where he seeks the divine he finds only primitive preconceptions and superstitions. From his mind, "darkness, as if an inherent positive quality, poured forth upon all objects of the moral and physical universe in one unceasing radiation of gloom," as Edgar Poe said of Roderick Usher.

And yet Ghelderode has successfully treated a resurrection in **Chronicles of Hell,** where the miracle, as in the Spanish plays, is a dramatic *fact,* an element in the conflict and the action, with neither obscure complications nor tiring metaphysics. A crime has been committed against Bishop Jan in Eramo, who saw the crime but was unable to prevent it. The criminal is Bishop Laquedeem, his assistant. Jan in Eramo rises from the dead, and there ensues a life-and-death struggle between the two bishops. There is no need to go into detail; the resurrected bishop dies again shortly after the epic combat. The events of this play are clear, the action compressed into a single act, the conflict is moving; the rapid succession of scenes allows no time for reflection.

If one reads Ghelderode attentively, it becomes clear that his best effects are due to his narrative and pictorial talents. Color plays a vital role. One has the impression of encountering a painter who expresses his vision with words instead of a brush. For this reason one cannot separate the scenic action from the pictorial whole. Often his characters give the feeling that they emerged from a painting to move under an incantation. The narrator complements the painter. Ghelderode's plays contain stage directions in which the portraits of the characters have intrinsic artistic value. In a few words, he evokes an atmosphere, delineates a character whose face haunts you. Upon the entrance on stage of most of his characters, he paints their physical features, their moral resonance, showing his gift for suggestion, economy, life, and color.

Bosch, Breughel, Tenier, Jordaens were his teachers and his inspiration, to a greater degree than the Elizabethans and the Spanish, and to an even greater degree than the fantastic writers of Germany and France. Of them all, it is Breughel who had the greatest influence upon him. In his paintings and etchings Ghelderode discovered a grotesque humanity, a mixture of suffering and surging joy, grotesque masques, hallucinatory visions, which one finds in his plays. However, when there are no crowd scenes, the Belgian writer sometimes moves away from what we may call popular vision, and Breughel's influence is replaced by a refinement drawn from other sources.

His farces, such as *The Ballad of the Great Macabre, About a Devil Who Preaches Marvels, The Strange Rider, The Farce of the Shadows,* contain matter to delight the popular spirit. These works put on the stage drunken, stinking monks, magicians, devils with their tricks and disguises, corrupt men, stutterers, lying ministers. *Red Magic* treats that popular type, the miser, whose exaggerated features have always delighted the masses. The characters of these plays are old friends; their superstitions have a long tradition of popular favor. But one has to go a long way from this popular art to understand Ghelderode's own spirit, for beneath these outbursts of vulgar, obvious humor hides a visionary, one who is obsessed and overtaxed. The public does not see this man, or cannot understand him.

There is nothing that springs from nature into his theatre without passing through his interior illumination, which transforms the aspects, the perspectives, the original meaning of things. He sees nature and man only through a kaleidoscope, at the bottom of which lies an infinite number of varying designs. Landscapes, men, or costumes may recall pictures seen somewhere, during trips through museums or through studios of painters. In the scenic directions of many of his plays there are references to a particular painter, etcher, or picture which recall similar scenes on his own stage. Breughel, Laermans, the Flemish primitives, Goya, Jacques Callot (who influenced Hoffmann so strongly) are *designated by name.*

This viewing of men and the world through pictorial art is one of the most curious features of Ghelderode's drama, which, worked out both plastically and poetically, is highly personal. However, the two ways of working are not simultaneous; the poet describes what is seen by the painter, engraver, sculptor, who, in turn, inspires the writer with his moral philosophy, and molds his perception of life. As a result, the writer no longer looks at life with his physical eyes or those of his imagination, but life is projected through painting. Inspiration does not move directly from object to image. But a dramatist should see things in terms of the stage: he discerns life in the development of the conflicts to which it gives rise, just as the painter or sculptor gives plastic form to life. These two kinds of perception are fundamentally different.

Paying no attention to the essential function of dramatic dialogue, Ghelderode repeats the weakness of many other writers, in giving the same language to all his characters. Whatever their education or social class, they all express themselves in the same stylized language. In *Hop Signor* for example, the sculptor, the gentlemen, the dwarfs, the executioner, the monk, the heroine all reason impeccably in fine flashes of insight, poetically expressed. The romantics were past masters in this sort of psychological confusion, and Villiers de L'Isle-Adam in *Contes cruels* has done something similar that probably inspired Ghelderode.

It is of some interest that one finds specifically dramatic dialogue in only one Ghelderode play, *Escurial.* More than any other of his plays, *Escurial* successfully combines the interest of an unusual plot with the poignancy of an anguished wait, while at the same time maintaining a high literary standard from beginning to end. The dramatic development is sure, the dialogue tight, the conflict all the more powerful because it is hidden beneath a dangerous game. The king and the fool change roles. The fool will pay with his life for the hour of truth.

In Ghelderode's comedies, death and evil are as omnipresent as in his serious drama, playing a primary role. Death, as in pictures of the late Middle Ages, sits astride man's shoulders, plays the fool, becomes comically theatrical. But the instinct of self-preservation in Ghelderode is powerless in and of itself, needing the stimulation of alcohol. It is alcohol that inspires the comic zeal and exaggerated outbursts of the heroes of his farces. Drunkenness is sovereign in Ghelderode's grotesque drama, and its effect on his plays' quality is unmistakable.

The first inescapable reflection after examining Ghelderode's theatre is that this view of the world reveals nothing new in art or thought. One can, of course, see the effort to create something new both in scenic conception and in form, but this effort leads to nothing distinguished, powerful, or significantly personal. His style degenerates into mannerism, arousing curiosity rather than real dramatic interest. His weakness lies rooted in the nature of his inspiration, which leads him to exploit the prejudices of a past age well-known for its intolerant fanaticism, for its dark superstition, and for its crimes. This shadowy period of history knew occasional bright moments, but the Belgian author does not seem to have noticed that. His feelings, his temperament, and his convictions bound him to the most absurd beliefs, to the most unreasonable superstitions. By seeking and cherishing them, he has sunk into the black clay from which he kneads his characters and moulds his fables, until he can no longer break free of it. Since these were his resources, he could be neither original, nor a true thinker. In spite of the humor of his farces, his drama leaves one uneasy. Tenderness, love, generosity, pure emotions are absent. He thought that he had put them into his mystery play, *Mademoiselle Jaïre,* but his resources betrayed his intentions. His faith has only bat-wings on which to soar into the vast spaces of thought and knowledge.

When one begins by reading or seeing *Escurial,* continues with *Hop Signor, Lord Halewyn,* and *The Ballad of the Great Macabre,* one senses an original talent, a powerful imagination full of remarkable visions. In spite of certain reservations that one may have, *Chronicles of Hell* does not contradict this impression. However, as soon as one goes on to other works and above all to those that claim to be philosophical, disenchantment and disappointment increase until our reaction is finally transformed into resistance and protest. The accumulation of absurdities becomes too great.

It is indeed disappointing to see on today's stage a revival of those gloomy textures and primitive eccentricities that tormented the lives of people for long, hard centuries. Ghelderode has created these works, not to derive from them a philosophy of human mistakes or of the disastrous effect of fanaticism, not to illuminate the thick fog of ignorance with a ray of light coming from above and beyond, not to show, through the dark paths of fate, the continuous human effort towards spiritual and moral progress, but he has created his drama to make us share his love for all these aberrations and to look at them with a tender and sympathetic eye. In the face of such weaknesses and deficiencies, the few merits of Ghelderode's theatre make it improbable that his drama will be judged favorably or that it will last.

George Wellwarth (essay date 1964)

SOURCE: "Michel de Ghelderode: The Theater of the Grotesque," in *Theater of Protest and Paradox: Developments in the Avant-Garde Drama,* New York University Press, 1964, pp. 98-113.

[*In the following essay, Wellwarth examines typical aspects of Ghelderode's grotesquerie.*]

Among modern dramatists Michel de Ghelderode stands by himself. If we must have a classification for him, then he can most nearly be compared to that group of novelists who have concentrated on the creation of a fictional world of their own, a microcosm in which to reflect their view of human behavior in the world as a whole. Like William Faulkner with his Yoknapatawpha County, Charles Dickens with his nineteenth century London, or James Joyce with his Dublin, Ghelderode has created an enclosed world that reflects and comments upon the larger world outside. Ghelderode's world is medieval Flanders, and his view of the world can best be described as savagely grotesque. His plays are sadistic caricatures shot through with a ribald scatological humor which reminds one of the pictures of his countrymen Hieronymus Bosch and Pieter Breughel and of the anonymous woodcuts of the danse macabre. Indeed, Ghelderode has specifically set some of his plays in a fictitious "Breughellande" where the painter's grotesque and ribald creations come to life. In all of his plays, with the exception of those written on specifically Biblical themes and set in the Holy Land, there is this quality of the painted, frozen grimace suddenly animated. Several of Ghelderode's plays are actually written for marionettes, and in these the sense of moment-to-moment transformation from still picture to moving picture is intensified. The marionettelike quality is retained in Ghelderode's plays for actors, which give the impression less of continuous movement than of a series of static tableaux in which the characters switch from one bizarre position to another, their faces seemingly permanently stretched into a sort of hysterical frozen rictus, their bodies reminding us more of Bosch's semihuman, basilisklike creatures than of human beings. Figures based upon a concentrated exaggeration of one particular physical trait recur constantly.

His characters, like spitefully caricatured puppets, are all lopsided in one direction: either enormously fat or unbelievably cadaverous, shriveled into deformed lumps of scabrous flesh (Ghelderode is particularly fond of inserting fiendish dwarfs into his plays) or stretched into lanky, stilt-supported scarecrows, saintlike guileless fools (a rare type in Ghelderode), or exaggeratedly sinister figures like the danse-macabre personifications of Death that he uses so frequently.

No better introduction to the atmosphere of the "Ghelderode country" could be given than this typical stage direction from *Marie la Misérable,* a modern miracle play that Ghelderode wrote in 1952 to be performed before the Church of St. Lambert in Woluwe, near Brussels:

> . . . enter an extraordinary procession to the sound of cacophonous music which is at the same time arhythmic and infinitely nostalgic—the music of some other, barbaric world, played upon baroque instruments. . . . This musical dragon (actually a camouflaged automobile with its headlights on containing a jazz band whose instruments have been altered to appear as if they did not belong to any particular period and whose Negro players have been disguised to look unreal) . . . pulls a ship, a sort of fourteenth century vessel—the Ship of Fools of the medieval moralists—with a raised forecastle and quarter-deck constituting practicable platforms. The mast, in the center, has only shreds of sail attached to it. Grim-looking black pavilions ornament the mast and poop. The quarterdeck is surmounted by a sort of arched ruin in which can be seen an admiral's skeleton. It is drinking and holding on its knees a woman covered with leprous sores. She has no nose and is naked under a shroud. Several scrawny and spastic couples are dancing together in front of the ship with signs of mutual disgust, as if they were fighting a merciless combat: a savage frolic, with the women's hair hanging down to their waists and flying round their rigid, sallow faces and the young men dressed in shrouds, their jaws bound shut with strips of cloth, dancing like robots to the hypnotic music. Their faces express disgust and dread, their dance shows the battle of the sexes. The middle of the ship is occupied by people wearing devil masks, pigs' snouts, animal muzzles, elephant trunks, asses' ears—a swarming menagerie, clucking, bellowing, whistling . . .[1]

Here we have a typical scene from the world of Ghelderode—fantastic, grotesque, bizarre, hypnotic: a subtle combination of the danse macabre with the lusty vulgarity of a Flemish peasants' kermess.

We can find this curious combination of demonism with ribaldry in all of Ghelderode's Flemish plays. As in the painting of Breughel, the world is seen as a place where the Devil is in control and moral perversity reigns. As in Breughel, this perversity takes the form of aimlessness and distraction in idle pursuits. Only the very few, like Marie la Misérable, see the purpose of life clearly and accomplish it through faith. Ghelderode's plays are almost all preoccupied, directly or indirectly, with Catholicism. However, their Rabelaisian attitude toward religion is not so much derisive of holy matters as a demonstration of his belief that sin has overcome the earth and that man's energies, instead of being concentrated on religion itself, are scattered and misdirected to the diabolic perversions of religion.

Several of Ghelderode's plays are taken *directly* from Breughel's paintings. Among these are *Les Aveugles* (***The Blind Men,*** written 1933), *La Pie sur le Gibet* (***The Magpie on the Gallows,*** written 1935), and *Le Cavalier Bizarre* (***The Strange Rider,*** written 1920). The first of these is a short sketch inspired by Breughel's painting "The Parable of the Blind," now in the Museo Nazionale, Naples. Breughel's picture shows six blind men walking along one behind the other and about to tumble into the ditch into which their leader has already fallen. Breughel based his picture on the Biblical proverb, "they be blind leaders of the blind. And if the blind lead the blind both shall fall into the ditch."[2] In Breughel's picture, as in Ghelderode's world, the blind men are the helpless victims of a system perverted by the Devil's ascendancy. If the Devil were not in control of the world, the men would not be blind, there would be no treacherously placed ditch for them to fall into, and they would not be instinctively led to disaster anyway, but rather to the church in the background of the picture. The literal presence of the Devil and his cohorts was a real concept to Breughel, as it undoubtedly is to Ghelderode as well. But Ghelderode makes the plan of the picture somewhat harsher. In Ghelderode's world the Devil makes men perverse: they are the victims not of their alien surroundings but of their own twisted and willful natures. The characteristic of the damned in religion, after all, is that they heed the promptings of the Devil instead of the voice of God. Ghelderode's blind men (reduced to three, presumably for convenience of staging) are pilgrims on the way to Rome, where they believe they have now arrived, although they have actually been wandering around in circles for weeks and are still in Flanders. A one-eyed man warns them that they are in dangerous country and offers to lead them to a monastery where they will be safe. The blind men refuse to believe him and scornfully reject his help. They trudge off and are swallowed up in a bog. Breughel's blind men are merely comically ducked in a ditch, but Ghelderode's deliberately turn down an offer of salvation and die.

In *La Pie sur le Gibet* Ghelderode has again dramatized a Breughel painting. "The Merry Way to the Gallows," now in the Darmstadt Museum, simply shows a gallows on a hill overlooking a countryside of extraordinary beauty. A magpie sits perched on top of the gallows, and a group of holidaying peasants is heedlessly dancing up the hill. Breughel here effects a double comment on the unfeeling stupidity of mankind, first in placing the gallows against a background of such idyllic tranquillity and secondly in having the peasants ignore both the beauty and the ugliness in the throes of their loutish dance. Ghelderode changes all this into a rollicking yet savagely contemptuous farce. The magpie becomes a sort of cynical croaking commentator on the action which here concerns a real

execution. The peasants come dancing up to the gibbet and then are replaced by a group of pompous officials (Ghelderode's professional men are invariably caricatured) who have come to hang Tyl Ulenspiegel. The strange location of the gibbet is now explained. The new ruler, wishing to temper justice with mercy, has decreed that death is to be made as pleasant as humanly possible for the condemned. They are to be hanged only after being permitted to get drunk on the best vintage wine. The ceremony is to be performed on a pink gibbet with a golden rope, and as the condemned man's eyeballs are extruded from his head by the force of strangulation his last view is to be of the most beautiful piece of countryside in Flanders. The condemned man drops dead just before he is to be hanged, and when the officials examine the body they find it is not Tyl Ulenspiegel at all. As the magpie croaks derisively, the carousing peasants return and the curtain falls.

Le Cavalier Bizarre is another short play and, if not directly taken from a Breughel painting like the two preceding ones, is inspired by the Flemish master's art. In his preface to the play Ghelderode states that his characters are taken from the brush of Breughel or the burin of Jacques Callot. A group of old people are living together in a large, dormitorylike room at a medieval Flemish hospice. They hear ghostly bells where none are supposed to be heard; one of them looks out of the window and sees a huge knight with large bells on his horse's bridle approaching. He says the horseman is Death, and the old people, believing him, go into a wild, kermesslike dance— their "last fling"—and then babble out their sins. They look like peaceful and innocent grandparents, and it is hard to imagine them once young and lusty and straight-backed. But the shriveled and bent old woman had sold her body when she was a beautiful young girl, one of the men had stolen, another fornicated tremendously, another had committed sacrilege, and still another had sinned so much that he feels only the pope in person could absolve him. After getting their sins off their chests, the ancients cease resigning themselves to their fate: "We want to live, no matter how—sick, suffering, covered with sores and vermin—but living!"[3] The whole thing ends with the watcher's revelation that Death has not come for them at all but has carried off a newborn child from another part of the hospice; and the audience is left in doubt as to whether the whole story proceeded from the watcher's imagination or not. The play ends with "a spasmodic dance of ancients, their mouths open, their fists clenched, like rigid marionettes."[4] After a moment's self-realization Ghelderode's ancients, teetering on the brink of death, fall back into the distraction from reality that is so typical of his people.

Demonism and Rabelaisianism are undoubtedly the two keynotes of Ghelderode's work: his plays combine the perversion of religious or political functions with scatological farce. Although the scatology often seems to be dragged in with willful vulgarity, it is really an extremely effective (because shocking) way of showing the author's disgust with the manner in which the world and the people in it have worked out. This element, too, Ghelderode seems to have got from Breughel, whose pictures, even the most idyllic ones, are full of hidden little scenes of defecation, urination, and animalistic fornication.

Two of Ghelderode's best plays, as yet unpublished in English, are *La Balade du Grand Macabre* (*The Grand Macabre's Stroll,* written 1934) and *Magie Rouge* (*Red Magic,* written 1931). In both of these ribald and unrestrained farces the demonism which suffuses Ghelderode's world takes the form of the primal satanic sin of belief in one's own divinity. In Ghelderode's view this leads to the creation of what may, literally, be described as monsters—persons who have become so obsessed by one of the more perverse possible phases of human character that they become in fact dehumanized personifications of it. This is, of course, essentially the same philosophy of dramatic construction as Ben Jonson's "humor" theory, except that Jonson uses it with satiric intent (i.e., he laughs at it from a position of superiority, thus implying that improvement is possible), while Ghelderode presents it as a literal picture of the world gone mad. Ghelderode's world is not populated by a few fools, as Jonson's is, but is collectively foolish.

In *Magie Rouge* Ghelderode has been influenced in about equal parts by Molière's *L'Avare* and Jonson's *The Alchemist.* Hieronymus is Sir Epicure Mammon taken seriously. He is avarice personified. He has the primary characteristic of the true obsessive in that he will not hesitate to sacrifice his own comfort to feed his obsession. For example, although he has a young and attractive wife (he himself being a filthy and unattractive old man in the best Molière tradition) he has kept her a virgin so that he will not be enchained by her and have to spend money on her. Naturally his wife can take just so much of this. She enters into a plot with one Armador, a sleight-of-hand artist, and two others to get all of Hieronymus's money. Armador is introduced to Hieronymus as one of the world's greatest alchemists. He promises to find the elixir of gold for Hieronymus and retires to the cellar with his paramour, ostensibly to begin his experiments. Meanwhile, Hieronymus sits upstairs in his counting-house planning, among other things, to buy the pope and the Holy Trinity once he has all the money in the world. On one of his trips up for air, Armador, pretending to be drunk, lets Hieronymus take a black stone off him which he says grants immortality to the wearer. Armador and his mistress escape after murdering their two fellow conspirators and leave Hieronymus with the bodies and a coffer full of counterfeit money. Arrested and led out to torture and execution, Hieronymus remains wrapped up in his grandiose self-delusion:

> I don't understand! What did you say? . . . The gallows? . . . The executioner? . . . (*He tears himself away*) It's enough to make one laugh! . . . (*He laughs*) Ho, ho! . . . You've been nicely tricked. I am the leader of the living. Bah! I'm every bit as good as the Emperor! . . . Me die? . . . I'll buy up Justice, ho . . . ho . . . ho! . . . Listen to me! . . . I'm the same

as God. Yes! Don't you realize yet that I'm immortal? . . . (*He laughs at the top of his voice. They drag him out to the hooting of the crowd.*)[5]

La Balade du Grand Macabre is a thoroughly unbridled farce that takes place in Ghelderode's Breughellande. Here the delusion of godhead is assumed by a strange, pilgrim-like figure calling himself Nekrotozar who thinks he is one of the archangels sent down to earth to announce the imminent end of the world—or at least of Breughellande. In Breughellande, or Brugelmonde as it is called in another play, the people have been twisted body and soul by the workings of the Devil and are taken up with the practice of one or another of the seven deadly sins.

The play opens with an idyllic and passionate love scene between two young lovers, the play's only innocents. They retire into an abandoned tomb to make love and are followed by a hollow laugh and chattering voice coming from "the clouds perhaps." The voice sardonically and gleefully predicts that the lovers' bones "will be dispersed in the folds of the earth among the rotting weeds and the clefts of the rocks. The passionate gestures will be imprinted in the oozing slime."[6] The voice turns out to be Nekrotozar's. He climbs down from the tree and proclaims that Breughellande will cease to exist at midnight. The rest of the play is taken up with the exploits of Nekrotozar as he goes around whipping everyone up into a frenzy with his news until the night ends in a tremendous drunken orgy. He is assisted in his efforts by Porprenaz, the town's chief drunkard, and Videbolle, the henpecked state philosopher of Breughellande, whose job it is to reflect, a habit which the other citizens are unable to contract, to declare (like Pangloss) that everything is good and could not be better, and to make agreeable forecasts exclusively while giving agreeable explanations for any disagreeable occurrences that may take place instead. The play ends as Nekrotozar expires of an excess of drink and exertion, and the lovers emerge from the tomb still totally wrapped up in each other and completely oblivious of all that has happened. They represent, presumably, the hope of better things for Breughellande.

The fortunes of Brugelmonde, as it is called this time, are continued in *D'un Diable qui prêcha Merveilles* (*Of A Devil Who Preached Wonders,* written 1934). Here the sins committed in this northern Gomorrah are revealed in a series of scenes in which all the leading citizens enter one after the other and confess their failings to each other. The occasion for this attack of communal breast-beating is not repentance but fear. The town has just received word that news of its dissoluteness has reached Rome and that a well-known hell-fire-and-brimstone preacher has been sent to clean the place up. And there is certainly plenty of cleaning up to be done: the bishop uses the poor-box money to finance his sybaritic banquets; the abbess is pregnant by her confessor, a young Italian of great ingenuity at thinking up new forms of erotica; the sheriff has embezzled the town funds so his wife can finance her orgies; and other prominent citizens all display an equal reluctance to earn an honest penny. Even the town's resident devil has grown neglectful of his duties and is just reading a letter from the infernal regions warning him that he will be turned into a hermit monk if he doesn't get cracking and produce some really first-class sinners. Capricant is in despair since he is old and no longer has any taste for devil's work. But Fergerite, the local sorceress, advises him to dress-up as the preacher and deliver the sermon in his place while she sees to it that the real preacher is led astray. The sermon is an enormous success since the devil simply advises everyone to go on living in sin—with the Church's blessing. At the end the devil and the preacher meet and go off to Rome together, the preacher believing that the devil-monk is the only just man he has met in Brugelmonde.

The tangible presence of death is always a very real concept to Ghelderode and several of his plays contain scenes in which either a personified Death is the protagonist or a character returns from the dead. *Le Cavalier Bizarre* has already been mentioned as a play in which Death is personified. *Mademoiselle Jaïre* (written 1934) tells the story of a girl who dies and is resuscitated by a sorcerer who is later crucified. The girl remains alive only until the following spring, when a root-covered corpse named Lazarus, who comes to visit her and whom she has apparently known in the world beyond, bursts into flower. The point of the play seems to be the paradox that death, even when it takes the form of the mildew-and-damp-earth-covered putrefying flesh of Lazarus, is purer than life. Lazarus, for all of his repellent appearance, is embraced by Jaïre and speaks lyrically of the beauties of death that will be theirs when his flesh bears fruit and flower in the spring. In dying, in passing out of the world as Ghelderode sees it, one is translated from chaos to order, from impurity to purity, from the Devil to God.

Although Ghelderode's genuinely religious feelings may be somewhat obscured by his emphasis on the reverse side of the coin—the diabolic aspects of religion—in such works as *Fastes d'Enfer* (*Chronicles of Hell,* written 1929) and *D'un Diable qui prêcha Merveilles,* they are expressed most explicitly in *Marie La Misérable.* In this play Ghelderode is entirely on the side of the angels, although the diabolic element is by no means absent.[7] The play tells the story of Marie la Cluse, a saintly and very beautiful young recluse who lives in the church precincts and devotes herself to good works. A young nobleman, Eglon d'Arken, is overcome by lust for her; but when she rejects him with the proper amount of scorn, he accuses her of witchcraft and with the help of his deformed, dwarfish servant makes her appear guilty of theft. Marie is martyred and the true source of the machinations against her is revealed when the dwarf is killed and "revolting fumes, as if Hell were coming out of his carcass" rise up from his body.[8]

What happens when the powers of hell gain the upper hand over religion may be seen in Ghelderode's most notorious play, *Fastes d'Enfer.* This work caused a minor

sensation when it was first produced by Jean-Louis Barrault in Paris in 1949—and no wonder. The main character is the Bishop of Lapideopolis, a titular see somewhere in Flanders. He is lying in state in an adjoining room, having just passed away to the great relief of every member of his staff. John of the Desert, as the bishop is called, is not even an ordained priest. Years before, he was washed up on the shore during a great plague, which was devastating the city. His appearance bearing a huge cross coincided with the end of the plague and he was elected bishop by acclamation, an act later confirmed by the Holy See, which knows a *fait accompli* when it sees one. As the priests, all of them grotesque, misshapen creatures, celebrate his passing, John suddenly appears in the doorway, apparently as alive as ever. It turns out he was unable to swallow the Host which he was given before dying and it is choking him. After an eerie battle with his successor and chief enemy, Simon Laquedeem, during which the room is wrecked as a tremendous thunderstorm crackles outside, he is finally able to spit out the Host and die. The priests, led by Laquedeem, celebrate his final passing by hopping about the room with their robes trussed up, gleefully breaking wind to express their relief.

Ghelderode turns the theme of the personification of Death into a hilarious farce in *La Farce des Ténébreux* (*The Farce of the Shadows,* written 1936). This play concerns Fernand d'Abcaude, a ridiculous fool worthy of rating with any of Ben Jonson's most extreme "humor" characters. D'Abcaude's pleasure is to imagine that he is dying of grief for his beloved Azurine. He spends all his time in darkness, starving himself and having his valet describe the extremely elaborate funeral procession he has planned for himself. He cannot wait to die so that the funeral oration he has written can be recited and the biography he has ghost written can be published. To disabuse Fernand of his wish to die in order to join Azurine in a mutually virginal eternity, his doctor hires an actress to play the fiancée's ghost. Failing this, the doctor plans to cure d'Abcaude by giving him a whale-oil enema. The ruse is effective, however, since the actress manages to persuade d'Abcaude that Azurine was not the virginal paragon he believed her to be but rather something little better than the town whore. After all sorts of misadventures in a brothel during a carnival, d'Abcaude finally loses his virginity and joy reigns.

All of the plays mentioned thus far are set in Ghelderode's home grounds—in the special world that he has created out of medieval Flanders and Brabant. Not all of his plays are placed in this setting, however. Some of them combine a Spanish setting with a Flemish setting, like *Escurial* (written 1927) and *Le Soleil se couche . . .* (*The Sun Sets . . . ,* written 1933), which take place in Spain but constantly refer back to the characters' former lives in Flanders; or *L'Ecole des Bouffons* (*The School for Buffoons,* written 1937), which reverses the process. None of these plays is particularly interesting, although *L'Ecole des Bouffons* has first-class theatrical qualities. *Le Soleil se couche . . .* is a short play about the last days of the

Emperor Charles V. *Escurial* views the famous Escurial as an old and dilapidated palace somewhere in Spain. The king, who appears to be in the last stages of febrile decay, is attended only by howling dogs, an executioner, a priest, and his Flemish jester. The play is purely and simply a mood piece—a study in decadence. It is unfortunate that this has been one of the few Ghelderode plays performed in English because it is one of his weakest works. *L'Ecole des Bouffons,* on the other hand, is one of Ghelderode's most successful exercises in grotesquerie. It is about a school of deformed dwarfs, which supplies jesters to the courts of Europe after having taught them that the secret of all buffoonery is cruelty.

Those of Ghelderode's plays which are completely out of his medieval Flemish world may be divided into two groups: those having a religious basis and those having a mythic basis.

Ghelderode is probably best-known to American audiences through his two specifically religious plays, *Barabbas* (written 1928) and *Les Femmes au Tombeau* (*The Women at the Tomb,* written 1928). *Barabbas* tells the story of the Passion and Crucifixion from the point of view of the robber who was released in Christ's place. Barabbas starts out as a defiant and unregenerate criminal reveling in his own toughness. He is to be crucified, but he promises the mob a good show when they come to see him nailed up. While he is in prison he meets Jesus, who never says a word and meekly accepts whatever abuse comes his way. Barabbas is greatly impressed by Jesus's behavior. He does not understand Christ's meekness, since it is entirely outside the bounds of his previous experience, and mistakes it for stoical courage, which he possesses to a high degree himself and therefore knows how to appreciate. When he is released in Jesus's place, not so much by the will of the people as by the cunning maneuvers of the high priest, he wanders aimlessly around the town, always stealthily followed by the high priest's spies, who plan to kill him as soon as they have an opportunity. Finally he comes to rest in an abandoned fair-ground. Here he listens to a mysterious watcher describe the agony of Jesus and gradually comes to think of himself as one of Christ's followers. At the end he dies just after Jesus, stabbed in the back by the clown:

> BARABBAS: Hey? (*He reels.*) They got me. In the back, eh? Pretty good work! (*He falls to his knees like an ox.*) No, no, they haven't got me yet. Got to do something first . . . (*He gets up painfully and cries, hoarsely:*) Hey there, beggars! Bear up! I'm coming. (*But he falls to his knees again.*) You'll make it all right without me. Yes, they've got me all right. Well, what of it? I was condemned to death anyway . . . It's all the same thing to me. I'm not scared anymore. And I'm bleeding. Hey! Jesus? I'm bleeding too. Sacrificed the same day . . . (*He collapses and half raises himself again.*) But you, you had something to die for. Me, I'm dying for nothing. It's for you all the same . . . for you . . . Jesus. If you like . . . And if I could . . . I'd give you my hand . . . and see you smile . . . Jesus . . . My brother.[9]

Both *Barabbas* and *Les Femmes au Tombeau* are flawed as theatrical works by being too static. *Barabbas* consists principally of the hero's comments—for the most part melodramatic, overwritten, and not particularly interesting—on the watcher's report of the doings on Calvary. Full of undramatic and awkward devices, *Les Femmes au Tombeau,* in which a group of women meet in a deserted house in Jerusalem to discuss the Crucifixion, is simply a discussion play that lacks the brilliance of dialogue and the intellectual acuity with which Shaw made the discussion play a workable drama. Lacking action, both *Barabbas* and *Les Femmes au Tombeau* are more like radio scripts than stage works.

Ghelderode's mythic plays are all based on well-known and frequently used literary myths. (By myth I mean a story, not necessarily untrue, that has been used repeatedly in literature and has attained a conventional form so that it can be used by writers as a commonly understood point of reference.) He uses the Don Juan and Faust myths, which are almost obligatory for any dramatic author with a large body of work to his credit, the guileless-fool myth in *Pantagleize,* and the Judith myth in *Sire Halewyn.*

Both *Don Juan* (written 1928) and *La Mort du Docteur Faust* (*The Death of Dr. Faust,* written 1925) are written in a semipuppet play style with Ghelderode's penchant for the grotesque very much in evidence. In *La Mort du Docteur Faust* Ghelderode plays with a technique that has consistently fascinated him: the Pirandellian double-exposure technique. In addition to *La Mort du Docteur Faust* he has written two other plays specifically to exemplify this technique—*Trois Acteurs, un Drame* (*Three Actors, One Drama,* written 1926), a short, melodramatic, and clumsy play about three players trying to solve their real-life entanglements by incorporating them into the play they are acting, the only result being that the author shoots himself, presumably out of exasperation; and *Sortie de l'Acteur* (*Exit the Actor,* written 1930), an equally melodramatic and oversentimental play commemorating the death at the age of twenty-six of the Flemish actor, Renatus Verheyen, which ends in farce as the dead man escapes from his grave and is recaptured by angelic gendarmes who force him to skip up a golden ladder to Heaven.

La Mort du Docteur Faust, which Ghelderode has called his first important theatrical work (it was written in 1925 when he was twenty-seven), is about the transposition of the real, original Doctor Faust to a modern Flemish town where a carnival is in progress. He meets a modern girl named Marguerite, who fancies herself the Marguerite of the story, and the Devil, who is, of course, ubiquitous in every century. All three watch a performance of the Faust legend in a booth set up in a tavern and become inextricably mixed up with the actors playing their characters. The play is lively but diffuse and pointless, while the technique is based mainly on tricks.

Don Juan, which Ghelderode dedicated to Charlie Chaplin, is probably his weakest play. He attempts to depict

Don Juan as an eternal figure with a heritage—the compulsion to make love—handed down from generation to generation. The current Don Juan realizes this when he meets a shriveled up little man—"the little green man," Ghelderode calls him—who tells him that he was the previous Don Juan and reveals that he, like all Don Juans, has retired from the lists because he has been overcome by the ailments which inevitably result from indiscriminate dalliance.

A more appropriate play for Ghelderode to have dedicated to Charlie Chaplin would have been *Pantagleize* (written 1929). In this brilliant retelling of the saga of the guileless fool, Ghelderode tells the story of Pantagleize, a harmless little man who innocently trots around town on May Day telling everyone what a lovely day it is. What he does not know is that the town is seething with social unrest and that the innocuous remark he has chosen to celebrate his joy in the beauty of the day is the password for the beginning of a revolution. Pantagleize continues to amble around the town throughout the day, totally unconscious of the strife he has started. Completely oblivious of danger, he goes from one hair-raising situation to another until at the end of the day he meets the fate of all innocents in a world governed by the Devil—that of being massacred. As he dies, still unaware of what is going on, he brings out for the last time the innocent phrase, which remains innocent only in the minds of those who have not lost their innocence: "What . . . a . . . lovely . . . day!"

Ghelderode has recorded that the character of Pantagleize was inspired by an anonymous inhabitant of the Rhineland whom Ghelderode observed reading a book while walking across a public square swept by heavy machine-gun fire during the Spartacist revolt of 1919. In the middle of the square he stopped, looked at the sky, opened an umbrella, and then went on his way, still reading.[10] Ghelderode's profound pessimism can be seen in the description of the character which the sight of the oblivious reader inspired him to create:

> . . . a fellow like Pantagleize remains an archetype, an exemplary man, and a fine example who has nothing to do with that dangerous thing, intelligence, and a great deal to do with that saviour, instinct. He is human in an age when all is becoming dehumanized. He is the last poet, and the poet is he who believes in heavenly voices, in revelation, in our divine origin. He is the man who has kept the treasure of his childhood in his heart, and who passes through catastrophes in all artlessness. He is bound to Parsifal by purity, and to Don Quixote by courage and holy madness. And if he dies, it is because, particularly in our time, the Innocents must be slaughtered: that has been the law since the time of Jesus. Amen![11]

Michel de Ghelderode has written several other short plays but none of them contains any significant additions to the main themes of his work. Ghelderode remains primarily the dramatist of his own personally created world of medieval Flanders, which is depicted not as a historical

recreation but as a convenient microcosm in which he displays his moral view. It is a world governed by diabolic forces which warp its inhabitants into grotesque, clownish forms as they prance about ignoring the beauties of the world and allowing instead some obsession based on one of the seven deadly sins to corrode and finally damn them. Ghelderode's wildly farcical grotesqueries and unbridled vulgarity is really the expression of a deeply pessimistic but sincere and completely orthodox Christian religious feeling.

Notes

1. Michel de Ghelderode, *Théâtre.* Copyright © Editions Gallimard (Paris: Gallimard, 1955), IV, pp. 288-89.

2. Matthew, XV:14.

3. Michel de Ghelderode, *Théâtre* (Paris: Gallimard, 1952), II, p. 21.

4. *Ibid.,* p. 25.

5. Michel de Ghelderode, *Théâtre* (Paris: Gallimard, 1950), I, p. 179.

6. *Théâtre,* II, p. 32.

7. Cf. *supra,* pp. 99-100.

8. *Théâtre,* IV, p. 264.

9. Michel de Ghelderode, *Théâtre* (Paris: Gallimard, 1957), V, pp. 172-73.

10. Michel de Ghelderode, *Seven Plays,* translated by George Hauger (New York: Hill & Wang, Inc., 1960), p. 147.

11. *Ibid.,* p. 148.

Helen Hellman (essay date 1965)

SOURCE: "The Fool-Hero of Michel de Ghelderode," in *Drama Survey,* Vol. 4, No. 3, Winter 1965, pp. 264-71.

[In the following essay, Hellman examines Ghelderode's use in his plays of the Renaissance buffoon character.]

Michel de Ghelderode frequently affirmed in his plays, prefaces, letters, notes and conversations that he was the heir of Brueghel, Bosch and Erasmus. He appeared to have inherited their vision of man's folly and wisdom which prevailed during the Renaissance. Like them he stressed the folly, rather than the sinfulness of human conduct, always recognizing, however, the dual aspect of man's nature. He was a cruel moralist and critic of human conduct, and he described himself in the preface to the first book-length study of his work as "resembling those preachers of the past who confounded Matter and Spirit, in the style of the good old days of Erasmus, that inventor of ideas, and of Bosch, that inventor of forms."[1] But it is primarily as a dramatist that we are here concerned with

Ghelderode, who felt himself a magician of the theatre and who believed that farce form was ideal for his purpose: the exposure and penetration of a ridiculous surface which masks the great mysteries beyond and "the wretched, sublime, eternal quandary of the soul."[2] The very violence and explosiveness of his farce may, by a law of opposites, be construed as a measure of his passionate faith in man. In a letter to Roger Iglésis, the director of **Mlle. Jaire,** he wrote: "What concerns me is the dramatic mystery which takes place like a liturgy. It is my final faith—faith in the human, *Eternal Man,* that the theatre must exalt, through archetypes and myths, what is great and ennobling—at the risk of showing men, by opposition, their vices, their defeat and ruin, as they are in their ugliness."[3]

Ghelderode explicitly referred to the importance of the Flemish tradition in his work, and his Flemish biographer, Jean Francis, has more than corroborated him by stating that Ghelderode's theatre actually sums up the genius of Flanders.[4] Perhaps the vision of man's dual nature which absolutely permeates the Flemish tradition had been best described by Erasmus in *The Praise of Folly*:

> For first 'tis evident that all human things, like Alcibiades' Sileni or rural gods, carry a double face, but not the least alike; so that what at first seems to be death, if you view it narrowly, may prove to be life; and so the contrary. What appears beautiful may chance to be deformed; what wealthy, a very beggar; what infamous, praiseworthy; what learned, a dunce . . . In short, view the inside of these Sileni and you'll find them quite other than what they appear . . .[5]

Even a brief examination of Ghelderode's cast of characters reveals to what a great extent the Sileni appeared to have been a basic symbol for him. As a matter of fact, the figure of the satyr, "given to riotous merriment and lechery",[6] bears a strong resemblance to the demonic aspect of Folial, the buffoon, who is perhaps the most typical Ghelderodian hero. Folial appears by this name in at least four plays and is the hero of two of them: *Escurial,* written in 1927, which the author felt was his first dramatic success, and *School for Buffoons,* written ten years later and which was the last of his really great plays for the stage.

Folial is a heroic archetype, who, in the unity of his deformed person, symbolizes the creative and form-making power of the artist analogous to the divine, as well as the destructive power characteristic of the demonic. Fools have always played a dual role in society, according to historical, literary and dramatic traditions.[7] They have embodied evil and moral baseness; they have also been inspired prophets and poets, entertainers, bearers of supernatural powers and critics of society with license to speak unwelcome truths and comment freely on events. Folial is this kind of multivalent character, who is a symbol of the artist by virtue of his dramatic genius, his craftsmanship and his artistic consciousness. He is certainly a projection of Ghelderode's image of the artist, alienated and on the periphery of society, cherishing his isolation and solitude. Ghelderode referred to himself as an old master buffoon.[8]

Escurial is subtitled a drama in one act by the author,[9] who preferred this short form in many cases, since it permitted an intensity of expression which a longer play might attenuate. In *Escurial,* Folial is the jester of a degenerate Spanish King, in love with the Queen and grieving over her imminent death. The King wishes Folial to amuse him, knowing all the while of the latter's grief. At the King's command they enact a farce in which they exchange roles. Folial is revealed as a noble lover, the King shows himself to be an able buffoon. In the course of this farce, the King-buffoon typically exposes Folial's true sentiments and vengefully causes him to be killed. In effect, Folial dies for love, while the King remains, at the death of the Queen and his fool, with nothing but the empty symbols of his royal power. Folial, the professional buffoon, is defeated in this play because he has permitted himself to be betrayed by his personal feelings which have destroyed the forms of his art. In his grief over the death of the Queen, he could not bring himself to complete the farce. The King, in his moment as buffoon, with the cruel detachment of an artist, played the fool's role more successfully than his jester, who has not yet learned the lesson of the master in *School for Buffoons.*[10]

This play was written in 1937, ten years after *Escurial,* and is also a drama in one act. Ghelderode believed it to be one of the two culminating moments of his theatre.[11] *School for Buffoons* was one of the last great plays he wrote before a series of illnesses and before the Second World War, and he evidently felt that it was particularly significant. Folial in this play is the master buffoon at the court of Philip II. He is described as follows:

> In truth Folial is not malformed; he might be a tall dwarf but in proportion and even graceful even though he probably wears a corset. His personality would express weakness and ruse were it not for his magnificent eyes, of a clear blue which sometimes shine with the metallic brilliance of a superior Volition. He also has the extraordinary hands of a mime, which seem to create form or direct musicians, like the makers of miracles.[12]

Folial has left Spain, however, and set up in Flanders a school for buffoons, whose two emblems are a ship of fools and a bier. His students, in their grotesqueness, incarnate many types of moral fools. Folial refers to them as parodies of human beings, malformed by nature but endowed with quick wits and rich imagination. They have been trained as masters of all the arts of entertainment, and at their commencement will receive from Folial the true secret of his art, of all great art. When they leave the school and go out into the world, they will be able to revenge themselves by the skill of their ridicule and mockery upon the society which has cast them out.

To celebrate the termination of their studies and to prove their artistry to Folial they perform a "play within a play", a farce in which they enact the tragic death of Folial's exquisite daughter. They attempt to destroy Folial by mocking his grief, and thus ironically put into practice the secret which Folial has promised to reveal to them. They do not succeed, however. Although Folial is genuinely overcome for a brief moment, he recovers his integrity as an artist and teacher and punishes them for their imperfect performance, imperfect because it did not succeed in destroying him. He rises up, subdues them and reveals what he had forgotten in his grief and rediscovers with joy—that the secret of all great art is *cruelty*. Folial affirms his vision of himself as an artist, but the final stage direction indicates the tragic ambiguity of his situation. "As his face lights up with joy, with the broad gesture of one who sows, he whips empty space and as his movement becomes broader, he whips himself mercilessly without feeling it . . . Like an automaton, tragically."[13]

Folial, the master, is thus able to do what the earlier Folial of *Escurial* could not. He is able to go to the end of his vision of art and resist the equivocation that life attempts to force upon the artist. His cruelty seems to consist in his putting aside and transcending his personal grief to face his artistic responsibilities as master buffoon.

Related to Folial among the other Ghelderodian heroes is Juréal, the sculptor in *Hop Signor*.[14] We have seen, in the characters of the two Folials, how the physical deformity of the dwarf/buffoon may cloak a genuine and noble humanity, how it may mask the great creative power of the artist. Juréal is also deformed and explicitly compares himself to the dwarf-buffoons of his household. He tells them that he is deformed like them and disgraced by nature but he has also received from her a quick and fanciful wit.[15] He adds that his soul redeems the mediocrity of his envelope. His speech to the dwarfs is a significant one, in which the buffoon, likened to the sculptor, is an artist in his own right and a symbol of the solitary and alienated artist on the periphery of humanity. Juréal speaks for Ghelderode when he tells the handsome courtiers who ask him to model beautiful antique forms, a young Bacchus, for example, or little angels: "Alas, I can only carve what is harsh and violent! I would distort marble like stone . . ."[16] His delight is to sculpt the buffoons in their horrible and burlesque poses, even though he knows that his art has become unfashionable. It would seem that Juréal, speaking for Ghelderode, shared this pleasure with Rabelais, that other great moralist, for as has been recently pointed out, the latter's art "is concerned with just that, the ridiculous and the monstrous ones—Gargantua, Pantagruel, Panurge—and the people may not like them."[17]

Juréal is literally the artist of the grotesque, who comes to a tragic end as he is martyred by the mob. In reality, he is destroyed like the Folial of *Escurial* by the failure of his will as an artist. He has permitted himself the human follies caused by the love and jealousy of his young wife.

It should be remembered that Ghelderode is always a moralist, and although he despised the didactic morality of "pedants and eunuchs",[18] he was constantly preoccupied with the battle between good and evil, flesh and spirit, Carnaval and Lent. He was well aware of the brutal nature of his theatre, and he wrote of *School for Buffoons* that it was a play which does not flatter but rather flagellates.[19] The purpose of his cruel farces is a moral one. He wrote in the directions to *A Devil Who Preached Marvels*:

> Because it is true that a coat turned inside out is still a coat and therefore useful, I maintain that morality upside down (or inside out) is still morality, which has only put on a mask; and that in showing characters in their peculiar actions on the little stage of the world, I can stimulate a nostalgia for virtue, for the contrary of what I am showing . . . To know the Devil well, one doesn't have to seek far nor in religious writings; it is only necessary to study oneself well, the shrewdness and triumphant principle which is the Devil always resembling men as much as possible.[20]

The cruelty of Ghelderode's farces may be said to fulfill the dramatic conditions outlined by Antonin Artaud, who was his contemporary, although it is extremely doubtful that the two men knew each other. Artaud claimed that real theatrical action can be attained through a theatre in which "violent physical images destroy and hypnotize the sensitivity of the spectator."[21] Folial is the hero *par excellence* of such a theatre, who in his double aspect as sage/fool and artist/scapegoat both attacks the spectator and suffers in his own person the cruelties of man's condition. He is at the summit of a hierarchy of fools in Ghelderode's theatre and the king of a world which is seen as a realm of folly. In Ghelderode's view, as in that of Erasmus, he is crowned by his cap and bells.

To say that life seems to have made fools of us all is simply another way of talking about the tragic absurdity of man's condition. But can it be so surprising that men act foolishly when, as Erasmus had said, "Nature has confined reason to a narrow corner of the brain, and left all the rest of the body to our passions?"[22] Since this may be too large a realm for reason to govern and for divine truths to penetrate, men frequently act from the impulsion of their baser parts. However, Ghelderode has always insisted on the duality of man's nature, and his theatre, in its cruel tragic farces, is precisely a revelation of and protest against man's folly. In a world of destructiveness, formlessness and chaos which are the expression of the demonic forces of the universe, he has created an archetypal hero whose personal vision of order through art, God or death, is powerful enough to penetrate the surface, the "ridiculous outside." His heroes are fully prepared to battle for the integrity of their vision. His heroic characters are many-faced projections of Ghelderode himself, and in their will to order, their rebellion and protest against destructiveness and folly, they embody what the author refers to as his faith in the "human, Eternal man."[23]

One of the most powerful of the Ghelderodian protagonists is that advocate of subjective faith in the divine, the bishop John of the Desert in *The Pomps of Hell*. The author has characterized this long one-act play as a "tragédie-bouffe."[24] It had orginally been written as a three-act play which the author condensed to achieve the violent intensity of form which characterizes it. It is a carefully structured work in which the tragic action seems to be enclosed and prefigured by the farce and in which John, the hero, seems to be conceived as "the fool in Christ," delighting in his simple savages, battling against the "Scribes and Pharisees and doctors of the law, but diligently defending the ignorant multitude."[25] Elements of farce and tragedy are not separated, however, but seem rather to be mingled by means of gesture and language, frequently symbolic of the communion and of Christ's Passion. They are used in an interplay of such seemingly disparate elements as the mystic and the digestive, the divine and the scatological. The play's complexities reside exactly in this interplay, in the debasement of holy symbols, on the one hand, and the sublimation, on the other, of the common, the lowly and the unclean.

The Pomps of Hell involves the struggle between the bishop John, who insists on the value of subjective faith, and his auxiliary bishop, Simon Laquedeem, who represents the power of the church as institution, a vast and hollow shell. Both the tragic and farcical action revolve around the offering of a poisoned host by Simon to the Bishop, which the latter is unable to swallow. The Eucharist is mocked in the clowning of the gluttonous monks at the beginning of the play, one of whom coughs up the meat he has greedily snatched and swallows it again. This wild burlesque prefigures the dying Bishop's agony, his inability to swallow the poisoned host, symbolic of the impure doctrine of a corrupt church, which sticks in his throat. There is a violent struggle on stage between John and Simon, at the conclusion of which the Bishop, through the intervention of Veneranda, his old mother, rejects the host and dies mercifully, absolving his enemies. His death is the signal for Simon's demoniac victory, celebrated in a very literal and physical catharsis after a final attack of cramps. The moral victory, however, belongs to the Bishop. His lonely rebellion against hypocrisy and pharisaism, his personal faith opposed to the church, his struggle against an infernal existence unillumined by the divine are vindicated in his death; his tears and the absolution of his enemies suggest charity, mercy and obedience to divine will. The buffoon, the corrupt clowns and the damned, hypocritical men of the church are in reality destroyed by ridicule and farce.

John of the Desert bears a close resemblance to the Folial of **School for Buffoons.** He is a monumental figure of lonely integrity in his opposition to the corruption and vices of the lower clergy. Like Folial he is in a position of authority over the subordinate monks who fear him and participate in a cabal against him, led by Simon Laquedeem, the auxiliary Bishop, just as Folial's apprentices take part in the attempt to destroy their master by ridicule and farce in an intrigue led by Galgut, the deacon. But most important, he particularly resembles Folial in the consistency of his faith and his powerful will.

John is related to Folial, Juréal, Pantagleize and Columbus—they are all alienated from the society of their time and suffer from the singularity of their vision or character. But with a typical irony, John's life story most resembles that of Capricant, the mischievous devil in **A Devil Who Preached Marvels.** This play is a hilarious farce in which Capricant replaces a stern preacher who is fearfully awaited by the bourgeoisie of Brugelmonde. He preaches a sermon to them, extolling them for their virtues rather than blaming them and threatening them with hell for their vices. He is like the goddess Stultitia in **The Praise of Folly,** who preaches her topsy turvy morality to a delighted audience of unconscious fools. Capricant subsequently becomes friendly with the preacher who duly arrives, and recounts his mysterious birth and early life, which in the context of the play is a parody of the life story of John of the Desert as recounted by Simon Laquedeem in **The Pomps of Hell.** Like John, Capricant is a performer of miracles, a topsy-turvy thaumaturge. He even refers to himself as a sort of religious buffoon, "thinking of Jesus, who was covered with garbage and treated like a fool."[26]

In Ghelderode's symbolic realm of folly, the sage/fool is king. It is undeniable, I think, that this king frequently bears a resemblance to the Christ figure, symbol of compassion, faith and suffering, who was forced to play the buffoon in those moments of mockery when the crown of thorns was placed upon His head by the hypocrites and the reed placed in His hand. Ghelderode has always made free use of the symbols of the church, using them for his own artistic purposes, and has written several plays dealing with specific events in the life of Christ. Very revealing indeed is his choice of words in a letter to André Reybaz, the French director who discovered Ghelderode, so to speak, after a long period during which the latter's theatre was silent: "Now . . . this silence will be broken like glass: and the stage will resound heavily under the weight of characters of flesh and blood, bearing my stigmata . . ."[27]

In investing the figure of the fool with responsibility as one of the principal archetypal heroes of his theatre, Ghelderode continued a literary and dramatic tradition which extends beyond Flanders and includes, in addition to Erasmus, both Rabelais and Shakespeare. There is hardly a type of character better able to contain and reveal the two aspects of man's nature, which Ghelderode referred to as the "mystic and sensuous"[28] than the fool, whose face is always ready with its theatrical grimace, ready to become the comic or tragic mask as the occasion requires and expose, betray even, the deepest possibilities of man's nature. His privileged position as an entertainer and a figure of fun, as well as his liberty to criticize and attack—many a true word is spoken in jest—make him an effective symbol of human nature as well as its severest critic. In a period when men seem to be overcome by events, and the anti-hero is popular, the bold *"défi"* of Ghelderode's heroes, both tragic and comic, is an inspiriting phenomenon.

Notes

1. Jean Francis, *Michel de Ghelderode* (Brussels, 1949), p. xv.

2. David I. Grossvogel, *Digs and Daisies* (New York).

3. See letter to Roger Iglésis, October 20, 1949, *Revue d'Histoire du Théatre (RHT),* 2 (1962), p. 134.

4. Jean Francis, p. 96.

5. Desiderius Erasmus, *The Praise of Folly* (Ann Arbor, 1960), p. 43.

6. Ibid.

7. Enid Welsford, *The Fool* (New York, 1961).

8. Letter to Marcel Lupovici, Brussels, 1953, *RHT,* 2 (1962), p. 146.

9. Michel de Ghelderode, *Escurial* (Paris, 1950), Vol. I, p. 67.

10. Ghelderode, *Ecole des Bouffons,* III, p. 285.

11. Letter to Lupovici, July, 1953, *RHT,* 2 (1962), p. 144.

12. Ghelderode, *Ecole des Bouffons,* III, p. 297.

13. Ibid., pp. 331-332.

14. Ghelderode, *Hop Signor,* I, pp. 8-65.

15. Ibid., p. 14.

16. Ibid., p. 18.

17. Walter Kaiser, *Praisers of Folly* (London, 1964), p. 116.

18. Letter to Lupovici, November 17, 1953, *RHT,* 2 (1962), pp. 147-148.

19. Ibid., pp. 147-148.

20. Ghelderode, *D'un diable qui prêcha merveilles,* III, p. 145.

21. Antonin Artaud, *The Theater and its Double.*

22. Erasmus, p. 26.

23. Letter to Roger Iglésis, (above, note 3).

24. Ghelderode, *Fastes d'enfer,* I, p. 265.

25. Walter Kaiser, p. 89.

26. Ghelderode, *D'un diable qui prêcha merveilles,* p. 212.

27. Letter to André Reybaz, April 5, 1948, *RHT,* 2(1962), p. 119.

28. Ghelderode, *Le soleil se couche,* V, p. 27.

Helen Hellman (essay date 1967)

SOURCE: "Hallucination and Cruelty in Artaud and Ghelderode," in *French Review,* Vol. 41, No. 1, October 1967, pp. 1-10.

[In the following essay, Hellman examines elements of the nightmarish and grotesque in the plays of Antonin Artaud and Ghelderode.]

C'est le Diable qui tient les fils qui nous remuent!

—Charles Baudelaire

I have chosen the domain of sorrow and shadow as others have chosen that of the glow and the accumulation of things.

—Antonin Artaud

Cette création vôtre tournait sur son axe comme la terre et les saisons, et montrait la folie et la sagesse, la vie et la mort, la Passion de l'homme et celle de Dieu, sans omettre nos fins dernières, ni les sept vertus, ni les sept péchés, ni enfin tout et l'opposite du tout!

—Michel de Ghelderode

Antonin Artaud's first manifesto and letters on the theater of cruelty resume the principle ideas in *The Theater and its Double,* which from the point of view of form are realized in the dramaturgy of Michel de Ghelderode. The resemblance of ideas, vocabulary and vision of both men suggest what Robert Brustein naively wrote of Genet and Artaud, but which is even more particular to Ghelderode and Artaud: "One of the most extraordinary coincidences in literary history."[1] It is generally believed that there was neither contact nor influence.

Artaud wrote in this manifesto that the theater will never find itself "except by furnishing the spectator with the truthful precipitates of dreams, in which his taste for crime, his erotic obsessions, his savagery, his chimeras, his utopian sense of life and matter, even his cannibalism pour out, on a level not counterfeit and illusory, but interior."[2] Herein is the fundamental matter of hallucination, and it is the hallucinatory tradition in art and literature which provides the clearest point of departure for a discussion of theater common to both Artaud and Ghelderode. The former believed that his vision of the theater suggested the best means to reveal and exteriorize the hallucinatory quality of our secret and unconscious life and to discover forms to "express that extreme tension of contemporary life where the dissolution of old values has given rise to a monstrous unleashing of appetites, a liberation of the basest instincts . . . to a state of conscious chaos into which events ceaselessly plunge us" (p. 18). He believed his theater would be the equal of and express that mythical and moving immediacy in the creation of myths relevant to modern life in its universal aspects.

Hallucination is both the experience and the expression of chaos, the permanent home of evil and the devil, while the idea of cruelty as defined by Artaud is "above all lucid, a kind of rigid control and submission to necessity, a condition of continuous creation" (p. 102). It is not a coincidence, therefore, that both Artaud and Ghelderode were concerned with this opposition. Both have acknowledged their debt to Flemish painting, particularly to the painters Bosch and Brueghel for their rendering of the secret and cruel world of hallucination; to Charles Baudelaire and to Goya and Greco, all of whose works form a part of the tradition of the cauche-maresque. Baudelaire understood perfectly the full power of Flemish painting when he wrote:

Or, je défie qu'on explique le carphanaüm diabolique de Brueghel le Drôle autrement que par une espèce de grâce spéciale et satanique. Au mot grâce spéciale substituez, si vous voulez, le mot folie, ou hallucination; mais le mystére restera presque aussi noir. La collection de toutes ces pièces répand une contagion; les cocasseries de Brueghel le Drôle donnent le vertige.[3]

Artaud, in his fourth letter on cruelty, describes in detail the special light and atmosphere of Brueghel's disquieting and mysterious painting "Dulle Griet," in language which recalls that of Baudelaire. He says it is "mute theater," but one which tells more than if it had received a language in which to express itself. Each of these paintings has a double sense, and beyond its purely pictorial qualities discloses a message and reveals mysterious or terrible aspects of nature and mind alike. Ghelderode felt that Brueghel was his "père nourricier." He acknowledged in the latter's painting exactly the same qualities as did Artaud, saying that the work was always present to him, "for it was not only wonderful painting but offered a vision of the world, a philosophy."[4] Bosch was also a source of inspiration to both men, with his cycle of terror beginning at midnight when his world is at the mercy of Nature's craziest whims and where objects assume a life and activity of their own. Artaud wrote that

> the nightmares of Flemish painting . . . originate in those half dreaming states that produce clumsy ambiguous gestures and embarrassing slips of the tongue: beside a forgotten child they place a leaping harp; near a human embryo swimming in underground waterfalls they show an army's advance against a redoubtable fortress.
>
> (p. 71)

Ghelderode said that

> Jèrome Bosch has depicted very well for us the inscrutable, redoubtable world of things. He shows you a knife, for example, an innocent and terrible knife, from which legs have suddenly sprung and which comes toward you hypocritically—today it would be called radio-controlled."[5]

Ghelderode's plays are filled with eloquent objects which are a source of powerful suggestion, and he has written several which are closely based on Brueghel's painting. He was privileged to have been born in Flanders and to have imbibed so naturally the Flemish tradition which is doubly rich, being both mystic and sensuous. Of it he said:

> The Fleming lives in a hallucinatory world. My mother before me had been conscious of the otherworldly manifestations which surround us. But our eye remains meticulously realistic: the keen awareness of the surface and of the great mysteries beyond—there you have the Fleming since even before Brueghel. Is this not Farce Form? The ridiculous outside and the wretched, sublime eternal quandary of the soul . . . I am not a revolutionary; I am merely writing in the tradition of my race.[6]

Brueghel also painted that sensuous, fleshly and orgiastic aspect of the Flemings, and this tradition seems to have left Ghelderode with a much freer if critical acceptance of man's "basest instincts" and monstrous appetites than Artaud found possible. The latter's obsession with evil, the "domain of sorrow and shadow," often seems to be an expression of his violent revolt, as poet and theoretician, against the oppressions of a rationalist tradition: a revolt in order to bring about a resurgence of the "primitive, prelogical mentality."[7]

Vital in the formulation of Artaud's ideas was the painting of Lot and his daughters by Lucas van den Leyden, which suggested his chapter on "Metaphysics and the Mise-en-Scène." He outlines here his idea of the stage as a concrete physical place to be filled by its own concrete language, intended to satisfy and captivate the senses. Technical ideas for the uses of theater are developed later in the sections on Oriental theater. In connection with those techniques of total theater, Ghelderode's ideas and intuitions were similar to Artaud's, and he was eminently successful in their dramatic realization. Although Ghelderode seems nowhere to have referred to Oriental theater, his own experience of hallucination, of fear and terror, seems to have confirmed his profound intuitions about the theater as the place to exorcise evil obsessions, chimeras, savagery. Permeated by the Flemish tradition, he recreated intuitively the hallucinatory quality of Flemish painting and was able by writing to fix to some extent "that fear of the night, the fear of that fear which took hold of him, which every man has on him and which has his odor."[8]

While Artaud theorized about these matters and described with enthusiasm the specters in Flemish painting and the terrifying dragon figures in Balinese theater, and analyzed precisely the effects produced, Ghelderode created his plays in which specters and effigies from the beyond are personified on stage: the vampire in *Sire Halewyn*; Larose, the handsome executioner (Death), in *Hop Signor!*; the intercessor Leroux in *Mlle Jaire*; the mischievous devil Capricant in *D'un diable qui prêcha merveilles*; the Bishop Jan in Eremo, neither dead nor alive, in *Fastes d'enfer.*

The techniques of the Balinese theater whose adoption Artaud proposed for metaphysical ends were based on the conception of theater as a "lieu physique" where

> every spectacle will contain a physical and objective element, perceptible to all. Cries, groans, apparitions, surprises, theatricalities of all kinds, magic beauty of costumes taken from ritual models; resplendent lighting, incantational beauty of voices, the charms of harmony, rare notes of music, colors of objects, physical rhythm of movements whose crescendo and decrescendo will accord exactly with the pulsation of movements familiar to everyone, concrete appearances of new and surprising objects, masks, effigies yards high, sudden changes of light, the physical action of light which arouses sensations of heat and cold, etc.
>
> (p. 93)

All such expressions would function as enchantment to capture the senses, to exorcise evil by act and effort which by their nature are cruel.

Any one of Ghelderode's plays fulfills the above prescriptions for theater. He applied these techniques intuitively in poetic plays in the western tradition, techniques to fulfill intentions seemingly identical to those of Artaud, if the following statement is any indication: "Without the verbal incantation which renders it dependent on Magic, the Theater disintegrates of itself, crumbles away in words, renounces its priority over other forms of literature and disclaims its obsessional or possessional power, its marvels."[9]

One of Ghelderode's most cruel plays is **Hop Signor!**, a part of whose action is described below as an example of the playwright's invention of gesture as symbol:

> Thus the farce of the dwarfs, who function as a chorus or as the masters of the revels, completes and encloses the drama which in reality expresses a conflict raging within the soul . . . The antics of the little buffoons have permeated the atmosphere of the play through language, gesture and use of objects, with hints, cries, statements, little songs, jokes about what the play is about—the struggle between order and chaos, life and death, high and low, pride and abjection and the symbolic limits of Carnival and Lent. So much so that all the images in the play combine to express the dynamic relationship between altitude and abjection and to create an atmosphere more significant than the actual décor.[10]

Another example are the opening stage directions in *L'Ecole des bouffons*:

> On entend le battement obstiné d'un tambourin. Venant de gauche, les bouffons entrent à la file, exécutant une marche de pèlerins. Ils sont treize, que dirige leur bedeau Galgut, celui qui frappe le tambourin pour tenir le rhythme de la grotesque procession. Les bouffons chantent sourdement. Leur déambulation s'accompagne de saluts et menus gestes ridicules . . . Nul d'entre eux qui n'offre de visibles tares: de répugnants déchets humains dont l'apparition suscite l'effroi plutôt que la gaité.[11]

These human rejects have by the end of the play been magically transformed from base human material into refined artists. *L'Ecole des bouffons* is a brutal and bizarre play and may be considered as Ghelderode's spiritual autobiography. It is remarkably close to Artaud's notion of cruelty, for in this play Ghelderode's master buffoon, Folial, speaking for the author, tells his students explicitly that the secret of all art is cruelty. Although Ghelderode nowhere defines what he means by this, an understanding of the exigencies of art and of the symbols and gestures of his theater indicate that Artaud's definitions were his own. In the latter's second and third letters on cruelty, he writes of the "cruel necessity of creation" by the hidden god who cannot "not create" (p. 102). Theater in the sense of continuous creation, a wholly magical action, obeys this necessity of "cosmic rigor" and "implacable" necessity.

At the beginning of *L'Ecole des bouffons,* the grotesque apprentices in their topsy-turvy headdresses, singing their parody of a mass, are still the incompletely formed artists but a great advance over what they had been. Folial has created them through the "cruelty" of his art, and at their graduation their attempt to apply the lessons of the master lead implacably to a rebellion and an effort to destroy him. Their creation recalls Artaud's image of Brahma rising into being—an example of sublime cruelty analogous to the artist's bringing into being form from chaos.

Ghelderode's letters about *L'Ecole des bouffons* reveal to what an extent this play exorcised in the theater a vision which he had had for a long time. Here again his vocabulary suggests Artaud's: "Oui, cette pièce contenait de quoi violenter le silence et l'immobilité qui sont les privilèges de la Mort: donc, il y avait théâtre, puisque geste et cri, puisque vie . . ."[12] In a final pantomime, after Folial has enunciated the secret of art, saying: "C'est la CRU-AU-TÉ!," he enacts the following stage directions in an ambiguous gesture which actually expresses both the title of the play and the secret of cruelty:

> Avec un large geste de semeur, il flagelle l'espace, et son geste s'amplifiant encore, il se flagelle lui-même, impitoyablement, et ne le sent . . . Comme un automate, tragiquement. Le rideau tombe, avec lenteur, tandis qu'aux environs, l'aube blémissant toute chose, l'heure sonne, inéluctable—et chante le coq . . .[13]

In his detailed directions for gesture, costumes, sounds, music, Ghelderode obviously felt, if not actually the limitations, then the inevitability and extension of language to gesture, sounds etc. For him as for Artaud the theater, the mise-en-scène was magic and sorcery. Its very multiplicity derived from the ceaseless invention of symbols and images which disturb and charm and continuously excite the mind. His theater is like the Oriental theater described by Artaud:

> [It] does not deal with the external aspects of things on a single level nor rest content with the simple obstacle or with the impact of these aspects on the senses, but instead considers the degree of mental possibility from which they issue, that it participates in the intense poetry of nature and preserves its magic relations with all the objective degrees of universal magnetism.

(p. 125)

Artaud refers to the director, creating such spectacles, as a kind of demiurge. Ghelderode described himself in a sort of mirror image as "cette sorte de demiurge qui avez ouvert des polyptiques inondés de feux bas et de hautes clartés, traversés d'astres chevelus, brulants d'incendies, résonnants de kermesses et de liturgies . . ."[14]

Even more violent than *L'Ecole des bouffons, Fastes d'enfer,* a tragedy-farce in one act, qualifies for Artaud's theater of cruelty, although Ghelderode would probably have rebelled at such a limited view of his work. The two ideas essential to the play of plague and cannibalism relate it to the hallucinatory matter of theater. However, while Artaud dealt with these ideas in a theoretical way, Ghelderode created a satanic spectacle based on the Eucharist. He created a "tragédie-bouffe" around the holiest symbol of the Christian church, which becomes the occasion for ceaseless play and speculation about the experience of cannibalism inherent in the Mass. In this connection it is interesting to observe what Jean Genet said about the ceremony of the Mass: "Beneath the familiar appearances—a crust of bread—a god is devoured. I know of nothing more theatrically effective than the elevation of the host . . ."[15]

The tragic and farcical action of *Fastes d'enfer* revolves around the offering of a poisoned host. The opening farce introduces the theme of cannibalism in its parody of Christ's commandment: "Except you eat the flesh of the Son of Man and drink his blood, you shall not have life in you . . . for my flesh is meat indeed and my blood is drink indeed." Carnibos, the Chaplain, spits up meat from the "last Supper," which he had wolfed and could not swallow and thus prefigures the tragic dilemma of the poisoned Bishop, who cannot swallow the Host lodged in his throat. By analogy, host and meat become one, and the symbolic ritual of the Mass is reduced to its most literal action. The farce is thus a profanation of the church's most sacred ritual and an ironic comment on the suggestion of cannibalism inherent in it. The dying Bishop is referred to as "gibier" and playful references to meat are made throughout the play. Jan in Eremo, who has always been the patron of the butchers, is taken by them back to the people when he dies. The idea of cannibalism is extended to the digestive processes whose end is purgation. While the death of the Bishop and his return to the people is a signal for celebration and triumph, as well as lamentation, the new Bishop suffers a final attack of wind. His intestinal pains and subsequent relief are the signal for the scatological farce which concludes the play which ends in the chorus of priests shouting "Caca! . . . Caca! . . ." As the clowning priests leap about in clouds of smoking incense to dispel bad odors, it is easy to see the inspiration of the "diableries" of Bosch and Brueghel. The final purification is a recapitulation of that of the plague, which Jan in Eremo had miraculously ended when he arrived in the city of Lapideopolis. During this plague "latent images became the most extreme gestures." Jan in Eremo, a humble missionary priest, usurped episcopal power and thenceforward lived in the hell of his compromised spirituality. And in the physical battle which takes place between the two Bishops, we can see how Ghelderode's play dramatically illustrates Artaud's conclusion about the theater as plague:

> The theater restores to us all our dormant conflicts and all their powers, and gives these powers names we hail as symbols: and behold! before our eyes is fought a battle of symbols, one charging against another in an impossible mêlée: for there is theater only from the moment when the impossible really begins and when the poetry which occurs on the stage sustains and superheats the realized symbols.
>
> (p. 27)

Most critics of modern theater have remarked on the similarities between Ghelderode and Artaud in a general way. This discussion is an attempt to demonstrate some of the basic similarities more precisely. Robert Brustein wrote in *The Theater of Revolt* that

> if Artaud never achieved his theater, then many of his successors practically did. Critics have seen his influence on almost every experimental dramatist after World War II. Artaud's desire to "theatricalize the nightmares of Flemish painting" was realized by the Flemish playwright Michel de Ghelderode in flamboyant crowded baroque plays, studded with Renaissance violence.
>
> (p. 376)

Mr. Brustein regrettably is not able to see the absolute modernity of Ghelderode's theater which is based on his form. He has rather adopted a conventional view implying a certain archaism on the part of Ghelderode.

Leonard Pronko, in his book *Avant-Garde: the Experimental Theater in France,* has written more to the point:

> . . . it seems apposite to recall here the name of Antonin Artaud, and to remember that he advocated a theater of cruelty. Ghelderode was writing at the same time as Artaud and probably was unfamiliar with his essays, but, in the spirit of the great surrealist, the Belgian poet also makes us aware that "the sky can still fall on our heads." He catches us through our skin and our viscera rather than through our minds, using a kind of 'total theater' that would have pleased Artaud.
>
> (p. 177)

The most perceptive critic is Michel Corvin, writing for the "Que sais-je" series, *Le Théâtre nouveau en France*:

> Les éléments matériels de la représentation sont mués par lui en objets agissants . . . C'est par cela, beaucoup plus que par les ruptures de ton et le mélange de l'anti-sublime à l'héroïque, que Ghelderode a véritablement inventé un langage nouveau, qui l'apparente aux dramaturges de l'après-guerre comme Beckett ou Adamov et le rapproche d'Artaud que, d'ailleurs, il ne connaissait pas . . . La scène devient ce lieu physique dont parle Artaud et le théâtre apprend à devenir spectacle, spectacle de cruauté.
>
> (p. 41)

Finally Professor Eric Sellin, the author of a recent dissertation entitled "The Dramatic Concepts of Antonin Artaud," wrote in a letter:

> And in all my reading of Artaud I have found no mention of Ghelderode and doubt if the latter influenced Artaud, although Artaud's great admiration of the kindred spirit Jérome Bosch makes it seem likely that he would have liked Ghelderode had he known his works, and probably would have spoken of him in that case. Artaud similarly was more influenced by the common ancestor Strindberg than he was by the German

Expressionists whom he seems to have known only slightly despite having lived in Germany awhile and collaborated on films there.

The points of resemblance then between the dramatic theories of Antonin Artaud as outlined in *The Theater and its Double,* and the ideas of Michel de Ghelderode, enunciated in interviews and letters and realized theatrically in a repertory of more than thirty plays, are so striking that all critics have remarked them. Although they were almost exactly contemporary, it is generally believed that there was no contact nor influence. Their major work appears to have been accomplished in the nineteen twenties and thirties. Both were involved with the Autant-Lara theater of Art and Action, Artaud as an actor, Ghelderode as a playwright, but no evidence is presently available of any possible contact. Jean-Louis Barrault, whose famous pantomime, *Autour d'une mère,* was so admired by Artaud, presented in 1949 three performances of Ghelderode's masterpiece **Fastes d'enfer.** The protests of the Marigny audience were so violent, however, he was forced to ring down the curtain. The players acted subsequently at Les Noctambules in a successful nine-month run. In any case, Artaud had died the previous year, "priest and victim,"[16] a tragic embodiment of the Ghelderode archetype of the fool as poet and "vates."

Notes

1. Robert Brustein, *The Theater of Revolt* (Boston, 1962), p. 378, note 11.

2. Antonin Artaud, *The Theater and its Double* (New York, 1958), p. 92. All subsequent references to Artaud are from this source with page numbers indicated in parentheses.

3. Charles Baudelaire, "Quelques Caricaturistes étrangers," *Œuvres complètes* (Paris, 1963), p. 1023.

4. George Hauger, "The Ostend Interviews," *Tulane Drama Review,* 3 (1959). p. 15.

5. *Ibid.,* p. 22.

6. David I. Grossvogel, *Digs and Daisies* (New York).

7. Paul Arnold, "The Artaud Experiment," *Tulane Drama Review,* 2 (1963), p. 16.

8. "The Ostend Interviews," p. 14.

9. *Ibid.,* p. 10.

10. Citation from the dissertation in progress (U. of Pennsylvania) by Helen Hellman, "The Fool Hero of Michel de Ghelderode."

11. Michel de Ghelderode, *L'Ecole des bouffons* (Paris, 1950), III, p. 291.

12. Ghelderode, "Lettres à Marcel Lupovici," *Revue d'Histoire du Théâtre,* XIV, no. 2, p. 148.

13. Ghelderode, *L'Ecole des bouffons,* p. 332.

14. Jean Francis, *Michel de Ghelderode, dramaturge des pays de par-deça* (Bruxelles, 1949), p. XIV.

15. Brustein, p. 379.

16. Maurice Saillet, "In Memoriam: Antonin Artaud," *The Theater and its Double,* p. 158.

Hollis T. Landrum (essay date 1974)

SOURCE: "Ghelderode's War of the Words," in *Southern Quarterly,* Vol. 12, No. 3, April 1974, pp. 273-83.

[*In the following essay, Landrum examines modern language as a barrier to experiencing reality in Ghelderode's plays, arguing that the playwright has much in common with absurdist dramatists.*]

"There would almost seem to be virtue in silence, if they could only be silent."[1] Thus John Killinger describes the confused state of characters in absurdist literature. The statement is equally applicable to the characters created by Michel de Ghelderode. Although this playwright is not ordinarily identified with the theatre of the absurd, Robert Brustein comments that he comes as close as any dramatist in this century to fulfilling Artaud's request for the realization of Breughel's grotesque paintings on the stage.[2] This connection to Artaud, metaphysical spokesman for the modern theatre of the absurd, has been surprisingly glossed over by most critics of Ghelderode.

Killinger maintains that words, because of their abstractness and their loss of potency in the modern world, actually inhibit man from directly approaching reality.[3] We shall see that this attitude is one of the chief traits of Ghelderode's plays. Killinger goes on to say that by using absurd speech, most absurdists are trying to point out the absurdity of the human situation. Our real speech is absurd because it reflects the absurdness of our existence. In absurdist drama, "speech is a condemnation, for it adds to the clutter and absurdity of existence."[4] This language devaluation is the result of a general dissatisfaction with reality that was expressed by Artaud. According to Brustein, Artaud's theatre of cruelty declares war on language. Words are germs of the theatre which must be reduced into submission to the role of gesture on the stage.[5]

One reason Ghelderode has received little recognition thus far in the theatre is that some critics do not consider his drama part of the modern milieu of the theatre of existential man. Aureliu Weiss, an example of this type of critic, attacks Ghelderode, claiming that he sought no illumination, no progressive structure in his plays. Weiss further claims that there is nothing new in Ghelderode's plays and that only a few of them are worth the time to linger over.[6]

George Hauger and Martin Esslin do not attack Ghelderode, but they do separate him from the modern absurdists. Hauger classifies Ghelderode as basically an expressionist and romantic.[7] Esslin distinguishes between the theatre of the absurd and the "poetic avant-garde" of Ghelderode, which he says differs from the absurd in several minor ways. There is more emphasis on dreams and fantasy in the "poetic avant-garde"; there is also less unity, less character development, less plot, and less violence or grotesqueness. But the major difference between the two, according to Esslin, is the use of language. The "poetic avant-garde" uses poetic language consciously to set a mood: "It aspires to plays that are in effect poems, images composed of a rich web of verbal association."[8] The absurdists, on the other hand, tend "toward a radical devaluation of language, toward a poetry that is to emerge from the concrete and objectified images of the stage itself."[9] The poetry is subordinate to the action in such a structure. In this situation, "what happens on the stage transcends, and often contradicts, the words spoken by the characters."[10]

Esslin is probably correct in this distinction, but he overstates his case in regard to Ghelderode. It is true that many of Ghelderode's plays are based on lyrical flights of fancy, employing poetry to evoke a mood. Some of Ghelderode's plays, however, also contain an element of language devaluation. Perhaps he does not emphasize the devaluation to the same degree as do Ionesco or Beckett, but it is there, lurking in the poetic images themselves. One might say that Ghelderode anticipates this devaluation of language. He has not yet reached the point of denouncing language by escaping from it; he still employs language in order to attack language, which to the absurdists would appear futile as well as damaging. But even Ionesco had to utilize language in order to ridicule it. That seems to be the dilemma of the modern playwright. How does he continue to communicate when he has attacked and destroyed communication?

Despite the dilemma, most of the absurd dramatists have made non-communicative speech a central point in their drama. This is more than word play in their case; it is a reflection of the existential emptiness that these dramatists see in the world. If their plays consist of dialogue, it is anti-dialogue. Words are attacked as being only another manifestation of the absurdity of the human condition.[11]

If one examines Ghelderode's plays carefully and considers Robert Brustein's definition of existential revolt, he can perhaps grant Ghelderode's achievement among the modern dramatists. According to Brustein, existential drama is marked by subhuman characters, a mood of helplessness, and a strong tendency toward the grotesque with a degrading description of human flesh.[12] The definition is remarkably like the description of Ghelderode's plays in *The Oxford Companion to the Theatre*, in which it is pointed out that the recurrent theme of Ghelderode's plays seems to be the "agonized appraisal of man's condition, seen as a crude and violent burlesque, where purity is engulfed by the obscene deformities of the flesh, and which ends in the eternal mystery of death."[13]

In determining whether Ghelderode belongs to an earlier tradition of the theatre or in part to the modern theatre of

the absurd, one must consider first the role of words or non-words in his plays. We include non-words because of the importance they also play in absurdist drama. Killinger states that "in a world where words have become mere things, quasi-physical projectiles that clutter life and landscape, it does not seem unusual that the silent person should come to have both preternatural dignity and authority."[14] He also points out that there are a number of mutes in absurdist drama and each of them is treated with more respect than those who verbalize. It is as if the authors are saying that it is better to be a mute than the most eloquent speaker in this insane world.[15]

Ghelderode's emphasis on silence is quite clearly shown in his own life of solitude. When asked to define what he was, he referred to himself as a man who wrote all alone in a room.[16] He said later that he loved solitude for its own sake. He called it a purifying agent, and a necessary element for creation; he believed no artist could ever do anything really great except in solitude.[17] In a letter, Ghelderode writes, "I have too great a need of solitude and silence, and Paris is a sort of fascinating hell from which I always come back physically and mentally exhausted."[18] Ghelderode writes in another letter, "Do as I do: keep silent, the silentium of the old church."[19]

This silence is not, however, just an empty silence for Ghelderode. Inanimate and speechless objects are totally possessed with life. He states that all such objects are alive and sensitive.[20] This is particularly true of Ghelderode's interest in marionettes. His delight in them, he confesses, stems from their silence and natural reserve. He states that marionettes console him "for the cacophony of the play and the crazy glibness of the impudent creatures that theatre people most often are."[21] Ghelderode writes in a letter, "The theatre is lost the moment it speechifies, discusses, analyzes, preaches. It is out of danger when it dreams, digresses, laughs, cries, tells startling stupidities, and commits a thousand follies and atrocities . . ."[22]

Ghelderode's silent objects thus have a language louder than words. Actualizing Artaud's philosophy of the stage as a restoring of magic to life, Ghelderode refers to the theatre as "an art of instinct."[23] He states, "For me, a theatrical work does not exist without the sensuousness proper to the plastic arts, or, in that case, exists only as a dialogue which can be read and does not call for realization on the stage."[24]

According to Ghelderode, it was painting which originally led him into the theatre.[25] He comments in a letter, "The only thing that could be useful to you is this: think of painting; this play is painting become theatre."[26] Hauger mentions that Ghelderode emphasized the visual in all of his plays. He calls them living paintings.[27] Another critic, Wellwarth, makes a similar observation. He says, "Ghelderode's theatrical sense was essentially a physical one (movement and appearance are far more important than speech in his plays) and he therefore adopted the medieval view that when man succumbs to sin his experience is reflected in his outer form."[28]

Less obvious than Ghelderode's emphasis on silence is his use of language devaluation. Ghelderode was a poet who sought a structure of poetic dialogue throughout his plays. He states at one point that he demands "a certain music in human speech."[29] Nevertheless, there is more than nice sounding language involved in poetic dialogue for Ghelderode. Musical speech is necessary to Ghelderode in order to keep language from dwindling to meaningless noise. He refers to this type of speech as "verbal incantation" and says that, without it, "the theatre disintegrates of itself, crumbles away in words, renounces its priority over other forms of literature, and disclaims its obsessional or possessional power, its marvels."[30] As he states in a letter, "Without shrieks, the theatre is merely chatter: words, words!"[31]

Thus poetry is not introduced simply because of the musical flow of the words, but in order to act as a buffer against the meaninglessness found in words used as just words. As Ruby Cohn states, "Particularly in his plays set in Christ's time or in the Flemish Middle Ages, Ghelderode energizes his drama with verbal shock."[32] It appears that Ghelderode uses poetry in order to attack language and that he amplifies the action on stage through physical movement or appearance. Ghelderode's poetry is both verbal and physical, and in each case it seems to denounce words as words.

In order, however, to discover what Ghelderode's own opinion of language is in the theatre, we must turn to his plays. We shall examine mainly four major plays of Ghelderode. These are considered his greatest achievements and illustrate his attack on language most clearly. Two other short plays will be considered briefly.

The Death of Doctor Faust, written in 1925,[33] is permeated by the confusion between art and reality. Each of the central characters has a corresponding character who is his actor. The confusion between art and reality spills over into the confusion of man himself. Man attempts an impossible task when he tries to find himself, since he is doing the looking. It is only when he acknowledges that his role is more real than himself that his search is ended. Faust admits at the end that he is only an actor who has somehow gone wrong, and when the devil admits that he too does not exist, but only sticks to his role, the actor Faust calls him a "phrasemonger."[34]

In the prologue, Faust attacks writers, saying, "Only the ocean will speak better than they. And if someone found out, it would be a joke beyond belief."[35] What Ghelderode seems to be saying is that just as the role a man elects is more real than the man, so his words fail to reach reality because of the fact that they are only words. The writer cannot hope to capture reality; the earth will always speak more clearly because it is more natural. The man who discovers this will find it ridiculous that man should even attempt to capture the world with words. Yet Ghelderode can find no other solution; that is the problem. As the devil states in the first part of this play, "I write in forty-seven languages, but I have put my self-respect elsewhere."[36]

In *Cristopher Columbus,* written in 1927, Ghelderode comments on the man of silence as well as the man of words.[37] Ghelderode labeled this play a "dramatic fairy tale."[38] Most of the play is weak and downright boring, but the conclusion makes up for all that went before. It is outside the scope of this paper to discuss the entire meaning embodied in the closing lines of this play. For our purposes it is enough to note that the Americans fail to recognize any of the humanity of Columbus. As the American says, "In the name of America, I come to salute you, Columbus—but not the great man, only the statue."[39] Ghelderode seems to be implying here that our speeches fail to describe the true man, only the hollow form. After this sequence of speeches, the statue climbs from its pedestal and weeps, "There is nothing you can do about anything. You have to be a statue to understand."[40]

This is both irony and tragedy at the close of the play. Ghelderode had built Columbus into a truly mortal form, complete with all the doubts and foibles of a human being. At the end his humanity is destroyed, and after four hundred years his statue is more real than his own life. There is savage irony in this innocent "fairy tale." Ghelderode seems to be standing aside and mocking our modern age, replete with up-to-the-minute newscasts and modern means of analysis, none of which seems to help man reach the humanity within himself or others.

Also, Ghelderode appears to imply in the closing lines of the play that in order to truly understand, man has to be speechless and motionless, like a statue. Only when one is truly still and above or outside the movement around him can he fully comprehend the life surging around him in all directions. The irony of this is that one can never communicate his understanding to others in such a situation. Thus one is forced to moan, "There is nothing you can do about anything."[41]

A year later, Ghelderode makes an even stronger distinction between the man of words and the man of silence in his play *Barabbas.* Before the play even begins, Ghelderode emphatically points out that Barabbas is a man "who talks a great deal," whereas Jesus is one "who says nothing."[42] Thus both of the central characters are distinguished by the amount of noise they make, one continuously talking and the other continuously silent.

The difference between the two goes deeper, however, than mere words. Barabbas thinks that Jesus knows more than ordinary men even though he won't speak.[43] Hence Ghelderode suggests that the men who know more than ordinary men speak less. Barabbas, on the other hand, is in a constant state of ignorance. In the second act he carries out the wishes of the priests without knowing what he is doing. When Caiaphas asks him if he knows what is going on, Barabbas replies, "Less and less."[44] At the end of the trial by the crowd, he asks, "In that case who is being deceived?"[45] Barabbas, until that point, thought he was fooling the crowd; suddenly, he begins to realize that the only one he was fooling with his words was himself.

Ghelderode implies that words only serve to confuse their users. The men who know more than ordinary men refuse to use words. It is significant to note that the clown who imitates Jesus and manages to slay Barabbas at the end of the play repeats in several places only the line, "What did he say?"[46] It is uttered entirely out of context since no one says anything worth repeating just before this question, and the clown is never answered. These words are uttered almost as an incantation just before the clown plunges the knife into the back of the unsuspecting Barabbas. It appears, then, that Ghelderode is using this question to emphasize the confusion which exists in the words of the characters. In effect, he seems to be using the statement as a sarcastic comment rather than an actual question. The point is that although the characters seem to be making sense when they speak, their words are actually only a parody masking their own confusion. As Barabbas remarks to the prisoners in Act I, "Sometimes it's good to talk nonsense."[47]

Although Jesus is condemned because of his silence, he is condemned by a crowd which do not realize that words fail them. Words actually confuse and mask reality, but the crowd are ignorant of that fact and equate words with reality. Thus they condemn an innocent man and free the guilty one on the basis of the degree of noise each makes.

But Ghelderode does not let it rest at that. The basis of the play is the struggle of Barabbas to understand what has happened. At the very end, when he is dying, he admits that Jesus, the silent, has died for something; while Barabbas, the talker, has died for nothing. But he calls Jesus his brother, saying that they have both been sacrificed, so they both share a common fate.[48] The difference is that there is a choice in silence and therefore a meaning for Ghelderode, but there is no choice in continuing to employ words as masks, so there is also no meaning in it.

One other point should be made here before we turn to the last major play. Crowds and background noise play a large part in *Barabbas* in that they add to the confusion of the characters. A background noise is present in most of Ghelderode's plays. It is normally composed of a crowd or a similar collective, and it is usually juxtaposed against the central character. The two best examples of this are the one act plays *Escurial* and *Chronicles of Hell*. In *Escurial,* the noise is a pack of dogs which the king eventually strangles.[49] In *Chronicles of Hell,* the noise is the howling mob that eventually breaks into the castle.[50]

These two are by no means the only instances of background noise in Ghelderode's plays. He seems anxious to parade noise and cacophony off stage to imply chaos and confusion. It is significant that in the two examples above, the noise is off stage and serves to antagonize or threaten the central characters. It is as if Ghelderode is implying that man is continuously haunted and threatened by a rabble of noise. In *Escurial,* the king laments, "My head is full of dogs and bells."[51]

The clearest example of Ghelderode's distrust of words is found in his last major play, *Pantagleize,* written the same year as *Chronicles of Hell,* 1929.[52] The entire structure of *Pantagleize* is based on irony. The names of the characters, for example, exhibit the opposite of the traits intended. Innocenti is the only figure of the play who truly knows what is happening to him. The poet's name, Blank, may be interpreted in several ways. It suggests that he speaks in blank verse and that his mind is a total blank. Ghelderode is probably making a bitter comment on modern poets through Blank. At the end of the play, during the trial, Blank confesses to be a modern poet, and the General replies, "Not content with overthrowing society, you must overthrow syntax in the bargain and sow confusion in healthy brains."[53] Blank's poetry makes no sense whatsoever, and his part in the revolution is equally cloudy.

As with Barabbas, Pantagleize is a victim of circumstances. He never comes to realize the part he is playing in the revolution and his position is entirely accidental. It is important to note that the entire action of the play is based on the misunderstanding of words. Intending only to make conversation in the beginning of the play, Pantagleize says, "What a lovely day!"[54] This phrase turns out to be the signal for the start of a revolution. Pantagleize repeats the phrase to all the revolutionaries, and they immediately assume that Pantagleize is their unknown leader. Pantagleize uses this phrase throughout the play without once realizing the consequences of what he is saying. Likewise, another innocuous phrase is the password for the government's treasure. The officials guarding the treasure are never sure when the soldiers mean to use the password or are using it literally.[55]

The very last line of the play emphasizes this irony of words. Pantagleize is dying, and he utters in a "gruesome and childish" tone, "What a lovely day."[56] The mocking use of words here is inescapable. This last phrase can be interpreted as a satiric comment on the entire play, a literal statement of fact by Pantagleize, or an ironic comment on the plight of Pantagleize. Ghelderode has based an entire play on the confusion to be found in words. Men are executed, revolutions begun, fortunes lost by the slippery use of "common" words. As Blank states, "Tonight, perhaps, I shall throw away my poet's mask and be a man among the others."[57] The use of a poet's mask could refer to the fact that Blank is an anarchist disguised as a poet in the play, or it could refer to the mask of words a poet uses to keep him from being a man among others. As Innocenti says to him, "If you could only guess for a minute what reality is like!"[58]

Ghelderode is attacking the falseness of words in this statement. Words are a mask which men use to hide from reality. Thinking their meaning is clear, men continue to exist in a state of stupidity, causing riots and calamities without knowing the slightest reason why. The farce is that the entire revolution is based on a mistake, a mistake which is fatal and thereby sad. Men play with words, hide behind them, and are finally executed by them. What is odd is that men never realize their plight. As Pantagleize says just before he is shot, "I can see less and less."[59] Apparently, no matter what his intentions, man cannot escape this mask of words as long as he employs them. If he fails to recognize the double meanings, the infinite interpretations, he is doomed by them.

All of this apparently makes a strong case for placing Ghelderode near the modern school of absurdity. His link with Artaud is inescapable, just as the existential meaninglessness in his plays is equally hard to overlook. His plays may not have consciously been designed to wage war on language, and Ghelderode would certainly deny belonging to any group of dramatists. However, his attack on words, his awe of silence, his use of the physical over the verbal, and his desire for a theatre based on instinct all seem to push Ghelderode close to the modern day absurdists. Regardless of whether we categorize him as an absurdist or a misplaced romantic, Ghelderode belongs to the present rather than to the past, and we must not make the mistake of shelving him in an antique closet and assuming that he has nothing to say about modern man. Rather than simply trying to escape the modern world, Ghelderode appears to use the past in order to show his deep existential feeling of despair of man in the twentieth century. As Wellwarth points out, "To a careful reader of his works there can be little doubt that Ghelderode is obsessed with a deep feeling of the inadequacy of the human condition."[60]

Notes

1. John Killinger, *World in Collapse* (New York: Dell, 1971), p. 100.

2. Robert Brustein, *The Theatre of Revolt* (Boston: Little, Brown, 1964), p. 376.

3. Killinger, pp. 92-93.

4. *Ibid.,* p. 100.

5. Brustein, p. 373.

6. Aureliu Weiss, "The Theatrical World of Michel de Ghelderode," *Tulane Drama Review,* VIII (Fall 1963), 60-61.

7. George Hauger, "The Plays of Ghelderode," *Tulane Drama Review,* IV (Fall 1959), 19.

8. Martin Esslin, *The Theatre of the Absurd* (Garden City, New York: Doubleday, 1961), p. 21.

9. *Ibid.*

10. *Ibid.*

11. Killinger, pp. 112-15.

12. Brustein, pp. 26-28.

13. Phyllis Hartnoll, ed., *The Oxford Companion to the Theatre,* 3rd ed. (London: Oxford University Press, 1967), p. 385.

14. *Ibid.,* p. 110.

15. *Ibid.,* pp. 110-11.

16. Michel de Ghelderode, *Seven Plays,* trans. George Hauger (New York, 1966), I, 3.

17. *Ibid.,* p. 14.

18. George Hauger, "Dispatches From the Prince of Ostrelande," *Tulane Drama Review,* VIII (Fall 1963), 26.

19. Michel de Ghelderode, "To Directors and Actors: Letters, 1948-1959," *Tulane Drama Review,* trans. Bettina Knapp, IX (Summer 1965), 53.

20. Ghelderode, *Seven Plays,* I, 24.

21. *Ibid.,* p. 23.

22. Hauger, *Tulane Drama Review,* VIII, 26.

23. Ghelderode, *Seven Plays,* I, 20.

24. *Ibid.,* p. 17.

25. *Ibid.,* p. 16.

26. Ghelderode, *Tulane Drama Review,* IX, 45.

27. Hauger, *Tulane Drama Review,* IV, 23.

28. George E. Wellwarth, "Ghelderode's Theatre of the Grotesque," *Tulane Drama Review,* VIII (Fall 1963), 21.

29. Ghelderode, *Seven Plays,* I, 9.

30. *Ibid.,* p. 11.

31. Ghelderode, *Tulane Drama Review,* IX, 56.

32. Ruby Cohn, *Currents in Contemporary Drama* (Bloomington: University of Indiana Press, 1969), pp. 56-57.

33. Hauger, *Tulane Drama Review,* IV, 30.

34. Michel de Ghelderode, *Seven Plays,* trans. George Hauger (New York, 1967), II, 142.

35. *Ibid.,* p. 101.

36. *Ibid.,* p. 105.

37. Hauger, *Tulane Drama Review,* IV, 30.

38. Ghelderode, *Seven Plays,* II, 151.

39. *Ibid.,* p. 174.

40. *Ibid.,* p. 175.

41. *Ibid.*

42. Ghelderode, *Seven Plays,* I, 50.

43. *Ibid.,* p. 70.

44. *Ibid.,* p. 88.

45. *Ibid.,* p. 92.

46. *Ibid.,* p. 122.

47. *Ibid.,* p. 61.

48. *Ibid.,* p. 123.

49. Eric Bentley, ed., *The Modern Theatre* (Garden City, N.Y.: Doubleday, 1957), V, 163-65.

50. Ghelderode, *Seven Plays,* I, 239-73.

51. Bentley, p. 165.

52. Hauger, *Tulane Drama Review,* IV, 30.

53. Ghelderode, *Seven Plays,* I, 211.

54. *Ibid.,* p. 157.

55. *Ibid.,* pp. 186-87.

56. *Ibid.,* p. 222.

57. *Ibid.,* p. 160.

58. *Ibid.*

59. *Ibid.,* p. 220.

60. Wellwarth, *Tulane Drama Review,* VIII, 22.

Paul M. Levitt (essay date 1975)

SOURCE: "Ghelderode and Puppet Theatre," in *French Review,* Vol. 48, No. 6, May 1975, pp. 973-80.

[*In the following essay, Levitt suggests philosophical and aesthetic reasons for Ghelderode's propensity for using puppets in his plays.*]

It should now be obvious that Michel de Ghelderode (1898-1962) is among the masters of modern theatre. If it was not obvious to his own contemporaries and is still not so obvious as it should be today, it is partly for the reasons that he lived as a recluse, eschewed realism in drama, and ideologically, as well as in practice, propounded an unpopular genre: puppet theatre.

Throughout his life Michel de Ghelderode was fascinated by dolls and marionettes. The inquiring few who visited him in his isolated home near Brussels invariably remarked about the number of puppets, statues, and dolls scattered about the house.[1] His visitors commented also on the frequency with which he introduced the idea of marionettes when talking about his problems as a playwright, and on his near veneration of puppets as important, exciting vehicles for dramatic expression.[2]

In fact, two of Ghelderode's plays—*Les Femmes au tombeau* and *D'un diable qui prêcha merveilles* are explicitly subtitled "Mystère pour marionnettes." And for good reason. There is no doubt that a play is potentially—and radically—different if produced (or imagined) with puppets instead of men acting the roles. To understand Ghelderode's plays, we must consider what particular needs he is attempting to satisfy by using puppets instead of actors. The two principal reasons for Ghelderode's attraction to puppet theatre are his dissatisfaction with living actors and

his inclination toward caricature.[3] Together they form the core of his theory on marionettes. There are, however, other reasons, admittedly more speculative and not easy to categorize, for his obsession with puppets. For example, there is Ghelderode's religious position.

A devout Pauline Catholic, Ghelderode sees man as the puppet and God as the puppet master. By employing the world-as-stage metaphor, Ghelderode is able vividly and dramatically to place man in the religious scheme of things: namely, at the end of a string drawn by the hand of God.[4] In the diction of puppetry, Ghelderode finds a vehicle to describe his own search for God and for personal meaning. "Cet art vaut ce qu'il vaut, mais il m'aide à vivre, tel que je me dépeins: cherchant toujours le montreur de marionnettes et le sens de la pièce que nous jouons" (p. 58). The language of puppetry provides a way to reify religious abstractions, and this apparently suits Ghelderode's personal needs, because he uses marionette metaphors in many of his most profound and introspective religious statements. "Je cherche encore, je cherche toujours celui que nul ne cherche, celui qui actionne les ficelles des poupées" (p. 55).

However, there is a more practical reason for Ghelderode to promote the use of puppets in place of actors: marionette theatre offers an inexpensive forum for young or unproven playwrights. "Elles offrent aussi la miraculeuse ressource aux infortunés dramaturges partout refusés, de risquer à peu de frais ces oeuvres non-conformes que les censures ou la stupidité des marchands de fesse qui dirigent les théâtres condamnent à l'asphyxie!" (p. 113). Marionette theatre provides a means of breaking away from stale dramatic conventions and of encouraging improvisation.

One of the most popular arguments against puppetry as a means of interpreting serious drama is that marionettes tend to destroy a play's seriousness, making a travesty of the artist's labor and a mockery of his dramatic vision. This view is the opposite of Ghelderode's and, in fact, underlies one of his principal reasons for advocating and practicing puppet theatre. Like Pirandello, Ghelderode believes that flesh and blood actors, popular opinion to the contrary, are the ones who destroy a playwright's creation through their inept, stumbling attempts to recreate the dramatist's conception of his characters. The problem is that the actors' own personalities, gestures, faces, voices, and histories are glaring reminders to the audience that what they are seeing is not an embodiment of the playwright's character, but only an imperfect look-alike, a feeble attempt by a man to be someone he is not. Ghelderode treats this problem of the actor's inherent duality of character in *Trois Acteurs, un drame.* In this play three actors virtually destroy a play in which they are acting because they cannot prevent their own personal complications from becoming inextricably involved with their acting. As the play progresses (degenerates would be more apt), the fictitious drama becomes hopelessly ensnared with the real-life problems of the actors. At the conclusion, the exasperated author commits suicide. To avoid the problem of "personality," Ghelderode recommends marionettes.

But how, one wonders, can puppets perform a play like **Trois Acteurs, un drame,** which proceeds from the assumption that plays fail because the actors *are* "human"? The answer to this seeming paradox is that Ghelderode's characters are never "human" in the modern sense of psychological realism. As Micheline Herz observes, "Ghelderode rejects all psychology."[5] His characters are reminiscent of those found in Medieval *mystère* plays. He sees man, according to Leonard Pronko, "in Manichaean terms of dark and light, good and evil, flesh and spirit."[6] Ghelderode, in fact, has said of himself: "I have an angel on my shoulder and a devil in my pocket."[7] Is it any wonder, then, that his characters are anti-realistic, stylized figures, fashioned, as it were, out of wood? It is precisely because his characters *are* puppet-like that Ghelderode has been criticized for failing to differentiate character by means of dialogue. He gives, as Auréliu Weiss remarks, "the same language to all his characters. Whatever their education or social class, they all express themselves in the same stylized language."[8] The practical result of creating one dimensional characters who speak alike is that virtually any play of Ghelderode's may be performed by marionettes.

A marionette, unlike its living counterpart, only suggests, and therein lies its art and its lesson for actors. Ghelderode would like actors to learn one fundamental lesson of puppet theatre, and that is, in the words of Bernard Shaw, "that very important part of the art of acting which consists of not acting, that is, allowing the imagination of the spectator to do its lion's share of the work."[9] Ghelderode is also dissatisfied with actors because they are, to use his metaphor, all too often puppets in the hands of the critics. In one of his typical, ambivalent remarks, he says: "En réalité il s'agissait de pièces écrites pour des acteurs vivants, ces oeuvres que je sous-titrais *pour marionnettes*; mais je ne pense pas que des comédiens de chair soient prêts à les jouer telles quelles, la lâcheté devant la critique et le public étant la marque des interprètes d'aujourd'hui" (p. 117).

Ghelderode also admires marionettes because they are *made* for their roles from non-living material, which gives them a magical quality. A marionette's very *raison d'être* is the play and in an important sense the marionette *is* the character and no one else. There can never be a problem of duality; once the play is over so is the marionette's life. It becomes again a heap of dead wood, cloth, and paint. When the curtain falls, the marionette does not go to a dressing room to remove its make-up, nor does its mind wander to critics and careers. It is forever frozen: its painted face to remain always distorted or beautiful, passive or flustered, virtuous or evil, as the case may be.

A logical retort to this argument might be that a marionette is, after all, controlled physically and vocally by an imperfect human being. But Ghelderode responds that the person pulling the strings is of minimal or no importance to the people in the audience as they perceive the play. The people see the marionette; they never stop to ask who is pulling the strings and is doing the speaking. The dramatic illusion is complete. The puppeteer is simply an intermediary of sorts who enables the characters in the play to spring to life from the written pages. His talent and artistry, although of paramount importance to a proper dramatic interpretation, do not prevent the audience from responding to the play imaginatively and creatively. The marionettes capture our attention. Their pathos and joy, for example, can be very real, affecting us as deeply as the play will permit. Paul Claudel, in a letter to Tsunao Miyajima, a famous Japanese puppeteer, sums up many of these ideas when he writes:

> L'acteur vivant, quel que soit son talent, nous gêne toujours en mêlant au drame fictif qu'il incorpore un élément intrus, quelque chose d'actuel et de quotidien, il reste toujours un *déguisé*. La marionnette au contraire n'a de vie et de mouvement que celui qu'elle tire de l'action. . . . Ce n'est pas un acteur qui parle, c'est une parole qui agit. Le personnage de bois incarne la prosopopée.[10]

Ghelderode's succinct, predictable response to Claudel's observation is, "Mais c'est cela même!"[11]

The second principal reason for Ghelderode's interest in puppet theatre—besides his dissatisfaction with living actors—is, as indicated earlier, that virtually all of his characters incline toward caricature. Perhaps another and more accurate way to say the same thing is that Ghelderode's characters have a great many affinities with marionettes. Traditionally, marionettes—and this is also true of Ghelderode's characters—are caricatures of human beings, not replicas. Their faces are painted and carved into one relentless expression. They represent essentially one unchanged aspect of human personality. Hence when Ghelderode speaks of marionettes and their influence on his work, he quite often emphasizes their potential for singular, extreme representation.

> Reflétant les deux clans grandioses de l'humanité, celui du vice et celui de la vertu, les poupées assument la continuité d'une double galerie de héros: ici les traîtres et là les justiciers, les mauvais et les bons, les ignobles et les nobles, les diaboliques et les providentiels.
>
> Dans un admirable mouvement, dans le jaillissement de sentiments absolus, le héros essentiel s'impose, intact, originel.
>
> Voici, en leur vérité, les traîtres, les rois félons et les vassaux hypocrites. Et voici les Salvateurs, les mousquetaires.
>
> [pp. 100-1]

Since marionettes lend themselves so easily and obviously to caricature, it is not difficult to understand how they influenced, and fit into, Ghelderode's dramatic world of archetypes, monsters, and personified sins. In all of Ghelderode's plays, whether written specifically for marionettes or not, his characters are grotesquely exaggerated to represent, both physically and mentally, single aspects of human nature.[12] For example, the seven priests in *Les Fastes d'enfer* represent the seven deadly sins. Each priest represents one sin and nothing more. Each has his own *idée fixe*. The passion of each priest is indicated by his name, much as in "humor characters."[13] Carnibos, for instance, represents the sin of gluttony. Continually eating, he can think of nothing but satisfying his craving for food.

Pantagleize, another of Ghelderode's plays with marionette-like characters, cannot be fully appreciated unless the hero, Pantagleize, is perceived as a dangling, jerky puppet. Oblivious to the revolution going on around him, Pantagleize is concerned only with telling everyone what a lovely day it is. Thus, the most convincing productions present him as Chaplinesque: happily bouncing around on the ends of strings, with a simple and innocent expression fixed on his face.[14] In General Macboom, Ghelderode captures the essence of the military type—obtuse and singleminded. Macboom, in a manner difficult or even impossible for a living actor to represent, is a fixed caricature of his mental aberrations. He is not unlike the secret police agent, portrayed by a Belgian puppeteer, whose hands ended in gun barrels instead of fingers, thus conveying his violent, savage nature.

In *Magie rouge* Ghelderode personifies greed and miserliness in the grotesquely distorted character of Hieronymus. In *Les Aveugles* Ghelderode dramatizes the miserable, lost souls of Pieter Bruegel the Elder's painting "The Parable of the Blind" to represent the spiritual emptiness of man. The blind men in the painting have faces frozen into expressions portraying, in turn, apathy, bewilderment, and fear. Puppets provide a perfect vehicle to capture their aimless spiritual wandering. In *La Pie sur le gibet* one of the main characters is a bird. The obvious difficulty is that when a person dresses up to look like a bird, he appears at best humorous and at worst foolish. A puppet in the role of the Magpie can provide the aesthetic distance needed to preserve the seriousness of the play. And in *D'un diable qui prêcha merveilles,* his longest single play written specifically for marionettes, Ghelderode personifies various sins and ridicules the so-called religious societies by having the Knight Capricant, a local devil, with the help of a sorceress, take the place of the town preacher in order to deliver a sermon. The sermon is well received, of course, because Capricant advocates the pursuit of behavior formerly considered sinful. He redefines sin, and the evil people gladly embrace the church's new definition. The play ends with the disguised devil going off to Rome with the preacher who is convinced that the devil is truly a good man. Ghelderode prefaces the play with an interesting paragraph entitled "Salutaire Avis du montreur de marionnettes" in which he explains the reason for such a characterization.

> Pour ce qu'il est vrai qu'un vêtement retourné reste un vêtement et partant utile, je prétends que la morale à rebours reste la morale, qui n'a fait que mettre un mas-

que; et qu'en montrant des personnages en leurs singuliers agissements sur le petit théâtre du monde, je puis provoquer la nostalgie de la vertu, du contraire de ce que je montre.[15]

The severity of Ghelderode's caricatures forces one to realize how close his characters are to puppets—and to clichés. It is, I think, because Ghelderode frequently fashions caricatures who approximate clichés of good and evil that he has been accused of anti-Semitic and anti-Negro attitudes, especially in *Pantagleize,* as well as anti-clerical sentiments in *Les Fastes d'enfer.*[16]

Ghelderode himself denies the charge of racism.[17] However, what can be adduced from the charge is that in creating caricatures instead of psychological characters, Ghelderode has come perilously close to cliché.

Given, then, Ghelderode's attitude toward live actors and his propensity for caricature, as well as his habitual use of tableau-like medieval and biblical settings, one should not be surprised to find him insisting that puppet theatre is the most appropriate interpretive medium for many of his plays. Those who have seen marionettes perform can understand, after reading Ghelderode's plays, why they are so important to him and what he means when he talks about their style.

> Non, ce qui m'a touché dans les marionnettes, c'est leur extraordinaire mouvement dramatique, c'est leur souffle qui n'appartient qu'à elles—c'est leur style, oui, leur très grand style proche du style roman et qui réside moins dans leur vocabulaire que dans leur esprit, leur tour d'esprit, et aussi dans cette exemplaire aisance d'allure et de propos qui leur est propre.
>
> [p. 116]

Although most plays written specifically for marionettes are puerile and devoid of literary or dramatic interest, the plays "pour marionnettes" of Ghelderode are serious and compelling drama. Inexplicably, there have been only a few important writers in this century, besides Ghelderode, who have written plays for puppet theatre—George Sand, Maeterlinck, and Shaw—and only a few theorists who have directed their attention to the puppet stage—Heinrich von Kleist, Arthur Symons, Gordon Craig, and Peter Arnott.[18] All too often, playwrights, critics, and public alike facilely dismiss marionette theatre as "children's theatre." As a result, with the exception of Peter Arnott's performances, there has been practically no serious drama in this country interpreted by puppets. It is generally believed that the function of marionettes is a narrow one: to entertain children, or to provide briefly and superficially an enjoyable distraction for "mature" individuals who need a cartoon-type of escape from an overbearing world. But Ghelderode finds much more in puppet theatre than medicinal solace for the depressed or a happy escape from our frenzied lives. He believes that marionettes can revitalize our inherent capacities for creativity and imagination. By regarding marionettes as the stuff of children, we are denying ourselves one of the most vital and effective vehicles for dramatic interpretation. If we want to understand the mysterious and magical world of puppets, we should, I think, follow Ghelderode's advice.

> Essayez, avec un peu de bois, d'étoffe et de fil de fer, même sans pousser beaucoup votre travail, essayez donc de fabriquer une poupée!
>
> Vous verrez comme elle naîtra rapidement sous vos doigts. Après cela, animez-la, attachez-lui un fil ou un petit crochet métallique et faites-la danser, faites-la marcher; vous verrez, vous sentirez combien la représentation humaine devient passionnante et fascinante.
>
> . . . . .
>
> Alors, la marionnette renaîtra, joyeuse et frondeuse, vivante, sage et gonflée de toute sa troublante poésie.
>
> . . . . .
>
> Mobile mandragore, elle peut faire rêver l'homme, comme elle a fait rêver les enfançons. Elle peut aider à vivre et surtout à rêver.
>
> Vous serez saisi de voir le résultat—peut-être même au-delà de votre intention. Sur quoi, le rideau!

[p. 130]

Notes

1. For a first-hand description of Ghelderode's home, see Samuel Draper, "Michel de Ghelderode: A Personal Statement," *Tulane Drama Review,* 8, No. 1 (Fall 1963), p. 37.

2. This same preoccupation with marionettes is found in the published interviews, *Les Entretiens d'Ostende* (Paris: Editions de L'Arche, 1956). In particular, the third interview of the series is devoted entirely to a discussion of marionettes and their influence on his thought and work. Citations from *Les Entretiens d'Ostende* in my text are to this edition.

3. A less convincing argument, I think, is the one proposed by David I. Grossvogel, *The Self-Conscious Stage in Modern French Drama* (New York: Columbia University Press, 1958). Grossvogel says that in addition to being a link with the Flemish past, "the puppets have still another significance: the mystery and power of the inanimate figure. The marionette is an ideal masque, suprahuman because it brooks no human familiarity and superhuman because it is able to embrace all human percepts as well as the shadows wherein they fade. . . . But more frequently, the Ghelderodian puppet is capable of greater transmutations. He shares with all inanimate objects in this curious world of the author, the ability to acquire prosaic life and to dispense the full measure of symbolism that comes from such metamorphosis. He then casts on the human thus born the mantle of his magic" (pp. 261-62).

4. For a similar comment, see Leonard Cabell Pronko, *Avant-Garde: The Experimental Theater in France* (Berkeley: University of California Press, 1962), p. 166.

5. Micheline Herz, "Tragedy, Poetry and the Burlesque in Ghelderode's Theatre," *Yale French Studies,* No. 29 (1962), p. 93.

6. Pronko, p. 165.

7. As quoted in Pronko, p. 165.

8. Auréliu Weiss, "The Theatrical World of Michel de Ghelderode," *Tulane Drama Review,* 8, No. 1 (Fall 1963), p. 59.

9. As quoted in Bil Baird, *The Art of the Puppet* (New York: Macmillan, 1965), p. 17.

10. Tsunao Miyajima, *Contribution à l'étude du théâtre japonais de poupées* ([Osaka: Sanyu-Sha] 1931), pp. 1-2.

11. Ghelderode, *Les Entretiens,* p. 105.

12. According to George Wellwarth, Ghelderode's practice of portraying single, morbid extremes of character has a religious basis. "To Ghelderode," writes Wellwarth, "life was the vehicle of sin—and sin, in the simple, straightforward (and therefore dramatic) popular thought of the Middle Ages, warped the body of the sinner. Almost all of Ghelderode's characters have some physical quirk to reflect the moral turmoil of their minds. Many of them appear to be in the grip of actual demonic possession; and in some of his plays Ghelderode symbolizes the total subservience of the body to the overwhelming and crippling power of sin by showing all of his characters as marionettes. In these latter plays sin has turned the human body into a grotesque puppet from which the soul has fled." (George E. Wellwarth, "Ghelderode's Theatre of the Grotesque," *Tulane Drama Review,* 8, No. 1 [Fall 1963], pp. 12-13.)

13. For a similar comment on Ghelderode's "humor characters," see Wellwarth, pp. 11-12.

14. A great admirer of Chaplin and the Chaplin style of acting—a style that is puppet-like in its flat-footed, jerky movements—Ghelderode had in mind Chaplin when he wrote *Pantagleize.* In the "Epitaph for Pantagleize," Ghelderode explains that "Pantagleize is a distant relative of the great circus . . . a fugitive from that circus which gave the world that other poet of actions called Chaplin. It is not so far from Chaplin to Pantagleize" (Ghelderode, "Epitaph for Pantagleize," in *Seven Plays,* v. 1, George Hauger [New York: Hill and Wang, 1960], pp. 146-47.)

15. Ghelderode, *Théâtre* (Paris: Gallimard, 1953), v. 3, p. 144.

16. Micheline Herz, among others, has commented on what she calls Ghelderode's "racism."

> Ghelderode's anti-Semitism may be explained, perhaps, as due to his preoccupation with magic. His characterizations of the children of Israel, for

all that, could have found a fitting place in such publications as *Le Pilori*. In *Fastes d'enfer* Simon Laquedeem, the wandering Jew transformed into a suffragan bishop, invents a new version of ritual murder, and as the curtain descends on his scene of triumph "his visage expresses a demoniacal glee." In *Pantagleize,* Rachel Silberschatz sets out to avenge her persecuted people by persecuting others, and Pantagleize describes the projected revolution in terms already familiar to readers of *L'Action Française.* Of all the Jewish figures evoked by Ghelderode only the Judas of *Barabbas* is treated with some measure of sympathy, and in much the same way as did Léon Bloy, who recognized the metaphysical necessity of the betrayal.

The Negroes Bam-Boulas and Beni-Bouftout are blacks that have been carefully filtered through a white consciousness, and not a single cliché is missing. Might not Ghelderode's [sic] racism be one aspect of the profound attraction he feels for evil?

[p. 100]

For a similar comment, see Grossvogel, p. 300.

17. Samuel Draper, "An Interview with Michel de Ghelderode," *Tulane Drama Review,* 8, No. 1 (Fall 1963), p. 45.

18. For a concise review of these theories, see Peter Arnott, *Plays Without People: Puppetry and Serious Drama* (Bloomington: Indiana University Press, 1964), pp. 75-77.

Gillian Farish (essay date 1978)

SOURCE: "Michel de Ghelderode: The Theatre of the Swerving Dream," in *University of Windsor Review,* Vol. 13, No. 2, Spring 1978, pp. 5-23.

[*In the following essay, Farish examines the states of dreaming and waking in Ghelderode's plays.*]

The search for truth among the rubble of reality and the debris of dreams is not new to the theatre nor is the effort to reconstruct the past and forecast the future from totems that have survived intact among such ruins. The fascinating aspect of this search is that no matter how the artist conceives the rubble, debris and totems, the truths which emerge are original in that they are discovered again and again. Thus, although the truths that Michel de Ghelderode uncovers in his theatre are not necessarily new, the conditions of his discoveries are startling, harrowing even, and render the terms of his drama newly convincing.

As his search for the truth of reality and dream spans two decades, it is often difficult to apprehend the significance of single plays taken out of the context of his other works.

Technically, his plays alter very little. He has a certain range of dramatic devices which he reuses with little variation. He relies heavily on dramatic monologue, the off-stage crowd, symbolic gestures, movements, properties and colours, and special lighting effects. He creates micro-dramas within his plays to intensify and expand the action. All these devices, however, acquire special meanings as Ghelderode establishes his own theatrical idioms to express his understanding of dream and reality which he develops and changes from play to play. The danger of misunderstanding Ghelderode arises when one ignores the subtle shifts which take place in the progression of his explorations and those equally subtle changes which occur in the meaning of his dramatic devices.

One play especially emerges as a pivot between the most outstanding differences in his work and marks a change in his interpretation of the experience of reality and dream. *Chronicles of Hell* (1929), which Ghelderode produced almost in the middle of his intensive playwriting period from 1918 to 1935, marks an important development in his art. Although the play has many characteristics of Ghelderode's theatre up to that point, *Chronicles of Hell* signals his departure from drama centered around Biblical and literary figures (Barabbas, Faust and Pantagleize) and historical figures (Christopher Columbus) to more abstract, fantastical drama based on those kinds of mystical, mysterious figures often found in fairy folktales. This shift frees Ghelderode to create major female characters who continue the search for truth between reality and dream in his later plays and gives him an entirely different perspective of the problems involved. To examine those details of dream and reality which Ghelderode sifts in his plays is to discover some truths of human existence. To trace the similarities and differences between his plays before and after *Chronicles of Hell* is to track the progression Ghelderode was making in his search for truth whose genesis is almost as fascinating as his ultimate conclusions.

Much of what happens in Ghelderode's plays involves a sleeping rather than a waking state and often results in the character's believing that he has been deluded. *Chronicles of Hell* introduces Ghelderode's audience to three terms which are unavoidable in a discussion of this aspect of his work. They are *comatose, chimera,* and *chiaroscuro.* In *Chronicles,* Simon Laquedeem describes Jan in Eremo as a "comatose, old man."[1] The comatose condition is quite common in Ghelderode's plays and takes many different forms. Sleep-walkers, zombies, catatonics, epileptics and drunkards are balanced by dreamers, visionaries and idealists who are all at different stages of realizing that the difficulty of distinguishing waking from sleeping frequently parallels the difficulty of distinguishing reality from illusion. Characters who recognize themselves as dreamers often consider that they are the victims of chimeras—impossible fantasies—that drive them to extraordinary behaviour. Ghelderode suggests that man so fears reality that he turns to the very thing that harms him—illusion—in whatever form best distracts him: inebriation, plays, spectacles, film, basic physical gratification. Further, the demand for illusion breeds unscrupulous pushers who augment man's awareness that there is a frightening chasm between reality and illusion and that one may not be in as much control of one's destiny as one thought. Ghelderode examines self will and external will in three plays which were written closely together: ***Christopher Columbus, Barabbas*** and ***Pantagleize.***

In ***Columbus*** (1927), Ghelderode has the title character comment on those people who discover truth in their sleep: "They know; but they only know in their dreams, and they wake up ignorant."[2] Here the characters approach truth in the reality of dreams: their waking state confuses them; numbs them. A year later, in ***Barabbas,*** Ghelderode's "dreamers" become those who are sensitive enough to discover the discrepancy between what appears to be and what is. More specifically, the characters discover that what they considered to be their true "selves" is often only a role played out behind an unrecognizable mask. Whereas the characters in ***Columbus*** have little or no control over their discovery of truth and cannot transfer their knowledge to their waking state, the characters of ***Barabbas*** not only contemplate the conditions of the truth about reality and illusion, they do this in their conscious waking state.

In ***Barabbas,*** Judas begs Christ for an explanation of what is happening:

> The kiss I gave you . . . I didn't know what I was doing, but an unknown force made me give you that kiss. Did I betray you? Yet you knew in advance that one of us would betray you. At that time you had an ineluctable expression that seemed to order me to betray you. Why did I do these things? What fate did I have to submit to?[3]

When Jocabeth, his wife, sees him, she says: "Judas! What is this horrible mask stuck on your face?"[4] Judas replies: "It is the true face, the imperishable face of Judas."[5] Judas has been cast into the role of villain, not against his will, but without his knowledge. No matter how much he protests that the mask isn't really him, no one will believe him. Finally, embittered by his position, he stops struggling to clear himself and no longer tries to understand what has happened. Ghelderode presents the issue of control through Judas: at times man is the victim of a higher volition and at times he victimizes himself by distorting his self image. More importantly, the discovery of the discrepancy between man and mask, between self reality and self illusion, causes man to question the reality and illusion of control. Whose will controls him? This question becomes an essential issue in all of Ghelderode's plays.

The following year, Ghelderode experiments with a variation of Judas's predicament in ***Pantagleize*** (1929) where the central character instigates a revolution, steals the national jewels, is tried for treason and executed without once becoming aware of the forces which control his behaviour. Both Judas and Pantagleize are manipulated by divine will and political wrangling respectively into roles

that the former rebelled against and the latter was ignorant of. It is not surprising that in his next play, ***Chronicles of Hell,*** Ghelderode considers the nature of the power that forces the characters to assume roles and the power structure which results. At the bottom of this structure, Laquedeem controls the priests:

> Laquedeem: Alter your faces! . . . Don't chuckle, don't get excited; assume the bearing of people overwhelmed by an infinite stupor; stick your noses out; let your arms hang down like Barbary apes after lovemaking; have your eyes lustreless and full of grey water, and from time to time raise them skyward like blind men counting the stars. . . . Compose your features into this circumstantial mask, which others will imitate . . .[6]

By commanding the priests to dissemble so, Laquedeem hopes to avoid arousing the suspicion that they were guilty of having expedited their Bishop's death struggle. However, the more the priests try to appear innocent, the more they appear demonic. Sodomati tells them:

> You make unsightly grimaces like men possessed. You are the suspect priests of a people of possessed souls![7]

Ghelderode accentuates the monstrous behaviour of the priests by uncompromising chiaroscuro lighting effects. He sets the action of ***Chronicles*** against a brewing storm (typical of his plays) that alternately illuminates the stage and leaves it gloomy. The source of the only sustained light is "the morbid light of a stormy summer dusk."[8] The only brilliant area of the stage is the Bishop's death chamber which is "blazingly illuminated by a hundred candles."[9] It is as if Ghelderode is suggesting that death in itself may not be a journey into darkness but into illumination. By contrast, Ghelderode depicts life as a dark hell. The dark areas on stage breed perversion, cruelty and chaos. The goatish behaviour of Krakenbus and Carnibos (suggested by their stamping on each other's feet and banging their foreheads together) activates the lewdness of the priests. The inhabitants of the gloom are grotesque: they are grimacing, misshapen, disabled, immoderate or cowardly. The devil-in-chief, Simon Laquedeem, is afflicted with a spastic bowel whose flatulence parallels the rumblings of the storm outside as he nervously awaits the arrival of the Nuncio. In fact, the intensity of Laquedeem's gastro-intestinal upset leaves the audience in no doubt that the Nuncio will be able to smell out his irregular behaviour literally and well as figuratively. However, Ghelderode quickly suppresses any promise of justice by substituting a young effeminate priest, Sodomati, whose very name declares his affinity for perversion.

Having established the demonic setting and the devilish behaviour of the priests, Ghelderode then asks the audience to consider the possibility that the Bishop himself had forced the priests into such grossness:

> Sodomati: You seem to be dreaming, Laquedeem. Are you entering into meditation when your clergy are not missing a mouthful?

Laquedeem: I was thinking about the inscrutability of the designs of Providence, the strangeness of certain destines. . . . Somebody! whose shadow weighs on us, in whose shadow we live crushed down. Somebody . . .

Krakenbus: He was called Jan Eremo.[10]

Laquedeem considers Jan Eremo a usurper, an anti-Christ, an impostor who gave the people the illusion that he possessed Christlike powers to save them from the plague and famine which were decimating them. Having established himself, Eremo refused to yield his power to the clerics and lay rulers when they returned from fleeing these dangers. Eremo's status is ambiguous: is he an original force who poses a threat to a corrupt established order, or is he an opportunist whose sense of the theatrical and good timing brings him the power he desires? When Eremo refuses to relinquish his power, he forces the clergy to play the villain to his saviour. If they have lost their part playing good, then their hellish, perverse antics, their preoccupation with noisome bodily functions, may be the only behaviour left to them. Ghelderode is not simply criticizing the clergy in *Chronicles*; rather, he is depicting the chaos brought about by disrupting the power structure. When an individual seizes power by adopting someone else's role, he displaces everyone else in the structure.

Up to this point in the play, Ghelderode has considered only the lower regions of the power structure. Now he considers the source of power itself. To do so he creates a moment of macabre that is nearly as terrifying to the audience as it is to the priests on stage: he resurrects Eremo who like a "jerkily moving athlete"[11] has all the characteristics of a galvanized corpse. What kind of will-power could (or would) force Eremo back to life in such a horrifying way? There are two alternatives: either Eremo was superhumanly tenacious of life and power, or some other force was at work on him. Here his jerky movements provide the clue. Possibly because Ghelderode was experienced in puppet theatre, the image of man the marionette appears frequently in his plays. Perhaps even more interesting than the image itself is the fact that Ghelderode's characters often simulate puppet movements; that is, they are incapable of movement, "wooden", or move frenetically with that jerkiness peculiar to puppets. Ghelderode's characters often appear afflicted with neurasthenic conditions which reduce them to zombie-like movements characteristic of the living dead and somnambulists who frequent his plays, or, conversely, propel them in spastic frenzy across the stage. Ghelderode depicted this latter state in his spider images which emerge as early as *The Death of Doctor Faust* (1925) when the title character laments: "Why go on living with all this mental mockery, this black spider in the brain?"[12] and later in *Pantagleize* through Bamboola who is described as a "tarantula, epileptic, wild Negro."[13] In neither state do the characters control their actions, and one concludes there is something sinister about an external will which would cause man to suffer paralysis or St. Vitus.

In *Chronicles of Hell,* the final image of Laquedeem squatting to evacuate his bowel, "his rabinical face expressing demonic bliss,"[14] would strongly suggest that the world has gone to the devil. At the moment when the priests are delivered from the living-dead Bishop, excrement triumphs over sacrament, leaving the audience to go home disgusted and dirty. Nevertheless, the final impression that one receives from *Chronicles* is that men are driven to perversity by their inability to withstand the cross-pressures of forces warring on a plane of existence just outside their range of apprehension. They can see manifestations of these forces in the physical world around them; they can feel themselves being shaped to some ulterior purpose; but they are denied an understanding of the experience, and, consequently, are driven mad. All Ghelderode's characters are similarly driven to make sense of experience; to distinguish reality from illusion; to be in control. These are difficult goals to attain especially as Ghelderode makes it increasingly clear that reality is illusion and illusion reality—a contradiction which one must accept if one is to understand anything.

In itself the reality of death can be an illusion. When Eremo first revives, Laquedeem cries out: "Not a genuine corpse! An impostor even in your death!"[15] Ghelderode introduces the idea that death is an illusion as early as 1926 in *Three Actors and Their Drama.* Three actors decide to end their tangled lives by committing suicide as a part of their performance in a play. However, they discover that they are so used to faking death that they are incapable of engineering their real deaths. Although the symbolism of the situation seems easy to understand, the implications inherent in the situation are not made clear until Ghelderode examines the necessity for executioners which he does in two of his last plays, *Lord Halewyn* (1934) and *Hop, Signor!* (1935). However, before he reached the state putting his characters to death, Ghelderode explored the possibilities of bringing them back from death.

In *Christopher Columbus,* Ghelderode transforms the title character into a self-commemorating statue before the audience's eyes. At the play's conclusion, the statue "comes back to life" just long enough to remark that now he understands life, he is no longer alive. Ghelderode develops the corpse-that-comes-back-to-life fully in *Miss Jairus* (1934), another of his last plays, where a young girl, Blandine, is forced back to life through the efforts of her lover and a necromancer. The catch is that Blandine is not grateful: she has been initiated into the beauty and purity of death and longs to return to that state. Blandine is visited by her male counterpart, Lazarus, who enters "draped in grey"[16] with little roots sprouting from his hands, feet and hair. These two initiates describe death joyously:

Blandine: . . . A spearhead will split the sealed skies. Dreams will be purple, bloodstained in holiness. Like bubbles to the surface we shall rise to burst. I only know these things by my dreams.

Lazarus: It was the approach of that spendid solemn sadness of the immortals. You are still made from the beds of the ocean. You will pass through many forms as you go back through past time, and when you are no more than a tiny salt star, you will melt under God's tongue. Reabsorbed you will become a little vibration of the universal light. A singing atom. And you will share in God's living dream, that wheel which dreams . . .[17]

This dialogue contains two images important to understanding Ghelderode's concept of death. In *Faust* and *Christopher Columbus,* Ghelderode presented the bubble image visually by having Faust do acrobatic tricks with a globe from his study and by having Columbus blow bubbles with a clay pipe throughout his opening monologue. Columbus discusses the significance of the image:

> I can't explain. I blow bubbles. They justify themselves and vanish. Little spheres, logical, perfect! Sphere, ideal volume, shape of my dreams, one must be like a child to understand you.[18]

To Columbus the bubble is a moment of perfection which gives him time only to appreciate it as an end in itself before it is gone. To Blandine the bubble is the moment of death which is to her a moment of perfection.

The image of the salt star melting under God's tongue leads in a different direction and helps explain another of Ghelderode's theatrical idioms; namely, the fits of choking that afflict certain characters. In *Chronicles of Hell,* Carnibos and Duvelhond choke themselves on the funeral meats set out for Eremo's wake. Considering the number of times in earlier plays that dead bodies are referred to almost instantaneously as dead meat, one might assume that the priests were, in a sense, choking on Eremo himself. This assumption is reinforced by the fact that Eremo has been choking on the host which, according to Roman Catholic dogma, *is* Christ's body. These acts of choking establish the power structure of the play: the priests choke on Eremo and Eremo chokes on God. The sacraments, the body and blood of Christ, are no comfort to them because they remind them of the noisome decay of the body which they fear and abhor. They equate death with decay. However, by *Miss Jairus,* Ghelderode's characters have progressed to the stage that those who have known death, long for it. Blandine and Lazarus can transcend decay which they accept as a condition necessary to their being reabsorbed in a mystical reversal of the communion rites where their bodies are taken under the tongue of God and restored to their cosmic state. *Chronicles* and *Jairus* reveal the characters (and possibly their creator) at different stages of apprehending the experience of death. Church ritual is of little solace to the clergy because it is only hocus-pocus against a much feared evil. Blandine understands death and accepts it because she trusts herself to die. When Lazarus remarks that: "humans in perdition clutch at the roughness and fissure of their confused reality,"[19] he is saying that man perpetuates his fear of physical death by reminding himself through his appetite for food and sex and his dwelling on the physical functions of his body that all purely physical existence must, sooner or later, be subject to decay. Perhaps, for this reason, Ghelderode

turns away from the church's morbid interest in the dead Christ's body which blocks man's understanding of the illusion and reality of death. Instead, in his late plays, he turns increasingly to secular mysticism which allows him to perceive the mystery of death in a different way.

Up to this turning point in his work, Ghelderode concerned himself with the male point of view which, by necessity of the dominant position of the male, forces him to consider the issue of power and will. Enraged by the convergence of opposites which confuse them, frustrated by false goals in their search for understanding life, it is no wonder that the majority of Ghelderode's male characters are men of violence. In his first play written in 1918, Ghelderode created a peasant who brutalizes and murders his wife not realizing, perhaps, that his savage treatment of her during her pregnancy probably resulted in the simple, blind child for which he drowns her. Jan Eremo, enraged by his untimely end, tries to behead Simon Laquedeem. Lord Halewyn, rapist and murderer, is looking for his eighth victim. Peasant, bishop, lord are violent because they are impotent and they are impotent because they have confused sexual gratification and political power with their failure to gain control of their own mortality. They confuse their ability to take life with their inability to take death—especially their own. If they knew they were really seeking their own deaths, they would be horrified. When Ghelderode turns to women characters, he makes a startling discovery; unlike men, women have the capacity, by necessity of their position in life, to look upon death as the ultimate seduction and enjoy it.

Like Blandine Jairus, Lord Halewyn's eighth intended victim, Purmelende, is infatuated by the man who comes to bring her to her death:

> I heard the magic song and fell into a very lucid sleep, where all my feelings were awake and only my will was fast bound in slumber. Like all my sinning sisters I obeyed his voice, and went to him as the bird flies to the trapper's lure. I moved as light as air in a new world where snow shone bright as crystal under the stars. Souls after death must all surely pass through that winter land. I doubted all creation, and myself. Words and thoughts no longer had meaning. I passed on, far from the beaten paths, beyond Good and Evil. . . . He was waiting for me, all ice and fire, and in his face shone a most baleful beauty, like that of a fallen archangel still glowing with the light of heaven, sweet with its odors, and yet already eloquent of Hell. I knew that I was lost and ran to him, the while his golden mouth sang songs of lust. His face shone with the light of rotting wood, and the sight of it brought tears into my eyes. I saw that he, for all his talk of bliss, was misery incarnate. I sought for tender words of consolation but none would come. I took his hands meaning to kiss them humbly.[20]

Despite her infatuation, Purmelende sees Halewyn as a man trapped by his actions and her pity for him gives her the strength to put him out of his misery. According to Purmelende's account, at the moment that Halewyn was struggling out of his coat of mail the better to seduce and murder her, she seizes his sword and beheads him. If Purmelende's audience is shocked by her account, it must be horrified by what she says next:

> She saw a man bent double, his head caught in a coat of mail, his arms imprisoned. She saw the hideous corpses and their hideous grimace. She saw the sword. Upward it whirled with a hissing sound, and I saw, for it was I who did the deed—a shrieking head bounding across the snow. I ran after it and caught it in mid-air. I wedged it between my knees and filled the gaping mouth with snow to stifle its blasphemies. And I said: "Pray to God now, my Lord, since you are dying . . ." The head still tried to sing, though very quietly. And, since the snow could not stifle it, I pressed my mouth to its mouth, and finally they died, both head and song, together.[21]

The fact that Ghelderode had the good sense not to dramatize this scene but have Purmelende recount it does not lessen its gruesome sexuality. The sword, the head wedged between Purmelende's knees, the snow which Halewyn pierces with his sword and Purmelende crams into the blaspheming head become the erotic details of the consummation of death. Halewyn has not sought a maiden to kill, but one who will kill him so that he too can participate in death. Ghelderode seems to suggest that men desire peace and grace but resist the necessity of achieving them through death and decay. Both Blandine and Lazarus revel in the earthy smell of their decay no less than Purmelende who "breathed in the smell of rotting flesh"[22] of the seven dead girls hanging from the trees around her until she is recalled to her revulsion of decay by the sound of her own name. Which aspect of death is reality and which illusion? Is the reality of death putrefaction or peace? Should man cling to life or yield to death? The vision of death that Ghelderode projects through his snow-maidens, Blandine and Purmelende, whose very names suggest whiteness and purity, may be nothing but a dream. Both girls say that they can only know their feelings of ecstasy in dreams from which they are rudely awakened and which are shattered as easily as bubbles by the rougher, coarser reality of physical experience. It would seem that the answer to this riddle does not lie with the dream or the dreamer but with the executioner. Because many of Ghelderode's characters are afraid to yield to the seduction of death, they spend a good part of their existence looking for their executioners under the pretext of looking for love or power or happiness. Nearly all of Ghelderode's characters are killed by their conscious and unconscious flirtations with their potential executioners—a fact which he emphasizes in his last play, *Hop, Signor!*, and *Red Magic* (1931) which he wrote four years earlier.

The two plays beg to be compared: they both deal with characters who abstain from the conditions of living—sex and death—in order to gain a little control of their destinies. In both plays, these abstainers become the victims of characters who deliberately fabricate false situations which implicate the former against their will. Both plays deal with the theme of the cuckolded husband. Both

deal with wives who are disillusioned with marriage. The situation of *Red Magic* is inverted in *Hop, Signor!*: in the former, the husband is a miser who is trying to abstain from life itself: from eating, drinking and making love; in the latter, the wife clings to her chastity refusing husband and suitors alike. In *Red Magic,* the miser is destroyed by his wife's passion for the sex which he has withheld from her. In *Hop, Signor!,* Ghelderode duplicates the situation in reverse. Ghelderode seems to be checking the validity of a truth he discovered in *Red Magic* by altering the variables of the conditions to that truth in *Hop, Signor!* Perhaps his caution springs from the reappearance of an earlier image, the spider, which he uses in both plays and which seems to have undergone a subtle shift in meaning that renders it infinitely more sinister than his earlier usage.

The gothic settings of both plays invite the appearance of spiders. The miser's house is haunted and built on a cemetery. The artisan's house in *Hop, Signor!* is situated in "an uncultivated garden. Among the bushes and rank weeds lie carved stones, statues of saints, basreliefs, capitals, pillars, sundials that make the garden look like a neglected yard or even like some forgotten cemetery."[23] Hieronymus, the miser, includes all things that fly over his land or crawl on his property in his possessions:

> I own a house with a ghost. . . . A bronze chest . . . in which gold pieces are breeding young. . . . A wife and her virginity . . . and the spiders watch over it . . .[24]

Hieronymus's parsimony is ironic: Gheldrodian spiders do indeed watch over Sybilla's virginity, for she develops an insatiable appetite for sexual gratification. Hieronymus doesn't want to lose control of the order he has imposed upon his life by abandoning himself to sex, yet, as he listens to Armador seducing his wife, he is seduced himself. Exciting himself with extravagant sexual fantasies, he rushes off to procure a whore with the money that Armador was supposed to be minting when he was seducing Sybilla. As in *Lord Halewyn,* eroticism ends in death: the lovers murder their two accomplices and Hieronymous, quite unjustly, is executed for the crime. This injustice invites a new consideration of the spider image. Sybilla, in her heightened sensuality says to Armador:

> Come, my ghost! Let us make love until dawn, and let us pretend we have all the abandonments, for dissembled thoughts are turning in the air like flies. I shall follow them on the wing for I too am a fly.[25]

Equally drunk on his new power, Hieronymus toasts himself:

> In your great honour, Hieronymus! I am very pleased with you! . . . Long life Hieronymus! (He laughs.) What a good joke I'm playing on death! . . . What? (He listens.) What quiet! It is as still as a spider's web . . . (He shivers.) What is there to be afraid of? The spite of the Almighty who is angry at my powers?[26]

With his usual talent for stumbling onto a truth he'd rather not know, Hieronymus's sudden nervousness fuses the images of the spider and fly in the audience's mind. Man the fly and God the spider. Written between ***Chronicles of Hell*** and ***Miss Jairus, Red Magic*** recreates the horror of the former through the concept that God is a spider who weaves his cosmic webs the better to ensnare and devour the characters, and falls short of the latter's beauty in the concept that God melts the tiny salt stars of men under his tongue, consuming them like consecrated wafers back into the cosmos. This is not to say, however, that somewhere between ***Red Magic*** and ***Hop, Signor!*** Ghelderode mellowed and began to contemplate the relationship between man and God in beatific terms. Spider images are equally strong in ***Hop, Signor!,*** but in this play, Ghelderode parallels arachnid detail with human rather than cosmic reality. To emphasize this new significance of the image, Ghelderode creates two dwarves who appear "like big insects"[27] as they creep along on stilts designed to raise them "to the level of men."[28] The dwarves refer to the husband, Jureal, as "an industrious spider"[29] and are referred to themselves as "spider's seed."[30] ***Hop, Signor!*** seems to be a nest of spiders all weaving webs to snare the recalcitrant heroine, Margaret Harstein. This lady is very much like Hieronymus: she tries to save herself from mindless animalism to gain clarity about and hence power over her own destiny. However, like Hieronymus, Margaret is drawn into a web and devoured by the people who resent her apparent escape from the coils of physical reality.

The significant difference between the plays is mood: although ***Hop, Signor!,*** like many of Ghelderode's plays, comes dangerously close to melodrama, it is dead serious; ***Red Magic*** is farcial. However, at some point Ghelderode stops laughing and despite the comedy, Hieronymus emerges a tragic character. Not only must he choose between unstable electives (sex and money), but the criteria of good and evil, pain and pleasure fail as Hieronymus begins to question the value of his abstemious existence when he witnesses the sudden blooming of his wife. Armador says: "It is my tragic privilege to command the two elements that activate the universe, Good and Evil."[31] Although he pretends not to, Hieronymus knows that Armador is an impostor. (Could an alchemist be anything but?) Perhaps, then, good and evil are counterfeit as well. When he hears Sybilla's moaning in his cellar, he asks: "Is it with pain? Is it with pleasure? . . . The two are so alike . . ."[32] Hieronymus is forced to reflect on the ultimate ambiguity: the nature of the volition which directs man to choose one course of action over another. He says to his "son"—a doll he makes Sybilla play with rather than give her a real child:

> Men have unhealthy dreams. They dream of being more powerful than nature, than its Creator. They want to make light out of darkness. When you grow up—if you grow up—you will be rich; but never wonder where the riches came from. Enjoy them stupidly. . . . From time to time say to yourself that your father was tortured and that he did away with his tranquillity for the happiness of his kin! . . . Sleep or I shall destroy you! . . . Do not whine Hieronymus. Be like your son, insensible and without complaint. What is taking place

had to be. It is solemn. It is grotesque. It is poignant. I am no doubt very happy . . . and I feel miserable.[33]

The "child" is also an illusion "born" out of his niggardliness to give anything of himself away. Suppose his own creator is equally ungenerous: could his being, his existence, be nothing more than a figment of imagination of some stingy deity? What meaning then could sex or money have? What is left when glands and power fail? What is left to Hieronymus is death. The paradox which teases man is that the meaning to his living is in his dying. The alternative to coping with this fearful truth is to live out one's life in mindless stupor; to sleep the time away. Even the alternative is false: the terrifying reality of the illogic of dreams catches man off guard, at his most vulnerable. He can only wake again to the terrible logic of conscious reality.

Ghelderode tackles this problem through the last major character of his sustained writing period—Margaret Harstein. Piqued and humiliated by his wife's celibacy, Jureal Harstein accuses her of having lovers. Flattered by this imaginary credit, the "lovers" do little to refute the accusation, and the world accepts the unfounded charge as fact. Seeing that her husband and his priest as well as her two suitors are determined to malign her, Margaret attempts to make falsehood a reality. She becomes lascivious and tries to seduce the priest as well as the suitors. Like Hieronymus, Margaret is increasingly aware that she is the victim of seduction. With each provocative turn of the plot, she becomes enmeshed in a dream-like existence which reduces her conscious will to determine her own destiny. She acknowledges her predicament:

> There are times when each dream swerves aside and disports itself for a moment in reality before recovering itself and making off as a dream. In fact the dream never stopped. Where is the dream? Where does it begin? Where does it end? On a road where the wolves run?[34]

Fully aware of the dangers of the dream—the disorientation; the spontaneous, unwilled shifts into truth: the "wolves"—Margaret decides that these are lesser evils than the frustration of being prevented from creating a light to illuminate the darkness of waking reality. She yields to the dream and becomes increasingly somnabulent as the play progresses. Her "awakening" is her death; she refuses to "wake" again to the irritations of life. Once again Ghelderode presents the need for an executioner. Swallowed up in the executioner's cape (like Blandine in Lazarus's), she is executed, like Hieronymous, on false charges of murder and witchcraft: for the way things *appear* to be; not the way they *really* are. The world is only too ready to snatch any excuse to relieve itself of the Eremos, Hieronymuses and Margarets who challenge the "truth" that all men are at the mercy of a divine control against which they are powerless. Each of these three characters marks a progression in Ghelderode's emergent resolution of the irreconcilable forces at work on man. Eremo's angry "rejection" of physical death, his terrible "resurrection", is a just punishment for tampering with illusion to gain his power. Hieronymus is full of self-recrimination and bitterness: he resents the spite of a creator who toys with his creations, but he *resigns* himself to this fate. Only Margaret who recognizes the injustice of waking reality and illusion and the perils of dreaming reality and illusion accepts the paradox. By *yielding* to it, she alone is not defeated by it.

If in **Miss Jairus** and **Lord Halewyn,** Ghelderode created snow maidens longing for death, in **Red Magic** and **Hop, Signor!,** he creates fire men to burn away deceit and corruption. True, Amador, in the comic terms of **Red Magic,** is a false fire man: he only pretends to mint coins from Sybilla's blood. Larose is a real executioner: he knows from the outset that he will execute Margaret Harstein. Once again Ghelderode probes the problem of death—this time through his executioner. Larose is Lazarus and Armador combined. His name (which even sounds like "Lazarus") associates him with a rose tree as Lazarus is associated with a sprouting plant. Lazarus is a kind of human compost feeding living plants. Larose is the plant who feeds on the decay—the death of his victims. He scents out Margaret's readiness for her execution:

Your flesh smells good, is in the right condition . . .

He briskly draws near to MARGARET *and goes around her, sniffing at her.* MARGARET *smiles, enraptured. But the executioner draws back.*[35]

Like Armador, he is the consummate lover, "a blond athlete, superbly molded in scarlet, beardless, with a nonchalant feline gait."[36] He inflames Margaret but refuses her seductive overtures knowing that the only true consummation of their relationship can occur at her moment of death in the flames of her execution. Margaret understands his affair with death and tells him so:

Margaret: Could you stop the crowd shouting when the whole of your scaffold rings at the outburst? Could you stop the condemned man's shout mingling with it, so weak and all-prevailing? Well, I too shout, with this crowd and the condemned man, and you . . .

(LAROSE takes a step. MARGARET draws back.) For the executioner cries out like his victim. . . . I know, I have heard him. No one hears it. Then you go pale, you stagger imperceptibly, your gaze wanders . . .

Larose: Be quiet! (He puts his hand over Margaret's mouth.)

Margaret: And that only lasts for . . .

Larose (pushing her away): Madwoman! (He spits.)

Margaret (bitter and sad): Nice executioner . . .

Larose (going toward the steps): And on the evenings after the executions women became pregnant. Not by me, no! I spit on them. (He spits again.)

Margaret (runs to Larose and prevents him from going down): Spit on me!

Larose: No!

Margaret: Why?

Larose: Because you, Lady Margaret . . . (Pause.) Because you . . . Margaret . . . are not a woman like the others. No. In a way you were a sister. Now you are becoming an accomplice, for you have come across a secret that God alone knows; God who probes the loins as well as the heart.[37]

Between them, Larose and Margaret eliminate love and passion as factors in the consummation of death. When Margaret begs Larose to "deliver"[38] her from the physical sexual frustration which is consuming her, he replies: "No pretense is possible. If I begin, I finish."[39] There will be no substitution of sexual passion for death passion; there will be no *coitus interruptus mortis* for Margaret as there was for Purmelende. Although he is tempted by Margaret's sexuality, Larose refuses to participate in such a deception, explaining:

I wasn't wanting anything. Take you away? No. Fate must lead you. Nothing is living, nothing is authentic unless fate has marked it with its indecipherable seal. Do you know that?[40]

Knowing a truth is not the same as accepting it; coping with it. Margaret has still to conquer the "animal horror"[41] which she says death awakens in her. Only when she succeeds in transcending this horror, when she falls asleep under the spell of death, does Ghelderode allow Larose to reveal the meaning of her death:

You shall be a poisonous flower flung into the purifying fire. I shall make your death agony fruitful, and from your ashes dreadful roses shall be born.[42]

For Ghelderode it seems that the ultimate mystery occurs at the moment when Life mates with Death: an act of cosmic procreation perpetuated by the living and dying of beings who were created as fuel for the process with no regard for their individual agony. Only the perpetuation of the cosmic forces matters. To prove this point one has only to consider that there are no children in Ghelderode's plays, only puppets, dolls, dwarves and dreadful roses. There are only interrupted matings: when Blandine and Lazarus would kiss, Jacquelin interrupts them; when Halewyn would ravish Purmelende, she kills him; when Margaret would seduce Larose, he resists. Through these terms of sex (life) and death, Ghelderode depicts the human condition: at the moment when man would be seduced by life, death interferes; at the moment he would be seduced by death, life intervenes. The reality of life cancels out the illusion of death; the reality of death cancels out the illusion of life. One force seems to cancel out the other leaving man forever suspended paralysed and waiting—like the fly in the spider's web. Until man learns to accept that he is only part of forces perpetuating a larger order which for all his poor struggles he will never understand and whose truths will manifest themselves to him in elusive moments, he will never transcend the animal fear of his own mortality. He must learn to yield to Life until it is time to yield to Death; until the inexorable, irreversible momentum of the forces that make the design require him for the procreation of the universe. Small wonder that Ghelderode's final image in **Hop, Signor!** is that of a "disjointed marionette"[43] tossed in a blanket by two dwarves "rising and falling like a wounded bird faltering between earth and sky."[44] If this was the truth that Ghelderode found in the shards of reality and illusion waking or dreaming, then it is a most dreadful rose indeed.

Notes

1. *Chronicles of Hell,* 1:260.

2. *Christopher Columbus,* 2:155-6.

3. *Barabbas,* 1:64.

4. *Ibid.,* 74.

5. *Ibid.*

6. *Chronicles of Hell,* 1:248.

7. *Ibid.,* 252.

8. *Ibid.,* 238.

9. *Ibid.,* 255.

10. *Ibid.,* 256.

11. *Ibid.,* 264.

12. *Faust,* 2:101.

13. *Pantagleize,* 1:161.

14. *Chronicles,* 1:273.

15. *Ibid.,* 263.

16. *Ibid.,* 253.

17. *Ibid.*

18. *C.C.,* 2:153-4.

19. *Miss Jairus,* 2:253.

20. *Lord Halewyn,* 1:302.

21. *Ibid.,* 303.

22. *Ibid.,* 302.

23. *Hop, Signor!,* 2:51.

24. *Red Magic,* 2:10.

25. *Ibid.,* 53.

26. *Ibid.,* 36.

27. *H.,S.!,* 2:51.

28. *Ibid.,* 52.

29. *Ibid.,* 54.

30. *Ibid.,* 74.

31. *Red Magic,* 2:15.

32. *Ibid.,* 37.

33. *Ibid.,* 19.

34. *H.,S.!* 2:85.

35. *Ibid.,* 81-2.

36. *Ibid.,* 77.

37. *Ibid.,* 78.

38. *Ibid.*

39. *Ibid.*

40. *Ibid.,* 85.

41. *Ibid.,* 93.

42. *Ibid.*

43. *Ibid.*

44. *Ibid.*

Bibliography

WORKS

Ghelderode de, Michel. Ghelderode: Seven Plays, Vol. 1 (tr. by George Hauger). New York: Hill and Wang, 1960.

———. Ghelderode: Seven Plays, Vol. 2, (tr. by George Hauger). MacGibbon and Kee, 1966.

Chronology of Plays found in the two preceding volumes:

1918 *Piet Bouteille*

1921 *A Night of Pity*

1925 *The Death of Doctor Faust*

1926 *Three Actors and Their Drama*

1927 *Christopher Columbus*

1928 *Women at the Tomb Barabbas*

1929 *Pantagleize Chronicles of Hell*

1931 *Red Magic*

1933 *Three Blind Men*

1934 *Lord Halewyn Miss Jairus*

1935 *Hop, Signor!*

CRITICISM

Abel, Lionel. "Our Man in the Sixteenth Century: Michel de Ghelderode," *Tulane Drama Review,* Vol. 8, No. 1, Fall 1963.

Beyen, Roland. *Michel de Ghelderode, ou la hantise du masque.* Bruxelles: Palais des Académies, 1971.

Deberdt-Malaquais, Elisabeth. *La Quête de l'Identité dans le Théâtre de Ghelderode,* 1967.

Decock, Jean. *Le Théâtre de Michel de Ghelderode: Une Dramaturge de l'Anti-théâtre et de la Cruauté.* Paris Editions-A.-G. Nizet, 1969.

Draper, Samuel. "An Interview with Michel de Ghelderode," *TDR,* Vol. 8, No. 1, Fall 1963.

———. "Bibliography," *Modern Drama,* Vol. 8, No. 3, Winter 1965.

———. "Discovery of Gheldrerode," *Commonweal,* LXXXVI, No. 7, May 1962.

———. "Infernal Theatre," *Commonweal,* LXXI, No. 10, New York, December 4, 1959.

Francis, Jean. *L'Eternal Aujourd'hui de Michel de Ghelderode.* Brussels, 1968.

Grossvogel, David. "Plight of the Comic Author and New Departures into Contemporary Comedy," *Romantic Review,* No. 45, New York, December 1954.

Guicharnaud, Jacques. *Modern French Theatre from Giroudoux to Becket.* New Haven: Yale University Press, 1961.

Hauger, George. "Dispatches from the Prince of Ostrelande," *TDR,* Vol. 8, No. 1, Fall 1963.

Pronko, Leonard, Cabell. *Avant-Garde: The Experimental Theatre in France.* Berkely and Los Angeles: University of California Press, 1962.

Weiss, Aurelui. "The Theatre of Michel de Ghelderode," *TDR,* Vol. 8, No. 1, Fall 1963.

Wellworth, George. "Michel de Ghelderode: The Theatre of the Grotesque," *TDR,* Vol. 8, No. 1, Fall 1963.

Renée C. Fox (essay date 1994)

SOURCE: "'Les Roses, Mademoiselle': The Universe of Michel de Ghelderode," in *American Scholar,* Vol. 63, No. 3, Summer 1994, pp. 403-19.

[*In the following essay, Fox provides a personal reminiscence of Ghelderode's life and career.*]

"Come preferably at five o'clock," Michel de Ghelderode had written to me. "The light changes then." And so it was late in the afternoon when I left the Brussels apartment where I was living in July 1961 to make my first visit to the renowned Belgian playwright, poet, storyteller, and writer of letters. My taxi moved swiftly down fashionable Avenue Louise, past the baroque Palace of Justice, and through the Place Royale of government ministries and the Société Générale, toward 71, rue Lefrancq, the house in Schaarbeek, a working-class district of Brussels, where Ghelderode and his wife Jeanne resided. As my cab proceeded along the Chaussée de Haecht, the domed basilica of the Eglise Sainte Marie loomed before me like a portal. Behind this church lay the address I was seeking.

The windows of their apartment were covered with green shutters when I arrived, and the big, green front door felt massively shut. But as soon as I pushed the brass bell marked "Michel de Ghelderode," his wife opened the door and ushered me into—I can think of it no other way—"the Ghelderodean universe."

Michel de Ghelderode was at his worktable in the salon, seated in a carved, thronelike Spanish chair, over which a crimson velvet cover, gold embroidered with some kind of ecclesiastical or royal insignia, had been draped. He was a large-boned man, made lean by illness. His straight, brown, maestro-style hair was combed neatly behind his big ears, accentuating his high forehead, prominent cheekbones, and long, ample nose. Although his mouth was thin, and drawn down by suffering, its sensual fullness in healthier, younger days was still discernible. His startlingly pale blue eyes, with their very dark pupils, dominated his hollowed-out and haunted face. His gaze came from some transfixing place inside of himself, and his eyes seemed to be hearing as well as seeing invisible things. His elegant artist's hands, of which he was not unaware, protruded gracefully from the sleeves of his velour jacket.

But Ghelderode's appearance was eclipsed by the "assault of images" that the furnishings of his salon and the spell of his words unleashed in me. "My little museum of inexpressible things, my collection of imponderables," was the way that he referred to the salon and the objects in it. We talked surrounded by masks from Belgian carnivals and kermesses; marionettes from the traditional puppet theaters of Brussels and Liège; seashells from the beaches of Ostend in Flanders; swords and scabbards; ancient Madonnas; crucifixes; Church hangings; a Gothic stone frieze reputedly a fragment from the sculptured face of Brussels's Hôtel de Ville; mannequins in various states of dress and undress; two carousel horses; and whole walls of Belgian paintings.

The antiquely musical sound of his voice made me think of a harpsichord. It filled the room with his exquisite, lavishly poetic and theatrical French—infused somehow with the enormous energy, the sensual joy, and the hallucinatory terror of Flanders. As he spoke, the objects in the salon took on life, as if animated by the enchantment of his words.

Before I left at sunset, Madame de Ghelderode served me many large cups of savory coffee and a whole platter of tastefully arranged, delicious pâtisserie. It must be she, I thought, the good Belgian housewife, who keeps the Ghelderodean museum so exquisitely neat, systematically arranged—and perfectly dusted!

Several days later, I received a handwritten letter from Michel de Ghelderode in response to my thank-you note. He had been reluctant to have me come, he admitted, because he was only beginning to emerge from a long and grave state of illness, and he feared that his appearance might cause me "some pain and disappointment." Arriving at his doorstep and entering his house at this point in his life meant that I would have to accept seeing him in the same state "as that of the objects that surround me, wounded, worn by age, scratched. . . . But they have their poetic resonance," he added, "these humble things that were beautiful at the beginning. Would they be *pathétiques* and worthy of tenderness if they did not carry the trace of their former existence?" In any case, he hoped that health was now "quickly returning" to him and that "it will not take many days before I lose this dilapidated style."

Ghelderode wanted me to know that whatever apprehension he may have had about my visit before I crossed "the threshold of [his] solitude" had been dispelled by my somewhat "immaterial . . . presence" and the "moving memory" with which my visit left his "companion" and himself:

> But no, you are not a stranger to me, and without ever having seen you I recognized you but from where, when? My wife felt the same sentiment, without being able to explain it. . . . It is not necessary to search; one must accept Destiny and the souls that Destiny sends us. . . . Do we know very much in this world?

"Your gentleness," Ghelderode continued, "your meditation, your sort of radiant wisdom express and reveal your rank in the poetic universe." He associated my aura, he said, with "the image of the rose, the most complete of flowers":

> . . . quasi-carnal and with a perfume that evokes angels—the roses of Ronsard that express passion and tenderness, forged together! It is the royal flower, more so than the lily, and I will teach you that in my ancient country of Flanders and of Brabant, it was the flower of Coronations, of joyous entrances, of princely marriages, of the triumphs of rhetoricians and artists: a chapel of roses [meaning a hat or a crown] was accorded to the personage on whom one wished to confer honor on pageant days. The victors in combats also, like Saint George or Saint Michael, enemies of the oriental Dragons in whom Claudel saw the devil in his last metamorphosis!

Ghelderode invited me to come and see them often, whenever I wanted, at any time it suited me. "You need never feel lonely or exiled," he declared, "because my house and my heart are open to you. We are, my wife and I, your spiritual and emotional family." "I will try," he promised, "to make your stay easier in this country which is very beautiful and contains more than one would dare to imagine."

His letter ended with a "vision" that he wished to impart to me. Although he was ill and "in the twilight of [his] destiny," he wrote, "so tenacious still is my love of life, my faith in men and their becoming, that I cannot abandon myself to bitter thoughts, to nocturnal philosophies without signs of hope from better skies, where human beings end by finding their redemption, their transfiguration of what was their primitive condition, perhaps that of angels, from their tragedy, crumbling into the abysses fortified by the infinite."

Because Ghelderode's letter, and the visit with him and his wife had touched things deep inside me, I sent them

twelve, long-stemmed Baccarat roses. One day later, the postman brought me another message from Ghelderode—the most extraordinary letter I have ever received. It was written in his eighteenth-century script, with an old wooden pen dipped in an inkwell, on four long parchment pages. The cover page, imprinted with a royal stamp and the date 1720, was filled with a pen-and-ink drawing he had made of a huge, single rose in a vase, around which strange forms—some with wings—floated. "Les Roses, Mademoiselle!" the text of the letter began on its second parchment page, bordered with another Ghelderodean sketch of a gigantic rose—this one, without a vase or phantasmagoric shapes:

> What a beautiful gesture of an artist yours was—and how you express the quality of my joy, I should say our joy—for are we not in my house but two souls in one . . . in a play of mirrors?
>
> You see me embarrassed before this gift from your hands, such as one finds painted on the shutters of ancient altar pieces.
>
> You will be happy when I state that you have been vested with Poetry, in a privileged way, as a second breath invigorating the world of learned truth with its corrective action—[Poetry] that precedes the Infinite and brings you revealed truth . . .
>
> These carnivalesque flowers impose the nostalgia of their imminent perishing! It is a law, is it not, ours and that of the pure, the poets, to give in the fashion of these roses of Holocaust, the best of their fervor, of their song, and of their vision even if this calls attention to how naked they are! Must we not very quickly return to ashes after having decreed to unknown persons, to possible hearts, our spiritual feast, our color, our perfume—it should be said, our virtues?
>
> There is the speech about the noble rose: a single one of them is sufficient to put me in a state of grace!
>
> [The roses] sumptuously light my hermetic room full of strange forms, impossible creatures, cosmic phantoms in a traveling theater décor where the Old Temptation of Saint Anthony is playing, that all our satiric painters of the centuries have evoked as much out of love of the Carnal Saint of the Angels as for the surrealistic devils who inhabited their nights with mad music and violent spectacles! . . . I forget my recent tribulations in [the roses], the physicians of Molière dancing their ballet, the *Danse Macabre* also that I must forget, and in which I failed to make my entrance, thank God!
>
> Scarcely had they arrived, when your flowers are scoured by a summer storm, and open up with a violent and provocative suddenness, pearled with celestial water, like curiously budding creatures! . . . Will they speak, in a sort of spasm, at the command of magicianly thunder? . . .
>
> *Belles comme le péché!*
>
> Michel de Ghelderode

At the bottom of the letter, alongside his description of the stormseized roses, Ghelderode had drawn another sketch:

a small vase, filled with roses that had become eyes, over which an ambiguous entity, more angelic than demonic, hovered.

This is the dramatic and mysterious way that one of the most profound and important relationships of my life began. Measured in calendar time, it was brief. Michel de Ghelderode died less than a year after I met him—on April 1, 1962, two days before he turned sixty-four. But viewed in a Ghelderodean perspective, what he called "our great friendship" spanned two generations and two different stages in the life cycle—his and mine—four seasons, and almost an entire liturgical year. It was perpetuated by his wife Jeanne and me, over the eighteen years that she survived him, through our correspondence, and our long visits during my annual trips to Belgium. My emotional and spiritual encounter with Michel de Ghelderode transported me into that frightening but strangely beautiful innermost place where my unconscious and the cultural symbolism of Belgium met. In a sense, he "took me to images" that I already knew but had never before dared to acknowledge or contemplate fully. In his letters to me, Ghelderode referred to Belgium as "this astonishing country of dream and action, of art and monuments, haunted by luminosity, by contrast, by meteoric spasms, which is ours and yours in sharing. Because you understand it," he said. "And people possess what they understand. You love it, too."

In part, Ghelderode was my teacher. He wanted to help me learn as much as possible about the "familiar by-streets" and the "buried strangeness" (a phrase from Richard Wilbur's poem "A Hole in the Floor") of his home country—about the shapes and odors, the voices and silences of its past, and their incarnation in its present. Some of his teaching was explicitly didactic. He encouraged me to spend time in Belgian museums. "There are many secrets inside our museums in Ghent, in Bruges, in Brussels!" In this "Country of Painting, so rich in hours of creative art," he said, he wanted me to "live a little of its hallucinatory past" through the works of historical and contemporary masters like Breughel and Bosch and Ensor—paintings that had led him "toward the art of theater," and inspired some of his plays. He also counseled me about how to derive the most value from these experiences. "Try to visit [the museum] in old Brussels before your departure. On your own. That is best. You are too much sovereign of your faculties to need a minister to help you prevail over this illusory world!" Occasionally, his instruction took the form of giving me some of his less-known works to read:

> I inscribe this little "*acte mystique*" [he wrote on the title page of his "mystical farce," **Les Vieillards**] which will tell you how much I am and continue to be close to the popular heart, in this Flanders of imagery. . . . You will see that the poet of this nation with such an intense past, metaphysically so rich, still produces realistic [works], close to the soil.

Ghelderode also taught me about Belgium through the "reality" dimensions of his plays and stories. An astute social observer and critic, he transposed his perceptions of current Belgian life, and his commentary on it, to Flanders and Brabant in the fifteenth and sixteenth centuries. The characters in his play, **Mademoiselle Jaïre,** for example, are "just as you might meet at random in the miniatures of the Burgundian period. Some wear turbans or preserve elements of orientalism in their dress," as they did in the port town of Bruges in a "bygone age." These characters "may seem to be invented," Ghelderode remarked, "but their voices betray inflections that could be caught nowadays by acute listening." When he wrote for the Toone Marionette Theatre of Brussels, Ghelderode made the puppets speak in the popular dialect, and with the folk humor of the men and women who lived in the city's working-class Marolles district. Not only did he capture the distinctive language and comedic sense of such local milieux, but he also ironically portrayed the particularism and the possessive love of things that he discerned in Belgians throughout the land.

Ghelderode made it plain that he did not read the works of social scientists. In his view, their analytic perspective was antithetic to the "instinct," "vision," and "divination" by which "the dramatic author must live." Yet he supported my own participant observation-based sociological research in Belgium, considering it analogous in some ways to his own observations of everyday life in Belgian society and his immersion in its culture, which were vital to his art. He even suggested that when I wrote about Belgium it might be more effective—and safer, too—if, like him, I transferred what I had noted and wished to say to a past century.

But it was primarily through the language of images and symbols that Ghelderode inducted me into the "ambiance" and the soul of the country that he inhabited and that inhabited him. He opened his salon to me, where the ancient and modern artifacts of Belgian culture that he had collected—what he called his "*objets étranges*" (strange objects)—were evocatively displayed. Under the spell of his theatrical genius and his magician-like qualities, the objects became live presences, sending messages that he helped me to perceive and decipher.

Ghelderode also gave me some of his "image-beings" as gifts—a wooden pen; a tiny, marionette-like doll; a watercolor portrait of him surrounded by objects and images from his salon and his plays; a photograph, in which he was mounted like a chevalier on his favorite carousel horse, Borax. "For Renée Claire Fox—wounded angel with tender eyes. . . . A flame that the wind can curve, but extinguish, no. . . . In offering her this image of my obsessions and phantoms, I offer her my friendship, always," is the way he inscribed the watercolor.

With romantic tenderness, mischievous humor, and skill, Ghelderode gave me the best of his vision, in ways that opened the inner chambers of Belgium—and of myself—to me. He recognized the yearning writer in me, asserting from the outset that I had been "vested with Poetry." He brought that part of me to the surface by releasing the imagery in me and making me less fearful of it. He counted me among those who were "sensitive to the supernatural," he said—"to the secret signal from a mystic country." And he linked this spiritual perception with the capacity to make, as well as to hear, poetry. I, in turn, responded to him both religiously and artistically.

Ghelderode was highly attuned to religious symbols, rituals, and signs: to old churches and chapels; to priestly vestments and liturgical chants; to religious offices, processions, and funerals (which he considered supreme, "stage-managed" performances); to statues of the Virgin Mary (the Notre Dame of Solitude and Sorrow, rather than "rosy" Madonnas, with self-satisfied expressions of "having so marvelously given birth"); and to the "everlasting language" that he said had accompanied him all of his life—the "aerial music" of the bells and the carillons of Flanders, "both the tragic bells with bloody mouths and the triumphant with golden tongues." Prophets and saints, priests and bishops, angels and devils, Mary, Joseph, and Jesus, and the many visages of Death crowd the pages of Ghelderode's stories and plays. Like the Primitive Flemish painters, he placed them in the houses, the villages, the towns, the squares, the courtyards, the streets, and the fields of Belgium "in olden times," and he gave them Belgian faces and garments. Ghelderode seemed to feel intimately acquainted with the members of the Holy Family and with certain saints like St. Francis and St. Anthony; his whole metabolism moved in the rhythm of the liturgical calendar.

Ghelderode was not a practicing Catholic, in the conventional sense of the term. He did not attend Mass. He was passionately critical of the "official Church" because of its emphasis on obedience and dogma rather than on "the eternal sob of prostrate man . . . at the foot of the incomprehensible Cross." The priests in the cast of characters of his plays were often more "ugly" and less holy than the unordained populace to whom they supposedly ministered, and they were suffused with a decaying "clerical odor." He was no more a Catholic author, Ghelderode insisted, than he was a national Belgian one. Rather, what he tried to write were "*patriale*" works that were "ancestral and traditionally of my home," while expressing "the man of my time everywhere . . . and through him man eternal." But the imagery of Belgian Catholicism was in Ghelderode and all around him. It pervaded his salon, his letters to me, his theater, and his being. My friendship with him made me see and feel the Catholicism of Belgian culture and the Belgianness of its Catholicism. And in the process, old churches, madonnas, carillons, and roses came to dwell in my Jewish-American soul.

I was at home in New York when I received Ghelderode's last letter. It was written on March 1, 1962, in the season when the "violet days" of Lent were approaching:

> Great Friend, faraway princess!
>
> There are silhouettes like yours, so intensely poetic, that traverse the Theatre of our friend Maeterlinck, the author of Pelléas and Mélisande! Slender, purebred,

far-reaching gaze, as far as the stars. . . . What is an ocean between our hearts? For Jeanne, for me, we stretch out our hand and we touch yours. In the fogs, you are a phosphorescent statue. . . . I pity you in that hallucinatory, glacial city, where humanity is no longer more than a frightened herd, that watches the sky, not in the direction of the angels, but for a rocket that this time transports a madman, [and] tomorrow will transport Death in person! Oh Poetry! And the solemn silence of my dear old room, at twilight. . . . And the look . . . of my companion, who holds you in such tender friendship! Thanks to God! I ask nothing else, except the spring—and a few radiant friendships like the one you devote to me and that lights my last years. . . . I have written very little to you, you who have spoken so much to me, from afar, from near—because you have remained close to us. . . . Sickness, yes. You knew it, no need to report it to you. Since January 1. And the cold, the ice! I shivered near the fire, poor little human being, contemplating the old black trees. And then sleep. . . . I forgot all . . . except you, friend, . . . and a few others—heralds of this Friendship as necessary as love. . . . I cannot maintain this muteness much longer. Hope is reviving, the sun mounts higher each day—our days are better—yes. . . . How much gratitude I owe you for all the signs of your vigilant affection . . . of very beautiful hours . . .

Jeanne, very tired, because of me! What sacrifices. There are days when I want to cry when I think of the poor lot I give her. She never complains. If she were not near me, I would let myself slide into nothingness, I confess to you; I would sleep forever. Exhausted from suffering, physically also; because these last months, I have undergone the anguish of being, of existing, and also the desire to no longer be. . . . But there is this creature who has fought so hard for me and my work: then there is my unfinished work . . . this Theater, still two more volumes. Some tales, Twilight Tales, you will like them I feel. It is very much me. It is Ghelderode, it is your friend, your "human brother," as Maître François Villon says to Louis XI in the ballads. . . . Condemned not to go out, I who do not ask to leave the room where I have all, my books, my paintings, my images, a vision of the garden, sometimes a visit, and letters coming from everywhere. You will have better news soon. Brussels-Capital gilds itself with sun—but what a winter. . . . They are playing me in Paris, *La Balade du Grand Macabre,* [put on] by the Free Theatre of the University of Brussels. . . . As for success, I scoff at it. Glory is a lie. Only the heart counts. The only thing that matters is to be loved, love, affection, outstretched hands . . .

Great friend, *au revoir!* lassitude overtakes me; I am still very weak! . . . The violet days of Christian liturgy are coming, the desolation of the empty Tabernacle, God absent! The churches are strange these holy days, Holy Thursday, Good Friday—and then, the Pascal explosion, the carillons of Flanders, the bells in the belfries that ring out: *Alléluia!* He is risen! Nature also! And the harvesters of Breughel arrive with flasks on their hips!

Don't let me leave you without speaking of you, of your work, of your projects. Jeanne embraces you, and I, your old friend of the heart, rich with childhood, I send you my most tender smile. . . . Come back to us, dear Renée Claire Fox; that will be festival and joy!

He did not live to hear the carillons of Flanders ring on Easter Sunday.

Ghelderode called me a friend, a younger sister, a wounded angel, a flame, a phosphorescent statue in the fog, and a faraway princess. He associated me with certain feminine "silhouettes" in the works of Edgar Allan Poe and Maurice Maeterlinck. My eyes, he said, were "not of this world, of a woman, a simple creature." He likened my hair, and the way I wore it—long, "loose" and "abundant"—to that of "The Women of the Tomb in our Primitives [paintings] of Flanders and Brabant." And in the letter that he wrote to me on the eve of my departure for the United States, he addressed me as "the Skinny Angel, ready for flight."

Authenticity and ardor, imagination and whimsy were commingled in the ethereally romantic way in which Ghelderode saw and wrote about me. He responded to certain of my personal qualities, embroidered artistically upon them, and projected me into the final acts of his theater and his life.

I came to his house bearing roses and crossed the threshold of his salon when he was mortally ill. I arrived there from the "faraway" land of New York City in America: a young, modern country that fascinated him, but frightened him, too, because it was so different from the Old Europe in which he dwelled. I was an emissary, from that foreign place where his plays were coming to be known, with whom he could communicate—a slender young woman, with long, dark hair and dark eyes, whose appearance pleased him, and an intellectual, whose speech and gestures were literary.

I was young, from a young country, but I had what Ghelderode felt was an "old soul," partly because I was Jewish. He never discussed my Jewishness with me, but it was important to him. In his eyes, it connected me with his favorite statue of "Our Lady," the *"Vierge noire"* (Black Virgin) in St. Catherine's Church in Brussels, whom he regarded as a more genuine and pure representation of Mary than the blonde-haired, blue-eyed Madonnas whom one usually saw in Belgian churches and paintings. Like her, I looked the way that Ghelderode thought a "granddaughter of King David" should.

I was an old soul, too, because I was already intimately acquainted with illness and death. At the age of seventeen, I had contracted a nearly fatal case of polio, which had left visible marks on me. In Ghelderode's words, I was "wounded" by illness, as he himself was. But "skinny" and "wounded angel" though I was, in Ghelderode's moral view I had demonstrated that I had tenacious hope and a supreme Belgian virtue—the *"courage"* to overcome adversity.

However serious and sincere Ghelderode was, if I had been so flattered by his romantic portrait of me that I failed to recognize its playfulness and humor, so awed by his dramatic self-presentation that I did not discern its staged aspects, or so out of touch with everyday reality that I could not participate in the down-to-earth dimensions of his life with Jeanne, our friendship would never have become what it was.

But from the beginning to the end, I was, above all, the Mademoiselle of the roses. In Ghelderode's emblematic universe, roses and death were associated. Death, he exclaimed, was as beautiful as "roses in the snow." In a letter to a fellow poet, Garcia Lorca, he declared that he was "now writing a kind of *opening-the-veins* poetry altogether averted from reality, with a feeling that reflects all my love for things and all my mocking of things. My love of death and poking fun at her." In his autobiographical *Ostend Interviews,* he went on to say: "I laugh at death . . . and make fun of her, but she will return, be certain of that. Although you do not love her, she remains with you, and she is the only person of whose fidelity you can be certain. Crown her with roses!" To this day I wonder whether, along with the other ways that he identified me, Michel de Ghelderode also thought I was a sign, if not a messenger, of his imminent death.

Jeanne de Ghelderode, Michel's wife and "companion," was part of every letter I received from him. Our friendship, he declared again and again, was a "luminous trinity," that united Jeanne and him and me and made us a "spiritual and emotional family." Jeanne reaffirmed this in her letters to me after Michel's death. "Even if we were never to see each other again," she wrote, "that marvelous message, *'Les Roses, Mademoiselle,'* . . . would remain a sign of union between us, . . . and every rose encountered would make me dream of you, of my faraway friend who is nevertheless so close to my thought."

Jeanne was an intelligent, shrewdly perceptive woman who was fiercely and lovingly protective of her husband and his work and acted as his gatekeeper. She considered herself to be (and undoubtedly was) less naively idealistic than Michel about the character and motives of the procession of writers, painters, sculptors, puppeteers, actors, publishers, literary and theatrical agents, journalists, public officials, students, professors and the like, from different parts of Belgium and Europe, and from many other countries in the world, who wished to meet and interview the great author, see his inner sanctum, and seek professional rights and favors from it.

It was Jeanne de Ghelderode, as much as Michel, who admitted me into their universe. Out of a combination of intuition and practical sense, she trusted me. Because I was a sociologist, rather than a literary, theater, or media person, she reasoned, I was less likely to have self-interested, careerist reasons for wanting to know her husband. Like Michel, she responded positively to my "aura," and she shared his sense of mysterious familiarity with my "silhouette." She also knew that I saw her as far more than Michel's devoted spouse, helpmate, and housekeeper. It was apparent to me that she typed all his manuscripts. She was an important in-house critic of the various drafts of his plays and stories. She also influenced the decisions that he made about whether a play was ready to be published or performed, and to whom the rights to produce it ought to go. I discovered, too, that she was not merely the guardian and duster of the Ghelderodean salon but also the one who helped Michel to choose and arrange its *objets étranges*. My recognition of her role and her awareness of the way I perceived her reinforced our friendship.

It was with anxiety as well as expectancy, however, that we anticipated our first visit *à deux* since Michel's death. "Your great friend Michel will not be there, unhappily, to welcome you," Jeanne forewarned me. "Both of us . . . live with his memory, and . . . [our] friendship . . . is placed under [his] protection."

My taxi pulled up in front of 7, rue Lefrancq and departed. A note written in Jeanne's hand had been slipped into the Michel de Ghelderode nameplate on the big, green front door. "Gone for five minutes," it read. Almost instantly, Jeanne was standing beside me. We embraced, kissing each other three times on alternate cheeks, *à la Belge*. Jeanne wept silently.

Inside the house, we entered the salon, and seated ourselves in chairs near the small, round table where Michel wrote, leaving the carved, throne chair, with its crimson and gold church hangings, empty, ready for his entrance. "I have left things just as they were," said Jeanne, weeping quietly again. Neatly laid out on his writing table, in their customary place, were Michel's green blotter, his old brown spectacles, his pipe in its stand, a small sword letter opener, an antique brass scale for weighing letters, and, in a special cup, all his *plumes*—wooden penholders, fitted out with steel pen points, arranged like a painter's brushes. In one corner of the desk stood a tall crystal vase, filled with simple garden roses. A book about Hieronymous Bosch and his paintings was propped on a nearby couch. A very large photographic portrait of Michel, that I had not seen before, had been placed in the center of the mantelpiece.

"I am not '*croyante*' or '*pratiquante*,'" Jeanne said, referring to the fact that she was not a believing, practicing Catholic. "I was baptized and had my First Communion," she continued, "but though I tried, I was never able to become '*croyante*.'" And yet, since Michel had died, she confessed, she had the sense of being "doubly strong," as though Michel's spirit had entered into her.

Jeanne felt his continuing presence in the apartment, and so did I. She had opened the shutters on the front windows of the salon and drawn back the curtains on the glass doors that framed the apartment's small, inner garden. An enchanted garden, Michel called it, and he wove it into some of his tales and plays. On this exceptionally lovely summer day, it was flooded with sunlight, very green, and

full of roses. The sun shone through the windows and panes of the French doors, illuminating the apartment as if an invisible stage director had turned a theatrical spotlight upon it. The light dispelled all the shadows in the house. It warmed the yellows, pinks, and reds of the roses in the crystal vase on the writing table. The bright-eyed carousel horses looked newly painted. The sequins on the red satin suit of the Gentleman-Devil puppet shimmered. The mantelpiece mirror gleamed. The crystal chandeliers sparkled. The amethyst necklace worn by one of the mannequins emitted a purple glow. And the paintings over the gold velvet settee were as radiant as a Flemish sky. Sunbeams fingered the green metal trunk filled with Michel's manuscripts and correspondence, and the old upright machine on which, for years, Jeanne had typed his manuscripts.

Jeanne smiled as she began to describe the visit she had received that morning from the notary. He admired the salon, Jeanne said, especially the religious objects in it, because he was a very pious Catholic. But, for that same reason, he did not understand why the crucifixes, the madonnas, the church candelabra, and the like were intermingled with masks, puppets, wooden horses, and semi-clothed mannequins. With a perfectly straight face, Jeanne explained to the notary that when the windows and shutters are closed, the house starts to smell like an old church, and so in order to offset this odor, the other objects in the salon are necessary. The notary listened respectfully to what he supposed was Jeanne's serious response, but he was clearly perplexed.

A visit that Jeanne thought would be comparable in its own way, and to which she was definitely not looking forward, she said, was the one she expected the assessors to make at the end of the year. They will come to estimate the value of all the furnishings and possessions in the house, in connection with the taxes that must be levied on them, she told me. How will the assessors appraise the objects in this salon, I wondered silently. What money value will they affix to the long-legged mannequin whom Michel named "Hamlet," with her scarlet lips and nails, bare breasts, a crown atop her lavender-tinted wig, and a sword hanging from the satin poncho that she wears? Or to Borax, the carousel horse, and Sire Mephistopheles, the "*Grand Seigneur*" Devil puppet?

Jeanne filled the afternoon and evening that we spent together with anecdotes and stories about Michel. He was cared for by three physicians, she recounted: one from Brussels, one from Ghent, and one from Bruges. They were all Flemish and Catholic. One of these physicians felt that it was important for Michel to see a priest during the last days of his illness. He asked a particular priest to visit Michel, but, Jeanne told me, this "wonderful priest" declined to do so. "Michel will find his way to Paradise by himself," the priest stated with conviction. Jeanne and Michel agreed that "the priest who never came to the house" was a "truly religious man."

Jeanne reminisced about her first meeting with Michel, their courtship, wedding, and honeymoon. They met when the two of them were working for the same stationer—she in the publicity department, he in school supplies. It was the beginning of the academic year, and the store was filled with children and their mothers coming to buy supplies for classes. All the employees of the firm were asked to help with the long line of customers. Jeanne and Michel were seated at the same table, dispensing merchandise and collecting cash. He was Adhémar Martens then, and in the course of the remarks they exchanged in the midst of the sales, Michel/Adhémar discovered that Jeanne had gone to school with his sister, Germaine Martens. Later, he asked Jeanne to type a tale for him, telling her that he was the literary executor for the works of a young author-friend who had recently died. The story was signed, "Michel de Ghelderode." Jeanne typed the manuscript, knowing full well that it was written by Adhémar Martens, because its style was so similar to the way that he spoke. "What do you think of it?" he asked her when she returned the typed story to him. "Not bad," she replied. "Not bad?" he responded with some indignation. "The boy has talent!"

Vowing to each other that they would never marry, Jeanne and Michel began going out together. Jeanne continued to type his manuscripts. She was also invited to his Saturday soirées. At the first of these evenings that she attended, she was greeted at the front door of the house by Michel, who was wearing a robe of some kind and whose hair, she said, was longer than mine. Michel was holding a candlestick in his hand. He led her up the staircase to the attic of the house where he had a bedroom-studio. There, by candlelight, with huge shadows flickering on the walls, Michel received his friends on Saturday nights. Jeanne was startled when she noticed that the pile of coats that had been thrown on the bed by the guests had begun to move with a strange, rocking motion. And then, from under the pile, a tiny dog, with a red face, emerged. It was Michel's dog!—one of the only "possessions" with which he entered marriage, she added.

Jeanne and Michel were married in a civil ceremony that lasted only a few minutes. She wore a very pretty black dress for the occasion, she said, and they went to Paris for their honeymoon, using the money that Michel had received from his first literary prize.

With a burst of candor, Jeanne told me that she knew her husband's faults well. He was "very influenceable," she said, and, during a certain period of his life, he drank too much in local cafés with writer, artist, and actor friends. At a critical point in their marriage, she had a very serious, "severe" discussion with Michel about the problem, particularly about the adverse way that it was affecting his writing. After that conversation, Jeanne alleged, Michel stopped drinking, and the problem never occurred again.

As Jeanne recalled past events, I learned more about Michel's parents. His mother, she told me, like her own father, was a "child of love," born out of wedlock. Michel's father, the son of a "good family" from Louvain, was the principal clerk at the General Archives of Belgium. It was

he who introduced Michel to "parchments, . . . faded writings, . . . great wax [and] metal seals," and antique objects; and like his father, Michel was employed for many years as an archivist (in the Communal Hall [Hôtel Communal] in the Brussels commune of Schaarbeek). Despite what they had in common in this regard, father and son "did not have a good understanding," Jeanne said. A major source of conflict between them was that Michel's father expected him to choose a "respectable" and "safe" occupation—preferably one in the civil service.

It was Michel's mother, Jeanne continued, from whom he received the "secret life" out of which he became a writer. She "grew up in a convent in Louvain [Michel wrote about his mother], and there she was taught the life of the saints. . . . She knew liturgical chant, spoke ecclesiastical Latin, and believed in the devil whom, she said, she had seen many a time. . . . She was rich in proverbs, in forgotten songs, . . . in ancient legends, . . . and in haunted stories," which she told "wonderfully well." Michel claimed that he was her one and only listener. Neither his siblings nor his father was interested in her tales. There was always something "celestial" about her face, Jeanne mused, her eyes filling with tears as she spoke of her mother-in-law.

Just before Jeanne and I had lunch together, the Ghelderodes' *femme de journée*, Madame Lambert, dropped by for a short visit. She had worked for Jeanne and Michel for more than thirty years, helping with the cleaning, laundry, and other chores around the house. They first met when she was the concièrge in the house where they lived before moving to 71, rue Lefrancq. In her earlier years, she was a singer and a dancer in the Flemish Art Theatre.

I had never been impressed with Madame Lambert's housekeeping abilities. When I watched her at work on previous visits, it seemed to me that there was no particular order in which she did things and that she spent quite a bit of time leaning dreamily on her mop, staring into space with a dust cloth clutched in her hand, or chatting animatedly with Jeanne and Michel—who always respectfully addressed her as *Madame* Lambert. Jeanne told me that Madame Lambert was Michel's confidante during the last days of his illness. He knew that he was dying, he said to Madame Lambert, and he asked her to look out for Jeanne. Artistically, as well as humanly, Madame Lambert fit into the décor and atmosphere of the Ghelderode house. With her tousled blonde hair drawn into a knot at the top of her head, her expressive light blue eyes, her long, upturned nose like those you see on carved wooden folk dolls, in the rumpled, shapeless dress, and huge carpet slippers that she donned for cleaning, she always gave me the impression of a comedienne, playacting the role of a servant or of a living, giant-sized marionette!

Jeanne had prepared a special lunch for me of Belgian dishes: small, fresh tomatoes, stuffed with tiny shrimp (*crevettes*), stewed rabbit, new potatoes, *petits pois,* a choice of cheeses, and for dessert a mixture of fresh strawberries, raspberries, and red currants (*groseilles*), accompanied by a glass of red wine, and a cup of her good, strong coffee. Over the meal, she discussed the problems that she was encountering to obtain permission for Michel to be buried in the Laeken cemetery. It was his ardent wish to join the renowned artists, war heroes, and noblemen who were interred in what he called this "necropolis," near the Royal Palace and Cathedral of Laeken, and the bronze cast of one of his favorite statues, Auguste Rodin's *Le Penseur.* Technical, bureaucratic, and political considerations were delaying the decision about whether the honor of being buried on the "Avenue of Artists" of this national cemetery would be accorded Ghelderode and his literary works. Meanwhile, his coffin remained on the Laeken cemetery grounds, in what Jeanne referred to as a "*cave d'attente,*" and the Belgian association of "The Friends of Michel de Ghelderode" was launching a public drive to collect funds to erect a special tombstone for him. (Michel de Ghelderode was finally buried in Laeken cemetery on December 6, 1964.)

After lunch, at about four o'clock in the afternoon, Jeanne's brother, Gérard, and his wife, Josette, came for the kind of long visit that they had been making at least once a week (usually Sunday) to Jeanne and Michel for many years. In appearance and manner, Gérard was a classical, almost vaudevillean "*Bruxellois/Brusselaar.*" He was a huge, rotund man, with a protruding stomach. His tremendous trousers were pulled all the way up to his chest and held there with suspenders; and he wore a very large, floridly printed tie. He was a jolly, fun-loving man, who loved good stories and jokes, food and drink, and the ladies: a *bon vivant, raconteur,* and *rigoleur* rolled into one. He held a minor civil service position in Brussels, from which he was now retired. He was a gifted amateur photographer, who had taken many outstanding artistic photos of Michel and the objects of his theater and salon. He was also an adroit practitioner of some of the more underground activities in Belgian community life. During World War II and the German Occupation, for example, he used both his photographic and forgery skills to produce false identity cards for endangered citizens, among them many Brussels Jews. He was not an educated man, but both Jeanne and Michel always considered him to be very intelligent, with a great deal of unused and, to some extent, misdirected talent. When I had heard them talk about Gérard in the past, they implied that what they regarded as the narrow, rather vacuous way in which he lived was largely attributable to Josette.

Josette was a "very proper woman," to use Jeanne's phrase, with perfectly set, graying hair, a rather doll-like pretty face, and an ample, tightly corseted, Rubensian body. She spoke in a singsong voice, with a thick Brussels accent like that of her husband. Jeanne said she was a compulsive housekeeper who spent hours every day dusting and mopping. She doted on Poupée, the little white fluff of a dog she and Gérard owned, whom she dressed up each day with a different colored ribbon.

Gérard and Josette's visit took place in the framework of an established routine. Josette unfolded a special cover that she had brought with her, spread it out on Jeanne's bed, and placed Poupée on it. The dog curled up comfortably and promptly went to sleep. Gérard and Josette chatted with Jeanne and me, watched some television, and, at an appointed time, unwrapped the cold cuts and sandwich supper that they had brought with them, and ate it on the kitchen table, while Poupée lapped up milk from a dish and nibbled on bits of chocolate. At about 10:00 P.M. they packed up all their belongings and their little dog and bid an affectionate farewell to Jeanne and me.

My visit with Jeanne did not end until very late in the evening. She was not accustomed to sleeping much during the night, because that is when Michel did most of his writing. We continued to converse, and I moved about the house with her as she made her rounds to put things back in their proper places and to touch some of the objects. For the first time I touched them, too, patting Borax's head and daring to shake the hand of the Gentleman-Devil puppet as if he were an old friend.

We called for a taxi. As Jeanne and I stood together in the doorway of 71, rue Lefrancq, waiting for the cab to come down the empty, silent street, both of us smelled roses.

Return to Rue Lefrancq: July 30, 1987

I am leaving Belgium the day after tomorrow. During the brief interlude of sunshine that appeared this afternoon, I made my first trip to 71, rue Lefrancq in years, to the house in the Brussels commune of Schaarbeek where Michel and Jeanne de Ghelderode lived in 1961, when I first met them.

Riding in the taxi, into the Schaarbeek world that exists behind the peeling and battered basilica of the Eglise Sainte Marie, I felt the same stirrings that I experienced when Michel and Jeanne were alive and I was approaching their house for a visit. Since that time, Schaarbeek has become a district that is inhabited principally by North Africans. I have been told that they tried, but did not succeed, in having the domed Eglise Sainte Marie converted into a mosque.

The streets were quiet at 3 o'clock in the afternoon. An occasional North African woman passed by, dressed in an ankle-length robe, her head covered in the Islamic way. A few children were playing summer games on the sidewalks. When I reached rue Lefrancq, it was totally devoid of people, and very still.

The windows of the Ghelderodes' ground-floor apartment were covered with green shutters, as they always were. And on the left side of the big green entrance door, attached to the faded brick wall, there is a white stone memorial plaque. "On April 1, 1962, Michel de Ghelderode died here," the plaque says in both French and Flemish. At the bottom, it reads, "*Les Amis de Michel de Ghelderode*" (The Friends of Michel de Ghelderode), exclusively in French. There is no mention of Jeanne.

On that momentarily sunny street, filled with the kind of light that Michel used to arrange for my visits, I sensed his presence. The carousel horses, the madonnas, the mannequins, the marionettes, the masks, the swords, the sea-shells, the walls of eloquent paintings, and the strange, secret garden might still be there, I felt, behind the green shutters. The enigmatic roses, too.

David B. Parsell (essay date 1997)

SOURCE: "The Renaissance Revisited," in *Michel de Ghelderode,* Twayne's World Authors on CD-ROM, 2000, pp. 1-33.

[*In the following essay, originally published in 1997, Parsell discusses Ghelderode's Renaissance and late-medieval themes in his plays.*]

Left to his own devices even as he remained nominally under contract to the declining VVT [Flemish Popular Theatre], Ghelderode returned in search of material to the time frame of his two previous "personal" efforts, *Christopher Columbus* and *Escurial.* Freed from any constraint of having to deliver a "message" the playwright's imagination actively sought, and readily found, in the late Middle Ages and early Renaissance a fertile source of archetypal characters and situations to represent the human "truths"—most of them negative or at least disquieting—that lie just beneath the surface of *Barabbas* and *Pantagleize.* Still young (in his early thirties), Ghelderode embarked on what appears to have been a near frenzy of creative activity. By the time his health began to fail in 1936-37, he would have turned out no fewer than five plays later recognized among his finest and most memorable—*Red Magic* (1931), *Lord Halewyn* (1934), *Miss Jairus* (1935), *Hop, Signor!* (1936), and *Chronicles of Hell* (1937), all set in the distant past, as was the remarkable "puppet" drama *Le Siège d'Ostende* (1933), regrettably not published until nearly 20 years after Ghelderode's death.

Also dating from this period but set in modern times is Ghelderode's impressive homage to Renaat Verheyen, *Sortie de l'acteur,* back-dated by the author to 1930 but actually composed, as Beyen has ascertained, between 1933 and 1935. Ironically, most of the plays dating from the 1930s would not be performed until at least 15 years later, by which time Ghelderode had, for all practical purposes, discontinued writing plays.

RED MAGIC

Among the first efforts normally assigned to the post-VVT period is *Red Magic,* written as early as 1931 but without the VVT in mind. One of Ghelderode's few plays of the period to be first performed during the 1930s (in Brussels in 1934 and in Paris during 1938), *Red Magic* confirmed the author's reputation for unorthodox and memorable drama, attracting the attention of those French actors and directors who would subsequently "remember" Ghelderode in the years after World War II. For many critics and observers, *Red Magic* remains among the most typical and

characteristic of Ghelderode's mature plays, both broadening and deepening the verbal and visual mastery present in *Escurial.*

Like the decrepit, half-mad monarch of *Escurial,* the main character of *Red Magic* is a late-medieval or early-Renaissance grotesque, in the present case an obese, obsessed miser known only as Hieronymus, the latin form of Jerome. In the course of a highly memorable opening scene consisting of a long soliloquy, Hieronymus takes inventory of his many possessions, including coins bearing both male and female likenesses. As he examines the coins he impulsively hatches a scheme to "breed" his "male" and "female" coins toward the procreation of innumerable shiny offspring. Hardly saner than the king of *Escurial,* Hieronymus, although not a ruler, is clearly a megalomaniac, seeking absolute power through absolute wealth. His ambition is to own the world, or at least all of the world that he knows, in order to maintain total control of his surroundings. Unlike other misers in literature as in life, Hieronymus has never, until now, sought to increase his wealth, preferring instead to savor its measure in an oft-repeated ritual of inventory. Indeed, what strikes him as most appealing about the "breeding" of his coins is that it offers him the prospect of return without investment.

Among his possessions Hieronymus counts also his wife and her clothes, a guard dog that saves money on food by eating its leash, and a ghost who presumably came with the house and helps to frighten off intruders. In time the spectator learns also that Hieronymus's wife, Sybilla, is still a virgin, Hieronymus having withheld himself from her as he has withheld his money from banks and bankers. In place of the child that Sybilla presumably wants, Hieronymus has given her a baby doll that, after all, costs nothing to feed. Last but by no means least, yet almost as an afterthought, Hieronymus counts among his possessions his immortal soul, which he has deliberately kept pure of the seven deadly sins, especially lust. Regarding the sin of avarice, Hieronymus prefers to describe himself as thrifty ("*économe*"). After all, he wonders aloud, who has ever seen a fat miser?

Oddly, Hieronymus has managed to grow fat without eating, as has the obnoxious monk who pays a daily call to remind Hieronymus of his mortality. When Sybilla rises from a sleepless night, interrupting her husband's inventory to tell him that she is hungry, he encourages her to feast with her eyes on the food depicted in his art collection, adding that he does not like fat women. Soon the Monk happens by on his morning rounds, and the two men trade insults regarding their shared, if unexplained, corpulence. Arguably, the Monk is Hieronymus's double as well as his antagonist, helping to bring about the miser's downfall.

Once he has crossed the threshold of reason by deciding to "breed" his money, Hieronymus easily falls prey to a scheme suggested to him by the local beggar, Romulus. Romulus, it seems, has a friend named Armador, an alchemist currently fleeing persecution for having transformed baser metals into gold. Again enchanted by the prospect of profit with little or no investment, Hieronymus agrees to shelter Armador under his roof, offering not only his basement as a laboratory but also his wife, as the virgin whose blood will be needed for Armador's experiments (hence the "Red Magic" of the play's title.)

By now, of course, the spectator has begun to suspect that Sybilla and Armador are already lovers, or would like to be, and that Romulus's outrageous suggestion is nothing more or less than a plot to bring the pair together under Hieronymus's roof and nose. Hieronymus, however, is so blinded by greed and the lust for power that he readily agrees, announcing, in a shorter soliloquy, his intention to "mend his ways"—in this case switching from virtue to vice—once he is assured of the absolute power that Armador's experiments promise to bring him: "What is happening to me? If it's a dream, it's stupendous, and I'm a dream better off. If it's real . . . then I shall be liberal, I shall live like a gentleman. I shall visit courtesans. The good time will have come, the end of hardship, fasting, calculation" (*SP,* 2: 13).

At the start of act 2 a full day has passed, and Hieronymus, his ear to the floor, anxiously awaits news of what is going on downstairs. In an extended soliloquy interrupted but not curtailed by dialogue with Romulus and with the Monk, Hieronymus begins to suspect, correctly, that he has been duped, even robbed, and threatens to kill Armador. Increasingly inflamed by imagination and resentment feeding off each other, Hieronymus ends by acting out the murder of Armador just as Armador himself arrives from the basement laboratory. Stagily outraged by the scene of his own death, Armador berates Hieronymus for his ingratitude. After all, he claims, his experiments have just made Hieronymus incredibly rich. Fawning, groveling, vainly trying to "eat" his words, Hieronymus curries favor with the alchemist, nearly bursting with delight when Armador hands over a sample of his "product," in fact a coin taken from Hieronymus's own coffers. Hieronymus is about to accuse Armador of counterfeiting when the latter sends him out to buy some wine, claiming that it is needed in the alchemical process.

During Hieronymus's brief absence, Armador is examining the miser's hoard when Sybilla appears, disheveled and clearly transformed by her night of love with Armador. Their conversation soon reveals that they are former childhood sweethearts. Reunited with Sybilla, Armador now proposes that they flee abroad with Hieronymus's stolen funds, operating a tavern and brothel in a port town until they are rich enough to retire to the countryside. Their conversation is soon cut short by the return of Hieronymus, now burdened with six flasks of wine. Armador quickly leaves, warning Sybilla to remain silent while he is out of the room. Faced with her husband's hated presence, Sybilla does even more than she has been told to do, credibly imitating a statue, or perhaps a member of the living dead. Hieronymus, increasingly outraged by Sybil-

la's refusal to answer his questions about Armador's experiments, denounces and strikes his wife, threatening to disrobe her in search of gold stains when Armador returns, bearing what appears—and sounds—to be a sack full of coins.

Breaking his long habit of abstinence, Hieronymus invites Armador to share the wine that he has just bought with the "sample" coin. Armador, feigning drunkenness, claims that he carries the alchemical formula on his person, together with a mystical black gem that confers and assures immortality. When Armador further feigns loss of consciousness, Hieronymus, increasingly intoxicated, predictably strips Armador of both document and jewel. When the Monk unexpectedly drops by, Hieronymus invites him to join in the celebration of a recent inheritance and announces his intention to leave all of his earthly possessions to the Church. After all, Hieronymus reasons, he has just obtained the gift of immortality, and the Church will have an eternity to wait. Unknown to Hieronymus, the Monk has been part of the scheme against him all along and can hardly wait for Hieronymus to succumb to his unaccustomed intake of wine.

Once Hieronymus has passed out, more or less on schedule, the Monk calls out to his three co-conspirators for help in heaving the miser's bulk atop the hoard inside his treasure chest, but only after they have substituted counterfeit coins for the real ones. Armador and Sybilla depart for another night of love before leaving town at dawn; the Monk departs too, leaving only the beggar Romulus to keep watch over the sleeping Hieronymus. Soon thereafter, the miser rouses briefly, raising the lid of his coffer as he revels in the tactile presence of his "gold" beneath him. As the curtain falls on act 2, Romulus laughs uproariously but silently, his presence unnoticed and unsuspected by the drunken miser as he recloses the lid of his trunk from inside.

At the start of the third and final act Hieronymus awakens and raises the lid of his coffer, indulging in another lengthy monologue as he prepares to reap the double benefits of immortality and absolute wealth. Hearing Sybilla's amorous shrieks and moans from below, he promises to begin his new "life" with a visit to prostitutes. Although he has told Sybilla that he detests obesity in women, he now vows to seek the fattest women he can find, the most "meat" for his money. Mistaking Romulus for the household haunt, Hieronymus exits quickly, whereupon Romulus summons his co-conspirators to discuss changes in their plan. Hieronymus's unexpected departure might well foil their scheme to have him arrested at dawn on charges of counterfeiting, after which they will divide the real gold into four equal portions and make good their escape. There is, however, no honor among thieves, and the Monk warns the lovers that Romulus is about to betray them in order to collect more than his share of the booty. Armador fatally stabs Romulus and hides his corpse in the coffer as the now-lascivious Monk follows Sybilla upstairs for an assignation tacitly approved by Armador.

Howling in anguish, fearing contagion and pursued by "enemies" both real and imagined, Hieronymus returns early from his "night of love." The experience has quickly turned disastrous, and he is now fleeing an angry brothel-keeper whom he paid with a coin instantly recognized as counterfeit. The Monk stumbles down from above, either drunk or (possibly) poisoned, just as the pimp and the law officers arrive all at once. Armador and Sybilla, disguising their voices as well as their faces, manage to slip down the back stairs before the officers find Romulus's body atop the counterfeit coins, charging Hieronymus with both crimes. (In a fit of pique, Hieronymus has stabbed the doll-child with a knife; the doll's presence at the scene suggests collusion with "dark forces," strengthening suspicion of his guilt.) As he is led away to certain condemnation and death, Hieronymus remains oddly detached from the experience, honestly believing himself to be immortal.

Inevitably compared to such legendary literary misers as Molière's Harpagon and Balzac's Grandet, Hieronymus nevertheless remains closer to symbol than to stereotype or archetype. Visibly and audibly approaching madness even as the play begins, never fully credible as can be discerned from his outrageous speeches, Hieronymus is memorable mainly for his almost palpable fear of the human condition, including both life and death. He is man in flight from himself, seeking in absolute power a refuge from the ravages wrought by the "seven deadly sins." Thus does Ghelderode, carefully avoiding the political "relevance" demanded by the VVT, manage still to question the maintenance of wealth for its own sake. As in his earliest effort, written in homage to Poe, Death still looks in at the window and takes what she (or he) can find. To be sure, Hieronymus, as he claims, is quite innocent of the charges leveled against him; still, it is hard to mourn his impending death. Having denied life in hopes of saving his own, he stands condemned in the eyes of both playwright and spectator as a member of the "living dead," outshone despite his eloquence by the vitality of Armador, Sybilla, and even the Monk.

Hieronymus's very real anguish, metaphysical more than "existential," continues to reach spectators and readers who find him hard to believe as a flesh-and-blood human being. Like Ghelderode, Hieronymus may well have been born onto the wrong planet, seeking a measure of security that, on planet Earth, is rarely to be found after birth. Threatened and eventually betrayed by the Monk, presumably God's earthly representative, Hieronymus proceeds toward the unknown, lulled, like many more credible mortals, into a false sense of security nourished by illusions held well into middle age.

Considered both as play and as document, **Red Magic** shows that Ghelderode had already learned much from his years with the VVT, even as he had disdained to watch over the production of his plays. The action of **Red Magic** is tightly condensed, well able to hold the attention of the average spectator. Only one stage set is needed, and there

are only six main characters, plus extras, to be cast. The character of Hieronymus, however, poses several real problems that are not easily surmounted. Hieronymus's soliloquies occupy nearly one-third of the text as printed; even those actors accustomed to playing Shakespeare's *Hamlet* in the title role would find it hard to maintain the breath and force, let alone the memory and command of lines, to play the role of Hieronymus as Ghelderode appears to have intended. Early productions of **Red Magic** tended to taper off toward the end for precisely that reason. In 1971 a production prepared for French television (not broadcast until 1973) was deliberately edited in "tapered" fashion, with the later soliloquies all but suppressed (see Beyen 1974, 61-62). Notwithstanding, **Red Magic** remains among Ghelderode's best-known and most frequently anthologized plays.

LE SIÈGE D'OSTENDE

Left to his own devices in his attic office, Ghelderode continued to write dramatic scripts at a prodigious rate in the early 1930s, with many scripts later deemed "disposable" by either the author or his critics. In 1933, however, he managed to turn out one true "masterpiece" which, however impossible to produce, began to attract favorable attention well before it appeared in print in 1980, nearly 20 years after Ghelderode's death. Initially planned and executed as homage to the Anglo-Belgian painter James Ensor (1860-1949), **Le Siège d'Ostende** (**The Siege of Ostend**), subtitled "A Military Epic for Marionettes," contains some of Ghelderode's most expressively poetic prose, together with some of his most memorable conceits.

Liberally "borrowed" from an episode in Flemish history, the plot and setting of **Le Siège d'Ostende** concern an invasion of the Flemish city by Spanish forces. Sir Jaime l'Ostendais, chosen to take charge of defending the city, is a supposed ancestor of James Ensor and is closely modeled on Ensor. Commanding the Spanish army based in Brussels (waggishly called "Brisselles" in the script) is one Duke Albert, whose duchess (*dussèche*) Isabella goads him on to victory by refusing to change her underwear (*chemyse*) until Ostend has been taken. Sexual and scatological humor abounds, as does biting satire of war, politics, nobility and the clergy. If performed, the action—divided into 19 scenes with nearly 50 characters—would last for approximately two hours. To Ghelderode's disappointment, the aging Ensor was less than honored by the "tribute" offered to him, and Ghelderode in time abandoned whatever further plans he might have had for the script. In retrospect, however, the writing of **Le Siège d'Ostende** seems to have served Ghelderode well in the development of his verbal and scenic talents—talents soon to be exercised again in such plays as **La Balade du grand macabre** (**Death Takes a Stroll**; 1934) and **La Farce des ténébreux** (**The Farce of the Dark Band**; 1936).

LORD HALEWYN

During his years with the VVT Ghelderode had considered writing a stage version of the Halewijn (or Halewyn) legend, a Flemish folk tale similar in theme and content to that of Bluebeard. At the time, however, another, lesser-known playwright claimed priority rights to the material, and Ghelderode would not begin work on his own version until 1933, having proposed the play as a radio project several months earlier.

A superior example of early radio drama, **Lord Halewyn** recounts the life and death of the title character, a noble-man whose lust for nubile virgins inevitably results in murder. As in the original legend, Halewyn will meet his match in the young countess Purmelende, arguably the one woman who could truly satisfy him. Like Halewyn, Pur-melende is haunted by strange needs and voices. As she deliberately rides off in search of Halewyn, she fully expects to meet death as have seven young maidens before her. At the "moment of truth," however, Purmelende awakens as if from a trance and severs Halewyn's head from his body with the sword that he had planned to use on her. Welcomed as a heroine on returning to her father's castle, Purmelende pours out her tale of ecstasy and death, Halewyn's name on her lips as she in turn suddenly dies, her heart "broken" by an excess of emotion.

As befits a play written for radio performance, the action of **Lord Halewyn** is narrated rather than portrayed. The text, however, has proved sufficiently tempting to actors and directors that the play has been staged more than once, with predictably ambiguous results; the actors, indeed, have little more to do than stand in place reciting their lines, more monologue than dialogue. The tale, however, is extremely well retold by Ghelderode, for whom the intermingled themes of sex and death were becoming something of a trademark.

By 1934, when he completed the manuscript of **Lord Halewyn,** Ghelderode was already well-launched on two other projects that would soon come to fruition as **La Balade du grand macabre** and **Miss Jairus**. The former effort seems to have offered Ghelderode some measure of recreation and respite while he worked with the "Jairus" material that he claims to have been haunted by since childhood (see Beyen 1974, 58). Although Death figures prominently in both plays, the portrayal of Nekrozotar in **La Balade du grand macabre** allows for a lightness of touch and tone that is quite absent from Ghelderode's brooding exploration of death and dying in **Miss Jairus**.

La Baldade du grand macabre

Earlier in 1933, presumably inspired by figures portrayed on an old tapestry, Ghelderode had composed **Adrian et Jusémina,** a pastoral "diversion" resembling a ballet with dialogue. The title characters and soon to be lovers are shepherd and shepherdess. The names Adrian and Jusémina would be retained to designate the "archetypal" lovers in **La Balade du grand macabre,** although the characters are no longer presented as shepherds. Once again, however, Ghelderode has clearly drawn his inspiration from visual models. The setting of **La Balade du grand macabre** is

described as "Breugellande," with scenes clearly recalling Brueghel paintings. It is into this rural setting that the Grim Reaper, Nekrozotar, drops from a tree, initially mistaken for a corpse by the local drunkard, Porprenaz ("purple nose"), who has himself climbed a tree to spy on Adrian and Jusémina.

Brandishing a scythe, Nekrozotar proceeds to announce the end of the world, enclosing the young lovers in a tomb and refusing Porprenaz's offer of his own life as a symbolic sacrifice to spare the people of Breugellande. Mounted on the drunkard's back, Nekrozotar then goes about his business, seeking and finding examples of abuse that more than justify his attentions. In a rapid succession of tableaux, characters and spectators will meet the henpecked astrologer Videbolle ("empty-head"), forced to dress as a woman while his insatiable wife, Salivaine, quite literally wears the pants, smoking a pipe as well. They will also meet the portly, benign Prince Goulave of Breugellande, whose ministers bore him to distraction by advising him to govern badly.

Notwithstanding the acknowledged debt to Brueghel, **La Balade du grand macabre** derives also from **Le Siège d'Ostende,** as from Ghelderode's earlier experiments with puppet theater. Here, however, the scenes and characters are expressly conceived for performance by human actors rather than puppets, convincingly capturing the tone and spirit of such late-medieval farces as *Pierre Pathelin* and *The Tub/La Farce du cuvier.* The latter play, in particular, looms large over Ghelderode's portrayal of Videbolle's troubled life with the salivating Salivaine, who forces him to choose between making love and getting flogged. Vide-bolle, whose astrological researches have foretold the end of the world, can hardly wait for the event and, in fact, has often prayed for death in order to get away from his shrew of a wife. Salivaine in turn prays to Venus for satisfaction, complaining that her first husband was no bet-ter in bed than Videbolle.

When Porprenaz arrives at his friend Videbolle's house bearing Nekrozotar on his back, Videbolle welcomes them with open arms, quite ready to be the first to die. Not so, says Nekrozotar; he will be among the last, because he deserves to witness the "purification" process that is soon to follow. Salivaine, asleep and dreaming, continues to cry out for satisfaction. Nekrozotar, addressing her by name, seizes Salivaine in a vampirelike embrace and bites her shoulder until she faints. In time it will become clear that Nekrozotar is none other than the maligned first husband of Salivaine, who sent him off years ago in search of a mysterious "red herring."

During the action to follow, rich in movement and "stage business" but in fact very tightly constructed, Videbolle, Porprenaz, and Nekrozotar will proceed about the latter's mission; Prince Goulave, who at first hides under a table to avoid the Grim Reaper, looks on with increasing admira-tion as his principality is purged of its least savory inhabit-ants. As Goulave will observe, the people in question die not from Nekrozotar's actions but rather from their own fear of what is about to happen. Gluttons, for example, have choked on their food, and misers have swallowed their money in a vain attempt to take it with them. Salivaine, however, remains alive to face a settling of scores, as do the ministers Aspiquet and Basiliquet. After Salivaine, held in place by three old soldiers who have also been spared, has received a ritual flogging at the hands of Videbolle, the two ministers stand revealed as her lovers, taking turns for her dubious affections. It is in fact none other than Salivaine who is responsible for the repressive government forced on Goulave by Aspiquet and Basiliquet, who compete in trying to please her.

In a climactic scene anticipating the end of Ionesco's *Bald Soprano,* Salivaine and her two "lovers" will trade insults and accusations, taking the art of name-calling to new extremes. As order is restored to Breugellande, the three will be left alive as a negative example, kept in a cage to yell and scream at one another for all eternity, or at least for the foreseeable future. Nekrozotar, his mission accomplished, at last feels free to die. As Porprenaz and Videbolle prepare to bury him, the lovers Adrian and Jusémina emerge from the tomb very much alive yet totally unaware of what has been going on around them. The continuity of life in Breugellande is thus assured, the couple signifying renewal and fertility as Videbolle and Proprenaz join hands with Goulave, their newly liberated and enlightened monarch, to celebrate the future.

Delicately (and not always successfully) balanced between fantasy and farce, *La Balade du grand macabre* remained unperformed for nearly 20 years after its composition. Its "ideal" audience would seem to be one already familiar with the twists and turns of Ghelderode's theatrical expression. Even then, in 1953, the recurrent theme and conceit of the "red herring," often mentioned but never seen, continued to pose problems for actors, director, and potentially for spectators. According to Beyen (1974, 75), Ghelderode agreed to sharpen or develop the theme in a revised acting script but in fact never managed to do so. Critics, meanwhile, continued to ponder the symbol on the basis of textual references. For Nekrozotar, the "red herring," once compared to the Holy Spirit, represents the philosopher's quest for the ideal or the absolute. Salivaine, however, quite obviously sees the herring as a phallic symbol, the idealized fulfillment of her insatiable and tyrannical lusts. Such conflicting views of the mythical, even mystical, fish lie at the heart of the "battle of the sexes" embedded in the dialogue. Postwar reviewers, however, seem to have had relatively little difficulty making sense of such references. More than one critic, in 1953, saw *La Balade du grand macabre* as derivative of the connubial farce in the works of Aristophanes, and badly derivative at that.

Other critics, meanwhile, saw in *La Balade du grand macabre* a correction or revision of the negative view of politics espoused in *Barabbas* and in *Pantagleize.* Arguably, however, the setting of *La Balade du grand macabre*

is fantastic from the start, an imaginary land harking back, through Goulave's yearnings, to an even more fantastic state of almost prelapsarian perfection, without strife and, perhaps most important, without women. For Beyen (1974, 77), the triumphant, seemingly affirmative final scene of *La Balade du grand macabre* has less to do with brotherhood, as some critics have supposed, than with male bonding, as Porprenaz celebrates the newfound freedom of both Videbolle (from Salivaine) and Goulave (from his ministers). Seen from such a perspective, *La Balade du grand macabre* falls far short of contradicting Ghelderode's earlier views on society and politics. Quite to the contrary, the play emerges as a baroque parable on the intertwined fortunes of politics and sex, either one of which would suffice to render a harmonious society quite impossible indeed.

Women, seldom treated kindly in Ghelderode's dramatic universe, take perhaps their strongest beating—figuratively as well as literally—in *La Balade du grand macabre.* Salivaine, her ugliness underscored by her predilection for masculine dress and mannerisms, is further characterized as cruel and oversexed. If the various images throughout the play are to be taken at face value, Salivaine's sex drive has ruined not only the lives of both of her husbands but also the peaceful society of Breugellande, thanks to her manipulation of the "statesmen" Aspiquet and Basiliquet. Significantly, Salivaine is treated throughout the play as a representative "daughter" of Eve, whose creation gave rise also to the invention of the rod and the whip. The only other female character portrayed is young Jusémina, whose coy words to Adrian hint at fickleness. For want of a better specimen of female humanity, Jusémina will simply have to suffice in order to assure the perpetuation of the human race.

Apart from the negative portrayal of women, a major problem with *La Balade du grand macabre* resides in the shifting role of Nekrozotar, who enters the action as a fearsome, other-worldly Grim Reaper figure only to leave it as yet another failed, henpecked "philosopher" who, sensing the approach of his death, has returned to his homeland on a final mission of "mercy." The resulting changes in tone remain hard to manage in performance, given the need for maintaining the rhythm of physical and verbal farce. Ideally, productions of *La Balade du grand macabre* should accentuate the visual and verbal "distractions" provided by the author, moving fast enough that spectators have little or no time to reflect on the more incongruous aspects of the plot.

Reduced to human scale, Nekrozotar memorably demonstrates the "human" side of death when his victims in fact die of fright, having feared life as much as they fear death. For Ghelderode, such a "demystification" of death helped to defer the more fearsome aspects of his next project, *Miss Jairus,* planned as early as 1929 but with roots reaching back into his earliest childhood. In the Interviews Ghelderode would recall hearing his mother tell of a girl nearly buried alive during the 1870s; although rescued from the grave, the girl would remain in a trancelike, other-worldly state until her actual physical death some years later. The premise of deferred death, recalling the biblical tales of Jairus's daughter and of Lazarus, had continued to grow and develop in Ghelderode's mind even as he seems to have procrastinated in committing his thoughts and feelings to paper. Finally, having "buried" Nekrozotar and temporarily exorcised his own demons, the still-young playwright began work on *Miss Jairus* during the fall of 1934, just one day after finishing *La Balade du grand macabre.*

MISS JAIRUS

Among the best-known and most frequently discussed of Ghelderode's plays, *Miss Jairus* is set during the late Middle Ages in the ancient city of Bruges. As their daughter Blandine lies on her deathbed, Jairus and his wife, otherwise unnamed, await the inevitable attended by such hangers-on as a witch, a doctor, a priest, professional mourners, and a cabinetmaker who boasts of his skill at constructing coffins. Jairus, ineffectual yet given to histrionics, searches in vain for the proper words and tone for such a crucial moment in his life. Also present, and greatly mistrusted by the other characters, is a mysterious *thaumaturge* (witch doctor) known only as Le Roux ("the redhead"), to whom Ghelderode has assigned, however incongrously, certain Christ-like attributes. Le Roux, it seems, has been summoned by Blandine's fiancé, Jacquelin, who, alone among those present, refuses to accept the fact of the young woman's impending death. In time Le Roux reluctantly agrees to work a miracle out of respect for Jacquelin's faith. He takes care, however, to warn both parents and fiancé that they will come to regret his action and, over time, to hate him for what he has done.

Resuscitated, Blandine awakens in a kind of trance, refusing Jacquelin's attentions and demanding to be left alone. Soon a strange, shrouded figure appears in the doorway to announce that he and Blandine will both die come springtime, some six months later. Dismissing Jacquelin from her presence, Blandine joins the stranger in an eerie, erotic dialogue mixing references to love, lust, and a common desire for death. The two are about to embrace when Jacquelin returns, brandishing a knife. Before long, however, he decides that both Blandine and the stranger are more dead than alive and leaves them alone. As the stranger makes good his escape, promising Blandine that they shall soon meet again, Blandine addresses him as Lazarus.

The fourth and final act of *Miss Jairus* takes place on Good Friday, as the people of Bruges prepare for the ritual execution of three "heretics," including Le Roux. Blandine, deceptively calm at first, breaks into a strangely disjointed monologue as soon as she is left alone. Her speech, anticipating Lucky's monologue in Beckett's *Waiting for Godot,* introduces the play's true climax. When the town crier arrives to announce the death of Lazarus, Blandine asks that her own name be added to the list; she then

proceeds to die, her last breath coinciding with that of Le Roux—who dies in the arms of the witch Mankabena, who may or may not be his mother. Jacquelin, returning to close Blandine's eyelids, appears to have undergone some kind of conversion experience and announces his imminent departure to spread the word. Blandine's parents, meanwhile, remain quite as bewildered as ever.

Among the more perplexing, if oddly fascinating, of Ghelderode's published plays, *Miss Jairus* would not be performed until 1949, amid the outbreak of Acute Ghelderoditis on the Paris stage. The play depended on an audience familiar with Ghelderode's work and its characteristic themes, but even such seasoned spectators were baffled by the mixture of sublime and grotesque elements, together with unexplained and seemingly gratuitous references to the New Testament. The three "paid mourners" in particular—three old women all named Marieke who carry onions to induce weeping and whose speech is a curious mixture of French, Dutch, and Latin—struck a discordant note with many observers, as did the ambiguous portrayal of Le Roux, seen by some as a parody of Christ. As with the first performances of *La Balade du grand macabre* some four years later, the irreducible Flemishness of Ghelderode's expression worked at cross-purposes with his total mastery of French poetic prose to keep Paris audiences at bay. Subsequent productions, both within and outside France, took liberties with Ghelderode's original instructions as to costumes and staging, usually in order to accentuate the "romantic appeal" of death embodied in Blandine and in Lazarus.

D'UN DIABLE QUI PRÊCHA MERVEILLES

Soon after completing *Miss Jairus* Ghelderode continued work on *Sortie de l'acteur,* begun as early as 1933 although back-dated to 1930, the date of Renaat Verheyen's early death. Late in 1935 he began work on a curious text to be known as *D'un diable qui prêcha merveilles* (*Of a Devil Who Preached Marvels*), designated, as was *Le Siège d'Ostende,* as a play for puppets. Roland Beyen is careful to point out, however, that by the mid-1930s the "puppet" designation had come to hold a somewhat different meaning for Ghelderode than it had during the 1920s when he actually rehearsed his scripts with marionettes. Beginning with *Le Siège d'Ostende,* the term had come to designate a kind of closet drama or reader's theater uniquely tailored to Ghelderode's own needs without regard for the specific demands of the stage. In the case of *D'un diable,* creative license permitted Ghelderode to invent approximately two dozen characters, involving them in one of his longest and most convoluted scripts.

Set in "Breugelmonde," the action of *D'un diable* recalls that of *La Balade du grand macabre* as well as *Miss Jairus* and *Le Siège d'Ostende.* The scene opens with the lamentations of the sorceress and beggar Fergerite, abandoned by her demon lover Capricant. The town of Breugelmonde, recalling both the Breugellande of *La Balade du grand macabre* and the Bruges of *Miss Jairus,* soon erupts into widespread panic as word travels that the Pope himself has sent an emissary to mend the people's ways. Corruption runs rampant, embodied in such colorful characters as the gluttonous, profane Bishop Bredemaag and the seductive Abbess Didyme, who is about to compound the sin of fornication by attempting an abortion.

Most of the action to follow, divided into three acts, revolves around a case of mistaken identity: Capricant, egged on by his former mistress, Fergerite, impersonates the dreaded monk Bashuiljus, preaching a "sermon" that, in effect, exhorts the townsfolk to remain just as they are.

The Pope, he claims, has been misinformed of their activities by inhabitants of rival villages envious of Breugelmonde's prosperity. When the real Bashuiljus at last appears, Capricant gains his confidence by passing himself off as Breugelmonde's purest and most virtuous soul. At the end of the play Capricant has persuaded the monk to leave with him for Rome, where both will be canonized. Life in Breugelmonde will continue just as before, while Capricant will in fact lead the unsuspecting Bashuiljus off to Hell, where he presumably belongs.

Despite rich lyrical and scenic possibilities similar to those of other Ghelderode plays written around the same time, *D'un diable qui prêcha merveilles* remains more often read than performed, notable mainly for its elaboration of Ghelderode's characteristic themes. As in *La Balade du grand macabre,* the intrusion of an other-worldly character serves to reaffirm, albeit in a warped way, the lusty joys of living. The late-medieval setting, meanwhile, provides just enough exoticism to blunt the sharpest edges of Ghelderode's anticlerical satire. Still, the liberal use of long-winded speeches—Capricant's bogus "sermon," for example, occupies the entire second act—tends to work against the text's playability.

LE FARCE DES TÉNÉBREUX

Ghelderode's subsequent effort, *La Farce des ténébreux (The Farce of the Dark Band)* is written in much the same vein as its predecessor, denouncing hypocrisy and exhorting the lusty enjoyment of life's transitory pleasures. For once, however, Ghelderode's characteristic anticlericalism is all but absent. He was saving his next full assault on the clergy for *Chronicles of Hell,* to be written the following year. Reminiscent of Baudelaire's prose poem "Laquelle est la vraie?" ("Which One Is for Real?"). The play opens with the monumental grief of one Fernand d'Abcaude, pining away after the sudden death of his fiancée, Azurine. Fernand's servants, including the physician Mops, have tired of their employer's sense of gloom and doom and will stop at nothing to lighten his mood.

With the help of a friend, the actress Emmanuèle, the servants stage an apparition of Azurine's ghostly remains, after which "Azurine" presents Fernand with her maggot-covered heart as a memento. Fernand, deep as ever in despair, fails to get the message, whereupon the conspirators, now including Emmanuèle, proceed to hatch an even bolder scheme. The play's second act takes place in the local bordello, where a most reluctant Fernand has been invited to attend a perverse "memorial service" for one Putrégina, "queen of whores." The other guests, first seen wearing masks, are the "dark band" of the play's title, a "brotherhood" of Putrégina's former customers that includes some of the town's most prominent inhabitants. As the service proceeds, the late prostitute's clothing and other relics are displayed for veneration. It is left to Fernand to unveil the dead woman's statue and thus to discover the true identity of his beloved Azurine. Emmanuèle comes quickly to the rescue, inviting the thunderstruck Fernand to dance with her as the curtain falls.

The third act of *La Farce des ténébreux* takes place, as did the first, in Fernand's room, where the valet Ludion will in time explain to Fernand that what he has recently experienced was no nightmare, but the truth. Pressed for details, Ludion will recall numerous instances of Azurine's lascivity, willfully inviting punishment from his master as he explains that all women are alike and that Fernand would no doubt have been cuckolded in marriage. Left to his own devices, Fernand repeatedly stabs the full-length portrait of Azurine that he has kept in her memory. When Emmanuèle returns, again playing the role of the shrouded Azurine, Fernand continues his interrogation, in time asking the young woman her true identity and profession. When Fernand recoils in horror at the presence of an actress in his house—at a time when actors are deemed unworthy of the sacraments or of Christian burial—Emmanuèle further admits to being a prostitute as well, with Azurine/Putrégina as her role model.

Faced with Fernand's indignation, Emmanuèle is about to leave when Fernand calls her back for further questioning: Why did she play the role of the dead Azurine? For the money, she replies, but also to cure Fernand of his disease, virginity. Patiently, she explains to an astonished Fernand that his rectitude has made him a laughingstock of the community, and that his honor depends on proof of his virility. In a reversal of traditional roles, Emmanuèle then drags a protesting Fernand offstage, presumably into an alcove where she proceeds to undress and seduce him, to the great delight of his entourage. *La Farce des ténébreux* thus comes to an end on a somewhat more disquieting note than Ghelderode seems to have intended. Perhaps, as certain of his critics suggest, Ghelderode unwittingly projected onto his main character some of his own anxieties about women, sex, and death. In any case, his portrayal of the grieving Fernand is shot through with ambiguities that tend to work against the mourner's ribald "liberation" in the final scene.

As developed throughout the action of *La Farce des ténébreux,* Fernand d'Abcaude is simply too complex a character to be set free from his inhibitions (or are they moral convictions?) in the manner described. The "pillars of the community" who comprise the "dark band" may well be hypocrites, but Fernand himself is not. As presented and developed, Fernand is either a pious man of principle or a case of arrested development. Perhaps, indeed, he is both at once—a dreamer truly obsessed with an ideal of purity equally binding on himself and on the woman he loves. His "liberation" therefore strikes something of a false note, as if Fernand were being punished for his chastity with what amounts to an act of rape.

Owing no doubt to ambiguities in the portrayal of Fernand, *La Farce des ténébreux* was among the last of Ghelderode's efforts to be staged during the "epidemic" of Acute Ghelderoditis in Paris. Jean-Louis Barrault, seldom daunted by the difficulties of a dramatic text, nonetheless abandoned plans to mount the play during the 1950-51 season at the Théâtre Marigny, having already had sets built and posters printed. The sets, constructed by Félix Labisse, were finally used in November 1952 when Georges Vitaly staged the play at the Grand Guignol, taking considerable liberties with the text in order to render it playable as comedy. Even so, the production was less than a rousing success, and nearly two decades would pass before a second attempt at production, in Brussels in 1970.

By 1936 Ghelderode's health was beginning to fail him, which may or may not help to account for the increasingly morbid concerns to be found in his plays of the period. True, the mingled themes of sex and death had characterized most of his plays from *Red Magic* onward; still, the paralyzing scruples—or inhibitions—of Fernand in *La Farce des ténébreux* sound a new, discomfiting note in Ghelderode's dramatic canon. Despite the author's avowed intentions, there is little or nothing to celebrate in Fernand's eventual "destiny." The affirmative spirit that came to Ghelderode's rescue in such efforts as *La Balade du grand macabre* somehow appears to have deserted him, replaced by strong intimations of mortality, sterility, and man's—or, more frequently, woman's—inhumanity to man.

Hop, Signor!

Soon after completing *La Farce des ténébreux* in July 1936, Ghelderode turned his attention to a project first outlined some 18 months earlier and loosely based, like *Lord Halewyn,* on folklore. The result, known even in translation as *Hop, Signor!,* would in time become one of the author's most notorious and frequently reprinted plays, even as the themes and tone expressed would, as in the case of *La Farce des ténébreux,* assure relatively few productions, at least in France.

Having attempted a comic treatment of lust and inhibition in *La Farce des ténébreux,* Ghelderode in *Hop, Signor!* would revisit the same themes in a tone rather delicately balanced between tragedy and melodrama yet partaking of the scenic vigor associated with *Red Magic.* If the earlier play, at least in intent, constituted an attack on hypocrisy, *Hop, Signor!* goes even deeper into perceived human

nature to show the basic incompatibility of the sexes—a perennial problem to which death would appear the only possible solution.

Based on the well-documented medieval punishment (or torture) of tossing an offender in a blanket or tarpaulin to break his bones—a tradition recalled down to the present day in the children's game known in Dutch as *Opsignoorke* and played with a doll—*Hop, Signor!* centers on the troubled career and marriage of the sculptor Juréal, deformed and aging, who hides his insecurities beneath a superficial arrogance that has earned him the sobriquet of Signor, or "milord." In constructing the play Ghelderode borrowed from yet another folkloric/historical source to present as Juréal's wife one Marguerite Harstein, executed for witchcraft during the sixteenth century.

Unable either to adapt his art to changing tastes or to consummate his marriage to the alluring, demanding Marguerite, Juréal easily falls prey to the blandishments of Helgar and Adorno, two handsome young noblemen who curry favor with him in hopes of getting closer to his wife. Marguerite, while expressing nothing but contempt for her husband and ridiculing his attempts to practice the manly art of fencing, keeps her two admirers at bay by playing them off against each other. As will soon become clear, Marguerite's inhibitions, similar to those of Purmelende in *Lord Halewyn,* are hardly less severe than those of her unfortunate spouse. Notwithstanding, her speech and actions exude a strong sexuality that helps to precipitate the play's dramatic, even tragic, action.

When Juréal, as proud as he is insecure, invites Marguerite to accompany him to a public procession in order to keep up appearances or at least to save face, Marguerite brutally informs him that there are no appearances to be kept up and no face to save. Everyone knows that he is virile only in his arms, she says, and only for the humble craft of carving tombstones. If only she were so inclined, she adds, she would already have betrayed him many times over. His pride mortally wounded, Juréal flies into an impotent rage, heaving an enormous carved stone that nearly hits and kills the monk Dom Pilar, who has been spying on him for Helgar and Adorno.

Close kin to the monk in *Red Magic,* as to the corrupt clergy in the forthcoming *Chronicles of Hell,* Dom Pilar plays both ends against the middle by arousing Juréal's jealous anger and then attempting, unsuccessfully, to receive Marguerite's confession. Juréal, meanwhile, alerted by the two dwarfs who work for him that the play being performed in the public square has to do with cuckoldry, takes the matter personally and goes off to avenge his honor, brandishing a sword. The focus then shifts to a curious scene between Marguerite and the executioner Larose, alternately described as strongly built, athletic, and catlike, who chews on an eponymous rose stem as others might chew on a blade of grass. Their dialogue and interaction is intensely sensual, even as both parties profess their chastity. Oddly uninhibited in the presence of Larose,

Marguerite admits to a kind of ecstasy when she watches his public beheadings, to which Larose evasively replies that many women become pregnant after watching him at work.

Soon thereafter curious sounds and silences announce the agony and death of Juréal, who has been tossed in a blanket and then dropped fatally to the ground when someone let go of the blanket. Marguerite, a less-than-bereaved widow, refuses to sign the cross on her late husband's forehead when Dom Pilar bids her to do so. She also asks that the corpse continue to be tossed in the air as it is carried out of town. Unable to attract Larose, who has conveniently made himself scarce, Marguerite then summons her two noble admirers, provocatively offering herself to the one who will claim greater responsibility for her husband's death.

As Marguerite leaves to wait in her room for her "deliverer," the two noblemen—identified by Dom Pilar as foreign spies—draw swords as they vie for the honor just offered to them by Juréal's widow. Adorno wins the duel and flees, leaving the dying Helgar to be comforted by Marguerite who, promising to love him "for the rest of his life," offers to close his mortal wound with her lips. Dom Pilar then emerges from yet another hiding place. Marguerite, covered in Helgar's blood, beside herself with anger and desire, presents one bare breast to the astonished Dom Pilar, offering to stuff it down his throat as she gives herself to the most monstrous bidder—himself. Pilar, unwillingly seized by lust, denounces Marguerite as possessed by the Devil, murmuring the *Agnus Dei* as he slips from her embrace onto the ground, covering his face. Marguerite is still trying to seduce the monk when the dwarfs reappear, closely followed by the executioner Larose.

In the sudden presence of Larose, Marguerite falls into a kind of stupor from which she will not awaken even when denounced by townsfolk and authorities for the violent deaths of Juréal and Helgar. Larose then leads her off to the only "consummation" in which either of them might find satisfaction, leaving the last words to the two dwarfs, Mèche ("Wick") and Suif ("Tallow") whose antics opened the play. Mocking the theater itself, Tallow observes that it is not only on the stage where several people die in one day. When Wick asks him if it is right to mourn a dead man, Tallow replies that it would be better to mourn him at birth, on his entry into this miserable world. The play then ends with the two dwarfs, ugly and deformed like their late master, tossing in a blanket a broken puppet dressed in Juréal's clothes, chanting "Hop, Signor!" as the puppet rises and falls.

Rich in sight and sound, *Hop, Signor!* as written is every bit as arresting as *Red Magic* and even more tightly constructed, hardly longer than the traditional one-act play. Having uncharacteristically indulged himself in prolixity and verbosity with such efforts as *La Balade du grand macabre* and *La Farce des ténébreux*, Ghelderode in *Hop, Signor!* returned to the procedure first used to advantage

in *Escurial,* allowing theme and subject matter to determine length and form instead of tailoring both to fit the perceived demands of traditional drama. The result is extremely stageworthy. If *Hop, Signor!* is less frequently performed than *Escurial* or *Red Magic,* this has less to do with its construction than with the audacity of its themes and the negations implied in its conclusion. It is likely, too, that many would-be directors or performers have shied away from the text because of what it seems to reveal about the author.

As Beyen observes, seldom did Ghelderode write himself into a text so visibly as he did in preparing and developing the character of Juréal, a sexual and social misfit whose art is anchored in the past and hopelessly out of touch with the prevailing taste. Denied the contrived, implausibly "happy" fate reserved for Fernand d'Abcaude, Juréal can only fall victim to an implacably hostile universe made even more hostile by the presence of his fellow mortals. Citing a letter written at the time by Ghelderode to a friend, the engraver Jac Boonen, Beyen shows that Ghelderode sought in *Hop, Signor!* to show the cruelty of man that religions have not only been unable to correct but have in fact tended to cultivate (Beyen 1974, 103).

Dom Pilar, to be sure, does considerably more harm than good, as do most clerics in Ghelderode's dramatic canon. He is, however, only a part of the problem so graphically set forth in *Hop, Signor!* Cruelty, it would seem, is embedded in the nature of the sexes, doomed to incompatibility by conflicting needs and demands. In Marguerite Harstein Ghelderode has managed to combine elements of Purmelende, Salivaine, and the charming but two-faced Azurine/Putrégina to provide his most disquieting, even unnerving, portrait of woman. Undeniably attractive, as Salivaine surely is not, Marguerite denounces Juréal for his impotence even as she proclaims her own disinclination toward extramarital affairs, and her continued "baiting" of the two young noblemen ends, not surprisingly, in Helgar's death. No man, it seems, can provide the ecstasy toward which her sexuality tends—a longing that can be satisfied only in her death at the hands of the equally "virginal" Larose, who bears, moreover, a feminine name.

Although infrequently staged since its first production (in French) in Brussels in 1942, *Hop, Signor!* remains among the most frequently read and discussed of all of Ghelderode's plays, notable, like *Escurial,* for its efficiency and economy of expression. Such autobiographical (or autopsychological) overtones as there may be are quite literally upstaged by the utter bleakness of the play's apparent "message," as by the author's scathing portrayal of the possible interactions among life, death, sex and art.

CHRONICLES OF HELL

Once he had, in a sense, dramatized his nagging distrust of women and, indeed, of the reproductive process itself, Ghelderode returned with a vengeance to yet another of his bêtes noires with *Chronicles of Hell,* in which all of the male characters are members of the Roman Catholic clergy. If, as his written statement to Jac Boonen implies, Ghelderode saw religion as fostering mankind's innate cruelty, he arguably set out to prove as much in his evocation of riot and celebration surrounding the death of a bishop murdered with a poisoned communion wafer.

Although dated 1929 in the Gallimard edition of Ghelderode's collected plays, *Chronicles of Hell* would appear, in Beyen's chronology, to have been composed, for the most part, during the fall of 1936 and the fall of 1937. While Ghelderode might well have framed or outlined the play's basic premise toward the end of the preceding decade, his technique and style tend to support, in Beyen's view, the documentary evidence favoring the later date (Beyen 1974, 104).

Chronicles of Hell begins in Flanders with an unseen crowd of worshipers clamoring to view the remains of the just-deceased Bishop Jan in Eremo of Lapideopolis, whom they revere as a saint. The bishop's fellow clergymen, meanwhile, indulge themselves in food and drink to celebrate their liberation from the bishop's strict rule. Six riotous scenes bordering on farce precede the arrival of the allusively named Sodomati, secretary to the papal nuncio. In Sodomati's presence, the auxiliary bishop, Simon Laquedeem, identified as a converted Jew, begins to eulogize the deceased cleric's life and career. Suddenly, amid thunder and lightning, Jan in Eremo rises from his deathbed brandishing his episcopal staff. All the clerics flee except for Laquedeem, who attacks the "dead man" with an ax. A brief struggle finds the ax in the hands of Bishop Jan, who is about to strike back when he "freezes" as if entranced, having recognized the aged servant Véneranda as his mother.

The bishop then tries to speak but cannot produce audible sound. When he points toward his throat, the old woman orders him to his knees and pulls from his throat a foreign object that turns out to be the poisoned Host. Faced with her son's abiding anger, Véneranda further orders him to pardon those who have sinned against him if he expects to be pardoned himself, then slaps him across the face when he is slow to respond, exhorting him to obey his mother. A dutiful son once more, the septuagenarian bishop, no doubt already dead, unclenches his fist to form the upraised palm of benediction. Véneranda then helps him back to his deathbed, where he can die in peace, the fact of his murder having been revealed.

Sure at last that his arch-enemy is dead, Simon Laquedeem, who administered the poison, takes back the wafer from the hands of Sodomati and, announcing Communion, force-feeds it to Véneranda, who predictably falls dead not long thereafter. Once the bishop's body has been removed by a team of "athletic" butchers, the clergymen once again celebrate their deliverance. Since all have eaten and drunk at least their fill, the "celebration" soon degenerates into a paroxysm of scatology, with the priests sniffing each other's backsides like dogs as they indulge in flatulence

and defecation. In the final scene Laquedeem squats suggestively before the audience, a fiendish smile on his "rabbinical" face as the curtain falls.

Although devoid of the sexual references that permeate *Hop, Signor!* and *La Farce des ténébreux, Chronicles of Hell* proved soon after its initial performances in 1949 to be Ghelderode's most controversial play, at least in France, defying not only good taste but also the ingrained Gallic sense of logic. Even in a country inured to anticlerical sentiment, Ghelderode's all-out attack on the clergy seemed gratuitous at best, offensive at worst, with strong overtones of anti-Semitism in the author's portrayal of Laquedeem, whose name recalls that often assigned to the Wandering Jew of legend (see Blancart-Cassou, 163). Still, the verbal and visual qualities of *Chronicles of Hell* would bring Acute Ghelderoditis to its height on the Parisian stage, assuring a ready, if temporary, audience for a number of Ghelderode's earlier work.

For Jacqueline Blancart-Cassou, *Chronicles of Hell* embodies a type of "solitary laughter" characteristic to Ghelderode's final phase, a grating laughter on the author's part that, by its nature, defies audience participation (168). It is clear in any case that Ghelderode by 1937 was writing increasingly "for himself," perhaps to exorcise his private demons. As in the case of *Hop, Signor!,* it is frequently difficult for an audience to share in the author's projected vision. Indeed, as Beyen has demonstrated, Ghelderode in the late 1930s feared the decline of his dramatic talents along with his health. On the evidence, he doubtless had cause for concern on both counts. Turning increasingly toward composition of the genre fiction to be collected in *Sortilèges,* Ghelderode would complete no more than three plays prior to being "discovered" by the French avant-garde soon after World War II, and only one play thereafter.

Late in 1937, after finishing *Chronicles of Hell,* Ghelderode returned to the general theme of a 1935 radio play to create *La Pie sur le gibet* (*Magpie on the Gallows*), portraying the arrest and execution of the legendary trickster Tyl Eulenspiegel against the background of an eponymous painting by Brueghel the Elder. *L'Ecole des bouffons* (*School for Jesters*) was outlined as early as 1937 but not actually written until 1942, after publication of *Sortiléges. Le Soleil se couche* (*The Sun Sets*) recalls the last days of the Hapsburg Emperor Charles V in a manner reminiscent of *Escurial* yet lacking that play's tight construction. Ghelderode was quite literally "played out" by the time he became famous as a dramatist. Acute Ghelderoditis would, however, lead not only to the Ostend Interviews but also to the composition of what turned out to be his final play, *Marie la misérable.*

MARIE LA MISÉRABLE

During the summer of 1950 the newly rediscovered Ghelderode received a request from the Belgian community of Woluwé-Saint-Lambert to dramatize the legend of the local martyr Lenneke Mare, the spectacle to be staged outdoors, on the actual site, in June 1952 to commemorate the six-hundred-fiftieth anniversary of her death. Although ill and frail, Ghelderode found the legend quite to his liking and took no more than two days to decide in the affirmative. He would not, however, actually begin work on the script until the fall of 1951, after taping the Ostend Interviews.

As first performed—on schedule—during the summer of 1952, *Marie la misérable* puts the virtuous, virginal Marie La Cluse, in her early thirties and known also as Lenneke Mare, in apposition to the hot-blooded young nobleman Eglon d'Arken, several years her junior, whose unrequited longing for Marie turns gradually to hate. Marie, who devotes her life to the poor and infirm although she has not actually taken the veil, harbors few illusions about men and treats her would-be suitor with candid scorn. He is, she points out, both rich and idle, lacking only the opportunity to prove his manhood in battle. Repeatedly rejected, d'Arken is about to renounce his suit when his jester Rostenduvel ("Red Devil") resolves to avenge his master's honor by "framing" Marie for the theft of a golden goblet belonging to Jean II, duke of Brabant. In time, the young woman is falsely accused, tried, convicted and sentenced to death for the crime, further accused by Rostenduvel of practicing witchcraft. At Marie's execution Rostenduvel is thrown onto the pyre as well, only to be resuscitated in the third and final act, where he exhorts his master, ostracized by the townsfolk for his part in Marie's death, to commit suicide.

The priest Adam Gherys, who tried in vain to save Marie's life, intervenes to show d'Arken that Rostenduvel was no more than an hallucination. When the duke arrives on the scene, d'Arken begs his forgiveness, admitting that he conspired in Marie's death out of love turned to hate, to destroy what he could not have. Marie then appears in a vision shared by the duke and all the townsfolk, whereupon d'Arken dons the garb of a pilgrim and prepares to leave for Jerusalem and Rome, accompanied by the mysterious Marie Cantilie, who may or may not be Marie La Cluse's mother. The action then ends on a decidedly affirmative note recalling that of Carnival as the duke drinks from the once-lost golden vessel, exhorting his loyal subjects to join him in commemorating Marie's exemplary life and sacrifice.

Among the longest—and wordiest—of Ghelderode's plays, *Marie la misérable,* although included in the Gallimard edition of his plays, is suitable for production only on the premises for which it was intended, and where it has indeed frequently been revived. In Beyen's view, however, it is markedly superior in verbal and scenic quality to the average run of historical pageants and "sound and light" spectacles commonly performed across Europe (1974, 117). Despite the necessarily archaic setting and tone, Ghelderode has managed to create vivid, credible characters who elicit and sustain the spectator's interest. Given

the exemplary nature of the legend, the "message" of *Marie la misérable* is rather more affirmative than those to be deduced from Ghelderode's last plays of the 1930s, in particular, *Hop, Signor!* and *Chronicles of Hell.* Unlike Marguerite Harstein, whose virginity masks a perverted lust, Marie La Cluse is presented as a prototypical saint who dies so that Eglon d'Arken and the other townsfolk might be saved. Unlike Bishop Jan in Eremo, she is thus shown not to have died in vain.

Ghelderode's ingrained pessimism might well have been held in check by the promise of a check. *Marie la misérable* was, after all, prepared in response to a commission, and the spectacle was meant to be somewhat uplifting. It would be misleading, however, to infer that Ghelderode here perjured himself as he refused to do for the VVT, when dealing with Barabbas or Saint Francis of Assisi. As in his earlier plays, the forces of evil are quite evident and credible. Indeed, it is hard to imagine another author bringing the material to life as convincingly as does Ghelderode. The effort, however, seems to have dealt a final blow to his creative energies even as it rekindled his interest in playwriting. Although new dramatic projects would be announced following the generally favorable reception of *Marie la misérable,* none would be completed.

Ghelderode's "return" to the late Middle Ages and early Renaissance in search of material appears to have assured his place in literary and dramatic history. Had his evolution as a dramatist stopped with his association with the VVT, Ghelderode might well be remembered—if at all— among the few expressionists who wrote in French, with the truly ground-breaking *Escurial* either overlooked or forgotten. By digging deeper into the vein that had produced *Escurial,* Ghelderode during the 1930s developed a singular dramatic voice and style that would resist assimilation into any school or movement, even as Acute Ghelderoditis helped to create a climate favorable to the reception of such Absurdist playwrights as Beckett, Ionesco, and the early Adamov. By the time Acute Ghelderoditis had run its course in the mid-1950s, the best of Ghelderode's plays, including *Red Magic, La Balade du grand macabre,* and *Escurial,* had passed into the worldwide dramatic repertory.

Ghelderode, working on his own and for himself, might well have returned to the medieval and renaissance period in search of private demons to exorcise. If so, it might also be argued that the demons finally got the better of him, particularly in *Hop, Signor!* and *Chronicles of Hell.* Although the language and style are forceful, Ghelderode's authorial voice in those two plays veers away from the universal toward the particular and even the personal, making it hard for the spectator or even the actor to take part in the experience portrayed. The universality of his earlier plays, however, continues to assure his place in the international dramatic canon.

THE DEATH OF DOCTOR FAUST

CRITICAL COMMENTARY

Douglas Cole (essay date 1966)

SOURCE: "Faust and Anti-Faust in Modern Drama," in *Drama Survey,* Vol. 5, No. 1, Spring, 1966, pp. 39-52.

[*In the following essay, Cole discusses* The Death of Doctor Faust *as a modernist interpretation of the Faust myth.*]

Damned or redeemed, tragical or travestied, noble, foolish, or darkly sinister, Faust has been a recurrent figure in European drama for nearly four centuries. Marlowe's tragic hero of the Elizabethan age, though transformed into a vehicle for burlesque and pantomime farce in the eighteenth century, was reincarnated with new grandeur by the life-long work of Goethe, who more than any other artist is responsible for endowing Faust with mythic proportions. Goethe's *Faust* has become the paradigm for the Faustian legend: it has managed to overshadow the dozens of imitations, continuations, and alterations that accompany it in the history of dramatic literature. But a mythic figure so closely tied to the intellectual history of Western man cannot rest in any one embodiment, no matter how impressive. Twentieth-century dramatists, whose recreations of the Greek myths are familiar enough, have also turned to Faust, forming him perhaps in their own image, but certainly in the image of our time. Three of them—Michel de Ghelderode, Paul Valéry, and Lawrence Durrell—have given us plays about Faust that are totally different in plot and atmosphere; but their conceptions of the tragic issues inherent in the Faustian character converge in striking ways to reveal a common central concern: Faust no longer strives for the absolute; he struggles to find himself, a self that is curiously at odds with the traditional Faustian personality.

Ghelderode's **The Death of Doctor Faust** (1925), though the earliest written of the three plays, is in some ways the most "modern." In theme it suggests the restless probing for self-identity so characteristic of the plays of Pirandello, who was then at the height of his success. In technique it reflects the militant anti-realism of the French *avant-garde* theatre. Calculated incongruities of time, space, and mood are immediately evident in the play's subtitle—*A Tragedy for the Music Hall*—and in its basic setting: "a city of the past and of the future in Flanders: in the sixteenth and twentieth centuries simultaneously."[1] Doctor Faust in his lofty and gloomy chamber belongs to the earlier age, but outside the window and around the house are the signs and sounds of a modern and garish city in carnival time. Within this deliberately anachronistic setting Ghelderode presents a Faust who undergoes an equally anachronistic experience. In his study he reveals himself as the familiar disillusioned and weary man of learning, who, in his own terms, has remembered everything but has a thorough knowledge of nothing. Oppressed by solitude, by an outside world he calls "dark, dirty, and vulgar," oppressed as well by the desire of the absolute ("this perpetual, sublime, and puerile drivel of the soul"), he sees himself as nothing, and even worse, as an actor playing a role. Ghelderode's stage direction underlines the basic incongruity of Faust's mental state: "Faust declaims and exaggerates all his gestures. His voice is forced. He is to appear to the spectator as a clown to whom a tragedian's role has been entrusted."

Seeking diversion rather than the devil, Faust rushes out to the fair, and we next see him in the twentieth-century carnival world, pursuing a naive, thrill-seeking servant girl costumed as Marguerite. In the tavern where they meet, two actors and an actress are performing a watered-down version of Goethe's *Faust,* which is ultimately broken up by the interruptions of Ghelderode's devil, a smooth-talking, wonder-working observer of the human scene dressed in an old red costume, a sword, and a bowler hat, and furnished with the improbable name of Diamotoruscant. In the carnival atmosphere, of course, everyone thinks he is an actor, and hence we are involved with a very complicated set of doubles: a sixteenth-century Faust who desperately wants to be a real person rather than a man playing a part, a twentieth-century actor playing Faust; two modern Marguerites—one a servant girl in costume, the other an actress in costume; and two devils: one an actor and the other a real one thought to be an actor. The Pirandello-like confusion of reality with illusion increases as the play goes on. Faust takes the servant girl to a cheap hotel, outside of which Diamotoruscant talks with a movie-theater barker advertising a melodramatic love-story, "the romance of everlasting illusion." The film is over at about the time that Faust, finished with his experience of common life, is trying to get rid of the distraught servant. The hysterical girl cries out to the theater crowd that she has been violated, and the mob is prevented from taking vengeance on Faust only by the wit of Diamotoruscant, who deludes them into thinking that the whole episode is only an advertisement for the local tavern production of *Faust.*

In the final episode, the tavern players are in flight before the populace, who seek to bring Faust to justice after the servant girl has committed suicide by throwing herself under a trolley. The actor Faust and the actress Marguerite seek shelter in what happens to be the sixteenth-century home of Faust, and are joined by the real Faust and Diamotoruscant shortly after. The confusion comes to a chaotic climax: the actor Faust rushes outside where he is executed by the crowd; the real Faust, disgusted with the self he has discovered in his experience with Marguerite, and urged on by Diamotoruscant, shoots himself. Exit Diamotoruscant, muttering, "Imbecile! Imbecile! Imbecile!" Faust's servant, Cretinus, dances around his master's corpse, struts in Faust's cloak, and hugs the actress Marguerite to him with lascivious laughter as the orchestra plays a frenzied funeral march.

Ghelderode's talent in mixing the tragic with the farcical is everywhere evident in this play. With his exploitation of improbabilities and irrationalities, his nightmarish combination of the clownish and the grotesque, his pervasive hints at the futility of knowledge and of experience, his exaggerated symbols of the impersonal quality of the modern world, it is no wonder that his name is now linked with the phenomenon of the theatre of the absurd. Certainly this Faust play is one of the most boldly experimental in dramaturgical terms: the actors are directed to perform like clowns or puppets, costumes are stylized in the manner of caricatures, a radio loudspeaker is strangled by the devil and utters a death speech, several scenes display simultaneous action and dialogue in two parts of the stage, the sensational headlines about the suicide of Marguerite are projected upon a movie screen before the vengeful crowd, and even the twenty-three pieces of the mangled girl's body are displayed before the curious populace. Why all this insane fantasy? The reasons are several.

One explanation lies with the reaction of the modern theatre against stale theatrical conventions. Ghelderode himself confesses to an early infatuation with the experimentalist novelties of the 1920's. And the 1926 publication of *The Death of Doctor Faust* was prefaced with remarks that allied it with the movement in France to purify the theatre by restoring to it the elements of spectacle, music, and fantasy which had been ignored by the conventions of the wellmade play and salon comedy. Ghelderode's name was linked with those of Jean Cocteau and Guillaume Apollinaire. Indeed, the musichall itself, with its variety acts of comic songs, acrobatics, conjuring, and dancing, was seen as a place where the basic elements of theatre were trying to assert their independence and vitality.

But there is more to Ghelderode's play than mere experiment with fresh dramaturgy. In changing the form of the Faust story, he makes it represent a new problem and a new world. From Goethe he borrows the basic plight of Faust in "Part One": dissatisfied with his knowledge and his respected stature, the doctor turns to new experience, and especially to the love of a simple girl. Goethe's Faust, despite his good intentions and nobler inclinations, becomes enmeshed in seduction and betrayal. So, too, Ghelderode's; but with an enormous difference in tone. For Ghelderode's Faust is a tragic clown, without the philosophic nobility of Goethe's, and indeed with a self-deflating antipathy for the principle that is the life-blood of the Goethian Faust: the desire of the absolute. Ghelderode's Faust is incredibly and pathetically naive. Driven, as he says, by "boredom, rain, stupidity, the need to be something else," he seeks the young Marguerite in a gesture of restless despair, and for a moment thinks he will experience a valued reality. But the twentieth-century context within which Faust enacts his adventure—a context of movies, taverns, cheap hotels, carnivals, sensationalistic journalism and advertising—serves as the immediate ironic contradiction to Faust's sentiments. The romantic Faust is

transported to a tawdry modern world where romance is offered only on the film screen. Ghelderode has transported Faust in time in order to exploit this irony, and also to suggest that Faust's futile adventure is a universal mistake endlessly repeated. The counterpointing of Faust's words to Marguerite in the hotel with the comments of Diamotoruscant and the movie barker is a vivid illustration:

> FAUST [*at the window*]. It is no longer raining! The clouds have vanished! Look at the stars appearing! You are trembling! It is the birth of spring! Let us be silent. Why are you blushing? Be free with yourself! One gets used to everything!

> THE BARKER [*sighing*]. My God, yes! [*He shouts.*] Walk up! The romance of everlasting illusion! The action takes place in a marvellous setting favorable to the blossoming of amorous feelings.

> FAUST. I am a sober, thoughtful man! And honorably known! You must not fear anything. Do not think of tomorrow. Life is so fleeting! You tell me I could be your father. How wrong you are! I have all my youth to consume. This is the first springtime of my life!

> THE BARKER. Come and see where unreasoned desire leads! This film will teach you that life is a constant recommencement, that lessons profit nothing, and that nothing happens but what must happen!

> FAUST. I feel you shivering, little rose! Is it from cold or love? Are you acquainted with love? I know nothing about it. But what does it matter? Being together is enough.

> MARGUERITE. How well you talk!

> DIAMOTORUSCANT [*comes forward and shouts toward the window*]. Look here! Will you soon be done?

> *The window is precipitately shut.*

> THE BARKER. Throbbing drama of sin and remorse! A film accessible to all intelligences. Walk up! [*To Diamotoruscant.*] The old fellow's not serious! You don't tell a woman tales like that.

The image of Faust is further degraded by his sudden renunciation of Marguerite. Afraid of scandal, suddenly fretful about his public reputation and honor, and, it would seem, disturbed at the discovery of a less respectable self than the one he had hoped to find in this adventure, he repudiates her and flees.

His final confrontation with the actor-Faust underscores in visual terms the inner conflict of the divided self that has been tormenting and confusing Faust. As a respected scholar Faust has a *public* identity but little sense of *personal* identity: he feels he is a fake; in search of his real self, he has found a dishonorable man, a seducer, a liar, a betrayer. In a confused but instinctive act of revulsion against that self, he destroys himself completely, and meets death still uncertain whether he possesses a soul. His suicide is curiously accidental: it is the act of the honorable self attempting to destroy the dishonorable self, not knowing that they are somehow one and the same man. Faust really thinks he is shooting someone else when he shoots himself. So, too, the ugly-faced crowd, led by gendarmes and judges, executes the actor-Faust, thinking they are punishing someone else. Out of the curious ironies of these deaths come two strong implications: first, that the crowd, fed on sensational headlines and thirsting for revenge, is an ugly, inhuman thing even when acting in the name of justice. Second and more important, that Faust, in attempting to slay the ugly, betraying self, is himself more noble than his adventure has hitherto indicated.

The theme of the divided self is certainly not rare in nineteenth-century literature, and indeed Goethe's own Faust laments the war of two spirits within his breast. But Goethe does not press the theme, indeed he distills most of the impurity from Faust and infuses it into Mephistopheles, who incarnates the negative elements in humanity. Ghelderode's Faust is less noble and harder to sympathize with because his negative side has not been severed from him; but we pity him nonetheless for the tragic confusion caused by his duality. He is a much smaller Faust than Goethe's, but perhaps no less universal. At the end of the first episode of the play, after the devil has tricked the tavern customers, they receive an exhortation that fits this Faust so roughly transported to the modern world: "Ladies and gentlemen, let us meditate on our smallness!"

Ghelderode has permitted his Faust to die in confusion and disillusionment after his single adventure with Marguerite, stressing the timelessness of this one segment of the career created for Faust by Goethe. Thus not only the stature of Faust but also the scope of his experience has been severely restricted. Paul Valéry, on the other hand, has modified the Faustian career by expansion rather than contraction. Like Goethe, he has written of a Faust in love and of a Faust in quest for some ultimate achievement, but Valéry's hero has already experienced all that Goethe's has lived through. Around the figure of this Faust, so thoroughly aware of his own mythical and literary tradition, Valéry has assembled two separate plays, both incomplete. In the first play, *Luste, or the Crystal Girl—A Comedy,* Faust is tempted by tenderness growing into love; in the second, *The Only One, or The Curses of the Cosmos—A Dramatic Fairy Tale,* he is tempted to relive the wealth of his experience with the added advantage of avoiding the mistakes of the past.

Valéry saw fit to publish both fragments under the title *My Faust,* explaining in his preface the origins of the work:

> It was one day in 1940 that I found I was talking to myself in two voices, and began to write accordingly. I sketched out these acts for two very different plays—if plays they are to be called—very rapidly and, I confess, with little care for plot, action, or ultimate scope. I had vaguely in the back of my mind the plan of a *Third Faust* which might comprise an indefinite number of works of a dramatic nature: melodramas, comedies, tragedies, pantomimes, according to the occasion; in verse or prose, as mood might require; a whole series of parallel yet independent productions which I knew, nevertheless, would never come into existence.[2]

Valéry's general idea suggests a kaleidoscopic projection of Faustian adventures, but with no single resolution or end in sight—and the two plays that began to materialize from this idea stop at the penultimate curtain. The last act of each was never written; there is no resolution, no death, no judgment for this enigmatic Faust of our time.

But by no means does this make him any less interesting a Faust. He is a fully realized figure—an articulate and sensitive human being, possessing a wry wisdom, a sense of humor, and a deep feeling that is far distant from the romantic enthusiasm of Goethe's hero. He is a Faust seeking unity rather than adventure, peace rather than passion, order rather than ordeals.

Luste, or the Crystal Girl, is a comedy of poignant, epigrammatic wit in the fashion of Giraudoux. The title refers to the young and open-hearted secretary whom Faust has hired to record his memoirs; more deeply, it suggests the qualities for which she stands: lucidity and delight, a delight that borders on the sensuous, but is not to be identified, as Mephistopheles identifies it, with sensuality. The central paradox of the play resides in the situation of Faust himself: he is not the restless spirit poised on the brink of a boundless and inviting future, but a spirit who has already been through it all, who has traversed all possible points of view, all possible feelings, and who now desires only to record this experience in a literary work of infinite styles and moods. This is, if you will, Faust turned artist after he has grown wise in experience. Wise, but not quite weary. He expresses a need for tenderness, for a warm and open presence that he finds in Luste, and in her presence he experiences a fullness of being which he calls his supreme achievement—simply to live, to be, to breathe, to see, to touch. For the traditional Faust the present moment is always a springboard to something greater and beyond; it is never sufficient in itself, and its insufficiency drives the Faustian spirit onward. Valéry's Faust finds his all in the present moment. And yet the moment cannot last—it is too fragile a thing, too evanescent. Even the delicate tenderness cannot last, for it seeks to express itself in love, and love for Faust has already proven itself many times over as a heart-breaking and illusory thing, an experience more disturbing than calming. To a young student who has made the pilgrimage to the Faustian study, Faust has given as his memento of wisdom, "Beware of Love." Faust himself, tempted to love by a girl who is already thoroughly in love with him, is caught in the dilemma of that memento. In Luste he finds a fruition of being and also a warning; the two are impossible to divide, and there is no last act to tell us Faust's final response.

Mephistopheles in this play, costumed as an English clergyman with goat's ears, scurries about in a futile sort of way. Unable to understand the nature of either Faust's human insights or of Luste's pure feelings, he attempts without success to have the young student seduce Luste. *His* counsel, a parody of Faust's, is "Love Thyself—Love All Thy Desires." His futility is underscored by the curious reversal of the traditional pact relationship. Faust does not seek the devil's aid so much as he wishes to teach the devil a lesson—to show him how obsolete he is in the modern world, which has rediscovered Chaos, in which Beauty is extinct and Evil no longer recognized, a world in which people are clever enough to damn themselves by their own devices. And yet this same Mephistopheles, this un-Lucifer-like devil whose self-proclaimed motto is "I SERVE," is given credit for the countless aberrations and disappointments that infect human love, and that convert it from a promise into a temptation. Obsolete in some of his forms, he still exists in others. Though never a threat to Faust, he remains a thorn.

Faust himself emerges as a kind of esthetic sage, ironically mocked by the insights of his own hard-won wisdom, concerned to preserve the integrity of the self against its weaker inclinations and against deceptions. His desire to sum up in adequate form the variety of his exhaustive past experiences may be read as an attempt to impose some unity upon the fragments and contradictions of one's past, an attempt, in short, to liberate the present self from the past. Finally, Faust's will to reject the love that beckons beyond the bounds of tenderness can be seen also as a move to preserve the identity and security of the self. This tendency toward *disengagement*—from the past, from illusory hopes, from the impulses of the lesser self—is in stark contrast to the outgoing, all-seeking spirit of the traditional Faust. But it is an essential element of what Valéry calls the pure self, *le moi pur*. When Faust rejoices in the present "I am" he is giving witness to the pure self, disengaged from past and future alike.

Valéry reminds us that his Faust plays began when he found that he was talking to himself in two voices. Perhaps one of those voices belongs to the title figure of his second Faust fragment, *The Only One, or The Curses of the Cosmos*. In the symbolic, dream-like atmosphere of this play Faust confronts in the first act a hideous, howling, prostrate recluse called the Only One, who rests atop a high mountain peak, the highest one can go.

The Only One is a grotesque caricature of the nihilistic hermit, who has climbed to his frigid solitary height to avoid all that smacks of mere human existence, and who revels in his own sense of superiority. He has climbed beyond the limits of ordinary life to a place where he can howl out the praises of nothingness, where he can invoke unseen spirits of negation:

> My great soulless, bodiless friends,
> Superior seraphim, ethereal concubines,
> Holding me safe from my own body and soul,
> Safe from time, safe from sex and sleep,
> Safe from life, from desire and regret,
> Safe from all that was and all that may be,
> Safe from what knows, and what feels,
> Safe from the self I hate as if it were a wife,
> Safe from any death but what One of You may be.
> Oh . . . splendid Winds, sweep into me!

Surely what Valéry has constructed here is a parody of the theme of disengagement that he has evoked elsewhere.

The Faust who has pushed beyond the limits of humanity, leaving even Mephistopheles at a lower and more habitable level, meets in the Only One a distorted image of the superhuman. He senses in the attitude of this strange creature a state of mind beyond madness, and hears echoes of his own Faustian impulses in the Only One's diatribe against the human mind:

> Yes, I used to be very intelligent, too. More than was needed to be an idolater of the Mind. My own (good as it was) offered me nothing but the wearisome ferment of its own malignant restlessness. The endless travail of an activity inventing, dividing, revising itself, exploring the narrow bounds of each single moment, only begets senseless longings, futile hypotheses, ridiculous problems, vain regrets, imaginary fears. . . . What else do you suppose it can do? . . . Give a glance up above . . . eh? Lovely sky, the famous starry sky overhead! Look at it and think! Think, you Minus Quantity of Muck, think of all the folly that handful of chaff and dust has sown in the brain, of all the imagination, declamation, supposition, incantation and calculation it has inspired in mankind . . .

The Only One resents Faust's presence (which stops him, of course, from being the only one), consistently calls Faust "Ordure" and castigates all things human. Faust's response is more curious than desperate; he judges the Only One as a monster of common sense, something worse than the devil—worse because he has more insight into what is wrong with the human condition. At last, the wolf-like Only One attacks Faust, and casts him from the heights into an abyss.

In the second act, Faust is awakened by fairy creatures who offer him the prospect of a renewed life on earth, a vigorous and heroic life, but one unmarred by the errors and waste of the past. Valéry's Faust declines the offer:

> All you know about me is nothing but fable.
> The truth within the truth remains ineffable:
> What can be recounted cannot count for much!
> The player hides in his heart the secret itch
> That lies beyond reach of losses and gains.
> All he knows is the fire running in his veins!
> The violence of being is his only good,
> And he'll throw anything on that fire to keep it red!
>   . . .
> You gave me back my breath to sigh, so you thought,
> For some still to be hoped-for pleasure or art,
> For some uttermost summit of the heart's empire . . .
> But the pride of my mind has undone desire.
> If the past was nothing but extravagant waste,
> What the future may promise moves me even less.
> Can you think my pride would accept the poor best
>   Of mounting the human stage once more
> To relive my legend with all mankind as witness,
> I, who can value nothing they adore,
> I, whom neither Heaven nor Hell could ever win,
> Whom love's melting warmth has left harder than
>   iron?
> No, I do not hate the immense bitterness I feel
> Never to have tracked the fire that burns in me still,
> Now that I am set free from every hope,

Set free from a past that has vanished in smoke,
From my crimes, my passions that could never find
Their mark, my carnal conquests, all that the world
    found
Fit to offer as rewards for my demon energies . . .
No . . . O no . . . do not waste your gifts on me,
    Fays . . .
However great the powers I'm supposed to possess,
They can't give me any taste for the Universe.
The devil I balked, the angel I fought and flung,
What other exploit can there be to tempt me?
I've known love and hate too well, they've left me
    empty,
And I am weary of being a created thing.

Faust refuses to be the traditional Faustian; he refuses to go on striving and achieving and striving again. Why? Because in one sense it would mean going round in the same circle. But more deeply, because he has seen that the traditional Faustian spirit is in some way specious and futile, that it thrives on illusions, that it masks a need which can never be met by energetic attainments. Though he is weary of being a created thing, Faust is neither despairing nor longing for transcendence. Though his proud spirit has defeated desire, he does not share with the Only One a perverse contempt for the human mind, the human heart, and existence itself. The fire of life runs in his veins, and burns in him still; he does not scorn this fire, but sees *it* as the important and central thing, and not the thousand and one ways in which man seeks to direct it, to contain it, to burn it up. He sees himself freed from his past, and free as well from the future. *In this freedom he finds self-possession,* just as in the other play he found it in the richness of the present moment. For a figure who has traversed the whole of experience, there can be no other resting point. To say this is not to say that Faust has found fulfillment and happiness: he attests his own feeling of weariness, of bitterness. But he cannot place his hope in a new illusion; he cannot, like Goethe's Faust, think that the sounds of the shovels digging his grave represent the building of a brave new world. Valéry's Faust suffers what one critic has called "the frustration of omniscience."[3] He is a Faust without an eternal feminine to draw him above, without a devil to drag him below. If he suffers damnation, it is the damnation of being human and wise at the same time. And Valéry has not written the final act.

Valéry's Faust fragments offer less of a prophetic perspective on the modern world than some of his early recorded ideas about the work suggest. At one time he had jotted down a list of items to be included at some point in *Faust*: among them were theoretical physics, mental and political catastrophe, a society of nations, science, Einstein, wars, machinery, finance, bolshevism, gravediggers, conquerors, ruins, and Mephistopheles as the spirit of objectivity. Instead, and more characteristically, his work turned into allegories of the individual spirit facing the internal crises of the self.

Psychological crisis lies at the heart of Lawrence Durrell's *An Irish Faustus* (1963) as well, but it is nearly over-whelmed by the exterior trappings of medieval romance. Durrell has chosen Ireland, he admits, to avoid clashing with the Germanic Faust of tradition; and his medieval setting provides him with a variety of colorful, if overly melodramatic, figures: a vampire-king; a mad and impassioned queen; a charlatan pardoner; a saintly chaplain; a philosophical hermit; and Doctor Faustus, a wise and kindly court physician who dabbles in white magic, tutors a young princess, and guards a magic ring made of alchemists' gold. These ingredients make possible a handful of sensational scenes, including the vampire's execution by a stake driven through his heart, and a descent into hell in which the traditional roles are reversed: a courageous Faustus drags down a cringing Mephistopheles.

Durrell's plot has two parts: the major part concerns Faustus' encounter with his dark self—symbolized in the play by Mephistopheles (who is Faustus' double); by the magic ring, which Faustus ought to have destroyed long ago; and by Faustus' pangs of conscience for having once informed upon his old black-magician master. The second part involves the passionate old queen and her vampire lover, and suggests that love is a violent, cruel, demonic, but strangely wonderful thing. Thus Durrell, unlike most other writers who take up the Faust figure, keeps his hero quite apart from the theme of sexual love. The major incidents of the action are few: the queen steals the ring from Faustus at the vampire's behest, and goes insane; Faustus tracks her to the vampire's hiding-place, recovers the ring, has the vampire killed, and cures the queen; then, to destroy the ring he must recite the magical "Great Formula" which is to open up the way to hell: this he does in the company of an unwilling Mephistopheles. *But Faustus comes back from his grim journey,* with a fresh and revitalized spirit. He now wishes to wander about, looking at life from his new perspective, and he visits his hermit friend on a mountain top, where they are joined for a card game by a comical pardoner and, as the last ironic surprise, by Mephistopheles.

Durrell calls his play "A Morality in Nine Scenes," and it is evident that he has tried to enrich the texture of his romantic fabric with several sententious lessons. One concerns the nature of wisdom, which Faustus defines in the opening scene as vision or awareness, beyond the confines of reason and mere knowledge. The play tries to dramatize one portion of such awareness in having Faustus face boldly his darker self and the decisions that must be made concerning it. The descent into hell represents a moral decision, the acting out of a dangerous responsibility, and with that decision comes an unexpected bonus: a glimpse of the hidden order in the apparent chaos of the universe. This insight, we are told, is born not of faith, but of despair wedded to imagination, and once grasped, it becomes the key to personal peace and the justification of the simple life: Faustus ends up, it is true, not wholly free of the presence of Mephistopheles, but nonetheless in association with congenial friends, playing the card game of Fortune, enjoying "a little music, a little wine" and conversation. The neighboring village below their mountain retreat just happens to be called Jerusalem.

Whether or not we agree with Durrell's moral, we must, I think, admit that it is not dramatically realized in the play—his symbols are obvious at one level, but loose, shifty, and vague at another. The concern with a vision of the order of the natural universe springs up in scene seven without any earlier preparation, and then becomes the major concluding theme. How or why it should have grown out of Faustus' previous concern with his moral being is never explained. The only inference seems to be that once you face the harsh reality of your total self, the whole order of the universe becomes meaningful.

Whatever the gap between action and meaning, it is clear that Durrell's Faustus, like Ghelderode's and Valéry's, is remarkably un-Faustian. Though he shares the romantic faith in the imagination, he bears none of the marks of the vigorous man in search of new boundaries and new experiences. He is rather a safe, calm, contemplative sort who becomes even calmer and more contemplative after his courageous journey to hell. His spirit is not restless but restful; though he is neither complacent nor slothful, he would probably be damned by Goethe's God for lack of *Streben.*

It should be clear by now, however, that the twentieth-century Faust does not live according to the Goethian principles. In an era that has given us the anti-hero in literature as a new conventional figure, it is not altogether surprising to discover an anti-Faust. Certainly that is what we have in the plays by Ghelderode, Valéry, and Durrell. The thirst for new experience and new achievements, the steadfast yearning to see and to move beyond the horizon, the romantic spirit undaunted by past mistakes or by remorse, all these are missing in the new Faust. Indeed, Valéry's Faust consciously rejects the career of this traditional, mythical Faust-figure. What we have instead is indicative of what has happened to humanity's vision of itself in the past decades. For Ghelderode, a confused and awkward Faust, ill at ease with the public role he must play, and dismayed by the actions of the true self he discovers before death. For Valéry, an ironic Faust who has seen and known too much in having experienced all human things, a Faust who has outgrown the immaturity of the uninitiated but is now the victim of his own sagacity. For Durrell, a moral Faust who has found a semblance of order only by coming to grips with his own worst decisions and evasions. In each case, the modern Faust exhibits a scrupulous self-consciousness that is foreign to Goethe's hero. He does not throw himself out upon the world, to savor all things and become one with all things; he turns within himself, to discover what lies within, and finds at times sweetness, at times bitterness, at times disgust. In our psychological age the Faustian pattern is not defined by the Self exploring the Universe, but by the Self exploring the Self. Faust becomes the symbol not for humanity seeking to transcend itself, but for humanity trying to understand itself, to live with itself. What rewards the modern Faust is neither heaven nor hell, but self-definition.

Identity, equilibrium, a tentative harmony—these become the goals of the new Faust. Goethe's Faust could never

rest with such, even in his union with Helen; Goethe's poem would not allow it. But dynamism and energetic achievement have taken on too destructive a tone in modern history to permit a contemporary writer to glory in them the way Goethe could. Meanwhile, what has happened to the quest for secret knowledge, the theme of forbidden magic that has been such an integral part of the Faust tradition? In the first place it has lost its association with the devil—even in Goethe the devil provides only utility, not knowledge. In the modern writers it is clear that man seems to have found out too much on his own, that knowledge and science do not get him very far. Indeed, knowledge and science are seen in these plays as substitutes for the devil, insofar as they are utilitarian things that continually force man into new dilemmas or new traps. The modern Faust wants wisdom instead, a sense of his own identity. And his modern creators have given him a greater capacity for self-questioning and self-recognition than Goethe ever gave to his hero. The old Faust gambled dangerously with his soul, challenging the supernatural powers; the new Faust wrestles with his complex self, struggling toward an awareness of his own nature. The Faustian myth has always been the test-pattern for exploring the bounds of human aspiration and achievement. It has always been tied to the urgent question, "What is the most valuable thing in human experience?" The modern answer provided in the drama of Ghelderode, Valéry, and Durrell is as ancient as it is enigmatic: KNOW THYSELF.

Notes

1. *Ghelderode: Seven Plays—Vol. II,* trans. by George Hauger, Mermaid Dramabook (New York, 1964), pp. 95, 98.

2. Paul Valéry, *Plays,* trans. by David Paul and Robert Fitzgerald, Bollingen Series XLV-3 (New York, 1960), p. 4.

3. Francis Fergusson, Introduction to *Plays,* xix.

ESCURIAL

CRITICAL COMMENTARY

Bettina Knapp (essay date 1978)

SOURCE: "Michel de Ghelderode's *Escurial*: The Alchemist's *Nigredo,*" in *Stanford French Review,* Vol. 2, No. 3, Winter 1978, pp. 405-17.

[*In the following essay, Knapp discusses the alchemical principle of* nigredo *as Ghelderode used it in* Escurial.]

Alchemy, frequently referred to as the "black art," requires a condition of *nigredo* before illumination or rebirth can ensue. In *Escurial* (1927), only the first stage of the alchemical process is experienced: *nigredo* with its accompanying phase of *mortificatio*. No renewal follows. No purification comes into being. There is no cleansing operation. Darkness hovers over the stage proceedings. *Escurial's* finale is as sinister and fetid as the outset of this dramatic ceremony.

Alchemists have made analogies between the *nigredo* phase of their operation and the seed implanted in the darkness of the earth. Each paves the way for creativity: the seed roots in the soil and the idea in the brain. Each feeds on surrounding nutritive agents; developing and enacting a specific role or function. Each battles its way into the light of day or consciousness—the manifest world. Rather than burgeoning and offering positive alchemical blends, however, Ghelderode's phantasms in *Escurial* remain in embryonic state. Like the seed which rots in the earth, so Ghelderode's creatures are stuck in the dark and regressive atmosphere in which they are embedded. *Escurial* is an alchemical drama, as are all of Ghelderode's plays. They delineate different phases involved in the decomposition of personalities, exposing in the process the nuances of decay and mephitism. Few, if any, of Ghelderode's characters are endowed with vision; fewer still with the strength to battle for their ideas and to pave the way for inner evolution. Their feeble natures, unhealthy psyches, and insalubrious conditions which surround them, impede normal growth. Their world is black; but not the rich blackness which offers a full range of harmoniously blended nutrients. Ghelderode's mixtures breed ghouls and gnomes; monsters endowed with distorted souls. His creatures befoul the air they breathe; revel in their own decay; delight in the sado-masochistic rounds; copulate with larvae and fungi; hiccup their strident grimaces and piercing screeches; rejoice in their sexual perversions. Reminiscent of the emanations of a Bosch, Grünewald, Breughel, and Ensor, or the excoriating depictions of Goya's crazed beings, Ghelderode's excrescences are stunted, malformed, degenerate creatures who have never grown beyond the *nigredo* phase.

Like so many tooled forms in a Goya mezzotint, so Ghelderode's monsters turn and churn, disrupt and disorient, but never resolve the chaos in their hearts. Instead, each brings further deterioration, greater ruin and despair. In *The Death of Doctor Faustus* (1925), audiences are not introduced to the Goethean construct—the man whose *descensus ad infernos* culminates with his redemption—but instead, to the anti-hero who fails in all spheres: religiously, philosophically, and socially. A "neurasthenic," Ghelderode's Faust sees no positive way in life and takes no affirmative stand. Life is absurd. To experience one's reality and individuality is impossible he concludes. Microbes alone exist for *Don Juan* (1928). Love is based on a lie. It is an illusion created by man to help him escape the horrors of life. *Christopher Columbus* (1927) dramatizes the plight of the idealist/poet who dreams of adventure and

beauty and instead becomes the prey of a jealous, covetous, and ungrateful populace dominated by political and religious fanatics. Christopher Columbus is imprisoned. When death finally beckons his way, he does not fear it. On the contrary, he welcomes that other realm. He loves adventure and so he loves death. *Barabbas* (1928) demonstrates the futility of sacrifice. Nothing positive can come to man through sacrifice. Nothing can stop humanity's lust for maiming and killing.

> Nous n'avons rien pu changer à tout ce que nous trouvions néfaste, révoltant et détestable. Et, après notre vaine mort, la Justice ne sera pas encore rendue, et le mensonge règnera non moins souverainement comme il règne depuis qu'il existe des humains. Voilà ce qui désespère cet homme, et voilà ce qui me désespère aussi. . . . Les fêtes commencent. Entendez les musiques. La foule est joyeuse. Et vraiment, ont-ils une raison de se réjouir? L'heure va venir. Bientôt, plus rien ne restera de ce que nous sommes. Il n'y a plus qu'à attendre et à se laisser faire, comme lui-même se laisse faire.[1]

Revolt itself is useless. The collective always wins. *Pantagleize* (1929) dramatizes the fate of the creative person. The sensitive and innocent poet is devoured by society. The miser's saga unfolds in *Red Magic* (1931). Gold, around which the spiritual and physical world revolves, absorbs Ghelderode's hero who finally couples with his shekels. Unlike Plautus's or Molière's misers who are finally punished for their possessive natures, Ghelderode's protagonist is defeated because he seeks to alter his condition: he wants to be generous. *Lord Halewyn* (1934) delineates the antics of an impotent man who pleasures in blood and gore. *Chronicles of Hell* (1929) focuses on death: a poisoned host, a noxious idea, kills individuals and societies.

That Ghelderode situates *Escurial* in sixteenth-century Spain is not surprising. He had always been absorbed by past eras. His father, a Clerk at the General Archives in Brussels, had encouraged him as a youth to study ancient documents, genealogies, history books, and engravings of all types. In *Les Entretiens d'Ostende,* Ghelderode writes: "Je me suis épris de choses inactuelles comme tout autre enfant s'éprend de ses jouets. Je ne voyais rien d'autre autour de moi! ces grands sceaux de cire ou de métal et ces contre-sceaux admirables dans leur boîte de buis; ces grandes feuilles onctueuses de parchemin; ces diplômes aux graphies fantastiques; ces lettres patentes adornées de blasons et au bas desquelles se déchiffraient les signatures prestigieuses de l'impératrice Marie-Thérèse, de Philipp II, de Charles-Quint et d'autres encore, d'un duc de Bourgogne parfois!"[2] Renaissance Spain, the historical climate in which *Escurial* is situated, was a period which in many ways reflected Ghelderode's penchant for the lugubrious; it concretized certain unregenerate forces within his subliminal world. Philip II was a formidable monarch. A colossal worker, he was endowed with a powerful personality. Somber and introverted, he surrounded himself with darkness; he even clothed himself in black. His shadow spread death and ruin wherever it was cast.

Although the Holy Inquisition had been established in Spain by Ferdinand and Isabella in 1478, Philip II had been instrumental in furthering its power. He had encouraged the clergy and the military to seek out Jews, Moors, or anyone accused of heresy, to convert them or to burn them at the stake. Death, murder, and horror marked his reign. In 1572, when he attempted to spread the spirit of the Holy Inquisition to the Low Countries, he was met with rebellion. As for his attempt to conquer England, his grandiose ideas resulted in the 1588 defeat of the Spanish Armada. It was his interest in this kind of "atmosphère méphitique, funèbre et féroce," Ghelderode wrote, that inspired *Escurial* (p. 32).

After having defeated the French at Saint-Quentin, Philip II's armies had inadvertently destroyed a church dedicated to the 3rd century martyr, Saint-Lawrence. Philip II built Escurial (1562-1584) in his honor. It housed a rich library, paintings by El Greco, among others, a convent, and a college. Philip II lived in one of the rooms in Escurial. It was virtually devoid of furniture. It opened on two alcoves: a study and a bedroom with a slit in the wall which allowed the monarch to follow the religious services from his bed. Philip II died in Escurial. Ghelderode's King, like the Spanish monarch, is a lonely being. Solitude helps the creative effort: "C'est une purification, une hygiène de l'âme," Ghelderode wrote in *Les Entretiens d'Ostende* (p. 46). A night spirit with a shadow personality, Philip II's smile resembled that of a vampire. So Ghelderode's King was also cruel. He was rigid in his ways and sinful in the sense that he was absorbed by his *idée fixe,* never varying the stranglehold he had on those whom he considered his enemies. Ghelderode's genius lies in his ability to dramatize his King's subliminal world; to bring his myopic creatures into the open; to compel his audiences to experience their chaos and *nigredo*. To increase the tension required for a theatrical spectacle, Ghelderode divided the King into two beings, each representing facets of the monarch's character: the King, an aged Father figure and the other, the Young Man Folial, the jester, whose function it was to entertain. *Escurial* enacts a blood sacrifice, Folial's immolation: the death of those functions—*love* and *feeling*—that he represents. The ruling principle, in the form of the King, survives: based on anger, hatred, and repression.

BLOOD SACRIFICE: AN ALCHEMICAL NIGREDO

Blood sacrifice, symbolically speaking, is part of the alchemical operation and the focal point of Ghelderode's dramatic ritual. The word *sacrifice* means "to make sacred." It requires the relinquishing of that object, or feeling, or thought with which one identifies. It is man's way of offering something that belongs to him (himself if need be) to that which transcends his offering. To sacrifice what is secure and comfortable (what eventually may engender a condition of stasis), is both a "threat" and a "challenge" to the ego-personality. It can be attempted only if the ego is strong and healthy. The alchemist has a dual view of sacrifice. For him sacrifice occurs on a physical plane as

he cooks his metals in his athanor. It also takes place in the spiritual sphere, when he transcends what he calls his base or leaden, instinctual condition, and attempts to ascend the ladder where he hopefully will attain the "golden" or "purest" of states. When blending, burning, and reshaping his metals, the alchemist destroys the present combinations of the *prima materia* with which he is working, to form the *ultima materia.* He sacrifices *what is* in order to bring about what *could be*: from the earthly to the celestial sphere; from the vulgar to the noble state.

Ghelderode's King is a God/Aged Father figure. Since the alchemist kills to vivify, the King should have been sacrificed as was the case in ancient times when the old King (or the old year) was ceremoniously killed, thus insuring seasonal fertility. With the King's demise a separation of the prevailing conscious attitude would have given way to new blendings, new solutions. In *Escurial,* however, the King is not killed. Thus, what he represents—the old, stayed, and limited views—prevail. As an aged Father figure, the King is identified with the planet Saturn (and the God), and with its metallic equivalent: *lead.* In *Escurial,* the King is in conflict with his double, Folial, who represents new ways and ideations; and he is reminiscent of the alchemist's Mercurius, the Son, and the Young Man. But Folial, that aspect of the King which loves and which relates to others, is weak. Relegated to a starvation diet, he cannot thrive in a climate of secrecy and terror. With his death, the positive elements are strangled by sinister forces. The hate factor smothers the love element. Youth is destroyed while old age pursues its narrow and negative course. Ghelderode's King is sick. He suffers from spiritual and physical sterility. He has reached an impasse. Viewed in terms of Christian dogma, to which Ghelderode was forever drawn in an ambivalent love/hate embrace, the King symbolizes God; Folial, Christ. Unlike Christ's crucifixion, which had been predicted and had been accepted, Folial's sacrifice went counter to his desire. Indeed, it was no sacrifice at all. It was murder. Folial was psychologically unwilling to relinquish his emerging ego—his feeling principle which manifested itself in his love for the Queen. Whereas Christ's death, according to dogma, resulted in his resurrection and the birth of new ideas and philosophies, thus compensating for the one-sided ruling principle of the time, Folial's murder merely prolonged an already decomposed atmosphere. By destroying Folial, the King was further repressing his love instinct; sacrificing kindness for cruelty; relatedness for hatred; understanding for authority.

King/Aged Father/Saturn figures are depicted in alchemical documents as carrying scythes, sickles, and sometimes hour glasses. In an 18th-century tract, *Philosophorum Praeclara Monito,*[3] he is featured as an old man with a scythe and cutting off Mercury's feet, thus attempting to fix and immobilize what could be developed. The scythe and the sickle are symbols of dismemberment: shearing, pruning, and others. To prune a tree helps conserve its vitality; it forces back the nutritive agents from the branches into the trunk and roots. Cutting (or cutting off), then, takes on a positive connotation in this regard. The hour glass carried by Saturn identifies him with Time, the Great Destroyer, the harbinger of Death, the spreader of Saturnine melancholia, and the darkness of the soul which poets such as Verlaine rendered in exquisite verse. For the alchemist, to experience such a condition paves the way to his second phase of endeavor, the cleansing and whitening process. Alchemists, therefore, are most always sought to "purge the horrible darkness of our mind" (*CW* 12, p. 167). But the King, like Saturn, is caught up in his own bile; suffers, agonizes, and is the victim of his own limited vision. He tends only to the needs of his inflated ego; all else in the world does not exist. Alchemists identify Aged Father/Saturn (the God) with the Titan Kronos. The Titans were primeval beings invested with anthropoid psyches. So Ghelderode's King also lives on an instinctual level and is likewise incapable of evaluating situations and people. More important was the fact that Kronos, fearful that his children would overthrow him, swallowed them. Such fear indicates an inability to accept the natural process of death and rebirth. Nature, however, in the form of Kronos's wife, Rhea, hid her son, Zeus, and replaced his body with a stone to which alchemists allude as the philosopher's stone.[4] Rhea forced Kronos to regurgitate the other children, thus bringing new life and blood to the land and restoring to Nature what was rightfully hers. The Aged Father figure then weakened progressively. No such outcome takes place in *Escurial.* The King kills Folial and there is no restitution to Nature. On the contrary, nature is impoverished. The loss adds to an already imbalanced situation. Since King/Saturn/Aged Father/Kronos was associated with lead, the basest of all metals, the lowest of common denominators, he was incapable, according to the alchemists, of bringing the light of consciousness to his acts, at least in his present condition. Like lead when exposed to moist air, his dark and somber personality traits became more obvious; their blackness and bleakness permeated the atmosphere. He was weighted down in every respect by the heaviness of the metal and its accompanying lugubrious tones. According to pseudo-Democritus, an alchemist, lead is "the generator of the other metals" and was used by the Egyptians and Babylonians to produce a variety of metallic substances; such reblendings resulted in the formation of fresh alloys. It could be said, then, that the King had the potential to create but failed in his endeavor. There were no new mixtures. Only the leaden factor remained. With prolonged contact, lead may act as a poison. In the King's case, he represented the noxious side of this element and destroyed everything and everyone with whom he came into continuous contact. Ghelderode accentuated the destructive and negative inner climate in *Escurial* through his lighting effects and decor. An eerie "subterranean" light emanated from the proscenium, like so many shadowy substances living their lives upon the stage and never to be seen again. The funereal hangings draped about the stage were described as being in a perpetual state of "agitation," thus mirroring both the King's fear of being overthrown and his horror of sterility and impotence. Even the rugs were worn and holey, further stressing the outdated and unregenerate ruling principle.

The stage room took on the contours of a cave. Cave cults, let us recall, were popular in ancient times. Sybils and oracles inhabited these dark and remote regions and from them predicted events. Initiates performed rituals (as in Eleusinian mysteries) in caves to earn redemption and inner transformation.[5] Many Christian martyrs found serenity in such protective areas. It is here that Nature and man worked together; that symbiotic relationships helped the maturation process. Mineral gestation, the alchemists believed, also took place in subterranean areas within the earth. The cave, like the Earth-Mother, permitted the contents of her uterus to grow and to burgeon. The King's room, however, was unhealthy. No air was allowed to flow; his mephitic realm led to further decomposition, ugliness, and decadence.

Folial, the buffoon, is Mercurius (Mercury). Alchemists looked upon Saturn as Mercurius's father and referred to the young man as "Saturn's child." Folial is a life force: he represents those character traits that are so weakly developed in the King: the feeling principle and the capacity to love. In *Tractatulus Alchimae,* Mercurius is described as "the universal vivific spirit" which "penetrates, exalts, and develops everything"; a "ferment to everybody with which it is united chemically." Such qualities are applicable to "metallic elixir, both to the white, or silver, and red, or gold producing degrees. Its potencies develop under the action of fire" (*CW* 13:53). Although Folial's dress as a buffoon is colorful, he mirrors only one of the above-mentioned tonalities at this stage of development: the dismal hue of pain. Folial was in love with the Queen and she with him. The love he had experienced brought about an inner change in him—that heat and fire—which altered his color from white, to silver, to red, to gold, that is, the alchemical operations which he needed to complete the *hieros gamos* or union with the Queen. It is he, as catalyst, who alters circumstances and moods; who brings about fermentation and forces the King's adventure to its dismal climax. Yet, it is he, who, had things been so organized, could have brought the events to a joyful conclusion and created a new orientation—a new center of gravity. But the Queen dies and the King cuts Folial down. Folial failed to earn happiness: to evolve into a higher state, a golden sphere. The root of his name indicates the reason for his deficiencies: *fool* or madman (*fou, fol* in French). He lacked the necessary mental attributes to compel a concerted effort on his part. When, for example, the King asked him to make him laugh, Folial was unable to comply with his wishes. He knew the Queen was dying and he felt his pain too acutely to overcome it. The King threatens him with death unless he obeys. Folial acquiesces and suggests they enact a farce together. The farce begins. Folial grabs the King's crown and scepter and assumes a regal stance. He then wraps his hands around the monarch's neck. His grip tightens. The King's strident cackle disorients him. Folial loosens his grip. Folial's momentary exchange of identity with the King was not sufficient to establish a new ruling principle. The thinking function, so well developed in the King, was dormant in Folial. His feelings were forever surging forth and disconcerting him at the most inappropriate moments. Because they had remained undeveloped and infantile (since they had been experienced only on a subliminal level, in secret, in hiding, in dark and remote corners of the palace and thus in unconscious spheres rather than on conscious levels), they could not strike hard and continuously when the need arose. Rather than attempting to understand Folial's contempt during the farce sequence, the King enjoys his buffoon's game of strangulation. He delights in his hatred of him and admires the power in his hands. In time, he muses, Folial could even become an "Executioner." But when Folial fails to strangle the King, he loses respect for the buffoon. The King derides the fact that Folial's feelings dominate and not his thinking factor. Worry, anguish, and despair appear on his face and not on the King's where they rightfully belong. The King suggests they carry their farce a step further. He asks Folial to don his vestments while he puts on the jester's. Folial is so weakly structured that when ordered to mount the throne, he barely has the strength to walk up the few steps necessary. The crown and scepter and clothes weigh too heavily upon him. The love and beauty he had once known in the Queen, and which had helped him find momentary fulfillment, are no longer. "Celle qui meurt, elle est belle, pure et sainte" (p. 82); killed by the "silence" and tenebrous nature of the palace.

It is not surprising that Ghelderode chose Folial as the sacrificial victim. Throughout history, jesters have been associated with goats who for many people were incarnations of evil. In the iconography of the Middle Ages, the devil was frequently portrayed as a goat. There was also the scapegoat; after evils were heaped upon him, this animal was then ejected from the tribe, thus purging the community of sin and assuring its fertility and well being. The goat was also a tragic figure. Indeed, the word tragedy is derived from *tragoidia* "the song of the goat." Members of the Greek chorus appeared as goats during dramatic performances. In Euripides's *Bacchantes,* the goat was divinity's choice victim and thus the perfect sacrificial agent. During certain religious ceremonies, Dionysus himself was metamorphosed into a goat. God became animal, with all of the negative implications and tragedy such a condition implies. So Folial, because he represented feeling and love—characteristics which the ruling principle of reason and authority considered objectionable—he had to be done away with. As a devotee of Aphrodite, too, the goat represented the Eros principle: instinct, sensuality, libido, and desire—those traits which religious ascetics considered unclean and thus worthy of destruction. "Il est défendu d'aimer dans ce palais!" the King declared (p. 83). That Folial should have suggested the enactment of a farce which included an exchange of identities, was ingenious. The farce is the supreme vehicle for the expression of bitterness, black humor, and iconoclasm. When pushed to the extreme, as in Ionesco's *The Chairs,* Pinter's *The Birthday Party,* and Mrozek's *The Police,* anger and hatred are siphoned out in spurts and gushes. The farce derides the concept of royalty and authority by pointing out the King's narrow views and his failures. Important

truths are spoken in the spirit of banter. The sacred is demeaned and ridiculed. Rather than the happy-go-lucky prankster of a Plautus and Molière, Chelderode introduces audiences to an exhausted and despairing jester whose laughter is marked with the rictus of pain, like the 19th-century Pierrot. When the King, in Folial's disguise, plays the buffoon, he confesses his suffering—the excoriating jealousy he experienced upon discovering his wife's love for another. It is at this juncture that he tells his rival that his wife has been poisoned. He then pursues his chatter in the most cavalier of manner, informing Folial that another wife will be found with great ease. He prances about the stage and admits he was really born to be a clown. "Je suis de nature grimacier, perfide, et dissimulé, semblable en cela aux femmes" (p. 81). His abandon seems complete. Now the King begins to whirl about like "un satyre ancien" during the *Walpurgisnacht* festivities. He is decidedly comfortable in the role he plays. The King jumps and dances, whirls about again. Alchemists used to dance around their athanors. Dancing is a liberation. "Je danse ma libération," the King declares (p. 81). Dancing, the most primitive of instinctual expressions, is man's way of becoming reabsorbed into the pleromatic world. The circles he weaves around the stage result in a loss of equilibrium and individuality. Once a *fixed* position (view of life) has been uprooted, a reblending may occur, new and fresh components may be constellated. Such is not the King's case. Unlike Shiva who danced the *tandava,* thus uniting time and space and in so doing creating the earth, the King's dance allows him to expel his hatred, lust, and anger, like the grimacing gargoyle that he is, but only temporarily. These instincts once again flood his being and dim his vision. On a stage with light piercing through the opaque atmosphere in glimmers, the King dances like those grotesque depictions which Goya delineated. Glorifying in the blood to be shed, feasting on the thought of a supernal feast, the proscenium becomes innundated with movement, flooded in the libidinous atmosphere of the King's perverse ways. "Assez, la farce est finie," the King tells Folial (p. 84). He asks his buffoon to return his crown and scepter—his identity. Folial refuses. A Monk enters and informs the King of his wife's demise. Folial is stunned. Taking advantage of his shocked condition, the King grabs his symbols of authority. He calls for the Executioner. "Après la farce, la tragédie," he says (p. 84). The Executioner, dressed in scarlet and wearing a hood over his head which allows only his eyes and nose to be seen, enters and strangles Folial. The King bursts out in hysterical laughter.

ALCHEMICAL SYMBOLOGY

Just as the alchemist wrote his formulae in complex symbols thereby hiding the enclosed arcana from the "vulgar" who might not only misunderstand it but who might also seek to destroy the material, so the playwright inserts signs into his drama that only the initiate may penetrate. *Escurial* opens to the sound of barking *dogs.* They "hurlent la mort," it says in the stage directions. The King cups his hands to shut out the sounds and the reality they force upon him: the Queen's demise is about to occur. The fear, horror, and torment leading up to the event is unbearable. He forbids the sounds. Once the Queen's death has occurred, however, the situation has become acceptable to the King who finally allows the baying of the dogs. In most mythologies, dogs are associated with the underworld. They are chthonic spirits (Anubis, Tien-k'uen, Cerberus). As psychopomps, their function is to guide man to the realm of the dead—to protect the underworld. Garm, in German mythology, guards the entrance to Nifleheim, a cold and tenebrous realm. In *Escurial,* dogs are the harbingers of death and not the positive and faithful creatures associated with St. Roch or the Dominican order (*Domini canes,* "dogs of the lord").

Not only do dogs spell death in *Escurial,* but as creatures of the night and, according to alchemical dictum, theriomorphic forms of spirit and the soul, they serve to blend with, and prolong, the *nigredo* atmosphere implicit in *Escurial.* As night animals, alchemists associate the dog with Hecate and the moon, that is, with the unconscious or the transpersonal sphere. Dark, quixotic, volatile, Hecate is depicted in drawings and paintings with a cortège of terrifying, barking dogs roaming about tombs and graveyards calling up the ghosts of the departed.[6] Pico della Mirandola considered the moon the most inferior of constellations, thus implying that the unconscious (or that irrational part of man) when allowed to act on its own, as in the King's case, without the light of reason or conscious orientation, is the promulgator of savage and brutal acts. Macrobius wrote: "The realm of the perishable begins with the moon and goes downwards" (*CW* 14:145).

Bells play an important role in *Escurial.* Ghelderode had always been sensitive to music, particularly to Medieval and Renaissance polyphonic compositions, such as those by Guillaume de Machaut, Dufay, Obrecht, Orlandus de Lassus, Palestrina and, of course, the greatest of them all for Ghelderode—Bach. In *Les Entretiens d'Ostende* he wrote: "Sachez encore qu'à certains moments, j'écoute une musique aérienne qui, pour moi, est encore un signe, un langage perpétuel dont toute une vie fut accompagnée: j'écoute vivre, respirer et divaguer les cloches, je suis un amateur de cloches! Une passion singulière n'est-ce pas? Non seulement les cloches religieuses, mais civiles aussi, ces carillons qu'inventèrent les Flandres et ces cloches tragiques à gueules sanglantes, et les triomphales à battant d'or" (p. 23). The collective tonalities which mark the striking bell sounds in consort with the howling of the dogs create celestial and infernal music: a composite of conflicting emotions, rhythms, and sonorities which not only transcend the limitations of man and thus merge with the cosmic, but add dynamism, tension, and *furor* to the drama itself. Bells are considered, in alchemical symbolism, as mediating forces between heaven and earth: a combination of spirit and matter. Their form (container) represents the woman, and, therefore, the feeling or Eros qualities with which she is identified. Their vaulted shape (heaven) represents the head and the thinking factor which dominates the stage proceedings. The primordial vibrations prelude the human activities; they announce in their

own language, that of subtle cosmic rhythms and the pain and anguish which will affect the human heart. In *Escurial,* bells prolong the religious and sinister atmosphere which marks the King's reign. Bells are so significant in this regard that at the outset of the play a Monk begs the King to let him sound them. "Ce serait une immense charité, une action sainte que de laisser sonner les cloches, de lever l'interdit que Votre Majesté a lancé contre les cloches . . . comme des criminelles qui ont heurté les tympans délicats de Votre Majesté, les cloches qui annoncent au Ciel joies et douleurs terrestres" (p. 73). The King relents. He knows he is powerless against an implacable destiny. And just as the bells howled and wailed in medieval mystery dramas—counting the hours of Christ's agony, making its progression—so they replicate the Queen's torment and Folial's by extension. Dogs and bells are the harbingers of Death, a figure which is virtually personified during the stage proceedings. Death, like the Medieval leader in the *Danse Macabre,* performs his gyrations in an inventive sado-masochistic round. Some in the audience are regaled by these antics while others are terrorized as death incises itself into the stage happenings: mysterious and stealthy at first, it slowly permeates the entire dialogue, thoughts, and sensations. "Vous aimez la Mort," the King tells the Monk, "et son odeur et ses fastes!" (p. 73).

For the alchemist, Death indicates an end to spiritual progress; a condition of degeneration and decay. Yet, such separation of soul from body is a prerequisite for the healing process, thus putting an end to the "affliction of the soul." Death means a finale to the old condition and the birth of new combinations, fresh alloys, avant-garde views. Thanatos, the son of Night and the brother of Sleep, represents the King. Impenetrable, insensitive, and grim, as was the Greek god, so he too is anchored in his solitude; caught up in his destructive ways, encapsulated in *nigredo.* Unlike alchemical symbolism which looked upon Thanatos as a precondition of renewal, Ghelderode's King bathes in the regressive first phase of the alchemical operation. To underscore the mephitic and decidedly uncomfortable condition of his protagonists thus adding to the play's visceral impact upon the audience, Ghelderode had recourse to images of fleas, carrions, and larvae. In Roman times, larvae were considered evil spirits which wandered about graveyards and near criminals. They grimaced and cackled as they made their way about in darkness terrorizing young and old. Images of skulls and craniums are interwoven into the dialogue semiotically, accentuating the disgust Ghelderode seeks to inject into the atmosphere. The King asks Folial whether "Ton crâne est rempli de larves" (p. 78), thus denigrating his thought processes. As the chief of his kingdom, the King was the head of his realm. Cranium cults have existed from time immemorial and are still popular today. Skulls of ancestors and saints are worshipped throughout the world. The crown of gold becomes the object of interchange during the farce episodes. Alchemists considered both the crown and the gold from which it was made the most splendid of substances. It was God's mouthpiece and the Sun's earthly counterpart. Since the crown is placed on the head it reaches closest to heaven; in that it is made of the noblest and the purest of metals, its rays shine throughout the cosmos, shedding light and illumination. The Kabbalists when depicting the *Sephiroth*, God's ten Emanations, considered the Crown the highest expression of the Absolute. Also the scepter exchanged between the King and Folial is a symbol of authority, power, and justice. The transference of crown and scepter during the enactment of the farce implies that the ruling authority is no longer a steady and stable force; that it neither dispenses justice nor any governing power; that it has lost solid footing. Rulership, then, is unsteady; stability and harmony are toppling. The edifice is about to crumble.

As an alchemical drama, *Escurial* enacts an inner experience. By slaying the new and vital forces in the *agon* (contest) and allowing the old and decayed forces to survive, the sacrifice serves no positive purpose. As a "primal rite," comedian and martyr are one in *Escurial*, as are "mocker and moralist," to quote from Plato's *Symposium*.[7] It is not noble metals that emerge, but ignoble ones. Rather than fostering love, a spirit of hatred is engendered; rather than health, sickness; rather than the avant-garde, the retrograde. Although the alchemical mixture was accompanied with brio and dexterity, it was aborted at the end. The weight of the leaden matter has crushed mercurial sprightliness; the subliminal realm has superseded consciousness. Terror, chaos, and *nigredo* reign. The *Aurora Consurgens*, allegedly written by Thomas Aquinus, sums up both the alchemical and the dramatic experience: "I saw a great cloud looming black over the whole earth, which had absorbed the earth and covered my soul . . . ."[8]

Notes

1. Michel de Ghelderode, *Théâtre*, 5 (Gallimard, 1957):102.

2. Michel de Ghelderode, *Les Entretiens d'Ostende* (L'Arche, 1956), p. 15.

3. C.G. Jung, *Collected Works*, 14 (New York: Pantheon, 1964):17; henceforth *CW*.

4. John Read, *Prelude to Chemistry* (London, 1936), p. 243.

5. Mircea Eliade, *The Forge and the Crucible* (New York: Harper Torchbooks, 1971), p. 31.

6. J. Tondriau et R. Villeneuve, *Dictionnaire du Diable et de la Démonologie* (Marabout Université, 1963), p. 93.

7. Wylie Sypher, *Comedy* (New York: Doubleday Anchor Books, 1956), p. 194.

8. Marie Louise von Franz, *Aurora Consurgens* (New York: Pantheon, 1966), p. 57.

RED MAGIC

CRITICAL COMMENTARY

Iska Fraidstern (essay date 1969)

SOURCE: "Ghelderode's *Red Magic*: Gold and the Use of the Christian Myth," in *Modern Drama*, Vol. 11, No. 4, February 1969, pp. 376-81.

[*In the following essay, Fraidstern analyzes the ways in which* Red Magic *differs from Ghelderode's other plays, which draw heavily on ancient themes and legends.*]

The vision of Michel de Ghelderode derives its theatrical vitality from the playwright's absorption in the anhistorical memories of the folk or the popular imagination, "about what the world was like before the appearance of homo sapiens. Through the primitive legends, poetry, and dream are revealed to us the existence of former human kinds, come from the stars and gone away again, leaving evidences in stone, astronomical, or esoteric symbols."[1] His dramatic preoccupation with the public manifestations of these archaic, frequently unconscious relics reveals an awareness of continuous human need for sacred objects, the ritual annulments of time, and the ceremonial repetition of certain exemplary gestures that demand participation in a reality greater than the limits enforced by the individual personality. Because he was haunted by physical mortality, Ghelderode became obsessed by the mortality of civilizations:

> The present is a fugitive which constantly escapes me. The past is more alive to me than this very day. I can feel the presence of the dead and their lost age more keenly than I can feel their opposites. . . . Legends of olden days, ancestral customs, the great centuries of violence . . . the brutal life and the religious wars.[2]

This cataclysmic view of history is partially conditioned by particular Flemish experience: the short reign as a commercial power at the beginning of the Renaissance, the swift decline during the fifteenth century "when Flanders staggered herself in war and danced in the orgies of the flesh,"[3] and the position of Belgium as the traditional battlefield where the forces of darkness and the angels of light contended for the soul of Europe. Ghelderode's own zest for living in spite of precarious health forced the personal recognition that the acceptance of death is the only valid hope of salvation. These widely varied perceptions coalesce to form a theater concerned with reenacting the archetypal truths present in the Christian myth. By utilizing the liturgical patterns of Christianity, stressing the Passion and Resurrection, Ghelderode can annihilate the present, inviting the spectator to enter a consecrated, time-less existence. But *Red Magic* is unusual in this regard. Unlike much of Ghelderode's work, this play uses the eschatological motifs to satirize an attitude peculiar to the modern temper—the sacralizing of money.

The other plays are clearly interested in the generalizing function of myth. In *Barabbas,* Ghelderode indicates the ecumenism of the rites surrounding the life and death of Christ by constructing a series of dramatic analogues around the figure of the thief as mock-Christ. *Miss Jairus* is a commentary on the belief that the Christian promise is a continuum with death as the bridge to a New Jerusalem. The structure of the play fuses the symbolic chronology of Christ's last year with the seasonal pattern of the vegetation myths, moving toward the necessary spring martyrdom of the god. Blandine moves through the play attempting to discover physical counterparts resembling death, waiting only for the Crucifixion to release her body. Pantagleize fulfills the Christian archetype because he completes his destiny in history in order to escape its temporal limitations, as Christ himself did. The *Chronicles of Hell* dramatizes, in a Christian context, the recurrent archetypal struggle between goodness and those demonic forces that would justify all excess. For Ghelderode, the outcome is inevitable: the Devil is enthroned as lord of this world; Christianity embodies hope in the realm outside the material present.

In these plays the symbolic pattern is redemptive. Individuals search for death, protagonists struggle for death, characters are led through secular experience to death and the life beyond time. *Red Magic,* however, is a play about the modern rejection of the idea of regeneration through death. It is an exploration of the psyche of contemporary man where the light of grace has been transformed into the mysterious glitter of gold, a false and unnatural sun. *Red Magic* concerns a successful temptation, an inversion of the Christian encounter in the wilderness, the triumph of the world, the flesh, and most especially, the devil. The title is significant because it not only describes the bloody results attendant upon the obsessive desire for money, but also presents the clue revealing the bias of the supernatural agency that impels the action of the play. *Red Magic* is, then, an ironic comedy about human behavior after the fall. Hieronymus inexorably moves toward damnation by denying the function of death, and substitutes, instead, the desexualizing drive for the power that would make man a god.

Hieronymus moves through a satanic world of illusion—"all in this universe is nothing more than seeming"[4]—created by the devil and his minions, Armador, Sybilla, Romulus, and the Monk: virgins who are bitches; alchemy that is, in fact, counterfeiting; the promise of immortality that is the cause of death. That these characters are functions of the demonic will is made clear by the imagery of the play. The "scarlet monk," haunted by the stench of hell existing within his own body, and Romulus, the begging opportunist, are lesser imps destroyed by their own greed.

Sybilla is a Lilith-figure, a succubus who is the devil's mate: "She is the lascivious, sumptuous and sordid woman dreamt about in nightmare."[5] And Armador, whose name may establish an anagrammatic link between the power of gold and the power of Satan, is depicted as the Devil himself by implication, by direct description, by ironic recognition. Romulus asserts that "the devil appears only to fools;"[6] and Hieronymus is nothing if he is not a fool. Sybilla declares passionately, "Yes, I shall follow you along the roads, across the plains, over the seas, as far as hell, which will burn less than your skin, the skin of a young devil."[7] Finally, Armador, attempting to seduce Hieronymus, tells him:

> If you betray me, you will die, die a horrible death, for I not only wield happiness in these hands, I work misery too. It is my tragic privilege to command the two elements that actuate the universe, Good and Evil . . . I have touched you. You are in my power.[8]

Alchemy, a crucial metaphor in the play, enhances the irony of these diabolically inspired misconceptions. This medieval science has an explicit spiritual content in which the purification of the metal parallels the purification of the human soul. It is a symbolic attempt to rescue nature from the consequences of the fall. To subvert the process, as does Armador, is to destroy a chance for salvation. But on a deeper level, alchemy bespeaks a commitment to lifelessness, an effort to endow gold which is in itself unproductive and non-creating with positive ritual significance.

Hieronymus is by no means a reluctant Adam. In translating all experience into possession, he willingly forfeits his humanity. The miser is concerned only with ownership. Even silence is defined as property:

> The constellations fill the sky. Who owns all these stars? I swar they burn away in sheer waste. And the moon is missing. It has been stolen. When it comes back it will have had a piece taken out of it. . . . Emptiness, everywhere! All the emptiness that the room contains is mine, too. Why can't I pick it up and store it? . . . The silence that reigns in here is mine also. What can I do with it?[9]

He views his soul as an entry in an account book, "I am the owner of my soul, and such I shall remain! That is something I had forgotten in the inventory. Item, one immortal soul, ornamented with diverse virtues."[10] And in his dreams, Hieronymus recites the litany of proprietorship:

> Item . . . I own a house . . . with a ghost. . . . A bronze chest . . . in which gold pieces are breeding young. . . . A wife and her virginity. . . . I own . . . a stomach . . . and a gullet . . . that I must . . . attend to . . .[11]

Rejecting nature, he has deflected his own physical impulses into the contents of his bronze chest. Ghelderode meant Hieronymus to be a lewd and big-bellied miser,"[12] an atypical stage figure, growing sleek and fat on sensuous dreams. Hieronymus shudders at the sun because gold has become the source of generative light in the miser's perverted cosmos:

> The moment the miser opens it [the coffer] to officiate, he is flooded with light. . . . The gold exists in its own right and burns like radium—and the miser takes on a supernatural look under this lighting. When he enters the coffer, he looks as though he has disappeared in an incandescent trap.[13]

If the universe is animated by sterility then the products of that world are barren. So his wife's supposed virginity is valued as a commodity: "No, not for anything in the world will I touch this priceless irreplaceable virginity that so few women can boast of possessing."[14] The child Hieronymus gives his wife must be a doll, not the result of intercourse between husband and wife. And his own sexuality, "A crown drops from your wallet at each spasm,"[15] is transmuted into inanimate coinage that is impotent:

> Tonight I shall mingle the male and female coins. . . . I shall marry them. Make love! Join together your golden bodies. . . . Let gold bring forth gold! . . . Conceive! Female coins, become so great that you almost burst! It is blessed, it is just, that your grand race should perpetuate itself, for yours is the domination of the world![16]

Hieronymus becomes the Devil's priest administering a black sacrament of marriage.

When alchemy enters to make his dream possible, Hieronymus is no longer concerned with possession for its own sake, but with power: "With my gold I shall buy the trinity!"[17] It is important that this change of attitude is depicted in terms of the Christian myth that he has, in fact, renounced: Romulus says ". . . in three days the sides of the chest will burst open;"[18] and Hieronymus becomes a crazy Jesus as he immolates himself in the coffer and is resurrected with a new vision of omnipotence.

But the process that Ghelderode illustrates in the course of the play is considerably more than a delineation of the corrupting force of money. *Red Magic* is, rather, a discussion of the way man commits Original Sin in the modern world. Hieronymus desires immortality only when he believes he can acquire an endless source of wealth because accumulating money is the primary method of accomplishing deification and the continuity of self. That money is a contingent manifestation of the impulse to attain the autogenic power of God is implied in Act I and directly stated in the remainder of the play. Hieronymus rarely sleeps because

> It is only at night that each thing takes on its full value. I am double at night. Rather than lose myself in incoherent and immediately forgotten dreams, I sleep on my feet. . . . I steal time, so that I shall have more waking hours than those people who sink themselves in useless sleep.[19]

There are no clocks in his house because they tick off the minutes of human mortality. And he does not indulge in sexual intercourse because that implies self-surrender. The gold florins are his promise of immortality, his account book the path to heaven. While Hieronymus awaits the results of Armador's experiments he asserts "Men have unhealthy dreams. They dream of being more powerful than the Creator. They want to make light out of darkness."[20] After he steals the amulet, he is convinced that he is both rich and immortal. Now he can safely will his house and possessions to the church certain that "I have robbed you jackal! . . . It serves you right. . . . I am immortal!"[21] Once released from the inevitability of death, Hieronymus becomes drunk—he can now afford to yield to the demands of his appetites. When he returns from the ritual entombment in the coffer, the miser's transformation is complete. Hieronymus believes he has short-circuited the Christian pattern; he has obtained eternity without self-extinction:

> I bought the globe and all that covers it, oceans, mountains, empires, peoples, and ruins. And the seasons, storms, and creation. . . . I bought Calvary . . . Jerusalem . . . Mecca and Rome. . . . Tonight I find myself flung outside time and law. . . . This old house will have crumbled and all the monks eaten by worms, when old Hieronymus is still laughing, and he will be the last to laugh. . . . What a transformation in my substance! Here I am, hungry and thirsty, wanting to do things, to speak out loud.[22]

He kills his non-human child because he no longer needs an heir. But this emphasizes the fact that Hieronymus' sexuality is still autoerotic—he is aroused by his own incantatory speech. When he attempts to find gratification outside his own body he becomes ill. The final moments of the play are an ironic coda to the entire action. Hieronymus is vigorously proclaiming "I am like God" at the very moment he is most human: he has gradually lost his house, his wife, his gold, and he will soon lose his life.

Ghelderode, in *Red Magic*, has not departed from his concern with the ritual function of archetypal theater: he allows the old symbols to criticize a more immediate problem, the dehumanization of the modern perspective through the quest for wealth. Gold does narrow man's vision to this world; it is the appropriate motif for a moribund civilization, "the proper symbol of sublimation, both as the death of the body and as the quest for a 'higher' life which is not of the body."[23]

Notes

1. Michel de Ghelderode, "Dispatches from the Prince of Ostreland" (trans. George Haugher, *TDR,* VII [Fall, 1963], 29).

2. Samuel Draper, "An Interview with Michel de Ghelderode," *TDR,* VII (Fall, 1963), 42.

3. *Ibid.,* 42.

4. Ghelderode, "Red Magic," *Seven Plays,* vol. 2 (New York, 1964), p. 33.

5. Ghelderode, "To Directors and Actors: Letters 1948-1959," *TDR*, IX (Summer, 1965), 59.

6. Ghelderode, *Red Magic*, p. 12.

7. *Ibid.*, p. 23.

8. *Ibid.*, p. 15.

9. *Ibid.*, p. 3.

10. *Ibid.*, p. 5.

11. *Ibid.*, p. 10.

12. Ghelderode, "To Directors and Actors," p. 42.

13. *Ibid.*, p. 58.

14. Ghelderode, *Red Magic*, p. 10.

15. *Ibid.*, p. 10.

16. *Ibid.*, p. 5.

17. *Ibid.*, p. 18.

18. *Ibid.*, p. 12.

19. *Ibid.*, pp. 3-4.

20. *Ibid.*, p. 17.

21. *Ibid.*, p. 34.

22. *Ibid.*, pp. 34-35.

23. Norman O. Brown, *Life Against Death* (New York, 1959), p. 281.

THE SPLENDORS OF HELL

CRITICAL COMMENTARY

Helen Hellman (essay date 1967)

SOURCE: "*Splendors of Hell*: A Tragic Farce," in *Renascence*, Vol. 20, No. 1, Autumn 1967, pp. 30-38.

[*In the following essay, Hellman discusses elements of* The Splendors of Hell *that outraged audiences at the time of its first performances, arguing that Ghelderode uses the play's profane aspects to emphasize a sense of faith.*]

The play *Splendors of Hell* is interesting from a biographical point of view because its success in Paris in 1949 brought wide public attention to the Belgian playwright, Michel de Ghelderode, who until then had lived in relative obscurity. Although he had chosen the life of a recluse, this somewhat belated success, and the recognition and acclaim by an admiring group of young actors and directors

in Paris amazed and delighted him. In the five or six years following the success of *Splendors of Hell,* which had won first prize in a theatrical competition, "Concours des Jeunes Compagnies," eight of his plays were produced in Paris and elsewhere in Europe.

Splendors of Hell opened in Paris at the fashionable Marigny Theater of Jean-Louis Barrault. The audience, scandalized by the scatological clowning and the apparent profanation of sacred rites, forced Jean-Louis Barrault to ring down the curtain and close the play after three nights. It then played with great success for nine months at the Théâtre des Noctambules.

Ghelderode's success prompted the publication of thirty plays in the years 1951-1957; a series of seven radio interviews in 1951, later published as *Les Entretiens d'Ostende*; and the publication of his correspondence with several of those young Paris directors in the French journal *Revue d'Histoire du Théâtre*. Since then two volumes of selected plays have appeared in English translation, and two or three have become standard works in American repertory.

Ghelderode has said remarkably little about *Splendors of Hell,* which some critics believe his most monumental and complex play. He has not commented on his intentions in writing it, nor has he discussed what some have construed as ambiguities in the play. In an interview in 1950, with *Figaro Littéraire,* he said that he never thought the play would be produced because of its violence and the Bishop's spitting up of the Host. If he had foreseen the possibility of its production, he would have made it not less violent but easier for the actors to perform. He added that for this "diabolical play, I have even received a sparging of holy water which I didn't ask for."

In the course of my exposition of this work, I shall attempt to deal with some of the play's complexities and establish the artistic function of what appears so shocking in the play, its scatological farce and profanation of the Mass. It is my belief that the play is about faith and that its murdered hero survives symbolically as the spiritual victor.

The tragedy of *Splendors of Hell* develops paradoxically in an atmosphere of wild farce and saturnalia, which liberate man's most perverse and profane possibilities. It moves into a crescendo of violence suggesting the fire and flames of the hell paintings of Bosch and Brueghel. But the most telling and revealing action is the play's dénouement in the sixteenth scene, which is a total reversal of the violence of the play up to this point. In contrast to the atmosphere of hell whose sounds are the roar of thunder, the moaning and lamenting of an invisible mob and the final diabolical laughter of the resurrected Jan in Eremo as he comes at his opponent Laquedeem with an axe, this scene takes place in total silence. Jan here reveals himself as the literal embodiment of the fool of faith, the fool in Christ.

As the old servant Veneranda, the Bishop's mother, is brought in, "the action is suddenly immobilized in space as the retributive hatchet is immobilized in air. The silence falls in the same way that thunder does—fatidically. And in this silence, this vacuum, rather, where nothing breathes—even the mob and the storm are quiet—one sees the old woman hop toward the Bishop and cry out in his face." The Bishop, despite his profound inner resistance, humbly obeys her command to pardon and absolve his enemies. He becomes like the little child, the babe to whom the mystery of salvation has been revealed. "In that hour Jesus rejoiced in spirit, and said, 'I thank thee, Oh Father, Lord of Heaven and earth, that thou hast hid these things from the wise and prudent, and hast revealed them unto babes . . .'" He thus rejoins his savages who were closer to the divine truth in their adoration of their fetishes than the monks and priests of the church who claim to love the true God.

In his final gesture of forgiveness and submission, he dies with tears of charity and mercy. He is thus revealed as the "fool of fools," defined by Walter Kaiser in *Praisers of Folly* as the "pious Christian who emulates the folly of Christ, who accepts as Christ did, human frailty. He is a fool because, in accepting the wisdom of Christ, he rejects the wisdom of this world . . .", or in the Erasmian sense, the foolish wisdom of the false doctors and churchmen.

Jan in Eremo, or John in the Desert, is the Ghelderodian hero as the fool of faith, the thaumaturge like Christ himself, who performs the miracles of curing the plague-ridden city of Lapideopolis and finding food for the hungry. Like the other Ghelderodian heroes, he is a Silenus figure whose very humanity necessarily contains the opposing elements of angelic and demonic. After his arrival in Lapideopolis as a mysterious figure of faith who has converted savages in distant places, he accomplishes miracles in the pest-ridden city. He remains there and usurps the power of the church when he remains as Bishop with the support of the populace. His power as head of the church corrupts the force of his faith and he remains to rule over an episcopal court of monks who are in reality gross, impious buffoons. They are obscene and sacrilegious and profane the symbols of the very church they serve. Jan is in conflict and in rebellion against the institution he represents, and his resistance is confirmed in his instructions for burial. He wishes to be placed "right into the earth, without a shroud and in the graveyard of the excommunicate . . ." He wants to remain, as he has always been, the incarnation of solitude, yet in communion with the most lowly. He is thus another form of the Silenus, whose episcopal trappings mask a spirit yearning for solitude, humility and simple faith. In his humble death, he rediscovers faith and humility and reverts to a state of unquestioning childlike obedience to his mother.

Opposed to him are the monks and priests over whom he rules. As in medieval drama, their names describe their distinctive characteristics. As the critic David Grossvogel has observed, "the symbolistic actor of the expressionists is nothing more than a renovation of the old morality figures." Jan in Eremo is the incarnation of solitude; Simon Laquedeem is the complex arch enemy of faith whose peculiarly Flemish scatological waggery is an expression of demonic forces. The name Isaac Laquedeem is one of the names for the Wandering Jew in Flanders. Simon represents also the church of Simon Peter; Carnibos is the glutton; Sodomati, the homosexual representative of the papacy. As Grossvogel remarked, Ghelderode's "monks, priests, vicars and clergymen generally are possessed by all the vices which that profoundly religious age ascribed to them while in the same breath he writes 'mystères' that reflect genuine religious transport."

Splendors of Hell was written in 1929, and can be considered Ghelderode's first really monumental play. Unlike *School for Buffoons* and *Hop Signor!* with which it has certain affinities of structure and characterization, it deals with the hero of religious faith rather than with the artist—but Folial, Juréal and Jan in Eremo are all projections of the traditional fool figure and of the author himself—the fool as *vates,* God-smitten, thaumaturge, seer and poet. They are, in Ghelderode's own words to one of his young directors, living characters who bear his stigmata.

Like *Hop Signor!* and *School for Buffoons,* it is a one-act play which had originally been conceived in three. In seventeen scenes, it suggests the continuous panorama of a medieval mystery play. Its three part structure is discernible in the development of the action and in the alterations of tone. The first seven scenes constitute the opening farce. The monks, who are the incarnation of gluttony, anger and foolishness, steal meat from the banquet table set up like the last supper for the vigil over the body of the dead bishop. They are frightened by his body which lies in state and clown among themselves as they await the arrival of Simon Laquedeem who will officiate at the burial services of the late Bishop, his rival.

In the seventh scene the tone changes when Sodomati, the papal representative, arrives. In the second group of scenes, Simon tells Sodomati the legend of the Bishop, which is also the true story of his life, or as much as is known about it. It is this part of the play, the exposition of the life of a man whom the "mob" has already canonized, which is reminiscent of the New Testament and hagiographic stories. And it is here that the character of the Bishop is created and defined, for in the play he never speaks. Jan in Eremo resembles the figure of Christ, who also performed miracles. The circumstances of Jan's birth are vague—it is rumored that he is the child of a mermaid and a monk. But Laquedeem describes them thus: "Jan in Eremo was his name. John in the desert, in memory of those sands where he was found—child of an unknown mother, child without a name—found by the monks of the Abbey of the Dunes, who had been awakened by his haunting cries. It is more than seventy years ago that he was born, John in the desert; John who was son of the sea and sand, John who used to say: 'I am solitude'—and he was!"

Just as the life of Christ is partially narrated by the evangelists and then told through his own words which reveal the events that had taken place, so, too, the legend of Jan in Eremo is recounted by his "false disciple," and the final events actually played out by Jan himself during the miraculous "resurrection." Christ, symbol of compassion and faith, was Himself forced to play the first buffoon in those moments of mockery when the crown of thorns was placed upon His head by the hypocrites and the reed placed in His hand. He knew Himself the scapegoat when He said: "For he shall be delivered unto the Gentiles and shall be mocked and spitefully entreated and spitted upon." As the body and blood of the sacrifical lamb are partaken of in continuation of the faith, Simon Laquedeem links Jan to Jesus when he rails out against the former during his struggle: "Let him not cross my path, your Jesus! . . . Wait, my people. You'll get your portion of flesh!"

The third part of the play consists of the struggle between Laquedeem and the Bishop, who rises up as if miraculously to attack his enemy. With superhuman strength he has survived and refused to swallow the poisoned host which Laquedeem had given him. He is in an agony of suffocation because of the host lodged in his throat and threatens to murder Simon. He is saved from his vengeance by Veneranda who draws the poisoned host from his throat and commands him to forgive his enemies, if he wishes forgiveness. At her command he submits to his true death.

The celebrated critic Charles de Tolnay, taking his cue from Erasmus' reference to the Silenus in *The Praise of Folly,* wrote in his study of Brueghel's drawings that these sheets on "mundane Folly are like the hermae of Silenus; they show a different face outwardly from that which is enclosed within them, that is, the truth. Their meaning becomes accessible to him who relies solely on the experience of form." So in *Splendors of Hell,* a tragedy-bouffe, the elements of farce and tragedy are often mingled, and the play's meaning in all its ambiguities is expressed in this very interplay. It begins and ends in a farce which both encloses and prefigures the tragic action, just as did *Hop Signor!,* written six years later.

The ceaseless repetition of farce in Ghelderode's plays is analogous to repetition of line and motif in Northern and Gothic art, where there is no intervention of desire for organic moderation and serenity. Wilhelm Worringer in *Form in Gothic* defines the will to form in Northern art in a remarkably illuminating passage which does much to explain why Ghelderode has been described as absolutely summing up the genius of Flanders:

> Our organically tempered sense of vitality recoils before this senseless rage of expression as from a debauch. When, however, finally yielding to compulsion, its energies flood these lifeless lines, it feels itself carried away in a strange and wonderful manner and raised to an ecstasy of movement, far outstripping any possibilities of organic movement. The pathos of movement which lies in this vitalized geometry—a prelude to the vitalized mathematics of Gothic architecture—forces our sensibility to an effort unnatural to it. When once the natural barriers of organized movement have been

overthrown, there is no more holding back: again and again it is forcibly prevented from peacefully ending its course, again and again diverted into fresh complications of expression, so that tempered by all these restraints, it exerts its energy of expression to the uttermost until at last, bereft of all possibilities of natural pacification, it ends in confused, spasmodic movements, breaks off unappeased into the void or flows senselessly back upon itself.

Thus the interplay of farce and tragedy in *Splendors of Hell,* of such seemingly disparate elements as the mystic and the digestive, the divine and the scatological are repeated and expanded until the very end when the guild of butchers come to take the body of the Bishop. The play's complexities reside exactly in this interplay, in the infernal debasement of holy symbols, on the one hand, and the sublimation, on the other, of the common, the lowly and the unclean. Thus Simon Laquedeem, seized by a stomach cramp, cries out: "My belly! . . . Calvary of my belly!" Whereas Jan in Eremo uses the idols of head hunters as symbols of faith, and he is himself the patron of the guild of butchers.

The key symbol in the play is the Host, the consecrated bread which, according to Catholic dogma, contains the body, the soul and the divinity of Christ. It is here a poisoned host, representing a corrupted doctrine, and it is administered by a cleric who is physically and spiritually corrupt. The dying bishop is unable to swallow the host, just as he was uable, during his lifetime, to swallow the impure doctrine of a poisoned church. The Church was an obstruction for him in the true exercise of his faith, and he has this to say of its practitioners: "Men of the Church, my savages in adoring these lying gods were closer to the divine truth than you, the anointed, who pretend to adore the true God." The Church of which he is bishop represents also his compromise of pure subjective faith, and it is a barrier between him and the people, his communicants, who had canonized him. Real-Temblor, the arch-deacon, says as much when he reports the attitude of the populace: ". . . the people were willing to march in honor of the bishop, but without priests or sacristans, in the sole company of the giants and dragons of carnival, and all in silence and with dignity." The poisoned host remains an obstruction in his throat, which he finally spits up and rejects. As a symbol of faith, he in turn may be construed as an obstruction barring the rise to power of the auxiliary bishop, whose relief, when the obstructive bishop is removed, is expressed in the scatological farce at the end of the play.

The Host, symbol of the most exalted mystery in the Christian religion, becomes an obstruction which cannot be swallowed and absorbed, nor regurgitated or expelled. It is the cause of the Bishop's final torment, which permits him neither to live nor to die. It is also a symbol of the tragic ambiguity, conflict and hell in which he lived as ruler over a corrupt clergy.

The play opens with a parody of Christ's commandment that "except you eat the flesh of the Son of Man and drink his blood, you shall not have life in you . . . for my flesh is meat indeed; and my blood is drink indeed." This first profanation by Carnibos, the chaplain, whose spitting up of meat from the "last supper" which he had wolfed and couldn't swallow, prefigures the tragic dilemma of the Bishop, who cannot swallow the Host lodged in his throat. By analogy the Host and the meat become one, and the symbolic ritual of the Mass is reduced to its most literal action. The farce is thus a profanation of the church's most sacred ritual and an ironic comment on the suggestion of cannibalism inherent in it.

Christian symbols and events from Christ's life and the lives of the saints serve as an inspiration for the tragic action as well as the buffoonery. They are so frequently referred to that an interpretation of the play in terms of Christian myth is inescapable. Such an interpretation of the play must derive from the struggle between the two protagonists, Jan in Eremo, the thaumaturge, who represents a state of subjective faith, albeit a faith he has compromised; and Simon Laquedeem, a faithless representative of the organized Church. The first crucial episode in this conflict has taken place before the play begins, and the audience is informed about it by one of the protagonists. Laquedeem tells the secretary of the papal ambassador how he had administered final communion to the dying Bishop. He tells how the bishop had watched him like an emaciated old eagle. "That eye, full of an unspeakable hatred, missed nothing of my gestures, followed my hands. And when I offered the host, the eye shot a glance of steel at me and the lips closed tight. But when I solemnly abjured him to receive the body and the blood of the living God, the eye was extinguished and the lips unsealed. He made his communion."

The play begins with a kind of Last Supper during which the sacrament of the Eucharist, which originated with Christ's Last Supper, is burlesqued by Krakenbus and Carnibos, the meat stealer, when the former shoves a piece of meat into Carnibos' mouth. Krakenbus thus plays out the tragic offering of the poisoned host, as he says: "Open your trap? *(Puts the meat in Carnibos' mouth.)* Give thanks, worm? Thanks!" Krakenbus, the hump-backed vicar, also parodies the symbol of the nails of the cross, as he constantly crushes the feet of his fellow monks with his heel. Another parallel which may be drawn with the Last Supper of Christ is the foreknowledge of betrayal by a false disciple. Carnibos, in recounting to Sodomati the occasion of the Bishop's death, quotes the latter as having said: "The hour is coming that I know of, forestalling that hour which God has fixed, and I accept it, since he permits it to be forestalled." This is a further example of Jan's faith and submission to the Divine spirit, and his words echo those of Christ in the garden of Gethsemane: "Father, if thou be willing, remove this cup from me: nevertheless not my will but thine be done."

The Bishop Jan in Eremo, or John in the Desert, is a hero who bears an ambiguous resemblance to Christ and to John the Baptist. To begin with, there is his legendary

birth: he leaves his own country and after many wanderings and a sojourn among the cannibals whom he has converted, he arrives, as if walking on the waters, to the pest-ridden city of Lapideopolis, city of stone, whose name suggests both the church of Peter and the lapidating of the Christian martyrs. Jan appears, bent under a huge cross, like Christ carrying the Cross to Calvary. But unlike Christ who dies upon the Cross, he throws his cross into the fires in which are burning the corpses of the plague-dead. The cross which Jan casts into the fire seems to purify the city; the atmosphere clears, the sick are healed, and Jan, like Christ, miraculously finds food for the hungry. This gesture may also be considered Jan's rejection of the cross, or a sacrifice to and appeasement of diabolic forces—a descent from pure subjective faith. Jan becomes the worker of objective miracles and a figure of authority in the city. Thenceforward his communion with the folk is direct, and the people become his disciples. Their love and faith sanctify him in effect. For them he has given up subjectivity and become a part of the only institution where he can effectively use his power. By main force he becomes Bishop of Lapideopolis, resisting the official clergy and nobility which returns to the city, and commits the "imposture" which, as Laquedeem says, is later consecrated by Rome.

Jan's assumption of episcopal power puts him into the false position of representing a church he can hardly believe necessary to the adoration of divine truth. From then on he exists in a state of hell, where, as the tormented upholder of subjective faith in the divine, he rules vengefully over an episcopal court of buffoons and clowns. His revolt against the church, his inner hell are represented by the decor of hideous idols, devils, witches' masks and fetishes of the barbarians he had converted. The grotesque monks in their devilish clowning are the living expression of these bizarre images.

Although there is a certain ambiguity in the bishop's character and in the significance of his throwing down of the cross, his railing against the priests and monks seems a fairly clear indication of the nature of his tragic dilemma. In Ghelderode's vision of religion, he seems very close to the attitudes of the sixteenth century as defined by Tolnay: "The fool and rogue literature of the sixteenth century developed out of the same spiritual attitude as the universal-religious theism and the new pantheism. In religion it was the apprehension of the *one* God, who despite all the diversities of the confessions, underlies them all as the ultimate truth in each; in pantheism it was the apprehension of the one vital force, the world-soul, which lies at the basis of all Nature despite the boundless diversity of its forms."

Jan's spiritual conflict finds its external expression in his struggle with Laquedeem. The latter had been a young deacon at the time of the plague, who had stayed with the people to comfort or bury them as the situation required. But as the Bishop's auxiliary, corrupted by ambition and revolt, as an incarnation of the devil who is absolutely devoid of faith, he betrayed the Bishop when he attempted to murder him with a poisoned host, although he had betrayed him and his God long before.

In the struggle between Jan and Simon, his assistant and false disciple, Jan's condition is ambiguous. Has he been miraculously resurrected? Or is he not yet dead? "His right hand ceaselessly tries to unknot invisible bonds about his throat, and sometimes he thrusts his hand into his mouth as if trying to pull out some obstruction which is suffocating him: Inexpressible torture! . . . Is he an old man forever agonizing and asking for death? Is he a resurrected corpse, rejected by death, struggling to live again?"

Through the intervention of Veneranda, his mother, the old Bishop is enabled to spit up the poisoned host. At her command, he absolves his enemies and pardons them albeit with regret. She commands him: "Lie down, my child! And die in your tears!" He dies, relinquishing his hatred of his enemies, the hypocrites and the faithless, in obedience to her love and devotion. He dies without Communion; he has rejected the Host. But his death, in charity and merciful tears, is an expiation of his compromised faith and, at the same time, a confirmation of his faith and his communion with the folk. His wish to rest with the excommunicated outside the Church is thus granted. He is now free from the oppression of the Church which he had suffered in his lifetime, and from that crushing oppression with which Laquedeem had threatened his corpse: "We'll dress him in iron, in lead, in oak; we'll hide him in the deepest crypt, and the cathedral will rest on his bones with all its weight."

The Bishop's death had freed him from the torment of the poisoned host. His spiritual conflict is over as he dies his merciful death, which is the signal for relief and catharsis, and which clears the menacing atmosphere of storm gathering outside the palace. His death in humility and obedience has dispelled the storm, just as his arrival with the cross which he threw into the flames drove out plague and storm in its pillar of fire.

The removal of the obstructive host, the relief of the Bishop, are parodied by Laquedeem as he joyfully squats after a final attack of cramps. All the monks are purged as well, and the curtain falls as they celebrate their demoniac victory in a profane farce. It is a simple matter to see in the image of these clowning priests, leaping about in clouds of smoking incense, the inspiration of the "diableries" of Bosch and Brueghel, to whom Ghelderode frequently referred as sources of inspiration. His theatrical invention is richly permeated with the sensuousness proper to the plastic arts, an essential attribute of his theater which he discussed in *Les Entretiens d'Ostende*. Every aspect of the decor he describes for **Splendors of Hell** is the visual correlative of the action and is an expression of the play of ambiguities and paradox inherent in the tragedy-bouffe: "The wall coverings hang in rags. On the walls, hung very high, are the portraits of priests; and along the bottoms of the walls, everywhere, stand a variety of baroque objects:

idols, suns, witch doctors' masks, motley devils, totems, stakes, and instruments of torture. But downstage there is a heavy table sumptuously laid with a crimson velvet cloth, silver service, and crystal glasses."

Before this table prepared for a last supper, framed by the portraits of mighty churchmen hung on torn and decayed tapestries, the low farce of the monks and the crucial struggle between Jan and Simon have taken place. The portraits hung on high constitute a typical Ghelderodian irony, whose other side is expressed by the idols, witches' masks and instruments of torture scattered about below. These diabolical images symbolize at the same time the pure faith of the savages. In their grotesqueness they carry out the theme and repeat in Gothic style the bizarre and demoniac postures of the clergy.

Although **Splendors of Hell** concludes almost immediately after the death of the Bishop with the apparent triumph of the buffoons and Laquedeem, the ultimate moral victory belongs to Jan in Eremo. His lonely rebellion against hypocrisy and pharisaism, against an existence without the divine, is vindicated in his death. His tears and the absolution of his enemies suggest charity, mercy and obedience to divine will, as well as the lesson that the usurpation of worldly power does not defeat that power. In **Splendors of Hell** the buffoons, the corrupt and the damned, the hypocritical "men of the church" are in reality destroyed by ridicule and farce, while Jan in Eremo remains as a triumphant fool of faith.

LA BALADE DU GRAND MACABRE

CRITICAL COMMENTARY

Alain Piette (essay date 1986)

SOURCE: " Michel de Ghelderode's *La Balade du Grand Macabre*: The Triumph of Life," in *Before His Eyes: Essays in Honor of Stanley Kauffmann*, edited by Bert Cardullo, University Press of America, 1986, pp. 51-55.

[*In the following essay, Piette argues that Ghelderode achieves his greatest thematic unity in* La Balade du Grand Macabre.]

Death is omnipresent in Michel de Ghelderode's theater, a recurrent theme that often betrays his inclination toward the gloomy and the gruesome. American audiences are probably more familiar with the dark and biting irony of **Pantagleize,** set, in 1929, "on the morrow of one war and the eve of another" and intended by the dramatist as "a farce to make you sad."[1] *Mademoiselle Jaïre,* written in

1934, presents an even darker embodiment of that theme: the sexual frenzy of the protagonist Blandine after she rises from the dead at times verges on necrophilia and is the epitome of natural horror. In the same year, Ghelderode wrote **La Balade du Grand Macabre**. Although this play also centers on the theme of death, it has little in common with **Mademoiselle Jaïre** or **Pantagleize**. As its subtitle, "Farce for Rhetoricians,"[2] suggests, the author's purpose is to present us with a surprisingly merry view of death.

The "Grand Macabre," the Grim Reaper of the title, is Nekrozotar. He introduces himself as the Angel of Death and says that he has come to earth to claim his toll: he announces the destruction of the world by a gigantic comet at midnight. In his peregrinations through Breugellande, where the play is set, he meets a series of colorful characters who never take him seriously: the charming lovers Adrian and Jusemina, the jocose drunkard Porprenaz, the philosopher Videbolle and his shrewish wife Salivaine, King Goulave of Breugellande and his two ministers Aspiquet and Basiliquet. After the characters have a night of revelry and frenzy in reaction to the impending end of the world, we witness what at first seems to be the predicted cataclysm. But Nekrozotar's efforts at destruction are not successful, because no one is killed. Ironically, the Angel of Death himself dies as the inhabitants of Breugellande start reorganizing their lives.

This inability to carry out his threats turns out to be the mark of Nekrozotar. When he appears on stage, he seems to be the embodiment of death itself, a tall figure whose outward appearance matches the darkness of his soul: he is bald and skeletal; he wears black clothing and heavy black boots. We are not meant to be deluded for long by this dismal apparition, however, since we see Porprenaz kick his bottom during their first encounter. Their initial conversation sets the tone for the rest of the play. Porprenaz makes us feel that there is nothing to be afraid of, despite Nekrozotar's declared intention to destroy the world at midnight:

NEKROZOTAR. Are you happy in this life?

PORPRENAZ. Immensely.

NEKROZOTAR. You will die.

PORPRENAZ. I know.

NEKROZOTAR. Your belly will burst.

PORPRENAZ. It will release a strong smell of beer.

NEKROZOTAR. You won't be hungry anymore and you will be eaten.

PORPRENAZ. The worms will feast.

NEKROZOTAR. You won't be thirsty anymore and the earth will swallow you.

PORPRENAZ. Stop! What are you saying?! Not thirsty anymore?[3]

Thirst is the only "evil" Porprenaz cannot bear to think of. Only this is capable of arousing his anger, and he prepares to beat Nekrozotar. As early as the first scene, then, Nekrozotar is portrayed as a clownish, totally harmless creature whose character sometimes verges on the grotesque. When the curtain rises, he is hiding in a tree, one of his legs hanging from the foliage. Seeing the leg, the facetious Porprenaz starts pulling it with all his strength, with the result that the sound of bells comes from the tree. Nekrozotar falls, and we discover that he wears bells around his waist: we are urged, therefore, to perceive this character as an eccentric court jester rather than as a potential threat.

This image of Nekrozotar is reinforced when he starts gathering the instruments he needs to carry out his mission. The scythe he brandishes has too often been associated with death to remain a significant symbol. He wears a ridiculous leather hat and a leather coat that is too long, and he plays the *Dies Irae* out of tune on his copper trumpet. Clearly, this shabby image of death is not to be taken seriously. On the contrary, as we witness the confrontation between the emaciated buffoon and the fat drunkard, we cannot help feeling that we are being presented with reincarnations of Don Quixote and Sancho Panza. And indeed, Porprenaz agrees to become Nekrozotar's servant. He even consents to be his mount, his Rosinante, for the fallen knight does not own a horse. As Nekrozotar and Porprenaz leave the stage, it seems that, instead of going off to trigger the predicted cataclysm, they are on their way to their own version of Cervantes' windmills.

The quizzical characterization of Nekrozotar does not come to an end with this ridiculous exit. Throughout the play, he is given comical names: Your Highness, Your Meagerness, Your Ugliness, Your Translucence, and Your Paleness, among many others, some of them invented by Ghelderode (and therefore untranslatable). These mocking names are perfectly in keeping with the protagonist's own name, which connotes his madness and ridiculousness. As Jean Decock has pointed out, the word "Nekrozotar" is an odd combination of ancient Greek, Flemish dialect, and Latin.[4] "Nekro-" is a Greek prefix meaning "death"; "-zot-" is a Flemish adjective meaning "mad"; and "-ar" is a Latin suffix that means "having the quality of."

Ghelderode, then, presents death as a potentially deranged character from the start. By the end of the last scene, Nekrozotar himself confirms our initial suspicions about his madness. The announced apocalypse has not taken place, and Nekrozotar piteously confesses that he is only an embittered, distracted senex who wanted to revenge himself on his former wife, Salivaine, a ruthless, mannish shrew who used to beat and scold him (and who is now married to Videbolle):

NEKROZOTAR. I was young and strong, loving life and my fellow man.

GOULAVE. Doesn't your head ache sometimes?

NEKROZOTAR. There are rocks in it. So many blows! It is cracked.

GOULAVE. How did it happen?

NEKROZOTAR. The whip . . . the broom. And my love died. And I ate the yeast of hatred.

(p. 121)

Exhausted by his confession and by events leading up to the aborted cataclysm, the old man dies and, in a puzzling peripeteia, all the characters show compassion for him. This death is dramatically prepared in the opening scene, when Porprenaz pulls Nekrozotar from the tree while uttering these ominous words: "Okay, I pull, and like the hangman I will swing with the convict" (p. 37). The figure of death is thus given a human dimension: the Angel of Death becomes a vulnerable mortal, and consequently is more easily demystified by us as well as by the characters.

Porprenaz and his friends never seem to feel threatened by Nekrozotar's presence. In fact, the atmosphere of the play is never gloomy, in contrast with the rest of Ghelderode's work. We are often reminded in *La Balade du Grand Macabre* of the Dionysian ambience that pervades a Flemish kermis as depicted by Breughel in many of his paintings, the influence of which Ghelderode always asserted. (In recognition of this quality in the play, the French director René Dupuy entitled his 1953 Paris production of it *La grande Kermesse.*) *La Balade du Grand Macabre* is set in Breugellande, and the stage directions describing the scenery are almost the colorful strokes of a painter:

GREEN. The grass, the bushes, and a round tree . . .

VIOLET. The sky . . .

WHITE. Left, a tomb falling into ruins. It is a whitewashed cube with a pediment and a door at the back.

FAR. The misty city of Breugellande, battlemented with domes and belltowers.

NEAR. A part of an abandoned yard at the end of a spring day. Proud loneliness.

(p. 31)

Even though death is always present in the canvases of Breughel, we derive from them a general impression of unrestrained joy and popular celebration, as we do from Ghelderode's play in spite of its protagonist and the tomb on stage. In Scene 1, Porprenaz walks on stage playing an accordion and singing an irreverent tune. Drinking bouts abound, and we are even presented with a mock circus parade advertising the performance:

PORPRENAZ. Alarm! He is arriving, he has arrived! Who? The Phantasmagoric, the Thread-Cutter, the Bogeyman, the Boneless, the Historian of Doom, the Producer of Cataclysms, the Director of the Ultimate Shindy, the Master of the Worms, the Piercer of Paunches . . . He is coming, the one that nobody expects . . . Book your seats. At midnight, the theater will burn, explode, collapse, and nothing will be grand anymore . . . Come and see what you have never seen and never will again. We play only once. There is room for everybody.

(p. 79)

"The Histrion of Doom, the Producer of Cataclysms, the Director of the Ultimate Shindy . . . At midnight, the theater will burn, explode, collapse . . ." In this almost surrealistic juxtaposition of theatrical and cataclysmic terms—a juxtaposition that applies to the clownish yet deathlike figure of Nekrozotar himself—lies an aspect of Ghelderode's artistry. He suggests here that we conceive of the whole play as a gigantic show, a grand spectacle, a treat for the eyes. The flourish of colors and forms, the movement of resplendently attired characters through a picturesque landscape, far from obliterating the thematic substance of the play, actually serves Ghelderode's purposes. The baroque beauty of the set and of the colorful costumes induces in us a feeling of bliss rather than fear, thus undercutting the potential horror of death. The dramatist is attempting in this play to "kill" death by ridiculing or demystifying it, while inviting us to share his philosophy of life, which strongly recalls Horace's "carpe diem."

In the *Ostend Interviews* Ghelderode declared, "All my life has been a dance around a coffin . . . In order to get rid of your specters, you have to write about them." But he was not simply trying to get rid of his private specters in *La Balade du Grand Macabre*. It was written in 1934, when the ghost of fascism was already beginning to threaten Europe and the world. The play is the striking visualization not only of the dark premonition of a lucid dramatist, but also of the deepest belief of a genuine humanist. For Ghelderode does not rest content to warn us against the impending catastrophe, he gives us an alternative to it, as every true artist can be said to do. The structure of the play is circular. It opens and closes with the same image: that of the young lovers Adrian and Jusemina, whose flirtation is interrupted at the start by Nekrozotar (who places them in confinement in the tomb) but resumes as if nothing had happened at the end of the last scene (when they walk out of the tomb). Their conversation at the close of the play is the exact continuation of their opening dialogue. The tomb has proved unable to imprison the two lovers for eternity; death has been deflated. The theme of love, as conveyed through the relationship of Adrian and Jusemina, the only really appealing couple in all of Ghelderode's plays, is meant to enclose *La Balade du Grand Macabre* in a parenthesis. As Jean Decock has observed, their lovemaking is the ideal antidote to the ravages of death: procreation and proliferation—underlined by the abundant vegetation that is slowly taking over the stage—annihilate the effects of destruction. Indeed, as Adrian takes Jusemina away, he speaks of birth and renewal. "Everything has been purified and washed. You walk slower because you have a treasure buried in your flesh. From now on, I shall listen to your silence to hear that minuscule heart beating under yours" (p. 127). The theme of rebirth and fertility is further emphasized by the time symbolism. The action begins on the evening of a misty spring day and ends as the sun rises on the following morning. As the parenthesis of love is being closed, we realize that we have been presented, not with the image of death contained in the title of the play, but rather with the triumph of life. Porprenaz himself is aware of this triumph, and at the sight of Adrian and Jusemina emerging from the tomb he voices the dramatist's innermost conviction: "The human race cannot perish" (p. 127).

In the *Ostend Interviews* Ghelderode said, "The only purpose of the theater is to portray man, the human being. I wanted to show man as he is now and, through him, the eternal man" (p. 79). *La Balade du Grand Macabre* does just that. In it, Ghelderode attained a unity of intent and expression that remained unequalled throughout his work. The play is, in my view, the major achievement of this important dramatist and true humanist. Like Cervantes' *Don Quixote, **La Balade du Grand Macabre*** has its roots in the anthropomorphism of the culture of the folk, but grows out of these roots to address universal and eternal concerns.

Notes

1. Michel de Ghelderode, *Pantagleize,* in *Ghelderode: Seven Plays,* trans. Georges Hauger (New York: Hill and Wang, 1960), I, p. 143 (2nd quotation), p. 150 (1st one).

2. Roger Iglesis and Alain Trutat, ed., *Les Entretiens d'Ostende* (Paris: L'Arche, 1956), p. 168. Hereafter referred to in the text by page number. All translations are my own.

3. Michel de Ghelderode, *La Balade du Grand Macabre,* in *Théâtre II* (Paris: Gallimard, 1952), p. 39. Hereafter referred to in the text by page number. My translations.

4. Jean Decock, *Le Théâtre de Michel de Ghelderode: Une Dramaturgie de l'Anti-Théâtre et de la Cruauté* (Paris: A.G. Nizet, 1969), p. 113.

FURTHER READING

Criticism

Ghelderode, Michel de. "To Directors and Actors: Letters, 1948-1959." *Tulane Drama Review* 9, No. 4 (Summer 1965): 41-62.

Collection of letters written by Ghelderode to various people in the theater community, most discussing interpretation of his plays.

Gilman, Richard. "Official Mediocrity." In *Common and Uncommon Masks: Writings on Theatre 1961-1970,* pp. 295-98. New York: Random House, 1971.

Offers a negative assessment of an American Repertory Theater's production of *Pantagleize.*

Merivale, P. "*Endgame* and the Dialogue of King and Fool in the Monarchical Metadrama." *Modern Drama* 21, No. 2 (June 1978): 121-36.

Includes *Escurial* in a discussion of the opposing characters of king and fool in the modern metadrama, exemplified by Samuel Beckett's *Endgame.*

Harold Pinter
1930-

(Also wrote under the pseudonym Harold Pinta and acted under the stage name David Baron) English dramatist, screenwriter, short story writer, novelist, poet, actor, and director.

INTRODUCTION

Regarded as a major playwright of the later twentieth century, Pinter first achieved renown in the late 1950s and early 1960s as the author of comedies peopled by ambiguously dangerous, intrusive figures and their victims. His plays are characterized by shifting patterns of domination and submission, linguistic minimalism, dialogue veiling the unsaid, anxious or ominous silences, verbal and physical brutality, individuals alienated from others, emotional longing, sexual pain, blocked communication, and an ambience of absurdity. The plays are superficially realistic and bear some resemblance to the working-class dramas of resentment, rebellion, and despair written by John Osborne, Shelagh Delaney, and the other English "angry young men" playwrights of the late 1950s. Pinter's art—a reflection of political terror and violence in the twentieth century—strips away the anchoring comforts of narrative realism, psychological motivation, social context, and rationality, presenting the stark present itself.

BIOGRAPHICAL INFORMATION

Born in 1930, Pinter grew up in Hackney, a working-class London neighborhood with a substantial Jewish population. His childhood was marked by two traumatic circumstances: the presence in Hackney of a large, active, violent ultra-rightist movement headed by Oswald Mosley, the British Fascist; and the Nazi bombing of London, which began in 1939. Pinter was a bookish boy, attracted to the works of Franz Kafka and Ernest Hemingway. He was an acclaimed actor in high school for his portrayals of Macbeth and Romeo. After high school, Pinter held a series of odd jobs. Refusing induction into the army because of a disallowance to "subscribe" to "the suffering and horror of war," he was minimally punished with a thirty pound fine. Pinter went on to acting school and pursued a career as an actor. He met and married the actress Vivian Merchant (who appeared in a number of his plays, and whom he

divorced in 1980 to marry the historian Antonia Fraser) and began writing poetry and a novel. He wrote his first play, *The Room* (1957), during a period of four afternoons between morning rehearsals for one play and evening performances in another. It was produced by the drama department at Bristol University. Although an amateur production, it was favorably reviewed in the *Times* of London, and that review led to a request by producer Michael Codron for a play. Pinter wrote *The Birthday Party* (1958) and *The Dumb Waiter* (1959) for him, beginning his theater career in earnest. Pinter also enjoyed considerable success as a film writer, especially for his collaborations with Joseph Losey. Their first film, *The Servant,* appeared in 1963. He also wrote *Accident* (1967), *The Go-Between* (1971), and *The Proust Screenplay* (1977), an unfilmed adaptation of Marcel Proust's *In Search of Lost Time* for Losey. Other film scripts include *The Pumpkin Eater* (1964) and adaptations of *The Last Tycoon* (1974), *The French Lieutenant's Woman* (1981), and *The Handmaid's Tale* (1990). Pinter also has directed his and other writers' plays including Robert Shaw's fictionalization of the Eichman trial, *The Man in the Glass Booth,* James Joyce's *Exiles,* and Noel Coward's *Blithe Spirit.* Pinter's own plays in the 1980s became overtly political, revealing his opposition to imperialism, war, governmental authority, and torture. His play *Mountain Language* (1988) grew out of his visit—as a representative of PEN, the international writers' league—with Arthur Miller to Turkey, where he became *persona non grata* for openly condemning Turkey's torture of political opponents.

MAJOR WORKS

With plays such as *The Room, The Birthday Party, The Dumbwaiter, The Caretaker* (1960), and *The Homecoming* (1965), Pinter established himself as a major figure in the theater. In such later plays as *Landscape* (1968), *Silence* (1969), and *Old Times* (1971), Pinter moved away from the minimalistic actions and the eerie tone of menace and personal disintegration that characterize his earlier plays. Pinter now found favor in the interactive ruminations of characters who do not speak directly to each other, although they people the same stage and meditate about the same events. Thematically the later plays excavate the drama of internal consciousness, memory, perception, and the unverifiability of either experience or reality.

CRITICAL RECEPTION

Pinter's first play to be professionally produced, *The Birthday Party,* was met with nearly universal disdain, and closed within a week. Critics panned it as being obscure and overly symbolic. Harold Hobson, the reviewer for the *London Sunday Times* was the exception, writing that "Pinter . . . possesses the most original, disturbing and arresting talent in theatrical London." Pinter's second full-length play, *The Caretaker,* enjoyed more critical acclaim. Kenneth Tynan in *The Observer,* backed away from his previous criticism, writing that "Pinter has begun to fulfil the promise that I singly failed to see . . . two years ago." In *The New York Times,* Howard Taubman proclaimed Pinter "one of the important playwrights of our day." *The Caretaker* won the Evening Standard Award in 1961, and the Newspaper Guild of New York Award in 1962. With successive plays, Pinter established a recognizable quality so native to him that Pinteresque became an adjective denoting a laconic, menacing force threatening to undermine established routines and identities. His plays, screenplays, and radio and television work have won numerous awards, and in 1996 he received the Laurence Olivier Award for a lifetime's achievement in the theater. Pinter has come to be considered by many critics and scholars as the most important British playwright of the twentieth century since George Bernard Shaw.

PRINCIPAL WORKS

Plays

The Room 1957
The Birthday Party 1958
The Dumb Waiter 1959
A Slight Ache 1959
The Caretaker 1960
The Dwarfs 1960
A Night Out 1960
The Collection 1961
The Lover 1963
The Homecoming 1965
Tea Party 1965
The Basement 1967
Landscape 1968
Night 1969
Silence 1969
Old Times 1971
No Man's Land 1975
Betrayal 1978
The Hothouse 1980
Family Voices 1981
A Kind of Alaska 1982
Victoria Station 1982
One for the Road 1984
Mountain Language 1988
The New World Order 1991
Party Time 1991
Moonlight: A Play 1993
Ashes to Ashes 1997
Celebration; and The Room 1999

Screenplays

The Servant 1963
The Pumpkin Eater 1964
Accident 1967
The Quiller Memorandum 1967
The Go-Between 1971
The Last Tycoon 1974
The Proust Screenplay 1977
The French Lieutenant's Woman 1981
Betrayal 1982
Turtle Diary 1985
Reunion 1989
The Comfort of Strangers 1990
The Handmaid's Tale 1990
Lolita 1997

Other Major Works

Various Voices: Prose, Poetry, Politics (collected works)
1998

OVERVIEWS AND GENERAL STUDIES

Kay Dick (essay date 1961)

SOURCE: "Mr. Pinter and the Fearful Matter," in *Texas Quarterly,* Vol. 4, No. 3, Autumn, 1961, pp. 257-65.

[*In the following essay, Dick examines the themes in Pinter's work and considers Pinter's plays in the context of the renaissance of English theater in the late 1950s and early 1960s.*]

> *"I think communication is a very fearful matter. . . ."*
>
> Harold Pinter: *Monitor* B.B.C. television interview,
> June 1960.

In three years, from 1957 to 1960, Harold Pinter has produced an astonishing volume of dramatic work. This consists of several radio and television plays, including the B.B.C.'s *succès d'estime, A Slight Ache* (also broadcast on the German radio), and *A Night Out,* a grim farce written for commercial television; many revue sketches, the most stylistically distinguished being those written for several London shows; two one-act plays, *The Room* and *The Dumb Waiter,* and two three-act plays, *The Birthday Party* and *The Caretaker.* What is possibly most astonishing is the crescendo of critical and material success that has paralleled this new contribution to the contemporary English theatre, particularly striking because Pinter's dramatic framework is uniformly and progressively idiosyncratic.

Pinter's plays have startled and baffled many, yet his best producer, and one of his first, James Roose-Evans, late of the Belgrade Theatre, Coventry, now Director of the Hampstead Theatre Club, says Pinter is one of the dramatists most easy to produce, because "there is so little for the producer to do." He is an author "who can be trusted"; one who has "an instinctive sense of the theatre and rhythm." It is enough to work to the Pinter script—extraneous embellishments obfuscate the work's basic clarity.

Certainly Pinter's basic obsession with clarity inspires the uniformity of his characters, who, socially, might be termed classless. They are not so much tramps in the Beckett sense—that is, dispossessed beggars—as persons without social security, which of course could be said of all of us in the wider sociological index. Their visual symbols relate to poverty, suggest the broken down, the

failure, the unemployable, the misfit, the slum dweller, the scavenger, the beachcomber. Their possessions are rubbish and cast-off properties, and yet they are not introduced as defeated. On the contrary, they are tremendously active, optimists even; ever alert and ready for the moment, simultaneously prepared for joy and grief. They are considerate and thoughtful people in that they clearly acknowledge each other's individuality even though fully conscious that clashes of personality are inevitable in all human relationships. They are brave and fearful, as we are all forced by circumstances to be brave about our personal experience (if only because we have no other kind of experience), and fearful of the social consequences of intimacy and communication.

Between this bravery and this fear, Pinter illuminates those tidal area of sympathy and understanding which stimulate intimacy and boastfulness between his characters. This intimacy provoked to excess, which is boastfulness, produces confusion and action, the last resort against those nameless and indefinable threats to individual security and survival which come not only from outside, but which are within each of us. Knowledgeable and questing are Pinter's characters, open to change and revolution, even though they compel themselves, almost automatically, to fight both for and against all change and its consequent revolution of the status quo. Their material assets are few. The stress on background poverty is a typical Pinter stress and is mainly a relative stress, underlining that all material assets have a fundamental paucity. That Pinter's materially impoverished characters cling so lovingly, passionately indeed, to their miserable, junkish possessions can be viewed as an act of faith, synonymous with the human race's belief in its continuity.

The physical impact of a Pinter play is generally conceded to be terrific, and is probably due to the author's technical proficiency in his handling of actual pace. Pinter was an actor for many years, and in this detail of pace he is a craftsman: moreover, acting is a delight for him, an exercise he much enjoys; hence his consenting to appear himself in a future production of *The Birthday Party.* So compulsive is the tempo of pace in a Pinter play that the audience's participation becomes almost a physical experience. The cunning syncopation of the ferocious and cajolable dialogue stuns the audience into accepting its offbeat reality and revelation. A Pinter play consistently threatens its audience as the play's characters react with hysteria and silence. This silence is that of wonder which comes from a reconsideration of accepted truths.

Mr. Leonard Russell of *The Sunday Times* recently questioned Pinter about the extraordinary hysteria which *The Caretaker* provoked in some audiences. Mr. Russell described his own experience as "a strangely menacing and disturbing evening," and he was puzzled that "a large majority" of the audience interpreted "a heartbreaking theme" as farce: "Gales of happy, persistent, and, it seemed to me, totally indiscriminate laughter greeted a play which I take to be, for all its funny moments, a tragic rendering of life."

Pinter replied that although he himself had indeed laughed while writing **The Caretaker,** certainly his humour had not been indiscriminate: "I did not intend it to be merely a laughable farce. If there hadn't been other issues at stake the play would not have been written. . . . From this kind of uneasy jollification I must, of course, dissociate myself. . . . As far as I'm concerned, **The Caretaker** is funny, up to a point. Beyond that point it ceases to be funny, and it was because of that point that I wrote it."

To interpret a Pinter play other than through literal paraphrase is a dangerous form of exposition. Even so, some comment must be risked. For instance, I would suggest that there is a traceable development of theme in the chronological progression of Harold Pinter's plays. This can best be described by stressing how victory is to the violent in **The Room, The Dumb Waiter,** and **The Birthday Party.** Loosely, this violence can be classified as the world outside: the intruder, the disruptive element, the potential destroyer of individual and local security. Perception of this drove Bert to his final brutish act in **The Room.** Rose, his devoted and humble wife, becomes tainted by the world outside when unexpected visitors (a young couple room-hunting and a blind Negro) stimulate her curiosity. Thereafter she feels and expresses a longing to know more. Bert wants Rose to remain as stagnant a quality as the room itself: he has his share of the world outside in his van driving, which he keeps apart from Rose, cherishing this as though it were a secret love affair. From the beginning Rose is potentially interested in the world beyond their room, and Bert, her taciturn jailor, makes no attempt to satisfy her curiosity. The blind Negro who insists on a private interview with Rose—he purports to be a messenger from her father—is the world outside, and the Negro's task is to persuade Rose to move away from The Room, which implies leaving Bert. Violence, as personified by Bert, whose animalism senses rather than knows, is allowed to triumph. The final effect of disaster is shattering.

The Dumb Waiter introduces Pinter's secondary main characteristic—his dreadful ability to introduce menace into the farcical. Again the theme of violence predominates, although it is more realistically presented. Ben and Gus (the only characters in this play) are two Cockney semiliterate thugs, petty gunmen hired for the killing—specific data are lacking about the extent and pattern of this killing in order to introduce the menace of the unknown. Closeted in a squalid hotel basement, they are harassed by the limitation of their joint intelligence and the gyrating activity of a dumb waiter that sends down a series of senseless orders for crazy meals. Tension is thus aggravated by the ridiculous. When the hour for the deed—still unspecified—approaches, nebulous instructions from an equally nebulous "boss" make themselves felt in the room. The final implication of Gus's being Ben's victim suggests that inevitably the violent man becomes his own prey. Again there is no escape from the violence.

With **The Birthday Party** a new stress is revealed and provides a climax to Pinter's illustration of violence. Liter-ally interpreted this play can be viewed as the drama of an ex-I.R.A. man finally trapped by two gunmen and taken off to his doom. What comes through is less simple. Stan, zany, tainted by mental disorder (the world was too much for him), is shown as a potentially perceptive and courageous individualist who battles ferociously against the evil from outside as represented by Goldberg, the merry grim executioner with a piquant line in sales-talk, and McCann, the dour manic-depressive killer. Stan the victim is protected. This is Pinter's first development of his theme.

Admittedly the protection as such is thin, represented as it is by Stan's doting, foolish, romantic-brained landlady and her slow-thinking, slow-moving husband. The local floosie also stands in as some kind of protection, although hers turns out to be the kind that can be bought. What is important is that there does exist some kind of protective solidarity for Stan, even though its combined action proves to be pretty ineffectual. In Goldberg and McCann we have all the gang pressure of the world outside; the propaganda, the hidden persuaders, the brainwashing. This is clearly established in their final word onslaught on Stan, whom they have almost completely demoralised. Pinter's clarity cannot be misinterpreted in this last pressure on Stan's will. Goldberg and McCann both speak in turn (a sentence from each one), but for the purposes of this illustration the dialogue of this scene is given as a continuity, which of course it is:

> It's about time you had a new pair of glasses. You can't see straight. It's true. You've been cockeyed for years. Now you're even more cockeyed. He's right. You've gone from bad to worse. Worse than worse. You need a long convalescence. A change of air. Somewhere over the rainbow. Where angels fear to tread. Exactly. You're in a rut. You look anemic. Rheumatic. Myopic. Epileptic. You're on the verge. You're a dead duck. But we can save you. From a worse fate. Undeniable. From now on, we'll be the hub of your wheel. We'll renew your season ticket. We'll take tuppence off your morning tea. We'll give you a discount on all inflammable goods. We'll watch over you. Advise you. Give you proper care and treatment. Let you use the club bar. Keep a table reserved. Help you acknowledge the fast days. Bake you cakes. Help you kneel on kneeling days. Give you a free pass. Take you for constitutionals. Give you hot tips. We'll provide the skipping rope. The vest and pants. The ointment. The hot poultice. The fingerstall. The abdomen belt. The ear plugs. The baby powder. The back scratcher. The spare tyre. The stomach pump. The oxygen tent. The prayer wheel. The plaster of Paris. The crash helmet. The crutches. A day and night service. All on the house. That's it. We'll make a man of you. And a woman. You'll be re-oriented. You'll be rich. You'll be adjusted. You'll be our pride and joy. You'll be a mensh. You'll be a success. You'll be integrated. You'll give orders. You'll make a decision. You'll be a magnate. A statesman. You'll own yachts. Animals. Animals. You'll be able to make or break, Stan.

What about the protection Pinter provides for his Stan? It goes the way of all well-meaning yet lazy protection; the landlady's husband makes a half attempt to prevent Stan's being taken away, and his wife willfully ignores the situation, immersing herself more deeply into her world of make-believe. A glimpse of hope has been shown, admittedly to be demolished almost immediately; even so, the Pinter theme is progressing.

The Caretaker continues from where the three previous plays left off, and with a shattering difference. Violence, as personified by Mick, the go-ahead spiv knock-you-down-as-soon-as-look-at-you buster, finally collapses, unable to pursue action (that is, violence) further, and it is passive resistance, embodied in Aston, the gentle, generous, thoughtful, previously sick brother, that triumphs. Aston refuses to compromise with the world outside as this comes through the tramp, whose insecurity and greed are geared for wanton destruction.

When *The Caretaker* opens Aston is shown mending a plug, and he is still concerned with the mending of this same plug at the end of the play. The following quotation illustrates Pinter's philosophical concept.

> ASTON: There's something the matter with it. I'm trying to find out what.
>
> DAVIES: Well, if you . . . persevere, in my opinion, you'll probably find out.
>
> ASTON: I think I've got a pretty good idea.

Creating tension is part of this dramatist's pattern, a suspense which superficially verges on the farcical but simultaneously hints at grim revelation. *The Room* opens with approximately ten minutes of monologue from Rose as she shuffles about, attending to the material comforts of the taciturn and ungrateful Bert. An extraordinary chain of commonplaces is woven, each item plain, almost insignificant, yet the juxtaposition produces chaos. Another notable characteristic is the way in which Pinter's characters are able to concentrate on their strangely limited topics of dialogue no matter how these may be at variance with what is being said by other characters at that particular moment. Pinter is well aware how devastating every word is in this business of communication and how impossible it is to cancel any spoken word. Life, he appears to be saying, is fascinatingly dangerous, and the need for extra care and consideration is consequently urgent.

Pinter's "fearful communication" becomes clearer with each new play. He has been compared to Beckett, and while he concedes that Beckett is a marginal inspiration, he will go no further because, as he correctly points out, everything read by a man must influence that man. Where Pinter differs from Beckett is in his final optimism (i.e., *The Caretaker* denouement). Beckett is frankly nihilistic in his pessimism. In *The Caretaker* Pinter shows hope, as this is expressed through an individual stand. What further developments will spring from *The Caretaker* remains one of the most interesting speculations in the contemporary English theatre.

In three years Pinter's plays have progressed from being choice noncommercial items to box-office, profit-making properties. Surrounded as he is by contemporaries similarly "hitting the jackpot" as new English dramatists, his financial gain is almost commonplace. In this particular Pinter's youth need not be stressed (he is thirty-one): John Osborne was five years younger when his *Look Back in Anger* hit the headlines; Shelagh Delaney, of *A Taste of Honey* fame, is still in her early twenties, and Arnold Wesker, author of the Jewish trilogy, *Chicken Soup with Barley, Roots,* and *I'm Talking about Jerusalem,* has not yet reached his thirtieth year. What is especially remarkable about Pinter's commercial success is the fact that his work, more than any produced by his contemporaries, makes so few concessions to audience reaction. In general terms he makes no concessions at all, as this is conventionally understood, in the matter of communication between the dramatist and his audience.

This has been possible only because of the theatrical climate of the last five years. Against such a climate Harold Pinter's fame must be reviewed, in the sense that he has benefited from circumstances which have combined to create a solid audience genuinely interested in original dramatic work.

Revolutionary is too definite and fashionable an adjective to describe the change of focus in the contemporary English theatre. To insist on this would be to ignore the past record of the little theatres, the regional organizations, and the university dramatic societies—all working as pioneers, extending the range of theatrical illustration, introducing new, if often imperfect, dramatic talent.

What has been headlined as a "renaissance" in English drama is in effect a culmination of prior communal dedication. These "New English Dramatists" were not created a species apart. They have benefited, like the proponents of any *art nouveau,* from the pattern set by their predecessors. Their originality and talent are not greater in essence than the gifts of those who succeeded or failed before them. All genuinely creative dramatists are concerned to perfect some aspect of the human comedy—all original talent has this basic inspiration. The difference today is that the "new" playwrights are in sympathy with the social mood of the fifties which has extended their potential markets. This is not because they mostly concentrate on social themes as distinct from sophisticated artifice: such a stress has always distinguished the creative dramatist, whose ultimate merit is assessed by posterity according to his ability to communicate the political, intellectual, and moral tone of his age in terms of human experience, as distinct from his skill as a propagandist.

Statistically, theatre audiences today interested in what is loosely called "the living theatre" are sufficient in numbers to guarantee a livelihood to the new dramatists, whereas in the thirties (the decade of the Unity Theatre, the Auden-Isherwood collaboration, the early T. S. Eliot verse plays) such audiences were in the minority. This progress in communication between the playwright and his audience is materially evident in the recent cooperation between noncommercial enterprises and large theatrical investment companies—a cooperation imposed by the social mood of contemporary audiences on the hitherto monopolistic, closed-shop commercial theatre.

This active contemporary theatre does not owe its popularity to the fact that Pinter and the rest have something to say that has not been said before. That they have something really new to say is an ever-debatable issue. What they have done is to add further illustration to an area of dramatic illustration that has long suffered from stagnation and creative erosion. What is really new is the audience's expanding curiosity and eagerness for this "living theatre," a fact substantially recognized by commercial theatrical managements who now look on noncommercial theatrical groups as talent-spotters for their box office.

Most of the press credit for this "renaissance" has been given—justifiably, to a large extent—to the Royal Court Theatre, in Chelsea, that is, to the English Stage Society, and to Joan Littlewood's remarkable achievement in Stratford's Theatre Workshop in London's East End. Between them they have produced most of the "star" names—John Osborne, Shelagh Delaney, N. F. Simpson, Brendan Behan, Frank Norman, Wolf Mankowitz, Nigel Dennis, Doris Lessing.

It is commonly assumed, especially abroad, that these two establishments are a sort of vortex of new dramatic talent: indeed, paradoxically enough, both are fast becoming the Establishment of the contemporary English theatre. This erroneous, and unfortunately voguish, assumption overlooks the vigorous and imaginative patronage of new talent by such regional theatrical groups as the new Belgrade Theatre in Coventry, which originally sponsored Arnold Wesker and his trilogy, the Bristol Old Vic, the Oxford Playhouse, the Cambridge Arts Theatre. Also much ignored is the very basic contribution made by the ever-maligned Arts Council of Great Britain, whose grants to both managements and individuals are seldom acknowledged except by way of criticism, in spite of the fact that the recent increase of Arts Council grants has been fairly considerable. It was an Arts Council award of £500 that enabled Bernard Kops to market so efficiently his *The Hamlet of Stepney Green,* and in the front rank of annual beneficiaries is the English Stage Society, that is, the Royal Court Theatre in Chelsea.

The groundwork has been laid for Harold Pinter's favourable reception for a longer period than is usually conceded, and what is more appropriate to this record of progress is the fact that Pinter cannot be introduced as another golden talent exclusive to the Royal Court's patronage. His apprenticeship has been served among wider landscapes, and his achievement expresses the practical victory of the enlightened intellectual policy which has inspired and governed those smaller noncommercial enterprises that have done so much to revitalize the commercial theatre in England.

Pinter's first play, **The Room,** was originally produced by Bristol University in May 1957. It had another showing at a *Sunday Times* Drama Festival in January 1958, by the Bristol Old Vic company and later was introduced to a wider public by James Roose Evans with Pinter's second play, **The Dumb Waiter,** at the Hampstead Theatre Club in January 1960. This double bill received a tremendous press reception and enjoyed the highly critical victory of a Royal Court run. **The Birthday Party** was originally produced by the Arts Theatre at Cambridge in April 1958, and later transferred to the Lyric Opera House in May of that same year. **The Caretaker** began at the Arts Theatre Club before it took the public by storm at the Duchess Theatre. These facts of production stress the variety and range of Pinter's audiences, especially when his radio and television work is taken into account.

When **The Caretaker** packed full houses in the commercial theatre, B.B.C. television's "Monitor" programme investigated Pinter's popularity in the form of a personal interview with the author. "Monitor" adopted a puzzled attitude, stressed the outcast nature of Pinter's characters, and introduced these as "derelicts" and "washed-up people." The author was urged to agree that his world was limited, his dialogue was bracketed with that of Simpson and Ionesco, and he was accused of symbolism.

Diffidently yet firmly Pinter denied limitation of scope. He accepted the "derelict" classification only in perspective: "We're all derelicts," he said, stating that there was no such thing as "a small world," because the man who might, superficially, appear to be socially confined was as much aware of the world as the best-informed among us. As to the matter of symbols, Harold Pinter expressed a ferocious distaste for the word:

> Categorically there is no direct symbolism in any of my work . . . one can't possibly start off with abstractions. . . . [I write a play with a particular thing in mind, a particular set of characters, possibly two characters in a room, and the circumstances grow, and, of course, the characters grow.] It's a very particular business, and this play, for instance, this play is not an abstraction, it's a very simple story about three people who encounter each other during the course of the action, and the situation is resolved at the end, there is a resolution. I think it's rather conventional myself. . . . I think there will be overtones in any work which has any kind of dimension at all . . . but there's no direct symbolic significance to anything at all that I've ever written, and I would like to say that it's the characters themselves who must grow . . . the author doesn't stand in the centre of the stage and tell the audience what to think about his characters.

What came out so precisely in the "Monitor" interview was Pinter's certainty of what he was about with his idiosyncratic use of dialogue. Mr. Hew Wheldon, the interviewer, tackled Pinter about this: "One of the things that is said about you is that you use this language in the mouths of the characters in order to write plays about people who can't communicate with each other, and what your plays are about in the end are about an absence of communication, not the other way round."

Pinter's reply was impossible to misinterpret: "I wouldn't say that was the case, and I wouldn't say that it was accurate as applied to my own work. I don't think there's an inability to communicate on the part of these characters. It's rather more that they communicate only too well in one sense. Their tentacles go out very strongly to each other, and I think communication is a very fearful matter, to really get to know someone, to participate with someone."

Harold Pinter trained as an actor, working in repertory for eight years, from 1949 to 1957. During that time he wrote no plays, but he wrote. Poetry especially was his first medium of expression, and much of this has been published in literary periodicals and anthologies. He also wrote a novel. He spent three years on this, and eventually decided that it was not good enough for publication. As a prelude to writing for the theatre he wrote a number of short pieces in which dialogue predominated. His training as a creative writer has been quite clearly as traditional and hard as is the natural convention.

Most gratefully, and without hesitation, Pinter expresses his indebtedness to the American Roger Stevens, whose fame as a theatrical impresario is international—this apart from Mr. Stevens' acknowledged work in the field of scholarship and international good-will politics. Pinter states that Roger Stevens made it practically possible for him to continue as a dramatist, because it was Stevens who commissioned three full-length plays from him. The first of these was *The Caretaker*, soon to be produced by Stevens in New York. Without this financial assistance, Pinter feels that he could not have written his plays, or rather that his plays would have taken him longer to write.

With a natural distaste for all interviews, Harold Pinter yet reveals his instinctive courtesy and grace of mind as he diffidently answers the useless questions—useless in the sense that all such off-the-cuff queries are arrows shot wildly into the air. What comes through the personal meeting with Pinter is the fine edge of his intelligence, which is most careful not to appear presumptuous. He hesitates to commit himself as to future work, and this adds to his value, because one realizes that here is a man who must first think and experience the matter personally before he can truthfully and creatively transform it into general terms of communication.

Not for him the easy line or the quotable quip; unlike some of his contemporaries, he has no ready-made aphorisms for the news of the day which will be lost before the day is out. What he has to say he will say through his work, at the right time, in the proper place—that is, in the theatre. "I'm beginning to find out. . . . I've a pretty good idea. . . ." Aston's words in *The Caretaker* are in effect a final summary of Harold Pinter's quest for "the fearful matter" of human communication.

Denis Donoghue (essay date 1961)

SOURCE: Review of *The Caretaker,* in *The Hudson Review,* Vol. 14, No. 1, Spring, 1961, pp. 94-5.

[*In the following essay, Donoghue strongly objects to the negative vision of life he sees conveyed in Pinter's plays.*]

Think of Harold Pinter. His published plays are ***The Room, The Dumb Waiter, The Birthday Party*** (all 1957) and ***The Caretaker*** (1959). In ***The Room*** Rose Hudd goes blind when her husband kicks and batters a blind negro who has insinuated himself into their lives with the admonition, "Come home, Sal." In ***The Dumb Waiter*** two gunmen, Gus and Ben, kill time in a basement room while waiting for their instructions; an envelope slides under the door, culinary orders arrive by dumb waiter, the final instruction is that Ben will kill Gus. In ***The Birthday Party*** two lodgers, Goldberg and McCann, interrogate and attack a third, Stanley Webber, on his birthday; at the birthday party, playing blind-man's-buff, Stanley, insane, tries to strangle Meg, who loves him. The following morning Goldberg and McCann take the imbecile away to be examined by a sinister and probably illusory figure called Monty. In ***The Caretaker*** an idiot, Aston, befriends an old man, Davies, gives him a bed and a corner of his room: words pass between them, words about negroes, soap, Sidcup, a pair of shoes, an insurance card, a jig saw, concealed identity, and the habits of women. Aston's brother, Mick, interrogates and attacks the old man: words pass between them, words about a leak in the roof, Sidcup, penthouses, clocks, décor. Davies draws a knife on Aston, proposes to change beds with him to avoid the draught, and is ejected, whimpering:

> I'll tell you what though . . . them shoes . . . them shoes you give me . . . they're working out all right . . . they're all right. Maybe I could . . . get down. . . . Listen . . . if I . . . got down . . . if I was to . . . get my papers . . . would you . . . would you let . . . would you . . . if I got down . . . and got my . . .

In these four plays there is not a single relationship for which an intelligent adult would give tuppence. What Pinter wrote four plays to say is not that life is sad, or that the heart is a lonely hunter, but that life is like two ambiguously connected figures who attack either each other or a third party. I mean to be prosaic about this. Such a view of life strikes me as untrue, not in accord with the facts insofar as I have encountered relevant facts, and—finally—arbitrary, unintelligent. During the first Act of ***The Caretaker*** at the Duchess Theatre I was reminded of Cummings' *HIM,* but the reminder was of contrast, for *HIM* is true and ***The Caretaker*** is false. *HIM* is more intelligent as well as more humane in disclosing the possibility of genuinely valuable relationships, of communication, of dialogue. There is in each play the blow of behaviour—yes, ***The Caretaker*** has striking moments of sheer gesture, when Davies says that he can't drink Guinness from a thick mug, when Aston talks about his head and the experience it has had, when Davies talks about shoes and says, "You can't beat leather . . ."—but *HIM* plays fair by life, and *The Caretaker* doesn't. *The Caretaker* lies when it says that people, their strictly essential selves (?), are morons, thugs, imbeciles, grunting their way through meaningless events. It is not enough to describe the play as a tragicomic parable of identity; it is falsely this, because the parable is rigged. A respectable playwright may argue that genuine communication is impossible—I don't believe him, but let him proceed in peace and goodwill—but he must not queer the issue by making Aston a headcase and his brother a moron. A modish dialectic is at work. The shadow of Samuel Beckett lurks behind Pinter's basements; indeed, to be England's Beckett may well be Pinter's role, a Watt-like walk down the Caledonian Road. By swift comparison with *Godot* and *All that Fall* even *The Caretaker* is rather thin; to assimilate is to masticate. At most, Beckett is guilty of bringing to the end of the line an insight which is good only as a marginal corrective. Pinter has the additional guilt of righteousness. It seems a proper moment to cite the massive commonsense of Henry James in the preface to *The Lesson of the Master*: elucidating the civic use of the imagination, James asks:

> How can one consent to make a picture of the preponderant futilities and vulgarities and miseries of life without the impulse to exhibit as well from time to time, in its place, some fine example of the reaction, the opposition or the escape?

Ruby Cohn (essay date 1962)

SOURCE: "The World of Harold Pinter," in *The Tulane Drama Review*, Vol. 6, No. 3, March, 1962, pp. 55-68.

[In the following essay, Cohn discusses the retributive role of villains in Pinter's plays]

Each of Harold Pinter's four plays ends in the virtual annihilation of an individual. In Pinter's first play, *The Room,* after a blind Negro is kicked into inertness, the heroine, Rose, is suddenly stricken with blindness. In *The Dumb Waiter,* the curtain falls as Gus and his prospective murderer stare at each other. Stanley Webber, the hero of *The Birthday Party,* is taken from his refuge for "special treatment." In *The Caretaker,* the final curtain falls on an old man's fragmentary (and unheeded) pleas to remain in his refuge.

As Pinter focuses more sharply on the wriggle for existence, each of his successive hero-victims seems more vulnerable than the last. Villain assaults victim in a telling and murderous idiom. Although Pinter's first two plays are in one act, and the second two in three acts, each successive drama seems to begin closer to its own end, highlighting the final throes of the hero-victims.

But who are they—these nondescript villains and victims, acting out their dramas in dilapidated rooms? Victims

emerge from a vague past to go to their ineluctable destruction. Villains are messengers from mysterious organizations—as in the works of Kafka or Beckett.

If Pinter has repeatedly been named as Beckett's heir on the English stage, it is because the characters of both lead lives of complex and unquiet desperation—a desperation expressed with extreme economy of theatrical resources. The clutter of our world is mocked by the stinginess of the stage-worlds of Beckett and Pinter. Sets, props, characters, and language are stripped by both playwrights to what one is temped to call their essence.

However, Pinter is not only Beckett's spiritual son. He is at least a cousin of the Angry Young Englishmen of his generation, for Pinter's anger, like theirs, is directed vitriolically against the System. But his System cannot be reduced to a welfare state, red brick universities, and marriage above one's class. Of all the Angries, John Wain approaches closest to Pinter's intention when he states that the artist's function "is always to *humanize* the society he is living in, to assert the importance of humanity in the teeth of whatever is currently trying to annihilate that importance" (*Declaration*). Pinter's assertion, however, takes a negative form; it is by his bitter dramas of *de*humanization that he implies "the importance of humanity." The religion and society which have traditionally structured human morality, are, in Pinter's plays, the immoral agents that destroy the individual.

Like Osborne, Pinter looks back in anger; like Beckett, Pinter looks forward to nothing (not even Godot). Pinter has created his own distinctive and dramatic version of Man vs. the System. Situating him between Beckett and the Angries is only a first approximation of his achievement.

The house as human dwelling is a metaphor at least as old as the Bible, and on the stage that house is most easily reduced to a room (e.g. Graham Greene's *Living Room,* Beckett's *Endgame*). Pinter's rooms are stuffy, nonspecific cubes, whose atmosphere grows steadily more stale and more tense. The titular Room of his first play is "A room in a large house"; in *The Dumb Waiter,* we descend to "a basement room"; in *The Birthday Party,* we have "The living room of a house in a seaside town," and, in *The Caretaker,* it is simply "A room." Unlike the tree and road of *Godot,* which suggest vegetation and distance; or the shelter of *Endgame,* which looks out on earth and sea; unlike the realistic "one-room flat . . . at the top of a large Victorian house" of *Look Back in Anger,* Pinter's rooms, parts of mysterious and infinite series, are like cells without a vista. At the opening curtain, these rooms look naturalistic, meaning no more than the eye can contain. But by the end of each play, they become sealed containers, virtual coffins.

Within each Pinter room, the props seem to be realistically functional, and only in retrospect do they acquire symbolic significance. Consider, for example, Pinter's treatment of such crucial details as food and clothing, in comparison with the casual realism of Osborne, or the frank symbolism of Beckett. The various preparations for tea in *Look Back in Anger* seem to be parallelled by the prosaic cocoa, tea, bread, sandwiches, crackers of Pinter's plays; in sharp contrast is the farcical and stylized carrot-turnip-radish "business" of *Godot*. So too, three men grabbing for an old man's bag in **The Caretaker** has few of the symbolic overtones of the slapstick juggling of derbies in *Godot*.

It is, however, in their respective use of that innocuous prop, a pair of shoes, that the different symbolic techniques of Beckett and Pinter are in most graphic evidence. Early in *Godot*, Vladimir establishes shoes as a metaphysical symbol: "There's man all over for you, blaming on his boots the faults of his feet." At the end of *Godot*, it is by virtue of being barefoot that Estragon admits he has always compared himself to Christ. In Pinter's **Caretaker**, the old man keeps trying on different shoes that might enable him to get on the road to Sidcup, where he claims to have left his identity papers. Each pair of shoes is rejected for specific misfit—"a bit small," "too pointed," "no laces"—before the curtain-lines of the play: "they're all right . . . if I was to . . . get my papers . . . would you . . . would you let . . . would you . . . if I got down . . . and got my. . . ." The finality of the fragments indicates that no shoes can ever fit, that the journey to Sidcup cannot be made. Thus, the symbolic significance of the shoes is instantaneous with Beckett, cumulative with Pinter.

Most crucial to an understanding of Pinter's theatre is the symbolism of his characters. For all their initially realistic appearance, their cumulative impact embraces the whole of humanity. In so generalizing, Pinter extends the meaning of his characters beyond such particulars as Osborne treats; nevertheless, he does not achieve the metaphysical scope upon which Beckett insists, from his opening lines: "Nothing to be done."

Pinter's defenseless victims are a middle-aged wife, a man who asks too many questions, an ex-pianist, a broken old man. Ruthlessly robbed of any distinction, they come to portray the human condition. And Pinter's villains, initially as unprepossessing as the victims, gradually reveal their insidious significance through some of the most skillful dialogue on the English stage today. For it is language that betrays the villains—more pat, more cliché-ridden, with more brute power than that of their victims.

Even hostile critics have commented on the brilliance of Pinter's dialogue, and it is in the lines of his villains that he achieves precise dramatic timing and economical manipulation of commonplaces. Representatives of the System, Pinter's villains give direct expression to its dogma. In the plays of Osborne and Beckett, which also implicitly attack the System, the oppressive forces are presented through the words of their victims.

Jimmy Porter of Osborne's *Look Back in Anger* garbs the System in contemporary corporate metaphors:

> JIMMY PORTER. . . . the Economics of the Supernatural. It's all a simple matter of payments and penalties . . . Reason and Progress, the old firm, is selling out. Everyone get out while the going's good. Those forgotten shares you had in the old traditions, the old beliefs are going up—up and up and up. There's going to be a changeover. A new Board of Directors, who are going to see that the dividends are always attractive, and that they go to the right people. Sell out everything you've got; all those stocks in the old, free inquiry. The Big Crash is coming, you can't escape it, so get in on the ground floor with Helena and her friends while there's still time. And there isn't much of it left. Tell me, what could be more gilt-edged than the next world! It's a capital gain, and its all yours.

Vladimir and Estragon, at the beginning of Beckett's *Godot*, describe the invisible deity figure in trivial human terms:

> VLADIMIR. Let's wait and see what he says.
>
> ESTRAGON. Who?
>
> VLADIMIR. Godot.
>
> ESTRAGON. Good idea.
>
> VLADIMIR. Let's wait till we know exactly how we stand.
>
> ESTRAGON. On the other hand it might be better to strike the iron before it freezes.
>
> VLADIMIR. I'm curious to hear what he has to offer. Then we'll take it or leave it.
>
> ESTRAGON. What exactly did we ask him for? . . . And what did he reply?
>
> VLADIMIR. That he'd see.
>
> ESTRAGON. That he couldn't promise anything.
>
> VLADIMIR. That he'd have to think it over.
>
> ESTRAGON. In the quiet of his home.
>
> VLADIMIR. Consult his family.
>
> ESTRAGON. His friends.
>
> VLADIMIR. His agents.
>
> ESTRAGON. His correspondents.
>
> VLADIMIR. His books.
>
> ESTRAGON. His bank account. . . . Where do we come in?
>
> VLADIMIR. Come in?
>
> ESTRAGON. Take your time.
>
> VLADIMIR. Come in? On our hands and knees.

In Pinter's **Birthday Party**, Goldberg and McCann express the System by echoing modern commonplaces of social success. Pinter damns them with their own deadly clichés.

> GOLDBERG. Between you and me, Stan, it's about time you had a new pair of glasses.
>
> McCANN. You can't see straight.

GOLDBERG. It's true. You've been cockeyed for years.

McCANN. Now you're even more cockeyed.

GOLDBERG. He's right. You've gone from bad to worse.

McCANN. Worse than worse.

GOLDBERG. You need a long convalescence.

McCANN. A change of air.

GOLDBERG. Somewhere over the rainbow.

McCANN. Where angels fear to tread. . . .

GOLDBERG. We'll make a man of you.

McCANN. And a woman.

GOLDBERG. You'll be re-orientated.

McCANN. You'll be rich.

GOLDBERG. You'll be adjusted.

McCANN. You'll be our pride and joy.

GOLDBERG. You'll be a mensch.

McCANN. You'll be a success.

GOLDBERG. You'll be integrated.

McCANN. You'll give orders.

GOLDBERG. You'll make decisions.

McCANN. You'll be a magnate.

GOLDBERG. A statesman.

McCANN. You'll own yachts.

GOLDBERG. Animals.

McCANN. Animals.

In comparing the three excerpts, we note that Osborne's sustained metaphors are almost lyrical with rebellion, but both Beckett and Pinter resort to pithy stichomythia. Although the passages are typical of the technique of each play, the respective tonal differences depend upon the dramatic structure. Osborne's satiric hostility recurs throughout *Look Back in Anger,* but Beckett's attitude towards Godot is ambivalent. The quoted excerpt occurs early in the play, when the tramps, in spite of their pathetic plight, can still attempt to define the System in familiar human terms. But by the end of the drama, man and diety are poignantly reduced to their compulsive, impossible, problematical interrelationship: "in this immense confusion one thing alone is clear," says Vladimir. "We are waiting for Godot to come."

In the Pinter play, the messengers of the System glibly mouth its pat phrases—increasingly pointed as the dehumanization of the victim progresses. In the quoted excerpt, which occurs towards the end of the drama, the seemingly irrelevant conclusion, "Animals," corrosively climaxes the process.

The central victim-villain conflict may be traced through Pinter's four plays. In the one-act *Room,* where the

presentation of the human dilemma is somewhat diffuse, victim and villain are recognized as such only at the final curtain. Rose and Bert Hudd, wife and husband, alone on-stage when the play begins, are almost alone when the curtain falls—except for the still body of the blind Negro, whose head Bert has kicked against the stove. But it is Rose who is Bert's victim, Rose whose suffering is sustained throughout the play, Rose who is suddenly and finally afflicted with the Negro's blindness.

When the play opens, Rose is busy preparing a realistic tea in their realistic room, while Bert Hudd quietly reads a realistic newspaper. Bert's silence in the face of Rose's disconnected rambling, seems to be a lower-class, marital-comedy silence. When Mr. Kidd, the landlord, enters to look at the pipes, to converse with husband and wife, Bert's persistent and insistent silence takes on a threatening quality. Mr Kidd talks about the house, about the time he used to live in their room. Quite suddenly, room and inhabitants lose their humdrum exterior, and take on new depth. When Rose asks how many floors there are in the house, Mr. Kidd replies, "Well, to tell you the truth, I don't count them now."

Close upon this rejection of the numerable, Mr. Kidd reminisces about his dead sister, his Jewish mother. There is a sporadic return to small talk, as Mr. Kidd admires Bert Hudd's van, his driving. After Mr. Kidd leaves, Bert Hudd, in increasingly sinister silence, goes down to his van. During his absence, a Mr. and Mrs. Sands come looking for a room; a man in the basement has told them there was one for rent. There is a confused conversation about the landlord, whom Mr. Sands mixes up with Bert, since the names Hudd and Kidd sound alike. Rose's security is shaken, and she denies the rumor of a vacancy. Mr. Sands insists that the man in the basement has offered them number seven—Rose's room.

When the Sands couple leaves, carrying with them all hint of social satire, the surface plausibility of the dialogue collapses completely. When Mr. Kidd reënters, Rose pounces upon him to affirm her claim to the room. But Mr. Kidd can talk only of a mysterious man in the basement, who has been waiting for Bert Hudd to leave, so that he can come up to see Rose. Even as she denies any knowledge of the man, she consents to see him. When a blind Negro enters, Rose screams that she doesn't know him, that his name is not Riley, as he claims. Riley announces his message: "Your father wants you to come home." Calling her Sal, Riley soon shifts to, "*I* want you to come home." [My italics] After Riley's final, "Come home now, Sal," Bert Hudd returns to the room, and speaks for the first time. In short, harsh sentences, he describes driving his van through the cold streets: "She took me there. She brought me back." When Riley addresses him, "Mr. Hudd, your wife—," Bert cries, "Lice!" He knocks Riley down and kicks his head until he lies still. Rose stands clutching her eyes, moaning, "Can't see. I can't see. I can't see."

Of the rival claimants for Rose, Riley and Bert, the latter bludgeons his way to triumph. Bert's role as villain explodes climatically, for it is Riley who first appears to menace Rose. But silence, conventional connubial demands, and a van (female in Bert's lines) are victorious over the blind Negro father-surrogate. Earlier, the landlord, Mr. Kidd, is nearly driven "off his squiff" by Riley's insistance on seeing Rose. With Bert, however, Mr. Kidd seems to have reached a *modus vivendi,* even though Bert never addresses him. Mr. Kidd admires Bert's driving ability; he too speaks of the van as a woman. Their very names, Kidd and Hudd, sound so much alike that outsiders such as the Sands, confuse them with one another. It is the presence of Riley against which both Kidd and Hudd react—the former with terror, the latter with violence. Although Riley is kicked unconscious by Bert, it is Rose-Sal who is Bert's ultimate prey. "A woman of sixty," garrulous and shuffling, she speaks disparagingly of foreigners, dwells on her physical comforts, is ungracious to the Sands, and hostile to Riley. At the last, she makes no attempt to defend Riley from Bert, but succumbs to her own blindness. Pinter has stripped her of all appealing qualities, so that any sympathy she inspires must be rooted in her plight.

Pinter's second play, the one-act *Dumb Waiter,* concentrates even more pointedly on the plight of the victim. As in *The Room,* it is not immediately evident who is victim and who villain. Sent by an offstage Wilson "to do a job," Gus and Ben, the play's two characters, await instructions in a basement room which contains two beds separated by a hatch—a dumb-waiter. While they wait, Gus busies himself with preparations for a realistic tea, and Ben reads the bloodier items from a realistic newspaper. Their life seems to lie in their Kafka-like career; as Gus summarizes it, "you come into a place when it's still dark, you come into a room you've never seen before, you sleep all day, you do your job, and then you go away in the night again."[1]

Despite the menace implicit in the job itself, early disquieting signs are plausible by their very triviality: the toilet has a deficient ballcock, the bed sheets are dirty, Gus and Ben cannot see a football game because all teams are playing "away." After an envelope of matches is mysteriously slipped under the door, they quarrel tensely about whether one can say "light the kettle," or must say "light the gas." Gus unobtrusively asks a few questions of Ben, "the senior partner." The gas goes out before their water boils, and Gus begins to have mutinous thoughts about Wilson, their boss. He thinks with distaste of their last job, a girl who was "a mess"; he wonders who cleans up after their jobs. "It was that girl made me start to think—," Gus reflects, and is interrupted by a sudden noise from the dumb-waiter. In a box is a note ordering "Two braised steak and chips." One by one, other notes are sent down the dumb-waiter, requesting an international series of delicacies. By the dumb-waiter, Gus sends up their meager tea supplies, comically and sadly prosaic in the vulgarity of modern brand names: "Three McVitie and Price! One Lyons Red Label! One Eccles cake! One Fruit and Nut!" Ben, "the senior partner," quickly corrects the Fruit and Nut to "Cadbury's."

This task accomplished, Ben conducts their preparations for the job; he superintends their attire and the cleaning of their revolvers. Through a suddenly discovered speaking tube, he appologizes that they have nothing more to send up the dumb-waiter. Humbly, he listens to the complaints about their service: "The Eccles cake was stale . . . The chocolate was melted . . . The milk was sour . . . The biscuits were mouldy." Then, triumphantly, Ben reports that they have been ordered to light the kettle: "Not put on the kettle! Not light the gas! But light the kettle!" However, there is still no gas.

In final rehearsal for the job, they recite their instructions about the victim:

> GUS. He won't say a word.
>
> BEN. He'll look at us.
>
> GUS. And we'll look at him.
>
> BEN. Nobody says a word.

Gus goes to the toilet a last time. "The lavatory chain is pulled . . . but the lavatory does not flush." When Gus returns, he reiterates his uneasy questions until Ben strikes him. The dumb-waiter tray clatters down; hysterically, Gus reads, "Scampi."

Ben returns to his newspaper, and Gus exits for a glass of water. As Ben waits, the toilet flushes belatedly, and Ben cries, "Gus!"

> The door right opens sharply. Ben turns, his revolver levelled at the door. Gus stumbles in. He is stripped of his jacket, waistcoat, tie, holster and revolver. He stops, body stooping, his arms at his sides. He raises his head and looks at Ben. A long silence. They stare at each other. Curtain.

It is because he has not been content to be a "dumb waiter" that Gus is destroyed. Although only a junior partner, perhaps *because* he is only a junior partner, he has complained about the job, and begun to ask questions; he has found Wilson "hard to talk to," has even meant to ask questions of him. But the organization turns upon Gus before he can probe or expose it.

Until his first three-act play, *The Birthday Party,* the threats in Pinter's drama emanate mysteriously from a vague apparatus of master-messenger-organization. But with his third play, Pinter not only defines the enemy more explicitly, but casts a retrospective light upon the villains of the earlier plays. Goldberg and McCann, who represent the System in *The Birthday Party,* do not appear on scene until the end of the first act, and until they do, the living room of the Boles' boardinghouse is Pinter's most photographically real set. Although Stanley Webber's reaction against the two prospective boarders seems disproportionate, and his review of his earlier concert career ambiguous, we do not definitively leave the realistic surface until Goldberg and McCann actually enter by the back door. Partners like Ben and Gus, they carry no revolvers, but pose as casual vacationers in the seaside boardinghouse where Stanley has taken refuge. Their first monosyllabic exchange establishes their relationship:

McCann. Is this it?

Goldberg. This is it.

McCann. Are you sure?

Goldberg. Sure I'm sure.

Their Jewish-Irish names and dialects suggests a vaudeville skit, and it is not long before we realize that that skit is the Judaeo-Christian tradition as it appears in our present civilization. Goldberg is the senior partner; he utters the sacred clichés of family, class, prudence, proportion. McCann is the brawny yes-man whose strength reënforces Goldberg's doctrine.

Although Meg and Petey Boles have sheltered Stanley in their home, they are unable to recognize that the sinister new guests threaten the welfare of their guest. Meg acquiesces joyously to Goldberg's suggestion of a birthday party for Stanley "to bring him out of himself." Villains and victim, Goldberg-McCann and Stanley are not brought face to face in Act I, but Stanley already begins to feel trapped.

Before the party that fills Act II, Stanley tries to convince McCann that he is not "the sort of bloke to—to cause any trouble," that it is all a mistake, that Goldberg and McCann have to leave because their room is rented. Having forced Stanley to sit down, Goldberg and, secondarily, McCann engage in a verbal fencing-match with Stanley, in which Pinter parodies the contemporary emptiness of the Judaeo-Christian heritage.

Interrupting Stanley's efforts at self-defense, Meg comes down ready for the party. In the maudlin mixture of drinking, pawing, and reminiscing that follows, a game of Blindman's Buff is played. An increasingly desperate Stanley tries to strangle Meg, a mother-surrogate, and rape Lulu, the sexy neighbor, but Goldberg and McCann advance upon him each time. As Act II closes, "[Stanley's] giggle rises and grows as he flattens himself against the wall. Their [Goldberg and McCann] figures converge upon him."

Act III is a virtual *post mortem.* Goldberg, McCann, and Petey talk about Stanley's "nervous breakdown." McCann complains to Goldberg about this job, and Goldberg encourages him by an interweaving of clichés, in which the Biblical tradition is the warp, and modern success formulas the woof: "Play up, play up, and play the game. Honour thy father and thy mother. All along the line. Follow the line, the line, McCann, and you can't go wrong."

When McCann finally ushers Stanley down, "dressed in striped trousers, black jacket, and white collar," the victim has lost the power of speech, and his glasses are broken. Again, Goldberg and McCann attack him verbally, in even pithier phrases, but this time they promise him worldly success if he complies. Stanley only gurgles unintelligibly.

"Still the same old Stan," Goldberg pronounces, and he and McCann start to lead Stanley to an unexplained Monty. When Petey Boles objects that Stanley can stay on at the boardinghouse, the macabre pair scornfully invite Petey to join them, "Come with us to Monty. There's plenty of room in the car." An automaton propped between the partners, Stanley is helped out while Petey, broken-hearted, calls, "Stan, don't let them tell you what to do!" But Goldberg's car is heard starting up, then fading into the distance. When Meg Boles comes down with a morning hangover, Petey does not even tell her Stan is gone, but encourages her to dream of the birthday party, at which she was the "belle of the ball."

The thread running through all Pinter's plays now appears more clearly. If we recall *The Room* in the light of *The Birthday Party,* we see resemblances between Goldberg and Mr. Kidd, who had a Jewish mother. Both emphasize the value of property, of progress, of family, of tradition. Similarly, the Irish names of Riley and McCann seem to indicate a Christian continuance of the Judaic legacy; in both plays, they are the weaker members, although never as weak as Gus of *The Dumb Waiter,* who is metamorphosed into a victim.

In *The Birthday Party* and *The Dumb Waiter,* there is a higher, invisible power behind the messengers, but Monty remains even more mysterious than Wilson, and more authority is invested in Goldberg than in Ben. In all the plays, the motor van becomes a clear symbol of modern power. In the first play, *The Room,* the van belongs to Bert Hudd, but is the object of Mr. Kidd's admiration. In *The Birthday Party,* as in *The Dumb Waiter,* the van is the property of one of the messengers—in each case, of the dominant and senior partner. It seems to be the older, crueler tradition which best embraces modern mechanization. Only the recalcitrant individual must be quashed.

As the victim-villain conflict in *The Room* is somewhat diffused by the socially satirized Sands couple, so the Boles couple in *The Birthday Party* provides a comic relief from the mounting tension. And yet the latter couple functions more directly in the symbolic context, for the Boles are not, like Mr. Kidd, mere landlords; they provide a temporary if tawdry refuge for Stanley. Distasteful as are the attentions of Meg-mother-mistress, impersonal as is Petey's presence, the Boles express affection and concern for Stanley. But human emotions are tricked or brushed aside by the ruthless team of a dogmatic system.

In Pinter's latest play, *The Caretaker,* as in the earlier *Dumb Waiter,* there are no deflections from the hunting down of victim by villain. Although none of Pinter's victims are sentimentalized—Rose is gruff, Gus has performed bloody deeds before he has begun to question them, Stanley is ungrateful to Meg—the old man of *The Caretaker* is perhaps the least sympathetic of all. He is ready to take anything from anyone, he feels superior to "them Blacks," he is suspicious of everyone, he repeatedly complains that the weather prevents his going to Sidcup for the papers which he left there during the war, and which can establish his identity.

After the opening tableau of *The Caretaker,* in which the leather-jacketed Mick slowly examines the miscellaneous objects in the room, Mick exits when he hears voices. Aston enters in worn but conventional clothes, and after him comes the ragged old man, "following, shambling, breathing heavily." Thrown out of his job and beaten up by a younger man, old Davies has been rescued by Aston and brought to the room. There seems to be no reason for this kindness. The old man takes stock of the scattered contents and inquires about the other rooms in the house. When Aston replies, "They're out of commission," we find ourselves in familiar Pinter country. Aston invites the old man to sleep with him in the room, until he gets "fixed up"; he gives him money and a key, lets him try on some old shoes.

After a night's sleep, the conversation is more erratic. When asked where he was born, the old man replies, "I was . . . uh . . . oh, it's a bit hard, like, to set your mind back . . . see what I mean . . . going back . . . a good way . . . lose a bit of track, like . . . you know. . . ." When Aston leaves, the old man examines the various objects in the room. Mick enters, watches silently, then suddenly springs and forces the old man to the floor. "What's the game?" he rasps at the old man, as Act I ends.

In Act II, Mick insistently questions the old man about his name, while the old man whines to Mick, "I don't know who you are!" Mick compares the old man to various outlandish relatives and acquaintances, refusing to believe the story of how he came to this room, of which he announces himself the owner, and his brother Aston the tenant. After Mick makes a long, caustic speech about the rent he intends to collect from the old man, Aston reënters. When Mick leaves the room Aston mentions his do-it-yourself remodeling plans for the house. Abruptly, Aston suggests that the old man become caretaker of the premises, but the old man thinks his assumed name may create difficulties.

When the old man next enters the room, it is dark, and he defends himself from an invisible enemy who proves to be Mick with an "electrolux." Friendly now, Mick confides to the old man that he cannot get Aston, his elder brother, to redecorate the premises. As owner, Mick offers the old man a job as caretaker. This time the old man quickly accepts, but Mick mentions the necessity for references. Reassuringly, the old man explains it is merely a question of getting down to Sidcup for his papers. If only he had a pair of shoes . . .

After a quick blackout, Aston wakens the old man so that he can start early for Sidcup, but the old man pleads that the weather is too bad. Aston closes Act II with a long monologue about his experiences in a mental hospital.

By Act III, the old man falls in with the wildly ambitious redecorating schemes of Mick. Since they have been living in the same room, Aston and the old man are mutual sources of irritation to each other. Feeling secure in his relationship with Mick, the old man carps at Aston's idiosyncrasies. When Aston suggests the old man find another place, he retorts, "You! You better find somewhere else." After the old man threatens Aston with a knife, the elder brother orders, "Get your stuff." Mumbling that Mick will protect him, the old man leaves temporarily.

But Mick turns on the old man, for Aston is his brother. Only if the old man is an interior decorator of great capability, can he stay. When the old man protests he is merely a caretaker, Mick accuses him of lying all the time, boasting about non-existent accomplishments. In the future, Mick intends to leave the house entirely in Aston's hands. "What about me?" pleads the old man. There is no answer as Aston enters and Mick leaves; when they pass each other, the two brothers smile briefly.

The old man attempts to make peace with Aston, and suggests various compromises to facilitate their living together, but to all of them Aston replies, "No." He does not need the old man's help, and will not have him as caretaker. More and more desperate, the old man begs to stay, but Aston turns his back on him. As the old man swears that he will go down to Sidcup for his papers so that he will have the proper references to be caretaker, "Aston remains still, his back to him, at the window," and the curtain falls on a "long silence" during which Aston is *as stone.*

Although Mick is slang for Irish, it is not clear in *The Caretaker* that Pinter is again designating the Christian tradition by an Irish name. Rather, the two brothers jointly seem to symbolize the family compatibility between a religious heritage and contemporary values. Thus, it is the elder, conventionally dressed Aston who is a carpenter, with its evocation of Christ, and it is the leather-jacketed Mick who is in the building trade and owns a motorized van. It is Mick who destroys a statue of Buddha, and who has grandiose schemes for redecorating the house. Aston's projects are humbler; he has been restored to competence by modern treatments for mental deviates; before the end of the play, he does manage to tar the roof of the room, so it no longer leaks. Although Mick is presumably the owner and Aston the inhabitant of the house, the possession is finally left in doubt. As Mick explains, "So what it is, it's a fine legal point, that's what it is."

In their attitudes towards the old man, the human derelict, the two brothers present only surface contrasts. Mick begins by knocking him down, whereas Aston, instead of allowing him to die in despair, rescues him, shares his room with him, and opens up hope to him. Both the brothers name the old man as caretaker, offer him a kind of security, which they both subsequently withdraw. Mick turns his back on the old man for failing to fulfill a role to which he never aspired, but Aston rejects him for what he is—cantankerous, self-deluded, and desperate.

Of all Pinter's plays, **The Caretaker** makes the most bitter commentary on the human condition; instead of allowing an old man to die beaten, the System insists on tantalizing him with faint hope, thereby immeasurably increasing his final desperate anguish. There is perhaps a pun contained in the title: the Caretaker is twisted into a taker on of care, for care is the human destiny.

Pinter's drama savagely indicts a System which sports maudlin physical comforts, vulgar brand names, and vicious vestiges of a religious tradition. Pinter's villains descend from motorized vans to close in on their victims in stuffy, shabby rooms. The System they represent is as stuffy and shabby; one cannot, as in Osborne's realistic dramas, marry into it, or sneak into it, or even rave against it in self-expressive anger. The essence of the Pinter victim is his final sputtering helplessness.

Although Pinter's God-surrogates are as invisible as Godot, there is no ambiguity about their message. They send henchmen not to bless but to curse, not to redeem but to annihilate. As compared to the long, dull wait for Godot, Pinter's victims are more swiftly stricken with a deadly weapon—the most brilliant and brutal stylization of contemporary cliché on the English stage today.

Note

1. Compare this description with that of Jimmy Porter's naturalistic Sundays in *Look Back in Anger:* "Always the same ritual. Reading the papers, drinking tea, ironing. A few more hours, and another week gone. Our youth is slipping away."

   On the other hand, observe Vladimir's clearly metaphysical routine in *Godot:* "Tomorrow, when I wake, or think I do, what shall I say of today? That with Estragon my friend, at this place, until the fall of night, I waited for Godot? That Pozzo passed, with his carrier, and that he spoke to us? Probably. But in all that what truth will there be?"

Walter Kerr (essay date 1967)

SOURCE: "Harold Pinter," in *Harold Pinter,* Columbia University Press, 1967, pp. 3-45.

[*In the following essay, Kerr argues that not only is Pinter an existentialist writer, but that his plays are written in an existentialist manner.*]

Harold Pinter seems to me the only man working in the theater today who writes existentialist plays existentially. By this I mean that he does not simply content himself with restating a handful of existentialist themes inside

familiar forms of playmaking. He remakes the play altogether so that it will function according to existentialist principle.

To show this it will be necessary to recapitulate briefly, and at the expense of some subtlety, the premises on which existentialist philosophy rests. At root, existentialism rejects the ancient Platonic principle that essence precedes existence.

What does this mean, practically speaking? Platonic theory, made more explicit by Aristotle and then accepted as a habit of thought by Western society in succeeding generations, proposed that before any one man, say, came into being there had to exist, somewhere in the mind of the universe, an idea of man—an immaterial essence which contained, bounded, dictated the nature of the species.

In this view, the essence Man exists before any one individual man. Individual men are, in effect, derived from it. They take their physical, mental, and moral capacities from it. Because individual men are concrete, idiosyncratic, and limited by having been incorporated in matter, no one of them perfectly expresses or realizes the abstract universal from which he has taken his name and shape. Pure being—including the pure essence "man"—is a sort of fountainhead, a reservoir, a pool of unadulterated spirit from which isolated individuals siphon off so much spirit as they have. Aristotle located this immaterial and universalized source in the mind of God. God thereafter, as it were, made man by die-stamp. From the concept "man," men took their existence. Existence became a hand-me-down. Men, as they walked the earth, were predefined. They conformed to an essence prior to themselves.

Viewed in a Platonic light, man was both inhibited and most helpfully guided. He was inhibited in the sense that he could not escape the boundaries set for him by his essential nature. Though he was obviously in some measure free, he was not free to behave as other than a man—and what a man was could be explicitly determined. Man was made to perform in a certain way, to pursue certain goals, to expect certain natural and logical rewards and punishments depending upon how well or ill he played out his assigned role.

The inhibition had its comforts. If man was predefined, he did have an identity. He was this, not that. He had a name, an address, a secure position in the universe. He was not altogether footloose in a void, he had instincts, a conscience, and an intelligence to tell him what steps to take. These tools were trustworthy precisely because they belonged to, or were drawn from, the essence "man." Listened to, or used properly, they could not very well lie. What was Of The Essence was bound to return to the essence, to echo it, to reflect it as a mirror reflects. Man could know himself by drawing deductions from the equipment he had been given.

Existentialist philosophy, moving from troubled speculation in the nineteenth century to aggressive assertion in the twentieth, reverses the Platonic order. It insists that existence precedes essence. That is to say, the notion of an original, immaterial archetype is jettisoned. There is no matrix from which individual men in the concrete are drawn. There are only individual men, born undefined. It is not even possible to say what a "man" is until we have seen how this man or that man actually behaves, until we see what this man or that man has done. Man does not come to the planet with an identity; he spends his time on the planet arriving at an identity.

As with the Platonic view, this new insistence has its comforts and its cruelties. Its principal comfort, which may in the first stages of discovery seem small comfort, lies in the unprecedented freedom now granted to man. Man is no longer to regard himself as confined by a "nature," by a given set of behavior patterns which are inbred and fundamentally inviolable. He is open, an experiment, a reaching, an adventure. There are no known limits to his possible activity. Man has no absolute face to be worn daily and Sunday; he can make as many faces as he likes, in something of the manner that Albert Camus' Caligula does.

At the same time he must walk through the world alone, without instructions from a central computer, without friends who share his nature, without confidence that his intelligence reflects anything absolute, without assurance that he fits into any discernible scheme. He is nameless, as yet featureless; he *is* footloose in a void; and his task, if he can be said to have one, is to create his identity by exercising his freedom to act. When he has done all that he can do, he may be able to say what *he* is. He may achieve his essence. Until the ultimate moment of actualization comes, however, he must move, with some vertigo, through a silent universe. Man is "condemned" to be free, Sartre says.

From these various corollaries of the proposition that existence precedes essence have come the characteristic dramatic themes of our time. Who am I? the man asks as he discovers that he has lost the wallet that contained his identity cards. Why can't we communicate? the stranger on the park bench snarls. Why has man no home? the vast, vacant settings on a hundred stages inquire. What are reasoning, logic, intelligence worth? demand the professors who contradict themselves word by word, line by line. What are we waiting for? wonder the nonentities who have been waiting so long for Godot. Is anything real or is everything illusion? anguish all of the people who cannot find themselves in mirrors. How silly conformity is when there is no essence to conform to!

Dozens of playwrights have made use of existentialist themes. What is surprising is that none of them—none but Harold Pinter, I think—has taken the fundamental proposition seriously enough to present his plays in the new existentialist sequence. Whether Mr. Pinter would wish to call himself a formal existentialist, or whether he has taken a creative leap intuitively, I do not know. Playwrights are

properly wary of labeling themselves, and it is in any case more important to know what plays do than what playwrights say they are meant to do. The philosophical impulse has, however, been the dominant experimental impulse during the time Pinter has been at work; Pinter is reported by Ronald Bryden as having been profoundly influenced by *Waiting for Godot* the year before he began his first plays; and the playwright's occasional remarks to interviewers, which we shall have to attend to shortly, strongly suggest that his rejection of Platonic sequence has been as deliberate in intention as it has been unique in practice.

In the current philosophical climate, the matter of sequence should be important. If existence does indeed precede essence, if an actual thing precedes an abstract concept of that thing, then it should also do so on the stage. Exploratory movement in the void, without preconception or precommitment, should come first. Conceptualization should come later, if at all.

But Samuel Beckett, for instance, does not really work that way. Mr. Beckett has been most influential in imposing upon contemporary theatergoers an awareness of existential loneliness, homelessness, facelessness; our strongest image of the void comes from the careful emptiness of his plays. Yet Mr. Beckett takes his curtain up upon a woman buried waist-deep in sand. Or upon an aged couple confined to ashbins. Or upon Didi and Gogo immobilized, already waiting.

The fact that Mr. Beckett does not make much use of the existentialist freedom to act is not the point here. A playwright is free to use one strand of available material to the exclusion of others; he is a temperament, not necessarily a doctor of philosophy. The point is that in each case—in all cases where Beckett is concerned, I would say—we are first offered a concept, a statement of essence. What the opening image of *Happy Days* says to us, immediately, is that man is essentially earthbound. Nagg and Nell in *Endgame,* lifting the lids of their ashbins occasionally but never leaving them, are essentially discards. In *Waiting for Godot* Lucky is seen as essential slave, Pozzo as essential master.

Lucky and Pozzo are not open, undefined figures who become slave and master, who arrive at their natures through exploratory action in the void. They appear fully formed, samples from their respective matrices: Pozzo with a rope, Lucky bearing a heavy load. Whatever Mr. Beckett's philosophical disposition may be, he builds plays as a Platonist. He forms an abstract concept of man's nature and role and presents it to us in its original conceptual form, individualizing it only very slightly. We are not concerned with persons forming themselves; we are concerned with persons inhabiting set forms they cannot escape.

Our habits of thought are so strong—after several thousand years of being trained in Greek method—that even when we wish to make an anti-conceptual statement, even when we wish to say that man has not been and cannot be defined, we do it by conceptualization, by starting from a definition. First we reach a conclusion, perhaps the conclusion that logic is a meaningless tool. Then we arrange a stage illustration to show that it is meaningless, as Ionesco does in *Rhinoceros*:

"The cat has four paws. Isidore and Fricot both have four paws. Therefore Isidore and Fricot are cats."

"My dog has got four paws."

"Then it's a cat."

Or perhaps we have reached the conclusion that words are essentially without valid content and that therefore communication by language is essentially illusory. Ionesco again, this time in *The Bald Soprano*:

"I've never seen her. Is she pretty?"

"She has regular features and yet one cannot say that she is pretty. She is too big and stout. Her features are not regular but still one can say that she is very pretty. She is a little too small and too thin."

These last cancellations—in which "too small and too thin" directly contradict "too big and stout"—are of course deliberately devised by the playwright in order to demonstrate an idea about the futility of verbal communication. There is no testing toward discovery. The playwright has reached his conclusion before beginning to write, and then has measured his illustration exactly to display that conclusion—precisely as another playwright might begin with the essential quality of Ambition and then manufacture a character to conform to it. Though Samuel Beckett holds very little in common with the medieval world-view of things, his actual method of composition is not radically different from that of the author of *Everyman*. A symbol—which is the sign of an essence—is hung up in plain view; later, some individualizing detail is added to it, though not so much as to obscure its continuing function as an abstract, almost immaterialized, concept.

Thus, though the drained-out and disjointed worlds which Beckett, Ionesco, and other contemporary playwrights place upon the stage may at first sight seem very strange indeed, the strangeness consists almost entirely in what is being said, in the inverted value-system that is carefully organized into an image. There is very little that is strange in the organizing process itself. The Platonic sequence keeps its grip on us: a concept precedes, and dominates, whatever we see existing on the stage.

"I don't conceptualize in any way," Pinter has said in an interview given to Lawrence M. Bensky for *Paris Review,* a statement which may well be taken at face value and which may help to explain why Pinter's plays seem strange to us through and through.

Watching a Beckett play, we immediately engage in a little game of "Concept, concept, who's got the concept?", no doubt because we sense that, beyond the play's opaque surface, there lies a conceptual nub. We want to get at this, to abstract it. We know that it was abstract to begin with.

Watching a Pinter play, we give over the scramble to stick pins in ideas and fix them forever to a drawing-board. We feel that the drawing-board isn't there and that our eager thumbs would only go through it. Instead of trying to bring matters to a halt by defining them, we permit them to move at will, understanding that we have been promised no terminal point. We give existence free rein, accept it as primary, refrain from demanding that it answer our questions, grant it the mystery of not yet having named itself.

To have drawn us into so complete a surrender of our ordinary, long-standing expectations and demands is a considerable achievement, and Mr. Pinter has taught us to follow the sequence his way by being strict in his presentation of it.

To begin with the matter of place. In his very first play, *The Room,* written in 1957, the existentialist challenge is formidable—and, within the limited confines of the piece, absolutely met.

Existentialism imagines man living in a void. At the same time it asks that we refrain from conceptualizing this void. How shall it be defined when it has not yet been fully explored? In short, we are asked to enter a void that is not an abstract void.

The Room completely satisfies this difficult—one would have thought impossible—requirement. Everything in "a room in a large house" is entirely tangible, concrete, present not as idea but as actuality. There is a gas-fire, a perfectly real one. A gas-stove and sink. A window. Table and chairs. A rocking chair. The foot of a double bed protruding from an alcove. The walls are solid, the dirty wallpaper has been firmly pasted up, the objects handled by a slatternly housewife as she moves in and about the aggressively dimensional furniture all have weight, texture, the density of experienced life.

These objects, and the actions involved in handling them, are given blunt importance in the stage directions—not as symbols of other values but in and for themselves. They are important because they are there, because they exist. Handling them is important because they are there to be handled, and because hands exist.

> Rose is at the stove. . . . She places bacon and eggs on a plate, turns off the gas and takes the plate to the table. . . . She returns to the stove and pours water from the kettle into the teapot, turns off the gas and brings the teapot to the table, pours salt and sauce on the plate and cuts two slices of bread. . . . She butters the bread. . . . She goes to the sink, wipes a cup and saucer and brings them to the table. . . . She pours milk into the cup. . . . Sits in the rocking-chair.

There is no comment in all of this, no suggestion that plate or teapot, salt or sauce, contains a meaning that will serve as metaphor for some larger value. The salt does not represent savor, or the loss of it; it is salt. The sauce is not poisoned, nor does the housewife's action in serving it signify the slavery of Woman. The rocking-chair does not mean to suggest that Rose has retired from life, or is a lulled prisoner of it. We are to attend to these things as things. The deliberateness, the patience, the concentration with which these companions in existence are listed and then handled breeds a kind of awed respect for them. Audiences tend to stare at the cup, at the stove, at the chair with an unfamiliar intensity. Each object seems more important than it would in another kind of play precisely because it is not a minor sign, a diminutive stand-in, for something of greater significance than itself but because all of the significance it has is its own. Everything that exists is self-contained. It does not derive from something prior to it, nor is it a marker indicating something to come. It *is* now. Handle with care.

Objects observed in a Pinter play tend to generate something like awe. They may be utterly commonplace, they usually are; yet they seem uncommon here because they have not been absorbed into a pattern that explains them away as mere tools of a narrative or as looming symbols of conceptual value. Sometimes these objects acquire such self-importance as to seem ominous, though that is not their initial function in a Pinter play. If we feel faintly startled to see how solid a cup is, or how shaped, we feel so—in the beginning—only because we are used to ignoring the solidity and shape of cups in our absent-minded lives. Normally we think of a cup as a means to an end, as an indifferent utility making a passing contribution to another, much more identifiable, purpose: our tea, our pleasure, our life-roles as wife, husband, host. Thinking of a cup in this way, we render it more or less invisible. In effect, we make it absent.

By suppressing the past and future of the cup, by refusing to name its origin or its destiny, Pinter increases its presence. It catches, and for the moment wholly occupies, our eye.

Whatever exists in the room is made to exist at its maximum intensity. Nothing within our view is in any way abstract, as, say, the landscape of *Waiting for Godot* is abstract. *Waiting for Godot* takes place Nowhere, or Anywhere. But in **The Room** we are Somewhere. Environment is utterly explicit; every piece on the premises could be sold at auction, the place as a whole could be rented.

At the same time that the tangible is insisted upon, literally thrust into our faces, the surrounding void is implied. The void is outside the room, upstairs, downstairs, everywhere beyond the walls. The real is real. The void envelops it. It is all rather as though a cyclone had picked up a still intact shed—as we used to see cyclones do in the movies—and were carrying it, still intact, through unknown air to an unknown end.

The outlying void is rhythmically described as Rose rocks. Does anyone live below Rose and her husband, in the basement? "I don't know who lives down there now. . . . I think there was one first, before he moved out. Maybe they've got two now."

Perhaps there's no one below. No matter. "If they ever ask you, Bert, I'm quite happy where I am. We're quiet, all right. You're happy up here. It's not far up either, when you come in from outside. And we're not bothered. And nobody bothers us."

Upstairs may be empty, too. When Mr. Kidd, the landlord, drops by, Rose asks him "Anyone live up there?"

"Up there?" Mr. Kidd ponders. "There was. Gone now."

"How many floors you got in this house?

"Floors. . . . Ah, we had a good few of them in the old days."

"How many have you got now?"

"Well, to tell you the truth, I don't count them now."

"Oh."

"No, not now."

Though the immediate room, the direct experience of life, is entirely dimensional, the universe in which it exists is unstructured. There is not even any knowing where Mr. Kidd lives, once he leaves these tight, tangible four walls. A prospective tenant asks Rose where the landlord might be:

"Well, say I wanted to get hold of him, where would I find him?"

"Well,—I'm not sure."

"He lives here, does he?"

"Yes, but I don't know—"

"You don't know exactly where he hangs out?"

"No, not exactly."

"But he does live here, doesn't he?"

". . . As a matter of fact, I don't know him at all. We're very quiet. We keep ourselves to ourselves. I never interfere. I mean, why should I? We've got our room. We don't bother anyone else. That's the way it should be."

Rose, who is only Rose and not Everyman, knows only what she experiences: her husband drives a van and enters and leaves the room at regular hours; a landlord drops in, but lives no defined existence once he has left; it is dark outside; it is cold inside; sitting down and getting up are important matters because they are events which truly happen as opposed to the mere rumor of events beyond the room; cups and saucepans can be touched.

Whatever impinges directly upon the consciousness is the sum total of what can be known. We share Rose's consciousness, knowing exactly as much as she does and no more.

Let alone, Rose would be content simply to exist.

Rose is not let alone, any more than the two hired killers in *The Dumb Waiter* are let alone. Quite soon Rose is disturbed by two discoveries. Apparently it is her room that is to let. Though the rest of the "building" may very well be unoccupied, the prospective tenants may be in the act of displacing her. And it would seem that someone does indeed live in the basement, someone who may intrude upon her at any moment.

As we move from the solid-inside-a-void environment of a Pinter play toward what we shall have to call the narrative movement of the people who have their being in that environment, we are instantly embroiled in threat. "Menacing" is the adjective most often used to describe the events in a Pinter play, "suspense" is considered one of the playwright's most satisfying effects.

It is almost shocking that this should be so. For narrative suspense in the past has almost always been derived from one clear source: known danger. Oedipus' fears are absolutely defined: the tyrant lives in dread that somewhere, somehow, it shall be proved that he has killed his father and married his mother. If Oedipus tries to blot these things from his mind, it is because they are so terribly present to his mind. Macbeth knows that it is Macduff he has to fear; no matter how much certain prophecies seem to support the notion that Macduff cannot be the man to best him, Macbeth trembles in apprehension. Willy Loman worries that he will not be liked. Charlie Chaplin worries that the cabin in which he is trapped will tumble over a precipice before he can get out of it. Watching these figures, we are frightened for them because we see—we are able to name and describe—the shape of the terror advancing upon them.

Yet the one thing Mr. Pinter steadfastly refuses to do is to offer his audience—or his characters—any information whatsoever about the forces they come to feel as hostile. We see no precipice; we are not told what may happen at the stroke of midnight; no oracle spells out, not even in ambiguous terms, the doom to be looked for. Ordinarily, danger is conceived in the future tense: this is what will happen if steps are not taken to avoid it. Apprehension rises as the future comes closer—while still remaining the future. Mr. Pinter writes exclusively in the present tense.

In *The Dumb Waiter*, written during the same year as *The Room*, two minor-league thugs are uneasily whiling away the time in a basement room. Presumably they have been sent there to do a killing. They do not know, however, who is to be killed. Neither do they seem to know who has hired them. This is simply the situation in which they find themselves: it is without an explicit beginning, it

looks forward to no explicit end. Once again the situation itself—everything that belongs to the experienced moment—is concrete. There are newspapers to be read, lavatories to be flushed, biscuits to be parceled out, gas-ranges to be lighted.

After they have waited a while, sometimes quarrelling over football matches and tea, an overlooked dumb-waiter in the wall gives off a sudden clatter. Opening the slot, the two men discover that an order for food has been sent down. "Two braised steaks and chips. Two sago puddings. Two teas without sugar," the order reads. But though the order itself is once again explicit, there is no telling who sent it down, or why. Was the building formerly a restaurant, and this the kitchen? Inside the basement flat, which is real, this sort of realistic speculation can be indulged. But it cannot continue to have meaning once it is applied to the world outside the flat: there can really be no restaurant which would send down orders to a "former" kitchen. Speculation is cut off in mid-breath, is plainly useless.

Yet orders continue to come down and the two men find themselves under immediate compulsion to fill them, however inadequately. Biscuits, crisps, a bar of chocolate, half a pint of milk—whatever catch-as-catch-can provisions they have brought to the flat with them—are loaded onto the dumb-waiter box and sent up. Still greater demands are returned ("Macaroni Pastitsio. Ormitha Macarounada.") and, in a frenzy of placation, the gunmen part with everything in their packs. In their inadequacy they are humble. Discovering a speaking-tube on the wall, one of them sends a message above "with great deference":

"Good evening. I'm sorry to—bother you, but we just thought we'd better let you know that we haven't got anything left. We sent up all we had. There's no more food down here."

They are not above resenting the sacrifice they have so willingly, so feverishly, made:

"We sent him up all we've got and he's not satisfied. No, honest, it's enough to make the cat laugh. Why did you send him up all that stuff? (*Thoughtfully*) Why did I send it up? (*Pause*) Who knows what he's got upstairs? He's probably got a salad bowl. They must have something up there. They won't get much from down here. You notice they didn't ask for any salads? They've probably got a salad bowl up there. Cold meat, radishes, cucumbers. Watercress. Roll mops."

But the sacrifice was swiftly and unquestioningly made at the time. Only when the moment has passed and the men have begun to exist in a succeeding moment can one of them ask his "thoughtful" question: "Why did I send it up?"

The question is central to the problem of Pinter's curious narrative power. For during all of the time that the gunmen have been desperately trying to meet the demands of the wholly mysterious dumb-waiter, suspense on the stage has grown in proportion to their ignorance of what they were doing. The suspense of **The Dumb Waiter** is in very small part due to our awareness that the two men are possibly waiting to kill someone. We are only half-certain that that is their function, their edginess is much more directly concerned with tea-kettles than with potential victims, we cannot fear very greatly for an unspecified victim in any case. The existence of the dumb-waiter is, in addition, apparently irrelevant to the task on which they are engaged; its commands are not necessarily the commands of the unnamed "he" who has hired them, indeed there seems no patterned relationship between the one kind of command and the other. Yet the intrusive, unlooked-for, in a narrative sense distracting activity of the dumb-waiter not only occupies the center of the play but markedly increases its tension.

The command "now" actually agitates the men more than the command "when." When a visitor taps at the door and enters, they are probably going to kill him. About such a matter they can be relatively casual. When a command, any command, is issued in the present tense—even though it has no recognizable source and even though they have no understood obligation—they are terrified.

Mr. Pinter exploits a contemporary form of terror. It would be easy to say that the author's unusual ability to create and maintain suspense in the absence of any defined threat was simply due to his possession of a narrative "gift." That is to say, some writers are born knowing how to tell a story, how to hold an audience—even when the story itself is not inherently fascinating and the audience is not certain that it has been promised any ultimate satisfaction. One kind of novelist, for instance, will write in such a way that the reader is desperately eager to turn the page, though what is on the other side of the page may only lead to the turning of yet another page; the syntax, the entirely personal sense of confiding something urgent, suggests movement. In effect, the pages turn themselves. Another kind of novelist will require conscientious assistance from the reader to keep the book, or the reader's hand, in motion. The pages need lifting, even though they may contain—paragraph by paragraph—arresting details of characterization, valid insights, finely tooled diction.

This is indeed a fact of life: there is such a thing as a narrative "gift." Graham Greene has it; Joyce Cary lacked it. Saul Bellow possesses very little of it, Truman Capote much more. The most ordinary writer of detective fiction probably has it in abundance, or he would not be successful at what he is doing; certainly his other qualities would not guarantee him readers. Yet having or not having a natural narrative power is not a means of distinguishing hacks from their betters, "commercial" writers from serious literary men. In the apocalyptic novels which constitute the literary avant-garde of the moment, the distinction continues to be felt: John Barth's pages turn slowly, Thomas Pynchon's or Gunter Grass's far more rapidly.

And, beyond doubt, Pinter is gifted in this sense: the fact that he has been an actor, and has worked inside the pressure chamber of stage production, may well have contributed to the development of such felicity at moving forward as he was born with. Yet the particular suspense he achieves is made of something more than a story-teller's lucky ability to make a listener say "And then?" or an actor's instinct for taking center stage and holding it by hook or crook.

A considerable portion of Mr. Pinter's suspense derives from the way that, in pursuing an existentialist method, he sets his plays in motion on a track that runs directly parallel to—or perhaps coincides entirely with—the track on which twentieth-century man feels himself running. It is a track quite different, in its tensions and apprehensions, from any most previous societies have found themselves pressed along.

All societies have found themselves driven by guilt. We find ourselves much more driven by what has been called *angst,* which the dictionary defines as "a feeling of dread, anxiety, or anguish." W. H. Auden has labeled our time "The Age of Anxiety," and the descriptive term has stuck; it was partly out of an effort to explain the prevalence of the sensation that existentialist philosophy came to birth.

There is a simple distinction to be made between the sensation of guilt and that of anxiety. The two are by no means identical. Guilt is felt for a specific crime or sin or failing; apprehension follows because man expects to be punished—in some way—for having permitted himself a particular, well-defined lapse. A man knows what he has done and lives in fear because he has done it.

Anxiety, on the other hand, rises from no single guilty act and fears no clearly spelled-out retribution. It is a general state of mind, a diffused sensation of spiritual and psychological unease which may have its roots in one or twenty of a thousand possible causes but which has no root in any one cause we can name. Anxiety lacks a clear origin. Lacking a clear origin, it lacks a clear ending. We cannot imagine atonement, or any means of freeing ourselves from the sensation, when we cannot say what initiated the sensation, or motivated our fear, to begin with. To use the dictionary again, anxiety—in its psychoanalytical reference—is "the expectancy of evil or danger, without adequate ground." A man who feels guilty always feels guilty about something. But a man in a state of anxiety is anxious about everything—his dread is not confined to responsibility for an act but is distributed throughout his environment and becomes his environment.

Pinter earns his special suspense by constructing his plays in such a way that we are forced to enter this state of mind in the theater. We have not always done so in the theater. When we watch Macbeth grow fearful, even to the point of hallucination, we can make a clear and objective judgment about his fear: he feels as he does because he is guilty of having killed Duncan. We are linking an observed effect to a known cause. We are not undefinably disturbed.

Even during the recent years of our mounting and thoroughly recognized *angst* we have not been accustomed to experiencing in the theater what we have experienced on the streets or at our desks. We may have felt a vague terror at the office, and not known where the animus was coming from. We then went to the theater, observed a man in terror, and saw plainly where his terror came from. The two experiences—one of life, one of art—have not generally coincided. We have felt anxiety on the subway, but seen guilt on the stage. Willy Loman is guilty of having bartered his soul for a smile and a shoeshine. His distress can be diagnosed. Blanche du Bois is to a serious degree guilty of misrepresenting her own nature. Simple exposure to the light will bring her screaming to heel. Such plays look for blame and find it, though the blame may not be confined to a single individual and may indeed attach to an entire social system; wherever it is lodged, the blame can be located. We stand outside the pattern, and know what to expect of it.

Pinter deprives us of our detachment—and our security—by taking us into the pattern. He does so by refusing to say what the pattern is, or by hinting very strongly that there is no pattern. Bewildered, we look about us for points of reference. Finding none, we begin to share the anxiety of the characters whose lives we can observe but cannot chart. We no longer judge their collective state of mind. We inhabit it.

The act of unpatterning is therefore of great importance in the working out of any Pinter scenario. Whatever action is taking place must have no clear beginning, which is to say it must not have originated in a guilty act. In this way the past is eliminated as a conscious source of worry and the two men of **The Dumb Waiter** are bound to the tense "now" of commands which are without cause or precedent. The two men become tense on the instant because the position in which they find themselves is, to them as to us, unintelligible. Instead of passing from past crime to future punishment, they stand trembling before all possibility.

Similarly, whatever action is taking place must have no foreseeable future, which is to say that there are no logical, deducible consequences coming from an earlier crime or event. The earlier crime or event has not been specified, and therefore cannot have preordained consequences. Thus the future is also eliminated, as we have seen, as a reasonable source of worry. There are no reasons why Rose should be dispossessed of her room—she has done nothing to deserve uprooting—or why she should expect a visitor from downstairs. A reasonable worry is, in a way, a comfort. It is only the altogether unreasonable, perched on the shoulder of the "now," that is altogether terrifying.

With the past gone from the pattern because no prior guilty act can be attributed to anyone, and with the future gone from the pattern because no deserved and identified threat looms ahead, the pattern itself disintegrates into a shapeless immediacy, a fearful moving-about among objects and persons that are directly present but are without histories

or discoverable essences. All persons, all objects are now to be feared—and revered, in the sense that they produce awe—because no one of them can be isolated as a single source of apprehension. A major part of Pinter's suspense, then, derives from his drawing us into the unpatterned *angst* which we know well enough in the dusty uncertainty of our days but which we normally keep at arm's length in the playhouse by insisting that the playwright show us cause and effect, crime and punishment. "Step into my parlor," Mr. Pinter says. We do so, feeling like so many flies, wondering where the spider is.

Perhaps it is easy enough to understand why we should feel effectively dislocated in rooms which may or may not have floors above or below them, or why we should feel a nameless anxiety in the face of commands being issued from wholly invisible sources in a restaurant above. These things are rumors, and rumors are always unsettling precisely because their origins cannot be traced or their effects anticipated.

But how is this faceless menace to be sustained as an effect in the theater when it acquires an actual face, when it is clearly and physically embodied in a character who walks in at the door to confront another, quickly quailing, character? If the threat is no longer a matter of hearsay, or of mysteriously delivered messages from nowhere, but an actual, breathing, talking, even obviously violent human being, hasn't the threat now been made concrete, tangible, defined on the spot? And aren't we back to regulation playmaking in which protagonist and antagonist face one another in broad daylight to thrash matters out?

In Pinter's first full-length play, **The Birthday Party,** also written in 1957, perfectly tangible confrontations of this sort are arranged. In outline, the play would seem to contain all of the standard paraphernalia of old-fashioned stage melodrama, or of the suspense film. We are concerned with a victim who is being hemmed in by apparent gangsters who mean to "take him for a ride," and the hemming-in is done openly on the stage. How shall this sort of danger remain nameless and faceless? And why?

We first meet Stanley, a man in his late thirties, some sort of concert pianist whose career has deteriorated, who now spends his time in a seaside boarding-house, sleeping late. He could probably still play piano on the local pier if he wanted to. If he doesn't want to, it is because he feels the effort would be futile. He has been systematically persecuted, driven from his profession. The last time he attempted a concert he found the hall closed, firmly shuttered up against him without so much as a caretaker about. He remembers the occasion as he would a nightmare. "They'd locked it up," he says, wiping his spectacles on his pyjama jacket, "A fast one. They pulled a fast one. . . . They want me to crawl down on my bended knees."

We next meet his enemies. "They" are no longer invisible hands sending peremptory messages by a dumb-waiter. "They" appear most tangibly in the persons of Goldberg and McCann, strangers carrying suitcases who wish to take rooms in the same boarding-house. Stanley tries to drive them away. They cannot be budged. Stanley defends himself before them. They cannot be won over. Ultimately, under their prodding and baiting and because of the sheer fact of their presence, Stanley suffers something like a nervous breakdown, becomes violent. Now Stanley is led off by Goldberg and McCann. The last thing we hear is "the sound of a car going away."

The confrontation is so direct and sustained that it is almost as though Rose had met her man from the basement early in the play, or as though the thugs of *The Dumb Waiter* were face to face, from the beginning, with the man they were hired to kill. We seem close to a play in which fear is reasonably motivated and in which the parties to the struggle are clearly identified. We are dealing with beginnings and ends, with patterns, again.

But are we? As it happens, no one in the play understands the pattern through which he is moving. Presumably, Stanley is being repaid for something he has done in the past, for some betrayal or other. But Stanley cannot quite remember his past, not even his father's address. Of one thing he feels certain: he's not the "sort of bloke to—cause any trouble." In the last place he lived, the place in which he might be thought to have done whatever it is Goldberg and McCann think he has done, he "never stepped outside the door."

Goldberg and McCann, though they seem to have a clear duty to carry out now, are no clearer about the impulses that have propelled them into motion. They are not personal enemies of Stanley, though they personally—and very viciously—rough him up. There is vague talk of an "organization" which Stanley has betrayed, but Goldberg and McCann give no indication of being insiders to that organization. They are emissaries, set on a certain course by an irresistible force outside them, but they are not intimates of the force at work nor are they even capable of thinking about it coherently. When Goldberg attempts to state his beliefs about the world and its patterning his mind stammers to a halt, becoming first "vacant," then "desperate," then "lost."

This is a blind collision. Existentially, it reports an experience we have not yet dealt with. Though each man exists uniquely in the void, straining to discover his identity and unable to relate intelligibly to other creatures like him, he is not sole inhabitant of the void. The void is like the vault of heaven in which shooting stars may, without warning and for no immediately discernible reason, cross paths and even crash into one another. Each shooting star follows its own orbit. It cannot help doing so. It is following the laws of the "organization." But two separate courses, initiated by two separate impulses, may come into conjunction at any time, and most tangibly. Two isolated forces enter an area simultaneously, behaving simply as they behave.

The principals in this central struggle—Stanley, Goldberg, McCann—exist. Because they exist, they act. They do not act out of prior definition; they are on the way to discovering themselves but they have not yet done so. Their gestures are not dictated by conscious roles, by a shared nature, by given melodramatic or metaphysical postulates. They are alive and free to do whatever they will do, but their activity is a probing process, not a disclosing one. They are finding out what they are by what they do and by what is done to them. There is no master-plan; there is only an experimental testing.

Any man who is in the process of achieving his identity is bound to meet, bump into, recoil from, affect, and be affected by other men engaged in the same process that occupies him. It is a historical accident that any two such orbits should coincide, since the overlapping paths are separately initiated and not logically related. But the overlapping, the collision, has consequences.

One man sets one foot into space, to see what it does. Another does the same thing at the same time. The two meet, and the meeting may be disastrous for one or the other or both. One thrust foot may prove stronger than another thrust foot. Each foot will contend for the space with the equipment it actually has, will struggle for what seems power but is actually definition. The encounter will end in some way or other. But it has not been a planned encounter, and it will not have an effect-from-cause ending. Only the encounter is recorded, in its suddenness, in its blindness, in its mystery. Yes, the encounter has a result. But the result is a fact, not an explanation or an interpretation. Pinter does not invite interpretation. "Sound of a car driving away."

This blind encounter is dramatized in a simpler and more literal way in a later full-length play, *The Caretaker,* written in 1959. Here a homeless, shiftless, scrofulous, exceedingly self-righteous old man encounters a younger man who voluntarily offers him living-space in his quarters. The generous act is not logically motivated; the old man cannot grasp why he has been taken in—though he is quick to come in, and quick to demand more than he has been offered—nor can he in any other way fathom the mind of his benefactor. His benefactor's mind is in fact unfathomable: he has earlier been subjected to a frontal lobotomy.

The old man next encounters his host's brother. This brother is sly, taunting, hostile—though again for no cause the old man can discover. The two encounters coincide in time but are not organically linked in the sense that they can explain each other; they are wholly baffling to the mind enduring them, and they are actual. The old man is given an actual pair of shoes, an actual bag is handed to him by one brother and snatched away by the other. The play confines us to the sensations of the man to whom these things happen, and for just so long as they are happening. At the end of the play they cease happening. The old man continues talking, but he is talking now to silence. He has had the experience of colliding with two other forces which exist precisely as he does: as self-determining isolates whose "natures" have not yet been resolved. There has been a meeting, a bumping, an abrasion. The meeting has been suspenseful because anything at all could happen. The three men in the room do not come from a common matrix which might enable them to predict one another. They go on finding themselves through what they cannot find in others.

Pinter maintains his mystery, even when his menacing forces are perfectly visible and in head-on confrontation, by carefully denying them psychological access to one another. They are face to face and still impenetrable. They have not yet acquired essences that can be detected.

Though there is a degree of violence, or of sensed menace, in every Pinter play, the plays are not straightforward melodramas. Comedy is the constant companion of threat, and sometimes the threat itself contains an elusive comic edge. The messages from the dumb-waiter make the gunmen who are receiving them apprehensive; they also make us laugh, sometimes openly, sometimes nervously.

Apart from the fact that the playwright himself has a knack for the curtly phrased retort that, read blandly, has an air of amusing insult about it—he has, in fact, written a group of revue sketches—the very methods he employs, and the shifting-sands vision of man's precarious existence which these methods record, tend naturally toward one kind of comedy.

Comedy has always made capital of mistaken identity. When one man is taken for another, or one thing taken for another, we are invariably surprised and most often delighted that such easy interchanges should prove to be so possible, that the universe should turn out to be so slippery. *The Comedy of Errors* is a root comic design: one looks into a face and cannot say whose face it is.

Existentialist uncertainty is, of course, not so blithe in tone as a mere tumbling about of twins. Not being able to tell one twin from another has a clear logic inside it to guide and comfort us: we know the "natural" cause of our confusion and can readily respond to it without any admixture of dismay. The Pinter approach is necessarily darker than this, for we look into a face and find ourselves unable to name it without being able to explain, on the spot, our bafflement. The effect is more closely related to another standard comic device: the business, say, of passing a graveyard at night, seeing an object moving among the tombstones and prickling in terror—only to have it turn out to be a cat. In *The Caretaker,* and in the dark, a buzzing, bright-eyed monster seems to move with seething teeth across a room: it turns out to be a vacuum-cleaner.

Mistakes of this sort always strike us as funny not only because, in the aftermath, we are relieved to find them unmenacing; fundamentally we are amused that, in a tangible world made up of sharply defined shapes and perfectly hard surfaces, any two unlikes should be able to blend into such a momentary like. A sensation of giddiness overwhelms us: what has frightened us shouldn't have, it is absurd that we should have responded so disproportionately; we have participated in an incongruity.

The fright is not forgotten, nor should it be: it is perfectly possible to be killed by a vacuum-cleaner or, for that matter, to be clawed by a cat. We never can know when vacuumcleaner or cat is going to turn on us. We might well be disturbed, in addition, by our awareness that we can make such mistakes. Our equipment for detecting reality is not all that it might be. Yet there is no getting away from the laughter that follows and was inherent in the situation all the time: we have used our eyes and been made fools of.

Following *The Caretaker,* Mr. Pinter turned his attention, in two shorter plays originally written for television, to what is lightly amusing in the ambiguity imbedded in his premises. *The Collection* (1961) and *The Lover* (1965) are both a great deal more than revue sketches: but here the scales are tipped to favor what is funny in our inability to define one another, or ourselves.

The Collection takes place in two simultaneously visible flats. One is shared by Harry and Bill, both dress-designers; though there are no explicit homosexual gestures, Harry is jealous of Bill. The other flat houses James and Stella, husband and wife, operators of a boutique. There has been a fashion display in Leeds the week before; both Stella, from the one flat, and Bill, from the other, have gone to it. Stella and Bill may have met in a hotel corridor, just outside an elevator, kissed on impulse, and spent the night together. Stella's husband thinks she has slept with Bill and he calls, unannounced, on Bill to get at the truth. Harry is equally concerned that Bill has slept with Stella; he calls upon Stella to urge her to break off the relationship.

But there is nothing to say—for certain—that there has been any relationship. Stella may be lying (boasting? teasing? tormenting?) when she seems to admit the affair to her husband. Bill, pressed to confess by James, may confess simply because he is expected to or because it amuses him to do so. All parties are sparring. No party knows the other well enough to say what he might or might not do. Around musical chairs the four contestants go; in a fashion reminiscent of Pirandello, each makes the other into the image he has of him.

There is no violent pressure here, simply an anxious—though generally polite—need to define. All are poised, self-controlled, in cool command of a situation that is endlessly open. James, intruding upon Bill, behaves as though he were in his own flat, not Bill's; he asks Bill what he would like to drink. Bill, at first dismissing the night in Leeds as a bit of pure fantasy Stella has invented ("Really rather naughty of her") pauses to ask her husband "Do you know her well?"

If neither of them can know Stella absolutely—is she a whore or is she putting it all on?—neither can they quite know themselves. James and Bill spend a moment, side by side, looking into a mirror, though James expects nothing to come of mirrors: "They're deceptive."

A degree of violence does obtrude before this psychological parlor game has run its course. Bill, backing away from James, tumbles over a piece of furniture and suddenly finds himself wondering whether James will permit him to rise again or whether he is about to lash out at him with his feet. During a subsequent meeting, James and Bill contemplate a duel with fruitknives, and there is in fact some minor bloodshed. But the comic emphasis is maintained even at knife's edge. Bill, ready to shrug the contest off, announces that he is putting his knife down.

> JAMES. Well, I'll pick it up.
>
> *James does so and faces him with two knives.*
>
> BILL. Now you've got two.
>
> JAMES. I've got another one in my hip pocket.
>
> *Pause.*
>
> BILL. What do you do, swallow them?

Ignorance has a preposterous side to it, and it is possible to be flippant about it. In the end, the play refuses to perspire over the problem of identity. James returns home to Stella, who is playing with her kitten. He has decided for himself, or rather he wishes to decide for himself, that Stella and Bill didn't really "do anything" in Leeds. If they met, they merely sat in the hotel lounge and chatted. If they discussed going to Stella's room, the discussion was hypothetical, the projected act unrealized.

> JAMES. . . . That's the truth, isn't it?
>
> *Pause.*
>
> You just sat and talked about what you would do, if you went to your room. That's what you did.
>
> *Pause.*
>
> Didn't you?
>
> *Pause.*
>
> That's the truth . . . isn't it?

End of play, with Stella looking at James, "neither confirming nor denying," her face "friendly and sympathetic." Uncertainty may be a tolerable condition of life if one has the patient good sense to cock an eye at it whimsically.

The Lover is even lighter, very close to extended vaudeville, though, in its existential playfulness, it opens the door to yet another aspect of the continuing proposition that existence precedes essence.

"Is your lover coming today?" Richard asks his wife, Sarah, as the curtain rises. Richard is leaving for his office, where he is pictured as slaving over ledgers all day, but he is concerned with Sarah's happiness and he wishes to be sure that she'll have a "pleasant afternoon." Returning in the evening, he solicitously inquires how the afternoon went. Sarah, equally considerate, supposes that Richard has a mistress. This, as it turns out, is not quite the case.

> RICHARD. But I haven't got a mistress. I'm very well acquainted with a whore, but I haven't got a mistress. There's a world of difference.
>
> SARAH. A whore?
>
> RICHARD. (*Taking an olive*) Yes. Just a common or garden slut.
>
> Not worth talking about. Handy between trains, nothing more.

Though Richard and Sarah pride themselves on "frankness at all costs" because frankness is "essential to a healthy marriage," Sarah confesses that she is surprised by the news that Richard has a whore. "Why?" Richard asks. "I wasn't looking for your double, was I?"

At this point—it is one of the few instances in which Pinter's surprises are not so surprising—we begin to leap ahead of the playwright. Yes, the lover who comes to visit Sarah in the afternoons is Richard. And Sarah is Richard's whore, her own double and not her double. Such a visit is dramatized and the two behave entirely differently to each other. Indeed, when Richard the lover speculates on whether or not he'd hit it off with Richard the husband, supposing their paths ever crossed, Sarah thinks not. "You've got very little in common," she points out.

What makes this relatively brief conceit more interesting than a simple, and fairly obvious, vaudeville "switch" is its introduction of the notion that both Richard and Sarah truly possess the two separate identities they assume. They are not children playing bawdy-house. They are adults who are other adults than themselves, unconfined by one or another social role. Looked at conventionally, ***The Lover*** might simply seem to be saying that married couples need to pretend a bit now and then in order to refresh their relationship. Or, conceivably, it might seem to be saying that in a highly structured society sexual impulses are rarely given free play and that some subterfuge is needed to release such impulses even in marriage. Looked at existentially, it says another thing altogether: no woman is essentially wife or essentially whore, she is potentially either or both at once; the same duality, or multiplicity, holds true for the husband-lover. Personality is not something given; it is fluid.

In the earlier ***The Collection*** no character could say what another was; but there was always the lingering assumption that, if only one could see clearly enough or probe persistently enough, a firm, fixed identity—a "truth"— might be uncovered. Here, in ***The Lover,*** we do see clearly enough, we walk directly into the situation as though we had walked into that hotel room in Leeds. And what we see, now that we see clearly, is that nothing human is fixed, everything human is mobile. The same woman can be a whore in a hotel room and an innocent playing with her kitten at home while remaining the same woman, without contradiction.

If existence precedes essence, and if plays are to be written in such a way as to reveal this sequence, then no character on a stage dares be essentially anything: husband, wife, lover, whore, brother, father, beggar, host. Instead, character is potency, possibility, movement.

We are touching now on that freedom of movement, without prior direction or definition, to which Sartre says man is "condemned" and which constitutes man's exploration of the void in search of his realized, until now unknown, self. Categories and traditional roles contain no man, unless he lets himself be contained by them, choosing to conform to a pattern that does not actually express his potency. Man cannot be described except in terms of motion: he is what he does next. And there may be another "next" after that, which means that there will then be a new, and still unfinished, "is."

In two thematically related plays, *A Slight Ache* (1961) and *The Homecoming* (1965), Pinter has gone on to examine identity as movement, not as category. In *The Homecoming* the issue is made most explicit, set forth in a single speech. The men about Ruth are debating categories. A table is a table, just as a wife is a wife.

> RUTH. Don't be too sure though. You've forgotten something. Look at me. I . . . move my leg. That's all it is. But I wear . . . underwear . . . which moves with me . . . it . . . captures your attention. Perhaps you misinterpret. The action is simple. It's a leg . . . moving. My lips move. Why don't you restrict . . . your observations to that? Perhaps the fact that they move is more significant . . . than the words which come through them. You must bear that . . . possibility . . . in mind.

The possibility is going to have consequences a few scenes later. But it may be best to glance at *A Slight Ache* first, not so much because it was written earlier, but because in it the contrast between category and movement is more simply and swiftly outlined.

A man—and for Pinter the male now tends to become the categorist—is baffled by the presence of an old, filthy match-seller who stands at the bottom of the lane near his house daily. There are very few passersby. The old man never sells any matches. Why does he come? The householder cannot let the question alone; he becomes feverish in his anxiety to know the answer. He invites the ragged presence into the house, offers him a drink, cajoles him, coaxes him, finally commands him to say who he is and what he is doing. The match-seller never utters a word. His inquisitor is now half-mad with frustration, distressed by his inability to define.

The householder's wife enters, and takes over. She asks no questions. She simply embraces the visitor. She is, that is to say, open to him and to his possibility. Shortly, she installs him in the house. The husband goes out to sell matches.

The woman here is readily seen as catalyst, as the agent of change. And she is. Through her the husband drops his "role" as husband and as categorist and finds himself assuming another role he could not have anticipated, cannot even now define. Through her the match-seller, still silent, becomes partner. But she is not merely an agent of action in the play, mistress of shifting possibilities. She is herself in motion, and it is her own assumption of a second identity—wife-mother to the match-seller—that is the central gesture of the play. She has been one thing; without hesitation, she moves forward to become another. Questions of identity—her own, or anyone else's—do not concern her, as they have so concerned her husband. She is what she finds it within herself to be, she is the movement she finds herself making.

The situation, with its altering relationships, is repeated in the climactic sequence of *The Homecoming.* Ruth is Teddy's wife and has come, after some years of marriage, to visit her husband's family. Teddy, her husband, is the categorist par excellence. He is a Doctor of Philosophy at an American university. For him, everything is fixed. He has seen stability. "To see, to be able to *see!*" he exclaims. "I'm the one who can see. That's why I can write my critical works." He is proud of his "intellectual equilibrium" and a shade contemptuous of those who move uncertainly about him. "You're just objects. You just . . . move about. I can observe it. I can see what you do. . . . But you're lost in it. . . . I won't be lost in it."

Teddy is rigid and detached, wedded to essences, a Platonist. Once more there are intruders with whom he cannot be comfortable: his father and two brothers. The father and two brothers, observing Ruth and her presence as motion, make Ruth a proposition. Let Teddy go back to America, let her remain with them as their "whore." They will give her a flat and furnishings, they will enable her to pay for these by leasing her out some nights to other men, they will take turns being with her and being whatever they can be to her. She will be whatever she can be to them. Ruth, having embraced one brother in a dance and the other in a copulative roll-about on the couch, accepts the proposition.

Teddy accepts Ruth's acceptance of the proposition. He is not so anxious about identities as the husband of *A Slight Ache*; he is certain that he has arrived at them, he is beyond becoming involved; he does, however, go into exile as surely as his predecessor does. As he leaves, there is no sign of animus, rejection, or even finality in Ruth. "Don't become a stranger" is the last thing she says to him.

The woman, Ruth, is the center of the play because she is the existential suppleness of the play. She continues to become her identity. She has been wife, mother, daughter-in-law, sister-in-law. But these roles are not terminal, they are not permitted to become absolutes. "Whore" is a part of her possibility, too. Neither is "whore" to be regarded as terminal, as defining. Who is to say what movement lies beyond, before the self comes to be the self? When does the movement of lips, legs, underwear cease, saying, in sum, "This is I"?

Pinter uses the "whore" image repeatedly—it has appeared in three out of the last four plays we have discussed—precisely because the whore, by definition, lacks definition. The whore performs no single social role, she is what each new man wishes to make of her. She is available to experience, and she is an available experience. She is eternally "between trains," she is known in passing and as something passing. In fact, she is simply unknown. Existentially speaking, we are all life's whores to the degree that we are in motion and have not arbitrarily codified and thereby stilled ourselves.

Rich man, poor man, beggar man, thief—the picaresque hero, who is generally something of a whore, is all of these in turn, which is no doubt why the picaresque hero has enjoyed a considerable revival under existentialist pressure. Viewed in an existentialist light, each of us is picaresque-hero-whore: permanently subject to unpredictable intrusion, to the unlooked-for event and the unthinkable proposition. Until we have actually responded to these things—actually moved and behaved in the circumstances they create—we cannot say what our response, or our very selves, might be. It is only when responsive movement has been exhausted that we can lay claim to knowing essence.

In the contemporary theater Pinter's work is original in method and unique in its effect upon the stage. An Arnold Wesker and a John Arden can be related in intention and style. Beckett and Ionesco have sunspots in common. It is possible to put John Osborne and Edward Albee side by side and see that they raise their disturbances with much the same lift of voice. But Pinter's territory is very private territory. He has drawn upon a philosophical disposition that is very much in the air and available to everyone, true. But he is the one man who has fought essence to a standstill, refused it houseroom until he has finished moving freely about.

"I don't know what kind of characters my plays will have until they . . . well, until they *are,*" he has said. "Until they indicate to me what they are. . . . Once I've got the clues, I follow them—that's my job, really, to follow clues. . . . I follow what I see on the paper in front of me—one sentence after another. That doesn't mean I don't have a dim, possible overall idea—the image that starts off doesn't just engender what happens immediately, it engenders the possibility of an overall happening, which carries me through. I've got an idea of what *might* happen—sometimes I'm absolutely right, but on many occasions I've been proved wrong by what does actually happen."

The play is discovery in the way that personality, under existentialism, is discovery. It has not been fashioned to fit a hard and fast idea about man, or society, or the nature of things. "I distrust ideological statements of any kind," the playwright adds.

He has been remarkably successful in constructing a series of felt realities that do not depend upon conceptual underpinning: the experience of entirely tangible places unmoored in a void, the experience of living and fearing and even laughing in the present tense without knowledge of past or future, the experience of encountering other objects just as impenetrable as we are as we jockey for position in a swarming, footloose universe, the experience of never being certain what gesture any man may make next because everyman is, at the present writing, incomplete.

These are not statements made in the plays. They are the movement of the plays. The play is only an event, not a logical demonstration; the event must speak, illogically but persuasively, for itself. The play persuades by existing, and in no other way. If it failed to persuade in this way, no theory—however correct, however contemporary—could save it. Pinter takes his uncertainty seriously.

Perfectly? Of course not. Playwrights have a habit of not being perfect, and in this case a writer is attempting a break not only with recently conventional modes of playmaking but with a kind of thinking that has simply been reflexive with us since Plato. It's not surprising that he doesn't entirely escape conceptualization, try as he may.

Clearly there is something schematic and preformed in his recurring use of the male as conceptualist, the female as existentialist, the male as rigid, the female as flexible. Such an observation may, of course, be true enough; it is even a very old one, echoing the ancient contrast between the male as rational, the female as intuitive. But it does suggest a return to a belief in essential natures—the mind of the universe has made man this way, women that way—which tends to contradict the author's own insistence that the moving lip is more important than the word it forms. There is also a shade of inadvertent irony here: Mr. Pinter, a male, is categorizing his own kind as somewhat incapable of the open and free action which he, the male playwright, is committed to exploring. No doubt he detects his inherited tendency to conceptualize when he doesn't want to.

The schematic pursues him in other ways. The frontal lobotomy which has been performed upon the benevolent brother in *The Caretaker,* for instance, very literally freezes that character into an essential position. This man is fixed, his patterns are determined, he cannot be further altered by any free forward movement of his own. The use of the lobotomy is, I think, a vulgarization in Pinter's terms: it is too easy, too expedient a way of saying that communication has been cut off. Instead of the mysteriously impenetrable we have here the symbolically impenetrable; the figure becomes a concept, as in Beckett, rather than an unpredictable, fluid force.

Actually, *The Caretaker* is a kind of battleground of styles, an unresolved tug-of-war between older methods of characterization and the newer method Pinter is reaching for. The play really functions in three degrees of perspective: we look at it as we might a toy theater in which three cut-out figures had been placed in different slots in the floor, at different distances from us. The caretaker himself, the garrulous and tenacious old man, is nearest to us, full-bodied in a familiar way, as rounded-out and complete as an ebullient whiner out of Dickens. We know him utterly. There is nothing unfinished or elusive about him. He is perfectly realized. But he is realized, in his wrapped-up complexity, in what here must be called an old-fashioned way.

The benevolent brother occupies the middle distance. He is symbolic man, two-dimensional, forever representing the same value, as he might in Beckett or certainly would in *Everyman.* He stands for an impasse, and has no other qualities, unless he can be said to have the quality of hinting that only the mentally destroyed are given to kindness in a violent universe intent upon exercising power to determine identity. He is a morality-play figure.

The inexplicably hostile brother, threatening even in his sporadic geniality, is placed in the far distance, nearest the shadows. He is the man Pinter's hand is most often after, all change and motion and indeterminateness, perpetual mocker of proposed stabilities. The others in the play have plans. So does he, in a whimsical and obviously untrustworthy way. But all plans dissolve as he touches them. His very presence destroys plan, exposes it for the mirage it is. He is the unfinished, the unascertainable, the existentialist man.

We are apt to like the caretaker most, simply because we are accustomed, in our theatergoing, to his sort of complex but firmly defined being. But the hostile brother, the taunting one who refuses us access to himself because the self is not ready to be named, is the presence in the play that leads us most directly into the Pinter landscape as a whole. He is, indeed, the only figure in the play to do the new thing most persistently and characteristically pursued by the playwright: behave before he has been pigeon-holed. Strictly speaking, the three men probably do not belong in the same play: each comes from a separate and somewhat isolated literary world; none can really move from one slot, one dimension, to another. This difficulty does keep the lines of communication down, which is an existentialist requirement. But it achieves that particular effect by a mixing of modes, and at some cost to stylistic unity.

Curiously, explicit violence is also a troubling, and not quite assimilated, element in the playwright's work. So long as violence is threatened, intimated, promised, the chill in the air is actual and the atmosphere of the play uncorrupted. But whenever the sinuous, seeking movement of the play breaks open into concrete deed, into physical definiteness, an aura of the stagetrick, the artificial climax, the merely surprising act-curtain intrudes. The sudden death at the end of *The Dumb Waiter* is surprising, and in that sense theatrically effective; but it also leaves us with a feeling of having been taken in by mere Grand Guignol.

The entrance of the Negro, the savage assault upon him, and the instant blindness of Rose at the end of *The Room* have a similar flavor of the startling for its own sake, or for the sake of getting the curtain down on a sufficiently defiant and baffling note. In *The Birthday Party* there is some feeling that we are losing the play as Stanley loses his self-control in the deliberately explosive nightmare of his attack upon Lulu.

Why is the deed sometimes less persuasive than the rumor of deeds to come? I suspect precisely because it is a defined act, which means that it terminates the groping forward that is the whole environment in an existentialist view of things. To kill someone is to put a name, a meaning, an identity upon the situation before us. The condition that is being dramatized has come to an end. But the end must be arbitrary because no existentialist is yet ready to say that he knows ends, that he can announce essences.

Pinter confesses that he likes "a good curtain," and some of his eruptions may simply come from a craftsman's passion for good stage-rigging. The stylistic problem remains unresolved, however. If existence is endlessly open, where is it to be closed? If movement is all, who dares stop it?

One last qualification. I find myself preferring the shorter plays—plays which may run anywhere from thirty minutes to an hour and a half—to the full-length extensions of Pinter's highly individual vision. *A Slight Ache,* for instance, seems to me to do the work of *The Homecoming,* or a very great deal of it, with a succinctness and a sustained tension that are distributed and seriously dissipated in the longer play.

In its last half hour, *The Homecoming* is going to feel its way to the same sort of unstable equation that keeps *A Slight Ache* poised on the edge of dissolving identities for as long as it lasts. But while *The Homecoming* is postponing its eventual plunge into movement, it has little to do but execute a delaying ballet of intimation, of carefully crossed legs and carefully concealed potentiality.

Marking time during the delay, Pinter tends to fill in with the near-exhausted devices of the conceptual Theater of the Absurd. In particular, he doesn't mind borrowing from Ionesco, spacing out his contradictions mathematically. Max, the father of the family, expands on the theme of his wife, who had "a heart of gold," and his "three fine grown-up lads." A minute later these same folk are "three bastard sons" and "a slutbitch of a wife." The device is more deeply imbedded in tangible character than it ever is in Ionesco, where two sides of a face pull apart as though they had been pasted together out of cut paper. It is also relevant to the infinite-identity theme. Nonetheless, it is an echo, too conceptually planned, transparently technical, wholly verbal. It is not life itself in unreined flux, as we shall find life behaving toward the end of the play.

Why should the longer plays delay, or circle, a situation that can be accounted for quite satisfactorily in a tight forty minutes? I suspect that it has not quite occurred to Mr. Pinter that it is possible to display more than a single altering step into the void, a single transposition of personality, a single throw of the existentialist dice, in any one play. There is nothing, really, to prevent him from moving forward again once the initial elision has taken place. Having moved from wife-mother to whore, Ruth may very well move to yet another extension of being. Since she is not predefined, she is free to go on taking steps without worrying about the kind of footprints she leaves or what prying detectives may make of them. One gesture is not definition, is not the end of things. A play might very well take us through three or four persons in one, as *Hamlet* does, before it chooses to curtail its possibly endless investigation of possibility. There is nothing in the method to say that we must stop at Stage Two. Thus far Mr. Pinter tends to confine himself to a first change of state, a practice which makes many of the shorter plays perfect but which attenuates, and makes repetitive, the longer ones.

I have mentioned *Hamlet,* which calls for a further remark. Mr. Pinter has described himself, and not necessarily baitingly, as "a traditional playwright." The fact of the matter is that there is a theatrical tradition of pursuing existence without being certain of essence—it came into being long before any philosopher elected to challenge Plato in so many words—and it has given us some of our most cherished, if hotly debated, masterpieces. It would seem very likely that Shakespeare traced Hamlet's course without any dead-certain concept in his head of where Hamlet's quest was to end. Death, yes, most likely, though in Shakespeare's source-legend Hamlet doesn't die. But precisely how the tangle of personality was to unravel itself, when and where it was to assert itself as defined, seems bafflingly open throughout Shakespeare's play. Now cruel, now kind, now dedicated, now dilatory, now—but we have gone over these unpredictable alterations in Hamlet forever. It is the very lack of a sensed master-plan, or a conceptual program for the play, that has led to the sort of exasperation with *Hamlet* for lacking "an objective correlative" that T. S. Eliot felt. In the end, Mr. Eliot controlled his exasperation and took his criticism back. Why? Because, "objective correlative" or no, Hamlet existed. Critics may quarrel about Hamlet's essential nature to the end of time. But Hamlet stirred first, and still stirs.

Thus, in a sense, Pinter is returning us to a "tradition" at the same time that he insists upon destroying what we call tradition. The stage has always been open, in spite of the rigors philosophers have imposed upon thought, to the tasting of experience experimentally. Its very nature tempts it to do so. The stage is an arena, a bear-bit, a bull-ring, an empty space until challengers enter it. Who is to say what all challengers are to do on the spur of the moment, in the heat of passion, under the pressure of the contest? Bear-pits and bull-rings breed surprises. Claw and cape behave differently on different days, in different winds. An arena is an open, initially empty, space not because it is a place for fighting but because it is a place for finding, for

discovery, for realization. It first gapes at us as though it were a great question mark. Then movement fills it and—perhaps—makes a shape.

We tend to forget that this is a possible theatrical tradition or a possible playwriting method because we have lately lived so long under another dispensation: that of the "well-made play," the play built of bricks selected to shore up a thesis, the play dominated by a writer's logic. This later, neater, more predictable method has wearied us for a considerable time. We have understood its virtues, its enclosed intellectual systems and its clear time-and-thought sequences well enough; but we have intuited, all along, that drama had something less reasonable and more impulsive to say to us, given its other voice.

Pinter might be called "traditional" in the sense that he has begun to restore, under the fresh questioning of a twentieth-century philosophical method, an old and neglected urge to enter the arena naked, without the support of tried-and-true tricks or proved propositions but with a firm determination to move as much as a man may move against whatever can be made to yield to him. When Euripides entered such an arena in *The Bacchae* it was probably without hope of fully resolving the contest between Dionysiac excess and Dionysiac rectitude. But in he went, all the way, giving every god and devil his due, to see what an uninhibited probing, an unrestricted invasion of the Greeks' very own void, might uncover. Conceptualization, prior commitment, would surely have stopped him short of the play's boundless frontier, its resolute pressing forward into the infinite. Asking only how extensively any one force might assert itself, he made—out of such a reaching—an ambiguous, deeply mystifying, blood-curdling masterpiece. He did not seek to devise or support a system, as Aeschylus had done in *The Eumenides*. Focusing his eyes beyond system, he sought instead to see all that was.

At the same time, Pinter is obviously untraditional in that he has almost fully freed himself from the realistic-naturalistic "problem-play" notion that drama is best constructed as a syllogism, with a conclusion following inevitably from known postulates. He is also untraditional in that he has accepted, for practical dramatic purposes, the post-Greek proposition that the lip moves first and that its "nature" as lip comes later—after the utterance and because of it. He does not particularly care whether "nature" or "essence" is absolutely arrived at within the confines of his activity as continuing observer. As a dramatist, he wishes to observe in the same way that, as man and householder, he wishes to live.

"I'm bored by what New York thinks of itself," he has said on one of his visits to the United States. "I wish it would shut up." Even cities are better off not trying to define themselves too precisely too soon. "There's a little village in Gloucestershire, in the Cotswold Hills, that I like better. The village is called Bibury. It's very English. It just exists."

R. F. Storch (essay date 1967)

SOURCE: "Harold Pinter's Happy Families," in *The Massachusetts Review,* Vol. 8, No. 4, Autumn, 1967, pp. 703-12.

[*In the following essay, Storch argues that Pinter's plays are about the anxiety and menace Pinter sees at the heart of the bourgeois family.*]

The shock-tactics of Harold Pinter's dramaturgy are so effective that his audience, cowed into the pit of irrationality, is afraid to ask why in the name of anxiety it has succumbed, and what it is in the plays that gives them such insidious power. To ask the question at all may seem silly, because Pinter, we know, deliberately destroys all clues for a rational appraisal: the irrationality is the major part of the meaning. Everyone has of course experienced the menace and terror and loneliness which are generally applauded as Pinter's chief dramatic effects. It is not only drama critics who by sheer repetition have made us accept anxiety and alienation as the final account of experience. And yet we are right to ask the question, because the very deliberateness with which Pinter befuddles us hints at an ordered meaning which will satisfy the rational levels of our minds. Anxiety is a word to conjure with these days, but what it pulls out of the hat is only the shadow of a meaning. And if we are honest with ourselves, we have to admit that the state of shock is enjoyable only if sooner or later rational relief is in sight.

In spite of the clever dislocation of common sense, Pinter's plays affect us because they are about the middle-class family, both as sheltering home longed for and dreamed of, and as many-tentacled monster strangling its victim. It does not, after all, surprise us that there is more menace and irrationality in this dramatic material than in any other. The London stage since 1945 (to look no further) has been very much occupied with the family as a trap-door to the underworld. Whether the angle of descent has been religious, as in Graham Greene, or social class, as in Osborne and Wesker, the game of Happy Families has provided the entertainment. Pinter, however, is by far the most radical in breaking with the naturalistic conventions of *drame bourgeois*. For he burrows into dark places where it is of little consequence whether a family is working-class or professional. If he is obsessed by the peculiar horrors of middle-class families, this is not within the larger view of social class, but simply because they epitomize everything that is horrifying in any family situation today. He makes us see that class distinctions are curiously out of date for today's theatre, and that a kitchen sink is no more enlightening than a coffee table. When such paraphernalia are made into class-symbols, they merely hide what Pinter knows to be the real drama. We cling to kitchen sinks in the belief that at last we have reached something solid and honest; but Pinter will have none of that. He destroys the predictable place of things, deliberately confuses and contradicts. As soon as a situation looks as if it were attaining a recognizable meaning,

he introduces some nonsense, wild improbability or verbal play, and we fall once more through the trap-door. His plays consist largely of his dogged attempts to destroy consistency and any clue to a rational pattern. The act of writing becomes, then, the work of the repressive censor as much as what is usually thought of as the creative imagination. This would seem to account for the taste of ashes, the sterility which pervades not only Pinter's plays but the whole Theatre of the Absurd in spite of its wildly fantastic ingredients. But the interesting point about this censorship is that it in fact underlines, or at any rate circumscribes, the very clues it destroys. As a result the audience is insidiously attacked at a level where it hurts most.

Pinter's plays are largely about the running away from certain family situations, and the faster the running, the clearer it becomes what he is running away from. Every trick in his repertory is supposed to distract our attention from those unappeasable furies haunting his mind. But their faces, or masks, leer and glower from the plays all the same. By dislocating our attention from the common sense view of things he makes us alive to primitive fears, destroys the rational façade of the adult mind, and lays bare regressive fantasies. He does not put to second-hand use ancient myths, in the manner of Cocteau or Sartre, but discovers the infantile fears that lie at the roots of those myths, and that are the ultimate nourishment of the poetic imagination.

There is another level to his plays, one he himself has drawn attention to. Much of what strikes us as irrational, comic or even idiotic, he says, he has merely set down as actually observed. The way people talk at or past each other, have breakfast together, or discuss the furnishing of a room is quite extraordinary enough if it is set down without embellishment or literary convention. But this strangeness of the ordinary Pinter uses as a way into the more fearful strangeness of the usually hidden.

The breakfast scene at the beginning of **The Birthday Party** (1959) is a brilliant example of inane small talk leading into fantasies and infantile terrors. This early play is one of the most concentrated, as it were single-minded, of Pinter's achievements. Stanley, in his role of boarder, is very clearly and lucidly at the psychological centre of the action. He has run away from home, only to hole himself up in another home-like shelter. And Meg, his landlady, sustains, more directly than a mother probably could, the ambivalent feeling of a mother towards her son. Stanley daydreams of his one and only concert, which has been a great success: "My father nearly came down to hear me. Well, I dropped him a card anyway. But I don't think he could make it. No, I—I lost the address, that was it." The dialogue moves through the neurotic realm of what could have been true into sheer invention. What emerges is that Stanley was not going to give his first concert in his father's presence. But the neurotic mind is honest in its own fashion: keeping away father must be followed by retribution: they carved Stanley up. He went down to his next place, but "the hall was closed, the place was shuttered up, not even a caretaker. They'd locked it up. . . . They want me to crawl down on my bended knees." Stanley's career as concert-pianist is effectively "blocked" and he, the guilty son, dare not leave his bolt-hole. "There is nowhere to go," he says to Lulu, the local bit of goods, but it really means that he is afraid to go, even to imagine somewhere to go. Father might turn up. As it happens, he does, in the shape of Goldberg, who makes up to the girl. When Goldberg and Mccann enter, there is at first some rather cheap mystification; they use the language of gangsters: "Is this it?"—"This is it." But the real threat they are to Stanley soon becomes clear. Goldberg reminisces of his childhood in a cosy, prosperous Jewish middle-class family. Uncle Barney had a house "just outside Basingstoke at the time. Respected by the whole community." The menace comes from this all-enveloping cosiness, the family culture served up in a heavy syrup of sentimentality. Mccann's version is of the familiar Irish kind. (James Joyce's young man had to escape from it too, though it continued to haunt him.) Goldberg and Mccann make a "team"—enterprising, loyal, and doing a job. Not necessarily a criminal job. The point is that any job done in this team spirit becomes sinister. They see each other as, respectively, "a capable man" and "a man in your position." And we know what skullduggery that sort of backscratching often hides. The team spirit belongs to the same world as family sentiment: both reach out their tentacles to strangle Stanley. The two visitors menace him with conformity, and the play shows how they crush him. The psychological lever is to make Stanley regress to the infantile state, where the need for security, mother, home and respectability—being "one of us"—becomes so overpowering that he is brainwashed of the last vestiges of an independent spirit. Goldberg is one long, sickening repertory of bourgeois make-believe, while Mccann is the bird-brained muscleman (all sentiment, too) who wields the truncheon, like a good storm trooper, when Stanley is not regressing fast enough into the infantile fold. The birthday party celebrates Stanley's infancy, something like his fifth year. The toy drum is unpacked, Stanley plays it, and the music possesses him. He beats the drum savagely. Motherly Meg asks for a kiss. She wants to keep him for her boy. Before he kisses her, his shoulders sag. But he is not yet defeated; he leaps at her throat.

Act II begins with the third temptation (the first is motherly Meg, the second treacly Goldberg): namely, Mccann's boyish truculence, daring you to step across the line he has drawn, or shouldering you in a crowd. He is the son Stanley should have been: go-ahead, tough, part of the team. The interrogation dramatizes the pressure from Stanley's background and upbringing; the world of respectability becomes a terrorizing cross-examination. It is not real moral problems that constitute the menace but petty trespasses and finally a childish puzzle: why did the chicken cross the road; and which came first, the chicken or the egg. This produces the kind of worry a child might have in facing the adult world. Goldberg's speech in Act III parodies prudential morality: the rule of thumb, the

decent way of life; but it is all meaningless. He is unable to finish his line beginning, "Because I believe that the world. . . ." A later parody of the code—work hard and play hard—is more than half way to idiocy. It prepares us for Stanley's final entrance, brainwashed and totally idiotic. He is now the suitable subject for the trite baits of the ad age: anything from an abdominal belt to a yacht. When he is about to be taken away, Petey pleads with him: "Stan, don't let them tell you what to do!" But it is too late, for Stanley, by way of infantile regression into the bosom of the family, has become the perfect victim for anyone who wants to tell him what to do.

The most devastating moment in the play is the last. Meg is completely oblivious of what had happened at the party, and quite unaware of the terrible things she has done to her Stanley. All she remembers is that she was the belle of the evening. At the end of the play hate of the female burns with a hot acetylene flame.

The Caretaker (first staged in 1960) does not have a woman in it, and apparently no one to take the place of father. And yet mother and father are like ghosts haunting the room, which is really the main character of the play. Its subject might be called: who is to occupy the room, and what sort of person is a caretaker—the substitute for parental care. Davies is as stupid as Meg, as garrulous and helpless. He is menaced, speaks of being maltreated and attacked. Put him into a pinafore and he is a housewife. He is always disgusted; it is the tenor of his dialogue. He nags like a woman: "My job's cleaning the floor, clearing the tables, doing a bit of washing-up, nothing to do with taking out buckets!" He is curiously epicene. Like Meg he is impervious to everything but his own needs, completely selfish and self-absorbed. The most powerful emotion emerging in the play is hatred of his kind of stupidity. His whining ungratefulness is particularly repulsive. "Can't wear shoes that don't fit. Nothing worse. I said to this monk, here, I said, look here, mister. . . ." His trying on a pair of boots becomes a nauseous spectacle.

Aston is also a weak character, fiddling about the room, making the bed. (Pinter's plays often have two contrasted male characters, one strong, one weak. Mick and Aston in this play; Ben and Gus in ***The Dumb Waiter***; Goldberg and Mccann in ***The Birthday Party***; Max and Sam in ***The Homecoming***.) Aston, unlike Mick, is not sure whether he has a right to occupancy. He had been betrayed by his mother into a serious brain operation that left him permanently disabled. The operation was performed with something like "pincers." As Act II ends with castration, so Act I had ended with a rape. Mick, the strong, threatening character, screws back Davies' arm and forces him to the floor, "*struggling, grimacing, whimpering and staring.*" Mick remains silent. His gesture of placing a finger on his lips and then on Davies' dramatizes this silence and at the same time underlines the sexual meaning of the struggle. Next Mick examines the bed and Davies' trousers. He presses him down with his foot. The first words he utters are equivocal: "What's the game?"

The opening of Act II is a good example of deliberate nonsense putting a blind between a vague feeling of menace and its cause in an obviously sexual tension. Mick cross-examines Davies—did you sleep in that bed, how did you sleep. This examination is repeated several times but interspersed with long monologues of utter nonsense. The bed becomes more significant: at first it was his, later it is his mother's. "Now don't get perky, son, don't get perky. Keep your hands off old mum."

One cannot push character-analysis very far in Pinter's plays. *The Caretaker,* for example, does not sort out motivation or lines of action by giving them consistently to one or the other character. Instead of an interplay of fixed characters we have a kaleidoscope of pieces of experience: of memories, fears and hatreds, which every now and then get shaken into configurations of character and situation. Even the division between the sexes is unstable. Davies' job comes close to a housewife's and he often talks like one: "You want me to do all the dirty work all up and down them stairs, just so I can sleep in this lousy filthy hole every night?" Mick at first seems to listen sympathetically, but consequently seems to enjoy all the more telling Davies with sheer and open cruelty that he is not wanted. The quarrel becomes violent (Mick smashes the Buddha) and sounds more and more like a marital fight. Davies: "All right then . . . you do that . . . you do it . . . if that's what you want. . . ." Mick: "Anyone would think this house was all I got to worry about. . . ." At the end the brothers unite and throw Davies out. At least half of him sounds like a deserted and maltreated woman.

Whatever situations and characters Pinter invents, the obsessive patterns will turn up. In *A Slight Ache* Edward has achieved respectability (like Goldberg) and wants to turn back to the point in his youth where he could have taken a different turning (like Stanley). His advice to the enigmatic dummy of a matchseller, who becomes whatever is most desired or feared or regretted, is very much like Goldberg's formula: keep your shoulder to the wheel, etc. Flora tells of her being raped, the one experience that seems to be meaningful to her, and makes up to the matchseller as Meg does to Stanley: "It's me you were waiting for, wasn't it? You've been waiting for me. You've seen me in the woods, picking daisies, in my apron, my pretty daisy apron, and you came and stood, poor creature, at my gate, till death do us part. Poor Barnabas. I'm going to put you to bed. I'm going to put you to bed and watch over you. But first you must have a whacking great bath. And I'll buy you pretty little things that will suit you. And little toys to play with. On your deathbed. Why shouldn't you die happily?" The role of woman, as Pinter sees her, put in a nutshell.

A Night Out is a dull play (BBC, 1960), because the theme is out in the open. Albert's mother is as nagging as Davies, as possessive as Meg and as deadly as Flora. The play becomes witty in Act III, when the prostitute turns out to be a respectable mother: at that Alfred explodes: "You are all the same, you see, you're all the same, you're just a dead weight round my neck. . . ." *The Dwarfs,* broadcast in the same year, is much more impressive because it belongs to the realm of disguised or displaced motivations. In many respects it resembles *The Caretaker,* except that it comes even closer to naked childhood obsessions, who are given the guise of dwarfs. The scene is again a domestic interior: there is talk of cleaning the place: "You'd think a man like that would have a maid, wouldn't you, to look after the place when he's away, to look after his milk?" And, "Still, he won't find much to come home to, will he? There's nothing in the kitchen, there's not even a bit of lettuce." And so on. The womanish complaints are given an irrational twist, but are still there—"I have to run downstairs to put the kettle on, run upstairs to finish what I am doing, run downstairs. . . ." This is the same Len who then meticulously and simplemindedly makes the room his own: "There is my table. That is a table. There is my chair. There is my table. . . ." The room is both an order and an ambush, a trap. A kingdom and an enemy. The imaginative pitch is so high that womanish chatter is reduced to a mechanical repetition: "What do I think of the cut? The cut? The cut? What a cut!" etc. The basic question is, "What are you doing in my room? What do you want here?" The answer comes from the king in his counting house: "I thought you might give me some bread and honey." But Len is afraid: "I don't want you to become too curious in this room. . . ." Indeed not, for rooms shrink, expand, and move. We have reached, very suddenly, the infantile fears and obsessions that will be embodied in the dwarfs. "But when the time comes, you see, what I shall do is place red hot burning coal in my own mouth." This cryptic statement is followed by *Silence* and "I've got some beigels." The situation becomes more clearly an anal fantasy. Len is told that he is not "elastic". "By elastic I mean being prepared for your own deviations." Pete's analysis of Len is highly suggestive of a very young child and is summed up very neatly in "You've got no idea how to preserve a distance between what you smell and what you think about. . . . How can you hope to assess and verify anything if you walk about with your nose stuck between your feet all day long?" The stage directions are clear enough: *Len begins to grunt spasmodically, to whimper, hiss, and by the end of the speech, to groan.* Pete's dream of peeling and blotched faces occasions Len's infantile whimpering. In the end it prompts the query of guilt: "Then I thought, Christ, what's my face like? Is that why she's staring? Is that rotting too?" Len, reduced to the infantile state, now sees the dwarfs in the cloaca: "They clock in very early, scenting the event. They are like kites in a city disguise." The cloaca then becomes the stock exchange: "All the same, it is essential that I keep a close watch on the rate of exchange, on the rise and fall of the market. . . . With due warning from them I shall clear my stocks, should there be a landslide." Here the obsession with fecal cleanliness comes very close to the surface. The obsession spreads. When the toasting fork drops on the hearth, Len shouts: "Don't touch it! You don't know what will happen if you touch it! You mustn't touch it! You mustn't bend!" His speech deteriorates into a child's perception of himself in a world he is not part of. The dwarfs are projections of his longing for "dirt": "One with a face of chalk chucks the dregs of the daytime into a bin and seats himself on the lid. He is beginning to chew though he has not eaten. Now they collect at the back step. They scrub their veins at the running sink, now they are gorged in the sud. . . ." And then the variations on "He sits. The other talks. He talks. The other sits. The other stands. I crouch." Len's fantasy continues until Mark asks: "What is up your nose now?" and Len answers: "I'm the centre of a holy plague." The plague is sent in punishment, and Len's occupancy of the room is threatened: "You are trying to buy and sell me . . . you're buying me out of house and home, you're a calculating bastard . . . I've lost a kingdom." (Again the nursery rhyme of the king in his counting house eating bread and honey.) The anal fantasy becomes more pronounced: "Always squatting and bending, dipping their wicks in the custard . . . then soothe each other's orifices with a local ointment. . . ." Lust and guilty fear become one: "It all came out, in about twenty-eight goes. I couldn't stop shivering and I couldn't stop squatting. . . ." Now the obsession with housecleaning at the beginning of the play is given meaning. At the very end, filth and disorder and the menace of change become identified: "And this change. All about me the change. The yard as I know it is littered with scraps of cat's meat . . . worms stuck in the poisoned shit heaps, the alleys a whirlpool of piss, slime, blood and fruit juice.—Now all is bare. All is clean. All is scrubbed. There is a lawn. There is a shrub. There is a flower."

To call *The Dwarfs* a *drame bourgeois* may seem stretching the term, but it is after all strictly accurate. For it deals with those infantile obsessions and fears which are the foundation of bourgeois virtues—cleanliness, order, four walls you can call your own. Many of the tensions in an Ibsen family are due to the frightful cost of taming the dwarfs, or to the reckless refusal to tame them.

Pinter's latest play *The Homecoming* (first performance, 1965) is an intriguing mixture of plain family drama at the naturalistic level and of obsessive fantasy which takes it out of the realm of the probable. At the naturalistic level Pinter has come into the open at last: the play deals with the tensions within a Jewish family. The central figure, the mother, is dead, and the father, Max, is the caretaker. The dead mother is still, however, the focus of all the emotions, even though she is not mentioned very often. Her ghost hovers in the background, and respect is paid to her memory. But that is only lip service. For the real emotions she has roused in her family are fear and hatred. The outrageously improbable plot—to set up Ruth both as communal concubine for the whole family and to make her a prostitute to bring in money—is simply the family's revenge against mother. Already in Act I, Lenny, with his stories of violence he has inflicted on women who threatened his health or had been inconsiderate, works off his hatred of Ruth as a mother figure. When they are introduced to each other, he won't accept the fact that she

is married to Teddy, his brother. Max, the father, behaves equally irrationally, by calling her a prostitute. Ruth is consequently initiated into the family. Joey goes upstairs with her for two hours (though he does not "go the whole hog" with her) while Lenny tells stories of exploits in the Paddington area. But in the end Max's scheme of turning the tables on the woman at last, of getting the most out of her, instead of letting her use the family, seems no longer so easy. His assurance dwindles. "She'll use us, she'll make use of us, I can tell you!" He collapses and crawls to her knees where she is sitting surrounded by her subdued boys. The woman has won again.

The real power of Pinter's plays does not lie in the shock-tactics of the dramaturgy but in the terribly familiar situations they are supposed to draw our attention away from. We may not be aware of the obsessive fears of childhood which dominate Pinter's characters (or shadowy configurations that take the place of characters), but we are never far from them, and a Pinter play can trip us over into that neurotic world. The very shadowiness of the characterization makes his world more real, and makes it easier for us to enter it, to "identify". Pinter gets through to the level of neurotic obsessions by a radical break with conventional images of reality. He parodies the bourgeois life which plays out the neurosis. But his most remarkable achievement is that at his best his vision is not a fanciful distortion of reality, but has the effect of a more direct, honest understanding of it. This honesty is the strength of all original art; with Pinter it often reaches the extreme point of seeming naïveté: the pouring of a cup of tea, the reading of a newspaper can become events fraught with climactic meaning. These are not, however, symbolic actions; their significance is genuinely in their being lived. Pinter has a very strong sense of what people really experience (as against what literary convention says they experience), as well as a sense of the mystery contained in the trite and banal. In *The Room* (1960) the blind Negro is not a symbol, but the real instance of extreme loneliness, of human weakness, who calls to the woman, and who must be kicked to death by the man unable to face such weakness in a human being. The idea of the room itself occurs in most of Pinter's plays. It does not have to symbolize some abstraction of anxiety. The actual four walls are part of our most important experience: to be inside a room, or to be outside in the open spaces—this elementary contrast is probably as closely worked into our emotions as anything we can think of. By way of such outrageously simple imaginings Pinter arrives at the most direct and also the most harassing view of things, and the banal is forced to reveal its mystery. Every poet knows that the world of mysterious dreams is to be found at the very centre of banality. But the obverse is also true: the most terrifying anxieties are caused by commonplace occasions. Pinter's plays are not about menaces and anxieties in some metaphysical realm, but take their life from the very heart of reality, the bourgeois family. And whether we like it or not, nothing could be more real than that.

Ray Orley (essay date 1968)

SOURCE: "Pinter and Menace," in *Drama Critique,* Vol. 2, 1968, pp. 125-48.

[*In the following essay, Orley examines the elements of horror and menace in Pinter's plays*]

Dramatically, as well as politically, terror and menace are most essential elements of Harold Pinter's vision of life: the horror of existence presented in truly threatening and frightening terms. Characters talk circles around each other, and frequently underlying a seemingly innocent speech is a savage threat; Mick chases Davies around in the dark with a vacuum cleaner in *The Caretaker* and nearly frightens the old man out of his wits; in *The Collection* one character makes threatening telephone calls to another and eventually begins to throw knives at him in a sort of "game"; Stanley Webber, in *The Birthday Party,* is driven out of his mind during an absurd and terrifying interrogation conducted by two seeming strangers; *The Room* ends on a most violent note, with one character killed and another blinded.

This treatment of the elements of menace in Pinter's plays will be limited to two areas. The first classification which I am making in Pinter's work I shall call menace of character and incident. In a Pinter play incidents are more clearly associated with the characters involved in them than with "what happens" in the play as a whole, since what happens tends to be of an episodic nature in any case. This classification operates on two levels. Most frequently the first, outward level of character-incident menace is driven forward by what John Pesta has called the "'usurper,' a menacing figure who, either actively or passively, undermines the existence of other characters, and who sometimes is himself undermined."[1] On the second level of menace in character and incident motivations for characters and actions are not easily apparent, if at all. What a character did or what he may have thought before he came on stage is rarely unfolded to us; origins are obscured. Pinter says of this: "A character on the stage who can present no convincing argument or information as to his past experience, his present behaviour or his aspirations, nor give a comprehensive analysis of his motives is as legitimate and as worthy of attention as one who, alarmingly, can do all these things."[2] Bernard Dukore equates the mystery in Pinter's works with menace, a menace aimed directly at the audience as well as at the other characters of the play, a menace which consistently deepens, just as every answer leads to a host of new questions.[3]

The second category of menace I find in Pinter's work I am calling, for lack of any more apt phrase, metaphysical menace. This is the menace engendered by an alien, incomprehensible universe, by the irrationality of life and even of rationality. This universe that Pinter sees and writes of is essentially the same one seen by Beckett and Genêt and other absurdist writers of genuine value. This metaphysical menace is the most terrifying of all, for it encompasses so vast a scope, it hits so close to the very foundations of our lives, and its specificity lacks a concreteness we can comfortably put our finger on. The audience is meant to be menaced at least as much as the characters within the plays, and by the very things we perhaps all come closest to believing true. And thus, an argument could perhaps be made for this shared menace and terror of our existence providing the sole ritualistic or communion bond to make today's theatre as communally meaningful and indeed religious an experience as that of, say, the Greeks or the Elizabethans.

This metaphysical menace will be seen in many obvious forms in the plays: the terror that comes from outside the security of one's "own place" in *The Room* or *A Slight Ache;* the unknown force, the "organization," that sends McCann and Goldberg after Stanley in *The Birthday Party;* the unknown being giving orders to Gus and Ben via the dumb-waiter; the many things from the outside world that irritate or terrify Davies in *The Caretaker.* Perhaps a remark Pinter once made will help to keep before us an image of how he sees his plays and the importance that menace has in them. When asked by a critic what his plays are *about,* Pinter replied: "The weasel under the cocktail cabinet."[4]

The Room, The Dumb Waiter, The Birthday Party, and *A Slight Ache* all take place in confined surroundings, in one room in fact, which represents for their protagonists at least a temporary refuge from the others (it is tempting, but not really necessary, to see it in terms of Freudian symbolism as a womb-substitute), something they have shored up against their ruins. The menace comes from outside, from the intruder whose arrival unsettles the warm, comfortable world bounded by four walls, and any intrusion can be menacing, because the element of uncertainty and unpredictability the intruder brings with him is in itself menacing.[5]

Thus John Russell Taylor, chief chronicler of the contemporary British drama, sums up what are the essential similarities of Pinter's earliest plays. Each revolves around a central character who has tried to escape from the metaphysical menace of the outside world by holing up in some seemingly safe burrow. For Rose in *The Room* it is a flat in a large and rather decrepit old house; for Stanley in *The Birthday Party* it is a seldom-frequented and, except for the owners and himself, unoccupied boarding-house by the seashore; for Gus and Ben, the two professional killers of *The Dumb Waiter,* it is a windowless and seemingly sealed-off basement room where they await instructions for their next "job"; for Edward of *A Slight Ache* it is his isolated country home. Into the sanctums of each of these characters comes some emissary from the outside, bringing with him the menace which the outside world represents; in each case the life of the recluse is changed drastically, even violently, by this arrival from the world beyond his haven.

The Room opens on *"A room in a large house. A door down right."*[6] Rose and the man who is probably her husband, Bert, are on stage. "When asked by a critic what his two people in his room are afraid of, Pinter replied, 'Obviously they are scared of what is outside the room. Outside the room there is a world bearing upon them which is frightening. I am sure it is frightening to you and me as well.'"[7]

In addition, there is an element of menace in Bert's continued silence. He maintains the silence even through the entrance of Mr. Kidd, the landlord, and does not speak a word before his own exit, about one-third through the play. There is something menacingly inscrutable about this man who sits reading a magazine and automatically consuming the food Rose sets before him—as he will show when he re-enters near the end of the play. Mr. Kidd's entrance provides Rose with an opportunity for a real duologue, as well as a whiff of menace from the outside.

Rose's first real brush with the menace from outside the room comes with the entrance of Mr. and Mrs. Sands, a young couple seeking a room for rent in the house. Mrs. Sands assures Rose, "Oh, it's murder out" (page 105). Rose reaffirms, "I never go out at night. We stay in" (page 107). The couple goes on to tell Rose that there is a strange man—or at least his voice, very polite—in the basement (a place Rose fears because it is damp and cold). The man told them there is a room for rent in the house:

> MR. SANDS. The man in the basement said there was one. One room. Number seven he said.
>
> ROSE. That's this room.
>
> (page 112)

"She ushers them out, but her sense of security has been shattered: the outer forces are beginning to encroach on her."[8]

Rose finds Mr. Kidd but gets only evasive answers to her questions about whether her room is to be let; he has something more pressing to tell her: a man has been lying in the basement all weekend waiting to see her. With a great deal of trepidation Rose at last agrees to see him. "Again the door becomes the focal point of a nameless menace."[9] The man is a blind Negro named Riley. He says he has a message for her: "Your father wants you to come home." Further, he begins to call her Sal, a name which seems to upset her, although she does not deny it belongs to her. At last he says, "I want you to come home" (page 118). As the reality shifts before the spectators' eyes and words become more and more ambiguous, the terror of the situation increases until at last Bert enters and speaks: "They got it dark out. . . . They got it very icy out" (pages 119, 120), revealing that he too mistrusts and fears some

mysteriously implacable force, some *they*. He sees the Negro and pushes him to the floor. Unaccountably he says only one word, "Lice!" to the blind man. *"He strikes the NEGRO, knocking him down, and then kicks his head against the gas stove several times. The NEGRO lies still."* There is a pause and Rose's curtain line is "Can't see. I can't see. I can't see" (page 120).

The ending of the play is surely laden with overt menace and terror; the outside powers that have been threatening with increasing intensity since the opening stage picture, since Rose first said, "It's very cold out, I can tell you. It's murder," have gained entrance into Rose's little bastion and done their worst in horror and violence. And yet there is something quite unsatisfying about this ending; whatever we may have expected to "get" Rose, it hardly would have been this. Taylor says of the artistry of *The Room* generally, "The hand is not yet entirely sure and the mystifications are often too calculated, too heavily underlined." He then proceeds to account for the unsatisfactory quality of the ending: "The melodramatic finale with its trappings of blindness and violent death (the blind negro is so like a parody of a Prévert embodiment of fate that one wonders how familiar Pinter can have been with the French cinema of the forties) appears in retrospect particularly out of place, since it makes the terrors which beset Rose all too actual and immediate."[10] Taylor, however, does not seem to have a completely firm grasp of the problem here: if there is anything Rose's terror is not, it is "actual and immediate." Despite the Negro's physical presence, he remains grossly unreal; he is almost an oracle, never speaking more than seven precious words at a time, making an almost *deus-ex-machina* entrance at the end of the play; he strains the audience's credulity to its limit. Esslin calls him "obviously an allegorical figure, a messenger of dark powers, of death." He states that "Pinter himself now criticizes this element in his first play for the over-obviousness of its symbolic machinery."[11]

None the less, it is possible to see in this first play at least the seeds of later developments of menace in Pinter's work. There is menace of character and incident in Bert's silence and violent beating of the Negro, in Mr. Kidd's erratic ways, and even in the Sands' fairly pedestrian manners; of metaphysical menace in the "tiny globe of light set in an immense and menacing void of darkness,"[12] and in Riley and his cryptic message.

If Pinter later found the character of Riley too overtly symbolic as Esslin states, it might be wondered why he introduced a seemingly very similar character as the agent of menace into the most recent play of the first group, *A Slight Ache*.[13] The Matchseller is even more laconic than Riley in *The Room*: he never utters a sound throughout the course of the play. The cast listing for the radio performance of the work names no actor in the part of the Matchseller—apparently on the air not even heavy breathing denoted his presence. This rather repulsive Matchseller has chosen a spot behind the country home of Edward and his wife Flora from which to vend his goods. Edward feels quite menaced by the man's presence at his gate, despite his bravado attempts to conceal the fact.

The Matchseller, however, because of his very different effect upon Edward and Flora, proves to be a much more effective character than is Riley in **The Room.** Plagued by the question of precisely what the Matchseller is up to and what he is like, the couple invites him inside, but he does not speak. "As though challenged by the stubborn absence of any reaction, Edward begins to tell the man his life story,"[14] during the course of which he reveals himself to be a quite pretentious, superficially urbane person, full of false notions of his own accomplishments and worth. Edward becomes more and more agitated by the menace of the Matchseller's hulking silent presence, all the time revealing more of his hypocrisy and the fatuous little dreams of himself he has been sheltering. At last he must leave the Matchseller's presence to get a breath of air. He says to Flora, "The man's an imposter and he knows I know it. . . . And I know he knows I know it. . . . And he knows I know" (page 29).

Flora goes to talk to the Matchseller and reminisces, not altogether ruefully, about being raped as a girl. She seems to develop a great fondness for the Matchseller and says she is going to give him a bath and keep him. Edward returns and begins to reveal still more of himself to the mute presence; becoming increasingly erratic, he falls to the floor, imagines the Matchseller is laughing at his revelations, and finally whispers, with great effort, his last words in the play: "Who are you?" (page 39).

Edward has surely been menaced to the extreme limits of his toleration by this man. Not so Flora, however, who returns, gives the Matchseller's tray of matches to Edward, and goes off together with the smelly old peddler, her Barnabas, as she has decided to name him.

Thus the Matchseller's role as the agent of menace can be seen to be much different from Riley's: "the nominal menace is completely passive and the real disruptive force exists in the mind of the menaced."[15] Esslin's analysis is that "the silent character acts as a catalyst for the projection of the other's deepest feelings. Edward, in projecting his thoughts, is confronted with his inner emptiness and disintegrates, while Flora projects her still vital sexuality and changes partners."[16] These views are essentially correct, but they perhaps do not go far enough; the menace of the Matchseller is more than "nominal" and it is more than "a catalyst." The Matchseller is the personification of what is potentially the ugliest bugaboo within each of our personalities. Vital to our well-being is the need to repress certain potential aspects of our selves, the killer, the rapist, the compleat idler, and to keep reasonably well-hidden from ourselves certain of the blackest facts of self-knowledge. Utter knowledge of the naked self, with all its failings and shortcomings and its potential for destruction, is not a viable situation. There also exists within each of us, however, a yearning to see ourselves as we really are, to throw off the repressions; this self-curiosity is usually pretty well stifled after childhood. We begin to build and believe in a superstructure of us-as-we-would-have-us. The Matchseller is the embodiment of the power to destroy the superstructure, the urge to know ourselves as we really are. This is a type of metaphysical menace, not of the world outside, but within our own minds. In *A Slight Ache* when this menace is realized, Edward destroys himself; Flora simply becomes promiscuous, releasing the sexual needs she has had to subjugate in her life with Edward—and there is abundant evidence in the play that the pair's sex-life is not all it might be.

Finally, we can agree with Taylor[17] in saying that the ending of *A Slight Ache* is much more satisfying than that of **The Room.** The violent melodrama of the latter is replaced in this work by the unexpected exchange of men by Flora, for the Matchseller at the end becomes suddenly only a man. And we realize that the consequences of this switch are undoubtedly more far-reaching, more central to the lives of the characters than the confused murder and blinding that close **The Room.**

In **The Dumb Waiter,** a one-act play written in 1957, Pinter dispenses altogether with a person as the agent or emissary of menace from the outside. Two hired gunmen, Ben, more forceful and domineering, and Gus, a bit weak at the knees, are waiting in a windowless basement room for the instructions to carry out their next job. Stage-left is a door leading to the kitchen and lavatory; stage-right is *"A door to a passage."*[18] Gus begins to grow impatient about the instructions: "What time is he getting in touch? What time is he getting in touch?" (page 88). Obviously the two are not to contact their boss in any way, but to wait for his orders. While Gus and Ben are passing the time with small talk about sports, an envelope with twelve matches inside is slid under the door to the passage. By the time the men open the door, whoever sent them the matches is gone. At first Ben and Gus are a bit agitated about this mysterious invasion of their room, but then accept it: Gus says, "Well, they'll come in handy," and Ben answers, "Yes you're always running out, aren't you?" (page 96).

Ben and Gus do not have the shilling to feed the gas meter, so even though they have matches, they cannot make tea: "I hope he's got a shilling, anyway, if he comes. He's entitled to have. After all, it's his place, he could have seen there was enough gas for a cup of tea" (page 101). The mysterious "he" is the man who gives the pair their orders.

Gus begins to discuss their last job: "I was just thinking about that girl, that's all. . . . It was a mess though, wasn't it? What a mess. Honest. I can't remember a mess like that one. They don't seem to hold together like men, women. A looser texture, like. Didn't she spread, eh? . . . Who clears up after we're gone? I'm curious about that" (pages 102-103). While the two are discussing this rather menacing subject, there is a clatter in the center of the room; there is a dumb-waiter there they had not noticed before. Inside is a piece of paper: "Two braised steak and chips. Two sago puddings. Two teas without sugar" (page 103). Another order comes down, both hilarious and menacing in its bald directness: "Soup of the day. Liver and onions. Jam tart" (pages 104-105). "The two gunmen, anxious not to be discovered, are pathetically eager to fill this mysterious order from above."[19] They send up the few scraps of food they have in their pockets in an attempt to appease whoever is upstairs. The orders get more exotic and demand Macaroni Pastitsio, Ormitha Macarounada, One Bamboo Shoots, Water Chestnuts and Chicken, One Char Siu and Beansprouts (pages 108, 110). The men become frantic at being unable to fill the orders; they find a speaking tube and say into it that they have nothing more. A reply comes: what they have already sent up was stale or moldy. Gus is now becoming really terrified.

To calm his panic Gus goes to the door to the kitchen to have a glass of water. Ben is called to the speaking tube: "Yes . . . Straight away. Right . . . Sure we're ready. . . . Understood. Repeat. He has arrived and will be coming in straight away. The normal method is to be employed. Understood. . . . Sure we're ready. . . . Right . . . Gus! . . . Gus!" (page 120). Gus stumbles in from the door *to the passage,* stripped of his jacket, tie, and revolver; Ben has his revolver leveled at Gus. They stare at each other as the curtain descends.

There is a great deal of farce in *The Dumb Waiter,* but the element of menace is unmistakable. It is the unknown, implacable *they* or *he* that Pinter's characters so often speak of. The dumb-waiter, as "their" instrument, takes on a menace of object of its own. It becomes the only visible thing Gus and Ben can deal with. Moreover, this object and the power behind it can turn one companion into a menace to the other: "it is no good simply keeping our minds closed to outside influence, for even inside there the seeds of destruction may already be planted."[20] *The Dumb Waiter,* however, is the last play in which we shall see the menace stated so overtly; it now begins to become more subtle—and more insidious.

Two hired gangsters, Goldberg and McCann, also appear in *The Birthday Party,* Pinter's first full-length play; however, here they are the agents of menace, rather than the menaced, as in *The Dumb Waiter.* Goldberg, parallel to Ben in that he is the dominant member of the pair, is on the surface "a stock East End Jew, replete with nostalgic memories of his Mamma's gefilte fish and sententious maxims about familial togetherness."[21] But under this outer guise is a brutal, acid-mouthed villain, who now and again shows his colors. At one point Goldberg asks Stanley Webber, the man he and McCann have come to get, to sit down; Stanley, being petulant, asks why he should. Goldberg answers him with a vituperation we are completely unprepared for: "If you want to know the truth, Webber, you're beginning to get on my breasts."[22] McCann, Goldberg's second, is a rather thick, brooding Irishman, who takes few pains to conceal either his menace or his density. Pinter does not miss an opportunity or two, however, to make the gangsters themselves the victims of a bit of

menace. Goldberg, giving McCann a string of platitudes about the conduct of life, ends up with:

Because I believe that the world . . . (*Vacant.*) . . .

Because I believe that the world . . . (*Desperate.*) . . .

BECAUSE I BELIEVE THAT THE WORLD . . . (*Lost.*) . . .

(page 80)

"Goldberg's desperation is perhaps a clue to Pinter's point of view—the world is inexplicable and more terrible than we think."[23] Goldberg also becomes rather apprehensive about the state of his health when he emits "a class of wheeze, like" (page 82), at first denying it was he that wheezed, and then inducing McCann to breathe into his mouth, as a sort of restorative measure. McCann, like Gus, is frequently apprehensive about their getting on with the job and is sometimes victimized in a rather minor fashion by Goldberg. We notice, then, that here for the first time the agents of menace are two quite realistically drawn characters. Gone are the blind Negro, the Matchseller, and the dumb-waiter—and Pinter has not again employed their ilk. It must be remembered, however, that despite the more realistic portrayal of these two, they still remain the agents of some mysterious outside force, or organization, or "Monty," and as such operate on a metaphysical as well as a personal level.

In line with Pinter's seeming contention that it is quite possible for the the same person to both menace and be menaced, Stanley has a few threatening moments himself. Early in the first act, foreshadowing what is about to happen to himself, Stanley says to Meg, "They're coming today. . . . They're coming in a van. . . . They've got a wheelbarrow in that van. . . . A big wheelbarrow. And when the van stops they wheel it out, and they wheel it up the garden path, and then they knock at the front door. . . . They're looking for someone. A certain person. . . . Shall I tell you who they're looking for?" (pages 24-25). Meg, obviously frightened, refuses to let him tell her. Similarly, at the end of the act, Meg gives Stanley for his supposed birthday a drum to replace the piano he no longer has. The act closes with Stanley playing the drum, at first normally, then "*halfway round the beat becomes erratic, uncontrolled. MEG expresses dismay. He arrives at her chair, banging the drum, his face and the drumbeat now savage and possessed*" (page 39). By the end of the second act, when McCann and Goldberg have had their way with Stanley, it is apparent that he has become something of a maniac. In the menacing game of blind man's bluff played in the dark at Stanley's birthday party, Stanley, when "it," finds Meg and begins to strangle her; McCann and Goldberg pull him away. A few moments later Stanley finds Lulu, a neighbor invited to the party: "*LULU is lying spread-eagled on the table, STANLEY bent over her. STAN-LEY, as soon as the torchlight hits him, begins to giggle. GOLDBERG and McCANN move towards him. He backs, giggling, the torch on his face. They follow him upstage, left. He backs against the hatch, giggling. The torch draws closer. His giggle rises and grows as he flattens himself against the wall. Their figures converge upon him. Curtain"* (page 68). Thus the second act closes with a menacing enactment of something that seems like a chilling primitive ritual, with the crazed Stanley acting both priest and victim. In the third act, however, which takes place the next morning, Stanley has fallen into an almost catatonic state, moves woodenly, and can only make animal-like sounds when Goldberg and McCann take him away in their car, of which Goldberg says ominously, "And the boot. A beautiful boot. There's just room . . . for the right amount" (page 73). Whatever menace Stanley had in him has been effectively removed; whatever life Stanley had in him has been effectively removed.

The second act of **The Birthday Party** is a tour de force of menace, the most concentrated, sustained example of it in all of Pinter's work to date. It is divided neatly into two parts, the events just prior to the birthday party,[24] including the grand interrogation of Stanley, and the party itself. It would be difficult to say which is the more frightening.

There is a tension built up from the act's opening tableau: McCann is industriously tearing a sheet of newspaper into five meticulously equal strips. Stanley enters and the two begin a conversation that is a masterpiece of cat-and-mouse. Stanley has unaccountably been frightened of Goldberg since the first act, when Meg told him a man of that name was coming to stay at the usually deserted boardinghouse. When he at last enters during Stanley and McCann's dialogue, Stanley is visibly further shaken. Goldberg and McCann waste little time maneuvering Stanley into a chair, with his back to the audience, and beginning their grueling, devastating inquisition:

> STANLEY. You'd better be careful.
>
> GOLDBERG. Webber, what were you doing yesterday?
>
> STANLEY. Yesterday?
>
> GOLDBERG. And the day before. What did you do the day before that?
>
> STANLEY. What do you mean?
>
> GOLDBERG. Why are you wasting everybody's time, Webber? Why are you getting in in everybody's way?
>
> (page 50)

Thus, the questioning, although unprovoked and unmotivated, begins seemingly reasonable enough. But as the interrogation progresses, the questions become more and more pointless, nonsensical:

> GOLDBERG. Why did you come here?
>
> STANLEY. My feet hurt!
>
> GOLDBERG. Why did you stay?
>
> STANLEY. I had a headache!
>
> GOLDBERG. Did you take anything for it?
>
> STANLEY. Yes.

> GOLDBERG. What?
>
> STANLEY. Fruit salts!
>
> GOLDBERG. Enos or Andrews?

Stanley becomes increasingly confused by these questions; the menace of the interrogation grows; finally the questions and accusations lose all sense.

> McCANN. You're a traitor to the cloth.
>
> GOLDBERG. What do you use for pyjamas?
>
> STANLEY. Nothing.
>
> GOLDBERG. You verminate the sheet of your birth.
>
> McCANN. What about the Albigensenist heresy?
>
> GOLDBERG. Who watered the wicket in Melbourne?
>
> * * *
>
> McCANN. Who are you, Webber?
>
> GOLDBERG. What makes you think you exist?
>
> McCANN. You're dead.
>
> GOLDBERG. You're dead. You can't live, you can't think, you can't love. You're dead. You're a plague gone bad. There's no juice in you. You're nothing but an odour! *Silence.*
>
> (pages 54-55)

Stanley at this point looks up slowly and kicks Goldberg in the stomach, and Meg enters soon afterward, halting a ritual-like circling with raised chairs that follows the kick. But Stanley is finished, the victim of a total breakdown; he has only one more intelligible line in the play, just after Meg's entrance: "Could I have my glasses?" (page 56).

Perhaps the most obvious question raised by what befalls Stanley at the hands of Goldberg and McCann is why does it happen to him, for what terrible fault is he being punished? In typical Pinter fashion, the question is unanswered. "To supply an explicit moral tag to an evolving and compulsive dramatic image seems to me facile, impertinent and dishonest. Where this takes place it is not theatre but a crossword puzzle. The audience holds the paper. The play fills in the blanks. Everyone's happy."[25]

There is a slippery shift of identity associated with Goldberg and McCann. Goldberg is usually called Nat, but refers to himself as having been called Simey by his mother and wife and Benny by his uncle (pages 46, 62, 81); when McCann in private calls him Simey, he becomes furious and seizes McCann by the throat; moreover, Goldberg ostensibly (that is, by his own telling) had a son named Emmanuel, whom he called Manny and sometimes Timmy (page 30). Goldberg refers to McCann once—and only once—as Dermot (page 73).

There are, in addition, some undertones of a sexual menace. Meg's relation to Stanley is at times that of a smothering mother; at others, it has the appearance of something quite different (Meg, by the way, is supposed to be in her sixties, Stanley in his late thirties, according to the cast of characters). When she goes upstairs to wake Stanley the stage directions indicate *"wild laughter from MEG"* (page 14), and when he complains of the condition of his bedroom, she says, *"(sensual, stroking his arm).* Oh, Stan, that's a lovely room. I've had some lovely afternoons in that room" (page 19). Whatever their relationship, Stanley's attitude alternates between an occasional dependence on the woman and a real cruelty toward her (witness his savage beating of the drum at the end of Act One and his trying to strangle her at the end of Act Two). At Stanley's party Goldberg makes a number of reasonably successful passes at Lulu, the neighbor girl, and she kisses him and sits on his lap. Stanley, as has been noted, is found standing over her "spread-eagled" form at the end of the party. Apparently there was an incident after the party as well.

Finally, when Stanley is brought down in bowler and morning suit, McCann and Goldberg, in a scene reminiscent of the inquisition, give him an ironic foretaste of what lies ahead of him. Whatever lies ahead of Stanley, it does not promise to be pleasant. Petey tries feebly to stop the pair. Goldberg says to him, "Why don't you come with us, Mr. Boles? . . . Come with us to Monty. There's plenty of room in the car." Petey can only call pathetically to Stanley as they leave, "Stan, don't let them tell you what to do!" (page 90).

There are certain very evident similarities between the treatment of menace in *The Caretaker* and that in the previous plays. Probably the most striking of these is the setting and its function: "The room is cluttered, dirty, and draughty. The roof leaks, the gas is disconnected, and the sanitary facilities are of the most primitive; but to the three people in the play it represents a haven in which they can hide from the world."[26] Although the implication that the room presents Mick with any sort of haven from the world is erroneous, the evaluation is quite valid in application to Aston and Davies. For Aston, the cluttered room is a refuge from a hostile world with which he found himself less and less able to cope; finally, after his mental breakdown, he has retired almost altogether from that world and has come to live within himself, dealing for the most part only with the room and the objects from the outside he has amassed within it. In Davies we see, for the first time in Pinter's stage works, "a man *seeking* for a place for himself, fighting for that little patch of light and warmth in the vast menacing darkness."[27] Mick owns the building in which his older brother lives, but he does not use it as a refuge; rather, he visits it upon occasion for reasons of his own, mostly generated by an interest in his brother and in Davies, his brother's strange guest.

As Taylor says, "again we have the room, but no outside menace, simply a clash of personalities on the inside."[28] This statement is true in its outline but needs modification in detail. Davies especially is menaced by the outside to some degree, but this outside menace does not assume the primary importance it had in the earlier plays. The *chief*

elements of menace in *The Caretaker* are provided by the interaction of the personalities of the three men upon one another, and it will be most valuable to study the menace in light of each of the three characters in turn.

James Boulton says that Aston's security is menaced by Davies[29] and George Wellwarth states that Aston lives in fear of being returned to the asylum and the electric shock treatments he was subjected to there.[30] A careful examination of the character of Aston as he appears in the play, however, seems to refute both of these opinions. Aston is a man who has been severely menaced in his life. It is difficult to imagine anyone undergoing a more harrowing experience than that through which Aston lived in the mental hospital. His recounting of the ordeal at the end of Act Two is "poetic creation in the plain unvarnished speech of reality."[31] He speaks simply, but very movingly of it: "The thing is, I should have been dead. I should have died."[32] But he did not die, and with his enduring came to him an almost absolute sense of resignation and tranquility, marred only by the fact that he needs still to retain some small illusions about his future. He is, in short, a rare man: one really beyond and above being menaced by anything. Nowhere in the play does he show any sign that he fears a return to the asylum. He has by no means, of course, forgotten the terrible experience of that place, and the memories of it are probably with him constantly (perhaps his mild complaints about Davies' groaning and jabbering in his sleep are caused by unpleasant memories of nights in the institution), but, as his long monologue demonstrates, the asylum no longer holds its terror for him and it is recollected with peace.

Aston frequently demonstrates that he is above fearing the host of things and people that menaces Davies from the outside world. He seems not even to notice Davies' wild accusations of "them Blacks" *et al.* He does, however, speak of a recent unpleasant encounter on the outside, thus providing the only hint of sexual menace in the play: "You know, I was sitting in a café the other day. I happened to be sitting at the same table as this woman. Well, we started . . . we started to pick up a bit of a conversation. I don't know . . . about her holiday, it was, where she'd been. She'd been down to the south coast. I can't remember where though. Anyway, we were just sitting there, having this bit of a conversation . . . then suddenly she put her hand over to mine . . . and she said, how would you like me to have a look at your body?" (page 26). The incident, however, held no menace for Aston himself, as evidenced by his evaluation of it: "Yes. To come out with it just like that, in the middle of this conversation. Struck me as a bit odd" (page 27). Thus we see, further, that Aston now does not try to cut himself off from the society of others, as so frequently do the chief characters of the earlier plays. The fact is, he *was* talking to the woman, his brother comes to see him, he mentions going to see people about getting various things—and we know he must do it because he brings Davies several articles of clothing, ostensibly from these contacts. He says, "I used to sit in my room. . . . And I never spoke to anyone any more" (page 60). But we know things have changed and he now speaks to people as much as he cares to.

It is most unfortunate, we feel, that in what must be Aston's first attempt since coming out of the asylum at making a full-fledged friendship, he should be so wrong as to choose Davies as the object. But never is Aston menaced even by Davies—irritated, yes, as perhaps only a Job could avoid being, so irritated, in fact that Davies eventually becomes too much of a trial to suffer and Aston is forced to ask him to leave, but even this is done by Aston in such understated terms that we cannot believe he feels *menaced* by Davies: "I . . . I think it's about time you found somewhere else. I don't think we're hitting it off. . . . I don't think you'd like it here" (page 71). When Davies tries to menace him with threats that Mick will throw Aston out and keep Davies on as caretaker—the one thing which might really frighten Aston—Aston says simply, "I live here" (page 72). When Davies threatens Aston by pointing a knife at his stomach, *"ASTON does not move"* (page 72).

Ironically, this gentle, good man, when presented on the stage, to the audience can seem to have an aura of menace about him. Perhaps it is that we are simply not accustomed to such calmness, such goodness of heart, such resignedness and peace, presented in these believable terms. There are constantly the nagging unstated questions: can he be sincere, what is his angle, should he be back in the asylum? And there is certainly much of our anxiety present in Davies, for he is distrustful of Aston in the extreme, especially following Aston's haunting revelations of his stay in the asylum. In fact, had Aston been seeking an enemy instead of a friend, he could have done no better than selecting Davies, for the personalities of the two are as opposed almost as those of two people can be. Whereas Aston is reserved, aloof, usually direct, Davies is garrulous and evasive. Aston is kind, Davies is spiteful, cruel. Aston is deliberate, slow to react, and tolerant, Davies is erratic and prejudiced. Aston is above being menaced. Davies is menaced by almost everything he meets. Nearly the first words he says are, "All them Blacks had it, Blacks, Greeks, Poles, the lot of them, that's what, doing me out of a seat, treating me like dirt" (page 8). In Davies' mind, everyone he meets is trying to treat him unfairly or to take advantage of him. He tells of going to a monastery, seeking a pair of shoes, and being told by a monk, "If you don't piss off, he says, I'll kick you all the way to the gate." To which Davies countered with, "I've a good mind to report you to your mother superior. One of them, an Irish hooligan, come at me. I cleared out" (pages 14-15). Offered the job of caretaker for Mick's house, Davies declines because he would have to answer inquiries and "Well, I mean, you don't know who might come up them front steps, do you? I got to be a bit careful" (page 46). When Aston gently wakes him the first morning, Davies sits up abruptly in a fright, and, of course, Aston says he makes noises in his sleep. When Aston goes out for the first time, Davies opens the door twice to assure himself that no one is outside, and then locks it. The objects which Aston has lovingly collected Davies finds menacing: the electric heater, the unconnected gas stove, the Buddha, the stacks of newspapers. The tramp seems at times paranoiac, so many and so varied are the things he fears.

Davies' conversation carries a strong element of menace on the metaphysical level, in that it is constantly evasive, destroying communication at its very roots. Often his non-sequiturs and attempts at evasion are wildly funny. But Pinter has said, "As far as I'm concerned, *The Caretaker* is funny, up to a point. Beyond that point it ceases to be funny, and it was because of that point that I wrote it."[33] Davies' speech is an excellent example; when one begins to perceive what the man is trying to make of communication, the humor begins to grow less, and menace creeps in. In fact, generally it seems true of *The Caretaker* that, with the element of external menace not so overwhelmingly present, Pinter was able to bring other smaller elements to perfection. Davies neither talks nor listens, and his "worn-out cliché creates its own horror, when we see its ineptness at the very moment of utterance."[34] Davies refuses to answer even so simple a question as that regarding the place of his birth—and does so in the absurd terms of not being able to remember back that far. "If it is terrifying to open the door to a strange knock, it is equally terrifying to open your mind to someone else, for once he is in you never know what he may do. . . . Consequently Pinter's characters twist and turn, profoundly distrustful of any direct communication."[35]

In truth, Davies is his own greatest menace; he is "so selfish, so overconfident, that he cannot resist the temptation of playing off the two brothers against each other—and so, at the end of the play he is expelled again into the cold outer darkness."[36] After Aston has told him of his incarceration in the asylum, Davies both fears Aston and at the same time tries to use his knowledge as a lever against this man who has tried to be his friend. The tramp speaks to Aston in terribly cruel terms: "They'd put them pincers on your head, they'd have you fixed! They'd take one look at all this junk I got to sleep with they'd know you were a creamer. That was the greatest mistake they made, you take my tip, letting you get out of that place. . . . You're up the creek! You're half off! You can tell it by looking at you. . . . I never been inside a nuthouse!" (pages 70-71). But Aston is beyond being menaced, and instead, very justifiably fed up with the old man, orders him to leave. Davies then tries to turn Mick against his brother, making thinly veiled insinuations about Aston's sanity, but finds Mick on Aston's side. He comes pleading back to Aston, but he has gone too far, and Aston remains adamant. Davies is the foolish, and at the same time pathetic, victim of his own devices, "a poetic image of the human condition itself: Man fighting for a place, for security, but at the same time deprived of it by the weakness of his own fallible, selfish nature."[37]

By far the most enigmatic of the three men in *The Caretaker* is Mick. From one point of view he seems to be a somewhat shiftless overgrown Teddy Boy, complete with black leather jacket, who delights in frightening old men; from another he seems almost the direct descendent of the agents of menace, especially Goldberg and McCann, in the earlier plays. He is most reminiscent of the earlier plays in the two incidents in which he surprises the easily-frightened Davies. In the first, at the end of Act One, he creeps up behind Davies, who has just carefully locked the door of the flat, twists the tramp's arm up behind his back, and, when he has reduced the old man to a huddled fearful little mass, asks inscrutably, "What's the game?" to lower the curtain. The second incident occurs in approximately the middle of Act Two: Davies enters the flat at night and finds the light will not go on; as he fumbles with some matches, something with an eery glow and a hum starts to pursue him around the room. Davies falls to the floor in fright and pulls out his knife. Just then the light comes on and reveals Mick with a vacuum cleaner. He says, "I was just doing some spring cleaning" (pages 46-47).

Yet there is this difference from the earlier plays: both of these bizarre happenings are at base very easily traced, whereas the blinding in *The Room,* say, is not. Moreover, Mick is not the emissary of any greater outside power of menace, as are all the earlier agents. What then is the explanation of Mick's behavior? Taylor seems to think that Mick is engaged in a rather subtle program of therapy for his brother, finds Davies an unhealthy influence, and thus tries to drive him out.[38] Wellwarth, on the other hand, posits Mick's fear of being dispossessed of his share of the room by Davies—thus his menacing campaign to scare the old man off.[39] Neither of these explanations, however, seems to be very well substantiated by the text. With regard to the first, never in the play does Mick show any real concern for Aston's condition, and in the last act he seems genuinely upset that Aston is so long procrastinating in the projected remodeling of the place. As for the second, Mick clearly lives somewhere other than in the room and does not appear to have a great deal of interest in it, except perhaps as it would be after the remodeling.

The explanation, I think, is simply that Mick recognizes Davies for a hypocritical, evasive old phony and takes great pleasure in puncturing his balloon. How better to explain his needling of Davies about his assumed name, the identification papers he never manages to get down to Sidcup to get, the place where he does his banking? These are all darts he knows will get to the base of Davies' sham, as is his needling Davies in Act Three about claiming to have experience as an interior decorator. Mick masterfully caps the whole business in the same act by slyly leading Davies on to make insinuations about Aston's sanity—only then to turn on him and force Davies to try to make good his insinuations. Mick's menace toward Davies, then, seems as cleverly designed as Goldberg's in *The Birthday Party* and, with the vacuum cleaner, its weird hum and light in the darkened room, even smacks a bit of the preternatural. But it is conducted merely to satisfy Mick himself, not the implacable outside forces that we find in the plays of the first group. And when the light comes on, we see only a vacuum cleaner after all.

In Pinter's development of menace, then, as far as it can be traced at this time, *The Caretaker* very definitely is the step toward greater realism, the evoking of menace in more commonplace situations and in a much subtler way, that Taylor has posited it to be. Yet, as Esslin notes, it is far above the mere "kitchen-sink" level of playwriting, for there is in it a mirror of the human condition, man's search for a place in the world, and his own self-defeat.[40] It is a most effective concretion of the universal. Pinter has analyzed his own development as a dramatist in this way: "I think that in this play . . . I *have* developed, that I have no need to use cabaret turns and blackouts and screams in the dark to the extent that I enjoyed using them before. I feel that I can deal, without resorting to that kind of thing, with a human situation. . . . I do see this play as merely . . . a particular human situation, concerning three particular people and not, incidentally . . . symbols."[41]

The trend in Pinter's plays toward what Taylor calls a closer approaching of realism and what Pinter himself has referred to as a lesser dependence upon "cabaret turns" and "screams in the dark" has continued into his most recent plays, *The Collection,* first presented on British television in 1961 and on the stage in 1962, and *The Homecoming,* which was first presented by the Royal Shakespeare Company at the Aldwych Theatre, London, in June 1965, and in New York in 1967. So too, the menace in these plays, as we found for the most part in *The Caretaker,* tends to be more understandably motivated, and its agents are merely human beings, not representatives of some outside power or force. A human menace, however, can be just as chilling as an inexplicable one from the outside—if not moreso.

Moreover, the menace in both of these plays arises out of interpersonal relationships, almost exclusively sexual and familial ones. Thus we find in them a good deal of menace on the metaphysical level, for Pinter is probing here at some of the most basic relationships in man's pattern of existence: those between man and woman, man and man, father and son, brother and brother.

The central action about which *The Collection* revolves has taken place the week before the time of the play itself. Bill and Stella either did or did not sleep with each other while in Leeds for a dress designers' show. Now, James, Stella's husband, and Harry, the older man who keeps Bill in his elegantly furnished house in Belgravia, are trying to ascertain whether or not the pair did spend the night together. But in Pinter's vision of the world,

> We don't carry labels on our chests, and even though they are continually fixed to us by others, they convince nobody. The desire for verification on the part of all of us, with regard to our own experience and the experience of others, is understandable but cannot always be satisfied. . . . Apart from any other consideration, we are faced with the immense difficulty, if not the impossibility, of verifying the past. I don't mean merely years ago, but yesterday, this morning. What took place, what was the nature of what took place, what happened?[42]

Such a view makes of the past a real menace. For we are constantly attempting to verify "facts" about the past, but it is the past itself which thwarts us, menaces us, by its very pastness, its inability to make itself known to us. It is often difficult enough to evaluate—even to know—what has happened to ourselves in the past; how much moreso when we come to someone else, whose mind we cannot enter, whose past we did not experience.

Bill and Stella do not prove terribly reliable witnesses for Harry and James's little inquests, and thus are really quite menacing to them; out of this fact grows much of the dramatic tension with which the play is filled. The relationship between Harry and Bill was undoubtedly already very tense long before the opening of the play, for Bill is young and handsome and Harry obviously fears losing him. When James keeps telephoning the house, asking for Bill, Harry seems to fear that Bill has picked up a new boyfriend in Leeds.

Harry apparently at last finds out the reason for James's visits and he then visits Stella, ostensibly to request her to ask James to stop bothering Bill. In the course of Harry's visit Stella rather too glibly agrees that James has made the whole adultery business up. Whether Harry is jealous of Stella and Bill's heterosexual exploits, whatever they may have been, is not made clear. In any case, Harry returns home and finds James there talking with Bill; he assures James that the whole story was made up by Bill and Stella. Harry, then, becomes clearly menaced by Bill's too casual attitude toward their relationship and is highly jealous about the younger man. He responds in kind by speaking very menacingly to and about the man he loves. He is far too superficially genteel to be overtly menacing toward James and Stella, but most of what he says to them reveals heavy undertones of menace. We can suppose that if he found James a real threat to his keeping Bill he would act much more overtly toward him. Harry's attitude toward Stella is not precisely clear; we are not sure whether he feels a woman could be a real menace to his relationship with Bill.

James's problem is a bit more straightforward: he simply wishes to know if Bill has made him a cuckold. He finds Bill a menace to his marriage and, like Harry, responds to menace with menace. Taylor calls this "the menace of the earlier plays given background: to Bill, James is at first a nameless and inexplicable terror from outside, but we know why he is doing what he is doing."[43] Bill, of course, is no help to James and he "describes how he and Stella talked of what they would do if they went to bed together, and Pinter's *expertise* with menace is such that the words seem far more obscene than any possible deed."[44] Bill repeatedly denies that he and Stella slept together, but when James, having knocked Bill to the floor, accuses him of "sitting on the bed, next to her," there is a silence and Bill closes the scene with a terse "Not sitting. Lying."[45]

It seems to be the same sort of thing when, on his second visit to the house, James starts praising Bill's cheese knife; but then he picks up the fruit knife as well.

BILL. Now you've got two.

JAMES. I've got another one in my hip pocket. (*Pause*).

BILL. What do you do, swallow them?

JAMES. Do you? (*Pause. They stare at each other. Suddenly*).

Go on! Swallow it!

(page 75)

"Harry gets back just as James is getting threatening and indulging in a little knife-throwing (none too successfully; again, the menace is humanized)."[46] James has only nicked Bill's hand, and Harry goes on to tell James about his visit with Stella and how she assured him the whole thing was made up, "for some odd reason of her own" (page 77). James seems convinced, but the play closes with his confronting Stella, begging her to reassure him that it *was* all a fabrication. Stella says not a word, and only "*looks at him, neither confirming nor denying. Her face is friendly, sympathetic*" (page 80).

The play ends repeating the theme of the menace of the past in all its unconfirmable slipperiness. James is, by the conclusion, so completely unsure of whether the act of adultery actually took place that we can feel nothing will ever dispel the doubt from his mind. This is certainly a menacing position to be in, when the "truth" makes as much difference as it obviously does to James. Moreover, the audience can be no more certain than James is, even though they, for instance, have witnessed the Harry-Stella interview, while James has not. Perhaps this might seem like something of a lady-or-the-tiger ending, but in a wider sense Pinter seems to be telling us the issue is that this sort of nagging doubt is a fact of human experience. We go to our graves without the ultimate answers to what are, in fact, the most central questions.

The corollary theme is a wry one of the menace inherent in the most intimate of human relationships. In this case Pinter is examining the dominance that one partner in a sexual relationship frequently gains over the other through one means or another; in *The Collection* there is the added twist gained from the fact that Stella gains her dominance through being perhaps an *offender* in an adulterous liaison. Once her dominance is achieved, she can use it to menace the man she ostensibly promised to cherish. Harry, on the other hand, is menaced by the shakiness of the dominance he holds in his love relationship with Bill. The game, it would seem, is to the ficklest.

Unlike *The Collection, The Homecoming* again is set in a single room, much as were the earlier plays; no longer, however, can the room be considered any sort of haven from the outside world; it is, rather, a distillation of the most concentrated menace, mystery, and viciousness. Without the intrusion of any external forces or their agents, the characters of the play set about to menace, tear apart, and destroy each other. The characters, moreover, are members of one family: Max, the father; Sam, his brother;

Lenny, Joey, and Teddy, Max's sons; and Ruth, Teddy's wife. Pinter's vision of the family seems to be one of a jungle, with the animal-like members forever at one another's throats.

Max, age seventy, is without a rival for being the most detestable character in all of Pinter's plays. Like Davies he is irascible, erratic, and nearly paranoiac in his fears that others are out to do him in. But the "others" are his own sons and his brother; further, he reacts with more vitriol, more menace, than Davies could ever muster. He fondly remembers his wife: "I've never had a whore under this roof before. Ever since your mother died. My word of honour."[47] On another occasion he recollects his home life: "A crippled family, three bastard sons, a slutbitch of a wife—don't talk to me about the pain of childbirth—I suffered the pain, I've still got the pangs—when I give a little cough my back collapses—and here I've got a lazy idle bugger of a brother won't even get to work on time" (page 47). The most alarming facet of Max, however, is his alternation of this viciousness with playing the role of the loving, doting father and grandfather. Just before calling her a slutbitch, Max recalls of his wife Jessie, "And she had a heart to go with it. What a heart. . . . That woman was the backbone to this family . . . with a will of iron, a heart of gold and a mind" (page 46). He savors a memory of relaxing one evening with Jessie and the boys, their faces rosy after a bath: "I tell you, it was like Christmas" (page 46).

When, near the end of the play, it becomes fairly certain that Max actually followed his father into the business of managing prostitutes and has Lenny and perhaps Joey following in *his* footsteps, the lines about being a butcher, about "meat" and the "slab," take on a gruesome, repulsive aspect; the menace of the old man's euphemisms is truly appalling. Significantly, it is Max who suggests that Ruth remain in the house with him, Joey, and Lenny when Teddy returns to America: "Where's the whore? Still in bed? She'll make us all animals. . . . Perhaps it's not a bad idea to have a woman in the house. . . . Maybe we should keep her" (pages 69, 70). And when Lenny suggests that they put Ruth "on the game" as well, to earn her keep, Max joyfully agrees: "That's a stroke of genius, that's a marvellous idea. You mean she can earn the money herself—on her back? . . . Wonderful. The only thing is, it'll have to be short hours. We don't want her out of the house all night" (page 73). When Teddy has gone, leaving his wife to his father and brothers, the play ends with Max disgustingly groveling before Ruth, trying to assure his share: "I'm not an old man. . . . Do you hear me? . . . Kiss me" (pages 82-83). In truth, Max's menace is not taken very seriously by the others on stage, although at one point he violently punches Joey in the stomach, and with his ever-present stick he does seem to wield some semblance of authority over his sons still. But on the whole, the "boys," like Ruth, find Max too old, too sexless, a harmless haranguer. Max's real menace is aimed at the audience, who, not living with the old man all the time, should find him more than disturbing. A disgusting, truly frightening epitome of the dirty old man.

Lenny is certainly his father's child: he apparently now runs the business; he retorts to the names Max calls him with ones equally vile. He truly has a sadistic streak in him as well and relates to Ruth two long and menacing stories of how he has beaten two women, one a diseased prostitute who made him a proposal, and the other an old lady whose mangle he was trying to move for her. There is a constant menacing tension underlying Lenny's relations with his brother Teddy; he tries to engage Teddy in a philosophic duel (Teddy is a professor of philosophy in America), but Teddy will have none of it and fends his brother off with "That question doesn't fall within my province. . . . I'm afraid I'm the wrong person to ask" (pages 51-52).

Joey, although much less quick-witted than Lenny, has a good deal of menace—especially the brute sexual—within him. He lies on Ruth on the sofa and on the floor in Teddy's presence. He takes Ruth upstairs for two hours, but perhaps he is not such a sexual menace after all, for somehow he does not "go the whole hog" (page 67). But Joey's chance for real menace comes when he, Lenny, and Max discuss before Teddy how they are going to keep Ruth and what they are going to do with her.

Teddy, the recipient of so much menace, seems to retaliate with none of his own. Why he almost meekly allows Ruth to stay with his father and brothers and their organization is an unanswerable question. Why, indeed, having escaped to America for six years, does he ever bring Ruth to his old home in the first place? Although he may well not have expected what is the final development of his return, he surely knew beforehand the nature of his father and brothers. It would seem that, having once got away, he could not be induced to return by fascination or for any reason whatever. But Pinter gives us no clue to the answers to any of these questions; we simply see Teddy drawn in almost total passivity. Perhaps the implication is simply that Teddy is not the type to survive in the sort of jungle made by his father and brothers. Not that he is shown as being any better than the stock from which he comes; he is simply different and cannot cope. So, after the casual little amenities of good-byes to his father and brothers, Teddy just goes, back to his classes in America, leaving his wife and the mother of his children in this sexual jungle of his old home.

Ruth becomes the character about whom the entire play revolves, and she seems well-equipped for the life she elects to lead. Somewhat like Stella of *The Collection,* she almost exudes a menace of the dark, mysterious allure of primitive sexuality. She is enigmatic, ambiguous, in almost all that she says, and there are undertones of the seductive in everything. Thus we are not too surprised when Ruth chooses to stay with the English branch of the family, haggling only over the kind of conveniences she will be supplied with in her new setup. Her primitive nature is doubtless better attuned to Max and sons' jungle than to the probably rather sterile life at the university in America with the empty Teddy. Perhaps after being married to her for six years, Teddy himself realizes this and thus puts up for her no more fight than he does. The cliché with which Ruth bids Teddy (or Eddie, as she calls him just this once) good-bye is devastating in its effectiveness: "Don't become a stranger" (page 81). Teddy goes in silence.

In this last of Pinter's stage plays to date we see a profound change from the menace we found in his earliest works. No longer is the room a haven, a refuge from the menace of the outside world, the alien universe; it has become the arena where character-related menaces do battle. The menace is no longer undefinable, obscure; it is now fairly explainable, based upon traits we can recognize in people. It does not spring from mysterious outside sources but from the characters themselves. The characters are not emissaries of an "other" menace; rather they contain threats within themselves, in their personalties. Whereas Pinter was at first examining the dark forces of the universe of which we are a part, in his last two plays, and to a great extent in **The Caretaker,** he has found forces just as black within the individual human psyche that can menace the man of whom they are a part as well as others. Sex, marriage, and the family, as the primary human relationships, have thus come to absorb his attention; in the earlier plays they were never of more than secondary interest. The early Pinter hero was merely alone, naked to the menace of the world; the later is, more paradoxically, alone in the company of his intimates, those whom society and tradition tie most closely to him, and he is subject to them as well.

Notes

1. "Pinter's Usurpers," *Drama Survey,* VI (Spring-Summer, 1967), 54.

2. "Pinter Between the Lines," (Transcript of a speech delivered at Bristol University), *The Sunday Times,* (London, March 4, 1962), p. 25.

3. "The Theatre of Harold Pinter," *Tulane Drama Review,* VI (March, 1962), 43-44.

4. Quoted in John Russell Taylor, *Anger and After: A Guide to the New British Drama,* (London, 1962), p. 231.

5. Taylor, p. 236.

6. Harold Pinter, "The Room," *The Birthday Party and The Room: Two Plays by Harold Pinter,* (New York, 1961), p. 95. All subsequent references to the play are from this edition and will appear parenthetically in the text.

7. Quoted in Martin Esslin, *The Theatre of the Absurd,* (Garden City, N.Y., 1961), p. 199.

8. George Wellwarth, *The Theatre of Protest and Paradox: Developments in the Avante-Garde Drama,* (New York), 1964), p. 199.

9. Esslin, *Theatre of the Absurd,* p. 200.

10. Pages 235, 236.

11. Martin Esslin, "Godot and His Children: The Theatre of Samuel Beckett and Harold Pinter," *Experimental Drama,* ed. William A. Armstrong, (London, 1963), p. 141.

12. Wellwarth, p. 199.

13. Harold Pinter, "A Slight Ache," *Three Plays,* (New York, 1962), p. 29. All subsequent references to the play are from this edition and will appear parenthetically in the text.

14. Esslin, *Theatre of the Absurd,* p. 208.

15. Taylor, p. 246.

16. Esslin, *Theatre of the Absurd,* p. 208.

17. Page 246.

18. Harold Pinter, "The Dumb Waiter," *The Caretaker and The Dumb Waiter: Two Plays by Harold Pinter,* (New York, 1961), p. 86. All subsequent references to the play are from this edition and will appear parenthetically in the text.

19. Esslin, *Theatre of the Absurd,* p. 202.

20. Taylor, p. 240.

21. Wellwarth, p. 203.

22. Harold Pinter, "The Birthday Party," *The Birthday Party and The Room: Two Plays by Harold Pinter,* (New York, 1961), p. 49. All subsequent references to the play are from this edition and will appear parenthetically in the text.

23. H. R. Hays, "Transcending Naturalism," *Modern Drama,* V (1962), 35.

24. McCann and Goldberg have arranged this party for Stanley, despite the fact that he assures Meg at end of Act One that it is not his birthday. This is another of the many cases in which Pinter leaves the audience maddeningly in doubt as to what would seem to be an easily verifiable fact. This is, of course, an intentional technique and a kind of menace, both of speech and metaphysical. Pinter states ("Pinter Between the Lines," p. 25), "I suggest there can be no hard distinctions between what is real and what is unreal, nor between what is true and what is false. A thing is not necessarily either true or false; it can be both true and false."

25. "Pinter Between the Lines," p. 25.

26. Wellwarth, p. 206.

27. Esslin, "Godot and Children," p. 142.

28. Page 246.

29. Page 138.

30. Page 206.

31. Kenneth Muir, "Verse and Prose," *Contemporary Theatre,* ed. John Russell Brown and Bernard Harris, (New York, 1962), p. 113.

32. Harold Pinter, "The Caretaker," *The Caretaker and The Dumb Waiter: Two Plays by Harold Pinter,* (New York, 1961), p. 60. All subsequent references to the play are from this edition and will appear parenthetically in the text.

33. Letter to *The Sunday Times,* (London, August 14, 1960), p. 21.

34. Valerie Minogue, "Taking Care of the Caretaker," *The Twentieth Century,* CLXVIII (Sept. 1960), 243-244.

35. Taylor, pp. 241-242.

36. Esslin, "Godot and Children," p. 142.

37. Ibid.

38. Pages 247-248.

39. Page 206.

40. "Godot and Children," p. 142.

41. Quoted in Esslin, *Theatre of the Absurd,* p. 212.

42. "Pinter Between the Lines," p. 25.

43. P. 254.

44. Cohn, p. 374.

45. Harold Pinter, "The Collection," *Three Plays,* (New York, 1962), p. 59. All subsequent references to the play are from this edition and will appear parenthetically in the text.

46. Taylor, p. 255.

47. Harold Pinter, *The Homecoming,* (London, 1965), p. 42. All subsequent references to the play are from this edition and will appear parenthetically in the text.

Francis L. Kunkel (essay date 1968)

SOURCE: "The Dystopia of Harold Pinter," in *Renascence,* Vol. 21, No. 1, Autumn, 1968, pp. 17-20.

[In the following essay, Kunkel explores the grim alienation Pinter's characters represent.]

Harold Pinter mounted the challenge to Broadway for two years in a row. *The Homecoming* (1965), written after *The Birthday Party* (1958) but produced on Broadway before, was the best play of the 1966-67 season, winning the Tony Award and the New York Drama Critics Prize. *The Birthday Party,* which opened two weeks before the first play closed, was one of the best plays of the 1967-68 season.

The Birthday Party is fully as obscure as *The Homecoming,* and a bit more mysterious, if less absurd. The most stimulating parlor game among theater buffs in the spring of '67 was called "What Does *The Homecoming* Mean?" Six months later, the meaning of *The Birthday Party* became another hip conversational diversion. The precise fixed meaning of either play, even if available, is of prime interest only to those who regard a work of art as a univocal cerebral puzzle rather than an equivocal felt experience. In the latter view, an enthralling play will send out multiple reverberations. These two dramas contain many diverse implications, of course, but together they vividly communicate, as I see it, at least one shareable experience. The two combine to form a portrait of modern society as degenerate. And so the two Broadway seasons in question witnessed the Pinter of discontent.

The Homecoming dramatizes a single situation. Teddy, a Ph.D., who teaches philosophy at an American University, returns after an interval of six years with his wife Ruth to his father's house in North London. Ruth behaving like a prostitute, before the father Max, the uncle Sam, and two brothers Lenny and Joey, is soon treated like one. She receives a brusque proposition to stay on as a family "retainer." Eagerly she accepts even though it means abandoning her husband and three children whom she has left behind in the U.S.A. Ruth is to be given a room in the house on the condition that she shall make her services freely available to all the residents and, so that she shall prove no expense to them, she even agrees to make those same services available at a fee to the community at large. Her acceptance of this immodest proposal leaves Teddy curiously unruffled.

The Birthday Party, another chilling fantasy, also dramatizes a single situation. Two men of mystery, Goldberg and McCann, descend for a one night stand upon a sleazy boarding house run by an elderly couple, Meg and Petey, in a seaside resort town. One boarder, a young man, Stanley, is systematically harrassed by these two intruders, before, during and after a terrifying birthday party. The other boarder, a young woman, Lulu, is seduced by or perhaps she seduces—here as elsewhere the evidence is equivocal—Goldberg. Finally Goldberg and McCann having reduced Stanley, the target of their inexplicable visitation, to the status of a gibbering idiot, whisk him off to an undisclosed, sinister destination. Six characters in search of identity constitute the dramatis personae in each play.

Pinter projects a "dystopian" vision in both plays. Homecomings and birthday parties, the signal in a healthy civilization for joy, are in our sick culture occasions for dread. We are in a process of devolution: hell is all around us. Women are damned. Mothers (Ruth) and sweethearts (Lulu) are whores; old ladies (Meg) are senile. Men are fragmented. The brothers in *The Homecoming* form a triad on the order roughly of the brothers Karamazov—roughly, since they are a debased version. Teddy, the talkative professor, is a disembodied brain who lives outside his emotions. Lenny, the witty procurer, is a wanton spirit whose religious faculty is maimed but still alive. Joey, the naive pugilist, is the "id" wallowing in the life of the senses.

Teddy, the epitome of detached cerebration, is so dehumanized that he reduces people to the level of objects. "It's a way of being able to look at the world," he says in response to a question concerning his philosophical allegiance. "It's a question of how far you can operate on things and not in things. . . . You're just objects. You just . . . move about. . . . It's the same as I do. But you're lost in it. You won't get me being . . . I won't be lost in it." Goldberg and McCann, *The Birthday Party* bullies, wall off their humanity and shut out their feelings with brutal consequences. With the passionless precision of automatons they strip human dignity from Stanley and shrink him to the condition of a thing. They have no quarrel with him: they destroy him beyond the power of rehabilitation simply because they sense that his intimidation potential is high while their potential for senseless destruction is unlimited.

Stanley has his inning as a victimizer as well as a victim, however. He directs his hostility against women: at the birthday party in his honor he tries to strangle Meg and ravish Lulu. In treating women as pure and simple sexual objects and knockabouts, he anticipates Lenny. The latter's stable of prostitutes provides him with a comfortable, if not a luxurious, livelihood. And Lenny also assaults women with gay abandon. He likes to boast about an occasion when he stopped just short of killing a girl under a bridge. Getting rid of the corpse would have been too much bother and so he left it at two belts in the nose "and a couple of turns of the boot." His deportment with regard to old ladies, while short of Boy Scout standards, is less brutish. He spares them the full "workover": he dispatches one of their number with a mere "short-arm jab to the belly."

Communication between the sexes is poor. When Stanley, for example, queries Lulu as to whether she would like to go away with him, she responds by wondering where they would go. It is as if he were speaking for every displaced person, every alienated soul on earth when he answers: "Nowhere. There's nowhere to go. So we could just go. It wouldn't matter."

In our time, Pinter implies, the family has degenerated into a ghastly institution; men and women are beastly; and so we are faced with a crisis of personhood. Worst of all, perhaps, God is dead. Lenny, wearing a mask of reptilian cool, smirks at the tomb as he baits his philosopher brother. "Do you detect a certain logical incoherence in the central affirmations of Christian theism?. . . . How can the unknown merit reverence? . . . How can you revere that of which you're ignorant? At the same time, it would be ridiculous to propose that we *know* merits reverence." Unable to love, Lenny falls into hate indiscriminately. He abhors man as well as God—perhaps that is why he abhors God. In the person of Lenny, Pinter depicts a nihilistic society that has become post-Christian and post-humanistic; anti-theocentric and anti-anthropocentric. In such a society, it is not startling that theologians should be recruited from the procurer ranks. The best pimp becomes the best theologian.

When Goldberg sneeringly asks Stanley, "Do you recognize an external force, responsible for you, suffering for you?" he attests to the same thing: where a religious consciousness still exists it is bound to be corrupted. Lenny, like Goldberg, is interested in knotty metaphysical problems. Lenny frets the "business of being and not-being" without shedding much light on the subject. Goldberg utters pretentious gibberish. "We admit possibility only after we grant necessity. It is possible because necessary but by no means necessary through possibility." And in his topsy-turvy hierarchy of values, fact is superior to truth. With regard to a commonplace statement, Goldberg assures McCann that "It's more than true. It's a fact." Paradox in our contemporary global village: the immoralist, the atheist, and the sophist are the custodians of ethics, theodicy, and ontology.

To orchestrate the plight of man—self-absorbed and alienated from the loves and sufferings of people around him—and God—shunned—in a weary satiated world, Pinter uses reverse rhetoric. Neither *The Homecoming* nor *The Birthday Party* seek to achieve versimilitude: the improbable is dramatized in both.

Routine matters are treated as though they were bizarre. Ruth and Lenny clash over a glass of water he has given her. He threatens to take it back before she has finished it. She counters with another threat, "If you take the glass . . . I'll take you." Teddy and Lenny clash over a cheese sandwich Lenny prepared as a snack for himself but which Teddy ate. Lenny sees the trivial action as the moment of truth for the two of them. "It's a real cards on the table stunt. I mean we're in the land of no holds barred now."

This escalation of the trivial issue into a cosmic one carries over from *The Birthday Party,* where it occurs repeatedly. Goldberg and McCann over-vehemently press Stanley to sit down as though his refusal to do so would plunge the world into some instant calamity. And the glowering chips-down confrontation between Stanley and Meg over a cup of tea that she has taken from him foreshadows the glass of water set-to between Lenny and Ruth.

Consistent with this Swiftian rhetoric, genuinely shocking incidents, on the other hand, are treated as though they were prosaic. The pact with Ruth is handled as though it were a perfectly natural arrangement. What is more predictable than a woman with deadly calm using incest in order to cuckold her knowing, complaisant husband? What is more normal than the family's annoyance at Sam's collapse and apparent death on the floor, in the midst of the delicate negotiations with Ruth? Max is loath to have his floor cluttered with a corpse. In his best matter-of-fact fashion Teddy is disappointed, because "I was going to ask him [Sam] to drive me to London Airport."

These inappropriate reactions to significant events copy not only the distorted reactions of the guests to the macabre goings-on at the birthday party, but they also ape the evasive reactions of Petey to the spiriting away of Stanley.

Petey is reluctant to get involved, even though he knows that Goldberg and McCann have aggravated Stanley to the point where he has parted with his senses. Far from interfering in their diabolical scheme, Petey actually abets it. He becomes a passive accomplice by lying to his apprehensive wife when, unaware of what has happened, she inquires after Stanley. Petey assures her that Stanley is safely asleep upstairs. By employing such incidents, Pinter graphically illustrates the way in which modern man, isolated and estranged, is fearful of committing himself to anything real. If you can make yourself indifferent enough or sham sufficient anger, there will be no need to take sides, make decisions, resist pressures, and withstand criticism.

Halfway through ***The Birthday Party***, Goldberg directs a blistering diatribe at Stanley. "You're dead. You can't live, you can't think, you can't love. You're dead. You're a plague gone bad. There's no juice in you. You're nothing but an odour!" Later he unburdens himself before McCann. "My father said to me, Benny. . . . come here. He was dying. I knelt down. . . . Forgive, Benny, he said, and let live. . . . I lost my life in the service of others, he said, I'm not ashamed. Do your duty . . . Always bid good morning to the neighbours. Never, never forget your family, for they are the rock, the constitution and the core!" Could the first quotation be Pinter's diagnosis of the multitudinous ills that modern man is heir to? Could the second quotation be the unpopular cure prescribed by the playwright?

Kirstin Morrison (essay date 1969)

SOURCE: "Pinter and the New Irony," in *The Quarterly Journal of Speech*, Vol. 55, No. 4, December, 1969, pp. 388-93.

[*In the following essay, Morrison argues that Pinter developed a new form of dramatic irony, not the classical irony where the audience knows things the characters do not, but an irony resulting from the characters' knowing things the audience does not.*]

At the heart of all irony lies a discrepancy, some surprisingly consequent change of meaning or reversal of expectation, an apposite contrast of appearance and reality. One of its specialized forms, dramatic irony, has frequently been described as a disparity between the real situation in a play and the way that situation appears, a significant incongruity that is understood by the audience but not, in time, by the characters of the play. This has been a useful way to define situational or dramatic irony because the description does coincide with the way irony is handled in many dramas: The audience, but not Oedipus, realizes how true and how congruent are the two prophecies of Apollo; the audience, but not Othello, knows of Iago's machinations. However, this description of dramatic irony is not complete. There are plays in which the audience's

discovery is simultaneous with the character's: Only in the Epilogue to *Saint Joan* does the audience—and Joan—realize the comic irony of what sainthood really means to an admiring but ill-at-ease world. Furthermore, there is an important qualitative difference in the way the audience and character realize irony: Othello's anguish is for him destruction but for the audience catharsis; what is for Joan a cry of lament—"How soon, O Lord, how soon!"—strikes the audience as philosophical Shavian humor.[1]

Certainly what the audience knows and what the characters know, how the audience reacts and how the characters react, is integral to the workings of irony in a play; but the ironic formulation need not involve the audience's understanding the "real" situation. In fact, a new kind of dramatic irony seems to have evolved recently that depends for its effectiveness on the fact that the audience does not understand. Some of the finest examples of this kind of irony are found in the work of Harold Pinter.

There is a sense in which Pinter's irony is itself ironic, a significant reversal of expectation: Ordinarily the audience understands to some extent the true meaning of words and events while a character or characters may not; Pinter has turned tables on his audience and left them uncertain of what the characters understand only too well. This in itself need not be ironic—just a simple maneuvering for suspense—were it not that this state of uncertainty carries with it a lurking sense of doom, an ill-defined menace the audience feels may threaten itself. In traditional dramatic irony, the protagonist is, in one way or another, the unwitting victim of himself; in Pinter's irony, the spectator comes to fear that he may himself be an unwitting victim. Traditionally an exempt audience watched the character bring himself to destruction, a superior audience that saw and understood what the character did not, an audience that thus freed itself vicariously from pity and fear. Pinter's spectator, however, has no such catharsis because he has no superior or exempt status. He does not fear for the character, even at the end of the play when he has more understanding than he did during the process of it; his real fear is for himself.

Pinter's first play will serve to illustrate this reversed dramatic irony. The sense of impending disaster that is built up in ***The Room*** is typical of Pinter's work; so too is the pattern of event; something from "outside" invades the "inside" and displaces the occupant, turning him out from safety, usurping his place in the world, forcing him to a symbolic equivalent of death. The dialogue is filled with traditional verbal irony. The opening words are Rose's remark as she gives her husband something hot to eat, "Here you are. This'll keep the cold out. It's very cold out, I can tell you. It's murder." The significance is, of course, not immediately realized; but as the play progresses, and remarks of this kind continue, it becomes clear that "the cold" and "outside" are more than usually terrible and do in fact constitute for Rose her own "murder." She says, it would seem, more than she realizes; and what she unwittingly says indeed actually occurs.

This ordinary verbal irony might seem, as in *Oedipus Rex*, to be building the usual kind of dramatic irony; there is, however, one important difference. In *Oedipus Rex* the problem is clear; the irony lies in Oedipus' blindness regarding how the pieces fit together; the audience knows there is ample cause for all that has happened and is happening. In *The Room* there is no such clear causality. Why indeed should the audience find anything terrible in the cold or the outside? Rose's remark that it's murder is almost too trite to notice. Except for the final few moments of the play, there is nothing apparent in events themselves to warrant the degree of fear that is generated within Rose. Whatever sense of fear the audience develops is communicated to it from something Rose sees and understands; the spectator "catches" her anxiety. This anxiety is not the same as the concern an audience has for an Othello or an Oedipus who do not realize where events are leading or what the hidden causes are. In *The Room* it is the character—not the audience—who sees what is coming, who knows the hidden causes, and this makes a profound difference.

What is coming is, quite simply, death. Not a particular fate, not a specific kind of death, but the utterly inescapable fact of death itself, *my own death*, that absolute certainty no one really believes. This is a genuinely difficult problem for a human being to consider at any level of activity; to write about it is particularly difficult because of the need to preserve one of death's essential elements, mystery: to make an image, to contrive an "experience" of the as-yet-unexperienced in such a way that it is both meaningful and yet remains "unknown." Much of modern drama is engaged in precisely this attempt and it is not coincidental that the kind of irony that is the subject of this essay developed in plays of that sort. Elsewhere I have discussed in some detail the various ways death has been treated in modern British drama;[2] here I would like to confine discussion to analysis of the irony employed in this treatment and to concentrate on one of the finest playwrights in Britain today, who is a master of this type of irony. But what is said in regard to Pinter applies as well to several of his fellow-writers, John Whiting, N. F. Simpson, James Saunders, David Rudkin, as well as a number of continental playwrights, who have also been concerned with explicating the unique menace of death.

The entire play *The Room* is a dramatic analogue for the problem of death in a man's life. Although Pinter has denied being conscious of using symbols, that does not prevent his play from functioning like one; nor does it prevent the spectator from asking that most human question, what does the thing mean? It is quite clear from retrospective analysis of *The Room* that the invader from without is death. But at the surface level of the drama there is no adequate reason for Rose's extreme agitation. A stranger in the basement wants to see her, having said that her room is vacant. She is terrified out of all proportion because she sees in these events a meaning that is not directly presented to the audience; the audience knows the event is fearful because she responds fearfully, but the audience does not yet know the cause of her fear, which only gradually becomes apparent. Rose, a woman of sixty, expresses fear that the man is old (aging threatens her life); she is informed that the man wants to see her alone, has been waiting a long time for her (death waits for everyman during the whole course of his life, and everyman dies alone). Finally, the menace of death is made most specific in the presence of the man himself; he is a blind Negro (the dark, in darkness); he has come up out of the cold darkness of the "grave"; he has brought a message from her father, "come home." When Burt, her stolid husband who is incapable of realizing the fact of death, strikes out at the Negro and seems to have killed him, he has not "saved" Rose from death because her death is not really something "outside" her—though she has feared it as that—but is something integrally part of her, something she has carried with her a long time, something that has been intrinsic to her origin, her home, her life. Rose does not need to be carried away by the Negro or to die on stage; this would be too inept. Her final cry "Can't see. I can't see. I can't see" is equivalent to her death.

By the end of the play considerable dramatic tension has been built up; Pinter's brilliant comic mood has modified slowly into terror (in later plays he will come to coordinate these into a wonderful simultaneity). Rose's mounting fear has communicated to the audience a sense of imminent doom; and part of this feeling of menace is that until the very end the audience does not really know what the threat is: As certainty over the presence of danger increases, uncertainty over the nature of the danger adds to the anxiety. Rose, in her bones, knows what the threat is but tries desperately to evade her own knowledge (as I have demonstrated elsewhere, she and Burt are perfect types of the Heideggerian "Everyday" attitude toward death);[3] but the audience has no such knowledge. This kind of irony, in which the character knows the nature of the danger and the audience does not, has a peculiarly unsettling effect on spectators. They are used to a dramatic structure in which disaster is the result of the character's not seeing hidden relationships; now suddenly they are in the uneasy position of not understanding causes and thus being open to unforeseen results. Some doom is there but they cannot locate it.

This ironic reversal of situation is more than just a device of suspense. The play is concerned with death, not death as a plot event but death as a personal reality; it is an exploration of the experience of facing death not as something that happens to someone else but as *my death*. Rose has acted out this image of death but the audience has undergone its mystery. Oedipus and Othello had their moments of realization that doom was theirs and they had been blind to it, that they had complicity in it. In *The Room* it is the audience that is led toward a moment of insight, that is suddenly confronted with the fact that the play is about the inevitability and abiding presence of death. After seeing *Oedipus Rex* and *Othello* the audience might have occasion to reflect anxiously on its own unwitting participation in its own particular doom; but in Pinter's form of irony the audience has actually experienced its own blindness in the presence of doom. It did not realize what Rose realized, and when it suddenly in the last moments understands the meaning of the play, the cause of Rose's fear, its own sense of lurking menace is increased: The audience, faced with its own blindness, realizes with anxiety its own liability to doom; there is a moment, however ill-defined and brief, in which it sees the falsity of the security that brought it to the theatre in the first place, comfortably to witness from an exempt position the fate of another.

I have used **The Room** for illustration because Pinter's theme of death and his inverted ironic situation are so clear. What he has done with a rather contrived obviousness in this first and rapidly written play is carried off with greater subtlety in **The Birthday Party** and **A Slight Ache.** In both of these plays there is a similar terror generated in the central character, a terror out of all proportion (it would seem) to the actual circumstances, a terror communicated to the audience, which does not understand the meaning of events the main character understands only too well; once again the theme is the presence of death and once again the audience is shocked by its own blindness to that presence, and menaced by its own realization of consequent vulnerability. Once again the dramatic effectiveness of the play is based on a reversed irony, the audience not seeing what the protagonist sees.

Pinter, like Beckett, does tend to write the same play over and over again. There are, however, some pieces that make use of a more traditional kind of irony. Both **The Lover** and **A Night Out,** for example, are conventionally clever comedies that depend for their final stroke of amusement on the audience's being informed of a fact it had not previously known, the revelation that the lover is really the husband and that the son has not really murdered his mother. But there is no contrast here between audience-ignorance and character-knowledge, and the final revelation is not so much a vehicle for significance as it is the punch line of a joke.

The Homecoming is probably the most puzzling play Pinter has written, though its recent performance in the United States shows him ten years after **The Room** still utilizing a reversed ironic situation. Once again he uses the theme of displacement, losing one's "home," and once again the audience is mightily confused—or would be if it had not picked up a certain sophistication toward Pinter's particular method—the audience is confused by events the characters accept as utter normalcy; the audience leaves the theatre wondering "*what* happened?" while the characters seem all along to have understood.

The Room—and, with more subtle variation, **The Birthday Party, A Slight Ache, The Dumb Waiter,** and even **The Caretaker**—are all studies of death. **The Homecoming** represents something of a departure from this earlier theme. Here Pinter has so successfully developed the relationship among characters that although this play fol-lows a pattern similar to the earlier pieces it seems to exist as a series of unique relations and not as a statement. Furthermore, in **The Homecoming,** the usual pattern, which focuses on the one displaced, is interestingly modified. The intruder, Teddy, who has come home for a visit, loses his place in two ways; he quits his paternal home in part because he only intended to stay a short time but also because he is driven from it by the behavior of his wife, his brothers, and his father; and he loses his own home because his wife chooses to stay behind with his relatives and to function as a prostitute. But his departure is not surrounded by the terror that attended Rose, Stanley, and Edward; he leaves rather quietly, the atmosphere is one of normalcy. The last moments of the play focus on Ruth, who has gained, not lost a place; in a grotesque tableau strangely reminiscent of Michelangelo and Faulkner together, Ruth sits, Madonna-like with Joey's head on her lap while Max, old and impotent Popeye, looks on with desire. One intruder has lost his home; the other remains in complete control.

The balanced compound of amusement and revulsion that this entire play, and especially its conclusion, produces in the spectator only adds to, does not resolve, the uncertainty he has experienced all along. Whatever this play is saying about the stability and genuineness of relationships between men and women, among members of a family, about the uncertainties concerning what really is appearance and what reality, one effect is clear: Once more the audience finds itself in a much greater state of ignorance than any of the characters. There is a certain uneasiness generated among the spectators by their realization that their ignorance is not the result of information withheld, a kind of cheating on the part of the author; rather, they are unable to perceive and to interpret the relationship among events that the characters seem to have no trouble understanding. The only character in the play who is at all disturbed by the bizarre household is Ruth, and she quietly, unobtrusively before the very eyes of the audience undergoes a shocking—yet highly comic—metamorphosis which is taken entirely for granted not only by the residents of the house but also by her husband. Indeed, the audience can only wonder, *what* has happened and, even more inexplicable, *why?*[4]

This uncertainty might be ineptitude on the part of the writer or obfuscation for its own sake; but Pinter is anything but inept, and the charge of willful obscurity is too easy a way to dismiss any new development in drama. What Pinter seems to be doing, among other things, is contributing to the formation of a new kind of irony, a reversal in audience-expectation, a surprisingly consequent contrast between what the audience knows and what the characters know. In his plays of menace this kind of dramatic irony shifts the fear of being an object of fate from the stage and into the audience; in the new turn of comedy that **The Homecoming** represents, this kind of dramatic irony if not leaving the audience feeling threatened at least leaves it anxious over the possibility of there being hidden relationships it does not discern; it knows from a traditional dramatic irony that a man who does not understand what he sees is liable to pull his destiny over him disastrously.

In one of the first essays to use the term "comedy of menace," Irving Wardle comments that this treatment of fateful disaster in comic terms is an appropriate sign of modern man's situation: "Destiny, handled in this way— not as an austere exercise in classicism, but as an incurable disease which one forgets about most of the time and whose lethal reminders may take the form of a joke—is an apt dramatic motif for an age of conditioned behavior in which orthodox man is willing collaborator in his own destruction."[5] The dramatic irony of classic tragedy has shown man as victim of himself, a "willing" but unwitting collaborator in his own destruction. Modern comedy of menace reverses the ironic relationship and suggests to the audience that it perhaps has forgotten its own "incurable disease" or is only willing to face it in the guise of a joke or entertainment. This audience is brought to a kind of fear not because it has seen the workings of Oedipus' blindness but because it has had experience of its own.

Notes

1. For an interpretation of irony as not merely an objective trope but also a subjective experience see Alan Reynolds Thompson, *The Dry Mock: A Study of Irony in Drama* (Berkeley, 1948).

2. See my article in the special issue on death, *Continuum*, V (Autumn 1967), 538-549.

3. Kristin Morrison, "Death in Modern British Drama, 1914-1964" (Ph.D. dissertation, Harvard University, 1966), pp. 149-152 and 159-169.

4. Retrospective analysis can find an answer to these questions, of course, just as it does for *The Room.* The menace in *The Homecoming* is the Omnivorous Lap, the challenge every man must meet and, in so many of Pinter's plays, the challenge he regularly fails. Tomb and womb appear to be equally threatening in Pinter's work; but that is a subject for another article. The point here remains that the experience of ironic confusion on the part of the audience is the same in *The Homecoming* as it is in *The Room* despite the differences between these two plays.

5. "Comedy of Menace," *Encore*, V (September-October 1958), 33.

Francis Gillen (essay date 1970)

SOURCE: "'. . . Apart from the Known and the Unknown': The Unreconciled Worlds of Harold Pinter's Characters," in *Arizona Quarterly*, Vol. 26, No. 1, Spring, 1970, pp. 17-24.

[*In the following essay, Gillen examines the division between the known and the unknown worlds in Pinter's plays.*]

The current Broadway success of Harold Pinter's *Tea Party* with its clear emphasis on the division between a world which the major character knows because he can touch it and a world whose reality he occasionally glimpses but cannot prove by any of his instinctual criteria for reality provides an appropriate occasion for a discussion of those divided worlds in two of Pinter's major works. To isolate a theme in Pinter is not, of course, to suggest that Pinter's highly complex and dramatic vision can be reduced or limited to an abstract schema. Yet the fact remains that both plays highlight what may well be the philosophical core of Pinter's work, the division, to use E. M. Forster's convenient terms, between the prose and the passion of life. Indeed, Forster's impassioned plea in *Howards End*, "Only connect," may well be taken as an implied meaning of Pinter's drama. For the horror and menace of his plays arise from no external force but from the lack of wholeness, from the characters' inability to locate their position as men.

In the *Tea Party* Disson, a self-made manufacturer of bidets, attempts to wed culture in the person of his new wife, Diana, "a woman of taste, discernment, sensibility and imagination."[1] (Bidets and Brahms!) A practical man who is most at ease when he is using his hands to work with wood, Disson is unsure of himself in his relationships with his wife. His uncertainty is heightened by the fact that at his wedding, Diana's brother Willy, after lavishly praising Diana's family and position, pays only the most perfunctory compliment to Disson, and spends the time which should have been devoted to the bridegroom in his continued adulation of the bride. On their honeymoon, Disson must frequently ask if he makes her happy. Yet Disson's wish to acquire that which he senses Willy and Diana have is shown when he offers Willy a job in his firm and when he allows Diana to become Willy's secretary, thus bringing both sister and brother to his place of business.

The day before his marriage, Disson had engaged an attractive young secretary named Wendy, who ominously confesses that she had been forced to leave her former job because her employer couldn't stop touching her. Wishing to be related to Diana, but at home only with what he can actually touch, Disson begins to toy with Wendy:

> DISSON: Is this you? This I feel?
>
> WENDY: Yes.
>
> DISSON: What, all this I can feel?
>
> WENDY: You're playing one of your games, Mr. Disson. You're being naughty again
>
> (p. 72).

His double vision, for which there is no physical cause, is the symbol of his unwillingness to belong exclusively to the world of either Wendy or Diana, and his inability to discover a means of fusing them. When Disson suddenly sees two ping-pong balls while he is playing that game with Willy, the one may be said to represent that world associated with Wendy whose reality he can touch, and the other, associated with Diana, a world which remains unexplained. Perhaps his anguished question about whether he makes Diana happy also suggests that, ill at ease as he is with her, he can find little sexual satisfaction with Diana, only with Wendy in whose presence he can be himself. In this case, the division between mind and body is complete; they remain the separate, disjointed facets of his vision.

Unable to enter into Diana's world (Pinter may wish us to recall the mythological reference—Diana is the chaste and unattainable goddess of the hunt), Disson can only reconstruct that which he cannot feel in terms of that which he knows, the physical. So he translates his fear of that which he cannot know about Diana into the belief that she is being "touched" and seduced by her brother Willy. In the movie script of the *Tea Party* the closing scenes are shot from two points of view, objective scenes which include Disson, and scenes which are purely from Disson's point of view. The scene in which Diana and Wendy lie on cushions on Disson's desk and Willy caresses Diana's face is thus clearly meant to be solely a representation of Disson's diseased imagination. The very tea party at which the scene takes place adds a further dimension of irony. Disson, who had boasted that he "used to down eleven or nine pints a night. . . . Me and the boys!" (p. 74) feels constrained to celebrate the first anniversary of his marriage in a form which he feels will be more acceptable to Diana, a tea party. The party intended to be a celebration of union is instead the perfect, bitter symbol of the division in Disson.

Disson's situation is created in part, Pinter suggests, by his inability to live with unresolved ambiguity in others. His rationalistic culture has taught him to value "the ability to operate lucidly upon our problems and therefore be in a position to solve them" (p. 53). "I don't like self-doubt. I don't like fuzziness. I like clarity. Clear intention. Precise execution. Black or white?" he tells Willy (p. 53). Such a person will naturally expect that his "disease" is physical and will fail to understand why his friend Disley cannot provide glasses to cure his double vision. In one of the most moving scenes of the play, hearing giggles coming from Willy's office and knowing that Wendy and perhaps Diana are there with Willy, Disson squats and tries vainly to peer through the keyhole, yet it is ironically Disson himself who in his uncertainty had insisted on the divided offices and Disson himself who had bolted the door and turned the key.

In **The Homecoming,** the audience is first introduced to a houseful of men. Max, the widowed father, had been a butcher; Sam, Max's brother, is a chauffeur; Joey, a boxer; and Lenny, a pimp. With the exception of Sam, who is mocked by the others for his seeming ineptitude with women, the members of this family encounter life and each other primarily on a physical level which Pinter strips of all social disguise with which civilized persons clothe their natural animosities and desires. When Max interrupts

Lenny who is cutting something out of a newspaper, Lenny, for instance, warns: "Plug it, will you, you stupid sod, I'm trying to read the paper." Max replies: "Listen! I'll chop your spine off, you talk to me like that! You understand? Talking to your lousy filthy father like that!"[2] The family has discovered only one acceptable alternative for such unmitigated naturalism, a maudlin sentimentality which is completely unrelated to reality. In this mood, Max, who has earlier admitted that "it made me sick just to look at her rotten stinking face" (p. 9), tells that his wife "taught those boys everything they know. She taught them all the morality they know. I'm telling you. Every single bit of the moral code they live by—was taught to them by their mother. And she had a heart to go with it. What a heart. Eh, Sam? Listen, what's the use of beating round the bush? That woman was the backbone to this family . . . a woman at home with a will of iron, a heart of gold and a mind" (p. 46). Moments later, as the sentimentality passes, Max's family becomes "a crippled family, three bastard sons, a slutbitch of a wife" (p. 47).

Once again, then, we observe the same division between that which can be experienced on a sensual level and an ideality which cannot be realized but only hinted at in flashes of sentimentality which falsify it. Clearly Max cannot reconcile his idealized picture of what a wife should be with his gnawing doubts about his wife's marital fidelity. Like Disson in the **Tea Party** Max is described by his son Lenny as being "obsessed with order and clarity. He doesn't like mess" (p. 33). Thus, like Disson, these characters are confronted with two unreconciled worlds and have only the futile tools of "order and clarity" to deal with this mystery.

The family's problem is compounded by the fact that the "things" which alone they can know because they alone are capable of being physically experienced don't remain things. "Things" take on a sinister aspect in Pinter's plays because they point to something beyond themselves, to a meaning which somehow isn't included in their "thingness," and hence to the agony of the characters' uncertain groping for meaning. As Lenny states it: "I mean there are lots of things which tick in the night, don't you find that? All sorts of objects, which, in the day, you wouldn't call anything else but commonplace. They give you no trouble. But in the night any given one of a number of them is liable to start letting out a bit of a tick" (p. 28). His speech reminds one of Caliban's in Shakespeare's *The Tempest*. His nights too are full of noises:

> And then, in dreaming
> The clouds methought would open and show riches
> Ready to drop upon me, that when I waked,
> I cried to dream again.

Indeed, Pinter's characters may aptly be compared to Calibans who are tortured by dreams of Ariels who have absented themselves and remain unattainable. In Pinter's wasteland as in Eliot's, "April is the cruelest month."

To this home return Max's other son, Teddy, and his wife, Ruth. Teddy had married Ruth without his family's knowledge and had lived with her in America for the past six years. Teddy, a philosopher at a university, brings with him the sign of the highest cultural achievement which America can grant, a Ph.D.; Ruth it would seem might be the softening feminine influence, the mother whom Lenny and Joey seem at times to seek in Max. Instead there is no fusion, no real homecoming. In his relationship with Teddy, Max alternates between the same bitter cynicism and mawkish sentimentality that had marked his attitude toward his wife. He accuses Teddy of having "a stinking pox-ridden slut in my house all night" (p. 41) only to invite him moments later to "have a nice cuddle and kiss, eh? Like the old days? . . . You want to kiss your old father?" (p. 43). Instead of becoming a mitigating force, Ruth is reduced to the level of the occupants of the home. First she is "touched" by Lenny, then she substitutes her very attractive leg as a reminder of the concrete during an abstract philosophical discussion. After this reduction to the physical, she is kissed, fondled, and possessed by Lenny and an attempt to "go the whole hog" is made by Joey. When Teddy decides he must return to America, the rest of the family agree to keep Ruth on for their pleasure if she will agree to help support herself by spending four hours a night in one of Lenny's flats.

The failure to fuse, however, is not solely the family's but Teddy's as well. Teddy's philosophy, which might be expected to confer meaning, is totally divorced from reality. Like American technology (and even the humanities are becoming increasingly dominated by technical methodology) his philosophy is so complex that it moves beyond the layman whose life it nevertheless shapes. As Teddy scornfully tells the rest of the family: "You wouldn't understand my works. You wouldn't have the faintest idea of what they were about. You wouldn't appreciate the points of reference. You're way behind. All of you. There's no point in my sending you my works. You'd be lost" (p. 61). Ironically, all that Teddy does reveal about his works is that they're about "how certain people can maintain . . . intellectual equilibrium" (p. 62). Teddy's divorce from reality is comically symbolized in the play by his casual attitude toward his wife's seduction by his brothers. Though perhaps seduction is too strong a word, for there is a suggestion in the play that Ruth so easily acquiesces because she too has been able to effect no really personal contact with her husband. Like Max's sentimentalized picture of his wife, Teddy's picture of Ruth is too cliché ridden to convince anyone that he accepts her as a complex person: "She's a great help to me over there. She's a wonderful wife and mother. She's a very popular woman. She's got lots of friends. It's a great life, at the University . . . you know . . . it's a very good life. We've got a lovely house . . . we've got all . . . we've got everything we want" (p. 50). Ruth affirms: "I was . . . different . . . when I met Teddy . . . first" (p. 50).

The other seeming idealist in the house is Sam. The two brothers Max and Sam seem to complement one another as two parts of something which was once whole. Max is aggressive, Sam passive; Max succeeds with women, Sam has never married; Max is vulgar, Sam respectful; Max takes, Sam gives. In love with Max's wife Jessie all his life, Sam nevertheless carries with him the guilty knowledge that Max's friend and drinking companion MacGregor had Jessie in the back of his cab as he drove them along. Yet Sam's long-suffering, effeminate idealism is no more related to reality than is Teddy's philosophy. All Sam can do is utter this truth once in a single gasping breath, croak, and fall to the floor as if dead. He has no impact; Max dismisses his statement as the product of a "diseased imagination" (p. 79) and the others step gingerly over his body as they go about preparing for Ruth's permanent residence.

Thus in the play there is no homecoming. Man, reduced to an object, deserted by the intellectual tradition to which he might turn for answers, is left alone with his "things" which can't satisfy: "All right, I say, *take it, take* a table, but once you've taken it, what are you going to do with it?" (p. 52). Yet "things" without meaning take on a sinister life of their own and rise up to menace those who have collected them. This is what the family feel at the end of the play when they express their fear that the woman they've reduced to an acquired object represents a vaguely intuited threat: "You understand what I mean? Listen, I've got a funny idea she'll do the dirty on us, you want to bet? She'll use us, she'll make use of us, I can tell you!" (p. 81). In such dread, devoid of meaning, Pinter's characters must remain in their wasteland. Lenny again states their problem most expressly: "How can the unknown merit reverence? In other words, how can you revere that of which you're ignorant? At the same time, it would be ridiculous to suppose that what we know merits reverence. What we know merits any one of a number of things, but it stands to reason reverence isn't one of them. In other words, apart from the known and the unknown, what else is there?" (p. 52).

Our observations on these two plays of Pinter suggest possible insights into some of his other dramas. Could *The Caretaker,* for example, be read on one level as symbolizing man's effort to live with these two aspects of himself (Mick the dreamer, and Aston the practical one at home in the world of things), and not knowing which he is or which side of himself to choose (Aston is vulgar but do Mick's visions of apartment houses bear any relation to reality?) gradually loses his own identity as man (as Davies has lost his papers).

We must be careful, of course, not to over-allegorize Pinter, lest we commit the very fault of his characters who are damned. We can only hope that these observations send the reader back to the plays with a renewed conviction that Pinter is a major dramatist not only because of his puzzling and innovative technique but because his vision and warning are extremely relevant to those of us who must live in that divided world which he portrays.

Notes

1. Harold Pinter, "Tea Party" in *The Lover, Tea Party, The Basement* (New York, 1967), p. 41. Since the

printed version of the Broadway play is not available, all quotations from this play are taken from the film script prepared for British television and reprinted by Grove Press in the edition cited above. All page references in the text are to this edition.

2. Harold Pinter, *The Homecoming* (New York, 1966), p. 9. All page references in the text are to this Grove Press edition.

Lois G. Gordon (essay date 1971)

SOURCE: "Harold Pinter—Past and Present," in *Kansas Quarterly,* Vol. 3, No. 2, Spring, 1971, pp. 89-99.

[*In the following essay, Gordon traces the manner in which Pinter moves from the analytic to the lyrical form of language in his plays.*]

In the remarkably short time between 1957 and 1965 Harold Pinter established himself as the most gifted playwright in England. Prominent not only as the author of nearly a dozen plays, including **The Birthday Party, The Caretaker,** and **The Homecoming,** he is also an accomplished poet, TV and film scriptwriter (**The Servant, The Quiller Memorandum, Accident**), actor, and director. It is therefore of interest that in his prolific career, a four-year silence separated his last stage play, **The Homecoming,** from the most recent **Silence** and **Landscape** (1969).

Pinter has created an idiom peculiarly his own, often miscalled "theatre of the absurd" or "drama of menace," labels which describe the so-called forces of terror, evil, or the absurd, which visit his characters and cause their breakdown. Actually, the "Pinteresque" consists of a much more frightening visitation. Pinter's comfortable people are, at least up until **Silence** and **Landscape,** besieged by internal fears and longings, and it is these which inevitably wage successful war against the tidy life styles they have constructed in order to survive from day to day.

Pinter elicits a unique response from these displays of inner violence, these eruptions of blind anger and sexuality within the seemingly stable routines of daily conversation and activity—simultaneous humor and horror. His characters (usually couples), enclosed in a room, play the "games people play," during which they say one thing but really feel and often communicate another. During their exchanges—where the verbal level is only the most superficial facet of a multi-level communication—the connotations of their words and their accompanying gestures, or pauses, or double-entendre, really communicate a second level of meaning often opposed to the first. Pinter has said of language:

> The speech we hear is an indication of that which we don't hear. It is a necessary avoidance, a violent, sly, and anguished or mocking smoke screen which keeps the other in its true place. When true silence falls we

are still left with echo but are nearer nakedness. One way of looking at speech is to say that it is a constant stratagem to cover nakedness.[1]

To be sure, Pinter's characters start out using language as that "necessary avoidance," but in the course of the plays, language breaks down. Ultimately Pinter's plays are stratagems to *uncover* nakedness. His characters may try to conduct their lives by routine, but their ordinary interchanges and activities are inevitably inadequate to clothe their untidy undersides.

Any interruption (i.e., a blind and mute old matchseller behind their house, a finicky old landlord inquiring about a rocking chair, a change of climate to cold or damp, a broken toaster, a malfunctioning w.c.) becomes a threat to their carefully measured routine, because their life games are ultimately a lie designed to submerge a darker, less social, more violent aspect of self.

Two questions arise: Why do Pinter's people become so upset by the seemingly trivial appearance of an old man or a change in weather? How do they handle the gratuitous appearance of these inner drives? We may think the appearance of any of the above "intruders" at most a minor inconvenience, but Pinter makes it clear that they are frightening *because* the characters view them as such. Within the Pinter world, the only "reality" is the reality of individual perception or behavior, whether to the outsider it appears as reality, distortion, or fantasy. Again Pinter writes:

> The desire for verification on the part of us all, with regard to our own experience and the experience of others, is understandable, but cannot always be satisfied. I suggest there can be no hard distinctions between what is real and what is unreal, nor between what is true and what is false. A thing is not necessarily either true or false; it can be both true and false.[2]

As to the release of violence beneath the word games, Pinter's characters project upon their visitors their own irrationality. In a sense, the so-called victimizers—Goldberg and McCann, the old matchseller, even the dumbwaiter—are screens upon which Pinter's characters externalize their inner selves, that side of them which the games have been ultimately inadequate to hide. What is, of course, simultaneously funny and horrific is that the games constructed—and even the "intruders" or screens, which are mirror images of the characters—contain within them the boring lives already lived *and* the violence struggling for expression.

What never ceases to fascinate us is the manner in which Pinter portrays the games people play and allows us to share his people's hopes and fears. After all, we know, rationally, that the blind, old matchseller in **A Slight Ache** and the two businessmen in **The Birthday Party,** let alone the mechanical dumbwaiter in the play of that name, are hardly forces of evil bent upon destruction of the innocents. But, long before their appearance, we also know that Pinter's people are not that innocent, that any intrusion into their carefully formulated patterns of living will transform comfort into disaster. In a word, what ultimately intrigues us—and this is "the Pinteresque"—is the artist's delicate yet profound awareness of the fragility of human relationships and communication, his insight into the terror and frustration that emerge from man's everyday experience rather than from cosmic forces. Pinter knows that most men spend their lives worrying about how to live with family, friends and employers—not national or international crises. His brilliance lies in his portrait of the devastating loneliness and fear that pervade both the ordinary and extraordinary individual, despite the variety of life styles erected to barter the internal furies.

In the plays preceding *Silence* and *Landscape,* Pinter's people are all of a type, and so are the objects of their homes and conversation. The men are emasculated and childish, usually given to little speech and silent recollections of a happier past; the women are childless and a combination of domineering-mother, coquette, and emasculating bitch. Whether the men or the women are responsible for this irreconcilable enmity between the sexes is really beyond speculation, for not only do both bring to the other unresolved problems from an earlier experience, but their current rivalry has something of a circular quality about it. That is, the women, who find no emotional or physical fulfillment in their husbands, have infantilized and castrated their men; but the men, either because they were so treated or because they have brought an older anger into their marriages, are passive and often impotent. Both, in turn, then project upon strangers or their spouse their fantasies for fulfillment. Whether or not each has a lover in fact little matters, for in his own mind he enacts a continuous infidelity.

Pinter's men and women often invest objects with emotional significance. Their rooms take on the qualities of a haven, a protection from inner upheaval; since their minds are filled with what to them are unclean thoughts, it is necessary that both they and their rooms always be tidy; they come to fear strangers or the cold, the damp, and both darkness and bright light; the women insist upon strong tea but proffer weak tea to their husbands, who more often than not have weak eyesight. Trucks or vans appear as sexual and threatening; appliances often need repair; and ordinary activities, the morning tea and dull meals, must be maintained with all the fervor of religious ritual so that the ravages of free time and possible introspection can be avoided.

Rose, in Pinter's first play, *The Room,* is the prototype of the Pinter woman. She coddles, feeds, clothes, and emasculates her husband, Burt, who is not only virtually silent throughout, but who is portrayed as a child, wearing a silly hat and reading comic books: "That's right. You eat that. . . . [She butters his bread.] Eat it up. It'll do you good. . . . Nice weak tea. Lovely weak tea. Here you are. . . . I'll wait for mine. Anyway, I'll have it a bit stronger. . . . You'd better put on your thick jersey." She treats her

landlord, whose name, fittingly, is Kidd, similarly, when he visits and announces that a blind black named Riley is waiting in the basement to visit her.

Rose's "game" involves protecting herself from what she calls the cold, the damp, the dark. If she can merely guarantee her room, her internal dark and cold can be contained. "This is a good room. You've got a chance in a place like this," she cries, and "It's very cold out. . . . It's murder . . ."

A young couple enters Rose's domain thinking that the room is to be let, and by the time they leave, she is so threatened about dislocation that the black stranger from the basement, whose arrival has been imminent and who has some connection with her childhood, becomes the final catalyst (and screen) for her dramatic breakdown. She reveals that the reason for her present games of ritual emasculation have to do with some childhood sexual experience. Riley calls her "Sal," and says, "I want you to come home," and she embraces and caresses him. Burt returns from his van and speaks for the first time, as if he has at last achieved some sexual advantage: "I drove her down, hard. . . . I sped her. . . . I bumped him. . . . She was good. She went with me." He then attacks Riley, and in so doing, acts out Rose's hidden wishes, murdering the primal figure. But Rose is unable to sustain the guilt of literally assaulting the male—she can endure the fantasy and game of it but not the reality—and she is then struck blind.

The same need to protect the self against sexual drives and guilt characterizes Pinter's brilliant *The Birthday Party.* But where Rose's relationship to Riley remained somewhat mysterious, Pinter now works out a Freudian treatment of the Oedipus story. The landlady, Meg, now treats her young male boarder, Stanley, exactly as Rose did Bert: "I made him [drink the tea]. I stood there till he did. I tried to get him up then. But he wouldn't, the little monkey. . . . Stan! Stanny! I'm coming up to fetch you [from bed]. . . . I'm coming to get you!"

Stanley allows Meg to mother him, but the games are never one-sided: Meg allows Stanley to court her. She is content to sustain the flirtation as long as it remains a word-game in which the reality—the fact that she really enjoys believing she is "the belle of the ball"—is never articulated, and in which she can simultaneously insult and infantilize her partner. When Stanley calls her toast "succulent," she replies, "Don't say it! . . . You shouldn't say that word to a married woman." Even before Goldberg and McCann arrive, we see Stanley's growing fear that someone or something is going to arrive to disturb the precarious happiness he has in this house through Meg.

Stanley suffers from a sense of sin and guilt that has to do with his mother. The mere presence of the two businessmen—who have their own word-game of comraderie that sustains a relationship opposite to Stanley's and Meg's, in which they talk happily of their childhood and past, among other things—is so threatening to Stanley that before too long he admits that he has driven his mother to a sanatorium and is now trying to do the same to Meg. He begins insisting that his room be straightened, as if this could cleanse his buried self, he announces his identity as "Joe Soap," and there follows his condemnation: "You stink of sin. . . . You contaminate womankind . . . Mother defiler! . . . You verminate the sheet of your birth."

Similarly, the deaf-blind matchseller in *A Slight Ache* becomes the screen upon which the sophisticated Flora and Edward project their deepest fears and longings. Not only are they gratuitously cruel to a bee which has been buzzing around their morning marmalade and interrupting their well-designed, chic chitchat, but by the end of the play, the marriage-game that so precariously permitted the oversexed Flora and the impotent Edward to remain together breaks down and Edward changes place with the old man whom Flora takes into the house as her baby-lover. Where Flora had earlier taunted Edward with "Oh, Weddie. Beddie-Weddie," she at last says to Barnabas, the old man, "All you need is a bath. A lovely lathery bath. And a good scrub. A lovely lathery scrub." Edward's identification with the matchseller is interesting: "The bastard isn't a matchseller after all. He's an impostor. He can go and ply his trade somewhere else. Instead of standing like a bullock [castrated bull], a bullock outside my gate."

After Pinter finished *The Room,* he said:

> Well, it's very peculiar. When I got to that point in the play, the man from the basement had to be introduced, and he just *was* a blind Negro. I don't think there's anything radically wrong with the character in himself, but he behaves too differently from the other characters; if I were writing the play now I'd make him sit down, have a cup of tea.[3]

As Pinter's career develops, a greater realism marks the portrayal of this "third party," whose very presence promises the dislocation of the room-bound characters. In addition, the more "ordinary" this screen figure appears, the more humorous its effect. The early Riley in *The Room* and the blind matchseller in *Slight Ache* are among Pinter's most mysterious apparitions; so are the mechanical dumbwaiter and misfunctioning w.c. in *The Dumbwaiter*—the "intrusions" into the life styles of the two hired killers who can function only because they have perfected their routines of murder and small talk. By the time Pinter gets to *The Caretaker,* however, he creates a totally realistic figure in Davies, and focuses upon the insecurities that develop, and the breakdown of loyalties and workable relationships, when a very ordinary man pits two brothers against one another and forgets the "care" that must be taken of the games honored by men.

The suggestion of homosexual relationships in *The Dumbwaiter* and *The Caretaker* returns in *The Homecoming,* but here Pinter is primarily concerned with the continuing enmities between both sexes. The academic Teddy and his wife Ruth return to the all-male household of Teddy's childhood where through a series of ritual castration games, Ruth gradually becomes identified with Teddy's mother—as the father puts it, an unfaithful, pox-ridden slut. By the end of the play, she remains behind to fill the shoes of that first progenitor: She will tempt each of the sons and fathers but then reduce them to whimpering children.

The four Pinter plays most recently produced in New York reflect a radical transformation in the Pinter style and the subject matter. The same violence, sexuality, and fear lurking behind the comfortable games of existence mark *The Basement* and *Tea Party,* but in *Silence* and *Landscape* Pinter puts aside the stripping of his characters. No longer concerned with the stratagems or the nakedness, he focuses upon the isolation and total incommunicability between couples who have long since tired or perhaps never bothered to play the games people play.

What Pinter seems to be exploring is his belief that "verification" remains impossible, that a "thing is not necessarily either true or false; it can be both true and false." Where in the earlier plays it was possible to discern bare motivation (and the contradictions between wish and act, the discrepancy between conscious and unconscious desire), Pinter now presents his characters in a number of guises *simultaneously* without even attempting to account for motivation. If man acts in contradictory and bizarre ways because he is motivated by contradictory and bizarre forces, the playwright can be faithful to human experience only by dramatically representing the seeming ambiguities and contradictions that result. If the truth of experience is the combination of both actual and fantasied behavior, the playwright must communicate this totality without judging his people or encouraging us to do so.

Both *The Basement* and *Tea Party* were originally written for TV. When transferred to the stage (Pinter assisting in direction), Pinter made no changes in the many quick cuts, overlapping dialogue, multiple set changes, and crosscuts—structural details that contribute to the sense and pace of real and imagined experience. In *The Basement,* specifically, rapid changes in season and decor (with the stage bare at the end) are the structural counterparts of the games played and the characters' final stripping of all external paraphernalia. Many of the Pinter emblems recur: the struggle for possession of the warm room (most like *The Caretaker*), the multiple personalities that each person enacts (*Lover*), the self-seeking and castrating woman and the fight for sexual identity through heterosexual and homosexual interchanges (*The Homecoming*).

The main ambiguity in the play concerns who is fighting with whom and what the prize to be won represents. The plot is very simple: Stott, a young man, comes to visit his old boyfriend (lover?), Law, but he brings a girl (Jane) along too. Almost immediately, they undress and proceed to an amorous adventure in Law's bed, while Law sits by and reads his Persian love manual. Rivalries, jealousies, and tensions mount, and by the end of the play, Stott and Law, undressed, battle with marbles and duel with broken milk bottles. In the final scene, Jane and Law are out in the rain waiting to visit Stott, now in possession of the room.

Is *The Basement* a satire of "proper" as opposed to "natural" behavior? Law is a man who acts "lawfully"; he is a caretaker of propriety and he follows the rules of the game; Stott, however (a stoat is a weasel), is sly and underhanded, but he seems to have the advantage through much of the play. After all, in this cycle of their game, he wins the room.

Is this an Oedipal triangle in which Law's and Jane's betrayal of Stott leads to their guilt-ridden projection of Stott on his deathbed? Is Jane only a pawn in the homosexual rivalry of the two men, or are they genuinely competing for her? Is each battling independently for the room, and is Jane the only real winner in the end? Were, as Jane suggests, she and Law actually married, or is Pinter writing a coda to *The Lover?* Are the two men wooing and/or destroying each other through Jane? Is she each man's lover and is this another *menage à trois,* or even *à quatre?* Is Jane a real character or a screen, a projection of their desires?

Not indicating an answer to any of the above, the play is Pinter's first dramatization of the multiple and simultaneously conflicting truths of experience. Interesting, *Basement* goes one step further than *Accident* and *The Servant,* which also focus upon the multiple sexual identities of a couple who invade a friend's house for the purpose of lovemaking. Now Pinter anatomizes the complex undercurrents that give rise to such sexual confusion.

Tea Party is the last of what we have called "the Pinteresque" to date. Robert Disson, a self-made British businessman, is the epitome of Pinter's characters who equate cleanliness and order: he manufactures bidets and toilets. Dependent upon precision and efficiency, Disson rejects any sexual impulses and what he calls "indulgence," but like so many of Pinter's other men, these overwhelm him and he is driven to blindness and paralysis.

The play deals with Disson's marriage to the cold, aristocratic Diana (goddess of chastity?) and his simultaneous attraction to his miniskirted, spikeheeled secretary, Wendy. A number of incidents upset Disson's well-planned life—i.e., his best friend, interestingly enough an ophthalmologist, fails to deliver the tribute-to-the-bridegroom speech at his wedding (in his mind an affirmation of masculinity) and Diana's brother Willy "replaces" Disley, the friend, in the role. But instead of praising Disson, Willy flaunts Diana's power over him (goddess of the hunt?):

> . . . he has married a girl who equals, if not surpasses, his own austere standards of integrity . . . who, in all probability, has the beating of her husband in the two hundred metres breast stroke.[4]

Disson, however, invites Willie into the firm, and by the end of the play, Willie becomes Disson's more than literal partner in all of his personal and professional possessions. Disson fantasizes that his sons have rejected him for Willie, that Willie and Diana have been incestuous, that Willie and Wendy have had an affair, that Willie has rejected his own homosexual needs—that everyone is persecuting and emasculating him. At the final tea party, really a ritual castration ceremony, with Disson's sons, parents, best friend and wife, and the two serving ladies present, Willie acts out Disson's fantasies: he caresses, alternately, both Diana and Wendy, who lie head to toe on a desk. Disson, who literally and figuratively sits holding the (ping-pong) ball (Willie has defeated him at ping-pong twice in the play), sits blind and mute (and even drops his teacup), as his mother reduces him to "Bobbie."

Tea Party is clearly a new form of monodrama. Pinter specifies in the text—and of course some of his instructions are impossible to transfer from TV to the stage—that we see the action from Disson's point of view. For example, in the final party scene, he writes "Disson's point of view. No dialogue is heard in all shots from Disson's point of view. Silence. Figures mouthing silently, in conspiratorial postures, seemingly whispering together." Pinter similarly asks us to share Disson's perception of Wendy: "Her buttocks fill the screen," as well as his "double vision": As he plays ping-pong with Willie, the text specifies: "From Disson's point of view see two balls bounce and leap. . . ."—a rather obvious representation of his conflicting sense of order and of lust. In addition, where the threats or screens in the early plays were harmless, Pinter now creates an extraordinary ambiguity about these figures. Is Wendy a sexual threat in fact or only in Disson's fantasy? Pinter again seems to be saying that something can be false and true at the same time, that any reflection of the totality of experience must contain the multiple contradictions of perception and external reality.

Needless to say, these basic "ambiguities" provoke enormous humor. For example, after speaking of Wendy's secretarial expertise, Disson mentions that Wendy's previous employer made untoward advances. Diana, however, who has just said, "Well [she is] perhaps not quite as accomplished as I am," adds, "Well, if we're to take it that that's general practice, I think it's safer to stay in the family, don't you? Mind you, they might not want to touch me in the same way they wanted to touch her." Exactly who is Diana referring to? She continues, "But Robert, you must understand that I not only want to be your wife, but also your employee. I'm not embarrassing you, am I, Willie? . . . I can help to further your interests, our interests." Is this the comment of an innocent, or a confession of incest? Diana works for Disson generally, but for Willie specifically. This beautiful ambiguity, one of the play's funniest moments, is but one detail that points ahead to the *menage à trois* tableau at the end.

Although these changes mark new techniques in Pinter's work, by and large he still concentrates upon how language, as a reflection of orderly and controlled behavior, breaks down to reveal a truth of character beneath. For example, when Disson sits drinking with Diana and Willie, the question of their incest still unresolved, Willie asks them to tell him how they "played at being brother and sister." Diana, perhaps aware of what he means by "played," aggressively replies: "Stop drinking," and Disson, confusing alcohol with masculinity, admits his castration, cuckoldry, and possible homosexuality. He also explains the significance of the many hobbies he has constructed to organize his life:

> Drinking? You call this drinking? This? I used to down eleven or nine [the reversal is interesting] pints a night! . . . Me and the boys! The boys! And me! I'd break any man's [not woman's] hand for . . . for playing me false. That was before I became a skilled craftsman.[5]

The recent *Silence* and *Landscape* (1969) indicate an entirely new direction in Pinter's work. *Basement* and *Tea Party* really went as far as possible in revealing the discrepancy between what man does and what he feels. They were nevertheless marked by a conspicuous thinness in texture, their psychology was somewhat obvious, and their plots were almost predictable; the tea, warmth of the room, failing eyesight, aggressive women, and passive men gave one the feeling that he had seen these Pinter plays before. Although the multiple ambiguities were interesting, we expected more intrigue in Pinter's stripping of character and we missed the usual provocation of fear coupled with humor.

In *Silence* and *Landscape,* however, Pinter continues his examination of the matter of verification, of what we called the ambiguities of *Basement* and *Tea Party.* Now, however, rather than present "screens" on to which his people project their needs, he instead focuses upon their words alone—their consciously articulated personal testaments—as if this were the only measure of identity knowable.

The same childless couples inhabit these plays, but they have long tired of playing games to assure their identity. Nothing is certain in their isolated rooms, and least of all their identity. Each one not only fails to understand himself and to distinguish fantasy from actual experience, but he can never know the stranger who calls himself his spouse. There is a kind of finality in these plays, but there is also a poignance about these people so inextricably locked within themselves.

Although *Silence* and *Landscape* have been published separately, they may well be parts of a single whole. Actually, in both London and New York the theatre program contained a slip of paper announcing that *Silence* would precede as well as follow *Landscape.* One does have the sense that, just as Beckett's unspoken Third Act of *Waiting for Godot* is Act I, *Silence* is the inevitable conclusion to *Landscape,* which in a sense is Act II. Pinter, in both plays, manipulates a series of circles: *Landscape* itself has a circular design (really a *da capo* musical structure, for

the play's last lines echo its first), and its husband and wife (and her remembered lover) seem to be the same three people from *Silence.* Interestingly, in at least the New York production the same actor played in both.

The plays (each about twenty minutes long) are poetic images of growing old age and desolation. They tell of brief and unfulfilled love affairs, their details are of walks in the country, moments in pubs, and flights of birds; recollections are illuminated by memories of fading sunlight or grey clouds or gusts of rain. In both, the speakers interrupt their wistful thoughts with lusty outbursts about the most mundane of matters. Every word reverberates, each character's reveries define the others', and although their conversation is not directed to the other, each one explains the way in which life has passed the other by, although to him that insight remains unfathomable.

The two men and women of *Silence* sit in a triangle, each character occupying his own time and space. Rumsey, a successful farmer of forty, proposed to a girl, but for some reason they never married. Now he recalls walking with her, although, as he puts it, "My heart never bangs." Bates, in his middle thirties, once asked the girl to go away with him, but he is uncertain why the affair was aborted. Once a farmhand, he now lives in the city in a boarding-house where he is tortured by the sounds of lovemaking that cross the thin walls of his rented room. Ellen, who is in her twenties, and who sits between the two, also recalls a youthful love. Although she says, "There are two, one who is with me sometimes and another," it is unclear if she is thinking of two separate men or the various facets of a single man—i.e., what he was and what he has become, what she wished him to be, and so forth. It even seems at times that Ellen is recalling her father, who finally took her home again. (Rumsey: "Can you remember . . . when you were here last? . . . You were a little girl"; Bates: "Once I had a little girl.")

The dynamic of the play, however, does not lie in unraveling a single line of plot. It lies rather in each character's rationalizations, hopes, fears, and fantasies that are true at one and the same time. It is the texture of the play, therefore, rather than its recollected incidents, that warrants discussion.

Each speaker's cadences and diction are particularly his own: Rumsey, whose girl dresses to please him, speaks in a way that reflects his own passive yet palpable pleasure in the world about him. Bates's speech, on the other hand, is more aggressive, as were his intentions with her. Ellen, who drifts between both men, wavers between hope, frustration, and despair. The only constant is their loneliness and ignorance of why things are as they are: "Around me sits the night. Such a silence." Their memories and fantasies, rather than human contact, are their only verification that they exist. And, as the fragments at the close of the play indicate, those memories are fading to silence.

Like any Symbolist poem, *Silence* is difficult to analyze; the total mosaic, as in human experience, constitutes its life. In the tradition of Joyce, Woolf, and Beckett, Pinter mirrors the simultaneous levels of thought—the mixtures of fantasy and real experience—that are the truth of experience. A few lines from the opening give some indication of the way in which an accretion of meaning grows from the positioning of all the details (i.e., clouds, hills, dogs, the pubs, rain, color):

> RUMSEY: I walk with my girl who wears a grey blouse when she walks and grey shoes and walks with me readily wearing her clothes considered for me. Her grey clothes.
>
> She holds my arm.
>
> On good evenings we walk through the hills to the top of the hill past the dogs the clouds racing just before dark or as dark is falling when the moon.
>
> . . . .
>
> I tell her my life's thoughts, clouds racing. She looks up at me or listens looking down. She stops in midsentence, my sentence, to look up at me. Sometimes her hand has slipped from mine, her arm loosened, she walks slightly apart, dog barks.
>
> ELLEN: There are two. One who is with me sometimes, and another. He listens to me. I tell him what I know. We walk by the dogs. Sometimes the wind is so high he does not hear me. I lead him to a tree, clasp closely to him and whisper to him, wind going, dogs stop, and he hears me.
>
> But the other hears me.
>
> BATES: Caught a bus to the town. Crowds. Lights round the market, rain and stinking. Showed her the bumping lights. Took her down around the dumps. Black roads and girders. She clutching me. This way the way I bring you. Pubs throw the doors smack into the night. Cars barking and the lights. She with me, clutching.[6]

Beth, in *Landscape,* occupies the same relationship to two men (though only one is on stage) as Ellen. She, however, speaks of a man on the beach with whom she wished to have a child. Exquisitely quiet and unutterably delicate, she recalls: "I walked from the dune to the shore. My man slept in the dune. He turned over as I stood. . . . Would you like a baby? I said."

Seated across from Beth sits her husband Duff, who in addition to his comments about their past employer and the rather casual mention of his one-time infidelity to Beth, discusses the routine of his normal day—his walks in the park, a drink in a pub, and even his annoyance at the excrement of dogs and ducks. Again, the gorgeous mosaic of the play creates a sense of multiple ambiguities. Is, for example, Beth's fantasy of her lover on the beach her revenge upon Duff? Is it her projection of herself as Duff's lover? Is this her memory of Duff when he (and she) was young? Or, did she in fact have an affair? The extraordinary irony, of course, is that as Duff addresses her, she performs a continuous infidelity in the pursuit of her memory or fantasy.

Again the language is lyrical, but there is something unspeakably moving about the dialogue and the way in which the monologues mesh and revive the echoes of *Silence*: Duff: "I never saw your face. You were standing by the windows. One of those black nights. . . . It was black outside. I could just see your shape in the window, your reflection"; Ellen in *Silence*: "One time visited his house [Rumsey's or Bates's?]. He put a light on, it reflected the window"; Rumsey: "Look at your reflection"; Ellen: "It's very dark outside. . . . Does it get darker the higher you get? . . . Around me sits the night. Such a silence. I can hear myself. Cup my ear. My heart beats in my ear. Such a silence beats."

Ultimately *Silence* returns to Duff and Beth, as Ellen repeats, "I turn. I turn. I wheel. I glide. I wheel. In stunning light. The horizon moves from the sun. I am crushed by the light." But her tones are soon overtaken by such melodies as "Sometimes I see people. They walk toward me, no, not so . . . never reaching me" (Rumsey); "I walk in my mind. But can't get out of the walls, into a wind" (Bates); and the final "I can't remember anything I'd actually thought, for some time" (Ellen).

This has been Pinter's last statement thus far. In projecting the direction of his future work, it may well be that Pinter has moved on to an entirely new form, the poetic cameo; it is of some interest then that his first volume of *Collected Poems* (a limited edition) has just appeared, although the poems were written as early as his first plays. Considering his vision, however, at least from what he has given us thus far, it seems that Pinter's characters have two alternatives in coping with the ordeal of ordinary experience: They can attempt the games that people play, but if they do, a kind of breakdown ultimately results. Or, they can abandon themselves to the world of fantasy and silence, in which case they must suffer total isolation.

Our preference for the earlier or more recent Pinter depends upon our fascination with the dramatic portrayal of pure being, as opposed to the complex unraveling of multiple motivation. Pinter's earlier work is more analytic, the later more poetic. His talent in both these styles, however, suggests that whatever direction he pursues will promise an elegant art work.

Notes

1. "Writing for the Theatre," *Evergreen Review,* 8 (Aug.-Sept., 1964), 82.

2. Program note at the Royal Court Theatre, London, for the March, 1960, performance of *The Room* and *The Dumb Waiter.*

3. Quoted in John Russell Taylor, *Anger and After* (Baltimore, 1962), p. 297.

4. (New York, 1967), pp. 48-49. All quotations cited in this article are taken from Grove Press's editions of Pinter's work.

5. *Ibid.,* p. 74.

6. (New York, 1970), pp. 33-34.

Alfred E. Rickert (essay date 1971)

SOURCE: "Perceiving Pinter," in *The English Record,* No. 2, Winter, 1971, pp. 30-35.

[*In the following essay, Rickert argues that contrary to Pinter's assertions, he is not a conventional playwright, and does not have the traditional aim of exploring social forces or analyzing social order, but is concerned with investigating the problems of identity and communication.*]

Pinter is not particularly easy to understand. He admits that "the theatre is a large, energetic, public activity," but he goes on nonetheless to say that for him "writing is . . . a completely private activity . . . What I write has no obligation to anything other than to itself."[1] There is a paradox here—the obvious conflict between the public aspect of the theatre and the private side of the drama. No matter how private the activity is, we, the audience, want to be able to make sense of what we see. And indeed Pinter's plays always seem to be about something. Yet almost immediately we recognize that each play's statement must be in terms of an allegory presented. We are inclined to seek an allegory or some deep symbolic significance in the work for two reasons. First, the action we understand seems too trivial not to have some deeper meaning—there must be something beyond the apparent. Second, the action we do not understand must have been included for some reason, otherwise, why is it there. For both of these reasons there is a growing body of Pinter criticism full of contradiction. Everyone has his explanation of a Pinter play, and the problem of puzzling Pinter has become so great that some critics have taken the position that it is impossible for us to know a Pinter play. We cannot explicate his work; we can only react to it, because he consciously and deliberately constructs his plays to create an unknowable world. This is done by giving incomplete information, by giving contradictory information, and by creating a highly personal symbol pattern and developing private myths.

For Pinter, as well as for most writers of the new drama, the conventional structure of a play was not acceptable. Plays written prior to World War II followed a specific pattern based on the concept of the well-made play. The structure of a play was discussed in terms of exposition, complication, rising action, crisis, and denouement. Using this traditional pattern, the playwright built a chain of events. The separate events were causally related so that at the end of the play a complete action was revealed. Every action was fully understood by the audience because the author related the events and provided motivation. This kind of play is essentially narrative. The audience is interested in the action—"What is going to happen next?" and "How is it going to end?" And, when the play ends, all the loose pieces have been properly fitted into the final picture. We have understood what has happened.

Pinter does not write this kind of play. He is only incidentally concerned with a story situation. His focus is not narrative and the events in the play are not causally related, at least not in the traditional sense. Undoubtedly each character has his motivation, that is to say he has reasons for doing what he does and saying what he says even though we may not be able to determine just what those reasons are. Pinter has said, "I have usually begun a play in quite a simple manner; found a couple of characters in a particular context, thrown them together and listened to what they said, keeping my nose to the ground. The context has always been, for me, concrete and particular, and the characters concrete also."[2]

The play Pinter writes is essentially lyrical and the focus shifts from "What is going to happen next?" to "What pattern is unfolding?" The wholeness of the work then is judged not on understanding the action, for in his plays the action is invariably slight. What is important is the pattern, not the events themselves, and the wholeness of the work is judged on the basis of seeing the pattern unfold—of discovering the pattern and thereby the "meaning" of the play. The response to such a work then is highly emotional rather than intellectual, a proper response to a lyrical work, and the response is very personal, again a proper response to a lyrical work.

Now Pinter has identified himself as a "traditional" playwright. "I *am* a very traditional playwright . . . For me everything has to do with shape, structure, and over-all unity."[3] He also observed, "I pay meticulous attention to the shape of things, from the shape of a sentence to the overall structure of the play."[4] But the fact is that he is not at all traditional. What he says about his interest in shape and structure is quite true, but he is misleading us. The "traditional" play is not determined only by its elements of construction. After all, the orthodox dramatists of the twentieth century were also interested in shape and structure. What identifies them as traditional and Pinter as non-traditional is not a matter of form but rather a matter of thematic interest. Interested in man and his society, earlier writers sought to analyze the social order, to understand the social forces. These are the essential features of traditional realism and not either a manner of play construction or even pictorial verisimilitude.

Pinter is not in this tradition. Pinter is not a "social writer." Lois Gordon quite correctly observes that Pinter is not the creator of "an Everyman on the road of life, awaiting and confronting larger forces. Instead, Pinter focuses upon an Everyman who exists in his ordinary activities at home or at work, making the seemingly insignificant decision to eat cornflakes for breakfast, contending with the threat of a cold, and combating a bee in his morning tea."[5] Further, he does not see himself as a social writer. He has said, "I'm not a theorist. I'm not an authoritative or reliable commentator on the dramatic scene, the social scene, any scene . . . a play is not an essay."[6] Although the social order does not interest him, he is interested in looking at man, in viewing the nature of man, and the essential question Pinter asks is "Who are you?" All of his plays concern themselves with this problem of identification. The answers he provides are varied perhaps, and, admittedly, some plays focus on the problem more sharply than others, yet the questions "Who am I" and "Who are you" are always central to his dramaturgy.

In addition to his interest in the problem of identification, at least three other motifs dominate Pinter's world: 1. the problem of threat, 2. the problem of communication—not the inability to communicate but the unwillingness to communicate, and 3. the problem of control.

A phrase which identifies the first of Pinter's plays—the comedy of menace—was coined by Irving Wardle, British theatre critic. Although Wardle has changed his mind and stated that the phrase should not be used to describe the later plays, the comedy of menace label seems rather fixed. In the early plays a great deal of attention was paid to the menace motif. The characters felt threatened and, indeed, were threatened. It was their knowledge or suspicion of impending disaster that created much of the dramatic intensity. Pinter never identified the nature of the threat yet there was never any doubt in either our minds or the character's mind that it existed. In each case the character is prey to unknown dangers, to unspoken threats and to an unpleasant fate. The characters live in fear because they do not know who they are. They have lost or never had any identity. Each lives in confined surroundings—suggesting that each is trying to escape life, to find a shelter. In each case the menace comes from without. The characters hope they have found an escape and, thus, the security they seek but, of course, they have not. The intruder finds them; there is no escape. Rose, Stanley, Edward clearly are victims. But left to our imagination—absolutely undetermined by Pinter—is the answer to the question "Who forces the threat?" "Who gives the order?" Goldberg, McCann and Stanley in *The Birthday Party* all speak of "the organization," evidently they know not only that it exists but that it is vastly powerful. Because we do not know who gives the order, and there are virtually no clues, Pinter has been able to create "an unnerving atmosphere of doubt and uncertainty . . . [which] helps to generalize and universalize the fears and tensions to which Pinter's characters are subject."[7] In the later plays the nature of the threat shifts: it no longer need come from without, and it no longer need act the role of an intruder. But the characters in the later plays feel just as threatened as the characters in the earlier works and for the same reason—they do not know who they are. The difference is that now the menace need not be a separate entity, an external force, for it may well exist in the mind of the character only. Parenthetically we might note that in the early plays violence accompanied the sense of menace; for the most part, violence has disappeared from the later plays. The conflict has moved from the threat from the outside world, from the organization, to a conflict of control. The struggle for control is seen clearly in *The Caretaker.* Mick seeks to remove Davies so that his relationship with his brother can continue without outside interference. Davies, in playing one brother against the other, is seeking to find security for himself, a place where

he can command. Aston, while a less dramatic example, nonetheless at the end of the play, will no longer tolerate Davies' attempt to usurp his place.

Another major motif is the problem of communication, a traditional problem. Playwrights for many years have stated that man has difficulty communicating with his fellow men. Pinter, however, looks at the problem in a somewhat different fashion, for of greater interest than the inability to communicate, the traditional position, is the unwillingness to communicate. This problem, of course, is quite apart from any consideration of ability. In addition to the evidence he has presented in his plays, Pinter has observed, "I feel that instead of any inability to communicate there is a deliberate evasion of communication. Communication itself between people is so frightening that rather than do that there is continual cross-talk, a continual talking about other things rather than what is at the root of their relationship."[8] Pinter relies very heavily on pause and silence in his plays. Both words are used in the texts to suggest different communication situations. The direction "pause" or the elipse is used to indicate pauses in a given speech which are supposed to be and, indeed, in performances are filled with non-verbal communication—that is to say that a kind of communication is taking place through the gesture and glance of one actor to another. The term "silence" is used to indicate no communication at all, a void.

> There are two silences. One when no word is spoken. The other when perhaps a torrent of language is being employed. This speech is speaking of a language locked beneath it. That is its continual reference. The speech we hear is an indication of that we don't hear. It is necessary avoidance, a violent, sly, anguished or mocking smokescreen which keeps the other in its place. When true silence falls we are still left with echo but are nearer nakedness. One way of looking at speech is to say it is a constant stratagem to cover nakedness.[9]

But still another observation must be made about Pinter's characters and the communication situation. John Russell Taylor has observed that although "no character really wants to communicate with the others in Pinter's plays he nearly always wants the others to communicate with him."[10]

Coupled with the problem of communication is Pinter's theory of non-verification.

> The desire for verification is understandable, but cannot always be satisfied. There are no hard distinctions between what is real and what is unreal, nor between what is true and what is false. The thing is not necessarily either true or false; it can be both true and false. The assumption that to verify what has happened and what is happening presents few problems, I take to be inaccurate. A character on the stage who can present no convincing argument or information as to his past experiences, his present behaviour or his aspirations, nor a comprehensive analysis of his motives is as legitimate and as worthy of attention as one who, alarmingly, can do all these things. The more acute the experiences the less articulate its expression.[11]

Without a doubt Pinter's statement sheds light on at least one major aspect of his dramaturgy. It is, of course, the antithesis of the orthodox dramaturgy of the well-made play type that has dominated the realistic drama since Ibsen. The technique of casting doubt upon everything by matching each clear and unequivocal statement with an equally clear and unequivocal statement to the contrary is found in all of the plays. The technique serves Pinter in three ways. First it demonstrates the difficulty one has with communication. Second it provides a realistic cast to the dialogue—and it is the dialogue more than any other element that permits some critics to classify him a realist. And thirdly, it creates the air of mystery and uncertainty (most often identified as menace) for which he has become so famous.

Some critics have observed that the question of verification, as well as the problem of character motivation, does not arise in the later plays although there is general agreement that both are significant factors in the early plays. It seems to me these critics are only partially correct. In some plays, admittedly the later ones, we are perhaps less interested in verifying what a character has said because of the nature of the play. Because the threat does not come from an undetermined external source, we feel perhaps that we do not need to comprehend or to verify what has been said; we accept it on face value. And it is just as well, because we cannot substantiate the information or arrive at a definitive statement about the characters in the later plays any more than we can for Stanley or Davies or Rose or anyone else. We should also note that we virtually never have the opportunity to probe the inner thoughts of a Pinter character. Some critics make the point that we get to know Aston in *The Caretaker* because of his speech at the end of act II. This soliloquy is often viewed in the traditional sense—that is as a stage convention used to reveal a character's inner thoughts. Pinter, however, warns us against this judgement. "And the one thing that people have missed is that it isn't necessary to conclude that everything Aston says about his experiences in the mental hospital is true."[12]

If the early plays emphasize the idea of menace, particularly the menace from the unknown, the later plays explore the conflict of will—the struggle for control, particularly as shown in both *The Caretaker* and *The Homecoming*. But the sense of menace, although diminished in the later plays, is still present, and the struggle for control is found in the earlier works although it is not emphasized.

The struggle to dominate may be understood more easily if we consider the three kinds of characters Pinter writes, i.e. assailants, victims, and bystanders. Pinter's interest in the last category, the bystander, is minimal and need not concern us. In the early plays the focus is almost entirely on the victims. But the force of the assailant and the control of the assailant are from an outer world and thus are unidentified. This constitutes the threat motif. In the later plays the assailant is a character we have seen; we see him function within the action of the play rather than

as an intrusion from outside or as the representative of some unidentified force, i.e. the organization. Because we know or we think we know him he appears as less of a threat. He becomes a real and identifiable force and one which the other characters can do combat with, as is the case in *The Homecoming.* For some critics the roles of victim/assailant are not all discrete, with several characters taking on dimensions of either role. The crucial question for these critics is who threatens whom. For those who see Ruth in *The Homecoming* as a whole person, who knows who she is and who accepts the various dimensions of her personality, mother, wife, and whore, there is no problem. It is Ruth who comes home and in doing so is in complete command. As such she poses a considerable threat to the male characters in the play. Ruth is absolutely sure of herself. At no point, either by action or statement, does she suggest she is lost. The only real threats that exist for her are the almost no contest struggle between herself and Max and herself and Lenny. Ruth, of course, wins hands down. She is whole; her mind and body constitute a single unit and there are no contradictions. She emerges the victor. The male who has not yet found his unity, his identity, remains fragmented and, therefore, is lost.

Understanding the kinds of play he writes, the devices he uses, and his thematic concern, of course, will not explicate any play. It does serve, however, as a beginning point for a discussion of Pinter which, unless there is an understanding of this overview. Pinter's *Weltanschauung,* may lead to a deadend and frustration. Thus the basic search in any play is for identification; the basic conflict is in terms of menace or control, and the basic theme is alienation via the loss of identity as exemplified by Stanley or a coming to knowledge through an acceptance of one's fate, via the knowledge of one's identity as exemplified by Ruth or Flora. The unknowable world of Pinter given these guideposts then can be explored and an understanding attained.

Notes

1. Harold Pinter, "Writing for the Theatre," *Evergreen Review,* 8 (1964) 80.

2. Pinter, p. 80.

3. Lawrence M. Bensky, "Harold Pinter: An Interview" *Paris Review,* No. 39 (January, 1967), pp. 36-37.

4. Pinter, p. 82.

5. Lois G. Gordon, *Stratagems to Uncover Nakedness: The Dramas of Harold Pinter,* Missouri Literary Frontiers Series, No. 6 (Columbia: University of Missouri Press, 1969), p. 2.

6. Pinter, pp. 80-81.

7. John Russell Taylor, *Anger and After: A Guide to the New British Drama* (London: University Paperback. Methmen, 1969), p. 328.

8. Taylor, p. 334.

9. Pinter, p. 82.

10. Taylor, p. 334.

11. Program note to the Royal Court production of "The Room" and "The Dumb Waiter," cited by Taylor, p. 339.

12. Bensky, p. 30.

Andrew K. Kennedy (essay date 1975)

SOURCE: "Pinter," in *Six Dramatists in Search of a Language: Studies in Dramatic Language,* Cambridge University Press, 1975, pp. 165-91.

[*In the following essay, Kennedy surveys Pinter's use of language, examining how he abstracts it from concrete meaning and makes language a dramatic rather than discursive element in his plays.*]

'I am pretty well obsessed with words when they get going', Pinter once said when an interviewer asked whether his creative imagination was not more visual than verbal. Pinter went on to stress the doubleness of drama: 'It is a matter of tying the words to the image of the character standing on the stage. The two things go very closely together.'[1] This dual stress is important, for Pinter has explored the whole scale of verbal-visual power in the different dramatic media: film scripts as well as plays for radio and television flank his major plays for the theatre. Yet one is entitled to single out that obsession with words. It is impossible to think of a Pinter play in terms of mime, for the groping attempt of two or more characters to mark out contested territory with indefinite words—as animals, we learn from Lorenz and Tinbergen, mark out territory with definite posture, movement, colour and sound—is central.[2] The new patterns of dialogue can be regarded as the principal interest in each play. All other interests—including structure and insight into character—are inseparable from the 'transactions' in the dialogue. Pinter has worked out his plays, and the plays work on us, through words.

On the level of artistic creation this means that Pinter has a particularly acute sense of the 'blank page' as 'both an exciting and frightening thing. It's what you start from.'[3] The words on the page *are* the shaping medium of the play, occasionally showing a strain of inbreeding, words multiplying words in scenes that seem autonomous.[4] On the level of 'audience impact' the words compel patient listening, attention to *how* things are being said, sometimes against *what* is being said. For certain patterns in a Pinter play may gain an almost hypnotic hold on ear or mind, even though they do not inform, have no emotional charge, and offer only neutral clues to the speaker.

On the linguistic level proper Pinter's dialogue is precise enough to provide samples for a work on the Varieties of Contemporary English; and the conversational rhythms alone could be used to train 'aural perception' in foreign students of spoken English. (It would be a much less mechanical primer than the one that inspired Ionesco's *The Bald Primadonna.*[5]) The precision is matched by the social-cultural range of the dialogue across Pinter's entire work (only once, in *The Homecoming,* within the texture of *one* play): from the 'non-standard' and inarticulate speech that keeps recurring in *The Room, The Dumb Waiter, The Birthday Party* and *The Caretaker,* to the euphemistic props of 'U-speech' in *A Slight Ache,* and to the sophisticated urban word-consciousness in plays like *The Collection, The Lover* and *Old Times.* Pinter has a facility for starting with a particular speech-style at a level of mimesis which Beckett found uncongenial and which Eliot could only achieve with strain. Yet a particular speech-style is not left 'to speak for itself', each is gradually made to exhibit its 'absurd' potentiality; the tramp's inarticulateness is intensified; the genteel phrases of Edward and Flora in *A Slight Ache* turn into a disturbed, mock-euphemistic litany by the end of the play; the mannered verbal games enacted by the married couple as adulterous lovers are underlined: 'To hear your command of contemporary phraseology, your delicate use of the very latest idiomatic expression, so subtly employed' (Richard in *The Lover,* p. 75). Not only is the dialogue 'idiomatic', it is saturated with idioms 'played' to show up their idiocy.[6] Similarly, jargon is used to draw attention to the misuse of language as a comic-aggressive smokescreen (Goldberg's cliché-patter, Mick's finance and interior-decorator terms; the academic jargon of Teddy, the cellar-manship of Duff).[7] The low slang in *The Homecoming* is arranged to sound as if the cloaca of language had been dredged to exhibit the 'underground' of ceremonious family talk. The words 'get going' with obsessive patterns.

One characteristic of Pinter's dramatic language has become so familiar that terms like 'Pinterish' and 'Pinteresque' have come to denote—as Ronald Hayman reminds us—the irrationality of everyday conversation, its 'bad syntax, tautologies, pleonasms, repetitions, *non sequiturs* and self-contradictions'. Hayman goes so far as to claim that 'Pinter has capitalised in a way that no playwright had ever done before . . . on the fact that real-life conversations don't proceed smoothly and logically from point to point.'[8] Pinter certainly is an innovator, yet it needs to be stressed that what is original in his dialogue is the fusion of the minimal language in naturalism (Chekhov) and the aesthetic expressiveness found in implicit speech from the Symbolists to Beckett.[9]

Most important of all: we experience—and can only experience—the plays through listening to the way everyday language gets deflected by—and the way it alienates—the speakers from one another. In James Boulton's words:

> Evocative or disturbing speech, language which is an accurate reflection of colloquial English and yet reflects the mystery that Pinter sees as an inevitable feature of human relationships: this is a starting point for a consideration of his vision. It leads directly to what is

perhaps the chief irony in his plays: the discrepancy between the implicit claim in any *patois* that it is the currency accepted and understood by all its users, and the dramatic fact that all such language in actual usage reveals not complete communication between man and man but their essential apartness.[10]

Pinter has, then, invented a drama of 'human relations at the level of language itself'. The phrase just quoted is taken from Jean Vannier's definition of what is really new in the theatre of Beckett and Ionesco: while the traditional theatre, says Vannier, presents 'psychological relationships which language only *translates*', in the new drama the characters' language is 'literally *exposed* upon the stage' so that there appears '*a theatre of language* where man's words are held up to us as a spectacle'.[11]

Yet Pinter stands in sharp contrast to Beckett and Ionesco.[12] Beckett—who seems to have been present at some latter-day Fall or Babel of literary language—has created his dialogue out of the stylised breakdown of hyper-literary styles.[13] Pinter, to develop the image, has taken the linguistic Babel for granted (perhaps too glibly at times) at the level of everyday exchanges, talk, chat, verbal games—with an ear for local usage, or rather abusage and verbiage. He seems to carry no literary 'burden of the past'. He has created his dialogue out of the failures of language that might occur *as* English is spoken, by frightened or evasive or sadistically playful characters. The words come much less from 'eavesdropping'[14]—that naive picture of the dramatist in the bus queue—than is sometimes supposed. The patterning in the dialogue frequently goes with violent or mannered distortion. Yet a Pinter character's speech can, eventually, be 'pinned down' to an identifiable person even when it is used to conceal identity. In sum, Pinter's dialogue tends to 'correspond' to what we hear outside the world of the play, even though it is made to 'cohere' with the overall rhythm of the play.

Consider a simple contrast, something like a paradigm. *The Caretaker* opens with a micro-naturalistically presented conversation between the host and the invited tramp (Aston and Davies) and after some Uuh-ing and Huh-ing the tramp bursts into this 'life-like' narrative: 'Ten minutes off for tea-break in the middle of the night in that place and I couldn't find a seat, not one. All them Greeks had it . . .' While *Waiting for Godot* begins with the stylised duologue of two literary tramps (or traditional clowns or questers) whose lines could be swapped around.[15] 'Nothing to be done'—Estragon's classical opening line—at once creates a 'gesture to the universe', with that literate non-personal passive voice. (No wonder that one down-to-earth producer insisted that the correct English must be 'Nothing doing'.[16]) Or take the exchange between Stella and James, the married couple in *The Collection* (1961), at one of the points where they are teasing out the verbal tangle created around Bill as a potential or hypothetical adulterous partner.

> STELLA: He dosn't matter.
>
> JAMES: What do you mean?

> STELLA: He's not important.
>
> JAMES: Do you mean anyone would have done? You meant it just happened to be him, but it might as well have been anyone?
>
> STELLA: No.
>
> JAMES: What then?
>
> STELLA: Of course it couldn't have been anyone. It was him. It was just . . . something . . .
>
> JAMES: That's what I mean. It was him. That's why I think he's worth having a look at. I want to see what he's like. It'll be instructive, educational.[17]

This sounds like a fusion of three areas of language: real-life conversation; conventional comedy of manners; and a certain elicitation technique (James's 'What do you mean? . . . Do you mean . . . You mean . . . That's what I mean'), suggesting a light parody of linguistic philosophers or 'linguisticians'. As conversation between a couple probing into their marital insecurity—with a slight comedy of manner sharpening—it is nearer to early scenes in Eliot's *The Cocktail Party* than to anything in Beckett. (It is, however, less rhetorical than the 'angry scene' verbal duel between Edward and Lavinia which we contrasted with Beckett's adulterous triangle.[18]) At the same time, James' questions amount to a language game, or, more exactly, Pinter makes use of a layman's half-knowing, half-playful semantic test: can these evasive words (which seem to say nothing yet may imply too much: 'It was him . . . It was just . . . something . . .') be pinned down, can they 'mean' an action? How different is Hamm's broken, still religious quest for meaning in *Endgame*—a question placed between Clov's report of a 'zero' sun and a surviving flea—'We're not beginning to . . . to . . . mean something?' A speculative question derided by Clov: 'Mean something! You and I mean something?' For Beckett 'the meaning of meaning' is ontological, a leftover quest for essence; for Pinter it is linguistic, word-clues crossing word-clues.[19]

In the present context what matters is to see that the texture of Pinter's dramatic language is quite different from Beckett's. Yet clearly this is related to other important differences which can only be listed here. The structure of many Pinter plays—notably *The Caretaker* and *The Homecoming*—can be plotted as a half-submerged but otherwise forward-moving action (*implicit* exposition, denouement, and so on), while Beckett's plays turn in a static-perennial cycle. A Pinter character can nearly always be extrapolated (the dots can be connected to draw a familiar figure, as in the child's puzzle), and hours can be spent discussing quite traditional questions of motive and psychological interaction. The time-scale for a Pinter play can be measured by the clock; there are no 'timeless moments', and no openings to time lost beyond redemption. Pinter's silences are perfectly timed to fit characterisation and to create a rhythm, but we do not feel—as we do in Beckett—that language is created out of a silence that is, in the end, all-consuming. (Though *Landscape* and even more *Silence* are Pinter's attempt at reaching this dimension.)

In sum, Pinter has little of Beckett's intense 'metaphysical' anguish; and, again, little of the sheer intensity of feeling—that to speak is to suffer and that all language is exhausted. But Pinter has learnt to exploit his own sense of language-nausea:

> Such a weight of words confronts us day in, day out, words spoken in contexts such as this, words written by me and by others, the bulk of it stale and dead terminology; ideas endlessly repeated and permutated, become platitudinous, trite, meaningless. Given this nausea, it's very easy to be overcome by it and step back into paralysis. I imagine most writers know something of this paralysis. But if it is possible to confront this nausea, to follow it to its hilt, then it is possible to say something has occurred, that something has been achieved.[20]

In his most authentic work Pinter succeeds in just that: in 'making something occur' out of the felt paralysis of words. He can re-create the rhythms of difficult or failing utterance with a detached, almost ego-empty method of writing, in a dialogue 'not subjected to false articulation'. This is a specialised, reduced version of one of the aims of classical naturalism:

> Given characters who possess a momentum of their own, my job is not to impose upon them, not to subject them to false articulation, by which I mean forcing a character to speak where he could not speak, of making him speak of what he could never speak.[21]

Paradoxically, the pursuit of this aim can also lead Pinter to indulgent pattern-making, and mannerism.[22] (I have refrained from using capital M, though in using this term here and elsewhere I do have in mind the style which has been so clearly identified in the realm of pre-Baroque architecture and painting, and applied in literature to the study of Metaphysical and Modernist poetry. The main point is that Mannerism is not just the sum total of 'mannerisms', but an inherent and consistent tendency to exploit 'conceits', linguistic complexity or modish *jeux d'esprit,* which a 'sophisticated' public can be expected to understand and enjoy. At the same time Mannerism is clearly parasitical on an earlier 'classical' art: it can develop 'line by line' or through richly ambiguous local scenes and texture only because the underlying structure is grasped with reference to an earlier form—in Pinter's case classical naturalism.)

In the early plays (as in **The Room**) it is the patterns of 'non-communication' that sometimes become decorative or facile. In the later plays, particularly in the 'sophisticated' television plays, the verbal games with their 'intriguing' sexual ambiguity are too dependent on the linguistic equivalent of 'suspense'—once the code is deciphered, we are left with a cliché.

Yet the progression of Pinter's work as a whole shows a determination to avoid cliché and self-repetition. Each of the four major stage plays has attempted to do something different—and the urge to innovate, to re-create the language in and for each new play is something Pinter shares with Eliot and Beckett. Pinter keeps renewing his dramatic form and language, at the cost of what looks like increasing critical self-consciousness. He himself has complained of the relative difficulty of writing **The Homecoming** and when that play was written he felt once more: 'I want to write a play, it buzzes all the time in me, and I can't put pen to paper.'[23] He connects this with the difficulty of avoiding 'the searchlights' in contrast with his direct concern with *writing*—'completely unselfconsciously'—when he wrote his first three plays. We may assume that writing against 'the searchlights' means, among other things, the dramatist writing with intensified stylistic consciousness: aware of his own achieved work—and the public's attitude to it—as something inhibiting (the taboo on repetition colliding with the expectation of something 'Pinteresque'). But in the narrower sense of scrupulous attention to the words on the page Pinter has been a highly self-conscious writer from the outset. The price is recurrent mannerism. The achievement: the shaping of an essentially mimetic dialogue towards a new kind of expressiveness in a 'theatre of language'.

PINTER'S 'DOUBLE THING': SHAPES FOR LISTENING

Ideas concerning his own dramatic language take up a good third of Pinter's tentative yet firmly thought-out article 'Writing for the Theatre'.[24] There are comments here on the ambiguity of dialogue, on the growth of language out of human indeterminacy, out of what is 'inexpressive, elusive, evasive, obstructive, unwilling' in the characters. This goes with a conscious exploration of a 'language where under what is said another thing is being said'. These points define genuine discoveries, and they remain essential keys to Pinter's dialogue. But so much has been heard of these ideas in our over-communicative time that they have become critical commonplaces (Pinter's 'failure of communication', 'subtext').[25] There is need for new questions, and a fresh inquiry, and it might as well start with a neglected point from Pinter's statement on playwriting:

> The function of selection and arrangement is mine. I do all the donkeywork, in fact, and I think I can say I pay meticulous attention to the shape of things, from the shape of a sentence to the overall structure of the play. This shaping, to put it mildly, is of the first importance. But I think a double thing happens. You arrange *and* you listen, following the clues you leave for yourself, through the characters.[26]

Just how does this 'double thing' happen—in particular dialogue sequences and across a whole play? How does Pinter solve the tension between 'spontaneity' and 'design' in language? In the context of this study this is to test, once more, a persistent tension in post-naturalist drama: between the diffuseness and fragmented banality of most 'conversation', and the need for dialogue to concentrate and express, to quicken the beat in the action—so that in under two hours a pattern of experience may be felt upon our pulses. There is here an affinity between Pinter's 'double thing' and Eliot's early hope for 'a new form . . . out of colloquial speech' (first attempted in *Sweeney Agonistes*). But Pinter has no interest in formal 'verse drama', and he seems to be free from the pains of Eliot's linguistic dualism: that partial taboo on 'the language of the tribe', the hollowness of words against the Word.[27]

We may first define the two poles of Pinter's dramatic language: moving from the seeming record of eavesdropping towards rhythmic abstraction. One can point to two distinct, as it were nuclear, styles, to be seen at their simplest in Pinter's revue sketches (each sketch being homogeneous enough to make us perceive the 'shape' of the dialogue instantly). Contrast, for example, the rambling, inane, yet humanly authentic conversation of two old women in an all-night café:

SECOND: Yes, there's not too much noise.

FIRST: There's always a bit of noise.

SECOND: Yes, there's always a bit of life.

(where the pattern is woven 'along with' and 'from within' the conversation) with the comic-parodic build-up of the cross-examination of the Applicant by a secretary, equipped with nerve-testing electrodes and earphones:

After a day's work do you ever feel tired? Edgy? Fretty? Irritable? At a loose end? Morose? Frustrated? Morbid? Unable to concentrate? Unable to sleep? Unable to eat? Unable to remain seated? Unable to remain upright? Lustful? Indolent? On heat? Randy? Full of desire? Full of energy? Full of dread? Drained? of energy, of dread? of desire?[28]

The applicant is caught up in a crescendo of bewilderment, he 'can't get a word in edgeways', and finally collapses—after trying to cover up his earphones—to the sound of drum-beat, cymbal, trombone and a piercing buzz. Such a simple situational convention (aptly called, in relation to Pinter's early plays, 'comedy of menace') is enough to enable Pinter to exploit the energies of rhythmic formalisation, in this instance a question-catalogue.

In *The Dumb Waiter* (a one-act play, much more complex than any revue sketch, but more immediately 'transparent' than any of the major plays) the guided inconsequentiality of the dialogue between Ben and Gus is transformed into a sharper pattern when—following the comic food orders received through the dumb waiter—the speaking tube is introduced. That ill-functioning instrument of communication 'dictates' a parodic ritual, with its own rhythm of pauses, as Ben listens, holds the tube to his ear and to his mouth, alternately:

BEN: The Eccles cake was stale.

The chocolate was melted.

The milk was sour.

GUS: What about the crisps?

BEN: The biscuits were mouldy.

Well, we're very sorry about that.

What? What? Yes. Yes. Yes certainly. Certainly. Right away.[29]

Such 'shapes for listening' are several removes from casual conversation, from some putative 'tape-recording ear'. (One could make a rough analogy: Pinter's speaking tube is nearer to Eliot's telephone in *Sweeney Agonistes*[30] in its function than to the concealed tape-recorder of the descriptive linguist.) And it can hardly be an accident that it is immediately after the little food-litany induced by the unseen and unheard presence in the speaking tube that the play reaches a rhythmic crescendo: the ritualistic reiteration of orders:

Shut the door behind him.

Shut the door behind him.

Without divulging your presence.

Without divulging my presence (. . .)

[A]nd the anguished litany of the victim's unanswered questions (ending with 'What's he playing these games for?').[31]

Through his entire work Pinter has been working out different kinds of dialogue 'shaping'. In the early plays, particularly in *The Birthday Party, The Dumb Waiter* and *A Slight Ache,* quasi-ritualistic patterns are used repeatedly to give a rhythmic intensity to climactic scenes. Yet the rhythms of ritual—responses, catechismic cross-examination, litanies—are used parodistically or playfully to dehumanise speech. (One is reminded of what Huizinga said about the *formal* similarity of 'ritual' and 'play': 'Formally speaking there is no distinction between marking out space for a sacred purpose and marking it out for sheer play.'[32]) Then, in *The Caretaker*—as I shall try to show—a language of lived encounter is created out of the fragmented speech of two inarticulate persons: Aston and Davies set against the sadistically elaborate jargon-speeches of Mick. To that extent *The Caretaker* is Pinter's most valuable achievement in unified 'listening' and 'shaping', in fusing the human and abstract attributes of dramatic language.

'Design' is more palpably or ingeniously imposed in all the later plays, in which we may distinguish three dominant interests, pressing to shape the dialogue. There is the ritualised interplay between decorum and scatological violence in *The Homecoming* (the language of the tribe in para-animal display within one family). Then there are the highly patterned, though colloquially based, verbal games people play,[33] taken from and presented to a psychosexually 'sophisticated', knowing society: in *The Collection* and *The Lover* (1961, 1963), later in *The Tea Party* and *The Basement* (1965, 1967), all originally written for television, and so exploiting visual clues (devices of close-up, mixing, fading and quick scene-shift) to intensify the omission of verbal clues. In all these plays the conventional comedy of manners is 're-packaged' as a modish language of hints and guesses, nourished by the energies of imagined or potential adultery. Such patterns of verbal fantasy and near-farcical titillation make up much of the texture of **Old Times** (1971), where the mannerist dialogue—the many-coloured bubbles of talk from three corners of the triangle—is shaped to re-enact a still unpurged trauma, with gathering intensity. The third way of shaping dialogue can be seen in the 'word-painting' and 'sound-painting' patterns of **Landscape** and **Silence** (1968, 1969): a semi-abstract scoring of speech fragments in a small-scale 'musical' design, as precise as Webern or Boulez.

I propose to discuss the essential features in this spectrum of styles by concentrating on three full-length plays—**The Birthday Party, The Caretaker** and **The Homecoming**—and then looking at the 'new direction' in **Landscape** and **Silence.**

When **The Birthday Party** was first performed,[34] critical response included the feeling that there was a violent yet imperfectly controlled style-switch in the play. This seemed to amount to an abrupt change from microscopic naturalism (typified by the opening exchanges of Meg and Pete on cornflakes and 'nice bits' from the newspaper), to highly stylised 'absurdist' patterns reaching a climax in the Goldberg-MacCann brainwashing patter of Act II, and the final incantation with its orchestrated clichés in Act III. The two styles then actually seemed to work negatively against one another, instead of creating a theatrical counterpoint: for Stanley's situation as a persecuted and guilty figure was never worked out on the human level 'promised' by the seeming naturalism, while the Goldberg-MacCann variations stood out too blatantly as an already familiar theatre style. Now, with repeated hearing and reading, one can see that Pinter does in fact control his 'two styles' with skill, but the controls are precariously dependent on performers (and auditors) having learned the 'codes' of early Pinter. And, in later plays, Pinter developed a subtler and more unified 'shaping' for the dialogue.

One way in which Pinter controls the two styles can only be appreciated when seeing the play whole—in practice, seeing it twice or reading it backwards. One then sees, with sudden clarity, that the 'ordinary' conversational opening and ending are a frame for, a connivance at, the 'extraordinary' events in the house. The empty, natural-seeming but denatured talk—which goes with stupor, with Meg's sentimental naiveté and Pete's good-natured impotence—makes the atrocious inquisition possible.

Another kind of control turns on emphasis. Take, for example, the phrase 'This house is on the list', repeated like a *leitmotif* four times, in increasingly alarming contexts, and amounting to gradual intensification. First we have the casual-seeming exchange between Meg and Pete:

> MEG: This house is on the list.
>
> PETE: It is.
>
> MEG: I know it is.

The pattern is next used in a teasing exchange between Meg and Stanley, when the latter is trying to cast doubt on Meg's talk of 'visitors':

> STANLEY: (. . .) I'm your visitor.
>
> MEG: You're a liar. The house is on the list.
>
> STANLEY: I bet it is.
>
> MEG: I know it is.

And it re-emerges in Stanley's first anxious questioning about the visitors ('Why?' 'This house is on the list.' 'But who are they?') and in his panicky questions after the arrival of Goldberg and MacCann:

> STANLEY: (*turning*) But why here? Why not somewhere else?
>
> MEG: This house is on the list.
>
> STANLEY: (*coming down*) What are they called? What are their names?[35]

On the simplest level these are just signals (don't miss 'the list'—it is sinister like a 'black list'.) But something else is also happening: the gradual stylisation—in the last two examples an insistent, 'catechismic' questioning—prepare the way for the fully stylised ritual inquisition later in the play.

Then there is the rather simple yet often effective heightening: the chain of idiomatic—and idiosyncratic—phrases, where the 'chain' amounts to a stylised verbal smoke-screen, what Pinter himself calls that other silence, a 'torrent of language'.[36] Here is Goldberg, on arrival in the house:

> (*sitting at table*) The secret is breathing. Take my tip. It's a well known fact. Breathe in, breathe out, take a chance, let yourself go, what can you lose? Look at me. When I was an apprentice yet, MacCann, every second Friday of the month my Uncle Barney used to take me to the seaside, regular as clockwork, Brighton, Canvey Island, Rottingdean—Uncle Barney wasn't particular. After lunch on Shabbus we'd go and sit in a couple of deck chairs—you know the ones with canopies—we'd have a little paddle, we'd catch the tide coming in, going out, the sun coming down—golden days, believe me MacCann.. . .
>
> (Act I, p. 27)

We recognise here, on the naturalistic level, the complacent clichés and rhythms of a semi-educated Jewish dealer with a flair for 'flannelling'. ('What can you lose?', and the raconteur's use of *would*: 'on Shabbus we'd go . . .') Yet it is highly patterned, and the cumulative effect of Goldberg's speeches (and they tend to dominate the play) is to parody a type of culture-patter: the sinister complacencies of the successful Head of Family and Business. So a highly individual language is used to expose the way elements in our language compel conformity. In Act II the function of Goldberg's speeches is quite clear: the farcical paean about the joys of boyhood ('I'd tip my hat to the toddlers . . .')

and the fit man's cheerful waking to sunshine ('all the little birds, the smell of grass, church bells, tomato juice . . .') amount to a verbal limbering up for the verbal torture of Stanley; and the birthday celebration speeches, after the inquisition inflicted on the victim, are experienced as a black ritual.[37] But by Act III Goldberg's patterned loquacity becomes more arbitrary. In particular, Goldberg's speeches when left alone with MacCann seem to have little function apart from 'creating a scene' and reinforcing the cultural bankruptcy of Goldberg through making him mouth a medley of slogans—Judaic, British and miscellaneous culture-props—with the dramatic breakdown over 'Because I believe': logorrhoea into vacancy. There is a strong local interest here but the connection with the context of the whole play is tenuous. It is, more than anything else, a verbal and rhythmic bravura act.[38]

In the cross-examination of Stanley, and, even more clearly, in the Goldberg-MacCann incantation in the penultimate scene of the play, we see the extent of Pinter's attraction to the patterns and rhythms of ritual—apparently without wishing to evoke (as Eliot wished to do)[39] a primitive or sacred rhythm of sacrifice. Nor do these scenes have the human pressure—the political—religious terror—which we find in such a work as *Darkness at Noon,* and in authentic documents of persecution. The pressure is induced through rhythmic intensification, through the paralysing spell of a disconnected language, for example the jump from random cliché-questions to random fantasy-questions ('What about the Albigensenist heresy? / Who watered the wicket at Melbourne?'). But the cross-examination scene at least externalises that sense of 'meaningless proceedings' which Kafka's K.[40]—never interrogated—so resents. The final incantation is, however, more gratuitous:

GOLDBERG: We'll watch over you.

MacCANN: Advise you.

GOLDBERG: Give you proper care and treatment.

MacCANN: Let you use the club bar.

GOLDBERG: Keep a table reserved.

MacCANN: Help you acknowledge the fast days.

GOLDBERG: Bake you cakes.

followed by those spell-unbinding parodic responses: 'We'll provide the skipping rope. / The vest and pants. / The ointment. / The hot poultice. / The fingerstall. / The abdomen belt. / The ear plugs. / The baby powder . . .'

We do respond here to the violent parody of institutionalised caring. But the detail of the mumbo-jumbo is so far-fetched (or farcical) that it is only in performance—through the image of the helpless victim and his reduction to gurgling speechlessness—that we connect this ritual with any pattern of felt persecution. The 'shaping' is preponderant, the texture of the language mannerist.

The only difference between *The Birthday Party* and *The Caretaker,* Pinter has pertly suggested, is that in the latter he has cut out the dashes and used dots instead. Neither dash nor dot can be heard in performance, yet the critics can 'tell a dot from a dash a mile off'.[41] One may not always be sure about those dots, but one can see a difference: in *The Caretaker* Pinter moves much nearer to dialogue 'in character'. The shaping is now all in the gradual intensification of the given—ultra-naturalistic—language; it is inseparable from the structure of the play. Moreover, such patterning is used for quite traditional aims: to express a character's life on the stage through speech—speech that is the signature of a mind, unmistakable, unique, even if it takes some time to decipher. So even the dots (those graphic-psychological-musical signs) are used and developed in the two patterns of hesitancy which meet, interact, and part company in the verbal encounter of Davies and Aston. For most of Act I these two characters are interlocked in a groping conversational exploration of one another, which reaches its first intensity when Aston offers the tramp a bed to sleep in:

DAVIES: How long for?

ASTON: Till you . . . get yourself fixed up.

DAVIES: (*sitting*) Ay well, that . . .

ASTON: Get yourself sorted out . . .

DAVIES: Oh, I'll be fixed up . . . pretty soon now . . .

This between two pauses; and the whole sequence takes up about a quarter of an hour of slow playing time. (Pp. 16-21. The effect of tempo is an essential factor in the rhythmic structure.) The pattern is further intensified—the groping reaches its own regressive climax—in Act II, when Davies is offered the job of caretaker:

ASTON: Well, there's things like the stairs . . . and the . . . the bells . . .

DAVIES: But it'd be a matter . . . wouldn't it . . . it'd be a matter of a broom . . . isn't it?

ASTON: You could have a duster . . .

DAVIES: Oh, I know I could have that . . . but I couldn't manage without a . . . without a broom . . . could I?

ASTON: You'd have to have a broom . . .

DAVIES: That's it . . . that's just what I was thinking . . .

ASTON: I'd be able to pick one up for you, without much trouble . . . and of course, you'd . . . you'd need a few brushes.

DAVIES: You'd need implements . . . you see . . . you'd need a good few implements . . .

ASTON: I could teach you how to use the electrolux, if you . . . wanted to learn . . .

DAVIES: Ah, that'd be . . .

(p. 45)

Out of context, this looks like the simple stylisation of comedy—underscoring the fumbling style of two 'hesitators'. But in the movement of the whole play this is taken further, to reveal—through that groping for clues, through the linguistic pattern—the hidden psychological pattern: Aston's pathological slowness after electric current treatment; Davies' paranoid suspiciousness. But the essential point is this: we continue to experience—to 'work out'—all this through the language; we listen to the words *as* symptoms, the diagnosis or aetiology is contributed by us. There is a double movement. Aston, in his ill-timed confession about mental illness, re-creates the feel of breakdown (as if speaking out of his illness and not after it). The pattern of hesitancy is at the same time movingly transformed at the end of Act II:

> They used to come round with these . . . I don't know what they were . . . they looked like big pincers, with wires on, the wires were attached to a little machine. It was electric. They used to hold a man down, and this chief . . . the chief doctor, used to fit them on either side of the man's skull. There was a man holding the machine, you see, and he'd . . . he'd do something . . . I can't remember now whether he pressed a switch or turned something, just a matter of switching the current . . . I suppose it was.. . . .
>
> (p. 59)

Against this, there is the transformation in Davies: the manic fluency of his 'pecking' speeches (when he thinks he can exploit the sickness of Aston, his benefactor) culminating in the rhythms of violent rejection, in the long outburst that ends with 'I never been inside a nuthouse!' Then, with the punitive intervention of Mick[42] and the expulsion of Davies, his wave of fluency breaks again, and the play ends—in a complete fusion of the psychic and rhythmic pattern—with the tramp's broken words.

In **The Homecoming,** the next major play, there is a shift away from the human-artistic balance of **The Caretaker**—to greater ingenuity in the 'shaping', with a language at once more violent and more mannered. A black family ritual—the initiation of the new mother-whore, with all due ambivalence—provides the climax for the meeting between hosts and homecomers; and the action—more indirect, more fragmented, and more dependent on gradual clue-assemblage than the earlier plays—is almost entirely verbal. True, one character, Ruth, warns her stage audience that her lips move and 'Perhaps the fact that they move is more significant . . . than the words which come through them' (pp. 52-3). But words are used to underscore those lips, and for the rest, every character is a speech-maker. Pinter himself has implied that there is less 'writing' (in the sense of wordy or gratuitous writing) in this play than in **The Birthday Party** or **The Caretaker,** saying that it is the only play that comes 'near to a structural entity which satisfies me'.[43] But we may add that this 'structural entity' goes with a highly elaborate texture woven out of the dehumanising abuses of speech.

The ritualised language of the family lies at the centre of the play, and it is arranged in broadly juxtaposed patterns

of ceremony and its violation.[44] It can best be seen in Max's schizoid-seeming shifts from the language of celebration to verbal defecation (and the other way round). There is something like a key-change at the end of Act I when Max suddenly switches from the abuse of Ruth as a whore ('We've had a smelly scrubber in my house all night. We've had a stinking pox-ridden slut in my house all night.') to the mother-ceremony ('You a mother? . . . How many you got?') and then to the father-ceremony: 'You want to kiss your old father? Want a cuddle with your old father? . . . You still love your old Dad, eh? . . . He still loves his father!' The repetition, the rhythmic intensity—as much as the change from bawdy to baby-talk—alerts us. By the opening of Act II the contraries become quite clear. Max's long, decorative speech (that rare thing, a subtle, comic pastiche) intensifies the ceremony: 'Well, it's a long time since the whole family was together, eh? If only your mother was alive . . .'

The speech (too long to quote in full) draws on a whole thesaurus of sentimental clichés in its evocation of 'fine grown-up lads', 'a lovely daughter-in-law', grandchildren who—if only they were present and Jessie, the first mother-figure, were alive—would be 'petted', cooed over', 'fussed over', 'tickled'. The mother-figure herself taught the 'boys' 'every single bit of the moral code they live by', she was 'the backbone of this family . . . with a will of iron, a heart of gold and a mind', to be attended in her lifetime with tribal ceremonies:

> she put her feet up on the pouffe and I said to her, Jessie, I think our ship is going to come home, I'm going to treat you to a couple of items, I'm going to buy you a dress in corded blue silk, heavily encrusted in pearls, and for casual wear, a pair of pantaloons in lilac flowered taffeta. Then I gave her a drop of cherry brandy. I remember the boys came down, in their pyjamas, all their hair shining, their faces pink, it was before they knelt down at our feet, Jessie's and mine. I tell you, it was like Christmas.

The counter-images follow at once, in the just as elaborately patterned, and comically violent, speech abusing his brother Sam and the whole 'crippled family, three bastard sons, a slutbitch of a wife', with retroactive curses (pp. 44-51). There follows an immediate switch-back to the celebration of the homecoming pair—as if they were newly wed and in need of paternal blessing—in an almost orientally ornate tone (beginning 'But you're my own flesh and blood . . .'). Such sudden switches not only make up a whole scene but clarify the 'shaping' in the play; and they foreshadow Max's final great contraries, the wish to expel and then incorporate the new mother—whore:[45]

> A.: Where's the whore? Still in bed? She'll make us all animals.
>
> B.: But you . . . Ruth . . . you're not only lovely and beautiful, but you're kin. You're kith. You belong here.

The point to stress here is that these rites of transformation are enacted entirely through *naming,* through a switch in the evocative range, as if using language magically. This resembles the way Othello transforms Desdemona's room into a brothel by going through the 'appropriate' gestures and naming (*Othello*, IV, ii, 24-96). But in *The Homecoming* the to-and-fro shifts of language cumulatively create a playful mood, a series of *as if* situations or simulated transformations, including the central transformation of the home into a family brothel. The effect is that of 'op art': rapidly flickering style signals which yield this or that pattern, depending on the angle of vision. It is only in retrospect that the spectator or reader can see that each of those shifts in language has been as precisely coded as traffic signals—green into red and so on—and it is only then that the 'shaping', and with it the meaning of the play, is seen.

This account underlines the virtuosity—and the mannerism, once more—in the structure and texture of the dialogue. And there are other aspects of the dialogue that support this reading. First, the excessive use of pastiche not so much in Max's speeches just discussed, as in Lenny's. There are too many of these, and it is only late in the play that we are able to make the connection between the pimp and the style-monger. Then we see the point of these appropriately centreless pastiches: the facility in assuming any tone, in using words seductively, as in the three 'stories' of his initial encounter with Ruth in Act I (pp. 28-33), or in the manner of a glossy ad, as in the taunting of Ted in Act II (p. 64). Secondly, conventional comedy-of-manner lines seem to be over-distributed. Max's manic slips of the tongue ('I gave birth to three grown men.'—p. 40) and comic antithesis ('I've never had a whore under this roof before. Ever since your mother died.'—p. 42) match his ornate ceremony speeches; and Lenny's elaborate inquiry into the facts of his conception (p. 36), may be justified as father-baiting; but even a deliberately low-toned and barely articulate character like Joey becomes a goonish phrase-maker on sexual intercourse, ringing speculative changes on 'going the whole hog' (rising to 'Now and again . . . you can be happy . . . without going any hog at all').

Cumulatively, such effects tilt the play too far towards parody and away from empathy or the shock of recognition. There is a 'too-muchness' on the surface. This may be the price of an over-conscious ingenuity in the post-naturalist idiom of the play, where the links between the overall shape and the detail of the dialogue are deliberately teasing and tenuous.

The compensating achievement of the play is the subtly worked out counterpoint which brings different kinds of dehumanised speech into collusion. The grossly perverted vernacular of Max and Lenny is balanced by the homogenised academic jargon of Teddy, which goes with an attitude ('It's a question of how far you can operate on things'), and provides a stylistic clue (the only one we get) to his at once clinically detached and voyeurish connivance at his wife's imagined prostitution. Between these two patterns hovers Ruth, whose gradual transformation is shown through the transformation in her language: from the slow, desultory marital conversation of her arrival, to the seductive innuendos and the fragmented story of her modelling in the two key encounters with Lenny, and then, at the end of the play, switching to the farcically clear-cut mercenary jargon of her professional terms, a mark of triumphant self-assertion. In the final effect, the play language of a comedy of manners is weighted by the cumulative imagery of flesh: Max's butcher-talk, Lenny's pimp-talk. Their scatological invective saturates the play with an almost Jacobean exposure to corruption of the body, and its vocal organ—the tongue.[46] And after such exposure Pinter is flexible enough to end the play with what comes over as an authentic human voice: 'I'm not an old man. Do you hear? Kiss me.' moans Max, crawling on the floor as his verbal fantasies collapse.

After *The Homecoming* Pinter turned from such large-scale and complex shaping to scene-plays with minute inner 'shaping' in the dialogue of *Landscape* and *Silence* (and the bagatelle *Night*). It seems clear that the miniature scale—probably influenced by Beckett's late plays for radio[47]—has been deliberately chosen so that the musical and rhythmic pattern—the sound of words emerging out of timed pauses and silences—may be played out, may become the play.

Despite the general move towards a 'musicalising' of language *Landscape* still has a clear, *dramatic* counterpoint: the interweaving of the two contrasted voices of Beth and Duff.[48] The classic female/male 'Yin and Yang' opposites provide the overall design; and it is worked out on every level—structure, image and rhythm.

Beth's interior monologue—almost psychotically withdrawn and regressive—reconstructs the fragmented memory of gentle love-making in the sand; Duff—addressing Beth and unsuccessfully attempting to engage her in colloquy (p. 21)—moves from two aggressively recounted episodes (a walk with the dog, an argument in the pub) to the fantasy of violently possessing Beth in the hall, against the banging of a gong. They are antithetical in every utterance: she is all inwardness, he a verbal Tarquin.

Their opposed 'stories' and psychic patterns are communicated through indirect 'word-painting', or through one of the basic principles of drawing invoked by Beth: 'as objects intercepting the light cast shadows' (pp. 27-8). Beth's words are taken from a 'landscape' of lyrical images: sea, sand, unremembered faces, light touch of arm and neck or withdrawal from touch, standing in the mist, in the sun; while Duff talks of walking through the 'racket' made by the birds, on paths covered 'with all kinds of shit' before he gets to boasting of his cellarmanship, of forcing Beth after violent complaining and swearing. In places the rhythmic pattern clearly supports this divergent 'duet'. For example:

> BETH: Still misty, but thinner, thinning.
>
> DUFF: The bung is on the vertical, in the bunghole. Spile the bung. Hammer the spile through the centre of

the bung. That lets the air through the bung, down the bunghole, lets the beer breathe.

BETH: Wetness all over the air. Sunny. Trees like feathers.

(p. 25)

where Duff's aggressive jargon, with its emphatic stress on action words and on 'bung' (the repetition, the plosives, the back vowels, the suggestion of dung and bang, the slang sense, all working together) is intercepted by Beth's low-toned and broken phrases, with their sibilants and front vowels. The two patterns culminate in the poetic inversions and vocatives given to Beth at the end of the play, while the rhythmic crescendo of Duff's verbal attack can only be shouted or barked. The nine silences—one of them marked *long* silence—insulate the speakers from one another, and create an inner space in the 'soundscape'— time for the inwardness of Beth's words to work on the listener.[49]

Silence lacks this contrapuntal strength. The dream-like 'stream of consciousness' that is only one part in the opposed voices of *Landscape* is now extended to two speakers—to Rumsey, the older man, and Ellen—and the more violent slangy language of Bates tends to get submerged in the dominant minor mode. ('I walk in my mind. But can't get out.'—p. 39). The shaping of the whole playlet is intricate. There are three fragmented sequences, each giving the 'tone' of a mind; three episodes are enacted in minimal dialogue; and in the final section the memory-fragments are further fragmented and re-played until the three tones are gradually diminished and engulfed by silence. It makes good listening; and it does suggest the gradual fade-out of memory or the conversion of 'events' into barely traceable verbal smudges in the mind. Yet, it lacks the subjective power—the sense of suffered action— which gives even Beckett's most abstract pieces (from *Play* to *Cascando*) an emotional immediacy. So, even though Pinter retains his mastery of concrete words—the mental landscapes, for example, can be visualised, the residual dialogue might be 'overheard'—it is as if the play had been written for the sake of the rhythmic pattern.

Landscape and *Silence* can be seen as a concentration—or distillation—of Pinter's concern for 'shaping', both as overall design and as insistent patterns of sound and rhythm. At the same time these plays point, once more, to one of the polar extremes of modern drama: the 'infolding' of language, at once reduced and musicalised, within a miniature play. The urge against explicit or rhetorical language which was first expressed by the Symbolist poets ('De la musique avant toute chose')[50] and by certain modern novelists ('I begin to long for some little language . . . broken words, inarticulate words . . .' says a character in *The Waves*)[51] has finally found expression in a carefully limited dramatic language.

Notes

1. 'Harold Pinter Replies', *New Theatre Magazine* (Jan. 1961), p. 9.

2. A similar analogy is offered by Ronald Hayman in *Harold Pinter*, London, 1969, p. 91. (It occurred to me independently.)

3. 'Between the Lines', *The Sunday Times* (4 March 1962), p. 25, subsequently published in a revised form as 'Writing for the Theatre', *Evergreen Review* (Aug.-Sept. 1964), pp. 80-3. All further references will be to the second version.

4. Pinter himself says: 'Too many words irritate me sometimes, but I can't help them, they just seem to come out—out of the fellow's mouth. I don't really examine my words too much, but I am aware that quite often in what I write some fellow at some point says an awful lot.' Interview with Lawrence Bensky, *The Paris Review*, no. 39 (Fall 1966), p. 26. Cf. Shaw on letting 'the play write itself and shape itself', Ch. 1, p. 75. See also Richard Schechner's unqualified gloss on Pinter as the 'disinterested artist . . . He is meticulous in scenic structure and dialogue for their own sake.' 'Puzzling Pinter', *Tulane Drama Review* (Winter 1966), p. 184.

5. The contrast can be tested by setting the banal conversational opening of, say, *The Dumb Waiter* or *The Collection* against the opening scene of *La Cantatrice chauve*. Pinter's patterns, though 'empty', are at once casual-seeming and humanly authentic. Ionesco *starts* with the denatured logic of language, the talking machine. Cf. also 'La Tragédie du langage', *Notes et contre-notes*, Paris, 1962, pp. 155-60. The essay confirms Ionesco's primary interests: 'la démarche tout à fait cartésienne de l'auteur de mon manuel d'anglais' and 'les automatismes de langage', for example. By contrast Pinter *starts* with a seemingly 'raw' language, as if untouched by schooling. See also n. 12.

6. Some examples: the idiom-catalogue of Edward on his wife in *A Slight Ache* (p. 24); Ben and Gus in sustained dispute over the phrase 'light the kettle' in *The Dumb Waiter* (pp. 47-8); Bill fencing with James over the extent to which he is a 'wow' at parties in *The Collection* (p. 22); or the variations rung on 'going the whole hog' in *The Homecoming* (p. 68) until Joey concludes that 'Now and again . . . you can be happy . . . without going any hog at all.' See also Martin Esslin's amusing account of 'Pinter Translated', *Encounter* (March 1968), and *Brief Chronicles*, pp. 190-5. The translators' howlers are all due to Pinter's dialogue being steeped in English idioms. Cf. Shaw on idiom and translatability, Ch. 1, n. 15.

7. *The Birthday Party*, Act III (2nd ed.), pp. 77-8; and below: pp. 180-1; n. 42; p. 187; p. 189. *The Caretaker*, Act II, pp. 37-8; Act III, pp. 63-4, used again, with dramatic irony, p. 76; *The Homecoming*, Act II, pp. 51-2 and 61-2; '*Landscape*' and '*Silence*', pp. 25-7. (All page references to Methuen paperback edition.) See the main section in this chapter for further discussion of these points.

8. *Harold Pinter,* London (2nd ed.), 1969, pp. 1-2 (a play-by-play discussion which *starts* with language). Attentive listening and systematic linguistic description both confirm that spoken English, at most levels of usage, is *inexplicit* - broken or jumbled-up syntax, word-searching, unrelated repetitions and overlaps are frequent. See David Crystal and Derek Davy, *Investigating English Style,* London, 1969, Part II, Ch. 4. The linguistic features are there, but not the dramatic shaping.

9. Cf. my Introduction, pp. 21ff in particular.

10. James T. Boulton, 'Harold Pinter: *The Caretaker* and Other Plays', *Modern Drama* (Sept. 1963), pp. 131-40. But Boulton does not develop this point on dialogue.

11. Jean Vannier, 'Theatre of Language', *Tulane Drama Review* (Spring 1963), p. 182. (Paraphrase with extracts.)

12. Pinter has explicitly stated: 'I'd never heard of Ionesco until after I'd written the first few plays.' *The Paris Review,* no. 39, p. 19. For this reason, and in keeping with the limits of this study, I shall not develop the brief contrast offered in n. 5. By contrast, the debt to Beckett is repeatedly acknowledged: in *The Paris Review* (p. 20); in 'Harold Pinter Replies' (*loc. cit.* p. 8); and in a cheerful private letter, in *Beckett at 60, A Festschrift,* London, 1967, p. 86.

13. Cf. Ch. 3, pp. 138-52.

14. Pinter on 'eavesdropping': 'I spend no time listening in that sense. Occasionally I hear something, as we all do, walking about. But the words come as I'm writing the characters, not before.' *The Paris Review,* no. 39, p. 26. That stress on *writing the characters* (here and elsewhere) accords with what we find in the dialogue.

15. As Gessner has done. See p. 156 and n. 52 above.

16. See Colin Duckworth (ed.), *En attendant Godot,* London, 1966, p. 91.

17. '*The Collection*' and '*The Lover*' (1963), London, 1966, pp. 29-30. Earlier, in the 'comedies of menace', 'what do you mean?' is always just that - comic evasion of threat. It is the question that greets a statement like 'tch, tch, tch, tch' (*The Birthday Party,* 2nd ed., p. 16; an imperative 'Pick it up' ('*The Room*' and '*The Dumb Waiter*', p. 45) and, most memorably, a question like 'Where were you born then?' (*The Caretaker,* p. 27).

18. Kennedy, Andrew K. *Six Dramatists in Search of a Language: Studies in Dramatic Language.* London: Cambridge University Press, 1975 Pp. 131-3.

19. Walter Kerr sees Pinter as the only dramatist today who 'writes existentialist plays existentially'; Beckett builds his plays conceptually as a Platonist: *Harold Pinter,* New York, 1967, pp. 3-9. The affinity between Beckett and Pinter was, I think, overstated by Martin Esslin in 'Godot and his Children . . .' (*Experimental Theatre,* ed. W. Armstrong, London, 1963, pp. 128-46), though he did distinguish Beckett's 'highly stylised classical mode' from Pinter's 'tape-recording fidelity' which has 'opened up a new dimension of stage dialogue' (*op. cit.* p. 46). In a later article Esslin himself stresses the fusion of 'realism' and 'the absurd' in Pinter's work: 'Epic Theatre, the Absurd, and the Future', *Tulane Drama Review* (Summer 1964), p. 46, reprinted in *Brief Chronicles,* London, 1970, p. 231.

20. 'Writing for the Theatre', *loc. cit.* p. 81.

21. *Ibid.*

22. See pp. 177-8; 181-2; 187 below. For an illuminating definition of Mannerism see *The Styles of European Art* (introduced by Herbert Read), London, 1965, pp. 248ff. For a critical attempt to relate the poetry of Donne to Mannerism in painting and music, see Daniel B. Rowland, *Mannerism—Style and Mood,* New Haven, 1964. Giorgio Melchiori finds a 'New Mannerism' in the early poetry of Eliot, and in the dramatic verse of Christopher Fry, but he sees Eliot the dramatist as increasingly in search of 'Classical' form and language. See *The Tightrope Walkers,* London, 1956 (especially Introduction, pp. 133-49; and pp. 150-74). At the end of this work there is an interesting note on a passage from E. R. Curtius (*European Literature and the Latin Middle Ages,* London, 1953, p. 273) which suggests that Mannerism is a stylistic constant running through all periods of unbalance.

23. *The Paris Review,* no. 39, pp. 35-6. Contrast Pinter on his early plays: 'It was a kind of no-holds barred feeling, like diving into a world of words.' 'In an Empty Bandstand', *The Listener* (6 Nov. 1969), p. 631.

24. *Evergreen Review,* no. 33 (cf. also n. 3 above).

25. The most sustained study on 'subtext' is John Russell Brown's 'Dialogue in Pinter and Others', *Critical Quarterly* (Autumn 1965), pp. 225-43, later used in the same author's *Theatre Language,* London, 1972, Ch. 1. See also Introduction, pp. 21-2. In 'Writing for the Theatre', Pinter himself has objected to the 'grimy, tired phrase, failure of communication' as applied to his work. Victor Amend points to the inherent dramatic limitations of 'demonstrating failure of communication through man's chief means of communication' in 'Harold Pinter—some Credits and Debits', *Modern Drama* (Sept. 1967), p. 173. In sum, the devices of non-communication tend to get obvious, contrived and self-exhausting.

26. 'Writing for the Theatre', *loc. cit.* p. 82.

27. See Ch. 2, pp. 108ff. Raymond Williams draws an evolutionary line from Eliot's early comic-strip characters, and the first scene of *The Cocktail Party,*

to *The Birthday Party*—Pinter taking further the stylisation of 'the dead phrases, the gaps of an accepted articulacy', etc., in the context of ordinary English speech. *Drama from Ibsen to Brecht,* London, 1968, p. 325.

28. Quoted, respectively, from *The Black and White* and *The Applicant,* in *'A Slight Ache' and Other Plays* (1961), London, 1966, pp. 126 and 135. Among the other revue sketches *Request Stop* and *Last to Go* resemble the first, *Trouble in the Works* the second pattern.

29. *'The Room' and 'The Dumb Waiter'* (1960), London, 1966, p. 62.

30. Cf. Ch. 2, pp. 110-11, Dusty's telephone conversation.

31. *Loc. cit.* pp. 64-5.

32. Johan Huizinga, *Homo Ludens,* London, 1949, pp. 19-20.

33. I am alluding to Eric Berne's book *Games People Play* (1964), London, 1966, because these plays by Pinter seem to be working exactly on that level of serio-sophistication. Also, Pinter's 'games' can be seen—as in Berne's work—as open-ended forms of ritual. If ritual provides fixed rhythmic patterns, 'games' are a source of half-ritualised ambiguity—in situation and language. I think that *Old Times* (1971)—first performed after the completion of this chapter—is comparable in approach and method, in a sustained and complex way.

34. Arts Theatre, Cambridge, April 1958. The response here recorded is based on a note I wrote after the first performance.

35. *The Birthday Party,* 2nd revised ed., London, 1965, pp. 12, 17, 20 and 34 respectively. (I note that the build-up of the 'catechism' is slightly more marked in the first edition—'I mean, why . . . ?' following 'But who are they?' in the third 'list' exchange. (Cf. 1963, p. 21 and 1965, p. 20.) More significantly: the third exchange is followed (in both editions) by Stanley's onslaught of Where/What/What/Who/Who questions over his tea. The whole sequence is rhythmically heightened and in effect establishes Stanley himself as the first inquisitor.

36. 'Writing for the Theatre', *loc. cit.* p. 82.

37. *The Birthday Party,* pp. 43, 44-5, 56.

38. *Ibid.* pp. 77-8. As far as I am aware no published criticism has seen this dialogue-sequence in context. A critic friend, Christopher Gillie, has suggested to me one possible function of this scene: Goldberg and MacCann are demoralised in and by the absence of Stanley, the victim they need.

39. See Ch. 2, pp. 97 ff.

40. *The Trial,* Ch. II (especially pp. 54-5, Penguin ed.).

41. 'Writing for the Theatre', *loc. cit.* p. 80.

42. The economy of Mick's jargon speeches needs to be stressed. It is doubly effective: as a voice, a 'torrent of language' counterpointing the speech of both Davies and Aston, and in the way Mick's interior-decorator patter is used again in a comic but sadistic climax (cf. n. 6). Contrast the speech-torrents of Goldberg (p. 180 above) and of Lenny (p. 187 below).

On the affinity of these monologues with the monologues of Dan Leno and other music hall artists, see Peter Davison, 'Contemporary Drama and Popular Dramatic Forms', in *Aspects of Drama and the Theatre,* Sydney University Press, 1965, pp. 160ff.

43. *The Paris Review,* no. 39, p. 26.

44. See also Kelly Morris: 'Within the format of excessive decorum, the idiom is aggression.' 'The Homecoming', *Tulane Drama Review* (Winter 1966), p. 186.

45. The ensuing quotes: pp. 68 and 75 respectively. For a full discussion of the theme of Ruth as queen-bee, mother and whore, see Hugh Nelson, *'The Homecoming: Kith and Kin'* in *Modern British Dramatists* (ed. John Russell Brown), Englewood Cliffs, N.J., 1968, pp. 145-63.

46. Hugh Nelson draws a parallel between *The Homecoming* and *Troilus and Cressida* (*loc. cit.* pp. 157-60); and Ronald Hayman says about the play: 'In mood, it's rather like a *Troilus and Cressida* taken over entirely by Thersites and Pandarus.' (*Op. cit.* p. 67.) Perhaps the language of the play, 'coming from below', releases one of Wilson Knight's 'Dionysian' powers: 'some dialect that has not been attenuated by modern sophistication'—though the sophistication is there in the shaping. (See Wilson Knight, 'The Kitchen Sink', *Encounter* (Dec. 1963), pp. 48ff., written before *The Homecoming* appeared.) One can understand why Pinter objects to 'this scheme afoot on the part of many "liberal-minded" persons to open up obscene language to general commerce. It should be the dark secret language of the underworld.' (*The Paris Review,* no. 39, p. 34.) Pinter's attitude to 'the dark secret language' is thus the opposite of what D. H. Lawrence wanted.

47. Cf. Ch. 3, pp. 152 and 163-4. *Landscape* and *Silence* were given a distinguished stage performance by the Royal Shakespeare Company (July 1969) which has, however, only confirmed that the dialogue is for the ear.

48. What follows is a reassessment of what I wrote about the first radio performance of *Landscape* for *Modern Drama* vol. 11, no. 4 (Feb. 1969), pp. 445-6. I now think that I then overstated Pinter's move to abstraction.

49. Martin Esslin states: 'When Pinter asks for a *pause* . . . he indicates that intense thought processes are

continuing, that unspoken tensions are mounting, whereas *silences* are notations for the end of a movement, the beginning of another, as between the movements of a symphony.' *The Peopled Wound,* London, 1970, p. 220.

50. Verlaine's *Art Poétique* opens with these words. The affinity between *Landscape* and *Silence* and certain pieces of modern music would have occurred to many people. Pinter himself says: 'I feel a sense of music continually in writing, which is a different matter from having been influenced by it. Boulez and Webern are now composers I listen to a great deal.' *The Paris Review,* no. 39, p. 20.

51. Virginia Woolf, *The Waves* (1931), London, 1955, p. 169: preceded by 'How tired I am of stories, how tired I am of phrases that come down with all their feet on the ground!' For further discussion, see Introduction, pp. 22ff.

Peter Thomson (essay date 1978)

SOURCE: "Harold Pinter: A Retrospect," in *Critical Quarterly,* Vol. 20, No. 4, Winter, 1978, pp. 21-28.

[*In the following essay, Thomson provides an overview of Pinter's plays, declaring the earlier ones authentic and superior to the later, which he finds formula-driven and lacking in dramatic drive.*]

With the publication, in 1978, of *Poems and Prose 1949-1977,* Pinter has vigorously reminded us that he is not merely a playwright. He may even, in a mood of declared disaffection, be saying that he is no longer a playwright. His first performed play, in 1957, was *The Room,* and the sixties was his triumphant decade. Something about the seventies—the declared violence on the one hand, a personal anguish on the other—has made his recent plays as secret and reclusive as he is himself. The production at the National Theatre of his latest play, *Betrayal,* scheduled for the autumn of 1978, may well be decisive. It seems unlikely that he has finished his career as a playwright, but the possibility has to be recognised.

It is a career that began effectively in 1958, with the London production of *The Birthday Party.* Most loyal theatregoers tried to dismiss the piece, but it wouldn't go away. You could say that the world of the play was unreal, but it was insistently analogous with the real world. What was missing from the plot was a clear *motive,* and, in a country dominated for two hundred years by the novel, motive had become a dramatic convention too. By ignoring, or at least obscuring, motive, Pinter concentrated his audience's attention on behaviour. The result is an uncomfortable diminution of human stature, and an equally uncomfortable analysis of human cruelty. The finest production I have seen was directed by George Roman, a Hungarian Jew who was a boy in Budapest during the

Nazi occupation and a young revolutionary in 1956. The sinister stranger and the knock at the door were visceral images for him, and he understood that a Jew and an Irishman might delight in destroying an English bully. Stanley is certainly a bully. He is also a boaster (the 'boast' in Pinter merits special attention), a liar, a sneak, prurient, prejudiced, and probably racist. Even so, he alarms and affects us by succumbing so grovellingly to two men equally devoid of endearing qualities. Goldberg and McCann owe a lot to Beckett's character-pairs, whose symbiotic relationship is gratuitously parodied in the breathing sequence. They conduct their comic and terrifying interrogation of Stanley in a moral void. Precisely because it lacks a context, because its malignity is motiveless, it stands for all persecutions. The birthday party, with choreography by Goldberg, is the first stage in the systematic reduction of a man who seems to deserve nothing, and yet deserves better than this.

It is the entry of Goldberg and McCann that shatters the play's scrupulously imitated normative triviality. The change of tone is shockingly abrupt. But Pinter has, in fact, prepared us for the moral confusions from the start. After Meg has given Petey his cornflakes, the adjectives have to be attended to:

MEG. Are they nice?

PETEY. Very nice.

MEG. I thought they'd be nice. [*She sits at the table.*] You got your paper?

PETEY. Yes.

MEG. Is it good?

PETEY. Not bad.

MEG. What does it say?

PETEY. Nothing much.

MEG. You read me out some nice bits yesterday.

PETEY. Yes, well, I haven't finished this one yet.

MEG. Will you tell me when you come to something good?

PETEY. Yes.

We are immediately in a world of impoverished values, where the nice is indistinguishable from the good, and where either adjective is applied indiscriminately and exclusively to such things as cornflakes, newspapers, and the weather. The lack of determinate values is a common feature of Pinter's plays. His characters flounder among approximations and hopeless enquiries (has no one ever counted the question marks in Pinter?). Pinter's cruelly accurate observation of the dialogue that surrounds a moral vacuum conveys his horror of it. Ben's question in *The Dumb Waiter,* 'What's one thing to do with another?', reverberates eerily through all the plays.

However perverse it may have seemed to its first audiences, *The Birthday Party* is governed by a ruthless narrative logic. It begins in a room, where a man sits at a table to read a newspaper. It ends with the same man sitting at the same table holding the mutilated copy of the next day's paper. On the floor beside him, an image of the past day's destruction, lie the equal strips of newspaper that McCann has torn—a precision job. The intervening day has been characterised by two movements—and these two movements are variously present in every one of Pinter's plays. The first is the movement towards deprivation, and the second a sterner, Hebraic movement towards the fulfilment of justice in punishment. Stanley is a victim, but he is neither an innocent nor a hero. Nor is Gus in *The Dumb Waiter*, Edward in *A Slight Ache*, Davies in *The Caretaker*, Max in *The Homecoming*, Disson in *Tea Party*. In a familiar context, they are acted on strangely. We are made witnesses of deeds whose motive is withheld. But the general point is psychologically persuasive. Invaded by unease, people take refuge. The typical refuge in Pinter is a room. But the room is not secure.[1] The shortest ghost story I know tells of the old woman, living alone, who went round the house bolting and barring all the doors and windows, until, as she turned the last heavy key, she heard a voice say, 'Now we're shut in for the night.' Pinter's rooms promise to their agorophobic occupants a protection which they fail finally to provide. They offer asylum, but, except for lunatics (and Pinter rarely excludes that possibility), an asylum is temporary—a resting-place for traitors, escaped prisoners, debtors, murderers on the run. And outside, *they* are searching. The refugee will be deprived of his safety. Justice will be done. Or injustice. There is no clear enough system of values to enable us to determine which. The interrogators are as motiveless as the prisoners. In a welter of effects, the cause remains mysterious.

The Birthday Party, it seems to me now, is a brilliantly appropriate theatrical statement of a social nervousness whose subtext was the enigmatic Cold War. It is also a comedy of manners, constructed according to principles quite as cruel as its Restoration forebears, and with an equivalent linguistic precision. At the comic end of its spectrum, Pinter's dialogue deploys inanity with zestful resourcefulness. Inane conversations, like those of Gus and Ben in *The Dumb Waiter*, are funny if the speakers are serious. It is a technique familiar to writers of revue sketches, and Pinter may well have learnt from Herbert Farjeon among others.[2] His contributions to the revues *One to Another* and *Pieces of Eight* are written with distinct ease, like the improvisations of actors when they surrender, in class, to the temptation to be funny. At the other end of the spectrum, though, Pinter's dialogue presents with critical incisiveness the tendency of conversation to camouflage meaning. A generation of actors has learnt, through performing Pinter, to speak with conviction lines that are not intended to convince. The high point in this style is *The Homecoming*. Since then, Pinter has become increasingly interested, or sidetracked, by the more overtly poetic possibilities of monologue. I recently attended a professional production of Pinter's *Landscape* on a double bill with Samuel Beckett's *Krapp's*

Last Tape. Director and actors had evidently assumed that *Landscape* is a masterpiece. On the contrary, it was tired and boring, verbose as Beckett's *Play*, a model for this kind of contiguous soliloquising, never is. The flat tone, the reliance on rhythm without counterpoint, and the lack of urgency to contact an interlocutor or confuse him deprived the play of Pinter's peculiar poetry. I suspect that *Landscape* lacks it anyway. But that night, in a full theatre and in front of a respectful audience, Pinter's status was extremely vulnerable. His feeling for the rhythms of deceptively 'ordinary' dialogue has been appreciated by all his critics. To some extent, he has an actor's sensitivity to the sounds of meaning; but it is the punctuation of his dialogue by silence and by stress that best expresses his poetry *of* the theatre. Poetry *in* the theatre is different altogether. If he returns to writing plays, I hope he will have abandoned it.

The four plays that conclude the first phase of Pinter's dramatic career may be loosely grouped with *The Room* and *The Birthday Party* as black comedies, or even comedies of menace, though they vary in quality. *The Dumb Waiter* (1960) is a small gem, the most certain of Pinter's plays to survive in the theatre. Such comprehending use of stage properties is rare, and modestly beguiling. Posterity may confirm it as the neatest and most engaging example of the 'comedy of menace'. It has escaped the excesses of critical explication. *A Slight Ache* (1959), alas, has not. This is an imperfect play, in which Pinter begins to apply the theme of threatened possession with the stiffness of a formula.

Katherine Burkman[3] buries it in an extended analogy with the *Bacchae*. I have no eagerness to exhume it, however inappropriate the cemetery. *The Caretaker* (1960) was better received by theatre critics than any previous or subsequent play. Donald McWhinnie had directed it finely, and Donald Pleasence's playing of Davies (tramp, bully, victim, Stanley gone further to the dogs) clarified for me the curious tug on an audience's sympathies when a whining opportunist with a taste for dominance loses all that he has. Now that Pinter's work is so familiar, *The Caretaker* wears an almost perfunctory air, but the skill that sustains through three acts a largely undeclared struggle for the mastery of a bleak room has to be admitted. Pinter aims to arouse our curiosity by disguising mystification as exposition. Instead of learning what of real significance has already happened, as we must have the patience to do in Ibsen, we are tested with possibilities and fed with vanities. The search for something as solid as a motive is further complicated by Aston's mental instability. We can rely on nothing but what actually happens, and that can be briefly summarised. Davies, a down-and-out, gets a lucky break when he is offered work as a caretaker by two brothers, then loses the job partly because he has mishandled it, and partly because the brothers have problems of their own. He is both scapegoat and *agent provocateur*. I choose those words carefully. *The Caretaker* is wide open to ingenious interpretation, and may be as readily linked with ancient ritual as with the precarious world of modern espionage. As the film version made very clear, it is a play firmly rooted in London. Pinter's fondness for place-names is in the tradition of revue-writing—until *The Caretaker* is forgotten, 'Sidcup' will always be good for a laugh—but there is more to it than that. The illusory certainty of place-names intrigues him, their ring of definition and their failure to define. The rhythm of a sentence or a whole speech gathers round them. The two long and unnerving 'recollections' with which Mick challenges Davies at the opening of Act Two are composed of a tissue of names and circumstantial detail, none of which is, in any useful sense, informative. There are obvious parallels here with the two 'Odd man out' speeches in *Old Times* and Briggs's 'Bolsover Street' reminiscence in *No Man's Land.* The names, the detailed qualifications, and the apparent determination to get the facts absolutely right are nothing to do with the real action of the play. On the contrary, they mask that action, and the masking is itself a transparent threat to the on-stage auditor. The apparently innocuous—names of places or people, food (there is almost always food in Pinter), inset narratives—is consistently invested with noxious undertones. To say, then, that *The Caretaker* is a London play or Pinter a London playwright is to succumb to his deceptive particularity. The city is important because it feeds the kind of panic (about over-population, about immigration, about 'the other') that turns the wish for secure possession into an obsession with it.

In *A Night Out* (1960), the final play in the series of black comedies with which Pinter established his reputation, a mother's boy teeters on the edge of matricide after an encounter with nubile office-girls and a prostitute. It is an introduction to the theme of sexual rivalry which dominates the second phase of Pinter's career. In *The Dwarfs* (1960), the theme is oddly focused. Virginia, a leading character in the early novel which Pinter is here translating into a play, has disappeared from the cast. Only the three young Londoners, whose competitive friendships are the novel's centre, remain. There is a strong sexual component in their rivalry, and in the various bids to unsettle the relationships. More revealing is Pinter's obvious relish in withholding from his theatre audience information and insights that he was prepared to allow his novel's readers. *The Dwarfs* is mysterious in a way I find irritating. Nor do I relish, as some critics have, its purple passages. *The Collection* (1961), which restores a woman to inflict further mayhem on the three men who complete the cast, is much more satisfying. Like *The Lover, Tea Party, The Homecoming,* and *The Basement,* it reveals Pinter's interest in the sexual and social games that people play.[4] Each of these plays provided Pinter's wife, Vivien Merchant, with a challengingly erotic central role. Each is composed of a sequence of competitive dialogues, in which victory (or, perversely, defeat) is pursued with a determination bordering on obsession. But it would be a mistake simply to lump them together. *The Lover* (1963) and *The Basement* (1967) look, in retrospect, like exercises. They have very little to say, and because they are unusually explicit, their shallowness declares itself. *Tea Party* (1965), however, survives vividly in my memory from its original television

presentation. Like *The Basement,* also a television play, it exploits close-up and angle-shot to create suggestively repeated images. The destruction of Disson, his descent from dependence to nonentity, touches on another theme that continues to disturb Pinter. Simply by depriving Disson of the reassurance he needs, his wife and his secretary accelerate his collapse. Pinter's women are often intuitively predatory. Diana, one might say, is less overtly a schemer than her brother Willy. But *Tea Party* has a carefully placed scene in which Diana and Wendy, wife and secretary, arrange to have lunch together, like manifest conspirators against the crumpling Disson. The indifference of his twin sons drives Disson further towards a sense of non-being, the catatonic death-in-life which is his condition at the end of the play. If the cruel permutations of family life are graphically illustrated in *Tea Party,* it is in *The Homecoming* (1965) that they are fully explored. I am one of those who believe that this play is Pinter's finest. The game-playing remains,[5] but the context is rich and desperately truthful. There is nothing that need not be there.[6]

With the final phase of Pinter's dramatic writing, I confront my gravest doubts. In a lecture delivered as early as 1962, he reminded his audience that: 'Apart from any other consideration, we are faced with the immense difficulty, if not the impossibility, of verifying the past.'[7] In a shifting universe, where the effect of the observer on the thing observed is an acknowledged fact, that has all the authority of truism. It does not have the promise of an alterable future which encourages us to commit ourselves to the insistent present tense of the dramatic mode at its best.[8] Even the title of *Old Times* (1971) implies its defiance of the thrust into the future that is Drama's peculiar arrogance. Of the other recent plays, *Landscape* (1968) and *Monologue* (1973) carry neutral names, *Silence* (1969), *Night* (1969), and *No Man's Land* (1975) are negatives. Not only the titles, but the plays themselves, suggest that Pinter has decided to occupy the stage in order to tell us what he can no longer tell us. In *Old Times,* Deeley and Anna compete, if not for the possession of Kate, then certainly for her acquiescence in their alternative versions of her place in their past. In addition to the many minor uncertainties in the play—did Deeley know Anna in the old times? was it her skirt he looked up? was it he who looked up her skirt?—there are two major ones. The first concerns a visit to the cinema, and is major only because of the stage-time devoted to it. Deeley's long account of his first meeting with Kate, in a fleapit in some remote part of London where they saw 'Odd man out', is undermined but not totally discredited by Anna's account of the visit she paid together with Kate to see the same film. Kate might have gone twice, Deeley may be wrong, or Anna may be inventing a wicked fiction. Any speculation is idle, since Pinter neither knows the 'truth', nor cares about it. The second major uncertainty attaches itself to an image that permeates the play. A horizontal figure (or perhaps two) lies on a bed beside a standing figure (Deeley? not necessarily), and later someone (who must surely, but need not, have been one of the participant figures) slumps on a chair to cry. This is a play that floats on the surface of language and silence. It is mysterious only because Pinter has chosen to mystify us. He has taken something very small, and let it stand for something larger by cleverly diverting our attention from it. The longer *Old Times* goes on, the smaller the subject becomes.

No Man's Land is a sophisticated development of the same technique. In all probability, the play is an elaborate spoof. Always mindful of the speculation aroused by the names Beckett gives to his characters, Pinter has provided surnames from *Wisden*. Hirst, Spooner, Foster, and Briggs all played cricket for England between 1890 and 1914. We can make more of it than that. Hirst was a Yorkshireman, Spooner and Briggs Lancastrians, and Foster exempted from the ancient rivalry by his adherence to the county of Worcestershire. Names have to come from somewhere, and it would be silly to base an attack on *No Man's Land* on the author's decision to pluck them from the pages of cricket history. I find in the play a puckish self-concealment, a casual marriage between the motiveless bullying of *The Birthday Party* and the memory music of *Old Times.*

In the conclusion to the 1962 speech from which I have already quoted, Pinter acknowledges a debt to Beckett by quoting from *The Unnamable*:

> The fact would seem to be, if in my situation one may speak of facts, not only that I shall have to speak of things of which I cannot speak, but also, which is even more interesting, but also that I, which is if possible even more interesting, that I shall have to, I forget, no matter.

Yes; but this faltering on the brink of definition is part of Beckett's philosophical buffoonery. If the deliberate cultivation of obscurity ceases to be a joke, it quickly becomes something much more reprehensible. It is possible, by seeming to be about to say something, to distract an auditor's attention from the fact that you have so far said nothing. The strategy is deployed with supreme fecklessness in Chekhov's 'lecture' on *The Harmfulness of Tobacco,* and Chekhov is another influence Pinter has reckoned with. Michael Anderson seems prepared to approve the technique which he shrewdly analyses:

> The idea of the subtext lurking behind the spoken words and revealing the characters' inner feelings has been with us at least since the time of Chekhov; but Pinter carries the process one stage further. The unconscious workings of the mind revealed (if that is the right word) in Pinter's subtext clarify nothing for his audiences. Their language systems hint at mysteries which even the author does not claim to be able to unravel.[9]

It is a style of writing that Cyril Connolly provokingly categorised as 'mandarin': 'It is the style of all those writers whose tendency is to make their language convey more than they mean or more than they feel.' And Connolly goes on to make another point which seems to me worryingly apposite:

> A writer who thinks himself cleverer than his readers writes simply (often too simply), while one who fears they may be cleverer than he will make use of mystifications: an author arrives at a good style when his language performs what is required of it without shyness.[10]

In the cruelly public world of the theatre, it is easy to lose confidence. Pinter has done so. More and more, his plays read like stretched lyrics or memory shocks ingeniously elaborated. Am I unfair? It is probably because I have admired Pinter for years, have grown up with him, and I feel let down. If I were to try to mount a case in his defence, it would be along the lines indicated by Yeats in his essay on 'A people's theatre':

> I desire a mysterious art, always reminding and half-reminding those who understand it of dearly loved things, doing its work by suggestion, not by direct statement, a complexity of rhythm, colour, gesture, not space-pervading like the intellect but a memory and a prophecy.[11]

Notes

The dates given in brackets after the title of the plays are those of the first major performance.

1. Philip Larkin's poem 'Mr Bleaney' (collected in *The Whitsun Weddings*) offers some fascinating insights into the ambience of a room. Its relationship to early Pinter is worth investigating. Mr Bleaney, protected by habit, none the less died in the room. 'They' moved him.

2. Particularly irresistible in view of Pinter's love of cricket is 'The less sporting spirit', which can be found in *Herbert Farjeon's Cricket Bag* (London, 1946), pp. 110-12.

3. Katherine H. Burkman, *The Dramatic World of Harold Pinter: Its Basis in Ritual* (Ohio, 1971), pp. 47-64.

4. Cf. Eric Berne, *Games People Play* (Harmondsworth, 1967).

5. Ruth's provocative display of her leg is a startlingly literal version of 'The stocking game' as described by Berne in *Games People Play,* pp. 113-14.

6. *A Casebook on Harold Pinter's The Homecoming,* edited by John and Anthea Lahr (London, 1974) is a useful collection of critical responses to this remarkable play. I have found myself unable to do it justice within the scope of this retrospect.

7. The lecture forms the Introduction to *Plays: One* (London, 1976), pp. 9-16.

8. For an extended discussion of the primacy of the present tense in the dramatic mode, see chapter 17 of S. Langer, *Feeling and Form* (New York, 1953).

9. Michael Anderson, *Anger and Detachment* (London, 1976), p. 101.

10. Cyril Connolly, *Enemies of Promise* (Harmondsworth, 1961). The first quotation is from p. 25, the second from p. 29.

11. W. B. Yeats, *Explorations* (London, 1962), p. 255.

Arnold P. Hinchliffe (essay date 1981)

SOURCE: "Comedies of Menace," in *Harold Pinter,* revised edition, Twayne Publishers, 1981, pp. 38-76.

[*In the following essay, Hinchliffe offers synopses of Pinter's works and of critical responses to them.*]

The title of this chapter was first applied to Pinter by Irving Wardle in *Encore* (September 1958), though it had appeared as the subtitle of a play by David Campton called *The Lunatic View* in 1957. Campton explicitly devoted the Absurd to social comment—as a weapon against complacency and in his "sick" comedies the source of menace is clear enough. In Pinter it has been universalized without losing its power. Pinter's terror is outside every door. In the "Tempo" program about his adolescence in Hackney Pinter denied that the atmosphere of violence was attributable to his Jewishness, though that must have contributed to his recognition of it. Trussler has objected to the use of "comedy" on the grounds that comedy throws into relief the eccentricities of everyday life whereas Pinter's plays are too devoid of social setting; but his alternative—tragic farce—seems no better. In fact the early plays have more precise settings than appeared at first, and if Pinter's themes are loneliness, menace, communication, and verification, his characteristic mode of expression is comedy, though, as Alrene Sykes aptly remarks, that comedy is frequently built "on the quicksands of fear."[1] Either description reminds us of the mixed nature of the plays—comedy that causes pain, and the peculiar misery of changing sides during the action, which in retrospect is hardly as novel as it seemed at the time. And since Pinter seldom stands still, but always develops, the first plays are the best place to start, those plays written about 1957 which enjoyed little success: *The Room, The Birthday Party,* and *The Dumb Waiter.*

All the time Pinter was acting (or "resting") he was writing, not plays but poems and short prose pieces, many of which were in dialogue form and anticipated his revue sketches, and the plays. He also wrote a novel based on his youth in Hackney which was never published but which later appeared transformed into *The Dwarfs.* The basic form for Pinter remains a series of images which, as Esslin observes, "never aspire to be arguments, explanations or even coherent stories."[2] His plays do, however, seem to be constantly aspiring to the condition of a poem!

I POETRY

Some of his poems were published, particularly in *Poetry London,* where they are sometimes ascribed to a Harold Pinta.[3] A selection by Alan Clodd was published by the Enitharmon Press in 1968 and in 1978 Methuen published *Poems and Prose: 1949-1977,* selected by the author and dedicated to Antonia Fraser. It is difficult to judge these poems without taking into account Pinter's successes elsewhere. They could not fail to be interesting, and critics have found in them all the characteristic themes: "the relativity of truth, mortality, dreams, the past, the intruder, dominance and subservience, and the sexual condition of men and women," though the techniques are fairly orthodox.[4] The early poems have echoes of Dylan Thomas, though they are mainly concerned with low-life in the city, as in "New Year in the Midlands," published in November 1950, which suggests that Pinter already has his themes and a great delight in language:

Now here again she blows, landlady of lumping
Fellows between the boards.
Singing "O Celestial Light," while
Like a T-square on the
Flood swings her wooden leg.
This is the shine, the powder and blood and here am
    I,
Straddled, exile always in one Whitbread Ale town,
Or such.
Where we went to the yellow pub, cramped in an al-
    ley bin,
A shoot from the market,
And found the thin Luke of a queer, whose pale
Deliberate eyes, raincoat, Victorian,
Sap the answer in the palm.
All the crush, camp, burble and beer
Of this New Year's Night; the psalm derided;
The black little crab women with the long
Eyes, lisp and claw in a can of chockfull stuff.
I am rucked in the heat of treading; the wellrolled
Sailor boys soon rocked to sleep, whose ferret fig
So calms the coin of a day's fever.
Now in this quaver of a roisty bar, the wansome lady
I blust and stir,
Who pouts the bristle of a sprouting fag—
Sprinkled and diced in these Midland lights
Are Freda the whimping glassy bawd, and your splut-
    tered guide,
Blessed with ambrosial bitter weed.—Watch
How luminous hands
Unpin the town's genitals—
Young men and old
With beetle glance,
The crawing brass whores, the clamping
Red shirted boy, ragefull, thudding his cage.

More obviously significant is the prose poem *Kullus* (1949), where the narrator allows an outsider, Kullus, into his room. Kullus at once starts to take over, calling in a girl who is waiting outside and without pausing they climb into the narrator's bed. Before long the girl invites the narrator to reverse the roles and the characters of the narrator and Kullus seem to blur; the past blurs, too, in a mysterious and ambiguous present. This sets the pattern of room, intruder, possession, but also the suggestion that in seeking the comfort of a room a young man gives up the chance of a girl. It was the first set of ideas, however, that occurs in the early plays which, Pinter claims, grew imaginatively out of a situation or image:

> I went into a room one day and saw a couple of people in it. This stuck with me for some time afterwards, and I felt that the only way I could give it expression and get it off my mind was dramatically. I started off with this picture of two people and let them carry on from there. It wasn't a deliberate switch from one kind of writing to another. It was quite a natural movement. A friend of mine, Henry Woolf, produced the result—*The Room*—at Bristol University, and a few months later in January 1958 it was included—in a different production—in the Festival of University drama. Michael Codron heard about the play and wrote to me at once to ask if I had a full-length play. I had just finished *The Birthday Party*. . . .

II *THE ROOM*

The Room was written in four days and begins with what Pinter saw as a very potent question: what is going to happen to these two people in a room? Will someone come in? Noticeably Pinter is equally aware of the image as both verbal and visual: "I see things pretty clearly, certainly, but I am continually surprised by what I see and by what suddenly happens in the play while I am writing it. I do not know, however, that the visual is more important to me than the verbal, because I am pretty well obsessed with words when they get going. It is a matter of tying the words to the image of the character standing on the stage. The two things go very closely together."[5] The words, as has been frequently recognized, are the language of cliché, but concentrated and organized so that the short period of the play produces the fullest impact on an audience. If the language is naturalism it is very much orchestrated naturalism. *The Room* contains the style, setting, and themes for Pinter's work up to and including *The Caretaker,* and noticeably the language is used to conceal rather than reveal. Pinter enlarged upon the initial image in *Time* (November 10, 1961) when he recalled seeing two men at a party—the little man feeding an enormous lorry driver with bread and butter and talking all the while. This image has been translated into Rose and Bert. In a shabby room in a large house, Rose, a woman of sixty, is fussing over her husband, Bert, a man of fifty, a van driver, who appears to be rather simple-minded but who never speaks to her, not even to reply to her monologue on the virtues of the room they live in. Outside the weather is cold and wintry (the second line of the play is, ominously, "It's murder"). Pinter is already *using* weather, here to emphasize the protective envelope or womb the room appears to provide for the characters. Rose's motherly solicitude for Bert is *partly* justified by the fact (?), suggested later in the play, that he has been ill; and her praise of the room is *partly* justified by the later suggestion that they have just moved into the area, though neither of these "facts" can be taken as necessarily true or false. The room for Rose is comfortable, representing, as it does, her only security; and it is just right for her—it is not in the basement (which is cold and damp) nor too far up. Also nobody bothers them:

> This is a good room. You've got a chance in a place like this. I look after you, don't I, Bert? Like when they offered us the basement here I said no straight off. I knew that'd be no good. The ceiling right on top of you. No, you've got a window here, you can move yourself, you can come home at night, if you have to go out, you can do your job, you can come home, you're all right. And I'm here. You stand a chance.[6]

Pinter's plays are about people bothering people who want to keep to themselves; who find communication too alarming. The first intruder is the landlord, Mr. Kidd, who arrives, talks, but tells us nothing. He and Rose do, however, confirm each other's opinion that this room is the best in the house—the downstairs is damp and upstairs the rain comes in. But even Mr. Kidd seems vague about the extent of the house—which room was what in the past—and his own parentage since he cannot decide whether his mother was a Jewess or not. Although he suggests that the house is full at the moment he also says that he can take his pick of the rooms for his own bedroom. When he leaves, he is followed out a little later by the silent Bert. Rose begins to tidy up, but on opening the door to empty the garbage can, she finds a young couple in the dark on the landing and invites them in. Clarissa and Toddy Sands are looking for a room and have been told that there is one vacant in the house, but they have been unable to find the landlord or explore the house, which is in darkness. As a married couple (presumably) they, too, seem on edge with each other; indeed the verbal battles between these two introduce a note of comedy into the play, though it is tinged with unease. They, for example, know the landlord by another name; and their bickering over whether Toddy should or should not sit down, whether Clarissa did or did not see a star, makes for uneasy laughter. When Toddy accidentally does sit down, Clarissa pounces:

> MRS. SANDS: You're sitting down.
>
> MR. SANDS: (*jumping up*): Who is?
>
> MRS. SANDS: You were.
>
> MR. SANDSS: Don't be silly. I perched.
>
> MRS. SANDS: I saw you sit down.
>
> MR. SANDS: You did not see me sit down because I did not sit bloody well down. I perched!
>
> MRS. SANDS: Do you think I can't perceive when someone's sitting down?
>
> MR. SANDS: Perceive! That's all you do. Perceive.
>
> MRS. SANDS: You could do with a bit more of that instead of all that tripe you get up to.
>
> MR. SANDS: You don't mind some of that tripe!
>
> MRS. SANDS: You take after your uncle, that's who you take after!
>
> MR. SANDS: And who do you take after?
>
> MRS. SANDS (*rising:*) I didn't bring you into the world.
>
> MR. SANDS: You didn't what?

MRS. SANDS: I said, I didn't bring you into the world.

MR. SANDS: Well, who did then? That's what I want to know. Who did? Who did bring me into the world?[7]

Even if we do not accept Gabbard's contention that this episode can be interpreted as penis envy and the desire to castrate it does contain arguments and fears that are still reverberating in the last plays; yet the mysteries seem irrelevant to the plot here and now, and indeed these exchanges delay the information that Rose desperately wants: which room is vacant? It turns out that a man sitting in the dark in the basement has told the Sandses that Room Seven is vacant. Since this is Rose's room she is naturally alarmed and gets rid of the couple, but Mr. Kidd bursts in. While she tries to question him about her room and what the Sandses told her, he, too, tries to tell her something, something he can only tell her when Bert is away. This information *partly* explains the inconsequential nature of his first visit but raises further questions in doing so—namely, why must Bert be out of the way before he can tell her? There is, he says, a man in the basement who is waiting to see her, who will not go away without seeing her, and who just sits there waiting, not even willing to play a game of chess to pass the time. Rose is finally convinced that she must see the stranger because he might turn up when Bert was there (again, why her panic?), so, she tells Mr. Kidd to send him up quickly. A blind Negro enters (so sitting in the dark is explained?) who says that his name is Riley and whom Rose immediately attacks for upsetting her landlord. But her dialogue contains one or two curious phrases—"you're all deaf, dumb and blind, *the lot of you*"; "oh, these *customers*" (italics mine)—that are obscure. And why does Rose deny that his name could be Riley? Her harangue culminates in a denial that is also a request:

ROSE: You've got what? How could you have a message for me, Mister Riley, when I don't know you and nobody knows I'm here and I don't know nobody anyway. You think I'm an easy touch, don't you? Well, why don't you give it up as a bad job? Get off out of it. I've had enough of this. You're not only a nut, you're a blind nut and you can get out the way you came. *Pause.* What message? Who have you got a message from? Who?

RILEY: Your father wants you to come home.[8]

The Negro repeats this message, calling her "Sal"—a name she does not deny; indeed, since she says, "Don't call me that," she almost admits to it. As she is feeling his face with her fingers (the action of a blind person rather than of a seeing one), Bert returns. He describes, in one short, violent speech, his furious drive back, how the one car that got in his way got "bumped," and how the van (which is feminine) goes well with him. Then he sits down and looks at the Negro for a few minutes. Suddenly he throws the Negro on the floor with the single world: "Lice." Then Bert beats him to death against the gas stove while Rose screams and announces that she is blind.

III CRITICISM OF *THE ROOM*

The Room drew an admiring notice from Harold Hobson at its performance at Bristol University and *The Times* compared Pinter to Webern because both incline "to etiolated pointilliste textures, forever trembling on the edge of silence, and to structures elusive, yet so precisely organised that they possess an inner tension nonetheless potent because its sources are not completely understood."[9] If the play is not finally successful the fault lies in its melodramatic ending and the portentous Negro. Such a character inevitably invites a symbolic response—is he Death, the woman's past, or some hidden guilt?—summarized by Esslin as follows:

He has been lying down below and had foreknowledge of the future—that room number seven would soon be vacant—he must therefore be a being from beyond the confines of this world: a dead man or a messenger of death, perhaps Rose's own dead father. His blackness and blindness reinforce these allegorical implications. The blindness which strikes Rose at the end belongs to the same category of symbolism—it must mean the end of her relationship with Bert, but probably more than that: her own death.[10]

But Esslin supports this by transferring Bert's sexual energy to the van—which, surely, overlooks the fact that they are sixty and fifty, respectively.

Quigley has little sympathy for this interpretation of the Negro as a symbol of anything: he sees the process of adjustment as central to the play, not a symbol or message. The Negro is not merely feared but also desired by Rose and the play explores both fear and curiosity, change and resistance to change. But the appearance of the Negro is too suggestive to be simply ignored. As Clifford Leech astutely remarked, we are "conscious of being invited to look for allegory and yet not sufficiently impelled to conduct the search,"[11] while Trussler has pointed out that in a physical sense at least this Negro is nonsymbolic: he is black and blind—so we sense Pinter's Jewishness in the subtext. Rose is recalled to her race, and her father might even be Irish. At any rate the mixture of an Irish name and a black face makes Riley an ideal image for the "foreign" that so terrifies Pinter characters; and if he is a cousin to the One Eyed Reilly who appears as a means of redemption in T. S. Eliot's *The Cocktail Party* then his daughter has had a very full sex life indeed!

Some puzzles can be explained (a blind man sits in the dark) and some motives can be provided (Sal has become Rose and as Sal she led a life which would appall Bert). Mr. Kidd's musings about his Jewish origins are, however, mechanical—suggesting he is either a liar, a deliberate mystifier, or, perhaps, just forgetful in old age? Is the father from whom the message comes the kind of Father we meet in T. S. Eliot? Intruders are repelled, but has a room which stifles any value? The imagery of warm/cold, light/dark which runs through the play might mean something. We cannot, however, complain of and praise the multiple possibilities simultaneously, though it is human nature to do so. The basic Pinter device of contradiction appears here in full play: "The technique of casting doubt upon everything by matching each apparently clear and unequivocal statement with an equally clear and unequivocal statement of its contrary . . . is one which we shall find used constantly in Pinter's plays to create an air of mystery and uncertainty."[12]

If the suppression of motive is often arbitrary the central theme, surely, is that even one who acts cannot know what impels action. A Freudian interpretation may provide insights, but they will be no more valuable than Stanislavski's specifics. The question being asked is: can we ever know the truth about anyone or anything? Is there, in fact, an absolute truth to be known? In *The Room* it is not so much, we feel, that motives are unknowable as that the author will not let us know them. The play remains a good piece of theater, if weak as drama: the final explosion occurs rapidly, stunning the audience. But the mature Pinter said he would have had the characters sit down and drink a cup of tea—which is even more disturbing.

IV *The Birthday Party*

Pinter recalls that *The Birthday Party* was written while he was touring in some kind of farce:

> It was sparked off from a very distinct situation in digs when I was on tour. In fact the other day a friend of mine gave me a letter I wrote him in nineteen-fifty something. Christ knows when it was. This is what it says, "I have filthy insane digs, a great bulging scrag of a woman with breasts rolling at her belly, an obscene household, cats, dogs, filth, teastrainers, mess, oh bullocks, talk, chat, rubbish shit scratch dung poison, infantility, deficient order in the upper fretwork, fucking roll on. . . ." Now the thing about this is *that* was *The Birthday Party*—I was in those digs, and this woman was Meg in the play, and there was a fellow staying there in Eastbourne, on the coast. The whole thing remained with me, and three years later I wrote the play.[13]

Before we "explain" in terms of allegory and symbol we should perhaps consider that it might simply be true. Audiences certainly could not, and although it was successful at the Arts Theatre in Cambridge it was disastrously unsuccessful when it was presented at the Lyric in Hammersmith.

The Birthday Party opens with another breakfast scene, this time at the Boles's. Meg and Petey Boles live in a run-down boarding house at the seaside (Petey is apparently a deck-chair attendant), and they have only one guest, Stanley. The opening scene is reminiscent of both *The Room* (Meg mothers Petey and hates going out) and *The Dumb Waiter* (which also starts with items read out from a newspaper). From the news items read out by Petey— that Lady Mary Splatt has had a baby, a girl—emerges the possible fact that Meg needs a son and that the lodger, Stanley, fills that role as well as that of a young lover.

Petey announces the possible arrival of two new guests, and Meg goes up to waken Stanley—a noisy game from which she appears panting and rearranging her hair. Stanley enters "unshaven, in his pyjama jacket and wearing glasses." Over breakfast he teases Meg—calling her fried bread "succulent," a word she is certain is an improper comment on herself. Stanley, apparently, was a great concert pianist stopped short in his career by "them." He is alarmed and unbelieving when told that two new guests are coming and pretends, with ironic cruelty, that they will cart Meg away in a wheelbarrow.

A young girl, Lulu, who comes in with a mysterious parcel tries to get Stanley to pull himself together and come out with her. After she has gone, he moves to the kitchen to wash himself, hiding there and observing the arrival of the two guests, Nathaniel Goldberg and Dermot McCann, who are looking for a particular place in which to do a specific job. These two strangers resemble the two gunmen in *The Dumb Waiter,* particularly in that McCann, the younger of the two, feels that the organization they represent no longer trusts him—with some reason it appears, for he is questioning its orders. He is, after much pressing, answered by Goldberg, in a "quiet, fluent, official tone":

> GOLDBERG: The main issue is a singular issue and quite distinct from your previous work. Certain elements, however, might well approximate in points of procedure to some of your other activities. All is dependent on the attitude of our subject. At all events, McCann, I can assure you that the assignment will be carried out and the mission accomplished with no excessive aggravation to you or myself. Satisfied?
>
> McCANN: Sure. Thank you, Nat.[14]

When Meg joins them she insists that it is Stanley's birthday, and Goldberg immediately suggests that they should have a party, though Stanley protests that it is not really his birthday. Stanley seems a little depressed after the strangers have gone upstairs, and to cheer him up Meg gives him the mysterious parcel, his birthday present. It is a toy drum (to replace his piano!), and the first act ends with Stanley marching around the room beating his drum—the beat growing more and more savage until, in the end, he is completely and frighteningly out of control.

Act Two opens with McCann alone, tearing a newspaper into five strips slowly and painstakingly—surely a reasonable dramatization of the insecurity betrayed in Act One.[15] Stanley comes in and tries to find out what Goldberg and McCann have in common, and what associations the two strangers have with his previous life in either Basingstoke or Ireland. He also tries to get rid of them by saying there is no room; and, after a little "game" of sitting down and standing up, he finds himself being questioned in return. McCann and Goldberg begin an interrogation that takes the form of a kind of litany in which serious and frivolous charges are balanced in the syntax of denunciation:

> GOLDBERG: Where is your lechery leading you?
>
> McCANN: You'll pay for this.

GOLDBERG: You stuff yourself with dry toast.

MCCANN: You contaminate womankind.

GOLDBERG: Why don't you pay the rent?

MCCANN: Mother defiler!

GOLDBERG: Why do you pick your nose?

MCCANNN: I demand justice!

GOLDBERG: What's your trade?

MCCANN: What about Ireland?

GOLDBERG: What's your trade?

STANLEY: I play the piano.

GOLDBERG: How many fingers do you use?

STANLEY: No hands!

GOLDBERG: No society would touch you. Not even a building society.

MCCANN: You're a traitor to the cloth.

GOLDBERG: What do you use for pyjamas?

STANLEY: Nothing.

GOLDBERG: You verminate the sheet of your birth.

MCCANN: What about the Albigensenist heresy?

GOLDBERG: Who watered the wicket in Melbourne?

MCCANN: What about the blessed Oliver Plunkett?

GOLDBERG: Speak up Webber. Why did the chicken cross the road?[16]

The mounting violence and ugliness of this scene is deflected only by the arrival of Meg in her party dress beating Stanley's drum. The party follows, whose central event is a speech by Goldberg (echoing Meg's evocation of her childhood pink room with its night light) in which he regrets the loss of love, which was so comfortably present in those nursery days: "How can I put it to you? We all wander on our tod through this world. It's a lonely pillow to kip on."[17]

At first Stanley will not join in his own party; but when Lulu suggests a game of blindman's buff, he is drawn in. At this point we detect echoes of **The Room;** there is even a song about Reilly. As the blind-folded Stanley picks his way across the room (McCann removes his spectacles first and quietly breaks them), McCann pushes the drum in his way, and Stanley crashes his foot through it. There is great merriment until he catches Meg and tries to strangle her. At this point all the lights go out. In the ensuing melee, McCann drops his flashlight (Goldberg's orders were apparently that Stanley should be kept spotlighted all the time), and, when it is found, Lulu "is lying spreadeagled on the table, Stanley is bent over her." When Goldberg and McCann approach him with the light, he retreats giggling to the wall.

The third act opens once more with breakfast at the Boles's. Meg and Petey (who could not attend the party) discuss both the party and Stanley's illness. His friends are looking after him, and Goldberg's large car waits outside to take him away. Stanley has had some sort of breakdown. Petey offers to help—to get a doctor or to find tape to repair the broken glasses—but such offers are brushed aside by the smoothly professional Goldberg. However, when McCann comes down from Stanley's room, he seems upset and begins to tear the newspaper into strips; but this time rapidly. In the tension of this scene and because McCann inadvertently calls Goldberg "Simey," a quarrel breaks out. The fight between Goldberg and McCann is terminated by Goldberg's statement of faith: never change and always do what you are told:

Because I believe that the world . . . *(Vacant)*. . . .

Because I believe that the world . . . *(Desperate)*. . . .

BECAUSE I BELIEVE THAT THE WORLD . . . *(Lost)*. . . .[18]

This uneasiness also appears to be physical. Goldberg has to have a kind of medical check-up and the "kiss-of-life" treatment to reassure himself that he is in perfect condition.

Lulu arrives, and after the events of the last night is surprised to find that Goldberg is leaving:

LULU: You're leaving?

GOLDBERG: Today.

LULU *(with growing anger):* You used me for a night. A passing fancy.

GOLDBERG: Who used who?

LULU: You made use of me by cunning when my defences were down.

GOLDBERG: Who took them down?

LULU: That's what you did. You quenched your ugly thirst. You took advantage of me when I was over-wrought. I wouldn't do those things again, not even for a Sultan!

GOLDBERG: One night doesn't make a harem.

LULU: You taught me things a girl shouldn't know before she's been married at least three times!

GOLDBERG: Now you're a jump ahead! What are you complaining about?[19]

The return of McCann, who has gone to get Stanley ready, darkens the scene and turns this comic game into another potential interrogation, but when Lulu is ordered to confess, she wisely leaves. Stanley is brought in transformed: striped trousers, black jacket, white collar, carrying a bowler hat and his broken glasses.[20] He is clean, neat, and shaven and the two men begin to woo him with relish. But Stanley is also dumb and their promises only produce a wordless wail. Petey makes one last attempt to intervene, but on being invited to go along, he, too, retreats, and the two men take Stanley away to "Monty." The play closes with Meg still unaware that Stanley has gone, remembering how she was the belle of the ball.

V Criticism of *The Birthday Party*

Reviews of **The Birthday Party** were almost unanimously dismissive. Milton Shulman, in the *Evening Standard,* thought the play would be best enjoyed by those who thought obscurity was its own reward; *The Times* found madness in Act One, delirium in Act Two, while the third act "studiously refrains from the slightest hint of what the other two may have been about"; the *Manchester Guardian* advised Pinter to forget Beckett, Ionesco, and Simpson and he might do better next time. The inclusion of Simpson is interesting, particularly as Milton Shulman thought that the play was not nearly as witty as Simpson's *The Resounding Tinkle.* But who, now, remembers N. F. Simpson? Harold Hobson came to the defense of the play in *The Sunday Times* (May 25), claiming that Pinter possessed "the most original, disturbing and arresting talent in theatrical London." He also pointed out that if unfavorable notices do not help the box office (by the time his review appeared the play had closed) their lasting effect is nothing. Pinter was in the best of company—Beckett, Osborne, Shaw, and Ibsen. But, of course, in the theater notices and the box office do matter. Is Pinter going to be encouraged to write more plays? The story of Pinter's development as a dramatist is very much also a story of education of the critics and by the critics. This need for education of audiences was stressed by Irving Wardle in his sympathetic review in *Encore:*

> Nowadays there are two ways of saying you don't understand a play: the first is to howl it out with the word "obscurity," once so popular in poetry reviews; the second way is to say that the seminal influence of Ionesco can be detected.

> Mr. Pinter received the full treatment. As well as standing for x in the formula above, he was described as inferior to N. F. Simpson, a lagging surrealist, and as the equal of Henry James. Remembering James's melancholy affair with the theater this last one carries a nasty sting; and within a couple of days of receiving it, **The Birthday Party** was over.

But Wardle observed that it was Pinter's "instinct for what will work in the theater that prompted hostility" and he pointed to the example of McCann tearing up strips of paper as a device that introduces a theatrical idea and lets it find its own road back to common sense. There was, moreover, a theme, namely that the man who has withdrawn to protect his illusions will not be helped by being propelled into the outside world. In the protected world a memory or two remain and when the intruders arrive they seem "as much furies emerging from Stanley's night thoughts as physical creatures. His downfall is swift. Scrubbed, shaved, hoisted out of his shapeless trousers, and stuffed into a morning suit he is led away at the end in a catatonic trance."[21]

Six years later **The Birthday Party** was revived in the Aldwych Theatre Summer Repertoire for 1964 with Pinter as director. The critical attention this time was more respectful. There were still, naturally, those who continued to believe that they had been right in 1958. Philip Hope-Wallace, in the *Guardian* (June 19), conceded that "a mild but palpable theatrical excitement is distilled and hangs in the air like an indefinable odor of holiness" while W. A. Darlington, in *The Daily Telegraph* (of the same day), found the play more enjoyable but still wanted to know, exactly, what it was that Stanley had done. For Bamber Gascoigne, in the *Observer* (June 21), Pinter's direction had made the situation too plain and ordinary for characters who were not ordinary, and the second cast failed to produce a gallery of fascinating grotesques in the way the first cast had. This plainness was no real gain since the meaning remained ordinary: "the pressures and guilt brought to bear by ideas of family and success (Goldberg), politics and religion (McCann) on a second-rate artist who has opted out of society and just wants to vegetate."

In fact, this second production, by holding off the horror aspects and allowing itself to be taken as broad comedy (which broadened noticeably as the production got into its stride), left little for the critic to say, as John Russell Taylor whimsically suggested in his review in the August issue of *Plays and Players:* if less than an ideal reading the production was "something unique in the contemporary Theater" and should not be missed. The production had a rightness about it, the sense of which became clearer with reseeing. Because the "explanation" was clearer the menace became all the more unreasonable. Pinter also threw emphasis upon certain aspects the text cannot. Stanley was stronger as a character, bandying words with the strangers, tormenting Meg with the idea of her being carted away in a wheelbarrow which haunts her still at the end of the play. The extremely slow pace of the play gradually justified itself. Thus McCann's irritatingly slow tearing up of the newspaper in Act Two was matched by the swift tearing up in Act Three. The comedy of the opening darkens very slowly, and if we did not feel much sympathy for anyone by the end of the play we were frightened into recognizing that we could not dismiss our fears by turning the play into an allegory about the artist in society, that here was something we might apply, if we dared, to our own lives—a feeling that matures later in **The Caretaker,** where we recognize that we all have a Sidcup—and if it is no cosmic Sidcup it is, nevertheless, frightening and not without eschatalogical implications.

VI Some Interpretations of *The Birthday Party*

Bert O. States has called the present game "filling Pinter pauses with O'Neill psychology";[22] we seek to explain our responses and we do so in terms of allegory and footnotes. Let us take the famous interrogation in which Goldberg and McCann attack Stanley; in 1962 Bernard Dukors saw this as part of a general reflection in Pinter's plays of the tensions and attitudes of an England that was no longer a colonial power. The plays show man being reduced to a cipher, and his vain fight against that reduction. Principally rebels must be crushed, and of these the artist is the chief. In this context Dukors examines the two henchmen of society who bring the pressure to bear, pointing out that they represent the two traditional religions of Western civilization, Judaism and Catholicism (it would be inappropriate to send a Protestant):

> Each has several given names, and these carry connotations of tradition and religion. McCann is sometimes called Dermot (Diarmaid) and sometimes Seamus (James); Goldberg is called Nat (Nathan) but his wife used to call him Simey (Simon or Simeon), and his father called him Benjamin (Benny); and Goldberg has a son named Emmanuel whom he calls Timmy. Their names change according to the function they perform. For example, although Goldberg's father called him Benny (Benjamin was Jacob's youngest son and the favorite of his old age), he is in his present capacity called Nat, and just as Nathan the prophet, commanded directly by God, rebuked King David for having sinned against the Lord, and brought him back to the paths of righteousness, so does Nat, commanded directly by the organization, bring Stanley back to the paths of conformity. While Goldberg supplies the brains, McCann supplies the muscle (the Church Militant), and at one point exhorts a young lady to get down on her knees and confess.[23]

This takes the names very seriously. But if Pinter is using punning names, what of Boles and Webber? The process is erratic and inexhaustible. Yet we remember Vivien Merchant's comment that David was hiding Harold and Vivien was hiding Ada, and that Pinter's agent Emmanuel Wax is always called Jimmy!

The same kind of detail is provided by Stephen Gale on the contents of the interrogation. But surely the name "Oliver Plunkett" was chosen as much for sound as for the fact that he was the last Catholic martyr to die in England? Similarly we are told that Drogheda "was the stronghold first of the Danes and then the Anglo-Normans and the site of several parliaments. In a rebellion in 1641 the town was besieged but relieved, only to fall to Oliver Cromwell in 1649, when the inhabitants were massacred." There follows a list of ruins in the vicinity. We almost expect a note directing us to Chapter 13 of *Oliver Cromwell* by Antonia Fraser! Does Pinter work like this? Not according to Quigley, who comments, rather clumsily:

> Their function is to overcome Stanley by the quantity of accusation not by the truth-quality of any particular accusation. Here again the language is primarily used in the negotiation of the relationship between Stanley and his visitors rather than for its overall referential possibilities. If anything, the diversity of potential referential usage is subordinated to and organized by an interrelational motive and goal.[24]

In calling the interrogation a litany I was trying to pin down a halfway house between these viewpoints. The details are meaningful but blurred by repetition; but repetition suggests practice. Goldberg and McCann perform the ritual like professionals, they have done it before and they make a great team. But they are frightening also because they exhibit doubt and fear—when Petey opens his newspaper at the end of the play five carefully torn strips flutter out, reminding us how ill at ease Goldberg and McCann have been. It is true that Pinter in his poem on the play, "A View of the Party" (it is *a* view not *the* view), does suggest that Goldberg is the center of the play and might be more than an agent of the power. The second part of the poem also hints that they are essentially forces in the mind of Stanley, but if so they are embodied furies. They promise Stanley a new birth:

> GOLDBERG: We'll make a man of you.
>
> McCANN: And a woman.
>
> GOLDBERG: You'll be reoriented.
>
> McCANN: You'll be rich.
>
> GOLDBERG: You'll be adjusted.
>
> McCANN: You'll be our pride and joy.
>
> GOLDBERG: You'll be a mensch.
>
> McCANN: You'll be a success.
>
> GOLDBERG: You'll be integrated.
>
> McCANN: You'll give orders.
>
> GOLDBERG: You'll make decisions.[25]

Of course Meg has invented the birthday because she wants to give Stanley a present: the drum. A present, friends, a party—even if rape, attempted murder, and a nervous breakdown ensue—are suggestive, as is the play's title, of coziness. R. F. Storch claims that the menace comes precisely from family feelings "served up in a heavy syrup of sentimentality":

> McCann's version is of course the familiar Irish kind (James Joyce's young man had to escape from it too, though it continued to haunt him). Goldberg and McCann make a team—enterprising, loyal, and doing a job. Not necessarily a criminal job. The point is that any job done in this team spirit becomes sinister. . . . The team spirit belongs to the same world as family sentiment: both reach out their tentacles to strangle Stanley.[26]

This is possibly an American viewpoint (though the British public school springs to mind as an equivalent) and is certainly a more indigenous interpretation than comparison with Kafka. It is true that in *The Trial* the hero has guilt feelings and is taken away to be executed by two respectable-looking gentlemen. To a Polish critic like Gregorz Sinko Kafka is the obvious key: "One feels like saying that the two executioners, Goldberg and McCann, stand for all the principles of state and social conformism. Goldberg refers to his 'job' in a typically Kafkaesque official language which deprives the crime of all sense and reality." As for his removal at the end of the play: "Maybe Stanley will meet his death there or maybe he will only receive a conformist brain-washing after which he is promised . . . many other gifts of civilization. . . ."[27] This may be appropriate to a Polish reader for whom the world of Kafka is not entirely fictional but in the context of an English seaside resort? Such a context suggests Graham Greene's *Brighton Rock* and the contrast between the vicious adult world and the safe night-lighted world of childhood recalls Greeneland—seediness, professional thugs, and traitors. And Kafka and Greene must coexist with another layer since Meg's illusions as belle of the ball are reminiscent of, say, Tennessee Williams. It is the number of layers that fascinates even if they may not have been too perfectly molded together: simultaneously we have "an allegory about the rise of fascism, a seaside social comedy, and a sexual farce."[28] What is interesting about the "allegory" is the reversal of racial sterotypes: here the Jew and the Irishman become instruments of vengeance on the Englishman! We may find it hard to accept Baker/ Tabachnik's contention that Stanley's special treatment is probably circumcision but their interpretation of the play as being about Pinter, the assimilated Jewish artist with feelings of guilt over his betrayal of the group, is plausible. Goldberg's fury when he is called Simey occurs because the name gives him away and disturbs his harmony with the Christian world:

> Goldberg flees from his position as a marginal man, a Jew in a Christian world, into an ethnic past of family, food and Fridays that may never have existed for him particularly. Such happy reminiscence of the past becomes a Pinter medium in later plays. . . . But the past offers Goldberg no escape, although he progressively retreats into it as the play moves. . . . At best it affords him some communication at the universal level with the equally maudlin memories of the other characters.[29]

This interpretation, then, sees Stanley turned into a renegade Jew just as McCann accuses him of the same crime in Irish terms, betrayal of the IRA. Stanley accepts the role and acts out on Meg and Lulu the sex and violence of which he stands accused. Such pressures only reappear so intensely again in *The Homecoming.* The party is, of course, a Bar Mitzvah (which means "Son of Duty"), the ritual that marks the age of responsibility, of Stanley's becoming a man.

What Stanley's crime or punishment is we simply do not know, nor do we need to: our critics are all more or less plausible:

> Something for everyone, in fact: somewhere, the author seems to be telling his audience, you have done something—think hard and you may remember what it is—which will one day catch you out. The next time you answer a door to an innocent-looking stranger. . . .[30]

VII *The Dumb Waiter*

Although written in 1957, *The Dumb Waiter* was not produced until 1959, and then in Germany. Its first English

production was at the Hempstead Theatre Club and later at the Royal Court, in 1960. It takes as its subject the two agents in *The Birthday Party,* or their counterparts, and explores the predicament of the victimizers, not the victim, who while menacing others can themselves be menaced. As Sinko puts it:

> When the functionary begins to reflect on the meaning of his job, he must die. The mechanism is a self-regulating one, hence the appropriateness of the ambiguous meaning of the Polish title: Samoobsluga, Self-service. Whatever one might think, the job has to go on. Just as in *The Birthday Party* we have not come close to the secret Court or the Authority living in the castle or at the top of the lift: we have just seen it work from another side.

This play explores the uneasiness expressed by a questioning McCann and a faltering Goldberg. *The Dumb Waiter* is a genuine comedy of menace set in a basement in Birmingham and in it Pinter begins to use silence as part of the dialogue, playing off a loquacious character against a silent one. Gus cannot bear silence and Ben resents talk.

The basement room has no windows and only one door leading out into the unknown; the other door opens into a defective lavatory. Here, two men of no particular age, called Ben and Gus, are waiting. Ben has a newspaper from which he occasionally reads out diverting passages and from behind which he watches irritably as Gus moves restlessly about the room or makes frequent visits to the faulty toilet. Their rambling conversation is about trivial matters—items in the newspapers, the crockery they have been provided with, who is playing whom at football next Saturday—trivia interrupted by questions from Gus about the length of the job they are on and what time "he" is likely to get in touch with them. Ben resents this kind of question, excessively, it seems, just as Gus's annoyance with the room seems excessive. Gus likes to have "a bit of a view." Ben, with his woodwork and model boats, replies that Gus ought to have a hobby, though its usefulness in the present situation hardly seems pressing. Gus goes on asking questions. Why, for example, did Ben stop the car early that morning when he thought Gus was asleep? These occasional remarks, running through the ordinary conversation on football and everday events, combine with the tension that obviously exists between Ben and Gus, and gradually build up a sense of something sinister behind the casual presence of two men waiting to do a job in Birmingham.

When an envelope containing twelve matches is pushed under the door and a revolver is snatched from under a pillow, we become more and more certain that these cannot be ordinary working men, that their job is no everyday job, that, in fact, they are two hired assassins, part of a large and mysterious organization, and that their occupation is traveling up and down the country killing people to order. Thus the seemingly trivial argument over the phrase "light a kettle" is more than a semantic quibble. It summarizes the relative positions of the two men, and when

Ben, wearily, forgets and says, "Put on the bloody kettle," the inadequacy of his position of not asking questions is revealed. Such arguments lay a comic foundation for the main question of the play. Moreover, Gus's irritation over smelly sheets, crockery that is not so good as it has been, not having a window, and being permanently on call are really symptoms of his disquiet about the job itself:

> GUS: I was just thinking about that girl, that's all. (GUS *sits on his bed.*) She wasn't much to look at, I know, but still. It was a mess though, wasn't it? What a mess. Honest, I can't remember a mess like that one. They don't seem to hold together like men, women. A looser texture, like. Didn't she spread, eh? She didn't half spread. Kaw! But I've been meaning to ask you. (BEN *sits up and clenches his eyes.*) Who clears up after we've gone? I'm curious about that. Who does the clearing up? Maybe they don't clear up. Maybe they just leave them there, eh? What do you think? How many jobs have we done? Blimey, I can't count them. What if they never clear anything up after we've gone.
>
> BEN *(Pityingly):* You mutt. Do you think we're the only branch of this organization? Have a bit of common. They got departments for everything.
>
> GUS: What cleaners and all?
>
> BEN: You birk!
>
> GUS: No, it was that girl made me start to think. . . .[31]

Further thought, however, is prevented by a clatter from the back of the room, where there is, after all, another entrance to this room: a serving hatch or dumb waiter, which suddenly starts to descend with orders on it for food. The gunmen, anxious not to be discovered, try to fulfill those orders with what food they have brought with them: an Eccles cake, a bar of chocolate, half a pint of milk, and a packet of potato chips. When Ben accuses Gus of hiding the one Eccles cake from him, it is, in view of the end of the play, a rather ironic reproach. But we could explain a great deal of edginess on Ben's part because he knows or suspects what he will have to do. The knowledge that he will have to get rid of his mate could account for his resentment at the beginning of the play and subsequently.

The orders for food continue to arrive, becoming more and more exotic, from macaroni pastitsio and ormitha maca-rounda to scampi. The two men shout up the serving hatch that they have sent everything up. Since this has no effect, they decide to send a written message. At this point, they notice a speaking tube, but it will only work for Ben, who speaks into it with great deference and is told something. Ben and Gus then rehearse the killing in a duologue that, significantly, leaves out the order for Gus to take out his gun. After this, the two men return to the newspaper game, but on a more muted level. While Gus is once more in the defective lavatory, Ben gets his orders—to shoot the next person to come in—and when Gus enters through the door, Ben is facing him, gun in hand, and, presumably, shoots him at the end of the slow curtain.

The main element of comedy is provided by the dialogue—talk to pass the time while Ben and Gus wait, not for Godot, but for orders. Their moral indignation over items in the newspaper (about a man of eighty-seven who crawled under a truck and was run over or the child of eight who killed a cat) contrasts with their own job; it also implies that they are just doing a job, like any other job; and, as long as they regard it as that, they are adequate gunmen. The discussions on football, making tea, and what to do on Saturday become terrifying when we see what these men are. But Gus is no longer a good gunman; he has begun to think about the victims and question the orders and efficiency of the organization. We suspect that the orders from above will lead to tragedy, but this tragedy clearly satisfies the postulate of Ionesco that tragedy should always be fused with hilarious farce. The play is much more comic than either of the preceding plays, though there is, presumably, a victim. The play is about the difference between Ben (the dumb waiter) and Gus (who by asking questions is rebelling). Whereas Ben accepts orders and is an almost perfect cog in the larger machine, Gus is becoming an individual and must be eliminated. Ironically, this very elimination might in turn unsettle Ben, who might, in turn, have to be eliminated also.

VIII CRITICAL INTERPRETATIONS

The end of the play is open, a device that Pinter is to use frequently in later plays. We assume that Gus will be shot and this assumption confirms the serious element of the play. But it is a very comic play, too. The sight of two serious gunmen trying to answer heavenly demands for exotic food is hilarious, and possibly this larger comic element has suggested that the piece is slight. It is certainly less "symbolic" than, say, its companion one-act play, ***The Room***. Critics have complained that it has the air of a dramatized anecdote, but it is not without significance even as a footnote to ***The Birthday Party***. There the "team spirit" was sinister. Martin Esslin asks whether the army (which Pinter so strenuously refused to join) is very different to the organization that sends out Gus and Ben; both require obedience and killing. Dumb obviously means mute, but it may also indicate a certain lack of intelligence, or sensitivity to the job in hand:

> This picture of a job for everyone and everything, with everyone performing his own speciality is close enough to a description of modern society for the correlation to be drawn. Here, then, the play becomes a depiction of the fate of a sensitive man . . . presenting a threat to society because he questions rather than accepts, and who must therefore be destroyed before he destroys.[32]

But we must not overload the play with significance; suggestions about the twelve matches (the Apostles?) and a Trinity of gas rings on the stove are surely far-fetched. J. W. Lambert's introduction to the play in the Penguin edition sums up the play admirably:

> This glimpse of two hired killers is told not merely without heightened prose but in the lowest common denominator of human speech—a dialogue in which

every phrase is drawn straight from life at a level of intellectual vacancy which might seem the death of drama; but which is handled with such a sure command of pause and repetition that evokes simultaneously the laughter of contemptuous recognition and a shiver of dread. As within ourselves, on the one hand open up abysses of bottomless inanity, and the other loom the fearful crags of an irrational, implacable cruelty.

Bizarre and claustrophobic as it is, Mr. Pinter's exploration of the lower depths has an unmistakeable, if indefinable relevance to life as we live it. But it is not, of course, explicitly sociological.[33]

IX *A Slight Ache* and Other Plays

Besides these three stage plays, Pinter's early work includes plays for the radio and revue sketches: *A Slight Ache* (1959), broadcast by the BBC; sketches for two revues; and two plays for radio, *A Night Out* (completed in 1959 and broadcast in 1960) and *The Dwarfs,* broadcast by the BBC Third Program, also in 1960. In these works Pinter explored his techniques and themes but also shifted the tone of his treatment.

A Slight Ache is a play for which Pinter has a very great affection. Written in the post-*Birthday Party* period of failure it established, for him, the right to write as he pleased. Its setting is different: a country house with a garden. If the opening scene between Edward and Flora at breakfast reminds us of *The Room* and *The Birthday Party,* Edward and Flora are obviously from a different social class, they are more articulate, and their room opens out on to a large garden. It is this garden and its plants which is the subject of the argument that opens the play and which is crystallized by the arrival of a wasp which Edward kills with great satisfaction by trapping it in the marmalade pot and pouring boiling water on it.

Once the wasp has been despatched Edward begins to reveal what his real worry is, a matchseller who has been standing at the back gate for two months. Both Edward and Flora use the word "bullock" to describe him, and in some way, he is a catalyst for the inadequacy of the relationship between Edward and Flora. Thus, when Flora calls her husband "Beddie Weddie," Edward's annoyance is surely only partly because she is treating him as a baby. Finally, Edward insists that Flora invite the matchseller in; and the rather revolting but totally silent creature becomes the focus of the histories of both characters. From these histories, which may or may not be true, the play builds up on the antagonisms between Edward and Flora—the inadequacy of Edward and the desires of Flora (her Laurentian rape speech is so elegantly told it must be fantasy).

Edward begins to emerge as the more significant character because he is asking questions. To ask questions is always dangerous, as we have seen in *The Dumb Waiter,* and here questioning the appearance, motives, or implications of the matchseller invites disaster. For Flora the matchseller is no problem—she gives him a name, Barnabas

(son of exhortation), and in naming him solves the problem of his identity. Barnabas becomes, for her, the desirable combination of child, husband, and lover that the apparently dominant Edward never could be. Edward, however, begins to show what is behind his bullying, self-sufficient facade. Pinter gives him two long speeches. His first speech is a history, as is Flora's long speech; but the second one is less a history and more a probe in which he tries to define the matchseller, put a name on him, and put him into a context which is comprehensible. He uses such questions and statements as what game do you play, or, you remind me of Cavendish. He contrasts this lack of definition with yesterday's clarity:

> Yesterday, now it was clear, clearly defined, so clearly.
>
> *(Pause.)*
>
> The garden, too, was sharp, lucid, in the rain, in the sun.
>
> *(Pause.)*
>
> My den, too, was sharp, arranged for my purpose . . . quite satisfactory.
>
> *(Pause.)*
>
> The house, too, was polished, all the bannisters were polished, and the stair rods, and the curtain rods.
>
> *(Pause.)*
>
> My desk was polished, and my cabinet.
>
> *(Pause.)*
>
> I was polished. *(Nostalgic.)* . . .[34]

Now all this brightness and clarity merely dazzles Edward into blindness. At this point the opening argument over the names of flowers becomes more understandable. So does the significance of Flora's last entrance, when she offers Barnabas an orderly polished house: her husband has been reduced to the silence of the matchseller (just as Rose became blind and Stanley dumb). Edward asks questions in search of information, but when Barnabas says nothing, Edward is obliged to invent questions for him. Before this silence, his crisp English middleclass reticence crumbles and he moves into an orgy of confession and self-examination that is concerned, from the beginning, with the basic question, who or what *is* the matchseller? Desperately, Edward tries to pin him down: for over two months he has looked at the matchseller in all weathers from all angles and in all lights. The examination breaks down the examiner—there is no answer to the question, who are you? The play ends with the substitution of Edward for the matchseller.

Basically, there are the usual properties in *A Slight Ache:* a room, uneasy inhabitants, and an intruder who will destroy the precarious if unhappy coziness. But here the "threat" is more completely located inside the characters; indeed, a radio audience could not verify whether or not the matchseller really exists outside the imagination of Edward and Flora. Gale feels this is an irrelevance since he does exist in the stage version and anyway the other two characters act as if he does exist, but this indecisiveness does help to point to the true source of the action: the unfulfilled needs of the man and the woman—psychological rather than physical menace. Trussler has objected that the play suffers badly "from never being about a middle-class couple and a matchseller. It is all symbol and no substance, with quite a few footnotes thrown in to make up the weight."[35] John Russell Brown, on the other hand, finds it Pinter's simplest play! It must be remembered that as a radio play the language has to carry all the weight of the action; and this at least illustrates Pinter's ability to write dialogue outside the vernacular of low life, to capture the class differences that still matter so much in English life and which, as Shaw observed in *Pygmalion,* are frequently a matter of how we speak.

Here Pinter's room has a window and a view (anticipating *The Lover* in theme and setting) and the menace is invited in for examination and plays a completely passive role, to become, in fact, no more than the object in relation to which Edward and Flora act out their fantasies and inadequacies. The venom of the action suggests that the inadequacies are sexual, though whether we feel it as a version of the *Bacchae,* as Burkman suggests, in which Flora, the earth mother, sacrifices the old god for the new is another matter. She is certainly the central character, because whether earth goddess or not she is the one in motion taking on the new role as wife and mother; whereas Edward breaks down when confronted with the silence of the matchseller, a subject explored in the short story written in 1955, "The Examination," and developed still further in another short story, "Tea Party."[36]

X "THE EXAMINATION"

This short story, first published in the summer 1959 issue of *Prospect* (reprinted with *The Lover* and *The Collection* in 1963), is, obviously, not an academic examination in spite of the presence of chalk and a blackboard. It could be compared with the interview sketch "Applicant" and it recalls the prose poem "Kullus": it involves the situation basic to *A Slight Ache* and *The Basement.* The story contains three favorite motifs: a room, domination, and silence. In the examination of Kullus by the Examiner (the "I" of the story) we watch a gradual shift of the dominant to the dominated, which was the theme that attracted Pinter to the film of *The Servant*:

> That short story dealt very explicitly with two people in one room having a battle of an unspecified nature, in which the question was one of who was dominant at what point and how they were going to be dominant and what tools they would use to achieve dominance and how they would try to undermine the other person's dominance. A threat is constantly there; it's got to do with this question of being in the uppermost position, or attempting to be. That's something of what attracted me to do the screenplay of *The Servant,* which was someone else's story you know. I wouldn't call this violence so much as a battle for positions, it's a very common everyday thing.[37]

Of course, in the film, Pinter has the advantage of class warfare and sex; Kullus's sole weapon here seems to be his silence:

> When Kullus was disposed to silence I invariably acquiesced, and prided myself on those occasions with tactical acumen. But I did not regard these silences as intervals, for they were not, and neither, I think, did Kullus so regard them. For if Kullus fell silent, he did not cease to participate in our examination. Never, at any time, had I reason to doubt his active participation, through word and through silence, between interval and interval, and I recognised what I took to be his devotion as actual and unequivocal, besides, as it seemed to me, obligatory. And so the nature of our silence within the frame of our examination, and the nature of our silence outside the frame of our examination, were entirely opposed.

The difference between the two characters is also illustrated, as in *The Basement,* by differences in their rooms; by the end of the story Kullus has not merely noticed the differences between his room and that of the Examiner, he has removed them. The Examiner does not object. He continues, however, to try to understand the nature of Kullus's silences, and his anxiety to do so leads him finally to accept his own Examination by Kullus. By the end he has changed places and rooms with Kullus.

The language in this story is reminiscent of the philosophical content of *The Dwarfs* and later *The Homecoming* as well as *A Slight Ache.* It must be remembered, however, that both *A Slight Ache* and *The Dwarfs* were written for radio, plays that gave scope (too much, perhaps) to Pinter the poet. *A Slight Ache* also marks the end of Pinter's first period, one of relative obscurity. It was commissioned by the BBC Third Program, which serves a minority audience; *The Dumb Waiter* was first produced in Germany; and neither *The Room* nor *The Birthday Party* had been particularly successful. Henceforth audiences and critical approval will grow, and the description "Comedies of Menace" ceases to be useful.

XI REVUE SKETCHES

Writing these revue sketches not only helped Pinter financially, but they also helped him to perfect the comic side of his art, although all of them are tinged with sadness, the pathetic, or the sinister. Pinter has not published two of them, **"Special Offer"** and **"Getting Acquainted"**; indeed, the latter, apparently a farcical episode built round a civil defense practice, is, according to him, lost. The former, however, is a brief account of a BBC lady disturbed by a special offer in a leading London store which Mr. Pinter has allowed to be printed here:

> SECRETARY (*at desk in office*): Yes, I was in the rest room at Swan and Edgars, having a little rest. Just sitting there, interfering with nobody, when this old crone suddenly came right up to me and sat beside me. You're on the staff of the B.B.C. she said, aren't you? As a matter of fact I am, I said. What can I do for you? I've got just the thing for you, she said, and put a little card

into my hand. Do you know what was written on it? MEN FOR SALE! What on earth do you mean? I said. Men, she said, all sorts shapes and sizes, for sale. What on earth can you *possibly mean?* I said. It's an international congress, she said, got up for the entertainment and relief of lady members of the civil service. You can hear some of the boys we've got speak through a microphone, especially for your pleasure, singing little folk tunes we're sure you've never heard before. Tea is on the house and every day we have the very best pastries. For the cabaret at teatime the boys do a rare dance imported all the way from Buenos Aires, dressed in nothing but a pair of cricket pads. Every single one of them is tried and tested, very best quality, and at very reasonable rates. If you like one of them by any of his individual characteristics you can buy him, but for you not at retail price. As you work for the B.B.C. we'll be glad to make a special reduction. If you're at all dissatisfied you can send him back within seven days and have your money refunded. That's *very* kind of you, I said, but as a matter of fact I've just been on leave, I start work tomorrow and am perfectly refreshed. And I left her where she was. Men for Sale! What an extraordinary idea! I've never heard of anything so outrageous, have you? Look—here's the card.

(Pause)

Do you think it's a joke . . . or serious?

An extraordinary idea indeed; but what's sauce for the goose ought, perhaps, to be sauce for the gander. Implicit in this slight sketch is precisely the reversal of roles that audiences found so shocking in **The Homecoming.**

Two of the sketches in print are about interviews: **"Trouble in the Works"** and **"Applicant."** The first grew out of a job that Pinter held for half a day in a factory service department where he had to copy down the names of machine parts. It is a skit on terminology in heavy engineering with splendid sexual overtones. A works manager receives complaints from the workers' representative about certain objects they are making and to which they have taken a dislike:

WILLS: They've just taken a turn against the whole lot of them, I tell you. Male elbow adaptors, tubing nuts, grub screws, internal fan washers, dog points, half dog points, white metal bushes—

FIBBS: But not, surely, my lovely parallel male stud couplings?

WILLS: They hate and detest your lovely parallel male stud couplings, and the straight flange pump connectors, and back nuts, and front nuts, *and* the bronze draw off cock with handwheel and the bronze draw off cock without handwheel![38]

When Fibbs asks, despairingly, what the men do want to make, the answer is brisk and to the point: Brandy Balls. This, for some curious reason, was changed, in the NBC television production "Pinter People," to Love.

"Applicant" apparently comes from the unpublished **The Hothouse** (q.v.) and concerns the fate of an applicant for a

job who is fitted with electrodes and bombarded with impossible questions (for example: Are you virgo intacta? Have you always been virgo intacta?) until he suffers a complete collapse, a situation halfway between the interrogations in **The Birthday Party** and the shock treatment in **The Caretaker.** The other three sketches show two or more characters allowed to interact: **"The Black and White"** (two old tramp women compare notes on how to pass the night), **"Last to Go"** (a newspaper seller and the proprietor of a coffee stall discuss which paper is the last to be sold),[39] and **"Request Stop"** (a slightly mad woman pesters a man at a bus stop with a question and then insists, loudly, that he has made an improper suggestion to her).

XII *A NIGHT OUT*

This radio play was almost immediately transferred to television, where it had a record audience of between 15 and 18 million viewers. Like the revue sketches it is a simple play. Pinter felt there was no real difference between sketch and play: "In both I am interested primarily in people: I want to present living people to the audience, worthy of their interest primarily because they *are,* they exist, not because of any moral the author may draw from them."[40]

Looking at *A Night Out* it is tempting to see Pinter as moving toward a greater realism, but, in fact, the menacers in **The Birthday Party** belong to the normal world and behave more like ordinary people than not, while the gunmen in **The Dumb Waiter** are shown as ordinary people with an extraordinary job; in both plays violence has been toned down. If we exclude the wasp episode violence in the physical sense has also been excluded from *A Slight Ache,* a trend that continues in **The Caretaker,** where menace is a practical joke; it is obviously a clash of personalities that causes displacement. *A Night Out* occurs within a varied and normal context, contains no symbols or any mystery, though Esslin, rather oddly, insists that it ends on a question: is he free? It shows the new directness and simplicity we see in **Night School** and **The Caretaker.** Esslin's view of the ending is odd because though the title does suggest a note of defiance it also confirms that this is a rare if not unique occasion: Albert breaks out of his room, but room service is soon restored.

The play opens with Albert Stokes trying to escape from a possessive mother who will not admit that her husband is dead or that grandma has been dead for ten years—will not admit these facts linguistically, at any rate—and whose principal worry is that Albert will grow up and leave her for another girl:

MOTHER *(following)*: Albert.

ALBERT: What?

MOTHER: I want to ask you a question.

ALBERT: What?

MOTHER: Are you leading a clean life?

ALBERT: A clean life?

MOTHER: You're not leading an unclean life, are you?

ALBERT: What are you talking about?

MOTHER: You're not messing about with girls, are you? You're not going to go messing about with girls tonight?

ALBERT: Don't be so ridiculous.

MOTHER: Answer me, Albert. I'm your mother.

ALBERT: I don't know any girls.

MOTHER: If you're going to the firm's party, there'll be girls there, won't there? Girls from the office?

ALBERT: I don't like them, any of them.

MOTHER: You promise?

ALBERT: Promise what?

MOTHER: That . . . that you won't upset your father.

ALBERT: My father? How can I upset my father? You're always talking about upsetting people who are dead!

MOTHER: Oh, Albert, you don't know how you hurt me, you don't know the hurtful way you've got, speaking of your poor father like that.

ALBERT: But he is dead.

MOTHER: He's not. He's living! (*Touching her breast*) In here! And this is his house![41]

The scene shifts to a coffee stall where two of Albert's colleagues from the office, Seeley and Kedge (the former played by Pinter), are talking about Albert's recent depression, which is spoiling his game of football. At this point, Pinter shifts to a short scene that shows Albert escaping from his mother. He comes to the coffee stall, where his colleagues tease him about a girl (who, they say, is attracted to Albert), his poor game of football, and his mother. The final shot of the act shows the mother laying out a game of patience, the clock ticking on the mantelpiece.

The second act shows the firm's party to say good-bye to an old and trusted member of the company, Mr. Ryan. Here another colleague asks his girl friend's friend, Eileen, to pretend to be friendly with Albert for a joke. Eileen agrees. During the formal speech of farewell, however, Eileen lets out a scream, claims that she has been interfered with, and Albert is blamed. When the firm's accountant, Sidney, taunts Albert with being a mother's boy, Albert hits him and leaves the party. In the television production it was made quite clear that the man who pinched Eileen was old, trusty Mr. Ryan. On the radio such identification was, of course, not possible. The second scene shows Albert's mother asleep in a disorder of playing cards, the clock at twelve, and Albert creeping in. She immediately wakes up and, seeing his disheveled appearance, assumes that he has been messing about with girls. She launches into a long speech on his wickedness in which leaving her alone to go and mess about with girls is confused with

leaving his dinner uneaten. Albert breaks down and the act ends when he raises the clock above her head as if he were going to hit her with it.

Act Three shows Albert back at the coffee stall, which is now closed, where he meets a tart who takes him back to her flat. There she insists that she is really a lady of refinement with a daughter attending a select boarding school in Hereford. She complains when Albert swears, insists that he take off his shoes, use the ashtray, and show other marks of respect, or domesticity. Albert retaliates by pretending to be an assistant director in films, which stimulates the girl to reveal her own longing for the violent, sexual, glamorous life she thinks he must lead as a film director. Albert, ignoring this rambling monologue, suddenly picks up the clock. Alarmed, the girl starts to psychoanalyze him, but he deliberately stubs a cigarette out on the carpet, threatens her with the clock, breaks the photograph of the daughter, exposing it as a lie, and, having made her put his shoes on for him, leaves, casually throwing her half a crown. The final scene shows his return to mother, who welcomes him back:

Listen, Albert, I'll tell you what I'm going to do. I'm going to forget it. You see? I'm going to forget all about it. We'll have your holiday in a fortnight. We can go away. *She strokes his hand.* It's not as if you're a bad boy . . . you're a good boy . . . I know you are . . . it's not as if you're really bad, Albert, you're not . . . you're not bad, you're good . . . you're not a bad boy, Albert, I know you're not. . . .

(*Pause*)

You're good, You're not bad, you're a good boy . . . I know you are . . . you are, aren't you?[42]

Unfortunately for Albert, she is right: the night out is over.

There is really no ambiguity or mystery in the play; the dreams of the tart and Albert are only dreams, the photograph is identified by the inscription on the back, and even the person who interfered with Eileen is identified. The play does bring together the multiple possibility of a woman: mother, girl friend, and tart—but this is not explored; indeed it is deliberately excluded from the next play, *The Dwarfs*. Basically the play is about the relationship between a mother and her son, almost a documented case history of an Oedipus complex;[43] and widening out from that situation the need for lonely or insecure people to have illusions: the *need* to lie. Albert and his mother remind us of the Stanley/Meg situation, but since Albert has not chosen it he resents it; and he is too inadequate to be able, as Stanley can, to turn his mother's stupidity to his own advantage. He feels guilty about going to the party, and so the party is bound to be disastrous. Even when he resorts to violence he has to be content with what Taylor calls "a substitute victory" against a substitute victim—he reproaches the girl, for example, for endless talking, as he does his mother. The mother's willingness to forget and the fact that she remains unharmed at the end of the play suggest that nothing that Albert can do now really matters.

XIII The Dwarfs

Finally, in 1960, the BBC Third Program broadcast Pinter's play **The Dwarfs,** which was subsequently staged, with Pinter directing, at the New Arts Theatre in September 1963. Of this play Taylor comments that it is the most difficult and daunting to popular taste,[44] while Wellwarth concludes that it was impossible to make anything definite of it.[45] The reactions of the critics and audiences in 1963, in spite of a very sensitive performance by John Hurt in the main part, support these judgments. It is a very private play, written for the radio, a medium that allowed Pinter freedom to experiment and to take risks with words. Thus **The Dwarfs** was an extremely valuable play for Pinter, although he admits that it may have been incomprehensible to the audience.[46]

The play is based on an unpublished novel written sometime between 1950-56, with four characters, three men and a girl called Virginia. In the play only the three men appear, Len, Pete, and Mark. The novel was, apparently, partly autobiographical, about growing up in the East End of London. Len and Mark were Jewish while Pete was not; and Mark was also an actor with Portuguese ancestors. Written over too long a period, in too many styles, and possibly showing too many signs of enthusiasm for Beckett's *Watt,* the only things Pinter felt worth exploring were used in the radio play.[47]

XIV The Action of the Play

The play opens with two typical Pinter characters, Pete and Len, who are waiting in Mark's flat for his return. Initially they remind us a little of Gus and Ben because of their desultory conversation (mainly about food and Mark), and particularly because of Len's incessant questions and Pete's irritation at them. We learn nothing about Pete, but we do gather that Len has a casual job as a porter at Euston station and prefers night work. The excitable nature of Len's interest in things justifies Pete's early remark, "You'll be ready for the looney bin next week if you go on like this." Pete, in contrast, is thoroughly noncommittal; even when Len examines his palm and pronounces Pete a homicidal maniac, he remains unperturbed.

The arrival of Mark ends this scene and the next takes place in Len's room. The text does not prescribe a particular room but the production showed that Len's room was old, inherited from the family, and reminiscent of Edgar Allan Poe in furnishing and decor. Here Len tries to establish his existence by defining, in a manner reminiscent of Ionesco's language-primer dialogue, his table, his chair, his bowl of fruit, and so on.[48] Against this fixed existence, which makes all "clear and abundant" but which is also a "manacle," runs the idea that the room moves (ironically, "to a dead halt"!). At the moment all is ordered, in its place; and Len is wedged: "There are no voices. They make a hole in my side." Since **The Dwarfs** is a play for voices and is certainly "poetic," the hole-in-the-side image could have a religious significance—it is repeated later—

but it does not make Len a Christ figure. It reminds us of certain connections, just as Wellwarth may be suggestive in seeing Mark as a papal symbol.[49]

The soliloquy is interrupted by the arrival of Mark in a new suit described (or defined?) in a music-hall patter played out between Len and Mark. Once more the talk is desultory, but behind it is a desire to put a label or price on everything—a desire that holds together statements like "There is a time and place for everything" and "The price of butter is going up."[50] But Mark's presence in the room constitutes a challenge: Len insists that he wants no curiosity there. Since curiosity is a mark of the Pinter victim and liberally displayed by Len and rarely, if ever, by Mark, this statement is both ironic and self-commentary. It leads into Len's second statement about the room. In his first description, while conceding mobility (the room rearranges itself if one stops watching it), he emphasizes the quality of "fixture"—albeit an imprisoning one. Len now stresses "mobility" or change. One cannot, he asserts, rely on the natural behavior of a room, however much one wants to. He uses the analogy of sitting in a railway compartment to show unknowability. From his window he can see lights moving that he knows are still and move only because he moves; or rather because he is still but being moved. Only when moving can he know objects, yet only objects in stillness can be known. This is a complicated way of saying that what we think we know can be false, and in the following scene, Pete suggests putting the troublesome furniture in a boat and parking it (that is, not moving it!). Pete delivers a lecture to Len summed up in the line, "Giving up the ghost isn't so much a failure as a tactical error."

Pete insists that Len pull himself together, or he will be locked up. When Len protests that things change every minute, Pete replies that he should discriminate:

> You've got no idea how to preserve a distance between what you smell and what you think about it. You haven't got the faculty for making a simple distinction between one thing and another. Every time you walk out of this door you go straight over a cliff. What you've got to do is nourish the power of assessment. How can you hope to assess and verify anything if you walk about with your nose stuck between your feet all day long?[51]

Pete then warns Len that Mark is no good for him and follows this with an account of a strange dream: of himself, in a subway station in which everybody's face was peeling off, rotting and blistering—which reduces Len to groans. It is possible that Pete's nightmare, deliberately thrust on the unstable Len, acts like Goldberg's speeches on Stanley. If, in fact, Pete and Mark are another form of menacers, their powers are ironically extended to the dwarfs themselves. Who or what the dwarfs are, we are not told; they simply organize, carry out a job of some sort, and leave (like fantastic Goldbergs and McCanns?). They are skilled laborers, and their trade is not without risk. Thus they might be phantasmal representatives of the organization that employs Ben and Gus or Goldberg and McCann. We know that in some way Len's standing with them depends on Pete and Mark.

In the next scene, Len, possibly influenced by Pete's dream, asks Mark about his face, and Mark warns Len that Pete is no good for him. Len interrupts this to state once more the close involvement of Len, Pete, Mark, and the dwarfs, using the conjugated verb "he sits, I sit; they stand, I squat." As the dialogue becomes more and more interior, the play seems to consist of a steady progression into Len's private world. Often scenes with Pete and Mark seem more presented by Len than directly experienced by us. The dwarfs, according to Len, have gone off on a picnic, leaving him to clean up their garbage. In another soliloquy he visualizes his two friends as seagull and spider:

> Pete walks by the—gull. Slicing gull. Gull. Down. He stops. Stone. Watches. Rat corpse in the yellow grass. Gull pads. Gull probes. Gull stamps his feet. Gull whinnies up. Gull screams, tears, Pete tears, digs, Pete cuts, breaks, Pete stretches the corpse, flaps his wings, Pete's beak grows, probes, digs, pulls, the river jolts, no moon, what can I see. . . .
>
> Mark lies, heavy, content, watches his smoke in the window, times his puff out, his hand fall, *(with growing disgust)* smiles at absent guests, sucks in all comers, arranges his web, lies there a spider.[52]

In a later conversation with Mark, Len tries to question him, but has as little success as with Pete. Important questions like "Do you believe in God?" are bypassed until Len forces the point:

> The point is, who are you. Not why or how, not even what. I can see what, perhaps, clearly enough. But who are you? It's no use saying you know who you are just because you tell me you can fit your particular key into a particular slot which will only receive your particular key because that's not foolproof and certainly not conclusive. Just because you're inclined to make these statements of faith has nothing to do with me. It's not my business. Occasionally I believe I perceive a little of what you are but that's pure accident. Pure accident on both our parts, the perceived and the perceiver. It's nothing like an accident, it's deliberate, it's a joint pretense. We depend on these accidents, on these contrived accidents, to continue. It's not important then that it's conspiracy, or hallucination. What you are, or appear to be to me, or appear to be to you, changes so quickly, so horrifyingly, I certainly can't keep up with it, and I'm damn sure you can't either. But who you are I can't even begin to recognize, and sometimes I recognize it so wholly, so forcibly, I can't look, and how can I be certain of what I see? You have no number. Where am I to look, where am I to look, what is there to locate, so as to have some surety, to have some rest from this whole bloody racket? You're the scum of so many reflections. How many reflections? Whose reflections? Is that what you consist of? What scum does the tide leave? What happens to the scum? When does it happen? I've seen what happens. But I can't speak when I see it. I can only point a finger. I

can't even do that. The scum is broken and sucked back. I don't see where it goes. I don't see when, what do I see, what have I seen? What have I seen, the scum or the essence? What about it?[53]

Mark is unmoved by the questions about personality until his vanity is pricked when Len, accidentally or deliberately, lets slip that Pete thinks Mark is a fool. After this incident Len is in a hospital, visited by Mark and Pete, who are clearly at odds with each other while, at the same time, realizing that in some curious way they need each other. When Len comes out of the hospital, the dwarfs are preparing to leave him, and at the end of the play they have left. So also, apparently, have Pete and Mark. The yard is clean and bare—except for a redeeming flower:

> Now all is bare. All is clean. All is scrubbed. There is a lawn. There is a shrub. There is a flower.[54]

XV CRITICAL REACTION TO *THE DWARFS*

The difficulties of staging a radio play are always interesting, but the critical response to this play, in print, and possibly heard previously, was disappointing. It was staged with **The Lover,** also in print and previously seen on television. The easier play to watch and write about was, obviously, **The Lover,** and it was that play that predominated in reviews; but, with the exception of *The New Statesman,* which simply gave a garbled version of the plot in two lines, most reviewers tackled **The Dwarfs** fairly, as far as the number of lines given to it.

David Nathan, in the *Daily Herald* (September 19), decided that he "had not got the password to Mr. Pinter's private though poetic world. Shortly afterwards I lost even the wish to enter it, and dreamed my own dreams while waiting passively for the curtain to fall." In varying degrees of agreement with Nathan were the critics of the *Daily Telegraph,* the *Guardian,* the *Spectator, Punch,* and even Harold Hobson in *The Sunday Times.* The critic of *The Times* (September 20) connected both plays with an "incurable obsession with the elusiveness of reality" and out-Pintered Pinter with a final comment: "The resolution of the play comes when Len discovers a flower in his backyard: an undeniable object."

T. C. Worsley, in the *Financial Times,* seems to have been right when he suggested that the play demanded more of an audience, including critics, than the average one was prepared to give. But he suggested that there was a reward in listening to the "heightened prose of a quite remarkable quality." He also pointed out that the play was not quite adjusted to the stage, a point raised by Bamber Gascoigne, in the *Observer,* who found the images muffled and blurred. Taylor, however, in *Plays and Players* (November 1963), felt that the transfer from radio to stage had come off better than one could have hoped for because of the density of the writing and the switches from subjective to objective moods. For a critic, Taylor offered an unusual conclusion: "The result is that one does not finally care about whether the play is or is not in theory "theatrical"; it is a riveting experience in the theater, and that, after all, is what really counts."

But the play was not new, and, even if it had been it is the job of a critic to express an opinion that will guide those people who have to pay for their tickets. We have a right to expect, even in a daily newspaper, more than a brief glance at the plot or a tentative foray into symbolic logic. Most of the reviewers who recognized that the play was "poetic" failed to give the language the attention such a recognition predicates. It is fascinating, for example, to connect the "bullock" image in *A Slight Ache* with the "bullock" image in *The Lover.* The language of *The Dwarfs* is less vernacular than we expect from Pinter; and of all his plays hints at a foreign origin. Kitchin remarked on the coincidence between *The Dwarfs* and the crabs in Sartre's *Altona* (1959): ". . . There is the feeling that this is tapping a big continental thing, and not just a parochial, though you bring it . . . you make it English that for me is a pleasure . . . you absolutely digest it."[55] This Englishness is crucial. But the work that springs to mind is, of course, Sartre's *Nausea,* and we might do well to take Iris Murdoch's advice on the interpretation of that novel:

> The rich overabundance of reality, the phantasmagoria of "disordered" sensation, seem to the author of *La Nausée* a horrifying rather than a releasing spectacle, a threat to the possibility of meaning and truth. The more surprising contents of our consciousness are to be interpreted as distorted versions of our deep intentions and *not as dependent symbols* [italics mine], and certainly not as strays from a subterranean region of supreme power and value. Sartre fears, not loves, this notion of a volcanic otherness within the personality.[56]

Transferring the play from radio to the stage solved certain problems: the stage production makes clear which speeches are soliloquy and which are monologues with Pete or Mark present. Pinter's production also cleared up Taylor's difficulty over the end of the play. Taylor, comparing Len with Aston in *The Caretaker,* suggested that Len still has Aston's desperate remedy to come, hovering as he is on the brink of mental insanity: ". . . When we leave him [he] is perhaps already in a mental home. (Or is he? It depends whether Pete is being evasive when he says that Len is in hospital suffering from 'kidney' trouble, or simply stating a fact.)"[57] Pinter's production showed the last speech spoken by a Len discharged from the hospital and back home (cured?)—a fact that may color our interpretation of the last speech; which certainly, to me, gave the end an upward shift—a sense of peace, beauty, and hopefulness.

XVI THE MEANING OF *THE DWARFS*

Was this sense of uplift appropriate? The meaning of *The Dwarfs* depends on how you answer two questions: is the end a victory or a defeat for Len, and who or what are the dwarfs? Both questions are essentially the same, and an optimistic answer may be simply Bad Faith.

Trussler sees Pete's speech as more important than Len's because Pete knows when a dream is a dream whereas

Len is losing his power of discrimination, failing to keep his distance. But if we trace philosophers from Edward through Len to Teddy in *The Homecoming* keeping ones distance is no good thing. Lenny is a cheerful and pragmatic philosopher; Teddy becomes a stranger. And by the end Len has become a stranger—at least to his friends and the dwarfs. For Gabbard, on a Freudian interpretation, Len is "a new man . . . born into an unlittered life. The new life promises to be empty of dark old houses without the light bulbs. The new life is bright. It promises to be empty of leaky old houses filled with junk. The new life is renovated."[58] But Stanley was promised a new life at the end of *The Birthday Party.* For Burkman, Len is reborn, emerging from his ordeal into a new kingdom; for Baker/Tabachnik, Len has scored a victory by ridding himself of intruders, the dwarfs who are "compounded of the threats and hatred of the 'friends'";[59] for R. F. Storch the dwarfs are "naked childhood obsessions"—the foundations of bourgeois virtues—cleanliness, order, four walls you can call your own: "Many of the tensions in an Ibsen family are due to the frightful cost of taming the dwarfs, or to the reckless refusal to tame them."[60]

Whether we accept that this play (according to Baker/Tabachnik) teems with Jewish nuances it is clearly more autobiographical than any previous play. Martin Esslin, who has read the novel version, sees the ending as a young man emerging "from the wild whirlpool of steaming adolescence into the bare, ordered world of respectability"[61] and suggests that the girl, Virginia (who anticipates Sally in *Night School* because she is a school teacher *and* a frequenter of night clubs), was excluded because she would provide a chance motivation for what must be seen as an inevitable change, part of growing up. The dwarfs, then, represent not unseen powers or poetic imagination but simply the misery of change, the end of a relationship which leaves Len—unable to move with the times—in an antiseptic world of dead emotions.

Mark and Pete may, of course, be projections of conflicting selves in Len. Yet they are also typical Pinter characters—inconsequential in conversation, avoiding real communication or real questions as much as possible. They shun the truth, ignoring Len's unusual behavior until Mark's vanity is pricked. Each thinks, or says, that the other is bad for Len and both gull and spider are, in their different ways, predators, scavengers, feeding on corpses. Len, as the central character, may possibly be the only character. He seems to be nearly mad, anticipating what, we assume, Aston was like before his operation and echoing previous examiners—like Edward in *A Slight Ache.* The question remains, who are you?

Len cannot bear relativity: his love of mathematics, his almost Freudian concern with his bowel movements, his worry about flux in nature bring him to some kind of breakdown. We ordinarily presume that beneath the spurious permanency naming confers upon objects, there is a more absolute kind of permanency, what Miss Murdoch calls "a subterranean region of supreme power and value"—but is there? It is not so much that Len has lost poetry or sanity but that by standing still he has refused the new roles—to grow up and on. Sex would have made the recognition of this too obviously; it would have distracted the audience from a natural change which is being observed, regretfully, but implacably. Pinter is dealing with characters trying to make the crucial adjustment to society and the people they meet. If they can adjust there will be time for them to play adult games (like sex or even politics), as we shall see in *The Collection* or *The Lover.* But so far the characters have not succeeded; as is illustrated in Pinter's first really successful long play, *The Caretaker,* which is still about a room and three people.

Notes

1. Sykes, p. 27.

2. Esslin, p. 43.

3. The *Observer* profile (September 15, 1963) attributed the name "da Pinta" to Pinter's Portuguese ancestry. But Pinter himself, in a letter to me dated April 28, 1964, pointed out that this was very remote.

4. Baker/Tabachnik, p. 18.

5. "Harold Pinter Replies."

6. *The Room* (New York, 1961), p. 99.

7. Ibid., p. 110.

8. Ibid., p. 118.

9. Quoted in Esslin, p. 21.

10. Ibid., p. 66.

11. Clifford Leech, "Two Romantics: Arnold Wesker and Harold Pinter," in Brown and Harris, *Contemporary Theater,* p. 26.

12. John Russell Taylor, *Anger and After,* p. 287.

13. Bensky, reprinted Ganz, p. 20.

14. *The Birthday Party* (New York, 1961), p. 32.

15. Cf. the gloss of this device in Jack Kerouac, *The Town and the City* (New York, 1950), pp. 375 ff.

16. *The Birthday Party,* p. 54.

17. Ibid., p. 59.

18. Ibid., p. 80.

19. Ibid., p. 84.

20. Pinter has since changed this to less formal wear.

21. Irving Wardle, *Encore* (July-August 1958), 39-40.

22. Bert O. States, *Irony and Drama* (Ithaca, N. Y., and London, 1971), p. 127.

23. Bernard Dukore, "The Theater of Harold Pinter," *Tulane Drama Review* VI: 3 (March 1962), 55-68.

24. Quigley, p. 66.

25. *The Birthday Party,* p. 88.

26. R. F. Storch, in Ganz, pp. 138-39.

27. Gregorz Sinko, "Stara i Mtoda Anglia," *Dialog* LX: 4 (April 1961), 97-99.

28. Simon Trussler, *The Plays of Harold Pinter* (London, 1973), p. 46.

29. Baker/Tabachnik, pp. 57-58.

30. Taylor, *Anger and After,* p. 290.

31. *The Dumb Waiter* (New York, 1961), pp. 102-103.

32. Steven H. Gale, *butter's going up: a critical analysis of Harold Pinter's work* (Durham, N.C., 1977), p. 59.

33. Tom Maschler (ed.) *New English Dramatists,* No. 3, Introduction by J. W. Lambert (Harmondsworth, Middlesex, 1961) pp. 9-10.

34. *A Slight Ache* (New York, 1962), p. 35.

35. Trussler, p. 64.

36. See Chapter 6 for discussion of "Tea Party."

37. Bensky, reprinted Ganz, p. 29.

38. *A Slight Ache and Other Plays* (London, 1961), p. 121.

39. Recorded by Kenneth Williams. See bibliography.

40. Quoted in Taylor, *Anger and After,* p. 296.

41. *A Slight Ache and Other Plays,* p. 47.

42. Ibid., p. 87.

43. Burkman, p. 97.

44. Taylor, *Anger and After,* p. 307.

45. Wellwarth, *The Theater of Protest and Paradox,* p. 208.

46. "Writing for Myself."

47. Ibid.

48. Cf. the following extract from Sartre's *Nausea,* p. 169.

> I murmur: "It's a seat," a little like an exorcism. But the word stays on my lips: it refuses to go and put itself on the things. It stays what it is, with its red plush, thousands of little red paws in the air; all still, little dead paws, this belly floating in this car, in this grey sky, is not a seat. It could just as well be a dead donkey tossed about in the water, floating with the current, belly in the air in a great grey river, a river of floods; and I could be sitting on the donkey's belly, my feet dangling in the clear water. Things are divorced from their names. They are there, grotesque, headstrong, gigantic and it seems ridiculous to call them seats or say anything at all about them: I am in the midst of things, nameless things. Alone, without

words, defenceless, they surround me, are beneath me, behind me, above me. They demand nothing, they don't impose themselves: they are there.

49. Wellwarth, *The Theater of Protest and Paradox,* p. 208.

50. Phrases like "butter's up" and "gentleman's gentle-man" recur in *The Servant.* It is surely the poet in Pinter that savors these phrases.

51. *The Dwarfs* (New York, 1962), p. 91.

52. Ibid., pp. 99-100, 101.

53. Ibid., pp. 103-104.

54. Ibid., p. 108.

55. BBC Transcript, *New Comment* (this accounts for the oddness of punctuation and the erratic grammar of the passages quoted).

56. Murdoch, *Sartre,* p. 35.

57. Taylor, *Anger and After,* pp. 307-308.

58. Gabbard, p. 140.

59. Baker/Tabachnik, p. 44.

60. Storch, in Ganz, p. 144.

61. Esslin, p. 119.

Arnold P. Hinchliffe (essay date 1986)

SOURCE: "After No Man's Land: A Progress Report," in *Harold Pinter: Critical Approaches,* edited by Steven H. Gale, Fairleigh Dickinson University Press, 1986, pp. 153-63.

[*In the following essay, Hinchliffe provides an overview of Pinter's plays from* No Man's Land *to* Players.]

No Man's Land opened on 23 April 1975 and marked the culmination of twenty years' work in the theatre, work interspersed with other kinds of writing—poetry, plays for radio and television, adaptations and film scripts—and other kinds of work—acting and directing. The longest gap between stage plays was that between *The Caretaker* (1960) and *The Homecoming* (1965), but during that time Pinter produced plays for television and two, if not three, film scripts. In short, Austin Quigley is probably correct when he suggests that of all the dramatists who came to the fore in the middle fifties in the British theatre only Pinter has consistently maintained a momentum of achievement:

> Where Osborne, Wesker, Simpson, Arden, and even Beckett have gradually faded as playwrights, Pinter increasingly attracts the attention of scholars, critics and audiences alike.[1]

The plays for the theatre were, it is true, getting shorter. Pinter confessed in 1969 that all he seemed to write were one-act plays: "I doubt if I will ever write something mammoth."[2] *Old Times* (1971) was certainly not *mammoth,* if that word implies five acts and a large canvas; nor, for that matter, was *No Man's Land,* but the texture and complexity of both rendered them formidable experiences in the theatre. *No Man's Land,* in particular, seemed to gather together in its bleak fashion the strands of Pinter's previous work—a room, power, violence, sex, memory, and language—in such a way as to leave us with the question: where can Pinter go after this? There was, of course, some difficulty in separating the play from the performance, since Sir Ralph Richardson and Sir John Gielgud could make anything memorable. Was it, after all, only, as Peter Thomson suggests, "an elaborate spoof"?[3]

In the period after *No Man's Land* Pinter worked on the film script of *The French Lieutenant's Woman,* which took over a year to write. Film scripts have nourished his stage plays, and filmic effects have been noted in *The Homecoming* and *Old Times. No Man's Land* itself surely owes much to *The Go-Between.* But film scripts, however rewarding, are time-consuming and, however distinguished, are works of translation rather than creation. The opening of *Betrayal* at the National Theatre on 15 November 1978, was, therefore, more than usually interesting, particularly as, for the first time, the title of the play was ominous rather than cozy. The play was striking in other ways too. In it, for the first time, Pinter abandoned the use of a single set in favor of several sets. The nine scenes require seven sets, which the National Theatre solved with a rather clumsy and very cramped revolving stage. The use of sets rather than a single, composite set had hitherto been restricted to the more fluid medium of television. Second, the nine scenes were all dated, and the play begins in 1977 and moves backward to 1968, an arrangement that is listed in the program (the alternative would have been, presumably, Brechtian slides announcing time and place, which might have been difficult since a revolve was being used). Each scene also has a season as well as a time and place.

Betrayal opens in the spring of 1977 in a pub where Emma has asked Jerry to meet her. Emma runs an art gallery and has been married to a publisher called Robert for more than fourteen years. Jerry is also married, though his wife, Judith, a doctor, never appears in the play. Both couples have children, and Jerry, a literary agent, has been Robert's best friend and best man since they were both at college (Jerry at Cambridge and Robert at Oxford). Emma had a seven-year affair with Jerry, which had ended two years ago (scene 3), may be having an affair with a writer-artist called Casey (whose name is actually Roger), and has asked Jerry to meet her not so much to recall old times as to tell him that her marriage is now finished, that Robert has been betraying her for years with other women (as she and Jerry betrayed him for years) and that it is now all out in the open. So she has told Robert about her affair with Jerry.

Jerry immediately calls Robert (scene 2) only to discover that Emma told him about the affair four years ago (scene 5). Jerry is upset and points out that he and Robert have seen one another a great deal over the last four years (though, as Robert observes, they have never played squash). Jerry tries to recall their relationship by saying that he is reading Yeats but has to remind Robert that he read Yeats at Torcello four years ago (scene 7). Scene 3 is set in the flat in Kilburn in the winter of 1975 when the affair is ending. It has proved difficult to get away to make love in the afternoon!

The play now catches up on the relationship between these three characters at crucial points in the story: the summer in Venice (1973) when, according to Emma, they did not go to Torcello and according to Robert he did, when Emma is trapped by a letter and discloses all about her affair with Jerry but insists that their son is Robert's; followed by Emma's meeting with Jerry in the flat after the Venice holiday when she mentions nothing about the discovery (though Jerry, too, has had a fright concerning a letter and thus offers her the opportunity to tell him); and a scene between Robert and Jerry in a restaurant, also after the Venice trip, when Robert does not mention Jerry's affair with his wife. Scene 8 is the summer of 1971 and shows the beginning of the affair in the flat at Kilburn when Emma assures Jerry that her son is Robert's, not his, and throws in the suggestion that Jerry's wife is not always at the hospital when he thinks she is. Finally, in scene 9, we see the true beginning of the affair, in the winter of 1968, when a drunken Jerry declares his love for Robert's wife and Robert accepts that Jerry, as his oldest friend and best man, can do just that.

The play is as loaded with detail as the room in *The Caretaker* is cluttered up with objects, but are any of the details significant? Is squash a game you only play with friends (does Robert stop playing squash with Casey because Casey is having an affair with Emma?)? Who is Casey? Who is Ned's father? In Judith, that busy doctor, busy betraying Jerry? What significance can we attach to the novel by Spinks that is read in Venice and that may be about betrayal ("not much more to say on that subject, really, is there?")? Is the journey to Torcello, if it took place, a clue—and should it recall Ruskin or even *Howard's End?* And during the discussion on Venice in the restaurant is there some clue in the fact that Robert orders Corvo Bianco, a wine from Palermo? But such questions seem rather teasing than resonant.

Critical reception was puzzled, too, and on the whole disappointed. Robert Cushman, in *The Observer* (19 November 1978), retitled the play "Harold Pinter's Revenge" because here was a dramatist who has always been accused of giving us no details about his characters now giving us everything and it does us no good:

> We learn a lot about the world of the three characters, and Mr. Pinter is as adept as ever in slipping immensely suggestive details on to a bland canvas. These details, however, are merely sociological; we learn almost nothing about the characters as individuals and thus—since their situation is hardly original—can take no very lively interest in them.

B. A. Young, in *The Financial Times* (17 November 1978), found "no complexities in the straight-forward tale of multiple adultery and the object of it seems to be to put forward the rival claims of wife and mistress." The characters were uninteresting presumably because Pinter wanted them to be uninteresting, and the colorless performances were, presumably, as Peter Hall required. Milton Shulman (*The Evening Standard,* 16 November 1978) also found nothing difficult or obscure in this Chinese box of deceit and thought that many women's magazines would be prepared to print it without changing a line. Noting that Pinter's concerns have gone up in the world, he suggested that the play was about something more important than the betrayal of a husband by his wife or vice versa—it was about "man's betrayal of his best friend." John Barber (*The Daily Telegraph,* 16 November 1978) came out feeling that he had seen "an intricate and unimportant machine" rather than a play, while Michael Billington, in *The Guardian* (16 November 1978), was distressed by "the pitifully thin strip of human experience it explores and its obsession with the tiny ripples on the stagnant pond of bourgeois-affluent life." Here Pinter has betrayed his talent "by serving up this kind of high-class soap-opera (laced with suitable cultural brand-names like Venice, Torcello, and Yeats) instead of a real play." Billington conceded that there was technical finesse in starting the play in the present and running it backward, but though he felt this would make for interesting discussions in a drama faculty it provided thin pleasure for the playgoer.

Bernard Levin, in the *Sunday Times* (19 November 1978), has never been an admirer of Pinter's very small talk—indeed he describes the Pinteresque elements in *The Caretaker* as "nothing but devices which cover a desperate poverty of thought and feeling"! Levin, therefore, was disheartened to find that he did not like the new, plain Pinter either. Here Pinter has written "a real play instead of a series of trivial dramatic acrostics" but he found "the content empty, and on its surface, dull":

> There is no sign of any interest, on the part of Mr Pinter, in these people, their lives or their feelings; not surprisingly, they therefore arouse no interest of their own.

He concluded that Pinter's new ground turns out to be a quicksand into which he sinks without a struggle.

Was this a new, plain Pinter? Martin Esslin asks that question, too (*Plays and Players,* January 1979), pointing out that here was a realistic account of adultery in London middle-class intellectual circles with one unusual feature—the story is told backward, and the sting is in the tail:

> Throughout the first eight scenes we might still have believed that it was the end of a great tragic passion that we witnessed at the beginning. Here it is revealed

that it arose casually, out of drunkenness, and, above all, that the husband who burst into the room just as it was happening not only remained blind to what was going on but actually encouraged the affair by taking the confession of his friend's affection for the wife as no more than politeness and withdrawing leaving the two together.

The colorlessness of the characters is according to Esslin the point of the play. There is very little human emotion between them—the relationship on "a personal, intellectual, spiritual plane is shown as totally arid, in fact, nonexistent. That, to my mind, is the point the play is making. And it is by no means a trivial point. It is central to the sickness of our society." Possibly; but we cannot have the impression of a great tragic passion if the characters are colorless and uninvolved.

The play, it seems to me, is more suited to television. The clumsy revolve at the National Theatre may have been intended to suggest a roundabout (as in *La Ronde*), but it reduced the sets to one cramped space losing the distinction between the spacious elegant surroundings of their married lives and the narrow conditions of adultery. The actor Daniel Massey, in fact, was far from colorless, and the text supports his knowing, ironic treatment of his character. Robert may not "give a shit," but he is a man who enjoys the violence of squash and who gives Emma "a good bashing" once or twice *because* he feels like it. He is also witty. Penelope Wilton made what she could of Emma, which is not very much, while Michael Gambon caught exactly a Jerry who doesn't know very much about anything and runs round trying to find out without being found out. But it is a comedy Pinter could have written any time before or after *No Man's Land;* it boils the pot nicely, and resonances may emerge with time. Reading the text again in 1982, I no longer found that the word *dull* applied.

Pinter's next play was no indication of the route he would take, either. *The Hothouse* opened on 1 May 1980, but according to Martin Esslin it was a play written for radio in 1958 and discarded in favor of the style and methods of *The Caretaker,* which incorporates some of its material. Another episode from the play appears as the revue sketch **"Applicant."** In an interview with Laurence M. Bensky in 1966 Pinter explained why he had discarded it:

> It was heavily satirical and it was quite useless. I never began to like any of the characters, they didn't really live at all. So I discarded the play at once. The characters were purely cardboard. I was intentionally—for the only time I think—trying to make a point, an explicit point, that these were nasty people and I disapproved of them. And therefore they didn't begin to live.[4]

Perhaps, however, in the mechanical world of *Betrayal* such characters struck their creator more sympathetically? At any rate, in an interview with John Barber (*Daily Telegraph,* 23 June 1980), he said that he had come across the script in 1979, read it as a stranger, and found himself laughing a lot: "Nothing about it seemed to be 22 years old. I could have written it yesterday, so far as I could see." He also added that it was more pertinent now than in 1958:

> . . . when we didn't know anything about the Russian psychiatric hospitals, did we? Now we do. But then, it might have been dismissed as fantasy. No, I certainly had no special knowledge of such things. Of course I knew Koestler's "Darkness at Noon" and so on, but in 1958 I don't think there was general knowledge that these things were being refined, as they are to this day. Not that I consider this play to be a grim piece of work. I don't think it is. An odd mixture of "laughter and chill" if you like.

Again we must qualify the comment about special knowledge with the comment in the *Radio Times* for the television production of the play:

> Way back in the 50s, Pinter became a guinea-pig in a psychiatric hospital, subjected to a test for "ten bob a time." And that was an experience, involving electrodes in the head, which stayed with him ever since.[5]

This would certainly explain material that runs through *The Hothouse* (1958), *The Dwarfs* (1960), and *The Caretaker* (1960).

The Hothouse is a psychiatric hospital run by the Ministry and staffed with characters who have names like Roote, Gibbs, Lamb, Lush, Tubb, and Lobb (Hogg, Beck, Budd, Tuck, Dodds, and Tate are also mentioned). It is Christmas Day and the snow is falling fast as Colonel Roote and his deputy, Gibbs, discuss the problems of the institution, one of which is the death of 6457 (patients have no names, only numbers). Does Gibbs want to replace Roote as Roote may have replaced his predecessor? Certainly Roote's hesitant use of the word "retired" seems to suggest that it does not exactly described what happened to his predecessor. The lights fade and come up on another part of the establishment, suggesting that Pinter did not need film work to write the opening scene of *Old Times* and that the text as we have it was certainly not written for radio. Lamb has just played a game of table tennis with Miss Cutts (as in *Tea Party?*). Although Lamb has been at the hospital for over a year he has made no contacts nor has he realized his ambitions for promotion, so he is delighted to meet Miss Cutts and play with her. We are also told that his job is to go round and round the hospital checking that all gates and doors are locked. The scene fades back to Roote's office where the second problem is being discussed: 6459 has given birth to a baby boy! Miss Cutts enters and having noted that Gibbs seems frightened of her proceeds to comfort Roote and ask him whether he finds her feminine enough (as in *The Lover?*). Gibbs, meanwhile, is playing patience! Lush enters and challenges him about paternity and death, but he responds by summoning Lamb to the No. 1 Interview Room where he can assist at an experiment (as his predecessor did). Lamb is fitted up with earphones and electrodes, interrogated, and left there.

Act 2 opens again in Roote's office. It is night, the snow is turning to slush, and the heat is intolerable (though higher up in the building, we are told, it is very cold). Roote is drinking with Lush, who challenges him (as he challenged Gibbs) and gets a violent response. Gibbs arrives to announce that Lamb is the father of the child (though as *virgo intacta* this can hardly be true), and over the intercom we hear the sounds of the understaff's Christmas raffle in which all the prizes go unclaimed (including the duck won by Lamb). Tubb arrives with a cake for the Colonel and a request that he will give his Christmas address. Before that happens, however, we have a series of scenes: one between Miss Cutts and Gibbs who is trying to offer him the same "comforts" that she gives to Roote, provided that he kills Roote; a scene in which Roote insists that Gibbs has come to murder him, and the three men (Roote, Lush, and Gibbs) draw knives and circle one another (as in **The Collection?**); and, finally, a scene in which Miss Cutts arrives for bed wearing a negligee given to her by 6459, when it is strongly suggested that Roote is the father of the baby. After the Christmas address, which is suitably platitudinous, the stage is filled with the murmur of madness and the lights go up on an office at the Ministry where Gibbs is offered Roote's job. It appears that all the staff have been killed when the patients escaped—possibly because the locktester was absent. Roote, as Gibbs says, was unpopular because he had murdered 6457 and seduced 6459. But all the staff have not been killed: the final scene of the play reveals locktester Lamb still sitting in Room 1 wearing electrodes and earphones and as if in a catatonic trance.

The Hothouse was played in a composite set from which most of the color had been drained—it was unnerving to see the familiar *Sunflowers* by van Gogh painted in creams and browns. Clearly, too, the play has been quarried for subsequent work.

James Fenton, in the *Sunday Times* (4 May 1980), asked the obvious questions: why reject the play in the first place and why resurrect it now? The answer to the second question he finds easy: it is a work of comic invention that clearly occupies an important transitional role in the development of the writer. The answer to the first question lies in the faults of the play:

> There is too much here which yields, or seems about to yield, to the more intrusive spirit of criticism. At the centre is the struggle between the two men, but at the periphery there are distracting figures and scenes waving to attract our attention.

When Pinter says in his program note that he put it aside and then went on to write **The Caretaker,** this shows, Fenton remarks, that he already knew he could do better. Robert Cushman, however, in *The Observer* (4 May 1980), sees Pinter as a major talent producing minor plays and suggests that this play shows that **The Caretaker** was not progress but rather "a glorious sidetrack." **The Hothouse,** he points out rightly, looks forward to **The Collection** and **The Homecoming** and beyond, where "the honing gets

finer, and the people thinner." The theme is state-subsidized terror: "It isn't a particularly interesting statement, but the author is clearly more hooked on the mechanics anyway." The play was directed by the author and televised on 27 March 1982. The composite set was replaced by a large mansion with an enormous, bare, classical staircase, long whispering corridors, and snow falling against leaded panes of glass. Pinter is reported to be happier with this version than with the stage production. Certainly in the theatre I found the play less funny than the audience seemed to find it, mainly because so much in it had been done better in subsequent plays. The television version was remarkably gray and unfunny: more chill than laughter—and the power struggle between Roote and Gibbs was intensified by making the nervousness of Gibbs clear. The close-up of his face wearing a genuinely haunted look when he says that something is happening and he cannot define it suggested that he will be as unstable as Roote when the time comes and matched the bleak passionless atmosphere of the play—even sex takes place in the control room of the interrogation center! A play, here, then, as unnerving as **The Homecoming** and as unlikeable as **Betrayal.** Pinter said that he did not like any of these characters, and it showed.

Pinter's next play, **Family Voices,** was written for radio in 1980. It was first broadcast by the BBC Radio 3 on 22 January 1981 and later given a concert performance at the National Theatre. Radio has always been a favorite medium for Pinter—it was radio that rescued him after the disaster of **The Birthday Party**—so in writing this play Pinter felt that he was coming home. In the *Radio Times* (17 January 1981) he spoke of the purity he finds in writing for the radio: "It reduces drama to its elemental parts and enforces the sort of restraint, simplicity and economy I strive for anyway." **Family Voices** is a dialogue between a young man and his mother. The young man has left his home (somewhere by the sea) to live in a boarding house in a big city run by a Mrs. Withers. Although the dialogue begins as a series of letters, the letters are never sent and, indeed, since the third voice is that of his father who speaks from the grave, the whole play may take place in the mind of the protagonist. The mother misses her son and wonders what is happening to him—and with reason, for as the boy explores the house and meets its strange inhabitants, he grows more and more uncertain. His mother, on the other hand, grows more and more angry until she finally threatens to denounce him to the police as a spineless character who has fallen into the hands of underworld figures who use him as a male prostitute. At the end the boy announces his homecoming, but if it takes place it will be too late since his father is dead and what he had to say can never be spoken. The son may be happy or unhappy, he may seduce the landlady's daughter or be seduced by a homosexual policeman in a house that may be charming and aristocratic or little more than a bawdy house. Such uncertainty is Pinter at his enigmatic best, and we would no more trust this young man than we would trust Stanley in **The Birthday Party.** For this family play about a homecoming (and as disturbing as **The**

Homecoming), Peter Hall directed a splendid cast with Peggy Ashcroft, Mark Dignam, and Michael Kitchen, who captured this experience of knowing nothing, expecting much, and fearing everything splendidly. With a different cast, *Family Voices* was included in a triple bill at the National Theatre on 14 October 1982 under the title *Other Places.*

The second sketch, *Victoria Station,* is short and comic, but comic only in the surreal sense that, say, *The Hothouse* was comic. A radio-car controller is trying to get hold of car 274 to go to Victoria Station to pick up a passenger coming from Boulogne. This passenger is an old friend of the controller, a Mr. MacRooney, who has a limp and a feather in his hat, is carrying fishing tackle, and wants to go to visit an old aunt at Cuckfield who will probably leave him all she possesses. So the trip would be worthwhile. But, 274 seems to be in a fog and neither knows nor cares about Victoria Station but thinks he is stuck outside Crystal Palace. The controller tries to humor him, then gets angry with him, but finally admires him and threatens to join him for a nice celebration, for 274 confesses that he has a Passenger On Board, a girl with whom he has fallen in love. We cannot see a girl on the back seat so, like the Matchseller in *A Slight Ache,* she may not exist or 274 may have killed her and kept her body on the back seat. Pinter leaves the sketch open and vague.

By contrast, *A Kind of Alaska* is founded on fact and gives us another country where, indeed, they do things differently. A note to the text acknowledges that the source is a book called *Awakenings,* published by Oliver Sacks in 1973, recounting his experiences as a doctor with a new drug, L-DOPA. Between 1916 and 1917 there was an epidemic of sleeping sickness, and fifty years later those still alive were treated with L-DOPA and "erupted into life once more" after a sleep that had lasted in some cases for twenty or thirty years. Pinter's play dramatizes the awakening of Deborah after her first injection. Deborah fell asleep when she was sixteen and awakens after 29 years at the age of 45, caught between an adult body and an adolescent mind. Critics compared the play to Luigi Pirandello's *Henry IV,* but Pinter eschews both melodrama and fancy dress, allowing the play to happen only as Deborah can tell it. She speaks, of course, with remarkable fluency and presents the memories the playwright needs to recapture her lost world. When she awakens she meets her doctor and her younger sister Pauline, who are married. But Pauline calls herself a widow because her husband has devoted his life to caring for the sleeping Deborah, keeping the body supple and ready to move should awakening take place. Deborah now has to adjust to her new world. She sees her sister as some old aunt who has come to visit her and keeps asking about her boy friend Jack or whether her elder sister Estelle married the ginger boy from Townley Street. She has been away, in a kind of Alaska, an arctic territory not unlike no man's land, which she recalls as "a vast series of halls. With enormous interior windows masquerading as walls. The windows are mirrors, you see.

And so glass reflects glass. For ever and ever."[6] Shall I tell her lies or the truth, asks Pauline. Hornby, her husband, suggests that she tell Deborah both. So Pauline says that the family is away on a world cruise and has stopped off at Bangkok. But Hornby tells Deborah that her mother is dead, and her elder sister never married because she has had to look after her father who is blind. And Pauline married him so that he could look after her. Martin Esslin claims that Deborah adjusts to and accepts her new reality, but at the end it is Pauline's version of reality that she chooses.

James Fenton, reviewing this triple bill in the *Sunday Times* (London; 17 October 1982), noted how difficult it is to distinguish between Pinter the gag writer and Pinter the poet. The whole experience of *Other Places* was, somehow, greater than the parts—a disturbing experience, though one that could as well take place on the radio as in a theatre.

At this stage we can, therefore, offer only an interim report. Martin Esslin sees *Betrayal* as something like a new beginning: a realistically told tale of trivial adultery among the London literary establishment. Jerry, a literary agent, has an affair with Emma, the wife of his best friend, Robert, which starts in 1968 and ends in 1975. Emma yields to Jerry because she resents Jerry's relationship with her husband and what she sees as a betrayal leads to a whole series of betrayals. The special touch, apart from the factual background each character is given, is that the tale is told backwards so that we see each "truth" happening after the "truth" that followed it. The idea of a collection of "truths" is not new (*The Collection,* after all, dates from 1961), and characters have always been free to invent any past or memory that suits them. Linguistically, too, nothing about *Betrayal* is new. The characters now are socially superior to the characters in the early plays and are both intelligent and literate, but whether it is Robert from *Betrayal* or Gus from *The Dumb Waiter* who is talking, the result is still just chatter. *Betrayal* may demonstrate that causality is fictititous, or that facts about characters are useless, but the characters here are, for Pinter, unusually empty. Adultery produces no resonance of guilt. What went wrong in the lives of Stanley or Davies is replaced here by an oddly anodyne feeling. The play is certainly the first that has been directly aimed at the audience that Pinter can expect at the National Theatre and turns out to be his most commercially successful play in America. The film, directed by David Jones and starring Jeremy Irons, Ben Kingsley, and Patricia Hodge has, apparently, been very successful in America and will, presumably, be so when it opens in England. A production of *Betrayal* at the Greenwich Theatre showed, in 1983, that it could sparkle in a Noel Coward sort of way, though one wonders what the Chinese made of it since this production was sent in 1982 as part of a British Council Tour and was the first modern Western play seen in China since the Cultural Revolution. Presumably, it confirmed their worst suspicious about Western society, for the characters are shallow and seem to be exclusively preoccupied with sexual relationships, which are shown to be casual and superficial. Esslin contends that this aridity is deliberate and satiric. Pinter presents us with a sardonically bitter portrait of the world of literary commerce and ladies who manage art galleries, none of whom have any deep commitment to culture, literature, or art. This, he suggests, is mature and distilled Pinter.[7] Certainly, Pinter after *No Man's Land* is distilled. The qualities that he most admires and strives for—restraint, simplicity, and economy—are strongly evident in all his recent work, and it is tempting to see him writing for radio and theatre in a deliberately spare verbal way to balance his work for films, where his words (often translations after all) exist only as part of an opulent whole. He certainly preserves the distance and anonymity of the camera.

All the more pleasing, then, to end with *Players,* which opened at the National Theatre on 7 September 1983. A dramatic monologue delivered by Edward de Souza gave us Pinter's memories of Anew McMaster and Arthur Wellard. The cliché "fondly remembered," used in the advance publicity, was, for once, quite accurate. Here Harold Pinter celebrates the two games in his life, acting and cricket, and recalls, with great affection, two old timers.

Notes

1. Austin E. Quigley, *The Pinter Problem* (Princeton: Princeton University Press, 1975), p. 273.

2. Harold Pinter, *The Times* (London), 11 April 1969.

3. Peter Thomson, "Harold Pinter: A Retrospect," *Critical Quarterly* 20 (Winter 1978): 21-29.

4. The interview with Lawrence M. Bensky was for the *Paris Review.* It is printed in *Writers at Work: The Paris Review Interviews,* Third Series, ed. George Plimpton (1967). It is reprinted by Arthur Ganz in *Pinter: A Collection of Critical Essays,* Twentieth Century Views (Englewood Cliffs, N.J.: Prentice-Hall, 1972), pp. 19-33. This quotation appears on p. 28.

5. *Radio Times,* 27 March-2 April 1982.

6. "A Kind of Alaska," *Other Places* (London: Methuen, 1982), p. 39.

7. Martin Esslin, *Pinter the Playwright* (London: Methuen, 1982), pp. 214-16.

Ewald Mengel (essay date 1990)

SOURCE: "'Yes! In the Sea of Life Enisled': Harold Pinter's *Other Places,*" in *Harold Pinter: A Casebook,* edited by Lois Gordon, Garland Publishing, Inc., 1990, pp. 161-88.

[*In the following essay, Mengel examines the themes of isolation and loneliness in* A Kind of Alaska, Victoria Station *and* Family Voices.]

Harold Pinter's *Other Places* opened at the National Theatre on 14 October 1982 in London, under the direction of Peter Hall.[1] *Other Places* is a trilogy that combines three short plays of a different character: *A Kind of Alaska* dramatises the awakening of a patient after twenty-nine years of comatose or trance-like sleep; in *Victoria Station,* the controller of a radio-taxi station tries in vain to persuade one of his drivers to pick up a customer; in *Family Voices,* a son, a mother and a father express their feelings after the son has gone away from home.

On the surface, the title *Other Places* refers to the three different settings of the plays. Secondly, the characters of the individual plays live, either in reality or in their minds, in "other places," so that communication between them has become difficult or problematic. The title of this paper, in quoting the first line of Matthew Arnold's "To Marguerite," alludes to a deeper, symbolic meaning of *Other Places.* The common underlying theme of all three plays is the isolation and loneliness of man in modern mass society, a theme that Pinter has already dealt with in some of his earlier plays, for example in *Landscape* or in *Silence.*

In the following, I shall first interpret the plays individually. My focus will be on the question of how Pinter succeeds in dealing with such a basically lyrical theme in dramatic form. In conclusion, I shall try to describe the relevance of *Other Places* with reference to Pinter's other plays, and chart his development as a dramatist.

A KIND OF ALASKA

A Kind of Alaska may be compared to a modern version of *Sleeping Beauty.* Pinter's "Sleeping Beauty" is called Deborah; the part of "Prince Charming" is played by Hornby, the doctor; Deborah's sister Pauline, who has no counterpart in the fairy tale, completes the cast.

As Pinter has admitted in a foreword to *A Kind of Alaska,* something which is quite unusual for him, the play was inspired by Oliver Sack's *Awakenings:*[2]

> *A Kind of Alaska* was inspired by *Awakenings* by Oliver Sacks M.D., first published in 1973 by Gerald Duckworth and Co.
>
> In the winter of 1916-1917, there spread over Europe, and subsequently over the rest of the world, an extraordinary epidemic illness which presented itself in innumerable forms—as delirium, mania, trances, coma, sleep, insomnia, restlessness, and states of Parkinsonism. It was eventually identified by the great physician Constantin von Economo and named by him *encephalitis lethargica,* or sleeping sickness.
>
> Over the next ten years almost five million people fell victim to the disease of whom more than a third died. Of the survivors some escaped almost unscathed, but the majority moved into states of deepening illness. The worst-affected sank into singular states of 'sleep'—conscious of their surroundings but motionless, speechless, and without hope or will, confined to asylums or

other institutions. Fifty years later, with the development of the remarkable drug L-DOPA, they erupted into life once more.

(3)

At first sight, this foreword seems to have a fictional quality: the many forms of the illness, the claim that it cost millions of people their lives, the peculiar name of the physician, Constantin von Economo, and the miraculous drug L-DOPA seem to owe their existence to the imagination of the author. A closer investigation reveals, however, that Pinter is remaining true to the facts. Everything he claims with reference to Sacks is accurate. What seems to have fascinated him is that the facts to be represented fall already into the pattern of a fantastic story, and that there was no need to invent something additional. All he had to do was to bring reality into a shape that could be used for dramatic purposes.

The full extent to which Pinter was inspired by *Awakenings* is revealed by a reading of the book. The neuophysiologist-chemist's account pays attention not only to the medical, but also to the psychological, philosophical and ontological implications of this ominous illness. *Awakenings* consists of a number of case studies in which the consequences of the sleeping sickness and its effect on the mind and the body of the patients is described. The majority of these cases concern female patients who were treated by Oliver Sacks with the drug L-DOPA between 1969 and 1972, when he was Director of the closed asylum of Mount Carmel near New York. Almost all of these patients had had an attack of *encephalitis lethargica* shortly after the epidemic had started in 1916. Subsequently, they had developed grave psychosomatic behavioural disturbances, so that they had to be hospitalised. The symptoms of sleeping sickness described by Sacks vary. They are similar to those of Parkinsonism, and comprise insomnia, different forms of tics or involuntary and repeated movements, spasms, respiratory crises, hyperkinesis, echolalia, serious neuroses, and catatonic trances in which the patients sometimes remain for hours or every days.

Sacks reports how patients who had been suffering very badly from *encephalitis lethargica* and who were treated with L-DOPA, a drug discovered by a physician named Cotzias early in the sixties, began to recover consciousness and part of their normal physical abilities. Some improved so much that they became able to lead a fairly normal life. Others, however, became even worse after a short period of recovery, and the treatment with the drug had to be discontinued, the patients falling back once again into their usual state of coma or unconsciousness. In most cases, Sacks claims, it was possible to stabilise the patients by a skillful dosing of the drug, so that the overall effect was more positive than negative. All of these patients went through three successive stages: first, there was the moment of their awakening; secondly, after some weeks, their awakening was followed by a crisis during which the symptoms of their illness grew worse; thirdly, this crisis overcome, they entered a phase of accommodation during

which they learned to live with their disease and control its more negative effects.

What can be shown is that Deborah's return to the world also has three stages, only that Pinter has compressed what in reality takes weeks and months into just a few minutes. Of course, *A Kind of Alaska* is not a case study, but rather a skillfully structured one-act play written for aesthetic purposes. Pinter obviously realised that the moment of awakening to the world after years and years of trance or semi-consciousness would have an enormous dramatic quality, and be particularly suitable for being turned into a play. Consequently, what interests us in *A Kind of Alaska* is the process of awakening itself and the patient's re-encounter with reality. Also, we are curious to know in what regions the patient's mind has travelled, and what feelings and memories are connected with her state. The form of Pinter's play is expressive of this double interest. The action taking place in the present has a progressive and teleological structure. After her awakening, Deborah is confronted with reality. What follows is a short moment of crisis. Having overcome this crisis, Deborah enters the phase of accommodation, during which she begins to adjust to the new situation.

In contrast to this present-related action, the characters' memories have the function of embedding the past into the present. Pauline's and Hornby's memories basically have expositional functions. They elucidate Deborah's fate and the history of her family, forming a narrative context that gives meaning to the past and to the present for both Deborah and the audience. Deborah's memories are lyrical in character. Her childhood memories serve to define her self, her identity, in a subjective way. The memories connected with her illness conjure up the phantasmagoric "no man's land" Alaska, in which her consciousness has travelled in the meantime.

With regard to the interaction of the characters, Pinter's play acquires its dramatic character through a discrepancy of awareness between Hornby and Pauline, on the one hand, and the patient Deborah on the other, through the juxtaposition of two conflicting interpretations of reality, a subjective and an objective one. The audience is presented with two mutually exclusive views, but from the beginning it is obvious that Deborah's physical appearance, which indicates her age, proves her wrong, whereas it supports Hornby's and Pauline's interpretation of reality.

At the beginning of the play, Deborah, who looks like a woman in her forties, is sitting in a bed covered with white sheets and is staring ahead. The "kiss of life," the injection with the drug L-DOPA, has obviously just taken place, and Deborah begins to speak. Her first words, "Something is happening" (5), are indicative of a beginning process of self-reflection, although she still ignores Hornby's questions "Do you know me?" "Do you recognize me?" "Can you hear me?" (5). Her counter-question, "Are you speaking?" (6), is her first goal-oriented, purposeful act of communication. It shows that she is beginning to rediscover reality, but has no firm grasp on it as yet, her thoughts still dwelling in "a kind of Alaska."

Gradually, however, the presence of Hornby seeps into her consciousness. She begins to notice him, a fact which is underlined by the stage direction: "She looks at him for the first time" (7). However, this explanation that she has slept for a long time and is now awake does not make sense to her. It becomes clear that, in her mind, she is still living in the world of her childhood, in the world as it was before she fell ill. She remembers the games she played with her father, recalls her mother, her sisters Pauline and Estelle, and her friend Jack, and believes herself to be fifteen or sixteen years old. Her language is partly that of a young girl, and in her memories she mixes earlier and later stages of her childhood. It seems that, for her, time came to a standstill years ago.

A similar phenomenon is noticed by Oliver Sacks with regard to his patient Rose R.:

> But I also have the feeling that she feels her "past" as her present, and that perhaps it has never felt "past" for her. Is it possible that Miss R. has never, in fact, moved on from the "past"? Could she still be "in" 1926 forty-three years later? Is 1926 now?[3]

Deborah's subjective construction of reality comes into conflict with another reality that is objectively defined by her age and by her outer appearance. This does not mean, however, that Deborah's definition of reality is less true, or less authentic than what Hornby or the audience hold to be correct. Deborah's subjective and Hornby's objective views are both valid, because they refer to different realities.

An especially dramatic moment in the course of Deborah's "awakening" is reached when she is confronted with her sister Pauline. On the one hand, Pauline is connected with the past; on the other hand, she is also part of the present. For Deborah, therefore, Pauline visibly demonstrates the flow of time, the process of ageing. This process has also changed Deborah, and when she regains consciousness, her own body feels alien to her, and Pauline appears as a stranger.

One of Pauline's functions is to confine and complete Hornby's story. In this way, his story gains an objective validity. Hornby and Pauline contradict each other only once: whereas Pauline claims that her father and mother are taking a cruise in the Indian Ocean, Hornby tells Deborah that her mother has died, and that her father has turned blind. For a moment, it seems that Pinter is making use of a technique of mystification that is characteristic of his earlier plays and that leaves the audience in the dark about the truth. The apparent contradiction may be resolved, however, when the situation is considered in which Hornby's and Pauline's conflicting stories are brought forward. Obviously, it is Pauline's intention to spare her sister the full truth, for she is afraid that Deborah, who has just regained consciousness, cannot take the impact of it.

Pauline's story emphasises that her family is doing well, at the same time explaining their absence. Hornby's version comes a bit later in the course of Deborah's "awakening." It is part of a longer explanation which is caused by Deborah's reaction to Pauline's story—"This woman is mad" (33). By being completely open to her and giving her an unpleasant piece of information, Hornby wants to make her face reality.

It is Pauline's function to tell Deborah—and the audience—what really happened in the past. Among other things Pauline recalls the moment when Deborah was overtaken by her illness:

> No it was you—
>
> *PAULINE looks at HORNBY. He looks back at her, impassive.*
>
> *PAULINE turns back to DEBORAH.*
>
> It was you. You were standing with a vase of flowers in your hands. you were about to put it down on the table. But you didn't put it down. You stood still, with the vase in your hands, as if you were . . . fixed. I was with you, in the room. I looked into your eyes.
>
> *Pause*
>
> I said, "Debbie?"
>
> *Pause*
>
> I said, "Debbie?"
>
> *Pause*
>
> But you remained . . . quite . . . still. I touched you. I said: "Debbie?" Your eyes were open. You were looking nowhere. Then you suddenly looked at me and saw me and smiled at me and put the vase down on the table.
>
> *Pause*
>
> But at the end of dinner, we were all laughing and talking, and Daddy was making jokes and making us laugh, and you said you couldn't see him properly because of the flowers in the middle of the table, where you had put them, and you stood and picked up the vase and you took it towards that little sidetable by the window, walnut, and Mummy was laughing and even Estelle was laughing and then we suddenly looked at you and you had stopped. You were standing with the vase by the sidetable, you were about to put it down, your arm was stretched towards it but you had stopped.
>
> *Pause*
>
> We went to you. We spoke to you. Mummy touched you. She spoke to you.
>
> *Pause*
>
> Then Daddy tried to take the vase from you. He could not . . . wrench it from your hands. He could not . . . move you from the spot. Like . . . marble.
>
> *Pause*
>
> You were sixteen.
>
> (29ff)

Pauline's tale is reminiscent of that passage in *Sleeping Beauty* where the cook wants to box the boy on the ear, but is overtaken by sleep at that very moment. As was mentioned above, this motif was inspired not so much by the fairy tale, but rather by Oliver Sacks's *Awakenings*. What Pauline describes is a typical symptom of the sleeping sickness. According to Sacks, however, this symptom is typical of an advanced stage of *encephalitis lethargica,* and does not appear right at the beginning. By thus deviating from reality, Pinter achieves a dramatic effect, for Deborah's illness acquires a mythical quality. Again, Pinter, for dramatic purposes, has condensed and accelerated a process that in reality takes weeks and months.

Whereas Pauline narrates what happened to Deborah in the past from the perspective of an eye-witness, Deborah's memories elucidate her illness from a personal point of view. She compares her experiences with those of the protagonist of *Alice in Wonderland:* "I've been dancing in very narrow spaces. Kept stubbing my toes and bumping my head. Like Alice . . ." (24). Deborah's statement is indicative of an active consciousness behind a seemingly inactive and lifeless front. A similar conclusion is suggested by the following passage, in which the audience can witness Deborah's illness *in actu* and from an inner point of view:

DEBORAH

Now what was I going to say?

She begins to flick her cheek, as if brushing something from it.

Now what—? Oh dear, oh no. Oh dear.

Pause

Oh dear.

The flicking of her cheek grows faster.

Yes, I think they're closing in. They're closing in.

They're closing the walls in. Yes.

She bows her head, flicking faster, her fingers now moving about her face.

Oh . . . we . . . oooohhhhh . . . oh no . . . oh no . . .

During the course of this speech her body becomes hunchbacked.

Something panting, something panting. Can't see. Oh, the light is going. The light is going. They're shutting up shop. They're closing my face. Chains and padlocks. Bolting me up. Stinking. The smell. Oh my goodness, oh dear, oh my goodness, oh dear, I'm so young. It's a vice. I'm in a vice. It's at the back of my neck. Ah. Eyes stuck. Only see the shadow of the tip of my nose. Shadow of the tip of my nose. Eyes stuck.

She stops flicking abruptly, sits still. Her body straightens. She looks up. She looks at her fingers, examines them.

(37ff)

Like Sacks's patients, Pinter's Deborah has to live through a crisis during which the symptoms of her illness become worse, only Pinter has compressed a process into a few minutes that in reality lasts several weeks. Deborah's flicking is an imitation of the spastic tics which Sacks describes in *Awakenings.* The same applies to the fact that her eyes seem to be frozen to a certain object ("Eyes stuck"), imitating an occulatory crisis. The many repetitions of words and sentences are characteristic of patients suffering from echolalia, and patients with hunchbacked bodies are shown in some of the photos in Sacks's book.

What is perhaps even more important than these physical similarities is the fact that Deborah's feelings also correspond to those of Sacks's patients. In the passage quoted above, her utterances refer to both an objective and a subjective reality. Her feeling of being "closed in," against which she fights in vain, refers to both the "closed institution" in which she had to live, and to the illness that is taking possession of her. From the beginning of his career as a dramatist, Pinter has shown a special predilection for "closed institutions" and the effects they have on their patients' psyches. Deborah's remarks—"Chains and padlocks. Bolting me up. Stinking. The smell"—may be taken to refer to the undignified circumstances under which patients in closed asylums sometimes have to exist. Her feeling that the walls are closing in on her, or that she is helplessly stuck in a vise, is characteristic of how patients subjectively experience their illness. The "objective correlative" for this experience can be seen in the catatonic trances into which patients suffering from *encephalitis lethargica* fall every now and then. The stronger the patients exert their willpower not to be overcome by their illness, the more they develop an inner resistance against their own willing, so that they have the feeling of being squashed by two opposing forces. What looks like a freezing of their movements, a ceasing of all their life-entertaining functions, is in reality a severe inner conflict the patients fight out with themselves:

> Patients so affected find that as soon as they "will" or intend or attempt a movement, a "counter-will" or "resistance" rises up to meet them. They find themselves embattled, and even immobilized, in a form of physiological conflict—force against counter-force, will against counter-will, command against countermand.[4]

Immediately after her crisis, Deborah is ready for the first time to accept her situation as it is, although she still refuses to face the full truth. This is shown by the ending of the play:

DEBORAH

I must be quite old. I wonder what I look like. But it's of no consequence. I certainly have no intention of looking into a mirror.

Pause

No.

She looks at HORNBY.

You say I have been asleep. You say I am now awake.
You say I have not awoken from the dead. You say I
was not dreaming then and am not dreaming now. You
say I have always been alive and am alive now. You
say I am a woman.

She looks at PAULINE, then back to HORNBY.

She is a widow. She doesn't go to her ballet classes
any more. Mummy and Daddy and Estelle are on a
world cruise. They've stopped off in Bangkok. It'll be
my birthday soon. I think I have the matter in proportion.

Pause

Thank you.

(39ff)

Deborah's refusal to look into the mirror amounts to an
evasion of reality. Her automatic way of speaking shows
that she has not quite accepted Pauline's and Hornby's
definitions of reality, although she is acknowledging them
now. One gets the impression that she is not convinced of
what she is saying, and is just recapitulating something
she has learned by heart. Especially relevant in this context
is the fact that she prefers Pauline's version of the "truth,"
at the same time ignoring Hornby's, which is much more
unpleasant. Again, this is indicative of her evasion of reality. When she therefore finally claims: "I think I have the
matter in proportion," this does not sound very convincing. The new "reality" to which she begins to adjust herself
is still illusory in character, so that her final words "Thank
you" appear in an ironic light.

Pinter's Hornby, about whom nothing has been said so far,
is another of those ambivalent "caretaker-figures" in whom
positive and negative qualities coincide. Although Hornby
succeeds in calling his patient back to life, the final
outcome of his medical manipulation is doubtful. Because
the play ends with Deborah's accommodation to reality,
the further physical and psychological consequences of her
"awakening" do not become clear, but what Pinter's play
suggests is that Deborah is also a guinea pig and victim of
a medical science whose methods and results can be dehumanising. Whereas it is Sacks's intention in *Awakenings* to
celebrate the success of his psychopharmacological experiments, the dramatist Pinter is much more skeptical about
the "rebirth" of his Deborah. The reason for this is that
both have different concepts of reality. For Pinter, the
empirical world is as shifting, ambivalent, and unreal as
the phantasmagoric "Alaska" which Deborah has left
behind. Conversely, Deborah's "no-man's land" is for him
a concrete reality. Deborah's "awakening" therefore
produces a conflict between two different kinds of reality,
which, although they exclude each other, are both valid
and authentic. The result is a mutual relativisation of both
concepts of reality, the subjective and psychological on the
one hand, and the objective and empirical on the other, so
that a final answer to the question of what the "actual"
reality consists of can no longer be given.

VICTORIA STATION

Victoria Station, which comes second in *Other Places,* is
much shorter than *A Kind of Alaska* and reminds one of

Pinter's early revue sketches. In many respects it is a very
funny play, but its underlying theme is also the isolation,
anonymity and loneliness of man in modern mass society.

The two characters of the play, the controller and the
driver, are not introduced by their names. Man is reduced
to his role, his function, or number. The controller's vain
attempts to convince his driver via radio to pick up a
customer form the action of this play.

The isolation of the two characters from each other and
from their environment is already underlined by the play's
setting. The controller is sitting alone in his office. His
only connection with the driver and with the outside world
is his radio equipment. The driver is sitting alone in his
car (although he claims later in the play that he has
company). His exact location within London remains
uncertain.

From the start, communication between the driver and the
controller prove to be problematic. At first, Pinter leaves it
open whether this is due to a bad radio connection, or
whether it is the fault of the driver, who ignores the
controller's question "274? Where are you?" (45), then
asks "What?" (45). The comedy of the dialogue throughout
the play is produced by the fact that the driver refuses to
act according to his role, and disappoints the controller's—
and the audience's—role expectations. What develops is
one of Pinter's well-known battles for positions, the
purpose of which is to decide who can dominate whom.[5]

Pinter's driver employs various strategies in order to
achieve this goal. He asks puzzling questions ("Who are
you?" 46), parries questions with counter-questions,
pretends ignorance, or just keeps silent, which may be
understood as a passive form of resistance.

In the course of the play's action, the driver's statements
become more and more unlikely. When he claims that he
is "cruising about" (47), he still sounds plausible because
"cruising about" is something that taxi drivers searching
for customers usually do. But when he claims that he does
not know Victoria Station, we no longer have confidence
in him, for this seems rather unlikely. Additionally, he
increasingly contradicts himself. When he claims that he
has parked his cab "underneath Crystal Palace" (55), from
where he can see the building, this is an obvious lie, for
Crystal Palace was destroyed by fire in 1936. As a result,
the statements he makes from now on become questionable. He affirms that he has a wife and children, for
example, but one is no longer inclined to believe him. A
bit later he asserts that he has a passenger on board.
Although he initially uses the personal pronoun "he" ("He
doesn't want to go anywhere," 57), he finally states that
the passenger is a woman, that he has fallen in love with
her, and that they plan to get married—this in spite of his
previous claim to be a married man with children.

As is the case of many other Pinter characters, the truth of
most of what the driver says cannot be finally verified.

The driver's behaviour, however, allows us to draw conclusions with regard to his mental and psychological constitution. By refusing to act in accordance with the controller's role-expectations, he succeeds in breaking out of the routine-like form of communication and starting a more or less private conversation which guarantees him the controller's attention. This is also emphasised by the fact that the driver takes the initiative as soon as the controller tries to talk to somebody else: "It's me, 274. Please. Don't leave me" (54). Interpretations which merely insist that Pinter's taxi driver has gone mad stop short of the truth, because they do not reveal anything about the motives underlying his behaviour.[6] What Pinter wants to emphasise, with the help of his taxi driver, is the location and anonymity of the individual in modern mass society, and his desire for attention and recognition.

For his part, the controller employs various tactical manoeuvres in order to make his obstinate driver change his mind. He appeals to his reason and understanding, explains the circumstances and promises him a remunerative job. When he realises the fruitlessness of his attempts, he gets more and more excited and resorts to veiled and open threats and insults.

Accustomed to having his orders carried out without much ado, he is presented with a great problem by the peculiar behaviour of his driver. Since his only connection with the outer world is his radio, he cannot rely on his own senses, but is dependent on the information given by his driver. Soon he is forced to realise that the driver's statements are unreliable and incomplete. To the same extent to which the driver refuses to function according to his role, that is, to drive, the controller loses control of the situation. At first he tries to be patient, but then his latent aggressiveness erupts:

CONTROLLER

Do you have a driving wheel in front of you?

Pause

Because I haven't, 274. I'm just talking into this machine, trying to make some sense out of our lives. That's my function. God gave me this job. He asked me to do this job, personally. I'm your local monk, 274. I'm a monk. You follow? I lead a restricted life. I haven't got a choke and a gear lever in front of me. I haven't got a cooling system and four wheels. I'm not sitting here with wing mirrors and a jack in the boot. And if I did have a jack in the boot I'd stick it right up your arse.

(50)

Passages like this one suggest that frustration is partly responsible for the controller's verbal bellicosity. The driver's refusal to obey is only a random event that triggers it off. The real cause of this frustration has something to do with his job. The controller's work is characteristic of modern mass society. Although communication with others is part of his task, he leads an isolated life in the anonymity of his office. The role he has to fill is relatively undemanding, so that he cannot realise himself or find fulfillment in his job. It becomes clear that it is not only the driver with the number 274 but also the controller who is suffering from alienation. In this way, Pinter shows that it is not the position of the individual within the social system, but rather the system as such which is to be held responsible for the alienation of people from each other and from themselves.

When the controller forgets himself and his role for a moment and drops his mask, this is caused by the deficient role behaviour of the driver: "You're beginning to obsess me. I think I'm going to die. I'm alone in this miserable freezing fucking office and nobody loves me. Listen, pukeface—" (58). These words are characterised by self-pity and sentimentality on the one hand, and violence on the other, a mixture which gives him a complex and ambivalent character.

In the following passage, the controller exchanges the role of boss for that of friend and colleague:

CONTROLLER

You know what I've always dreamed of doing? I've always had this dream of having a holiday in sunny Barbados. I'm thinking of taking this holiday at the end of this year, 274. I'd like you to come with me. To Barbados. Just the two of us. I'll take you snorkelling. We can swim together in the blue Caribbean.

Pause

In the meantime, though, why don't you just pop back to the office now and I'll make you a nice cup of tea? You can tell me something about your background, about your ambitions and aspirations. You can tell me all about your little hobbies and pastimes. Come over and have a nice cup of tea, 274.

(59)

It is generally characteristic of Pinter's plays that a friendly invitation often contains a hidden menace. This also applies to the above passage. The text shows a characteristic ambivalence that makes it difficult to describe what is really going on. The idea of the two men spending their holiday together snorkelling in Barbados has hints of homosexuality. The real intentions of the controller are revealed by the last sentence. He still wants to reassert his authority and get the driver, who is not functioning properly, back under his control. What is really going on, therefore, is a battle for positions, its purpose being the undermining of the position occupied by the partner in the interaction in order to dominate in the end.

As it turns out, the tactical manoeuvres of the controller are unsuccessful. The obstinate driver refuses to come to the office; on the contrary, at the end, the controller offers to visit the driver in his car. Who comes to whom is always very important in a Pinter play. Whether they will meet at all remains uncertain, however, for the actual position of the driver is unknown, so that the controller's intention—"I'll be right with you" (62)—cannot be realised.

The play's effect is partly due to the fact that it is impossible to verify the truth of what the characters say. This suggests that Pinter initially must have intended *Victoria Station* to be a radio play. For the listener of a radio play, the characters gain reality only by their voices, something that makes it even more difficult to verify their statements. As far as the driver is concerned, the listener is in the same position as the controller, who has to depend on the driver for information. On the stage, however, the characters are physically present. When the driver, who is sitting in his car, claims that he is cruising about, this statement is contradicted by the fact that he does not move. The same applies to his claim that he has a passenger on board. The theatregoer knows that this is not true, because there is nobody in the car besides himself. That the driver is a liar, therefore, is much clearer on the stage than on the radio, where reality is much more ambivalent. This additional information which the audience gets because of the setting is not contributive to the overall effect of the play. It becomes clear, then, that a reality that is ambivalent or undefined and the impossibility of verification are important ingredients of Pinter's dramaturgy.[7]

FAMILY VOICES

Pinter's *Family Voices,* the third play of *Other Places,*[8] was written for the radio and first broadcast on BBC Radio 3 on 22 January 1981. The theatre version was first performed in a "platform performance" under the direction of Peter Hall by the National Theatre on 13 February 1981. In the theatre version, the three characters still bear the name VOICE 1, VOICE 2, and VOICE 3, but in a stage direction Pinter has defined them by mentioning their age and their sex. Their relationship is revealed by what they say. They are father, mother and son, and in their monologues they give expression to their feelings after the son has left the family home. All three characters are separated from each other. Whereas the mother has remained at home, the son is now living in a big city, and the father, who plays a minor role, even speaks out of his grave.

Pinter has already dealt with the theme of the family in some of his earlier plays. The mother-son relationship has especially interested him. Early examples of this are Meg and Stanley in *The Birthday Party,* or Albert and his mother in *A Night Out.* The repressiveness of a dominating mother-figure, who threatens the ego-identity of her son, and the son's incapability of becoming emotionally independent and forming a family of his own, are characteristic of these relationships. Pinter's son-figures are therefore torn between the conflicting impulses of coming home and leaving home, and there is no solution to this dilemma.

The impossibility of a satisfying emotional relationship between mother and son is also characteristic of *Family*

Voices. The play dramatises "the agonized isolation of the individual 'living pretty much alone' at the same time that he lives in the midst of family, in this case a newfound family and his original one."[9]

Although Pinter's characters do not communicate with each other directly because of their local separation, their monologues are all addressed in their minds to a specific partner: that is, they are dialogic in character.[10] The monologues of father and mother are addressed to the son, whereas those of the son exclusively address his mother. The behaviour of all three *dramatis personae* is characterised by a high degree of self-monitoring;[11] they are extremely careful of what they say, hide their actual feelings behind false claims and masks, and invent stylised self-images. Their statements are "other-determined," insofar as they can be related to the assumed expectancies of their imaginary partners. Behind their pretensions, however, is hidden a completely different emotional reality: "And there is a total contradiction between what is said and what is felt. So in order to show reality, one has to show the mask and the distorted vision."[12] The longer one listens to them, the clearer their contradictions become. Their masks begin to crumble, and their true faces show through. Their high self-monitoring partly breaks down, but only to be substituted by new attempts at self-stylisation and role-playing.

Family Voices begins with a monologue from the son, who has a room in a house inhabited by strange people who leave a more than dubious impression.[13] The imaginary letters he addresses to his mother inform us that the family he lives with and whom he gets to know by and by is called Withers. It consists of a "Mrs. Withers," who is seventy years old, a certain "Lady Withers," and a girl who answers to the name of Jane, aged fifteen. In addition, there is a bald-headed old man, who is also called Withers but has no contact with the others, and Riley, who confesses to be homosexual, but also claims to be deeply religious.

The intercourse of these people with each other and with the son is characterised by a peculiar and puzzling mixture of intimacy and indifference. Although the son gets to know all the people in the house as time goes by, he can define neither their actual identities nor their relationships. Riley claims to be a policeman but rarely leaves the house to go to work. Lady Withers is at night visited by strange, anonymous people whose dealings remain unknown. She wants him to call her "Lally." Jane puts her feet into his lap. He is visited by Riley in the bathroom while he is sitting naked in the tub. Last but not least, the Withers have given him the pet name "Bobo" and thereby a new identity.

At the beginning of the play, the son claims to be happy with his new situation—"I am having a very nice time" (67); "I like walking in this enormous city, all by myself. It's fun to know no-one at all" (68); "I get on very well with my landlady, Mrs. Withers" (69)—but, because of the frequency with which they turn up, these affirmations

sound forced and uneasy. His monologues are characterised by a high degree of self-monitoring because his intention is to convince his imaginary addressee—that is, his
mother—that he is leading a totally happy and fulfilled
life.

The climax of this development—some time passes
between the individual monologues—is reached when he
finally claims in a very emotional speech that he has found
a new family and a new home: "Oh mother, I have found
my home, my family. Little did I ever dream I could know
such happiness" (77).

After his encounter with Mr. Withers ("Mother, mother,
I've had the most unpleasant, the most mystifying
encounter, with the man who calls himself Mr. Withers
. . ." 77) and with Riley ("And who is Riley?" 80) at the
latest he begins to have some doubts. Even if he still says:
"But if you find me bewildered, anxious, confused,
uncertain and afraid, you also find me content. My life
possesses shape. The house has a very warm atmosphere
. . ." (80), his assertions turn out to be desperate attempts
at convincing his mother and himself of their truth. In
reality, just the opposite is the case. He has to admit this at
the end, when he declares his intention to return home,
thus accepting defeat:

> I'm coming back to you, mother, to hold you in my
> arms.
>
> (82)
>
> I am coming home.
>
> (82)
>
> I am on my way back to you. I am about to make the
> journey back to you. What will you say to me?
>
> (83)

Although the son is still self-monitoring his utterances at
this point, because he is not completely open and honest
but is hiding his doubts with regard to his possible return,
he can no longer maintain his initial pose of independence
and contentment. He also implicitly acknowledges his
emotional needs. Whether he will actually return home,
however, remains completely open.

The character of the mother develops in the opposite direction. At the beginning, she admits her need for love and
attention. Her questions directed to the son—"Darling.
Where are you? . . . Why do you never write?" "Do you
ever think of me?" "Have you made friends with anyone?"
(69)—show that she misses him and wants him near her.
Her letters (which are never written) inform us that her
husband has died, and that she is alone in the house. Her
monologues create the impression of total loneliness and
isolation, of life lived in a kind of "no man's land," which
reminds one of Deborah's "Alaska":

> I hear your father's step on the stair. I hear his cough.
> But his step and his cough fade. He does not open the
> door.

Sometimes I think I have always been sitting like this.
I sometimes think I have always been sitting like this,
alone by an indifferent fire, curtains closed, night,
winter.

> You see, I have my thoughts too. Thoughts no-one else
> knows I have, thoughts none of my family ever knew I
> had. But I write of them to you now, wherever you are.
>
> (76)

Out of the loneliness and senselessness of her life grow
frustrations, which by and by come to the surface and give
her monologues a different tone. At the end of the play,
she even shows her hatred towards her son openly,
although she is still asking him to come home. It becomes
clear that her feelings toward him are ambivalent, and that
the longing for him which she expressed at the beginning
was only part of the truth. As she emphasises at the end,
she has even put the police on his track: "You will be
found, my boy, and no mercy will be shown to you" (82).
With her last words in the play, she breaks with him
completely: "I'll tell you what, my darling, I've given you
up as a very bad job. Tell me one last thing. Do you think
the word love means anything?" (82).

The voice of the father, which comes out of the grave,
makes itself heard towards the end of the play. His
"ghostly" appearance underlines that *Family Voices* is not
a realistic representation of an empirical reality, but that
Pinter is interested in the secret inner life and the psychology of his characters, forming a drama out of imaginary
wishes and thoughts that are never spoken and do not
reach their addressee.

Psychologically speaking, Pinter's procedure takes account
of the fact that somebody's inner thoughts and feelings do
not necessarily correspond to what he or she actually says,
that important things remain unsaid because courage is
lacking, and that the intention to tell them to somebody is
realised too late, or never at all, as is the case with the
father.

Although the mother claims that, on his deathbed, the
father has condemned the son, the father still sends "Lots
of love" (81) from the grave and tries to give him courage
for his future life. One cannot say with certainty how serious he is, and whether he has changed his mind about his
son. But even if he is serious, the son will never know
what his father had to say. The chance to improve their
relationship has gone forever. Only the listening audience
gets an insight into the thoughts of the dead father and can
realise that he wanted to say so many things to his son.
The image of the father who addresses his son *post mortem* from the grave effectively emphasises the actual isolation of the characters and the silence that surrounds them.

All in all, the father is a less important character in the
context of the play, whereas the relation between the
mother and son is the play's focal point. If the changing
positions of mother and son are related to each other, there
is something like a dramatic development, which is chias-

tic in structure. Whereas the son at the beginning empha-sises his satisfaction with the situation and pretends to be thrilled with his new family, he grows increasingly uneasy in the future course of the play, and finally admits his desire to return home. His development is therefore char-acterised by the fact that in his thoughts he is drawing ever nearer to his mother. The development of the latter, however, points in exactly the opposite direction. Whereas she admits at the beginning that she is missing her son, thereby showing her emotional dependency, anger and frustration break out at the end. The irony of this double development, therefore, lies in the fact that the mother is rejecting her son exactly at the moment when he is trying to draw closer to her. The characters themselves are not aware of this process, for their letters are never written or sent, or the partners do not hear the words addressed to them in their imagination. In contrast to the characters, the audience is in a privileged position, for it is informed about both characters and can relate their development to each other. Therefore, the conclusion has to be drawn that the actual drama takes place in the minds of the audience. Seen from their point of view, the dramatic character of the mental and emotional processes is created by the fact that for a moment there seems to be a chance of a satisfac-tory communication between mother and son, which is then given away. Pinter's **Family Voices** is a drama of the mind in a double sense of the phrase. On the one hand, the form Pinter has chosen for his play allows him to elucidate mental processes which take place in the imagination of the characters and make them visible and audible. On the other hand, the dramatic process is transposed into the minds of the audience, for here the mental and emotional development of the isolated characters can be related to each other, and the above mentioned chiastic, dramatic structure evolves. All in all, this is a new and innovative form of drama for Pinter, since plays like **Landscape** and **Silence,** which resemble **Family Voices** in many respects, are still comparatively lyrical and static. In **Family Voices,** therefore, Pinter succeeds in creating a form of dramatic monologue that is suitable to both the basically lyrical character of the theme of isolation and the genre of drama which relies on action and interaction as its most important constituents.

Conclusion

It is certainly not easy to describe the development that Pinter has gone through over the past ten years,[14] but, in my opinion, there are two clear trends that can be recog-nised. As Pinter's critics have observed, **Betrayal** (1979) was an uncommon play for him insofar as he no longer employed the techniques of mystification that were characteristic of his previous plays.[15] The alienation of reality is achieved not by a deficit of information on the part of the audience, but by a surplus of information in comparison to the characters on stage. This is effected by a reversal of chronology. Pinter begins with a portrayal of the present, then blends back into the past. Whereas the characters are of course blind to what the future has in store for them, the audience knows where it will end. This is a kind of parallel to **A Kind of Alaska** and to **Family**

Voices. Here too the audience knows how the characters are doing, whereas the latter lack this information. The first effect which is achieved by this distribution of information is that the action on the stage appears less mysterious, more probable and therefore more "realistic" than that of Pinter's earlier plays. Secondly—and this ap-plies to both **Betrayal** and **Family Voices**—the actual drama takes place in the minds of the audience, so that there is a shift of focus from the mimetic towards the re-ceptional pole of Pinter's dramaturgy.

The other trend concerns the relation between fictional and empirical reality. Pinter's **The Hothouse** (1980) must be mentioned in this connection. **The Hothouse** was actually written as early as 1958, but then put aside. It was first staged more or less unchanged in 1980. Pinter himself has explained the late date of publication by pointing out that, in 1980, the play appeared much more modern than in 1958,

> when we didn't know anything about the Russian psychiatric hospitals, did we? Now we do. But then, it might have been dismissed as fantasy. No, I certainly had no special knowledge of such things. Of course I knew Koestler's *Darkness at Noon* and so on, but in 1958 I don't think there was general knowledge that these things were being refined, as they are to this day. Not that I consider this play to be a grim piece of work, I don't think it is. An odd mixture of "laughter and chill" if you like.[16]

In the light of those revelations Pinter is talking about, **The Hothouse,** which in 1958 might have been read as a fantastic satire on society, becomes disconcertingly realistic. Pinter shows himself especially satisfied about the fact that the disclosed political reality *a posteriori* confirms the fictional reality of his play, or, to put it the other way round, that the fictional reality of **The Hothouse** had always been more than a mere invention, and what at first seemed to be a fantastic creation of the brain existed in reality.

If this is conceded, an interesting parallel between **The Hothouse** and **A Kind of Alaska** can be discovered. In Ol-iver Sacks's *Awakenings* Pinter found the "objective cor-relative" for the fictional "kind of Alaska" which already plays an important role in plays like **Old Times** (1971) and **No Man's Land** (1975). Although reality in **A Kind of Alaska** still seems strange, mysterious and even a bit absurd, this impression is not created by a willful alienation of reality but rather, paradoxically, by its imita-tion. Basically, Pinter's dramaturgy in **A Kind of Alaska** is still founded on a kind of realism that is characteristic of some of his earlier plays, for example, **The Caretaker** or **The Homecoming.** That this realism did not exclude interesting innovative experiments and could be developed, Pinter has shown in his later plays.

Notes

1. All quotations are based on the Methuen paperback edition (London, 1982), to which the page numbers in parentheses in the text also refer.

2. Harmondsworth, 1976.

3. *Ibid.,* p. 110.

4. *Ibid.,* p. 24.

5. About this motif compare, among others, Rüdiger Imhof, *Harold Pinters Dramentechnik. Gestalterische Mittel im Kontext des Gesamtwerks,* p. 19 and *passim;* Ewald Mengel, *Harold Pinters Dramen im Spiegel der soziologischen Rollentheorie* (Frankfurt, 1978), 36ff.

6. This is overlooked by Fenton and Barber in their reviews. See James Fenton, "The Miniature Masterpiece of Harold Pinter," *The Sunday Times,* October 17, 1982; John Barber, "The Disturbing Pinter," *The Daily Telegraph,* October 15, 1982.

7. But see also my observations on Pinter's development as a dramatist in the conclusion of this article.

8. On the first night of *Other Places* in the National Theatre, however, *Family Voices* came first, whereas *A Kind of Alaska* concluded Pinter's trilogy.

9. Katherine H. Burkman, "*Family Voices* and the Voices of the Family in Pinter's Plays," in *Harold Pinter: Critical Approaches,* ed. Steven H. Gale (London: 1985), 164-170, here 164.

10. About this and other Pinter monologues in general see Paul Goetsch, "Die Tendenz zum Monologischen im modernen Drama: Beckett und Pinter," in *Das Hörspiel im Englischunterricht,* ed. Horst Groene (Padenborn, 1980), 73-98.

11. About the concept of self-monitoring, see Mark Snyder, "Cognitive, Behavioral, and Interpersonal Consequences of Self-Monitoring," in *Perceptions of Emotion in Self and Others* [Advances in the Study of Communication and Affect, 5] (New York/London, 1979), 181-201.

12. Daniel Salem, "The Impact of Pinter's Work," *Ariel,* 17 (1986), 71-83.

13. In this respect, Pinter's *Family Voices* is also reminiscent of the early play *The Room.*

14. This is emphasised by Joachim Möller, "Neueres zu Harold Pinter (1975-85): Kritik als Kaleidoskop," *LWU,* 19 (1986), 142-155, here 155.

15. About *Betrayal* see also Ewald Mengel, "Unterschiedliche Formen der Bewußtseinsdiskrepanz und ihre dramatische Funktion in Harold Pinters *Betrayal*," *GRM,* 32 (1982), 333-44.

16. Quoted by Arnold Hinchliffe, "After *No Man's Land:* A Progress Report," in *Harold Pinter,* ed. S. Gale, 153-163, here 157.

Susan Hollis Merritt (essay date 1990)

SOURCE: "Pinter and Politics," in *Harold Pinter: A Casebook,* Duke University Press, 1990, pp. 129-60.

[*In the following essay, Merritt examines Pinter's shift towards political drama in his works of the 1980s.*]

Though acknowledging a "shift" toward political drama in Pinter's recent dramatic works *One for the Road, Precisely,* and *Mountain Language,* some critics question whether it is genuine. Judging the authenticity of any such change of direction is more complex than giving an account of Pinter's views or of his dramatic plots. Such judgments are contingent on the perspectives of the critics, on their particular politics or ideologies. From different critical vantage points, Pinter's politics can seem to have undergone a radical shift on the one hand, while maintaining a somewhat conservative stance on the other. This double perspective on Pinter's shift to political drama reflects current conflicts in cultural studies between those writing from mainstream positions and those espousing Marxist, neo-Marxist, and post-Marxist views.

A feature of the academic study of drama and theater may have engendered the problem of assessing Pinter's position and classifying his plays. As Marvin Carlson documents, "a continuing point of debate in modern theatre theory has been over whether the theatre should be viewed primarily as an engaged social phenomenon or as a politically indifferent aesthetic artifact; a significant amount of contemporary theoretical discourse can still be oriented in terms of this opposition" (454). Carlson's own historical account of twentieth-century theater details the opposition between theater based on Brechtian theory and practice ("political theatre") and theater based more on the theory and practice of Artaud ("absurd theatre," "theatre of cruelty").

Critics have difficulties "placing" Pinter and his drama because he crosses the "standard" boundaries delineated by such binary oppositions. At various stages throughout his career, Pinter himself has characterized his work in some of these terms, and Pinter's plays have been championed by one "camp" or another, leading to early critical claims that he is *either* a "social realist" *or* an "absurdist," *or* that his work is an oddly idiosyncratic mixture of *both* strains. It has been commonplace to quote Pinter's statement "what goes on in my plays is realistic, but what I'm doing is not realism" ("Writing for Myself," 174). Critics' different responses to this "paradox" inform controversies about how to assess any developments in his career.

The social realism perceived in his most recent work complicates the problem. Though Pinter dramatizes political concerns more overtly in *One for the Road, Precisely,* and *Mountain Language,* this "new interest" has strong roots in Pinter's early "comedies of menace" with their representations of individuals anxiously confronting the forces of social authority. What *political position* Pinter represents through his plays is difficult to situate on a conventional Left/Right spectrum. As we will see, Pinter gravitates less toward specific political ideological affiliations (rejecting even their terminology) than toward thinking matters out on his own, though he does ally himself with organizations that support his particular inclinations.[1] If a label is necessary for purposes of identification—and I am not so sure one is—I would call Pinter a social democrat and an advocate, even an activist, for peace, international human rights, and freedom of expression; his current political activities and his plays dramatize concerns with the protection of human rights and unilateral disarmament. Perhaps the most conspicuous shift, however, involves his characterization of the source of these concerns as an unquestionable political "reality."

Throughout most of his career it has been "against the grain" to discuss Pinter's drama as "political." For example, Henkle points to the relative isolation of Pinter's characters; "[t]he possible political dimensions of plays like *The Birthday Party* are remarkably abstract, and the sources of our response to them lie much more in our *personal* anxieties" (185). But, in Germany, where *The Dumb Waiter* premiered in 1959 and *The Caretaker* was performed in 1960, the initial critical popularity of Pinter's plays was partly due to an appreciation of their social relevance. Describing the first performance of Ionesco's *Rhinoceros* at the Düsseldorf Schauspielhaus, where *The Caretaker* also played, Esslin observes: "the German audience instantly recognized the arguments, used by the characters who feel they must follow the trend, as those they themselves had heard, or used, at a time when people in Germany could not resist the lure of Hitler. . . . Rhinoceritis is not only the disease of the totalitarians of the Right as well as of the Left, it is also the pull of conformism" (*Theatre of the Absurd,* 150-51). Though Pinter has recalled spectacular choruses of "boos" accompanying his opening night curtain calls in Düsseldorf ("Between the Lines"), some Germans, focusing on the lower-class status of Davies, regarded *The Caretaker* as relevant socioeconomically. In England, following *The Caretaker,* Taylor grouped Pinter with the "Kitchen Sink" playwrights—social realist and working-class drama of "the Angry Young Men" John Osborne and Arnold Wesker—in *Anger and After,* first published in May 1962 (cf. Anderson, "Harold Pinter").

Yet, in talking about the politics of such drama with Harry Thompson in 1961, Pinter rejected its dramatic viability (9). When Bensky gave him another opportunity to discuss his political concerns in 1966, Pinter himself tended to de-emphasize their importance to his early work. Though qualifying the impression that he was "indifferent" to politics and indicating that his political consciousness was still developing, he nevertheless questioned the relevance of politics to his social role as a playwright, focusing on his violent dislike of politicians and political ideologies and how such violence characterized his life and work. Perhaps as a result, the theme of violence has been discussed repeatedly in Pinter criticism.[2]

By the late sixties Esslin was still trying to sort out connections between Pinter's personal act of conscientious objection in 1948, when he was eighteen years old, and political aspects of his drama (*Peopled Wound,* 24-27; *Pinter: The Playwright,* 36-39). In 1971, when Mel Gussow raised similar questions about his political

(ir)relevance, Pinter replied by criticizing the "totally meaningless, hypocritical" language of "politicians": "Politicians just don't interest me. What, if you like, interests me, is the suffering for which they are responsible. It doesn't interest me—it horrifies me!" He offered comments on Vietnam, South Africa, and China as evidence that he is "very conscious of what's happening in the world. I'm not by any means blind or deaf to the world around me. . . . I'm right up to the minute. I read the papers. I have very strong objections to all sorts of things" ("Conversation," 133-34). Yet these objections still did not enter his plays directly.

Anderson compares Pinter with Arnold Wesker and Edward Bond in terms of their similar lack of popularity in England ("This," 447). In 1979 Pinter alluded to the "very, very strong *young* wave of political playwrights" currently popular in England to help explain what he saw as his poor critical reception there (Gussow, "I Started," 7). The next year Pinter told Barber that he found himself in the "odd position" for a writer of being "really quite unpopular" in his own country, when he is apparently of interest elsewhere. "I have a suspicion," he said, "that fashion at the moment is with the young political Left. I'm never going to be a young political Left. I'm afraid it's a bit too late!" As Pinter also told Gross, "my last three full-length plays [*Old Times, No Man's Land,* and *Betrayal*] have hardly been performed at all in this country, outside London" (27). About this time (1980) Pinter produced and published *The Hothouse,* a "heavily satirical" play which he had "discarded" as worthless earlier (Bensky, 28-29). Though Pinter described his decision to produce *The Hothouse* "rather quietly—at the Hampstead Theatre Club" in terms of having "a bit of fun" (Gussow, "I Started," 5), later remarks suggest that (for a variety of reasons perhaps) Pinter was also now ready to produce more overtly political work.[3]

At the University of East Anglia in 1981, ending his brief talk, Pinter directly addressed the difficulty that he was encountering as a "nonpolitical" writer: "I think it must be very much easier for other people, particularly people, writers who write from a very political point of view and are able to incorporate their politics in one way or another into their work. I do happen to have strong political views but they simply do not come into my work as far as I can see." Asked whether this avoidance of politics as a subject in his plays was "deliberate," Pinter said, "Of course not. It simply doesn't work out that way," adding: "I am myself a convinced nuclear unilateralist but I don't see there is any—there is no way I can write a play about it. It's simply something that would never occur to me, I suppose, any of these considerations. . . . I am sure that some writers do—can very easily and properly sit down and write plays from a political kind of ideology. I am unable to do that." Yet, as another audience member suggested in East Anglia, after having "obviously achieved what [he] set out to," Pinter can now "use the success . . . to help" dramatize sociopolitical and ethical issues.

Pinter began to "help" first by reassessing publicly the political implications of the work that he had suppressed earlier and then by writing and producing new plays. Talking about the 1982 American premiere of *The Hothouse,* he told William Gale that whereas *The Hothouse* "would have been taken as a fantasy, as something remote and surrealistic" when it was written in 1958, "I felt that was not the case then, and I *know* it is not the case now. In 1982 it cannot be denied that it fits in with the facts of life today. The real political hypocrisy and brutality are now blatant. We cannot be fooled by them any longer" (A-16).

Pinter's most recent dramas—*One for the Road, Precisely,* and *Mountain Language*—present today's political "facts of life" more starkly. *One for the Road,* written in 1983 and first produced and directed by Pinter in 1984, dramatizes political torture. *Precisely,* a dramatic sketch that Pinter read before an audience at New York University upon accepting the Elmer Holmes Bobst Award in Arts and Letters in December 1984, satirizes nuclear war bureaucracy. *Mountain Language,* first published and produced in 1988, dramatizes institutionalized abuses of sociopolitical prisoners and their distrust of their guards' perhaps feigned ultimate tolerance, satirizing effects of censorship curtailing individual freedoms.

Pinter's more recent perceptions of the political relevance of his early work further counterbalances the critical commonplace that it lacks such relevance. In "A Play and Its Politics," a conversation between Pinter and Nicholas Hern in 1985 published in the Grove Press edition of *One for the Road* the next year, Pinter explicitly discusses the change in his attitude toward authoritarianism between his early plays, (e.g., *The Birthday Party, The Hothouse,* and *The Dumb Waiter*), all written in 1957-60, and *One for the Road* and *Precisely.* Though he actively considered "the abuse of authority" in writing the earlier plays, he says, they "use metaphor to a great extent, whereas in *One for the Road* the deed is much more specific and direct": "I don't really see *One for the Road* as a metaphor. For anything. It describes a state of affairs in which there are victims of torture. You have the torturer, you have the victims. And you can see that two of the victims have been physically tortured" (8). *One for the Road* is "brutally real: my earlier plays were perhaps metaphors for states of affairs in various respects. This is not a metaphor about anything—it's just a brutal series of facts" (back cover). As when discussing the germination of his earlier plays in other interviews, in "A Play and Its Politics" Pinter further explains the impetus for such violent acts of "actual physical brutality" as rape and murder in *One for the Road.* As well as citing the general context of torture "quite commonly" practiced in "at least ninety countries now" throughout the world, both "Communist and non-Communist," he recounts the more particular circumstances stimulating him to write it: his knowledge of torture and inhumane prison practices in Turkey and his anger at the insensitivity of two young Turkish women toward their own country's violation of human rights. His own active membership in Campaign

for Nuclear Disarmament led to his awareness that members of a counterpart organization in Turkey (the Turkish Peace Association) have been inhumanely treated (12-14).

This "new direction" in Pinter's playwriting grows out of Pinter's long-standing engagement in some social activities against human rights abuses. As early as 1974 Pinter wrote a letter to the London *Times* to draw attention to the plight of Soviet internee Vladimir Bukovsky. Pinter told Gross, in 1980, "While we're talking now . . . people are locked up in prisons all over the place, being tortured in one way or another. I'm quite rattled with these kinds of images, with the sense that these things are ever-present" (25). Several months after his 1981 visit to the University of East Anglia, in the summer of 1982, with his wife, Lady Antonia Fraser, Pinter helped to coordinate "The Night of the Day of the Imprisoned Writer," described as "a charity occasion to benefit the all-too-many writers of the world who are now in prison" (Owen, 24). Pinter's claim for the "very positive effect" that this International PEN benefit could achieve seems deflated by his account of a previous benefit for the imprisoned Czech writer Vaclav Havel: "On my 50th birthday last year [10 October 1980] the National Theatre were kind enough to put on a play of mine [*Landscape*] for one night and the proceeds from that were for Havel's family. The awful thing is that now, a year later, nothing has changed for him" (Owen, 25). Despite this recognition, Pinter persisted in his efforts.[4]

Pinter represented International PEN again on behalf of imprisoned writers in March 1985, when, as vice presidents of English and American PEN, Pinter and Arthur Miller visited prisons in Turkey. On 23 March 1985 the two writers held a joint news conference in Istanbul to protest Turkish human rights abuses. During the five-day visit to Turkey, they talked with over "100 Turkish intellectuals, with former prison inmates, politicians and diplomats," expressing International PEN's concern with "'the dignity of its members throughout the world'" (Gursel; cf. Kamm). At the opening ceremonies of the 48th International PEN Congress in New York, on 12 January 1986, it was reported that "almost 450 writers on nearly every continent are known to be confined" (McDowell).

In a postscript to the interview with Hern, written after he returned from Turkey, Pinter points to support that the United States gives military regimes like Turkey (24). While he clearly protests human rights violations in *One for the Road,* those abused in the play comprise a family (a man, his wife, and their young son) whose national and social identity is not specified. Going beyond the imprisoned writer, the play embraces all prisoners of conscience and others whose rights are being violated by "the State" throughout the world. The play "could take place in totalitarian countries in Eastern Europe or South America," but, Dukore argues, "the many approving references to religion ironically exclude Communist countries, where the interrogator would be unlikely to call himself a religious man, to declare that God is on the side of the state not the dissidents, or to claim that the state's business is to cleanse the world for God" (132-33). To me Nicholas's religious references seem fanatical (not merely "approving"), as associated these days with Middle Eastern countries; yet, I would stress that the setting could still be almost anywhere in the world today, where, unfortunately, such religious, ideological, and other "anti-intellectual" fanaticism is all too widespread.

Vis-à-vis his own recent experiences and concerns as a social activist, it appears Pinter's perspective on the political themes of his earlier plays has sharpened. In the February 1985 interview with Hern, comparing those plays with *One for the Road,* Pinter alludes to a "run-through" of a television production of *The Dumb Waiter:* "It was quite obvious to the actors that the chap who is upstairs and is never seen is a figure of authority. Gus questions this authority and rebels against it and therefore is squashed at the end, or is about to be squashed. The political metaphor was very clear to the actors and directors of the first production in 1960. It was not, however, clear to the critics at the time . . . that it was actually *about* anything" (7).[5] "*The Birthday Party,*" Pinter tells Hern, "which I wrote more or less at the same time, in 1957, again has a central figure who is squeezed by certain authoritarian forces"; and "*The Hothouse*—which actually followed quite shortly, the next year, I think—is essentially about the abuse of authority" (8). (Pinter told Bensky that he wrote *The Hothouse* after *The Caretaker* [28], but his note to the published text confirms his statement to Hern.) When Hern suggests that, retrospectively, the early plays would appear to reflect Pinter's "unease about the Hungarian Revolution and the Soviet annexation of East Europe," Pinter qualifies this view somewhat: "Except that one doesn't normally write about today, but yesterday—or even the day before yesterday" (9). His own "political act" of conscientious objection resulted from being "terribly disturbed as a young man by the Cold War. And McCarthyism. . . . A profound hypocrisy. 'They' the monsters, 'we' the good. In 1948 the Russian suppression of Eastern Europe was an obvious and brutal fact, but I felt very strongly then and feel as strongly now that we have an obligation to subject our own actions and attitudes to an equivalent critical and moral scrutiny."

Even though *One for the Road* did not represent "a sudden crystallisation of [Pinter's] political sensibility" as Hern first thought, since Pinter had been a conscientious objector as a teenager and thus "involved in political acts from early on," nevertheless, "in 1958," critics saw Pinter's plays "as having no relation to the outside world at all"; his plays were, Pinter recalls, "dismissed as absurd rubbish" by most critics (10). "[F]or many people," Hern speculates, "it must have seemed that you've been operating on this political level invisibility" (11). Pinter recapitulates his political attitude: "I wouldn't say that my political awareness during those years was dead. Far from it. But I came to view politicians and political structures and political acts with something I can best describe as

detached contempt. To engage in politics seemed to me futile. And so, for twenty years or so, in my writing I simply continued investigations into other areas" (12).

As Gussow has observed more recently, "In retrospect . . . [Pinter] can identify the political content in his plays, which he can trace back to *The Birthday Party* and *The Dumbwaiter.* Linking *The Birthday Party* to *One for the Road* and *Mountain Language,* he said they all dealt with 'the destruction of an individual.'" The idea for the "knock" on Stanley's door in *The Birthday Party,* Pinter said, "came from my knowledge of the Gestapo. The character of the old man, Petey, says one of the most important lines I've ever written. As Stanley is taken away, Petey says, 'Stan, don't let them tell you what to do.' I've lived that line all my damn life. Never more than now" ("Pinter's Plays," C22; cf. Dukore, 143-46). Whereas, retrospectively, Pinter presents his most recent plays as a more overt development of a generally underestimated aspect of his earlier ones in "A Play and Its Politics," in another more recent interview Pinter further explains the change that *One for the Road* signifies more emphatically: "It certainly represents a permanent change in me as a citizen of this country . . . a man living in this world. It's been happening for a very long time. In other words, I've become more and more political over the last 10 years—more politically engaged. And now I'm profoundly engaged" (Drake, 6).

Whether or not this "change" will indeed prove "permanent" remains to be seen. So far what Gussow calls Pinter's "politicization" ("Pinter's Plays," C17) has raised "anxious murmurings from his devotees that, by taking on the mantle of Amnesty International, he may lose the touch of genius with which he illumines the despair and the power games of less obviously charged situations" (Carne). In assessing this "new phase in Pinter's oeuvre, a departure into the realm of political debate, even propaganda," Esslin still asks, "To what genre do Pinter's anti-torture tracts belong?" To consider *Mountain Language* "straightforward *documentary drama*" is problematic because "the aestheticism . . . the beautiful way in which it is done, undercuts the documentary quality. Real torture is much more messy, much more sordid" ("Mountain Language," 76, 78).[6]

PINTER'S SHIFT TO POLITICAL DRAMA: AN ALTERNATIVE CRITICAL VIEW

As if anticipating these concerns, in *British and Irish Political Drama in the Twentieth Century,* David Ian Rabey observes: "The merging of social drama into political drama is an easy transition and may cause problems of classification (as in the work of Osborne and Wesker)" (2). Rabey makes no mention of Pinter. Though *British and Irish Political Drama in the Twentieth Century* was probably in press at the time that Pinter published *One for the Road* and *Precisely,* even on the basis of these short works and *Mountain Language,* Rabey still might not have included Pinter, given this definition of the aims and styles of the genre:

"*Political* drama" emphasizes the directness of its address to problematic social matters, and its attempt to interpret these problems in political terms. Political drama communicates its sense of these problems' avoidability, with implicit or explicit condemnation of the political circumstances that have allowed them to rise and continue to exist (just as Brecht identifies *The Rise of Arturo Ui* as Resistable). In perceiving social problems as avoidable, political drama is necessarily diverging from the worldview that the agents of the status quo would seek to impose for the continued smooth running of society in its present form.

(1-2)

Whereas Rabey takes "*social* drama as that which purports to act as an impartial report on social relations, or to focus on specific social abuses, without stepping over into an attack on the fundamentals of the society in question," he takes "*political* drama as that which views specific social abuses as symptomatic of a deeper illness, namely injustice and anomalies at the heart of society's basic power structure" (2). Whereas it might seem that *One for the Road, Precisely,* and *Mountain Language* could be classified as political drama, Pinter's attitude toward social change, as he describes it to Hern, does not fit "Leftist" concepts of the attitude and kinds of change that a political dramatist advocates.

Pinter does not seem to perceive social problems of the kind he dramatizes as "avoidable." When Hern asks "whether a play like *One for the Road* can really have any effect," Pinter explains: "[R]eason is not going to do anything. Me writing *One for the Road,* documentaries, articles, lucid analyses, Averell Harriman writing in the *New York Times,* voices raised here and there, people walking down the road and demonstrating. Finally it's hopeless. There's nothing one can achieve. Because the modes of thinking of those in power are worn out, threadbare, atrophied. Their minds are a brick wall" ("A Play," 20). Whereas Pinter recognizes hegemonic paradigms governing institutional abuses—"the modes of thinking of those in power"—he gives no indication that solving the problem must involve a change in what Rabey identifies as the "basic . . . structure" of power; indeed, he denies that *any* solution is even plausible. "But," he adds, "still one can't stop attempting to try to think and see things as clearly as possible."

In her interview with Pinter, Drake observes that Pinter "feels artists don't influence politics much." "The only thing that will influence politics," Pinter said, "certainly in this country [America], and in my own country, is the voters. I do take the point that if I say something someone might listen. At the same time, I don't talk as an artist; I talk as a man. Everyone has a quite essential obligation to subject the society in which we live to moral scrutiny" (6). Pinter defines his own position quite clearly: "My own view is that the appalling danger that the world is in at the moment has to do with a schism that has actually been manufactured. I'm referring to Them and Us. To inhabit rigid and atrophied postures like these has led to the

present danger." The McCarthyite distinctions between political-economic systems (Communists and non-Communists) that he objects to in "A Play and Its Politics"; national alliances (Eastern Bloc and Western Bloc); classes (bourgeois and working class, or, more generally, the Haves and the Have-nots); and even political ideologies (Left and Right): Pinter rejects all such polarizing binary oppositions. "I was 15 when the war was over, so that one emerged out of that and lurched through adolescence into manhood as it were, with the weight of all that and the further reverberations—such as The Bomb and the Iron Curtain. McCarthyism here, repression in Eastern Europe. There seemed to be no end to it. But there is an end to it. There's an end all right. My view, incidentally, is that that end is going to come. . . . I think it's inevitable, yes." Ironically, he concludes, with (mock?) upper-class panache: "And on that note I shall have a glass of champagne."

In contrast, Günther Klotz defines the "internationalism" of "recent progressive British drama" to include such recurrent themes as "the combined efforts of monopolies, governments and military commanders to keep themselves in power and to enlarge their control by enforcing maximum profits" and "socialist reality" (36, 39). There are "a new strategy of anti-imperialist drama and a new type of production as well as reception in the British theatre, a new type of play which offers something constructive for people to identify with, the feeling of a prospective integration of the individual in a new common cause which is not an abstract idea but, in some parts of the world, tangible reality" (39-40). This is not the same "tangible reality" that Pinter has been describing and dramatizing.

For Pinter, altering his earlier emphasis on reality as relative and unverifiable: "All we're talking about, finally is what is real? What is real? There's only one reality, you know. You can interpret reality in various ways. But there's only one. And if that reality is thousands of people being tortured to death at this very moment and hundreds of thousands of megatons of nuclear bombs standing there waiting to go off at this very moment, then that's it and that's that. It has to be faced" ("A Play," 21). Thus intending to confront his audience with this "one reality," Pinter has been critical of their unwillingness to face it, despite his own awareness of "that great danger, this great irritant to an audience" of "agit-prop" ("A Play," 18). Pinter has not suggested any "constructive" measures for his audience to take against the atrocities dramatized in *One for the Road* and *Mountain Language* or those implied in *Precisely.* He may feel, as he has said about spectators' responses to his other plays, that any response is their own individual responsibility.

Several people walked out midway through performances of *One for the Road* that I attended in New York City and Portland, Oregon (see *Other Places* and *No Holds Barred*). Apparently, some could not tolerate the physical and verbal abuse on stage. Portland's Sumus Theatre management received complaints about the play's language, not the political issues it raised. Since the performance of *One for the Road* that I saw in Portland was a benefit for Amnesty International, it was preceded by a short speech about the aims of this organization, delivered by its local president, Arden Benson, who encouraged the audience to sign petitions in behalf of individual political prisoners, directing us to such petitions, as well as leaflets, in the lobby. In this way the theater management provided opportunities for purposive political action that Pinter's play does not directly prescribe, though they are activities likely to merit his approval, since Pinter himself is a member of Amnesty International (Drake, 6).

Rabey further distinguishes "the comparative aims and styles of political *dramas* (plays) and political *theatre*" by citing Sandy Craig's "working definition," which attributes the difference to a playwright's stance toward the audience:

> the important feature which distinguishes political plays from political theatre is this: *political plays* seek to appeal to, and influence, the middle class, in particular that section of the middle class which is influential in moulding 'public opinion.' The implication of this is that society can be reformed and liberalized, where necessary, by the shock troops of the middle class— and, of course, such people are influential in campaigns for reform. But further, political plays in bourgeois theatre implicitly realize that the middle class remains the progressive class within society. *Political theatre,* on the other hand, as embodied in the various political theatre companies, aims—with varying degrees of success—to appeal to, and be an expression of, the working class. Its underlying belief is that the working class is the progressive class within society.

(Rabey 6, quoting Craig, 30-31; emphasis added)

Political theater tries "to produce plays that arouse a wider and deeper awareness of the necessity and of the possibility to change the present society," Günther Klotz also observes. "In its struggle against imperialism and against the set-up of the commercialized institutions and media of communication, the progressive drama had to change from the social criticism of the breakthrough [e.g., Osborne's *Look Back in Anger*] to a theatre looking for alternatives. . . . No longer can a progressive drama be effective if it continues to imitate life in a naturalistic way, in serving the old liberal aims of education and entertainment, or moralizing and edifying. What is required is a drama as medium of social movement" (40).

Though Pinter himself comes originally from a working-class background (his father was a tailor), he has, through his own professional success and his second marriage to Lady Antonia Fraser, risen through the middle class into the upper class of English society. Though his first few plays featured working-class characters loosely modeled on people encountered during his experiences as a struggling actor, these dramas were presented first to university audiences. After *The Caretaker* Pinter became more

upscale, appealing to upper middle-class audiences. Some of his later characters could *attend* what Rabey calls "the legitimate, established theatre" (ix). If Pinter's political plays do not count as political theater, it is also because his customary audiences—"bourgeois" or "elitist"—are not politically progressive.

The distinguishing "political" issue involved in "cultural analysis on the left" is "how to acknowledge and comprehend the tremendous capacity of patriarchal and capitalist institutions to regenerate themselves not only in their material foundations and structures but in the hearts and minds of people, while never losing sight or despairing of the power of popular organization and struggle to resist and transform them" (Batsleer et al., 5). Joining the "professional" classes (as an actor, writer, and director), Pinter has worked within our "patriarchal and capitalist" cultural institutions (what Klotz calls "the commercialized institutions and media of communication"—theater, radio, film, television, and print) and become a phenomenal commercial success. This success is sometimes cited as a symptom of Pinter's "cop-out"; he has become a symbol of the "mainstream," the kind of theater to which "alternative theatre" is an alternative.[7] Yet "whilst the tradition of academic Marxism which is now a familiar feature of literary criticism provides an ideology, a vocabulary and enough internal disputes for the committed critic of political theatre, the alternatives to *that* alternative are less clearly formulated and the continuities between one group and another largely uncharted" (Anderson, "This," 452).

Unlike most other Leftist critics, who regard Pinter as a mainstream, commercial playwright and would term him "*boulevard,*""West-End," or "Broadway bound," Klaus Köhler argues that Pinter's position is "the position of a bourgeois dramatist at variance with the sacrosanct beliefs of his class[;] the direction of his criticism is clearly anti-bourgeois. Rather than invite compliance with an untouchable status quo[,] [Pinter] discredits the illusion of possible harmony and integrity under imperialist power structures." With their "individual activities of consciousness warped by the ideologic strategies of the 'Welfare State,' [Pinter's characters] are unable to take stock of themselves and the world around them." Their alienation and "estrangement" result from "a repressive canon of bourgeois ethics and politics." But there is an important difference between Pinter's "distancing effects" and Brecht's contention that "'the present-day world can only be described to present-day people if it is described as capable of transformation.'" With other "congenial late bourgeois writers," Köhler argues, Pinter "shares . . . an unresolved dualism of rejection and doubts as to the alterability of what is rejected" (324-25).

Köhler concludes "The Establishment and the Absurd" (published before Pinter's *One for the Road* and the interview on its politics) by citing Pinter's repeated expressions of "his indifference to political issues" (326). But in both his plays and his public pronouncements Pinter has never been unequivocally indifferent to politics (Cf.

Dukore). Köhler's more specific contention that "[c]rucial problems of the present-day class struggles in Britain are absent from [Pinter's] plays" is even qualified by rereading *The Caretaker* from the perspective of Sahai, for whom it dramatizes consequences of urbanization for the lower and would-be middle classes. Yet, as Köhler recognizes, "[Pinter] has also stressed the general social significance of his theatre" (326). Pinter presents "model situations from a micro-sociological perspective. Beyond all ambiguities they set forth a perpetual fight of opposites, not so much between the privileged and the unprivileged as among the representatives and camp-followers of the bourgeois regime today." From this perspective, "[b]y exposing [his characters'] fruitless navel inspection, self-laceration and incapacity for purposeful action[,] [Pinter] analyses the social and moral make-up of a class destined to perish by its own contradictions." But despite this "[t]renchant debunking," Pinter still refuses "to envisage any constructive commitment," Köhler concludes, and "this basic inconsistency . . . narrows the extent and impact of Pinter's critique." This opinion of Pinter's social and political range suggests a current strategy of some cultural criticism "on the Left": to devalue any author who does not espouse a Marxist and/or feminist ideology. Pinter is being "rewritten" by critics sympathetic to Marxism and feminism. To become successful "social strategists" themselves, these critics rewrite Pinter so as to enact their own scenarios for social change.[8]

A position somewhat different from Köhler's informs C. W. E. Bigsby's "Politics of Anxiety: Contemporary Socialist Theatre in England." Melmoth defines Bigsby's perspective succinctly: "the truly subversive dramatist is relativistic and anarchistic rather than programmatic, a farceur rather than a commentator or, as Bigsby puts it, 'not Arden but Orton, not McGrath but Pinter'" (Melmoth, 954). As neither Bigsby nor Melmoth was able to take into account *One for the Road, Precisely,* and *Mountain Language,* I wonder how these plays might modify their views. In all three plays Pinter suggests no particular solution to problems of culturally institutionalized oppression that they dramatize; but he does implicate his audience in these problems viscerally. Finding solutions (if there are any) is up to us—audiences and voters—and our governmental officials (elected or not). Pinter may have placed little stock in our ability to solve such social and political problems, but at least he has given us the opportunity to "try to think and see things as clearly as possible" too, to subject "reality" to intense "moral scrutiny."

While accepting Pinter's viewpoint that *One for the Road* is "not metaphorical in the same way that *The Dumb Waiter* and *The Birthday Party* are," Judith Roof points out that "the concreteness of the portrayal of abuse also conveys larger ideological metaphors (the family, the father). Its realism, thus, is not only a realism of detail and behavior, but also a rendering of the context, of the ideas in whose name horrors are perpetuated" (11). If, in *One for the Road,* "[t]he central place of the subversive stare . . . suggests that an unauthorized watching—a kind of

seditious theatre—is a way of opposing political oppression" (17), so the final silence of the Elderly Woman in *Mountain Language*—an unauthorized *refusal* to speak—subverts linguistic oppression by "the State."[9] Though Pinter suggests that an impetus for *Mountain Language* was his visit with Arthur Miller to Turkey, the play was advertised falsely as "a 'parable about torture and the fate of the Kurdish people'"; while Pinter accepts that it is about torture, he denies both that it concerns "'the fate of the Kurdish people'" and that it is "'a parable'" (Pinter, "'Mountain Language'"; cf. Gussow, "Pinter's Plays," C17). From Pinter's own "point of view, it is about suppression of language, and the loss of freedom of expression . . . [and] therefore . . . as relevant in England as it is in Turkey" (C17).

"While the 'clear vision' Pinter proposes may make a more intelligent populace," Roof argues further, "it too is complicit in the maintenance of the power relations it dissects. Awareness must be accompanied by a look back at the forces which conspire to construct us all within a dominant ideology which obscures problems in the interest of maintaining status quo" (17). Yet in "[u]rging a different way to see"—and different ways to hear and to feel as well, I would add—like Beckett's *Catastrophe,* Pinter's political plays do "propose a theatrical model for that seeing different from the analytical disengagement of Brecht's alienation-effect. Committing theatre to political action in a most direct way, Pinter and Beckett involve both stage and audience in an enactment of the oppression theatre embodies and exposes."

PINTER'S FUTURE AS A POLITICAL DRAMATIST

We do not know how Pinter's own beliefs in the political prospects of vast social change will develop. We do not know, as he himself has said that he does not know, how long he will continue to write political plays, or anything else ("A Play," 18-19). "I won't, I'm sure, continue to write plays about politics," he has insisted, "unless an authentic image comes into my mind which demands to be written. But I've no such plans and I can't write out of ideological *desire*. That, almost invariably, is artificial. Dry. Manufactured. In other words, I've no idea what I'm going to write and I don't anticipate that I shall continue to write political plays as such. I don't know what my future is as a writer" (Drake, 6). But while he may not know his "future as a writer," Pinter does predict his "future . . . as a man," and that is: "To continue to ask some very straight questions about the society in which we live, without fear or favor. In other words, I don't give a damn how many people I offend."[10]

"My attitude toward my own playwriting has changed," Pinter told Gussow. "The whole idea of a narrative, of a broad canvas stretching over a period of two hours—I think I've gone away from that forever. I can't see that I could ever encompass it again. I was always termed, what is the word? 'minimalist.' . . . Maybe I am. Who knows? But I hope that to be minimal is to be precise and focused.

I feel that what I've illuminated is quite broad—and deep—shadows stretching away." Reporting his answer to a Sussex University student's question about whether he could ally his current interests with "characters as [he] used to write them, people called Meg and Max"—"I don't think I can any longer"—he reserved this opening: "I don't want to cut myself off from all experiences likely to come" ("Pinter's Plays," C22).

On 3 October 1989, after his reading at the 92nd Street Y, when asked by Gussow if he had reconsidered the change in his attitude, Pinter said: "It is not a matter for me to reconsider. Nothing would give me greater pleasure than to write any play, of whatever length. I don't think length is in any way so important anyway, but one thing about the act of writing is that it is an act of—essentially an act of freedom, as I understand it, so it's great to write any way, if you can do it. I just find it more and more difficult." "I'm only concerned at the moment with *accurate* and *precise* images of what is the case," he added. In response to Gussow's opening statement that Pinter has "always been a political playwright" and his question about whether Pinter could trace "a serious interest" in the world of politics" from **The Birthday Party** through **Mountain Language,** Pinter replied:

> In the early days, which was thirty years ago, I was a political playwright of a kind. But I then took a break from being so for about seventeen years. And I wrote a lot of plays between 1970 and 1985 which can't be said to be political plays—things like **Old Times, Betrayal, Landscape,** and **Silence,** which were concerned with memory and youth and loss and so on . . . they didn't take place and didn't concern themselves with social or political structure, whereas the earlier plays did. . . . My early work was I think full of games and jokes and so on, but I think the distinction I would make between those plays then and these plays now is that I'm afraid that for me the joke is over. I can't see any more jokes. I can't play any more games. So I therefore find that I'm writing shorter and shorter pieces which are more and more brutal and more and more overtly naked, you see.

Though admitting that the theater may "affect the world in which we live" only a "little," Pinter explained: "But that little is something, and I respect the power, the correspondence between theater and audience. . . . I always have hated propaganda plays . . . agit-prop. . . . But I still feel that there is room, there is a role somewhere, for a work that is not following, pursuing, the normal narrative procedure of the drama, and it's to be found, and I'm trying to find it." Criticizing the "debased language" pervading American and English governmental statements about Central America, Pinter stated: "I just want to make the facts *absolutely clear,* and it's as I see myself not only as an actor and an entertainer, but . . . I'm also a citizen of the world in which I live, and I take responsibility for that, I really *insist* upon taking responsibility and *understand* my responsibility quite precisely as *actually* trying to find out what *the truth is.* And what actually happens. And so [what] I've found is that we're really at the bottom

of a *blanket* of lies which unfortunately we are either too indifferent or too frightened to question."[11]

If Pinter does keep on writing plays—however minimalist, serious, and factually truthful—critics cannot rule out further developments that might alter assessments of what Köhler terms "the extent and impact of Pinter's critique" (326). Pinter may continue to widen his breadth while further deepening his insight into human social relations and global politics.

Signaling such a development perhaps, Pinter has written some new screen adaptations dealing with a variety of sociopolitically relevant subjects: **Reunion** (based on Fred Uhlmann's novel about Stuttgart in the 1930s and 1980s), **The Heat of the Day** (based on Elizabeth Bowen's novel about wartime London), and **The Handmaid's Tale** (based on Margaret Atwood's novel about a Christian fundamentalist regime in America).[12] **Reunion** is "a story of friendship between two boys—one a German aristocrat, the other a German Jew, beginning in 1932 and ending a half century later, when the Jewish man comes to terms with his belief that his friend has let him down"; the film's American director, Jerry Schatzberg describes "the relationship" between them as the project's appeal (Van Gelder, "Togetherness"). According to writer-director Paul Schrader, Pinter has also written a screenplay adapting Ian McEwan's *Comfort of Strangers,* a novel "set in Venice—about a vacationing young British couple whose lives are sort of taken over by a local couple," reminiscent of **The Servant** (1963); "full of innuendo and subtext," it is reportedly "quite close to the kind of thing Pinter writes for himself. Though it's an adaptation, it has the same themes and cadences of his original work, that element of dominance in relationships between men and women that is very Pinteresque" (Van Gelder, "Pinteresque Pinter"), that is, in the broadest sense, very political.

On 3 October 1989, when Pinter related his current project of writing a screenplay of Kafka's *The Trial* to people's distorted memories of it "as a political book" reminiscent of Arthur Koestler, he explained: "I simply wouldn't be interested in writing a screenplay of *Darkness at Noon* because it's so specifically of its time and place"; whereas "the nightmare of [Kafka's] world is precisely in its ordinariness, and that is what I think is so frightening." But, though chairman of the Arts for Nicaragua Fund in Great Britain, Pinter says that writing "a specific play about such a[n immediate political] situation" as Nicaragua "is not something I could possibly do." Yet, like many of Pinter's past remarks, this one should not be taken as "final and definitive": what Pinter foresees now that he could not "possibly do" does not rule out what he may actually do in the future.

Notes

1. For a context of some of Pinter's current activities, see Atlas.

2. See Bensky, 30-31; Bosworth; and Gross, 25. For a more recent discussion of violence in Pinter's work, especially *Hothouse,* see Mengel.

3. See Pinter, "Author's Note," in *Hothouse;* cf. Bensky, 28-29. See also Gillen, "Nowhere," 86-87 and 96 n.5; cf. Knowles, "Hothouse," 134.

4. As a result of such efforts on his behalf, Havel's situation improved both politically and financially. Though Havel was released after the benefit in which the Pinters were involved, early in 1989 he was incarcerated again, becoming the focus of intense worldwide protests for his release, which finally occurred on 17 May. As a result of the remarkable national uprising in December 1989 ("the Velvet Revolution"), Havel became president of Czechoslovakia and was nominated for the Nobel Peace Prize (for the second time) on 28 January 1990. In February "[t]he Pinters [will] visit Havel to share his triumph" (Angelo, 66).

5. Concerning the premiere of *The Dumb Waiter* on American television in 1987, cf. Pinter's telephone remarks to Farber about the play's topical relevance: "I think it also has a serious subject. I always considered it a political play, though it's not overt. But it is a play about dissidence. It's a play about questioning and criticizing powers that remain complaisant and sure of themselves and somewhere upstairs. I think that's still a timely subject."

6. For other reviews of the London premiere, see *London Theatre Record.* See also Gussow, "Pinter's Plays."

7. James regards "alternative theatre" as "political theatre" (in Craig's sense, as quoted above). Cf. Anderson, "This," 450, 456 n.11.

8. On "the notion of the critic as social strategist," as exemplified by Terry Eagleton, see King, 60-61.

9. Cf. Gillen, "From Chapter Ten," 4.

10. Williams finds it "impossible to believe [Pinter's] assurances [on *Saturday Review* (BBC-2)] that 'I'm no longer interested in myself as a playwright.' There was something willed, media-ridden, even schizoid about [Pinter's] assessment that 'I've got an awful lot under my belt. It's no great loss.'" Cf. Pinter's remark to Gussow: "I understand your interest in me as a playwright. But I'm more interested in myself as a citizen" ("Pinter's Plays," C17). On Pinter's role as a "citizen," see Knowles's forthcoming article.

11. Cf. Pinter, "Language and Lies" and the refutation by Nyholm.

12. The parenthetical descriptions are all quotations from "Harold Pinter: Growth of an Angry Playwright." See also Canby; and Gussow, "Pinter's Plays," C17. Pinter has also adapted Joseph Conrad's anti-war novel *Victory* for the screen.

Works Cited

Anderson, Michael. "Harold Pinter: Journey to the Interior." Chap. 4 in *Anger and Detachment: A Study of Arden, Osborne and Pinter.* London: Pitman, 1976.

———. "This, That and the Other: The Critic and the Alternative Theatre." *Modern Drama* 24 (1981): 445-57.

Angelo, Bonnie. "Profile: Not Quite Your Usual Historian." *Time,* 15 Jan. 1990, 66-68.

Atlas, James. "Thatcher Puts a Lid On: Censorship in Britain." *New York Times Mag.,* 5 Mar. 1989.

Barber, John. "Precise Words of Pinter." London *Daily Telegraph,* 30 June 1980, 11.

Batsleer, Janet, and Tony Davies, Rebecca O'Rourke, and Chris Weedon. *Rewriting English: The Politics of Gender and Class.* London and New York: Methuen, 1985.

Bensky, Lawrence M. "The Art of the Theater III: Harold Pinter: An Interview." *Paris Rev.* 10 (Fall 1966): 12-37. (Excerpted in "Pinter: 'Violence Is Natural.'" *New York Times,* 1 Jan. 1967, Sec. 2: 1, 3.)

Bigsby, C. W. E. "The Politics of Anxiety: Contemporary Socialist Theatre in England." In *Modern British Dramatists: New Perspectives,* ed. and intro. John Russell Brown, 161-76. Englewood Cliffs, N.J.: Prentice-Hall, 1984.

Bosworth, Patricia. "Why Doesn't He Write More?" *New York Times,* 27 Oct. 1968, Sec. 2: 3.

Canby, Vincent. "Critic's Notebook: Old Favorites Are No More at Cannes." *New York Times,* 18 May 1989, Sec. C: 23, 29.

Carlson, Marvin. *Theories of the Theatre: A Historical and Critical Survey, from the Greeks to the Present.* Ithaca and London: Cornell Univ. Press, 1984.

Carne, Rosalind. "Theatre: Space Probe." *New Statesman,* 23 Mar. 1984, 31.

Craig, Sandy. "Unmasking the Lie: Political Theatre." In *Dreams and Deconstructions: Alternative Theatre in Britain,* ed. Sandy Craig, 20-48. Ambergate, Derbyshire, Eng.: Amber Lane, 1980.

Drake, Sylvie. "Acting Is Just like 'Old Times' for Pinter." *Los Angeles Times,* 29 Oct. 1985, Sec. 6: 1, 6.

Dukore, Bernard F. *Harold Pinter.* Grove Press Modern Dramatists. New York: Grove, 1982. 2d ed. Macmillan Modern Dramatists. London: Macmillan, 1988.

Esslin, Martin. "Mountain Language Opens in London." Rev. of National Theatre (Lyttelton) production of *Mountain Language. Pinter Rev.* 2 (1988): 76-78.

———. *The Peopled Wound: The Work of Harold Pinter.* Garden City, N.Y.: Doubleday, 1970. 4th ed. Repr. as *Pinter: The Playwright.* London and New York: Methuen, 1982. Corrected repr. 1984.

———. *The Theatre of the Absurd.* Garden City, N.Y.: Doubleday, 1961. Rev. ed. London: Pelican, 1968. Repr. Garden City, N.Y.: Doubleday, Anchor Books, 1969.

Farber, Stephen. "Topical Relevance." Telephone interview with Harold Pinter. *New York Times,* 10 May 1987, Sec. 2: 25.

Gale, William K. "Pinter Believes Trinity Rep. Will Do 'Damn Well' in Staging His 'Hothouse.'" *Providence Jour.,* 12 Feb. 1982, A1, 16.

Gillen, Francis. "From Chapter Ten of *The Dwarfs* to *Mountain Language:* The Continuity of Harold Pinter." *Pinter Rev.* 2 (1988): 1-4.

———. "'Nowhere to Go': Society and the Individual in Harold Pinter's *The Hothouse.*" *Twentieth Century Literature* 29, no. 1 (1983): 86-96.

Gross, Miriam. "Pinter on Pinter." London *Observer Rev.,* 5 Oct. 1980, 25, 27.

Gursel, Mustafa. "Turkey Censors Blast on Rights by Two Authors: Miller, Pinter Say Torture a Fact in Turkey." *Washington Post,* 24 Mar. 1985, A27.

Gussow, Mel. "A Conversation [Pause] with Harold Pinter." *New York Times Mag.,* 5 Dec. 1971.

———. "Harold Pinter: 'I Started with Two People in a Pub.'" *New York Times,* 30 Dec. 1979, Sec. 2: 5, 7.

———. "Pinter's Plays Following Him out of Enigma and into Politics." *New York Times,* 6 Dec. 1988, Sec. C: 17, 22.

"Harold Pinter: Growth of an Angry Playwright." London *Observer,* Oct. 1988, 13.

Henkle, Roger B. "From Pooter to Pinter: Domestic Comedy and Vulnerability." *Critical Quart.* 16 (Summer 1974): 174-89.

James, Alby. "Alternative versus Mainstream." *Gambit* 9, no. 36 (1980): 7-9.

Kamm, Henry. "Two Playwrights Deplore Turkish Rights Record." *New York Times,* 28 Mar. 1985, A17.

King, Noel. "Rewriting Richardson." *Jour. of the Midwest Modern Language Association* 18 (Spring 1985): 42-61.

Klotz, Günther. "Internationalism and Present British Drama." *Zeitschrift für Anglistik un Amerikanistik* 27 (1979): 35-42.

Knowles, Ronald. "'The Hothouse' and the Epiphany of Harold Pinter." *Jour. of Beckett Studies* 10 (1985): 134-44.

Köhler, Klaus. "The Establishment and the Absurd: Trends, Ideologies and Techniques in Non-Realistic Drama from Beckett to Pinter (Part II)." *Zeitschrift für Anglistik und Amerikanistik* (Leipzig, E. Ger.) 32, no. 4 (1984): 315-29.

London Theatre Record 21 (1988): 1467-71.

McDowell, Edwin. "PEN Talks on Freedom of the Word." *New York Times,* 16 Jan. 1986, Sec. 3: C17.

Melmoth, John. "Theatre: Subversives and Hooligans." *Times Literary Supplement,* 30 Aug. 1985, 953-54.

Mengel, Ewald. "The 'Closed Society': Structural Violence in the English Drama to the Present." Photocopy.

No Holds Barred. Precisely. By Harold Pinter. Stage production directed by Robin Stone. With Douglas Mace and Megan Taylor. *The Dumb Waiter.* By Harold Pinter. Stage production directed by Keith Scales. With Gary Brickner-Schulz and Ken Colburn. *One for the Road.* By Harold Pinter. Stage production directed by Gary O'Brien. With Daniel Kalapsa, Douglas Mace, Keith Scales, and Megan Taylor. MetroNorthwest Productions, Sumus Theatre, Portland, Ore., 16 and 28 Aug. 1986. Performance of *One for the Road* on 28 Aug. dedicated to Amnesty International.

Nyholm, Per. "Language and Nicaragua." Letter to the editor. *Index on Censorship* 17, no. 7 (1988): 6.

Other Places. Three Plays by Harold Pinter. Stage production directed by Alan Schneider. *Victoria Station.* With Henderson Forsythe and Kevin Conway. *One for the Road.* With Caroline Lagerfelt, David George Polyak, George Hosmer, and Kevin Conway. *A Kind of Alaska.* With Caroline Lagerfelt, Dianne Wiest, and Henderson Forsythe. Manhattan Theatre Club, New York, 18 May 1984. (From 3 Apr. to 20 May 1984.)

Owen, Michael. "Harold Pinter and His Lady and a Great Erotic Experience." London *Standard,* 11 Sept. 1981, 24-25.

Pinter, Harold. *Complete Works.* 4 vols. New York: Grove, 1976-81.

———. *The Hothouse.* Incl. "Author's Note." New York: Grove, 1980.

———. "Language and Lies." *Index on Censorship* 17, no. 6 (1988): 2.

———. Letter to the Editor. London *Times,* 22 Mar. 1974, 17.

———. "'Mountain Language.'" Letter to the Editor. *Times Literary Supplement,* 7-13 Oct. 1988, 1109.

———. *Mountain Language.* New York: Grove, 1989.

———. *One for the Road.* New York: Grove, 1986.

———. "A Play and Its Politics: A Conversation between Harold Pinter and Nicholas Hern" and "Postscript." In *One for the Road,* 5-24.

———. *Precisely. Harper's,* May 1985, 37.

———. Readings of an excerpt from *The Hothouse* and of *One for the Road* and discussion with Mel Gussow, reading selected questions from the audience. The Poetry Center of the 92nd Street Y, New York, 3 Oct. 1989.

———. Talk presented at the Univ. of East Anglia, East Anglia, Eng., 29 Oct. 1981.

———. "Writing for Myself." Comp. Richard Findlater. *Twentieth Century* 169 (Feb. 1961): 172-75. (Repr. in Pinter, *Complete Works* 2: 9-12.)

Rabey, David Ian. *British and Irish Political Drama in the Twentieth Century: Implicating the Audience.* New York: St. Martin's, 1986.

Roof, Judith. "Staging the Ideology behind the Power: Pinter's *One for the Road* and Beckett's *Catastrophe.*" *Pinter Rev.* 2 (1988): 8-18.

Sahai, Surendra. "Pinter's *The Caretaker:* A Treatise on Urbanization." *Indian Jour. of English Studies* 19 (1979): 69-79.

Taylor, John Russell. *Anger and After: A Guide to the New British Drama.* London: Methuen, 1962. 3d ed. London: Methuen, 1969.

Thompson, Harry. "Harold Pinter Replies." *New Theatre Mag.* 2 (Jan. 1961): 8-10.

Van Gelder, Lawrence. "At the Movies: Pinteresque Pinter." *New York Times,* 28 July 1989, B4.

———. "At the Movies: Togetherness." *New York Times,* 22 Jan. 1988, C6.

Williams, Hugo. "Mumbo Gumbo." Rev. of *Saturday Review* (BBC2). *New Statesman,* 4 Oct. 1985, 36.

Benedict Nightingale (essay date 1990)

SOURCE: "Harold Pinter/Politics," in *Around the Absurd: Essays on Modern and Postmodern Drama,* edited by Enoch Brater and Ruby Cohn, The University of Michigan Press, 1990, pp. 129-54.

[*In the following essay, Nightingale examines Pinter's political commitments and argues that their expression in his later plays lessens the quality of those plays.*]

Ten or twenty years ago Harold Pinter was the very last British dramatist one would have expected to find publicly crusading against nuclear weapons, state torture, America's domination of the lands to her south, and other actual or supposed ills. The idea that this activism might extend to his plays would have been even more unthinkable.

True, a few alert critics, notably Martin Esslin and Ruby Cohn, detected political resonances in his work, especially his early work; but they knew that these were resonances and reverberations only. Pinter's primary emphasis was the embattled individual in his or her personal relationships. More than any of his British contemporaries, he seemed concerned with the primary drives and needs: for a place to sleep, belong, and be secure; for status and attention; for influence and power; for emotional and sexual bonds and attachments. At a time when most British playwrights felt some responsibility to address public issues, and many were content to see their characters in their social and political roles alone, Pinter concentrated his attention on the human animal in its most intimate dealings. He seemed the most private of writers—and, as would-be interviewer after would-be interviewer was pained to discover, the most private of men as well.

What a reversal there has been! It now seems that there is scarcely a liberal or radical cause that Harold Pinter does not espouse, and espouse loudly. He is an active supporter of Amnesty International, the Campaign for Nuclear Disarmament, Arts for Nicaragua, the Index on Censorship, and International PEN. Indeed, it was in behalf of the last of these organizations that he went to Turkey with Arthur Miller in 1985, a visit whose principal events the American dramatist was memorably, and suggestively, to describe in the *Observer.*[1]

The two men became convinced that human rights were being systematically abused in that country. They heard stories of mass arrests, beatings, and torture. By the time they arrived at the American embassy for a dinner in Miller's honor, they were finding it difficult to observe diplomatic niceties. It was Miller who made a short speech calmly questioning U.S. support for a military dictatorship, but it was Pinter who became the center of one verbal fracas after another. In the end he reportedly told the ambassador that diversity of opinion was difficult "if you've got an electric wire hooked to your genitals," was angrily informed that his remark was a breach of hospitality, concluded he was being thrown out, and left. Back in London a few days later, Pinter and Miller discovered that their parting press conference had been retroactively "banned" and that an investigation was to be held into their entire trip.

That Turkish trip was a significant one, both for Pinter himself and for those interested in his personal and professional evolution. It still provides the most vivid illustration of the indignant, vociferous, and demonstrative man he became, and has remained, in the 1980s. It clearly reinforced his own growing political skepticism and sense of alienation, particularly in relation to the United States. And it led eventually to the composition of the short play *Mountain Language.* But neither the visit nor the events in Pinter's political life immediately preceding and following it should be seen as precisely representing an "awakening." It would be better to talk of a reawakening after what Pinter himself has called a longish period of "sleepwalking."[2]

It would, after all, be difficult for a Jewish boy to grow up in the east London of the 1930s and 1940s without developing a political consciousness. "The sense of the Gestapo was very, very strong in London, in England," he said recently. "We knew about them as children . . . we knew the German force was a very, very strong one."[3] And he has several times told interviewers of the resurgence of violent anti-Semitism in the East End itself with the reappearance of the English fascists after the war. He had a number of physical fights. Others he managed to avoid, with displays of the kind of verbal legerdemain his characters were frequently to employ in his plays.[4]

By 1948 the eighteen-year-old Pinter was prepared to risk imprisonment for the sake of his political convictions. He refused military service, announcing at various tribunals and trials that he regarded himself as a conscientious objector, not because he was a pacifist, but because he disapproved of the emergence of McCarthyism in America and of the growing rift between Britain and her former ally, Soviet Russia. Why, he asked himself, should he be party to "the tragic forces of starting the Cold War almost before the last war had finished"?[5] As he said in an interview in 1980, "I've always had a deeply embedded suspicion of political structures, of governments, and the way people are used by them. I was determined not to be used in that way."[6]

These feelings may have helped shape the plays he wrote in the late 1950s—more of this in a moment—but their longer-term effect was quite different. That suspicion, that determination not to be used, led to withdrawal, not protest or implied protest. Pinter the man had by now lapsed into what he recently called a "detached contempt" for politics and politicians, a belief that any political engagement was futile. And Pinter the writer, in his own words, "simply continued investigations into other areas."[7] When the magazine *Encounter* asked British people involved in the arts what they thought of their country's entry to the Common Market, his reply was the most succinct: "I have no interest in the matter and do not care what happens."[8] Explaining this statement in 1967, he declared that politicians left him variously irritated, indignant, indifferent, bored, and confused. "Generally I try to get on with what I can do and leave it at that," he said. "I don't think I've got any kind of social function that's of any value, and politically there's no question of my getting involved because the issues are by no means simple." He did, however, admit that although political structures did not alarm him personally, they caused "a great deal of suffering to millions of people"—and added the following, often quoted words:

> I'll tell you what I really think about politicians. The other night I watched some politicians talking about Vietnam. I wanted very much to burst through the screen with a flame-thrower and burn their eyes out and their balls off and then inquire from them how they would assess this action from a political point of view.[9]

The impression one gets from what Pinter said during this "sleepwalking" period, and from what he has added since then, is that his political feelings were still alive, and that he was to some extent still conscious of them; but that a combination of ennui and helplessness had driven them underground, where they remained dormant until 1973. The overthrow of President Allende, in Pinter's opinion at the behest of the United States, told him "that I couldn't sit back and not take responsibility for my actions and thoughts, and act upon them." It was necessary, in his words, to "make a bit of a nuisance of myself."[10] And that is what he began to do—though not with evident impact either on the public at large or on his own work until the 1980s.

As early as 1974 he joined the campaign for the release of Vladimir Bukovsky, telling the *Times* that the dissident Russian had been imprisoned "effectively for criticising the Soviet government's use of psychiatric hospitals for political prisoners,"[11] and he has never hesitated to attack abuses of human rights in the Eastern bloc. But increasingly he has taken the view that the West emphasizes communist injustices in order to distract its citizens from wrongs nearer home, and has come to regard it as his duty to fight those supposed wrongs. Indeed, his suspicions of the United States in particular now appear to have few bounds. In 1984 he told a *Times* interviewer that the Americans were preparing to wage a limited nuclear war in Europe, and that civilization as a whole would be "very lucky to get to the end of this century."[12] Since then he has taken more and more interest in what he describes as the "dungeons" of South and Central America, accusing the United States of supporting repression and torture in El Salvador, Chile, and elsewhere. Recently he paid a visit to Nicaragua, met President Ortega, was deeply impressed by Ortega's social achievements, and left the country enraged by American attempts to destabilize what he had become convinced was the only decent regime in that part of the world.[13]

His opinion of Britain under Margaret Thatcher's Conservative government is not exactly high, either. In 1984 he told an interviewer that the country had become the compliant victim of U.S. military ambition, "as much a satellite of America as Czechoslovakia is of Russia,"[14] and more recently he has inveighed against what he sees as an increase in police power, official secrecy, and state censorship. He has publicly expressed anxiety about the future of broadcasting, the free press, and the arts generally in Britain, and in 1988 he acted on his fears. He and his wife, the historian Antonia Fraser, invited to their house several other prominent writers, including David Hare, Margaret Drabble, and Salman Rushdie, and organized a sort of literary think tank, the June Twentieth Group, dedicated to countering conservative ideas. They were much mocked in some newspapers as champagne radicals; but then, as Pinter told the BBC, "derision and mockery are staple weapons of the British establishment and always have been—and I must say I find that kind of complacent malice and self-congratulatory spite beneath contempt."[15]

It has indeed been an astonishing turnabout. The hermit Pinter is now enough of a public irritant to have become the butt of conservative columnists and leader-writers, and seems, if anything, to relish the fray. Now he is decrying poverty and homelessness in London; now he is attacking a government law prohibiting municipalities from giving sympathetic publicity or financial support to homosexual organizations. As he told the BBC in late 1988, "The homosexual is an alien force, someone to be feared and therefore to be rejected and repressed."[16] And who was it leading a delegation to Downing Street to demand action in defense of Salman Rushdie after Rushdie had been threatened with death by Iran in early 1989 for his book *The Satanic Verses*? By then the answer was almost inevitable: Harold Pinter.

He has carried his libertarian message to universities and international conferences and public meetings—and, to a much more limited extent, also to the place that won him the status and authority to become an effective campaigner in the first place: the stage. The year 1983 saw the first production of *One for the Road,* a short play involving a gloating apparatchik and the family he is in the process of destroying: a man who has been brutally tortured; his wife, who has been repeatedly raped; and their small son, who ends up murdered, presumably for committing the only offense anyone mentions, spitting and kicking at some unnamed dictator's military personnel.

Two years later, in 1985, *Harpers* published Pinter's dramatic fragment *Precisely,* which embodied his feelings about nuclear weapons. This showed one bureaucrat complacently assuring another that just twenty million people would be killed in a future war, and the two of them agreeing that those who claimed the final count would be much higher were communist subversives and "bastards" who should be shot, or (better) hung, or drawn and quartered.

> A: I want to see the colour of their entrails.
>
> B: Same colour as the Red Flag, old boy.[17]

And in 1989 the National Theatre produced Pinter's *Mountain Language,* a play that derived from his discovery in Turkey three years earlier of "the real plight of the Kurds, which is quite simply that they're not allowed to exist and certainly not allowed to speak their language."[18]

What one would call the main plot, if the play didn't run some seventeen minutes only, involves an old woman and her prisoner son. First, her thumb is half bitten off by a police dog. Then she's denied the right to speak to the young man in the only tongue she understands, and has to sit silently while he's taken away for a beating offstage. Finally, she proves unable to take advantage of a sudden, arbitrary reversal of government linguistic policy. Though she's now permitted to speak as she wishes, she has lost the power to speak at all. These events are intercut into a subplot involving a young woman who offers her sexual favors to some unseen bureaucrat in hopes of helping her husband, whom she (and we) have just seen hooded and half-collapsed at the end of a corridor in the prison camp where the play is set.

At the time this chapter was written, in mid-1989, these were Harold Pinter's only new dramatic works since *A Kind of Alaska* in 1982. During the same period he has directed Donald Freed's *Circe and Bravo* for London's Hampstead Theatre. He has appeared occasionally as an actor in his own work, playing Goldberg in *The Birthday Party* for BBC-TV and Deeley in his own American stage production of *Old Times.* He has made film adaptations of other people's work, and seems likely to continue doing so. His latest screenplays, again at the time of this writing, are based on Fred Uhlman's *Reunion,* Elizabeth Bowen's *The Heat of the Day,* and Margaret Atwood's *The Handmaid's Tale,* all novels with political connotations, the last of them about a Christian fundamentalist regime in America. But his own theatrical output has dwindled to a trickle, and may well dry up altogether. "I'm no longer interested in myself as a playwright," he informed the BBC in 1985.[19] "I don't think I'll be writing plays much more." "I understand your interest in me as a playwright," he repeated to the *New York Times* in 1988, "but I'm more interested in myself as a citizen."[20]

The obvious retort is: Are the roles of playwright and citizen incompatible? The example of Bernard Shaw, above all, is there to remind us that they need not be. *One for the Road, Mountain Language,* and the shard *Precisely* would seem themselves to emphasize the point. Indeed, they show a closer, or at least a clearer, link between the onstage and the offstage Pinter than was ever apparent before he took to writing directly on political subjects. What the citizen-playwright is telling us is not merely that the most terrible abuses of human rights are occurring, but that we're fooling ourselves if we believe they could never occur in his own country, England. Indeed, there is much in all three plays to suggest that we are watching people who could be British trapped in situations that could occur in a Britain of the not-very-distant future.

In *Precisely,* bureaucrat *A* is addressed as Stephen and bureaucrat *B* as Roger. They use phrases like "old boy" and "bloody cheek" and see their opponents' estimate of the total number of victims of nuclear war, between forty and seventy million, as "almost the entire population"— which in Britain it clearly would be. The characters of *One for the Road* are called Nicolas, Victor, Gila, and Nicky, names that singly might be found in some other European country, but collectively suggest an English location, especially when some of the language they use is taken into account. The torturer's sentimental reference to nature, trees, "a nice blue sky," and "blossom" would seem to evoke Kent or the Cotswolds more than Central America, the Middle East, or the Mediterranean. His cricket slang—"I open the batting," "you're on a losing wicket"—obviously has a similar but stronger effect.

Mountain Language may have derived from Pinter's experience of Turkey and his knowledge of the Kurds, but the production of the play he himself directed at the National Theatre suggested a location far nearer home. The women forlornly waiting outside the prison wore the kind of cardigans and raincoats you would find in any town or village from Dover to Belfast, and the uniforms of the soldiery were recognizably British too. The name of the wife of the hooded internee was Sarah Johnson, her husband was called Charley, and the bureaucrat with whom she offered to have sex was Joseph Bokes. A reference to Babycham, a perry very popular in Britain, and such distinctive argot as "Lady Duck Muck" added to the impression that the "mountain language" being banned might be Welsh or Gaelic, and that the prison itself might be in Northern Ireland or in one of the more desolate mainland shires.

That is not of course the whole truth. The prevalence of English names could after all be regarded as a convenience, the kind of liberty a translator might take when adapting a foreign play for an English audience. It would be pretty literal-minded to conclude that their use meant that Pinter's "political" plays had no relevance to any other country or countries. Indeed, it's evident that both *Mountain Language* and *One for the Road,* which he wrote immediately after an angry conversation with some young Turkish women he regarded as remarkably complacent about events in their country, are supposed to be comprehensive in their scope.[21] They are meant to evoke Turkey and all or any of the ninety countries that Amnesty International believes practice torture—and a potential and to some extent even an actual Britain.

Pinter himself made the point explicitly when he spoke about *Mountain Language* to the BBC in 1988. He agreed that the play concerned the Turks and their treatment of the Kurds. He went on to say that the Basques, the Estonians, the Irish, and the Welsh had all seen their languages banned at one time or another. He added that the abuses he was showing were "serious facts throughout the world, which most people prefer understandably to ignore, to pretend don't exist." He went on: "The people who have been through these appalling deprivations and awful assaults, they're exactly the same as you and me. If they're 3,000 miles away, people say, why don't you look at England? Well, we are looking at England. In other words, do not ask for whom the bell tolls, it tolls for thee." In his opinion, he concluded, the play was "very, very close to home."[22]

It would seem, then, that the concerned citizen and the committed playwright are not merely compatible: the playwright has become an extension, almost an instrument, of the citizen—and, in Pinter's own view, not the most important extension or instrument. That does, however, raise some interesting and troubling questions for those of us who admire his past accomplishments as a dramatist. What, if anything, can we say about the quality of his new "political" work—and, indeed, how "new" is it? It is one thing to integrate the roles of playwright and citizen. It is quite another to reconcile the role of the citizen and the role of what, while recognizing the difficulty of defining those adjectives, one might call the good playwright or the effective playwright.

Pinter himself has gone to some pains to suggest a link—indeed, a consistency of feeling and attitude—between his recent work and his first plays. What some of his original critics "dismissed as absurd rubbish," he has said, actually embodied a "political metaphor."[23]

To some extent this seems a revisionist view. In his earlier public statements, such as they were, he tended to disclaim any moral intention, let alone one so specific, and to avoid interpreting his work in any way at all, let alone one so relatively limited. "I'm not committed as a writer in the usual sense of the term, either religiously or politically," an interviewer quoted him as saying in 1961. "And I'm not conscious of any particular social function. I write

because I want to write. I don't see any placards on myself, and I don't carry any banners. Ultimately, I distrust any definitive labels."[24] He actually walked out of Peter Brook's *US,* explaining later that he disliked being subjected to propaganda, detested "soapboxes," and thought the play was presumptuous in its apparent desire to shock and ineffective in its attempt to inspire opposition to the Vietnam War. "It's impossible," he concluded, "to make a major theatrical statement about such a matter when television and the press have made everything so clear."[25]

The conclusion a critic could reasonably have drawn from Pinter's comments about his own writing during this period was that his function as a dramatist was to "find" interesting characters, give them their freedom, and edit their words and deeds into a play with all the impersonality he could muster. "I've got an idea of what *might* happen," he explained in 1967. "Sometimes I'm absolutely right, but on many occasions I've been proved wrong by what actually does happen."[26] And the function of individual members of an audience was to listen, ponder, and come up with their own interpretations if they wished, always confessing to an educated uncertainty when, as was often the case, the evidence seemed incomplete or ambiguous.

Did it follow, then, that there could never be any consensus about at least part of a play's thrust or meaning, and that such a consensus could never receive Pinter's imprimatur? If you read parts of the letter he wrote to the director Peter Wood back in 1958, you might indeed conclude that he took this somewhat extreme view at that time. "Where is the comment, the slant, the explanatory note?" he asked Wood, who wanted to clarify his production of *The Birthday Party.* "In the play. Everything to do with the play is in the play." And he went on: "Meaning begins in the words, in action, continues in your head and ends nowhere. There is no end to meaning. Meaning which is resolved, parceled, labeled and ready for export is dead, impertinent—and meaningless."[27]

Yet there are contradictions here, as Pinter himself recognized at more than one point in the same letter. The play "dictated itself," yet he wrote it "with intent, maliciously, purposefully, in command of growth." And though his opinion of his protagonist, Stanley Webber, was not "the point of the play," he nevertheless did hold an opinion about him and his predicament. Indeed, he went so far as to offer an interpretation of *The Birthday Party* as a whole:

> The hierarchy, the Establishment, the arbiters, the socio-religious monsters arrive to effect alteration and censure upon a member of the club who has discarded responsibility . . . towards himself and others . . . he collapses under the weight of their accusation—an accusation compounded of the shitstained strictures of centuries of "tradition."[28]

Nor was this the only occasion on which the younger Pinter emphasized his early work's social and political aspects. In an interview he gave the BBC as long ago as 1960, he talked of the false security of the main characters of both *The Birthday Party* and *The Room,* and of the intruders who came to upset it: "This thing, of people arriving at the door, has been happening in Europe in the last 20 years. Not only the last 20, the last two to three hundred."[29] Again, he recalled in 1984 that "the political metaphor" of *The Dumb Waiter* was "very clear to the actors and director of the first production in 1960," even if it was missed by critics at the time.[30] Yet again, he told the *New York Times* in 1988 that the original idea of two men invading Stanley's home in *The Birthday Party* "came from my knowledge of the Gestapo."[31]

So one cannot quite accuse Pinter of post-hoc rationalization when he says, as he has done recently, that his early plays "seemed to have to do with authoritarian structures of one kind or another,"[32] or "dealt with the individual at the mercy of an authoritarian system,"[33] or "were political plays [that] were talking about society as I understood it at the time in certain manifestations,"[34] or took "an extremely critical look at authoritarian postures . . . power used to undermine if not destroy the individual or the questioning voice or the voice which simply went away from the mainstream and refused to become part of an easily recognisable set of standards and social values."[35] Nor can one altogether accuse him of revisionism when he claims, as he did in 1988, that "one of the most important" lines he's ever written is the one delivered by Petey to the waxen Stanley as he is taken away to some unmentioned and probably unmentionable fate at the end of *The Birthday Party*—"Stan, don't let them tell you what to do"—and adds that he himself has "lived that line all my damn life, never more than now."[36] On the other hand, looking at his comments overall, one may reasonably wonder whether Pinter isn't now offering us a less complete and balanced view of his early plays than he would have done before he committed himself so thoroughly to politics. What he's giving us, in short, is a post-hoc *emphasis.*

Perhaps this hardly matters. After all, a dramatist surrenders control of his plays with their performance or publication. And as Pinter himself implied in the letter to Peter Wood, his own explanations, interpretations, and conclusions are no more than that: his own. The important thing is what audiences and readers make of his plays; and even without his prodding, they should be able to see their political implications. Indeed, some of them did so even in the relatively early days, notwithstanding Pinter's own belief that he was regarded as a cross between N. F. Simpson and Ionesco. As early as 1962 Ruby Cohn suggested there was a connection between his work and that of the Angry Young Englishmen of his generation. "Pinter's anger, like theirs, is directed vitriolically against the System," she wrote; his plays were "bitter dramas of dehumanization"; "the religion and society which have traditionally structured human morality are, in Pinter's plays, the immoral agents which destroy the individual."[37] In 1963 James T. Boulton actually complained that *The Birthday Party* over-obviously evoked specific organiza-

tions "such as the IRA."[38] And in 1970, about the time Pinter was writing *Landscape* and *Silence,* Martin Esslin was able to argue that basic political problems lurked within his plays' private worlds. "The use and abuse of power, the fight for living space, cruelty, terror," he explained. "Only very superficial observers could overlook this social, this political side of the playwright."[39]

It is indeed difficult to overlook the contrasting reactions to authority of the two assassins in *The Dumb Waiter*— Ben's unerring need to obey, Gus's impulse to question and challenge—and the contrasting results of those reactions. In effect, one is offered a worm's-eye-view of power: invisible, inscrutable, unaccountable, arbitrary, brutal, absolute. Again, one can hardly overlook some of the things said by the intruders, Goldberg and McCann, in *The Birthday Party.* Now their conversation consists of officialese—"certain elements might well approximate in points of procedure to some of your other activities"; now it turns into inquisition—"You betray our land"; "We can sterilise you"; "Stick a needle in his eye"; and so on. They and their sinister colleague or chief, Monty, might almost be working from the police headquarters of *One for the Road* and preparing Stanley for an even more unsettling reception there. Certainly, they know how to dominate and disorient; to terrify, brainwash, and destroy.

It is even more difficult to overlook the thrust of the play Pinter wrote in 1958 but did not allow to be performed until 1980, *The Hothouse.* It is, after all, set in a government-run asylum. The men in charge are an insecure, blustering incompetent, a sly and malicious opportunist, and an icily ambitious bureaucrat. Their "patients" are known by their allocated numbers only, and, may, it seems, be raped or killed without complaints from outside or inside. "It's supposed to be a mental home, but I don't think it is," Pinter recently told the BBC. "It's a home for political dissidents."[40] That was a somewhat anachronistic claim, since the play was written before the West had become aware of the misuse of psychiatry in Soviet Russia; but there is little if anything in the text to contradict it.

Esslin did not, however, seem to be referring only to the early plays when he wrote about "this social, this political side" of Harold Pinter. His suggestion was that the concerns of the so-called "sleep-walking" period were less exclusively private than they might at first appear. And certainly Roote, Gibbs, and Lush, the men at the center of *The Hothouse,* have more than a little in common with Mick, Davies, Ruth, Anna, Spooner, and several other characters Pinter created both before and after 1970. They want people or places, or both, under their control, in their power. They know, many of them, how to manipulate situations to their advantage; they maneuvre, some of them, with great flair and cunning. Mick, Ruth, and Spooner have an instinct for politics, even if the politics they practice are of the living room, bedroom, or attic. As Pinter himself pointed out in 1988, "How power is used, how you terrorise someone, how you subjugate someone, has always been alive in my work."[41]

There is, of course, a danger of stretching the word *political* so far beyond its obvious sense that it becomes meaningless. After all, not every play involving acquisitive people and their shifting relationships can usefully be described with such a term. Yet in Pinter's case one does often feel that characters are bringing more than private skills to their highly private worlds. Their goals may be domestic merely; their methods are more broadly pertinent. Consider the guile with which Mick, having failed to frighten away the tramp Davies in *The Caretaker,* wins the slavish allegiance of the old man, allows him to alienate his true friend Aston, lures him into making a damaging admission, and then rejects him. It's a plot that a Renaissance courtier and a modern government executive would find equally instructive.

There are Pinter plays, then, that are obviously political because they deal, explicitly or implicitly, literally or metaphorically, with the structures and substructures that exercise control over the individual; and there are Pinter plays, occasionally the same ones, that may perhaps be called political, since they anatomize individual yet exemplary power struggles. And it might, I suppose, be argued that there is yet another variety of Pinter political play, close to the first category but broader in its implications. Such work doesn't necessarily involve authoritarian structures. It does, however, have something to say or suggest about the outer worlds in which the characters lead their embattled lives.

In an interesting recent article for *Theatre Journal,* for instance, Graham Woodroffe discusses one particular play in relation to the racial tensions in the changing Britain of the 1950s. Indeed, he actually titles his essay "Taking Care of the 'Coloureds': The Political Metaphor of Harold Pinter's *The Caretaker.*" In it, he notes Davies's anger at the "Greeks, Poles and Blacks, all them aliens" who have failed to acknowledge his superiority. He notes the old man's distaste for the new Commonwealth residents, a family of Indians, who live next door to Aston and Mick's house. And he notes how evasive Davies himself becomes when he's questioned about his own ethnic background. "On the one hand he espouses the kind of racist attitudes that accompanied the call for immigration controls," writes Woodroffe, "but on the other hand he is the indignant victim of racial prejudice."[42]

As is often the case with distinct and limited interpretations of Pinter's work, Woodroffe does somewhat labor the unobvious. The water leaking through Aston's roof into his bucket metaphorically suggests an "anxiety about the flow of immigrants into the country"; the smile exchanged at one important point by Aston and Mick hints at the complicity of Labour and Conservative parties, tacitly colluding in the exclusion of unwanted intruders from abroad. But Woodroffe's approach is refreshing in that it emphasizes, to a degree rare in Pinter scholarship, that by no means all the plays occur in a social vacuum. On the contrary, there are those that leave one with a strong and somewhat discomfitting sense of the environment beyond the rooms in which they are characteristically set.

The Caretaker is a good example, with its junk shops and cheap cafés and public toilets and rainy streets, not to mention the asylum where Aston was given electric shock treatment. So is *The Homecoming,* with its constant evocations of an urban underworld: a violent confrontation involving a pimp and a prostitute under an arch near the docks; a near-rape on a bombed site near Wormwood Scrubs prison; sexual encounters to come in the Soho flat where the female protagonist, Ruth, can expect to "get old . . . very quickly." In this sordid city even the local swimming-baths are "just like a urinal, a filthy urinal." The impression cumulatively left by *The Room, Night School, A Night Out,* the revue sketches *The Black and White* and *Last To Go,* and the recent radio plays *Family Voices* and *Victoria Station* is also of a seedy and dilapidated London, a place where lonely people slump in milk bars or stand at coffee stalls or sit in gaunt terrace houses watching the all-night buses trundle from the unfashionable south or east to the desolate north or west.

Max, Lenny, and Joey in *The Homecoming,* Mick and Aston in *The Caretaker,* Rose and Bert in *The Room,* and Wally and Solto in *Night School* seem inseparable from this world. They belong to it as much as cockroaches to a decaying tenement. At all events, one certainly feels that there's a strong link between the individual and his or her environment—and yet one also feels that the nature of that link is shadowy. One cannot say, as one can (for instance) of Edward Bond's *Saved,* that the cultural and economic deprivation the characters have endured in London has shaped their attitudes, feelings, and behavior. One knows nothing about how or why Davies became a tramp beyond his eccentric claim that one day he found his wife's underwear in a saucepan, walked off, and (presumably) kept walking. There is not the strong sense of socioeconomic determinism you find in Bond, Howard Brenton, David Hare, Trevor Griffiths, Barrie Keeffe, Nigel Williams, Stephen Poliakoff, and John McGrath, among many other contemporary British playwrights.

Indeed, one might almost argue that there's a reverse determinism in Pinter. Nature seems more influential than nurture. The world is what it is because people are what they ineluctably are. We can, no doubt, say that Ruth and Lenny were to some extent formed by the sinister and dangerous subworld of hustling, pornography, and sex-for-sale that they appear to have inherited. But don't we feel still more strongly that there's something deep in their glands and bowels, some innate and unalterable need, that makes them glad to perpetuate it? Indeed, doesn't one feel that it was just such animal instincts that first created this shabby, sleazy London, this visceral "home" for the returning Ruth? Other dramatists may owe philosophic allegiance to Marx: Pinter's approach would seem to have more in common with Konrad Lorenz.

Seen from this point of view, then, some of the plays Pinter wrote before *One for the Road* are "political" partly because they tacitly invite us to speculate about the relationship of individuals to their society, and partly, and more important, because they present a striking and disturbing picture of the raw material with which politicians must deal. That is to say, they look at the human animal in a way, and perhaps at a level, alien to most "political" dramatists. That is also (of course) to say that they are much more than "political."

But no one can seriously claim that the great majority of Pinter's plays can be adequately discussed in terms of their political resonances and implications only. If *The Caretaker* did not involve a great deal more than tensions during a period of racial change in Britain, it would scarcely be revived as often and internationally as it now is. Again, *The Birthday Party* would surely lose, not gain, in texture and interest if it more clearly concerned a dissident and representatives of some "political" establishment.

As it is, Pinter seems at pains to make both Stanley's alleged sins and his persecutors' accusations as wide-ranging as possible. Indeed, his Goldberg tends to emphasize the private, leaving more public complaints to McCann: "When did you last have a bath?," "Where's your old mum?," "You verminate the sheet of your birth." Given the nature and abundance of the play's references to parents and children, one might as or more plausibly argue that the play's subject is the cruelty of growing up, being forced finally to cut the umbilical cord, and having to face the adult world. Hence the contrast between Stanley as he is at first, untidy, irresponsible, churlishly dependent on the possessive Meg, and the Stanley of the end, scrubbed, shaved, and transformed into a pin-striped, bowler-hatted zombie, ready for the office or the grave. As Martin Esslin puts it, the play may be seen as a metaphor for the process of "expulsion from the warm, cosy world of childhood."[43]

Yet Esslin is the first to acknowledge that this, too, is an excessively precise interpretation. Perhaps *The Birthday Party* is better seen as involving everyone's repressed guilts and unspoken fears, everyone's dim suspicion that one day his past may catch up with him and punishment be exacted for what he has done or is thought by someone, somewhere, to have done. It defines an insecurity the more unsettling for involving nothing specific. Though it is by no means his best play, there is about it that sense of mystery that, surely, goes far toward explaining the hold Harold Pinter has long maintained over our imaginations; that feeling that people aren't quite saying what they mean or meaning what they say; that peculiar combination of intensity of emotion and social obfuscation, animal instinct, and inscrutability of motive. To define most of the dramatist's work closely is to limit it. To insist strongly on its "political" relevance is to diminish it.

Conversely, a Pinter play that is to be seen solely or mainly in one way, or interpreted on a single level only, is likely to be an inferior Pinter play. That is not just a personal opinion. It was in effect Pinter's own view when he revealed to an interviewer back in 1967 that there was a play, called *The Hothouse,* that he had withheld from production. "It was heavily satirical and it was quite useless," he said.

The characters were so purely cardboard. I was intentionally—for the only time, I think—trying to make a point, an explicit point, that these were nasty people and I disapproved of them. And therefore they didn't begin to live. Whereas in other plays of mine every single character, even a bastard like Goldberg, I care for.[44]

If that is even remotely a fair assessment of *The Hothouse*—and it is hard altogether to refute—what are we to make of his recent "political" plays? *Precisely* can perhaps be discounted, since it is only a sketch, delivered by Pinter in place of an acceptance speech when he received the Elmer Holmes Bobst Award in Arts and Letters at New York University in late 1984. But it is pretty evident he does not "care for" the interrogator Nicolas in *One for the Road* or the salacious, bullying sergeant of *Mountain Language.* The former may perhaps be conceived with a kind of appalled empathy, since Pinter has acknowledged that he too has "violent" feelings and firmly believes that the play's audiences saw something of themselves in the character: "Think of the joy of having absolute power."[45] On the other hand, he was clearly signaling that both Nicolas and the Sergeant are "nasty people" of whom he "disapproves." And he was, it would seem, "trying to make a point, an explicit point" about them and their kind.

The new Pinter would, however, probably quarrel with this conclusion. On several occasions he has suggested that both *One for the Road* and *Mountain Language* were composed in much the same unplanned way as his earlier work. He started with a character or image and "let rip and [didn't] think."[46] After his confrontation with those complacent Turkish women, he went home and, still in a state of "rage,"[47] launched immediately into *One for the Road,* finishing it in three days. "I wanted to see how detestable [Nicolas] could be," he recalled later. "I think by the end I found him detestable enough."[48] *Mountain Language,* too, he has described as an intuitive exploration of images troubling his mind: "They shocked me into life and into the act of writing." And it, too, "went like a bomb" when he eventually composed it in 1988.[49]

Yet that play's genesis was suggestively different from *One for the Road.* Pinter actually began it three years earlier, after his trip with Miller to Turkey, but found it impossible to continue. As explained to the BBC at about that time, he thought of writing about a mother forbidden to speak to her imprisoned son, but "my annoyance and revulsion was so strong I knew there was no play to be written."[50] "I knew what I felt, which was a sense of outrage," he said in a public forum in 1984. "There was no real life in it, I would have done better just to speak . . . about it."[51]

In this same interview he went further, radically questioning "political" drama and his own talent for it: "The problem with writing a play from a particular point of view is that the play is written before you've written it, and therefore is in a certain sense dead." And he amplified this thought for the BBC in 1985:

One of the joys of writing is in fact not knowing how the thing is going to turn out; but when I know perfectly well what I think about something, as I do in these cases of nuclear weapons and torture, I therefore know what's going to happen in the play. It's as if I'd already written the play. The play has come to its conclusion before I've written it.[52]

Again, his example was the then-unfinished *Mountain Language,* a piece he clearly thought even more "useless" than *The Hothouse.*

One detects in Pinter's recent utterances a great and understandable need to believe in his recent work while keeping faith with his artistic principles; and the strain sometimes shows. His new plays are "political": well, so were his old ones. His new plays have something intellectually and emotionally preplanned about them: nevertheless, they "dictate" themselves and, he hopes, have an authentic life of their own.

Again, his new plays have, he has insisted, no specific didactic aim. When he wrote *One for the Road,* he "wasn't thinking then of my audience."[53] *Mountain Language* is not an "ideological piece of work, it's simply a series of short, sharp, brutal encounters" about which spectators must "make up their own minds."[54] Nevertheless, he clearly wants to instruct. He wants to face his audience with uncomfortable truths, and he wants to draw their attention to abuses "which most people prefer understandably to ignore and pretend don't exist."[55] He wants those leaving *One for the Road* to feel that "this is an accurate state of affairs that exists all over the world. I will at least contribute to Amnesty International. I will investigate and find out what's going on in the world."[56]

But Pinter's contradictions, if such they be, obviously matter less than the questions they raise. Has he in fact found a way of injecting firsthand life and energy into politically constructive drama? Or is *Mountain Language* as "dead" as he feared it would be before he decided to disinter and refashion it in 1988—and does *One for the Road* smell somewhat of the dramatic charnel house too? What are the qualities of what, to repeat, are the only remotely substantial plays Pinter has written since 1982?

The similarities between the two are obvious enough. In each, state power seems as whimsical as it is oppressive, unscrupulous, and irresistible. A brutalized man is released while his wife remains under arrest, and his seven-year-old son is killed; in every case the action is without explanation. One day people may be "badly punished" for speaking their language, and the next the prohibition is lifted, again without apparent cause. In each play, both torture and sexual exploitation seem commonplace. In each, any unsolicited reference by the victims to family relationships of their own is absolutely taboo. Nicolas gets openly angry once only, when the abused Gila refers to her father. In *Mountain Language,* the reason the old woman's son is beaten is that he remarks that, like his prison guard, he has a wife and three children. These

people are not permitted to share the bonds of humanity. Their status is that of "shitbags," an insult directed at them in each play.

In each, the persecutors themselves combine a contemptuous sadism with anti-intellectualism and a certain religiosity. Nicolas disingenuously apologizes to the battered Victor ("You're a man of the highest intelligence") for the damage his men have done to his "lovely house" with its "lots of books." The sergeant in *Mountain Language* calls Sarah Johnson "a fucking intellectual" and, when his commander reminds him that her buttocks wobble, says that "intellectual arses wobble the best." Nicolas describes himself as "a religious man," twice declares that "the voice of God speaks through me," calls his troops "soldiers of God," and defines his job as to "keep the world clean for God." No such claim is explicit in *Mountain Language;* yet the sergeant, as crude a character as Pinter has ever created, can still point out that people who have committed no crime may not be "without sin." The "socio-religious monsters," as Pinter called them in his letter to Wood, are clearly still alive and capable of destruction.

Again, those monsters are still fulfilling what one might call their zoological imperatives. They are only too eager to deprive others of their loved ones, security, freedom of movement, self-respect, and sanity. The old mother, like Stanley in *The Birthday Party* and Lamb in *The Hothouse,* ends up in a kind of catatonic stupor. But now the assault goes further. Life itself is at risk—and so, less drastically, is something of particular importance to Pinter: language. Throughout his oeuvre people have used words simultaneously as camouflage and weapons, disorienting and dominating their victims from behind their private smokescreens. Now speech itself has also become an object of attack. In both plays it is clearly dangerous to volunteer any but the most carefully considered words, and in *Mountain Language* a whole word-system has been proscribed, stolen. As if to emphasize the iniquity of this, the soldiers' language is brusque, cold, and cliché-ridden when it is not coarse and insulting. Again and again we get such words as "not permitted," "outlawed," "military decree," and, no less than eight times in the course of the play's seventeen minutes, "forbidden." Clearly we are meant to contrast these loveless repetitions with the loving ones the prisoner's mother thinks aloud, presumably in her mountain language: "When you come home there will be such a welcome for you. Everyone is waiting for you. They're all waiting for you. They're all waiting to see you."

That, no doubt, is a gain; but it is difficult to ignore the artistic loss that's surely also apparent in *One for the Road* and *Mountain Language*—of characterization, for a start. If the not-uninteresting Roote of *The Hothouse* is, by Pinter's admission, made of "cardboard," the principal characters of both these plays must consist of see-through paper. Their place and purpose in the moral scheme are what's important about them, and in each case that is entirely obvious. They are set and stuck, foredoomed to play the roles of vices and victims in homilies about political oppression. It could certainly be argued that Nicolas is rather more complex than, say, the sergeant with his cruel sneers, his combination of grandiloquence and foul-mouthed slang, his musings about death and nature and madness, his wild laughter and heavy drinking. But all this seems externally and even rather melodramatically conceived, a luridly impressionistic case study of a torturer rather than the torturer himself. In spite of (or perhaps partly because of) those exaggerated invocations of a punitive God, one is not left with the impression that Pinter has done what would be genuinely enlightening: that is, felt his way into the psychopathology of a modern monster. There are even times when one wonders if Nicolas's artistic ancestry is not the caricatured SS officer of the B-movies.

Not all these criticisms—judging by the play's mostly warm reception in England in particular—will command general consent. They can anyway hardly be "proved." But when Nicolas says to his tattered, bruised quarry, "I've heard so much about you, I'm terribly pleased to meet you," it is surely all too easy to hear the echo of the kind of Nazi sadist who informs his quivering victim, "I zink ve are going to get to know each other very, very well." This is not altogether a facetious comparison. What has given so many of Pinter's plays much of their distinctiveness is, again, their characters' tendency to express themselves on more than one level at once. A speech about the complexities of a one-way street system in *No Man's Land* is also a warning to an intruder that he may be venturing into an emotional situation he cannot handle. Mick's bizarre description of the London bus system in *The Caretaker* carries a rather similar message for Davies. But with Nicolas the verbal ruse is too transparent; oblique threat has become obvious, formulaic sarcasm.

That dramatizes what is surely the central problem with both *One for the Road* and *Mountain Language.* Pinter's originality has to do with his rich use of subtext, with suggestiveness and that mystery of which I spoke before. If there is violence in his plays, and there often is, it is generally to be found beneath the words and behind the actions, adding to the tension and sense of danger. The description of his work that he himself offered and then withdrew some years ago, that its subject was "the weasel under the cocktail cabinet," is actually very apposite.[57] But in these two plays the terror is up front, on the surface, and, perhaps as a result, curiously banal. The characters and situations are what they seem, and that is that.

Pinter's own answer to these objections might be roughly the same as his riposte to a critic who worried about his lack of "perspective": neither perspective nor subtext matter much to someone who is being tortured. Aesthetic qualms must cede to moral urgency. But that raises, and perhaps begs, several questions. Are these objections aesthetic only? Isn't one of the merits of Pinter's best work that it promotes a kind of creative paranoia in the spectator? If people are in emotional disguise, warily

circling each other, maneuvering, plotting, then wisdom is to learn to sniff out what is really happening. The experience of a good Pinter play is a lesson in ontological self-defense. But with *Mountain Language* and *One for the Road* there is little if any work for the spectator to do, little if anything for him or her to discover. The weasel has, so to speak, been taken out of the cabinet, stuffed by a taxidermist, and put on public view.

Actually, a rather similar analogy was made by Pinter himself when he recalled his meeting with the Turkish women who provoked him into writing *One for the Road.* "[They] saw reality in a totally different way," he said.

> They saw a table which had a very striking tablecloth on it and vases of flowers on it, striking and beautiful and worth preserving. They didn't look under the table at any time and find what the people who are being tortured find: mess, pain, humiliation, vomit, excrement, blood.[58]

What has made so much of his past work so disturbing is its implicit invitation to us to sniff out the blood beneath the tablecloth. What makes his new work so much cruder is that the blood, excrement, and vomit are under our noses, in our faces. At its best, his past work took up permanence resident in the mind, troubling it, haunting it, maybe reshaping its opinions, *including* its political ones. His new plays take direct aim at the stomach and rely on short-term shock.

But Pinter would doubtless argue that crudeness and shock may actually be constructive, partly because they bring home that the world's political wrongs need immediate attention and not leisurely contemplation, and partly because they prevent people from doing what they're all too inclined to do: avoid unpleasant facts. The question, however, is whether they do indeed accomplish these ends. Pinter himself has observed that many members of his audiences, precisely the people he most needed to reach, walked out of the New York production of *One for the Road,* rather as he himself had walked out of *US.*[59] As he might have remembered, it is a human instinct, if not a very praiseworthy one, to wince away when being bludgeoned with cruel and ugly truths. Such spectators, if they are worth reaching at all, may need approaching with more of that guile, that subtlety Pinter once inimitably possessed.

But there were and are hardier spectators, both for *One for the Road* and for *Mountain Language.* What has been the impact of the plays on them? Each must naturally speak for him- or herself; and it must be admitted that some have been extremely enthusiastic. That has especially been the case in England, where more than a few critics have come to expect a sociopolitical slant to the drama and are even inclined to attack as "irrelevant" dramatists who fail to offer it. *One for the Road* won a major award there. And the influential Michael Billington of *The Guardian,* for example, found *Mountain Language* "masterly"— "It distils the daily barbarism of military societies with painterly precision."[60]

But even if that claim is true, it raises yet another worrying question. As we've seen, Pinter wishes to evoke "military societies" in the plural, with perhaps some emphasis on a putative Britain of the future. But generality can also betoken vagueness, a matter of some concern when the subject is as real and pressing as that of his "political" work. One wonders if it is possible to universalize the topical at all. Certainly, it is difficult to do so without dissipating point and impact. A play can easily end up by being about everywhere, and therefore about nowhere at which we are able to direct our feelings of outrage. That is surely the case with both *One for the Road* and *Mountain Language.* Both tell us that terrible oppression exists, but they lack not only the informativeness but also the front-line authority of, say, a TV program, a newspaper article, or even a stage documentary chronicling particular yet characteristic examples of injustice. Kenneth Brown's *The Brig,* dated though it now may be, surely tells us more about what it is like to be in a military jail than does *Mountain Language.* The film *Midnight Express* is even more limited in scope, a case study of prison life, specifically involving Turkey. But Pinter's "political" plays, derived though they both are from that country, tell us less about Turkish prisons without telling us more about violence, victimization, and the abuse of power in any other country or countries.

How useful can these plays then be? What can they achieve beyond reminding us that appalling things continue to happen in our world—and giving the cognoscenti an interesting insight into the mind of a major dramatist as it has evolved over the years? What change can they bring about? The answer is "not a lot," as Pinter himself has ruefully acknowledged. "Not very much, no," he replied when he was asked that very question about *One for the Road.* "I don't think it has a great effect, no."[61] We might also parenthetically remember what we've noted before, that his work as a whole implicitly suggests that his pessimism is deep-rooted. If human beings themselves are innately fearful and acquisitive, what hope is there of changing their society or their political systems for the better? There is, perhaps, a curious contradiction in Pinter writing "political" plays at all.

At all events, it seems possible to conclude that Pinter has abandoned a kind of play he wrote uniquely well for a kind of play lesser dramatists continue to do better; he has, so to speak, assiduously rowed his way into the narrows and shallows; and all with no great likelihood of political usefulness. Yet what else could he do, given a "reawakening" that is clearly as passionate as it is principled? How could such a firsthand work as he now writes not be "political," given the images of political horror that are crowding his head? How could he not be true to emotions that are, for better or worse, manifestly central to his life?

Notes

1. *Observer* (London), 21 July 1985.
2. Public interview with Benedict Nightingale at the Institute of Contemporary Arts, London, in 1984.
3. Television interview with Anna Ford, BBC, 1988.
4. In an often-quoted section of an interview with Lawrence Bensky ("Harold Pinter," in *Writers at Work: The Paris Review Interviews,* 3d ser. [New York: Viking, 1967; London: Secker & Warburg, 1968]), Pinter spoke of men persistently lurking with broken milk bottles under a railway arch on the way to a Jewish club he frequented: "The best way was to talk to them, you know, sort of 'Are you alright?' 'Yes, I'm alright,' 'Well, that's alright then.' And all the time keep walking towards the lights of the main road." See this interview as reprinted in *Pinter: A Collection of Critical Essays,* ed. Arthur Ganz (Englewood Cliffs, N.J.: Prentice-Hall, 1972), 29.
5. Ford interview.
6. Interview with Miriam Gross, *Observer* (London), 5 October 1980.
7. Interview with Nicholas Hern, published as an introduction to Pinter's *One for the Road* (London: Methuen, 1984).
8. Quoted in Martin Esslin, *The Peopled Wound: The Work of Harold Pinter* (Garden City, N.Y.: Anchor, 1970), 25.
9. Bensky interview.
10. Interview with Michael Dean, BBC-TV, 1985.
11. Letter to the *Times* (London), 22 March 1974.
12. Interview with Bryan Appleyard, *Times* (London), 16 March 1984.
13. Ford interview.
14. Nightingale interview. See also Appleyard interview and an interview with Sue Summers in the *Independent* (London) on 18 October 1988.
15. Ford interview.
16. Ibid.
17. *Harpers,* May 1985.
18. Ford interview.
19. Dean interview.
20. Interview with Mel Gussow, *New York Times,* 6 December 1988.
21. Pinter has described the inception of *One for the Road* in his interviews with Hern, Nightingale, and Dean.
22. Ford interview.
23. Hern interview.
24. Harold Pinter, "Writing for Myself," *Twentieth Century Magazine,* 168 (February 1961), 172-75.
25. Bensky interview.

26. Ibid.

27. Letter to Peter Wood, 30 March 1958, published in *Drama,* Winter 1981, and republished in *Harold Pinter:* The Birthday Party, The Caretaker, *and* The Homecoming: *A Casebook,* ed. Michael Scott (London: Macmillan, 1986), 79-82.

28. Ibid.

29. Interview with John Sherwood, BBC European Service, March 1960.

30. Hern interview.

31. Gussow interview.

32. Dean interview.

33. Ibid.

34. Ibid.

35. Ford interview.

36. Gussow interview.

37. Ruby Cohn, "The World of Harold Pinter," *Tulane Drama Review* 6, 3 (March 1962). Reprinted in *Pinter: A Collection of Critical Essays,* 78-92.

38. James T. Boulton, "Harold Pinter: *The Caretaker* and Other Plays," *Modern Drama* 6 (September 1963). Reprinted in *Pinter: A Collection of Critical Essays,* 93-104.

39. For an elaboration of this point, see Martin Esslin, "Language and Silence," in *Pinter: A Collection of Critical Essays,* 34-59.

40. Ford interview.

41. Gussow interview.

42. Graham Woodroffe, "Taking Care of the 'Coloureds': The Political Metaphor of Harold Pinter's *The Caretaker,*" *Theatre Journal,* December 1988, 498-508.

43. Esslin, *The Peopled Wound,* 84.

44. Bensky interview.

45. Hern interview.

46. Ford interview.

47. Hern interview.

48. Dean interview.

49. Ford interview.

50. Dean interview.

51. Nightingale interview.

52. Dean interview.

53. Hern interview.

54. Ford interview.

55. Ibid.

56. Nightingale interview. See Pinter's speech, made in Hamburg, on being awarded the 1970 German Shakespeare Prize, reprinted as an introduction to *The Complete Works of Harold Pinter,* vol 4. (London: Methuen; New York: Grove, 1981).

57. Nightingale interview.

58. Dean interview.

59. Hern interview.

60. Review by Michael Billington, *Guardian* (London), 22 October 1988.

61. Nightingale interview.

Martin Esslin (essay date 1991)

SOURCE: "Harold Pinter's Theatre of Cruelty," in *Pinter at Sixty,* edited by Katherine H. Burkman and John L. Kundert-Gibbs, Indiana University Press, 1993, pp. 27-36.

[*In the following essay, Esslin traces the depiction of cruelty in Pinter's plays from the metaphysical realm in his early plays to the actual realm in later plays as Pinter became more politically aware.*]

What has happened to Harold Pinter the playwright—as distinct from the screenwriter who is as busy as ever?

Since 1982, when *A Kind of Alaska* opened as part of a triple bill, he has published only two short plays, *One for the Road* and *Mountain Language,* and a tiny sketch, *Precisely.* And, while all his previous work dealt with problems such as identity, verification, the nature of reality, existential angst, the concerns of Beckett and Kafka rather than those of the committed political playwrights of his and a later generation, since 1982 his work has become entirely political, devoted to attacks on dictators who torture their subjects and civil servants who are unperturbed by the menace of a nuclear holocaust.

Whereas all his previous work was enigmatic, multilayered, relying on pauses, silences, and a subtext of far greater importance than what was actually being said, these later pieces operate unambiguously on the surface, even relying on voice-overs to make the characters' thoughts crystal clear and proclaiming a message of blinding simplicity, a message which is a call to political action.

And at the same time Pinter has assumed a very visible political role as one of the sponsors of Charter 88, a group of British left-wing intellectuals clamoring for a bill of rights and a written consitution for the United Kingdom.

So, how has a previously confessedly unpolitical playwright become a political pamphleteer?

Of course, while his plays were free from an openly political slant, Pinter himself has never been a politically undefined personality. A good deal has recently been written on this question: from Pinter's own utterances in interviews, speeches, and other incidental autobiographical material, it is fairly clear that he has always been politically conscious and committed to a variety of libertarian causes—his registering as a conscientious objector in his youth, because he was disgusted with the cold war, is a case in point; so are his repeated interventions on behalf of political prisoners in various parts of the world, East and West. At the same time he has repeatedly proclaimed his distrust of establishment politics of all kinds, left or right, and his contempt for politicians. That he is now involved in a movement of intellectuals that stands outside the traditional structure of politics further consolidates that impression. In the light of his recent, more openly political output he has also, himself, pointed out that much of his earlier work was, if not on the surface, at least subtextually political: were not the two killers in *The Dumb Waiter* clearly manipulated by a higher authority upstairs, and did not *The Caretaker* and *The Homecoming* describe social conditions in a debased postwar London?

All this is clearly true and relevant. Yet, it seems to me that it poses the question the wrong way round: the question is not whether Pinter's politics engendered certain aspects of his work, but on the contrary, how and in what forms Pinter's basic existential experience, his manner of perceiving the world, his individuality as a human being and an artist activate his imagination and creativity and in turn determine his politics—both his former seeming abstention from direct political involvement in his early work and his open commitment to politics in his latest work.

For what so many of the early, ostensibly unpolitical, and the later, openly propagandist, works have in common is the image of the torturer, the terrorist: Nick in *One for the Road* and the brutal torturers in *Mountain Language* are directly related to, say, Ben and Gus in *The Dumb Waiter,* who are discussing the mess created by the girl they killed: "They don't seem to hold together like men, women. A looser texture, like. Didn't she spread, eh? She didn't half spread . . ." (146-47). Or the genteelly middle-class Edward in *A Slight Ache,* who revels in the agony of the wasp he is killing in a jar of marmalade. "What a horrible death," exclaims his wife. "On the contrary," he replies (172).

A preoccupation with cruelty in all its varieties and possible manifestations, physical as well as verbal, with the recurring figures of terrorists, torturers, and executioners pervades Pinter's oeuvre and constitutes one of the main thematic strands of its total texture—indeed, it might be argued that it stands at its very center. In this Pinter is a true representative of his century, the century of the Holocaust, genocide, the nuclear bomb.

In his early novel *The Dwarfs* (1990), written between 1952 and 1956 but unpublished for more than a quarter

century, Pinter has one of the characters, Pete, a young East London intellectual from the very circles Pinter comes from, express his despair of the world as it exists and his desperate desire to put distance between himself and "them":

> I am of a mind to abdicate. When my sense of distance has been proved wrong. And no one but me can eliminate it. When I have proved distance malleable I shall lay down this sword. Got to prove they exist, then lay down the sword. Because I am the axiom I will not escape. In the act of proof, after all, is the proof. The gas chamber, I won't deny it, is a ripe and purposive unit. I look into my garden and see walking blasphemies. A blasphemy is a terrible thing. They cut the throat of a child over the body of a naked woman. The blood runs down her back, the blood runs between the cheeks of her arse. In my sight the world commits sacrilege . . .

> (111-12)

Here the images of heaped corpses at Belsen and other concentration camps that peopled the imagination of the generation growing up in the late forties are brutally present. How were the young people of that generation to deal with these images?

Another of the three main male characters in the book, young intellectuals in postwar East London, Mark, the actor who claims descent from a Portuguese Sephardic background and thus outwardly is the one most like Pinter himself, cultivates a sovereign attitude of indifference to these horrors:

> —The world's got nothing on me, Mark said. Where's the bother?

> —You're a marked man, said Len.

> —Possibly. Marked, but indifferent.

> —Would you be indifferent to the torturing wheel? Pete asked.

> —Oh no.

> —So you're not indifferent to everything? asked Virginia.

> —All I'm trying to say is that everything's a calamity, Mark said. There are items within the fact of that fact that I am unable to accept. But I accept that I can't accept them. I accept that which I can't accept. I accept the fact within which I act. In other words I carry on merrily.

> (116)

Pete's despair and Mark's show of indifference can thus be seen as two sides of the same coin—and these attitudes reappear in many of the characters of later plays, who like, for instance, Mick in *The Caretaker* or Lenny in *The Homecoming* nonchalantly accept the horrible facts of life in this world and try to stand aloof from and above them.

The label of "comedies of menace" that has been applied to Pinter's plays is correct as far as it goes, yet behind the menace there stands the consciousness of an anxiety about the cruelty of the post-Holocaust, postnuclear world itself. In the same way the frantic search for a territory of one's own, a safe haven from which that world can be excluded—the territorial element of Pinter's work—also emerges as merely an aspect of that basic realization of the ruthless brutality of the times, a panic-stricken desire to shelter from a world pervaded by terror and torture.

Pinter's earliest play, **The Room,** can thus be seen as a post-Holocaust nightmare: is Rose, whose real name seems to be Sal—the Nazis forced all Jewish women to carry the second name Sarah—a Jewish woman sheltering in a marriage with a non-Jew? The emissary who has come to remind her of her family is a black man with an Irish name, Riley, thus representing two other despised minority races. In the end he is brutally beaten down by Rose/Sal's racialist husband, who screams "lice!" (inferior races, in his mind, being no more than vermin). "You verminate the sheet of your birth" is one of the taunts hurled at Stanley, another shelterer from the world, in **The Birthday Party.** In **The Room,** moreover, the anxieties of Jewishness are also introduced in Mr. Kidd's musings about whether his mother might have been a "Jewess."

The professional torturers and terrorists make their first appearance in **The Dumb Waiter;** unlike the impulsive racialist Bert Hudd in **The Room,** they are part of an organization—the twentieth century world is one of organized cruelty on a large scale; and terrorist organizations are so intricately and cunningly structured that the executive organs at the bottom, the members of terrorist cells, have only a vague knowledge of the forces above them, the deeper connections and policies that govern their orders. Pinter's period of acting in a touring Shakespearean company in Ireland at the very beginning of his career as an actor has also obviously furnished many echoes of the IRA and its brand of terrorism and terrorist organization to him.

In **The Birthday Party** the outcast hiding from the brutal world and the torturers who are part of a large and mysterious organization are brought together in the same play—and here another aspect of the cruel totalitarian twentieth-century world comes to the fore: the ruthless interrogation that accompanies the application of the instruments of torture. "The third degree" was familiar to boys from Pinter's generation from American gangster pictures of the period, which represent another aspect of the cruelty of the epoch, the corrupt policemen, as well as the Mafia, organizations closely akin to the Kafkaesque secret-police organizations of the totalitarian world that use torture to extract confessions from possible traitors.

Goldberg and McCann, the Jew and the Irishman (here Pinter used stock comic characters from the repertoire of popular drama as he did with Ben and Gus, the stock cockneys of the London East end music hall), are masters of the third degree, verbal torturers, who bombard their victim with an endless stream of verbiage until he is ut-

terly confused and befuddled. "You betrayed the organization . . . we can sterilise you . . . you betray our breed . . . you are a plague gone bad . . . you're nothing but an odour"—these apostrophes, that I have picked out at random from the stream, emphasize the racialist flavor of the assault in the second act (58-62), while in the third act the already brainwashed and blinded victim (his glasses have been broken) is pressed into the new mold of the cowed subject, a preprogrammed cog in the wheel of the organization, the society of whatever kind it might be (rather like Winston Smith in Orwell's *1984*): "From now on we'll be the hub of your wheel"—"We'll watch over you"—"Advise you"—"Give you proper care and treatment"—"Let you use the club bar"—"Keep a table reserved"—"Help you acknowledge the fast days"—"We'll make a man of you"—"And a woman"—"You'll be reorientated"—"You'll be rich"—"You'll be adjusted"—"You'll be our pride and joy"—"You'll be a mensch" (92-93). These are but a few of the verbal punches under which the victim is made to reel.

Here the horror is precisely that this type of totalitarian third degree is designed to produce the preprogrammed, zombie-like ideal subject of any conformist society, whether totalitarian or bourgeois, conditioned like one of Pavlov's dogs to follow the strictly preordained pattern. There is also here a striking analogy drawn between the terrorism of the secret police, the Gestapo, or the Mafia on the one hand, and the terrorism of bourgeois conformism on the other: the brilliance of the image in **The Birthday Party** is precisely the indeterminacy of the terrorist characters: they may be the emissaries of an underground terrorist organization, or they may merely be the agents of a society that forces Stanley, the potential artist, into the straightjacket of a bowler-hatted, nine-to-five job that effectively castrates his creative impulses.

This image is even more drastically present in **The Hothouse,** a play Pinter wrote shortly after **The Birthday Party,** in 1958-1959, but then decided to withhold until 1980. Here Pinter went further in showing a world in which human beings—the inmates of a bureaucratic institution that might be a mental hospital—are reduced to numbers and subjected to a third degree. Wired to an electrical apparatus that can give them an electrical shock when they answer wrongly, the patients are in a clinical environment devoted to the systematic torture and degrading of its members. It is significant that in explaining why he had decided to put this play—so long withdrawn—before a public more than twenty years after it had been written, Pinter pointed out that reality had caught up with his fantasy: when he had written the play he was unaware of the fact that in Russian mental hospitals actual dissidents were subjected to this kind of torture. (On the other hand it must not be forgotten that in the late fifties there was much talk about the brainwashing techniques used by the Chinese and North Koreans in the Korean war, so the subject of psychological techniques to produce zombie-like conformity was certainly in the air then.) Moreover, that it was not then as topical as it had become twenty years later does not explain why he decided in 1959 to keep this play out of public view. (He lent me a copy of the manuscript when I was writing my book about him: it had a note on the title page that it was not to be performed.) It seems to me much more likely that at the time he felt that this play fell too much into the stereotype of what by then had become know as a "Pinteresque" play, that it merely repeated earlier works, exaggerating some of their characteristics—i.e. a preoccupation with the grotesquely comic aspect of mechanized torture.

The Caretaker, which constituted his breakthrough into worldwide success (it reached Broadway in 1961), can be seen as dealing with the same subject matter in a far more subtle and less "mechanical" manner. Here the grotesquely comical electrified third degree of *The Hothouse* has become the very realistic electro-shock treatment to which Aston has been subjected in the mental hospital, where his mother sent him because he had been too excitable and emotional. In other words, to rid him of the artistic side of his personality and make him conform to the standards of bourgeois existence. In this play, the verbal third degree of *The Birthday Party* as well as *The Hothouse* has become the sadistic teasing to which Mick, Aston's brother, subjects the intruder Davis, by immersing him in endless streams of difficult language that is beyond his comprehension.

Torture through electro-shock within the everyday situation of a National Health Service Hospital allows the preoccupation with such cruelty to be taken into a much more realistic, less grotesquely caricatured framework. With *The Caretaker,* that is, Pinter abandoned the surrealist, Kafkaesque stage machinery of his earlier plays, to enter an outwardly far more realistic style of representation, while still preserving, under the seemingly traditionally realistic surface, his main thematic preoccupations and the poetic, metaphoric quality that underlay his main concerns as an artist—the evocation of a world awesome in its unfathomable impenetrability, its senseless cruelty and evanescence.

If the grotesque electrical torture chamber of *The Hothouse* has been transformed into the clinical equipment of the mental hospital in *The Caretaker,* the verbal third degree of *The Birthday Party* and *The Hothouse* reemerges in the linguistic teasing and torture Davis is subjected to by Mick. Language as an instrument of torture, language as a medium through which power is exerted between individuals, becomes ever more prominent in Pinter's later work—it was already present in *The Dumb Waiter's* discussions about linguistic minutiae and very much foregrounded in *The Birthday Party* and *The Hothouse.*

In *The Caretaker,* the more articulate can play cat and mouse with the more inarticulate, befuddle him with questions he cannot understand, and terrify him by using words beyond his comprehension, subject him, that is, to a veritable third degree. In the end, it is the interpretation of the word "caretaker" that decides the fate of the unfortunate outcast Davis.

Torture is the most blatantly visible exercise of power by one human being over another. The "third degree" is verbal torture. But all verbal confrontations, all dialogue in fact, contains an element of a power struggle. One of the interlocutors will dominate, the other will have difficulty in getting a word in edgewise; one will have the wider vocabulary, a quicker response reaction than the other. This is the most prominent characteristic of Pinter's use of dialogue. All verbal interchange may not be a "third degree," but it certainly is at least a "second degree," a struggle for momentary, local power—dominance. And as Elias Canetti, the Nobel-Prize writer who has also produced one of the unknown masterpieces of social analysis of our time, *Crowds and Power,* has brilliantly shown, all power, even its most seemingly mild forms, as the power of the parent over the child, the teacher over the pupil, the bus conductor over the traveler, the employer over his worker, is in the last resort reducible to the ultimate sanction: all power is an aspect of the power over life and death. Verbal cruelty, which always lurks in any dialogic situation—all dialogue being a fencing for positions in a pecking order—is thus only different by degrees from physical cruelty as exercised by the torturer and executioner.

The dialogue of Pinter's plays is, more plainly than that of most other dramatists, always a struggle for linguistic dominance, a power struggle, which, in this sense, always ultimately is a life-and-death matter. The terrorist, the torturer thus always lurks behind the verbal exchanges in Pinter's plays.

Harry's diatribe against Bill in *The Collection* is an excellent example:

> Bill's a slum boy, you see, he's got a slum sense of humour. That's why I never take him along with me to parties. Because he's got a slum mind. I have nothing against slum minds *per se,* you understand, nothing at all. There's a certain kind of slum mind, which is perfectly all right in a slum, but when its kind of slum mind gets out of the slum it sometimes persists, you see, it rots everything. That's what Bill is. There something slightly putrid about him, don't you find? Like a slug. . . .
>
> (154-55)

Because Harry is speaking in the presence of the victim of this outburst, his diatribe is verbal torture—and contains a threat of physical execution, for if Bill is expelled from his cohabitation with Harry, that might be the end of him.

The verbal duels in *The Homecoming* are of an even fiercer and more deadly nature: In this play also the connection between cruelty and sexuality comes very strongly to the surface, more strongly than in earlier plays, where, however, it was always present in the subtext. The prostitution ring Lenny is running is, after all, another version of the Mafia organization, with its torturers and executioners: in Lenny and Joey, the pattern of the pairs of executioners, the slick, intelligent one and the dumb strong man, reappears in a new but very clearly recognizable variation. Lenny's description of his chastising of one of his prostitutes, with which he confronts Ruth at the beginning of the play, is a case in point; so is the story of Lenny's and Joey's rape of two girls on a derelict bombsite. Lenny's verbabl torture of his father is another deadly game of power. And Ruth establishes her dominance over Lenny precisely by taking these descriptions of brutality with the coolness of a professional. There is a life-and-death struggle also going on in the dialogues between Lenny and his father and between Max and Sam. The milieu of **The Homecoming** is the world of terrorist organizations like the IRA or the SS, the world of gas chambers and the nuclear menace projected into a domestic setting: the final tableau, with Sam lying lifeless on the floor and Max vainly begging for recognition of his status as a man, is a graphic illustration of that fact.

What a harsh universe this play presents us with—in its subtle combination of physical cruelty and sexuality. Characters like Lenny clearly derive erotic pleasure from inflicting pain. It is an essentially loveless world. There is sex, but very little tenderness in this and most other plays by Pinter.

It is surely significant that in Pinter's entire oeuvre there is hardly a single genuine love scene: even in **The Lover** the nearest point that the protagonists can reach to love is by playing a game of prostitute and paying client; in **Land-scape** the love scene is a wholly one-sided fantasy in the mind of a woman, while the man is an aggressive bully. In **Silence** and **Betrayal** love is shown to have been no more than a fleeting illusion, a cruel self-deception.

And here another of Pinter's main preoccupations enters the picture: the ever recurring problem of verification, the fact that the individual can never be entirely sure that what others tell him is true, that it can be subjected to the test of verification. The most unverifiable statement of all is a profession of love: love, by its very nature, is beyond verification; it can be faked, pretended. And one partner, the one who loves with greater intensity, will always be deceived. There is one exception, as the Marquis de Sade, that archetypal philosopher of torture, has argued: the evidence of suffering, which is always genuine, cannot be faked. The only genuine evidence that an individual can obtain of having true impact on another individual is through the first-hand evidence of suffering, physical suffering inflicted in full view. This Sadian "touch," as Mario Praz has convincingly argued in *The Romantic Agony,* is a topic subtextually present in much of romantic and postromantic literature. It is most openly approached in Brecht's *Jungle of Cities,* where Shlink finally confesses that not even a life and death struggle can establish genuine contact:

> The infinite isolation of human beings makes even enmity an unattainable goal. . . . I have observed the animals. Love, warmth from the proximity of our bodies, is the only grace in our darkness. But the union of organs is the only one possible, it does not bridge the separation created by language. . . . If you stuff a ship full to the point of bursting, with human bodies, there will be such loneliness there, that they will all turn to ice.

> (307-308)

The sadistic torturers and executioners of Pinter's universe, the characters seeking domination through verbal fencing, are thus engaging in a sadomasochistic quest for human contact; there is a distinctly erotic element in the various forms that cruelty, the striving for dominance and power over the other, is taking in Pinter's plays. This is not to say that he does not show the processes of torture, domination, and struggle for power as reprehensible; he is merely depicting, as a detached and neutral observer, how it is, what he sees. But there can be no doubt also about the fact that he is fascinated by the spectacle.

As the social milieu of Pinter's world is gradually raised in his work of the late sixties and seventies, the power struggles and the cruelty they entail become less overt. Although still powerfully present in the subtext of plays like **Tea Party, Old Times,** or **Betrayal,** these struggles again powerfully rise to the surface in **No Man's Land,** where the two executioners reappear in the guise of Foster and Briggs, who conduct the final ceremony of Hirst's entombment in an eerie parody of a third-degree session, with the executioners pronouncing the sentence:

> BRIGGS: The trees—

> FOSTER: Will never bud

> HIRST: I must ask you—

> BRIGGS: Snow—

> FOSTER: Will fall forever. Because you've changed the subject. For the last time.

> (151)

Uncertainty—the difficulty, or indeed, impossibility of verification, and the anxiety that must accompany such an absence of certainties; the relentless life-and-death struggle for power, linguistic as much as crudely physical; the presence of vast, mysterious organizations threatening torture and execution; the structure of the world itself experienced as such a vast machine of senseless cruelty— these images form the backdrop to Pinter's universe, however grotesquely comic some of the ludicrous proceedings in the foreground might be. As he himself once said, much in his plays may be funny, but there comes a point where it ceases to be funny—and that, indeed, is the point of it all.

Kafka and Beckett are the patron saints of this vision, with the Marquis de Sade powerfully lurking in the background. The power of a writer like Pinter derives to a large extent from the degree to which his work embodies the *Zeitgeist,* the cultural, ideological, and philosophical undercurrents of his time. The contemporary philosopher who seems to correspond most closely to the existential experience embodied in Pinter's vision seems to me, whether Pinter is aware of his work or not, Heidegger, in whose philosophy the Cartesian definition of being—I think therefore I am—is replaced by "I fear nonbeing—therefore I am."

To point up these connections and to draw these parallels with other writers and philosophers is to situate Pinter's work within a wider context as the expression of a world-view, an *Existenzgefühl*. What this ultimately amounts to saying is that his work, as that of a major poet and artist, embodies its own metaphysics, its own cosmic perspective, which, however far removed from any established or codified body of doctrine, is akin to something like his own "myth," his own metaphor for his experience of the world as a place of awful—in both senses of the word—impenetrable mystery.

What strikes me in Pinter's latest work is, in fact, that this "mythical" element present in his previous works, which all, ultimately, can be seen as metaphors, generalized visions of the world, has now become, as it were, secularized, taken from the general, metaphorical, and ultimately poetic plane to a level of the specific and particular, from the contemplative detached embodiment of general truths to short-term calls for action on a practical, almost immediately topical level. The material is still that of his first vision—the torturers, the executioners, the victims—but now they have lost the metaphorical dimension; they simply are what they are.

Yet even here Pinter still shuns the specific: it has been said that the people deprived of the use of their language in **Mountain Language** are Kurds in Turkish Kurdistan. He has denied this specificity. Nor is the torturer in **One for the Road** identifiable as a member of a particular secret police in a particular totalitarian regime: the setting might be the then still repressive world of Eastern Europe, or Central or South America, or indeed, a country like Iraq. It is the unidimensional nature of the proceedings, however, the clearcut purposiveness of what is depicted that separates these later works from the earlier ones. There is no uncertainty here about what is being shown, nor why it is shown, no multiplicity of levels of possible meanings and interpretations; everything is on the surface, immediately verifiable as what it is and what it intends.

Is this a loss? Or is it a gain? The elegance of the language, the suavity of the style are still there. It is the penumbra, the chiaroscuro, the intriguing opacity of characters and action, that are absent.

On the other hand there is the clear moral and political purpose, the "saeva indignation" about injustice and suffering, the courage to get actively involved in campaigns to combat them, that constitute a breakthrough into the real world. Mark, the character in **The Dwarfs** who is an actor like Pinter, proclaimed himself indifferent even to the threat of the torturing wheel.

—Do you enjoy life? said Virginia.

—Up to the neck, Mark said. But I don't ask questions.

(117)

Clearly now Harold Pinter has reached a stage where *he* does feel compelled to ask questions and to abandon the attitude of the suave, elegant, indifferent onlooker. It is a step from *l'art pour l'art* to *engagement,* which, whatever else one may think of it, certainly deserves respect and admiration.

Brian Rose (essay date 1992)

SOURCE: "The City Beyond the Door: Effects of the Urban Milieu in Pinter's Early Plays," in *Theatre Studies,* Vol. 37, 1992, pp. 57-65.

[*In the following essay, Rose explores the influence of the interior and exterior urban environment on Pinter's plays.*]

Mother Ann Lee, founder of the Shakers, often used the maxim, "Every force evolves a form."[1] The force of Pinter's dramaturgical vision led him to the crafting of the distinctive form of the Pinteresque drama, one of indoor menace[2], to use Bert O. States' phrase. But one might with equal validity cite Sartre's thought as Mother Lee's: "Every technique leads to metaphysics."[3] States, a phenomenologist, postulates that Pinter is to Strindberg as Beckett is to Chekhov—that the work of the more recent pair of playwrights reflects the logical development of the epistemological stance of the realistic theatre. "Strindberg's characters," writes States,

> at the dawn of the new psychology, are very 'forthcoming,' to use a Pinter word; they tells us what is on their minds, and of course it must have been very shocking. . . . But by the time we get to Pinter all this is old psychology—perhaps not the psychology itself as much as the drama of its revelation—and we are left with the bare fact of menace into which one can read all sorts of Freudian and post-Freudian motives.[4]

This "shortcutting in the display of persuasion" is an instance of "[t]he growing fascination with the forms of violence [that] leads to a corresponding atrophy in the motivational psychology behind violence."[5]

I view this process of shortcutting as an aspect of the absorption by Pinter's earlier work of the socio-cultural effects of the City, or urban milieu, as the self-referential cultural backdrop against which the action of modern theatre unfolds. As Lewis Mumford wrote of a period during which the effects of the City as process were less felt than was the case in the days when Pinter wrote his early work, and far, far less so than we perceive them from our contemporary vantage point,

> Under the peaceful and orderly the metropolis became more and more a device for increasing the varieties of violent experience, and every citizen became a connoisseur in the arts of death.[6]

This phenomenological perspective on the nature of the City represents a revisionist, modern view of its effects upon human social experience, and is a far cry from the long-held and, to some extent, illusory vision of the City as described by one scholar of Victorian urbanism: "The city is the literal representation of the progressive humanization of the world."[7] However, as that same scholar went on to comment, "Life in the city is the way in which many men have experienced most directly what it means to live without God in the world."

Much of the modern theatre concerned itself with the social and personal ramifications of crafting a life within an urbanized society that has lost the presence of centralizing, moral structure—God, or whatever name it may be given. The purpose of this essay is to explore briefly the urban milieu as a structuralizing element of the Pinteresque form: to highlight, as it were, the translation of technique into metaphysic by noting the impact upon Pinter's characters and aspects of his dramaturgical structure of the overarching presence and influence of the Urban Milieu as an organizing principle. It will do so by examining several areas gravid with possibilities as gateways into deeper, more extended discussion: the concept of the auto-creation of the dramatic character (or, to use Stephen Greenblatt's phrase, their "self-fashioning"); the retreat of the character into both the literalism of the interior space and the internality of personal representation; and the effect of the City as the NeoGothic backdrop against which unrolls the actions of the world of the Pinteresque.

It should not be assumed by the placing of the urban milieu at the center of this analysis that I am positing that those plays of Pinter's that most reflect the effects of urbanicity could not take place in a non-specific environment; the plays could have been written, and would have been just as powerful, without specific references to Birmingham, Sidcup or the West End. Rather, the use of the City as a paradigm of reference and source of structural influence is to be seen, not so much as a specific geographic locale, but as a symbolic distillation of the total set of cultural elements that signify the translation from post-Enlightenment culture to that of the modern. And the use of the City as a collective symbol of the transition of society into its more modern forms is certainly not new: Ralph Waldo Emerson wrote,

> In our large cities, the population is godless, materialized—no bond, no fellow-feeling, no enthusiasm. These are not men, but hungers, thirsts, fevers and appetites walking. How is it that people manage to live on—so aimless as they are?[8]

Or, as Stjepan Mestrovic has more recently written:

> In sum, modernity in its broadest sense represents the many dimensions of that massive social change from Tönnie's *Gemeinschaft* (community) to *Gesellschaft* (society); traditional economics to industrialization and capitalism; Riesman's traditional-directed societies to inner-directed or other-directed societies. . . . Modernity is the permanent end to humankind's innocence, and despite acknowledgement of the obvious benefits of modernity (mainly technological gadgetry), for most

writers, it represents something pejorative, negative, decadent or otherwise abhorrent. Postmodernism seems to be an extension and exacerbation of *Gesellschaft* values, other-directedness, anomie, and other elements of modernity . . . not a genuine rebellion nor reaction against modernity.[9]

An examination of Pinter's early work reveals the manner in which many of his plays gauge and display the effects of this anomie of modern culture, evoked, in part, by what may be read as the corporatization of violence and structures of personal life. I have chosen certain of the earlier plays to focus attention upon because the reflexive relationship between The City Without and the famous Pinteresque action within the closed room is more overt; after **The Homecoming,** Pinter the playwright moved on to explore other aspects of interpersonal relationships and political themes utilizing techniques that can, in the context of dramatic form, be cited as more post-modern than modern. His early work more closely reflects many of the concerns that the late-modern period of dramaturgy in the middle part of the twentieth century found itself expressing, and in a manner that can be designated as more socially reactive than purely or essentially existential: the problems of language as a device of effective communication; the exploration of the true nature of the self; and the relationship of the isolated self to the corporate, social body. All of these themes found reflections in the way that the City, which, in Pinteresque terms, may be positioned as being the threatening world outside of the structured domain of the Room (usually held at bay by a Door that one always fears will open) reached into the sacral space to affect existence, essence and action.

As a relief from the rigors of scholarship, I took a break not long ago to read the latest novel by P.D. James, and serendipitously chanced upon a passage that provides ingress to these aspects of Pinter's world. She wrote:

> It was in London that you could live anonymously, could create your own ambience, could deliberately fabricate the persona which you chose to present to the world. In the country you lived as a social being and at the valuation of others.[10]

It is this tendency toward self-creation as part of the necessary posture of denizens of the modern urban space that provides insight into the process by which Pinter's characters become complex, living icons of urbanicity.

One dramaturgical result of the Pinteresque character's assumption of self-creation is the ambiguity of his or her relationship to the past; nor can we, when in Pinter's world, rely upon the ultimate epistemological substrate of the process of disbelief suspension—that we will, at some point in the dramatic narrative, however late or inversely through a *via negativa,* be told the truth by the play's characters. With Pinter, of course, that should not surprise us; "There are," says Pinter, "no hard distinctions between what is real and what is unreal, nor between what is true or what false. The thing is not necessarily either true or false; it can be both true and false."[11] He leads us deeply here into the metaphysics of quantum mechanics, where the operation of complimentarity (the definitional, ontological denial of the "either/or" dichotomy) denies the opportunity of ever relaxing into the assumption of truth or of the completeness of vision. This quantum ambivalence of character and situation may be the phenomenological core of Pinter's work, certainly of the early work, until *The Homecoming.* "The explicit form," said Pinter in an interview,

> which is so often taken in twentieth-century drama is . . . cheating. The playwright assumes that we have a great deal of information about all his characters, who explain themselves to the audience. In fact, what they are doing most of the time is conforming themselves to the author's own ideology. They don't create themselves as they go along . . . we know no more about them than I know about you. . . .[12]

The Dumbwaiter is paradigmatic of the imposition of urbanization on character and on structural aspects of the play. Ben and Gus are placed by circumstances in a basement and in communication with an unknown number of upper layers of space through a dumbwaiter shaft and speaking tube. They don't seem to know precisely what city they are in: is it Birmingham? They reflect upon the similitude of all individual examples of City, and it is clear that their operations (whatever they may be) are reflections of a generalized urbanization process, rather than being city-specific. And just as the definitive nature of their urban placement is in doubt, an indication of the similitude and homogenization of the urban milieu, so is the nature of their interior space: all rooms are the same for them, all the places within which they operate, the same. The unknown number and nature of the upper levels of interior space impose themselves upon Ben and Gus through the repeated requests for foods to be sent up the dumbwaiter: English, Chinese, Greek, high-class, low-class: a litany of culinary types ideogrammatic of the City's internal heterogeneity, as opposed to the homogeneity of its external form. Charles Carpenter cites *The Dumbwaiter* as a an example of the "nutty, unlifelike, non-analogical world of farce" due to the manner in which "mechanical objects suspend nature's law and follow theirs,"[13] but this Bergsonian analysis, however correct for an understanding of how Pinter blends the farcical and the horrific, undercuts the terror implicit in the play, and ignores the function of the dumbwaiter as a conduit that connects the subterranean sacral space with the corporate terror without. The very emplacement of the central action in the now-famous "room" outside of which whirls the imposing and threatening action of the world separated from the room's "safe" or, at least, established, interior by a single door is a symbolization of the withdrawal of *homo urbanus* into the defensible terrain of the interior, a theme Pinter would explore in many works. In this play, however, Ben and Gus have brought the indiscriminate, corporate violence of the world into the sacral, interior space, only to discover by the last moment/image of the play, that one of them is to be the slated victim of the other. Their ac-

tions are routinized, ritualized, expressed in stichomythic and repetitive recitations to be undertaken in a certain order. The expected result of those actions is the committing of murder upon unknown and unknowing victims, faceless individuals to which the men struggle to assign individuation. As George Wellwarth has recently written, it is a play "about hierarchical domination, a universal aspect of the human condition as shown by the menacers menaced, the butcher butchered, and the potential rebel cut down."[14] The play thus combines the themes of sacralization of interior space as a reaction to the Gothicization of exterior urban environment, with that of the auto-foundation of the characters, as Ben and Gus struggle for hierarchical dominance through the manipulation of the every-day language (in this case, among other instances, the struggle to determine the exactly proper way to define the putting up of a pot of water for tea) that marks Pinter's masterful use of vernacular for the establishment and defining of existential role.

The Birthday Party, too, presents a vision of the murderous intent of a corporatized world intruding upon an interior that is presented as a route of escape—in this case, for Stanley, who has created a self-ordered collection of fantasies and lies to justify his withdrawal from the world outside the boarding house. The very nature of the professionalization, the depersonalization, of the violence that has sought out Stanley, or that Ben and Gus bring into their victims' interior refuges, is an imposition of the hierarchical domination and ordering of experience inherent in the operation of the City Without. Here is a linkage between the defensive structuring of personal identity, and the concurrent intensification of the importance of the interior space, with the reflexive sense that the world without the room is being escaped from: that, as Marybeth Inverso has noted in her recent analysis of modern drama as a powerful and active reinscription of the techniques and structures of the Gothic narrative, "The characters of the NeoGothic drama are, like their narrative counterparts, engaged in a frantic search for shelter."[15]

One of the most gripping moments in *The Birthday Party* is the diatribe by Goldberg to which Stanley is submitted during Goldberg and McCann's extended torturing. He is questioned with stichomythia that is overtly threatening in form but seemingly nonsensical in content; beneath the nonsense is a deadly concern on the torturers' part to establish origins, where Stanley has come from, been, and done. It is one of the definitional qualities of The City Without that it provides us with the opportunity of escaping our origins, as countless millions have done, and, as P.D. James reminds us, forging new identities free from prior reference. But it is this very process that threatens Stanley: the City (McCann and Goldberg) has reached out to grab Stanley, haul him back for punishment or destroy him. One critic has noted that Goldberg's use of ethnicity and quasi-nonsensical ethnic references is for the purpose of establishing color for the character and comic relief for the audience[16], but this analysis, while perhaps correct from the point of view of performance phenomenology, certainly does not explain the depth of the threatening evocations of the scene. Rather, as Alice Rayner notes, the ethic speeches of Goldberg can be seen as a way of "tracing a genealogy . . . in line with what I believe are Pinter's consistent concerns for the unspeakable in origins. . . ."[17] The agents of corporatized violence dispatched by the City have as their task not only the punishment of the victim, but the establishment of origins, which may be seen as a technique of expelling the sacrificial victim from the social fold: if the City is the place within which we have no origins, to have an origin is to place one outside of the City, as either torturer (Goldberg knows his origins) or tortured (the purpose of the torture is to affix the origins of Stanley). And Stanley's defense, of course, must be to create his persona anew through auto-creation.

The process of character auto-definition is more explicitly explored in **The Caretaker,** where Davies varies back and forth between names that label the construction of his identity extended over time. The papers in Sidcup, which, he claims, will establish his definitive identity, are never retrieved, and become symbolizations of his capacity to auto-establish and shift that identity. The sacral interior of the acting space powerfully mirrors Aston's auto-establishment of self through the accumulation of definable, physical objects (often useless and non-working, evoking Jan Kott's concept of the clothes iron with a spike driven into its face as the rendering of that object into an icon of itself); and although, as Ronald Hayman points out, the setting of Pinter's plays are "nearly always a realistic representation of a room,"[18] the room in this play is, as Inverso notes, "a miniaturized version of the urban scrap-heap . . . [that] makes no pretense at being inhabitable, let alone comfortable."[19] The room therefore becomes, in Kott's sense, an icon of itself, functioning as a symbol of the escape from, and reinscription of, the Gothic horror of the external world which is itself symbolized by the electric shocks of societal domination suffered by Aston, and by the eternal tramping from city to city to which Davies is condemned. He is finally consigned, condemned, to that fate by his very inability to successfully establish his identity, his selfhood, in a manner consonant with the hierarchical requirements of the relationship between the brothers. This inability to solidify his own identity or the expression of it proves the ultimate undoing of Davies; Mick, mirroring the implicit violence of the exterior world, baits and attacks Davies as he struggles to form the alignments of his relationships to Mick and Aston. Finally, he is expelled once again into the exterior space outside the sacral interior as a penance for his misjudgment, which may be read as his inability to establish an interior identity that properly reflects the hierarchical needs of the world of relationships that constitute this play's dramatic core.

The Homecoming, among Pinter's most powerful and disturbing plays, utilizes, recombines and refines all of the structural elements of urban imposition cited above. The house is Gothic in its darkness, in the words of a Polish critic, Ewa Byczkowska-Page, "impossible to explore, incomprehensible, mysterious and terrifying,"[20] and serving as both a refuge from and symbol of the Urban Outside, the violence of which has partially structured the play's characters and their relationships.

Lenny, certainly, may be cited as a character caught, *media res,* in the process of creating himself, or his own legend, as he monologizes to Ruth of a menacing past that, lies or truth, evokes the horror of the implicit, senseless violence of the urban Outside. His speech on the unwieldy mangle (evocative word in this context) is particularly noteworthy as being double-edged, invoking the theme of nascent violence growing out of impersonal contact and the power of mechanical, technological objects to both spark and symbolize this violence. Max, too, is constantly restructuring the past in an almost Orwellian manner, only to be brought up short by the alternative views of his past, associations and character possessed by Lenny; and Ruth is the most mysterious character in the play. She is, from the point of view of this analysis, citable as the most urban of the characters in the play, as we watch her being molded, remolded, and finally, reflexively affecting and controlling the other characters and action.

But Wellwarth comments that it is Teddy who disturbs him the most, writing that, were it not for the fact that the internal evidence is to the contrary, and that Teddy is actually who he says he is,

> one would be tempted to suggest an alternative and more credible background for the pair . . . the marriage, the children the Ph.D., the professorship, and the publications would all be part of a cover story intended to aid Teddy's carefully planned revenge on his family . . . he has become head of the underworld or chief pimp in, say, Blackpool or Scunthorpe with Ruth as his chief helper. The 'homecoming' is a plot between him and Ruth . . . to destroy his family . . . and Teddy, as he thinks, will be vindicated, revenged, and liberated.[21]

But it is not for theatrical credibility in the traditional sense that we refer to Pinter; instead, his power grows out of the very fact that his characters and situations must be encountered with the same sense of impotence of absolute knowledge and *mysterium tremendum* with which we encounter situations and people in life. That *mysterium* is, to a great extent in the early plays of Pinter, bound up with that which is among the most dangerous, unwieldy, complex and evocative of our human creations: the City Beyond the Door.

Notes

1. Qtd. by Guy Davenport, *Every Force Evolves a Form* (San Francisco: North Point Press, 1987), ix.

2. Bert O. States, *Great Reckonings in Little Rooms: On the Phenomenology of Theatre* (Berkeley: University of California Press, 1985), 194.

3. Qtd. by Jerzy Grotowski, *Towards a Poor Theatre* (New York: Simon and Schuster, 1968), 1.

4. States, 194.

5. States, 192-193.

6. Lewis Mumford, *The City in History* (New York: Harcourt, Brace and World, 1961), 532.

7. J. Hillis Miller, *The Disappearance of God* (Cambridge: Harvard University Press, 1963), 5.

8. Ralph Waldo Emerson, *Selections From Ralph Waldo Emerson,* ed. Stephen E. Whicher (Boston: Houghton Mifflin, 1960), 204.

9. Stjepan G. Mestrovic, *The Coming Fin De Siècle: An Application of Durkheim's Sociology to Modernity and Postmodernism* (London: Routledge, 1991), 29.

10. P.D. James. *Devices and Desires* (New York: Alfred A. Knopf, 1990), 29.

11. Pinter qtd. in Ronald Hayman, *Harold Pinter* (London: Heinemann, 1980), 9.

12. Interview with John Sherwood, B.B.C. European Service in the series "The Rising Generation," March 3, 1960; qtd. by Martin Esslin in *The Peopled Wound: The Work of Harold Pinter* (Garden City, N.Y.: Doubleday Anchor Books, 1970), 31.

13. Charles A. Carpenter, "The Absurdity of Dread: Pinter's *The Dumbwaiter*", in *Modern Drama* 16 (1973), 281.

14. George E. Wellwarth, *"The Dumb Waiter, The Collection, The Lover* and *The Homecoming:* A Revisionist Approach," in *Harold Pinter: A Casebook,* ed. Lois Gordon (New York: Garland Publishing, 1990), 100.

15. Marybeth Inverso, *The Gothic Impulse in Contemporary Drama* (Ann Arbor, MI: UMI Research Press, 1990), 120.

16. Kristin Morrison, *Canters and Chronicles: Use of Narrative in the Plays of Samuel Beckett and Harold Pinter* (Chicago: University of Chicago Press, 1983), 150.

17. Alice Rayner, "Pinter: Narrative and Presence," *Theatre Journal,* Vol. 40, No. 4 (December, 1988), 487.

18. Ronald Hayman, *Theatre and Anti-Theatre: New Movements Since Beckett* (New York: Oxford University Press, 1979), 128.

19. Inverso, 126.

20. Ewa Byczkowska-Page, *The Structure of Time and Space in Harold Pinter's Drama, 1957-1975* (Wroclaw, Poland: Wydawn. Uniw. Wrocławskiego, 1983), 29. Qtd. in Inverso, 126-7.

21. Wellwarth, 106-7.

Joseph Hynes (essay date 1992)

SOURCE: "Pinter and Morality," in *Virginia Quarterly Review,* Vol. 68, No. 4, Fall, 1992, pp. 740-52.

[*In the following essay, Hynes explores Pinter's visions of morality and values.*]

Viewers and critics have applied any number of adjectives to Pinter and his plays. Among the terms used, usually but not always by way of offering compliments, are "absurdist," "existential," "anti-humanistic," and "amoral." Each of these labels makes its own kind of sense, I think, but none of them, alone or in combination with others, says about Pinter's plays what it seems to me ought finally to be said about the achievement of any writer who has written so much and whose work has been so widely valued. I should therefore like to look at the terms cited here and to go beyond them, with an eye to defining the view of morality or the moral life to be derived from a number of his most renowned plays. We instinctively make this effort when we read, teach, publish on Shakespeare or Shaw, and indeed such an attempt at coming to grips with a body of prominent work by a single author would appear essential to any eventual placing and understanding of what that author is about and thus of whether, how, and why his works should matter to us now and in the future. Presumably, without an attempt at placing a writer morally, we cannot in the end know what we are talking about when we discuss him or her. Without this effort we would seem confined to discussing this or that isolated characteristic of a drama. We would seem inevitably prevented from having a context within which to place that particular writer's works. I sense a good deal of such floundering at present in the treatment of Pinter and his plays.

Is Pinter's world—the world of his plays—absurd or absurdist? Yes, of course it is if we mean that events occur without evident explanation, or that we are confronted with hopelessness when we set about waiting for or looking for some kind of reasons sufficient to answer our questions. If we take Ionesco as the archetypal absurdist, we can say that Pinter's work is much like Ionesco's, and that it is also quite different. On the similar side, we experience blankness when we look for reasons. Why does the clock strike 13 or 15 in Ionesco? Who are Goldberg and McCann, and why do they search out Stanley? Ionesco and Pinter share the absurdist's code in making us want to know and in refusing to entertain our need at all seriously. Indeed, both dramatists deliberately leave us puzzled and frustrated. On the different side, however, Ionesco makes no sense at all *except as* an absurdist, whereas Pinter crafts a realist-rationalist's moves consistently, only to change the subject, cast doubt on possible resolutions that may occur to us, and otherwise dampen our Holmesian quest. So: yes, Pinter and absurdism fit in some way that fails to get at what he is finally after.

Is he, then, an existentialist? Again the answer is partial and unsatisfying, rather like some weight-watching diets. Pinter is an existentialist if the term means one who focuses on choices made by the individual rather than on choices made by that individual with an eye to matching or defying any code like the Ten Commandments or the laws of the United Kingdom or the received tradition found in Emily Post or Dear Abby. Pinter's characters would seem to be on their Sartrean own. Yet on the other hand, where Sartre typically insists that his characters should do or—more likely—should have done something else, and thus presents us with an implicit if theoretically denied standard for morality, Pinter offers nothing like so specifiable a standard, nor does he follow Sartre in playing up our responsibility to others for the choices we make. The reason why "existential" is not a comfortable fit for Pinter's plays is that he so commonly and regularly upsets our attempts to find out and label his moral universe. It is simple for us to know what Sartre means by the bad faith of the trio in *No Exit.* My experience is that readers and viewers fall fairly silent when asked to be similarly precise about a Pinter play. Thus, if existentialism refers to Sartre's brand thereof, Pinter seems to lie only partially within this labeled circle.

Does the term "anti-humanistic" better describe the plays in question? In a sense the term works. Like Sartre and Robbe-Grillet before him, Pinter seems anxious to avoid associations with long and respected traditions of literature, in his case those of tragedy, comedy, problem play. Lear and Oedipus *should* have chosen otherwise. Choices and circumstances bail out or redeem Beatrice and Benedick, John Tanner and Ann Whitefield, and most of Ayckbourn's characters. We know where Nora and Torvald went wrong and what options the future may hold out to them, just as we know that we are left with the need to clean up the mess shown or implied at the end of *Ghosts* or *The Wild Duck.* That is, Ibsen shows us that we can and should change ourselves and our world in order to stop doing wrong and start doing right. Pinter, on the other hand, not only avoids such classic outcomes, but leaves us asking what this or that play is about. With Robbe-Grillet, we have sense enough to know that there's no point in asking for meaning, while in Pinter we are compelled to look for answers. Why did Teddy and Ruth marry and become responsible and respectable parents and citizens, and why does Teddy make no fuss when Ruth and his family agree to separate Ruth from Teddy and the children and to set up a business and domicile of their own? What holds together that household in *No Man's Land*? Can anyone find the past in *Old Times,* and thereafter specify its accurate importance to Kate, Anna, and Deeley? I think we can and must speculate about answers to these questions, and furthermore that Pinter wants us to do so even as he compels us to admit that he's done a splendid job of preventing our coming up with anything like convincing answers. Because the plays raise such questions, those of the usual humanist inquirer, Pinter cannot in my opinion be simply regarded as anti-humanistic.

Well, then, can we use "amoral," that old familiar critical standby term, that nomenclatural dodge, to describe this writer and his plays? The problem with this label, applied to Pinter or to anyone or anything else human, is that it would appear to make no sense at all. I can of course understand that someone might wish to make the point that Pinter does not conform to the morality or to the moral point of view on display in *Agamemnon,* or *Measure for Measure,* or *The Master Builder,* or *The Flies,* or any other work. But I think it is in the long run impossible for any writer or for any work really to be amoral, that is, without or beside the point of morality. For this reason, I must necessarily rule out the use of "amoral" as appropriate to anyone's actions, whether in life or in art. Rather than merely ignore the whole notion of morality, then, we have to bear down and find out the particular way in which particular persons suggest moral questions or imply a moral frame, different as those questions or that frame may be from our own. Going through this workout may have the advantage of forcing us not to use "amoral" to describe others and ourselves. My basic premise is that morality of some sort is inevitably in human beings and their works. Morality comes with the human territory.

II

So much for what Pinter and his works are not, and about what they are only in a limited sense. I should like now to consider what most people do see in Pinter's plays that would steer one away from moral considerations, to think about Pinter's dramatic universe in comparison to that of other modern playwrights, and finally to suggest what I mean in Pinter's case when I say that he must be implying morality of some sort.

For one thing, viewers and readers find Pinter's characters stupid or brutal or pointlessly motivated in what they do. Meg and Petey are nearly moronic, if arguably good-hearted; Goldberg and McCann are cruel for no discernible reason. Stanley is presented as a victim, although we are unable to say what has made him into such a type. Moreover, we cannot prove that Goldberg and McCann were even looking for Stanley in particular, apart from what he may have done or what prompts their quest. A complementary quality inherent in most Pinter plays is that of menace. It may be embodied in Goldberg and McCann or just be present in the dialogue or the physical arrangement—as in *The Dumbwaiter,* but it hovers and inheres and is most effective in keeping audiences on their chair-edges.

Allied with these unaccountable qualities is the dialogue typical of Pinter. The *non sequitur* may be the best-known Pinter speech pattern. Discussion of Kate's casserole in *Old Times* and Lenny and Ruth's water-glass conversation in *The Homecoming* are cases in point. Typically, audiences don't know what such moments may eventually come to signify. The result is that we laugh and shudder, or at least tighten up a bit, at the same time. We sense that we may be manipulated for some reason or for no reason, and we are therefore uneasy. But, on the other hand, we do not want to think ourselves inattentive to something that may be coming along later in the play, and we certainly don't want to think ourselves lacking in awareness of the comic dimensions of the seemingly purposeless: so we laugh and wonder what's going on; we laugh and wonder what we're laughing at.

This uncertainty, carefully crafted, is only one reason for our finding Pinter's work unpleasant or discomforting. I suspect we may be thinking that he's mocking us when he forces us to laugh at what we fail to comprehend, although seeming inappropriateness of cause to effect is perhaps the commonest source of laughter, whether friendly or unfriendly. We also tend often to find Pinter implausible or mystifying, just as we find his work absurdist. That he can be so frightening, so incomprehensible, and also so funny is unsettling, and may account in part for our thinking him amoral.

Incidentally, one charge against Pinter is that he is not really a top-notch writer and won't be until he can move us. I take it that this means we demand to be moved in certain ways, and especially to laugh and cry or feel compassion where we are accustomed to behaving in these ways. However, it seems to me impossible to deny that Pinter moves us. It's just that he commonly moves us in a manner that we don't understand or like very much. Our hearts are most unlikely to open or to bleed for Pinter's characters. But feelings of tenderness and empathy are hardly the only expressions of emotion. If we can guffaw and become frightened, we are decidedly being moved. And, in fact, in some instances (as in **Betrayal** and **Old Times**) we can be moved to more conventional forms of pity.

One additional trait that I want to specify is the toughness on view in Pinter's work. He is eminently anti-sentimental, anti-nostalgic. **Old Times** is probably the clearest example of this stance. Another sure signal of his position is the titling of a number of his dramas. Titles like ***The Homecoming, Old Times,*** and ***The Birthday Party*** automatically start up the violin background in the halls of our memories, and obviously make use of such inevitability to bring on the confusion and laughter and mystification. One emotion he will not settle for is nostalgia. Our supposed homecomings, birthday parties, and old times are virtually certain to clash with what Pinter dramatizes under those titles.

What, then, are we to say about Pinter and about his place in the line of dramatists from Ibsen to the present? I believe that a look at Ibsen and Shaw provides a useful insight into what makes Pinter tick and thus eventually into Pinter's relationship with morality.

Ibsen famously rocked the traditional boat of drama by arranging for the curtain to fall on Nora's door-slamming and on the Alvings' confrontation at dawn. Uproar, shock, embarrassment attended upon such moments because audiences knew perfectly well that they were being struck in their collective and individual morality. When all the screaming and outrage diminished, reasonable people could and did see that Ibsen was out to make them face something that they preferred not to notice or admit. Ibsen's implicit morality assaulted what he knew to be the moral foundation of his audience. He dramatized the problems, dropped the curtain, and left viewers with the need to cope with what they had been forced to realize. He did not tell them what to do; he merely showed them what they were in the habit of doing and by implication

asked them whether they were content with the *status quo* or saw the urgency of changing things. Nobody could or can doubt Ibsen's morality: he was for change, and the change should be for the better.

Of course here is the nub of the morality discussion. Anyone talking about or acting on moral terms means that we should act in some ways and should avoid acting in other ways. The reasoning behind admonishing us may be religious or theological, or it may be merely that underlying the so-called social contract. That is, we may advise others to do as God wants them to do, or we may rely upon the conviction that all good persons have always agreed upon the betterness of this or that behavior and the worseness of that other.

In England the dominant Ibsenian realist was clearly Shaw. He was by no means like Ibsen temperamentally, but he was decidedly like Ibsen in knowing what he wanted, and his conviction (unlike Ibsen's) was that humans are perfectly capable of achieving what he thought good for them. Thus he wrote comedy for the most part, rather than Ibsen's brand of dour problem play. However, the point here is that Shaw and Ibsen both knew what was wrong and that we ought to strive for what is right. About these matters they were sure of themselves. John and Ann could and would marry and produce children superior to themselves. Shaw knew what was wrong with English politics and politicians, and was just as confident in recommending against it and them as was Caesar in putting Cleopatra to school so that she would become an able and good ruler. Shaw found no reason, apparently, to doubt that Vivie Warren was in for a splendid life as a spinsterish accountant, and laughed at any suggestion that Higgins and Eliza might have developed anything more than a frantically amusing relationship designed to establish Shaw's theories of politics, phonetics, and the superiority of the unattached life. In the same way, Undershaft's reasoning is finer and pragmatically better than that of Christianity, and Saint Joan, whatever Catholicism may suppose, is the first Protestant. About the moral position being recommended in these Shaw plays there can be no doubt, no matter how we may receive them.

Whatever may be Pinter's moral stance, it is plain that he cannot be Ibsen's or Shaw's sort of modernist. Realism in that sense is impossible for him, very likely because he lives in the later 20th century rather than at the turn of the century. What characterizes Pinter, in addition to what we have already spelled out, is either fundamental doubt that we can know anything for sure beyond the tips of our fingers, or an absolute certainty that such is our human condition. That is, he may be either an atheist or an agnostic with respect to the question of truth, or what one can know beyond the sensible. If this intransigence makes him very much like Robbe-Grillet and other phenomenologists, it nonetheless fails to divorce him entirely from Ibsen and Shaw in their modernism, and it certainly leaves him in the moral realm.

Where Ibsen and Shaw were iconoclasts of their world, and knew what the morally better life should be, Pinter, I suggest, is an iconoclast of both the world that they assaulted and the one that supposes itself to have learned their lessons and profited from them. I suggest that Pinter's force is in no small part traceable to the fact that his audience is much the same one that Ibsen assaulted. We can be and often are scandalized in our bourgeois roots by what Pinter does to us, and this despite our frequent (not universal) assumptions that we have learned from the modernist masters and have lost all the old illusions. I suggest that Pinter is masterful at playing on our sitcom softness, our hypocrisy, and our assumption that, since the time of Ibsen and Shaw, we have known what's good or bad, what's what morally speaking. Again, some examples from the work of these three playwrights will demonstrate this point.

In retrospect it is obvious that Ibsen had a discernible mindset and a program. At least in his renowned middle period, he regularly exposed what he saw as weaknesses in the culture of Western Europe. In his attacks upon the institution of marriage, upon democracy and freedom of the press, upon the abstract virtue of duty *per se,* he clearly assumed that when the audience's wrath subsided, they would understand that he was not the immoral wretch he was consistently accused of being, but someone who wanted to get rid of pretense and human wastefulness of human potential, in favor of something better, morally speaking. He left it to us to agree that he was right about what he saw as wrong and to find some remedy. We have by no means grappled successfully with all of the issues stated and implied by his plays, but the attention given over the past century to liberal individualistic development, to love rather than duty as the foundation of marriage (or of "relationships"), to honesty in public and private life alike—all of these emphases show that Ibsen has had remarkable influence, though by no means total success at cleaning things up from his perspective. The point, however, is that we could figure out what was under attack and that we were being called upon to do something about fixing things or acquiescing in them.

Shaw also knew what he liked and disliked, and he let us know in terms often amusing and sometimes annoying. Political systems had to get better if society was to be improved, marriage was essential in our present state of civilization if the race was to be satisfactorily sustained and strengthened (but not for any other reason, seemingly), strong economy and full employment outweighed anyone's objections to whatever might be the basis of these fruits, personal growth and development rooted in intellect and imagination were superior to arguments in favor of submerging the individual for the group's welfare. Shaw was Ibsen with a comic flair and boundless optimism, for the most part. A long time after the fact, Ibsen seems the sounder writer in his declining to spell out the ways to achieve morally better ends. But even so, the point about Shaw is still that he was sure of himself and of others, individuals and institutions alike, and did not hesitate to preach his meliorism.

III

What strikes me about Pinter's plays is that they sometimes arouse resentment precisely because they assault the same sets of values that Ibsen and Shaw worked on. *The Homecoming* derives from someone who knows full well that we all think and feel fondly about returns home— which is to say that we have a fixed notion of such events, whether or not that notion conforms to our personal experience of homecomings. Pinter thus puts us into a reliable frame of mind, wherein we probably expect certain experiences, and then he gives us the gang of thugs and psychological bullies on view in his play. To the extent that we may be shocked or offended (not merely puzzled), we can safely say that we remain the same audience that Ibsen and Shaw went after. Pinter had done this same thing to us in *The Birthday Party,* where the characters themselves mock rituals denoted by the title of the play. In one way or another, persons leaving this play may be heard to mutter variations on the question, "Is nothing sacred?" Or look at *Old Times* as another instance of our dismay at how things turn out. Nobody knows better than Pinter how we select and reinvent the past. He delights in compelling Deeley and Anna to alternate in singing bits from popular tunes of the Twenties and Thirties, because he knows that we're out there in the theatre humming and singing along in our hearts. Such a trick goes hand-in-hand with the attempts of all three of the characters to get straight what in fact did happen in their lives. Because they cannot remember for sure, or because they have created the past deliberately or unintentionally, they cannot ascertain what in fact happened. And because they cannot do this, they do not know who they are. To paraphrase Lambert Strether, If you haven't had your past, what have you had? Unless we know who we have been, we cannot know who we are. Ignorance of who they are is more than enough to account for the despondency and tears on which the curtain falls. But surely the nostalgia and self-delusion responsible for such a state of affairs is akin to the self-delusion that Ibsen and Shaw jumped on nearly a century ago. We seem to have learned little. Much the same point emerges from *Betrayal.* By writing and presenting events backwards, Pinter allows himself and us to examine love, marriage, adultery, friendship, commitment from the other end, so to speak. Clearly we (like the audiences addressed by Ibsen and Shaw) regard these virtues and attitudes and relationships in set ways. Usually, Pinter supposes, we make much of them and take them seriously: that is our official morality. What he gives us is an opportunity to observe that these familiar issues come to very little in the long run—and it is the long run that his method allows us to entertain. Thus, the involvement of Jerry, Emma, and Robert with themselves and others would be thought of, in the abstract, as importantly affecting their own lives and the moral fabric of their society. Abstractly, we might well observe that the title refers to what they have done, out of stray passion, to two marriages, two kinds of friendship, and parental commitment—these at least. What Pinter shows us, however, is that their behavior is easily and commonly blown out of proportion and dignified beyond its paltry significance. By showing us the aftermath first and then working back to the start of an adulterous affair, Pinter suggests that much of what we assume about grand passion and the glory of love is as phony and small as the "memories" shared in *Old Times*. The play appears to be asking questions about the true worth of our oldest values, or the values to which we give at least lip-service. In other words, he deflates our received ideas in much the same manner employed by Ibsen and Shaw in a day that we tend to think of as long ago and far away, well before the dawn of our own sophisticated time.

Thus far Pinter would seem to be doing the same old job of iconoclasm. There are of course differences, which we may now address. For one thing, Pinter strikes me as one who hits us in more fundamental ways than do Ibsen and Shaw. They strike at our institutions and at our involvement in those institutions. Pinter gets at our human nature itself. His plays implicitly ask the question: what's left to be moral about, since we cannot trust the intellect, the memory, the beauty of love, family ties, marriage, friendship, social contract, and in view of our seeming inability to know our present, past, or future?

Well, Pinter certainly doesn't go for any long-range values or abstractions. Instead, he gives up on mind and stresses appetite or will. What he dramatizes is a conviction that we do in fact live for now and take what we need or want in order to satisfy this or that appetite. He shows that we will likely lie to ourselves or to others if we try to go beyond that admittedly primitive level to one of altruism, virtue for its own sake, etc. Or we may even hurt ourselves and others and suffer pain by misremembering or by presuming to follow principles or ideals. Moreover, even one who does speak for mind and principle (one like Teddy in *The Homecoming*) is likely pursuing a need or an appetite for what he regards as real.

The characters of Teddy and Lenny in *The Homecoming* may come as close as anything in Pinter to demonstrating the moral stance in these plays. Teddy, the philosopher, tells Lenny and the rest of the family that they wouldn't understand Teddy's philosophical publications because the family are incapable of getting outside the immediate and of seeing the world objectively. Importantly, Teddy remarks that he and the others are alike in some ways, but that he is different from them in being able to transcend that which he is simultaneously involved with. In fact, he says, he refuses to immerse himself in the world as the family do. He considers this a matter not of intelligence but of attitude. Salvation, he implies, lies in distancing oneself. He trusts the mind to reach conclusions somehow superior to appetite.

Lenny, on the decided other hand, would appear to speak for everyone else on stage in asking the kind of question that Pinter's plays always raise:

> Well, look at it this way. How can the unknown merit reverence? In other words, how can you revere that of which you're ignorant? At the same time, it would be

ridiculous to propose that what we *know* merits reverence. What we know merits any one of a number of things, but it stands to reason reverence isn't one of them. In other words, apart from the known and the unknown, what else is there?

This passage gets at the heart of Pinter's moral position, not because we need identify Lenny with Pinter, but because what Lenny says so plainly echoes what we see and may infer from other Pinter does not so much prescribe as describe. This, then, is how he divides good from bad, authentic from inauthentic. The result is conclusiveness on a pretty primitive level, but it is assuredly conclusive. It is also perhaps no less painful in the pursuing—both because of and in spite of its stark reductionism, and it is certainly a moral vision—that is, one which emerges from a view of what is better or worse, morally, for human beings. In this view people are basically animals and the right (moral) thing to do is to accept this premise and its consequences, whatever the cost. In short, just get on with meeting our needs, rather than think and fret about consequences, since he finds no foundation for sweating of principles.

Pinter makes us uneasy, I think, because he gets us in the guts, where he implies we live. Ibsen and Shaw are softer, being concerned as well with mind. The tone and flavor of Pinter's work suggest that of course we are free to deny the accuracy of his vision if we can do so convincingly and can suggest something more plausible in the way of morality. Can we do so?

David Z. Saltz (essay date 1992)

SOURCE: "Radical Mimesis: The 'Pinter Problem' Revisited," in *Comparative Drama*, Vol. 26, No. 3, Fall, 1992, pp. 218-36.

[*In the following essay, Saltz examines the difference between concept and meaning in the language of Pinter's plays.*]

When Goldberg grills Stanley in *The Birthday Party* about whether "the number 849" is "possible or necessary,"[1] or Gus challenges Ben in *The Dumbwaiter* about whether one should say "light the kettle" instead of "light the gas" (I, 141), or Lenny battles with Ruth in *The Homecoming* over whether he will "relieve" her of her water glass (III, 49), the objects of the characters' discourse—a number, a figure of speech, a glass—hardly seem to warrant the intense interest the characters invest in them. One might try to explain the objects' significance by positing details of the characters' biographies that Pinter fails to make explicit. Perhaps Lenny's mother used to beat him severely for leaving dirty glasses around the house; perhaps Gus is compiling an English language guide for foreign chefs in his spare time; perhaps Goldberg and Stanley once collaborated on a treatise about mathematical logic. I set to one side the question of whether this kind of exercise might ever be helpful as a rehearsal strategy. As a critical strategy, however, it is patently absurd. An obvious problem is that since such speculations lack textual support, one could generate an indefinite number of equally plausible (or implausible) alternatives. Recognizing this problem, very few critics indulge in such flagrant flights of invention (though more restrained forms of "filling in" are not uncommon).[2] Nonetheless, some critics feel a need for more information than the texts supply to explain the action and so portray Pinter's plays as ineluctably enigmatic, a portrayal that, depending on the critic's sensibility, may be a compliment or a complaint.

Most critics, however, recognize that Lenny may want the glass simply because Ruth currently has it in her possession, and that Gus may object to the expression "light the kettle" simply because Ben uttered it. Much criticism makes the point that in Pinter's plays *what* the characters are discussing is often a pretext. To understand Pinter is to be sensitive to the language's impact within the here-and-now of the dramatic moment. Martin Esslin, for example, writes that Pinter draws attention to "what people are *doing* to each other through" language; John Russell Brown proposes that Pinter "is interested in speech as barriers and as bridges between people, as elements in a social combat"; Bernard Dukore suggests that "present activities, interrelationships, and strategems are more dramatically important than past actions"; Ewald Mengle describes Pinter's drama "as a socio-pathological phenomenon . . . arising immediately from the interactions of people in 'face-to-face' situations"; and Austin Quigley argues that "the language of a Pinter play functions primarily as a means of dictating and reinforcing relationships."[3]

This insight recurs like a refrain throughout Pinter criticism, from the earliest to the most recent. Undoubtedly, these critics are underscoring something essential about Pinter's language. To account clearly for what is distinctive about the kind of drama Pinter creates, however, we need a clear account of how the aspect of language that Pinter highlights differs from the one he subordinates. Quigley has felt the importance of this question most urgently and has undertaken the most rigorous attempt so far to answer it. "The barrier to progress" in understanding Pinter's drama, he contends, "is the seeming impossibility of finding a controllable second term with which to contrast what is felt to be characteristic of non-Pinter language" (p. 34). Actually, critics have been surprisingly consistent in their description of this "second term"—that is, in their positive characterization of Pinter's language. Esslin and Brown (whose comments pre-date Quigley's book), Mengle and Dukore (whose comments post-date it), and Quigley himself all agree that in Pinter's texts language first and foremost functions as action within a social context. Quigley's carefully-chosen appellation, "the interrelational function," nicely fits all these depictions of Pinter's language. The real problem, as I see it, is how to define the *first* term. Pinter privileges the "interrelational" function of language as opposed to . . . what?[4]

The answer that comes most naturally to mind—or at least that has come naturally to many minds—is something like

"meaning" or "reference." Esslin distinguishes between what language "does" and its "conceptual content," and Brown between language as "social combat" and as "statement."[5] Quigley himself ultimately offers the "referential function" as the alternative to the "interrelational function," though he also provides an extensive and often penetrating critique of "dualistic" models that involve "the separation of meaning and use" (p. 46). Pinter's plays, he suggests, cause problems for critics blinded by what he calls the "reference theory of language" because the characters use language to do things beside referring. Stymied by language that does not function primarily to refer, critics "cast Pinter into a series of limbos of language" (p. 36) and proclaim that "Pinter's language conveys something other than the meaning of his words, that Pinter shows that language can be used to convey what it cannot say, that it is not the words that count but the subtext, that Pinter has transcended the boundaries of language" (p. 46).

Significantly, however, Quigley does not dismiss the reference theory as entirely bankrupt but only as limited.[6] As he puts it, the problem with earlier criticism has been the "implicit belief that language is *primarily* referential," while in fact "other language functions *can* predominate" (p. 50; italics mine). Presumably Pinter's texts baffle critics by being among the few to exploit this possibility. When Quigley comes to defining the predominant function of Pinter's language, he leaves his definition wide open. "The coining of a name for this function of language does not reduce it or Pinter's plays to something single or something that is simply repeated from one play to the next," he assures us (p. 55). But clearly, if the concept of the "interrelational function" is so elastic as to encompass *any* use of language, it is of no help in characterizing Pinter's language in particular. Wittgenstein once observed that when we make a claim such as that "Every word in language signifies something," we have said "*nothing whatever* unless we have explained explicitly *what* distinction we wish to make."[7] The claim that Pinter's language is "interrelational" must meet this challenge. Ultimately, however, Quigley identifies only one sure mark of the interrelational function: it is not the referential function. Despite appeals to the "countless" uses of language, his own model carves out space for only two: the "referential" function, and everything else. The opposition between use and meaning, now called interrelation and reference, is as integral to his position as to those he attacks.[8]

We are still confronted, then, with the need to define what exactly this "referential" function is that Pinter's language purportedly subordinates. After all, it is manifestly not the case that Pinter's language "is stripped bare of reflective or conceptual thought, so that the play could be just as effectively performed in Finno-Ugric," as Brustein once suggested.[9] Following Quigley's lead, let us look to Wittgenstein for help here. In *Philosophical Investigations,* Wittgenstein describes "a particular picture of the essence of human language. It's this: the individual words in language name objects—sentences are combinations of such names. . . . In this picture of language we find the roots of the following idea: Every words has a meaning." Wittgenstein observes, however, that the words used in many utterances are not "names of objects" at all. Among the examples he suggests are "Water! Away! Ow! Help! Fine! No!"[10] This simple insight is remarkably powerful and produced what even so understated a philosopher as J. L. Austin felt justified calling a "revolution in philosophy."[11] But is it the elixir for the "Pinter Problem" that Quigley supposes it to be? The answer, unfortunately, is no. To be sure, Pinter's plays are replete with the sorts of non-referential utterances that Wittgenstein adduces. The same, however, is true of virtually any play; one needn't turn to Pinter to find characters who cry "Help" or "No!" More significantly, words that *do* refer to objects permeate the utterances of Pinter's characters, and these include the very utterances that best exemplify the "interrelational" function of language. When Lenny says, "Just give me the glass" (III, 50), he wants Ruth to give him not just any object, not even just any glass, but *that* glass, the glass on the table in front of her. The word "glass" has an absolutely specific reference.

Perhaps we should understand "the referential function" in a narrower sense than Quigley's arguments suggest. Rather than simply being a function of *words* naming mental or physical *objects,* let us consider it a function of *sentences* expressing *propositions,* an interpretation implied, for example, by Brown's suggestion that nothing is "stated" in Pinter's plays. Lenny's imperative about the glass is not a statement and so falls outside the scope of this more narrowly interpreted function, but Pinter does not as a rule begrude his characters their assertions. In fact, assertions referring to the past, present, and future comprise the larger part of Lenny's considerable verbal output earlier in the same scene:

My name's Lenny.

(III, 43)

We haven't got a drink in the house.

(III, 44)

I clumped her one.

(III, 47)

Well, the old man'll be pleased to see you, I can tell you.

(III, 45)

These assertions do not mark deviations from interrelational language use. They are part and parcel of it. Obviously, in recounting past incidents that evince his violent and unpredictable behavior toward women, Lenny is not *merely* conveying information to Ruth; he is negotiating the terms of their relationship. But the "referential" function of the language—what the language refers to—is not tangential to this act. The meaning matters. The impact of Lenny's speeches derives precisely from *what Lenny is asserting.*

One of Wittgenstein's key points is that asserting is itself a language game. It is something that people *do* for diverse reasons and with diverse effects. This observation about language, which subsequent philosophers such as Austin, Strawson, and Grice rapidly picked up and developed in different ways,[12] applies to assertions made by Pinter's characters, characters in other plays, and people in real life. One can read Austin's *How to Do Things with Words* as dramatizing the futility of any effort to draw a line between "referential" and "interrelational" language. As is well known, Austin begins by observing that certain utterances constitute actions in their own right; for example, "if I utter the words 'I bet . . .', I do not state that I utter the words 'I bet', or any other words, but I perform the act of betting."[13] After trying unsuccessfully to locate a criterion for separating utterances that perform actions—"performative utterances"—from those that simply convey information—"constative utterances"—he concludes that *all* utterances have both a referential and an interrelational aspect.[14] These he dubs an utterance's locution and illocution, respectively. Language is always "use"; the question is only what we are using it for in any given situation. The "referential function" is not an *alternative* to the "interrelational function," but *one aspect* of it.

If *all* language is interrelational, then the insight that Pinter's language is interrelational—and consequently much of the thirty years of criticism that this observation has fueled—seems otiose. In fact, I believe there is something essentially right—and important—about this insight. We will not be able to define clearly what it is, however, unless, to use Teddy's often-quoted words, we "appreciate the points of reference" and "operate on things and not in things" (III, 77). We must distinguish clearly between the way the characters use language within the fictional universe of the plays, and the way the plays themselves as narrative representations use language.

Instead of the exchange of signs between characters, let us concentrate on the exchange of signs between the stage and the audience. When we adopt this perspective, a question comes into focus that for the time being I do not propose to address though it is important to distinguish clearly: whether the plays as a whole assert anything—in other words, convey "messages"—to the audience. Many critics, along with Pinter himself until relatively recently, have insisted that they do not. A primary difference between Pinter's earlier plays and his more recent ones (*Precisely, One for the Road, Mountain Language,* and *Party Time)* is that the latter adopt a clear moral stance toward the action and more specifically encourage a critical attitude toward agents of political power. By contrast, Pinter once said of his earlier work: "I want to present living people to the audience, worthy of their interest basically because they *are,* they exist, not because of any moral the author may draw from them. . . . I want as far as possible to leave comment to the audience."[15] Note, however, that whether or not the *plays* constitute assertions is a distinct issue from the one I have been considering so far, which specifically involves the function of the *language* in the plays. One can interpret a play as promoting an idea that none of its characters assert; for example, *The Threepenny Opera* critiques capitalism by representing characters who relish in it. Of course, in some cases a character's meaning does seem to coincide with the play's meaning. Many people, for instance, perceive John Tanner to be Shaw's mouthpiece in *Man and Superman*. But surely the critics who stress that Pinter's language is "interrelational" are not simply making the point that Pinter is not Shaw. If Pinter seldom speaks explicitly through his characters, he is hardly unique in this.[16] The bulk of dialogue in the vast majority of plays—even in Shaw's plays—functions not to set forth an idea for the audience's consideration but to advance a narrative storyline. To lend substance to the proposal that Pinter's use of language is distinctively "interrelational" we need to focus specifically on the role Pinter's language plays in the process of narrative representation.

An assertion uttered in the course of a performance can represent narrative content in two fundamentally different ways. First, performers can use assertions to narrate stories. The assertion, then, *describes* a narrative event; it is *about* the event. Or, more precisely, it *projects* the event in the sense proposed by the philosopher Nicholas Wolterstorff.[17] It defines a fictional world to which spectators might subsequently refer. The existence of the assertion itself, however, is not part of that world. Alternatively, performers can enact a *character's* use of an assertion. In this case, the performance as a whole and not the assertion itself is the medium of narrative representation. The assertion does not assert the story but asserts *within* the story. The making of assertions is simply one among many kinds of actions, verbal and non-verbal, in the narrative world that the performance projects.

The opposition between narrating and enacting recalls the ancient distinction between diegesis and mimesis: telling and showing.[18] To represent narrative content mimetically defines the activity we call "acting" and is, as Northrop Frye puts it, drama's radical of presentation. The philosopher Kendall Walton addresses the mimetic nature of acting when he describes dramatic performance as a "reflexive" form of representation: an actor playing Hamlet does not merely represent Hamlet but represents *himself* as Hamlet. The reflexivity of mimetic representation underlies the spatial and temporal *presence* that many writers have held to be integral to drama. Drama is, in Joyce's words, "the form wherein [the artist] presents the image in immediate relation to others."[19] Goethe and Schiller stress the temporal dimension of mimetic reflexivity when they characterize "the dramatic poet" as one who presents events "as totally present," in contrast to "the epic poet" who "presents the event as totally past"—a characterization that Brecht self-consciously adopts when he attacks the conventions of drama and envisions an epic theater.[20] Peter Szondi is calling attention to the reflexivity of drama when he emphasizes drama's "primacy"; Drama, Szondi writes, "is not a (secondary) representation of something else (primary); it presents itself, is itself."[21] Hence, absolute

drama must be "purely relational"; "it must break loose from everything external" (p. 8). It can represent only what it can show: the immediacy of the human interaction that actually takes place on the stage. "The absolute dominance of dialogue—that is, of interpersonal communication, reflects the fact that the Drama consists only of the reproduction of interpersonal relations" (p. 8).

That Szondi's characterization of Drama with a capital "D" bears an uncanny resemblance to common critical characterizations of Pinter's drama is not a coincidence. The insight that Pinter subordinates language's "meaning" to its "use" becomes both coherent and important *if* we understand "meaning" to designate *diegetically represented narrative content* and "use" to designate *mimetically represented language use* (which includes the use of assertions, with story-relative reference, in the narrative[22]). The distinction between "meaning" and "use" is still misleading, however, since both mimesis and diegesis involve both use and meaning: actors *use* language, diegetically or mimetically, to project narrative *meaning*. Hence, in the interest both of economy and clarity, we should retire the meaning/use opposition once and for all and speak instead simply of diegesis and mimesis. My proposal is that Pinter's plays are instances of almost, though not entirely, pure mimesis. They are radically dramatic in Frye's sense: they are "radically acting scripts."[23] (I stress that "mimesis" here corresponds simply to the mode of signification that semioticians call "ostension." One should not take it to imply "imitation" and even less "imitation of reality"— ideas commonly associated with the term.[24])

Most plays are a hybrid of diegesis and mimesis. Sometimes the relationship between the narrative and its representation is purely diegetic, such as when plays begin with a prologue spoken by a performer in a neutral narrative voice (*Troilus and Cressida,* for instance). Fictional characters also adopt a purely diegetic relation to the narrative whenever the fact that they are narrating or commenting on the story is not itself an event within that story. The aside is a convention that allows fictional characters to shift from a mimetic to a diegetic mode of representation in mid-scene. Most commonly, however, diegesis is embedded in mimetic dialogue. For example, in his first speech in *Hamlet,* Claudius recounts his brother's death and his own marriage to his former sister-in-law. This assertion provides the audience with important information about past events in the narrative (diegesis) and also functions as an action in the dramatic present (mimesis). Not atypically, the diegetic function in this case is primary and the dramatic significance negligible since within the play Claudius is merely reiterating what his listeners already know.

The pressure to house diegetic representation in mimetic dialogue derives from the generic demands of drama. As Szondi suggests, with the advent of neo-classicism this pressure became especially acute. "In the Renaissance [specifically on the continent], after the exclusion of prologue, chorus, and epilogue, dialogue became perhaps for the first time in the history of the theater . . . the sole constitutive element in the dramatic web."[25] At the same time as closing off non-mimetic avenues of representation, the normative rules of neo-classicism limited what could be represented mimetically by imposing the unities of time and place, thereby placing an even greater diegetic burden on the dialogue. The conventions of late nineteenth-century realism added to this burden by demanding, as Charles Lyons has observed,

> that the realistic drama present a complex and yet plausible explication of determination and consequence working through time. . . . Consequently, within the brief period of time that could be played out plausibly within these mundane spaces, the dialogue had to reveal the impact of the past upon the present. Consequently, the revelation of the past, which has presence only as the material of language, became the actual stuff of dialogue.[26]

Such diegetic extensions of the narrative into the past mitigate what Szondi calls the "primacy" of drama. Pinter reifies drama's generic impulse, untethering drama from its diegetic ties to the past and restoring to it its radical presence. In Pinter's plays, as he himself once said, "we are only concerned with what is happening then, in this particular moment of the people's lives."[27]

Pinter's dialogue is not absolutely devoid of embedded diegesis. For example, most spectators and critics accept that in the world of the **Homecoming** Ruth and Teddy moved to America six years prior to the action of the play, where they have three children, all boys, and where Teddy teaches philosophy, and that in **The Caretaker** Aston spent time in a mental hospital and received shock treatment. This information comes exclusively through the dialogue. In general, an audience will infer diegetic information whenever it interprets a character to be making a true assertion about the past, and there are times when Pinter's characters make assertions about themselves that the audience has no reason to doubt.

One thing that is striking about Pinter's plays, however, is how rare such occasions are. (An exception in this regard is **Betrayal,** which projects a singularly complete and stable narrative picture and makes the lies easy to spot.) In such early plays as **The Dumbwaiter** and again in more recent plays such as **One for the Road,** characters are completely mute about key elements of their past. For whom exactly do Ben and Gus work? What is the crime for which Victor and his family are being punished? The absence of such information provoked the infamous letter in which a woman asked Pinter to "kindly explain to me the meaning of your play **The Birthday Party.** These are the points which I do not understand: 1. Who are the two men? 2. Where did Stanley come from? 3. Were they all supposed to be normal? You will appreciate that without the answers to my questions I cannot fully understand your play." The lack of such information frustrated her ability to formulate the kind of deterministic explanation of the present in terms of the past that naturalistic texts

encourage. However, as an early reviewer of **The Caretaker** remarked, this lack of knowledge is only felt retrospectively; "strangely enough, while the play is on, it never occurs to us to worry about not knowing."[28]

In a scene from Pinter's screenplay for **The Last Tycoon,** which draws closely on Fitzgerald's novel, the successful filmmaker Monroe Stahr instructs Boxley, a novelist, on the art of writing dramatically. Boxley's attempt at a screenplay, Stahr complains, "Is just talk. We'd lose the audience." Suddenly, Stahr launches into the following story:

> STAHR: Suppose you're in your office. You've been fighting duels all day. You're exhausted. *(He sits.)* This is you. *(He stands.)* A girl comes in. *(He goes to the door, opens it, comes back in, shuts it.)* She doesn't see you. She takes off her gloves, opens her purse, and dumps it out on the table. *(He mimes these actions.)* You watch her. This is you. *(He sits.)* She has two dimes, a nickel, and a matchbox. She leaves the nickel on the table, puts the two dimes back into the purse, takes the gloves to the stove opens it and puts them inside. *(He mimes all this while talking.)* She lights a match. Suddenly, the phone rings. She picks it up. *(He mimes this.)* She listens. She says, "I've never owned a pair of black gloves in my life." She hangs up, kneels by the stove, lights another match. *(He kneels, mimes lighting another match, then quickly jumps up and goes to the door.)* Suddenly, you notice there's another man in the room, watching every move the girl makes . . .
>
> *Pause*
>
> BOXLEY *(intrigued):* What happens?
>
> STAHR: I don't know. I was just making pictures.[29]

Stahr does not explain who this girl is or where she comes from, and provides us with no reason to care about her situation. And yet the performance arrests our attention. Stahr's anecdote describes a paradigmatic dramatic performance. He is not "withholding" anything; even he himself only knows what is happening in the moment. If this scene were in one of his films, eventually he or someone else would need to fill in the blanks, but this demonstration reveals that the missing narrative detail would be merely an afterthought; it is superfluous and to a large extent arbitrary. Pinter's plays—and this applies equally to his recent "political" plays as well as his earlier, ostensibly "apolitical" ones—eliminate all such dramatically inert padding and provide only what is necessary, and everything that is necessary, for the dramatic event to take place.[30]

Of course, even when Pinter's characters do provide information about their past—and plays like **Old Times, Monologue,** and **Landscape** consist mostly of such material—one is always wary of accepting this information at face value. Consider this excerpt from Esslin's synopsis of **The Birthday Party:**

> Stanley, we learn, had come to the seaside resort in question as the pianist of a concert party who appeared at the pier. He even tells the story of an occasion when, *so he claims,* he gave a concert on his own in London; in Lower Edmonton to be exact. . . .[31]

With the phrase "we learn" and the use of the past perfect tense ("had come"), Esslin acknowledges that the play represents Stanley's concert at the pier diegetically and not mimetically, but he nonetheless incorporates this information directly into his own version of the narrative. He is careful, however, to represent Stanley's Lower Edmonton concert only as an event that Stanley *claims* to have occurred.[32] There is no reason in particular not to believe Stanley here; on the contrary, Esslin's observation that Lower Edmonton is "anything but a major centre of artistic activity" speaks on behalf of the story's credibility. But in Pinter's plays, one cannot simply take the truth of a character's description of the past for granted. Pinter's texts embrace the always implicit problematic of embedded diegesis—that, as the narratologist Didier Coste has remarked, "a tale told in words on stage is heresay."[33] In a Pinter play, we can accept with confidence only what we actually see happening before us.

This problem (if it is a problem) has persuaded Almansi and Henderson that Pinter's is a language of deceit, obfuscation, and lies. "Pinter has systematically forced his characters to use a perverse, deviant language specialized in concealing reality."[34] Once again, we must distinguish between the characters' use of language and the plays'. Our inability to verify the claims that Pinter's characters make about their off-stage lives is not a consequence of Pinter's having created a particularly deceitful assortment of characters. After all, no Pinter character is more mendacious than, say, Volpone or Iago. On the other hand, it is not quite right to say that Pinter's plays as a whole conceal the fictional reality from the audience, or that, as many critics have suggested, they thematize the fundamental unverifiability of the past in the way that many of Pirandello's plays do.[35] *Cosi é (se vi pare),* like the Japanese story *Rashomon,* confronts us with a series of incompatible versions of the past and challenges us to choose between them. Such texts focus our attention on the diegetically represented past by enticing us to construct a consistent narrative picture and then frustrating our efforts to make that picture cohere.

Pinter, by contrast, circumvents the problem of verifiability altogether by calling on assertions about the past to function exclusively as events in the dramatic present. Whether we happen to believe an assertion or not is incidental. Lenny's boast that he gave an old woman "a short-arm jab to the belly" (*Homecoming,* III, 49), for instance, is equally useful to him whether it is true or not. Did Stanley really perform the concert at Lower Edmonton? Did Hirst really have an affair with Spooner's wife Emily, as Spooner accuses (*No Man's Land,* IV, 134)? For that matter, did Spooner even have a wife named Emily—or any wife at all?[36] Did Harry really find James "in a slum" (*The Collection,* II, 147)? Did Mick really know "a bloke . . . in Shoreditch" who "lived in Aldgate" and who, aside from being a "bit bigger round the nose," was a "dead spit" of Davies (*The Caretaker,* II, 41)? The answers to these questions are impossible to determine precisely because they *do not matter* in a way that the

answer to the question "Who is Signora Ponza?" (in *Cosi é*), inaccessible though it may be, does matter. We have no conclusive evidence that any of these assertions is false, and indeed many of them are perfectly plausible. But if they were not true, the characters might just as well have invented them. In one of the landmark documents of New Criticism, L. C. Knights in 1933 exposed the folly of questions such as "how many children had Lady Macbeth."[37] Since the text of *Macbeth* is silent about this issue, there *is no answer.* The answer falls outside the scope of what the text represents. To contemplate virtually any question about the past in Pinter's plays, even those questions about which the texts (or, more accurately, the characters) are *not* silent, is like fretting about the number of Lady Macbeth's children. The answers simply fall outside the scope of what the plays represent.

In *The Collection,* Pinter comes closest to Pirandello in making the diegetic unreliability of dramatic dialogue an issue for the audience. He does so, however, only by making this unreliability an issue for the characters and implicating it in the mimetic action. Even in this case, the "truth of the matter" is dramatically immaterial. The play is not about an affair that may or may not have taken place in Leeds but about James and Stella's failure to provide Harry and Bill with a consistent account of the past *in the present.* The narratives that the characters themselves project within the fictional world—in other words, the narratives that the play mimetically represents the characters projecting—become tangible forces in the dramatic action.[38] As Anna remarks famously in *Old Times,* "there are things I remember which may never have taken place, but as I recall them so they take place" (IV, 28).

Far from obfuscating, Pinter radically minimizes narrative uncertainty by never asking us to assimilate the content of character's claims into the world the plays project. In Pinter, all we need to know is that the tale is being told, and this knowledge is not susceptible to epistemic doubt because its truth is not a matter of epistemology but hermeneutics. We know it is true because whatever a drama represents mimetically *is* true, by definition, in the fictional world. The representation is what makes it true.

Some critics have suggested that form and content are one in Pinter. Quigley has astutely highlighted the problematic nature of such claims (p. 44); once again, however, this suggestion becomes meaningful if we take it to refer specifically to the form and the content of the narrative representation—in other words, to what some narratologists call the "discourse" and the "story." In purely mimetic theater, the difference between story and discourse collapses. The "story" of the play is not something that is told but something that happens. The events that transpire on the stage, the real interactions between living human beings, *are* the story. By bracketing the question of whether a character's claims about the past are "true" in the character's world, mimetic theater places the actors in the same relation to the fictional past as it places the characters themselves. As Pinter once proposed in reference to **Old Times,** "the fact that they discuss something that he says took place—even if it did not take place—actually seems to me to recreate the time and the moments vividly in the present, so that *it is actually taking place before your very eyes*—by the words he is using. By the end of this particular section of the play, they are sharing something in the present."[39] When the *characters* discuss the fictional past, they are sharing something in the *fictional* present, but in exactly the same way the *actors* are sharing something in the *theatrical* present.[40]

In *Radical Theatre,* Arthur Sainer reflects on his involvement with the theater avant-garde of the 1960's:

> We began to understand in the '60's that the words in plays, that the physical beings in plays, that the events in plays were too often evasions, too often artifices that had to do not with truths but with semblances. At best they were *about* something rather than *some* thing; they were ideas describing experiences rather than the experiences.[41]

Sainer is discussing American ensemble groups such as the Living Theater, the Open Theater, the Performance Group, and the Bread and Puppet Theater. But the impulse he articulates also formed the basis of Peter Brook's attempts to create "Immediate Theatre" in England, Mnouchkine's environmental productions in France, and, most influentially Grotowski's "Poor Theatre" in Poland. It underlay the Happenings that artists like Cage and Kaprow began to devise in the 1950's. And this same impulse is manifested, more subtly but in some ways most "radically" of all, in the plays that Harold Pinter began writing in 1957.

Pinter, of course, never represented himself as a radical. "I am a very traditional playwright," he maintained in a 1966 interview. "All this jamboree in 'Happenings' and eight hour movies is great fun for the people concerned I'm sure."[42] And as I have tried to show, Pinter's work is indeed "very traditional." "Radical," after all, derives from the Latin *radicalis,* "having roots": Pinter gets to the root of what makes theater, in its most popular, bourgeois form, engaging. He simply pushes the normative conventions of drama to their limits. As John Russell Taylor has suggested, a play such as **The Birthday Party** is "a well-made drawing-room drama complete in every detail, even down to the meticulously realistic dialogue, *except that the exposition is left out altogether.*"[43] In drama, the past is always a pre-text. In a recent interview, Mnouchkine remarks that "when I see young students work on what they call the 'Stanislavski method,' I am surprised to find how much they go back to the past all the time. . . . I always tell them, 'You enter leaning backwards, weighted by all this past, while in the theatre only the moment exists'."[44] Pinter discards the pre-text; or rather, he exposes it for what it is. If, as Bert O. States has proposed, plays "are efficient machines whose parts are characters who are made of actors,"[45] the diegetic details merely provide an excuse to set the machine in motion (as "translations" of classic texts into contemporary contexts such as *West Side*

Story, The Flies, Mourning Becomes Electra demonstrate). If Pinter's dramatic technique, which once seemed startlingly original, now seems dated it is because the kind of radicalism that it exemplifies is itself dated. Pinter's work—like, in different ways, that of Beckett and Handke—responds to the High Modernist impulse to strip every art form down to its "essence." (The growing recognition that these "essences" are themselves social constructions, of course, has mitigated the urgency of this impulse.) Hence, at the same time as he participates in the movement toward "immediacy" and "presence" that characterized the dominant wave of experimental theater in the sixties—and that subsequently provoked a postmodern reaction—Pinter demonstrates that this movement is already inherent in the conventional forms that the avant-garde of the sixties purported to oppose. Considered in the context of the 1960's, Pinter is at once quintessentially mainstream and quintessentially radical—*radically mainstream.*

Notes

1. Harold Pinter, *The Birthday Party,* in *Complete Works* (New York: Grove, 1976), I, 60. All subsequent references to Pinter's plays are to the *Collected Works,* and will appear in parentheses in my text with the volume followed by the page number.

2. Cf. Ronald Knowles' suggestion that "one of the great ironies of Pinter's plays in general is that in proportion to the absence of explanation for motive the auditor's intuition is called on to reconstruct psychologically the underlying cause of behaviour" (*Text and Performance: The Birthday Party and The Caretaker* [London: Macmillan, 1988], p. 75). For a forceful denouncement of the practice of "filling in" Pinter's narratives, see Thomas Van Laan, "*The Dumb Waiter:* Pinter's Play with the Audience," *Modern Drama,* 24 (1981), 494-502.

3. Martin Esslin, *Pinter: A Study of his Plays* (New York: Methuen 1976), p. 215; John Russell Brown, *Theatre Language: A Study of Arden, Osborne, Pinter and Wesker* (London: Allen Lane, 1972), p. 25; Bernard Dukore, *Harold Pinter* (New York: Grove Press, 1982), p. 25; Ewald Mengle, *Harold Pinters Dramen* (Frankfurt: Peter Lang, 1978), pp. 273-75, as quoted in Susan Hollis Merritt, *Pinter in Play* (Durham: Duke Univ. Press, 1990), pp. 189-90; Austin Quigley, *The Pinter Problem* (Princeton: Princeton Univ. Press, 1975), p. 52. Subsequent references to Quigley appear in my text. Naturally there are a number of crucial differences between the positions of these critics. An important matter concerns whether Pinter challenges language's ability to convey information (as, for example, Brown suggests) or simply de-emphasizes that function of language (as Esslin holds).

4. Of course, to define one of these two "terms"—either what Pinter's language is, or what it isn't—entails defining the other, and so the two issues are complementary. Cf. Quigley, pp. 36, 40, 45.

5. Esslin, p. 215; Brown, p. 23.

6. Actually, Quigley offers both a strong and a weak interpretation of "the reference theory" at various points of his discussion without explicitly distinguishing between these versions and their implications. The strong version is that the *sole* function of language is to refer, and the weak version is that the *central, normal,* or *primary* function of language is to refer. The former theory is truly binary: it allows only for the presence or absence of a single language function, while the latter theory allows for any number of language functions. See Quigley's critiques of I. A. Richards, Jakobson, and Halliday (pp. 41-45) for his objections to weak versions of the reference theory. Quigley concludes that "the common approach to multifunctioning language is still governed by attempts to divide up what is left of language when the central component, the referential component, or the basic content, has been extracted under a newly coined name. Such an approach to linguistic meaning is as much rooted in error as ever, and the lessons of Wittgenstein's work have not been learned" (p. 45). Quigley's own approach is vulnerable to the same critique. In the end, the only thing that distinguishes the model of language Quigley advocates from a weak reference theory is his rejection of "the notion of a *central* function" (p. 46; italics mine)—a notion that, in fact, Quigley never defines.

7. Ludwig Wittgenstein, *Philosophical Investigations,* trans. G. E. M. Anscombe (Oxford: Blackwell, 1953), p. 13.

8. Quigley's emphatic rejection of the meaning/use distinction serves an important function: it dispels the temptation to pronounce Pinter's language *meaningless.* Quigley usefully traces this temptation to the critic's implicit espousal of a reference-based (or truth-conditional) theory of meaning. However, this point, which concerns the theory of meaning *in general,* does not itself contribute to a positive understanding of how Pinter's language *in particular* functions (that is, as opposed to any other playwright's language). With respect to this latter issue, Quigley ends up in the same position as previous critics: dividing language into two categories— language that ("centrally") refers, and language that does not—and placing Pinter's language in the second category.

9. Robert Brustein, "A Naturalism of the Grotesque," *New Republic,* 145 (23 Oct. 1961), 29, as quoted in Quigley, p. 35.

10. Wittgenstein, pp. 2, 13.

11. J. L. Austin, *How to Do Things with Words* (Cambridge: Harvard Univ. Press, 1962), p. 2.

12. The seminal works are Austin's *How to Do Things with Words,* P. F. Strawson, *Logico-Linguistic Papers* (London: Methuen, 1971), pp. 1-27 ("On Referring"), and H. Grice, "Logic and Conversation," in *Speech Acts,* ed. P. Cole and J. L. Morgan, Syntax and Semantics, 3 (New York: Academic Press, 1975), pp. 41-58. These works all were first produced in the 1950's (in Austin's case, in the form of lectures). At the same time (1952-53) but independently, Bakhtin advanced a similar view of language in essays that are only now becoming available in English. See M. M. Bakhtin, "The Problem of Speech Genres," in *Speech Genres and Other Late Essays,* ed. Caryl Emerson and Michael Holquist (Austin: Univ. of Texas Press, 1986), pp. 60-102. For explicit applications of "discourse analysis" (including the models proposed by Austin and Grice) to Pinter, see Deirdre Burton, *Dialogue and Discourse: A Sociolinguistic Approach to Modern Drama Dialogue and Naturally Occurring Conversation* (London: Routledge and Kegan Paul, 1980); Kripa K. Gautam, "Pinter's *The Caretaker*: A Study in Conversational Analysis," *Journal of Pragmatics,* 11 (1987), 49-59; Deborah Tannen, "Ordinary Conversation and Literary Discourse: Coherence and the Poetics of Repetition," in *The Uses of Linguistics,* ed. Edward H. Bendix (New York: New York Academy of Sciences, 1990), pp. 15-32.

13. Austin, p. 63.

14. Actually, the locution of an utterance incorporates both its sense *and* reference, terms that Austin does not define but almost certainly allude to Frege's *Sinn* and *Bedeutung.* Austin, then, might consistently maintain that certain speech acts have sense and illocutionary force but no reference.

15. "Mr. Harold Pinter—Avant-Garde Playwright and Intimate Revue," *London Times,* 16 Nov. 1959, p. 4, as quoted in Merritt, p. 14.

16. Nothing that I will maintain in this paper about the function of Pinter's language is inconsistent with the possibility that a character might make a statement that the play as a whole supports. In fact, there are a number of passages that critics habitually, and plausibly, present as if the texts endorse them, such as Ruth's suggestion in *The Homecoming* that "Perhaps the fact that [my lips] move is more significant . . . than the words which come through them" (III, 69) and Len's speech about identity in *The Dwarfs* (II, 111-12).

17. Nicholas Wolterstorff, *Works and Worlds of Art* (Oxford: Oxford Univ. Press, 1980).

18. Plato sets forth the distinction between mimesis and diegesis in Book III of *The Republic.* Aristotle also distinguishes between narrating and enacting, but in his terminology both are species of mimesis. Nonetheless, enacting remains for Aristotle mimesis in its purest form. For a discussion of the relationship between Aristotle and Plato's positions, see Gerald F. Else, *Aristotle's Poetics: The Argument* (Cambridge:

Harvard Univ. Press, 1963), pp. 97-98. Narrative theory has recently put the Platonic distinction back into circulation. See, for example, Gerald Prince, *A Dictionary of Narratology* (Lincoln: Univ. of Nebraska Press, 1987), pp. 52-53.

19. Northrop Frye, *Anatomy of Criticism* (Princeton: Princeton Univ. Press, 1957), pp. 246-47; Kendall L. Walton, *Mimesis as Make-Believe: On the Foundations of the Representational Arts* (Cambridge: Harvard Univ. Press, 1990), pp. 117-21; James Joyce, *A Portrait of the Artist as a Young Man* (New York: Penguin, 1977), p. 214.

20. See Martin Esslin, *Brecht: A Choice of Evils,* 4th ed. (New York: Methuen, 1984), p. 113.

21. Peter Szondi, *Theory of the Modern Drama,* trans. Michael Hays (Minneapolis: Univ. of Minnesota Press, 1987), p. 9.

22. I allude here to Strawson's concept of "story-relative reference" or "identification" in *Individuals: An Essay in Descriptive Metaphysics* (1959; rpt. Garden City, N. Y.: Doubleday, 1963), p. 18. For theoretical discussions of how reference operates within theatrical performance, see Jean Alter, "Waiting for the Referent: Waiting for Godot? (On Referring in Theatre)," and Michael Issacharoff, "How Playscripts Refer: Some Preliminary Considerations," both in *On Referring in Literature,* ed. Anna Whiteside and Michael Issacharoff (Bloomington: Indiana Univ. Press, 1987), pp. 42-56, 84-94. Also see Benjamin Bennett, *Theater as Problem* (Ithaca: Cornell Univ. Press, 1990), pp. 196-208.

23. Frye, p. 247. That Pinter's plays are eminently actable is widely affirmed by both critics and theater practitioners (including some who otherwise find little to recommend the plays). See, for example, David T. Thompson, *Pinter: The Player's Playwright* (London: Macmillan, 1985), *passim;* Knowles, *Text and Performance, passim*; Simon Trussler, *The Plays of Harold Pinter: An Assessment* (London: Gollancz, 1973), pp. 187-88.

24. For a discussion of acting as ostension, see Umberto Eco, "Semiotics of Theatrical Performance," *The Drama Review,* 21 (1977), 107-17. For a general account of ostention, see Ivo Osolsobe, "On Ostensive Communication," *Studia Semiotyczne,* 9 (1979), 63-76.

25. Szondi, p. 9; subsequent citations appear in my text.

26. Charles R. Lyons, "Shepard's Family Trilogy and the Conventions of Modern Realism," in *Rereading Shepard: Contemporary Essays on the Drama of Sam Shepard,* ed. Leonard Wilcox (Basingstoke, forthcoming).

27. Quoted in Martin Esslin, *Theater of the Absurd,* 2nd ed. (Garden City, N. Y.: Doubleday, 1969), p. 256. Michael Hinden is describing the radical presence of Pinter's narratives when he states that "characters who enter these rooms bring versions of the past but never histories; nor do they move through time as if the future had a palpable reality. . . . When they are not on stage, they truly seem to disappear; that is, they do not go 'off' into imaginary rooms but rather into the wings" ("To Verify a Proposition in *The Homecoming,*" *Theatre Journal,* 43 [1982], 30). Hinden's main argument, however, is that Pinter's texts are centrally concerned with the problem of verification.

28. Esslin, *Pinter,* pp. 22, 37-38.

29. Harold Pinter, *The French Lieutenant's Woman and Other Screenplays* (Boston: Little, Brown, 1981), pp. 227-29.

30. The one real exception here, and indeed to all of my claims about Pinter's drama, is *A Kind of Alaska.* This play provides a great deal of information about the past, and this information is integral to the narrative that the play as a whole represents. Significantly, this work is unique among Pinter's plays in being a direct adaptation of another text, Oliver Sacks' *Awakenings.* Consequently, I believe it to be more akin to Pinter's screenplays than to his original stage, radio, and television plays.

31. Esslin, *Pinter,* p. 76 (italics mine).

32. Meg mentions the concert at the pier to Goldberg on p. 41; Stanley describes the concert at Lower Edmonton to Meg on p. 32.

33. Didier Coste, *Narrative as Communication* (Minneapolis: Univ. of Minnesota Press, 1989), p. 267.

34. Guido Almansi and Simon Henderson, *Harold Pinter* (London: Methuen, 1983), p. 12.

35. See, for example, Hinden, pp. 27-39, and also Barbara Kreps, who suggests that all of Pinter's plays elaborate on a "single idea," namely, the relativity of truth ("Time and Harold Pinter's Possible Realities: Art as Life, and Visa Versa," *Modern Drama,* 22 [1979], 47).

36. Hirst first refers to Spooner's wife, as if they all were old acquaintances, soon after he enters in Act II, though throughout Act I he had given no indication of having any knowledge of Spooner's life prior to their present encounter.

37. L. C. Knights, "How Many Children Had Lady Macbeth," in *Explorations* (New York: George W. Stewart, 1947), pp. 15-54.

38. Cf. Steven Gale's reading of *The Collection,* which construes the play as "an attempt to expose the tenuousness of relationships because of the inability of the participants to verify those things which constitute the basis of their relationship." In the end, however, "in terms of the play, the truth of what hap-

pened at Leeds is not significant. . . . What is important is how and why people react to what they consider the truth" (*The Butter's Going Up* [Durham: Duke Univ. Press, 1977], pp. 126, 128).

39. "A Conversation (Pause) with Harold Pinter," *New York Times Magazine,* 5 December 1971, p. 126 (italics mine).

40. For a discussion of the theoretical obstacles to performing real actions and in particular real speech acts within a theatrical context, see David Z. Saltz, "How to Do Things on Stage," *Journal of Aesthetics and Art Criticism,* 49 (1991), 31-45.

41. Arthur Sainer, *The Radical Theatre Notebook* (New York: Aron, 1975), p. 15.

42. Thompson, p. 37.

43. John Russell Taylor, *The Rise and Fall of the Well-Made Play* (New York: Hill and Wang, 1967), p. 163 (italics mine).

44. Josette Féral, "Building Up the Muscle: An Interview with Ariane Mnouchkine," *The Drama Review,* 33 (1989), 91.

45. Bert O. States, *Great Reckonings in Little Rooms* (Berkeley: Univ. of California Press, 1985), p. 149.

Ronald Knowles (essay date 1995)

SOURCE: "Plays, 1984-93: *One for the Road, Mountain Language, Party Time, Moonlight,*" in *Understanding Harold Pinter,* University of South Carolina Press, 1995, pp. 183-208.

[*In the following essay, Knowles surveys the plays written between 1984 and 1993, emphasizing the continuity of themes from Pinter's earlier, detached period to the later, overtly engaged plays.*]

The context for the political plays—*One for the Road, Mountain Language,* and *Party Time*—is the world of public events in the 1980s, in both national and international terms. Events in the United Kingdom, the United States, South America, Turkey, and elsewhere, forced upon Pinter an urgent awareness of the imperative need for public commitment both in life and art. This chapter will survey Pinter's public engagement, with particular stress on his own statements in the period, as background to the passionate indignation that gives rise to the plays.[1]

Political awakening was not a sudden conversion. As a young man, Pinter refused to do his national service after the war on political, not moral, grounds. His refusal was not as a pacifist but because of the postwar political situation: "I disapproved of the Cold War and wasn't going to join the Army in order to help it along as a boy of 18."[2] If he had been older, he would have fought in the war. In the 1970s Pinter became a member of the Campaign for

Nuclear Disarmament, and for many years he has been a member of PEN International, the organization concerned with the rights and welfare of writers throughout the world, a supporter of Amnesty International, and a subscriber to the Index on Censorship. An action that anticipated Pinter's public commitment was his attempt to deliver a letter of protest concerning the imprisonment of the Russian dissident Vladimir Bukovsky to the Russian ambassador in London and then his outlining of his concern in a letter to the *Times* (22 March 1974, 17). In relation to Pinter's later political reassessment of *The Hothouse* as reflecting the political abuse of a totalitarian society, Bukovsky's "crime" was "for criticizing the Soviet Government's use of psychiatric hospitals for political prisoners." The "Letter to Peter Wood" concerning the first production of *The Birthday Party* was published in 1981,[3] anticipating the full political revision of Pinter's views in recent interviews.

Looking back on the early plays, Pinter saw them as "metaphors" for political situations,[4] but in a television interview with John Tusa, a leading political journalist, Pinter was more explicit: "Well, they seemed to do . . . all of them seemed to do with various kinds of abuses. First of all descriptions of authoritarian systems of one kind or another, authoritarian structures. *The Hothouse* went even further and could be defined as a totalitarian society. In other words, each of the plays, I would say, dealt with the individual at the mercy of a certain authoritarian system."[5] Further comment in another television interview clarifies this: "When you look at them, they're much closer to an extremely critical look at authoritarian postures—state power, family power, religious power, power used to undermine, if not destroy the individual, or the questioning voice, or the voice which simply went away from the mainstream and refused to become part of an easily recognizable set of standards and social values."[6] It was in the Tusa interview that Pinter stated more explicitly than anywhere else the catalyst for his changed political attitudes: "The military coup in 1973 in Chile which overthrew a democratically elected government was brought about, I believe, by the United States of America . . . [this] told me without any further ado that I could not sit back and not take responsibility for my own actions, my own thoughts and act upon them which I've been doing ever since, making a bit of a nuisance of myself, in fact."

The conscientious self-examination contrasts markedly with earlier attitudes—"I came to view politicians and political structures and political acts with something I can best describe as detached contempt."[7] The reverse of this patrician aloofness eventually impelled Pinter to a point of self-recriminating candor. A TV news item covering a show at the Barbican London, on behalf of imprisoned writers, briefly interviewed Pinter, who was performing, and recorded this statement:

> I in common with a great body of people have been sleepwalking for many years, really, and I remember years ago I regarded myself as an artist in an ivory tower—really when it comes down to it a rather classic

nineteenth century idea. I've now totally rejected that and I find that the things that are actually happening are not only of the greatest importance but [have] the most crucial bearing on our lives, including this matter of censorship of people and writers' imprisonment, torture, and the whole question of how we are dealt with by governments who are in power . . . and essentially to do with the nuclear situation.[8]

The facts of torture were really brought home when Pinter joined Arthur Miller for a week-long visit to Turkey, sponsored by PEN, where he confronted the full horror of systematic torture of prisoners held for forty-five days incommunicado. Amnesty International eventually included Pinter and Miller's findings in a report, which the press summarized with the statement: "More than a quarter of a million people have been arrested on political grounds in Turkey since the 1980 military coup, and almost all have been tortured."[9] Pinter subsequently became president of the Friends of Turkey in the United Kingdom, protesting in a letter to the *Guardian* the torture, during their five-year custody, of trade unionists for engaging in basic trade union activities. More immediately germane to *Mountain Language* was Pinter's discovery of the plight of the Kurds in Turkey: "They're not really allowed to exist at all and certainly not allowed to speak their own language."[10]

In his protest at the abuse of human rights in the 1980s Pinter was frequently impelled to defend Nicaragua against the activities of the United States administration. At the end of 1987 Pinter launched an Arts for Nicaragua Fund at the Royal Court Theatre, having published the previous day a full statement of his criticism of the United States' support for the Contras: "The US Elephant must be stopped."[11] Pinter draws immediate attention to the judgment of the International Court of Justice at The Hague, in June 1986, which found that, in Pinter's words: "The US, by training, arming, equipping, financing and supplying the Contra force or otherwise encouraging, supporting and aiding military activities in and against Nicaragua, had breached its obligations under international law not to intervene in the affairs of another state." Pinter points out that the Nicaraguan revolution overthrew "a dictatorship which had been supported by the US for 40 years." The 1984 free elections were witnessed by seventy-nine observers from all over the world. Moreover, Amnesty International found that in the new Nicaragua, the systematic torture carried out in the majority of South American countries did not take place. Far from the Sandinistas being "Marxist-Leninist anti-religious devils," Nicaragua is a Catholic country with three priests as government ministers, and, while hundreds of priests had been killed in Central America in the last ten years, not one had died in Nicaragua. Pinter indicts the United States for bringing down the legally elected democracies of Guatemala in 1954 and of Chile in 1973, and the article closes with his fears for the country in which the United States-backed Contras, compared by President Reagan to the Founding Fathers, "have murdered and mutilated. . . . Thousands of Nicaraguan men, women and children"—"They have been raped, skinned, beheaded, castrated."

All this could be construed as simply anti-American propaganda were the facts not so blatant, but behind Pinter's stance there is something broader, something that was just touched on at the end of the 1984 TV news item. Apart from a piece on El Salvador, the Barbican program on imprisoned writers focused on Eastern Europe. The final exchange was as follows:

> PINTER: The horrors which are going on in Central America actually at this very [moment] . . . there's nothing to choose between one side or the other really.
>
> INTERVIEWER: You're not lined up politically to East or West, Left or Right?
>
> PINTER: Not at all.
>
> INTERVIEWER: It's totalitarianism?
>
> PINTER: And hypocrisy . . . which is to do with both Russia, America and this country.

In the Tusa interview Pinter discussed an impulse behind *One for the Road.* Both in Turkey and throughout the world there were those who would not face the reality of torture, those who "were looking at a table which had a very strong table cloth on it and vases of flowers on it": "It looked strong, that's right, and beautiful, worth preserving. They didn't look under the table at any time. Under the table they would have found what the people who are being tortured find. Mess, pain, humiliation, vomit, excrement, blood." In the same interview, as an example of "the distinctions between one reality and another," Pinter quoted the U.S. physicist Peter Hagelstein, who saw nuclear weapons as "an interesting physics problem." To Pinter the "reality" of the U.S. submarine force's nuclear capacity of destroying twenty-three thousand Hiroshimas is "death but more and more and more and more": "Other people see it in terms of strategic principles and so on. I see it in terms of annihilation." Statistics, logistics, and theoretical strategy, to Pinter, are abstract misrepresentations of the unequivocal facts of suffering and death. A graphic illustration of this was his reply to the U.S. ambassador in Turkey, who remarked that there were many opinions on any given issue: "Not if you've got an electric wire hooked to your genitals."[12] In political terms, for Pinter: "There's only one reality, you know. You can interpret reality in various ways. But there's only one. And if that reality is thousands of people being tortured to death at this very moment and hundreds of thousands of megatons of nuclear bombs standing there waiting to go off at this very moment, then that's it. . . . It has to be faced."[13]

Another kind of pressing reality that had to be faced was that of the United Kingdom itself under the ten-year rule of Thatcherism, which Pinter saw as "becoming very, very close to any other damn police state."[14] For all the significance of the visit to Turkey as "background" for *Mountain Language,* Pinter remarked: "In fact the play isn't about Turkey at all. I think the play is very much closer to home and I believe it reflects a great deal that is happening in this country."[15] He continues by indicating areas in which "the present government is turning a stronger and stronger vice on democratic institutions that we've taken for granted for a very long time"[16]—namely, Clause 28 (making "promotion" of homosexuality illegal), the Official Secrets Act, police powers, antiunion legislation, the independence of the universities, broadcasting, and the press.

Given all this, a growing sense of public dismay, frustration, and anger culminated in Charter 88, to which, along with some six thousand others, Pinter added his signature. It is ironic that the values Pinter would most support, as Charter 88 indicates, are those of the Constitution of the United States, which derive, like those of the playwright's fierce moral stance, from the values of the Enlightenment—freedom from any form of oppression, liberty of conscience, and equality before the law—in a word, democracy. This is the all-informing principle against which the plays of this period should be seen.

ONE FOR THE ROAD (1984)

Pinter was recently dubbed a "Foucauldian *avant la lettre*,"[17] and it is not difficult to see why. The French sociologist and philosopher Michel Foucault, from the 1970s on, was particularly concerned with power in society, particularly the way in which various discourses operate both on and within individuals as a form of defining coercion. From an English point of view the seventeenth-century political philosopher Thomas Hobbes had anticipated Foucault in his conviction that, for all the appearances of man in society, the reality beneath was that of egoistic striving for power. Pinter's writings have always shown a consistent concern with direct and indirect forms of power—physical, social, and oral—and their criticism has always recognized the topic of power-subservience relationships.

One for the Road is a study not so much of torture as of the torturer, and, though ostensibly the play is concerned with the power of the torturer over the tortured, it is more subtle than that. The pathological power to corrupt the mind is made manifest, and the torturer himself is always the first victim.

In a sparse formal office that could be anywhere Nicolas interviews, in succession, a father, son, and mother—Victor, Nicky, and Gila—and then the father once more. Characters names have been chosen for their indeterminacy, and no particular country is ever mentioned. No physical violence takes place onstage. Both Victor and Gila have been beaten offstage and the latter raped several times. We do not learn of Victor's supposed offense beyond the fact that he seems to be out of step with "the man who runs this country" and his regime. "We are all patriots, we are as one, we all share a common heritage. Except you, apparently" (373), Nicolas alleges.

The victims say very little; the power of the play has to derive from the actors' ability to create a palpable sense of fear and terror. This was so much the case with Alan Bates's performance as Nicolas in the first production that the actress playing Gila, Jenny Quayle, almost underwent a nervous breakdown. Yet a corrosive, sardonic humor comes from the sick mind of Nicolas. For Pinter the politics of the 1980s were "past a joke."[18] The action takes place after the victims' torture and interrogation, demonstrating Nicolas's particular sort of sadism, which is not to actually give physical pain but, instead, to relish the broken figures before him, as his interrogation serves no practical purpose at all. "One for the Road" is Nicolas's toast as he drinks constantly throughout the interview, and this action becomes a shocking manifestation of the self-willed intoxication of power: "I love death," he says. "The death of others. Do you love the death of others, or at any rate do you love the death of others as much as I do? . . . Death. Death. Death. Death. As has been noted by the most respected authorities, it is beautiful. The purest, most harmonious thing there is" (370-71). Absolute for death, with the power to take or give life, Nicolas even goes in for a little fascist pleasantry: "Everyone else knows the voice of God speaks through me" (368).

Invoking civilization and civility, friendship and respect, the corruption of his mind is in the corruption of his language, as he also talks of "wet shit," of his agents, who "pissed on the rugs" (369). Nicolas's strategy becomes apparent in Victor's eventual comment, "Kill me" (373). To reduce life to a condition worse than death and then to refrain from actual killing is the last refinement of the sadist.

Gila is simply bludgeoned verbally by Nicolas's hatred until she inadvertently mentions her father, which draws a revealing outburst from Nicolas, who celebrates the father's patriotism, his heroism, and his faith: "He would die, he would die, he would die for his country, for his God. . . . How dare you speak of your father to me? I loved him, as if he were my own father" (381). It is a fascism like that of Robert's in *The Comfort of Strangers* in the association of death, the death wish, and God with the loved/hated father figure. When he interviews Nicky, Nicolas is fatherly and talks of airplanes and toys. As in the interpretation of the father figure in **The Birthday Party,** so here the father figure sacrifices his namesake. Answering Victor's pained inquiry, Nicolas's closing line is: "Your son? Oh, don't worry about him. He was a little prick" (387).

MOUNTAIN LANGUAGE (1988) AND "NEW WORLD ORDER" (1991)

Mountain Language concerns a group of women who have been waiting all day outside a prison in the hope of seeing their menfolk inside. They have to endure abuse from an intimidating sergeant, and in one case an elderly woman has almost had a thumb severed by a guard dog. On admission to the prisoners "mountain language" is forbidden, and prisoners and visitors must use the language of the capital. It was assumed that Pinter had written a barely veiled critique of Turkey's suppression of the Kurds and their language, but he resisted the identification, suggesting that the play has a certain significance for an English audience. Pinter's very short work of less than a thousand words can be seen in both a literal and metaphorical way.

From a literal point of view an audience is likely to make the connection with the plight of the Kurds, though Brian Friel's play of 1980, *Translations,* reminded a British audience of the English encroachment on the Irish language in the nineteenth century. Friel's play was well attended in Wales, where it is not forgotten that England attempted to prohibit the speaking of Welsh in the last century. Throughout the performance of **Mountain Language** Pinter, as director, created a particular uneasiness in the audience by exploiting a specific condition of audience reception. The soldiers are dressed in regular battle fatigues, and the foul-mouthed sergeant spoke with a strong London accent. British television screens have made British audiences long familiar with such images—in the Northern Ireland of the "H" blocks, no-go areas, proscription on broadcasting interviews with representatives of the IRA. By having political and geographical reference undetermined, but suggested, Pinter creates a polemical space in which the question arises just how far the United Kingdom could be said to have taken such a direction.

Pinter signals this in a fashion that is peculiarly his own. No British dramatist has used names and naming so consistently throughout a whole career as Pinter has.[19] Let one example stand for many. In **Betrayal** the only time that the married name and titles of Robert and Emma are mentioned is precisely when Robert comes across Jerry's letter to Emma in the American Express office in Venice and intuitively realizes the nature of the contents: "I mean, just because my name is Downs and your name is Downs doesn't mean that we're the Mr. and Mrs. Downs that they, in their laughing Mediterranean way, assume we are" (218). Approximately halfway through **Mountain Language** one of the women reveals that her name is the very English "Sara Johnson." In contrast to the names in **One for the Road,** this comes as a shock if it is automatically assumed that such abuses could only happen in places like Turkey.

The first word of **Mountain Language** is "Name?" and this aspect of bureaucratic officialdom is cruelly parodied when one of the women complains of the older woman's injury from the dog. The officer in charge insists that he can only initiate disciplinary procedures if he is given the name of the animal: "Every dog has a *name!* They answer to their name. They are given a name by their parents and that is their name, that is their *name.* Before they bite they *state* their name. It's a formal procedure" (393). Beyond this overt bullying there is a certain kind of profundity.

The old woman is forbidden to speak her mountain language, and, unlike her prisoner son, she does not speak the language of the capital. Then the decision is reversed, and mountain language is allowed. But now the old woman is traumatized by the sight of blood on her son's face and her own pain and is speechless. At this the son is reduced to a voiceless shuddering. The logic of totalitarianism always seeks to suppress speech—by book-burning, torture, murder, or exile—because speech is itself symbolic of freedom. To speak is to name things like truth and tyranny, to speak is to give one's voice in a vote, in antiquity, or to mark a ballot paper in modern democracies. The final tableau of mother and son indicates the end of democracy—the body politic made speechless. Thankfully, after sound mountains echo; that is their "language."

The sketch **"New World Order"** appeared as a curtain raiser for Ariel Dorfman's acclaimed play *Death and the Maiden.* Set in post-Pinochet Chile, Dorfman's work concerns a woman's revenge against her past torturer. In Pinter's sketch two interrogators gloat over their blindfolded victim, swapping obscenities, until the almost sexual sadistic climax with one sobbing and the other congratulating him for "keeping the world clean for democracy" (3). These words were those used by the youthful Pinter and friends in ironic response to the dropping of atom bombs on Japan.[20] As in **Mountain Language,** the victim is rendered literally and symbolically speechless: "Before he came in here he was a big shot, he never stopped shooting his mouth off, he never stopped questioning received ideas. Now—because he's apprehensive about what's about to happen to him—he's stopped all that, he's got nothing more to say" (2). Similarly, upon Victor's second entrance in **One for the Road** he has difficulty speaking because his torturers have mutilated his tongue.

PARTY TIME (1991)

Another figure who wishes "to clean up . . . wash the place clean," is the Commander in the biblical dystopia of **A Handmaid's Tale,** a film from Margaret Atwood's novel. Pinter's name was kept in the credits, but he decided not to publish the screenplay, which differed in several places from the final shooting script. The handmaids are fertile young women coerced into becoming the bearers of children for a ruling elite, whose wives are sterile. The puritanical totalitarian state rejects any dissidence, and in the background of a particular handmaid's story the military regime is carrying out a violent purge against a rebellion. Atwood's slightly futuristic setting nevertheless recalls actualities of history. In 1976 Joseph Losey made *Mr. Klein,* the backdrop of which was the Vichy government's roundup of Jews in 1942. History and film provide a context for Pinter's most recent play, **Party Time,** along with the reality of increasingly autocratic government of the United Kingdom in the 1980s.

Party Time is like the obverse of the public world of these films. In Gavin's flat a party gets under way, with just a few remarks intimating that something is taking place outside. Dusty, a guest, twice tries to raise the question of her brother's where-abouts, but "it's not on anyone's agenda" (18), she is told. Dame Melissa, arriving at the party, is rather bewildered by "soldiers": "My driver had to stop at a . . . you know . . . what do you call it? . . . a roadblock. We had to say who we were . . . it really was a trifle . . ." (7). It is the measure of the distance from reality of such a character that she has to search for the word *roadblock*. Her reality is the reality of a trifling delay on the way to a party. What the reality of a roadblock is for those presumably under curfew can be imagined.

In due course, after a symbolic exchange of clenched fists and a simultaneous declaration—"A bit of that"—Fred asks: "How's it going tonight?" "Like clockwork" (13), Douglas replies. In a slightly expanded version of the play for television, additional characters, Sam, Smith, and Harlow, discuss a musician called Stoddart: "I met a man at a party the other day—I couldn't believe it—He was talking the most absolute bloody crap—his ideas about the world, that kind of thing—he was a complete and utter and total arsehole." Smith replies: "Don't worry about Stoddart. We've seen him off," and Harlow adds, in comic idiom, "We've had him for breakfast."[21] In other additional exchanges for the television production we learn that Emily's husband cannot be present, as "he's busy . . . down there" on the streets outside. What this means becomes clear when another character later lets drop that Emily's husband, the equestrian sportsman they are discussing, jumps, "for the army." All these hints culminate in Gavin, a personage of undisclosed power and influence, declaring: "Now I believe one or two of our guests encountered traffic problems on their way here tonight. I apologize for that, but I would like to assure you that all such problems and all related problems will be resolved very soon. Between ourselves, we've had a bit of a round-up this evening" (36-37). Such euphemism is chilling.

These remarks are interspersed among snatches of conversation largely revolving around the benefits of a new leisure club. Comfort, luxury, fashion, and sex alternating with a dash of fascist morality reflect the wealthy and powerful "society of beautifully dressed people," of "elegance, style, grace, taste." Yet it would be hard to find such a collection of saloon bar pieties, obscenity, crassness, and vulgarity. All are embodied in Terry, friend of the great and arbiter of "real class" (21), who recounts of his wife, Dusty: "The only thing she doesn't like on boats is being fucked on boats" (17).

Three times in the course of the play a light "*burns into the room*" through a partly opened door. Finally, Dusty's brother Jimmy enters in spectral disarray, standing in the light of the doorway. In his closing speech Pinter attempts to find language and utterance for what is left of a person after torture and deprivation, when identity, consciousness, and the senses have been pulverized and only darkness is left: "The dark is in my mouth" (38), Jimmy says.

Party Time is a punning title of great relevance for the 1980s, in which the deregulation of the money markets in England meant great wealth and one long party for the

well placed few. In that decade champagne imports doubled, while it was discovered that in economically blighted areas of the country scavengers picked on rubbish heaps for a living. In reviews of the play Michael Billington, a leading critic and Pinter's forthcoming biographer, made the most incisive and just comment on the play: "a packed, swift indictment of blunted modern sensitivities . . . private relationships echo public brutality . . . an image of style-conscious, narcissistic, bourgeois society cut off from and culpably indifferent to the intolerance and squalor of the outside world."[22]

MOONLIGHT (1993)

The genesis of **Moonlight,** the first full-length work since **Betrayal,** is more unusual than Pinter's customary engendering creative process. The play was written intensively over the Christmas holiday period of 1992-93 and the third and final draft finished at the end of January. Pinter completed the work while immersed as actor, since October 1992, in a very successful revival of his own earlier play of 1974, **No Man's Land.** Pinter played Hirst, the alcoholic writer who has retreated into the representations and misrepresentations of delusive memory. As Pinter recorded: "When I was acting in **No Man's Land** every night, saying those words every night, and however nerve-racking an event acting is, it's also enjoyable if you get it right, I was stimulated by the act of saying these words and getting a few laughs. And one day while I was still acting at night, I started to scribble away and so something in me was released by saying all these damned words."[23]

Pinter has always maintained an absolute and objective distance from artistic creativity, as if writing involved an abnegation of self while the process takes place. Thus, he has always denied any omniscient superior knowledge of a play beyond what appears in the text itself, and characters take on a life of their own onstage—speech now theirs, no longer the author's. Paradoxically, Pinter acknowledged: "I have learned more about my own play by acting in it."[24] This position is perhaps not strange to modern audiences familiar with Pirandello's *Six Characters in Search of an Author* (1921). But, with Pinter returning to his play as an actor, there is a crucial difference from Pirandello. A group of characters are not seeking an author, but the playwright himself returns as a character and reenters his play of twenty years ago to find "pools within it that [he] hadn't known were there: as if the light hit it": "I just saw that image, I don't know why, of light hitting dark pools and illuminating those pools."[25] In returning to the 1970s— before the decade of his political involvement—with an actor's imaginative projection and immersion, Pinter found seven characters bathed in moonlight, waiting for their story to be told.

There is little action in **Moonlight.** Andy, a man in his fifties, lies in bed awaiting his death, with his wife, Bel, in attendance at his bedside. In another area of the stage two young men, Andy's estranged sons, Jake and Fred, develop endlessly prevaricating word games. Intermittently, in a third stage area there appears the wraithlike figure of a young girl, Bridget, the daughter, speaking lyrically of light and dark and the moon. On three occasions Maria and Ralph, old family friends of Andy and Bel, appear with stories of the past.

Pinter acknowledged: "Obviously as you're older you think about death more; you have it on your body; but there's so much death about," observing, "My mother died last year, she was 88." He was quick to add, "But I'm not at all sure the play comes from that fact," pointing out that he had in his possession notes from 1977: "I was writing the same thing . . . it was a man dying; a man saying, 'Where are they?'"[26] The date 1977 is significant, since that was the year his schooldays mentor and lifetime friend, Joseph Brearley his English master, died. Ten years after this death Pinter wrote a commemorative poem invoking the presence of his friend, revealingly: "You tall in moonlight." Darkness and light, moonlight and loss, separation and death, all reemerge in the creation of *Moonlight*.

David Leveaux's direction of *Moonlight* was his third of a Pinter play at the Almeida Theatre, London, following that of *Betrayal* (1991) and *No Man's Land* (1992). Common to all three productions was visual austerity—from the white of *Betrayal* to the gray of *No Man's Land* to the pallor of *Moonlight*. The small Almeida stage created a visually telling irony by necessarily having to place the beds of Andy and Fred side by side: physical closeness and yet an insurmountable emotional distance, a mode that recalls the memory plays. But then a greater irony still, whereas so many of Pinter's earliest characters had been threatened with dispossession by another person, here Andy awaits the final dispossession of all—of room, of memory, of speech, and of life itself—by the silence of death.

Although generally the play was very well received, audiences and critics had some difficulty in absorbing the play as a whole. After a long absence from the stage Ian Holm won a prestigious award for his portrayal of Andy. All critics seized on the unambiguous passion of grief and anger in Holm's flashes of rage, several quoting Dylan Thomas's "Do not go gentle into that good night / Rage, rage against the dying of the light." Pinter certainly does not provide the algebraic stepping stones of the well-made play, but on the other hand he does give what is the case with many playwrights—an evocative title. If the play is considered retroactively with this in mind, its formal coherence emerges.

In the middle of the play Bel suggests, "Death is your new horizon." Andy's reply is a major turning point in the play and is thus given extensively here:

> That may be. That may be. But the big question is, will I cross it as I die or after I'm dead? Or perhaps I won't cross it at all. Perhaps I'll just stay stuck in the middle of the horizon. In which case, can I see over it? Can I see to the other side? Or is the horizon endless? And what's the weather like? Is it uncertain with showers or

sunny with fogpatches? Or unceasing moonlight with no cloud? Or pitch black for ever and ever? You may say you haven't the faintest fucking idea and you would be right. But personally I don't believe it's going to be pitch black for ever because if it's pitch black for ever what would have been the point of going through all these enervating charades in the first place?

(46)

Bob Crowley, the designer, emphasized the crepuscular, throughout stressing gray, white, and black, so much so that the light fades themselves become an integral part of the play. Above all, Andy's bed/deathbed, with its silver-white covering, became a visual correlative to his state. This was taken one emphatic and revealing step further in the design for the advertising poster and the cover of the text. The poster featured the bed—empty—photographed from directly above, the canopy lit to appear silver, while on either side was blackness. A variant on this clear symbolism appeared on the book cover.

If death is a "pitch black" nothingness, as Andy ponders, then "unceasing moonlight with no cloud" precedes it as a final limbo of guilt-ridden consciousness, anticipated by the moonlit white of Andy's deathbed. This situation provides a context for the expressionist function of Bridget. She is the ghostlike projection of Andy's grief and guilt. In rehearsal, when David Leveaux asked whether Bridget was dead, Pinter replied, "That would seem to be the case."[27] Thus, as the play opens, the benign spirit of Bridget emerges in darkness: "There's no moon. It's so dark. . . . It's so dark" (1), while at the close she tells us of waiting, "I stood there in the moonlight" (80), separate from a house, which was "dark."

Bridget is the emotional core of the play. Her death is never discussed, but what she means to each of the characters through the circumstance of death—hers and Andy's—is the source of compromising pain. In contrast, the scene between Jake, Fred, and Bridget (29-33) might seem inconsequential and redundant. It is played in the "third area" of the stage, which is largely allocated to Bridget. Crucially, the printed text indicates that this is ten years ago; the boys are eighteen and seventeen, respectively, and Bridget is fourteen, just two years younger than her ghostlike appearance elsewhere in the play, since the dramatis personae gives her age as sixteen, presumably her age at death. The youthful scene simply depicts Bridget listening to music (forebodingly, Elton John's elegiac "Song for Guy" was chosen), while Fred pesters Jake to join him on a lift to a gig. Just enough is given to bring out that peculiar combination of devotion and dislike perhaps unique to siblings of both sexes. In short, the scene reminds us of the ordinariness of young people at home—all that Bridget's death destroyed. Later in the play, in the midst of mutually defensive charades, we suddenly find the following:

> FRED: Bridget would understand. I was her brother. She understood me. She always understood my feelings.
>
> JAKE: She understood me too.

Pause.

She understood me too.

Silence.

(53)

Earlier Andy, pugnaciously seeking an illicit drink, searches for a bottle in the third stage area, which now doubles as part of his house. As he drinks, the area reverts to the moonlit space for Bridget, who appears, still, in the background—of both the stage and of Andy's conscience, as he laments: "Ah darling. Ah my darling" (49). Joined by Bel in silence, they complete a mute tableau of three. Guilt, grief, and delusion have become so intermixed that Andy not only resurrects Bridget but also her unborn children. "Where is she?" Andy asks and evokes the fatherly memory of comforting her as she was falling asleep. Bel weakly remonstrates: "Please. Oh please." But after a pause Andy persists, "Is she bringing my grandchildren to see me?" as Bel "*sits frozen*" (45), while he rehearses his death and their loss. Toward the close Maria and Ralph enter, ten years after moving away, which was two years before the death of Bridget. Unknowingly, Maria recalls: "Your lovely little girl! Bridget! (*She laughs.*) Little girl! She must be a mother by now." To which Andy replies: "I've got three beautiful grandchildren (*To* BEL) Haven't I?" (71).

The "past is a mist" (20) for Andy because he cannot bring himself to confront whatever degree of responsibility, of either omission or commission, was his in Bridget's death, even at the point of his own demise. He protests, "I've never harmed a soul" (4), but his conscience belies the claim. Stories of Bel's lesbian affair with Maria in the past show that she is not beyond reproach, which is presumably the basis for Jake's "Don't talk dirty to me," when asked by Fred, "Tell me about your mother" (62). The sons' estrangement is as complete as their love must have been, since the whole of their time is spent in an obsessive parodic roll call of civil service figures—all proxies for the father they cannot name without mockery—culminating in the mock consolation for one "Silvio D'Orangerie." "I loved him like a father" (79), says Fred.

In following through these affective ramifications the serious emotional core of the play is revealed—but, of course, this is literary exposition, not the play that Harold Pinter wrote. These concerns are just part of the total experience of the play, much of which consists of hilarious foulmouthed exchanges from Andy, as part of the fascinating collocation of the class registers of English idiom ironically giving such vibrancy and life to the subject of death. Once again Pinter resists the conventional alliance of subject and sentiment, of death and pathos. Andy subverts the sentimental as he watches Bel embroider, querying: "Oh, I've been meaning to ask you, What are you making there? A winding sheet? Are you going to wrap me up in it when I conk out? You'd better get a move on. I'm going fast" (34).

Unsympathetic critics once again saw Pinter as repeating himself, whereas it can be said that, in the peculiar

psychology that lies beneath the creation of *Moonlight,* Pinter returned to his imaginative roots and did indeed compose a work that offers something of a retrospective. Menace, as we have seen, teams up with the intruder death. The whole play could be said to be about the evasion of communication concerning Bridget. Even in death and at a distance, Andy exercises power over his sons. Memory reacts once more as the past jostles with the present. Again, the theatrical vies with realism, seriousness with laughter.

Furthermore, actual dramatic contexts are evoked constantly. The bond of isolated brotherhood, seen here between Jake and Fred, recalls that of Mick and Aston in *The Caretaker.* Andy's vulgar power in travestying the family is occasionally close to Max in *The Homecoming.* Such emotional distance between husband and wife recalls *Landscape.* The two women-one male triangle of the past, and mutual betrayal, is like a combination of *Old Times* and *Betrayal.* Andy is no Hirst, but there is something about that moonlit canopy which relates it to *No Man's Land.* Pinter's delight in rococo character and language almost throughout recalls the stylized extremes of *Family Voices.* Finally, in the bed and bedside attendant we have something of a reverse of *A Kind of Alaska.* Yet, for all this, *Moonlight* adds to Pinter's oeuvre significantly. Nowhere else is found such expression as Andy's grief and rage—not in Hirst and not in Deeley. And *finally* is most certainly the wrong word. Pinter—vituperative, passionate, and committed—remains avidly engaged with whatever the work in hand is, be it acting, directing, writing screenplays or drama, or taking part in political activity.

Pinter changed the nature of theater experience because he intuitively grasped that the conventional representation of the individual and society on the stage was no longer a reflection of what humanity had become in the course of the twentieth century. The positivist enthronement of universal human nature, an essentialist humanism, was displaced by the less palatable truths of humanity as limited and contingent. The moral assurances of the literature of tragedy, heroism, and romance were no longer tenable for Pinter, and neither was the security of human beings in a metaphysically contained universe. In Pinter's theater humanity is stripped to the barest speech in the barest silence, against which laughter resonates uneasily.

As an individual, Harold Pinter has made a major contribution to British cultural life in the second half of the twentieth century. But he has never allowed success to soften his responses to life around him. Rigorous, challenging, and radical, his work always insists on the examination of self and society. A Socratic gadfly on the body politic—long may he remain so. A recent tribute by Pinter's contemporary, the playwright John McGrath, provides a fitting conclusion: "We ought to be glad that we've got Harold Pinter because he handles words, he believes in words and the power of words in the theater, and he has the ability to make them work."[28] Where there is comedy and there is truth, they combine to make an art that is, as Pinter once put it, "a kind of celebration."[29]

Notes

1. The factual details which follow are taken from a fuller article by the author, "Harold Pinter, Citizen," *The Pinter Review* (1989).

2. "Radical Departures," *The Listener* 120, no. 3086 (27 October 1988), 6.

3. In Michael Scott, ed., *Harold Pinter: "The Birthday Party," "The Caretaker," and "The Homecoming,"* (London: Macmillan, 1986).

4. "Radical Departures," 6, and "A Play and Its Politics. A Conversation between Harold Pinter and Nicholas Hern," preface to *One for the Road* (London: Methuen, 1984), 8.

5. "Harold Pinter Plays and Politics," BBC 2, *Saturday Review,* 28 September 1985. See Knowles, "Harold Pinter, Citizen."

6. "Radical Departures," 6.

7. "A Play and Its Politics," 12.

8. Channel Four 7 o'clock News, 9 January 1984.

9. *The Independent,* 2 November 1988, 13.

10. "Radical Departures," 4.

11. *The Guardian,* 5 December 1987, 10

12. *The Guardian,* 22 October 1988, 9.

13. "A Play and Its Politics," 21.

14. "The New Light that burns within Harold Pinter," Bryan Appleyard (an interview with Pinter), *The Times,* 16 March 1984, 13.

15. "Radical Departures," 6.

16. *Ibid.*

17. By Terry Eagleton in a review of *Party Time, Times Literary Supplement,* 15 November 1991, 20.

18. "A Play and Its Politics," 11.

19. See Knowles, "Names and Naming in the Plays of Harold Pinter," in *Harold Pinter: You Never Heard Such Silence,* edited by Alan Bold (London and Totowa, N.J.: Vision Press, Barnes and Noble, 1985).

20. "The 22 from Hackney to Chelsea," 14.

21. Typescript courtesy of Harold Pinter.

22. *The Guardian,* 7 November 1991, 32.

23. "HP Source," *Time Out,* 15-22 September 1993, 19.

24. *The Observer,* 14 February 1993, 22.

25. "Harold's New Baby," *The Guardian,* 3 February 1993, 3.

26. "HP Source," 19.

27. "Angry Old Man of the Theater," *The Observer,* 12 September 1993, 9.

28. *The Late Show,* BBC 2, 7 November 1991.

29. "Writing for the Theatre," *Plays One* (London: Faber, 1991), xiv.

Ronald Knowles (essay date 1996)

SOURCE: "*A Kind of Alaska*: Pinter and Pygmalion," in *Classical and Modern Literature,* Vol. 16, No. 3, Spring, 1996, pp. 231-40.

[In the following essay, Knowles explores Pinter's use of the Pygmalion-Galatea myth as a theme in several of his plays.]

The printed text of **A Kind of Alaska**[1] is preceded by a note indicating the source for the play, Dr. Oliver Sacks's book *Awakenings,* published in 1973. *Awakenings* records case histories of sufferers of sleeping sickness, *encephalitis lethargica,* who were treated with the drug L-DOPA which brought them back to life after decades in a trance-like limbo. Pinter took some details from the case of "Rose R."[2]

"Rose R" was a New Yorker, born in 1905, who lived an adventurous partying life until the age of twenty-one when in 1926 she was struck down by what Dr. Sacks describes as a "virulent form"[3] of the disease. For forty-three years "Rose R" remained in her kind of Alaska until L-DOPA made a partial recovery possible. In fact Pinter took very little from Sacks's account. "Rose R" in the early stages of recovery declared "I love you, Dr. Sacks, I love you, I love you."[4] Her speech was often very salacious and she developed a physical tic of flicking her right hand across her chin. More significant is that, on awakening, though now in later middle age, Rose was still immersed in the world of 1926.

In **A Kind of Alaska** Deborah is a London girl who succumbed to the sleeping sickness aged sixteen. On coming to consciousness, at one point she says to her physician Dr. Hornby, "I think I love you" (20). Occasionally her language has teenage crudity. At a later stage Deborah appears to be going into remission as she begins compulsively flicking her fingers across her face (37-38). Again, on awakening it becomes apparent that Deborah's mind is still confined to the local London world of twenty-nine years ago. Apart from these details the rest of the play comes from Pinter's imagination. Bernard Dukore has drawn attention to thematic antecedents of **A Kind of Alaska** in Pinter's work but there is a further detail in the account of "Rose R" which suggests an alternative way of situating the play within the oeuvre.[5] Victims of sleeping sickness often had premonitory dreams, and Rose "dreamed that she had become a living, sentient statue of stone."[6] The relationship of Hornby to Deborah and Pinter to his play may be reconsidered in terms of the enduring myth of Pygmalion.

The story of Pygmalion existed before Ovid's defining portrayal in book ten of the *Metamorphoses* and the fable has since undergone varied hermeneutic and representational metamorphoses from *Ovide moralisé* to J. Hillis Miller, in poetry, painting, drama, and aesthetics.[7]

Ovid's story of Pygmalion is amongst the most well-known of the *Metamorphoses*.[8] In revulsion at the Propoetides, the first prostitutes, Pygmalion chose to live a celibate life. He falls in love with the statue of a beautiful girl he has made. His caresses and kisses, following his adoring gaze, treat ivory as a live human body. Pygmalion pays court to the statue with presents and clothes eventually installing it in his bed. At the festival of Venus he prays for a wife like the ivory girl. The goddess responds, recognizing his real love, and the statue is transformed, becoming warm and human as he kisses her. She, in return, now gazes upon her lover. Venus presides over their marriage, and from their union comes a child Paphos whose name is given to the island.

The story of Pygmalion is commonly considered in terms of the artist outdoing nature, a parable of the supremacy of art. But this was not always so. Early church fathers condemned Pygmalion for perversity. Shakespeare's redemptive version in *A Winter's Tale* is rather exceptional since at that time Pygmalion's statue signified whoredom.[9] The fourteenth-century *Ovide moralisé* christianises the story as an allegory of the relationship between God and his creation of humanity. Secondly, this medieval French poem anticipates Frank Wedekind's *Earth Spirit* (1895), no less, with another story of Pygmalion as lordly householder who dignifies an uncouth but beautiful serving maid, grooming her to become his wife.[10] The idealist view of the perfection of art was vigorously attacked by Georg Büchner in *Dantons Tod* (1835). In act two, scene three, Camille lambasts the escapist puppetry of high art theatre which turns its back on the reality of everyday life. Büchner contradicts an element of Ovid's myth by ascribing sterility to such art with the charge: "The Greeks knew what they were talking about when they said that Pygmalion's statue came to life but bore no children."[11] Büchner was in revolt against the neoclassical idealism of such figures as Lessing and Winckelmann.[12]

In his *Pygmalion* (1770) Jean-Jacques Rousseau gave a name to the statue—Galatea.[13] In the nineteenth century Galatea took on a new lease of life with a post-Gothic affinity to tales of Frankenstein's monster and the Golem: she turned against or away from her creator-lover-husband. In such works as Hazlitt's prose, the Rossettis' poetry, in W.S. Gilbert's *Pygmalion and Galatea* (1871) and George Bernard Shaw's *Pygmalion* (1912) human psychology supervenes in a word also bequeathed to us by the ancient world—narcissism. Mystical interpretations of Pygmalion and Galatea as a compound of religion, love, and art persisted in paintings such as Burne-Jones's *Pygmalion and the Image* series but not without this psychological dimension. As a theoretical development from this subjective view two contemporary scholars, the classicist John

Elsner and the literary critic J. Hillis Miller, independently reinterpret the Pygmalion myth in a complementary way.

Seeing himself as "The New Pygmalion" Hazlitt elevated his lowerclass lover, Sarah Walker, into a Galatea in his *Liber Amoris* (1823). As a "mirror image of his desire"[14] Hazlitt reflects his own narcissism in the idealised image he has created. Martin A. Danahay compares Dante Gabriel Rossetti's poem *The Mirror* and comments:

> The nineteenth-century twist on the Pygmalion myth . . . is the way in which the woman as mirror image of the male viewer refuses to conform to his desire. . . . Both *Liber Amoris* and "The Mirror" depict a situation in which the masculine subject's search for a complementary self-image has been thwarted by the woman's refusal to reflect accurately the artist's self-image.[15]

Christina Rossetti's poem *In an Artist's Studio* in part reads as a comment on her brother's paintings as a kind of Pygmalion obsession:

> , every canvass means
> 　The same one meaning, neither more nor less.
> He feeds upon her face by day and night,
> 　　　. . . . .
> Not as she is, but as she fills his dream.
>
> 　　　　　　　　　　　　(7-9, 14)[16]

Ironically, Dante Gabriel Rossetti's complementary poem *The Portrait* suggests that what he gazes on is the painting as mirror reflecting the artist himself:

> This is her picture as she was:
> 　It seems a thing to wonder on,
> As though mine image in the glass
> 　Should tarry when myself am gone.
>
> 　　　　　　　　　　　　(1-4)[17]

The implied recalcitrance of the image to adequately mirror its creator is developed comically by G. B. Shaw and tragically by Frank Wedekind. As Shaw noted of Eliza Doolittle in his prose conclusion, "Galatea never does quite like Pygmalion: his relation to her is too godlike to be altogether agreeable."[18] Wedekind's Lulu, on the other hand, can be related to the destructive femme-fatale figures from Rossetti's Lilith to Maeterlinck's Melisande, for she finally destroys her Pygmalion "creator" Dr. Schön. Analysing the Pygmalion theme in *Earth Spirit*, Edward P. Harris observes that his interpretation "rests upon the associative connections with the unconscious constellation of effects of the fable" and "transposition of motifs . . . inversion, duplication, the splitting of one figure into other manifestations."[19] This is precisely the case in an analysis of Pinter's dramas in relation to the hermeneutics of the historical mutations of Ovid's myth. In *Earth Spirit* Wedekind included a parody of the Pygmalion fable with the inclusion of Schwarz, the venal and lubricious painter of Lulu chasing her round his studio. In the drama of another sculptor and another beautiful statue, Luigi Pirandello reapplied the Pygmalion myth in *Diana and Tuda* (1927) in which the dichotomy between art and life finds a tragic outcome. Tuda is the beautiful model for the statue of Diana sculpted by Sirio Dossi who believes in the consummate achievement of ideal art and thus intends suicide on completion of his work. The vibrant Tuda comes to believe that indeed the statue will immortalize her beauty and that Sirio should absorb her life-energy into his art. As she embraces the statue, another sculptor Giuncarlo, a rival in love and art, kills Sirio, and Tuda is left to "nothingness." As we shall see, Pinter is drawn to the analogue of art and artists in varying forms throughout his work. A. R. Sharrock interprets the myth of Pygmalion as a paradigm of "woman perceived is woman as art-object."[20] John Elsner takes this a crucial step further. Pointing out how little of Ovid's story is devoted to the sculpting of Galatea, and how much is given to Pygmalion as viewer, he writes:

> This suggests that Ovid's focus is not on the myth of the creative artist as such (as critics have invariably assumed), but on the role of Pygmalion as author of his own love, creator of his own desire. In other words, Ovid's picture of Pygmalion as artist-sculptor is itself a metaphor for Pygmalion as artist-viewer. . . . This theme of Pygmalion as viewer is itself a metaphor for the reader as creator of his own narrative, his own reality, out of the text of the *Metamorphoses*.

This statement appeared in 1991 in a double article by Elsner and Alison Sharrock entitled "Re-viewing Pygmalion."[21] Presumably this went to press before either could consider J. Hillis Miller's *Versions of Pygmalion*[22] which sees in the Pygmalion myth an ur-trope underlying all culture. In principle Miller extends Elsner's point to all literature. Put simply, for Miller writers, readers, narrators, and critics are all Pygmalions in that they share in the fundamental personification that takes place in literary creation and re-creation. Miller's examples are primarily taken from nineteenth-century fiction, but his approach is even more compelling for drama, and Pinter's drama in particular.

To return to the beginning and recapitulate: the distinguishing features in Ovid's story and the shifts in interpretation I wish to stress are prostitution, the artist constructing the female, eroticism and narcissism, gazing upon the beloved, and Galatea turning against her creator-master-lover. Complementary to these in Pinter's plays, either read or in performance, are the playwright's constructing character and play paralleled by the interior analogue and internalized construction of a surrogate artist. In performance this is duplicated by the auditor struggling towards a rounded understanding of what is taking place: as Pinter does not offer the "Well Made Play" the auditor has to discern the shape of meaning. This dialectically complements what is happening on stage in the duplication of the gaze—in characters and auditors—all gazing upon the same object whose own gaze back resists responding.

In 1990, honouring Pinter's sixtieth birthday the BBC devoted a whole evening of Radio Three to his work including a production of *A Kind of Alaska* in which the dramatist himself took the part of Dr. Hornby. A whole new metaphorical perspective arose here in the complex of Pinter as artist, Pinter as actor, actor as character, Dr. Hornby, and finally Hornby as interior analogue of the artist. Further, Pinter does not regard his characters as fictions he has created but, in Pirandellian fashion, as existences having an independent life: "They observe you, their writer, warily," he once said.[23] Thus Pinter as Hornby observing the comatose Deborah became an allegory of Pinter attending the impulses of creative imagination, awaiting the engendering process which brings new life. The Pygmalion parallel is further duplicated by directors who have to breathe life into the page to embody performance on stage. Further, the condition of Deborah-Galatea symbolizes so much of Pinter's particular preoccupation with a kind of humanity: the alienated individual isolated in space and time struggling with fragments of memory.

A Kind of Alaska as Pinter's Pygmalion makes manifest what had been developing throughout his dramatic writing. The second half of this essay will examine *Alaska* and then look back to show the development of the myth as metaphoric palimpsest, bearing in mind those "transportations of motifs . . . inversion, duplication, the splitting of one figure into other manifestation."

Galatea's beauty derives from consummate art. Awakening into life her spontaneous love is virginal and innocent, in contrast to the prostitute Propoetides who eventually turned to stone. Struck by sleeping sickness Deborah was "Like . . . marble" (30) in contrast to her father's rumoured mistress and the prostitution of the white-slave traffic she recalls later. Dr. Hornby, like Dr. Schön in *Earth Spirit,* was a friend of the young girl and the family. For twenty-nine years Hornby has gazed upon Deborah, Like Pygmalion his life is celibate, having seemingly ceased relationships with his wife Pauline, Deborah's sister.

> Your sister Pauline was twelve when you were left for dead. When she was twenty I married her. She is a widow. I have lived with you.
>
> (35)

Hornby's feelings are never explicitly stated but they are implicitly suggested by the *Silences* in the following sequence:

> I have never let you go.
>
> *Silence*
>
> I have never let you go.
>
> *Silence*
>
> I have lived with you.
>
> (34)

Pygmalion falls in love with a statue he has made and is rewarded with love when the statue becomes human. Hornby has devoted most of his life to Deborah, nourished her, exercised her, cared for her. Devotion and self-sacrifice foster the image of a reciprocated love. Oliver Sacks noted of "Rose R" that although in her sixties she looked half her age.[24] Hornby confirms Deborah's beauty, and she suggests the comparison with Prince Charming and the Sleeping Beauty (19). The professional and personal have merged in Hornby's life. Throughout twenty-nine years desire and longing have been projected onto the sleeping figure as Hornby has created her as the object of his devotion. At least this seems to be the case as the director-auditor-reader enacts that enabling prosopopeia by which we construct motive, cause, and effect. In the same way, Hornby has to construct Deborah as something more than a sick comatose body.

The forty-five-year-old Deborah awakes as the sixteen-year old she was. She cannot fulfil Hornby's imagination and emotions. Every word she utters is full of the implacable otherness of youth, gender, and history. Like the nineteenth-century Pygmalions mentioned above, Hornby had inscribed himself upon her, "Not as she is, but as she fills his dream."

In *The Room* (1957), *The Birthday Party* (1958), and *A Night Out* (1960) Pygmalion is seemingly reversed as the female apparently constructs the male, but in each case it is finally patriarchy which constructs the female. In *The Room* Bert is passive and statuesque as Rose projects upon him "his" feelings, wants, and desires. Yet the audience becomes aware that it is she who acts on his silent behalf and is reclaimed by patriarchy and offered a new identity as "Sal." *The Birthday Party* introduces the figure of the artist in Stanley as pianist. Celibate and in flight from the world Stanley's "statue" is himself as the international concert pianist he fantasises upon. But Meg reconstructs him as a pre-pubescent little boy, with the gift of a drum. Again Goldberg and McCann refashion him as the mute image of patriarchal conformity: "We'll make a man of you," "And a woman" (83),[25] they say. Albert's mother in *A Night Out* unwittingly acts as the agent of Pygmalion-patriarchy by insisting that Albert model himself on his virtuous dead father—"Are you leading a clean life?" (47). The virginal Albert's frustrated revenge is to bully a prostitute under the pretence of being an assistant film director, an artist manqué. Pygmalion's retreat from the Propoetides is really a retreat from his own pornographic desire which is sublimated in Galatea. Albert rages against the prostitute before returning to enforced celibacy and his mother's "love."

In *Night School* the Pygmalion-Galatea theme begins to take shape as the celibate ex-convict Wally returns from prison to find a beautiful young schoolteacher installed in his bed like a realised fantasy. Walter is an artist-forger of post-office books. His imagination becomes divided between Galatea and the Propoetides, between purity and pornography, between Sally as innocent schoolteacher and Sally as the nightclub "hostess" he discovers in a photo. Wally finally declares the photo a "fake" and another of Sally as games mistress is discovered.

Ruth in *The Homecoming* relates that she had been "a photographic model for the body" (57). On returning to the East London home of Teddy's family, as respectable wife she combines Galatea and the Propoetides. In flight from the "filth" (55) of his East End neighbourhood and the association of his mother with prostitution, Teddy had taken Ruth to the cleanliness of the United States where as the Pygmalion figure of the learned Doctor of Philosophy he had remodelled her new life free from the suspect slur of her modelling past. Teddy's family wish to return Ruth to prostitution. Some productions draw on Ruth as a former model to direct the actress's self-conscious movements particularly at those intense moments when she makes herself become the object of the male gaze (e.g., "Look at me. I . . . move my leg" [52]). Like the nineteenth-century Galateas Ruth refuses to become a mirror for her Pygmalion who is effectively rejected. Teddy had wished her to go back to her male-ordered role as mother, wife, and helpmeet, back to his narcissistic image—"You can help me with my lectures when we get back" (55), But Ruth chooses to stay on, statuesquely taking her place centre stage, enacting a composite role which a patriarchal society has created yet can only accept as divided and polarised into pornographic desire and puritanical revulsion; fear, loathing, and adoration.

The dramaturgy of *Landscape* combines Galatea and Pygmalion as one in the figure of Beth. Visibly before us on stage Beth's posture and speech make her seem remote. Physically she becomes like a statue, particularly at the close, as in narratives like W. S. Gilbert's comic version, where Galatea returns to sculpture. Verbally, as artist Beth makes herself a figure in a landscape of memory. Duff is not directly associated with prostitutes, but he is with excremental filth, sexual betrayal, and sexual crudity. Beth's memory recreates ideal love, gentleness, and delicacy. All experience is aestheticized as she rejects the external world and worships at the altar of her own imagination, "I am beautiful" (10). As Pygmalion's love for the beautiful statue expressed itself in touch, so Beth transfers her sensitivity to her recreated lover who "touched the back of my neck. His fingers, lightly, touching, lightly touching, the back, of my neck" (13).

"I touched her profoundly all over" (31) are the words used about another poised figure who rejects Pygmalion: Kate in *Old Times*. Deeley, her husband, is a film director whose artistic business is framing the female image for, to use Laura Mulvey's word, the "scopophilic" gaze.[26] Framed against a window at the rear of the stage, her back to the audience, is Anna, Kate's old friend visiting after twenty years. This image recalls the tradition of painting, domestic yet mysterious, in such works as Caspar David Friedrich's *Woman at the Window*.[27] Anna's pose anticipates the way in which the audience is later encouraged by both herself and Deeley to gaze upon Kate as a beautiful but inert object—"You talk of me as if I were dead," Kate says (34). Ironically it is their symbolic interment which Kate rehearses later. Living in a converted farmhouse on the coast Deeley has turned his back on the "prostitutes of all kinds" (42) in his professional world. Deeley had found Kate "a classic female figure" with "classic female posture" lacking in "understanding" (36) and thus "compliant" (35) to the male remoulding of body and mind. His sexual experience has shaped the beautiful but innocent Kate—"he thought I had profited from his teaching" (73)—who is now kept protectively like an object in a gallery.

Anna's visit makes apparent that, it is hinted, as a lesbian Pygmalion she had shaped Kate in her own artistic image aestheticizing their relationship with poetry, ballet, concerts, film, and painting. Thus between them Anna and Deeley split the Pygmalion sequence of art to eroticism, adoration to desire. Kate's Galatea-like turning away from Anna in part takes the form of a comic rejection of art, "I was interested once in the arts, but I can't remember now which ones they were" (37). Anna and Deeley vie with each other in seeing Kate as a preraphaelite "dreamer," "floating" (23-24). Deeley attempts to subvert Anna's adoring gaze with his own pornographic gazing at black stockings and white thighs (51-52), but Anna's retaliation sees Kate as a kind of etherial nude Aphrodite "float[ing] from the bath" (54).[28] Both discuss her not as a person but as an object, "Doesn't she look beautiful" (59). However, Kate's disaffection is signalled long before the final rejection in the way in which, like Beth, her self-sufficiency is indicated by her making herself a figure in a landscape (20, 24).

Robert Newton in *Odd Man Out* brought them together Deeley claims (*Old Times*, 29-30). Ironically, in F. L. Green's novel of 1945 the demonically driven character Newton plays, Lukey (possibly recalled by "Luke" in *Old Times*? [49]), is a painter. In the film he insists on painting the fugitive IRA gunman Johnny, in order to reveal the wounded and dying man's soul, a curious anticipation of Pinter's favourite painter's [Francis Bacon's][29] studying and painting wounds and beaten figures. In the novel Lukey feels that his painting has failed but that nevertheless he has discovered something within himself—a dialectical internalisation of the narcissism within the Pygmalion myth.[30] Kate's speech reflects both Deeley's and Anna's at different times, but in her rejection as she finally stares out at the audience, she freezes into Galatean otherness.

Whatever that otherness is we cannot know as we can't with any Pinter character. The reader as Pygmalion engaging in prosopopeia has equally as much to "read" as "misread" in J. Hillis Miller's deconstructive terms. The epistemological and ontological distance between Pygmalion and Galatea is realized at its extreme in *A Kind of Alaska,* as we have seen. Re-examining Pinter's work in this way, as a coherently developing oeuvre, it becomes clear that the familiar power-subservience theme is particularly built into the myth. Furthermore, Pinter's portrayal can be seen as a descendent of nineteenth-century artists' disquiet at the emergence of the rebellious New Woman, while currently, with the preeminence of gender studies, it can clearly be seen that the Pygmalion myth has metamorphosed into a version of patriarchy.

Notes

1. Harold Pinter, *A Kind of Alaska* is printed with *Family Voices* and *Victoria Station* under the title *Other Places* (London: Methuen, 1982).

2. Oliver Sacks, *Awakenings,* rev. ed. (London: Pan Bks, 1982), 67-79; originally published London: Duckworth, 1973.

3. Ibid., 67.

4. Ibid., 73.

5. Bernard Dukore, "Alaskan Perspectives," in Alan Bold, ed., *Harold Pinter: You Never Heard Such Silence* (Totowa, N.J.: B&N, 1984), 166-178.

6. Sacks (above, note 2) 68.

7. As an introduction to a voluminous literature see Jane M. Miller, "Some Versions of Pygmalion," in *Ovid Renewed: Ovidian Influences on Literature and Art from the Middle Ages to the Twentieth Century,* ed. Charles Martindale (Cambridge: Cambridge U Pr, 1988), 205-214.

8. Ovid, *Met,* 10, 243-297.

9. See Barbara Roche Rico, "From 'Speechless Dialect' to 'Prosperous Art': Shakespeare's Recasting of the Pygmalion Image," *Huntington Library Quarterly* 48 (1985): 285-295.

10. See Edward P. Harris, "The Liberation of Flesh from Stone: Pygmalion in Frank Wedekind's *Erdgeist,*" *Germanic Review* 52 (1977): 44-56.

11. *Georg Büchner: Sämtliche Werke und Briefe* (Hamburg: Christian Wegner, 1967), 1: 37. For a convenient translation, see *The Plays of Georg Büchner,* trans. Victor Price (Oxford: Oxford U Pr, 1971), 33.

12. See M. B. Benn, "Anti-Pygmalion: An Apologia for Georg Büchner's Aesthetics," *Modern Language Review* 64 (1969): 597-604.

13. See J. L. Carr, "Pygmalion and the Philosophes," *Journal of the Warburg and Courtauld Institutes* 23 (1960): 242.

14. J. Hillis Miller, *Versions of Pygmalion* (Cambridge: Harvard U Pr, 1990), 4. The quote is from Miller's description of Ovid's account of the Pygmalion story.

15. Martin A. Danahay, "Mirrors of Masculine Desire: Narcissus and Pygmalion in Victorian Representation," *Victorian Poetry* 32 (1994): 35-53; 37-38. For most of the above Victorian references I am indebted to this essay. For a specific parallel study of Browning, see Catherine Maxwell, "Browning's Pygmalion and the Revenge of Galatea," *English Literary History* 60 (1993): 989-1013.

16. *The Complete Poems of Christina Rossetti,* ed. R. W. Crump (Baton Rouge: La State U Pr, 1990), 3: 264.

17. *The Poetical Works of Dante Gabriel Rossetti* (Boston: Little, 1906), 1: 128.

18. *The Complete Plays of Bernard Shaw* (London: Odhams Pr, 1934), 757.

19. Harris (above, note 10) 48.

20. A. R. Sharrock, "Womanufacture," *Journal of Roman Studies* 81 (1991): 36.

21. John Elsner and Alison Sharrock, "Re-viewing Pygmalion," *Ramus* 20 (1991): 149-182. Pages 149-153 introduces the Ovid with Latin text and translation by Alison Sharrock; "Visual Mimesis and the Myth of the Real: Ovid's Pygmalion as Viewer," by John Elsner, 154-168 (my quotation is on 159); A. R. Sharrock, "The Love of Creation," 169-182.

22. Miller (above, note 14).

23. "Harold Pinter: Speech, Hamburg 1970," *Theatre Quarterly* 1 (1971): 4.

24. Sacks (above, note 2) 69.

25. Page references in the text are to the following Methuen, London, editions: *The Birthday Party* (1965); *A Night Out,* in *A Slight Ache and Other Plays* (1968); *The Homecoming* (1965); *Landscape and Silence* (1969); *Old Times* (1971).

26. Laura Mulvey, "Visual Pleasure and Narrative Cinema," in *Feminism and Film Theory,* ed. Constance Penley (New York: Routledge, 1988), 57-68.

27. Nationalgalerie, Berlin. See William Vaughan, *German Romantic Painting* (New Haven: Yale U Pr, 1980), 100, plate 16.

28. The October 1991 BBC2 TV production of *Old Times* stressed the painterly aspect here with Kate's nudity "framed" by the open doorway of the bathroom and the interior lighting. See Ronald Knowles, "From London: Harold Pinter 1991," *Pinter Review* (1991); 67-69.

29. Steven H. Gale, *Butter's Going Up: A Critical Analysis of Harold Pinter's Work* (Durham, N.C.: Duke, 1977), 15.

30. F. L. Green, *Odd Man Out* (London: Michael Joseph, 1945), 209.

THE ROOM AND *THE DUMB WAITER*

PRODUCTION REVIEW

A. Alvarez (essay date 1960)

SOURCE: "Wanted—A Language," in *New Statesman,* Vol. 59, January 30, 1960, pp. 149-50.

[*In the following review, Alvarez states that* The Room *and* The Dumb Waiter *are about the "impossibility of communication."*]

Harold Pinter is . . . a playwright without a language, b deliberately so. Both **The Room** and **The Dumb Wait** (Hampstead Theatre Club) are about the impossibility communication. In **The Room** a married couple sit cosi together over their evening meal; the wife is having lively conversation, cajoling, complaining, encouragin sympathising and politely answering; and all the time h husband is silent as stone. All through the play peop come and go without ever properly meeting or understan ing each other. The only person who can get anythi across to the wife is a blind Negro intruder; her husba kills him. It is much the same in **The Dumb Waiter:** tv odd little cockney killers try to pass the time while waitin to do a job (in Pinter's plays, everyone is always obse sively asking the time). And gradually the killers the selves are victimised by inconsequentiality. The blankne through which they hopelessly peer is so total that, mu of the time, it is extremely funny. But out of this nothin ness, these queer silences and comic misunderstanding Pinter generates terror. As in a dream, the logical unreas leads to violence and horror.

In a way it is the reverse of O'Neill; Pinter seems to wri out of an obsession with the murderous size and indiffe ence of mass society. So it is an achievement despi language, something that happens in the silences betwee the lines. As such it demands a great deal of the actors ar director; they need resources of silent implication tha luckily, Vivien Merchant, Nicholas Selby and Georg Tovey can provide, though the author's direction of *Th* **Room** was far too slow-paced. At the moment, Pint seems less concerned with imaginative statements tha with an unchanging state of mind, a kind of artist hypnosis like the rhythm of *Hiawatha*. It will be interes ing to see if anything less specialised will come out of it

---

THE BIRTHDAY PARTY

PRODUCTION REVIEWS

T. C. Worsley (essay date 1958)

SOURCE: "A Dramatist, or Two," in *New Statesman,* Vo 55, May 31, 1958, pp. 692, 694.

[*In the following review, Worsley describes Pinter as a off-beat playwright of considerable promise.*]

A new play by a new playwright, **The Birthday Party,** the Lyric, Hammersmith, invited us to peer between th lines of the seedier reports of the *News of the World.* In run-down boarding house in some windy seaside tow Meg and Petey crumble inarticulately together. Petey i the man who sets out the chairs on the front, and then gloomily collects your threepence. Meg, like a character out of a John Bratby painting, feeds him on a diet of corn-flakes—when she remembers to buy any. In the last two years there has been one 'guest' and he has become a 'permanent', a fat, pudgy, short-sighted young man, Stanley—not so young now either, a little backward evidently, but Meg has made him her spoiled boy, and her meagre life is brightened by the indulgence she lavishes on him.

The first act which establishes this situation is wryly, sadly, rather terribly, funny, making play in the very latest contemporary manner with the pathos of clichés softly and repetitiously reiterated, over and over. It reveals the author, Mr Harold Pinter, as an off-beat comic writer of very considerable promise, and the whole odd maddeningly elusive play is shot through with quality. But like so many writers who are 'young' and 'promising', Mr Pinter is unable to resist the temptation to fly off into the symbolic. What a pity it is that German is not better known among young writers—they might learn by innumerable examples from that literature how fatal that temptation is! And what a pity that *Waiting for Godot* was so successful that others think they can repeat the unrepeatable (when even Mr Beckett can't!).

Two mysterious, inexplicable strangers, Goldberg and Mc-Cann, a slick Jew and a renegade Irish priest and/or gun-man, arrive to persecute the pudgy Stanley. They are Death or Doom or Conscience or Something or Other. They organise a party for Stan and drive him to a murderous breakdown and then carry him off in a very large car with a very large back part, that we must suppose to be a hearse. We do not know exactly, and by this time we do not frankly much care. The Symbols have broken up the party in every sense and an arrestingly comic beginning has become a fashionable mess.

A highly talented cast under Mr Peter Wood, who so brilliantly directed *The Iceman,* play the piece with an assurance and finesse which convinces us that they and he understand it, and almost persuade us that we should. Miss Beatrix Lehmann has a wonderful way of getting for her awful croaking, angular moron sympathy as well as laughs. Twitching, twining, preening, with sudden dips into terror and sudden hops into elation, she is the thing itself, unaccommodated, slatternly housewife. Mr Richard Pearson, all blubber and spite, is the nasty child experiencing its first dose of love late in life and dangerously uncertain, now grasping and now rejecting. Mr John Slater gives edge and assertion to his unexplained Jew, Mr John Stratton a sinister sliminess to his gunman jackal, and Mr Willoughby Gray is tenderly real as the chair man. Mr Peter Wood does a very great deal to keep this collection of oddities within the bounds of the credible. This was a play which deserved an Arts theatre audience, who are prepared to indulge a young author in the belief that they are sitting in at the birth pangs of an undiscovered talent. The gamble with Mr Pinter would be a good one.

Henry Hewes (essay date 1961)

SOURCE: "The Frisco Kids," in *Saturday Review,* Vol. 44, No. 34, August 26, 1961, p. 26.

[*In the following review, Hewes commends the San Francisco Actor's Workshop for maintaining a roster of quality offerings, and praises its production of* The Birthday Party.]

What happens to most idealistic young artists who attempt to set up theatres around the United States is that they begin by producing Yeats's *A Full Moon* in March and end up by finding themselves obliged to present F. Hugh Herbert's *The Moon is Blue.* It is therefore a heartening surprise to discover that the San Francisco Actor's Workshop, now in its tenth year of operation, is offering a repertory of plays by Genet, Beckett, O'Neill, Albee, Shakespeare, Shaw, and Pinter. Particularly surprising is the last named, for Harold Pinter is a new English playwright not generally known elsewhere in this country. His first full-length play, which the Actor's Workshop alertly acquired before Broadway started to become interested, is called **The Birthday Party** and is the product of several discernible influences. Its protagonist, a John Osborne cadhero named Stanley, is a sensitive young pianist who finds an apathetic and conformist England pushing him into an intolerable existence. The play begins with a hilarious sketch of British domesticity that reminds one of Ionesco, but reveals an ear for dialogue and a sensitivity to speech rhythm that are closer to Gertrude Stein. Then it moves into something like a Kafka nightmare as two mysterious and threatening boarders named Goldberg and McCann move in. And a wonderful scene in which Stanley receives the shock treatment of a birthday party owes something to Eliot's "Sweeney Agonistes."

The production here is exciting, expert, and full of intelligence. It reveals a company of actors professional in their discipline and their craft but amateur in their spirit and obvious pleasure of participating in art rather than merely supplying it on demand. Most impressive in the company is Robert Symonds, who plays Goldberg. Mr. Symonds, who has chosen to develop within the Workshop company instead of aspiring to Broadway recognition, is not a luminous personality who turns the role into a projection of himself, but just a fine actor capable of employing his superb skill and coordination to create any character an author or a director has devised. And in general this appears to be true of the other actors, most of whom have been with the Actor's Workshop for several years. While one can argue about the actors' interpretation of their roles, there can be no quarrel with the quality of their performances.

John Beaufort (essay date 1964)

SOURCE: "Pinter's Words Cut Through," in *The Christian Science Monitor,* June 24, 1964, p. 6.

[*In the following review, Beaufort praises the mood of "macabre menace" Pinter evokes in a production of* The Birthday Party, *which he also directed.*]

MEG: What do they do then?

PETEY: They just talk.

To the unconverted, these two lines from Harold Pinter's *The Birthday Party* describe—more in annoyance than admiration—the nonobjective play. To those who have welcomed Mr. Pinter and comparable others, *The Birthday Party* speaks with an eloquence that transcends its talk. I found it fascinating.

This first full-length Pinter play said nothing to most of London's critics when it was introduced in 1958 and ran for a week. Since then, it has been done on stage and television in many parts of the world, and is scheduled for production by the Lincoln repertory company in New York. Since then, too, Mr. Pinter has not only enjoyed fame, but also cultism.

The revival at the Aldwych offers an opportunity to examine the approaches to *The Caretaker, The Servant,* and the remainder of the relatively small output on which Mr. Pinter's relatively large reputation has been established. (Incidentally, the reviews of the Aldwych production reflect a perceptibly improved climate of critical opinion.)

The Birthday Party, like *The Caretaker,* presents the human predicament: the individual in conflict with overpowering forces. In what is now a familiar rather than an avant garde manner, the author builds from a casually realistic situation a weird, surrealist nightmare. There is no precharted course through the dangerous shoals and rippling banalities of *The Birthday Party.* Unseen currents draw the situation and the spectator toward deep waters and dark. Weird, violent storms break and subside.

Nor can we "by indirectious find directions out." Yet the situation itself, while bizarre, does not baffle description. Stanley, a loutish boarder at a shabby seaside rooming house, is visited by two menacing, malignly mysterious intruders who brutally subdue, paralyze, and in the end abduct him. The birthday party of the title is given to celebrate an anniversary which Stanley unavailingly disclaims.

Apart from his virtuosic skill with dialogue, his theatricalism, and the mood of macabre menace he evokes, Mr. Pinter employs a succession of symbolic devices to startle, prod, and frequently amuse the spectator, and to excite his imagination. Conspicuous examples include a newspaper (as meaningless when Petey reads it over breakfast as when the sinister McCann tears it meticulously into long shreds); the toy drum which Meg gives Stanley and which he inadvertently puts his foot through; Stanley's eyeglasses, which McCann cruelly breaks; the near fatal game of blind man's buff at the party; and the neat, sober suiting in which the helpless Stanley makes his final exit—the uniform of conformity, the vesture of status-manship.

Acted with authoritative ease under Mr. Pinter's direction, the Aldwych production is a provocative and disturbing experience. The absence of well ordered plotting and clearcut statement doesn't mean that there is no method in this fantastic madness.

The Birthday Party offers no retreat from the surrealist nightmares of the everyday world (apartheid, Cyprus, southeast Asia, the Congo, automation, to name a few). It does offer one of the half dozen most stimulating entertainments on the London stage at the moment.

CRITICAL COMMENTARY

Simon O. Lesser (essay date 1972)

SOURCE: "Reflections on Pinter's *The Birthday Party,*" in *Contemporary Literature,* Vol. 13, No. 1, Winter, 1972, pp. 34-43.

[*In the following explication of* The Birthday Party, *Lesser compares Pinter's worldview to that of Kafka's.*]

One cannot, and probably should not, write about Pinter without facing his similarity to Kafka and his acknowledged indebtedness to him.[1] In the course of telling stories which are apparently objective and up to a point even pretend to be realistic, both writers tap subjective concerns, many of which go back to infancy. Both deal with experiences which at first glance seem commonplace, even paltry, but which turn out to be battles for high stakes, sanity, for example, or sometimes life itself. Both share a conviction that the essential aspects of experience are ambiguous if not unknowable, yet both write simply and lucidly. Both achieve drama and poetry, without too many departures from colloquial speech and material that may appear to lack depth. Pinter is the more colloquial of the two, in part of course because he is a dramatist but also because a larger proportion of his characters are inarticulate or barely articulate and he has a sure ear for the diction of these characters, including their vulgarisms, neologisms, and slang.

Another similarity is too important to ignore: both men are preoccupied with our fears—our anxieties really—rather than our hopes. This is even more true of Pinter than of Kafka, one of whose two great novels is concerned with man's aspirations and strivings. Curiously, we are less likely to become aware of this preoccupation with anxiety than we are with one of its qualities, its abstractness. It is this abstractness which gives almost any situation in a Pinter play the effect of ambiguity, but this word is here scarcely adequate. In addition to permitting the viewer or reader to interpret the presented situation in an almost infinite number of ways, the abstractness provides a mold into which each reader can pour his own expressive content, in particular his free-floating anxieties, the kind which are intolerable precisely because they can be mobilized by so many different things. A further advantage of the abstractness is that the anxieties do not have to be specified even as one reexperiences them and tries to cope with them. The word "overdetermined" is also inadequate to describe a work which evokes this kind of response: it conveys a work's openness to multiple interpretations but not its power to impel a reader to become a covert coauthor. Whatever name one gives this quality, it does much to explain both the breadth and intensity of the appeal of Pinter's plays. In *The Angry Theatre* John Russell Taylor writes: "The ambiguity . . . not only creates an unnerving atmosphere of doubt and uncertainty, but also helps to generalize and universalize the fears and tensions to which Pinter's characters are subject."[2] It achieves this effect of generalizing and universalizing, paradoxically, by permitting the reader to individualize the content.

Some of Pinter's borrowing from *The Trial* in *The Birthday Party* must have been deliberate. Like *The Trial*, the play opens on the hero's birthday and it ends with two men taking him away—but the next day, not a year less a day later—perhaps to put him to death. Here a difference between Kafka and Pinter asserts itself. We know that K. is put to death; we witness his execution. We expect that Goldberg and McCann, who in effect abduct Stanley, are going to exploit him in some way for their own purposes—and we feel that they would not balk at murder. But we are not certain about either of these things and can only surmise what their exact plan is. Are they going to kill Stanley as a way of getting hold of some money he possesses, perhaps without being aware of it? Do they plan to put him in a corrupt and run-down rest home, where he will have scant chance of recovering, in order to divert some income to which he is entitled to their own pockets? Or do they have some quite different plan or motive for taking him away? We do not know. A Pinter play is like a Thematic Apperception Test. On the basis of scanty, obscure, and ambiguous evidence—a picture in the case of a TAT, puzzling dialogue and hazy glimpses of more puzzling people in the case of the play—we must decide the exact nature of the story being told: in this way also we are put in the author's chair. And specifying the story being told, we find, is just a warmup for the more arduous task of deciphering its meaning.

Like Kafka, Pinter is apparently candid. The setting of *The Birthday Party* is a shabby living room in a seaside town in England, a room too appallingly real to question. Both the shabby woman who takes care of this establishment, Meg, a woman in her sixties, and her husband, Petey, a deck chair attendant, seem firmly, indeed inescapably, moored in the world of everyday being. Both speak about commonplaces in a dreary, flat, usually hackneyed way. Despite these reassuring indications, before long we find that we are in a strange world, a world where there are no signposts, where nothing is clearly defined. In some respects Pinter's plays are more continuously puzzling than Kafka's stories. In the end there is no significant difference: eventually in Kafka also one thing melts into another and everything dissolves into mystery and uncertainty. But provisionally Kafka may develop a

character or a place with great solidity. Pinter weaves more loosely. He carefully—determinedly, it sometimes appears—leaves everything vague and fluid. Situations never assume a definite shape; either their outlines are left hazy and obscure or we are given two flatly contradictory versions of something and never told which one (if either) is correct. The development of the situations is no less enigmatic. We seldom feel that we have a sure grasp of the "whatness," much less the significance, of the happenings in a Pinter play. Of course, much of this holds for Kafka also. The similarities between the two writers are more important than the differences. And one feels that the similarities were there to begin with, that the British Jewish dramatist apprehended reality in very much the same way that the Central European Jewish novelist did and that Pinter, however unconsciously, was searching for someone like Kafka. If this is so, his appropriation of Kafka was not a matter of emulation but of seizing upon something helpful in defining and rendering his own vision of the human situation. This may explain the fact that, clear as the debt to Kafka is, not even *The Birthday Party*, Pinter's first full-length play, seems derivative. It is like Kafka but different. It bears Pinter's special stamp and, we feel certain, expresses his own vision.

It seems peculiarly difficult to specify the meaning of *The Birthday Party* primarily or largely in psychological terms.[3] In this respect it differs both from most of Pinter's other plays and Kafka's stories. In *The Birthday Party* Pinter appears to be using psychological devices to make some melancholy comments on our society. A social reading will come to grips with more facets of the story and explain the play more comprehensively, I believe, than any of the interpretations advanced thus far.

From one point of view the play's six characters constitute a microcosm of society. In particular, they mirror the fundamental economic division in society, the division between exploiters and exploited. Goldberg and McCann are of course the exploiters—symbols both of the anonymous forces that control life and the managers, operators, and decision makers who understand those forces well enough to use them for their own ends. The reference is chiefly to economic forces, but the men's purposiveness, authority, and strength are vaguely enough defined to symbolize power in any form or area.

Despite—or because of—the kempt facade under which the power lies hidden, it is as cruel and remorseless as that of any primeval despot. Goldberg's bromides and moral platitudes help make him menacing: we feel defenseless before him because he has appropriated the decencies on which we thought we could rely for protection and perverted them to his own purposes—thus our pity and fear for Stanley, the borderline psychotic who in one day's harassment Goldberg and McCann are able to drag over the line, in all probability irreversibly. Without pity, but with some vague apprehension, we observe that the cruelty of the exploiters is not confined to the exploited group. When McCann shows the slightest trace of insubordination, Goldberg makes him say "Uncle." Dog eats dog.

At a still deeper level Goldberg and McCann may be responded to as surrogates for or agents of the father—the male who has first claim on the mother and seems almost omnipotent to a little boy, hence is hated, envied, and feared. The evidence for this is inferential but persuasive. Before Goldberg and McCann appear, we learn that Stanley regarded the "they" who blocked his second concert as agents of retribution for his failure to invite his father to his first concert, and this supposition is significant whether the concerts were pure fantasy or had some basis in reality. Morever, from the time Meg mentions the fact that she is expecting two new roomers, we see that Stanley fears them. It seems reasonable to suppose that a feeling that the newcomers are also emissaries of the father is the ultimate source of this fear—and of the hostility which quickly manifests itself once the men appear.

Pinter's constellation of the exploited provides if anything a still sadder commentary on our society. As we have seen, one member of the group is completely unqualified for life: by his entire pattern of behavior Stanley is pleading *nolo contendere*. Meg is not much more competent or effective. Intellectually, she is a cretin, either illiterate or not up to the strain of reading. She is disregarded and treated contemptuously by her husband, Petey, and hardly seems to notice much less contest this. She thinks she has been well served if her husband condescends to read her a juicy item or two from the tabloid he always carries to hide in. Still, she feels his lack of love. Her libidinized though mainly maternal love for Stanley is born, we feel, of her desperate loneliness and lack of love. The exploited, Pinter is saying, for all their economic and emotional poverty are sometimes capable of giving. Even though Stanley is not all there and grumbles a great deal, he is aware of Meg's love and, in one of the most moving moments of the play, shows that he returns it.

Lulu, the girl next door but hardly the cleanly girl next door of American movies and situation comedies, is also capable of love. Lulu is Sex, she has been around, she is clearly there to satisfy sexual needs and to have her own needs satisfied. It might seem that she could be placed with the exploiters as well as with the exploited, and during the birthday party which climaxes the play she pairs off with Goldberg. But even the sexual practices to which he introduces her do not corrupt her, and we feel that nothing can. While she is far more sensual—and real—than Dostoevsky's Sonia, she shares her impregnable innocence. Her limitations must be noted, but they are in a sense, if not her virtues, her defenses against corruption. She is not much brighter than Meg; perhaps by the time she is as old as Meg she will be equally dull. She is not interested in, and probably not capable of understanding, anything which is even slightly abstract. But in part because she is simple-minded, she refuses to notice that Stanley is ill. With the slightest encouragement, we feel, she could love him. She is kind to him, helpless as he is, until the party, when, lacking even the ability to discriminate immediately between good man and bad, she responds to Goldberg. But once she knows him, revulsion follows

swiftly. Lulu will not join the exploiters unless she becomes corrupted and she will not become corrupted. She sleeps with Goldberg, but we feel sure she will not stay with him.

At first meeting, Petey, who completes the exploited group, is far from prepossessing. He is without love, warmth, or purpose. He teaches us the saddening lesson that there is exploitation among the exploited as well as among the exploiters. In Act One, the furtiveness with which he transfers his earnings from one place to another suggests that he tells his wife no more than is good for her, gives her as little as possible, and stows away the rest for himself. And just as Meg retreats from life into infantile narcissistic daydreams, he, though better endowed, retreats from it into the meaningless but distracting jumble of his newspaper.

Nevertheless, in certain respects Petey is at the "desirable" end of the spectrum among the exploited group. (To be sure, it is a narrow spectrum.) He is the most alert representative of the group Goldberg and McCann must deal with and manipulate. Moreover, he possesses a measure of courage. He stands up to Goldberg and protests his appropriating control of Stanley. Goldberg quiets his first objection by assuring him that arrangements have been made to take Stanley to a doctor. When Petey intervenes again, just as Goldberg and McCann are preparing to leave with Stanley, Goldberg uses a variant of this same "don't you worry" formula. In addition, he puts down a bill that one feels is more than ample to cover his and McCann's overnight stay. After some hesitation Petey pockets the bill, as his previous handling of money made us expect he would, and his resistance subsides.[4] The exploited, Pinter seems to be saying, accept their place in the pecking order without serious fuss. Those with a will to power do not experience too much difficulty either in seizing or remaining at the controls.

Meg has given Stanley a birthday present, which is lovingly wrapped. It turns out to be a toy drum—bought, she tries to explain, to make up for his not having access to a piano. Though nothing which is told us about the characters is firmly established, it seems reasonably certain that at one point Stanley at least felt that he was a promising pianist. The drum is a well-intentioned but stupid present. If one does not have time to foresee the effects it will have on Stanley, as soon as they appear one feels one should have foreseen them. Stanley puts the drum around his neck and begins to beat on it rhythmically, perhaps wanting to show his appreciation to Meg and taking pleasure in once again making music. But bitterness overcomes him: soon he is beating on the drum angrily, vindictively. Music turns into cacophony as the first act curtain falls.

That evening there is a party, presumably to celebrate Stanley's birthday, though it is still not certain that it is his birthday and he steadfastly denies it. A party means fun and games, and the group decides to play blindman's buff.

No selection could have been more apposite for symbolizing the cruelty inflicted upon Stanley during the "party" without provoking the attention of Meg and Lulu, much less any remonstrance from them. Only Petey is absent and this seems appropriate: he is neither totally blind nor, except with Meg in certain areas, interested in deceiving others.

We have already seen Goldberg and McCann treat Stanley with the utmost cruelty, subjecting him to a tattoo of questions and crazy accusations and insults which eventually make him scream in rage, terror, and helplessness. Now when Stanley is blindfolded, McCann deliberately snaps the frame of his glasses and then puts the drum before him so that he steps on it, stumbling and breaking it. At intervals Goldberg and Lulu embrace and kiss, quite openly. We are not surprised when Stanley breaks down completely. Nor are we surprised at the first indication of this—he tries to strangle Meg. We have seen that he is too easily irritated by her stupidity and slovenliness and at some level have even sensed the underlying source of his hostility: his fear of the way Meg satisfies his desire to be infantilized. Unconsciously he must realize that her babying reinforces his reluctance to resume life as an adult. His act gives Goldberg and McCann the excuse they have been looking for to also use physical force to subjugate him.

An unexplained blackout now occurs. McCann shines his torch, but it is knocked out of his hand, probably by Stanley. While Goldberg and McCann look for the torch, Stanley "picks up Lulu and places her on the table" (stage direction). Shortly afterwards McCann finds his torch and "shines it on the table and Stanley." The next sentence in the stage direction which ends Act Two reads: "Lulu is lying spread-eagled on the table, Stanley bent over her." Even a critic as astute as Martin Esslin is misled by this description—in particular, I suspect, by the word "spread-eagled"—and refers to Stanley's action as an attempt at rape.[5] But surely Stanley's treatment of Lulu is fueled chiefly by anger and jealousy arising from her behavior with Goldberg. Stanley may also be trying to show Lulu and himself, and possibly the other three people present, that he could be a good sexual partner also, perhaps a better one than Goldberg. But a spectator or reader has good reason to view such a claim with mistrust. It seems possible that Stanley is impotent. His Act One rejection of Lulu's invitation to go on a picnic with her provides firmer evidence that he is probably too shy to make a sexual advance to a woman, much less attempt rape. Moreover, anyone who had empathized with Stanley during the torment which is the party as he experiences it must sense that he is at low ebb and feels little inclination for sex. What lies under your dreary social occasions, Pinter seems to be asking throughout this second act, but eroticism and aggression? But Goldberg's complacent and sometimes insulting replies to Lulu's ingenuous expressions of admiration suggest that eroticism plays a minor role. The act ends with cruelty firmly in the saddle: Goldberg and McCann are again converging upon Stanley.

We never learn the exact nature of the going-over Stanley was probably subjected to that night, but the next morning the brutal McCann is loath to return to Stanley's room and even Goldberg is edgy. Eventually McCann does fetch Stanley, who is now clean-shaven and dressed for departure. Once again Goldberg and McCann subject him to an unendurable rapid-fire verbal barrage. But it is superfluous. Stanley's will to resist has vanished and he can only make meaningless sounds.

The Birthday Party does not promise Stanley, or any of the rest of us, a happy year or a happy life. The ending of the play provides no catharsis for the pity and fear it has aroused. It is more depressing than the ending of *The Trial*, largely because the conclusion of the play does not terminate our thinking about Stanley. This is not to minimize the grimness of the ending of *The Trial*. It will be recalled that K. suffers a cruel death at the hands of the two executioners he awaits on the eve of his thirty-first birthday, though he has had no notice of their coming: while the hands of one of the men are at K.'s throat, "the other thrust the knife deep into his heart and turned it there twice."[6] But Kafka does much to soften this ending. He has prepared us throughout the novel for the probability that K. will ultimately surrender to his guilt and become reconciled to the need for punishment. Moreover, K. is reminded of his guilt in the concluding scene: he glimpses Fraulein Burstner, though it "was not quite certain that it was she."[7] It does not matter: K. acquiesces to the sentence of death. The ceremonial quality of the scene and the pervasive suggestion that it is a subjective experience also help to make the scene palatable.

So does the relative definiteness of the ending. In contrast, the ending of *The Birthday Party* is provisional. Since Stanley has been pushed over the line into psychosis and is completely at the mercy of the men who inflicted this injury, no happy ending is conceivable, but the involved reader or spectator is likely to extrapolate and supply some ending, or endings. Since whatever particulars he supplies are the work of his imagination, they are likely to be especially vivid and moving. No matter what shape the ending takes, it is likely to be hard to accept.

Amazingly, inexplicably, *The Birthday Party* does not suffer seriously from the failure to supply any information or use of form which would reconcile readers or viewers to what lies ahead for Stanley. To the contrary, for a long time the play—in particular, the ending and the surmises the reader or viewer supplies to round out the ending—has continued to haunt anyone whom *The Birthday Party* has put under its distinctive spell.

Notes

1. "Pinter, who acknowledges the influence of Kafka and Beckett, is, like these two writers, preoccupied with man at the limit of his being." Martin Esslin, *The Theatre of the Absurd,* revised ed. (Garden City: Doubleday, 1969), p. 255. See also Esslin's recent book, *The Peopled Wound: The Work of Harold*

Pinter (Garden City: Doubleday, 1970), p. 29, for a statement of Pinter's sense of affinity with Kafka and Beckett.

2. *The Angry Theatre* (New York: Hill & Wang, 1962), p. 238.

3. It may be significant that Dr. Abraham Franzblau, who advanced a perceptive psychological interpretation of *The Homecoming*, was far less successful in my judgment in discussing *The Birthday Party*. See the *Saturday Review*, 8 Apr. 1967, and 28 Oct. 1967. One of the three interpretations of the play Esslin advances in *The Peopled Wound* is also psychological: "*The Birthday Party* might also be seen as an image, a metaphor for the process of growing up, of expulsion from the warm, cosy world of childhood" (p. 84). This interpretation is invalidated, I believe, by the fact that at the end of the play Stanley is psychotic and the captive of the two men who have destroyed his sanity. There is little prospect that he will regain his sanity, much less grow up.

4. Both this business about the bill and the earlier business about the stealth with which Petey handles his own money are evidently additions made before or during the New York performance of *The Birthday Party* in the 1967-68 season. There is no reference to them in the Grove Press edition of the play. To ascertain whether these changes and additions represented second thoughts of Pinter's or in any case had been approved by him, I wrote him a note of inquiry, to which he was kind enough to reply. Mr. Pinter has no memory "of Petey handling his money with stealth in Act One." And he feels that Petey's ultimate acceptance of the money Goldberg throws on the table as he leaves does nothing to characterize him.

> "I think your memory has misled you in your reference to the passing of money from Goldberg to Petey in the third act. It was intended in no way to be a reassurance or bribe. Actually I introduced this piece of business myself when I directed the play at the Aldwych in 1964 (I think!). What actually happens or should have happened was this: Goldberg makes his point about Monty to Petey and Petey falls silent, as always. Goldberg then simply places a bill or two onto the table, as a final courteous insult, if you like. Petey does nothing. The action continues. After they have all gone Petey, on his return to the table, automatically puts the money into his pocket. There's no point in his leaving it lying around. What has taken place is merely an added punctuation to the action. It has no further significance in my view—I mean to be applied to the character of Petey."

With all respect to Mr. Pinter, I must add that *after* seeing the bit of business about money in Act One I could not help thinking that the money Goldberg left was immediately perceived to be more than enough

to cover the overnight stay of himself and his hatchet man and thus that bribery, as well as reassurances and threat, helped to overcome Petey's resistance to his "guests" taking Stanley with them. The "intentional fallacy" is not at issue here. My reaction to the significance of the money exchange in Act Three, which I assume was shared by some members of the audience, was born of the earlier bit of business about money evidently added by the director or producer.

5. *The Peopled Wound*, p. 77.

6. *The Trial*, definitive ed. trans. by Willa and Edwin Muir, rev. and with additional materials trans. by E. M. Butler (New York: The Modern Library, 1956), p. 286.

7. *Ibid.*, p. 282.

Michael W. Kaufman (essay date 1973)

SOURCE: "Actions That a Man Might Play: Pinter's *The Birthday Party*," in *Modern Drama*, Vol. 16, No. 2, 1973, pp. 167-78.

[*In the following essay, Kaufman argues that the game of blindman's buff, central to* The Birthday Party, *provides an expressive structure for what Pinter sees as inherent human traits: a struggle for mastery and hostility.*]

Although Harold Pinter has been writing for the theatre for more than fifteen years, his achievement is still very much in question. The reasons for this uncertainty are complex, and to a large extent the complexity stems from the plays themselves: from the carefully contrived ambiguities that refuse to offer ultimate coherence; from the minimal plots, adumbrated characters, and the multiplicity of inferences his dramatic actions excite. Early in his career Pinter acknowledged Kafka and Beckett as the major influences in his treatment of plots and characters. But perhaps even closer in spirit to Pirandello, Pinter exhibits the same contempt for absolute Truth and Reality. He can speak of the real and the unreal in an almost Pirandellian manner as indistinguishable,[1] and he has specifically emphasized the incredible problem inherent in interpreting experience:

> There are at least twenty-four possible aspects of any single statement, depending on where you're standing at the time or on what the weather's like. A categorical statement, I find, will never stay where it is and be finite. It will immediately be subject to modification by the other twenty-three possibilities of it.[2]

An enigma in itself, Pinter's theatre reflects the spiritual and philosophical enigmas of our age, and no criticism can presume to penetrate its ultimate mysteries.

But it is not enough simply to say that Pinter presents disturbing images of man's problematic existence and leave it at that. "Between my lack of biographical data about [the characters] and the ambiguity of what they say," Pinter significantly warns, "lies a territory which is not only worthy of exploration but which it is compulsory to explore."[3] In fact, close exploration reveals a remarkable coherence in Pinter's art. The continuing interplay between the characters and the objects and experiences that surround them which critics such as John Lahr, Martin Esslin, and James Hollis[4] have rightly seen as the creative power of Pinter's theatre, serves to intensify what has always been Pinter's primary concern: to make manifest "an individual's otherwise inaccessible and inexpressible experience of living."[5]

The Birthday Party, Pinter's first full-length play, is typical of his work and thus affords a clear insight into the dynamics of his theatre. Here external reality, created through casual conversations and ordinary encounters between characters, seems from the first nothing more than insipid dialogue and innocuous actions. But beneath the placid surfaces seethes the chaotic world of human emotions, and it is in this tension between society's ritualized conventions and men's violent impulses that the essential drama inheres. In ***The Birthday Party*** this seminal tension is epitomized in the games his characters play. In the various forms and contexts Pinter devises the game emerges as a subtle theatrical metaphor, a complex rite of language and action through which the characters can play out their fantasies, avoid their deepest fears, or find acceptable outlets for their hostile impulses. In this play particularly, the idea of the game with its corollary attitudes of playing and acting crystallize in blind man's buff. Everything in the play points toward and moves away from this crucial complex of events. Now in Pinter's recurring figure of the blind man Stanley shatters the ritual framework of the game and with violent and passionate gestures of murder and rape he releases his repressed frustrations against Meg and Lulu, unwitting victims of his aroused frenzy.

This bizarre and violent action has been variously interpreted. While the prevailing tendency is to understand Stanley's fury as his emphatic rejection of Meg's suffocating maternalism,[6] or to see it as the inevitable consequence of society's repression of the individual,[7] Pinter seems to be posing a more fundamental insight into human nature and its relations. For if ***The Birthday Party*** makes us uncomfortably aware of the brutality of societal coercion, it also demands that we recognize the need for civilized restraints to control our primitive natures. Simply put, the crisis in Pinter's plays arises when his characters realize that their own inner impulses are in irreconcilible conflict with the role society expects them to play. By the conclusion of the second act those games which initially appeared to represent the tawdry rituals and civilized deceits of modern living now seem to have a more positive function. In fact, they present the only restraint on man's innately violent and brutish nature, relatively harmless means of containing the anarchy of his inner urges which must be contained if he is going to live in society. By isolating the

birthday party, especially its celebratory blind man's buff, I want to suggest the rich density of Pinter's art, and to illuminate what I take to be the thematic center of this play.

It is a tribute to Pinter's skill as well as a significant growth in his dramaturgy that he allows the metaphorical implications of the action to expand from the realistic surfaces of his dramas. Blind man's buff is, of course, a traditional party game and therefore perfectly appropriate to the plot of a play that converges on the celebration of a birthday. But Stanley's birthday, so easily accepted by the literal-minded Meg as the anniversary of his nativity, becomes in the course of the festivities associated with his metaphoric regeneration as Goldberg and McCann bring Stanley "out of himself," and he emerges in the final act "a new man." Consequently, the birthday celebration focuses attention on the play's deeper issue: the perplexing question of human identity. This possibility is strengthened when we consider the name of the game the characters play. Literally, blind man's buff means the blows the blindfolded pursuer inflicts on those who seek to avoid his tag. But Pinter's deeper meaning becomes clearer when the punning alternative is understood, for the etymology of buff conveys the notion of nakedness. Within the economic metaphor of the game with its simultaneous images of aggressive hostility and helpless alienation, blind man's buff expresses Pinter's understanding of human activity as a perpetual "stratagem to cover nakedness."

Because this party game requires that the players be blindfolded and that the game proceed in silence, Pinter may exploit two of his recurring motifs. The first is the figure of the blind man[8] which variously relates to the dark mysteries of human experience or to the character's refusal or inability to penetrate beyond the surfaces. The second motif, more properly a technique, is silence. In blind man's buff the silence necessary to avoid being "it" corresponds to the notorious Pinter pauses, revealing stillnesses that essentially serve the same protective function outside the game. Because the players know as they reach out to touch each other that in Lulu's words "you mustn't be touched . . . if she touches you then you become blind,"[9] this game is the perfect vehicle for Pinter's view that people fail to communicate, not because they are unable to, but because they are afraid to.

But blind man's buff is even more suggestive than these parallels allow. Since the one blindfolded—the "it"—is physically alienated and helpless, he feels obliged to defend his vulnerability. Consequently, he assumes the offense, aggressively stalking his silent antagonists. Fearfully estranged from the rest of the community, reduced to the cipher of an impersonal pronoun, the "it" simultaneously gropes and strikes, seeks and attacks those he believes have rendered him so solitary. In all its complexity the stage game reflects Pinter's paradigm of the human condition; human relations are expressed in terms of the game: through the inchoate forces that pursue man; through the rhythms of thrust and withdrawal, flight and pursuit that characterize personal relations; through the vying and sparring of competitors in a struggle for mastery; and through the dominating hostility that emerges as the central passion in Pinter's universe.

Still more generally, but of particular importance to this play, the game becomes in its largest sense a metaphor for civilized society, representing the need for structure in human affairs. Playing allows the characters to assume a variety of roles necessary to quell their ontological insecurity; it provides a system of rules and regulations which temporarily lend order to an otherwise chaotic existence; and finally, by regulating competition and providing sanctioned outlets for their hostility, games offer ritualized schema that protect the characters from their inner violence. Consequently, *The Birthday Party* depicts man's life in society as a game, and the game to borrow Johan Huizinga's phrase, as "the living principle of civilization."

The sequence begins abruptly when Meg rises to announce, "I want to play a game." Although Meg's desire to play seems spontaneous, a *non sequitur* interrupting Goldberg's conversation with Lulu, actually it emerges organically from the characters' unconscious impulses, which the preceeding dialogue and action imply. Pinter has carefully written this scene to be acted "spatially." By symmetrically grouping the characters in pairs—Lulu and Goldberg moving together to the left of the table; Meg and McCann joining downstage to the right—Pinter forces emphasis on Stanley who all the while sits silently at center stage, an outsider to this company. Now this grouping and the ensuing dialogue and gestures work together to reveal emotions of which the characters' are not completely aware:

MEG. Let's have some of yours.

McCANN. In that?

MEG. Yes.

McCANN. Are you used to mixing them?

MEG. No.

McCANN. Sit down. Give me your glass.

[*Meg sits on a shoe-box, downstage, right. Lulu at the table, pours more drink for Goldberg and herself, and gives Goldberg his glass.*]

GOLDBERG. Thank you.

MEG. [*to McCANN*] Do you think I should?

GOLDBERG. Lulu, you're a big bouncy girl. Come and sit on my lap.

McCANN. Why not?

LULU. Do you think I should?

GOLDBERG. Try it.

MEG. [*sipping*] Very nice.

LULU. I'll bounce up to the ceiling.

McCANN. I don't know how you can mix that stuff.

GOLDBERG. Take a chance.

MEG. [*to McCANN*] Sit down on this stool.

[*Lulu sits on Goldberg's lap.*]

(p. 61)

The suggestive movements extend the verbal impressions of the counterpointed dialogue permeated with *double entendres* and together gestures and words communicate the characters' deeper passions. Consequently, the idea of the game, already introduced in Goldberg's suggestion that he might have known Lulu while playing "pop goes the weasle," or "piggy back," now seems the appropriate focus for the guilty urgency the characters only sense, an idea reinforced by the reference to the vanished Eden about which McCann sings immediately prior to the sequence.[10] Thus the game serves as an established ritual translating their chaffing sexual energies into acceptable social form.

Stanley's silence which he maintains throughout the game is paradoxically the most concentrated aural effect of this boisterous scene, as his physical separation is its most notable visual focus. This emphasis on Stanley's singular isolation has been present from the play's opening where Meg and Petey had repeatedly commented on his absence. In fact, Stanley's presence at this lonely resort and his emphatic uniqueness seem to imply for most readers his assertion of individuality, the result of his rejection of the engulfing conventions that stifle self-expression. The difficulty with this interpretation is that it disregards the more complex aspects of Pinter's construction. The play's exposition, ambiguous at best, still suggests that Stanley's retreat has been prompted not by *his* rejection of social conformity, but rather by his radical failure in society, a defeat he relates to Meg amidst the inflated fantasies of his artistic career:

My next concert. Somewhere else it was. In winter. I went down there to play. Then, when I got there, the hall was closed, the place was shuttered up, not even a caretaker. They'd locked it up. [*Takes off his glasses and wipes them on his pyjama jacket.*] A fast one. They pulled a fast one. I'd like to know who was responsible for that. [*Bitterly.*] All right Jack, I can take a tip.

(p. 23)

Moreover, Stanley's actual condition qualifies immensely any positive assertion of individuality his withdrawal from society might imply. During the first act his manner suggests that far from the rejuvenation of his self, isolation has resulted only in the loss of his sense of belonging; alienation from society's ritual forms and functions has produced merely anxiety and emptiness, and as he confides to McCann he longs to be "back home." Early in the play Stanley reveals the intense emotional strain his self-doubt has produced when he questions Meg: "Tell me Mrs. Boles, when you address yourself to me, do you ever ask yourself exactly who you are talking to?" What seems at the moment only a casual remark of bravado is immediately underscored when Stanley "groans" and falls forward holding his head in his hands.

Rather than rejuvenescence of the spirit, Pinter associates Stanley's isolation through a number of visual and verbal motifs with a state of living death. His refusal to go outdoors, his continual fatigue and dishevelled appearance, and his hasty retreat when Lulu suggests he have a look in her mirror,[11] are symptomatic of the crisis Stanley suffers, a confusion of self he tacitly admits to McCann when he asserts, "I suppose I have changed but I'm still the same man I always was." But more importantly, Pinter introduces a verbal pattern that moves toward a definition of Stanley's moribund emotional state. Early in the first act Lulu suggests that Stanley have a wash, and concludes from his morose silence that he is "a bit of a washout." Pinter skillfully weaves several repetitions of this idea into the text until their accumulated force becomes associated with Stanley's spiritual death. Prior to the celebration Goldberg proclaims a birthday to be a great occasion:

> What a thing to celebrate—birth! Like getting up in the morning. Marvelous! Some people don't like the idea of getting up in the morning. I've heard them. Getting up in the morning, they say, what is it? Your skin's crabby, you need a shave, your eyes are full of muck, your mouth is like a boghouse, the palms of your hands are full of sweat, your nose is clogged up, your feet stink, what are you but a corpse waiting to be washed?
>
> (p. 48)

These lines unite a whole series of earlier resonances—Stanley's irritable petulance, his unwashed and unshaven appearance, his repeated rubbing of his eyes, his sour sense of taste, and most pertinently, his emphasized reluctance to rise in the morning—and implicitly connect Goldberg's remarks to Stanley. Consequently, when Goldberg, echoing Lulu, questions "when did you last have a bath?" Pinter has prepared us to accept his climactic assessment of Stanley's fatal alienation:

> You're dead. You can't live, you can't think, you can't love. You're dead. You're a plague gone bad. There's no juice in you. You're nothing but an odour!
>
> (p. 55)

The arrival of Goldberg and McCann, bringing with them societal platitudes and reminders of communal allegiance, effectively sharpens Stanley's inner desolation. On the one hand, their mysterious appearance and the slick patter they weave around questions of the betrayal of organizations, the supremacy of the necessary or the probable, and the existence of an external force only heightens Stanley's anxiety regarding the menacing world in which he exists. On the other hand, their appearance is inexorable for as Goldberg reminds Stanley, "if we hadn't come today we'd have come tomorrow." Goldberg and McCann are most clearly significant within the play's structure as they define Stanley's emotional turmoil and concretize his inevitible confrontation with the personal annihilation which he continually dreads. Specifically, these two so supremely confident about their selves exacerbate Stanley's anxiety by asking over and over again questions of identity—"Who do you think you are," "Where do you come from,"

"What's happened to your memory," "Webber, you're a fake," "Who are you Webber," "What makes you think you exist"—accelerating Stanley's insecurity until blind man's buff becomes the nightmarish analogue of his most passionate fears.

Goldberg and McCann, moreover, represent an idea of culture; together they present a way of thinking about our life in society. For them, as Ruby Cohn and others have noted,[12] traditional values and prescribed traditions have meaning and validity. Not only do their names signify the two dominating orthodoxies of Western civilization, but their actions and speech reveal a deep and pervasive allegiance to all facets of community. That Goldberg has a respected position and several good names, that he can define himself according to the shifting functional role of family, organization, and profession indicates the multiple frames-of-reference necessary to play the game of human identity.[13] Most important, Goldberg's self-assurance provides a valuable contrast to Stanley's mordant fears about himself, throwing into high relief the anxious predicament of the individual who attempts to exist outside the pale of society's organizing rituals.

Not, however, until the game of blind man's buff are the connections between rituals of social behavior and the passional violence that underlies them finally made clear. Significantly, the two most self-assured characters, Lulu and Goldberg, are the only ones who are never "it," yet they most actively establish the rules and guide the procedure of the game. Although their assertive aggressiveness effectively contrasts with the others' ineffectual passivity, Pinter's focus is even thematically sharper. Lulu and Goldberg present a mirror reflection of the relationship between Meg and Stanley. Just as Stanley finds in Meg a disturbing embodiment of mother and mistress, so does Lulu see Goldberg simultaneously as father and lover. Immediately after meeting Goldberg, Lulu confesses that she trusts him, that she has always liked older men because "they can soothe you." And after inquiring whether Goldberg might have known her as a little girl, Lulu confides that he is "the dead image of the first man I ever loved."

During the playing of blind man's buff Goldberg and Lulu engage in their own private game—kissing and fondling each other. These contrapuntal actions—Lulu and Goldberg upstage and the game proceeding downstage—create a visual analogy and a revealing comparison. When the game begins all the characters "move about": at the same time that Meg reaches out to touch McCann within the game, Goldberg reaches out to fondle Lulu. The effect of the parallel gestures is twofold: on the one hand, reaching out indicates the need men have for affective human contact. On the other hand, the stylized and duplicated gestures accentuate the ceremonious rituals that ultimately shape all human relationships.

Nevertheless, up to this point the characters' hostile and lustful impulses have been restrained, controlled by the acceptable ritual of the game. But when in the same motion used by the others Stanley reaches out, it is to strangle Meg. Now the repetition of visually analogous actions establishes a fundamental relationship between the apparent polarities of Stanley's aggressive hostility and Goldberg's sexual caresses. These interchanges are neither personal nor affectionate and are thus linked together by the violations they effect on another human being. Moreover, when taken together they summarize the conflicting forces that drive nature, emotions that are simultaneously intimate yet impersonal, tender yet violent, rationally perceived yet blindly instinctual. But equally important, the visual equation between Stanley's murderous aggression and Goldberg's loveless play relate hostility and sexual urgency at the core of man's nature, an inner violence that threatens to erupt to the surface at any time. In this context Stanley's passionate attack on Meg must remind us of the game recently ended which with its harmless rites now seems the necessary outlet for man's dangerous impulses. Stanley has broken the rules and in so doing he has destroyed the game—the imperative need for order and restraint in human affairs.

If Pinter's man must play a role and embrace ritual to survive, the theatre would seem his appropriate milieu, and this pertinent analogy might explain Pinter's profound attraction to the drama after his hasty production of *The Room*. Indeed, the theatrical form has special relevance to Pinter's established themes, and in *The Birthday Party* he exploits these correspondences to their fullest. The first analogy Pinter draws is that of the theatrical performance as ritual. Drama is a rite acted out with a ceremoniousness of attitude and gesture. People posing as actors impersonating characters play out their proscribed roles, and speech and action is regulated by a script which demands faithful adherence to its cues and conventions. Consequently, the stage for Pinter is emblematic of essential reality; the world is a theatre where the artifice of roles and rituals and the ceremoniousness of games and playing shape men's lives.

This comparison between the stage and the world is made the more significant through Pinter's use of playing-within-the play. Not only does blind man's buff necessarily call attention to the actor as player, but it serves as a mirror image for the audience in which we glimpse our own role. As Goldberg and Lulu direct the festivities of the party they move up-stage watching the game from the perspective of an on-stage audience, and thus linking them and their roles to that of the real theatre audience. Thus, the play engages us in its action and forces us into an uncomfortable identification with the actors, a closure which undermines the audience's critical detachment and blurs the distinction between reality and role-playing. In the theatre the spectator's reality is, after all, his role; in a very significant sense he is part of the game of the drama.

Through the implied relation between life and its games, man and his masks, Pinter suggests the problematic nature of the self beneath the role. But in still another way he draws tighter the analogy between the world and the stage,

audience and actors. In formal realism the audience is physically and emotionally detached from the ritual action on stage. This detachment and the audience's superior awareness are of course traditional features of the drama, providing the perspective of critical alienation necessary to foster the dramatic irony so characteristic of the form. But in *The Birthday Party* Pinter turns that dramatic irony on his audience. At that moment during the theatrical game when Stanley reaches out for Meg—that moment of inexplicable violence—the lights mysteriously go out, and the blindness and ignorance that shrouds the stage characters envelops the audience as well.

By involving the audience in the mystery of blind man's buff, Pinter forces us into the play demanding that we see our own perplexities mirrored in the characters' anxious panic. And our clearest reflection comes from Goldberg. Rather than the confident, detached spectator he was, Goldberg now emits a series of frantic questions. In the confusion that follows the characters ask questions of identity, and the ensuing silence underscores Pinter's deepest strategy in this game. If within the regulated order of blind man's buff questions such as "Who is it?" and responses such as "It's me," are logical and sufficient, outside the game they are absurd and irrelevant. From the play's first speech—Meg's "Is that you Petey?"—Pinter establishes an interrogative mood and a problem of identity. And in a play that explores the mysterious imponderables of the question, "Who are you Webber?" the simple game of tag brilliantly underscores the necessarily reductive way in which human nature must define itself.

The Birthday Party, then, invites a closer and more serious consideration than it has received, since it embodies the basic techniques of Pinter's craft as well as the primary thematic patterns of his later work. While it is true that Pinter explores the standardization of modern life—an aspect of the play's design traced in Stanley's helpless capitulation to his antagonists, and epitomized when he emerges in the last act dressed in striped suit and bowler hat, a visual punning reference to the uniform of uniformity—the lasting impression of the total dramatic experience must dwell on the unpredictible, hidden violence of which human nature is capable, and the ways man must deal with this underside of his being.

And these ways are introduced in verbal and visual motifs of game-playing which culminate in the final act. The arousal and ultimate outburst of Stanley's hostility climaxing at the end of the second act, leave Goldberg and McCann, agents of order, decorum, and propriety perceptibly shaken. Goldberg's earlier assurance that "the assignment will be carried out . . . with no excessive aggravation" to either is ironically erroneous for during their last appearance both he and McCann are nervous and irritable. What for Goldberg had seemed the incontestable props of his life now no longer sustain his unquestioned confidence, and he seeks reassurance from McCann:

> All my life I've said the same. Play up, play up, and play the game. Honour thy father and thy mother. All along the line. Follow the line, the line, McCann, and

you can't go wrong. What do you think, I'm a self-made man. No! I sat where I was told to sit. I kept my eye on the ball. . . .

Because I believe that the world . . . [*Vacant*]

Because I believe that the world . . . [*Desperate*]

BECAUSE I BELIEVE THAT THE WORLD . . . [*Lost*]

(p. 80)

What has shaken Goldberg's belief in the truth and justness of his world is presumably what his subverting interrogations of the previous act uncovered: the lust and cruelty that underlie all civilized customs. By reducing Stanley to a radical object, Goldberg and McCann arrive at the stark image of human nature. In their last verbal duet, as they hold before Stanley the promise of a new life, McCann suddenly breaks the ritual stychomythia, and the fracture underscores the naked truth of Stanley's rejuvenescence neither can now resist:

GOLDBERG. We'll make a man of you.

McCANN. And a woman.

GOLDBERG. You'll be re-oriented.

McCANN. You'll be rich.

GOLDBERG. You'll be adjusted.

McCANN. You'll own yachts.

GOLDBERG. Animals.

McCANN. Animals.

(p. 88)

The ensuing and final action, punctuated by Stanley's inarticulate howls, provides Pinter's uncomfortable dramatic terms for the brute animality of unaccommodated man.

The existence of this final act suggests that Pinter is equally concerned with how human nature accommodates itself to this actuality; how only elaborate immersion in ritual keeps these characters from facing their fearful selves. Immediately after McCann's decisive rupture of their verbal game, Goldberg reasserts his authority ("*I said* animals"), and now the order and balance return which allow them to complete their job and bring the play to a close. This thrust lays bare the whole point of the play: that form and structure are essential to contain the utterly chaotic and disordered inner life. This same ritualistic pattern is repeated when Meg and Petey return to their seemingly irrelevant conversation of the opening scene. The linking ties the play's opening and conclusion in what appears to be a ceaseless ritual of gesture and speech. But the more basic importance of this repetition is that it dramatically emphasizes the significance of the change that has occurred. What had begun as ceremonial irrelevancy is now associated with the characters' desperate need to shut out the terrifying actuality that has interceded between the play's opening and its conclusion.

The grotesque tableau with which the second act concludes, presenting Stanley giggling over the spread-eagled figure of Lulu, is, in part, the result of the aggravated tension to which he has been subjected, and, in part, a dramatic embodiment of the deepest, unchartered passions of human nature. Stanley is an exaggerated anticipation of the central theme in Pinter's later plays which one critic sees epitomized in Ruth who in *The Homecoming* represents "the force not merely of sexuality but of all those blind, brutal, hostile impulses which, sweeping aside the restraints of intellect and morality make their own fearful claims to be part of any vital existence."[14] In *The Birthday Party*, however, Pinter is more dubious about the results of sweeping aside those restraints. In this play man's only protective ambiance is the game which alone may provide a viable identity and may transform those instinctive urges into regulated and civilized forms.

Notes

1. "There are no hard distinctions between what is real and what is unreal, nor between what is true and what is false. The thing is not necessarily either true or false; it can be both true and false." Quoted by Walter Wager, *The Playwrights Speak,* New York, 1968, p. 174.

2. Quoted by James R. Hollis, *Harold Pinter: The Poetics of Silence,* Carbondale, Ill., 1970, p. 36.

3. Quoted by Martin Esslin, *The Peopled Wound: The Work of Harold Pinter,* New York, 1970, p. 38.

4. John Lahr, "Pinter the Spaceman," *Up Against the Fourth Wall,* New York, 1968, pp. 175-94. See also Hollis and Esslin cited above.

5. Esslin, p. 252.

6. Lois G. Gordon, *Stratagems to Cover Nakedness: The Dramas of Harold Pinter,* Columbia, Missouri, 1969, pp. 19-29 *passim.*

7. Bernard Dukore, "The Theatre of Harold Pinter," *TDR* 6, March, 1962, pp 43-54. Dukore describes Pinter's dramas as depicting "contemporary man beaten down by the social forces around him," an idea Jacqueline Hoefer explicitly relates to *The Birthday Party* in "Pinter and Whiting: Two Attitudes Towards the Alienated Artist," *MD* 4, February, 1962, pp. 402-408.

8. See especially *The Room, A Slight Ache,* and *Tea Party.*

9. *The Birthday Party* and *The Room,* New York, 1961, p. 65. All quotations are taken from this edition and will subsequently be incorporated into the text.

10. That Pinter's characters exist in a fallen state is suggested by their secluded alienation from the natural world. John Lahr has characterized his plays as "urban fables in which . . . man's earthly garden . . . is cluttered with lifeless, alien objects." But even more significant are the characters' constant

nostalgic references to the security, simplicity, and innocence of childhood. In *The Birthday Party* each character brings a wistful romanticism to his reminiscence of youth, what Goldberg remembers as a time of "Hot water bottles, Hot milk, Pancakes, Soap suds." For Stanley it represents the quiet life, when he "lived well away from the main road," self-sufficient in his home. For Meg, childhood is epitomized by a night-light, a pink room and a father who nursed and protected her. Thus, when McCann reminisces about "Mother Nolan's in Roscrea" where he spent his youth only to ask, "Now where am I," Pinter draws our attention to the irreconcilible falling off man's initiation into adulthood brings.

11. Pinter has provided an interesting gloss on the scene in which Stanley shrinks from Lulu's suggestion that he have a look at himself in the mirror (*The Birthday Party*, p. 26). Walter Wager, p. 181, reports the following remark Pinter made: "I had—I have—nothing to say about myself, directly. . . . Particularly since I often look at myself in the mirror and say, 'Who the hell's that?'"

12. Cohn, "The World of Harold Pinter," *TDR* 6, March, 1962, pp. 55-68. Dukore, p. 52, follows this line of argument calling Goldberg and McCann "representatives and symbols of tradition and conformity."

13. Dukore, p. 52, rightly points out that both Goldberg and McCann use several given names which "carry connotations of tradition and religion." But more significant is his later remark that "their names change according to the function they perform."

14. Arthur Ganz, "A Clue to the Pinter Puzzle," *ETJ* 22, May, 1969, p. 187.

Mary L. Bogumil (essay date 1992)

SOURCE: "Gameplaying: Conventional and Narrative Games in Pinter's *The Birthday Party*," in *Massachusetts Studies in English*, Vol. 11, Nos. 1 & 2, Summer, 1992, pp. 72-83.

[*In the following essay, Bogumil looks at the role and meaning of games in* The Birthday Party.]

The sense of post-war malaise and uncertainty is evoked through the use of gameplaying in Harold Pinter's ***The Birthday Party.*** Historically, this play was composed in 1957 during the "Diminishing Age" in English Literature (1940-1965), a time when this beleaguered nation was desperately struggling to re-establish itself, to re-assert its sense of nations and tradition after post war carnage. In the play, the characters are bewildered, and the plot seems incidental. The characters, particularly Stanley, struggle with the irrationality of experience while Meg, Petey, Goldberg, McCann and Lulu initiate games as a way to counteract or hold at bay their sense of detachment in a

seemingly meaningless universe. Such games, whether narrative or conventional, create a sense of order and certainty in a cultural environment in which traditions have been emptied of all significance and value.

In his essays "Six Asides about Culture," Vaclav Havel, a playwright and author who has been greatly influenced by his reading of and friendship with Pinter, states that "If there is a sphere which precludes all prognostication, it is that of culture, and especially of the arts and the humanities" (123). Havel elaborates that one may to a certain extent feel certain about what one knows and about what one may come to know in the natural sciences, but such certainty does not exist in culture or the arts. In relation to his own country of Czechoslovakia, Havel can only make predictions of contingency:

> There is a countless number of possibilities for culture in our country: perhaps the police pressure will intensify, perhaps many more artists will intensify, perhaps many more artists and scholars will go into exile, many others will lose all desire to do anything and the last remnants of imagination with it, and the entire so-called 'second culture' will gradually die out while the 'first culture' will become entirely sterile. Or again, perhaps that second culture will suddenly, unexpectedly blossom to an unprecedented extent and form . . . Or massively awaken, perhaps wholly improbable 'new waves' will arise within it and the second culture will quietly, inconspicuously and gladly merge into its shadow. Perhaps wholly original creative talents and spiritual initiates will suddenly emerge on the horizon, expanding somewhere in a wholly new space between the two present cultures so that both will stare in amazement. Or again, perhaps nothing new will come up at all, perhaps everything will remain as it is. . . .
>
> (123-24)

This sense of perhaps . . . and perhaps . . . and perhaps is more than likely still part of Havel's consciousness despite the dramatic changes in his country over the past year. It is in what Havel calls the "sphere" of art that Pinter captures the sense of perhaps and perhaps through characterization, action, and dialogue in ***The Birthday Party.*** In a program note, Pinter addresses his mode of characterization and the role of contingency and uncertainty in his plays:

> The desire for verification is understandable but cannot always be satisfied. There can be no hard distinctions between what is real and what is unreal, nor between what is true and what is false. A thing is not necessarily either true or false; it can be both true and false. a character on the stage who can present no convincing argument or information as to his past experience, his present behavior or aspirations, not give a comprehensive analysis of his motivations is as legitimate and as worthy as one who, alarmingly, can do all these things. The more acute the experience the less articulate its expression.
>
> (qtd. in Esslin, *Theatre of the Absurd,* 243)

Here, Pinter is interested in the problems of personal identity and personal motivation. He suggests that human beings are opaque to one another. He implies as well that the playwright who attempts to create non-fictional characters or to establish some kind of intrinsic understanding between "real" people is falsifying reality. Thus, the game motif in the play is a way to reveal a character's desire to "create" or fabricate relationships, to make transparent a connection between himself or herself and others. Accordingly, Pinter's use of language games is one way to comprehend his style of characterization. Pinter says that we use language not to communicate, but to imply that we have a grasp on what is incidental in life. In other words, language, at times, attempts to convey things about which we have no knowledge, and games, fictional constructs, become a way to fabricate that knowledge.

In "Names and Naming in the Plays of Harold Pinter", Ronald Knowles states that the act of naming in Pinter's plays is a relevant aspect of characterization. He states: "It is as if knowledge and the use of a name form is a kind of articulated power" (116). Knowles provides illustrations to substantiate his point, including one in which he addresses Meg's relationship to Stanley.

> After his breakdown Stanley is reduced to a speechless cipher of surface respectability, his real identity is quite lost. In *The Birthday Party* Pinter dramatizes the way in which first names are used by the individual or others to protect or negotiate versions of self. Meg's maternal possessiveness is expressed by the diminutive "Stanny". Her version of Stanley is one of a boy who needs mothering, or as someone to clearly flirt with.
>
> (115)

As one reads *The Birthday Party,* one recognizes that naming becomes a way to confer or verify a character's existence, a metaphor for characterization in narrative games; the tenor being the name and the vehicle being the character. Yet a problem arises in the utterance of a name in Pinter's play as Knowles remarks. For example, Goldberg is mainly "Nat" to McCann, "Simey" to his late wife and mother, and "Benny" to his father. Certainly, naming sheds light upon character development, but the pathological "tormentor" Goldberg the audience knows does not parallel this personable character as Knowles suggests, for names reflect "an exclusive aspect of Goldberg's past identity which he jealously guards, rejecting McCann's appropriation [Simey] with 'NEVER CALL ME THAT'" (Knowles 115). Simply put, when McCann calls Goldberg 'Simey', prior to their removal of Stanley from the premises, he is encroaching upon intimate territory, Goldberg's past, and in doing so violates the prerequisite rules of Goldberg's narrative game with Petey, and with the Boles, where he is in the position of dominance.

Narrative games, instances of interaction between characters through dialogue, often are moments of confrontation in this Pinter play. Thompson in his chapter entitled "Revaluation: Movement and Dialogue" says that Pinter's mode of characterization is unique in that "Characters,

[Pinter] insists, are not fixed and 'given' but open to negotiation, "and one's sense of the character is solely contingent upon interpretation. (113) Accordingly, it is this mode of characterization, drawn almost exclusively from language, and the way that one interprets that language, the clues to a character's identity, which Pinter plays upon:

> Language, under these conditions, is highly ambiguous commerce. So often, below the words spoken, is the thing known and unspoken. . . . You and I, the characters which grow on the page, most of the time we're inexpressive, giving little away, unreliable, elusive, evasive, obstructive, unwilling. But it's out of these attributes that language arises. A language, I repeat, where, under what is said, another thing is being said.
>
> (qtd. in Brown 25)

This language of uncertainty and the games which ensue entail a risk factor according to Jean Francois Lyotard in his book *Just Gaming,* for any narrative game "is interesting in itself insofar as the interesting thing is to play moves. And to play moves means precisely to develop ruses, to set the imagination to work" (61). Examples of such gameplaying abound in Pinter's play: the role of Petey and Meg as Stanley's parents, the invention of Stanley's birthday party, Stanley as the dejected artist—the pianist, Goldberg and McCann as members of nefarious "organization" headed by the enigmatic Monty, and Lulu as a "nice little girl," among others. Lyotard further postulates about the creation and need for such narrative games:

> . . . it is certainly not because one thinks that one game is better than another; it is because one has several kinds of games at one's disposal. There are even some that are not invented yet and that one could invent by instituting new rules; and that is quite interesting. It is in this way that something like the imagination, or the will, I do not know, could develop. And when I say "develop," I do not mean it in the sense of progress; I mean the fact that one can introduce into the pragmatics, into our relations with others, forms of language that are at the same time unexpected and unheard of, as forms of efficacy. Either because one has made up new moves in an old game or because one has made up a new game.
>
> (61)

Lyotard's point is that most people continue to play the same games over and over again without any sense of inventiveness. Artists, on the other hand, attempt to play the "master strokes" and invent new games and propose new rules for the medium in which they work.

Pinter proposes some new rules by playing with the old ones. He combines and undercuts traditional dramatic genres through parody, yet another form of gameplaying, in order to show their boundaries or limited applicability in regard to portraying "human nature." Pinter creates a hybrid play, utilizing the dramatic implications and conventions of various dramatic forms in hopes of exploring modern man's predicament whereby man must create himself by the choices that he makes in life. To paraphrase Bernard F. Dukore's comments in *Where Laughter Stops: Pinter's Tragi-Comedy,* Pinter's play could be seen as a tragi-comedy in his use of humor to heighten the tragic sense, although it falls short of the conventional comedy thematically because it does not contain a resolution typical of comedy. The sense of renewal, or rebirth, in the character of Stanley is frustrated in respect to a cathartic epiphany. Rather than encourage the reader to anticipate a "happy" transformation or re-birth in Stanley's character, Pinter plays upon the tragic sense of resolution as an ironic renewal in terms of comedy. Stanley's mourning attire and autonomous state are appropriate to the theme at the conclusion of the play in that his rebirth is paradoxically his death, as Pinter's character Goldberg reiterates ironically in Act III: "Still the same old Stan. Come with us, come on, boy" (85).

The Birthday Party could also be described as a hybrid play as Pinter conflates many genres, avoiding any one particular genre or form. He frustrates the reader's attempt to classify the play, to place it within the confines of a particular genre. He employs the elements of conventional drama without rigidly adhering to the structure of any specific genre. The play is a tragi-comedy because Pinter uses humor to heighten Stanley's tragic dilemma. It could be classified as a tragedy in part because Stanley's loss of individuality invokes a sense of empathy within the audience in that this loss is a fear that everyone recognizes but is unwilling to admit. The play contains naturalistic elements because Stanley's existence is shaped by his environment over which he has little or no control. The play could also be perceived as an expressionistic drama because the characters of Goldberg and McCann first appear as a representation of thought or impression of some form of social repression when Meg first mentions them to Stanley. It could be a realistic piece because Pinter's use of language or paralanguage is riddled with cliches, which is a realistic aspect of everyday speech. In addition, the play contains an existential element emblematic of Absurdist drama in that Stanley resides in a world of angst as a result of his lack of faith and precarious notion of progress. Finally, the confrontation scene that occurs near the end of Act II between Stanley and the other characters, except Petey, could be described as a harlequinade: Goldberg is the pantaloon, an avaricious older man who is the harlequin's master; McCann is the clown, Goldberg's knave who serves his master; Lulu and, in some cases, Meg represent the columbine, a maid servant, a sweetheart; and, Stanley is the harlequin, part trickster, part buffoon, and certainly the central performer in the game of Blind man's bluff. Simply put, any attempt to classify the play in a traditional manner is consistently truncated by Pinter.

As one examines Pinter's play, one comprehends that the efficacious power that the other characters wield over Stanley through gameplaying is startling. Pinter's use of dialogue in the play perpetuates this uncertainty aspect of language, this risk factor in narrative games. Thus, his dialogue becomes increasingly stylized in such a way to simultaneously capture the stilted conventional qualities manifest or apparent in everyday speech. Each character articulates in a cliched manner what is invariably inarticulate—inexpressible in the confines of language. One specific example of this uncertainty aspect of language occurs in Act II where Goldberg, with McCann present, involves Stanley in a mock interrogation, a variation on the game of twenty questions, that begins with the question "Webber, what were doing yesterday?" (47) These questions range from pseudo-biographical information about Stanley and his philosophy on life riddles, non sequiturs, and quasi-equations he is asked to solve. When the reader attempts to decipher these codes, to disclose some pertinent information about Stanley's relationship to these men, Pinter, through dialogue, involves the reader in a game of interpretation where fragmentary clues to Stanley's identity lead nowhere, and Stanley's final response is inarticulate, "Uuuuuhhhh!"

David T. Thompson comments upon the importance of the staging of the game in *Pinter: The Player's Playwright* and calls the reader's attention to the mock interrogation scene, often referred to as the inquisition:

> The 'mystery and strangeness' of Goldberg and McCann's bizarre questioning is enhanced by such use of an unusual stage direction. Stanley has his back to the wall, and, as the audience is in a sense the forth wall of the proscenium stage, it is in effect more involved: it both receives Goldberg and McCann's questions more directly, owing to the interrogators' stage position, and represents an immediate final barrier, cutting off possible way of escape for Stanley.
>
> (102)

Thus, through stagecraft, Pinter includes the audience, which represents "the forth wall," unknowingly, as players in the game as well. In other words, the audience's reaction as spectators and, in turn, as players because of their proximity to the events taking place on stage, demonstrates how Pinter's staging of the interrogation scene involves an unsolicited invitation to the game.

Martin Esslin in his article entitled "Language and Silence" discusses Pinter's technique of playing upon the context of the questionable meaning of language:

> Only when it was recognized that the verbal element need not be the dominant aspect of drama, or at least it was not the content of what was said that mattered most, but the action which it embodied, and that inarticulate, incoherent, tautological, and nonsensical speech might be as dramatic as verbal brilliance when it could be treated as an element of action, only then did it become possible to place inarticulate characters in the center of the play and make their unspoken emotions transparent. Pinter is among the discoverers of this highly significant aspect of drama.
>
> (143-44)

Although every character is searching for the *mot juste* and in turn for the right game in order to impress his or her ideas upon others, these attempts are rendered as absurdly futile aspirations in Pinter's drama. In a narrative game such as this, cliches, jargon, and repetition become the substantive elements in the language and are, in turn, used to verify one's power over another in the game, which reveals not so much a breakdown in communication as a character's inability to communicate with other characters. Perhaps, it is this sense of truncated communication that gives rise to each character's need to change the game. The reader is presented with a language laden with inorganic metaphors, conceptually stilted mannerisms, ironic rhetorical phrases, and fossilized cliches (i.e. dead metaphors) that collectively become an affirmation of the ambiguity, the uncertainty, that filters, or imposes upon, all attempts at communication.

For instance, Meg and Petey's constant repetition of the word "nice" in the beginning and throughout the play is one substantial case in point. "Nice" simply becomes an adage, a form of inclusion and affirmation in that "nice" as an adjective is used to describe both subjects and objects: the weather, cornflakes, Petey's chores, fried bread, news articles, Stanley's present (the drum), Meg's appearance in a dress, McCann and Goldberg, Stanley's birthday party and more.

Accordingly, one witnesses Stanley who is always puzzled by each character's notion that every moment is somehow a well of intrinsic meaning—one which they create artificially through gameplaying where things are made to be important or unimportant, where action is beginning only to be truncated or erased, and where winners and losers are defined. According to Havel, art is a reflection of the culture and a distinctive way of seeking the truth; thus, it is Pinter's character who is on the periphery of the cultural stratum in that Stanley is the character who epitomizes the "existential crisis" because of his autonomous position in the games.

That is not to say that Stanley does not participate in their games, but that he is forced to play the games. His sense of free will repeatedly thwarted and, in turn, enveloped by the context created by the other characters. Meg, Petey, Lulu, McCann, and Goldberg fix themselves upon desired archetypal roles whereas Stanley's identity remains indeterminable in that he apprehensively acquiesces to the notion of creating an identity. Frequently, Meg is an absurdist version of the Madonna figure with lascivious inclinations, Petey the sighted Virgil, Lulu the dumbfounded *ingenue,* McCann a parody of a Kafka character, and Goldberg a caricature of the Mosaic lawgiver. But Stanley, unlike the other characters, refrains from conceptualizing a sense of purpose, a role, in that existential void. Correspondingly, one perceives that an epistemological crisis occurs for Stanley whenever an imposed reality is questioned, whenever games are fabricated at a moment's notice, especially by Meg and Goldberg: to Meg, Stanley is the son she longs for, and to Goldberg he is that mentally unbalanced young man who needs order in his life.

Still, throughout Acts I and II, Stanley countermands their impositions of identity as the willing participant in their

games with bouts of anger and ruminations of a womb-like retreat. Because he is not in the "process of creating" an identity, Stanley cannot actually engage in a dispute arising from the other's concept of his nature, but can only make tacit assumptions about their intent. He is the participant, ofttimes unwilling, who always disrupts the game.

In Act II, a game of musical chairs commences except that the music is provided by Goldberg's intimidating voice. In a game in which the players walk around a row of chairs, with one chair less the number of players, the players typically rush to sit down before the music stops. In Pinter's version it is Stanley, under the insistence of Goldberg and McCann, who is a hostile participant in the game in order to find the purpose of their visit, or so he thinks:

> GOLDBERG. Mr. Weber, sit down a minute.
>
> STANLEY. Let me—make it clear. You don't bother me . . .
>
> GOLDBERG. Mr. Webber, sit down.
>
> STANLEYy. It's no good starting any kind of trouble.
>
> GOLDBERG. Sit down.
>
> STANLEYy. Why should I?
>
> GOLDBERG. If you want to know the truth, Webber, you're beginning to get on my breasts.
>
> STANLEY. Really? Well, that's—
>
> GOLDBERG. Sit down.
>
> STANLEYy. No.
>
>   * * *
>
> GOLDBERG. Ask him to sit down.
>
> McCANNn. Yes Nat . . . Do you mind sitting down?
>
> STANLEY. Yes, I do mind.
>
>   * * *
>
> McCANN. He won't sit down.
>
> GOLDBERG. Well, ask him.
>
> McCANN. I've asked him.
>
> GOLDBERG. Ask him again.
>
> McCANN. Sit down.
>
> STANLEY. Why?
>
> McCANN. You'd be more comfortable.
>
> STANLEY. So would you.
>
> McCANN. All right. If you will I will.
>
> STANLEY. You first.
>
>   (Act II 46-7)

After Stanley has managed to coax McCann to sit, McCann and Goldberg are both seated, and Stanley thinks in this version of musical chairs that he has won; Goldberg arises, and McCann is angered that he has been made sport of by Stanley in a perverted power play, and now Goldberg, his boss, is inappropriately standing: "McCann. You've made Mr. Goldberg stand up" (47). Suddenly, Mc-Cann orders Stanley to sit, and Goldberg reiterates his command: "Weber . . . SIT DOWN . . . ," and Stanley sits (47).

Yet, even after this version of musical chairs with three players, Stanley plays a version by himself:

GOLDBERG (*crossing to him*). Webber. (*Quietly.*) SIT DOWN. (*Silence.* STANLEY *begins to whistle "The moun-tains of Morne". He strolls casually to the Chair at the table. They watch him. He stops whistling. Silence. He sits.*) (47)

Control in the game is essential in narrative games as well as traditional games, albeit an absurd version of musical chairs, interpretation on the part of the participants leads to a risk factor in the outcome of the game. This risk or uncertain outcome is apparent in the game Meg wishes them all to play later in Act II, blind man's buff.

MEG. I want to play a game!

GOLDBERG. A game?

LULU. What game?

MEG. Any game.

LULU. Yes, let's play a game.

GOLDBERG. What game?

McCANN. Hide and seek.

LULU. Blind man's buff.

MEG. Yes! . . .

(61-65)

In blind man's buff, one player is designated to be blindfolded, and this player attempts to catch and identify any one of the others. Meanwhile, the other players push, buffet and make sport of the blindfolded player. Of course, it is Stanley who is blindfolded and doubly blinded in the game because McCann seizes his glasses, breaks them, and then situates Stanley's present, the toy drum, in his path so that Stanley Stumbles upon it. What is significant about this game is that the other players seem to act like a tragic Greek chorus conspiring against doubly blind Stan-ley: There is a powerless participant in the game, a pawn. Moreover, one notices that Petey is absent from the game. Petey, the one who plays chess, is also the one who at the conclusion of the play seems most disturbed by Gold-berg's and McCann's treatment of Stanley. Perhaps, Pinter left Petey out of this scene because one who knows the rules of chess would perceive that control over Stanley is the object of their games—that is, to place Stanley in check-mate, which in the game of chess signals the end of the game and foreshadows the autonomous transformation of Stanley in Act III. The burlesque party scene also entails

games of seduction: a lascivious encounter between Lulu and Goldberg takes place when Lulu sits on Goldberg's lap; Meg, prior to Stanley's stranglehold, capitalizes upon her "succulent" nature in her conversation with McCann; and when the lights go out Lulu is spread-eagle on the table with Stanley standing over her.

Every time Stanley takes off his glasses this signals a change in perception. One of these radical changes in perception occurs when the two guests, Goldberg and Mc-Cann, are about to arrive. They symbolize Stanley's fear of the unknown, those "visitors" from outside "this house on the list" (20). Stanley's anxiety, triggered by their impending arrival, projects itself like some "menace" inadvertently onto Meg through fits of anger. Stanley's drum, a significant prop in the play, could be construed as a symbol of breaking the membrane of his conceptual womb room that Meg, Petey and Stanley, through initia-tion, have fabricated. He thinks that he has seen these two intruders before in Maidenhead as he mentions to them. There is elaborate punning on Pinter's part here because Lulu the maiden wants Stanley to break-out in a connota-tive sense. So, the play entails the story of boy meets girl, and the girl has some affect. Thus, it is conceivable why Pinter has Stanley wash his face and remove his spectacles repeatedly when he encounters Lulu, for she is considered to be an option, an alternative game, in which to escape the likes of Goldberg and McCann, those who have games of their own in mind.

Pinter's Goldberg might be seen as a gold mountain, mount Sinai in a tragi-comic sense where Judaism begins (the Mosaic code), and also where Christianity begins. To Stan-ley, Goldberg and McCann allegorically represent "Monty," the figurative *mont* in French that refers back to the source or back to Biblical patriarchal figures. Here, Pinter dramatizes the human condition by using this allegory paradoxically, for in post-war existential thought man resides in a Godless universe where he must create mean-ing in order to rationalize his existence, and games, a disparate attempt to create meaning, are man made; therefore, the metaphysical connection attributed to Bibli-cal, essentially patriarchal, figures is absent, as a passage from Goldberg indicates:

. . . All my life I've said the same. Play up, play up, and play the game. Honour thy father and thy mother. All along the line. Follow the line, the line, McCann, and you can't go wrong. What do you think, I'm a self made man: No! I sat where I was told to sit. I keep my eye on the ball. School? Don't talk to me about school. Top in all subjects. And for why? Because I'm telling you, I'm telling you, follow my line? Follow my mental? Learn by heart. Never write down a thing. And don't go too near the water. And you'll find—what I say is true. Because I believe that the world . . . (*Vacant*) . . . Because I believe that the world . . . (*Desperate*) . . . BECAUSE I BELIEVE THAT THE WORLD . . . (*Lost*). . . .

(78)

The principle conflict in *The Birthday Party* seems to oc-cur when Stanley, who cannot or does not want to change, to be reborn, encounters Goldberg and McCann, who come along wanting (even demanding) him to change or they will change him. As Meg exclaims, "It's his birthday today," his so-called nativity (32). He summoned Goldberg and Mccann into "being" there, but when they come, he is devastated. McCann represents through his tearing of the newspaper a literal breakdown in communication. He causes Stanley to experience a birth trauma at the party. McCann is Irish because to an English audience he symbolizes violence and terrorism despite the fact that he is a defrocked priest. Along with Goldberg, he attempts to stop Stanley from being a "wash-out," or having no identity according to their context.

Some may interpret Stanley's dilemma as analogous to the artist torn between bourgeoisie existence and the bohemian life. In this vein, McCann and Goldberg represent that "external force," society, as they forcibly attempt to make Stanley respect and acknowledge the status quo, that conventional construct called society. Hence, all their questions are designed to break Stanley down, to make him become a "decent human being." Meg too attempts to make Stanley her little boy, along with Petey as the perfect surrogate father. These fictional identity constructs are possible because Stanley's identity as the artistically frustrated pianist is fallible. In contrast to Stanley, every character believes in his or her vision of the world—or as Goldberg says, "I believe in the world"—without which they contrive for themselves. All believe in the world except for Stanley who remains an outsider, for indecision seems to be his primary attribute. He resorts to a primal sense of self by banging on the toy drum or by fleeing to the womb room to escape their games. The room is an important thematic motif in Pinter's play in that it signifies distance or a retreat from uncertainty, or that unseen element of chaos, a menace. During this breakfast scene in Act I, as soon as Stanley finds out about the two gentlemen coming to visit, he complains about his dreary situation to Meg. Then, suddenly, he demands his tea which is symbolically a traditional custom in Britain. Through his overtly hostile conversation with Meg, one can perceive his inner tension over said convention such as social decorum. An instance of his reluctance to "play the game" or any game occurs when Meg asks him when he is going to start playing the piano again, and he attempts to contrive the most lame excuses for his lost career, his "lost" identity as a concert pianist. He must fabricate and nurture his ego by saying that his first concert was unjustly panned by the critics and that before his second concert he was locked out. Pinter punningly recants Stanley's present lack of motivation and his sense of a somewhat fleeting identity crisis by having Meg tell Goldberg that Stanley's main problem is that he was "locked in," subjectively speaking.

As previously mentioned, the newspaper is an important motif in many ways. Petey's newspaper is used as a refuge from Meg, from the reality of their environment. The newspaper separates one from reality in that it represents organized information, both in graphics and construction, thereby allowing the reader to think he/she is in control.

Within this orthographic structure, the newspaper, there is a juxtaposition of images that force the reader to contend with the implied relationships amongst narrative, metaphorical, and iconographic images. Therefor, Mccann's tearing of the newspaper is an unnerving torture to Stanley, the sight and sound of disorder, it reflects the breakdown of Stanley, of his sense of reality, as well as the overall breakdown of communication which Pinter wishes to reveal. For the reader knows when a piece of paper falls from Petey's morning newspaper in Act III that the Stanley who Meg and Petey fabricated ceased to exist.

Pinter undercuts the possibility of tragedy in the conventional sense, for he impresses upon the reader that what is perceived as intrinsically good could also be seen as unfortunately bad. Gameplaying, whether traditional games or narrative games, contribute to one's knowledge of ambiguity, of uncertainty, of risks. He plays upon conventional motifs in *The Birthday Party* by obscuring such ideals as heroism, power, mortality and the extent of catharsis. When tragedy is conceived as incidental rather than formulaic such as the result of the character's motivation and action, then what language can express and what it inadvertently impresses upon the characters and the reader alike demonstrates this problematic situation. Nothing is resolved, not even the plot, in terms of revealing some "intrinsic meaning"; only the cacophonous sounds such as Petey's cornflakes crackling in milk or McCann's tearing of the newspaper become things in the realm of certainty.

At the end of the play, Pinter plays upon the tragicomic sense of renewal by making Stanley's pantomime bowel movement his last rebellious gesture expressing the "caaahhh . . . caaahhh" prospect of rebirth. Perhaps Petey's advice to Meg in the beginning of the play that she should let Stanley sleep was not such a bad idea because a change in Stanley's lethargic routine, one brought on by gameplaying, can sometimes cause dire consequences.

As so succinctly stated by John Russell Brown in "Words and Silence: *The Birthday Party,*" Pinter's characters use language to subvert their sense of detachment in a seemingly meaningless universe, albeit a run down English coastal resort, and Pinter as playwright discloses that language as a means to communicate with others or to assert control over one's destiny is at best the only means of communication and, unfortunately, the least reliable:

> At the center of Pinter's plays is a skepticism about language of unusual tenacity. Can anything ever be said to be corrected stated in words? Can anything ever be said to be "stated?" We play with words, and words play with us. We can neither say what we know, nor know what we say. When we stop to think, we do not trust words.

(23)

Perhaps this is why the issue of gameplaying becomes a dominant motif in *The Birthday Party,* because through games, whether narrative or conventional, Pinter enables us to view characters who attempt to project a sense of certainty in a post war cultural environment where traditions need to be resurrected or re-invented.

Works Cited

Brown, John Russell. "Words and Silence: *The Birthday Party*." *Harold Pinter: Modern Critical Views*. Ed. Harold Bloom. New York: Chelsea, 1987.

Esslin, Martin. *The Theatre of the Absurd*. Hammondsworth: Penguin, 1961.

————. "Language and Silence." *Harold Pinter: Modern Critical Views*. Ed. Harold Bloom. New York: Chelsea, 1987.

Havel, Vaclav. *Living in Truth*. Ed. Jan Vladislav. Great Britain: Faber, 1987.

Knowles, Ronald. "Names and Naming in the Plays of Harold Pinter." *Harold Pinter: You Never Heard Such a Silence*. Ed. Alan Bold. Totowa, NJ: Vision and Barnes and Noble, 1984.

Lyotard, Jean-Francois, and Jean-Loup Thebaud. *Just Gaming*. Minneapolis: U of Minnesota P, 1985.

Pinter, Harold. *The Birthday Party*. New York: Grove, 1959.

Thompson, David T. *Pinter: The Player's Playwright*. London: Macmillan, 1985.

THE DUMB WAITER AND THE COLLECTION

PRODUCTION REVIEW

Edith Oliver (essay date 1962)

SOURCE: "Comedies of Terror," in *The New Yorker*, Vol. 38, No. 42, December 8, 1962, pp. 148-51.

[*In the following review, Oliver gives high praise to* The Dumb Waiter *and* The Collection.]

The problem this week is to give you some idea of the brilliance and originality and wild humor of *The Dumbwaiter* and *The Collection,* two one-acters by Harold Pinter at the Cherry Lane, without at the same time revealing too many of the surprises. *The Dumbwaiter* is one of his early plays; *The Collection* is his most recent. On the evidence of both, and of last year's *The Caretaker,* it seems to me that Mr. Pinter, right from the start, has broken comedy

into its components and taken for himself the element of cruelty to probe and explore and juggle around. All three plays are comedies about torture and menace—about, I guess, practical jokes. (That is not all they are, of course.) The victims in *The Dumbwaiter* are a pair of matter-of-fact Cockneys, Ben and Gus, who are waiting on a pair of sagging cots in the basement of a deserted building somewhere in Birmingham for a signal from their boss telling them that the time has come to do "the job." That "the job" is one they have done many times before becomes apparent in their sketchily reminiscent conversation, in their casual deportment, and in the off-hand way they handle and examine their pistols. They are so matter-of-fact when we meet them that it takes some time to discover that their nerves are shot, but this becomes plain when they are subjected to a series of what appear to be nutty pranks, chief among them a dumbwaiter that repeatedly comes down to a hatch in the wall bearing orders for meals, which grow more and more elaborate. Frantically, Ben and Gus pile their own provisions—tea, biscuits, chocolate, potato chips—onto the dumbwaiter, and then get word through a speaking tube that their food is unsatisfactory. Their panic rises. They feel that they are being put to a test, but they can't figure out why. Toward the end, their conversation becomes a stencil of their conversation at the beginning—same form but no content. The ending is as surprising and loony as all that has gone before it.

The Dumbwaiter is a farce about cruelty in which the tricks are physical—the dumbwaiter and its freakish orders, offstage plumbing that doesn't work and then whooshes away on its own, a gas burner that doesn't light, mysterious envelopes under the door, and the mysterious voice over the speaking tube. *The Collection* is high comedy about cruelty in which the tricks are verbal. The action alternates between the two sides of the stage. At stage left is an elaborate house in Belgravia inhabited by a pair of homosexuals—an elegant, gray-haired man and a young man he once picked up in a slum and has trained to be a dress designer. At stage right is the modern and fashionable Chelsea flat of a husband and wife; the wife is also a dress designer, and the husband runs their shop. Except for the wife and the young man, who do not meet onstage but whose encounter at a fashion show at Leeds the week before sparks the plot (did he sleep with her or didn't he?), the characters combine and recombine in a series of lethal tête-à-têtes. These dialogues are duels, really, in which the playwright displays infinite and comic variations on psychological torture—the unanswered question, the smile that goes dead, the surprise shift from camaraderie to menace, the false security that ends in fright, the purposely irrational behavior, the threat of physical violence that comes to nothing, the easy game that ends in pain. It is all civilized and funny on the surface and diabolic and funny underneath. Each of the characters becomes the victim of the hypnotic malice of one of the others, just as the audience becomes the victim of the hypnotic Mr. Pinter. His theatrical talent seems to me the strongest that has come along in years. Every prop, every movement, every word has meaning; nothing goes to waste. It is interesting to trace his path from *The Dumbwaiter* to *The Caretaker* to *The Collection*. (I don't think progress comes into it much; they are all splendid plays.) In *The Dumbwaiter,* the mischief is spooky and comes from offstage. In *The Collection,* it is sane and concrete—no longer free-floating, as it was in *The Caretaker,* but firmly anchored in the nature of the people involved. The play is absolutely tight; there are no chinks this time for the allegorical interpreters, and no mistakes. Also, Pinter seems to have sloughed off all trace of the influence of Samuel Beckett, a man with one-eighty-fifth of his ability.

Dana Elcar and John C. Becher do beautifully as Ben and Gus in *The Dumbwaiter.* For the first few minutes, their Cockney accent sounded a little off, but either it got better or I got used to it. In *The Collection,* James Ray is the husband, Patricia Roe the wife, Henderson Forsythe the elderly homosexual, and James Patterson the young man. Their acting is flawless. Alan Schneider staged both plays, but the performance was so magnetic that I couldn't step back even far enough to notice his direction. William Ritman's settings are fine, too.

THE CARETAKER

PRODUCTION REVIEWS

A. Alvarez (essay date 1960)

SOURCE: "Olivier among the Rhinos," in *New Statesman,* Vol. 59, May 7, 1960, pp. 666-67.

[*In the following review, Alvarez complains that, despite an excellent production,* The Caretaker *is disappointing because, in it, Pinter repeats what he has "already done better in other plays."*]

Harold Pinter's new play, **The Caretaker** (Arts) is rather disappointing. Donald McWhinnie's direction could not be better; he squeezes every last drop of meaning from the play and gains a whole extra dimension of meaning from his handling of sounds: rasping breath, terrible, screaming nightmares, ominous bumps in the dark and perfectly timed, equally appalling silences. It is not for nothing that McWhinnie has the reputation of being the BBC's most intelligent drama producer; at this rate, he will soon have the same standing on the legitimate stage. The cast of three, Donald Pleasence, Peter Woodthorpe and Alan Bates, respond to this treatment with an equal intelligence. They recreate the rather stock characters from the ground

up in their own fresh terms. As an example of sheer theatrical skill, the production could scarcely be bettered.

The play, however, is less assured. Pinter is a master of the single scene, but he seems to have great difficulty in spinning a work out for three acts. Aston (Peter Woodthorpe) rescues a tramp (Donald Pleasence) from a café brawl, takes him home and gives him clothes, money and a job as caretaker. He does it all with scarcely a word, motivated only by a kind of indifferent charity. Mick (Alan Bates), Aston's practical, tough-boy brother, bullies the tramp, terrifies him but treats him as an equal man of the world. The tramp is driven almost mad with anger by Aston's blank goodness; he tries to set brother against brother, fails and is thrown out. The action develops, then languishes. It reaches a tremendous climax when Aston, in a trance of remembered horror, describes his spell in a mental home where he had been given shock treatment; this is the finest single speech I've heard in a very long time. Then the action spurts forward again, languishes and fades away. It is bitty, haphazard, too long by about a third.

The trouble is that Pinter repeats himself from play to play. He is concerned always with the same human derelicts who, as they continually say, 'don't stand a chance'. He is, of course, mining a vein of Beckett's, and I don't believe Beckett, who writes out of his martyrdom to his own limitations, is rich enough to stand so extensive a working. After a certain point (and this is the fourth Pinter I've seen in a few months), the controlled inconsequentiality seems more mannered than funny and the unspoken terrors are too easily implied. But in Aston's long speech the terrors are at last spoken. If only Pinter would go on from there and not just lapse back into what he has already done better in other plays!

John Simon (essay date 1961)

SOURCE: Review of *The Caretaker,* in *The Hudson Review,* Vol. 14, No. 4, Winter, 1961, pp. 590-91.

[*In the following review, Simon can find nothing of value in* The Caretaker.]

Not since Joanna Southcote announced that she would give birth to the Messiah, have there been such public pangs and heaving—and such a failure to produce even a *ridiculus mus*—as the Lyceum (operating) Theatre, where Harold Pinter's *The Caretaker* tossed and moaned like a parturient Ingmar Bergman heroine. We have heard this play explained by assorted mystagogues as a tragicomic excursion into the Kafkaesque realms of human non-communication; as a salty satire on the British middle class with all its prejudices, pretensions, and absurdity; as a Manichaean parable of man's existence; and as an insoluble conundrum full of fascinating and funny details. One of the producers freely admitted that he does not understand it, which, however, did not keep him from producing it; the reviewers, though they admitted nothing, gave ample evidence in their reviews of equal incomprehension, which, however, did not prevent them from praising the play to the skies.

One trouble with the various explications is that they are either too parochial or too cosmically vague; another is that they do not fit. The play abounds in every kind of mystification: disconnected speeches, non sequiturs, red herrings, paradoxes for the sheer hell of it, withheld information, unexplained oddities, and, above all, unimpregnated silences. Most of the time, the speeches seem to be carefully constructed so as to have all the superficies of sense, but a big hole where the meaning ought to be; and whatever connecting thread may have held the minuscule incidents together, has been carefully allowed to rot away. When the language happens to deviate into sense, as in the elder brother's description of how he was given shock treatment, the drabness and triviality of the writing become manifest in spite of Robert Shaw's immaculate reading of the lines.

The Caretaker, I am afraid, is very much the work of an actor who relies on his knowledge of the externals of theatre and his shallow awareness of contemporary trends in drama. For whereas the better experimental writers in today's theatre have mastered the uses of language and symbol, Mr. Pinter, a once and future thespian, though occasionally amusing and sometimes resourceful in thinking up effective things for his three brilliant actors to do, has no style, no ideas, no poetic fantasy with which to hold us. "Vacant and idiotic as an actress," Lawrence Durrell says of a mirror in one of his poems. This is unfairly discriminatory. For it can be applied with equal rights to most *actors,* at least when they overstep the narrow boundaries of their competence.

CRITICAL COMMENTARY

Valerie Minogue (essay date 1960)

SOURCE: "Taking Care of the Caretaker," in *The Twentieth Century,* Vol. 168, No. 1003, September, 1960, pp. 243-48.

[*In the following essay, Minogue argues that reviewers of* The Caretaker *focused too much on Pinter's style and ignored the content of the play.*]

A man went rushing into a building. 'Fire! Fire! Fire!' he cried. 'Hell! the flaming house is on fire!' Those who lived in the house had been trained in the New Criticism. 'Splendidly vivid. Lower-class idiom,' said one. 'Repetitive but racy,' said another. 'Over-emotional of course, but dramatic,' said a third. And they all went on with what they were doing. The funeral was a quiet affair.

This fable aptly represents the relations between Harold Pinter's play *The Caretaker,* and its critics. Although many have praised the production, the evocation of atmosphere, and the accurate reflection of lower-class talk, most have seen it as a sort of specialized sociological document. Few have explored the content and ideas of the play—these have been 'taken care of' by being attributed to a 'special belt of English suburbia'.

Now that the play has been published (together with *The Birthday Party* and other plays in a companion volume[1] we have little excuse for refusing to explore further. The plays require to be read by the mental vocal-chords rather than by the eye alone, but they are worth the effort.

In an interview on 'Monitor' Pinter expressed his admiration for the lower-class speech with which he appears to have hypnotized the critics. He also objected, as I think justifiably, to the attitude of mind which relegates all the import of the play to a remote limbo solely inhabited by derelicts. What he admired about the idiom was its 'muscularity'—and this seems to involve an attachment to the muscles of thought and feeling, from which the impulse to speak derives. This kind of talk is not formalized or pre-thought, not made into useful counters exchangeable at standard rates. Despite its apparent air of banality, and its inconsequences (or because of them) the effects are fresh and revealing. Even the worn-out cliché creates its own horror, when we see its ineptness at the very moment of utterance:

'I never had enough time to go into it,' [says the tramp, or again, watching Aston fiddling with a plug]:

'You getting to the root of the trouble are you?'

'I've got a suspicion.'

'You're lucky.'

The difference between this and middle-class speech seems less one of kind than of degree. Middle-class speech less often reveals its lacunes, and though it also derives from the rag-bag and pot-pourri of jargon and cliché, appearances are better kept up. The merest twitch of a toe may be the only expression of the sudden discomfort. In *The Caretaker,* discomforts, evasions, and pretensions flash like headlights on a dark road.

In the three characters, the illusions are less expertly integrated, the supposed realities less solidly entrenched, the fears, confusions, and delusions of grandeur nearer the surface than they are in most of us. Clearly this idiom, and this group of people served Mr Pinter's purpose particularly well—but what purpose? Only the writer himself can tell us; but we can at least examine what he has done, and discuss his achievement.

Three men are trying, by means of language, to surmount barriers and find common ground. Their language itself, because of its imperfections—and their lack of expertise—reveals the fears, needs, and inadequacies they struggle to conceal. All three co-operate to cover up things which are embarrassing not merely to one but to all. They attempt to close the abyss—silence is the great enemy—generally understanding too much rather than too little. Their talk shows, as Mr Pinter said, not so much a failure as an evasion of communication. In silence, the questions they avoid are deafening, and silence in this world becomes a catalyst of action, even action itself. Talk seems an expedient, a means of evasion. In silence and in the dark is the nonentity against which they all precariously struggle.

The fight against nonentity, or simply non-being, is something that echoes over and over through the Pinter plays. In *The Birthday Party,* Goldberg and McCann taunt Webber with

> 'Who are you, Webber? What makes you think you exist?'

and this is a repetition of Stan's enquiry, early in the play (moving typically from the phrase 'who do you think you're talking to?'):

> 'Tell me, Mrs Boles, when you address yourself to me, do you ever ask yourself who exactly you are talking to?'

In the case of the tramp of *The Caretaker,* who has left all his papers at Sidcup, the theme is worked out against the background of the other two men, who have a slightly stronger grip on identity. Aston achieves this by clinging tightly to the very little he has left, and Mick by refusing to let anything come between him and his 'I'll-make-this-place-into-a-penthouse' delusions of grandeur.

Pinter's analytical use of the idiom, betraying at each moment the bare bones of motive and emotion, is often funny, but also embarrassing, and at times, unbearable. Kenneth Tynan, reviewing the play, wrote 'one laughs in recognition; but one's laughter is tinged with snobbism.' This seems to indicate an enviable certainty of being out of reach. It would be comforting if this picture of humanity had nothing to do with the world we know, but it seems to concern not an isolated group of institutionalized eccentrics, but Man in general. If my laughter was tinged with anything, it was embarrassment, and occasionally horror, a feeling of having been caught out, and exposed to a chill wind.

To relegate this comment on life to a special and defined area is in many ways a sensible protective reaction; it is difficult to live without some regard for mental comfort. Pinter's view may be salutary, but it is far from pleasant. It forces upon us standards of judgement by which we cannot live, awareness that we would sooner avoid. To see human helplessness, to recognize the vainglorious weakness with which we habitually meet facts and situations that appal if seen too clearly—this is to hold up a mirror to an aspect of life (not total but none the less true) which it is easier to ignore than contemplate.

Does no one wonder, hearing Aston's description of his experiences in a mental hospital, and seeing the curious half-life he leads, whether there is not something wrong, and perhaps a little cocksure about our treatment of those we regard as of unsound mind? Does no one recognize in himself the hapless turning from attitude to attitude in order to entrench a position, or see, in the desperate claims to knowing what goes on, his own baffled attempts to lay claim to at least a partial understanding of what life is all about? Does no one share the feeling that 'if only the weather would break', if only everyone and everything would stand still for a tick of time (in fact if only things were different) then one might have a chance? Does no one see in Aston's sad monologue, his own reduction by the shocks of living; does no one feel appalled at the difficulties of disinterested kindness in a world that lives not by charity but by politics?

We have all left our references and papers somewhere. We mostly feel we have 'cards of identity' somewhere even more inaccessible than Sidcup. Sidcup seems to derive from the same myth-making impulse as the Garden of Eden, where we mislaid our innocence and our nobility, but if the weather would break, we might dash back and get them—but,

> The glass is falling hour by hour, the glass will fall for ever, But if you break the bloody glass you won't hold up the weather.

One sees in the play the frenzied attempt to feel important, and to be 'in' on things. We must know the right responses whether to jig-saws, fret-saws, 'Blacks', work-shy people, the latest 'ism' or the newest West End play. We must know what 'they' are saying, even if we choose to disagree. 'Oh, they're handy,' says the tramp, and we recognize the awful futility of it all. The terrible thing about the dialogue is that it has the authentic ring of the stop-gap. Behind it lies the awareness of another world of meanings, a plane on which defeats are being acknowledged, and where there is a fight for the right to exist, an endless apology for existence, a fierce assertion of rights, and a hideous plea for forgiveness of what is known to be unforgivable, and irremediable. When silence begins to leak through the battered pores of the speakers, they point to the obvious, to the bucket for instance, catching the drips from the roof. They distract each other's attention away to the mundane realities, that are at the same time a symbol of the unsatisfactory state of things which will, of course, be put right in time, when the shed is built in the garden, when we get back from Sidcup with our papers.

Or again, when the silence threatens, one may ask 'What's your name?' and continue the fight against nonentity. No matter that it's been asked before, and given before; it's still a symbol of stability, especially if we know not only the assumed name, but the *real* name as well. Yet it tells us nothing. Anonymity remains, and the papers are still at Sidcup. We are all in some sense dispossessed, frightened, ridiculous, like the tramp who, in the bravado of fear, pulls out a knife against Mick. Mick sits beside him when he is bored with baiting him, and offers him a sandwich. They sit together, getting chummy over shared views, while the tramp, who appears to have no views, tries to commit himself to views acceptable to Mick. Mick, taking the intention as sufficient, says 'I can see you're a man of the world', thus acknowledging the tramp's right to exist in the world he is a man of. And we are all in this sense 'men of the world' claiming to know what is going on in a world dominated by 'them'. We too have our fingers on the imaginary pulse of things, we know there is a 'crying need' for this, that, and the other. We have to have some pipe-line to 'in-ness' if not to infinity. We like to tap our heads significantly like Mr Pinter's tramp implying that 'they' haven't got *us* fooled. And it all underlines our helplessness in a world even more obviously out of control than usual.

We pretend to know what it all means, and jockey for position in a competitive world whose rules are baffling. We resemble the tramp whose shifts of allegiance, whose endless search for the expedient are pitilessly laid bare. We see his vain efforts to discover exactly where his dependence lies; he wants clearly to know 'which way the wind is blowing', and spends a great deal of time trying to find absolute answers to the question—who has the power to kick him out? Whose support does he need most? It seems ultimately his servility that defeats him, for servility implies at least some knowledge of whom it is worthwhile to placate. When this proves impossible to discover, he has no means of living with the others. He goes off at the end of the play, presumably to find other people on whom to impose his failures, his trailing clouds of vainglory, others to whom he can justify himself—perhaps searching for a day of judgement, but unable to find a judge. It is interesting that at the end, Aston stands with his back to him, refusing to speak, refusing to see him, and slowly the tramp's efforts to talk himself into recognition twitter away into the long silence in which he recognizes defeat.

No one is much interested in forgiving or condemning him, no one wants to know the 'truth' about him, no one wants his excuses or promises, for they have their own, and so have we all.

While Mick, the younger brother, is a bundle of undirected energies, flexing his muscles, but achieving nothing, it is Aston, the gentle elder brother who has authority. This appears to derive from his having his silences under control. He has accepted defeat, recognized limitations, and impotence, as though he had been surgically detached from his life, while Mick and the tramp are still shadow-boxing with theirs. When, at the end of a fierce scene with the tramp, he announces quietly, 'I don't think we're hitting it off', it seems not merely understated, but under-experienced, only half-felt. He seems almost emotionless, though he recognizes occasional discomforts and seeks to remove them. He accepts the abyss as normal, nonentity as a mode of existence, and lives in a permanently shell-shocked state where his own reality is without importance.

He seems more able to cope with immediate things than the other two, perhaps because he is so uninvolved. One may well ask whether reality is so terrible that one can only accept it by losing half one's life. The half that is left is capable of registering surprise; he has some sense of the fitness of things, while the tramp, completely enclosed in fantasy, does not even have this. Aston's concern about building the shed before he begins to decorate is far less aggressive than the excuses of the other two. One feels that he knows he's beaten before he begins, but it doesn't much matter anyway. The shed-illusion seems at times a polite piece of conformism—a way of sharing the life and idiom of the others.

Now all of this seems far more than a specialized sociological study, and involves more than the pleasure of recognizing conversations overheard in buses and public places. Certainly it is possible we may ultimately have to avoid the issue, but we might first look at what we are about to evade.

There is little point in pretending that Mr Pinter had nothing to say to us anyway. When someone shouts 'Fire!' it's fun to analyse the style, but it may not be prudent to ignore the content.

Note

1. *The Caretaker* and *The Birthday Party and Other Plays,* by Harold Pinter. (Methuen, 1960).

Robert P. Murphy (essay date 1972)

SOURCE: "Non-Verbal Communication and the Over-looked Action in Pinter's *The Caretaker,*" in *The Quarterly Journal of Speech,* Vol. 58, No. 1, February, 1972, pp. 41-7.

[*In the following essay, Murphy focuses on* The Caretaker, *explaining the importance of attending to action indicated by the stage directions as much as to the dialogue in Pinter's plays.*]

Few modern dramatists manage to employ dialogue and gesture without emphasizing one at the expense of the other; and even fewer critics seem able to appreciate non-verbal communication in the context of a basically verbal play. Non-verbal communication, in particular gesture, is of special importance in the plays of Harold Pinter. Emphasis on Pinter's dialogue—especially the mysteries, fragments of information, red herrings, and obvious contradictions—to the exclusion of the various gestures and *seemingly* inconsequential actions had led to misinterpretations of his plays, notably *The Caretaker* (1960). The richness of Pinter's dialogue makes it all too tempting to overlook the non-verbal aspects of *The Caretaker.* These are clearly spelled out, however, for the careful reader. Failure to include the gestures and "minor" actions in a performance—i.e., failure to follow exactly Pinter's printed directions—is another matter altogether, for even the most attentive playgoer cannot see what is not there. *The Caretaker* hinges on the non-verbal communication between the brothers Mick and Aston and on the audience being enabled to perceive their communications.

The obvious objection to my argument is that I am making too much of a few stage directions; however, the man who is perhaps the most perceptive and acute of all Pinter's critics has convincingly shown that every stage direction in Pinter's plays—without exception—is vital and charged with meaning. John Russell Brown reminds us that Pinter was an actor long before he was a playwright and that he is particularly aware of the power and importance of subtle gestures and actions. Pinter is perhaps the only modern playwright who orchestrates gestures, pauses, and silences, and he carefully distinguishes between slight pauses, pauses, and long pauses.[1]

In *The Theatre of the Absurd* Martin Esslin writes that the final scene of *The Caretaker* "is almost unbearably tragic. After Davies has been shown in all his abject unreliability, clearly undeserving of the charity offered to him by the brothers, his ejection from the dingy room that could have become his world assumes almost the cosmic proportions of Adam's expulsion from Paradise. Davies's lying, his assertiveness, his inability to resist any chance to impose himself as superior, are, after all, mankind's original sin—hubris, lack of humility, blindness to our own faults."[2] Esslin goes on to quote a letter of Pinter's to the London *Sunday Times*: "'As far as I'm concerned *The Caretaker* is funny up to a point. Beyond that point it ceases to be funny, and it was because of that point that I wrote it.'"[3] The questions I would like to consider are, first, whether the play is in fact tragic, and if so, why and for whom. The second is whether there is some recognizable point in the play—some gesture, action, or speech—which informs the entire play and makes it cease to be funny.

Critics agree that one character is the victim or potential victim of a cruel game played by one or more of the other characters, although opinions vary widely as to the identity of the victim. In the most prevalent interpretation, which relies heavily on understanding *The Caretaker* in terms of Pinter's entire canon, Aston is the victim. According to this theory, Aston, who lives in a huge, cluttered room at the top of a large house which belongs to his younger brother Mick, is victimized by Davies, a tramp whom he has rescued from a café fight. Aston, who is kind and considerate but slow-witted as the result of electric shock treatments at a mental institution, brings Davies home, gives him money, and offers to let him stay. Once he is entrenched, Davies' true personality surfaces: he is belligerent, demanding, fawning when it suits his purposes, and convinced that the world owes him a living. Aston, despite Davies' arrogance and presumptuousness, offers him the job of caretaker while he redecorates the house, a job concocted by Mick to occupy Aston. After Aston has revealed his electric shock treatments to Davies, Davies tries to play off one brother against the other and succeeds

to the point that Mick—independently—also offers him the job of caretaker. In an attempt completely to replace Aston, Davies oversteps himself by suggesting to Mick that his brother be reinstitutionalized. This brings the brothers closer to one another and the play ends with Davies pleading not to be thrown out.

This interpretation is very reasonable in terms of Pinter's other plays. Davies would certainly seem to be the usual usurper, the character from outside who comes into the warm, lighted, secure room in order to sow discord and disruption and either replace one of the inhabitants of this island of security or carry him away. Despite its shabbiness, Mick's house is an island of safety and security. The backyard is described as a dense, overgrown jungle, inhabited by "them Blacks." The house is a refuge in a menacing, hostile world, a world that is both literally and figuratively a jungle, a world of threatening foreigners, café fights, and shock treatments at mental institutions. Certainly for Aston it is a place where he does not have to cope with the complexities of modern life and a place where he can live "normally" in his own muddled way. Davies would seem to menace Aston's security by attempting to usurp his place. This is very similar to the way in which Mr. and Mrs. Sands in *The Room* (1960) menace the security of Rose. Rose's room is a place of warmth and light in a world of cold, ice, and darkness. The Sands insist that her room is for rent. It is the blind Negro, Riley, who finally destroys Rose's security, however, by transferring his blindness to her. The shabby seaside boarding house of Petey and Meg in *The Birthday Party* (1958) is a place of refuge and hiding for Stanley from the institution or organization from which he has escaped until Goldberg and McCann take him back to Monty. The dumb Matchseller in *A Slight Ache* (1959) succeeds in usurping Edward's place in the comfortable country house in which the play takes place and at the end of the play Edward exits with the tray of sodden, useless matches. Thus, *The Caretaker* may be read as another play of usurpation.[4]

In a modification of this interpretation Aston remains the victim, but the role of Davies as usurper is de-emphasized. Aston is the artist, poet, rebel, or simply a person who persists in asking embarrassing questions who is crushed into conformity by society. This reading emphasizes Aston's great speech at the end of the second act in which he tells of his talking too much and his hallucinations which preceded his commitment. Aston might indeed have been some sort of militant idealist or reformer. The governments on neither side of the "iron curtain" have ever hesitated to declare such people insane and tuck them safely away in mental institutions. Now, after the electric shock treatments, Aston claims—with Davies—that he has never dreamed. This reading, too, draws ready support from other plays in the canon: Stanley in *The Birthday Party* is a pianist at odds with the tastemakers; Gus, one of the hired gunmen in *The Dumb Waiter* (1960) wonders, among other things, why they kill their various victims and who cleans up after them; and Len in *The Dwarfs*

(1960) questions most of the values of modern, materialistic society. All of these questioners are crushed or killed, and Aston may be simply one more such rebel.[5]

In yet another variation of this basic interpretation, in which Aston is kind and slow-witted and Davies a potential usurper, Mick manipulates Davies. Mick becomes jealous of Davies' having usurped his relationship with Aston but in order to get rid of Davies without upsetting Aston's delicate mental balance he must manipulate Davies so that he oversteps himself and Aston thinks getting rid of Davies is his own idea. Aston is a potential victim, Davies is both usurper and victim, and all the real vitality and initiative belong to Mick.[6]

A second group of critics sees all three characters as victims—all engaged in an endless quest for acceptance, security, identity, and lost innocence,[7] or else victims of "the System," or simply of the human condition itself. Mick wants to achieve success and security for himself and Aston through his carpentry business. Most of all, he wants to provide a refuge for Aston. Aston speaks wistfully of the ready acceptance of his mates in the factory and pubs that was his before his hospitalization. Davies wants to go to Sidcup to get the papers, left there years ago, that will prove his identity. Aston and Mick might indeed be the representatives of a repressive "System" which includes the detritus of a corrupt religious tradition, a meaningless and destructive technology, an emphasis on physical comforts, and a deadening brand-name aesthetic. The flat itself is literally a junk heap of modern civilization. The subtlest intellectual distinction of which the three men seem capable is the difference between a fret saw and a jig saw. Mick's scheme for decorating the flat is a compendium of all the worst tastes in our modern, mass-produced plastic world: teal-blue, copper and parchment linoleum squares, with the colors echoed in the walls; off-white rug; plastic-topped coffee table; and a table of afro-mosia teak veneer. Mick and Aston are the spokesmen and representatives of this "System," even if Aston might at one time have questioned it, and they try to impose it on Davies, who is a kind of archetypal tramp. Although Mick and Aston are representatives of the "System" which victimizes Davies, they, too, are victims because they are unable to escape it themselves.[8] One version of this interpretation emphasizes that the three characters are less the victims of a consciously repressive "System" than of the human condition itself, which is implacably and gratuitously cruel.[9] The dirt, disorder, and futile activity of the flat symbolize man's condition. Outside is the jungle, with its threatening "Blacks," café fights, and monks who offer no succor to the needy. The only possible change inside is the creation of a world of tawdry creature comforts totally devoid of any real beauty or warmth. Civilization is a junk heap, inhabited by men who think only of themselves, ready always to deprive their fellow men of whatever shabby and meager security they might have achieved. Certainly there is overwhelming gratuitous cruelty in *The Caretaker,* but it is directed by Aston and Mick toward Davies alone.

A third group of critics, all of whom seem much closer to the mark, recognizes either the essential game structure of *The Caretaker* or that Davies alone is the victim of the games; however, none seems willing to recognize the degree of cruelty and gratuitous maliciousness involved in the games Aston and Mick play with Davies. One critic who recognizes the basic game structure of the play insists that Aston is as much a victim or attempted victim of Davies as Davies is of Mick,[10] and still another critic recognizes Davies as the only victim of a cruel game but dismisses the entire play in which such gratuitous cruelty exists as psychologically untrue.[11] Finally, one critic recognizes and accepts Davies as the sole victim of a gratuitous game perpetrated on him by Aston and Mick but feels that Aston is a passive member of the team which reduces Davies to babbling helplessness.[12] Aston is slow-witted, perhaps even kindly, and participates completely unknowingly in the cruel games planned and executed by Mick. This makes Mick into a double villain; he victimizes Davies and, more cruelly, uses his mentally deficient and completely dependent brother to do so.

All of the critics whose interpretations I have reviewed rely on analysis of dialogue and gross actions and ignore the non-verbal communications Pinter carefully incorporates in the form of gestures and "stage business." Davies is indeed the victim of a cruel game, a game consciously and maliciously played on him by both Aston and Mick. The single action of the play is the game in which Aston brings Davies home, after having "rescued" him from a café fight, where he and Mick, using classic Pavlovian and police state methods and rarely appearing together, torment him to distraction for no apparent reason by constantly destroying the expectations of security and acceptance which they themselves have planted in him.

The consciousness of the game and the co-ordination between the two brothers is obvious from the opening scene of the play. When the curtain rises Mick alone is silently and expressionlessly surveying the contents of the room. When he hears Aston and Davies below he quietly goes out before they enter. If he were really concerned about Aston's condition he would have stayed to see whom Aston was bringing home, but in fact he has been making a final check of the preparations for the game he and Aston are about to play. After Aston brings Davies in he almost immediately begins drawing Davies out in order to find out where he is vulnerable. He does this in typical Pinter fashion by refusing really to communicate and creating a conversational void which Davies feels compelled to fill. This is similar to *A Slight Ache,* in which Edward and Flora reveal themselves completely when confronted by the dumb Matchseller. *Tea Party* (1965) also contains conversational voids which various characters compulsively fill with highly revealing chatter. Aston's usual responses to Davies in the opening minutes of the play are "Yes," "Would be," "Mmnn," and "Ah." Aston learns that Davies is violently xenophobic and racially prejudiced, sensitive to draughts, fastidious to the limits of his ability in matters of personal hygiene, deeply concerned with proper respect for old age and people who take "liberties" with their elders, in desperate need of a decent pair of shoes, and confused or concerned about his identity. It is precisely this information that Aston and especially Mick use again and again to torment Davies in the second and third acts. The first act ends with a classic setup. Aston insists that Davies remain in the room alone, knowing full well that Davies will begin rummaging around through the piles of litter and junk as soon as he is alone. Besides setting-up Davies to be "caught" by Mick, Aston's exit serves the additional purpose of allowing him to communicate to Mick Davies' areas of vulnerability. The first act ends with Davies' being caught by Mick in a very compromising situation. The final words of the act are Mick's cruelly ironic, "What's the game?"[13]

The second act is a series of cruel games, mental and physical, which Mick and Aston separately and together play on Davies. Mick begins with an interrogation which attacks Davies in all of his areas of mental vulnerability (i.e., all but his sensitivity to draughts and need of shoes—which he saves for Aston later in the act). Mick's method of interrogation is classic police technique designed to keep the victim off-balance; however, instead of having two people, one of whom is a "tough guy" and the other a "good guy," Mick assumes both roles and shifts with dizzying speed from seeming genuine concern for Davies' welfare to accusations of the most serious kinds of crime. The questions and accusations are interrupted by bewildering elliptical speeches which serve to confuse Davies even more, and by the drip which sounds in a bucket suspended overhead, reminiscent of a Chinese water torture. Davies is confused about his name (is it Mac Davies, or Bernard Jenkins, the assumed name he has used for years?); Mick repeatedly asks him his name. Davies is violently xenophobic (he hates Scots, Greeks, Poles, and especially Blacks); Mick asks him whether or not he is foreign—or perhaps Welsh. Davies is quite fastidious (he is never without a piece of soap, and he left his wife because she put her unwashed underclothing in the pan for vegetables) and he is very concerned about the respect that youth should show to their elders (the youth must not take "liberties"). Mick tells him, "Listen, son. Listen, sonny. You stink" (p. 35). Toward the end of the second act Aston, too, has the chance to attack Davies where he is most vulnerable. Aston—whom Pinter carefully notes wears long underwear—insists that the window cannot be closed despite the wind and rain which blow on Davies; and he promises to look for a pair of shoes for Davies, a promise which he keeps in the third act by bringing a pair of shoes which not only do not fit, but have no laces.

Mick and Aston make Davies the butt of a variety of physical games in the second act. Mick snatches Davies' trousers from him and he and Aston play keep-away with Davies' bag. This childhood game is of particular significance since it is usually played by a group of larger children against a single, comparatively helpless victim who is unable to retaliate individually against any of those who are keeping-away some object of value from him.

They also demean Davies by dressing him in an outlandish costume, a red velvet smoking-jacket covered by a pair of white overalls. The most terrifying game played on Davies is that in which Mick chases him in the darkened room with the "electrolux." There is no question that the sole purpose of this simultaneously hilarious and frightening incident is utterly to unnerve Davies. Davies comes into the darkened room and lights a match. The matchbox falls and "*The box is kicked*" (s.d., p. 44). Davies, reduced to complete helplessness in the dark and cluttered flat, is the ideal victim of opportunity for cruelly imaginative Mick. The second act, like the first, ends with Aston setting-up Davies to overstep himself, to place himself in a compromising position of which Mick can take the utmost advantage. Act Two ends with Aston's great speech on his mental illness and the electric shock treatments he has undergone.

In the third act the games continue, but perhaps with a bit less intensity. Davies must be made to feel as secure as possible so that the final expulsion can be all the more cruel. Mick pretends to take Davies into his confidence and share his dreams for redecorating the house with him. Like Aston in the second act, Mick offers Davies the job of caretaker. He later turns this into an "understanding" that Davies has represented himself as an experienced interior and exterior decorator. Aston brings the pair of wrong-size, laceless shoes and tells Davies that he has "been stinking the place out" (p. 69). This is the goad that makes Davies finally overstep himself and sets him up for the expulsion. Mick comes in and Davies complains that Aston has said he stinks. Mick assures him that he does not stink and tells him that if he did he would be the first to tell him (which, in fact, he was). This reassurance from Mick prompts Davies to suggest to him that Aston be recommitted to the mental institution because he is "nutty" (p. 73). This, in turn, is the opening Mick has been waiting for and he calls Davies a liar, violent, erratic, unpredictable, a wild animal, and a barbarian. He also mentions Davies' inability to establish his identity and says that he stinks "from arse-hole to breakfast time" (p. 74). The play ends with Mick and Aston kicking out Davies, leaving him far worse off than when he was "rescued" by Aston from the café fight. Davies is a broken, unnerved, babbling wretch whose psyche has been completely destroyed by the conscious and concerted games of Aston and Mick.

Davies seems strangely aware of his role as gratuitously chosen victim of a cruel game. He notes at the end of Act One that Aston "Had a sheet and pillow ready in here" (p. 28). He tells Mick that "I was brought here!" (p. 34)—which, of course he was, quite literally—and he rhetorically asks Aston if Mick is not "a bit of a joker" (p. 39). Finally, he tells Mick, "You been playing me about, you know. I don't know why. I never done you no harm" (p. 47). Significantly, Mick makes no rejoinder because Davies is indeed a completely gratuitous victim. Despite Davies' awareness of his role as victim—the kind of awareness that Stanley in ***The Birthday Party*** does not have—he is unable to act on his knowledge. Thus, he finds it impossible to shift ends of his bed to keep the wind and rain off his head. Davies' self-awareness is further evidence of the gratuitous viciousness of the games of Mick and Aston.

That Aston is not a passive and unwitting member of the team is made absolutely clear in two stage directions. After the game is essentially over (i.e., after Davies has been tricked into overstepping himself by suggesting to Mick that Aston be readmitted to the mental hospital) Mick throws a half-crown at Davies, then picks up a figure of Buddha and smashes it against the disconnected gas stove. Mick's smashing the Buddha, like his chasing Davies in the dark room with the "electrolux," is designed completely to unnerve and terrify Davies. This is not a chance or extemporaneous gesture, but has been carefully prepared for. About one-third through Act Two "ASTON *stands, goes to the sideboard drawer, right, picks up the statue of Buddha, and puts it on the gas stove*" (p. 40). This, like the kicked matchbox, shows the absolute cruelty and malice of Aston and Mick, and it shows that they are conscious partners in the game. The second significant stage direction occurs immediately after Mick smashes the Buddha. After a passionate speech Mick pauses and Davies asks, "What about me?" . . .

> *Silence. They do not move.*
>
> ASTON *comes in. He closes the door, moves into the room and faces* MICK. *They look at each other. Both are smiling, faintly*

(pp. 74-75).

After this stage direction the play quickly ends with Davies incoherent and helpless. This faint smile absolutely validates both the game structure and the vicious, conscious cruelty of the game. This, I believe, is the point at which the play ceases to be funny. The faint smile that passes between Mick and Aston informs the entire play. The tragedy of **The Caretaker** is not that of a modern Adam or Everyman expelled from a shabby plastic paradise because of original sin or the human condition. It is the tragedy of man existing in an implacably cruel world in which the norm is that of small boys who bring home stray cats to torture and abuse. Outside the flat is the jungle—the world of menacing foreigners, dirty wives, café fights, shock treatments at mental institutions, and corrupt religious orders. Inside there are chaos, humiliation, and shattered hopes. Nowhere in the play are there normative values posited other than those of an implacably cruel and absurd universe in which any man may become the anonymous victim of opportunity for the games of others.

Notes

1. "Dialogue in Pinter and Others," *Critical Quarterly,* 7 (1965), 225-243.

2. Garden City, New York: Doubleday, 1961, p. 211. In his recent full length study, *The Peopled Wound: The Work of Harold Pinter* (New York: Doubleday, 1970),

Esslin not only affirms these ideas, he embellishes them. Aston "is good-natured and ready to help his fellow human beings" (p. 96), and the actions of Davies, who has a "sour, querulous nature," (p. 98) are a translation of the *hubris* of Greek tragedy to the lower levels of contemporary society (p. 100). Davies "is within sight of salvation and then is driven out of Paradise by his own original sin" (p. 102). The embellishment is in Esslin's suggestion that Mick "plays the role of the snake in this re-enactment of Adam's expulsion from Paradise: by apparently accepting Davies' inane boasts, his complaints about Aston, he has deliberately provoked him into revealing the worst side of his nature" (p. 107).

3. *Ibid.,* p. 212.

4. See George Wellwarth, *The Theater of Protest and Paradox: Developments in the Avant-Garde Drama* (New York: New York University Press, 1964), pp. 205 ff.; John Pesta, "Pinter's Usurpers," *Drama Survey,* 6 (1967), 54-65; and Dick Kay, "Mr. Pinter and the Fearful Matter," *Texas Quarterly,* 4 (Autumn 1961), 257-265.

5. See *The Theatre of the Absurd,* pp. 210-214 and Bernard Dukore, "The Theater of Harold Pinter," *Tulane Drama Review,* 6 (March 1962), 43-54.

6. John Russell Taylor, *Anger and After: A Guide to the New British Drama* (London: Methuen, 1962), pp. 245-250.

7. James J. Boulton, "Harold Pinter: *The Caretaker* and Other Plays," *Modern Drama,* 6 (1963), 131-140. James R. Hollis, in *Harold Pinter: the Poetics of Silence* (Carbondale, Illinois: Southern Illinois University Press, 1970) explores this interpretation extensively. He reads this play and *The Collection* (1961) as struggles for possession, possession of both the truth and "the real person, the embodiment of the truth" (p. 70). He emphasizes the quest motif and notes that "each of the characters of *The Caretaker* nurses a private illusion" (p. 89).

8. Ruby Cohn, "The World of Harold Pinter," *Tulane Drama Review,* 6 (March 1962), 55-68.

9. Florence Jeanne Goodman, "Pinter's *The Caretaker: The Lower Depths* Descended," *The Midwest Quarterly,* 5 (1964), 117-126.

10. Kent G. Gallagher, "Harold Pinter's Dramaturgy," *QJS,* 52 (1966), 242-248.

11. Victor E. Amend, "Harold Pinter—Some Credits and Debits," *Modern Drama,* 10 (1967), 165-174.

12. Richard Schechner, "Puzzling Pinter," *Tulane Drama Review,* 11 (Winter 1966), 176-184.

13. Harold Pinter, *The Caretaker and The Dumb Waiter* (New York: Grove Press, 1961), p. 29. All subsequent quotations from *The Caretaker* are from this edition.

THE HOMECOMING

PRODUCTION REVIEWS

Ronald Bryden (essay date 1965)

SOURCE: "A Stink of Pinter," in *New Statesman*, Vol. 69, No. 1787, June 11, 1965, p. 928.

[*In the following review, Bryden praises Pinter's skill as a playwright but wonders about the depth of his concerns, or of his accomplishment.*]

With a click of lights, a room jumps into being. An echoing grey chamber, reminiscent of that lichened brain-dungeon where, last year at the Aldwych, Beckett's Hamm and Clov railed against the dying of the light in *Endgame*. Only these walls are bare as chalk, these furnishings a blackened, broken-backed three-piece and dresser, remnants of some Seven Sisters Road auction. They lessen the scene's bareness no more than the chewed stools and duckboards in one of the larger animal-houses at the Zoo. An old man in flat cap and dirty tennis shoes is quarrelling with a younger over the newspaper. He wants to snip out an advertisement for cut-price Navy surplus flannel vests. His son, a sullen little Carnaby Street dandy, hogging the racing page, snarls back. The battle for mastery of the cage is on; will continue, you know, until some intruder has either conquered or slunk away, defeated. A pungent smell of cats, decay and hostility, of cheap toiletries and enigma assails your ringside nostrils. It is the smell of Pinter.

Increasingly during the past year, its perfume has risen faintly from lesser British drama. From thriller and comedy, *Travelling Light* and *Entertaining Mr Sloane,* you suddenly detect a whiff of the familiar odour: a touch of Pinter dabbed over the proceedings as you might rub a salad bowl with garlic. To re-encounter the thing itself is like stepping abroad after a diet of Soho ersatz; entering a French café after months of sniffing other people's imported Gauloises. The sense of authenticity, of the authority of an original, is overwhelming. All the same, you find yourself wondering whether it amounts to more than a flavour, a fashionable spice? After its imitations, genuine Pinterism comes over strong, rank, rawly individual. Beside it, most new playwriting seems tasteless. But is it in fact more than a taste? Is it more than garlic?

Of the playwrights who came out of the Fifties, Pinter is undeniably the master-technician. He uses the stage as an acrobat his trampoline; as a wrestler exploits the ropes, he converts its limitations into strength. His construction is tight and polished as marquetry; despite its appearance of studied irrelevance, his dialogue is the sparest in the theatre today—each calculated wamble steers toward a line which pivots the whole play, on a sixpence, in a new direction. This has been wholesomely infectious. But historically, as much has been true of many minor influences. A Shakespeare or Ibsen takes decades to sink in. It is the Beaumonts, Fletchers, Sardous, Anouilhs, Rattigans, who fasten their tone, manner and craftsmanship on their periods. Will Pinter turn out to be more than a theatrical trend-setter? Or is he merely the Sardou of the Absurd?

His new full-length play *The Homecoming,* at the Aldwych, provides a fair test. It is the most he has done so far: funniest, best-constructed, most characteristic, most explicit. The last may sound a presumptuous claim after all the reports of angry and baffled patrons stalking out of the theatres where, on a swing round the provinces, Peter Hall honed his production to its present razor-sharpness. Possibly they were more angry than baffled; had discerned the intention some of London's sophisticated symbol-hunters seem to have missed. At the interval in last Friday's performance, an indignant lady stalked into the foyer behind me, fuming: 'They're exactly like animals!' She obviously considered that she had missed the point. In fact, she had encapsulated it in four words.

Pinter's characters have always had an animal instinct for 'territory', spatial possession. The strength of his stagecraft is that their obscure warfare, however verbalised, is over the stage itself: for possession of the actual area on which they battle. To have the last word coincides with dominating the stage; the actor who ends upstaging the rest has established his barnyard dominion over them like a cock on a dunghill. In *The Birthday Party* and *The Caretaker,* this manoeuvring is implicit. It is flesh and bone of *The Homecoming.* The whole point, structure and joke of the play is its gradual disclosure that what these actors, with their modern clothes and slightly Golders Green accents, are unfurling is most readily and recognisably described in the language of a zoologist reporting the mating-customs of fighting seals on the beaches of Sakhalin.

Two elderly males, offspring of the same mother, share a lair on the northern scarp of the Thames valley—Kilburn, perhaps, or Camden Town. One, the feebler, has grown neuter with age and been forced to wait upon his stronger sibling. He, a mangy, widowed old bull, is failing too, but still powerful enough to provide food and occasionally to savage the two young bulls of his engendering who also use the lair. Snarling, they recognise his mastery to the extent that they do not bring females there. A third male offspring, however, after several seasons' absence on the east coast of America, returns to the family breeding-ground with a mate: a meek young female of tantalising sleekness. The household of deprived males gang jealously against him. One of the young bulls makes a mating-display to the female; when she responds, the younger and stronger mounts her. She, foreseeing greater sexual freedom and comfort with a multiplicity of providers, acquiesces in the rape. Her mate, recognising defeat, retreats whence he came with an unconvincing show of dignity.

Pinter translates this zoo story to human dress with considerable wit and, ultimately, some cold power. He's helped by a production tuned like a racing-car: every line has been pointed, every silence charged. Paul Rogers, as the father, and Ian Holm, as the peacocking son, deal beautifully with their scenes of surly cohabitation, established in Pinter's best vein of bickering non-sequitur, flowering when a woman arrives into baroquely genteel fantasy. Sentimentally, Rogers recalls how he promised his wife 'a dress in pale corded blue silk, heavily encrusted with pearls, and for casual wear a pair of pantaloons in lilac flowered taffeta.' Michael Bryant makes the returning son's hectoring of his wife a brilliant amalgam of human and animal nervousness, and Vivien Merchant, in a part mainly requiring enigmatic passivity, is wonderfully apt at riveting attention on each crossing and uncrossing of her legs.

The gradual shift of emphasis to animality is achieved deftly. There's a shock of poetry in the fact that the wife's only statement about America contains nothing human:

> It's all rock. And sand. It stretches . . . so far . . . everywhere you look. And there's lots of insects there. (*Pause*) And there's lots of insects there.

The final metamorphosis, too, comes with gruesome force. Before her husband's eyes, the wife and her brutish brother-in-law roll, locked together, from the sofa to the floor. As the curtain falls, the father, crawling like an old beast, thrusts his white head up at her, bellowing desperately for a kiss. But something has gone wrong in this second half, and the failure tells much about what's lacking in Pinter.

The shape of the play is the unfolding of a metaphor. It should show the gradual convergence of two separate logics, animal and human. But in fact it works the other way round. It is the early scenes, where the characters growl and sniff around each other like dogs on a corner, which, while funny, seem truthful. The further they lapse into zoology, the more the logics diverge. Either you can claim seriously that men are at bottom animals (one can imagine O'Neill carrying through such a demonstration) or you can present the notion as a surrealist whimsy, like David Garnett in *Lady into Fox*. It is Coleridge's distinction between imagination and fancy. Choosing humour and shock, Pinter has chosen the lesser of the two. In spite of some superficial philosophising about people and 'objects', he has elected to exploit his metaphor's exoticism. He has written a stylish entertainment, but not much more. All that remains at the end is a flavour. Still, it is a strong, individual one. Perhaps it is enough for him that, like the beasts which fascinate him, he has staked out a territory with his personal odour.

David Benedictus (essay date 1965)

SOURCE: "Pinter's Errors," in *The Spectator*, London, June 11, 1965, pp. 755, 758.

[*In the following review, Benedictus suggests that* The Homecoming *is a metaphorical representation of Pinter's relation to playwriting and to his audience.*]

Surely Mr. Harold Pinter is something more than a practical joker. His new play *The Homecoming* is surely something more than the squalid scenario which a synopsis suggests—unless the confusion over *The Homecoming* is not simply in the minds of his critics, but a confusion in his own mind as well? Surely not.

There is no confusion about the narrative. Teddy, who has been six years at an American university, where he has acquired a doctorate of philosophy, returns for a brief visit to his family in their sordid but spacious house in London. The family consists of Max, the irascible paterfamilias, Sam, the chauffeur uncle, and Teddy's two brothers, Lenny, the sly one, the pimp, and Joey, the stupid one, the failed boxer. Teddy has left his three children in America, but has brought with him his wife, Ruth, who blatantly and sexually teases both his brothers before agreeing to prostitute herself both with and for them. Unenthusiastic about his wife's behaviour, Teddy returns to America alone; Sam and Max have heart attacks.

This summary inevitably excludes much that is important, but even in its simplest form the synopsis seems capable of a reasonable interpretation which it would be craven not to attempt.

Let us assume then that Teddy is Pinter. He has been away six years (it is nearly six years since Pinter last wrote a full-length play); in that time he's become, in Lenny's words, 'a bit inner.' Let his wife represent his work as a playwright and film-writer, for writers are traditionally 'married to' their work. His family must be his public and/or his critics ('they're very warm people; they're my family; they're not ogres'). So let us discover, as in an algebraic equation when all the symbols are known, whether x does really equal x.

His wife teases his family but won't 'go all the way.' She seems perfectly prepared to prostitute herself for them in the future but Teddy doesn't want to be there; he will return to his sons and his philosophical research 'in America.' You take the point? My tentative solution is not without internal evidence, for Teddy does have one very big speech, quite explicit, harking back to the theme of *The Dwarfs*, which speech, delivered directly at the audience, says: 'I'm the one who can see, that's why I write my critical works. . . . You're just objects. You just move about. . . . I can observe you.' It seemed not insignificant that the blackout after this outburst was not illuminated by any applause. We sat in silence, in angry silence. I find it hard to see how Mr. Pinter, given his macabre imagination and the allegorical nature of his fancies, *could* be any more explicit than he is here—or much more personal. And if I am right, this personal play is a fascinating and vital thesis on the relation between an author's development and the reactions of his audiences, the sort of ironical game which Mr. Nabokov plays so well in his novels. For our acceptance or otherwise of the play—and on the second night it was very much otherwise—becomes an integral part of the play itself. Again, *if I am right*, the very title would seem to be a supreme irony. Pinter has not come home. He has gone to a different continent and left behind his fancies to console us.

The acting of the parts is nauseously first-rate, but Mr. Peter Hall's direction seemed frequently at fault. There were long duologues in which both parties were wilfully tethered to a single spot on the stage—needlessly puritanical, I thought—and of the two moments of real action, one in each act, only the eroticism in Act 2 came off, for the violence in Act 1 was a damp squib. The weakness of the final curtain (a weakness in the play itself) was embarrassingly prolonged. But one should not carp. It's a good nightmare as nightmares go.

CRITICAL COMMENTARY

Kelly Morris (essay date 1966)

SOURCE: "*The Homecoming,*" in *The Tulane Drama Review*, Vol. 11, No. 2, Winter, 1966, pp. 185-91.

[*In the following essay, Morris discusses* The Homecoming *as a comedy of manners with a tragic theme.*]

> PEER GYNT. . . . You seem busy here today—a christening? Or a wedding feast?
>
> MAN IN MOURNING. I'd call it, rather, a homecoming party; the bride is sleeping with the worms.
>
> *Peer Gynt,* Act V

Eliot, speaking of Jonson, said that poetry dealing with the surface of life requires great deliberateness and simplicity of effect. Pinter is a poet of the surface. His manipulation of performance conventions suggests the "comedy of manners" in its dependence on standard theatrical devices and tightly constructed exploitation of speech and gesture patterns, disabused of conscious causality and motivation data. He differs radically from most comic theatre in two important respects: his plays do not aim (or pretend) to reflect or represent society in a typical, satiric, or parodic way; and he effectively eliminates plot as even a structural element (which is one of his similarities to Beckett).

The notion of plotless comedy of manners accounts for the remarkably opaque or noninformative quality of Pinter dialogue. The characters are grotesques, rather like Humours (which, as Eliot points out, are *not* types). They are (quite literally) circumscribed and defined by the Scene or total image-structure. They live only insofar as their facts and acts contribute to that Scene, giving it shape and animation, changing its perspective. They do not act *upon* one another but *with* each other. (They *do* communicate—as Pinter insists—and, from a performance standpoint, constantly. Since so much of the activity is sheer performance, the result is not mechanical: the dynamics of the dialogue is readily grasped by actors and the plays are

splendidly actable.) *Why* does not matter, as all of the false clues and irrelevancies are integral to the surface, to filling out the form. The "simple effect" depends on how actions fit into the Scene as constituents. The Scene itself is an internally consistent non-specified symbol. It is not a metaphor, and the plays are not allegorical. Hence the repetition and "rote" quality of the dialogue, and hence the blatant poetic artifice of extended passages.

One peculiar difficulty with Pinter is that the specific Scene uses a realistic stage set, the locus of mid-Ibsen dramaturgy. (Pinter *does* show the *theatre* in typical, satiric, and parodic forms.) Pinter's famous Room is a drawing room affected by the "suction of the absurd." Each of his plays produces a bizarre clash of conceptual expectations with Pinter's asocial intentions (in any morally corrective sense) and his nonrealist techniques. This confusion can be avoided by viewing Pinter's work as an ingenious composition of constricted situational modes—i.e., a comedy of manners.

In his most lucid and complex play, **The Homecoming,** the set is in fact a parlor, and the themes are favorites of Ibsen-Strindberg realism—Generation, Heredity, Family, Home. The matrix of the humor is contradiction, the bald irony of the family as a civilization-unit—at once a "natural" group and an artificial apparatus for social repression. The family in **The Homecoming** is associated or identified with animals and parasitic insects: horses, dogs, maggots, ticks. The menagerie is bounded by the "social institution" of family values, and the resultant mode of behavior is an ineffectual violence obeying a ludicrous code of propriety. (There are several congruences with Arden's *Live Like Pigs.*) The prim and the primitive coexist, usually through socially-sanctioned, *institutionalized* violence. Joey, descended from butchers, is a demolition worker and a boxer ("a gentleman's game"). Lenny is vicious in fantasy and language. Within the format of excessive decorum, the idiom is aggression.

The family, for all its internal homicidal intent, is also self-perpetuating. Max, head of the brood, keynotes the play in the opening moments: "One lot after another. One mess after the other. . . . Look what I'm lumbered with. One cast iron bunch of crap after another. One flow of stinking pus after another." But the situation is desperate; Jessie, the mother, deserted years before. ("Mind you, she wasn't such a bad woman. Even though it made me sick just to look at her rotten stinking face, she wasn't such a bad bitch.") The fracture is imaged in the set: a naked door-arch, where the back wall has been ripped down, frames the action. The loss of the mother aggravates a radical confusion of roles, within and between generations: Max, unsure of his paternity, plays the mother, "dandling the kids" (as *his* father had)—"A crippled family, three bastard sons, a slutbitch of a wife—don't talk to me about the pain of childbirth—I suffered the pain, I've still got the pangs." In this sexually chaotic situation, the men fiercely call each other "bitch" and "tit." It is by such perverted readjustment that the family maintains its integrity, as Lenny says: "We do make up a unit, Teddy, and you're an integral part of it." This tangle of identities and duties is "the normal course of events," the "order and clarity" of their weird domesticity.

Following Kenneth Burke [T32], "tracking down the implications" of this play's title pays off. "Homecoming" is a fruitful pun: 1. Jessie, in Ruth, returns home; 2. the Mother brings Home back to the family; 3. Ruth is returning to her birthplace (as is Ted); and 4. the play erupts in a veritable household orgasm (or tribal rite) just before the final curtain. The provocative event is Ted bringing his wife into the house. Since the family was cuckolded by Jessie, women have been anathema, constantly reviled as "pox-ridden whores." Ruth's entrance is an overt challenge to this "normal course." She almost immediately becomes queen of the zoo. She simply takes her rightful place in the restored matriarchy. That is the simple action of the play, the event around which Pinter builds a poem on family themes.

Ruth's first scene with Lenny, moments after her arrival, stands in synecdochic relation to *The Homecoming* as a whole. Lenny is preoccupied with a clock when she enters. He's been kept awake by "ticks" and has threatened a violent solution: "Well, if it's the clock I'd better do something about it. Stifle it in some way, or something." Lenny has the pimp's suave menace; he is impotent, but a sadistic rapist in spoken fantasy. The logic of his eroticism: women must be shown *seduceable*—which obviates actual seduction. If Ruth can be proven a whore, "the normal course of events" will be preserved.

Lenny's opening gambits are stock Pinter: offering the drink that isn't there, asking a question when he knows the answer. Then he uses the tick problem to confuse Ruth. His philosophical discourse on things that "start letting out a bit of a tick" serves warning that he suspects "a bit of a rough time" with her. He ignores her refusal, and gives her a glass of water. "*She takes it, sips, places the glass on a small table by her chair. Lenny watches her.* LENNY: Isn't it funny that I've got my pajamas on and you're fully dressed." This is a close approach and the game is going well for Lenny. His next tactic is an example of Pinter's use of abstracted speech patterns: Lenny reacts with seeming surprise at the most commonplace details. The very rhythm of interrogation charges the data with disproportionate significance and throws it into question, rattling Ruth.

RUTH. We're on a visit to Europe.

LENNY. What, both of you?

RUTH. Yes.

LENNY. What, you sort of live with him over there, do you?

RUTH. We're married.

LENNYY. On a visit to Europe, eh? Seen much of it?

RUTH. We've just come from Italy.

LENNY. Oh, you went to Italy first, did you? And then he brought you over here to meet the family, did he? Well, the old man'll be pleased to see you, I can tell you.

RUTH. Good.

LENNYY. What did you say?

RUTH. Good.

Pause.

LENNY. Where did you go to in Italy?

This buffeting is so successful that Lenny abruptly asks to hold Ruth's hand, to cinch the job:

RUTH. Why?

LENNY. Just a touch. *He stands and goes to her.* Just a tickle.

RUTH. Why?

LENNY. I'll tell you why.

Lenny relishes the chance to shift from the actual to the imaginary, wheeling into a long story about "a certain lady" who made "a certain proposal." Richard Schechner is correct to note the similarity between this speech and Mick's handling of Davies in *Caretaker,* but I strongly disagree with his assessment of intent and effect. These speeches *are* self-revelatory and *are* directed to the victim. Lenny's speech is an overt sexual threat: this lady was "taking liberties with me down under this arch." (Ruth and Lenny are framed by the empty door arch.) She was "falling apart with the pox" (an image of Jessie); her chauffeur was "an old friend of the family" who wouldn't interfere (Ted brought Ruth, as Sam had chauffered for Jessie).

. . . liberties which by any criterion I couldn't be expected to tolerate, the facts being what they were, so I clumped her one. It was on my mind at the time to do away with her, you know, to kill her, and the fact is, that as killings go, it would have been a simple matter, nothing to it.

Lenny concludes his narrative of scorn, placing Ruth beneath erotic notice: "But . . . in the end I thought . . . Aah, why go to all the bother . . . you know, getting rid of the corpse and all that, getting yourself into a state of tension." The speech is self-revelatory because *what* Lenny is doing (not why) is so transparent. Ruth's perception of this marks the turning point of the scene, and, indeed, of the play:

RUTH. How did you know she was diseased?

LENNY. How did I know? *Pause.* I decided she was.

Silence.

From this point on, Ruth settles into her place as the new Jessie, the Mother. She turns the interrogation technique on Lenny: "Have you? . . . Could you?" Lenny's second long tale reflects his loss of control and his realization of

Jessie's return. This time it is "an old lady" who makes "unreasonable demands" and the concluding violence springs from frustration. He senses that the whole household is in danger. As often happens in Pinter, the game focuses on an insignificant object, gives it *formal* importance (Davies' bag, the Buddha, etc.). Lenny moves Ruth's ashtray: "I'm rather worried about the carpet. It's not me, it's my father. He's obsessed with order and clarity. He doesn't like mess." Now the glass of water becomes the trophy.

> RUTH. I haven't quite finished.
>
> LENNY. You've consumed quite enough, in my opinion.
>
> RUTH. No, I haven't.
>
> LENNY. Quite sufficient, in my own opinion.
>
> RUTH. Not in mine, Leonard.
>
> *Pause.*
>
> LENNY. Don't call me that, please.
>
> RUTH, Why not?
>
> LENNY. That's the name my mother gave me.

Lenny threatens to take the glass; Ruth replies "If you take the glass . . . I'll take you." Lenny backs down. She offers herself, she offers the water, then she drinks it.

The rest of the play presents farcical variations on this movement, in terms of the constituent behavior modes of Home. Ruth's method is a feminine paradigm: she is victor through her own victimization—i.e., she uses passivity to dominate: she submits to Max's praises and his sons' pawing, then suddenly becomes peremptory: "I'd like something to eat . . . I'd like a drink. . . . Well, get it . . . Put the record off."; she willingly goes upstairs with Joey, but

> JOEY. I didn't get all the way.
>
> LENNY. You didn't get all the way? *Pause. With emphasis.* You didn't get all the way? But you had her up there for two hours.
>
> JOEY. Well?
>
> LENNY. You didn't get all the way and you've had her up there for two hours!
>
> JOEY. What about it?

She blandly agrees to prostitution (her former profession), but sets her own conditions—three rooms and bath, "all conveniences," a personal maid, a wardrobe, and a contract.

Max calls Ruth "a woman of feeling," and that is precisely her contribution: she is physical, sensual. She proceeds by body ("I was a model for the body"), guided by appetite, seeking only comfort and adornment. She restores potency to the tribe (home-coming).

Her root attitude, the core of her mode, is presented in the philosophical forum on the subject: "What do you do with a table once you've taken it?" It is Lenny, of course, who poses the question and then speculates all around it, devoid of judgment apparatus: he is the arranger, the poet-philosopher. The question is not in Ted's academic "province"—nor, apparently, is anything else: he is simply a chauffeur, standing blankly by until dismissed, the family outrigger. Max, the provider: "sell it." Joey, the sexless muscle, the family eunuch: "chop it up." Ruth ends all discussion with this extraordinary statement:

> Don't be too sure though. You've forgotten something. Look at me. I . . . move my leg. That's all it is. But I wear . . . underwear . . . which moves with me . . . it . . . captures your attention. Perhaps you misinterpret. The action is simple. It's a leg . . . moving. My lips move. Why don't you restrict . . . your observations to that? Perhaps the fact that they move is more significant . . . than the words which come through them. You must bear that . . . possibility . . . in mind.

I know of no Pinter speech so likely to be an "author's note," so explicit in its warning. It seems to say: beware the suggestive rustle which accompanies the real action, beware dead ends and non-questions, beware distraction by ornament, beware extrapolation. The action in Pinter is always "dressed" and often elaborately, always affords glimpses of its "underwear," but clothing is not the core. The pertinent facts are the ones you see onstage; you should "restrict . . . your observations" to the simple movement. Likewise, it is not the discursive connotations of the dialogue which matter ("the words which come through"), but the fact and pattern of speech—how it sounds, and how it is made, and the response it provokes.

This root concern for "simple action" with "simple effect" locates Pinter in a special type of modern comedy of manners. No ideas but in acts: wisdom lies in the discovery of immediate theatrical means. In intentions and method, Pinter may be linked with William Carlos Williams, who concluded *Paterson V* with:

> We know nothing and can know nothing but
> the dance, to dance to a measure
> contrapuntally,
> 　　Satyrically, the tragic foot.

Bert O. States (essay date 1968)

SOURCE: "Pinter's Homecoming: The Shock of Nonrecognition," in *The Hudson Review,* Vol. 21, No. 3, Autumn, 1968, pp. 474-86.

[*In the following essay, States examines the use and significance of irony in characterization, situation, and language in Pinter's* The Homecoming.]

> TEDDY: You wouldn't understand my works. You wouldn't have the faintest idea of what they were about. You wouldn't appreciate the points of reference. You're

way behind. All of you. There's no point in my sending you my works. You'd be lost. It's nothing to do with the question of intelligence. It's a way of being able to look at the world. It's a question of how far you can operate on things and not in things. I mean it's a question of your capacity to ally the two, to relate the two, to balance the two. To see, to be able to *see!* I'm the one who can see. That's why I can write my critical works. Might do you good . . . have a look at them . . . see how certain people can view . . . things . . . how certain people can maintain . . . intellectual equilibrium. Intellectual equilibrium. You're just objects. You just . . . move about. I can observe it. I can see what you do. It's the same as I do. But you're lost in it. You won't get me being . . . I won't be lost in it.

BLACKOUT

I want to consider [*The Homecoming*] on what seems to me its most interesting level: that is, as a fiction about a group of people so *different* from us, while in certain obvious respects resembling us, that they are fascinating to watch. As a start, I propose to explore my recognition of the play in this speech which strikes me as being *there* in a peculiar way. It is, first, what we may call a genuine idea in a play that contains almost no ideas at all. Moreover, it is the only place in the play where Pinter permits a character to be undevious, "forthcoming" as Lenny would say, and that is a privilege most Pinter characters never get. Finally, as the penultimate break in the play, it is spoken with an almost thematic inflection. In fact, in the early throes of Critic's Rapture, I wondered whether Pinter wasn't very deliberately telling us more about *his* homecoming here than about Teddy's.

Basically, the speech is Pinter's only pass at motivating Teddy's unusual capacity to "observe" with "equilibrium" the degeneration (or more correctly, the re-degeneration) of his wife to the level of his family. Applying it with a little imagination to *the rest* of Teddy, moreover, we can arrive at a coherent explanation for all of his actions: why he married a girl like Ruth, why he risked stopping off here en route back to the Campus from Venice, why he is willing (anxious, if you like) to return to the children without their mother, thus living out the pattern of his father's luck with Jessie. You can even predict, come twenty years, what intellectual barbarians the children will be, the eldest perhaps coming to a bad end in some dark form of father rejection. A New York psychoanalyst has suggested that Teddy is an example of a "totally withdrawn libido" troubled by a basic hatred for women and a tendency toward homosexuality (a family problem); he therefore substitutes intellectual equilibrium for a proper sex life. Michael Craig, who played Teddy, says he is the most violent of all the brothers, a veritable "Eichmann" underneath who has "rationalized his aggressions." Pinter, with characteristic simplicity (if not pure disinterest), says he walks out in the end to avoid a "messy fight," and anyway his marriage was on the rocks. All of these ideas (see *Saturday Review*, April 8, 1967) do not arise from the speech alone, of course, but the speech authorizes them: it puts the lid, so to speak, on Teddy's possibilities.

My feeling is that it is more a case of the play's not contradicting such ideas than of its actually containing them. Here is the one example of character "psychology" we get in the whole play and it directs us toward nothing definite in the character's experience but rather toward his *way of dealing* with whatever *happens* to be in his experience. In this respect, the speech bears out an impression confirmed by the rest of the play: the Pinter character's complete lack of interest in "things," in obligations, social or moral transactions, past "sins," future "goals," the whole world of palpable reality which Pinter is paradoxically so good at evoking in his dialogue; and his obsession with "points of reference," means, style, what can be *made* out of what is passing at any particular moment. In short, Teddy's philosophy of equilibrium is simply a more academic page out of the old family album.

In a more general sense, this helps to account for the powerful impression of the play's having been spun outward from an invisible center of complicity which clearly beckons the Interpreter to try his hand at supplying objective correlatives. On one hand, therefore, we explain the play as a study in psychic ambiguity: under the banal surface a massive Oedipal syndrome (like the part of the iceberg you can't see) bumps its way to grisly fulfillment. Or, beneath Freud lurks Jung and the archetypal: the father-sons "contest," the "fertility rite" on the sofa, the Earth Mother "sacrifice," the tribal sharing of her body (a Sparagmos for sure), the cyclical "return," and so on. But before the play is any or all of these things, it seems to be something much different and much simpler.

Perhaps the best way to pin it down is to try to say why psychology and myth seem unsatisfactory as explanations. The trouble with them is that they bring to the fore a purposiveness which seems at odds with the nature of the imagination we are dealing with. They assume that the play is *about* these things, whereas I think they come much closer to being by-products, as we would be dealing with by-products of, say, a story by Poe in the themes of crime-does-not-pay, or man-is-evil, or even in the mythic structures which I am sure there are plenty of in Poe, as there always are in tales of victimization. As for the psychological drives themselves, one somehow doubts that Pinter's characters, deep down, are any more troubled by appetites of the sexual kind than Dostoevsky's people are troubled by finding suitable jobs. They seem far more interested in manipulating the idea of sexuality, for its effect on others, than in their own performance. As for the mythic elements, it is simply hard to see what they prove, other than that Pinter deals in some pretty raw urges, hardly a distinction these days. To be "primitive" is not to be Pinteresque.

I suggest that it is in the peculiar way the story is told and in the liberties it takes with the reality it posits. For instance, if we reduce the play to its main turns of plot we have something like this: a son and his wife return to the family home on a visit abroad. Almost immediately, the father and brothers make open advances on the wife. She seems to tolerate, if not encourage, them and the husband makes no effort to protect his interests. In fact, it is the husband in the end who makes the family's proposal to the wife that she stay on as mother, mistress to everybody, and as prostitute. She accepts (!) and he goes back to their three children. We anticipate that it will be the wife who now controls the family.

It would be hard to conceive an action, in modern "family" terms, which violates so many of our moral scruples with so little effort and so little interest in making itself credible. You may read causes *into* it, but the causes pale beside the facts, like the page of repentance at the end of a dirty book. The whole thing has about it a blatant improbability and artifice which depends not upon our sympathizing, or understanding its origins, but upon our seeing how far it has taken its own possibilities. Moreover, it is all so harmless. As Eliot said of Ford's incest, the fact that such outrageous vices are defended by no one lends a color of inoffensiveness to their use. At any rate, the reaction one has to the play comes nowhere near Pity and Fear, or any of their weaker derivatives, but is better described as *astonishment at the elaboration.* And it is precisely this quality of astonishment that is apt to disappear from any thematically oriented recovery of the play.

So the idea I want to develop here is that *The Homecoming* may be about homecomings of all kinds but it is not ultimately about ours. We witness it, it even coaxes us to grope for connections among our own realities (and find them), but it does not, as its primary artistic mission, refer us back to a cluster of moral or existential issues we care very much about. What astonishes about the play is its taking of an extraordinarily brutal action, passing it through what is perhaps the most unobtrusive and "objective" medium since Chekhov's, and using it as the host for a peculiar activity of mind. We have invented special words for this activity ("Pintercourse," "Pinterism," "Pinterotic," etc.), which Pinter understandably detests, but it seems we have needed them as semantic consolation for his having hidden from us the thing they refer to.

And it is, I think, a thing—something all the characters *do* (in this play at least), with varying degrees of genius. To come back to my epigraph, what attracted me to Teddy's "philosophy" is that it offers the best explanation of this thing Pinter has given us. It is not particularly recondite, or mysterious; in fact, it goes under the household label of Irony, or the making of ironies, the art of being superior to things by disposing of them without passion or involvement. The best way to make the connection is to set Teddy's speech against this more clinical description of the ironic temper by Haakon Chevalier:

> The Ironist is committed to the search of a more and more exterior point of view, so as to embrace all contradictions and behold the world from a point of vantage to which nothing else is superior. The indefinite extension of his field of vision to the furthest attainable reaches is implied even in the point of view of the Ironic observer of a simple human situation. The Ironic

reaction is exterior to both elements of the contrast observed. And this necessarily leads to a progressive extension of the point of view. Beyond the Ironist's perception of a situation is his Ironic perception of himself Ironically perceiving the situation, etc.

Now this fits and it doesn't fit, and I am ultimately more interested in the sense in which it fits Pinter's own perspective (and he, in turn, the contemporary perspective) than in its application to specific characters. It is a gentle kind of irony M. Chevalier deals with in his book about Anatole France, whereas ours is a more subterranean variety based in cruder contrasts. But it is the same operation, in essence, and as Chevalier goes on to observe, it accompanies a peculiar relationship to "everyday reality" and is "stimulated and encouraged to expression in a special environment." If you wish to think of it as the collective "motive" of the characters, and get your psychology in that way, it would certainly do no harm; but I think it has more aesthetic ramifications. For it seems to me that character is here usurping—rather wholesale—a privilege that has traditionally belonged to the audience (superiority to the situation) and that when irony is practiced to this degree of exclusiveness it might more properly be considered as a form of *audience* psychology designed by the author to meet the expectations of the "special environment" in which he writes, more about which later. This, in my opinion, is the source of our consternation and fascination with Pinter—our quest for the lost superiority of knowing more than the characters who now know more than we do, the very reverse of the familiar "dramatic" irony in which *we* know but they don't. To put it crudely, it is the goal of the Pinter character, as agent of his author's grand strategy, to stay ahead of the audience by "inventing" his drama out of the sometimes slender life afforded him (glasses of water, newspapers, cheese-rolls, etc.). His motto, in fact, might well be Renan's remark (which I also crib from Chevalier): "The universe is a spectacle that God offers himself; let us serve the intentions of the great choroegus by contributing to render the spectacle as brilliant, as varied as possible." To this end, he becomes, as it were, a little Pinter, an author of irony, sent into his incredible breathing world scarce half made-up, morally, to work on the proper business of his author's trade—to "trump" life, to go it one better by going it one worse. This, I think, is what Teddy is doing in his repressed, tweedy way in escorting his wife to the rank sweat of the family bed (which she, in turn, negotiates into a still greater triumph of "perspective") with all the possession of someone passing the salt. It is a similar triumph of perspective that moves Max to take one look at his eldest son and his wife, newly arrived from Independence America, the World's Bandwagon, and call her tart, smelly scrubber, stinking pox-ridden slut, a disease, sensing with uncanny instinct that his son is, at this moment, *bigger* than the family, outside it yet condescending to "visit," that his superiority is somehow vested in this woman and that an insult in the form of an imitation (not too convincing) of moral indignation will do the trick. It is, again, another triumph that his apology for this outrage should descend to an equally ludicrous imitation of fatherly sentimentality ("You want to kiss your old father? Want a cuddle with your old father?"). And so on, through his repertoire of sudden reversals of sentiment calculated to demonstrate that his perception of a situation includes all possible positions. For instance:

> He was fond of your mother, Mac was. Very fond. He always had a good word for her.
>
> *Pause.*
>
> Mind you, she wasn't such a bad woman. Even though it made me sick just to look at her rotten stinking face, she wasn't such a bad bitch. I gave her the best bleeding years of my life, anyway.

Finally, it is the pleasure of irony that moves the play's least gifted character, Sam, to spit out the priceless secret he has been nursing for years ("MacGregor had Jessie in the back of my cab as I drove them along") at a moment so right, so symmetrical, that the beauty of it almost kills him.

Pinter's best and most continuous irony, however, arises not from situation but from language, and on this point he reminds me a good deal of Chekhov and Beckett with whom he shares powerful affinities in imagination. Putting aside their differences, I think they are ironists in the same tradition, they hold similar fascination for us, and give us, on the whole, similar critical problems. They are probably the three least discursive playwrights one could name; in fact, their silence before the questions they raise—their Socratic smile, you might say—is so extreme that it qualifies as their special *excess*, like Genet's devout immorality, Brecht's social consciousness, Pirandello's cerebration. Such detachment is very rare in the theatre because it tends to produce the sort of play Hamlet might write, one that hovers on the verge of motionlessness (a quality for which all three have been variously praised or damned). Obviously their success with such essentially undramatic materials has a good deal to do with their preoccupation with words, silence (as anti-words), and with what we might broadly call the *expressive* aspect of life. And in each case it seems to me that even language functions in an ironic way, that our interest is centered upon a tension between the words and the situation. I was interested in Richard Gilman's article on *The Homecoming* in *The New York Times* (Jan. 22, 1967) in which he said that "language can itself be dramatic, can *be* the play, not merely the means . . . etc.," a remark which Mr. Simon trounced in *The Hudson Review* (Vol. XX, No. 1, Spring, 1967) as intellectual cant. Now I don't think language can *be* the play any more than the medium can *be* the message, but there is something in Mr. Gilman's idea. I think he touches upon a habit of composition which Pinter has cultivated more and more as he goes along—a habit which is, in a technical sense, analogous to Chekhov's highly controlled practice of putting language out of proportion to the "content" (the almost *elegant* expression of near-suicidal desperation), and which we find again in Beckett's insistence on putting the significant things in the guise of insignificance ("What about hanging ourselves?").

The equivalent technique in Pinter—and especially in *The Homecoming* where it reaches a kind of *tour de force* intensity—is a direct and almost satirical formalism of expression which is, putting it mildly, inappropriate to the situation. The whole technique might be presampled in a remark Pinter himself recently made to a *Paris Review* reporter about politicians:

> I'll tell you what I really think about politicians. The other night I watched some politicians on television talking about Vietnam. I wanted very much to burst through the screen with a flamethrower and burn their eyes out and their balls off and then inquire from them how they would assess this action from a political point of view.

I checked this on first reading because it was so interesting to see Pinter being, as it were, Pinteresque on a *real* issue he obviously felt strongly about, brilliantly satirizing the politician's habit of converting ugly reality to pure rhetoric—an almost perfect description of what he is doing in *The Homecoming*. Listen to this same politician's language now in the mouths of Max and Lenny:

> SAM: . . . You know what he said to me? He told me I was the best chauffeur he'd ever had. The best one.
>
> MAX: From what point of view?
>
> SAM: Eh?
>
> MAX: From what point of view?
>
> LENNY: From the point of view of his driving, Dad, and his general sense of courtesy, I should say.

Or this passage taken from the family discussion of how Ruth is to be treated in her "various" roles:

> MAX: Lenny, do you mind if I make a little comment? It's not meant to be critical. But I think you're concentrating too much on the economic considerations. There are other considerations. There are human considerations. You understand what I mean? There are the human considerations. Don't forget them.

Or take the peripety itself, in which the play arrives at its greatest gulf between manner and matter, a small masterpiece of collective one-upmanship:

> TEDDY: Ruth . . . the family have invited you to stay for a little while longer. As a . . . a kind of guest. If you like the idea I don't mind. We can manage very easily at home . . . until you come back.
>
> RUTH: How very nice of them.
>
> *Pause.*
>
> MAX: It's an offer from our heart.
>
> RUTH: It's very sweet of you.
>
> MAX: Listen . . . it would be our pleasure.

Altogether, it is an irony that disappears at times into pure comedy, reminding one of that old cartoon about the cannibal sporting the bowler and umbrella of the English gentleman he is about to eat.

Perhaps the most spectacular example of Pinter brutality to date is the scene in which Lenny recites his deeds to Ruth, his brother's wife (whom he has known less than five minutes):

> Well, this lady was very insistent and started taking liberties with me down under this arch, liberties which by any criterion I couldn't be expected to tolerate, the facts being what they were, so I clumped her one. It was on my mind at the time to do away with her, you know, to kill her, and the fact is, that as killings go, it would have been a simple matter, nothing to it. Her chauffeur, who had located me for her, he'd popped round the corner to have a drink, which just left this lady and myself, you see, alone, standing underneath this arch, watching all the steamers steaming up, no one about, all quiet on the Western Front, and there she was up against this wall—well, just sliding down the wall, following the blow I'd given her. Well, to sum up, everything was in my favour, for a killing. Don't worry about the chauffeur. The chauffeur would never have spoken. He was an old friend of the family. But . . . in the end I thought.. Aaah, why go to all the bother . . . you know, getting rid of the corpse and all that, getting yourself into a state of tension. So I just gave her another belt in the nose and a couple of turns of the boot and sort of left it at that.

Now there is a serious question here as to whether Lenny really did this at all, much less with such terrifying indifference; but that is beside the point, just as it is beside the point to inquire whether the family is capable of having sex with Ruth. The main thing is the conception and framing of the possibility, the something *done to* the brutality that counts. The genial minimization of it, you might say. And Lenny accomplishes this by satirizing his act in the language his "betters" habitually use to sanitize themselves from dockside realities of just this sort. The effect, of course, is to make him superior to his brutality, to the class morality he is mimicking, and to his freshest opponent in what his soul-brother Mick, in *The Caretaker,* calls "the game." In a sense I think the actor will appreciate, life is *all* performance for Lenny, a veritable charade of politesse.

The question is, what does it mean to an audience? Is Pinter our Molière of the bullock-pen? Is he saying that insofar as language is supposed to correspond to deed and intent it is being "spilled," and the entire moral structure along with it? That the Family is taking out its spite against society by imitating it to its own "diseased" specifications (each character being an aspect of, first English, then "modern" decay), and that in order to avoid such corruption as theirs, as one critic has pointed out, we have got to pull together somehow, wake up to our encroaching dehumanization? Or, what seems a more commonly held view, that the play is simply descriptive of a condition we can do nothing about, given the persistence of the beast in the genes, but which it is the artist's instinct and duty to portray, in the belief that an aesthetic triumph over life is better than none at all? In short, what does the presence of such Irony, as the very *process* of the play, signify on our scene?

In the *Paris Review* article, Pinter was asked if he considered the world "an essentially violent place." Yes, it was violent all right, he said, but the violence was "really only an expression of the question of dominance and subservience," the repeated theme (he thought) of his plays. There is about Pinter's remarks on himself a very refreshing sense of the craftsman in his shop (or rather, *out* of it, and wanting to get back), and none of the displaced philosopher taking his chance to talk (art being mute). All questions, if possible, are converted to matters of technique—*"writing the bloody play!"* In his remark I think he has converted *our* world into his own artistic frame of reference very thoroughly: a question of dominance and subservience, a "common everyday thing." Reflecting it against the plays, the telling thing about it is its fixation on *the fact* of violence as a kind of source, or quarry to be mined, and its unconcern for the consequences of violence on the human scene. Does it not, in fact, bespeak a certain detachment that comes with accommodation to, or indifference toward, an "old" problem?

Now one might easily invoke here Chekhov's famous comeback to the accusation of indifference—"We don't have to be *told* that stealing horses is bad." In other words, the objective, no-comment depiction of malevolence carries its own power of denial and opposition, its own unfurled sympathy with health. And it undoubtedly does—when the artist *wants* it to and sees to it that the ironies are leaned in that direction. But I have never been convinced that Chekhov wanted it to and that he was not absolutely fascinated by the blackest possibilities of the void out of which Shestov said he created. Moreover, questions of this sort occur: Do we not underestimate the attractiveness of evil? Is not one of the pleasures of art evil's power to arrest for our delight certain bold lines of force which goodness simply doesn't possess? To bring it up to date, could we not be arriving at a kind of art (of which Pinter is our most daring example) which is showing signs of restlessness with its content and is therefore shifting its focus from an attention to the content for its own sake (our Absurd "condition") to the interesting symmetries inherent in it?

I seem to be suggesting that Pinter is callously producing what Mr. Wimsatt calls "vile art," art which presents immoral acts irresponsibly, if not with approval and joy (as we are told our movies are doing these days). I am not really prepared to argue that question; but I feel obliged to put Pinter into the context he deserves most and that amounts to considering him as a craftsman rather than a thinker, a maker of theatre out of "accepted" materials. In short, I find the question of whether he sees the world as "essentially violent" about as interesting and relevant to his art as whether, let us say, John Constable sees the world as essentially peaceful. And I would enlarge this idea along the following line:

It would appear that Absurdist violence, like all forms of radical experience "used" and then "used up" by artists, may be passing into its twilight or "aesthetic" stage and that our reactions to it are changing in subtle and remarkable ways, impossible to assess. We know very little about this strange passage in the arts in which moral actions figure powerfully as the content, but we are learning something about how greatly it influences the course of the graphic arts; and there seems no reason to exempt the drama from the implications of Wölfflin's well-known idea that paintings owe more to other paintings than they owe to nature; nor from E. H. Gombrich's more recent expansion of that general idea that it is "the power of expectation rather than the power of conceptual knowledge that molds what we see in life no less than in art." We see reality, in other words, in terms of our formulations of it.

It is not appropriate to develop this far-ranging idea in very great detail here, but one of the ways in which the power of expectation would seem to operate on the dramatic artist is in adjusting his field of vision between "what has been done," to put it simply, and "what is left to do," or, if you prefer, between the images of other artists (in and out of his medium) and the suggestions they carry for further expansion. Since violence is the natural content of all "serious" drama, it seems reasonable to assume that violence (to personify it) goes a progress through the available possibilities in a constant struggle to recapture its power of fascination; one of the ways it appears to do this, as I trust the history of drama will show, is to take daring permissions with its inherited conceptions of itself, to become by turns more particular, more inward, more subtle, more "free," more "immoral," more "real," more indifferent, more sophisticated, more paradoxical (a standard device for eluding discovery); to parody itself, to offer as much sensation as the traffic will bear, and so on, until it is finally performing with only a side glance at Nature herself, the reality observed being mainly the already formulated realities of the tradition to which it belongs. Fidelity to experience, moral qualm, truth, these are indeed perpetuated, but in the terms of the medium. Something of this sort seems to have been happening in the later Greek plays (*Orestes* comes to mind) and again in those chain-reactive monstrosities of lust and cruelty of the Jacobeans—the sort of plays, in other words, which our theatre is rapidly discovering as "surprisingly playable" and which critics are busy writing down as remarkable prefigurations of the existential view of life, or—if not that—as clear proofs of the author's disillusion with his age.

To what extent all this is reflective of external changes in moral patterns and tolerances it is probably not possible to say; certainly the interplay is greater than I am suggesting in this one-sided presentation and I am stating the whole case badly in forcing a separation of the insoluble marriage of Morals and Aesthetics. But it does seem to me that the incidence of irony on our scene (and I have discussed only one particular, if not rare, variety)—which has led Northrop Frye and others to conclude that irony is the characteristic fictional mode of our century—might be reckoned in our criticism as a somewhat less depressing thing than our loss of spiritual security. Does it not open also the possibility of irony's appeal as a form of more or less pure patterning, of the manipulation of "experience" into certain kinds of symmetries (the predictable operation of dissonance) which the mind finds innately interesting because (1) it appreciates symmetry of any kind, irrespective of its bearing on human ideals, and (2) at certain times in the flux of art traditions it craves the release of the ironic variation, the art, as Frye says, which has "no object but its subject" (or, as Empson says, the art which enables the artist to say "a plague on both your houses"). Thus, we might theorize that irony has two aspects: it is, in the moral sense, a defense against the failure of any single option to convince, the loss of a clear stake in an ideological inheritance; and, in the aesthetic sense, it is a defense against the exhaustion of a set of inherited images. No doubt there is an intricate relationship between the two (if *two* there are); the point I wish to make here is that in such movements there are such things as artists who are less interested in revealing us than in amazing us.

Getting back to Poe for a moment, I am reminded of a recent essay in *Kenyon Review* by Terence Martin who makes a case for Poe's "play habit," the "desire to astonish by boundless exaggeration or confusion of proportions." He is "our one author," says Mr. Martin, "who makes an absolute commitment to the imagination—who releases the imagination into a realm of its own where, with nothing to play *with*, it must play *at* our destruction. He shows us insistently that the imagination at his kind of play is not only anti-social but anti-human. To do justice to his contemporaries, perhaps we should say that what Poe undertook was not to be looked at without blinking."

That is more or less how I feel about Harold Pinter. In fact, with just a little transposing, we could probably derive most of the old Gothic essentials from our play: the nightmare setting, the double vision of the real and the super-real, the lurking fatality and inexplicable tyranny, the mysterious inspecificity and yet *utter* relevance of everything. Even—allowing for an unfortunate degeneration in our heroine—the central Gothic theme of the pale and lovely maiden *dominated* by the inscrutable sadist of the "nameless vice." This is not intended as a dismissal of either Pinter or Gothicism. If anything, it is a plug for art which produces reactions other than the shock of recognition, art in which the very limitedness of the artist to relatively outré kinds of experience and his ability to arouse the precise *sense* of that experience are the things to be praised. To me, Pinter falls brilliantly into this category and it is with considerable respect for him that I subscribe to his own evaluation of himself as "overblown tremendously" by people who "tend to make too much of a meal." This is not at all to deny the good chance that he may come out in the end as the Poe or Huysmans of the Absurdist theatre—a better fate, perhaps, than the one in store for some of our sterner moralists.

Hugh Nelson (essay date 1968)

SOURCE: "*The Homecoming*: Kith and Kin," in *Modern British Dramatists: A Collection of Critical Essays,* edited by John Russell Brown, Prentice-Hall, Inc., 1968, pp. 145-63.

[*In the following essay, Nelson explicates* The Homecoming *by associating it with the biblical stories of the Prodigal Son and Ruth, and with Shakespeare's* Troilus and Cressida.]

Without exception, Harold Pinter's plays have titles which seem neither enigmatic nor evocative. Casually scanned, they seem not to merit a second look, since they simply abstract a central object, person, or event from the context of the play. This is again true of his most recent play, **The Homecoming.** The title would seem at first glance to indicate nothing but the central event around which the action pivots, or, to put it in the terminology of the well-made play, its inciting incident.

In the first act, the stage is set for the bizarre but logical consequences of the second act. We see a family, two pairs of brothers a generation apart, a family which has a certain routine of daily living. Within this routine, signs of strain and stress are writ large. Max and his son Lenny are involved in a predatory struggle for dominance. Unable to conquer Lenny, Max turns on his own brother, Sam, a fellow creature less capable of offering direct resistance, and impugns his masculinity on the one hand while accusing him of being a secret lecher on the other. Joey, Lenny's brother, is treated with a mixture of condescension and coddling. A boxer and a demolition worker, he appears to have the physical means at hand to dominate all of them, but a certain slow-wittedness prevents his taking the opportunities available to him.

In earlier Pinter plays, we have become accustomed to seeing family situations in which such stresses were apparent. We have also become accustomed to seeing these stresses revealed through the small rituals of family living: breakfasts, tea, dusting, opening and closing windows, repairing broken stair rods and leaks in the ceiling. Pinter is interested in these trivia not for their own sake but for the opportunities they afford him to expose much deeper states of unrest, boredom, and resentment. In **The Homecoming,** the same technique is used. Max is furious because he has to fix dinner for his family: "Honest. They walk in here every time of the day and night like bloody animals. Go and find yourself a mother."[1] Lenny criticizes his cooking: "You're a dog cook. Honest. You think you're cooking for a lot of dogs." Apparent inconsequence always comes home to roost in Pinter. After the homecomers have come home, Max makes several crucial inquiries of his oldest son's wife:

MAX. You a mother?

RUTH. Yes.

MAX. How many you got?

RUTH. Three.

* * *

MAX. I've got the feeling you're a first rate cook.

RUTH. I'm not bad.

MAX. No, I've got the feeling you're a number one cook. Am I right, Teddy?

TEDDY. Yes, she's a very good cook.

The real problem then is that the family we see at the beginning of the play is womanless, hence unbalanced, out of phase. There is no cook, no mother, no sexual partner, or, rather, inadequate substitutes for all of these necessities. Max is the cook at night and Sam the cook in the morning; neither is happy with his role; both the feeders and the fed use this issue to "get at" each other. In place of the woman they need, they have a memory, Max's late wife, Jessie. From the various descriptions we get of her, she seems to have been all things to all men. Sam speaks of her with reverence but reveals at a climactic moment that he had acted as her procuror. Max speaks of her as an ideal wife and mother at one moment; and the next, she becomes a "slutbitch." Eventually, Ruth, the intruder, will also find herself compelled to take on such apparently opposed tasks and roles, but not until she has fathomed the family and its needs and, in turn, been fathomed by them.

The homecoming initiates the forward movement. Teddy and Ruth arrive late at night. There are clear indications of stress and imbalance in their relationship as well. Ruth wants to go out for a walk; Teddy demurs, then goes out for a walk himself. Lenny appears, draws his own conclusions, and operates on them. His acceptance of Ruth as Teddy's wife is perfunctory at best. Clearly, he sees something more in her. She sees that he sees and brings the issue to him. (As Edward says of the Matchseller in *A Slight Ache:* "The man's an impostor and he knows I know it. . . . And I know he knows I know it. . . . And he knows I know.") Again, the means is trivial, a glass of water. But the subtext is loaded:

RUTH. Have a sip. Go on. Have a sip from my glass. Sit on my lap. Take a long cool sip. Put your head back and open your mouth.

LENNY. Take that glass away from me.

RUTH. Lie on the floor. Go on. I'll pour it down your throat.

LENNY. What are you doing, making me some kind of proposal?

The following morning, Ruth and Teddy, two ethereal apparitions in dressing gowns, come downstairs with the family morning in full career. Max decides that Ruth is a whore. After taking out his violence on Sam and Joey, he greets the returning prodigal and his new daughter-in-law in a curtain scene dripping with sarcasm. Like Lenny, he is not so easily dislodged from his first conclusions.

The second act is a shocker, but those critics, like Walter Kerr, who have implied that it could or should stand by itself as a one-act play are misled. None of the events in this act would be supportable without the first act foundation. It is also important to see that the central movement of this act and of the play is Ruth's process of self-discovery. Teddy's victimization and his presumably lonely return to America and to the fall semester are only of peripheral interest. In addition, the play does not seem to be about the victimization of Ruth. At its conclusion, she is the queen bee, as Flora is at the end of *A Slight Ache,* as Meg is at the end of *The Birthday Party,* as Stella is at the conclusion of *The Collection.* It is a much stronger play when viewed as a process of self-discovery in which Ruth remembers things about herself, discovers things she had not known, weighs the needs of Teddy against those of the group, and makes an amoral but none the less logical choice. Max, Lenny, and Joey may have a certain hypnotic effect upon her, but it is a hypnosis which she chooses to undergo. (Stanley's "victimization" in *The Birthday Party* should be viewed in the same way as pointed up by Petey's poignant warning: "Stan, don't let them tell you what to do.")

But we, the audience, need more time to evaluate the strength of needs than Ruth, the character, does. Thus, the first act is crucial in allowing us to see the motherless, wifeless, sexless family in operation and in allowing us to see the essential sterility of Ruth's relationship to Teddy (three children notwithstanding). Her description of America is telling: "It's all rock. And sand. It stretches . . . so far . . . everywhere you look. And there's lots of insects there. (*Pause.*) And there's lots of insects there." The only vision that Teddy can muster with which to hold her is one of swimming pools and lecture halls. This is not enough. Teddy's "intellectual equilibrium" upon which he prides himself finally excludes Ruth as well as his "blood" family: "You're just objects. You just . . . move about. I can observe it. I can see what you do. It's the same as I do. But you're lost in it. You won't get me being . . . I won't be lost in it." Ruth chooses to lose herself and, like the Biblical prodigal, is found. Or, rather, she finds herself—as mother, whore, manageress, cook, housekeeper, and brood mare. Very early in the play, Max had mentioned his way with horses, particularly the fillies:

> But I was always able to tell a good filly by one particular trick. I'd look her in the eye. You see? I'd stand in front of her and look her straight in the eye, it was a kind of hypnotism, and by the look deep down in her eye I could tell whether she was a stayer or not. It was a gift. I had a gift.

In the play's final moments, Max tries to fathom the Ruth they have helped to bring to life and finds that his "gift" has deserted him.

Thus, the title of the play, seemingly obvious, must be re-examined. Again, this is true of all of Pinter's plays. "The birthday party" is a central event in the play which bears its name, but it is much more than a birthday party; it is also an initiation and a rebirth. "The dumb waiter" is a physical object and a state of being. "The caretaker" is a specific function offered to Davies and also a deep pun on man's responsibility for his fellow man. "The homecoming" like "the birthday party" is an event that occurs in the play: Teddy comes home. But the truer of the "homecomings" is Ruth's. She comes home to herself, to all of her possibilities as a woman. What she comes home to may not be very pleasant and the experience of watching the return may be lacerating, but in Pinter's world, as in that of Sophoclean tragedy or in the equally fatal universe of Ibsen, the human truth will always out. In fact, it is interesting that Pinter's titles are similar to those of the early Ibsen. As titles, *A Doll's House, Ghosts, Pillars of Society,* and *The Master Builder* have a double-edged ironic thrust to which Pinter's titles simply add an ingrained affinity for the play on words.

II

Pinter has frequently referred to himself as an extremely traditional playwright. This warning has generally been ignored. In the fashionable rush to see him as a playwright of the "absurd" (whatever that may mean) or as Chekhov's heir in the contemporary theatre, it is seldom realized that his form may be closer to the well-made play in its Ibsenite incarnation than to any other structural source. In a recent interview, he was quoted as saying:

> I *am* a very traditional playwright—for instance I insist on having a curtain in all of my plays. I write curtain lines for that reason. . . . For me everything has to do with shape, structure, and over-all unity.[2]

The Homecoming an Ibsenite play? Only if we see that exposition, development, and resolution have been driven underground through a healthy distrust of language. The surface of any one of Pinter's plays may seem chaotic, arbitrary, and illogical. Short passages of stichomythia about apparently irrelevant subjects may be succeeded by massive speeches recounting personal experience, plans, dreams, bus routes which seem not to fit into the context in which they appear. This pattern is even truer of *The Homecoming* in which Pinter's increased daring in the manipulation of dramatic dialogue is readily apparent. But to react to this dialogue as arbitrary absurdity is to miss the true excitement of a Pinter play. For in Pinter, far more than in many playwrights credited with tightness of construction and dramatic economy, every word is chosen so that in the final analysis, nothing in the design shall seem arbitrary. Apparently trivial differences of opinion over cheese rolls, cigars, glasses of water, routes to the airport, are, in fact, Pinter's somewhat unique means of exposition and development. What we lack in precise information about the characters' backgrounds and motives is made up for by a very complex knowledge (if we are alert to it) of the nature of their shifting emotions in regard to each other. What they do *not* say becomes as important here as what they do say. Thus, the pause, the silence, can take on an expository and developmental function. In addition, there are physical indicators. Pinter has stated that he begins his plays with a vision of certain physical relationships between people in a room: sitting, standing, lying, kneeling. A careful look at his final curtains will reveal a significantly altered physical relationship which makes a statement beyond the power of words. Other individual moments allow us to chart stages in the development again by purely physical means.

The Homecoming with its sinister family history (*à la Rosmersholm*), its clear division between exposition and development incited by the homecoming (*à la Ghosts*), its withheld facts from the past suddenly revealed in a climactic scene (*à la* almost any Ibsen play), and its emphatic resolution, is structurally a very traditional piece of playwrighting. What Pinter mainly adds is a distrust of language, a belief that language is more often used as evasion than as revelation. Only if we are committed to charting structural unity in a play through what is said, only if we are unwilling to try to see through layers of subterfuge to the emotional truth of individual moments, shall we be induced to believe that the structure of the play is arbitrary or that deliberate obfuscation is a motivating force.

In Pinter, development is internalized. In his earliest play, *The Room,* we are only mystified by the events that occur if we fail to realize that what we see on the stage is the gradual revelation of one character's inner life, her inner geography, first through monologue, later through the dramatic action itself. We are first given hints about her fears, her conflicting desires for security and for knowledge, which the action, culminating in the appearance of a mysterious blind visitor, forces into the open where she must make a decision. As Pinter's technique has developed, he has eschewed approaching his material through the inner life of a single character and has worked towards a balance in which various individual needs and fears may all be answered, if not satisfied, by a single resolution. The major turning point came in Act Three of *The Birthday Party,* where Pinter, having disposed of his ostensible hero, moved on to examine the conflicting needs of the group which had disposed of the victim. But the concept of inner geography remains valid in the subsequent plays. Exposition, development, and resolution can not be open in Pinter because he refuses to compel any character to say more than he wants to say or can say at a given moment. But what the characters do say is always to the point in that it exposes more and more what the characters fear, anticipate, and cherish. In this respect, it often does not matter whether what they say is, in fact, true. An invented past can be as telling as a true one. Thus, it makes little difference whether Ruth was or wasn't a photographic model for the body, or whether she was or wasn't a whore when Teddy married her. It makes little difference whether Jessie did or didn't sleep with MacGregor, whether Lenny's stories of his violence towards women are highly exaggerated or complete fabrications, or whether Teddy and Ruth have three children or not. The play does not operate at a level of facts. As Pinter has said: "The desire for verification is understandable but cannot always be satisfied."³ All we are to expect from the play is a gradu-

ally expanding knowledge of the inner lives of the characters. This knowledge almost always reveals an imbalance which we can count on the resolution to bring to a new equilibrium. Pinter's vision of human relationships is basically dialectical. Contradictions lead to new syntheses which in turn may break apart. While the family is discussing Ruth's new position and making plans for an advertising campaign to put the product across, Teddy interjects a telling reservation:

> TEDDY. She'd get old very quickly.
>
> MAX. No . . . not in this day and age! With the health service? Old! How could she get old?

The resolution of *The Homecoming* is not to be taken as final, but it has resolved one set of contradictions.

The play is full of extraordinary moments. One of the most striking is Sam's last-minute revelation which seems for a moment to have provoked his decease:

> SAM. (*in one breath*) MacGregor had Jessie in the back of my cab as I drove them along. (*He croaks and collapses. . . .*)
>
> MAX. What's he done? Dropped dead?
>
> LENNY. Yes.
>
> MAX. A corpse? A corpse on my floor? Get him out of here! Clear him out of here!
>
> JOEY. He's not dead.
>
> LENNY. He probably was dead, for about thirty seconds.
>
> MAX. He's not even dead!

This scene interrupts the forward momentum of the dramatic action, the snowballing plans for setting Ruth up in business and for "finalizing" the deal. A moment later, the participants return to the business at hand leaving Sam to remain stretched on the carpet (dead or alive) until the final curtain. What is this but proof reasonably positive of some of the points made above? It is the old Scribean *scene à faire* wedged into a situation where death becomes a farce. Poor Sam's carefully concealed fact, his delayed exposition, his last-minute message, is of no importance and never was of any importance. The characters have made their decisions on the basis of what each wishes to remember of the past, what each wants to see in the present, what each needs, desires, and fears. That decision is inevitable, irrevocable. For his trouble, Sam gets an abbreviated eulogy:

> MAX. You know what that man had?
>
> LENNY. Has.
>
> MAX. Has! A diseased imagination.

III

And Ruth said, intreat me not to leave thee, or to return from following after thee: for whither you goest, I will go: and where thou lodgest, I will lodge: thy people shall be my people, and thy God my God.

The Book of Ruth, I.16

And he arose and came to his father. But when he was yet a great way off, his father saw him, and had compassion, and ran, and fell on his neck and kissed him. And the son said unto him, Father, I have sinned against heaven, and in thy sight, and am no more worthy to be called thy son. But the father said to his servants, Bring forth the best robe, and put it on him; and put a ring on his hand, and shoes on his feet: And bring hither the fatted calf, and kill it; and let us eat and be merry: For this my son was dead, and is alive again; he was lost, and is found. And they began to be merry.

St. Luke, XV. 20-24

Bi-fold authority! Where reason can revolt
Without perdition, and loss assumes all reason
Without revolt: This is and is not Cressid!
Within my soul there doth conduce a fight
Of this strange nature, that a thing inseparate
Divides more wider than the sky and earth;
And yet the spacious breadth of this division
Admits no orifex for a point as subtle
As Ariachna's broken woof to enter.

Troilus and Cressida, v.ii.141-49

There are two frames of reference in Pinter's plays which have not been sufficiently explored, the Biblical (or Judaic) and the Shakespearean. The influence of the strictly modern, particularly of Beckett and Ionesco and their literary forbears, Kafka, Proust, and Joyce, carries us a certain distance into the early plays, although from the very beginning Pinter is doing absolutely unique and personal things and, in many ways, is in complete contrast to Ionesco's techniques and aims.

Pinter's statements about his methods seem to indicate a controlled but essentially intuitive approach:

I merely write and characters create themselves. I don't arbitrarily impose a characterisation upon someone, and say you're going to be like this to prove a point that I'm going to make. The stage opens, the curtain goes up and characters move along with it.[4]

Such an approach is even more open than normally to a certain degree of unconscious influence based on deeper layers of background and experience. Two vital facts in Pinter's biography are that his family was Jewish and that he was a Shakespearean actor. Beyond the testimony of the plays themselves, this is the only solid justification for the remarks which follow. But even if this critic's tenuous notions about parallels and narrative sources at conscious or subconscious levels are in error, they may still open up new perspectives on the work at hand.

The narrative and thematic source which *The Homecoming* most immediately suggests is Christ's parable of "the prodigal son." Indeed, it would be difficult to explore the idea of "homecoming" without suggesting this narrative sequence in one way or another, so deeply imbedded is it in the Christian consciousness. In an age which seems to have few myths which can act as common denominators

for human experience, the myth of "the prodigal" stands out as one of the few having a fairly universal coinage.

Nevertheless, there are elements in the play which suggest that the relationships are particular and not general. The prodigal son returned, it will be remembered, having "wasted his substance with riotous living" and "devoured his living with harlots": "And when he had spent all, there arose a mighty famine in that land; and he began to be in want." Teddy and Ruth have conflicting stories to tell about America. Teddy refers to the good life, the sun, their lovely house, and the "stimulating" environment. But, for Ruth, it is something else entirely. Her description suggests a land of famine, a land of plagues, such as those visited upon the Egyptians. The "cuddle and kiss" which Max insists upon at the Act One curtain suggests the compassion which the father in the parable showed towards his son (though Max's feelings here are clearly not compassionate), and Max's occupation as a butcher and his constant emphasis on blood suggests the killing of a fatted calf. There is no evidence that Teddy has wasted his substance in riotous living; nevertheless, he has had to do with "harlots," has even married one, and for this sin he is in due time forgiven with rather alarming consequences.

The real significance of the "prodigal" theme, however, lies not in the comparison but in the contrast. Teddy's fate is opposed to that of the figure in the parable; we wonder, in fact, if he is not perhaps the fatted calf in this version of the celebration. At the conclusion of the play's "merry-making," Teddy is lost and not found, dead and not alive. In fact, Ruth seems to have forgotten his name in the last line she speaks to him: "Eddie. Don't become a stranger." The ostensible hero is transformed into a *pharmakos,* or scapegoat, a transformation with which we are familiar from Pinter's earlier plays.

There seems to be, however, a more complex Biblical parallel involved which relies on a less familiar narrative sequence. Ruth's name may suggest the Biblical Ruth, but few of us are conversant enough with the Old Testament story to make the proper connections. At most, we shall probably recall that she was a Gentile who returned to Israel with her mother-in-law, Naomi, saying: "Thy people shall be my people, and thy God my God." Even this, however, particularly the relevance of her statement to the action of the play, ought to alert us to the possible significance of the parallel.

In the Biblical narrative, Ruth is a Moabite and the widow of Mahlon, Naomi's son. Upon her return to Bethlehem with Naomi, she goes into the fields to work, where she meets Boaz, a kinsman of her late husband, who speaks kindly to her. According to Israelite law, the brother-in-law of a childless widow, or the next nearest of kin, was required to marry her in order to insure the perpetuation of the family strain. Ruth, at her mother-in-law's instigation, goes to the threshing floor where Boaz is working and, while he is asleep, lies down at his feet, asserting her claim to him by means of an old custom:

And it came to pass at midnight, that the man was afraid, and turned himself: and, behold, a woman lay at his feet. And he said, Who art thou? And she answered, I am Ruth thine handmaid: spread therefore thy skirt over thine handmaid; for thou art a near kinsman.

He agrees to perform the "kinsman's part" for her, if another, who is yet more closely related, refuses. The nearer kinsman declines, saying: "I cannot redeem it for myself, lest I mar my own inheritance." Boaz and Ruth are married:

And Boaz said unto the elders, and unto all the people, Ye are witnesses this day, that . . . Ruth the Moabitess, the wife of Mahlon, have I purchased to be my wife, to raise up the name of the dead upon his inheritance, that the name of the dead be not cut off from among his brethren, and from the gate of his place: ye are witnesses this day.

If the parable of the prodigal son helps us to understand Teddy's role in the dramatic fable, the history of Ruth provides clues to Ruth's actions and to the strange behavior which her appearance seems to induce in the other characters. Both Ruths are aliens; both seem to make a "claim" upon their kinsmen; and the midnight encounter with Boaz on the threshing floor parallels Ruth's strange midnight encounter with Lenny in *The Homecoming* which concludes with Lenny aware that "some kind of a proposal" has been made.

Besides illuminating the motives which are operating behind some of the play's more difficult moments, the comparison makes clear the ambivalence of Ruth's position. In terms of the family, she is, like the Biblical Ruth, a Gentile and a heathen, by definition unclean and contaminated. Since such religious distinctions have no place in the play, an objective correlative must be found to express her "Gentility." She becomes, therefore, a whore, a "smelly scrubber," a "pox-ridden slut," in order to be redeemed from that state and accepted as "kith and kin" of the chosen people. (Again, the ironic inversion: Ruth becomes a whore in order to truly belong.) At the conclusion of the play, the redemption has taken place. In fact, Ruth sits enthroned like a queen among her subjects, repository of the seed from which kings will emerge. In this guise, she has also saved the family from sterility and will perpetuate the strain. Max seems to be unpleasantly aware of this transformation; hence, his final agonized concern over whether she has understood what they expect from her, and his attempt to re-establish the functional bond which was the basis of the agreement. Which is Ruth? The subservient whore? Or the frozen mythic princess whom the characters have unwittingly created and to whom they have unwittingly ceded their male dominion?

Whether or not these Biblical parallels are operative, there is little question that the dramatic world which Pinter conjures up has unusual affinities with the Judaic tradition—just as Kafka's world has. The family unit, as something to be revered and feared, lies at the center of this world. It acts both as a secure haven and as a threat from within, asserting its claim upon its members, frequently with violence. Pinter's world is equally a world of commandments, laws, and rules which one breaks only at one's peril.

The comparison between *The Homecoming* and Shakespeare's *Troilus and Cressida* could be made simply on the basis of a resemblance in tone and attitude. Both plays are unequivocal in their unmasking of hypocrisy and false value. Shakespeare takes a heroic and romantic story and proceeds to write an intensely anti-heroic and anti-romantic play. The noble Achilles murders a defenseless Hector and ties the corpse to his horse's tail. The Greek leaders are portrayed as buffoons and perverts, and Helen as a vapid nonentity. Pinter's play is not ostensibly heroic, but it is decked in the full regalia of cherished values, memories, and traditions which are exposed to an equally dyspeptic scrutiny.

Beyond this, however, there are again points of comparison which seem more than accidental. Most striking is Cressida's welcome to the Greek camp as a hostage:

AGAMEMNON. Most dearly welcome to the Greeks, sweet lady.

NESTOR. Our general doth salute you with a kiss.

ULYSSES. Yet is the kindness but particular; 'Twere better she were kissed in general.

In accordance with Ulysses' punning suggestion, she is passed from Greek to Greek, and each claims a kiss from her. (Ruth, as a hostage of Teddy's family, undergoes a similar initiation with equal willingness.) Later, Troilus and Ulysses spy on Cressida as she flirts with the Greek, Diomedes, with the omnipresent Thersites providing ironic commentary:

TROILUS. Cressid comes forth to him.

DIOMEDES. How now, my charge?

CRESSIDA. Now, my sweet guardian! Hark, a word with you. (*Whispers.*)

TROILUS. Yea, so familiar?

ULYSSES. She will sing any man at first sight.

THERSITES. And any man may sing her, if he can take her cliff; she's noted.

DIOMEDES. Will you remember? . . .

CRESSIDA. In faith, I cannot: what would you have me do?

THERSITES. A juggling trick,—to be secretly open.

Similar scenes in which the sexual urge is exposed in a cruel and unromantic light are to be found in *The Homecoming:*

JOEY. Christ, she's wide open. Dad, look at that. (*Pause.*) She's a tart.

* * *

MAX. Where's the whore? Still in bed? She'll make us all animals.

LENNY. The girl's a tease.

* * *

LENNY. I've got a better idea. Why don't I take her up with me to Greek Street? (*Pause.*)

MAX. You mean put her on the game? (*Pause.*) We'll put her on the game. That's a stroke of genius, that's a marvelous idea. You mean she can earn the money herself—on her back?

Teddy, like Troilus, is compelled to witness scenes which must curdle his blood, scenes in which the woman he calls wife is pawed, kissed, prostituted, and profaned. Ruth, like Cressida, is a Trojan among the Greeks (again the "alien" theme), and a Trojan who makes herself a Greek by using her sex as bait. At the play's conclusion, she is relegated, like Cressida, to Greek Street.

Out of a discussion between Lenny and Teddy on the subject of being and non-being, a matter which Teddy says "doesn't fall within my province," comes an opaque and disturbing statement by Ruth:

Don't be too sure though. You've forgotten something. Look at me. I . . . move my leg. That's all it is. But I wear . . . underwear . . . which moves with me . . . it . . . captures your attention. Perhaps you misinterpret. The action is simple. It's a leg . . . moving. My lips move. Why don't you restrict your observations to that? Perhaps the fact that they move is more significant . . . than the words which come through them. You must bear that . . . possibility . . . in mind.

Is she referring to a language of the body, a sensual communication which words cannot approximate? Ulysses ascribes just such a language to Cressida in startlingly similar terms:

Fie, fie upon her!
There's language in her eye, her cheek, her lip,
Nay, her foot speaks, her wanton spirits look out
At every joint and motive of her body.
O these encounterers, so glib of tongue,
That give a coasting welcome ere it comes,
And wide unclasp the tables of their thoughts
To every ticklish reader! set them down
For sluttish spoils of opportunity,
And daughters of the game.

It is worth noting in passing that "the game" in Pinter and Shakespeare has a similar reference, and that both Ruth and Cressida play by the same rules.

Earlier, I remarked upon the state of trance in which Ruth seems to drift through so much of the play, a kind of hypnosis presumably imposed upon her by the naked wills of the men among whom she moves. Early in the first scene of the play, Max remarks upon his "instinctive

understanding of animals," particularly of fillies, and suggests that some hypnotic effect is involved. Cressida uses hypnosis as an excuse for her unavoidable wantonness:

Troilus, farewell! one eye looks on thee,
But with my heart the other eye doth see.
Ah, poor our sex! this fault in us I find
The error of our eye directs our mind:
What error leads must err; O, then conclude
Minds swayed by eyes are full of turpitude.

There would seem to be sufficient evidence that the two plays are preoccupied with similar images and concerns and that the atmosphere which they generate and the attitude which they project seem to have much in common. In addition, we can see that Cressida among the Greeks, Ruth among the Israelites, and the heroine of *The Homecoming* among her husband's family are all wanderers who, to borrow a phrase from Keats, stand "in tears amid the alien corn."

It would perhaps be better to discard the idea of narrative parallels in the play as having altogether the wrong implications. If the prodigal son, the Biblical Ruth, and Shakespeare's Greeks and Trojans are all validly related to Pinter's latest play, the notion of "parallels" becomes difficult to support. In the myth of the prodigal, there is no place for Ruth. In the story of Ruth, there is no place for Teddy. In *Troilus and Cressida* there is room for both, but this "parallel" excludes the Judaic frame of reference which seems so vital to the play.

What is perhaps most important is the recognition that Ruth is a "fractionized" image forced into completely contradictory roles: mother and whore, wife and sister, matriarch and handmaiden, guardian and hostage. At the height of his agony, while watching Cressida betray him, Troilus suddenly sees her as two Cressida's, one his and one Diomedes':

This she? no, this is Diomed's Cressida: . . .
If there be rules in unity itself,
This was not she. O madness of discourse,
That cause sets up with and against itself!

Erich Kahler in *The Tower and the Abyss* speaks of the "disintegration of the individual" as being characteristic of our age. The "unity and integrity of the human form," which is perhaps the primary value which we have been bequeathed by Greek and Jewish antiquity, has been broken down, subjected to a "dissolution of coherence and structure."[5] What Kahler refers to as "fractionized universe" and "fractionized consciousness" is evident not only in contemporary art but also in a host of Shakespearean characters, Hamlet, the two Richards, Cressida, among others who, submitted to "bi-fold authority" and conflicting claims upon them, divide "more wider than the sky and earth," although "the spacious breadth of this division / Admits no orifex for a point as subtle / As Ariachna's broken woof to enter." Pinter's characters frequently show the same divisions, and it is this fact, in addition to a similarly powerful verbal complexity and sense of structure, which gives his plays their texture and vitality.

IV

"But you . . . Ruth . . . you're kin. You're Kith. You belong here."

In effect, what **The Homecoming** finally illustrates is the triumph of function over blood tie. As early as **The Birthday Party,** a struggle-to-the-death between the community (or family), and the collectivity (or organization) seemed to be a central issue in Pinter's work. The family bases its judgment of belonging on blood. The collectivity bases its judgment of belonging on function. In **The Caretaker,** Davies' attempt to take on a function as "caretaker" is defeated by his inability to deal with the blood tie between the two brothers. **The Homecoming** illustrates the process in reverse. The blood tie is set aside; the family has no "need" for a Ph.D.: what it does need is a woman and it simply takes what it needs. A prodigal attempts to reclaim his family and is turned away, but his wife is initiated into the tribe, becoming "kith" and "kin."

The idea represented by the phrase, "kith and kin," is of immense importance to the play. "Kin," of course, denotes blood relationship. Originally, however, "kith" denoted countryman rather than blood relative; it stems from the same root as "couth," and both refer to what is "known" by the beholder. It may not be wide of the mark to say that Teddy is kin but not kith (related but not known), and Ruth kith but not kin. At the end of the play, Teddy has been rejected from both circles, but Max warmly accepts Ruth as "kith" and "kin," separating the phrase into its two component parts to make a significant effect.

"Blood" also runs through the play as a persistent image. It serves a double function, since it is the strongest expression of the family tie and also a by-product of the butcher's trade. The curious scene in which Ruth offers Lenny a drink from her water-glass may be a distortion of the Jewish marriage rite; it can also be viewed as a reference to the traditional proverb: "Blood is thicker than water."

Related to the play's immersion in the world of the family is its ironic contemplation of values. Max and Lenny talk about values constantly. Both—but particularly Lenny—speak on this subject with such confidence that we tend to be taken in. The very mention of "values" tends to intimidate us. Pinter, however, places these references in juxtaposition with actions by the same characters which refute any notion of moral ultimatums. Max refers to Ruth as a woman of "quality" and "feeling" as she is in the process of rolling off the couch with Joey. Max's description of his dead wife as a "slutbitch," is succeeded by the statement that "she taught them [i.e., Teddy, Lenny, Joey] all the morality they know."

In the second act, Lenny launches into the play's fullest statement of family values, in response to Teddy's admission that he has stolen Lenny's cheese roll. Since the family is already well advanced in the process of stealing Teddy's wife, concern over a cheese roll at this moment seems somewhat profane. There is an ironic displacement involved here; by all rights, this should be Teddy's speech in response to the gross indignities to which he has been submitted:

Barefaced audacity. (*Pause.*) What led you to be so . . . vindictive against your own brother? I'm bowled over.

* * *

Well, if that's the kind of thing they teach you over there, you're welcome to it, Ted. But I think in that case you'd better cut your visits to this country down to a bare minimum. After all, we're talking about kith and kin, aren't we? I mean that's what we're talking about.

* * *

Because we know something about the values which have been handed down to us. . . . Our little community, our little group, our team, you might say, our unit, made up of, I'll admit it, various and not entirely similar component parts, but which, put together, do nevertheless make up a whole. An organization, which, though we're not exactly a sentimental family, we do recognize as such. And you're an integral part of it, Ted. . . . And so when you at length return to us, we do expect a bit of grace, a bit of liberality of spirit, to reassure us. We do expect that. But do we get it? Have we got it? Is that what you've given us?

There is no question that Lenny is upset about his cheese roll; the act of theft has disordered his world; chaos has been invited to institute its reign. Again, an echo from *Troilus and Cressida* is helpful, Ulysses' much quoted speech on "degree," a speech which is also a defense of traditional values and which comes from just as unlikely a source:

The heavens themselves, the planets and this centre,
Observe degree, priority and place,
Insisture, course, proportion, season, form,
Office and custom, in all line of order: . . .
Take but degree away, untrue that string,
And, hark, what discord follows! each thing melts
In mere oppugnancy: . . .
Force should be right; or rather, right and wrong,
Between whose endless jar justice resides,
Should lose their names, and so should justice too.
Then every thing include itself in power.
Power into will, will into appetite;
And appetite, an universal wolf . . .
Must make perforce an universal prey,
And last eat up himself.

The last three lines seem a fitting précis for **The Homecoming.**

The concept of family which Max and Lenny have is clearly a collage of empty clichés. Responsibility, democracy, morality, quality, standards, feeling, values, liberality of spirit, and generosity of mind: words, words,

words. But beneath the verbal gloss, as beneath a politician's panaceas, what we see in the attitudes and responses of the characters and in their relationships to each other is a reality which is prehistoric and primitive, a world where appetite reigns. Max's stick defends him against the murderous impulses of his sons; a woman is dragged into the cave and the inhabitants argue over their share in her as if she were a piece of meat; images of blood and butchery predominate; any respect for the value of human life is belied. Beneath the stated values of the play, there is a total absence of values, a void which is filled by the human family's animal struggle to survive and perpetuate itself. That such an environment should spawn a Doctor of Philosophy is one of the more brutal ironies of a play which exposes the powerlessness of rationality. *The Homecoming* makes us aware that Pinter is again showing us nothing more surprising or mystifying than man's primitive nature reasserting itself, naked and demanding, from beneath the layers of intellectual and ethical sophistication with which it has been so carefully covered.

Notes

1. All quotes from *The Homecoming* were originally drawn from an unpublished manuscript which I wish to thank Mr. Harold Pinter for the privilege of reading and the permission to quote from. The last speech quoted, from "Well, if that's the kind of thing . . ." to "Is that what you've given us?", occurs in a different version in the published text; all other quotations conform in essentials to the printed version.

2. Interview with Lawrence Bensky abstracted from the forthcoming issue of *The Paris Review.* Quoted from *The New York Times* (January 1, 1967).

3. Program note for performances of *The Room* and *The Dumb Waiter,* Royal Court Theatre, London, March, 1960.

4. Harold Pinter and Hallam Tennyson, Interview, B.B.C. General Overseas Service (August 7, 1960).

5. Erich Kahler, *The Tower and the Abyss* (New York: George Braziller, Inc., 1957), p. xiv.

John M. Warner (essay date 1970)

SOURCE: "The Epistemological Quest in Pinter's *The Homecoming,*" in *Contemporary Literature,* Vol. 11, No. 3, Summer, 1970, pp. 340-53.

[*In the following essay, Warner argues that* The Homecoming *asks the audience to reevaluate their expectations and values.*]

No one denied the brilliance of the Royal Shakespeare Company's production of *The Homecoming* when it was first produced in London in 1965 or later in New York in 1967. Harold Pinter's mysterious play elicited, however, responses that ranged from bafflement to outrage. One English critic found the key to the meaning of the play in the chance remark of a member of the audience that the characters all "behaved like animals." Ronald Bryden concedes that Pinter "has written a stylish entertainment, but not much more. All that remains is a flavour. Still, it is a strong, individual one. Perhaps it is enough for him that, like the beasts which fascinate him, he has staked out a territory with his personal odour."[1]

The ease with which Pinter disregards or even inverts our ordinary values undoubtedly caused this agitated criticism. The play opens with a father talking with (or rather, at) a son; but the locus of authority has mysteriously shifted from father to the son who callously remarks: "Plug it, will you, you stupid sod, I'm trying to read the paper."[2] When Max tries to reassert his parental power, Lenny only casually retorts: "You know what, you're getting demented." Not only is the role of the father out of joint in the Pinter world; the whole family situation reeks of perversity. An elder son, Teddy, who has become a philosophy professor in America, brings his mysteriously cool yet sensual wife back to his family home for a visit. Ruth, the wife, sexually arouses Teddy's father and his two younger brothers, Lenny, a pimp, and Joey, an erstwhile boxer. After making love with the brothers in front of Teddy, Ruth decides to stay on in England to care for the family's sexual needs (in the meantime agreeing also to join Lenny's string of prostitutes in order to pay her own way). To all of this, Teddy quietly acquiesces.

So baldly stated, the action of the play does indeed seem animalistic, a further illustration of a modern decadence made all the more shocking by the casual attitude the central protagonists retain throughout. Pinter may, however, be seeking another, and redemptive, kind of "shock." Indeed, he uses an extreme metaphor (for such we may construe the whole family situation he describes) in an effort to force his audience into a recognition of a spiritual poverty more terrible than any affront to its conventional morality. Moreover, Pinter's spectators have nearly lost the capacity to be critical of this spiritual desiccation because it arises from something so innate to their way of thinking, their way of creating values. For this reason Pinter must resort to metaphors replete with violent inversions of conventional morality to make his audience see the decadence of its whole materialistic, rationalistic culture; for *The Homecoming* is a drama which describes man's plight in the godless world of science and reason.

As such, Pinter's play becomes a significant document in that broad movement labelled existentialism. If existentialism is such a diversified phenomenon that no simple definition can be conceived, perhaps the roots or causes for the generation of this widespread attitude can be agreed to. These have been well summarized by William Barrett, whose book, *Irrational Man,* remains the most important survey of existentialist thought. According to Barrett, modern man has entered upon a secular phase of his history, and he has "found himself for the first time *home-*

less." His chief tool, science, has "stripped nature of its human forms and presented man with a universe that was neutral, alien, in its vastness and force, to his human purposes." Religion, which "had been a structure that encompassed man's life, providing him with a system of images and symbols by which he could express his aspirations toward psychic wholeness," has lost its force, and with the "loss of this containing framework man became not only a dispossessed but a fragmentary being." Barrett continues:

> In society, as in the spiritual world, secular goals have come to predominate; the rational organization of the economy has increased human power over nature, and politically also society has become more rational, utilitarian, democratic, with a resulting material wealth and progress. The men of the Enlightenment foresaw no end to this triumphant expansion of reason into all areas of social life. But here too reason has foundered upon its opposite, upon the surd and unpredictable realities—wars, economic crises and dislocations, political upheavals among the masses. Moreover, man's feeling of homelessness, of alienation has been intensified in the midst of a bureaucratized, impersonal mass society. He has come to feel himself an outsider even within his human society. He is trebly alienated: a stranger to God, to nature, and to the gigantic social apparatus that supplies his material wants.[3]

Such are the roots of modern man's sense of alienation and estrangement against which his reason seems curiously impotent.

It has been worthwhile to quote Barrett's summary so extensively since it provides the exact context for Pinter's play. As other existential thinkers have tried to find a way out of modern man's dilemma, so Pinter's **Homecoming** suggests his response to the prevailing sense of homelessness in our century. Pinter uses not the precise categories of the philosopher but the symbols of the artist to demonstrate his idea. Nevertheless, the affinities between the dramatist and the philosophers are again apparent. Like Heidegger, Pinter suggests that the way out of the tragic box which modern, rationalist man has gotten himself into may be a return to an analysis of the sources of his being. **The Homecoming** provides dramatic exploration of the epistemological possibilities open to man in his efforts to overcome his crippling alienation from his own self.

Some apparently rambling conversation about horse racing between Max and Lenny in the opening scene adumbrates the play's epistemological theme. Lenny asks his father what he thinks are the chances for a horse called Second Wind at Sandowne Park. His inquiry leads to Max's fulminations:

> He talks to me about horses. You only read their names in the papers. But I've stroked their manes. I've held them, I've calmed them down before a big race. I was the one they used to call for. Max, they'd say, there's a horse here, he's highly strung, you're the only man on the course who can calm him. It was true. I had a . . . I had an instinctive understanding of animals.
>
> (p. 10)

As a prototype of modern man, Lenny experiences the horses only as names in the papers. Hence, his knowledge remains abstract, in some ways unreal. (". . . the fillies are more highly strung than the colts, they're more unreliable, did you know that? No, what do you know? Nothing," Max remarks in the same scene.) Max by no means represents Pinter's ideal mode of perception, but he is clearly less tainted by abstract knowledge than is Lenny. Max has an "instinctive understanding" of the horses that goes beyond the rational organization of knowledge according to the racing forms to a full experience of the horse itself—an experience that does not reduce the horse to some form of abstraction: "The times I've watched those animals thundering past the post. What an experience. Mind you, I didn't lose, I made a few bob out of it, and you know why? Because I always had the smell of a good horse. I could smell him" (p. 10). Max "knows" the horses more fully than Lenny because he has experienced them existentially. It was, he remarks, "a gift. I had a gift" (p. 10). Modern man, caught in the fabrications of his abstracting intellect, has lost that gift.

Ironically, however, it is Lenny who hopes for the victory of Second Wind. Speaking from his fuller knowledge, Max gives the horse no chance. The symbolic implications of the horse's name are, on one level, immediately clear. It implies some kind of renewal, a second chance for a dispirited world. Indeed, the word "wind" was once, as its etymology reveals, synonymous with the word "spirit." Hence, Lenny's desire for Second Wind's victory might be construed, on a subtler level, as reflecting his unconscious desire to achieve Max's "instinctive understanding" and thus rid himself of the spiritual aridity of his abstract knowledge. Along this line we must note Ruth's desire, later in the act, for a "breath of air" (p. 23). Teddy, the abstracting philosopher, responds: "The last thing I want is a breath of air. Why do you want a breath of air?" (p. 24). (The word "breath" bears the same etymological relation to "spirit" as "wind.") The products of a tradition which uses language in such a way as to split up single meanings into a number of separate and often isolated concepts, Lenny and Ruth may be unconsciously revealing their desire to return to a more unified perception of reality.[4]

Indeed, Lenny and Ruth, like the other characters in the play, are obsessed with the question of knowing, of how reality is perceived.[5] When Ruth returns from her "breath of air," she meets Lenny. In the course of their conversation, he describes a meeting with a certain lady who was "falling apart with the pox." He then discusses in detail his impulse to kill the woman and the reasons he "only gave her another belt in the nose and a couple of turns of the boot and sort of left it at that" (p. 31). Ruth's only reaction to this gory detail is to ask calmly: "How did you know she was diseased?"

> LENNY: How did I know?
>
> *Pause*
>
> I decided she was.
>
> *Silence*

Lenny's answer could simply express his brutishness, but the symbolic configuration of the play suggests more is involved. For Lenny there is an essentially subjective basis to cognition. The lady's disease is not something simply to be scientifically or objectively verified; rather it is a reality imparted by his mind. What attracts Ruth is not his callous brutality but this capacity for subjective awareness in contrast to her husband's apparently sterile objectivity.

Other examples of this concern with "knowing" abound in the text. Angry with his brother Sam, Max berates him:

> Listen, Sam. I want to say something to you. From my heart. I want you to get rid of these feelings of resentment you've got toward me. I wish I could understand them. Honestly, have I ever given you cause? Never. When Dad died he said to me, Max, look after your brother. That's exactly what he said to me.

Sam's answer is simply: "How could he say that when he was dead?"

> MAX: What?
>
> SAM: How could he speak if he was dead?
>
> *Pause*
>
> (p. 39)

Sam's concern for knowing could be seen simply as a Pinterean device for comedy—an illustration of Bergson's idea of the comic arising from the substitution of a mechanical response where one would expect an organic one. But that is precisely Pinter's point. Sam, associated always with his Super Snipe automobile, substitutes a weakly sense of scientific curiosity for the violently insistent, yet more human "knowing" of his brother. (Such a scene could easily degenerate into a kind of low comedy. The Royal Shakespeare Company, presumably at the author's instance, caught remarkably well the weighted insistence of Pinter's prose which pushes the action onto another level altogether.)

A degenerate patriarch, Max nevertheless continues to command a grudging respect from his family because of the strength of his affirmation of the passional life over economic or rational values. (He tells Lenny: "I think you're concentrating too much on economic considerations. There are human considerations. You understand what I mean. There are human considerations. Don't forget them"; p. 71). This commitment to the "blood consciousness" has given him a productiveness which his family envy yet apparently cannot achieve:

> I respected my father not only as a man but as a number one butcher! And to prove it I followed him into the shop. I learned to carve a carcass at his knee. I commemorated his name in blood. I gave birth to three grown men! All on my own bat. What have you done? (*Pause*) What have you done? You tit!
>
> (pp. 39-40)

Max has opened himself to a way of knowing through the blood; and this has given him a certain sacramental power which is rejected yet desired by his sons, to whom ritual has become an empty abstraction.

This power is most clearly revealed in Pinter's association of Max with meals and cooking. The implications of the "sacred meal" have been described by Louis Bouyer:

> a common meal makes men appreciate their relation with the cosmos which provides the natural resources for their life. Eating in common is the human act *par excellence,* where society is built up from within, while each man perfects himself by integrating himself with the universe. It is moreover the first and supreme act in which man apprehends himself in his living relationship with God. Man undoubtedly comes to the meal to secure this relationship, and, in a way, to secure everything, since he there receives nourishment for his life. But he also goes there to give, to give himself. In other words, he realizes, not in thought, but in a decisive act, that his life is not his own, that it depends upon God alone. And thus, at last in sacrifice the life of man comes, or comes again, to participate in the life of God.[6]

Because of his power of knowing "through the blood" Max retains some limited power to ritualize the meal. The spiritual nourishment of such meals is both rejected and longed for by Max's children. In the first act, Lenny speaks to his father:

> I want to ask you something. That dinner we had before, what was the name of it? What do you call it?
>
> *Pause*
>
> Why don't you buy a dog? You're a dog cook. Honest. You think you're cooking for a lot of dogs.
>
> MAX: If you don't like it get out.
>
> LENNY: I am going out. I'm going out to buy myself a proper dinner.
>
> (pp. 10-11)

Lenny, the economic man who thinks he can buy whatever he needs, might seem to be rejecting the ritualistic aspect of dinning at Max's table, yet he perceptively, if ironically, remarks later in the scene: "What the boys want, Dad, is your own special brand of cooking, Dad. That's what the boys are looking forward to. The special understanding of food, you know, that you've got" (p. 17). Max's "special understanding" of food depends on his ability, as he remarks to Ruth who has complimented him on his lunch, to "put my heart and soul into it . . ." (p. 45). In whatever attenuated way, Max retains the ability to give, and this differentiates him from his sons, who are thereby alienated from such capacity for spiritual communion. (Note the altercation between Teddy and Lenny over the cheese roll in Act Two. Teddy refuses to apologize for taking the roll, saying only: "I saw you put it there. I was hungry, so I ate it"; p. 64. Such cool logic Lenny can only interpret as sheer vindictiveness.)

The sons are not uniform in their incapacity, however, but reflect gradations of responsiveness dependent upon their commitment to reason and science as keys to man's understanding of his existence. Although an utilitarian entrepreneur, Lenny is, as we have seen, fascinated by more subjective, spiritual ways of knowing. Thus, we can interpret his questioning Max about the night of his conception as reflecting his desire to know whether man can be reduced simply to a mechanistic impulse:

> That night . . . you know . . . the night you got me . . . that night with Mum, what was it like? Eh? When I was just a glint in your eye. What was it like? What was the background to it? I mean, I want to know the real facts about my background. I mean, for instance, is it a fact that you had me in mind all the time, or is it a fact that I was the last thing you had in mind?
>
> (p. 36)

Lenny maintains that he asks about this only out of an almost scientific curiosity ("I'm only asking this in a spirit of inquiry, you understand that, don't you?"; p. 36); yet his persistence in worrying at Max suggests an inner dissatisfaction with his own way of knowing reality and the search for something else.

Indeed, Lenny is an existential quester, the proverbial armchair philosopher who enjoys sitting "round the Ritz bar having a few liqueurs" and asking questions about the "logical incoherence in the central affirmations of Christian theism" and the "business of being and not-being" (pp. 51f.). In contrast with Lenny's freewheeling pursuit of philosophic inquiry, Teddy, the professional philosopher, can only stiffly reply that such questions don't fall within his province. Pinter satirizes the academic philosopher whose profession has become so specialized that he can no longer respond to basic questions about the nature of man's existence. In this regard, Pinter's insight is confirmed by other thinkers. Barrett, for example, feels the "modern university is as much an expression of the specialization of the age as is the modern factory." And the academic philosopher, anxious to conform to his peer group, also turns increasingly to a specialization that "leads away from the ordinary and concrete acts of understanding in terms of which man lives his day-to-day life," and toward an "extraordinary preoccupation with technique . . . with logical and linguistic analysis, syntax and semantics; and in general with the refining away of all content for the sake of formal subtlety."[7]

Teddy symbolizes such specialized, academic philosophy. He likes the cleanness of America:

> TEDDY: It's so clean there.
>
> RUTH: Clean.
>
> TEDDY: Yes.
>
> RUTH: Is it dirty here?
>
> TEDDY: No, of course not. But it's cleaner there.
>
> *Pause*

> Look I just brought you back to meet the family, didn't I? You've met them, we can go. The fall semester will be starting soon.
>
> RUTH: You find it dirty here?
>
> TEDDY: I didn't say I found it dirty here.
>
> (pp. 54f.)

But Teddy quickly belies this last statement: "Here, there's nowhere to bathe, except the swimming bath down the road. You know what it's like? It's like a urinal. A filthy urinal!" (p. 55). What Teddy likes is the purity, the cleanliness, of a scientific methodology and technology that have been purified of the stink of human emotion. He would, in fact, prefer to be rid of emotions. Curiously, he responds quite passively to his brothers' making love to his wife. He only becomes charged with feeling when Ruth, breaking off from embracing Joey, asks if Teddy's family have read his critical works.

> You wouldn't understand my works. You wouldn't have the faintest idea of what they were about. You wouldn't appreciate the points of reference. You're way behind. All of you. There's no point in my sending you my works. You'd be lost. It's nothing to do with the question of intelligence. It's a way of being able to look at the world. It's a question of how far you can operate on things and not in things. I mean it's a question of your capacity to ally the two, to relate the two, to balance the two. To see, to be able to *see!* I'm the one who can see. That's why I write my critical works. Might do you good . . . have a look at them . . . see how certain people can view . . . things . . . how certain people can maintain . . . intellectual equilibrium. Intellectual equilibrium. You're just objects. You just . . . move about. I can observe it. I can see what you do. It's the same as I do. But you're lost in it. You won't get me being . . . I won't be lost in it.
>
> (pp. 61-62)

The central importance of the epistemological theme to the play becomes obvious here. As Teddy says, it is not a question of intelligence, but a "way of being able to look at the world." Curiously, Teddy posits an ideal form of cognition which he then emotionally repudiates. He suggests the need to relate or balance the capacity to operate *on* things (the mechanistic, objective basis for knowing) and the ability to operate *in* things (a subjective form of experiencing reality). His ideal, then, constitutes something very similar to a romantic epistemology. In "Tintern Abbey" Wordsworth speaks of what we "half create, and what perceive" as reality. Similarly, Teddy would find his capacity to "see" dependent upon his ability to balance, to ally the subject and the object.

Unfortunately, Teddy, like the whole specialized, scientific, materialistic, academic tradition he represents, has gotten out of whack. The emotional explosion at the end of his speech clearly reveals that he would rather "operate on things and not in things." His "intellectual equilibrium" is not the result of a balanced capacity to perceive reality but the rationalizing defense of a person intensely afraid of subjective involvement: "You won't get me being . . . I won't be lost in it."

Operating "on" things permits the creation of a materially rewarding scientific technology. America becomes the symbol of a country given over to such a technology. (It was painful to see how easily—simply with two shining suitcases and two brand new raincoats—the Royal Shakespeare Company could mock our whole society.) But America's material riches do not lead, as Lenny points out to Teddy, to a greater liberality of spirit.

> . . . I'd have thought that in the United States of America, I mean with the sun and all that, the open spaces, on the old campus, in your position, lecturing, in the center of all the intellectual life out there, on the old campus, all the social whirl, all the stimulation of it all, all your kids and all that, to have fun with, down by the pool, the Greyhound buses and all that, tons of iced water, all the comforts of those Bermuda shorts and all that, on the old campus, no time of the day or night you can't get a cup of coffee or a Dutch gin, I'd have thought you'd have grown more forthcoming, not less.
>
> (p. 64)

But the promise of America proves hollow. Its materialistic, rationalistic foundations seem sterile—at least to Ruth.

> I was born quite near here.
>
> *Pause*
>
> Then . . . six years ago, I went to America.
>
> *Pause*
>
> It's all rock. And sand. It stretches . . . so far . . . everywhere you look.
>
> And there's lots of insects there.
>
> *Pause*
>
> And there's lots of insects there.
>
> *Silence*
>
> *She is still.*
>
> (p. 53)

Viewed in this context, Ruth may seem something more than the London *Sunday Observer's* "tarty, bourgeois wife who contemplates promiscuity as evenly as if she were counting the doilies. . . ." Like her biblical namesake, she seeks out a home among her husband's people. If it would be going too far to say that she also sought thereby greater spiritual fulfillment, Ruth's decision to stay with Teddy's family ought to be seen not as a sign of ultimate decadence but as a life-seeking attempt to return to a greater wholeness of experience, of existence in face of the barrenness of her life in America. If it comes to a question of choosing between the "stink of being" and the aridity of abstraction, Ruth prefers to be. "My lips move," she tells the family. "Why don't you restrict . . . your observations to that? Perhaps the fact that they move is more significant

. . . than the words which come through them. You must bear that . . . possibility . . . in mind" (p. 53). The evolution of language has resulted in the movement toward greater and greater abstraction.[8] What Ruth suggests is that there may be more significant ways of human communication than the abstractions of words can permit. In rejecting her husband, whose province is words, and in staying with his family, she seeks not simply promiscuous pleasure but greater existential wholeness.

To seek, however, is not to find; and the ambivalence of Pinter's attitude toward Ruth's decision must be recognized. Undoubtedly, he creates an ending replete with violent inversions of conventional morality to make his audience see the decadence of its culture (our original point). Whether he finds Ruth's means of seeking existential wholeness valid is another question. The reversion to a more passionate, physical kind of existence may be an effort to reawaken the answers of the past. But "history has never allowed man to return to the past in any total sense. And our psychological problems cannot be solved by a regression to a past state in which they had not yet been brought into being."[9] Lenny invokes the spirit of Second Wind, but Max more wisely knows that the horse can not win.

Certainly the immediate consequences of Ruth's decision to stay do not offer much hope that either she or the family have come to a more fruitful way of "knowing" reality. The relationship, first of all, intensifies an inclination toward commercialization already noted in Lenny. Indeed, the men become almost like little boys playing at being American capitalists:

> LENNY: No, what I mean, Teddy, you must know lots of professors, heads of departments, men like that. They pop over here for a week at the Savoy, they need somewhere they can go to have a nice quiet poke. And of course you'd be in a position to give them inside information.
>
> MAX: Sure. You can give them proper data. You know, the kind of thing she's willing to do. How far she'd be prepared to go with their little whims and fancies. Eh, Lenny? To what extent she's various. I mean if you don't know who does?
>
> *Pause*
>
> I bet you before two months we'd have a waiting list.
>
> LENNY: You could be our representative in the States.
>
> MAX: Of course. We're talking in international terms! By the time we've finished Pan-American'll give us a discount.
>
> (p. 74)

Curiously, it is Teddy who raises a key existential issue: "She'd get old . . . very quickly," he remarks (p. 75). In response, Max speaks with all the confidence of one attuned to the jargon of a scientific technocracy. "No . . . not in this day and age! With the health service? Old! How could she get old? She'll have the time of her life"

(p. 75). It is unlikely that a free sexuality, even bolstered by the health service, will prove any more effective than analytic philosophy in coping with such matters as "anxiety, death, the conflict between the bogus and the genuine self, the faceless man of the masses, the experience of the death of God. . . ."[10]

Nor will the sexuality be that free. Ruth demonstrates her own sense of economic imperialism, telling the men: "I'd need an awful lot. Otherwise I wouldn't be content" (p. 77). And she gives every indication of turning into a real bitch, exploiting her sexual power over the men (cf. pp. 60-61) in such a way as to confirm D. H. Lawrence's worst predictions. The sexual effect she has on the men is also debilitating. Rather than expanding into full manhood, they exhibit alarmingly regressive tendencies. Joey, the most virile member of the family, fails to gain full sexual satisfaction with Ruth. Undue emphasis on love-play, the psychiatrists tell us, reveals immaturity. "Love play? Two bleeding hours? That's a bloody long time for love play!" Max remarks with some truth (p. 73). Moreover, Max's behavior at the end of the play can only be considered some form of infantile regression as he whimpers about on the floor, moaning that he is "not an old man."

The reversion to operating "in" things is, apparently, no more satisfactory a route to existential wholeness than to operate "on" things. The answer will depend on man's learning "how to look at the world." But modern, rationalist man will not be able to turn the clock backward; he will not be able to revert to his past. Ruth remarks to the family:

> I was . . . different . . . when I met Teddy . . . first.
>
> TEDDY: No you weren't. You were the same.
>
> RUTH: I wasn't.
>
> MAX: Who cares? Listen, live in the present, what are you worrying about? I mean, don't forget the earth's about five thousand million years old, at least. Who can afford to live in the past?
>
> (p. 50)

If one is to seek wholeness, one must run the risk of "living in the present." The risk for modern man, cut off from the sanctuaries of the past, is the danger of becoming the existential "stranger" (and it is this that Ruth, in her last words to her husband, cautions him against: "Don't become a stranger"; p. 80). But if the risk is great, at least there is the chance of authentic selfhood.

This possibility may explain the paradoxical quality of Pinter's attitude toward Teddy. For Teddy, of all the members of the family, most lives in the present. It is he alone who has accepted the challenges and risks involved in modern life. The calculated ambiguity of Pinter's response to Teddy leaves the spectator doubtful whether the character (or any man) can survive these challenges in a meaningful way. His seeming callousness as he departs for America, leaving his wife as concubine for his family,

suggests a total corruption by modern materialism. On the other hand, it is possible that Teddy's seeming indifference to his wife's prostituting herself reflects rather a determination not to impose his will on her, a desire to let her "be" herself and not the object of his will. Teddy may have gained at least some partial insight into Buber's idea that "meaning in life happens in the area between person and person in that situation of contact when one says *I* to the other's *Thou*. . . ."[11] Moreover, it is Teddy who perceives the need to balance the demands of the abstracting intellect and the concrete self. Teddy's "success," like Ruth's, is left doubtful, but Pinter seems to suggest that he is at least looking in the right direction. At any rate, it is Teddy who most clearly articulates, if he does not successfully enact, the epistemological possibility through which modern man might come to know himself in his homelessness.

Notes

1. Ronald Bryden, "A Stink of Pinter," *New Statesman,* 69 (June 11, 1965), 928. Forewarned, some of the American critics were forearmed. The critic of *Time* noted with some insight: "Baffling the intellect while it stirs the instincts, *The Homecoming* operates in the realm of myth. Myth frequently proclaims the dark primacy of what D. H. Lawrence called 'the blood consciousness' over the light of reason, clearly one of Pinter's intentions in the play." "Land of No Holds Barred," *Time,* 89 (January 13, 1967), 43. Most perceptive of all were the remarks of Richard Gilman in *Newsweek.* He noted that "the characters of *The Homecoming* are incarnations of human faculties, dividing among themselves the great possibilities of attitude and approach to existence." "Mortal Combat," *Newsweek,* 69 (January 16, 1967), 93. Gilman's view of the play as existential drama parallels in general outline that of my essay although, of course, he could only baldly state his thesis because of the space limitations of his review.

2. Harold Pinter, *The Homecoming* (New York: Grove Press, 1965), p. 9; references hereafter cited within the text.

3. William Barrett, *Irrational Man* (New York, 1958), pp. 35-36.

4. The relationship of the history and origins of language to epistemology is too complex to enter upon within the limitations of this essay. Those interested in this field should see the brilliant study of Owen Barfield, *Poetic Diction.* Barfield's description of a true metaphor may illuminate my all too tenuous remarks about Lenny and Ruth. "It is these 'footsteps of nature' whose noise we hear alike in primitive language and in the finest metaphors of poets. Men do not *invent* those mysterious relations between separate external objects, and between objects and feelings or ideas, which it is the function of poetry to reveal. These relations exist independently, not indeed of Thought, but of any individual

thinker. And according to whether the footsteps are echoed in primitive language or, later on, in the made metaphors of poets, we hear them after a different fashion and for different reasons. The language of primitive man reports them as direct perceptual experience. The speaker has observed a unity, and is therefore himself conscious of *relation*. But, we, in the development of consciousness, have lost the power to see this one as one. Our sophistication, like Odin's, has cost us an eye; and now it is the language of poets, in so far as they create true metaphors, which must restore this unity conceptually, after it has been lost from perception. Thus, the 'before-unapprehended' relationships of which Shelley spoke, are in a sense 'forgotten' relationships. For though they were never yet apprehended, they were at one time seen. And imagination can see them again." *Poetic Diction* (New York, 1964), pp. 86-87.

5. The word "know" occurs sixty times in the play while the word "understand(ing)" occurs thirteen times. Other related words dealing with this problem of perception are "think" (in the sense of "what do you think of"), "mean," "curious," "ask," and "realize." The repeated occurrence of all these words forms an underlying pattern of meaning in the play. The 440 questions in the play emphasize its interrogative rather than affirmative tenor.

6. Louis Bouyer, *Rite and Man,* trans. M. J. Costelloe (Notre Dame, Ind., 1963), p. 90.

7. Barrett, pp. 6-7.

8. See Barfield, *Poetic Diction,* especially pp. 93-101.

9. Barrett, p. 26.

10. *Ibid.,* p. 9.

11. *Ibid.,* p. 17.

SILENCE AND *LANDSCAPE*

PRODUCTION REVIEWS

Catharine Hughes (essay date 1969)

SOURCE: "Pinter Is as Pinter Does," in *The Catholic World,* Vol. 210, No. 1257, December, 1969, pp. 124-26.

[*In the following review of* Silence *and* Landscaping, *Hughes discusses Pinter's ideas about fear of communication and examines the significance of silence in his plays.*]

Harold Pinter surely must be the easiest of all playwrights to imitate. One can imagine him someday doing as Graham Greene did: entering a contest for the best parody of his own work—and, of course, pseudonymously winning it.

Pinter's latest plays, *Silence* and *Landscape,* recently premiered by the Royal Shakespeare Company and due in New York later this season, though even more sparse than his earlier work, and somewhat more poetic, are not really an exception. Fragments from the past, a past that as easily may be imagined as it may be real, one filtered through years of hopes, dreams and frustrations, come drifting to the surface. In a sense, all that occurs, more accurately, all that is said, is said at a moment outside time. There is a past, but it can never be other than guessed at; if there is a future, it is only hinted. What is real, if anything is real, is the moment, what occurs or fails to occur in the seventy minutes that are the plays' duration.

A great deal of space has been expended on the "meaning" of Pinter's plays, their symbols, their metaphysics and their ambiguities. But the dedicated symbol hunters, for all the light reading they provide, are missing the point: Pinter is as Pinter does. The importance of his work is in what takes place *on the stage.* "Pinter started his career as an actor," Ronald Bryden of *The Observer* recalled in his review of a revival of *The Birthday Party.* "The Pinter world is a stage, with nothing in the wings. It has no previous life, no outside influences; people may tell life-stories, give names and addresses, but these are not necessarily to be believed, usually turn out to be inventions. All that is credible is what passes on the stage."

What passes on the stage in *Silence* is a complex, slowly unfolding trio of interwoven monologues from somewhat atypical Pinter people, voices that are rural rather than urban or suburban. Rumsey is a farmer and Bates a farmhand, Ellen the girl both once loved. As their monologues move back and forth among the years, at some moments young, at others old, bits of their relationship emerge. They are speaking more to the audience than to each other, more to themselves than to the audience. Only twice do they move from their row of chairs to speak directly to each other in their West-country accents.

In their youth they lived in the country, walked in the fields, watched birds at rest on the limb of a tree. There was a time when Rumsey might perhaps have married Ellen, but did not, another when Bates sought to induce her to go away with him, only to be refused, though she was not really able to tell him why. Somewhere along the line, for reasons unknown or at least unacknowledged, all three have missed their opportunities for happiness. Now aging, living in town, cut off from love's possibilities, they react in differing ways—the farmer in perplexed puzzlement, Bates with resentment, Ellen in something approaching despair. In time, or perhaps at the end of time, the shadows that have loomed behind them merge and disappear. "Around me sits the night," says Ellen, "such a silence." It has all been inconclusive, a remembrance of things past, perhaps merely an imagining of them, thrown up in defense against the absence of things present. In their loneliness and their isolation, there is no place to go and even the words that seek to fill the void have begun to lose their resonance and their flavor. The rest is **Silence.**

And silence is something Pinter has used with stunning effectiveness almost from the first. Frank Marcus, critic of the London _Sunday Telegraph_ and author of _The Killing of Sister George,_ tells of a time when Pinter agreed to write a one-hour television play. At the first reading everything went well until the producer asked for the timing. "The girl looked at her watch," Marcus relates. "'Exactly twenty-eight minutes and thirty-four seconds', she said. Awkward silence. Then the author cleared his throat: 'You see, there are quite a lot of pauses. . . .'"

For Pinter, silence plays many roles. At one moment it may convey the passage of time, at another an inability, more accurately a failure, to communicate, at yet another simply an emptiness. Often it has been an integral factor in the atmosphere of menace that engulfs the characters in such earlier plays as **The Birthday Party, The Dumb Waiter** and _A Slight Ache._ Elsewhere it is employed to evoke an aura of uncertainty, of mystery—**The Caretaker, The Homecoming, The Collection.** Always, it is as calculated as the words it surrounds, and, frequently, as important.

"Often, below the word spoken, is the thing known and unspoken," Pinter said in a BBC interview. "There are two silences. One when no word is spoken. The other when perhaps a torrent of language is being employed. . . . The speech we hear is an indication of that which we don't hear. It is a necessary avoidance, a violent, sly, anguished or mocking smoke screen which keeps the other in its place. . . . I think that we communicate only too well in our silence, in what is unsaid, and that which takes place is a continual evasion, desperate rear-guard attempts to keep ourselves to ourselves."

The two characters in _Landscape,_ the second and more substantial of the two plays, are surely doing just that. Beth, a woman in her late forties, and Duff, a man in his early fifties, are sitting in the kitchen of a country house. It is evening, whether an evening like many others or an evening unique, unknown and, in a sense, almost irrelevant. Though Duff appears to address his wife normally, he does not seem to hear her voice. For her part, she never looks at him, and does not appear to hear him. Somehow, it all seems very natural, a situation they appear to accept and live within. Whatever once passed between them, whatever the extent of their sometime love or their sometime hate, it is all past. What remains is memory, fantasy, an echo of what was and shadows of what might have been.

Beth speaks of a day by the sea, a day of love and dreams and possibilities, of an unnamed lover who may have been Duff or may not have been. She recalls asking him whether he would like a baby—their own child; recalls that she was beautiful. Duff begins to tell of a downpour that afternoon as he walked near the pond on his way to the pub. She speaks of a time long gone, of dreams, and arranging flowers in a bowl, of a deserted beach where she wore a white robe and underneath was naked, of waves that were light and delicate as they touched the back of her neck, of drawing a face in the sand. He tells her the dog is gone, that a man and a woman were on the other side of the pond when the downpour began, of the fact that there was "dogshit, duckshit . . . all kinds of shit . . . all over the paths," and that the rain simply made it more treacherous. He describes how he left the park and went to the pub, where he found another man, who criticized the beer. "He didn't know I'd been trained as a cellarman," he tells her. Then, unfolding the intricacies of his one-time trade, he repeats his description of how "a cellarman is the man responsible," how he is the one who "could speak with authority" about the quality of the beer and how it got that way. He alludes to their past together, in which she was the housekeeper and he the chauffeur and handyman. He recalls how he returned one night after driving their employer to the North and told her of his infidelity and how she "didn't cry," but put her hands on his face and kissed him.

"Do you like me to talk to you?" he asks at last. "Do you like me to tell you about all the things I've been doing? About all the things I've been thinking?" And, when she does not respond: "I think you do."

Now, their employer is dead and they have the house all to themselves. But what matters, he tells her, is that "We're together. That's what matters." For brief moments, their parallel monologues echo each other, seem almost on the brink of intertwining, only to separate and return to their independent lines of thought or dreaming. Was he her idealized man by the sea and she his infidelity? Are they remembering an unacknowledged shared past, perhaps, or inventing phantoms to make it seem there was another one? Pinter is not about to tell us, not even when Beth, still caught up in her reverie, remembering how she felt the sand on her skin, the kiss on her cheek, the "silent sky" in her eyes and "gently the sound of the tide," utters the play's final words: "Oh my true love I said."

There are things we remember and things we forget, things certainly that we try to forget. In Pinter's plays those things are seldom really defined. They exist as fragments, images, moments, with no clear context and no automatic progression, bottles floating on the sea. Where did they come from? Why? Where are they going? If there are three questions Pinter is not about to answer, it is they. "There are no hard distinctions between what is real and what is unreal," he has written, "nor between what is true or false. The thing is not necessarily either true or false; it can be both true and false. The assumption that to verify what has happened and what's happening presents few problems I take to be inaccurate. A character on a stage who can present no convincing argument or information as to his past experience, his present behavior or his aspirations, nor give a comprehensive analysis of his motives, is as legitimate and as worthy of attention as one who, alarmingly, can do all these things."

Even in *Silence* and *Landscape,* so steeped in reverie and remembrance, in the moments from the past that help to ward off the present or, at best, to make it livable in its isolation, it is not so much that past that is important as its effect on the present. The past which each of the five characters muses on is, after all, a compendium of fantasies and tired dreams, of events selected or imagined to permit one to go on, sometimes almost joyous in its reflected joy, sometimes simply adapting, sometimes resenting without really knowing what to resent. They do not speak to each other not because they cannot but because they will not. The barriers that protect them are too fragile to attempt it, the risks too great. Like figures on a bleak and deserted landscape, they are alone, inaccessible and, one suspects, more than a little afraid both of where they are and of where they might be. If the choice is between love and safety, between making the connection with another human being and ensuring that some core of the self will remain inviolable, Pinter's characters almost invariably will choose the latter. "I feel that instead of any inability to communicate, there is a deliberate evasion of communication," Pinter told an interviewer. "Communication itself between people is so frightening that rather than do that there is continual cross-talk, a continual talking about other things, rather than what is at the root of their relationship."

In *Silence* and *Landscape* that refusal to make contact has been carried to its farthest extreme thus far. The contrapuntal monologues in both plays are heavily interpersed with troubled silences (one critic has estimated that the playing time of the pauses in *Silence* adds up to more than that of the dialogue). Gradually, as Ronald Bryden has noted, Pinter has been "saying less and less about more and more." There is a point where it becomes risky, and Pinter would seem to be approaching it. Without the tensions and progression of the earlier plays, *Silence* and *Landscape* are obviously less inherently dramatic. And, in the former, which was the last to be completed, he has written as much an elegy, a staged poem, as a play. Inevitably, it raises the question of where he is to go. Somehow, it is difficult to envision a return to the intricacies, the non sequiturs and the often quirky humor of the earlier "comedies of menace," which, for all the craftsmanship and superbly tuned ear they displayed, were at times a little too reflective of the games playwrights play. In blending the static and the poetic he now has ventured onto a terrain that seems inevitably limited. Doing so, he resolutely goes his own way, ignoring the trends toward opening up the theater to ever-wider involvement for the audience and ever-increasing reliance on flamboyant assaults on the senses. His world remains the world of words, and of the silences that sometimes speak louder than words. If it is a world that is ending, he is not about to let it go out without a fight.

Stanley Kauffmann (essay date 1970)

SOURCE: "*Landscape* and *Silence,*" in *The New Republic,* Vol. 162, No. 2887, April 25, 1970, pp. 20, 31.

[*In the following review, Kauffmann applauds the "gentleness" he sees in* Silence *and* Landscape.]

Harold Pinter's new short plays reveal a new Pinter. He doesn't produce much, but usually a new Pinter work means some sort of development. Each of his successive long plays, *The Birthday Party, The Caretaker, The Homecoming*—has shown, within the realm of Pinter's temperament, differences in control and interest. These two new short pieces are Pinter's first works of gentleness.

Neither play has a story, not even a logically eccentric one like *The Homecoming.* It's possible, retrospectively, to put together something of a story for each, but it has to be done merely as outline, not explanation. Otherwise the implication is that Pinter thought up a plot, then jigsawed it into a puzzle, and scattered the bits out of sequence for us to rearrange. This approach brutalizes two sensitive plays. In essence they are not coded stories, they are evocations from certain lives that have been lived in certain juxtapositions, and the evocations include silence. The plays are not concerned with alienation or difficulty of communication, two facile Pinter "labels" that have already been trotted out by people who finally got a pigeon-hole carpentered for Pinter and keep trying to shove this changing man back into it; the silences in these plays are between people who *have* communicated.

Silence has three characters, two men and a woman who sit on widely spaced chairs. (The woman approaches one man at one point.) They are presumably older people (no make-ups are worn). One man lives quietly in the country with animals, the other man lives surlily in a noisy rented room in town. Both of them focus on the woman as an object of affection—as woman, as girl, even as child—and time flows back and forth for all of them as carelessly as light flickers. The two men address the woman only occasionally but each other never. Pinter lifts out segments of three lives as they may have brushed and entwined now and then, and from them draws quintessences of moments and moods, not narrative. At the Forum Theater in New York, the evening begins with *Silence,* which is repeated in its entirety after *Landscape,* and this gives the evening a double design since *Silence* is itself cyclical in shape.

With the very first line of *Silence,* a different language comes from Pinter. The quiet man begins:

> I walk with my girl who wears a grey blouse when she walks and grey shoes and walks with me readily wearing her clothes considered for me. Her grey clothes.

Later, the woman remembers a younger day in the country:

> I turn. I turn. I wheel. I glide. I wheel. In stunning light. The horizon moves from the sun. I am crushed by the light.

Pinter has always *placed* words exactly: for verisimilitude, for rhythm, for silhouettes of banality that enclose horror or, very often, humor. Now his language is evolving new lyric qualities, poignant, still, compassionate. Most of his characters have been on their own, fighting for prerogatives of self against others, fighting even for their desires against the persons desired. In these two new plays there are acknowledged weaknesses and dependencies.

It is further apparent in *Landscape.* In the kitchen of a large country house sit two characters, presumably man and wife, presumably a "pair" in service there. He addresses her throughout, she never addresses him and never seems to hear him; her utterances are all memories. Neither person rises during the play. Again it is possible to reconstruct something of a "story," more than in the other play. We can infer that she has had some mental trouble, that it had something to do with a confession of unfaithfulness by him, that her devotion to him—exemplified by a day on a beach when they made love to have a child—is where she still resides; that his devotion to her, suggestive of contrition, consists of telling her details of his daily doings on the farm and in the pub. He speaks in rather more expected Pinter terms, in detail made large, like Oldenburg's sculpture—all excellently molded. The play's effect is of a protector caring for an injured person whom he injured, but without anguish. She and he take their lives as they have happened, and the last line is hers, spoken to the man no longer present, the man on the beach that day: "Oh my true love I said."

The Forum is the small "experimental" theater underneath the large Vivian Beaumont at Lincoln Center, where I have gone frequently in the past few years only to be disappointed frequently. Not so with these Pinter plays: they are small, delicate additions to our drama. The Forum production itself is another matter. The settings and lighting do little, which would not matter if the performances did more. (I read the plays after seeing them and now have a better idea of what they might mean in performance.) Peter Gill, a young English director, has a sense of phrase and seems to have worked with his actors on the essential imaginative foundation to "base" their lines, to govern their tempos and pauses. But these plays depend greatly on the very flavor of the performers, and these casts are insufficient. James Patterson, as the unquiet man in *Silence,* has the greatest chance for flamboyance and can make something of it; but his part is easier than the others. Barbara Tarbuck, the woman in *Silence,* is blandly adequate. Robert Symonds, both the quiet man in *Silence* and the "husband" in *Landscape,* is one of the Lincoln Center reliables. Here again he is competent and intelligent, but he is insufficiently rich. The two roles together emphasize how much Symonds relies on that rustic dryness which was good in Kit Carson (*The Time of Your Life*) but is getting to be something of a prop for him.

The chief disappointment is Mildred Natwick as the "injured" woman in *Landscape.* But then Miss Natwick's career is, sad to say, a disappointment. She began some thirty-five years ago as one of the most original and creative young actresses of her generation and has since given good performances (Madame Arcati in *Blithe Spirit,* for instance). But in general she has not developed and, in fact, has diminished. Her recent performance in the New York production of *Our Town* was like an entry in the Helen Hayes Sweepstakes for Audience Love. Here she is straining for color, but the depths that might provide it are not there.

Pinter, on the other hand, does develop. These new plays are not works of major scope and force, like *The Caretaker* and *The Homecoming,* but they are lovely, and they certify that he continues to inquire his way through experience of the world and of imagination. *Silence,* in particular, sounds haunting chords, made of three lives combined like notes of music. "Elected Silence, sing to me," said Hopkins in one of his best poems. Pinter has elected a rather different silence, but it sings to him.

Henry Hewes (essay date 1970)

SOURCE: "Thought Games," in *Saturday Review,* Vol. 53, No. 17, April 25, 1970, p. 16.

[*In the following review, Hewes finds that* Silence *and* Landscape *lack dramatic tension and development.*]

Ten years ago when British playwright Harold Pinter first came to this country with his wonderful play *The Caretaker,* he was asked which playwright he most admired. His reply was, "Samuel Beckett. But not so much his plays as his novels."

Now several impressive plays of his own later, Pinter has departed from Pinteresque (a word he loathes) to attempt a couple of very short works in a style that, although it is not a copy of Beckett, emanates the quality of Beckett's novels.

Called *Silence* and *Landscape,* they are currently being presented by the Repertory Theater of Lincoln Center in its intimate thrust-stage playhouse, The Forum. This is an important and appropriate service for this company to render, particularly if, as the distinguished critic Richard Watts reports, they "come off better" here than in the original London production he saw last summer.

However, on the basis of this performance and a persual of the texts, Pinter's experiment seems desperately lacking in dramatic excitement. In *Silence,* two men and a woman sit in front of a background that suggests hills and open country. Pinter deliberately tells us little about them. One, Rumsey, owns horses and other animals, and seems quite contented with the walks he takes with his girl, Ellen, who dresses to please him and listens to him talk. He enjoys the natural environment around him and the comfort of feeling unnecessary in it. Happily he tells us, "There is no one to tell me what is expected or not expected of me. There is nothing required of me."

The second man, Bates, is desperately unhappy. He lives in a rooming house where his landlady asks him, "Are you nothing but a childish old man, suffocating himself?" He apparently has the same girl as Rumsey, but he takes her to pubs or to his room for more aggressive companionship.

The woman, Ellen, is sad about getting old and being unmarried, but she drifts passively between the two men. The silent impersonality of her life vaguely troubles her. She says, "After my work each day, I walk back through people, but I don't notice them. . . . I'm quite wide awake to the world around me. But not to the people."

One suspects that in this play Pinter is concerned with how people move from the more fully engaged prime of life into the silence of old age. But as directed by Peter Gill, Robert Symonds as Rumsey, Barbara Tarbuck as Ellen, and, to a lesser extent, James Patterson as Bates are much too glib. What drama there is to *Silence* probably depends upon the actors' seeking to relate their dialogue to remembered sensory experience so that the silences in the script detonate as emotional explosions.

The second play, *Landscape,* has a bit more story to it. An old man named Duff and his wife, Beth, seem to be the caretakers of an empty house. While Duff rambles on in commonplaces about his trivial and somewhat insensitive life, Beth speaks her private reminiscences about the day the late master of the house made love to her on the beach.

Here, Mildred Natwick as Beth beautifully realizes the performance style these plays require. Yet, the counterpoint makes little dramatic progress. It is the distilled essence of a play, and, like Beckett, Pinter may have lost interest in creating theatrical journeys and is now satisfied merely to present final destinations.

LANDSCAPE

CRITICAL COMMENTARY

Brian Richardson (essay date 1991)

SOURCE: "Pinter's *Landscape* and the Boundaries of Narrative," in *Essays in Literature*, Vol. 18, No. 1, Spring, 1991, pp. 37-45.

[*In the following essay, Richardson considers whether the two apparently separate narrators in* Landscape *form one integrated narrative, and if "narrativity" is the result of chronology, causality, or juxtaposition.*]

It is both curious and unfortunate that narrative theorists rarely address the experiments in story construction frequently present in modern drama. It is also unfortunate that interpreters of innovative playwrights like Beckett, Stoppard, and Pinter generally neglect the critical perspectives afforded by narrative theory.[1] In what follows I suggest that a comprehensive poetics needs to address the unusual questions posed by dramatists like Harold Pinter, and that some of Pinter's distinctive achievements, traditionally so difficult to articulate, can be effectively described and appreciated within the context of narrative theory.

Pinter has exposed and transgressed most of the fundamental elements and conventions of narrative. Several of his dramas at some point lay bare the construction of temporality. Both *The Caretaker* and *The Collection* contain abrupt time shifts that foreground the undramatized periods between scenes. *The Basement* has irreconcilably contradictory chronologies, and in *Betrayal* the scenes are presented to the audience in the opposite order of their actual occurrence: as the play moves forward, the story goes backward; here, the drama's *sjuzhet* (*recit*) is entirely antichronological.[2]

The Basement, a rather neglected drama originally written for television and subsequently produced on stage, violates traditional concepts of space, cause, and character as it deforms narrative time. While the dialogue suggests that a few hours or a couple of days have passed, the furnishing of the room undergoes radical changes and the setting leaps back and forth between summer and winter. By the end of the play, the two male characters have exchanged roles completely. Such stark and apparently unmotivated reversals of time, space, and character are so extreme as to call into question the very notions of setting and self. After so many unexplained transformations, the audience may legitimately wonder whether (and in what sense) the same space or the same character continues to be presented. At some point it becomes equally plausible to suppose that "the" room is in fact several similar rooms, or that one actor portrays different persons. Here conventions of representation become exposed, as repeated alterations of setting gradually disrupt the coherence of the story that the setting is assumed to frame.

Pinter criticism on the other hand all too often attempts to "naturalize" these disturbing features by reducing them to allegory, gratuitous stylization, subjective fantasy, or the highly unlikely actions of demented or incomprehensible individuals.[3] Some degree of reductionism is to be expected: an author who plays on the edge of the possibilities of representation is always in danger of being forcibly placed back within the very limits his work seems designed to transgress. Too insistent a demand for interpretation leads to impoverished readings; it is necessary to resist both overly simple and needlessly vague accounts of this kind of theater.

Dialogue, frequently considered the distinguishing feature of drama, is also problematized by Pinter, who in *Mono-*

logue presents a man addressing a speech to an empty chair. In *Landscape,* Duff narrates events to Beth, who does not appear to perceive his words, and his speech is contrapuntally interrupted by what may be a vocalization of Beth's interior monologue. In *Family Voices,* the audience is treated to chronologically scrambled articulations of three sets of letters which, respectively, were never received, never mailed, or could never have been written. In these plays, the distinctions between narration and enactment, soliloquy and dialogue, and speech and writing are forced to collide. Once again, it is necessary to identify the most basic elements of drama in order to discern how meticulously Pinter conflates them.

What has been termed "the Pinter problem"—crudely stated, the fact that the same set of vague phrases continues to be applied indiscriminately to the varied corpus of Pinter's work—may in fact point to the revolutionary nature of the playwright's achievement rather than to unfortunate limitations of his critics.[4] If Pinter is actually challenging fundamental elements of narrative, we will have to look to the cornerstones of narrative theory in order to explain the nature of Pinter's undertaking. Contemporary narratology does not of course provide a stable set of basic axioms, in part because it tends to be grounded in the kind of High Modernist fiction produced by Henry James, Marcel Proust, and James Joyce. Perhaps for this very reason, an investigation from the perspective of poetics into one of Pinter's most experimental plays, *Landscape,* can simultaneously elucidate the work and shed light on the definition of narrative.

Although there is no consensus among narratologists over what constitutes narrativity, two rival conceptions are prominent, one of which stresses temporal succession while the other is more drawn to causal connection. Gerald Prince, Shlomith Rimmon-Kenan (18-19), and Jean-Michel Adam (12) argue for the former position. Prince states that "narrative is the representation of *at least two* real or fictive events in a time sequence, neither of which presupposes or entails the other" (4). Roland Barthes also inclines to this position, since he suggests that any causal attribution is inherently suspect (94). Todorov tries to find a middle ground, and implies that some narrative literature may be devoid of chronology and that other equally rare forms may lack causality (41-46). Boris Tomashevsky, on the other hand, argues that "a story [*fabula*] requires not only indications of time, but also indications of cause" (66). Descriptive poems and travel books may be chronologically arranged, he observes. Without some causal connection however these works are non-narrative: "[I]f the account is only about the sights and not about the personal adventures of the travellers, we have exposition without story. The weaker the causal connection, the stronger the purely chronological connection" (66). Seymour Chatman advocates a similar position: "If we were to extract randomly from cocktail chatter a set of events that happened at different times and at different places to different persons, we would clearly not have a narrative . . ." (21). Mere temporal succession is inadequate; some causal con-

nection, however oblique, is also necessary. "The events in a true narrative" always "manifest a discernible organization" (21); some connection, if only a contingent one, is needed to hold a text together (47).

What is especially intriguing about *Landscape* is that it brings this question—the definition of narrative—to the foreground, and can confirm or refute some of the theories outlined above. The play is set in the kitchen of a country home with the characters Beth and Duff seated at a table. The drama begins as Beth says:

> I would like to stand by the sea. It is there.
>
> *Pause*
>
> I have. Many times. It's something I cared for. I've done it.
>
> *Pause*
>
> I'll stand on the beach. On the beach. Well . . . it was very fresh. But it was hot, in the dunes. But it was so fresh, on the shore. I loved it very much.
>
> *Pause*
>
> (177)

The precise status of Beth's speech is ambiguous. First, she expresses a desire for the future, then she indicates that that scene is present, presumably in her mind—or at least present as narrative. She then delves into the past, revealing that she has often been by the sea, in some sense or another. Next we move from what Genette calls the iterative to the historical past proper: "it was very fresh." In this opening section, one feels a tension between memory and invention, personal experience and wish-fulfillment, the past tense and the subjunctive. As her monologue continues, it becomes more precise, concrete, and descriptive: "I walked from the dune to the shore. My man slept in the dune. He turned over as I stood. . . . Would you like a baby? I said. Children? Babies? Of our own? Would be nice" (177, my ellipsis). Despite a couple of incursions into what may be the present (e.g., "I am beautiful"), the past tense predominates and a narrative starts to emerge.

At this point Duff's speech begins. He recounts events from the immediate past in a tone and vocabulary totally different from Beth's:

> The dog's gone. I didn't tell you.
>
> *Pause*
>
> I had to shelter under a tree for twenty minutes yesterday. Because of the rain.
>
> I meant to tell you. With some youngsters. I didn't know them.
>
> (178)

The most striking feature of Duff's speech is its complete irrelevance to the lines spoken by Beth. The two narrations have nothing in common; any audience would be hard-pressed to imagine a possible context that could frame such disparate locutions. The interpretive situation is further complicated by the fact that (as the stage directions indicate) Duff refers normally to Beth though he does not appear to hear her voice, while Beth never looks at Duff and does not appear to hear his words even though both characters sit in chairs at opposite ends of the same table.[5] As the play progresses, the two stories narrated by the protagonists remain autonomous and unconnected, even as the personalities of the characters appear increasingly antithetical. Beth is romantic and imaginative; her monologue is a series of arabesques that embellish and re-create her primal experience with the man on the beach. Duff's speech is terse, stark, direct, and crude; his narrative is relentlessly linear, obviously motivated, and addressed to a familiar auditor.

The question provoked by Beth's unheard monologue and Duff's semidialogue goes to the very basis of poetics: in what sense can these independent accounts be considered parts of a single narrative? Or are we being presented with two narratives disguised as one? Considered this way, Aristotle's animadversion toward episodic plots and Elizabethan playwrights' recklessness with subplots tend to pale into insignificance.[6] Here we are forced to decide what is and what is not a story [*fabula*].

To be sure, Pinter plants numerous hints—and perhaps a few red herrings as well. The naturalistic setting of the drama (the conventional country house) invites us to find a naturalistic explanation for the strikingly disjoined speeches. One may simply assert, as some critics do, that two people are engaged in ordinary conversation, though they consistently ignore each other's words.[7] It is equally possible that Beth is verbally articulating her stream-of-consciousness while Duff is telling her his story. The problem with either of these readings is that there is no indication, verbal or semiotic, that Beth ever hears a word spoken by Duff. Consider the following exchange:

> DUFF: I should have had some bread with me. I could have fed the birds.
>
> BETH: Sand on his arms.
>
> DUFF: They were hopping about. Making a racket.
>
> BETH: I lay down by him, not touching.
>
> DUFF: There wasn't anyone else in the shelter. There was a man and woman, under the trees, on the other side of the pond. I didn't feel like getting wet. I stayed where I was.
>
> *Pause*
>
> Yes, I've forgotten something. The dog was with me.
>
> (179)

Neither narration has a discernible effect on the speech of the other. If anything, Duff's admission that he had "forgotten something" suggests he may be responding to a comment that he alone is able to perceive. To maintain a "naturalistic" thesis it may well be necessary to imagine that Beth is in fact conversing with Duff, offering questions and promptings that only he can hear; or, alternatively, that Duff is mentally rehearsing a story he will tell Beth, complete with responses to her anticipated comments. But at this point the possible naturalistic recuperation becomes so byzantine that one is virtually forced to reject it altogether.

At the same time, it is equally difficult to dismiss the play as two juxtaposed but independent narratives. The counterpoint between the birds' vigor ("They were hopping about. Making a racket") and Beth's demureness ("I lay down by him, not touching") is too weak for causal connection, though too strong for mere coincidence. The same might be said of the parallel settings of the two narrations. Duff sees a man and a woman on the other side of the pond; Beth and her man at the beach can be seen by another fellow at a distance (181). The symmetry teases our understanding of narrativity such that we may be tempted to reinterpret the speeches as the same event viewed from two perspectives (in which case Duff would be the observer) or as two versions of the same event (in which case Duff perhaps displaces himself from participant to observer in his own "recounting"). On the other hand, radical differences in the timeframe and season work against this kind of identification.

As the play develops, another discrepancy arises. The man in Beth's monologue is one who reflects upon her gravity while she waters and arranges flowers. It is hard to imagine that this lover, in any avatar however romantically reconstructed, can be the figure Duff, who says, "Mind you, there was a lot of shit all over the place, all along the paths, by the pond. Dogshit, duckshit . . . all kinds of shit . . . all over the paths" (180). Throughout most of the play, disjunction reigns. The following passage is typical:

> DUFF: Anyway . . .
>
> BETH: My skin . . .
>
> DUFF: I'm sleeping all right these days.
>
> BETH: Was stinging.
>
> DUFF: Right through the night, every night.
>
> BETH: I'd been in the sea.
>
> DUFF: Maybe it's something to do with the fishing. Getting to learn more about fish.
>
> BETH: Stinging in the sea by myself.
>
> (182)

But just at the points where the speeches seem most unconnected, new parallels and symmetries emerge, depriving an audience of even the dubious consolation that the two narratives are in fact independent ones. Immediately after the passage just cited, Duff muses on the nature of fish, concluding that they are very shy creatures who need to be wooed (182), a thought that just might have been shared by Beth's consort on the beach. A further twist in this plot of connection and disjunction appears when Duff narrates his trip to a local pub, followed immediately by Beth's decision within her own narrative to visit the hotel bar with her friend (183). Once again the repetition is too obvious to be devoid of significance, but just what the significance might be is at this point indeterminable.

By juxtaposing apparently unrelated series of events, Pinter seems to be challenging the very preconditions of narrativity. And this, I believe, can illuminate the controversy over what constitutes a narrative. Up to this point, what we have are represented events in a temporal sequence. In fact, we have two levels of representation that occupy several periods of time. Beth's monologue recounts events in a remote past, while Duff narrates what happened "yesterday." Actors portraying the two characters take turns relating those events in sequence. Here, it seems, the criterion for narrativity set forth by Prince, Adam, and Rimmon-Kenan is scrupulously adhered to, and yet we cannot say we are in the presence of a single narrative. In fact, the opposite seems to be the case; at some level, the drama is about the suspension, deferral, or transgression of narrative. Temporal succession alone is inadequate; some causal connection is essential if the piece is in fact one drama, rather than two disparate ones forcibly yoked together. And it is just this ambiguity that Pinter exacerbates by hinting at and then denying causal connection between the two characters' accounts.

Roughly halfway through the play, the first real evidence for connection appears. Duff states vaguely "I was thinking . . . when you were young . . . you didn't laugh much . . . You were . . . grave" (186). He also mentions having planted flowers she might like (184), and still later observes, "I was very gentle to you. I was kind to you, that day. I knew you'd had a shock, so I was gentle with you" (190). These lines confirm the possibility that Duff just might have been the subject of Beth's narration, though this is by no means certain, particularly since her shock and Duff's gentleness are caused by his admission of infidelity.

A stronger case for connection is occasioned by the following metadiscursive commentary that Duff addresses to Beth:

Do you like me to talk to you?

Pause

Do you like me to tell you about all the things I've been doing?

Pause

About all the things I've been thinking?

Pause

Mmmnn?

Pause

I think you do.

(189)

Instead of reciting events to a person who does not seem to hear his words, Duff is now drawing attention to his act of narration, suggesting that he is partially aware of the monological nature of his discourse and that it is not as utterly unnatural as the audience might understandably perceive it to be. Duff's questions are rhetorical, demanding no response; consequently, Beth's silence during the pauses takes on an aura of naturalness, as some submerged form of connection between the two speakers grows increasingly plausible.

Some minutes later, Beth narrates another scene, this time in a different landscape. Now she works as a housekeeper exactly as Duff's wife does. She refers to a dog which could be Duff's dog. The day she describes is sunny but wet. "Wet, I mean wetness, all over the ground" (193). At this point the two narratives begin to converge. She talks about stroking the dog silently while looking through a window. Duff then says:

I never saw your face. You were standing by the windows. One of those black nights. A downfall. . . . You knew I'd come in but you didn't move. . . . What were you looking at? . . . I stood close to you. Perhaps you were just thinking, in a dream. . . .

(my ellipses, 195)

This passage also tends to "naturalize" the odd dialogical relationships between the two characters, making it possible that the representation might consist of Duff's actual speech juxtaposed to Beth's internal monologue—though if this were the case, Beth's ability to block out all of Duff's words is genuinely preternatural. Nevertheless, some such connection is further reinforced by Beth's admission that when she asked "him" to look at her, "he turned to look at me but I couldn't see his look" (197). This statement refers simultaneously to the hero of her private narrative, symbolically depicts her emotional estrangement from Duff (assuming that she is the wife addressed by Duff's speech), and articulates the position of the characters on stage—from where she is sitting, Beth cannot see Duff's eyes.

The forces of connection finally defeat the pattern of disjunction in the final speeches of the play. In a virtually fugal counterpoint, Duff narrates his sudden copulation with his wife as Beth reiterates details of her memory-fantasy encounter with the man on the beach. Here, the balancing of past and present, romance and carnality, "he" and "you" form a perfect architecture, and some interpretive fusion seems to be demanded. The final line of the play, Beth's "Oh my true love I said" (198), contrasting so starkly with Duff's naive vulgarity, leaves the audience with the perception that they have seen opposite perspectives of the same marraige. Although the play's precise temporal and spatial coordinates will always remain dubious (can they really be in the same room at the same time?), the causal connection, however vague or oblique, seems firmly in place. And for this reason, the two accounts form in the end a single narrative, albeit an ambiguous one. It is unfortunate that so many of Pinter's critics, sensing the connection implied by the ending, tend to downplay or ignore the "drama of disjunction" that precedes the moment of intersection.[8]

Pinter's achievement in *Landscape* is perhaps best appreciated when contrasted to similar experiments in story construction. Both *King Lear* and *Ulysses* contain two main co-plots that begin to affect each other toward the middle of each narrative and are fused together at the end of each work (though the fusion is more tenuous and deferred longer in Joyce's novel). *Light in August* employs several story-lines of varying complexity that touch one another without ever merging in a direct causal chain. In Middleton and Rowley's *The Changeling,* the main plot is almost entirely independent of the subplot until the play's final scene, although thematic parallels between the two abound. Beckett's *Molloy* juxtaposes a pair of suspiciously similar narratives, one purportedly by Molloy, the other about Moran's quest for Molloy (or perhaps Mollose; Moran is not entirely sure). There is no question *that* these two narrations are connected; just how they are conjoined, however, has vexed critics for decades. Finally, in Faulkner's *The Wild Palms,* two completely distinct narratives are juxtaposed chapter by chapter as different characters in different locations confront analogous dilemmas.

On this spectrum of works with increasingly divergent story-lines, *Landscape* might be placed somewhere between *Molloy* and *The Wild Palms.* While the Molloy and the Moran sections of Beckett's novel must be related in some way, Pinter leaves open the possibility that Beth and Duff might just be unknown to each other, though most of the rather scanty evidence does point to the opposite position. For this reason, there is a greater epistemological tension inherent in this work than is present in *The Wild Palms,* the stories of which do not and cannot affect each other. Pinter takes us to the limit of possible causal connection, which is also the boundary of narrative. Pinter's lesson makes it apparent that causality is in fact a necessary condition of narrativity, as Tomashevsky and Chatman have argued. Furthermore, the challenge of *Landscape* is so extreme that it calls for a re-thinking of the fundamental concepts of critical analysis, in particular those that are applied to the more experimental works of modern drama. As the example of *Landscape* should reveal, it is necessary to continue to probe ever deeper, even to re-examine the most basic principles of representation, in order to fully appreciate the achievement of Pinter.

Notes

1. Following the practice of most narrative theorists, I use the term "narrative" to describe the representation of events, regardless of genre. As Roland Barthes explains: "Narrative is first and foremost a prodigious variety of genres, themselves distributed amongst different substances—as though any material were fit to receive man's stories. Able to be car-ried by articulated language, spoken or written, fixed or moving images, gestures, and the ordered mixture of all these substances; narrative is present in myth, legend, fable, tale, novella, epic, history, tragedy, drama, comedy, mime, painting (think of Carpaccio's *Saint Ursula*), stained glass windows, cinema, comics, news item, conversation" (79).

   Those who prefer to limit the use of "narrative" to acts of narration need not be troubled, however: *Landscape* consists entirely of two extended, alternating narrations. The analysis of the text itself should be equally appropriate for either definition of the term.

2. Pinter's deployment of temporality is shrewdly analyzed by William F. Dohmen in "Time after Time: Pinter Plays with Disjunctive Chronologies."

3. The limitations of such kinds of reductionism are articulated by Quigley (7-20).

4. This conundrum was first set forth by Austin Quigley (see esp. 3-31). For a critical update on this topic, see Hinchliffe (21-30).

5. This work, though originally written for the stage, first premiered on radio, a medium that would exacerbate still further the disjunctions of the play.

6. For an excellent study of multiple plots in Elizabethan and Jacobean drama, see Levin.

7. Even Pinter's best critics tend to presume some level of personal interaction. Quigley states: "Not everything they say derives from what the other has said—indeed, it often derives from what they themselves said in their previous remark—but the words the other person speaks do affect the development of each individual's speech" (236). Steven H. Gale, while noting that the stage directions make it clear that the two figures "are not communicating, maybe not even talking to each other" (176), nevertheless asserts that "Beth has withdrawn from life into her imagination and Duff is still involved in living and trying to reinvolve her" (177). Similarly, Kristin Morrison affirms that "Beth exists for Duff (when he says 'you' he means Beth). . . . These two people are physically present now in the same room, have for many years physically participated in the same life, yet for all that proximity they are worlds apart" (129). Each of these readings assumes a naturalistic relation between the two characters that the dialogue consistently undermines.

8. To cite only one example, Martin Esslin states: "Beth thus does not even try to communicate. She has shut herself off from the present, the world that now surrounds her. Duff, on the other hand, *wants* to tell *her* what he has been doing, and also, clearly, wants to elicit an answer from her" (175). By contextualizing the characters' relationship within such a naturalistic frame, Esslin's account precludes the possibility of any play with the limits of narrative from ever aris-

ing. On the other hand, his observations concerning the identity of the man on the beach are quite astute, and he quotes from a letter by Pinter that suggests the man was actually Duff. See 178-180.

Works Cited

Adam, Jean-Michel. *Le Recit.* Paris: Presses Universitaires de France, 1984.

Barthes, Roland. *Image-Music-Text.* Trans. Stephen Health. New York: Hill and Wang, 1977.

Chatman, Seymour. *Story and Discourse: Narrative Structure in Fiction and Film.* Ithaca: Cornell UP, 1978.

Dohmen, William F. "Time after Time: Pinter Plays with Disjunctive Chronologies." *Harold Pinter: Critical Approaches.* Ed. Steven H. Gale. Rutherford, NJ: Fairleigh Dickinson UP, 1986.

Esslin, Martin. *Pinter the Playwright.* 4th ed. London: Methuen, 1984.

Gale, Steven H. *Butter's Going Up: A Critical Analysis of Harold Pinter's Work.* Durham: Duke UP, 1977.

Hinchliffe, Arnold P. *Harold Pinter.* Rev. ed. Boston: Twayne, 1981.

Levin, Richard L. *The Multiple Plot in English Renaissance Drama.* Chicago: U of Chicago P, 1971.

Morrison, Kristin. *Canters and Chronicles: The Use of Narrative in the Plays of Samuel Beckett and Harold Pinter.* Chicago: U of Chicago P, 1983.

Pinter, Harold. *Complete Works,* Vol. III. New York: Grove Press, 1978.

Prince, Gerald. *Narratology: The Form and Functioning of Narrative.* Amsterdam: Mouton, 1982.

Quigley, Austin E. *The Pinter Problem.* Princeton: Princeton UP, 1975.

Rimmon-Kenan, Shlomith. *Narrative Fiction: Contemporary Poetics.* London: Methuen, 1983.

Todorov, Tzvetan. *Introduction to Poetics.* Trans. Richard Howard. Minneapolis: U of Minnesota P, 1981.

Tomashevsky, Boris. "Thematics." *Russian Formalist Criticism: Four Essays.* Ed. Lee T. Lemon and Marion J. Reis. Lincoln: U of Nebraska P, 1965.

OLD TIMES

CRITICAL COMMENTARY

Tony Aylwin (essay date 1973)

SOURCE: "The Memory of All That: Pinter's *Old Times,*" in *English,* Vol. 22, No. 114, Autumn, 1975, pp. 99-102.

[*In the following essay, Aylwin reviews the way characters in* Old Times *determine their identities, and interact with each other on the basis of their memories of the past.*]

In the Sunday papers following the first performance of *Old Times* (1 June 1971), Ronald Bryden (*The Observer*) wrote: 'The techniques, the preoccupations are the same. There's no new departure from the ground he has made his own.' Harold Hobson (*The Sunday Times*) wrote: '*Old Times* is the most technically daring play that Harold Pinter has written . . . it is dangerous to suppose that the ambiguity of a new Pinter play is merely a development of the ambiguity of one that preceded it.' Pinter has said: 'There are at least twenty-four possible aspects of any single statement',[1] so it is perhaps understandable that two highly complimentary reviews should present contrasting aspects.

The play is indeed full of ambiguity as its characters seek to recall or discover what happened twenty years before, while, typically of Pinter, they try to reveal as little of themselves as possible.

From his earliest plays onwards, Pinter has let his stories grow out of a naturalistic framework, usually by the use of colloquial language, so that the extraordinary events which follow seem to arise out of really possible lives. *Old Times,* like *The Lover,* has the advantage of having characters who speak our type of language (that is, the speech of the majority of theatregoers). In a sense, then, Pinter may be said to be using techniques he has used before. The important difference in *Old Times* (I am ignoring *Landscape* and *Silence* which have no naturalistic stage furniture and so never ask us to accept the action in a traditionally realistic way) is that Anna is on stage from the start, although she is not present as far as Deeley and Kate are concerned. The dim light of the opening, before lights come up on the married couple, also adds to our feeling that we are not merely eavesdropping on a piece of life. Although the opening conversation between Deeley and Kate seems like a real-life conversation (even if somewhat laconic), we cannot fail to be influenced in our attitude to the play by the ambiguous presence of Anna. It might be worth examining what would change in our attitude if the play opened with Anna's entry, with the husband-and-wife dialogue following when she had gone out to change her clothes.

In Pinter's earlier play *The Dwarfs,* Len asks, 'What have I seen, the scum or the essence?' as he puzzles over the problem of trying to understand life in the present. Deeley's struggle to unravel the romantic/sordid past is a development of Len's confused efforts. When we talk of the realism of *Old Times* we must acknowledge also a different sort of realism from language which recalls real life speech in its rhythms, words, and silences. This is the realism of the experience common to mankind, in this case, the part memory plays in our lives in our efforts to understand the people we are closest to, and what we have been or might have been ourselves.

The play, then, is concerned with memory, but in its shifting between present and past we are inevitably faced with comparing the two, as we are in Virginia Woolf's *Mrs.*

Dalloway, where in connection with the Bourton of her life at twenty, Clarissa feels:

> If it were now to die,
> 'Twere now to be most happy.

The concern with death links the play further with the novel in which the young man Septimus Smith may, in dying instead of Clarissa (as Virginia Woolf originally intended), have a similar significance in relation to the heroine as Anna has to Kate. Kate says: 'You talk about me as if I am dead. Now.' This suggests that the moments of the past are of a time that is dead, and the closing moments of the play, when Kate tells Anna: 'I remember you dead', seem to confirm this. Perhaps our conclusion should be that only the Anna side of Kate is dead, and that her silent, still side lives on.

Anna enters the play with an outpouring of words which recall the exciting life of their London days, in contrast to the quiet conversation that Deeley has just had with Kate. Anna breathlessly refers to 'the looking-forwardness of it all'. If, however, we think back to Stanley's nervous anxiety about the future in *The Birthday Party,* we see another side to a young person's feelings. What we get from Anna would seem to be selected exhilarating moments seen in retrospect.

Another aspect of these memories appears after Deeley has recalled the first time he went to bed with Kate in such detail as to challenge all doubt. Anna says, 'There are some things one remembers even though they may never have happened. There are things I remember which may never have happened, but as I recall them so they take place.' This may help to explain Beth's comment in *Landscape,* 'Sometimes the cause of the shadow cannot be found', so that the later play shows a development in Pinter's writing that helps to explain earlier ambiguity. From this point especially, *Old Times* becomes not just a play about trying to recall the past, but also about trying to separate truth from fantasy. As long ago as 1960 Pinter wrote: 'There are no hard distinctions between what is true and what is false. The thing is not necessarily either true or false; it can be both true and false.'[2] Deeley learns from Anna's words here how to challenge her memories. In Act Two he says to her: 'Yes, I remember you quite clearly from The Wayfarers.' He re-establishes himself by bringing Anna down to his level. He insists: 'It's the truth. I remember clearly.' There is also something here perhaps of the instinctive recognition shown by Max in *The Homecoming* when he calls Ruth a whore at first sight. Deeley can identify Anna perhaps as the sort of woman he would see in The Wayfarers, and so his memory is truthful in a sense.

Anna has also taught Deeley that one way to recapture the past is to use its language. Both through the old songs and through words like 'gaze', the old times are relived. Deeley later remembers how he had 'gazed' up Anna's skirt. Later still, in telling the same incident to Kate, he uses the masculine slang of his own past, saying that Anna 'amiably allowed me a gander'. Deeley does in fact come to express doubts about whether he really had looked up Anna's skirt, but by this time, because Kate has intervened in saying that Anna had found him attractive, it is too late for Anna to regain the initiative. She admits that she remembers him, to which Kate replies, 'But I remember you dead'.

Kate's memory of Anna dead seems to represent the end of their youthful period, and Anna lying 'dead' at the end may have the same symbolic significance as Haggerty's coffin has for Bernard Link's young manhood at the end of David Mercer's *After Haggerty.* Deeley too seems to acknowledge both the enjoyment and the end of these times. Of the pub memories he says: 'That's something that's all over now, of course, isn't it, nothing like the same palpable profit in it now, it's all over. But it was worthwhile then.'

This past, for Anna and Kate at first, seems to have been associated with appreciating the arts. Now Kate can say: 'I was interested once in the arts, but I can't remember now which ones they were.' Surprisingly, in view of his coarser recollections, Deeley too emerges as having been a sensitive and artistic man. Anna says how pleased she had been to hear of their marriage because Kate had always been so interested in the arts. Later, when Kate tells him that Anna had been attracted to him because 'She found your face very sensitive, vulnerable', we are reminded of the second time that Anna and Kate relive the past in considering which men friends to invite round. When Kate says she likes Christy best, her reasons are: 'Hasn't he got a lovely sense of humour? And I think he's . . . so sensitive.' The young Deeley, with his ability to make Kate smile, seems to have had both these qualities. Deeley indeed joins in here to say that Christy is out of town, and the possibility that he is Christy even arises. It seems that the sensitive young Deeley has had to change as he leaves his youth, just as Stanley, in *The Birthday Party,* has to give up his piano-playing, or Aston, in *The Caretaker,* has had to lose his extreme sensitivity by shock treatment in hospital.

What Deeley fails to realize, however, is that the passing of these enjoyable times also takes away the special feeling he shared with Kate when they first fell in love. When he first recalls meeting her after the film *Odd Man Out,* he remembers having said something which made her smile at him in a way that made him think she was 'even more fantastic than Robert Newton'. Kate's smile can be seen to represent the love they felt at that time. Later, soon after she has got out of the bath, Kate smiles at a remark of Deeley's and he reacts: 'See that smile? That's the same smile she smiled when I was walking down the street with her, after *Odd Man Out,* well, quite some time after.' He asks Kate to do it again, to which she replies; 'I'm still smiling.' Deeley protests: 'You're not. Not like you were a moment ago, not like you did then.' Though Kate still smiles, what Deeley cannot recapture more than fleetingly is the love of their first meetings. Their married life is shown as something different. At the end, Kate recalls how she bent over the 'dead' Anna who tried to do the old 'slow smile' which was stopped by the dirt. The 'smile' of love for Deeley is to die with the past, it seems.

In 1966, referring to the violence between Gus and Ben in *The Dumb Waiter,* Pinter said, 'I wouldn't call this violence so much as a battle for positions, it's a very common, everyday thing.' Whether we consider Anna as a part of Kate, or as a separate person, the 'battle for positions' is still a prominent feature of *Old Times.* The contrasting memories of Anna and Deeley can be seen as their ways of laying a claim on Kate. At the risk of some repetition, it seems necessary to trace the struggle between these two to see what light it throws on Deeley's marriage.

In the opening lines of the play Deeley tries to find out more about Kate's friend, until he is startled to learn that the two girls had lived together before his marriage to Kate. This information marks a critical point in the play. Deeley remarks: 'Anyway, none of this matters', showing his first sign of irritation as Anna is established as a rival. Up to now Deeley has asked more than thirty questions. Such intensive questioning reveals doubts and, as Ronald Bryden writes: 'On Pinter territory, every question is an attempt to control and every answer a swift evasion.'

Anna appears as soon as Deeley stops wanting to know more. From then until the end of Act One, Anna is in command. The very way in which she speaks suggests she stands for a more exciting way of life, the words gushing out as she describes their life in London. One is reminded of Ruth's words in *The Homecoming:* 'My lips move. . . . Perhaps the fact that they move is more significant . . . than the words which come through them.'

Words, however, do take on great significance in the remainder of Act One, Anna chooses her words carefully, expressing admiration for their being so 'wise' and 'sensible' to live in this 'silence'. The words imply that the rash spontaneity of youth has been lost. Perhaps her slip in calling Kate 'a wonderful casserole' lacks subtlety, but it does lead to the contrast with how they 'guzzled' their food in London. Her old-fashioned words, 'lest', 'gaze', and 'beguilingly', show the distance between them.

Deeley's efforts to rival Anna seem crude by comparison. His memories about seeing *Odd Man Out* centre on the tough, manly Robert Newton as being the memory that he and Kate share, while the romantic café-visiting Kate is reduced in Deeley's memory to 'a trueblue pickup'. Not only does Anna alarm Deeley by raising doubts about the truth of memories, but later she too recalls seeing *Odd Man Out* in 'some totally obscure, some totally unfamiliar district'. So casually, she is able to undermine Deeley's claim to share a special memory with Kate.

At this point Deeley changes the subject to his own work, only to reveal a further fear of failure as a husband. When Anna asks him if he enjoys his travels, his repetition of

'Enormously' seems too insistent, and merely opens the way for Anna to wonder what happens then to 'poor Kate', and to threaten to replace him next time he is away. From this one feels that the play is dealing with the tensions of a marriage in the present. The worry for Deeley is that life is not as good for Kate as it might have been, and Anna's threat is that Kate might be tempted to return to the livelier ways of the past. In many of Pinter's plays, the wife/whore or mother/whore duality of the female, such as Sarah in *The Lover,* or Ruth in *The Homecoming,* seems to be created from a man's point of view showing his conflicting needs for a respectable social partner and a sexual partner. In *Old Times* most of the fears Deeley has about his wife seem created in himself, for Kate herself shows little enthusiasm for a return to the past. She says she prefers living in the country, because 'There aren't such edges here'. She shows greater interest in Anna's luxurious life in Sicily, which perhaps indicates another sort of life that she might have had, and which provokes Deeley's most open expressions of anger in the play.

At the end of Act One Deeley seems to have been forgotten by Anna and Kate, but, in the light of Kate's later description of the 'dead' Anna, the bath Kate takes, refusing Anna's offer to help, seems to signify a turning point. Indeed, in the second act, Deeley comes on more equal terms with Anna, first by recalling her in his memory of The Wayfarers Tavern, then by discussing how to dry Kate after her bath. Most effectively, he is able to comment on Anna's age. He says: 'If I walked into The Wayfarers Tavern now, and saw you sitting in the corner, I wouldn't recognize you.' Life at forty is now seen as something totally different from that of earlier days.

Anna regains the initiative by retelling the pub incident in front of Kate without mentioning Deeley. Finding this distasteful, Deeley is aroused to a furious attack on Anna's present life and a flippant description of his past knowledge of her. This effectively demolishes Anna, but it is an ambiguous victory for Deeley. Kate, who knows more than both the others, now recalls Deeley as a sensitive young man loved by Anna. Deeley's failure to understand the past is shown to be a failure to understand himself. Where Kate considered him as being sensitive, he looks back on his behaviour as 'crass'. Though less clearly contrasted than in *Landscape,* we again have the woman's sensitive memories of past love clashing with the coarseness of the man's present attitudes.

The final silent actions make a sad comment on everything that we have come to know. Anna 'dies' and Deeley, after getting no reaction from her, lies on Kate's lap. His final movement away from Kate to slump in an armchair explains to us why, twenty years after falling in love, he should have been so alarmed at recalling the past.

Have we seen a new Pinter? Undoubtedly. The old Pinter? That as well. The reviews of *Old Times* seem to have been true and false at the same time in a way that Pinter himself would appreciate.

1. 'Writing for the Theatre', in *New British Drama*, ed. H. Popkin, New York, 1964.

2. In a programme note to the double bill production of *The Room* and *The Dumb Waiter*, 8 March 1960.

THE HOTHOUSE

CRITICAL COMMENTARY

Rudolph Stamm (essay date 1981)

SOURCE: "*The Hothouse*: Harold Pinter's Tribute to Anger," in *English Studies*, Vol. 62, No. 3, June, 1981, pp. 290-98.

[*In the following essay, Stamm praises* The Hothouse, *an early play Pinter originally suppressed, but then produced in 1980.*]

The Hothouse was first presented at the Hampstead Theatre, London, in April 1980 in a production directed by the author and was transferred to the Ambassadors Theatre in June. In the printed text there is a note, saying: 'I wrote **The Hothouse** in the winter of 1958. I put it aside for further deliberation and made no attempt to have it produced at the time. I then went on to write **The Care-taker**. In 1979 I re-read **The Hothouse** and decided it was worth presenting on the stage. I made a few cuts but no changes.'[1]

If we want to understand some of the reasons for Pinter's original dissatisfaction with the play we can turn to his interview with Lawrence M. Bensky, printed in 1967 and reprinted in 1972.[2] When he was asked to define the relation of his art to politics he stated that he did not think highly of political plays and that his aim in making his own was simply to write as truthfully and well as he could. He confessed, however, that the ways of politicians could occasionally rouse his anger, and, when he was asked whether he would ever use this anger in a politically-oriented play, his answer was:

> I have occasionally out of irritation thought about writ-ing a play with a satirical point. I once did, actually, a play that no one knows about. A full-length play writ-ten after **The Caretaker**. Wrote the whole damn thing in three drafts. It was called **The Hothouse** and was about an institution in which patients were kept: all that was presented was the hierarchy, the people who ran the institution; one never knew what happened to the patients or what they were there for or who they were. It was heavily satirical and it was quite useless. I

never began to like any of the characters, they really didn't live at all. So I discarded the play at once. The characters were so purely cardboard. I was intention-ally—for the one time, I think—trying to make a point, an explicit point, that these were nasty people and I disapproved of them. And therefore they didn't begin to live. Whereas in other plays of mine every single character, even a bastard like Goldberg in **The Birthday Party,** I care for.[3]

Both quotations connect the play with **The Caretaker,** but the first has it that **The Hothouse** preceded, the second that it followed this work. It seems reasonable to accept the considered statement of 1980, which places **The Hot-house** between **The Birthday Party** and **The Caretaker.** What may appear surprising in this chronological arrange-ment is the relation between **The Birthday Party** and the lately produced play. Without the author's guidance specta-tors and readers would tend to consider **The Hothouse** as a preparatory exercise for **The Birthday Party.** It is a comparatively easy Pinter: his characteristic technique is used less economically and discreetly in it than in the other plays of the same period. One simple consequence of this appears in the length of the text. In the Methuen edition **The Hothouse** covers about 150 pages as against 30 for **The Room,** 40 for **The Dumb Waiter,** 80 for **The Caretaker** and 90 for **The Birthday Party.** It looks as if the play had not undergone the process of elimination and concentration that has led to the enigmatic compactness of the rest of his plays.

In spite of a number of loose ends there is a fairly complete and intelligible plot. The chief of what is a cross between a hospital, a mental home and a prison is gradually revealed to be a criminal, and the main members of his staff turn out to be not much better. After he has exasper-ated the so-called patients by a hypocritical Christmas ad-dress, composed of all the available platitudes and clichés, they break out of their cells and kill the whole staff with two exceptions, one of them the man who can carry the tale to the official in the Ministry and who seems to have engineered the whole catastrophe in order to become the successor of his liquidated chief. Thus a fairly well constructed crime story is neatly resolved in a concluding scene, and we are left with fewer questions to ponder than we have learnt to expect at the end of a Pinter play. Tak-ing the author's hint we may read it as an experimental excursion into Ben Jonson's ferocious mode of satire and as a reaction to the reception of **The Birthday Party** by critics and audiences, many of whom had loudly com-plained of the young author's opacity.

We realize what the targets of his satire are right at the start of the performance when we see the protagonist, Roote, sitting at his office table, bull-necked, crop-haired, a commanding military figure, speaking curtly to his subordinate, Gibbs, who answers with slightly exaggerated correctness:

ROOTE: Gibbs.

GIBBS: Yes, sir?

ROOTE: Tell me . . .

GIBBS: Yes, sir?

ROOTE: How's 6457 getting on?

GIBBS: 6457, sir?

ROOTE: Yes.

GIBBS: He's dead, sir.

ROOTE: Dead?

GIBBS: He died on Thursday, sir.

ROOTE: Thursday? What are you talking about? What's today?

GIBBS: Saturday, sir.

ROOTE: Saturday . . . Well, for goodness sake, I had a talk with him, when was it? (*Opens his desk diary.*) Recently. Only the other day. Yesterday, I think. Just a minute.

GIBBS: I hardly think yesterday, sir.

ROOTE: Why not?

GIBBS: I supervised the burial arrangements myself, sir.

ROOTE: This is ridiculous. What did he die of?

GIBBS: I beg your pardon, sir?

ROOTE: If he's dead, what did he die of?

GIBBS: Heart failure, sir.

ROOTE: *stares at him, then consults the diary.*

(13f.)[4]

Many of the play's themes appear in this brief exchange of curt questions and answers. The rules of the institution demand that the patients be deprived of their names and given numbers instead. The system does not seem to work too well since the chief himself is mixing up two numbers, one belonging to a patient that has died, the other to one who has given birth to a boy. Roote is far more shocked by the birth than by the death and, in an access of common sense, he even complains of the number system, saying: 'The whole thing's ridiculous! The system's wrong. (*He walks across the room.*) We shouldn't use these stupid numbers at all. Only confuses things. Why don't we use their names, for God's sake? They've got names, haven't they?' (19) From Gibbs comes the answer: 'It was your predecessor who instituted the use of numbers, sir.' Nevertheless, Roote continues to regret that he has failed to introduce changes in the system, not 'many changes' or 'drastic changes', but still something about this number business, for instance. When Gibbs politely asks: 'Would you like me to place further consideration of this matter on the agenda, sir?' he gets the sharp reply: 'Certainly not. We can't.' (22) And the reason given by Roote for this is that the number system was one of the rules of procedure laid down in the original constitution. Here his behaviour can for a moment recall Hector's change of mind in the Trojan council scene in *Troilus and Cressida*. The whole system we encounter is depersonalized, rigid, resisting change, and it is strictly hierarchical. Roote is the top man, Gibbs is his inferior, Lush is Gibb's inferior, and far down on the ladder stands Lamb, the unfortunate novice on the staff. Looking back to the time when his predecessor was the top man, Roote instructs Gibbs:

> ROOTE: I was standing where you're standing now. I can tell you that. Saying yes sir, no sir and certainly sir. Just as you are now. I didn't bribe anyone to get where I am. I worked my way up. When my predecessor . . . retired . . . I was invited to take over his position. And have you any idea why you call me sir now?
>
> GIBBS: Yes, sir.
>
> ROOTE: Why?
>
> GIBBS: Because you called him sir then, sir.
>
> ROOTE: Right!
>
> *Pause.*
>
> (20f.)

This is one of the many exchanges in the play that raise chuckles or even laughter in the audience; they occur before, but also after the spectators have recognized that what they are witnessing is anything but sheer comedy. As the play proceeds we realize that hot passions are lurking under the frozen surface of the hierarchical system: rivalry, envy, hatred, and that almost the whole staff is hardly better than a pack of wolves ready to jump at each other's throats and eventually destroyed by the most cunning specimen, the enigmatic Gibbs of the opening scene. As pointed out by the author in the interview quoted at the beginning of this paper, there is little information concerning the so-called patients. Roote and Lush intermittently indulge in plenty of double-talk concerning the benefits enjoyed by them, but a number of hard facts come to light and give away the brutality of the institution. The death of number 6457 was caused by Roote if we can trust Gibbs's final report, and we can trust it once we have discovered that he knows much more about his superior's devious ways than Roote, in his desperate isolation, imagines. Roote is also the cause of the birth the report of which shocks him so deeply, and how the patients feel about it all appears in the final massacre of the staff, the account of which is received quite calmly by Lobb, the representative of the ministry, who seems aware—to use a phrase of T. S. Eliot's—that this sort of thing has occurred before, and invites Gibbs to take over.

Pinter's satire is aimed at the *libido dominandi*; he has constructed a model of a vicious circle of power; we witness the fall of the tyrannical top man and are left with the certainty that his successor will be worse and that the wheel will continue to turn without alteration.[5] In a play of this type there is hardly any room for characterization in the traditional sense. We cannot trust what a figure says about himself or what other figures say about him. The information we get this way is mostly deceptions and lies. In his list of characters the author merely offers monosyllabic names and an age indication. In the case of Cutts the name is preceded by 'Miss'. Age and sex, like birth and death, are indubitable facts, for the rest we are referred to the behaviour of the figures and invited to draw our own conclusions. The main members of the gang show a remarkable family likeness. Their identity depends upon their place in the power game. Unless they have reached the top, they cringe to their superiors, whom they secretly hope to replace. In their dealings with inferiors they develop the very vices that disgust them in those they want to replace. Everybody is suspicious and ill at ease. Miss Cutts, the only female specimen, keeps harping on her femininity and is ready to sleep with all and sundry.

There is an extraordinary difference between seeing or reading this play for the first time and a second and third experience of it. The first viewing should be a treat for people who know their way about detective stories. But even they will not be able to catch all the clues to which we readily respond once we have seen the second act with its revelations and catastrophe. Then we have also gained an insight into the author's utterly pessimistic use of language. His figures cannot communicate through language. It is a weapon for them in their struggle for dominance, an instrument permitting them to disguise or hide their emotions and intentions. As a result of this the play moves on two different levels from beginning to end: the level of language, which is most deceptive when most florid, and the level below it, full of dark passions, plots, and secrets. In order to grasp what is going on down here we have got to listen and observe very carefully: an incoherence, a contradiction, a mere hesitation, a strange inflexion may be an important pointer. Pinter is following Freud where he turns lapses into the most revealing elements of speech.

An example of a telltale hesitation: in his account of how he worked his way up to his present position Roote mentions his predecessor: 'When my predecessor . . . retired . . . I was invited to take over his position.' When we come to the passage with a knowledge of the whole play, the three stops before and after 'retired' are full of sinister implications. His difficulty in finding the right word may hint that he had been responsible for his predecessor's death just as Gibbs will be responsible for Roote's death. The preceding sentence 'I didn't bribe anyone to get where I am', becomes overshadowed by a dark meaning, too, the negative statement calling for the positive complement 'but I had someone murdered to get where I am'. Another way of having hidden secrets manifest themselves may be observed in the very first section of the play when Roote is informed of the death of number 6457. He seems exasperated, exclaiming: 'This is ridiculous. What did he die of?' Gibbs's retort is: 'I beg your pardon, sir?' This request for the repetition of the question seems innocent enough at first sight and perhaps slightly funny. However, it points to Gibbs's thoughts, which tempt him to say at this moment: 'Why do you ask: you know better than anyone else how the man died.' Ironic innuendos of this

type are sprinkled over Gibbs's and, especially in the second act, over many of Lush's speeches.

Here speech functions in an indirect way, at least. But there are other passages where language is allowed to run riot. These come from Roote and the rest of the staff when they are on the defensive, mostly against their own feelings of isolation and insecurity. For such effusions Pinter knows how to assemble cascades of clichés, platitudes, palliations and downright lies. Rhetoric develops into an entirely self-sufficient intoxicant, being cut away from any roots language may have in reality. The supreme example of this is Roote's final Christmas speech. In its place I want to quote a shorter piece, his outburst when he hears that a boy has been born in his institution. Sinking on to the sofa, he indulges in a little self-pity: 'This has made my morning. It really has made my morning.' Then *he takes a pair of glasses out of his pocket, puts them on and looks across the room to Gibbs.* The glasses are necessary to support him in the role of the virtuously shocked governor. Now he opens the floodgates:

> I'm dumbstruck. Quite thunderstruck. Absolutely thunderstruck! This has never happened before. Never! In all the years I've been here, in all the years my predecessor was here. And I'm quite certain never before him. To spend years and years, winter after winter, trying to perfect the working of an institution so fragile in its conception and execution, so fragile the boundary between the achievement of one's aspirations and their collapse, not only one's own aspirations; rather the aspirations of a whole community, a tradition, an ideal; such a delicately wrought concept of participation between him who is to be treated and him who is to treat that it defies analysis; trying to sustain this fine, fine balance, finer than a . . . finer than a . . . . . . far, far finer. Year after year, and so refined the operation that the softest breath, the breath of a . . . feather . . . can send the whole thing tottering into chaos, into ignominy, to the death and cancellation of all our hopes. Goodness gracious. *He stands.*

(37)

Using the author's phrase we can call this speech 'heavily satirical', but we should not miss its tragic implications. It is haunted by the ghosts of Roote's former self, which was not unlike young Lamb. He, too, dreamt at one time of making the institution a better place to live in. When he tries to revert to his early idealism his words sound empty and hollow; growing painfully half-conscious of this, he is forced to lay it on thick and gets entangled in absurdities and rebellious figures of speech. Finally, before pocketing the glasses, he confides to Gibbs: 'I tell you quite frankly I smell disaster.' Premonitions of this type are frequent and help to create the feeling that some sort of catastrophe may happen at any moment.

Pinter knows other methods of presenting language that has become partly or wholly independent of meaning. He loves to arrange it in rapid question and answer games that are strikingly amusing and, at the same time, puzzling, ominous and, in one case, cruel. For an example we turn to the scene in the second act, where Roote, after having given a toast 'To our glorious dead', inquires what sort of man Lamb is. He calls him 'a rapist' as there seems to be a silent understanding among the top gang to saddle him with the fatherhood of the boy so unaccountably born. Roote's questions remind us that, beside sex and age, the physical characteristics of a human being should be indisputably ascertainable. But here is the outcome of his inquiries:

> ROOTE: What sort of man is he?
>
> GIBBS: Lamb, sir? Nondescript.
>
> ROOTE: Tall?
>
> GIBBS: No, sir. Small.
>
> LUSH: Tall.
>
> GIBBS: Small.
>
> *Pause*
>
> ROOTE: Do you know him, Lush?
>
> LUSH: I've seen him.
>
> ROOTE: Is he fat?
>
> GIBBS: Thin, sir.
>
> LUSH: Fat.
>
> GIBBS: Thin.
>
> *Pause*
>
> ROOTE: Brown eyes?
>
> GIBBS: Blue, sir.
>
> LUSH: Brown.
>
> GIBBS: Blue.
>
> *Pause*
>
> ROOTE: Curly hair?
>
> GIBBS *and* LUSH *eye each other.*
>
> LUSH: Straight, sir.
>
> GIBBS: Curly.
>
> LUSH: Straight.
>
> *Pause*
>
> ROOTE: What colour teeth?
>
> GIBBS: Lemon, sir.
>
> LUSH: Nigger.
>
> GIBBS: Lemon.
>
> LUSH: Nigger.
>
> *Pause*

> ROOTE: Any special peculiarities?
>
> GIBBS: None.
>
> LUSH: One.
>
> GIBBS: None.
>
> *Pause*
>
> ROOTE: These descriptions don't tally. Next time bring me a photograph.
>
> (99ff.)

This is a grotesque way of showing that the three interlocutors, out of sheer submerged antagonism, cannot agree on the simplest facts. But let us turn ourselves to Roote's question: what sort of man is Lamb?

We have called him an unfortunate novice low down on the hierarchical ladder. His position is so low that Roote has never seen him. He carries a speaking name whereas the names of the other figures seem to have been chosen at random for the sake of their brevity and sound quality in order to suggest that there is not much to distinguish the several products of the one bleak system. Roote's name may remind some spectators of 'the root of all evil', although this Biblical phrase does not refer to the love of power, but to the love of money. In contrast to the rest Lamb is not an enigmatic figure. In an early short scene with Miss Cutts he gives himself away as a naive and idealistic youngster. He has now worked in the institution for a whole year, his task being to see to it that the gates of the building and all the cells of the patients remain locked. He complains of his lack of contact with the rest of the staff, but speaks hopefully of a report he has written and sent up to the chief, in which he has expounded his ideas for the improvement of the whole establishment, without realizing for a moment that this is the unforgivable sin in the eyes of his superiors. We could almost accept him as a sympathetic figure, but he, too, is tainted because he is ambitious and dreams of promotion. This is why he becomes a victim. In the interrogation-and-torture scene he develops into an entirely grotesque figure. His deference and desire to make himself agreeable and useful to Gibbs and Cutts are such that he walks eagerly into the soundproof room where, according to his two suave tormentors, a scientific experiment will take place. While he continues to talk hopefully of the institution and his past and future work in it, he allows them to attach electrodes to his head and his hands, and in the end he finds himself seated in what looks desperately like an electric chair. He earnestly tries to respond reasonably to the incoherent questions coming from the two sadists, and he does not even get cured of his optimism when the following happens:

> LAMB *sits. Silence. He shifts and concentrates. The red light flicks on and off. Silence.*
>
> *Suddenly a piercing highpitched buzz-hum is heard.*

LAMB *jolts rigid, his hands go to his earphones, he is propelled from the chair, falls, stands, falls, rolls, still clutching his earphones, crawls under the table.*

The sound ceases. Silence.

The red light is still flickering.

LAMB *peeps up from under the table. He crawls out, stands.*

He twitches, and emits a short chuckle.

(68)

This chuckle and his readiness to continue playing his part in the disgusting game prove his inability or unwillingness to recognize malignity when it is the malignity of his superiors, from whom he expects promotion, and to recognize their torturing as torture although he is himself subjected to it. When he is finally left in the chair, speechless and motionless, we are reminded of Stanley in *The Birthday Party* after Goldberg and McCann have done with him. Unlike Stanley, Lamb is a willing victim. The scene is a fearful theatrical symbol, in which a prolonged process of deterioration, caused by social and psychological mechanisms, is concentrated. At its end Lamb will probably have developed into another potential successor of the Roote of the future. What happens to Lamb has a plot function, too. This is not clearly stated anywhere, but we can guess it at the end of the play. It seems that Gibbs puts Lamb out of action in order to prevent him from looking after the locks of the patients' cells, which renders the final killing possible. Secondly, we suspect the intention of turning Lamb into a willing instrument in the hands of Gibbs, the next chief, who will not be able to carry on without the help of, at least, one member of the old staff.

We return to Pinter's pointers to what is going on below the level of language. Those we have considered so far belonged to speech; quite often, however, it is a gesture that betrays the thoughts and emotions of a figure. When Roote wants to learn from Gibbs who is the new-born baby's father, and inquires what its mother had to say on this nice point, Gibbs answers: 'She was . . . noncommittal, sir. She said she couldn't be entirely sure since most of the staff have had relations with her in this last year.' (40) Roote, nonplussed, exclaims: 'Most of the staff?' And Gibbs confirms: 'According to her statement, sir.' There follows a stage direction: 'ROOTE *sits, rubs his mouth.*' This is the first hint to the spectator that Roote himself may have had relations with the patient in question. A more easily decipherable gesture strikes us earlier in the play and gets mirrored in speech. Roote is sitting at his desk examining his diary, and Gibbs, trying to help him, is leaning over his shoulder. All of a sudden Roote protests: 'Don't stand so close to me. You're right on top of me. What's the matter with you?' (17) And Gibbs steps away from the desk with an 'I'm sorry, sir'. The gestures hint at Roote's secret fear of Gibbs as well as at Gibbs's secret aspirations.

Together with the sometimes unaccountable pauses and the frequent staring of the interlocutors at one another the gestures unmask their deceitful language and help to create a sense of dubiety, of rottenness, and doom. In the second act the strains behind the correct relationship of Roote, Gibbs, and Lush lead to open outbreaks of hostility. The air is charged with violence. Roote complains more than once that he feels hot, that the room is overheated, and once he adds ominously 'like a crematorium'. (90) Lush appears over-fond of assuring him that the snow, which is the weather symbol of the first act, has now turned to slush. The playwright seems to enjoy having Lush harp on the slush outside. Whisky is another second act symbol. It is swallowed in increasing quantities, especially by Roote, who begins to act and talk wildly. He throws whisky in Lush's face; he hits him in the stomach several times in an attempt to convince him that he himself as the chief is delegated, entrusted, appointed and authorized. He accuses Gibbs openly of an intention to murder him, and before the final outbreak we see knives in the hands of the antagonists. Roote's speeches grow more and more incoherent as he is getting drunk, but he has his moments of insight, and then his recurrent theme is a gnawing sense of doom.

Sporadically, the rapidly deteriorating situation is saved by a recourse to convention. After all it is Christmas, the day of the exchange of wishes for health and happiness, a day of toasts and gifts. The understaff have their raffle. Tubb, their representative, brings their best wishes and a Christmas cake to Roote, and even pretends that everybody, including the patients, is eager to hear his Christmas address. Roote is delighted to receive the gift of a beautiful cigar from Lush, of all people, but when he lights it and settles down to enjoy it, it explodes. Thus all the Christmas motifs, above all Roote's final address, turn farcical in this world of deception and violence. If Pinter has deprived it of any means of salvation, he has generously equipped it with technical devices. As we have seen they are very much in evidence in the interrogation-and-torture scene; Roote uses an intercom, which renders his human relations more difficult, and there is an amplifier, through which terrifying noises—a sigh, a keen, and a laugh—make themselves heard three times. All this machinery has an important function in creating the appropriate setting for Pinter's dehumanized society.

The play as a whole is planned and executed with the meticulous care which is a mark of Pinter's genius. The author of so many polysemantic plays decided to write a monosemantic one in this case, and he knew how to pursue his one aim relentlessly and successfully. This required a large-scale use of some of his favourite devices, a fact that annoyed him at a time when his passion for the achievement of the intensest effect through the most unobtrusive means was growing. He was well advised when he decided in 1979 that his outcry against an hierarchical, bureaucratic and inhuman organization of society, and against the abuse of language for the contrary of communication, should be no longer left unheard. The most poignant part of his satire concerns Lamb and the why and how he gets absorbed into the dismal system. Beside writing a powerful satire Pinter has succeeded in creating a modern hell, worthy of taking its place beside his purgatory **The Birthday Party.**

Notes

1. Author's Note in *The Hothouse* (London, 1980).

2. *Pinter: A Collection of Critical Essays* in *Twentieth Century Views* (Englewood Cliffs, N.J., 1972), pp. 19-33.

3. *Ibid.*, p. 27ff.

4. All quotations are taken from the edition mentioned in note 1.

5. This type of model recurs in many works of the post-war period, cf. e.g. Jan Kott's interpretations of Shakespeare's histories and *König Johann*, Friedrich Dürrenmatt's version of Shakespeare's *King John*.

FURTHER READING

Bibliography

Gale, Steven H. *Harold Pinter: An Annotated Bibliography.* Boston: G.K. Hall & Co., 1978, 244 p.

A comprehensive bibliography of works by and about Pinter up to 1978.

Biography

Billington, Michael. *The Life and Work of Harold Pinter.* London: Faber and Faber, 1996, 414 p.

A blend of analysis and bibliography, placing Pinter's work in the developing context of his life.

Criticism

Baker, William and Stephen Ely Tabachnick. *Harold Pinter.* Edinburgh: Oliver & Boyd, 1973, 196 p.

Provides an overview of Pinter's early plays.

Brien, Alan. "The Guilty Seam." *The Spectator* 204 (January 29, 1960): 138.

A review of early plays, appreciating Pinter's ability to present dramas of people in a trap, but calling upon Pinter to address the question of how it is the trap exists.

———. "Something Blue." *The Spectator* 204 (June 10, 1960): 835.

A thumbnail analysis and review praising *The Caretaker.*

Brustein, Robert. "Thoughts from Home and Abroad." *The New Republic* 152, No. 2640 (June 26, 1965): 29-30.

Brustein complains that Pinter's plays usually are composed only of atmosphere, but that in *The Homecoming* the playwright does not show the skill even to develop a consistent and coherent atmosphere.

Diamond, Elin. *Pinter's Comic Play.* Lewisburg: Bucknell University Press, 1985, 241 p.

Analyzes Pinter's use of comedy as a disturbing rather than a liberating element.

Esslin, Martin. *Pinter The Playwright.* London: Methuen, 1992, 280 p.

An enlarged edition of Esslin's 1970 study of Pinter's plays, background, and methods of playwriting.

Lahr, John, ed. *A Casebook on Harold Pinter's The Homecoming.* New York: Grove Press, 1971, 199 p.

A collection of essays discussing various aspects of *The Homecoming.*

Merritt, Susan Hollis. *Pinter in Play: Critical Strategies and the Plays of Harold Pinter.* Durham and London: Duke University Press, 1990, 344 p.

Surveys and analyzes critical approaches to and visions of Pinter's plays.

Oliver, Edith. "The Room." *The New Yorker* 40, No. 44 (December 19, 1964): 68ff.

In an enthusiastic review of *The Room* and *A Slight Ache,* Oliver emphasizes how Pinter's vitality and talent counterbalance the "unpleasantness" of the material.

———. "'Landscape' and 'Silence.'"*The New Yorker* 46, No. 8 (April 11, 1970): 84.

Commends Pinter for his powers of investigating character and behavior without preset conclusions.

Panter-Downes, Mollie. "The Caretaker." *The New Yorker* 36, No. 21 (July 9, 1960): 60-1.

An enthusiastic recommendation for a first production.

Quigley, Austin E. *The Pinter Problem.* Princeton: Princeton University Press, 1975, 295 p.

Views the problem of understanding Pinter's use of language as the key to developing an adequate critical methodology for understanding his plays.

Scott, Michael, ed. *Harold Pinter.* The Birthday Party, The Caretaker, The Homecoming *A Casebook.* London: Macmillan.

A collection of essays discussing Pinter and various aspects of *The Birthday Party, The Caretaker,* and *The Homecoming.*

Sykes, Arlene. *Harold Pinter.* St. Lucia, Queensland: University of Queensland Press, 1970, 135 p.

Critical analyses of Pinter's plays through 1970.

Trussler, Simon. *The Plays of Harold Pinter: An Assessment.* London: Victor Gollancz, 1973, 222 p.

Critical approaches to Pinter's work through 1973.

Taylor, John Russell. *Harold Pinter.* Essex: Longmans, Green & Co Ltd, 1969, 31 p.

A monograph arguing that the strength of Pinter's plays lies in their self-contained actuality and integrity rather than in verbalized and reductive analyses.

Additional coverage of Pinter's life and career is contained in the following sources published by the Gale Group: *Concise Dictionary of British Literary Biography 1960 to Present; Contemporary Authors,* **Vols. 5-8R;** *Contemporary Authors New Revision Series,* **Vols. 33, 65;** *Contemporary Dramatists; Contemporary Literary Criticism,* **Vols. 1, 3, 6, 9, 11, 15, 27, 58, 73;** *Dictionary of Literary Biography,* **Vol. 13;** *DISCovering Authors; DISCovering Authors 3.0; DISCovering Authors: British; DISCovering Authors: Canadian; DISCovering Authors Modules: Dramatists, Most-studied Authors; Drama for Students,* **Vols. 3, 5, 7;** *Major 20th-Century Writers,* **Vols. 1, 2; and** *World Literature Criticism.*

How to Use This Index

The main references

Calvino, Italo
1923-1985 .... CLC 5, 8, 11, 22, 33, 39,
73; SSC 3

list all author entries in the following Gale Literary Criticism series:

BLC = *Black Literature Criticism*
CLC = *Contemporary Literary Criticism*
CLR = *Children's Literature Review*
CMLC = *Classical and Medieval Literature Criticism*
DA = *DISCovering Authors*
DAB = *DISCovering Authors: British*
DAC = *DISCovering Authors: Canadian*
DAM = *DISCovering Authors: Modules*
    DRAM: *Dramatists Module;* *MST:* *Most-Studied Authors Module;*
    MULT: *Multicultural Authors Module;* *NOV:* *Novelists Module;*
    POET: *Poets Module;* *POP:* *Popular Fiction and Genre Authors Module*
DC = *Drama Criticism*
HLC = *Hispanic Literature Criticism*
LC = *Literature Criticism from 1400 to 1800*
NCLC = *Nineteenth-Century Literature Criticism*
NNAL = *Native North American Literature*
PC = *Poetry Criticism*
SSC = *Short Story Criticism*
TCLC = *Twentieth-Century Literary Criticism*
WLC = *World Literature Criticism, 1500 to the Present*

The cross-references

See also CANR 23; CA 85-88;
obituary CA116

list all author entries in the following Gale biographical and literary sources:

AAYA = *Authors & Artists for Young Adults*
AITN = *Authors in the News*
BEST = *Bestsellers*
BW = *Black Writers*
CA = *Contemporary Authors*
CAAS = *Contemporary Authors Autobiography Series*
CABS = *Contemporary Authors Bibliographical Series*
CANR = *Contemporary Authors New Revision Series*
CAP = *Contemporary Authors Permanent Series*
CDALB = *Concise Dictionary of American Literary Biography*
CDBLB = *Concise Dictionary of British Literary Biography*
DLB = *Dictionary of Literary Biography*
DLBD = *Dictionary of Literary Biography Documentary Series*
DLBY = *Dictionary of Literary Biography Yearbook*
HW = *Hispanic Writers*
JRDA = *Junior DISCovering Authors*
MAICYA = *Major Authors and Illustrators for Children and Young Adults*
MTCW = *Major 20th-Century Writers*
SAAS = *Something about the Author Autobiography Series*
SATA = *Something about the Author*
YABC = *Yesterday's Authors of Books for Children*

Literary Criticism Series
Cumulative Author Index

Anaximander c. 611B.C.-c. 546B.C. .... **CMLC 22**

Anaya, Rudolfo A(lfonso) 1937- ...... **CLC 23; DAM MULT, NOV; HLC 1**
See also AAYA 20; CA 45-48; CAAS 4; CANR 1, 32, 51; DLB 82, 206; HW 1; MTCW 1, 2

Andersen, Hans Christian 1805-1875 .... **NCLC 7, 79; DA; DAB; DAC; DAM MST, POP; SSC 6**
See also AW; CLR 6; DA3; MAICYA; SATA 100

Anderson, C. Farley
See Mencken, H(enry) L(ouis); Nathan, George Jean

Anderson, Jessica (Margaret) Queale 1916- .... **CLC 37**
See also CA 9-12R; CANR 4, 62

Anderson, Jon (Victor) 1940- . **CLC 9; DAM POET**
See also CA 25-28R; CANR 20

Anderson, Lindsay (Gordon) 1923-1994 .... **CLC 20**
See also CA 125; 128; 146; CANR 77

Anderson, Maxwell 1888-1959 .... **TCLC 2; DAM DRAM**
See also CA 105; 152; DLB 7, 228; MTCW 2

Anderson, Poul (William) 1926- .... **CLC 15**
See also AAYA 5, 34; CA 1-4R; 181; CAAE 181; CAAS 2; CANR 2, 15, 34, 64; CLR 58; DLB 8; INT CANR-15; MTCW 1, 2; SATA 90; SATA-Brief 39; SATA-Essay 106; SCFW 2

Anderson, Robert (Woodruff) 1917- .... **CLC 23; DAM DRAM**
See also AITN 1; CA 21-24R; CANR 32; DLB 7

Anderson, Sherwood 1876-1941 ..... **TCLC 1, 10, 24; DA; DAB; DAC; DAM MST, NOV; SSC 1**
See also AAYA 30; AW; CA 104; 121; CANR 61; CDALB 1917-1929; DA3; DLB 4, 9, 86; DLBD 1; GLL 2; MTCW 1, 2

Andier, Pierre
See Desnos, Robert

Andouard
See Giraudoux, (Hippolyte) Jean

Andrade, Carlos Drummond de CLC 18
See also Drummond de Andrade, Carlos

Andrade, Mario de 1893-1945 .... **TCLC 43**

Andreae, Johann V(alentin) 1586-1654 .... **LC 32**
See also DLB 164

Andreas-Salome, Lou 1861-1937 ... **TCLC 56**
See also CA 178; DLB 66

Andress, Lesley
See Sanders, Lawrence

Andrewes, Lancelot 1555-1626 .... **LC 5**
See also DLB 151, 172

Andrews, Cicily Fairfield
See West, Rebecca

Andrews, Elton V.
See Pohl, Frederik

Andreyev, Leonid (Nikolaevich) 1871-1919 .... **TCLC 3**
See also CA 104; 185

Andric, Ivo 1892-1975 .... **CLC 8; SSC 36**
See also CA 81-84; 57-60; CANR 43, 60; DLB 147; MTCW 1

Androvar
See Prado (Calvo), Pedro

Angelique, Pierre
See Bataille, Georges

Angell, Roger 1920- .... **CLC 26**
See also CA 57-60; CANR 13, 44, 70; DLB 171, 185

Angelou, Maya 1928- .... **CLC 12, 35, 64, 77; BLC 1; DA; DAB; DAC; DAM MST, MULT, POET, POP; PC 32**
See also AAYA 7, 20; AMWS 4; AW; BW 2, 3; CA 65-68; CANR 19, 42, 65; CDALBS; CLR 53; DA3; DLB 38; MTCW 1, 2; SATA 49

Anna Comnena 1083-1153 .... **CMLC 25**

Annensky, Innokenty (Fyodorovich) 1856-1909 .... **TCLC 14**
See also CA 110; 155

Annunzio, Gabriele d'
See D'Annunzio, Gabriele

Anodos
See Coleridge, Mary E(lizabeth)

Anon, Charles Robert
See Pessoa, Fernando (Antonio Nogueira)

Anouilh, Jean (Marie Lucien Pierre) 1910-1987 .... **CLC 1, 3, 8, 13, 40, 50; DAM DRAM; DC 8**
See also CA 17-20R; 123; CANR 32; MTCW 1, 2

Anthony, Florence
See Ai

Anthony, John
See Ciardi, John (Anthony)

Anthony, Peter
See Shaffer, Anthony (Joshua); Shaffer, Peter (Levin)

Anthony, Piers 1934- .... **CLC 35; DAM POP**
See also AAYA 11; AW; CA 21-24R; CANR 28, 56, 73; DLB 8; MTCW 1, 2; SAAS 22; SATA 84

Anthony, Susan B(rownell) 1916-1991 .... **TCLC 84**
See also CA 89-92; 134

Antoine, Marc
See Proust, (Valentin-Louis-George-Eugene-)Marcel

Antoninus, Brother
See Everson, William (Oliver)

Antoninus, Marcus Aurelius 121-180 .... **CMLC 45**

Antonioni, Michelangelo 1912- .... **CLC 20, 144**
See also CA 73-76; CANR 45, 77

Antschel, Paul 1920-1970
See Celan, Paul
See also CA 85-88; CANR 33, 61; MTCW 1

Anwar, Chairil 1922-1949 .... **TCLC 22**
See also CA 121

Anzaldua, Gloria (Evanjelina) 1942-
See also CA 175; DLB 122; HLCS 1

Apess, William 1798-1839(?) .... **NCLC 73; DAM MULT**
See also DLB 175; NNAL

Apollinaire, Guillaume 1880-1918 .. **TCLC 3, 8, 51; DAM POET; PC 7**
See also CA 152; MTCW 1

Appelfeld, Aharon 1932- ... **CLC 23, 47; SSC 42**
See also CA 112; 133; CANR 86; CWW 2

Apple, Max (Isaac) 1941- .... **CLC 9, 33**
See also CA 81-84; CANR 19, 54; DLB 130

Appleman, Philip (Dean) 1926- .... **CLC 51**
See also CA 13-16R; CAAS 18; CANR 6, 29, 56

Appleton, Lawrence
See Lovecraft, H(oward) P(hillips)

Apteryx
See Eliot, T(homas) S(tearns)

Apuleius, (Lucius Madaurensis) 125(?)-175(?) .... **CMLC 1**
See also DLB 211

Aquin, Hubert 1929-1977 .... **CLC 15**
See also CA 105; DLB 53

Aquinas, Thomas 1224(?)-1274 ..... **CMLC 33**
See also DLB 115

Aragon, Louis 1897-1982 .. **CLC 3, 22; DAM NOV, POET**
See also CA 69-72; 108; CANR 28, 71; DLB 72; GLL 2; MTCW 1, 2

Arany, Janos 1817-1882 .... **NCLC 34**

Aranyos, Kakay 1847-1910
See Mikszath, Kalman

Arbuthnot, John 1667-1735 .... **LC 1**
See also DLB 101

Archer, Herbert Winslow
See Mencken, H(enry) L(ouis)

Archer, Jeffrey (Howard) 1940- ...... **CLC 28; DAM POP**
See also AAYA 16; BEST 89:3; CA 77-80; CANR 22, 52, 95; DA3; INT CANR-22

Archer, Jules 1915- .... **CLC 12**
See also CA 9-12R; CANR 6, 69; SAAS 5; SATA 4, 85

Archer, Lee
See Ellison, Harlan (Jay)

Archilochus c. 7th cent. B.C.- .... **CMLC 44**
See also DLB 176

Arden, John 1930- .... **CLC 6, 13, 15; DAM DRAM**
See also BRWS 2; CA 13-16R; CAAS 4; CANR 31, 65, 67; DLB 13; MTCW 1

Arenas, Reinaldo 1943-1990 . **CLC 41; DAM MULT; HLC 1**
See also CA 124; 128; 133; CANR 73; DLB 145; GLL 2; HW 1; MTCW 1

Arendt, Hannah 1906-1975 .... **CLC 66, 98**
See also CA 17-20R; 61-64; CANR 26, 60; DLB 242; MTCW 1, 2

Aretino, Pietro 1492-1556 .... **LC 12**

Arghezi, Tudor CLC 80
See also Theodorescu, Ion N.
See also CA 167; DLB 220

Arguedas, Jose Maria 1911-1969 .... **CLC 10, 18; HLCS 1**
See also CA 89-92; CANR 73; DLB 113; HW 1

Argueta, Manlio 1936- .... **CLC 31**
See also CA 131; CANR 73; CWW 2; DLB 145; HW 1

Arias, Ron(ald Francis) 1941-
See also CA 131; CANR 81; DAM MULT; DLB 82; HLC 1; HW 1, 2; MTCW 2

Ariosto, Ludovico 1474-1533 .... **LC 6**

Aristides
See Epstein, Joseph

Aristophanes 450B.C.-385B.C. .... **CMLC 4; DA; DAB; DAC; DAM DRAM, MST; DC 2**
See also AW; DA3; DLB 176

Aristotle 384B.C.-322B.C. .... **CMLC 31; DA; DAB; DAC; DAM MST**
See also AW; DA3; DLB 176

Arlt, Roberto (Godofredo Christophersen) 1900-1942 .... **TCLC 29; DAM MULT; HLC 1**
See also CA 123; 131; CANR 67; HW 1, 2

Armah, Ayi Kwei 1939- .... **CLC 5, 33, 136; BLC 1; DAM MULT, POET**
See also BW 1; CA 61-64; CANR 21, 64; DLB 117; MTCW 1

Armatrading, Joan 1950- .... **CLC 17**
See also CA 114; 186

Arnette, Robert
See Silverberg, Robert

Arnim, Achim von (Ludwig Joachim von Arnim) 1781-1831 ..... **NCLC 5; SSC 29**
See also DLB 90

Arnim, Bettina von 1785-1859 .... **NCLC 38**
See also DLB 90

Arnold, Matthew 1822-1888 ..... NCLC 6, 29, 89; DA; DAB; DAC; DAM MST, POET; PC 5
See also AW; CDBLB 1832-1890; DLB 32, 57

Arnold, Thomas 1795-1842 .... NCLC 18
See also DLB 55

Arnow, Harriette (Louisa) Simpson
1908-1986 .... CLC 2, 7, 18
See also CA 9-12R; 118; CANR 14; DLB 6; MTCW 1, 2; SATA 42; SATA-Obit 47

Arouet, Francois-Marie
See Voltaire

Arp, Hans
See Arp, Jean

Arp, Jean 1887-1966 .... CLC 5
See also CA 81-84; 25-28R; CANR 42, 77

Arrabal
See Arrabal, Fernando

Arrabal, Fernando 1932- ... CLC 2, 9, 18, 58
See also CA 9-12R; CANR 15

Arreola, Juan Jose 1918- .... SSC 38; DAM MULT; HLC 1
See also CA 113; 131; CANR 81; DLB 113; HW 1, 2

Arrian c. 89(?)-c. 155(?) .... CMLC 43
See also DLB 176

Arrick, Fran CLC 30
See also Gaberman, Judie Angell

Artaud, Antonin (Marie Joseph)
1896-1948 . TCLC 3, 36; DAM DRAM; DC 14
See also CA 104; 149; DA3; MTCW 1

Arthur, Ruth M(abel) 1905-1979 ..... CLC 12
See also CA 9-12R; 85-88; CANR 4; SATA 7, 26

Artsybashev, Mikhail (Petrovich)
1878-1927 .... TCLC 31
See also CA 170

Arundel, Honor (Morfydd)
1919-1973 .... CLC 17
See also CA 21-22; 41-44R; CAP 2; CLR 35; SATA 4; SATA-Obit 24

Arzner, Dorothy 1900-1979 .... CLC 98

Asch, Sholem 1880-1957 .... TCLC 3
See also CA 105; GLL 2

Ash, Shalom
See Asch, Sholem

Ashbery, John (Lawrence) 1927- .. CLC 2, 3, 4, 6, 9, 13, 15, 25, 41, 77, 125; DAM POET; PC 26
See also Berry, Jonas
See also AMWS 3; CA 5-8R; CANR 9, 37, 66; DA3; DLB 5, 165; DLBY 81; INT CANR-9; MTCW 1, 2

Ashdown, Clifford
See Freeman, R(ichard) Austin

Ashe, Gordon
See Creasey, John

Ashton-Warner, Sylvia (Constance)
1908-1984 .... CLC 19
See also CA 69-72; 112; CANR 29; MTCW 1, 2

Asimov, Isaac 1920-1992 ..... CLC 1, 3, 9, 19, 26, 76, 92; DAM POP
See also AAYA 13; AW; BEST 90:2; CA 1-4R; 137; CANR 2, 19, 36, 60; CLR 12; DA3; DLB 8; DLBY 92; INT CANR-19; JRDA; MAICYA; MTCW 1, 2; SATA 1, 26, 74; SCFW 2

Assis, Joaquim Maria Machado de
See Machado de Assis, Joaquim Maria

Astley, Thea (Beatrice May) 1925- .. CLC 41
See also CA 65-68; CANR 11, 43, 78

Aston, James
See White, T(erence) H(anbury)

Asturias, Miguel Ángel 1899-1974 .... CLC 3, 8, 13; DAM MULT, NOV; HLC 1
See also CA 25-28; 49-52; CANR 32; CAP 2; DA3; DLB 113; HW 1; MTCW 1, 2

Atares, Carlos Saura
See Saura (Atares), Carlos

Atheling, William
See Pound, Ezra (Weston Loomis)

Atheling, William, Jr.
See Blish, James (Benjamin)

Atherton, Gertrude (Franklin Horn)
1857-1948 .... TCLC 2
See also CA 104; 155; DLB 9, 78, 186; TCWW 2

Atherton, Lucius
See Masters, Edgar Lee

Atkins, Jack
See Harris, Mark

Atkinson, Kate CLC 99
See also CA 166

Attaway, William (Alexander)
1911-1986 .... CLC 92; BLC 1; DAM MULT
See also BW 2, 3; CA 143; CANR 82; DLB 76

Atticus
See Fleming, Ian (Lancaster); Wilson, (Thomas) Woodrow

Atwood, Margaret (Eleanor) 1939- ... CLC 2, 3, 4, 8, 13, 15, 25, 44, 84, 135; DA; DAB; DAC; DAM MST, NOV, POET; PC 8; SSC 2
See also AAYA 12; AW; BEST 89:2; CA 49-52; CANR 3, 24, 33, 59, 95; DA3; DLB 53; INT CANR-24; MTCW 1, 2; SATA 50

Aubigny, Pierre d'
See Mencken, H(enry) L(ouis)

Aubin, Penelope 1685-1731(?) .... LC 9
See also DLB 39

Auchincloss, Louis (Stanton) 1917- .. CLC 4, 6, 9, 18, 45; DAM NOV; SSC 22
See also AMWS 4; CA 1-4R; CANR 6, 29, 55, 87; DLB 2; DLBY 80; INT CANR-29; MTCW 1

Auden, W(ystan) H(ugh) 1907-1973 . CLC 1, 2, 3, 4, 6, 9, 11, 14, 43, 123; DA; DAB; DAC; DAM DRAM, MST, POET; PC 1
See also AAYA 18; AMWS 2; AW; CA 9-12R; 45-48; CANR 5, 61; CDBLB 1914-1945; DA3; DLB 10, 20; MTCW 1, 2

Audiberti, Jacques 1900-1965 .... CLC 38; DAM DRAM
See also CA 25-28R

Audubon, John James 1785-1851 . NCLC 47

Auel, Jean M(arie) 1936- .... CLC 31, 107; DAM POP
See also AAYA 7; BEST 90:4; CA 103; CANR 21, 64; DA3; INT CANR-21; SATA 91

Auerbach, Erich 1892-1957 .... TCLC 43
See also CA 118; 155

Augier, Emile 1820-1889 .... NCLC 31
See also DLB 192

August, John
See De Voto, Bernard (Augustine)

Augustine 354-430 .... CMLC 6; DA; DAB; DAC; DAM MST
See also AW; DA3; DLB 115

Aurelius
See Bourne, Randolph S(illiman)

Aurobindo, Sri
See Ghose, Aurabinda

Austen, Jane 1775-1817 ...... NCLC 1, 13, 19, 33, 51, 81, 95; DA; DAB; DAC; DAM MST, NOV
See also AAYA 19; AW 1; CDBLB 1789-1832; DA3; DLB 116

Auster, Paul 1947- .... CLC 47, 131
See also CA 69-72; CANR 23, 52, 75; DA3; DLB 227; MTCW 1

Austin, Frank
See Faust, Frederick (Schiller)
See also TCWW 2

Austin, Mary (Hunter) 1868-1934 . TCLC 25
See also Stairs, Gordon
See also CA 109; 178; DLB 9, 78, 206, 221; TCWW 2

Averroes 1126-1198 .... CMLC 7
See also DLB 115

Avicenna 980-1037 .... CMLC 16
See also DLB 115

Avison, Margaret 1918- .... CLC 2, 4, 97; DAC; DAM POET
See also CA 17-20R; DLB 53; MTCW 1

Axton, David
See Koontz, Dean R(ay)

Ayckbourn, Alan 1939- ...... CLC 5, 8, 18, 33, 74; DAB; DAM DRAM; DC 13
See also BRWS 5; CA 21-24R; CANR 31, 59; DLB 13; MTCW 1, 2

Aydy, Catherine
See Tennant, Emma (Christina)

Ayme, Marcel (Andre) 1902-1967 ... CLC 11; SSC 41
See also CA 89-92; CANR 67; CLR 25; DLB 72; SATA 91

Ayrton, Michael 1921-1975 .... CLC 7
See also CA 5-8R; 61-64; CANR 9, 21

Azorin CLC 11
See also Martinez Ruiz, Jose

Azuela, Mariano 1873-1952 . TCLC 3; DAM MULT; HLC 1
See also CA 104; 131; CANR 81; HW 1, 2; MTCW 1, 2

Baastad, Babbis Friis
See Friis-Baastad, Babbis Ellinor

Bab
See Gilbert, W(illiam) S(chwenck)

Babbis, Eleanor
See Friis-Baastad, Babbis Ellinor

Babel, Isaac
See Babel, Isaak (Emmanuilovich)

Babel, Isaak (Emmanuilovich)
1894-1941(?) .... TCLC 2, 13; SSC 16
See also Babel, Isaac
See also CA 104; 155; MTCW 1

Babits, Mihaly 1883-1941 .... TCLC 14
See also CA 114

Babur 1483-1530 .... LC 18

Baca, Jimmy Santiago 1952-
See also CA 131; CANR 81, 90; DAM MULT; DLB 122; HLC 1; HW 1, 2

Bacchelli, Riccardo 1891-1985 .... CLC 19
See also CA 29-32R; 117

Bach, Richard (David) 1936- .... CLC 14; DAM NOV, POP
See also AITN 1; BEST 89:2; CA 9-12R; CANR 18, 93; MTCW 1; SATA 13

Bachman, Richard
See King, Stephen (Edwin)

Bachmann, Ingeborg 1926-1973 .... CLC 69
See also CA 93-96; 45-48; CANR 69; DLB 85

Bacon, Francis 1561-1626 .... LC 18, 32
See also CDBLB Before 1660; DLB 151, 236

Bacon, Roger 1214(?)-1294 .... CMLC 14
See also DLB 115

Bacovia, George 1881-1957 .... TCLC 24
See also Bacovia, G.; Vasiliu, Gheorghe
See also DLB 220

Barth, John (Simmons) 1930- ... CLC 1, 2, 3, 5, 7, 9, 10, 14, 27, 51, 89; DAM NOV; SSC 10
    See also AITN 1, 2; CA 1-4R; CABS 1; CANR 5, 23, 49, 64; DLB 2, 227; MTCW 1

Barthelme, Donald 1931-1989 ... CLC 1, 2, 3, 5, 6, 8, 13, 23, 46, 59, 115; DAM NOV; SSC 2
    See also AMWS 4; CA 21-24R; 129; CANR 20, 58; DA3; DLB 2, 234; DLBY 80, 89; MTCW 1, 2; SATA 7; SATA-Obit 62

Barthelme, Frederick 1943- ...... CLC 36, 117
    See also CA 114; 122; CANR 77; DLBY 85; INT 122

Barthes, Roland (Gerard) 1915-1980 .... CLC 24, 83
    See also CA 130; 97-100; CANR 66; MTCW 1, 2

Barzun, Jacques (Martin) 1907- ...... CLC 51
    See also CA 61-64; CANR 22, 95

Bashevis, Isaac
    See Singer, Isaac Bashevis

Bashkirtseff, Marie 1859-1884 .... NCLC 27

Bashō
    See Matsuo Bashō

Basil of Caesaria c. 330-379 .... CMLC 35

Bass, Kingsley B., Jr.
    See Bullins, Ed

Bass, Rick 1958- .... CLC 79, 143
    See also CA 126; CANR 53, 93; DLB 212

Bassani, Giorgio 1916-2000 .... CLC 9
    See also CA 65-68; 190; CANR 33; CWW 2; DLB 128, 177; MTCW 1

Bastian, Ann CLC 70

Bastos, Augusto (Antonio) Roa
    See Roa Bastos, Augusto (Antonio)

Bataille, Georges 1897-1962 .... CLC 29
    See also CA 101; 89-92

Bates, H(erbert) E(rnest) 1905-1974 . CLC 46; DAB; DAM POP; SSC 10
    See also CA 93-96; 45-48; CANR 34; DA3; DLB 162, 191; MTCW 1, 2

Bauchart
    See Camus, Albert

Baudelaire, Charles 1821-1867 . NCLC 6, 29, 55; DA; DAB; DAC; DAM MST, POET; PC 1; SSC 18
    See also AW; DA3

Baudrillard, Jean 1929- .... CLC 60

Baum, L(yman) Frank 1856-1919 ... TCLC 7
    See also CA 108; 133; CLR 15; DLB 22; JRDA; MAICYA; MTCW 1, 2; SATA 18, 100

Baum, Louis F.
    See Baum, L(yman) Frank

Baumbach, Jonathan 1933- .... CLC 6, 23
    See also CA 13-16R; CAAS 5; CANR 12, 66; DLBY 80; INT CANR-12; MTCW 1

Bausch, Richard (Carl) 1945- .... CLC 51
    See also AMWS 7; CA 101; CAAS 14; CANR 43, 61, 87; DLB 130

Baxter, Charles (Morley) 1947- .... CLC 45, 78; DAM POP
    See also CA 57-60; CANR 40, 64; DLB 130; MTCW 2

Baxter, George Owen
    See Faust, Frederick (Schiller)

Baxter, James K(eir) 1926-1972 .... CLC 14
    See also CA 77-80

Baxter, John
    See Hunt, E(verette) Howard, (Jr.)

Bayer, Sylvia
    See Glassco, John

Baynton, Barbara 1857-1929 .... TCLC 57
    See also DLB 230

Beagle, Peter S(oyer) 1939- .... CLC 7, 104
    See also AW; CA 9-12R; CANR 4, 51, 73; DA3; DLBY 80; INT CANR-4; MTCW 1; SATA 60

Bean, Normal
    See Burroughs, Edgar Rice

Beard, Charles A(ustin) 1874-1948 .... TCLC 15
    See also CA 115; 189; DLB 17; SATA 18

Beardsley, Aubrey 1872-1898 .... NCLC 6

Beattie, Ann 1947- ..... CLC 8, 13, 18, 40, 63; DAM NOV, POP; SSC 11
    See also AMWS 5; BEST 90:2; CA 81-84; CANR 53, 73; DA3; DLBY 82; MTCW 1, 2

Beattie, James 1735-1803 .... NCLC 25
    See also DLB 109

Beauchamp, Kathleen Mansfield 1888-1923
    See Mansfield, Katherine
    See also CA 104; 134; DA; DAC; DAM MST; DA3; MTCW 2

Beaumarchais, Pierre-Augustin Caron de 1732-1799 . LC 61; DAM DRAM; DC 4

Beaumont, Francis 1584(?)-1616 .... LC 33; DC 6
    See also CDBLB Before 1660; DLB 58, 121

Beauvoir, Simone (Lucie Ernestine Marie Bertrand) de 1908-1986 .... CLC 1, 2, 4, 8, 14, 31, 44, 50, 71, 124; DA; DAB; DAC; DAM MST, NOV; SSC 35
    See also AW; CA 9-12R; 118; CANR 28, 61; DA3; DLB 72; DLBY 86; MTCW 1, 2

Becker, Carl (Lotus) 1873-1945 ..... TCLC 63
    See also CA 157; DLB 17

Becker, Jurek 1937-1997 .... CLC 7, 19
    See also CA 85-88; 157; CANR 60; CWW 2; DLB 75

Becker, Walter 1950- .... CLC 26

Beckett, Samuel (Barclay) 1906-1989 .. CLC 1, 2, 3, 4, 6, 9, 10, 11, 14, 18, 29, 57, 59, 83; DA; DAB; DAC; DAM DRAM, MST, NOV; SSC 16
    See also AW; BRWS 1; CA 5-8R; 130; CANR 33, 61; CDBLB 1945-1960; DA3; DLB 13, 15, 233; DLBY 90; MTCW 1, 2

Beckford, William 1760-1844 .... NCLC 16
    See also DLB 39,213

Beckman, Gunnel 1910- .... CLC 26
    See also CA 33-36R; CANR 15; CLR 25; MAICYA; SAAS 9; SATA 6

Becque, Henri 1837-1899 .... NCLC 3
    See also DLB 192

Becquer, Gustavo Adolfo 1836-1870
    See also DAM MULT; HLCS 1

Beddoes, Thomas Lovell 1803-1849 .... NCLC 3; DC 15
    See also DLB 96

Bede c. 673-735 .... CMLC 20
    See also DLB 146

Bedford, Donald F.
    See Fearing, Kenneth (Flexner)

Beecher, Catharine Esther 1800-1878 .... NCLC 30
    See also DLB 1

Beecher, John 1904-1980 .... CLC 6
    See also AITN 1; CA 5-8R; 105; CANR 8

Beer, Johann 1655-1700 .... LC 5
    See also DLB 168

Beer, Patricia 1924- .... CLC 58
    See also CA 61-64; 183; CANR 13, 46; DLB 40

Beerbohm, Max
    See Beerbohm, (Henry) Max(imilian)
    See also BRWS 2

Beerbohm, (Henry) Max(imilian) 1872-1956 .... TCLC 1, 24
    See also CA 104; 154; CANR 79; DLB 34, 100

Beer-Hofmann, Richard 1866-1945 .... TCLC 60
    See also CA 160; DLB 81

Begiebing, Robert J(ohn) 1946- .... CLC 70
    See also CA 122; CANR 40, 88

Behan, Brendan 1923-1964 ...... CLC 1, 8, 11, 15, 79; DAM DRAM
    See also BRWS 2; CA 73-76; CANR 33; CDBLB 1945-1960; DLB 13, 233; MTCW 1, 2

Behn, Aphra 1640(?)-1689 .... LC 1, 30, 42; DA; DAB; DAC; DAM DRAM, MST, NOV, POET; DC 4; PC 13
    See also AW; BRWS 3; DA3; DLB 39, 80, 131

Behrman, S(amuel) N(athaniel) 1893-1973 .... CLC 40
    See also CA 13-16; 45-48; CAP 1; DLB 7, 44

Belasco, David 1853-1931 .... TCLC 3
    See also CA 104; 168; DLB 7

Belcheva, Elisaveta 1893-1991 .... CLC 10
    See also Bagryana, Elisaveta

Beldone, Phil "Cheech"
    See Ellison, Harlan (Jay)

Beleno
    See Azuela, Mariano

Belinski, Vissarion Grigoryevich 1811-1848 .... NCLC 5
    See also DLB 198

Belitt, Ben 1911- .... CLC 22
    See also CA 13-16R; CAAS 4; CANR 7, 77; DLB 5

Bell, Gertrude (Margaret Lowthian) 1868-1926 .... TCLC 67
    See also CA 167; DLB 174

Bell, J. Freeman
    See Zangwill, Israel

Bell, James Madison 1826-1902 ... TCLC 43; BLC 1; DAM MULT
    See also BW 1; CA 122; 124; DLB 50

Bell, Madison Smartt 1957- ...... CLC 41, 102
    See also CA 111, 183; CAAE 183; CANR 28, 54, 73; MTCW 1

Bell, Marvin (Hartley) 1937- ...... CLC 8, 31; DAM POET
    See also CA 21-24R; CAAS 14; CANR 59; DLB 5; MTCW 1

Bell, W. L. D.
    See Mencken, H(enry) L(ouis)

Bellamy, Atwood C.
    See Mencken, H(enry) L(ouis)

Bellamy, Edward 1850-1898 ...... NCLC 4, 86
    See also DLB 12

Belli, Gioconda 1949-
    See also CA 152; CWW 2; HLCS 1

Bellin, Edward J.
    See Kuttner, Henry

Belloc, (Joseph) Hilaire (Pierre Sebastien Rene Swanton) 1870-1953 ...... TCLC 7, 18; DAM POET; PC 24
    See also AW 1; CA 106; 152; DLB 19, 100, 141, 174; MTCW 1; SATA 112

Belloc, Joseph Peter Rene Hilaire
    See Belloc, (Joseph) Hilaire (Pierre Sebastien Rene Swanton)

Belloc, Joseph Pierre Hilaire
    See Belloc, (Joseph) Hilaire (Pierre Sebastien Rene Swanton)

Belloc, M. A.
    See Lowndes, Marie Adelaide (Belloc)

Bellow, Saul 1915- . CLC 1, 2, 3, 6, 8, 10, 13, 15, 25, 33, 34, 63, 79; DA; DAB; DAC; DAM MST, NOV, POP; SSC 14
    See also AITN 2; AW; BEST 89:3; CA 5-8R; CABS 1; CANR 29, 53, 95; CDALB 1941-1968; DA3; DLB 2, 28; DLBD 3; DLBY 82; MTCW 1, 2

Braverman, Kate 1950- .... CLC 67
See also CA 89-92

Brecht, (Eugen) Bertolt (Friedrich)
1898-1956 .... **TCLC 1, 6, 13, 35; DA; DAB; DAC; DAM DRAM, MST; DC 3**
See also AW; CA 104; 133; CANR 62; DA3; DLB 56, 124; MTCW 1, 2

Brecht, Eugen Berthold Friedrich
See Brecht, (Eugen) Bertolt (Friedrich)

Bremer, Fredrika 1801-1865 .... **NCLC 11**

Brennan, Christopher John
1870-1932 .... **TCLC 17**
See also CA 117; 188; DLB 230

Brennan, Maeve 1917-1993 .... **CLC 5**
See also CA 81-84; CANR 72

Brent, Linda
See Jacobs, Harriet A(nn)

Brentano, Clemens (Maria)
1778-1842 .... **NCLC 1**
See also DLB 90

Brent of Bin Bin
See Franklin, (Stella Maria Sarah) Miles (Lampe)

Brenton, Howard 1942- .... **CLC 31**
See also CA 69-72; CANR 33, 67; DLB 13; MTCW 1

Breslin, James 1935-1996
See Breslin, Jimmy
See also CA 73-76; CANR 31, 75; DAM NOV; MTCW 1, 2

Breslin, Jimmy CLC 4, 43
See also Breslin, James
See also AITN 1; DLB 185; MTCW 2

Bresson, Robert 1901(?)-1999 .... **CLC 16**
See also CA 110; 187; CANR 49

Breton, Andre 1896-1966 .. **CLC 2, 9, 15, 54; PC 15**
See also CA 19-20; 25-28R; CANR 40, 60; CAP 2; DLB 65; MTCW 1, 2

Breytenbach, Breyten 1939(?)- .. **CLC 23, 37, 126; DAM POET**
See also CA 113; 129; CANR 61; CWW 2; DLB 225

Bridgers, Sue Ellen 1942- .... **CLC 26**
See also AAYA 8; AW; CA 65-68; CANR 11, 36; CLR 18; DLB 52; JRDA; MAICYA; SAAS 1; SATA 22, 90; SATA-Essay 109

Bridges, Robert (Seymour)
1844-1930 ... **TCLC 1; DAM POET; PC 28**
See also CA 104; 152; CDBLB 1890-1914; DLB 19, 98

Bridie, James TCLC 3
See also Mavor, Osborne Henry
See also DLB 10

Brin, David 1950- .... **CLC 34**
See also AAYA 21; CA 102; CANR 24, 70; INT CANR-24; SATA 65; SCFW 2

Brink, Andre (Philippus) 1935- . **CLC 18, 36, 106**
See also CA 104; CANR 39, 62; DLB 225; INT 103; MTCW 1, 2

Brinsmead, H(esba) F(ay) 1922- ...... **CLC 21**
See also CA 21-24R; CANR 10; CLR 47; MAICYA; SAAS 5; SATA 18, 78

Brittain, Vera (Mary) 1893(?)-1970 . **CLC 23**
See also CA 13-16; 25-28R; CANR 58; CAP 1; DLB 191; MTCW 1, 2

Broch, Hermann 1886-1951 .... **TCLC 20**
See also CA 117; DLB 85, 124

Brock, Rose
See Hansen, Joseph
See also GLL 1

Brodkey, Harold (Roy) 1930-1996 ... **CLC 56**
See also CA 111; 151; CANR 71; DLB 130

Brodsky, Iosif Alexandrovich 1940-1996
See Brodsky, Joseph
See also AITN 1; CA 41-44R; 151; CANR 37; DAM POET; DA3; MTCW 1, 2

Brodsky, Joseph CLC 4, 6, 13, 36, 100; PC 9
See also Brodsky, Iosif Alexandrovich
See also CWW 2; MTCW 1

Brodsky, Michael (Mark) 1948- .... **CLC 19**
See also CA 102; CANR 18, 41, 58

Brodzki, Bella ed. CLC 65

Brome, Richard 1590(?)-1652 .... **LC 61**
See also DLB 58

Bromell, Henry 1947- .... **CLC 5**
See also CA 53-56; CANR 9

Bromfield, Louis (Brucker)
1896-1956 .... **TCLC 11**
See also CA 107; 155; DLB 4, 9, 86

Broner, E(sther) M(asserman)
1930- .... **CLC 19**
See also CA 17-20R; CANR 8, 25, 72; DLB 28

Bronk, William (M.) 1918-1999 .... **CLC 10**
See also CA 89-92; 177; CANR 23; DLB 165

Bronstein, Lev Davidovich
See Trotsky, Leon

Brontë, Anne 1820-1849 .... **NCLC 4, 71**
See also DA3; DLB 21, 199

Brontë, Charlotte 1816-1855 ...... **NCLC 3, 8, 33, 58; DA; DAB; DAC; DAM MST, NOV**
See also AAYA 17; AW; CDBLB 1832-1890; DA3; DLB 21, 159, 199

Brontë, Emily (Jane) 1818-1848 ... **NCLC 16, 35; DA; DAB; DAC; DAM MST, NOV, POET; PC 8**
See also AAYA 17; AW; CDBLB 1832-1890; DA3; DLB 21, 32, 199

Brontës
See Bront

Brooke, Frances 1724-1789 .... **LC 6, 48**
See also DLB 39, 99

Brooke, Henry 1703(?)-1783 .... **LC 1**
See also DLB 39

Brooke, Rupert (Chawner)
1887-1915 .... **TCLC 2, 7; DA; DAB; DAC; DAM MST, POET; PC 24**
See also AW; BRWS 3; CA 104; 132; CANR 61; CDBLB 1914-1945; DLB 19; GLL 2; MTCW 1, 2

Brooke-Haven, P.
See Wodehouse, P(elham) G(renville)

Brooke-Rose, Christine 1926(?)- ...... **CLC 40**
See also BRWS 4; CA 13-16R; CANR 58; DLB 14, 231

Brookner, Anita 1928- . **CLC 32, 34, 51, 136; DAB; DAM POP**
See also BRWS 4; CA 114; 120; CANR 37, 56, 87; DA3; DLB 194; DLBY 87; MTCW 1, 2

Brooks, Cleanth 1906-1994 . **CLC 24, 86, 110**
See also CA 17-20R; 145; CANR 33, 35; DLB 63; DLBY 94; INT CANR-35; MTCW 1, 2

Brooks, George
See Baum, L(yman) Frank

Brooks, Gwendolyn (Elizabeth)
1917-2000 .. **CLC 1, 2, 4, 5, 15, 49, 125; BLC 1; DA; DAC; DAM MST, MULT, POET; PC 7**
See also AAYA 20; AITN 1; AMWS 3; AW; BW 2, 3; CA 1-4R; 190; CANR 1, 27, 52, 75; CDALB 1941-1968; CLR 27; DA3; DLB 5, 76, 165; MTCW 1, 2; SATA 6

Brooks, Mel CLC 12
See also Kaminsky, Melvin
See also AAYA 13; DLB 26

Brooks, Peter 1938- .... **CLC 34**
See also CA 45-48; CANR 1

Brooks, Van Wyck 1886-1963 .... **CLC 29**
See also CA 1-4R; CANR 6; DLB 45, 63, 103

Brophy, Brigid (Antonia)
1929-1995 .... **CLC 6, 11, 29, 105**
See also CA 5-8R; 149; CAAS 4; CANR 25, 53; DA3; DLB 14; MTCW 1, 2

Brosman, Catharine Savage 1934- ..... **CLC 9**
See also CA 61-64; CANR 21, 46

Brossard, Nicole 1943- .... **CLC 115**
See also CA 122; CAAS 16; CCA 1; CWW 2; DLB 53; GLL 2

Brother Antoninus
See Everson, William (Oliver)

The Brothers Quay
See Quay, Stephen; Quay, Timothy

Broughton, T(homas) Alan 1936- ..... **CLC 19**
See also CA 45-48; CANR 2, 23, 48

Broumas, Olga 1949- .... **CLC 10, 73**
See also CA 85-88; CANR 20, 69; GLL 2

Broun, Heywood 1888-1939 .... **TCLC 104**
See also DLB 29, 171

Brown, Alan 1950- .... **CLC 99**
See also CA 156

Brown, Charles Brockden
1771-1810 .... **NCLC 22, 74**
See also AMWS 1; CDALB 1640-1865; DLB 37, 59, 73

Brown, Christy 1932-1981 .... **CLC 63**
See also CA 105; 104; CANR 72; DLB 14

Brown, Claude 1937- .... **CLC 30; BLC 1; DAM MULT**
See also AAYA 7; BW 1, 3; CA 73-76; CANR 81

Brown, Dee (Alexander) 1908- . **CLC 18, 47; DAM POP**
See also AAYA 30; CA 13-16R; CAAS 6; CANR 11, 45, 60; DA3; DLBY 80; MTCW 1, 2; SATA 5, 110; TCWW 2

Brown, George
See Wertmueller, Lina

Brown, George Douglas
1869-1902 .... **TCLC 28**
See also CA 162

Brown, George Mackay 1921-1996 ... **CLC 5, 48, 100**
See also CA 21-24R; 151; CAAS 6; CANR 12, 37, 67; DLB 14, 27, 139; MTCW 1; SATA 35

Brown, (William) Larry 1951- .... **CLC 73**
See also CA 130; 134; INT 133

Brown, Moses
See Barrett, William (Christopher)

Brown, Rita Mae 1944- .... **CLC 18, 43, 79; DAM NOV, POP**
See also CA 45-48; CANR 2, 11, 35, 62, 95; DA3; INT CANR-11; MTCW 1, 2

Brown, Roderick (Langmere) Haig-
See Haig-Brown, Roderick (Langmere)

Brown, Rosellen 1939- .... **CLC 32**
See also CA 77-80; CAAS 10; CANR 14, 44

Brown, Sterling Allen 1901-1989 ...... **CLC 1, 23, 59; BLC 1; DAM MULT, POET**
See also BW 1, 3; CA 85-88; 127; CANR 26; DA3; DLB 48, 51, 63; MTCW 1, 2

Brown, Will
See Ainsworth, William Harrison

Brown, William Wells 1815-1884 ... **NCLC 2, 89; BLC 1; DAM MULT; DC 1**
See also DLB 3, 50

Browne, (Clyde) Jackson 1948(?)- ... **CLC 21**
See also CA 120

Browning, Elizabeth Barrett
1806-1861 ...... **NCLC 1, 16, 61, 66; DA; DAB; DAC; DAM MST, POET; PC 6**
See also AW; CDBLB 1832-1890; DA3; DLB 32, 199

Browning, Robert 1812-1889 . **NCLC 19, 79; DA; DAB; DAC; DAM MST, POET; PC 2**
See also AW; CDBLB 1832-1890; DA3; DLB 32, 163

Browning, Tod 1882-1962 .... **CLC 16**
See also CA 141; 117

Brownson, Orestes Augustus
1803-1876 .... **NCLC 50**
See also DLB 1, 59, 73

Bruccoli, Matthew J(oseph) 1931- ... **CLC 34**
See also CA 9-12R; CANR 7, 87; DLB 103

Bruce, Lenny CLC 21
See also Schneider, Leonard Alfred

Bruin, John
See Brutus, Dennis

Brulard, Henri
See Stendhal

Brulls, Christian
See Simenon, Georges (Jacques Christian)

Brunner, John (Kilian Houston)
1934-1995 .... **CLC 8, 10; DAM POP**
See also CA 1-4R; 149; CAAS 8; CANR 2, 37; MTCW 1, 2; SCFW 2

Bruno, Giordano 1548-1600 .... **LC 27**

Brutus, Dennis 1924- .... **CLC 43; BLC 1; DAM MULT, POET; PC 24**
See also BW 2, 3; CA 49-52; CAAS 14; CANR 2, 27, 42, 81; DLB 117, 225

Bryan, C(ourtlandt) D(ixon) B(arnes)
1936- .... **CLC 29**
See also CA 73-76; CANR 13, 68; DLB 185; INT CANR-13

Bryan, Michael
See Moore, Brian
See also CCA 1

Bryan, William Jennings
1860-1925 .... **TCLC 99**

Bryant, William Cullen 1794-1878 . **NCLC 6, 46; DA; DAB; DAC; DAM MST, POET; PC 20**
See also AMWS 1; CDALB 1640-1865; DLB 3, 43, 59, 189

Bryusov, Valery Yakovlevich
1873-1924 .... **TCLC 10**
See also CA 107; 155

Buchan, John 1875-1940 .... **TCLC 41; DAB; DAM POP**
See also AW 2; CA 108; 145; DLB 34, 70, 156; MTCW 1

Buchanan, George 1506-1582 .... **LC 4**
See also DLB 152

Buchanan, Robert 1841-1901 .... **TCLC 107**
See also CA 179; DLB 18, 35

Buchheim, Lothar-Guenther 1918- .... **CLC 6**
See also CA 85-88

Büchner, (Karl) Georg 1813-1837 . **NCLC 26**

Buchwald, Art(hur) 1925- .... **CLC 33**
See also AITN 1; CA 5-8R; CANR 21, 67; MTCW 1, 2; SATA 10

Buck, Pearl S(ydenstricker)
1892-1973 .... **CLC 7, 11, 18, 127; DA; DAB; DAC; DAM MST, NOV**
See also AITN 1; AMWS 2; CA 1-4R; 41-44R; CANR 1, 34; CDALBS; DA3; DLB 9, 102; MTCW 1, 2; SATA 1, 25

Buckler, Ernest 1908-1984 .... **CLC 13; DAC; DAM MST**
See also CA 11-12; 114; CAP 1; CCA 1; DLB 68; SATA 47

Buckley, Vincent (Thomas)
1925-1988 .... **CLC 57**
See also CA 101

Buckley, William F(rank), Jr. 1925- . **CLC 7, 18, 37; DAM POP**
See also AITN 1; CA 1-4R; CANR 1, 24, 53, 93; DA3; DLB 137; DLBY 80; INT CANR-24; MTCW 1, 2

Buechner, (Carl) Frederick 1926- . **CLC 2, 4, 6, 9; DAM NOV**
See also CA 13-16R; CANR 11, 39, 64; DLBY 80; INT CANR-11; MTCW 1, 2

Buell, John (Edward) 1927- .... **CLC 10**
See also CA 1-4R; CANR 71; DLB 53

Buero Vallejo, Antonio 1916-2000 ... **CLC 15, 46, 139**
See also CA 106; 189; CANR 24, 49, 75; HW 1; MTCW 1, 2

Bufalino, Gesualdo 1920(?)-1990 ...... **CLC 74**
See also CWW 2; DLB 196

Bugayev, Boris Nikolayevich
1880-1934 .... **TCLC 7; PC 11**
See also Bely, Andrey
See also CA 104; 165; MTCW 1

Bukowski, Charles 1920-1994 ... **CLC 2, 5, 9, 41, 82, 108; DAM NOV, POET; PC 18; SSC 45**
See also CA 17-20R; 144; CANR 40, 62; DA3; DLB 5, 130, 169; MTCW 1, 2

Bulgakov, Mikhail (Afanas'evich)
1891-1940 . **TCLC 2, 16; DAM DRAM, NOV; SSC 18**
See also CA 105; 152

Bulgya, Alexander Alexandrovich
1901-1956 .... **TCLC 53**
See also Fadeyev, Alexander
See also CA 117; 181

Bullins, Ed 1935- .... **CLC 1, 5, 7; BLC 1; DAM DRAM, MULT; DC 6**
See also BW 2, 3; CA 49-52; CAAS 16; CANR 24, 46, 73; DLB 7, 38; MTCW 1, 2

Bulwer-Lytton, Edward (George Earle Lytton) 1803-1873 .... **NCLC 1, 45**
See also DLB 21

Bunin, Ivan Alexeyevich
1870-1953 .... **TCLC 6; SSC 5**
See also CA 104

Bunting, Basil 1900-1985 ..... **CLC 10, 39, 47; DAM POET**
See also CA 53-56; 115; CANR 7; DLB 20

Bunuel, Luis 1900-1983 .. **CLC 16, 80; DAM MULT; HLC 1**
See also CA 101; 110; CANR 32, 77; HW 1

Bunyan, John 1628-1688 ... **LC 4; DA; DAB; DAC; DAM MST**
See also AW; CDBLB 1660-1789; DLB 39

Buravsky, Alexandr CLC 59

Burckhardt, Jacob (Christoph)
1818-1897 .... **NCLC 49**

Burford, Eleanor
See Hibbert, Eleanor Alice Burford

Burgess, Anthony CLC 1, 2, 4, 5, 8, 10, 13, 15, 22, 40, 62, 81, 94; DAB
See also Wilson, John (Anthony) Burgess
See also AAYA 25; AITN 1; AW; BRWS 1; CDBLB 1960 to Present; DLB 14, 194; DLBY 98; MTCW 1

Burke, Edmund 1729(?)-1797 .... **LC 7, 36; DA; DAB; DAC; DAM MST**
See also AW; DA3; DLB 104

Burke, Kenneth (Duva) 1897-1993 ... **CLC 2, 24**
See also CA 5-8R; 143; CANR 39, 74; DLB 45, 63; MTCW 1, 2

Burke, Leda
See Garnett, David

Burke, Ralph
See Silverberg, Robert

Burke, Thomas 1886-1945 .... **TCLC 63**
See also CA 113; 155; DLB 197

Burney, Fanny 1752-1840 .... **NCLC 12, 54**
See also BRWS 3; DLB 39

Burney, Frances
See Burney, Fanny

Burns, Robert 1759-1796 . **LC 3, 29, 40; DA; DAB; DAC; DAM MST, POET; PC 6**
See also AW; CDBLB 1789-1832; DA3; DLB 109

Burns, Tex
See L'Amour, Louis (Dearborn)
See also TCWW 2

Burnshaw, Stanley 1906- .... **CLC 3, 13, 44**
See also CA 9-12R; DLB 48; DLBY 97

Burr, Anne 1937- .... **CLC 6**
See also CA 25-28R

Burroughs, Edgar Rice 1875-1950 . **TCLC 2, 32; DAM NOV**
See also AAYA 11; AW; CA 104; 132; DA3; DLB 8; MTCW 1, 2; SATA 41

Burroughs, William S(eward)
1914-1997 .. **CLC 1, 2, 5, 15, 22, 42, 75, 109; DA; DAB; DAC; DAM MST, NOV, POP**
See also Lee, William; Lee, Willy
See also AITN 2; AMWS 3; AW; CA 9-12R; 160; CANR 20, 52; DA3; DLB 2, 8, 16, 152; DLBY 81, 97; MTCW 1, 2

Burton, SirRichard F(rancis)
1821-1890 .... **NCLC 42**
See also DLB 55, 166, 184

Busch, Frederick 1941- .... **CLC 7, 10, 18, 47**
See also CA 33-36R; CAAS 1; CANR 45, 73, 92; DLB 6

Bush, Ronald 1946- .... **CLC 34**
See also CA 136

Bustos, F(rancisco)
See Borges, Jorge Luis

Bustos Domecq, H(onorio)
See Bioy Casares, Adolfo; Borges, Jorge Luis

Butler, Octavia E(stelle) 1947- .... **CLC 38, 121; BLCS; DAM MULT, POP**
See also AAYA 18; AW; BW 2, 3; CA 73-76; CANR 12, 24, 38, 73; CLR 65; DA3; DLB 33; MTCW 1, 2; SATA 84

Butler, Robert Olen, (Jr.) 1945- ...... **CLC 81; DAM POP**
See also CA 112; CANR 66; DLB 173; INT 112; MTCW 1

Butler, Samuel 1612-1680 .... **LC 16, 43**
See also DLB 101, 126

Butler, Samuel 1835-1902 . **TCLC 1, 33; DA; DAB; DAC; DAM MST, NOV**
See also AW; BRWS 2; CA 143; CDBLB 1890-1914; DA3; DLB 18, 57, 174

Butler, Walter C.
See Faust, Frederick (Schiller)

Butor, Michel (Marie Francois)
1926- .... **CLC 1, 3, 8, 11, 15**
See also CA 9-12R; CANR 33, 66; DLB 83; MTCW 1, 2

Butts, Mary 1890(?)-1937 .... **TCLC 77**
See also CA 148

Buzo, Alexander (John) 1944- .... **CLC 61**
See also CA 97-100; CANR 17, 39, 69

Buzzati, Dino 1906-1972 .... **CLC 36**
See also CA 160; 33-36R; DLB 177

Byars, Betsy (Cromer) 1928- .... **CLC 35**
See also AAYA 19; CA 33-36R; CAAE 183; CANR 18, 36, 57; CLR 1, 16; DLB 52; INT CANR-18; JRDA; MAICYA; MTCW 1; SAAS 1; SATA 4, 46, 80; SATA-Essay 108

Byatt, A(ntonia) S(usan Drabble)
1936- ...... **CLC 19, 65, 136; DAM NOV, POP**
See also BRWS 4; CA 13-16R; CANR 13, 33, 50, 75, 96; DA3; DLB 14, 194; MTCW 1, 2

Byrne, David 1952- .... **CLC 26**
See also CA 127

Carr, John Dickson 1906-1977 .... **CLC 3**
See also Fairbairn, Roger
See also CA 49-52; 69-72; CANR 3, 33, 60; MTCW 1, 2

Carr, Philippa
See Hibbert, Eleanor Alice Burford

Carr, Virginia Spencer 1929- .... **CLC 34**
See also CA 61-64; DLB 111

Carrere, Emmanuel 1957- .... **CLC 89**

Carrier, Roch 1937- .... **CLC 13, 78; DAC; DAM MST**
See also CA 130; CANR 61; CCA 1; DLB 53; SATA 105

Carroll, James P. 1943(?)- .... **CLC 38**
See also CA 81-84; CANR 73; MTCW 1

Carroll, Jim 1951- .... **CLC 35, 143**
See also AAYA 17; CA 45-48; CANR 42

Carroll, Lewis NCLC 2, 53; PC 18
See also Dodgson, Charles Lutwidge
See also AAYA 39; AW; CDBLB 1832-1890; CLR 2, 18; DLB 18, 163, 178; DLBY 98; JRDA

Carroll, Paul Vincent 1900-1968 ...... **CLC 10**
See also CA 9-12R; 25-28R; DLB 10

Carruth, Hayden 1921- ..... **CLC 4, 7, 10, 18, 84; PC 10**
See also CA 9-12R; CANR 4, 38, 59; DLB 5, 165; INT CANR-4; MTCW 1, 2; SATA 47

Carson, Rachel Louise 1907-1964 ... **CLC 71; DAM POP**
See also CA 77-80; CANR 35; DA3; MTCW 1, 2; SATA 23

Carter, Angela (Olive) 1940-1992 ...... **CLC 5, 41, 76; SSC 13**
See also BRWS 3; CA 53-56; 136; CANR 12, 36, 61; DA3; DLB 14, 207; MTCW 1, 2; SATA 66; SATA-Obit 70

Carter, Nick
See Smith, Martin Cruz

Carver, Raymond 1938-1988 ..... **CLC 22, 36, 53, 55, 126; DAM NOV; SSC 8**
See also AMWS 3; CA 33-36R; 126; CANR 17, 34, 61; DA3; DLB 130; DLBY 84, 88; MTCW 1, 2; TCWW 2

Cary, Elizabeth, Lady Falkland 1585-1639 .... **LC 30**

Cary, (Arthur) Joyce (Lunel) 1888-1957 .... **TCLC 1, 29**
See also CA 104; 164; CDBLB 1914-1945; DLB 15, 100; MTCW 2

Casanova de Seingalt, Giovanni Jacopo 1725-1798 .... **LC 13**

Casares, Adolfo Bioy
See Bioy Casares, Adolfo

Casely-Hayford, J(oseph) E(phraim) 1866-1903 ...... **TCLC 24; BLC 1; DAM MULT**
See also BW 2; CA 123; 152

Casey, John (Dudley) 1939- .... **CLC 59**
See also BEST 90:2; CA 69-72; CANR 23

Casey, Michael 1947- .... **CLC 2**
See also CA 65-68; DLB 5

Casey, Patrick
See Thurman, Wallace (Henry)

Casey, Warren (Peter) 1935-1988 .... **CLC 12**
See also CA 101; 127; INT 101

Casona, Alejandro CLC 49
See also Alvarez, Alejandro Rodriguez

Cassavetes, John 1929-1989 .... **CLC 20**
See also CA 85-88; 127; CANR 82

Cassian, Nina 1924- .... **PC 17**
See also CWW 2

Cassill, R(onald) V(erlin) 1919- ... **CLC 4, 23**
See also CA 9-12R; CAAS 1; CANR 7, 45; DLB 6

Cassiodorus, Flavius Magnus c. 490(?)-c. 583(?) .... **CMLC 43**

Cassirer, Ernst 1874-1945 .... **TCLC 61**
See also CA 157

Cassity, (Allen) Turner 1929- .... **CLC 6, 42**
See also CA 17-20R; CAAS 8; CANR 11; DLB 105

Castaneda, Carlos (Cesar Aranha) 1931(?)-1998 .... **CLC 12, 119**
See also CA 25-28R; CANR 32, 66; HW 1; MTCW 1

Castedo, Elena 1937- .... **CLC 65**
See also CA 132

Castedo-Ellerman, Elena
See Castedo, Elena

Castellanos, Rosario 1925-1974 .... **CLC 66; DAM MULT; HLC 1; SSC 39**
See also CA 131; 53-56; CANR 58; DLB 113; HW 1; MTCW 1

Castelvetro, Lodovico 1505-1571 .... **LC 12**

Castiglione, Baldassare 1478-1529 ...... **LC 12**

Castiglione, Baldesar
See Castiglione, Baldassare

Castle, Robert
See Hamilton, Edmond

Castro (Ruz), Fidel 1926(?)-
See also CA 110; 129; CANR 81; DAM MULT; HLC 1; HW 2

Castro, Guillen de 1569-1631 .... **LC 19**

Castro, Rosalia de 1837-1885 ... **NCLC 3, 78; DAM MULT**

Cather, Willa
See Cather, Willa Sibert
See also TCWW 2

Cather, Willa Sibert 1873-1947 ...... **TCLC 1, 11, 31, 99; DA; DAB; DAC; DAM MST, NOV; SSC 2**
See also Cather, Willa
See also AAYA 24; AW; CA 104; 128; CDALB 1865-1917; DA3; DLB 9, 54, 78; DLBD 1; MTCW 1, 2; SATA 30

Catherine, Saint 1347-1380 .... **CMLC 27**

Cato, Marcus Porcius 234B.C.-149B.C. .... **CMLC 21**
See also DLB 211

Catton, (Charles) Bruce 1899-1978 . **CLC 35**
See also AITN 1; CA 5-8R; 81-84; CANR 7, 74; DLB 17; SATA 2; SATA-Obit 24

Catullus c. 84B.C.-c. 54B.C. .... **CMLC 18**
See also DLB 211

Cauldwell, Frank
See King, Francis (Henry)

Caunitz, William J. 1933-1996 .... **CLC 34**
See also BEST 89:3; CA 125; 130; 152; CANR 73; INT 130

Causley, Charles (Stanley) 1917- .... **CLC 7**
See also CA 9-12R; CANR 5, 35, 94; CLR 30; DLB 27; MTCW 1; SATA 3, 66

Caute, (John) David 1936- .... **CLC 29; DAM NOV**
See also CA 1-4R; CAAS 4; CANR 1, 33, 64; DLB 14, 231

Cavafy, C(onstantine) P(eter) TCLC 2, 7; DAM POET
See also Kavafis, Konstantinos Petrou
See also CA 148; DA3; MTCW 1

Cavallo, Evelyn
See Spark, Muriel (Sarah)

Cavanna, Betty CLC 12
See also Harrison, Elizabeth Cavanna
See also JRDA; MAICYA; SAAS 4; SATA 1, 30

Cavendish, Margaret Lucas 1623-1673 .... **LC 30**
See also DLB 131

Caxton, William 1421(?)-1491(?) .... **LC 17**
See also DLB 170

Cayer, D. M.
See Duffy, Maureen

Cayrol, Jean 1911- .... **CLC 11**
See also CA 89-92; DLB 83

Cela, Camilo Jose 1916- .... **CLC 4, 13, 59, 122; DAM MULT; HLC 1**
See also BEST 90:2; CA 21-24R; CAAS 10; CANR 21, 32, 76; DLBY 89; HW 1; MTCW 1, 2

Celan, Paul CLC 10, 19, 53, 82; PC 10
See also Antschel, Paul
See also DLB 69

Celine, Louis-Ferdinand CLC 1, 3, 4, 7, 9, 15, 47, 124
See also Destouches, Louis-Ferdinand
See also DLB 72

Cellini, Benvenuto 1500-1571 .... **LC 7**

Cendrars, Blaise CLC 18, 106
See also Sauser-Hall, Frederic

Centlivre, Susanna 1669(?)-1723 .... **LC 65**
See also DLB 84

Cernuda (y Bidon), Luis 1902-1963 .... **CLC 54; DAM POET**
See also CA 131; 89-92; DLB 134; GLL 1; HW 1

Cervantes, Lorna Dee 1954-
See also CA 131; CANR 80; DLB 82; HLCS 1; HW 1

Cervantes (Saavedra), Miguel de 1547-1616 .. **LC 6, 23; DA; DAB; DAC; DAM MST, NOV; SSC 12**
See also AW

Cesaire, Aime (Fernand) 1913- . **CLC 19, 32, 112; BLC 1; DAM MULT, POET; PC 25**
See also BW 2, 3; CA 65-68; CANR 24, 43, 81; DA3; MTCW 1, 2

Chabon, Michael 1963- .... **CLC 55**
See also CA 139; CANR 57, 96

Chabrol, Claude 1930- .... **CLC 16**
See also CA 110

Challans, Mary 1905-1983
See Renault, Mary
See also CA 81-84; 111; CANR 74; DA3; MTCW 2; SATA 23; SATA-Obit 36

Challis, George
See Faust, Frederick (Schiller)
See also TCWW 2

Chambers, Aidan 1934- .... **CLC 35**
See also AAYA 27; AW; CA 25-28R; CANR 12, 31, 58; JRDA; MAICYA; SAAS 12; SATA 1, 69, 108

Chambers, James 1948-
See Cliff, Jimmy
See also CA 124

Chambers, Jessie
See Lawrence, D(avid) H(erbert Richards)
See also GLL 1

Chambers, Robert W(illiam) 1865-1933 .... **TCLC 41**
See also CA 165; DLB 202; SATA 107

Chamisso, Adelbert von 1781-1838 .... **NCLC 82**
See also DLB 90

Chandler, Raymond (Thornton) 1888-1959 .... **TCLC 1, 7; SSC 23**
See also AAYA 25; AMWS 4; CA 104; 129; CANR 60; CDALB 1929-1941; DA3; DLB 226; DLBD 6; MTCW 1, 2

Chang, Eileen 1921-1995 .... **SSC 28**
See also CA 166; CWW 2

Chang, Jung 1952- .... **CLC 71**
See also CA 142

Chang Ai-Ling
See Chang, Eileen

Channing, William Ellery 1780-1842 .... **NCLC 17**
See also DLB 1, 59, 235

Chao, Patricia 1955- .... **CLC 119**
  See also CA 163
Chaplin, Charles Spencer
    1889-1977 .... **CLC 16**
  See also Chaplin, Charlie
  See also CA 81-84; 73-76
Chaplin, Charlie
  See Chaplin, Charles Spencer
  See also DLB 44
Chapman, George 1559(?)-1634 .... **LC 22;
    DAM DRAM**
  See also DLB 62, 121
Chapman, Graham 1941-1989 .... **CLC 21**
  See also Monty Python
  See also CA 116; 129; CANR 35, 95
Chapman, John Jay 1862-1933 .... **TCLC 7**
  See also CA 104
Chapman, Lee
  See Bradley, Marion Zimmer
  See also GLL 1
Chapman, Walker
  See Silverberg, Robert
Chappell, Fred (Davis) 1936- ..... **CLC 40, 78**
  See also CA 5-8R; CAAS 4; CANR 8, 33,
    67; DLB 6, 105
Char, Rene(-Emile) 1907-1988 .... **CLC 9, 11,
    14, 55; DAM POET**
  See also CA 13-16R; 124; CANR 32;
    MTCW 1, 2
Charby, Jay
  See Ellison, Harlan (Jay)
Chardin, Pierre Teilhard de
  See Teilhard de Chardin, (Marie Joseph)
    Pierre
Charlemagne 742-814 .... **CMLC 37**
Charles I 1600-1649 .... **LC 13**
Charriere, Isabelle de 1740-1805 .. **NCLC 66**
Charyn, Jerome 1937- .... **CLC 5, 8, 18**
  See also CA 5-8R; CAAS 1; CANR 7, 61;
    DLBY 83; MTCW 1
Chase, Adam
  See Marlowe, Stephen
Chase, Mary (Coyle) 1907-1981 .... **DC 1**
  See also CA 77-80; 105; DLB 228; SATA
    17; SATA-Obit 29
Chase, Mary Ellen 1887-1973 .... **CLC 2**
  See also CA 13-16; 41-44R; CAP 1; SATA
    10
Chase, Nicholas
  See Hyde, Anthony
  See also CCA 1
Chateaubriand, François Rene de
    1768-1848 .... **NCLC 3**
  See also DLB 119
Chatterje, Sarat Chandra 1876-1936(?)
  See Chatterji, Saratchandra
  See also CA 109
Chatterji, Bankim Chandra
    1838-1894 .... **NCLC 19**
Chatterji, Saratchandra **TCLC 13**
  See also Chatterje, Sarat Chandra
  See also CA 186
Chatterton, Thomas 1752-1770 ..... **LC 3, 54;
    DAM POET**
  See also DLB 109
Chatwin, (Charles) Bruce
    1940-1989 . **CLC 28, 57, 59; DAM POP**
  See also AAYA 4; BEST 90:1; BRWS 4;
    CA 85-88; 127; DLB 194, 204
Chaucer, Daniel
  See Ford, Ford Madox
Chaucer, Geoffrey 1340(?)-1400 .. **LC 17, 56;
    DA; DAB; DAC; DAM MST, POET;
    PC 19**
  See also AW; CDBLB Before 1660; DA3;
    DLB 146

Chavez, Denise (Elia) 1948-
  See also CA 131; CANR 56, 81; DAM
    MULT; DLB 122; HLC 1; HW 1, 2;
    MTCW 2
Chaviaras, Strates 1935-
  See Haviaras, Stratis
  See also CA 105
Chayefsky, Paddy **CLC 23**
  See also Chayefsky, Sidney
  See also DLB 7, 44; DLBY 81
Chayefsky, Sidney 1923-1981
  See Chayefsky, Paddy
  See also CA 9-12R; 104; CANR 18; DAM
    DRAM
Chedid, Andree 1920- .... **CLC 47**
  See also CA 145; CANR 95
Cheever, John 1912-1982 ..... **CLC 3, 7, 8, 11,
    15, 25, 64; DA; DAB; DAC; DAM
    MST, NOV, POP; SSC 1, 38**
  See also AMWS 1; AW; CA 5-8R; 106;
    CABS 1; CANR 5, 27, 76; CDALB 1941-
    1968; DA3; DLB 2, 102, 227; DLBY 80,
    82; INT CANR-5; MTCW 1, 2
Cheever, Susan 1943- .... **CLC 18, 48**
  See also CA 103; CANR 27, 51, 92; DLBY
    82; INT CANR-27
Chekhonte, Antosha
  See Chekhov, Anton (Pavlovich)
Chekhov, Anton (Pavlovich)
    1860-1904 .... **TCLC 3, 10, 31, 55, 96;
    DA; DAB; DAC; DAM DRAM, MST;
    DC 9; SSC 2, 28, 41**
  See also AW; CA 104; 124; DA3; SATA 90
Cheney, Lynne V. 1941- .... **CLC 70**
  See also CA 89-92; CANR 58
Chernyshevsky, Nikolay Gavrilovich
    1828-1889 .... **NCLC 1**
  See also DLB 238
Cherry, Carolyn Janice 1942-
  See Cherryh, C. J.
  See also AW; CA 65-68; CANR 10
Cherryh, C. J. **CLC 35**
  See also Cherry, Carolyn Janice
  See also AAYA 24; DLBY 80; SATA 93
Chesnutt, Charles W(addell)
    1858-1932 .. **TCLC 5, 39; BLC 1; DAM
    MULT; SSC 7**
  See also BW 1, 3; CA 106; 125; CANR 76;
    DLB 12, 50, 78; MTCW 1, 2
Chester, Alfred 1929(?)-1971 .... **CLC 49**
  See also CA 33-36R; DLB 130
Chesterton, G(ilbert) K(eith)
    1874-1936 . **TCLC 1, 6, 64; DAM NOV,
    POET; PC 28; SSC 1**
  See also CA 104; 132; CANR 73; CDBLB
    1914-1945; DLB 10, 19, 34, 70, 98, 149,
    178; MTCW 1, 2; SATA 27
Chiang, Pin-chin 1904-1986
  See Ding Ling
  See also CA 118
Ch'ien Chung-shu 1910- .... **CLC 22**
  See also CA 130; CANR 73; MTCW 1, 2
Chikamatsu Monzaemon 1653-1725 ... **LC 66**
Child, L. Maria
  See Child, Lydia Maria
Child, Lydia Maria 1802-1880 .. **NCLC 6, 73**
  See also DLB 1, 74; SATA 67
Child, Mrs.
  See Child, Lydia Maria
Child, Philip 1898-1978 .... **CLC 19, 68**
  See also CA 13-14; CAP 1; SATA 47
Childers, (Robert) Erskine
    1870-1922 .... **TCLC 65**
  See also CA 113; 153; DLB 70

Childress, Alice 1920-1994 .. **CLC 12, 15, 86,
    96; BLC 1; DAM DRAM, MULT,
    NOV; DC 4**
  See also AAYA 8; AW; BW 2, 3; CA 45-48;
    146; CANR 3, 27, 50, 74; CLR 14; DA3;
    DLB 7, 38; JRDA; MAICYA; MTCW 1,
    2; SATA 7, 48, 81
Chin, Frank (Chew, Jr.) 1940- ...... **CLC 135;
    DAM MULT; DC 7**
  See also CA 33-36R; CANR 71; DLB 206
Chislett, (Margaret) Anne 1943- ...... **CLC 34**
  See also CA 151
Chitty, Thomas Willes 1926- .... **CLC 11**
  See also Hinde, Thomas
  See also CA 5-8R
Chivers, Thomas Holley
    1809-1858 .... **NCLC 49**
  See also DLB 3
Choi, Susan **CLC 119**
Chomette, Rene Lucien 1898-1981
  See Clair, Rene
  See also CA 103
Chomsky, (Avram) Noam 1928- ..... **CLC 132**
  See also CA 17-20R; CANR 28, 62; DA3;
    MTCW 1, 2
Chopin, Kate **TCLC 5, 14; DA; DAB; SSC 8**
  See also Chopin, Katherine
  See also AAYA 33; AMWS 1; AW; CDALB
    1865-1917; DLB 12, 78
Chopin, Katherine 1851-1904
  See Chopin, Kate
  See also CA 104; 122; DAC; DAM MST,
    NOV; DA3
Chretien de Troyes c. 12th cent. - . **CMLC 10**
  See also DLB 208
Christie
  See Ichikawa, Kon
Christie, Agatha (Mary Clarissa)
    1890-1976 .... **CLC 1, 6, 8, 12, 39, 48,
    110; DAB; DAC; DAM NOV**
  See also AAYA 9; AITN 1, 2; AW; BRWS
    2; CA 17-20R; 61-64; CANR 10, 37; CD-
    BLB 1914-1945; DA3; DLB 13, 77;
    MTCW 1, 2; SATA 36
Christie, (Ann) Philippa
  See Pearce, Philippa
  See also CA 5-8R; CANR 4
Christine de Pizan 1365(?)-1431(?) .... **LC 9**
  See also DLB 208
Chubb, Elmer
  See Masters, Edgar Lee
Chulkov, Mikhail Dmitrievich
    1743-1792 .... **LC 2**
  See also DLB 150
Churchill, Caryl 1938- .... **CLC 31, 55; DC 5**
  See also BRWS 4; CA 102; CANR 22, 46;
    DLB 13; MTCW 1
Churchill, Charles 1731-1764 .... **LC 3**
  See also DLB 109
Chute, Carolyn 1947- .... **CLC 39**
  See also CA 123
Ciardi, John (Anthony) 1916-1986 . **CLC 10,
    40, 44, 129; DAM POET**
  See also CA 5-8R; 118; CAAS 2; CANR 5,
    33; CLR 19; DLB 5; DLBY 86; INT
    CANR-5; MAICYA; MTCW 1, 2; SAAS
    26; SATA 1, 65; SATA-Obit 46
Cibber, Colley 1671-1757 .... **LC 66**
  See also DLB 84
Cicero, Marcus Tullius
    106B.C.-43B.C. .... **CMLC 3**
  See also DLB 211
Cimino, Michael 1943- .... **CLC 16**
  See also CA 105
Cioran, E(mil) M. 1911-1995 .... **CLC 64**
  See also CA 25-28R; 149; CANR 91; DLB
    220

Cisneros, Sandra 1954- . **CLC 69, 118; DAM MULT; HLC 1; SSC 32**
See also AAYA 9; AMWS 7; AW; CA 131; CANR 64; DA3; DLB 122, 152; HW 1, 2; MTCW 2

Cixous, Helene 1937- .... **CLC 92**
See also CA 126; CANR 55; CWW 2; DLB 83, 242; MTCW 1, 2

Clair, Rene CLC 20
See also Chomette, Rene Lucien

Clampitt, Amy 1920-1994 .... **CLC 32; PC 19**
See also CA 110; 146; CANR 29, 79; DLB 105

Clancy, Thomas L., Jr. 1947-
See Clancy, Tom
See also CA 125; 131; CANR 62; DA3; DLB 227; INT 131; MTCW 1, 2

Clancy, Tom CLC 45, 112; DAM NOV, POP
See also Clancy, Thomas L., Jr.
See also AAYA 9; BEST 89:1, 90:1; MTCW 2

Clare, John 1793-1864 ... **NCLC 9, 86; DAB; DAM POET; PC 23**
See also DLB 55, 96

Clarin
See Alas (y Urena), Leopoldo (Enrique Garcia)

Clark, Al C.
See Goines, Donald

Clark, (Robert) Brian 1932- .... **CLC 29**
See also CA 41-44R; CANR 67

Clark, Curt
See Westlake, Donald E(dwin)

Clark, Eleanor 1913-1996 .... **CLC 5, 19**
See also CA 9-12R; 151; CANR 41; DLB 6

Clark, J. P.
See Clark Bekedermo, J(ohnson) P(epper)
See also DLB 117

Clark, John Pepper
See Clark Bekedermo, J(ohnson) P(epper)

Clark, M. R.
See Clark, Mavis Thorpe

Clark, Mavis Thorpe 1909- .... **CLC 12**
See also CA 57-60; CANR 8, 37; CLR 30; MAICYA; SAAS 5; SATA 8, 74

Clark, Walter Van Tilburg
1909-1971 .... **CLC 28**
See also CA 9-12R; 33-36R; CANR 63; DLB 9, 206; SATA 8

Clark Bekedermo, J(ohnson) P(epper)
1935- .. **CLC 38; BLC 1; DAM DRAM, MULT; DC 5**
See also Clark, J. P.; Clark, John Pepper
See also BW 1; CA 65-68; CANR 16, 72; MTCW 1

Clarke, Arthur C(harles) 1917- .... **CLC 1, 4, 13, 18, 35, 136; DAM POP; SSC 3**
See also AAYA 4, 33; AW; CA 1-4R; CANR 2, 28, 55, 74; DA3; JRDA; MAICYA; MTCW 1, 2; SATA 13, 70, 115

Clarke, Austin 1896-1974 ... **CLC 6, 9; DAM POET**
See also CA 29-32; 49-52; CAP 2; DLB 10, 20

Clarke, Austin C(hesterfield) 1934- .. **CLC 8, 53; BLC 1; DAC; DAM MULT; SSC 45**
See also BW 1; CA 25-28R; CAAS 16; CANR 14, 32, 68; DLB 53, 125

Clarke, Gillian 1937- .... **CLC 61**
See also CA 106; DLB 40

Clarke, Marcus (Andrew Hislop)
1846-1881 .... **NCLC 19**
See also DLB 230

Clarke, Shirley 1925-1997 .... **CLC 16**
See also CA 189

Clash, The
See Headon, (Nicky) Topper; Jones, Mick; Simonon, Paul; Strummer, Joe

Claudel, Paul (Louis Charles Marie)
1868-1955 .... **TCLC 2, 10**
See also CA 104; 165; DLB 192

Claudius, Matthias 1740-1815 .... **NCLC 75**
See also DLB 97

Clavell, James (duMaresq)
1925-1994 .. **CLC 6, 25, 87; DAM NOV, POP**
See also CA 25-28R; 146; CANR 26, 48; DA3; MTCW 1, 2

Clayman, Gregory CLC 65

Cleaver, (Leroy) Eldridge
1935-1998 . **CLC 30, 119; BLC 1; DAM MULT**
See also AW; BW 1, 3; CA 21-24R; 167; CANR 16, 75; DA3; MTCW 2

Cleese, John (Marwood) 1939- .... **CLC 21**
See also Monty Python
See also CA 112; 116; CANR 35; MTCW 1

Cleishbotham, Jebediah
See Scott, Walter

Cleland, John 1710-1789 .... **LC 2, 48**
See also DLB 39

Clemens, Samuel Langhorne 1835-1910
See Twain, Mark
See also AW 2; CA 104; 135; CDALB 1865-1917; DA; DAB; DAC; DAM MST, NOV; DA3; DLB 11, 12, 23, 64, 74, 186, 189; JRDA; MAICYA; SATA 100

Clement of Alexandria
150(?)-215(?) .... **CMLC 41**

Cleophil
See Congreve, William

Clerihew, E.
See Bentley, E(dmund) C(lerihew)

Clerk, N. W.
See Lewis, C(live) S(taples)

Cliff, Jimmy CLC 21
See also Chambers, James

Cliff, Michelle 1946- .... **CLC 120; BLCS**
See also BW 2; CA 116; CANR 39, 72; DLB 157; GLL 2

Clifton, (Thelma) Lucille 1936- .... **CLC 19, 66; BLC 1; DAM MULT, POET; PC 17**
See also BW 2, 3; CA 49-52; CANR 2, 24, 42, 76; CLR 5; DA3; DLB 5, 41; MAICYA; MTCW 1, 2; SATA 20, 69

Clinton, Dirk
See Silverberg, Robert

Clough, Arthur Hugh 1819-1861 ... **NCLC 27**
See also DLB 32

Clutha, Janet Paterson Frame 1924-
See Frame, Janet
See also CA 1-4R; CANR 2, 36, 76; MTCW 1, 2; SATA 119

Clyne, Terence
See Blatty, William Peter

Cobalt, Martin
See Mayne, William (James Carter)

Cobb, Irvin S(hrewsbury)
1876-1944 .... **TCLC 77**
See also CA 175; DLB 11, 25, 86

Cobbett, William 1763-1835 .... **NCLC 49**
See also DLB 43, 107, 158

Coburn, D(onald) L(ee) 1938- .... **CLC 10**
See also CA 89-92

Cocteau, Jean (Maurice Eugene Clement)
1889-1963 .... **CLC 1, 8, 15, 16, 43; DA; DAB; DAC; DAM DRAM, MST, NOV**
See also AW; CA 25-28; CANR 40; CAP 2; DA3; DLB 65; MTCW 1, 2

Codrescu, Andrei 1946- .... **CLC 46, 121; DAM POET**
See also CA 33-36R; CAAS 19; CANR 13, 34, 53, 76; DA3; MTCW 2

Coe, Max
See Bourne, Randolph S(illiman)

Coe, Tucker
See Westlake, Donald E(dwin)

Coen, Ethan 1958- .... **CLC 108**
See also CA 126; CANR 85

Coen, Joel 1955- .... **CLC 108**
See also CA 126

The Coen Brothers
See Coen, Ethan; Coen, Joel

Coetzee, J(ohn) M(ichael) 1940- ...... **CLC 23, 33, 66, 117; DAM NOV**
See also AAYA 37; CA 77-80; CANR 41, 54, 74; DA3; DLB 225; MTCW 1, 2

Coffey, Brian
See Koontz, Dean R(ay)

Coffin, Robert P(eter) Tristram
1892-1955 .... **TCLC 95**
See also CA 123; 169; DLB 45

Cohan, George M(ichael)
1878-1942 .... **TCLC 60**
See also CA 157

Cohen, Arthur A(llen) 1928-1986 ...... **CLC 7, 31**
See also CA 1-4R; 120; CANR 1, 17, 42; DLB 28

Cohen, Leonard (Norman) 1934- ...... **CLC 3, 38; DAC; DAM MST**
See also CA 21-24R; CANR 14, 69; DLB 53; MTCW 1

Cohen, Matt(hew) 1942-1999 .... **CLC 19; DAC**
See also CA 61-64; 187; CAAS 18; CANR 40; DLB 53

Cohen-Solal, Annie 19(?)- .... **CLC 50**

Colegate, Isabel 1931- .... **CLC 36**
See also CA 17-20R; CANR 8, 22, 74; DLB 14, 231; INT CANR-22; MTCW 1

Coleman, Emmett
See Reed, Ishmael

Coleridge, Hartley 1796-1849 .... **NCLC 90**
See also DLB 96

Coleridge, M. E.
See Coleridge, Mary E(lizabeth)

Coleridge, Mary E(lizabeth)
1861-1907 .... **TCLC 73**
See also CA 116; 166; DLB 19, 98

Coleridge, Samuel Taylor
1772-1834 . **NCLC 9, 54, 99; DA; DAB; DAC; DAM MST, POET; PC 11**
See also AW; CDBLB 1789-1832; DA3; DLB 93, 107

Coleridge, Sara 1802-1852 .... **NCLC 31**
See also DLB 199

Coles, Don 1928- .... **CLC 46**
See also CA 115; CANR 38

Coles, Robert (Martin) 1929- .... **CLC 108**
See also CA 45-48; CANR 3, 32, 66, 70; INT CANR-32; SATA 23

Colette, (Sidonie-Gabrielle)
1873-1954 . **TCLC 1, 5, 16; DAM NOV; SSC 10**
See also Willy, Colette
See also CA 104; 131; DA3; DLB 65; MTCW 1, 2

Collett, (Jacobine) Camilla (Wergeland)
1813-1895 .... **NCLC 22**

Collier, Christopher 1930- .... **CLC 30**
See also AAYA 13; CA 33-36R; CANR 13, 33; JRDA; MAICYA; SATA 16, 70

Collier, James L(incoln) 1928- .... **CLC 30; DAM POP**
See also AAYA 13; CA 9-12R; CANR 4, 33, 60; CLR 3; JRDA; MAICYA; SAAS 21; SATA 8, 70

Collier, Jeremy 1650-1726 .... **LC 6**

Collier, John 1901-1980 .... **SSC 19**
See also CA 65-68; 97-100; CANR 10; DLB 77

Delaney, Franey
See O'Hara, John (Henry)

Delaney, Shelagh 1939- .... **CLC 29; DAM DRAM**
See also CA 17-20R; CANR 30, 67; CD-BLB 1960 to Present; DLB 13; MTCW 1

Delany, Martin Robinson
1812-1885 .... **NCLC 93**
See also DLB 50

Delany, Mary (Granville Pendarves)
1700-1788 .... **LC 12**

Delany, Samuel R(ay), Jr. 1942- . **CLC 8, 14, 38, 141; BLC 1; DAM MULT**
See also AAYA 24; BW 2, 3; CA 81-84; CANR 27, 43; DLB 8, 33; MTCW 1, 2

De La Ramee, (Marie) Louise 1839-1908
See Ouida
See also SATA 20

de la Roche, Mazo 1879-1961 .... **CLC 14**
See also CA 85-88; CANR 30; DLB 68; SATA 64

De La Salle, Innocent
See Hartmann, Sadakichi

Delbanco, Nicholas (Franklin)
1942- .... **CLC 6, 13**
See also CA 17-20R; CAAE 189; CAAS 2; CANR 29, 55; DLB 6, 234

del Castillo, Michel 1933- .... **CLC 38**
See also CA 109; CANR 77

Deledda, Grazia (Cosima)
1875(?)-1936 .... **TCLC 23**
See also CA 123

Delgado, Abelardo (Lalo) B(arrientos) 1930-
See also CA 131; CAAS 15; CANR 90; DAM MST, MULT; DLB 82; HLC 1; HW 1, 2

Delibes, Miguel CLC 8, 18
See also Delibes Setien, Miguel

Delibes Setien, Miguel 1920-
See Delibes, Miguel
See also CA 45-48; CANR 1, 32; HW 1; MTCW 1

DeLillo, Don 1936- ..... **CLC 8, 10, 13, 27, 39, 54, 76, 143; DAM NOV, POP**
See also AMWS 6; BEST 89:1; CA 81-84; CANR 21, 76, 92; DA3; DLB 6, 173; MTCW 1, 2

de Lisser, H. G.
See De Lisser, H(erbert) G(eorge)
See also DLB 117

De Lisser, H(erbert) G(eorge)
1878-1944 .... **TCLC 12**
See also de Lisser, H. G.
See also BW 2; CA 109; 152

Deloney, Thomas 1543(?)-1600 .... **LC 41**
See also DLB 167

Deloria, Vine (Victor), Jr. 1933- ...... **CLC 21, 122; DAM MULT**
See also CA 53-56; CANR 5, 20, 48; DLB 175; MTCW 1; NNAL; SATA 21

Del Vecchio, John M(ichael) 1947- .. **CLC 29**
See also CA 110; DLBD 9

de Man, Paul (Adolph Michel)
1919-1983 .... **CLC 55**
See also CA 128; 111; CANR 61; DLB 67; MTCW 1, 2

DeMarinis, Rick 1934- .... **CLC 54**
See also CA 57-60, 184; CAAE 184; CAAS 24; CANR 9, 25, 50

Dembry, R. Emmet
See Murfree, Mary Noailles

Demby, William 1922- .... **CLC 53; BLC 1; DAM MULT**
See also BW 1, 3; CA 81-84; CANR 81; DLB 33

de Menton, Francisco
See Chin, Frank (Chew, Jr.)

Demetrius of Phalerum c.
307B.C.- .... **CMLC 34**

Demijohn, Thom
See Disch, Thomas M(ichael)

Deming, Richard 1915-1983
See Queen, Ellery
See also CA 9-12R; CANR 3, 94; SATA 24

de Molina, Tirso 1580(?)-1648 .... **DC 13**
See also HLCS 2

de Montherlant, Henry (Milon)
See Montherlant, Henry (Milon) de

Demosthenes 384B.C.-322B.C. ...... **CMLC 13**
See also DLB 176

de Natale, Francine
See Malzberg, Barry N(athaniel)

de Navarre, Marguerite 1492-1549 ..... **LC 61**

Denby, Edwin (Orr) 1903-1983 .... **CLC 48**
See also CA 138; 110

Denis, Julio
See Cortazar, Julio

Denmark, Harrison
See Zelazny, Roger (Joseph)

Dennis, John 1658-1734 .... **LC 11**
See also DLB 101

Dennis, Nigel (Forbes) 1912-1989 ...... **CLC 8**
See also CA 25-28R; 129; DLB 13, 15, 233; MTCW 1

Dent, Lester 1904(?)-1959 .... **TCLC 72**
See also CA 112; 161

De Palma, Brian (Russell) 1940- ...... **CLC 20**
See also CA 109

De Quincey, Thomas 1785-1859 ..... **NCLC 4, 87**
See also CDBLB 1789-1832; DLB 110; 144

Deren, Eleanora 1917(?)-1961
See Deren, Maya
See also CA 111

Deren, Maya CLC 16, 102
See also Deren, Eleanora

Derleth, August (William)
1909-1971 .... **CLC 31**
See also CA 1-4R; 29-32R; CANR 4; DLB 9; DLBD 17; SATA 5

Der Nister 1884-1950 .... **TCLC 56**

de Routisie, Albert
See Aragon, Louis

Derrida, Jacques 1930- .... **CLC 24, 87**
See also CA 124; 127; CANR 76; DLB 242; MTCW 1

Derry Down Derry
See Lear, Edward

Dersonnes, Jacques
See Simenon, Georges (Jacques Christian)

Desai, Anita 1937- ..... **CLC 19, 37, 97; DAB; DAM NOV**
See also BRWS 5; CA 81-84; CANR 33, 53, 95; DA3; MTCW 1, 2; SATA 63

Desai, Kiran 1971- .... **CLC 119**
See also CA 171

de Saint-Luc, Jean
See Glassco, John

de Saint Roman, Arnaud
See Aragon, Louis

Desbordes-Valmore, Marceline
1786-1859 .... **NCLC 97**
See also DLB 217

Descartes, Rene 1596-1650 .... **LC 20, 35**

De Sica, Vittorio 1901(?)-1974 .... **CLC 20**
See also CA 117

Desnos, Robert 1900-1945 .... **TCLC 22**
See also CA 121; 151

Destouches, Louis-Ferdinand
1894-1961 .... **CLC 9, 15**
See also Celine, Louis-Ferdinand
See also CA 85-88; CANR 28; MTCW 1

de Tolignac, Gaston
See Griffith, D(avid Lewelyn) W(ark)

Deutsch, Babette 1895-1982 .... **CLC 18**
See also CA 1-4R; 108; CANR 4, 79; DLB 45; SATA 1; SATA-Obit 33

Devenant, William 1606-1649 .... **LC 13**

Devkota, Laxmiprasad 1909-1959 . **TCLC 23**
See also CA 123

De Voto, Bernard (Augustine)
1897-1955 .... **TCLC 29**
See also CA 113; 160; DLB 9

De Vries, Peter 1910-1993 ..... **CLC 1, 2, 3, 7, 10, 28, 46; DAM NOV**
See also CA 17-20R; 142; CANR 41; DLB 6; DLBY 82; MTCW 1, 2

Dewey, John 1859-1952 .... **TCLC 95**
See also CA 114; 170

Dexter, John
See Bradley, Marion Zimmer
See also GLL 1

Dexter, Martin
See Faust, Frederick (Schiller)
See also TCWW 2

Dexter, Pete 1943- .. **CLC 34, 55; DAM POP**
See also BEST 89:2; CA 127; 131; INT 131; MTCW 1

Diamano, Silmang
See Senghor, Leopold Sedar

Diamond, Neil 1941- .... **CLC 30**
See also CA 108

Diaz del Castillo, Bernal 1496-1584 .. **LC 31; HLCS 1**

di Bassetto, Corno
See Shaw, George Bernard

Dick, Philip K(indred) 1928-1982 ... **CLC 10, 30, 72; DAM NOV, POP**
See also AAYA 24; CA 49-52; 106; CANR 2, 16; DA3; DLB 8; MTCW 1, 2

Dickens, Charles (John Huffam)
1812-1870 .... **NCLC 3, 8, 18, 26, 37, 50, 86; DA; DAB; DAC; DAM MST, NOV; SSC 17**
See also AAYA 23; CDBLB 1832-1890; DA3; DLB 21, 55, 70, 159, 166; JRDA; MAICYA; SATA 15

Dickey, James (Lafayette)
1923-1997 .... **CLC 1, 2, 4, 7, 10, 15, 47, 109; DAM NOV, POET, POP**
See also AITN 1, 2; AMWS 4; CA 9-12R; 156; CABS 2; CANR 10, 48, 61; CDALB 1968-1988; DA3; DLB 5, 193; DLBD 7; DLBY 82, 93, 96, 97, 98; INT CANR-10; MTCW 1, 2

Dickey, William 1928-1994 .... **CLC 3, 28**
See also CA 9-12R; 145; CANR 24, 79; DLB 5

Dickinson, Charles 1951- .... **CLC 49**
See also CA 128

Dickinson, Emily (Elizabeth)
1830-1886 ..... **NCLC 21, 77; DA; DAB; DAC; DAM MST, POET; PC 1**
See also AAYA 22; CDALB 1865-1917; DA3; DLB 1; SATA 29

Dickinson, Peter (Malcolm) 1927- .. **CLC 12, 35**
See also AAYA 9; CA 41-44R; CANR 31, 58, 88; CLR 29; DLB 87, 161; JRDA; MAICYA; SATA 5, 62, 95

Dickson, Carr
See Carr, John Dickson

Dickson, Carter
See Carr, John Dickson

Diderot, Denis 1713-1784 .... **LC 26**

Didion, Joan 1934- .... **CLC 1, 3, 8, 14, 32, 129; DAM NOV**
See also AITN 1; AMWS 4; CA 5-8R; CANR 14, 52, 76; CDALB 1968-1988; DA3; DLB 2, 173, 185; DLBY 81, 86; MTCW 1, 2; TCWW 2

Dietrich, Robert
See Hunt, E(verette) Howard, (Jr.)

Drabble, Margaret 1939- ...... **CLC 2, 3, 5, 8, 10, 22, 53, 129; DAB; DAC; DAM MST, NOV, POP**
See also BRWS 4; CA 13-16R; CANR 18, 35, 63; CDBLB 1960 to Present; DA3; DLB 14, 155, 231; MTCW 1, 2; SATA 48

Drapier, M. B.
See Swift, Jonathan

Drayham, James
See Mencken, H(enry) L(ouis)

Drayton, Michael 1563-1631 ..... **LC 8; DAM POET**
See also DLB 121

Dreadstone, Carl
See Campbell, (John) Ramsey

Dreiser, Theodore (Herman Albert) 1871-1945 .... **TCLC 10, 18, 35, 83; DA; DAC; DAM MST, NOV; SSC 30**
See also AW; CA 106; 132; CDALB 1865-1917; DA3; DLB 9, 12, 102, 137; DLBD 1; MTCW 1, 2

Drexler, Rosalyn 1926- .... **CLC 2, 6**
See also CA 81-84; CANR 68

Dreyer, Carl Theodor 1889-1968 ...... **CLC 16**
See also CA 116

Drieu la Rochelle, Pierre(-Eugene) 1893-1945 .... **TCLC 21**
See also CA 117; DLB 72

Drinkwater, John 1882-1937 .... **TCLC 57**
See also CA 109; 149; DLB 10, 19, 149

Drop Shot
See Cable, George Washington

Droste-Hulshoff, Annette Freiin von 1797-1848 .... **NCLC 3**
See also DLB 133

Drummond, Walter
See Silverberg, Robert

Drummond, William Henry 1854-1907 .... **TCLC 25**
See also CA 160; DLB 92

Drummond de Andrade, Carlos 1902-1987 .... **CLC 18**
See also Andrade, Carlos Drummond de
See also CA 132; 123

Drury, Allen (Stuart) 1918-1998 .... **CLC 37**
See also CA 57-60; 170; CANR 18, 52; INT CANR-18

Dryden, John 1631-1700 .... **LC 3, 21; DA; DAB; DAC; DAM DRAM, MST, POET; DC 3; PC 25**
See also AW; CDBLB 1660-1789; DLB 80, 101, 131

Duberman, Martin (Bauml) 1930- ..... **CLC 8**
See also CA 1-4R; CANR 2, 63

Dubie, Norman (Evans) 1945- .... **CLC 36**
See also CA 69-72; CANR 12; DLB 120

Du Bois, W(illiam) E(dward) B(urghardt) 1868-1963 ... **CLC 1, 2, 13, 64, 96; BLC 1; DA; DAC; DAM MST, MULT, NOV**
See also AMWS 2; AW; BW 1, 3; CA 85-88; CANR 34, 82; CDALB 1865-1917; DA3; DLB 47, 50, 91; MTCW 1, 2; SATA 42

Dubus, Andre 1936-1999 ..... **CLC 13, 36, 97; SSC 15**
See also AMWS 7; CA 21-24R; 177; CANR 17; DLB 130; INT CANR-17

Duca Minimo
See D'Annunzio, Gabriele

Ducharme, Rejean 1941- .... **CLC 74**
See also CA 165; DLB 60

Duchen, Claire CLC 65

Duclos, Charles Pinot 1704-1772 .... **LC 1**

Dudek, Louis 1918- .... **CLC 11, 19**
See also CA 45-48; CAAS 14; CANR 1; DLB 88

Duerrenmatt, Friedrich 1921-1990 ... **CLC 1, 4, 8, 11, 15, 43, 102; DAM DRAM**
See also CA 17-20R; CANR 33; DLB 69, 124; MTCW 1, 2

Duffy, Bruce 1953(?)- .... **CLC 50**
See also CA 172

Duffy, Maureen 1933- .... **CLC 37**
See also CA 25-28R; CANR 33, 68; DLB 14; MTCW 1

Dugan, Alan 1923- .... **CLC 2, 6**
See also CA 81-84; DLB 5

du Gard, Roger Martin
See Martin du Gard, Roger

Duhamel, Georges 1884-1966 .... **CLC 8**
See also CA 81-84; 25-28R; CANR 35; DLB 65; MTCW 1

Dujardin, Edouard (Emile Louis) 1861-1949 .... **TCLC 13**
See also CA 109; DLB 123

Dulles, John Foster 1888-1959 .... **TCLC 72**
See also CA 115; 149

Dumas, Alexandre (pere)
See Dumas, Alexandre (Davy de la Pailleterie)

Dumas, Alexandre (Davy de la Pailleterie) 1802-1870 ...... **NCLC 11, 71; DA; DAB; DAC; DAM MST, NOV**
See also AW; DA3; DLB 119, 192; SATA 18

Dumas, Alexandre (fils) 1824-1895 .... **NCLC 9; DC 1**
See also AAYA 22; DLB 192; EW 1

Dumas, Claudine
See Malzberg, Barry N(athaniel)

Dumas, Henry L. 1934-1968 .... **CLC 6, 62**
See also BW 1; CA 85-88; DLB 41

du Maurier, Daphne 1907-1989 .. **CLC 6, 11, 59; DAB; DAC; DAM MST, POP; SSC 18**
See also AAYA 37; BRWS 3; CA 5-8R; 128; CANR 6, 55; DA3; DLB 191; MTCW 1, 2; SATA 27; SATA-Obit 60

Du Maurier, George 1834-1896 ..... **NCLC 86**
See also DLB 153, 178

Dunbar, Paul Laurence 1872-1906 . **TCLC 2, 12; BLC 1; DA; DAC; DAM MST, MULT, POET; PC 5; SSC 8**
See also AMWS 2; AW; BW 1, 3; CA 104; 124; CANR 79; CDALB 1865-1917; DA3; DLB 50, 54, 78; SATA 34

Dunbar, William 1460(?)-1520(?) .... **LC 20**
See also DLB 132, 146

Duncan, Dora Angela
See Duncan, Isadora

Duncan, Isadora 1877(?)-1927 .... **TCLC 68**
See also CA 118; 149

Duncan, Lois 1934- .... **CLC 26**
See also AAYA 4, 34; AW; CA 1-4R; CANR 2, 23, 36; CLR 29; JRDA; MAICYA; SAAS 2; SATA 1, 36, 75

Duncan, Robert (Edward) 1919-1988 .... **CLC 1, 2, 4, 7, 15, 41, 55; DAM POET; PC 2**
See also CA 9-12R; 124; CANR 28, 62; DLB 5, 16, 193; MTCW 1, 2

Duncan, Sara Jeannette 1861-1922 .... **TCLC 60**
See also CA 157; DLB 92

Dunlap, William 1766-1839 .... **NCLC 2**
See also DLB 30, 37, 59

Dunn, Douglas (Eaglesham) 1942- .... **CLC 6, 40**
See also CA 45-48; CANR 2, 33; DLB 40; MTCW 1

Dunn, Katherine (Karen) 1945- .... **CLC 71**
See also CA 33-36R; CANR 72; MTCW 1

Dunn, Stephen 1939- .... **CLC 36**
See also CA 33-36R; CANR 12, 48, 53; DLB 105

Dunne, Finley Peter 1867-1936 ...... **TCLC 28**
See also CA 108; 178; DLB 11, 23

Dunne, John Gregory 1932- .... **CLC 28**
See also CA 25-28R; CANR 14, 50; DLBY 80

Dunsany, Edward John Moreton Drax Plunkett 1878-1957
See Dunsany, Lord
See also CA 104; 148; DLB 10; MTCW 1

Dunsany, Lord TCLC 2, 59
See also Dunsany, Edward John Moreton Drax Plunkett
See also DLB 77, 153, 156

du Perry, Jean
See Simenon, Georges (Jacques Christian)

Durang, Christopher (Ferdinand) 1949- .... **CLC 27, 38**
See also CA 105; CANR 50, 76; MTCW 1

Duras, Marguerite 1914-1996 . **CLC 3, 6, 11, 20, 34, 40, 68, 100; SSC 40**
See also CA 25-28R; 151; CANR 50; CWW 2; DLB 83; MTCW 1, 2

Durban, (Rosa) Pam 1947- .... **CLC 39**
See also CA 123

Durcan, Paul 1944- .... **CLC 43, 70; DAM POET**
See also CA 134

Durkheim, Emile 1858-1917 .... **TCLC 55**

Durrell, Lawrence (George) 1912-1990 .... **CLC 1, 4, 6, 8, 13, 27, 41; DAM NOV**
See also BRWS 1; CA 9-12R; 132; CANR 40, 77; CDBLB 1945-1960; DLB 15, 27, 204; DLBY 90; MTCW 1, 2

Dürrenmatt, Friedrich
See Duerrenmatt, Friedrich

Dutt, Toru 1856-1877 .... **NCLC 29**
See also DLB 240

Dwight, Timothy 1752-1817 .... **NCLC 13**
See also DLB 37

Dworkin, Andrea 1946- .... **CLC 43, 123**
See also CA 77-80; CAAS 21; CANR 16, 39, 76, 96; GLL 1; INT CANR-16; MTCW 1, 2

Dwyer, Deanna
See Koontz, Dean R(ay)

Dwyer, K. R.
See Koontz, Dean R(ay)

Dwyer, Thomas A. 1923- .... **CLC 114**
See also CA 115

Dybek, Stuart 1942- .... **CLC 114**
See also CA 97-100; CANR 39; DLB 130

Dye, Richard
See De Voto, Bernard (Augustine)

Dylan, Bob 1941- .... **CLC 3, 4, 6, 12, 77**
See also CA 41-44R; DLB 16

Dyson, John 1943- .... **CLC 70**
See also CA 144

E. V. L.
See Lucas, E(dward) V(errall)

Eagleton, Terence (Francis) 1943- .. **CLC 63, 132**
See also CA 57-60; CANR 7, 23, 68; DLB 242; MTCW 1, 2

Eagleton, Terry
See Eagleton, Terence (Francis)

Early, Jack
See Scoppettone, Sandra
See also GLL 1

East, Michael
See West, Morris L(anglo)

Eastaway, Edward
See Thomas, (Philip) Edward

Eastlake, William (Derry) 1917-1997 .... **CLC 8**
See also CA 5-8R; 158; CAAS 1; CANR 5, 63; DLB 6, 206; INT CANR-5; TCWW 2

Eastman, Charles A(lexander)
1858-1939 .... **TCLC 55; DAM MULT**
See also AW 1; CA 179; CANR 91; DLB
175; NNAL

Eberhart, Richard (Ghormley)
1904- .. **CLC 3, 11, 19, 56; DAM POET**
See also CA 1-4R; CANR 2; CDALB 1941-
1968; DLB 48; MTCW 1

Eberstadt, Fernanda 1960- .... **CLC 39**
See also CA 136; CANR 69

**Echegaray (y Eizaguirre), Jose (Maria
Waldo)** 1832-1916 .... **TCLC 4; HLCS 1**
See also CA 104; CANR 32; HW 1; MTCW
1

Echeverria, (Jose) Esteban (Antonino)
1805-1851 .... **NCLC 18**

Echo
See Proust, (Valentin-Louis-George-Eugene-
)Marcel

Eckert, Allan W. 1931- .... **CLC 17**
See also AAYA 18; CA 13-16R; CANR 14,
45; INT CANR-14; SAAS 21; SATA 29,
91; SATA-Brief 27

Eckhart, Meister 1260(?)-1327(?) ... **CMLC 9**
See also DLB 115

Eckmar, F. R.
See de Hartog, Jan

Eco, Umberto 1932- .... **CLC 28, 60, 142;
DAM NOV, POP**
See also BEST 90:1; CA 77-80; CANR 12,
33, 55; CWW 2; DA3; DLB 196, 242;
MTCW 1, 2

Eddison, E(ric) R(ucker)
1882-1945 .... **TCLC 15**
See also CA 109; 156

Eddy, Mary (Ann Morse) Baker
1821-1910 .... **TCLC 71**
See also CA 113; 174

Edel, (Joseph) Leon 1907-1997 .. **CLC 29, 34**
See also CA 1-4R; 161; CANR 1, 22; DLB
103; INT CANR-22

Eden, Emily 1797-1869 .... **NCLC 10**

Edgar, David 1948- .... **CLC 42; DAM DRAM**
See also CA 57-60; CANR 12, 61; DLB 13,
233; MTCW 1

Edgerton, Clyde (Carlyle) 1944- ...... **CLC 39**
See also AAYA 17; AW; CA 118; 134;
CANR 64; INT 134

Edgeworth, Maria 1768-1849 .... **NCLC 1, 51**
See also BRWS 3; DLB 116, 159, 163;
SATA 21

Edmonds, Paul
See Kuttner, Henry

Edmonds, Walter D(umaux)
1903-1998 .... **CLC 35**
See also CA 5-8R; CANR 2; DLB 9; MAI-
CYA; SAAS 4; SATA 1, 27; SATA-Obit
99

Edmondson, Wallace
See Ellison, Harlan (Jay)

Edson, Russell CLC 13
See also CA 33-36R

Edwards, Bronwen Elizabeth
See Rose, Wendy

Edwards, G(erald) B(asil)
1899-1976 .... **CLC 25**
See also CA 110

Edwards, Gus 1939- .... **CLC 43**
See also CA 108; INT 108

Edwards, Jonathan 1703-1758 .... **LC 7, 54;
DA; DAC; DAM MST**
See also DLB 24

Efron, Marina Ivanovna Tsvetaeva
See Tsvetaeva (Efron), Marina (Ivanovna)

Ehle, John (Marsden, Jr.) 1925- ...... **CLC 27**
See also CA 9-12R

Ehrenbourg, Ilya (Grigoryevich)
See Ehrenburg, Ilya (Grigoryevich)

Ehrenburg, Ilya (Grigoryevich)
1891-1967 .... **CLC 18, 34, 62**
See also CA 102; 25-28R

Ehrenburg, Ilyo (Grigoryevich)
See Ehrenburg, Ilya (Grigoryevich)

Ehrenreich, Barbara 1941- .... **CLC 110**
See also BEST 90:4; CA 73-76; CANR 16,
37, 62; MTCW 1, 2

Eich, Guenter 1907-1972 .... **CLC 15**
See also CA 111; 93-96; DLB 69, 124

Eichendorff, Joseph Freiherr von
1788-1857 .... **NCLC 8**
See also DLB 90

Eigner, Larry CLC 9
See also Eigner, Laurence (Joel)
See also CAAS 23; DLB 5

Eigner, Laurence (Joel) 1927-1996
See Eigner, Larry
See also CA 9-12R; 151; CANR 6, 84; DLB
193

Einstein, Albert 1879-1955 .... **TCLC 65**
See also CA 121; 133; MTCW 1, 2

Eiseley, Loren Corey 1907-1977 .... **CLC 7**
See also AAYA 5; CA 1-4R; 73-76; CANR
6; DLBD 17

Eisenstadt, Jill 1963- .... **CLC 50**
See also CA 140

Eisenstein, Sergei (Mikhailovich)
1898-1948 .... **TCLC 57**
See also CA 114; 149

Eisner, Simon
See Kornbluth, C(yril) M.

Ekeloef, (Bengt) Gunnar
1907-1968 ... **CLC 27; DAM POET; PC
23**
See also CA 123; 25-28R

Ekelöf, (Bengt) Gunnar
See Ekeloef, (Bengt) Gunnar

Ekelund, Vilhelm 1880-1949 .... **TCLC 75**
See also CA 189

Ekwensi, C. O. D.
See Ekwensi, Cyprian (Odiatu Duaka)

Ekwensi, Cyprian (Odiatu Duaka)
1921- ...... **CLC 4; BLC 1; DAM MULT**
See also BW 2, 3; CA 29-32R; CANR 18,
42, 74; DLB 117; MTCW 1, 2; SATA 66

Elaine TCLC 18
See also Leverson, Ada

El Crummo
See Crumb, R(obert)

Elder, Lonne III 1931-1996 .... **DC 8**
See also BLC 1; BW 1, 3; CA 81-84; 152;
CANR 25; DAM MULT; DLB 7, 38, 44

Eleanor of Aquitaine 1122-1204 ... **CMLC 39**

Elia
See Lamb, Charles

Eliade, Mircea 1907-1986 .... **CLC 19**
See also CA 65-68; 119; CANR 30, 62;
DLB 220; MTCW 1

Eliot, A. D.
See Jewett, (Theodora) Sarah Orne

Eliot, Alice
See Jewett, (Theodora) Sarah Orne

Eliot, Dan
See Silverberg, Robert

Eliot, George 1819-1880 ...... **NCLC 4, 13, 23,
41, 49, 89; DA; DAB; DAC; DAM
MST, NOV; PC 20**
See also AW; CDBLB 1832-1890; DA3;
DLB 21, 35, 55

Eliot, John 1604-1690 .... **LC 5**
See also DLB 24

Eliot, T(homas) S(tearns)
1888-1965 ...... **CLC 1, 2, 3, 6, 9, 10, 13,
15, 24, 34, 41, 55, 57, 113; DA; DAB;
DAC; DAM DRAM, MST, POET; PC
5, 31**
See also AAYA 28; AW; CA 5-8R; 25-28R;
CANR 41; CDALB 1929-1941; DA3;
DLB 7, 10, 45, 63; DLBY 88; MTCW 1,
2

Elizabeth 1866-1941 .... **TCLC 41**

Elkin, Stanley L(awrence)
1930-1995 .. **CLC 4, 6, 9, 14, 27, 51, 91;
DAM NOV, POP; SSC 12**
See also AMWS 6; CA 9-12R; 148; CANR
8, 46; DLB 2, 28; DLBY 80; INT
CANR-8; MTCW 1, 2

Elledge, Scott CLC 34

Elliot, Don
See Silverberg, Robert

Elliott, Don
See Silverberg, Robert

Elliott, George P(aul) 1918-1980 .... **CLC 2**
See also CA 1-4R; 97-100; CANR 2

Elliott, Janice 1931-1995 .... **CLC 47**
See also CA 13-16R; CANR 8, 29, 84; DLB
14; SATA 119

Elliott, Sumner Locke 1917-1991 ..... **CLC 38**
See also CA 5-8R; 134; CANR 2, 21

Elliott, William
See Bradbury, Ray (Douglas)

Ellis, A. E. CLC 7

Ellis, Alice Thomas CLC 40
See also Haycraft, Anna (Margaret)
See also DLB 194; MTCW 1

Ellis, Bret Easton 1964- ..... **CLC 39, 71, 117;
DAM POP**
See also AAYA 2; CA 118; 123; CANR 51,
74; DA3; INT 123; MTCW 1

Ellis, (Henry) Havelock
1859-1939 .... **TCLC 14**
See also CA 109; 169; DLB 190

Ellis, Landon
See Ellison, Harlan (Jay)

Ellis, Trey 1962- .... **CLC 55**
See also CA 146; CANR 92

Ellison, Harlan (Jay) 1934- ... **CLC 1, 13, 42,
139; DAM POP; SSC 14**
See also AAYA 29; CA 5-8R; CANR 5, 46;
DLB 8; INT CANR-5; MTCW 1, 2;
SCFW 2

Ellison, Ralph (Waldo) 1914-1994 .... **CLC 1,
3, 11, 54, 86, 114; BLC 1; DA; DAB;
DAC; DAM MST, MULT, NOV; SSC
26**
See also AAYA 19; AMWS 2; AW; BW 1,
3; CA 9-12R; 145; CANR 24, 53; CDALB
1941-1968; DA3; DLB 2, 76, 227; DLBY
94; MTCW 1, 2

Ellmann, Lucy (Elizabeth) 1956- ..... **CLC 61**
See also CA 128

Ellmann, Richard (David)
1918-1987 .... **CLC 50**
See also BEST 89:2; CA 1-4R; 122; CANR
2, 28, 61; DLB 103; DLBY 87; MTCW
1, 2

Elman, Richard (Martin)
1934-1997 .... **CLC 19**
See also CA 17-20R; 163; CAAS 3; CANR
47

Elron
See Hubbard, L(afayette) Ron(ald)

Eluard, Paul TCLC 7, 41
See also Grindel, Eugene

Elyot, Sir Thomas 1490(?)-1546 .... **LC 11**

Elytis, Odysseus 1911-1996 .... **CLC 15, 49,
100; DAM POET; PC 21**
See also Alepoudelis, Odysseus
See also CA 102; 151; CANR 94; CWW 2;
MTCW 1, 2

Emecheta, (Florence Onye) Buchi
1944- .. CLC 14, 48, 128; BLC 2; DAM MULT
See also BW 2, 3; CA 81-84; CANR 27, 81; DA3; DLB 117; MTCW 1, 2; SATA 66

Emerson, Mary Moody
1774-1863 .... **NCLC 66**

Emerson, Ralph Waldo 1803-1882 . **NCLC 1, 38, 98; DA; DAB; DAC; DAM MST, POET; PC 18**
See also AW; CDALB 1640-1865; DA3; DLB 1, 59, 73, 223

Eminescu, Mihail 1850-1889 .... **NCLC 33**

Empson, William 1906-1984 ... **CLC 3, 8, 19, 33, 34**
See also BRWS 2; CA 17-20R; 112; CANR 31, 61; DLB 20; MTCW 1, 2

Enchi, Fumiko (Ueda) 1905-1986 ..... **CLC 31**
See also CA 129; 121; DLB 182

Ende, Michael (Andreas Helmuth)
1929-1995 .... **CLC 31**
See also CA 118; 124; 149; CANR 36; CLR 14; DLB 75; MAICYA; SATA 61; SATA-Brief 42; SATA-Obit 86

Endo, Shusaku 1923-1996 ..... **CLC 7, 14, 19, 54, 99; DAM NOV**
See also CA 29-32R; 153; CANR 21, 54; DA3; DLB 182; MTCW 1, 2

Engel, Marian 1933-1985 .... **CLC 36**
See also CA 25-28R; CANR 12; DLB 53; INT CANR-12

Engelhardt, Frederick
See Hubbard, L(afayette) Ron(ald)

Engels, Friedrich 1820-1895 .... **NCLC 85**
See also DLB 129

Enright, D(ennis) J(oseph) 1920- .. **CLC 4, 8, 31**
See also CA 1-4R; CANR 1, 42, 83; DLB 27; SATA 25

Enzensberger, Hans Magnus
1929- .... **CLC 43; PC 28**
See also CA 116; 119

Ephron, Nora 1941- .... **CLC 17, 31**
See also AAYA 35; AITN 2; CA 65-68; CANR 12, 39, 83

Epicurus 341B.C.-270B.C. .... **CMLC 21**
See also DLB 176

Epsilon
See Betjeman, John

Epstein, Daniel Mark 1948- .... **CLC 7**
See also CA 49-52; CANR 2, 53, 90

Epstein, Jacob 1956- .... **CLC 19**
See also CA 114

Epstein, Jean 1897-1953 .... **TCLC 92**

Epstein, Joseph 1937- .... **CLC 39**
See also CA 112; 119; CANR 50, 65

Epstein, Leslie 1938- .... **CLC 27**
See also CA 73-76; CAAS 12; CANR 23, 69

Equiano, Olaudah 1745(?)-1797 .... **LC 16; BLC 2; DAM MULT**
See also DLB 37, 50

Erasmus, Desiderius 1469(?)-1536 ...... **LC 16**

Erdman, Paul E(mil) 1932- .... **CLC 25**
See also AITN 1; CA 61-64; CANR 13, 43, 84

Erdrich, Louise 1954- .... **CLC 39, 54, 120; DAM MULT, NOV, POP**
See also AAYA 10; AMWS 4; BEST 89:1; CA 114; CANR 41, 62; CDALBS; DA3; DLB 152, 175, 206; MTCW 1; NNAL; SATA 94; TCWW 2

Erenburg, Ilya (Grigoryevich)
See Ehrenburg, Ilya (Grigoryevich)

Erickson, Stephen Michael 1950-
See Erickson, Steve
See also CA 129

Erickson, Steve CLC 64
See also Erickson, Stephen Michael
See also CANR 60, 68

Ericson, Walter
See Fast, Howard (Melvin)

Eriksson, Buntel
See Bergman, (Ernst) Ingmar

Ernaux, Annie 1940- .... **CLC 88**
See also CA 147; CANR 93

Erskine, John 1879-1951 .... **TCLC 84**
See also CA 112; 159; DLB 9, 102

Eschenbach, Wolfram von
See Wolfram von Eschenbach

Eseki, Bruno
See Mphahlele, Ezekiel

Esenin, Sergei (Alexandrovich)
1895-1925 .... **TCLC 4**
See also CA 104

Eshleman, Clayton 1935- .... **CLC 7**
See also CA 33-36R; CAAS 6; CANR 93; DLB 5

Espriella, Don Manuel Alvarez
See Southey, Robert

Espriu, Salvador 1913-1985 .... **CLC 9**
See also CA 154; 115; DLB 134

Espronceda, Jose de 1808-1842 ..... **NCLC 39**

Esquivel, Laura 1951(?)- ... **CLC 141; HLCS 1**
See also AAYA 29; CA 143; CANR 68; DA3; MTCW 1

Esse, James
See Stephens, James

Esterbrook, Tom
See Hubbard, L(afayette) Ron(ald)

Estleman, Loren D. 1952- ..... **CLC 48; DAM NOV, POP**
See also AAYA 27; CA 85-88; CANR 27, 74; DA3; DLB 226; INT CANR-27; MTCW 1, 2

Euclid 306B.C.-283B.C. .... **CMLC 25**

Eugenides, Jeffrey 1960(?)- .... **CLC 81**
See also CA 144

Euripides c. 485B.C.-406B.C. .... **CMLC 23; DA; DAB; DAC; DAM DRAM, MST; DC 4**
See also AW; DA3; DLB 176

Evan, Evin
See Faust, Frederick (Schiller)

Evans, Caradoc 1878-1945 ... **TCLC 85; SSC 43**

Evans, Evan
See Faust, Frederick (Schiller)
See also TCWW 2

Evans, Marian
See Eliot, George

Evans, Mary Ann
See Eliot, George

Evarts, Esther
See Benson, Sally

Everett, Percival
See Everett, Percival L.

Everett, Percival L. 1956- .... **CLC 57**
See also Everett, Percival
See also BW 2; CA 129; CANR 94

Everson, R(onald) G(ilmour)
1903-1992 .... **CLC 27**
See also CA 17-20R; DLB 88

Everson, William (Oliver)
1912-1994 .... **CLC 1, 5, 14**
See also CA 9-12R; 145; CANR 20; DLB 212; MTCW 1

Evtushenko, Evgenii Aleksandrovich
See Yevtushenko, Yevgeny (Alexandrovich)

Ewart, Gavin (Buchanan)
1916-1995 .... **CLC 13, 46**
See also CA 89-92; 150; CANR 17, 46; DLB 40; MTCW 1

Ewers, Hanns Heinz 1871-1943 ..... **TCLC 12**
See also CA 109; 149

Ewing, Frederick R.
See Sturgeon, Theodore (Hamilton)

Exley, Frederick (Earl) 1929-1992 .... **CLC 6, 11**
See also AITN 2; CA 81-84; 138; DLB 143; DLBY 81

Eynhardt, Guillermo
See Quiroga, Horacio (Sylvestre)

Ezekiel, Nissim 1924- .... **CLC 61**
See also CA 61-64

Ezekiel, Tish O'Dowd 1943- .... **CLC 34**
See also CA 129

Fadeyev, A.
See Bulgya, Alexander Alexandrovich

Fadeyev, Alexander TCLC 53
See also Bulgya, Alexander Alexandrovich

Fagen, Donald 1948- .... **CLC 26**

Fainzilberg, Ilya Arnoldovich 1897-1937
See Ilf, Ilya
See also CA 120; 165

Fair, Ronald L. 1932- .... **CLC 18**
See also BW 1; CA 69-72; CANR 25; DLB 33

Fairbairn, Roger
See Carr, John Dickson

Fairbairns, Zoe (Ann) 1948- .... **CLC 32**
See also CA 103; CANR 21, 85

Fairman, Paul W. 1916-1977
See Queen, Ellery
See also CA 114

Falco, Gian
See Papini, Giovanni

Falconer, James
See Kirkup, James

Falconer, Kenneth
See Kornbluth, C(yril) M.

Falkland, Samuel
See Heijermans, Herman

Fallaci, Oriana 1930- .... **CLC 11, 110**
See also CA 77-80; CANR 15, 58; MTCW 1

Faludi, Susan 1959- .... **CLC 140**
See also CA 138; MTCW 1

Faludy, George 1913- .... **CLC 42**
See also CA 21-24R

Faludy, Gyoergy
See Faludy, George

Fanon, Frantz 1925-1961 ... **CLC 74; BLC 2; DAM MULT**
See also BW 1; CA 116; 89-92

Fanshawe, Ann 1625-1680 .... **LC 11**

Fante, John (Thomas) 1911-1983 ..... **CLC 60**
See also CA 69-72; 109; CANR 23; DLB 130; DLBY 83

Farah, Nuruddin 1945- .. **CLC 53, 137; BLC 2; DAM MULT**
See also BW 2, 3; CA 106; CANR 81; DLB 125

Fargue, Leon-Paul 1876(?)-1947 .... **TCLC 11**
See also CA 109

Farigoule, Louis
See Romains, Jules

Farina, Richard 1936(?)-1966 .... **CLC 9**
See also CA 81-84; 25-28R

Farley, Walter (Lorimer)
1915-1989 .... **CLC 17**
See also AW; CA 17-20R; CANR 8, 29, 84; DLB 22; JRDA; MAICYA; SATA 2, 43

Farmer, Philip Jose 1918- .... **CLC 1, 19**
See also AAYA 28; CA 1-4R; CANR 4, 35; DLB 8; MTCW 1; SATA 93

Farquhar, George 1677-1707 ... **LC 21; DAM DRAM**
See also DLB 84

Fitzgerald, Penelope 1916-2000 . **CLC 19, 51, 61, 143**
See also BRWS 5; CA 85-88; 190; CAAS 10; CANR 56, 86; DLB 14, 194; MTCW 2

Fitzgerald, Robert (Stuart)
1910-1985 .... **CLC 39**
See also CA 1-4R; 114; CANR 1; DLBY 80

FitzGerald, Robert D(avid)
1902-1987 .... **CLC 19**
See also CA 17-20R

Fitzgerald, Zelda (Sayre)
1900-1948 .... **TCLC 52**
See also CA 117; 126; DLBY 84

Flanagan, Thomas (James Bonner)
1923- .... **CLC 25, 52**
See also CA 108; CANR 55; DLBY 80; INT 108; MTCW 1

Flaubert, Gustave 1821-1880 .... **NCLC 2, 10, 19, 62, 66; DA; DAB; DAC; DAM MST, NOV; SSC 11**
See also AW; DA3; DLB 119

Flavius Josephus
See Josephus, Flavius

Flecker, Herman Elroy
See Flecker, (Herman) James Elroy

Flecker, (Herman) James Elroy
1884-1915 .... **TCLC 43**
See also CA 109; 150; DLB 10, 19

Fleming, Ian (Lancaster) 1908-1964 . **CLC 3, 30; DAM POP**
See also AAYA 26; AW; CA 5-8R; CANR 59; CDBLB 1945-1960; DA3; DLB 87, 201; MTCW 1, 2; SATA 9

Fleming, Thomas (James) 1927- ...... **CLC 37**
See also CA 5-8R; CANR 10; INT CANR-10; SATA 8

Fletcher, John 1579-1625 .... **LC 33; DC 6**
See also CDBLB Before 1660; DLB 58

Fletcher, John Gould 1886-1950 .... **TCLC 35**
See also CA 107; 167; DLB 4, 45

Fleur, Paul
See Pohl, Frederik

Flooglebuckle, Al
See Spiegelman, Art

Flora, Fletcher 1914-1969
See Queen, Ellery
See also CA 1-4R; CANR 3, 85

Flying Officer X
See Bates, H(erbert) E(rnest)

Fo, Dario 1926- .... **CLC 32, 109; DAM DRAM; DC 10**
See also CA 116; 128; CANR 68; CWW 2; DA3; DLBY 97; MTCW 1, 2

Fogarty, Jonathan Titulescu Esq.
See Farrell, James T(homas)

Follett, Ken(neth Martin) 1949- ..... **CLC 18; DAM NOV, POP**
See also AAYA 6; BEST 89:4; CA 81-84; CANR 13, 33, 54; DA3; DLB 87; DLBY 81; INT CANR-33; MTCW 1

Fontane, Theodor 1819-1898 .... **NCLC 26**
See also DLB 129

Fontenot, Chester CLC 65

Foote, Horton 1916- .... **CLC 51, 91; DAM DRAM**
See also CA 73-76; CANR 34, 51; DA3; DLB 26; INT CANR-34

Foote, Mary Hallock 1847-1938 .. **TCLC 108**
See also DLB 186, 188, 202, 221

Foote, Shelby 1916- ..... **CLC 75; DAM NOV, POP**
See also CA 5-8R; CANR 3, 45, 74; DA3; DLB 2, 17; MTCW 2

Forbes, Esther 1891-1967 .... **CLC 12**
See also AAYA 17; AW; CA 13-14; 25-28R; CAP 1; CLR 27; DLB 22; JRDA; MAICYA; SATA 2, 100

Forche, Carolyn (Louise) 1950- .... **CLC 25, 83, 86; DAM POET; PC 10**
See also CA 109; 117; CANR 50, 74; DA3; DLB 5, 193; INT 117; MTCW 1

Ford, Elbur
See Hibbert, Eleanor Alice Burford

Ford, Ford Madox 1873-1939 ... **TCLC 1, 15, 39, 57; DAM NOV**
See also Chaucer, Daniel
See also CA 104; 132; CANR 74; CDBLB 1914-1945; DA3; DLB 162; MTCW 1, 2

Ford, Henry 1863-1947 .... **TCLC 73**
See also CA 115; 148

Ford, John 1586-1639 .... **DC 8**
See also CDBLB Before 1660; DAM DRAM; DA3; DLB 58

Ford, John 1895-1973 .... **CLC 16**
See also CA 187; 45-48

Ford, Richard 1944- .... **CLC 46, 99**
See also AMWS 5; CA 69-72; CANR 11, 47, 86; DLB 227; MTCW 1

Ford, Webster
See Masters, Edgar Lee

Foreman, Richard 1937- .... **CLC 50**
See also CA 65-68; CANR 32, 63

Forester, C(ecil) S(cott) 1899-1966 ... **CLC 35**
See also CA 73-76; 25-28R; CANR 83; DLB 191; SATA 13

Forez
See Mauriac, Fran

Forman, James Douglas 1932- .... **CLC 21**
See also AAYA 17; AW; CA 9-12R; CANR 4, 19, 42; JRDA; MAICYA; SATA 8, 70

Fornés, María Irene 1930- . **CLC 39, 61; DC 10; HLCS 1**
See also CA 25-28R; CANR 28, 81; DLB 7; HW 1, 2; INT CANR-28; MTCW 1

Forrest, Leon (Richard) 1937-1997 .. **CLC 4; BLCS**
See also BW 2; CA 89-92; 162; CAAS 7; CANR 25, 52, 87; DLB 33

Forster, E(dward) M(organ)
1879-1970 ...... **CLC 1, 2, 3, 4, 9, 10, 13, 15, 22, 45, 77; DA; DAB; DAC; DAM MST, NOV; SSC 27**
See also AAYA 2, 37; AW; CA 13-14; 25-28R; CANR 45; CAP 1; CDBLB 1914-1945; DA3; DLB 34, 98, 162, 178, 195; DLBD 10; MTCW 1, 2; SATA 57

Forster, John 1812-1876 .... **NCLC 11**
See also DLB 144, 184

Forsyth, Frederick 1938- .... **CLC 2, 5, 36; DAM NOV, POP**
See also BEST 89:4; CA 85-88; CANR 38, 62; DLB 87; MTCW 1, 2

Forten, Charlotte L. TCLC 16; BLC 2
See also Grimke, Charlotte L(ottie) Forten
See also DLB 50

Foscolo, Ugo 1778-1827 .... **NCLC 8, 97**

Fosse, Bob CLC 20
See also Fosse, Robert Louis

Fosse, Robert Louis 1927-1987
See Fosse, Bob
See also CA 110; 123

Foster, Hannah Webster
1758-1840 .... **NCLC 99**
See also DLB 37, 200

Foster, Stephen Collins
1826-1864 .... **NCLC 26**

Foucault, Michel 1926-1984 . **CLC 31, 34, 69**
See also CA 105; 113; CANR 34; DLB 242; GLL 1; MTCW 1, 2

Fouque, Friedrich (Heinrich Karl) de la Motte 1777-1843 .... **NCLC 2**
See also DLB 90

Fourier, Charles 1772-1837 .... **NCLC 51**

Fournier, Pierre 1916- .... **CLC 11**
See also Gascar, Pierre
See also CA 89-92; CANR 16, 40

Fowles, John (Philip) 1926- .. **CLC 1, 2, 3, 4, 6, 9, 10, 15, 33, 87; DAB; DAC; DAM MST; SSC 33**
See also BRWS 1; CA 5-8R; CANR 25, 71; CDBLB 1960 to Present; DA3; DLB 14, 139, 207; MTCW 1, 2; SATA 22

Fox, Paula 1923- .... **CLC 2, 8, 121**
See also AAYA 3, 37; AW; CA 73-76; CANR 20, 36, 62; CLR 1, 44; DLB 52; JRDA; MAICYA; MTCW 1; SATA 17, 60, 120

Fox, William Price (Jr.) 1926- .... **CLC 22**
See also CA 17-20R; CAAS 19; CANR 11; DLB 2; DLBY 81

Foxe, John 1517(?)-1587 .... **LC 14**
See also DLB 132

Frame, Janet CLC 2, 3, 6, 22, 66, 96; SSC 29
See also Clutha, Janet Paterson Frame

France, Anatole TCLC 9
See also Thibault, Jacques Anatole Francois
See also DLB 123; MTCW 1

Francis, Claude 19(?)- .... **CLC 50**

Francis, Dick 1920- .... **CLC 2, 22, 42, 102; DAM POP**
See also AAYA 5, 21; BEST 89:3; CA 5-8R; CANR 9, 42, 68; CDBLB 1960 to Present; DA3; DLB 87; INT CANR-9; MTCW 1, 2

Francis, Robert (Churchill)
1901-1987 .... **CLC 15**
See also CA 1-4R; 123; CANR 1

Frank, Anne(lies Marie)
1929-1945 . **TCLC 17; DA; DAB; DAC; DAM MST**
See also AAYA 12; CA 113; 133; CANR 68; DA3; MTCW 1, 2; SATA 87; SATA-Brief 42

Frank, Bruno 1887-1945 .... **TCLC 81**
See also CA 189; DLB 118

Frank, Elizabeth 1945- .... **CLC 39**
See also CA 121; 126; CANR 78; INT 126

Frankl, Viktor E(mil) 1905-1997 ...... **CLC 93**
See also CA 65-68; 161

Franklin, Benjamin
See Hasek, Jaroslav (Matej Frantisek)

Franklin, Benjamin 1706-1790 .. **LC 25; DA; DAB; DAC; DAM MST**
See also AW; CDALB 1640-1865; DA3; DLB 24, 43, 73

Franklin, (Stella Maria Sarah) Miles (Lampe) 1879-1954 .... **TCLC 7**
See also CA 104; 164; DLB 230; MTCW 2

Fraser, (Lady)Antonia (Pakenham)
1932- .... **CLC 32, 107**
See also CA 85-88; CANR 44, 65; MTCW 1, 2; SATA-Brief 32

Fraser, George MacDonald 1925- ...... **CLC 7**
See also CA 45-48, 180; CAAE 180; CANR 2, 48, 74; MTCW 1

Fraser, Sylvia 1935- .... **CLC 64**
See also CA 45-48; CANR 1, 16, 60; CCA 1

Frayn, Michael 1933- .... **CLC 3, 7, 31, 47; DAM DRAM, NOV**
See also CA 5-8R; CANR 30, 69; DLB 13, 14, 194; MTCW 1, 2

Fraze, Candida (Merrill) 1945- .... **CLC 50**
See also CA 126

Frazer, Andrew
See Marlowe, Stephen

Frazer, J(ames) G(eorge)
1854-1941 .... **TCLC 32**
See also BRWS 3; CA 118

Frazer, Robert Caine
See Creasey, John

Frazer, Sir James George
See Frazer, J(ames) G(eorge)

Frazier, Charles 1950- .... **CLC 109**
See also AAYA 34; CA 161

Frazier, Ian 1951- .... **CLC 46**
See also CA 130; CANR 54, 93

Frederic, Harold 1856-1898 .... **NCLC 10**
See also DLB 12, 23; DLBD 13

Frederick, John
See Faust, Frederick (Schiller)
See also TCWW 2

Frederick the Great 1712-1786 .... **LC 14**

Fredro, Aleksander 1793-1876 .... **NCLC 8**

Freeling, Nicolas 1927- .... **CLC 38**
See also CA 49-52; CAAS 12; CANR 1,
17, 50, 84; DLB 87

Freeman, Douglas Southall
1886-1953 .... **TCLC 11**
See also CA 109; DLB 17; DLBD 17

Freeman, Judith 1946- .... **CLC 55**
See also CA 148

Freeman, Mary E(leanor) Wilkins
1852-1930 .... **TCLC 9; SSC 1**
See also CA 106; 177; DLB 12, 78, 221

Freeman, R(ichard) Austin
1862-1943 .... **TCLC 21**
See also CA 113; CANR 84; DLB 70

French, Albert 1943- .... **CLC 86**
See also BW 3; CA 167

French, Marilyn 1929- .... **CLC 10, 18, 60;**
DAM DRAM, NOV, POP
See also CA 69-72; CANR 3, 31; INT
CANR-31; MTCW 1, 2

French, Paul
See Asimov, Isaac

Freneau, Philip Morin 1752-1832 ... **NCLC 1**
See also AMWS 2; DLB 37, 43

Freud, Sigmund 1856-1939 .... **TCLC 52**
See also CA 115; 133; CANR 69; MTCW
1, 2

Friedan, Betty (Naomi) 1921- .... **CLC 74**
See also CA 65-68; CANR 18, 45, 74;
MTCW 1, 2

Friedlander, Saul 1932- .... **CLC 90**
See also CA 117; 130; CANR 72

Friedman, B(ernard) H(arper)
1926- .... **CLC 7**
See also CA 1-4R; CANR 3, 48

Friedman, Bruce Jay 1930- ...... **CLC 3, 5, 56**
See also CA 9-12R; CANR 25, 52; DLB 2,
28; INT CANR-25

Friel, Brian 1929- .... **CLC 5, 42, 59, 115; DC**
8
See also BRWS 5; CA 21-24R; CANR 33,
69; DLB 13; MTCW 1

Friis-Baastad, Babbis Ellinor
1921-1970 .... **CLC 12**
See also CA 17-20R; 134; SATA 7

Frisch, Max (Rudolf) 1911-1991 ... **CLC 3, 9,**
14, 18, 32, 44; DAM DRAM, NOV
See also CA 85-88; 134; CANR 32, 74;
DLB 69, 124; MTCW 1, 2

Fromentin, Eugene (Samuel Auguste)
1820-1876 .... **NCLC 10**
See also DLB 123

Frost, Frederick
See Faust, Frederick (Schiller)
See also TCWW 2

Frost, Robert (Lee) 1874-1963 .. **CLC 1, 3, 4,**
9, 10, 13, 15, 26, 34, 44; DA; DAB;
DAC; DAM MST, POET; PC 1
See also AAYA 21; CA 89-92; CANR 33;
CDALB 1917-1929; CLR 67; DA3; DLB
54; DLBD 7; MTCW 1, 2; SATA 14

Froude, James Anthony
1818-1894 .... **NCLC 43**
See also DLB 18, 57, 144

Froy, Herald
See Waterhouse, Keith (Spencer)

Fry, Christopher 1907- .... **CLC 2, 10, 14;**
DAM DRAM
See also BRWS 3; CA 17-20R; CAAS 23;
CANR 9, 30, 74; DLB 13; MTCW 1, 2;
SATA 66

Frye, (Herman) Northrop
1912-1991 .... **CLC 24, 70**
See also CA 5-8R; 133; CANR 8, 37; DLB
67, 68; MTCW 1, 2

Fuchs, Daniel 1909-1993 .... **CLC 8, 22**
See also CA 81-84; 142; CAAS 5; CANR
40; DLB 9, 26, 28; DLBY 93

Fuchs, Daniel 1934- .... **CLC 34**
See also CA 37-40R; CANR 14, 48

Fuentes, Carlos 1928- .. **CLC 3, 8, 10, 13, 22,**
41, 60, 113; DA; DAB; DAC; DAM
MST, MULT, NOV; HLC 1; SSC 24
See also AAYA 4; AITN 2; AW; CA 69-72;
CANR 10, 32, 68; CWW 2; DA3; DLB
113; HW 1, 2; MTCW 1, 2

Fuentes, Gregorio Lopez y
See Lopez y Fuentes, Gregorio

Fuertes, Gloria 1918-1998 .... **PC 27**
See also CA 178, 180; DLB 108; HW 2;
SATA 115

Fugard, (Harold) Athol 1932- . **CLC 5, 9, 14,**
25, 40, 80; DAM DRAM; DC 3
See also AAYA 17; CA 85-88; CANR 32,
54; DLB 225; MTCW 1

Fugard, Sheila 1932- .... **CLC 48**
See also CA 125

Fukuyama, Francis 1952- .... **CLC 131**
See also CA 140; CANR 72

Fuller, Charles (H., Jr.) 1939- .... **CLC 25;**
BLC 2; DAM DRAM, MULT; DC 1
See also BW 2; CA 108; 112; CANR 87;
DLB 38; INT 112; MTCW 1

Fuller, Henry Blake 1857-1929 .... **TCLC 103**
See also CA 108; 177; DLB 12

Fuller, John (Leopold) 1937- .... **CLC 62**
See also CA 21-24R; CANR 9, 44; DLB 40

Fuller, Margaret
See Ossoli, Sarah Margaret (Fuller marchesa
d')
See also AMWS 2

Fuller, Roy (Broadbent) 1912-1991 ... **CLC 4,**
28
See also CA 5-8R; 135; CAAS 10; CANR
53, 83; DLB 15, 20; SATA 87

Fuller, Sarah Margaret
See Ossoli, Sarah Margaret (Fuller marchesa
d')

Fulton, Alice 1952- .... **CLC 52**
See also CA 116; CANR 57, 88; DLB 193

Furphy, Joseph 1843-1912 .... **TCLC 25**
See also CA 163; DLB 230

Fuson, Robert H(enderson) 1927- .... **CLC 70**
See also CA 89-92

Fussell, Paul 1924- .... **CLC 74**
See also BEST 90:1; CA 17-20R; CANR 8,
21, 35, 69; INT CANR-21; MTCW 1, 2

Futabatei, Shimei 1864-1909 .... **TCLC 44**
See also CA 162; DLB 180

Futrelle, Jacques 1875-1912 .... **TCLC 19**
See also CA 113; 155

Gaboriau, Emile 1835-1873 .... **NCLC 14**

Gadda, Carlo Emilio 1893-1973 .... **CLC 11**
See also CA 89-92; DLB 177

Gaddis, William 1922-1998 ... **CLC 1, 3, 6, 8,**
10, 19, 43, 86
See also AMWS 4; CA 17-20R; 172; CANR
21, 48; DLB 2; MTCW 1, 2

Gage, Walter
See Inge, William (Motter)

Gaines, Ernest J(ames) 1933- ...... **CLC 3, 11,**
18, 86; BLC 2; DAM MULT
See also AAYA 18; AITN 1; AW; BW 2, 3;
CA 9-12R; CANR 6, 24, 42, 75; CDALB
1968-1988; CLR 62; DA3; DLB 2, 33,
152; DLBY 80; MTCW 1, 2; SATA 86

Gaitskill, Mary 1954- .... **CLC 69**
See also CA 128; CANR 61

Galdos, Benito Perez
See Perez Galdos, Benito

Gale, Zona 1874-1938 .... **TCLC 7; DAM**
DRAM
See also CA 105; 153; CANR 84; DLB 9,
78, 228

Galeano, Eduardo (Hughes) 1940- . **CLC 72;**
HLCS 1
See also CA 29-32R; CANR 13, 32; HW 1

Galiano, Juan Valera y Alcala
See Valera y Alcala-Galiano, Juan

Galilei, Galileo 1564-1642 .... **LC 45**

Gallagher, Tess 1943- ...... **CLC 18, 63; DAM**
POET; PC 9
See also CA 106; DLB 212

Gallant, Mavis 1922- .. **CLC 7, 18, 38; DAC;**
DAM MST; SSC 5
See also CA 69-72; CANR 29, 69; CCA 1;
DLB 53; MTCW 1, 2

Gallant, Roy A(rthur) 1924- .... **CLC 17**
See also CA 5-8R; CANR 4, 29, 54; CLR
30; MAICYA; SATA 4, 68, 110

Gallico, Paul (William) 1897-1976 ..... **CLC 2**
See also AITN 1; CA 5-8R; 69-72; CANR
23; DLB 9, 171; MAICYA; SATA 13

Gallo, Max Louis 1932- .... **CLC 95**
See also CA 85-88

Gallois, Lucien
See Desnos, Robert

Gallup, Ralph
See Whitemore, Hugh (John)

Galsworthy, John 1867-1933 .... **TCLC 1, 45;**
DA; DAB; DAC; DAM DRAM, MST,
NOV; SSC 22
See also AW; CA 104; 141; CANR 75; CD-
BLB 1890-1914; DA3; DLB 10, 34, 98,
162; DLBD 16; MTCW 1

Galt, John 1779-1839 .... **NCLC 1**
See also DLB 99, 116, 159

Galvin, James 1951- .... **CLC 38**
See also CA 108; CANR 26

Gamboa, Federico 1864-1939 .... **TCLC 36**
See also CA 167; HW 2

Gébler, Carlo (Ernest) 1954- .... **CLC 39**
See also CA 119; 133; CANR 96

Gandhi, M. K.
See Gandhi, Mohandas Karamchand

Gandhi, Mahatma
See Gandhi, Mohandas Karamchand

Gandhi, Mohandas Karamchand
1869-1948 .... **TCLC 59; DAM MULT**
See also CA 121; 132; DA3; MTCW 1, 2

Gann, Ernest Kellogg 1910-1991 ..... **CLC 23**
See also AITN 1; CA 1-4R; 136; CANR 1,
83

Garber, Eric 1943(?)-
See Holleran, Andrew
See also CANR 89

Garcia, Cristina 1958- .... **CLC 76**
See also CA 141; CANR 73; HW 2

Garcia Lorca, Federico 1898-1936 . **TCLC 1,**
7, 49; DA; DAB; DAC; DAM DRAM,
MST, MULT, POET; DC 2; HLC 2;
PC 3
See also Lorca, Federico Garcia
See also AW; CA 104; 131; CANR 81;
DA3; DLB 108; HW 1, 2; MTCW 1, 2

García Márquez, Gabriel (Jose)
1928- .... **CLC 2, 3, 8, 10, 15, 27, 47, 55, 68; DA; DAB; DAC; DAM MST, MULT, NOV, POP; HLC 1; SSC 8**
See also AAYA 3, 33; AW; BEST 89:1, 90:4; CA 33-36R; CANR 10, 28, 50, 75, 82; DA3; DLB 113; HW 1, 2; MTCW 1, 2

Garcilaso de la Vega, El Inca 1503-1536
See also HLCS 1

Gard, Janice
See Latham, Jean Lee

Gard, Roger Martin du
See Martin du Gard, Roger

Gardam, Jane 1928- .... **CLC 43**
See also AW; CA 49-52; CANR 2, 18, 33, 54; CLR 12; DLB 14, 161, 231; MAICYA; MTCW 1; SAAS 9; SATA 39, 76; SATA-Brief 28

Gardner, Herb(ert) 1934- .... **CLC 44**
See also CA 149

Gardner, John (Champlin), Jr.
1933-1982 ...... **CLC 2, 3, 5, 7, 8, 10, 18, 28, 34; DAM NOV, POP; SSC 7**
See also AITN 1; AMWS 5; CA 65-68; 107; CANR 33, 73; CDALBS; DA3; DLB 2; DLBY 82; MTCW 1; SATA 40; SATA-Obit 31

Gardner, John (Edmund) 1926- ...... **CLC 30; DAM POP**
See also CA 103; CANR 15, 69; MTCW 1

Gardner, Miriam
See Bradley, Marion Zimmer
See also GLL 1

Gardner, Noel
See Kuttner, Henry

Gardons, S. S.
See Snodgrass, W(illiam) D(e Witt)

Garfield, Leon 1921-1996 .... **CLC 12**
See also AAYA 8; AW; CA 17-20R; 152; CANR 38, 41, 78; CLR 21; DLB 161; JRDA; MAICYA; SATA 1, 32, 76; SATA-Obit 90

Garland, (Hannibal) Hamlin
1860-1940 .... **TCLC 3; SSC 18**
See also CA 104; DLB 12, 71, 78, 186; TCWW 2

Garneau, (Hector de) Saint-Denys
1912-1943 .... **TCLC 13**
See also CA 111; DLB 88

Garner, Alan 1934- ..... **CLC 17; DAB; DAM POP**
See also AAYA 18; AW; CA 73-76; 178; CAAE 178; CANR 15, 64; CLR 20; DLB 161; MAICYA; MTCW 1, 2; SATA 18, 69; SATA-Essay 108

Garner, Hugh 1913-1979 .... **CLC 13**
See also Warwick, Jarvis
See also CA 69-72; CANR 31; CCA 1; DLB 68

Garnett, David 1892-1981 .... **CLC 3**
See also CA 5-8R; 103; CANR 17, 79; DLB 34; MTCW 2

Garos, Stephanie
See Katz, Steve

Garrett, George (Palmer) 1929- .. **CLC 3, 11, 51; SSC 30**
See also AMWS 7; CA 1-4R; CAAS 5; CANR 1, 42, 67; DLB 2, 5, 130, 152; DLBY 83

Garrick, David 1717-1779 .... **LC 15; DAM DRAM**
See also DLB 84

Garrigue, Jean 1914-1972 .... **CLC 2, 8**
See also CA 5-8R; 37-40R; CANR 20

Garrison, Frederick
See Sinclair, Upton (Beall)

Garro, Elena 1920(?)-1998
See also CA 131; 169; CWW 2; DLB 145; HLCS 1; HW 1

Garth, Will
See Hamilton, Edmond; Kuttner, Henry

Garvey, Marcus (Moziah, Jr.)
1887-1940 ...... **TCLC 41; BLC 2; DAM MULT**
See also BW 1; CA 120; 124; CANR 79

Gary, Romain CLC 25
See also Kacew, Romain
See also DLB 83

Gascar, Pierre CLC 11
See also Fournier, Pierre

Gascoyne, David (Emery) 1916- .... **CLC 45**
See also CA 65-68; CANR 10, 28, 54; DLB 20; MTCW 1

Gaskell, Elizabeth Cleghorn
1810-1865 .... **NCLC 5, 70, 97; DAB; DAM MST; SSC 25**
See also CDBLB 1832-1890; DLB 21, 144, 159

Gass, William H(oward) 1924- . **CLC 1, 2, 8, 11, 15, 39, 132; SSC 12**
See also AMWS 6; CA 17-20R; CANR 30, 71; DLB 2, 227; MTCW 1, 2

Gassendi, Pierre 1592-1655 .... **LC 54**

Gasset, Jose Ortega y
See Ortega y Gasset, Jose

Gates, Henry Louis, Jr. 1950- .... **CLC 65; BLCS; DAM MULT**
See also BW 2, 3; CA 109; CANR 25, 53, 75; DA3; DLB 67; MTCW 1

Gautier, Theophile 1811-1872 .. **NCLC 1, 59; DAM POET; PC 18; SSC 20**
See also DLB 119

Gawsworth, John
See Bates, H(erbert) E(rnest)

Gay, John 1685-1732 .. **LC 49; DAM DRAM**
See also DLB 84, 95

Gay, Oliver
See Gogarty, Oliver St. John

Gaye, Marvin (Penze) 1939-1984 ..... **CLC 26**
See also CA 112

Gee, Maggie (Mary) 1948- .... **CLC 57**
See also CA 130; DLB 207

Gee, Maurice (Gough) 1931- .... **CLC 29**
See also CA 97-100; CANR 67; CLR 56; SATA 46, 101

Gelbart, Larry (Simon) 1928- .... **CLC 21, 61**
See also Gelbart, Larry
See also CA 73-76; CANR 45, 94

Gelbart, Larry 1928-
See Gelbart, Larry (Simon)

Gelber, Jack 1932- .... **CLC 1, 6, 14, 79**
See also CA 1-4R; CANR 2; DLB 7, 228

Gellhorn, Martha (Ellis)
1908-1998 .... **CLC 14, 60**
See also CA 77-80; 164; CANR 44; DLBY 82, 98

Genet, Jean 1910-1986 .. **CLC 1, 2, 5, 10, 14, 44, 46; DAM DRAM**
See also CA 13-16R; CANR 18; DA3; DLB 72; DLBY 86; GLL 1; MTCW 1, 2

Gent, Peter 1942- .... **CLC 29**
See also AITN 1; CA 89-92; DLBY 82

Gentile, Giovanni 1875-1944 .... **TCLC 96**
See also CA 119

Gentlewoman in New England, A
See Bradstreet, Anne

Gentlewoman in Those Parts, A
See Bradstreet, Anne

Geoffrey of Monmouth c.
1100-1155 .... **CMLC 44**
See also DLB 146

George, Jean Craighead 1919- .... **CLC 35**
See also AAYA 8; AW; CA 5-8R; CANR 25; CLR 1; DLB 52; JRDA; MAICYA; SATA 2, 68

George, Stefan (Anton) 1868-1933 . **TCLC 2, 14**
See also CA 104

Georges, Georges Martin
See Simenon, Georges (Jacques Christian)

Gerhardi, William Alexander
See Gerhardie, William Alexander

Gerhardie, William Alexander
1895-1977 .... **CLC 5**
See also CA 25-28R; 73-76; CANR 18; DLB 36

Gerstler, Amy 1956- .... **CLC 70**
See also CA 146

Gertler, T. CLC 134
See also CA 116; 121

Ghalib NCLC 39, 78
See also Ghalib, Hsadullah Khan

Ghalib, Hsadullah Khan 1797-1869
See Ghalib
See also DAM POET

Ghelderode, Michel de 1898-1962 ..... **CLC 6, 11; DAM DRAM; DC 15**
See also CA 85-88; CANR 40, 77

Ghiselin, Brewster 1903- .... **CLC 23**
See also CA 13-16R; CAAS 10; CANR 13

Ghose, Aurabinda 1872-1950 .... **TCLC 63**
See also CA 163

Ghose, Zulfikar 1935- .... **CLC 42**
See also CA 65-68; CANR 67

Ghosh, Amitav 1956- .... **CLC 44**
See also CA 147; CANR 80

Giacosa, Giuseppe 1847-1906 .... **TCLC 7**
See also CA 104

Gibb, Lee
See Waterhouse, Keith (Spencer)

Gibbon, Lewis Grassic TCLC 4
See also Mitchell, James Leslie

Gibbons, Kaye 1960- .... **CLC 50, 88; DAM POP**
See also AAYA 34; CA 151; CANR 75; DA3; MTCW 1; SATA 117

Gibran, Kahlil 1883-1931 .... **TCLC 1, 9; DAM POET, POP; PC 9**
See also CA 104; 150; DA3; MTCW 2

Gibran, Khalil
See Gibran, Kahlil

Gibson, William 1914- .. **CLC 23; DA; DAB; DAC; DAM DRAM, MST**
See also AW; CA 9-12R; CANR 9, 42, 75; DLB 7; MTCW 1; SATA 66; SCFW 2

Gibson, William (Ford) 1948- ... **CLC 39, 63; DAM POP**
See also AAYA 12; CA 126; 133; CANR 52, 90; DA3; MTCW 1

Gide, Andre (Paul Guillaume)
1869-1951 . **TCLC 5, 12, 36; DA; DAB; DAC; DAM MST, NOV; SSC 13**
See also AW; CA 104; 124; DA3; DLB 65; MTCW 1, 2

Gifford, Barry (Colby) 1946- .... **CLC 34**
See also CA 65-68; CANR 9, 30, 40, 90

Gilbert, Frank
See De Voto, Bernard (Augustine)

Gilbert, W(illiam) S(chwenck)
1836-1911 .... **TCLC 3; DAM DRAM, POET**
See also CA 104; 173; SATA 36

Gilbreth, Frank B., Jr. 1911-2001 .... **CLC 17**
See also CA 9-12R; SATA 2

Gilchrist, Ellen 1935- .... **CLC 34, 48, 143; DAM POP; SSC 14**
See also CA 113; 116; CANR 41, 61; DLB 130; MTCW 1, 2

Giles, Molly 1942- .... **CLC 39**
See also CA 126

Hoagland, Edward 1932- .... **CLC 28**
See also CA 1-4R; CANR 2, 31, 57; DLB 6; SATA 51; TCWW 2

Hoban, Russell (Conwell) 1925- . **CLC 7, 25; DAM NOV**
See also CA 5-8R; CANR 23, 37, 66; CLR 3, 69; DLB 52; MAICYA; MTCW 1, 2; SATA 1, 40, 78

Hobbes, Thomas 1588-1679 .... **LC 36**
See also DLB 151

Hobbs, Perry
See Blackmur, R(ichard) P(almer)

Hobson, Laura Z(ametkin)
1900-1986 .... **CLC 7, 25**
See also Field, Peter
See also CA 17-20R; 118; CANR 55; DLB 28; SATA 52

Hoch, Edward D(entinger) 1930-
See Queen, Ellery
See also CA 29-32R; CANR 11, 27, 51

Hochhuth, Rolf 1931- .. **CLC 4, 11, 18; DAM DRAM**
See also CA 5-8R; CANR 33, 75; CWW 2; DLB 124; MTCW 1, 2

Hochman, Sandra 1936- .... **CLC 3, 8**
See also CA 5-8R; DLB 5

Hochwaelder, Fritz 1911-1986 .... **CLC 36; DAM DRAM**
See also CA 29-32R; 120; CANR 42; MTCW 1

Hochwalder, Fritz
See Hochwaelder, Fritz

Hocking, Mary (Eunice) 1921- .... **CLC 13**
See also CA 101; CANR 18, 40

Hodgins, Jack 1938- .... **CLC 23**
See also CA 93-96; DLB 60

Hodgson, William Hope
1877(?)-1918 .... **TCLC 13**
See also CA 111; 164; DLB 70, 153, 156, 178; MTCW 2

Hoeg, Peter 1957- .... **CLC 95**
See also CA 151; CANR 75; DA3; MTCW 2

Hoffman, Alice 1952- ... **CLC 51; DAM NOV**
See also AAYA 37; CA 77-80; CANR 34, 66; MTCW 1, 2

Hoffman, Daniel (Gerard) 1923- . **CLC 6, 13, 23**
See also CA 1-4R; CANR 4; DLB 5

Hoffman, Stanley 1944- .... **CLC 5**
See also CA 77-80

Hoffman, William 1925- .... **CLC 141**
See also CA 21-24R; CANR 9; DLB 234

Hoffman, William M(oses) 1939- ..... **CLC 40**
See also CA 57-60; CANR 11, 71

Hoffmann, E(rnst) T(heodor) A(madeus)
1776-1822 .... **NCLC 2; SSC 13**
See also DLB 90; SATA 27

Hofmann, Gert 1931- .... **CLC 54**
See also CA 128

Hofmannsthal, Hugo von
1874-1929 ...... **TCLC 11; DAM DRAM; DC 4**
See also von Hofmannsthal, Hugo
See also CA 106; 153; DLB 81, 118

Hogan, Linda 1947- .. **CLC 73; DAM MULT**
See also AMWS 4; CA 120; CANR 45, 73; DLB 175; NNAL; TCWW 2

Hogarth, Charles
See Creasey, John

Hogarth, Emmett
See Polonsky, Abraham (Lincoln)

Hogg, James 1770-1835 .... **NCLC 4**
See also DLB 93, 116, 159

Holbach, Paul Henri Thiry Baron
1723-1789 .... **LC 14**

Holberg, Ludvig 1684-1754 .... **LC 6**

Holcroft, Thomas 1745-1809 .... **NCLC 85**
See also DLB 39, 89, 158

Holden, Ursula 1921- .... **CLC 18**
See also CA 101; CAAS 8; CANR 22

Hölderlin, (Johann Christian) Friedrich
1770-1843 .... **NCLC 16; PC 4**

Holdstock, Robert
See Holdstock, Robert P.

Holdstock, Robert P. 1948- .... **CLC 39**
See also CA 131; CANR 81

Holland, Isabelle 1920- .... **CLC 21**
See also AAYA 11; CA 21-24R, 181; CAAE 181; CANR 10, 25, 47; CLR 57; JRDA; MAICYA; SATA 8, 70; SATA-Essay 103

Holland, Marcus
See Caldwell, (Janet Miriam) Taylor (Holland)

Hollander, John 1929- .... **CLC 2, 5, 8, 14**
See also CA 1-4R; CANR 1, 52; DLB 5; SATA 13

Hollander, Paul
See Silverberg, Robert

Holleran, Andrew 1943(?)- .... **CLC 38**
See also Garber, Eric
See also CA 144; GLL 1

Holley, Marietta 1836(?)-1926 .... **TCLC 99**
See also CA 118; DLB 11

Hollinghurst, Alan 1954- .... **CLC 55, 91**
See also CA 114; DLB 207; GLL 1

Hollis, Jim
See Summers, Hollis (Spurgeon, Jr.)

Holly, Buddy 1936-1959 .... **TCLC 65**

Holmes, Gordon
See Shiel, M(atthew) P(hipps)

Holmes, John
See Souster, (Holmes) Raymond

Holmes, John Clellon 1926-1988 ...... **CLC 56**
See also CA 9-12R; 125; CANR 4; DLB 16

Holmes, Oliver Wendell, Jr.
1841-1935 .... **TCLC 77**
See also CA 114; 186

Holmes, Oliver Wendell
1809-1894 .... **NCLC 14, 81**
See also AMWS 1; CDALB 1640-1865; DLB 1, 189, 235; SATA 34

Holmes, Raymond
See Souster, (Holmes) Raymond

Holt, Victoria
See Hibbert, Eleanor Alice Burford

Holub, Miroslav 1923-1998 .... **CLC 4**
See also CA 21-24R; 169; CANR 10; CWW 2; DLB 232

Homer c. 8th cent. B.C.- .. **CMLC 1, 16; DA; DAB; DAC; DAM MST, POET; PC 23**
See also AW; DA3; DLB 176

Hongo, Garrett Kaoru 1951- .... **PC 23**
See also CA 133; CAAS 22; DLB 120

Honig, Edwin 1919- .... **CLC 33**
See also CA 5-8R; CAAS 8; CANR 4, 45; DLB 5

Hood, Hugh (John Blagdon) 1928- . **CLC 15, 28; SSC 42**
See also CA 49-52; CAAS 17; CANR 1, 33, 87; DLB 53

Hood, Thomas 1799-1845 .... **NCLC 16**
See also DLB 96

Hooker, (Peter) Jeremy 1941- .... **CLC 43**
See also CA 77-80; CANR 22; DLB 40

hooks, bell **CLC 94; BLCS**
See also Watkins, Gloria Jean
See also MTCW 2

Hope, A(lec) D(erwent) 1907-2000 .... **CLC 3, 51**
See also CA 21-24R; 188; CANR 33, 74; MTCW 1, 2

Hope, Anthony 1863-1933 .... **TCLC 83**
See also CA 157; DLB 153, 156

Hope, Brian
See Creasey, John

Hope, Christopher (David Tully)
1944- .... **CLC 52**
See also CA 106; CANR 47; DLB 225; SATA 62

Hopkins, Gerard Manley
1844-1889 .... **NCLC 17; DA; DAB; DAC; DAM MST, POET; PC 15**
See also AW; CDBLB 1890-1914; DA3; DLB 35, 57

Hopkins, John (Richard) 1931-1998 .. **CLC 4**
See also CA 85-88; 169

Hopkins, Pauline Elizabeth
1859-1930 ...... **TCLC 28; BLC 2; DAM MULT**
See also BW 2, 3; CA 141; CANR 82; DLB 50

Hopkinson, Francis 1737-1791 .... **LC 25**
See also DLB 31

Hopley-Woolrich, Cornell George 1903-1968
See Woolrich, Cornell
See also CA 13-14; CANR 58; CAP 1; DLB 226; MTCW 2

Horace 65B.C.-8B.C. .... **CMLC 39**
See also DLB 211

Horatio
See Proust, (Valentin-Louis-George-Eugene-)Marcel

Horgan, Paul (George Vincent O'Shaughnessy) 1903-1995 . **CLC 9, 53; DAM NOV**
See also CA 13-16R; 147; CANR 9, 35; DLB 212; DLBY 85; INT CANR-9; MTCW 1, 2; SATA 13; SATA-Obit 84; TCWW 2

Horn, Peter
See Kuttner, Henry

Hornem, Horace Esq.
See Byron, George Gordon (Noel)

Horney, Karen (Clementine Theodore Danielsen) 1885-1952 .... **TCLC 71**
See also CA 114; 165

Hornung, E(rnest) W(illiam)
1866-1921 .... **TCLC 59**
See also CA 108; 160; DLB 70

Horovitz, Israel (Arthur) 1939- ...... **CLC 56; DAM DRAM**
See also CA 33-36R; CANR 46, 59; DLB 7

Horton, George Moses
1797(?)-1883(?) .... **NCLC 87**
See also DLB 50

Horvath, Odon von
See Horvath, Oedoen von
See also DLB 85, 124

Horvath, Oedoen von 1901-1938 ... **TCLC 45**
See also Horvath, Odon von; von Horvath, Oedoen
See also CA 118

Horwitz, Julius 1920-1986 .... **CLC 14**
See also CA 9-12R; 119; CANR 12

Hospital, Janette Turner 1942- .... **CLC 42**
See also CA 108; CANR 48

Hostos, E. M. de
See Hostos (y Bonilla), Eugenio Maria de

Hostos, Eugenio M. de
See Hostos (y Bonilla), Eugenio Maria de

Hostos, Eugenio Maria
See Hostos (y Bonilla), Eugenio Maria de

Hostos (y Bonilla), Eugenio Maria de
1839-1903 .... **TCLC 24**
See also CA 123; 131; HW 1

Houdini
See Lovecraft, H(oward) P(hillips)

Hougan, Carolyn 1943- .... **CLC 34**
See also CA 139

Household, Geoffrey (Edward West)
1900-1988 .... **CLC 11**
See also CA 77-80; 126; CANR 58; DLB 87; SATA 14; SATA-Obit 59

Housman, A(lfred) E(dward)
1859-1936 .... **TCLC 1, 10; DA; DAB; DAC; DAM MST, POET; PC 2**
See also AW; CA 104; 125; DA3; DLB 19; MTCW 1, 2

Housman, Laurence 1865-1959 .... **TCLC 7**
See also CA 106; 155; DLB 10; SATA 25

Howard, Elizabeth Jane 1923- ..... **CLC 7, 29**
See also CA 5-8R; CANR 8, 62

Howard, Maureen 1930- .... **CLC 5, 14, 46**
See also CA 53-56; CANR 31, 75; DLBY 83; INT CANR-31; MTCW 1, 2

Howard, Richard 1929- .... **CLC 7, 10, 47**
See also AITN 1; CA 85-88; CANR 25, 80; DLB 5; INT CANR-25

Howard, Robert E(rvin)
1906-1936 .... **TCLC 8**
See also CA 105; 157

Howard, Warren F.
See Pohl, Frederik

Howe, Fanny (Quincy) 1940- .... **CLC 47**
See also CA 117; CAAE 187; CAAS 27; CANR 70; SATA-Brief 52

Howe, Irving 1920-1993 .... **CLC 85**
See also AMWS 6; CA 9-12R; 141; CANR 21, 50; DLB 67; MTCW 1, 2

Howe, Julia Ward 1819-1910 .... **TCLC 21**
See also CA 117; DLB 1, 189, 235

Howe, Susan 1937- .... **CLC 72**
See also AMWS 4; CA 160; DLB 120

Howe, Tina 1937- .... **CLC 48**
See also CA 109

Howell, James 1594(?)-1666 .... **LC 13**
See also DLB 151

Howells, W. D.
See Howells, William Dean

Howells, William D.
See Howells, William Dean

Howells, William Dean 1837-1920 .. **TCLC 7, 17, 41; SSC 36**
See also CA 104; 134; CDALB 1865-1917; DLB 12, 64, 74, 79, 189; MTCW 2

Howes, Barbara 1914-1996 .... **CLC 15**
See also CA 9-12R; 151; CAAS 3; CANR 53; SATA 5

Hrabal, Bohumil 1914-1997 .... **CLC 13, 67**
See also CA 106; 156; CAAS 12; CANR 57; CWW 2; DLB 232

Hroswitha of Gandersheim c. 935-c. 1000 .... **CMLC 29**
See also DLB 148

Hsi, Chu 1130-1200 .... **CMLC 42**

Hsun, Lu
See Lu Hsun

Hubbard, L(afayette) Ron(ald)
1911-1986 .... **CLC 43; DAM POP**
See also CA 77-80; 118; CANR 52; DA3; MTCW 2

Huch, Ricarda (Octavia)
1864-1947 .... **TCLC 13**
See also CA 111; 189; DLB 66

Huddle, David 1942- .... **CLC 49**
See also CA 57-60; CAAS 20; CANR 89; DLB 130

Hudson, Jeffrey
See Crichton, (John) Michael

Hudson, W(illiam) H(enry)
1841-1922 .... **TCLC 29**
See also CA 115; 190; DLB 98, 153, 174; SATA 35

Hueffer, Ford Madox
See Ford, Ford Madox

Hughart, Barry 1934- .... **CLC 39**
See also CA 137

Hughes, Colin
See Creasey, John

Hughes, David (John) 1930- .... **CLC 48**
See also CA 116; 129; DLB 14

Hughes, Edward James
See Hughes, Ted
See also DAM MST, POET; DA3

Hughes, (James) Langston
1902-1967 .... **CLC 1, 5, 10, 15, 35, 44, 108; BLC 2; DA; DAB; DAC; DAM DRAM, MST, MULT, POET; DC 3; PC 1; SSC 6**
See also AAYA 12; AMWS 1; AW; BW 1, 3; CA 1-4R; 25-28R; CDALB 1929-1941; CLR 17; DA3; DLB 4, 7, 48, 51, 86, 228; JRDA; MAICYA; MTCW 1, 2; SATA 4, 33

Hughes, Richard (Arthur Warren)
1900-1976 .... **CLC 1, 11; DAM NOV**
See also CA 5-8R; 65-68; CANR 4; DLB 15, 161; MTCW 1; SATA 8; SATA-Obit 25

Hughes, Ted 1930-1998 . **CLC 2, 4, 9, 14, 37, 119; DAB; DAC; PC 7**
See also Hughes, Edward James
See also AW; BRWS 1; CA 1-4R; 171; CANR 1, 33, 66; CLR 3; DLB 40, 161; MAICYA; MTCW 1, 2; SATA 49; SATA-Brief 27; SATA-Obit 107

Hugo, Richard F(ranklin)
1923-1982 .... **CLC 6, 18, 32; DAM POET**
See also CA 49-52; 108; CANR 3; DLB 5, 206

Hugo, Victor (Marie) 1802-1885 .... **NCLC 3, 10, 21; DA; DAB; DAC; DAM DRAM, MST, NOV, POET; PC 17**
See also AAYA 28; AW; DA3; DLB 119, 192; SATA 47

Huidobro, Vicente
See Huidobro Fernandez, Vicente Garcia

Huidobro Fernandez, Vicente Garcia
1893-1948 .... **TCLC 31**
See also CA 131; HW 1

Hulme, Keri 1947- .... **CLC 39, 130**
See also CA 125; CANR 69; INT 125

Hulme, T(homas) E(rnest)
1883-1917 .... **TCLC 21**
See also CA 117; DLB 19

Hume, David 1711-1776 .... **LC 7, 56**
See also BRWS 3; DLB 104

Humphrey, William 1924-1997 .... **CLC 45**
See also CA 77-80; 160; CANR 68; DLB 212; TCWW 2

Humphreys, Emyr Owen 1919- .... **CLC 47**
See also CA 5-8R; CANR 3, 24; DLB 15

Humphreys, Josephine 1945- ..... **CLC 34, 57**
See also CA 121; 127; INT 127

Huneker, James Gibbons
1860-1921 .... **TCLC 65**
See also DLB 71

Hungerford, Pixie
See Brinsmead, H(esba) F(ay)

Hunt, E(verette) Howard, (Jr.)
1918- .... **CLC 3**
See also AITN 1; CA 45-48; CANR 2, 47

Hunt, Francesca
See Holland, Isabelle

Hunt, Howard
See Hunt, E(verette) Howard, (Jr.)

Hunt, Kyle
See Creasey, John

Hunt, (James Henry) Leigh
1784-1859 .... **NCLC 1, 70; DAM POET**
See also DLB 96, 110, 144

Hunt, Marsha 1946- .... **CLC 70**
See also BW 2, 3; CA 143; CANR 79

Hunt, Violet 1866(?)-1942 .... **TCLC 53**
See also CA 184; DLB 162, 197

Hunter, E. Waldo
See Sturgeon, Theodore (Hamilton)

Hunter, Evan 1926- .... **CLC 11, 31; DAM POP**
See also AAYA 39; CA 5-8R; CANR 5, 38, 62; DLBY 82; INT CANR-5; MTCW 1; SATA 25

Hunter, Kristin (Eggleston) 1931- .... **CLC 35**
See also AITN 1; AW; BW 1; CA 13-16R; CANR 13; CLR 3; DLB 33; INT CANR-13; MAICYA; SAAS 10; SATA 12

Hunter, Mary
See Austin, Mary (Hunter)

Hunter, Mollie 1922- .... **CLC 21**
See also McIlwraith, Maureen Mollie Hunter
See also AAYA 13; AW; CANR 37, 78; CLR 25; DLB 161; JRDA; MAICYA; SAAS 7; SATA 54, 106

Hunter, Robert (?)-1734 .... **LC 7**

Hurston, Zora Neale 1891-1960 .. **CLC 7, 30, 61; BLC 2; DA; DAC; DAM MST, MULT, NOV; DC 12; SSC 4**
See also AAYA 15; AW; BW 1, 3; CA 85-88; CANR 61; CDALBS; DA3; DLB 51, 86; MTCW 1, 2

Husserl, E. G.
See Husserl, Edmund (Gustav Albrecht)

Husserl, Edmund (Gustav Albrecht)
1859-1938 .... **TCLC 100**
See also CA 116; 133

Huston, John (Marcellus)
1906-1987 .... **CLC 20**
See also CA 73-76; 123; CANR 34; DLB 26

Hustvedt, Siri 1955- .... **CLC 76**
See also CA 137

Hutten, Ulrich von 1488-1523 .... **LC 16**
See also DLB 179

Huxley, Aldous (Leonard)
1894-1963 .... **CLC 1, 3, 4, 5, 8, 11, 18, 35, 79; DA; DAB; DAC; DAM MST, NOV; SSC 39**
See also AAYA 11; AW; CA 85-88; CANR 44; CDBLB 1914-1945; DA3; DLB 36, 100, 162, 195; MTCW 1, 2; SATA 63; SCFW 2

Huxley, T(homas) H(enry)
1825-1895 .... **NCLC 67**
See also DLB 57

Huysmans, Joris-Karl 1848-1907 ... **TCLC 7, 69**
See also CA 104; 165; DLB 123

Hwang, David Henry 1957- .. **CLC 55; DAM DRAM; DC 4**
See also CA 127; 132; CANR 76; DA3; DLB 212; INT 132; MTCW 2

Hyde, Anthony 1946- .... **CLC 42**
See also Chase, Nicholas
See also CA 136; CCA 1

Hyde, Margaret O(ldroyd) 1917- ..... **CLC 21**
See also CA 1-4R; CANR 1, 36; CLR 23; JRDA; MAICYA; SAAS 8; SATA 1, 42, 76

Hynes, James 1956(?)- .... **CLC 65**
See also CA 164

Hypatia c. 370-415 .... **CMLC 35**

Ian, Janis 1951- .... **CLC 21**
See also CA 105; 187

Ibanez, Vicente Blasco
See Blasco Iba

Ibarbourou, Juana de 1895-1979
See also HLCS 2; HW 1

Ibarguengoitia, Jorge 1928-1983 ...... **CLC 37**
See also CA 124; 113; HW 1

Ibsen, Henrik (Johan) 1828-1906 ... **TCLC 2, 8, 16, 37, 52; DA; DAB; DAC; DAM DRAM, MST; DC 2**
See also AW; CA 104; 141; DA3

Ibuse, Masuji 1898-1993 .... **CLC 22**
See also CA 127; 141; DLB 180

Jefferson, Thomas 1743-1826 .... **NCLC 11**
See also CDALB 1640-1865; DA3; DLB 31

Jeffrey, Francis 1773-1850 .... **NCLC 33**
See also DLB 107

Jelakowitch, Ivan
See Heijermans, Herman

Jellicoe, (Patricia) Ann 1927- .... **CLC 27**
See also CA 85-88; DLB 13, 233

Jemyma
See Holley, Marietta

Jen, Gish CLC 70
See also Jen, Lillian

Jen, Lillian 1956(?)-
See Jen, Gish
See also CA 135; CANR 89

Jenkins, (John) Robin 1912- .... **CLC 52**
See also CA 1-4R; CANR 1; DLB 14

Jennings, Elizabeth (Joan) 1926- ...... **CLC 5, 14, 131**
See also BRWS 5; CA 61-64; CAAS 5; CANR 8, 39, 66; DLB 27; MTCW 1; SATA 66

Jennings, Waylon 1937- .... **CLC 21**

Jensen, Johannes V. 1873-1950 ...... **TCLC 41**
See also CA 170; DLB 214

Jensen, Laura (Linnea) 1948- .... **CLC 37**
See also CA 103

Jerome, Jerome K(lapka)
1859-1927 .... **TCLC 23**
See also CA 119; 177; DLB 10, 34, 135

Jerrold, Douglas William
1803-1857 .... **NCLC 2**
See also DLB 158, 159

Jewett, (Theodora) Sarah Orne
1849-1909 .... **TCLC 1, 22; SSC 6, 44**
See also CA 108; 127; CANR 71; DLB 12, 74, 221; SATA 15

Jewsbury, Geraldine (Endsor)
1812-1880 .... **NCLC 22**
See also DLB 21

Jhabvala, Ruth Prawer 1927- . **CLC 4, 8, 29, 94, 138; DAB; DAM NOV**
See also CA 1-4R; CANR 2, 29, 51, 74, 91; DLB 139, 194; INT CANR-29; MTCW 1, 2

Jibran, Kahlil
See Gibran, Kahlil

Jibran, Khalil
See Gibran, Kahlil

Jiles, Paulette 1943- .... **CLC 13, 58**
See also CA 101; CANR 70

Jimenez (Mantecon), Juan Ramon
1881-1958 .... **TCLC 4; DAM MULT, POET; HLC 1; PC 7**
See also CA 104; 131; CANR 74; DLB 134; HW 1; MTCW 1, 2

Jimenez, Ramon
See Jimenez (Mantecon), Juan Ramon

Jimenez Mantecon, Juan
See Jimenez (Mantecon), Juan Ramon

Jin, Ha
See Jin, Xuefei

Jin, Xuefei 1956- .... **CLC 109**
See also CA 152; CANR 91

Joel, Billy CLC 26
See also Joel, William Martin

Joel, William Martin 1949-
See Joel, Billy
See also CA 108

John, Saint 107th cent. -100 .... **CMLC 27**

John of the Cross, St. 1542-1591 .... **LC 18**

John Paul II, Pope 1920- .... **CLC 128**
See also CA 106; 133

Johnson, B(ryan) S(tanley William)
1933-1973 .... **CLC 6, 9**
See also CA 9-12R; 53-56; CANR 9; DLB 14, 40

Johnson, Benj. F. of Boo
See Riley, James Whitcomb

Johnson, Benjamin F. of Boo
See Riley, James Whitcomb

Johnson, Charles (Richard) 1948- .... **CLC 7, 51, 65; BLC 2; DAM MULT**
See also BW 2, 3; CA 116; CAAS 18; CANR 42, 66, 82; DLB 33; MTCW 2

Johnson, Denis 1949- .... **CLC 52**
See also CA 117; 121; CANR 71; DLB 120

Johnson, Diane 1934- .... **CLC 5, 13, 48**
See also CA 41-44R; CANR 17, 40, 62, 95; DLBY 80; INT CANR-17; MTCW 1

Johnson, Eyvind (Olof Verner)
1900-1976 .... **CLC 14**
See also CA 73-76; 69-72; CANR 34

Johnson, J. R.
See James, C(yril) L(ionel) R(obert)

Johnson, James Weldon
1871-1938 .. **TCLC 3, 19; BLC 2; DAM MULT, POET; PC 24**
See also BW 1, 3; CA 104; 125; CANR 82; CDALB 1917-1929; CLR 32; DA3; DLB 51; MTCW 1, 2; SATA 31

Johnson, Joyce 1935- .... **CLC 58**
See also CA 125; 129

Johnson, Judith (Emlyn) 1936- .... **CLC 7, 15**
See Sherwin, Judith Johnson
See also CA 25-28R; 153; CANR 34

Johnson, Lionel (Pigot)
1867-1902 .... **TCLC 19**
See also CA 117; DLB 19

Johnson, Marguerite (Annie)
See Angelou, Maya

Johnson, Mel
See Malzberg, Barry N(athaniel)

Johnson, Pamela Hansford
1912-1981 .... **CLC 1, 7, 27**
See also CA 1-4R; 104; CANR 2, 28; DLB 15; MTCW 1, 2

Johnson, Robert CLC 70

Johnson, Robert 1911(?)-1938 .... **TCLC 69**
See also BW 3; CA 174

Johnson, Samuel 1709-1784 . **LC 15, 52; DA; DAB; DAC; DAM MST**
See also AW; CDBLB 1660-1789; DLB 39, 95, 104, 142

Johnson, Uwe 1934-1984 .. **CLC 5, 10, 15, 40**
See also CA 1-4R; 112; CANR 1, 39; DLB 75; MTCW 1

Johnston, George (Benson) 1913- .... **CLC 51**
See also CA 1-4R; CANR 5, 20; DLB 88

Johnston, Jennifer (Prudence) 1930- . **CLC 7**
See also CA 85-88; CANR 92; DLB 14

Joinville, Jean de 1224(?)-1317 ..... **CMLC 38**

Jolley, (Monica) Elizabeth 1923- ..... **CLC 46; SSC 19**
See also CA 127; CAAS 13; CANR 59

Jones, Arthur Llewellyn 1863-1947
See Machen, Arthur
See also CA 104; 179

Jones, D(ouglas) G(ordon) 1929- ..... **CLC 10**
See also CA 29-32R; CANR 13, 90; DLB 53

Jones, David (Michael) 1895-1974 .... **CLC 2, 4, 7, 13, 42**
See also CA 9-12R; 53-56; CANR 28; CD-BLB 1945-1960; DLB 20, 100; MTCW 1

Jones, David Robert 1947-
See Bowie, David
See also CA 103

Jones, Diana Wynne 1934- .... **CLC 26**
See also AAYA 12; AW; CA 49-52; CANR 4, 26, 56; CLR 23; DLB 161; JRDA; MAICYA; SAAS 7; SATA 9, 70, 108

Jones, Edward P. 1950- .... **CLC 76**
See also BW 2, 3; CA 142; CANR 79

Jones, Gayl 1949- ..... **CLC 6, 9, 131; BLC 2; DAM MULT**
See also BW 2, 3; CA 77-80; CANR 27, 66; DA3; DLB 33; MTCW 1, 2

Jones, James 1931-1978 ...... **CLC 1, 3, 10, 39**
See also AITN 1, 2; CA 1-4R; 69-72; CANR 6; DLB 2, 143; DLBD 17; DLBY 98; MTCW 1

Jones, John J.
See Lovecraft, H(oward) P(hillips)

Jones, LeRoi CLC 1, 2, 3, 5, 10, 14
See also Baraka, Amiri
See also MTCW 2

Jones, Louis B. 1953- .... **CLC 65**
See also CA 141; CANR 73

Jones, Madison (Percy, Jr.) 1925- ...... **CLC 4**
See also CA 13-16R; CAAS 11; CANR 7, 54, 83; DLB 152

Jones, Mervyn 1922- .... **CLC 10, 52**
See also CA 45-48; CAAS 5; CANR 1, 91; MTCW 1

Jones, Mick 1956(?)- .... **CLC 30**

Jones, Nettie (Pearl) 1941- .... **CLC 34**
See also BW 2; CA 137; CAAS 20; CANR 88

Jones, Preston 1936-1979 .... **CLC 10**
See also CA 73-76; 89-92; DLB 7

Jones, Robert F(rancis) 1934- .... **CLC 7**
See also CA 49-52; CANR 2, 61

Jones, Rod 1953- .... **CLC 50**
See also CA 128

Jones, Terence Graham Parry
1942- .... **CLC 21**
See also Jones, Terry; Monty Python
See also CA 112; 116; CANR 35, 93; INT 116

Jones, Terry
See Jones, Terence Graham Parry
See also SATA 67; SATA-Brief 51

Jones, Thom (Douglas) 1945(?)- .... **CLC 81**
See also CA 157; CANR 88

Jong, Erica 1942- .... **CLC 4, 6, 8, 18, 83; DAM NOV, POP**
See also AITN 1; AMWS 5; BEST 90:2; CA 73-76; CANR 26, 52, 75; DA3; DLB 2, 5, 28, 152; INT CANR-26; MTCW 1, 2

Jonson, Ben(jamin) 1572(?)-1637 .. **LC 6, 33; DA; DAB; DAC; DAM DRAM, MST, POET; DC 4; PC 17**
See also AW; CDBLB Before 1660; DLB 62, 121

Jordan, June 1936- .... **CLC 5, 11, 23, 114; BLCS; DAM MULT, POET**
See Meyer, June
See also AAYA 2; AW; BW 2, 3; CA 33-36R; CANR 25, 70; CLR 10; DLB 38; GLL 2; MAICYA; MTCW 1; SATA 4

Jordan, Neil (Patrick) 1950- .... **CLC 110**
See also CA 124; 130; CANR 54; GLL 2; INT 130

Jordan, Pat(rick M.) 1941- .... **CLC 37**
See also CA 33-36R

Jorgensen, Ivar
See Ellison, Harlan (Jay)

Jorgenson, Ivar
See Silverberg, Robert

Joseph, George Ghevarughese CLC 70

Josephus, Flavius c. 37-100 .... **CMLC 13**
See also DLB 176

Josiah Allen's Wife
See Holley, Marietta

Josipovici, Gabriel (David) 1940- ...... **CLC 6, 43**
See also CA 37-40R; CAAS 8; CANR 47, 84; DLB 14

Joubert, Joseph 1754-1824 .... **NCLC 9**

Jouve, Pierre Jean 1887-1976 .... **CLC 47**
See also CA 65-68

Kyd, Thomas 1558-1594 .... **LC 22; DAM DRAM; DC 3**
    See also DLB 62
Kyprianos, Iossif
    See Samarakis, Antonis
La Bruyere, Jean de 1645-1696 .... **LC 17**
Lacan, Jacques (Marie Emile)
    1901-1981 .... **CLC 75**
    See also CA 121; 104
Laclos, Pierre Ambroise Francois Choderlos de 1741-1803 .... **NCLC 4, 87**
La Colere, Francois
    See Aragon, Louis
Lacolere, Francois
    See Aragon, Louis
La Deshabilleuse
    See Simenon, Georges (Jacques Christian)
Lady Gregory
    See Gregory, Isabella Augusta (Persse)
Lady of Quality, A
    See Bagnold, Enid
La Fayette, Marie (Madelaine Pioche de la Vergne Comtes 1634-1693 .... **LC 2**
Lafayette, Rene
    See Hubbard, L(afayette) Ron(ald)
La Fontaine, Jean de 1621-1695 .... **LC 50**
    See also MAICYA; SATA 18
Laforgue, Jules 1860-1887 . **NCLC 5, 53; PC 14; SSC 20**
Lagerkvist, Paer (Fabian)
    1891-1974 ...... **CLC 7, 10, 13, 54; DAM DRAM, NOV**
    See also Lagerkvist, Par
    See also CA 85-88; 49-52; DA3; MTCW 1, 2
Lagerkvist, Par SSC 12
    See also Lagerkvist, Paer (Fabian)
    See also MTCW 2
Lagerkwist, Pär
    See Lagerkvist, Paer (Fabian)
Lagerloef, Selma (Ottiliana Lovisa)
    1858-1940 .... **TCLC 4, 36**
    See also Lagerlof, Selma (Ottiliana Lovisa)
    See also CA 108; MTCW 2; SATA 15
Lagerlof, Selma (Ottiliana Lovisa)
    See Lagerloef, Selma (Ottiliana Lovisa)
    See also CLR 7; SATA 15
La Guma, (Justin) Alex(ander)
    1925-1985 .... **CLC 19; BLCS; DAM NOV**
    See also BW 1, 3; CA 49-52; 118; CANR 25, 81; DLB 117, 225; MTCW 1, 2
Laidlaw, A. K.
    See Grieve, C(hristopher) M(urray)
Lainez, Manuel Mujica
    See Mujica Lainez, Manuel
    See also HW 1
Laing, R(onald) D(avid) 1927-1989 . **CLC 95**
    See also CA 107; 129; CANR 34; MTCW 1
Lamartine, Alphonse (Marie Louis Prat) de 1790-1869 . **NCLC 11; DAM POET; PC 16**
Lamb, Charles 1775-1834 ..... **NCLC 10; DA; DAB; DAC; DAM MST**
    See also AW; CDBLB 1789-1832; DLB 93, 107, 163; SATA 17
Lamb, Lady Caroline 1785-1828 ... **NCLC 38**
    See also DLB 116
Lamming, George (William) 1927- ... **CLC 2, 4, 66, 144; BLC 2; DAM MULT**
    See also BW 2, 3; CA 85-88; CANR 26, 76; DLB 125; MTCW 1, 2
L'Amour, Louis (Dearborn)
    1908-1988 ...... **CLC 25, 55; DAM NOV, POP**
    See also Burns, Tex; Mayo, Jim
    See also AAYA 16; AITN 2; BEST 89:2; CA 1-4R; 125; CANR 3, 25, 40; DA3; DLB 206; DLBY 80; MTCW 1, 2

Lampedusa, Giuseppe (Tomasi) di TCLC 13
    See also Tomasi di Lampedusa, Giuseppe
    See also CA 164; DLB 177; MTCW 2
Lampman, Archibald 1861-1899 ... **NCLC 25**
    See also DLB 92
Lancaster, Bruce 1896-1963 .... **CLC 36**
    See also CA 9-10; CANR 70; CAP 1; SATA 9
Lanchester, John CLC 99
Landau, Mark Alexandrovich
    See Aldanov, Mark (Alexandrovich)
Landau-Aldanov, Mark Alexandrovich
    See Aldanov, Mark (Alexandrovich)
Landis, Jerry
    See Simon, Paul (Frederick)
Landis, John 1950- .... **CLC 26**
    See also CA 112; 122
Landolfi, Tommaso 1908-1979 .... **CLC 11, 49**
    See also CA 127; 117; DLB 177
Landon, Letitia Elizabeth
    1802-1838 .... **NCLC 15**
    See also DLB 96
Landor, Walter Savage
    1775-1864 .... **NCLC 14**
    See also DLB 93, 107
Landwirth, Heinz 1927-
    See Lind, Jakov
    See also CA 9-12R; CANR 7
Lane, Patrick 1939- ... **CLC 25; DAM POET**
    See also CA 97-100; CANR 54; DLB 53; INT 97-100
Lang, Andrew 1844-1912 .... **TCLC 16**
    See also CA 114; 137; CANR 85; DLB 98, 141, 184; MAICYA; SATA 16
Lang, Fritz 1890-1976 .... **CLC 20, 103**
    See also CA 77-80; 69-72; CANR 30
Lange, John
    See Crichton, (John) Michael
Langer, Elinor 1939- .... **CLC 34**
    See also CA 121
Langland, William 1332(?)-1400(?) ... **LC 19; DA; DAB; DAC; DAM MST, POET**
    See also DLB 146
Langstaff, Launcelot
    See Irving, Washington
Lanier, Sidney 1842-1881 ..... **NCLC 6; DAM POET**
    See also AMWS 1; DLB 64; DLBD 13; MAICYA; SATA 18
Lanyer, Aemilia 1569-1645 .... **LC 10, 30**
    See also DLB 121
Lao-Tzu
    See Lao Tzu
Lao Tzu fl. 6046th cent. B.C.-490 ... **CMLC 7**
Lapine, James (Elliot) 1949- .... **CLC 39**
    See also CA 123; 130; CANR 54; INT 130
Larbaud, Valery (Nicolas)
    1881-1957 .... **TCLC 9**
    See also CA 106; 152
Lardner, Ring
    See Lardner, Ring(gold) W(ilmer)
Lardner, Ring W., Jr.
    See Lardner, Ring(gold) W(ilmer)
Lardner, Ring(gold) W(ilmer)
    1885-1933 .... **TCLC 2, 14; SSC 32**
    See also CA 104; 131; CDALB 1917-1929; DLB 11, 25, 86, 171; DLBD 16; MTCW 1, 2
Laredo, Betty
    See Codrescu, Andrei
Larkin, Maia
    See Wojciechowska, Maia (Teresa)
Larkin, Philip (Arthur) 1922-1985 ... **CLC 3, 5, 8, 9, 13, 18, 33, 39, 64; DAB; DAM MST, POET; PC 21**
    See also BRWS 1; CA 5-8R; 117; CANR 24, 62; CDBLB 1960 to Present; DA3; DLB 27; MTCW 1, 2

Larra (y Sanchez de Castro), Mariano Jose de 1809-1837 .... **NCLC 17**
Larsen, Eric 1941- .... **CLC 55**
    See also CA 132
Larsen, Nella 1893-1963 .... **CLC 37; BLC 2; DAM MULT**
    See also BW 1; CA 125; CANR 83; DLB 51
Larson, Charles R(aymond) 1938- ... **CLC 31**
    See also CA 53-56; CANR 4
Larson, Jonathan 1961-1996 .... **CLC 99**
    See also AAYA 28; CA 156
Las Casas, Bartolome de 1474-1566 ... **LC 31**
Lasch, Christopher 1932-1994 .... **CLC 102**
    See also CA 73-76; 144; CANR 25; MTCW 1, 2
Lasker-Schueler, Else 1869-1945 ... **TCLC 57**
    See also CA 183; DLB 66, 124
Laski, Harold J(oseph) 1893-1950 . **TCLC 79**
    See also CA 188'
Latham, Jean Lee 1902-1995 .... **CLC 12**
    See also AITN 1; AW; CA 5-8R; CANR 7, 84; CLR 50; MAICYA; SATA 2, 68
Latham, Mavis
    See Clark, Mavis Thorpe
Lathen, Emma CLC 2
    See also Hennissart, Martha; Latsis, Mary J(ane)
Lathrop, Francis
    See Leiber, Fritz (Reuter, Jr.)
Latsis, Mary J(ane) 1927(?)-1997
    See Lathen, Emma
    See also CA 85-88; 162
Lattimore, Richmond (Alexander)
    1906-1984 .... **CLC 3**
    See also CA 1-4R; 112; CANR 1
Laughlin, James 1914-1997 .... **CLC 49**
    See also CA 21-24R; 162; CAAS 22; CANR 9, 47; DLB 48; DLBY 96, 97
Laurence, (Jean) Margaret (Wemyss)
    1926-1987 . **CLC 3, 6, 13, 50, 62; DAC; DAM MST; SSC 7**
    See also CA 5-8R; 121; CANR 33; DLB 53; MTCW 1, 2; SATA-Obit 50
Laurent, Antoine 1952- .... **CLC 50**
Lauscher, Hermann
    See Hesse, Hermann
Lautreamont, Comte de
    1846-1870 .... **NCLC 12; SSC 14**
Laverty, Donald
    See Blish, James (Benjamin)
Lavin, Mary 1912-1996 . **CLC 4, 18, 99; SSC 4**
    See also CA 9-12R; 151; CANR 33; DLB 15; MTCW 1
Lavond, Paul Dennis
    See Kornbluth, C(yril) M.; Pohl, Frederik
Lawler, Raymond Evenor 1922- .... **CLC 58**
    See also CA 103
Lawrence, D(avid) H(erbert Richards)
    1885-1930 .... **TCLC 2, 9, 16, 33, 48, 61, 93; DA; DAB; DAC; DAM MST, NOV, POET; SSC 4, 19**
    See also Chambers, Jessie
    See also AW; CA 104; 121; CDBLB 1914-1945; DA3; DLB 10, 19, 36, 98, 162, 195; MTCW 1, 2
Lawrence, T(homas) E(dward)
    1888-1935 .... **TCLC 18**
    See also Dale, Colin
    See also BRWS 2; CA 115; 167; DLB 195
Lawrence of Arabia
    See Lawrence, T(homas) E(dward)
Lawson, Henry (Archibald Hertzberg)
    1867-1922 .... **TCLC 27; SSC 18**
    See also CA 120; 181; DLB 230

Lermontov, Mikhail Yuryevich
1814-1841 .... **NCLC 5, 47; PC 18**
See also DLB 205

Leroux, Gaston 1868-1927 .... **TCLC 25**
See also CA 108; 136; CANR 69; SATA 65

Lesage, Alain-Rene 1668-1747 .... **LC 2, 28**

Leskov, Nikolai (Semyonovich)
1831-1895 .... **NCLC 25; SSC 34**

Lesser, Milton
See Marlowe, Stephen

Lessing, Doris (May) 1919- ... **CLC 1, 2, 3, 6, 10, 15, 22, 40, 94; DA; DAB; DAC; DAM MST, NOV; SSC 6**
See also AW; BRWS 1; CA 9-12R; CAAS 14; CANR 33, 54, 76; CDBLB 1960 to Present; DA3; DLB 15, 139; DLBY 85; MTCW 1, 2

Lessing, Gotthold Ephraim 1729-1781 . **LC 8**
See also DLB 97

Lester, Richard 1932- .... **CLC 20**

Levenson, Jay CLC 70

Lever, Charles (James)
1806-1872 .... **NCLC 23**
See also DLB 21

Leverson, Ada 1865(?)-1936(?) .... **TCLC 18**
See also Elaine
See also CA 117; DLB 153

Levertov, Denise 1923-1997 .. **CLC 1, 2, 3, 5, 8, 15, 28, 66; DAM POET; PC 11**
See also AMWS 3; CA 1-4R, 178; 163; CAAE 178; CAAS 19; CANR 3, 29, 50; CDALBS; DLB 5, 165; INT CANR-29; MTCW 1, 2

Levi, Jonathan CLC 76

Levi, Peter (Chad Tigar)
1931-2000 .... **CLC 41**
See also CA 5-8R; 187; CANR 34, 80; DLB 40

Levi, Primo 1919-1987 ...... **CLC 37, 50; SSC 12; TCLC 109**
See also CA 13-16R; 122; CANR 12, 33, 61, 70; DLB 177; MTCW 1, 2

Levin, Ira 1929- .... **CLC 3, 6; DAM POP**
See also CA 21-24R; CANR 17, 44, 74; DA3; MTCW 1, 2; SATA 66

Levin, Meyer 1905-1981 .... **CLC 7; DAM POP**
See also AITN 1; CA 9-12R; 104; CANR 15; DLB 9, 28; DLBY 81; SATA 21; SATA-Obit 27

Levine, Norman 1924- .... **CLC 54**
See also CA 73-76; CAAS 23; CANR 14, 70; DLB 88

Levine, Philip 1928- .. **CLC 2, 4, 5, 9, 14, 33, 118; DAM POET; PC 22**
See also AMWS 5; CA 9-12R; CANR 9, 37, 52; DLB 5

Levinson, Deirdre 1931- .... **CLC 49**
See also CA 73-76; CANR 70

Levi-Strauss, Claude 1908- .... **CLC 38**
See also CA 1-4R; CANR 6, 32, 57; DLB 242; MTCW 1, 2

Levitin, Sonia (Wolff) 1934- .... **CLC 17**
See also AAYA 13; AW; CA 29-32R; CANR 14, 32, 79; CLR 53; JRDA; MAICYA; SAAS 2; SATA 4, 68, 119

Levon, O. U.
See Kesey, Ken (Elton)

Levy, Amy 1861-1889 .... **NCLC 59**
See also DLB 156, 240

Lewes, George Henry 1817-1878 ... **NCLC 25**
See also DLB 55, 144

Lewis, Alun 1915-1944 .... **TCLC 3; SSC 40**
See also CA 104; 188; DLB 20, 162

Lewis, C. Day
See Day Lewis, C(ecil)

Lewis, C(live) S(taples) 1898-1963 .... **CLC 1, 3, 6, 14, 27, 124; DA; DAB; DAC; DAM MST, NOV, POP**
See also AAYA 3, 39; BRWS 3; CA 81-84; CANR 33, 71; CDBLB 1945-1960; CLR 3, 27; DA3; DLB 15, 100, 160; JRDA; MAICYA; MTCW 1, 2; SATA 13, 100

Lewis, Janet 1899-1998 .... **CLC 41**
See also Winters, Janet Lewis
See also CA 9-12R; 172; CANR 29, 63; CAP 1; DLBY 87; TCWW 2

Lewis, Matthew Gregory
1775-1818 .... **NCLC 11, 62**
See also DLB 39, 158, 178

Lewis, (Harry) Sinclair 1885-1951 . **TCLC 4, 13, 23, 39; DA; DAB; DAC; DAM MST, NOV**
See also AW; CA 104; 133; CDALB 1917-1929; DA3; DLB 9, 102; DLBD 1; MTCW 1, 2

Lewis, (Percy) Wyndham
1884(?)-1957 .. **TCLC 2, 9, 104; SSC 34**
See also CA 104; 157; DLB 15; MTCW 2

Lewisohn, Ludwig 1883-1955 .... **TCLC 19**
See also CA 107; DLB 4, 9, 28, 102

Lewton, Val 1904-1951 .... **TCLC 76**
See also IDFW 3

Leyner, Mark 1956- .... **CLC 92**
See also CA 110; CANR 28, 53; DA3; MTCW 2

Lezama Lima, Jose 1910-1976 .... **CLC 4, 10, 101; DAM MULT; HLCS 2**
See also CA 77-80; CANR 71; DLB 113; HW 1, 2

L'Heureux, John (Clarke) 1934- ...... **CLC 52**
See also CA 13-16R; CANR 23, 45, 88

Liddell, C. H.
See Kuttner, Henry

Lie, Jonas (Lauritz Idemil)
1833-1908(?) .... **TCLC 5**
See also CA 115

Lieber, Joel 1937-1971 .... **CLC 6**
See also CA 73-76; 29-32R

Lieber, Stanley Martin
See Lee, Stan

Lieberman, Laurence (James)
1935- .... **CLC 4, 36**
See also CA 17-20R; CANR 8, 36, 89

Lieh Tzu fl. 7th cent. B.C.-5th cent.
B.C. .... **CMLC 27**

Lieksman, Anders
See Haavikko, Paavo Juhani

Li Fei-kan 1904-
See Pa Chin
See also CA 105

Lifton, Robert Jay 1926- .... **CLC 67**
See also CA 17-20R; CANR 27, 78; INT CANR-27; SATA 66

Lightfoot, Gordon 1938- .... **CLC 26**
See also CA 109

Lightman, Alan P(aige) 1948- .... **CLC 81**
See also CA 141; CANR 63

Ligotti, Thomas (Robert) 1953- ...... **CLC 44; SSC 16**
See also CA 123; CANR 49

Li Ho 791-817 .... **PC 13**

Liliencron, (Friedrich Adolf Axel) Detlev von 1844-1909 .... **TCLC 18**
See also CA 117

Lilly, William 1602-1681 .... **LC 27**

Lima, Jose Lezama
See Lezama Lima, Jose

Lima Barreto, Afonso Henrique de
1881-1922 .... **TCLC 23**
See also CA 117; 181

Lima Barreto, Afonso Henriques de
See Lima Barreto, Afonso Henrique de

Limonov, Edward 1944- .... **CLC 67**
See also CA 137

Lin, Frank
See Atherton, Gertrude (Franklin Horn)

Lincoln, Abraham 1809-1865 .... **NCLC 18**

Lind, Jakov CLC 1, 2, 4, 27, 82
See also Landwirth, Heinz
See also CAAS 4

Lindbergh, Anne (Spencer) Morrow
1906-2001 .... **CLC 82; DAM NOV**
See also CA 17-20R; CANR 16, 73; MTCW 1, 2; SATA 33

Lindsay, David 1878(?)-1945 .... **TCLC 15**
See also CA 113; 187

Lindsay, (Nicholas) Vachel
1879-1931 . **TCLC 17; DA; DAC; DAM MST, POET; PC 23**
See also AMWS 1; AW; CA 114; 135; CANR 79; CDALB 1865-1917; DA3; DLB 54; SATA 40

Linke-Poot
See Doeblin, Alfred

Linney, Romulus 1930- .... **CLC 51**
See also CA 1-4R; CANR 40, 44, 79

Linton, Eliza Lynn 1822-1898 .... **NCLC 41**
See also DLB 18

Li Po 701-763 .... **CMLC 2; PC 29**

Lipsius, Justus 1547-1606 .... **LC 16**

Lipsyte, Robert (Michael) 1938- ..... **CLC 21; DA; DAC; DAM MST, NOV**
See also AAYA 7; CA 17-20R; CANR 8, 57; CLR 23; JRDA; MAICYA; SATA 5, 68, 113

Lish, Gordon (Jay) 1934- ... **CLC 45; SSC 18**
See also CA 113; 117; CANR 79; DLB 130; INT 117

Lispector, Clarice 1925(?)-1977 .... **CLC 43; HLCS 2; SSC 34**
See also CA 139; 116; CANR 71; DLB 113; HW 2

Littell, Robert 1935(?)- .... **CLC 42**
See also CA 109; 112; CANR 64

Little, Malcolm 1925-1965
See Malcolm X
See also BW 1, 3; CA 125; 111; CANR 82; DA; DAB; DAC; DAM MST, MULT; DA3; MTCW 1, 2

Littlewit, Humphrey Gent.
See Lovecraft, H(oward) P(hillips)

Litwos
See Sienkiewicz, Henryk (Adam Alexander Pius)

Liu, E. 1857-1909 .... **TCLC 15**
See also CA 115; 190

Lively, Penelope (Margaret) 1933- .. **CLC 32, 50; DAM NOV**
See also CA 41-44R; CANR 29, 67, 79; CLR 7; DLB 14, 161, 207; JRDA; MAICYA; MTCW 1, 2; SATA 7, 60, 101

Livesay, Dorothy (Kathleen)
1909-1996 . **CLC 4, 15, 79; DAC; DAM MST, POET**
See also AITN 2; CA 25-28R; CAAS 8; CANR 36, 67; DLB 68; MTCW 1

Livy c. 59B.C.-c. 17 .... **CMLC 11**
See also DLB 211

Lizardi, Jose Joaquin Fernandez de
1776-1827 .... **NCLC 30**

Llewellyn, Richard
See Llewellyn Lloyd, Richard Dafydd Vivian
See also DLB 15

Llewellyn Lloyd, Richard Dafydd Vivian
1906-1983 .... **CLC 7, 80**
See also Llewellyn, Richard
See also CA 53-56; 111; CANR 7, 71; SATA 11; SATA-Obit 37

Llosa, (Jorge) Mario (Pedro) Vargas
See Vargas Llosa, (Jorge) Mario (Pedro)

Lloyd, Manda
See Mander, (Mary) Jane

Lynx
See West, Rebecca

Lyons, Marcus
See Blish, James (Benjamin)

Lyotard, Jean-Francois
1924-1998 .... **TCLC 103**
See also DLB 242

Lyre, Pinchbeck
See Sassoon, Siegfried (Lorraine)

Lytle, Andrew (Nelson) 1902-1995 ... **CLC 22**
See also CA 9-12R; 150; CANR 70; DLB
6; DLBY 95

Lyttelton, George 1709-1773 .... **LC 10**

Maas, Peter 1929- .... **CLC 29**
See also CA 93-96; INT 93-96; MTCW 2

Macaulay, Catherine 1731-1791 .... **LC 64**
See also DLB 104

Macaulay, (Emilie) Rose
1881(?)-1958 .... **TCLC 7, 44**
See also CA 104; DLB 36

Macaulay, Thomas Babington
1800-1859 .... **NCLC 42**
See also CDBLB 1832-1890; DLB 32, 55

MacBeth, George (Mann)
1932-1992 .... **CLC 2, 5, 9**
See also CA 25-28R; 136; CANR 61, 66;
DLB 40; MTCW 1; SATA 4; SATA-Obit
70

MacCaig, Norman (Alexander)
1910-1996 .... **CLC 36; DAB; DAM
POET**
See also CA 9-12R; CANR 3, 34; DLB 27

MacCarthy, Sir(Charles Otto) Desmond
1877-1952 .... **TCLC 36**
See also CA 167

MacDiarmid, Hugh CLC 2, 4, 11, 19, 63; PC
9
See also Grieve, C(hristopher) M(urray)
See also CDBLB 1945-1960; DLB 20

MacDonald, Anson
See Heinlein, Robert A(nson)

Macdonald, Cynthia 1928- .... **CLC 13, 19**
See also CA 49-52; CANR 4, 44; DLB 105

MacDonald, George 1824-1905 .... **TCLC 9**
See also CA 106; 137; CANR 80; CLR 67;
DLB 18, 163, 178; MAICYA; SATA 33,
100

Macdonald, John
See Millar, Kenneth

MacDonald, John D(ann)
1916-1986 .. **CLC 3, 27, 44; DAM NOV,
POP**
See also CA 1-4R; 121; CANR 1, 19, 60;
DLB 8; DLBY 86; MTCW 1, 2

Macdonald, John Ross
See Millar, Kenneth

Macdonald, Ross CLC 1, 2, 3, 14, 34, 41
See also Millar, Kenneth
See also AMWS 4; DLBD 6

MacDougal, John
See Blish, James (Benjamin)

MacDougal, John
See Blish, James (Benjamin)

MacEwen, Gwendolyn (Margaret)
1941-1987 .... **CLC 13, 55**
See also CA 9-12R; 124; CANR 7, 22; DLB
53; SATA 50; SATA-Obit 55

Macha, Karel Hynek 1810-1846 .... **NCLC 46**

Machado (y Ruiz), Antonio
1875-1939 .... **TCLC 3**
See also CA 104; 174; DLB 108; HW 2

Machado de Assis, Joaquim Maria
1839-1908 ..... **TCLC 10; BLC 2; HLCS
2; SSC 24**
See also CA 107; 153; CANR 91

Machen, Arthur TCLC 4; SSC 20
See also Jones, Arthur Llewellyn
See also CA 179; DLB 36, 156, 178

Machiavelli, Niccolò 1469-1527 ..... **LC 8, 36;
DA; DAB; DAC; DAM MST**
See also AW

MacInnes, Colin 1914-1976 .... **CLC 4, 23**
See also CA 69-72; 65-68; CANR 21; DLB
14; MTCW 1, 2

MacInnes, Helen (Clark)
1907-1985 .... **CLC 27, 39; DAM POP**
See also CA 1-4R; 117; CANR 1, 28, 58;
DLB 87; MTCW 1, 2; SATA 22; SATA-
Obit 44

Mackenzie, Compton (Edward Montague)
1883-1972 .... **CLC 18**
See also CA 21-22; 37-40R; CAP 2; DLB
34, 100

Mackenzie, Henry 1745-1831 .... **NCLC 41**
See also DLB 39

Mackintosh, Elizabeth 1896(?)-1952
See Tey, Josephine
See also CA 110

MacLaren, James
See Grieve, C(hristopher) M(urray)

Mac Laverty, Bernard 1942- .... **CLC 31**
See also CA 116; 118; CANR 43, 88; INT
118

MacLean, Alistair (Stuart)
1922(?)-1987 .. **CLC 3, 13, 50, 63; DAM
POP**
See also CA 57-60; 121; CANR 28, 61;
MTCW 1; SATA 23; SATA-Obit 50;
TCWW 2

Maclean, Norman (Fitzroy)
1902-1990 .... **CLC 78; DAM POP; SSC
13**
See also CA 102; 132; CANR 49; DLB 206;
TCWW 2

MacLeish, Archibald 1892-1982 ... **CLC 3, 8,
14, 68; DAM POET**
See also CA 9-12R; 106; CANR 33, 63;
CDALBS; DLB 4, 7, 45; DLBY 82;
MTCW 1, 2

MacLennan, (John) Hugh
1907-1990 . **CLC 2, 14, 92; DAC; DAM
MST**
See also CA 5-8R; 142; CANR 33; DLB
68; MTCW 1, 2

MacLeod, Alistair 1936- .... **CLC 56; DAC;
DAM MST**
See also CA 123; CCA 1; DLB 60; MTCW
2

Macleod, Fiona
See Sharp, William

MacNeice, (Frederick) Louis
1907-1963 .... **CLC 1, 4, 10, 53; DAB;
DAM POET**
See also CA 85-88; CANR 61; DLB 10, 20;
MTCW 1, 2

MacNeill, Dand
See Fraser, George MacDonald

Macpherson, James 1736-1796 .... **LC 29**
See also Ossian
See also DLB 109

Macpherson, (Jean) Jay 1931- .... **CLC 14**
See also CA 5-8R; CANR 90; DLB 53

MacShane, Frank 1927-1999 .... **CLC 39**
See also CA 9-12R; 186; CANR 3, 33; DLB
111

Macumber, Mari
See Sandoz, Mari(e Susette)

Madach, Imre 1823-1864 .... **NCLC 19**

Madden, (Jerry) David 1933- .... **CLC 5, 15**
See also CA 1-4R; CAAS 3; CANR 4, 45;
DLB 6; MTCW 1

Maddern, Al(an)
See Ellison, Harlan (Jay)

Madhubuti, Haki R. 1942- . **CLC 6, 73; BLC
2; DAM MULT, POET; PC 5**
See also Lee, Don L.
See also BW 2, 3; CA 73-76; CANR 24,
51, 73; DLB 5, 41; DLBD 8; MTCW 2

Maepenn, Hugh
See Kuttner, Henry

Maepenn, K. H.
See Kuttner, Henry

Maeterlinck, Maurice 1862-1949 ... **TCLC 3;
DAM DRAM**
See also CA 104; 136; CANR 80; DLB 192;
SATA 66

Maginn, William 1794-1842 .... **NCLC 8**
See also DLB 110, 159

Mahapatra, Jayanta 1928- .... **CLC 33; DAM
MULT**
See also CA 73-76; CAAS 9; CANR 15,
33, 66, 87

Mahfouz, Naguib (Abdel Aziz Al-Sabilgi)
1911(?)-
See Mahfuz, Najib
See also BEST 89:2; CA 128; CANR 55;
CWW 2; DAM NOV; DA3; MTCW 1, 2

Mahfuz, Najib CLC 52, 55
See also Mahfouz, Naguib (Abdel Aziz Al-
Sabilgi)
See also DLBY 88

Mahon, Derek 1941- .... **CLC 27**
See also CA 113; 128; CANR 88; DLB 40

Mailer, Norman 1923- ... **CLC 1, 2, 3, 4, 5, 8,
11, 14, 28, 39, 74, 111; DA; DAB;
DAC; DAM MST, NOV, POP**
See also AAYA 31; AITN 2; CA 9-12R;
CABS 1; CANR 28, 74, 77; CDALB
1968-1988; DA3; DLB 2, 16, 28, 185;
DLBD 3; DLBY 80, 83; MTCW 1, 2

Maillet, Antonine 1929- .. **CLC 54, 118; DAC**
See also CA 115; 120; CANR 46, 74, 77;
CCA 1; CWW 2; DLB 60; INT 120;
MTCW 2

Mais, Roger 1905-1955 .... **TCLC 8**
See also BW 1, 3; CA 105; 124; CANR 82;
DLB 125; MTCW 1

Maistre, Joseph de 1753-1821 .... **NCLC 37**

Maitland, Frederic William
1850-1906 .... **TCLC 65**

Maitland, Sara (Louise) 1950- .... **CLC 49**
See also CA 69-72; CANR 13, 59

Major, Clarence 1936- . **CLC 3, 19, 48; BLC
2; DAM MULT**
See also BW 2, 3; CA 21-24R; CAAS 6;
CANR 13, 25, 53, 82; DLB 33

Major, Kevin (Gerald) 1949- . **CLC 26; DAC**
See also AAYA 16; CA 97-100; CANR 21,
38; CLR 11; DLB 60; INT CANR-21;
JRDA; MAICYA; SATA 32, 82

Maki, James
See Ozu, Yasujiro

Malabaila, Damiano
See Levi, Primo

Malamud, Bernard 1914-1986 .. **CLC 1, 2, 3,
5, 8, 9, 11, 18, 27, 44, 78, 85; DA;
DAB; DAC; DAM MST, NOV, POP;
SSC 15**
See also AAYA 16; AMWS 1; AW; CA
5-8R; 118; CABS 1; CANR 28, 62;
CDALB 1941-1968; DA3; DLB 2, 28,
152; DLBY 80, 86; MTCW 1, 2

Malan, Herman
See Bosman, Herman Charles; Bosman,
Herman Charles

Malaparte, Curzio 1898-1957 .... **TCLC 52**

Malcolm, Dan
See Silverberg, Robert

Malcolm X CLC 82, 117; BLC 2
See also Little, Malcolm
See also AW

Martinez, Enrique Gonzalez
  See Gonzalez Martinez, Enrique
Martinez, Jacinto Benavente y
  See Benavente (y Martinez), Jacinto
Martinez Ruiz, Jose 1873-1967
  See Azorin; Ruiz, Jose Martinez
  See also CA 93-96; HW 1
Martinez Sierra, Gregorio
  1881-1947 .... **TCLC 6**
  See also CA 115
Martinez Sierra, Maria (de la O'LeJarraga)
  1874-1974 .... **TCLC 6**
  See also CA 115
Martinsen, Martin
  See Follett, Ken(neth Martin)
Martinson, Harry (Edmund)
  1904-1978 .... **CLC 14**
  See also CA 77-80; CANR 34
Marut, Ret
  See Traven, B.
Marut, Robert
  See Traven, B.
Marvell, Andrew 1621-1678 .. **LC 4, 43; DA;
  DAB; DAC; DAM MST, POET; PC 10**
  See also AW; CDBLB 1660-1789; DLB 131
Marx, Karl (Heinrich) 1818-1883 . **NCLC 17**
  See also DLB 129
Masaoka Shiki TCLC 18
  See also Masaoka Tsunenori
Masaoka Tsunenori 1867-1902
  See Masaoka Shiki
  See also CA 117
Masefield, John (Edward)
  1878-1967 ..... **CLC 11, 47; DAM POET**
  See also CA 19-20; 25-28R; CANR 33;
  CAP 2; CDBLB 1890-1914; DLB 10, 19,
  153, 160; MTCW 1, 2; SATA 19
Maso, Carole 19(?)- .... **CLC 44**
  See also CA 170; GLL 2
Mason, Bobbie Ann 1940- ... **CLC 28, 43, 82;
  SSC 4**
  See also AAYA 5; AW; CA 53-56; CANR
  11, 31, 58, 83; CDALBS; DA3; DLB 173;
  DLBY 87; INT CANR-31; MTCW 1, 2
Mason, Ernst
  See Pohl, Frederik
Mason, Lee W.
  See Malzberg, Barry N(athaniel)
Mason, Nick 1945- .... **CLC 35**
Mason, Tally
  See Derleth, August (William)
Mass, Anna CLC 59
Mass, William
  See Gibson, William
Master Lao
  See Lao Tzu
Masters, Edgar Lee 1868-1950 .... **TCLC 2,
  25; DA; DAC; DAM MST, POET; PC
  1**
  See also AMWS 1; AW; CA 104; 133;
  CDALB 1865-1917; DLB 54; MTCW 1,
  2
Masters, Hilary 1928- .... **CLC 48**
  See also CA 25-28R; CANR 13, 47
Mastrosimone, William 19(?)- .... **CLC 36**
  See also CA 186
Mathe, Albert
  See Camus, Albert
Mather, Cotton 1663-1728 .... **LC 38**
  See also AMWS 2; CDALB 1640-1865;
  DLB 24, 30, 140
Mather, Increase 1639-1723 .... **LC 38**
  See also DLB 24
Matheson, Richard Burton 1926- .... **CLC 37**
  See also AAYA 31; CA 97-100; CANR 88;
  DLB 8, 44; INT 97-100; SCFW 2

Mathews, Harry 1930- .... **CLC 6, 52**
  See also CA 21-24R; CAAS 6; CANR 18,
  40
Mathews, John Joseph 1894-1979 .. **CLC 84;
  DAM MULT**
  See also CA 19-20; 142; CANR 45; CAP 2;
  DLB 175; NNAL
Mathias, Roland (Glyn) 1915- .... **CLC 45**
  See also CA 97-100; CANR 19, 41; DLB
  27
Matsuo Bashō 1644-1694 .... **LC 62; DAM
  POET; PC 3**
Mattheson, Rodney
  See Creasey, John
Matthews, (James) Brander
  1852-1929 .... **TCLC 95**
  See also DLB 71, 78; DLBD 13
Matthews, Greg 1949- .... **CLC 45**
  See also CA 135
Matthews, William (Procter, III)
  1942-1997 .... **CLC 40**
  See also CA 29-32R; 162; CAAS 18; CANR
  12, 57; DLB 5
Matthias, John (Edward) 1941- .... **CLC 9**
  See also CA 33-36R; CANR 56
Matthiessen, F(rancis) O(tto)
  1902-1950 .... **TCLC 100**
  See also CA 185; DLB 63
Matthiessen, Peter 1927- ... **CLC 5, 7, 11, 32,
  64; DAM NOV**
  See also AAYA 6; AMWS 5; BEST 90:4;
  CA 9-12R; CANR 21, 50, 73; DA3; DLB
  6, 173; MTCW 1, 2; SATA 27
Maturin, Charles Robert
  1780(?)-1824 .... **NCLC 6**
  See also DLB 178
Matute (Ausejo), Ana Maria 1925- .. **CLC 11**
  See also CA 89-92; MTCW 1
Maugham, W. S.
  See Maugham, W(illiam) Somerset
Maugham, W(illiam) Somerset
  1874-1965 ... **CLC 1, 11, 15, 67, 93; DA;
  DAB; DAC; DAM DRAM, MST, NOV;
  SSC 8**
  See also AW; CA 5-8R; 25-28R; CANR 40;
  CDBLB 1914-1945; DA3; DLB 10, 36,
  77, 100, 162, 195; MTCW 1, 2; SATA 54
Maugham, William Somerset
  See Maugham, W(illiam) Somerset
Maupassant, (Henri Rene Albert) Guy de
  1850-1893 . **NCLC 1, 42, 83; DA; DAB;
  DAC; DAM MST, NOV; SSC 1**
  See also AW; DA3; DLB 123
Maupin, Armistead 1944- ..... **CLC 95; DAM
  POP**
  See also CA 125; 130; CANR 58; DA3;
  GLL 1; INT 130; MTCW 2
Maurhut, Richard
  See Traven, B.
Mauriac, Claude 1914-1996 .... **CLC 9**
  See also CA 89-92; 152; CWW 2; DLB 83
Mauriac, François (Charles)
  1885-1970 .... **CLC 4, 9, 56; SSC 24**
  See also CA 25-28; CAP 2; DLB 65;
  MTCW 1, 2
Mavor, Osborne Henry 1888-1951
  See Bridie, James
  See also CA 104
Maxwell, William (Keepers, Jr.)
  1908-2000 .... **CLC 19**
  See also CA 93-96; 189; CANR 54, 95;
  DLBY 80; INT 93-96
May, Elaine 1932- .... **CLC 16**
  See also CA 124; 142; DLB 44
Mayakovski, Vladimir (Vladimirovich)
  1893-1930 .... **TCLC 4, 18**
  See also CA 104; 158; MTCW 2
Mayakovsky, Vladimir
  See Mayakovski, Vladimir (Vladimirovich)

Mayhew, Henry 1812-1887 .... **NCLC 31**
  See also DLB 18, 55, 190
Mayle, Peter 1939(?)- .... **CLC 89**
  See also CA 139; CANR 64
Maynard, Joyce 1953- .... **CLC 23**
  See also CA 111; 129; CANR 64
Mayne, William (James Carter)
  1928- .... **CLC 12**
  See also AAYA 20; AW; CA 9-12R; CANR
  37, 80; CLR 25; JRDA; MAICYA; SAAS
  11; SATA 6, 68
Mayo, Jim
  See L'Amour, Louis (Dearborn)
  See also TCWW 2
Maysles, Albert 1926- .... **CLC 16**
  See also CA 29-32R
Maysles, David 1932- .... **CLC 16**
Mazer, Norma Fox 1931- .... **CLC 26**
  See also AAYA 5, 36; AW; CA 69-72;
  CANR 12, 32, 66; CLR 23; JRDA; MAI-
  CYA; SAAS 1; SATA 24, 67, 105
Mazzini, Guiseppe 1805-1872 .... **NCLC 34**
McAlmon, Robert (Menzies)
  1895-1956 .... **TCLC 97**
  See also CA 107; 168; DLB 4, 45; DLBD
  15; GLL 1
McAuley, James Phillip 1917-1976 .. **CLC 45**
  See also CA 97-100
McBain, Ed
  See Hunter, Evan
McBrien, William (Augustine)
  1930- .... **CLC 44**
  See also CA 107; CANR 90
McCabe, Patrick 1955- .... **CLC 133**
  See also CA 130; CANR 50, 90; DLB 194
McCaffrey, Anne (Inez) 1926- .... **CLC 17;
  DAM NOV, POP**
  See also AAYA 6, 34; AITN 2; BEST 89:2;
  CA 25-28R; CANR 15, 35, 55, 96; CLR
  49; DA3; DLB 8; JRDA; MAICYA;
  MTCW 1, 2; SAAS 11; SATA 8, 70, 116
McCall, Nathan 1955(?)- .... **CLC 86**
  See also BW 3; CA 146; CANR 88
McCann, Arthur
  See Campbell, John W(ood, Jr.)
McCann, Edson
  See Pohl, Frederik
McCarthy, Charles, Jr. 1933-
  See McCarthy, Cormac
  See also CANR 42, 69; DAM POP; DA3;
  MTCW 2
McCarthy, Cormac CLC 4, 57, 59, 101
  See also McCarthy, Charles, Jr.
  See also CA 13-16R; CANR 10; DLB 6,
  143; MTCW 2; TCWW 2
McCarthy, Mary (Therese)
  1912-1989 .. **CLC 1, 3, 5, 14, 24, 39, 59;
  SSC 24**
  See also CA 5-8R; 129; CANR 16, 50, 64;
  DA3; DLB 2; DLBY 81; INT CANR-16;
  MTCW 1, 2
McCartney, (James) Paul 1942- . **CLC 12, 35**
  See also CA 146
McCauley, Stephen (D.) 1955- .... **CLC 50**
  See also CA 141
McClaren, Peter CLC 70
McClure, Michael (Thomas) 1932- ... **CLC 6,
  10**
  See also CA 21-24R; CANR 17, 46, 77;
  DLB 16
McCorkle, Jill (Collins) 1958- .... **CLC 51**
  See also CA 121; DLB 234; DLBY 87
McCourt, Frank 1930- .... **CLC 109**
  See also CA 157
McCourt, James 1941- .... **CLC 5**
  See also CA 57-60

Molnár, Ferenc 1878-1952 .. **TCLC 20; DAM DRAM**
See also CA 109; 153; CANR 83; DLB 215

Momaday, N(avarre) Scott 1934- ...... **CLC 2, 19, 85, 95; DA; DAB; DAC; DAM MST, MULT, NOV, POP; PC 25**
See also AAYA 11; AMWS 4; AW; CA 25-28R; CANR 14, 34, 68; CDALBS; DA3; DLB 143, 175; INT CANR-14; MTCW 1, 2; NNAL; SATA 48; SATA-Brief 30

Monette, Paul 1945-1995 .... **CLC 82**
See also CA 139; 147; GLL 1

Monroe, Harriet 1860-1936 .... **TCLC 12**
See also CA 109; DLB 54, 91

Monroe, Lyle
See Heinlein, Robert A(nson)

Montagu, Elizabeth 1720-1800 .... **NCLC 7**

Montagu, Mary (Pierrepont) Wortley 1689-1762 .... **LC 9, 57; PC 16**
See also DLB 95, 101

Montagu, W. H.
See Coleridge, Samuel Taylor

Montague, John (Patrick) 1929- ..... **CLC 13, 46**
See also CA 9-12R; CANR 9, 69; DLB 40; MTCW 1

Montaigne, Michel (Eyquem) de 1533-1592 .... **LC 8; DA; DAB; DAC; DAM MST**
See also AW

Montale, Eugenio 1896-1981 ... **CLC 7, 9, 18; PC 13**
See also CA 17-20R; 104; CANR 30; DLB 114; MTCW 1

Montesquieu, Charles-Louis de Secondat 1689-1755 .... **LC 7**

Montessori, Maria 1870-1952 ...... **TCLC 103**
See also CA 115; 147

Montgomery, (Robert) Bruce 1921(?)-1978
See Crispin, Edmund
See also CA 179; 104

Montgomery, L(ucy) M(aud) 1874-1942 .... **TCLC 51; DAC; DAM MST**
See also AAYA 12; CA 108; 137; CLR 8; DA3; DLB 92; DLBD 14; JRDA; MAICYA; MTCW 2; SATA 100

Montgomery, Marion H., Jr. 1925- .... **CLC 7**
See also AITN 1; CA 1-4R; CANR 3, 48; DLB 6

Montgomery, Max
See Davenport, Guy (Mattison, Jr.)

Montherlant, Henry (Milon) de 1896-1972 ..... **CLC 8, 19; DAM DRAM**
See also CA 85-88; 37-40R; DLB 72; MTCW 1

Monty Python
See Chapman, Graham; Cleese, John (Marwood); Gilliam, Terry (Vance); Idle, Eric; Jones, Terence Graham Parry; Palin, Michael (Edward)
See also AAYA 7

Moodie, Susanna (Strickland) 1803-1885 .... **NCLC 14**
See also DLB 99

Moody, William Vaughan 1869-1910 .... **TCLC 105**
See also CA 110; 178; DLB 7, 54

Mooney, Edward 1951-
See Mooney, Ted
See also CA 130

Mooney, Ted CLC 25
See also Mooney, Edward

Moorcock, Michael (John) 1939- ...... **CLC 5, 27, 58**
See also Bradbury, Edward P.
See also AAYA 26; CA 45-48; CAAS 5; CANR 2, 17, 38, 64; DLB 14, 231; MTCW 1, 2; SATA 93

Moore, Brian 1921-1999 ... **CLC 1, 3, 5, 7, 8, 19, 32, 90; DAB; DAC; DAM MST**
See also Bryan, Michael
See also CA 1-4R; 174; CANR 1, 25, 42, 63; CCA 1; MTCW 1, 2

Moore, Edward
See Muir, Edwin

Moore, G. E. 1873-1958 .... **TCLC 89**

Moore, George Augustus 1852-1933 .... **TCLC 7; SSC 19**
See also CA 104; 177; DLB 10, 18, 57, 135

Moore, Lorrie CLC 39, 45, 68
See also Moore, Marie Lorena
See also DLB 234

Moore, Marianne (Craig) 1887-1972 .... **CLC 1, 2, 4, 8, 10, 13, 19, 47; DA; DAB; DAC; DAM MST, POET; PC 4**
See also AW; CA 1-4R; 33-36R; CANR 3, 61; CDALB 1929-1941; DA3; DLB 45; DLBD 7; MTCW 1, 2; SATA 20

Moore, Marie Lorena 1957-
See Moore, Lorrie
See also CA 116; CANR 39, 83; DLB 234

Moore, Thomas 1779-1852 .... **NCLC 6**
See also DLB 96, 144

Moorhouse, Frank 1938- .... **SSC 40**
See also CA 118; CANR 92

Mora, Pat(ricia) 1942-
See also CA 129; CANR 57, 81; CLR 58; DAM MULT; DLB 209; HLC 2; HW 1, 2; SATA 92

Moraga, Cherrie 1952- .... **CLC 126; DAM MULT**
See also CA 131; CANR 66; DLB 82; GLL 1; HW 1, 2

Morand, Paul 1888-1976 .... **CLC 41; SSC 22**
See also CA 184; 69-72; DLB 65

Morante, Elsa 1918-1985 .... **CLC 8, 47**
See also CA 85-88; 117; CANR 35; DLB 177; MTCW 1, 2

Moravia, Alberto CLC 2, 7, 11, 27, 46; SSC 26
See also Pincherle, Alberto
See also DLB 177; MTCW 2

More, Hannah 1745-1833 .... **NCLC 27**
See also DLB 107, 109, 116, 158

More, Henry 1614-1687 .... **LC 9**
See also DLB 126

More, Sir Thomas 1478-1535 .... **LC 10, 32**

Moreas, Jean TCLC 18
See also Papadiamantopoulos, Johannes

Morgan, Berry 1919- .... **CLC 6**
See also CA 49-52; DLB 6

Morgan, Claire
See Highsmith, (Mary) Patricia
See also GLL 1

Morgan, Edwin (George) 1920- .... **CLC 31**
See also CA 5-8R; CANR 3, 43, 90; DLB 27

Morgan, (George) Frederick 1922- .. **CLC 23**
See also CA 17-20R; CANR 21

Morgan, Harriet
See Mencken, H(enry) L(ouis)

Morgan, Jane
See Cooper, James Fenimore

Morgan, Janet 1945- .... **CLC 39**
See also CA 65-68

Morgan, Lady 1776(?)-1859 .... **NCLC 29**
See also DLB 116, 158

Morgan, Robin (Evonne) 1941- .... **CLC 2**
See also CA 69-72; CANR 29, 68; MTCW 1; SATA 80

Morgan, Scott
See Kuttner, Henry

Morgan, Seth 1949(?)-1990 .... **CLC 65**
See also CA 185; 132

Morgenstern, Christian 1871-1914 .. **TCLC 8**
See also CA 105

Morgenstern, S.
See Goldman, William (W.)

Mori, Rintaro
See Mori Ogai
See also CA 110

Moricz, Zsigmond 1879-1942 .... **TCLC 33**
See also CA 165

Morike, Eduard (Friedrich) 1804-1875 .... **NCLC 10**
See also DLB 133

Mori Ogai 1862-1922 .... **TCLC 14**
See also CA 164; DLB 180

Moritz, Karl Philipp 1756-1793 .... **LC 2**
See also DLB 94

Morland, Peter Henry
See Faust, Frederick (Schiller)

Morley, Christopher (Darlington) 1890-1957 .... **TCLC 87**
See also CA 112; DLB 9

Morren, Theophil
See Hofmannsthal, Hugo von

Morris, Bill 1952- .... **CLC 76**

Morris, Julian
See West, Morris L(anglo)

Morris, Steveland Judkins 1950(?)-
See Wonder, Stevie
See also CA 111

Morris, William 1834-1896 .... **NCLC 4**
See also CDBLB 1832-1890; DLB 18, 35, 57, 156, 178, 184

Morris, Wright 1910-1998 .. **CLC 1, 3, 7, 18, 37**
See also CA 9-12R; 167; CANR 21, 81; DLB 2, 206; DLBY 81; MTCW 1, 2; TCLC 107; TCWW 2

Morrison, Arthur 1863-1945 .... **TCLC 72; SSC 40**
See also CA 120; 157; DLB 70, 135, 197

Morrison, Chloe Anthony Wofford
See Morrison, Toni

Morrison, James Douglas 1943-1971
See Morrison, Jim
See also CA 73-76; CANR 40

Morrison, Jim CLC 17
See also Morrison, James Douglas

Morrison, Toni 1931- . **CLC 4, 10, 22, 55, 81, 87; BLC 3; DA; DAB; DAC; DAM MST, MULT, NOV, POP**
See also AAYA 1, 22; AMWS 3; AW; BW 2, 3; CA 29-32R; CANR 27, 42, 67; CDALB 1968-1988; DA3; DLB 6, 33, 143; DLBY 81; MTCW 1, 2; SATA 57

Morrison, Van 1945- .... **CLC 21**
See also CA 116; 168

Morrissy, Mary 1958- .... **CLC 99**

Mortimer, John (Clifford) 1923- ..... **CLC 28, 43; DAM DRAM, POP**
See also CA 13-16R; CANR 21, 69; CDBLB 1960 to Present; DA3; DLB 13; INT CANR-21; MTCW 1, 2

Mortimer, Penelope (Ruth) 1918-1999 .... **CLC 5**
See also CA 57-60; 187; CANR 45, 88

Morton, Anthony
See Creasey, John

Mosca, Gaetano 1858-1941 .... **TCLC 75**

Mosher, Howard Frank 1943- .... **CLC 62**
See also CA 139; CANR 65

Mosley, Nicholas 1923- .... **CLC 43, 70**
See also CA 69-72; CANR 41, 60; DLB 14, 207

Mosley, Walter 1952- .... **CLC 97; BLCS; DAM MULT, POP**
See also AAYA 17; BW 2; CA 142; CANR 57, 92; DA3; MTCW 2

O'Brien, Richard 1942- .... **CLC 17**
    See also CA 124
O'Brien, (William) Tim(othy) 1946- . **CLC 7, 19, 40, 103; DAM POP**
    See also AAYA 16; CA 85-88; CANR 40, 58; CDALBS; DA3; DLB 152; DLBD 9; DLBY 80; MTCW 2
Obstfelder, Sigbjoern 1866-1900 .... **TCLC 23**
    See also CA 123
O'Casey, Sean 1880-1964 .... **CLC 1, 5, 9, 11, 15, 88; DAB; DAC; DAM DRAM, MST; DC 12**
    See also AW; CA 89-92; CANR 62; CD-BLB 1914-1945; DA3; DLB 10; MTCW 1, 2
O'Cathasaigh, Sean
    See O'Casey, Sean
Occom, Samson 1723-1792 .... **LC 60**
    See also DLB 175; NNAL
Ochs, Phil(ip David) 1940-1976 .... **CLC 17**
    See also CA 185; 65-68
O'Connor, Edwin (Greene)
    1918-1968 .... **CLC 14**
    See also CA 93-96; 25-28R
O'Connor, (Mary) Flannery
    1925-1964 .... **CLC 1, 2, 3, 6, 10, 13, 15, 21, 66, 104; DA; DAB; DAC; DAM MST, NOV; SSC 1, 23**
    See also AAYA 7; AW; CA 1-4R; CANR 3, 41; CDALB 1941-1968; DA3; DLB 2, 152; DLBD 12; DLBY 80; MTCW 1, 2
O'Connor, Frank CLC 23; SSC 5
    See also O'Donovan, Michael John
    See also DLB 162
O'Dell, Scott 1898-1989 .... **CLC 30**
    See also AAYA 3; AW; CA 61-64; 129; CANR 12, 30; CLR 1, 16; DLB 52; JRDA; MAICYA; SATA 12, 60
Odets, Clifford 1906-1963 ..... **CLC 2, 28, 98; DAM DRAM; DC 6**
    See also AMWS 2; CA 85-88; CANR 62; DLB 7, 26; MTCW 1, 2
O'Doherty, Brian 1934- .... **CLC 76**
    See also CA 105
O'Donnell, K. M.
    See Malzberg, Barry N(athaniel)
O'Donnell, Lawrence
    See Kuttner, Henry
O'Donovan, Michael John
    1903-1966 .... **CLC 14**
    See also O'Connor, Frank
    See also CA 93-96; CANR 84
J CLC 10, 36, 86; DAM NOV; SSC 20
    See also CA 97-100; CANR 36, 50, 74; DA3; DLB 182; DLBY 94; MTCW 1, 2
O'Faolain, Julia 1932- .... **CLC 6, 19, 47, 108**
    See also CA 81-84; CAAS 2; CANR 12, 61; DLB 14, 231; MTCW 1
O'Faolain, Sean 1900-1991 ...... **CLC 1, 7, 14, 32, 70; SSC 13**
    See also CA 61-64; 134; CANR 12, 66; DLB 15, 162; MTCW 1, 2
O'Flaherty, Liam 1896-1984 .... **CLC 5, 34; SSC 6**
    See also CA 101; 113; CANR 35; DLB 36, 162; DLBY 84; MTCW 1, 2
Ogilvy, Gavin
    See Barrie, J(ames) M(atthew)
O'Grady, Standish (James)
    1846-1928 .... **TCLC 5**
    See also CA 104; 157
O'Grady, Timothy 1951- .... **CLC 59**
    See also CA 138
O'Hara, Frank 1926-1966 .... **CLC 2, 5, 13, 78; DAM POET**
    See also CA 9-12R; 25-28R; CANR 33; DA3; DLB 5, 16, 193; MTCW 1, 2

O'Hara, John (Henry) 1905-1970 . **CLC 1, 2, 3, 6, 11, 42; DAM NOV; SSC 15**
    See also CA 5-8R; 25-28R; CANR 31, 60; CDALB 1929-1941; DLB 9, 86; DLBD 2; MTCW 1, 2
O Hehir, Diana 1922- .... **CLC 41**
    See also CA 93-96
Ohiyesa 1858-1939
    See Eastman, Charles A(lexander)
Okigbo, Christopher (Ifenayichukwu)
    1932-1967 ... **CLC 25, 84; BLC 3; DAM MULT; POET; PC 7**
    See also BW 1, 3; CA 77-80; CANR 74; DLB 125; MTCW 1, 2
Okri, Ben 1959- .... **CLC 87**
    See also BRWS 5; BW 2, 3; CA 130; 138; CANR 65; DLB 157, 231; INT 138; MTCW 2
Olds, Sharon 1942- ... **CLC 32, 39, 85; DAM POET; PC 22**
    See also CA 101; CANR 18, 41, 66; DLB 120; MTCW 2
Oldstyle, Jonathan
    See Irving, Washington
Olesha, Yuri (Karlovich) 1899-1960 .. **CLC 8**
    See also CA 85-88
Oliphant, Laurence 1829(?)-1888 .. **NCLC 47**
    See also DLB 18, 166
Oliphant, Margaret (Oliphant Wilson)
    1828-1897 .... **NCLC 11, 61; SSC 25**
    See also Oliphant
    See also DLB 18, 159, 190
Oliver, Mary 1935- .... **CLC 19, 34, 98**
    See also AMWS 7; CA 21-24R; CANR 9, 43, 84, 92; DLB 5, 193
Olivier, Laurence (Kerr) 1907-1989 . **CLC 20**
    See also CA 111; 150; 129
Olsen, Tillie 1912- .... **CLC 4, 13, 114; DA; DAB; DAC; DAM MST; SSC 11**
    See also CA 1-4R; CANR 1, 43, 74; CDALBS; DA3; DLB 28, 206; DLBY 80; MTCW 1, 2
Olson, Charles (John) 1910-1970 .. **CLC 1, 2, 5, 6, 9, 11, 29; DAM POET; PC 19**
    See also AMWS 2; CA 13-16; 25-28R; CABS 2; CANR 35, 61; CAP 1; DLB 5, 16, 193; MTCW 1, 2
Olson, Toby 1937- .... **CLC 28**
    See also CA 65-68; CANR 9, 31, 84
Olyesha, Yuri
    See Olesha, Yuri (Karlovich)
Ondaatje, (Philip) Michael 1943- .... **CLC 14, 29, 51, 76; DAB; DAC; DAM MST; PC 28**
    See also CA 77-80; CANR 42, 74; DA3; DLB 60; MTCW 2
Oneal, Elizabeth 1934-
    See Oneal, Zibby
    See also CA 106; CANR 28, 84; MAI-CYA; SATA 30, 82
Oneal, Zibby CLC 30
    See also Oneal, Elizabeth
    See also AAYA 5; CLR 13; JRDA
O'Neill, Eugene (Gladstone)
    1888-1953 .... **TCLC 1, 6, 27, 49; DA; DAB; DAC; DAM DRAM, MST**
    See also AITN 1; AW; CA 110; 132; CDALB 1929-1941; DA3; DLB 7; MTCW 1, 2
Onetti, Juan Carlos 1909-1994 ... **CLC 7, 10; DAM MULT, NOV; HLCS 2; SSC 23**
    See also CA 85-88; 145; CANR 32, 63; DLB 113; HW 1, 2; MTCW 1, 2
O Nuallain, Brian 1911-1966
    See O'Brien, Flann
    See also CA 21-22; 25-28R; CAP 2; DLB 231
Ophuls, Max 1902-1957 .... **TCLC 79**
    See also CA 113

Opie, Amelia 1769-1853 .... **NCLC 65**
    See also DLB 116, 159
Oppen, George 1908-1984 ...... **CLC 7, 13, 34**
    See also CA 13-16R; 113; CANR 8, 82; DLB 5, 165; TCLC 107
Oppenheim, E(dward) Phillips
    1866-1946 .... **TCLC 45**
    See also CA 111; DLB 70
Opuls, Max
    See Ophuls, Max
Origen c. 185-c. 254 .... **CMLC 19**
Orlovitz, Gil 1918-1973 .... **CLC 22**
    See also CA 77-80; 45-48; DLB 2, 5
Orris
    See Ingelow, Jean
Ortega y Gasset, Jose 1883-1955 ... **TCLC 9; DAM MULT; HLC 2**
    See also CA 106; 130; HW 1, 2; MTCW 1, 2
Ortese, Anna Maria 1914- .... **CLC 89**
    See also DLB 177
Ortiz, Simon J(oseph) 1941- . **CLC 45; DAM MULT, POET; PC 17**
    See also AMWS 4; CA 134; CANR 69; DLB 120, 175; NNAL
Orton, Joe CLC 4, 13, 43; DC 3
    See also Orton, John Kingsley
    See also BRWS 5; CDBLB 1960 to Present; DLB 13; GLL 1; MTCW 2
Orton, John Kingsley 1933-1967
    See Orton, Joe
    See also CA 85-88; CANR 35, 66; DAM DRAM; MTCW 1, 2
Orwell, George TCLC 2, 6, 15, 31, 51; DAB
    See also Blair, Eric (Arthur)
    See also AW; CDBLB 1945-1960; CLR 68; DLB 15, 98, 195; SCFW 2
Osborne, David
    See Silverberg, Robert
Osborne, George
    See Silverberg, Robert
Osborne, John (James) 1929-1994 .... **CLC 1, 2, 5, 11, 45; DA; DAB; DAC; DAM DRAM, MST**
    See also AW; BRWS 1; CA 13-16R; 147; CANR 21, 56; CDBLB 1945-1960; DLB 13; MTCW 1, 2
Osborne, Lawrence 1958- .... **CLC 50**
    See also CA 189
Osbourne, Lloyd 1868-1947 .... **TCLC 93**
Oshima, Nagisa 1932- .... **CLC 20**
    See also CA 116; 121; CANR 78
Oskison, John Milton 1874-1947 .. **TCLC 35; DAM MULT**
    See also CA 144; CANR 84; DLB 175; NNAL
Ossian c. 3rd cent. - .... **CMLC 28**
    See also Macpherson, James
Ossoli, Sarah Margaret (Fuller marchesa d')
    1810-1850 .... **NCLC 5, 50**
    See also Fuller, Margaret; Fuller, Sarah Margaret
    See also CDALB 1640-1865; DLB 1, 59, 73, 183, 223, 239; SATA 25
Ostriker, Alicia (Suskin) 1937- .... **CLC 132**
    See also CA 25-28R; CAAS 24; CANR 10, 30, 62; DLB 120
Ostrovsky, Alexander 1823-1886 .. **NCLC 30, 57**
Otero, Blas de 1916-1979 .... **CLC 11**
    See also CA 89-92; DLB 134
Otto, Rudolf 1869-1937 .... **TCLC 85**
Otto, Whitney 1955- .... **CLC 70**
    See also CA 140
Ouida TCLC 43
    See also De La Ramee, (Marie) Louise
    See also DLB 18, 156

Paulin, Tom CLC 37
See also Paulin, Thomas Neilson
See also DLB 40
Pausanias c. 1st cent. - .... CMLC 36
Paustovsky, Konstantin (Georgievich)
1892-1968 .... CLC 40
See also CA 93-96; 25-28R
Pavese, Cesare 1908-1950 .. TCLC 3; PC 13;
SSC 19
See also CA 104; 169; DLB 128, 177
Pavic, Milorad 1929- .... CLC 60
See also CA 136; CWW 2; DLB 181
Pavlov, Ivan Petrovich 1849-1936 . TCLC 91
See also CA 118; 180
Payne, Alan
See Jakes, John (William)
Paz, Gil
See Lugones, Leopoldo
Paz, Octavio 1914-1998 . CLC 3, 4, 6, 10, 19,
51, 65, 119; DA; DAB; DAC; DAM
MST, MULT, POET; HLC 2; PC 1
See also AW; CA 73-76; 165; CANR 32,
65; CWW 2; DA3; DLBY 90, 98; HW 1,
2; MTCW 1, 2
p'Bitek, Okot 1931-1982 .... CLC 96; BLC 3;
DAM MULT
See also BW 2, 3; CA 124; 107; CANR 82;
DLB 125; MTCW 1, 2
Peacock, Molly 1947- .... CLC 60
See also CA 103; CAAS 21; CANR 52, 84;
DLB 120
Peacock, Thomas Love
1785-1866 .... NCLC 22
See also DLB 96, 116
Peake, Mervyn 1911-1968 .... CLC 7, 54
See also CA 5-8R; 25-28R; CANR 3; DLB
15, 160; MTCW 1; SATA 23
Pearce, Philippa CLC 21
See also Christie, (Ann) Philippa
See also CLR 9; DLB 161; MAICYA;
SATA 1, 67
Pearl, Eric
See Elman, Richard (Martin)
Pearson, T(homas) R(eid) 1956- .... CLC 39
See also CA 120; 130; INT 130
Peck, Dale 1967- .... CLC 81
See also CA 146; CANR 72; GLL 2
Peck, John 1941- .... CLC 3
See also CA 49-52; CANR 3
Peck, Richard (Wayne) 1934- .... CLC 21
See also AAYA 1, 24; CA 85-88; CANR
19, 38; CLR 15; INT CANR-19; JRDA;
MAICYA; SAAS 2; SATA 18, 55, 97;
SATA-Essay 110
Peck, Robert Newton 1928- .... CLC 17; DA;
DAC; DAM MST
See also AAYA 3; AW; CA 81-84, 182;
CAAE 182; CANR 31, 63; CLR 45;
JRDA; MAICYA; SAAS 1; SATA 21, 62,
111; SATA-Essay 108
Peckinpah, (David) Sam(uel)
1925-1984 .... CLC 20
See also CA 109; 114; CANR 82
Pedersen, Knut 1859-1952
See Hamsun, Knut
See also CA 104; 119; CANR 63; MTCW
1, 2
Peeslake, Gaffer
See Durrell, Lawrence (George)
Peguy, Charles Pierre 1873-1914 ... TCLC 10
See also CA 107
Peirce, Charles Sanders
1839-1914 .... TCLC 81
Pellicer, Carlos 1900(?)-1977
See also CA 153; 69-72; HLCS 2; HW 1
Pena, Ramon del Valle y
See Valle-Inclan, Ramon (Maria) del
Pendennis, Arthur Esquir
See Thackeray, William Makepeace

Penn, William 1644-1718 .... LC 25
See also DLB 24
PEPECE
See Prado (Calvo), Pedro
Pepys, Samuel 1633-1703 ..... LC 11, 58; DA;
DAB; DAC; DAM MST
See also AW; CDBLB 1660-1789; DA3;
DLB 101
Percy, Thomas 1729-1811 .... NCLC 95
See also DLB 104
Percy, Walker 1916-1990 .... CLC 2, 3, 6, 8,
14, 18, 47, 65; DAM NOV, POP
See also AMWS 3; CA 1-4R; 131; CANR
1, 23, 64; DA3; DLB 2; DLBY 80, 90;
MTCW 1, 2
Percy, William Alexander
1885-1942 .... TCLC 84
See also CA 163; MTCW 2
Perec, Georges 1936-1982 .... CLC 56, 116
See also CA 141; DLB 83
Pereda (y Sanchez de Porrua), Jose Maria
de 1833-1906 .... TCLC 16
See also CA 117
Pereda y Porrua, Jose Maria de
See Pereda (y Sanchez de Porrua), Jose
Maria de
Peregoy, George Weems
See Mencken, H(enry) L(ouis)
Perelman, S(idney) J(oseph)
1904-1979 .. CLC 3, 5, 9, 15, 23, 44, 49;
DAM DRAM; SSC 32
See also AITN 1, 2; CA 73-76; 89-92;
CANR 18; DLB 11, 44; MTCW 1, 2
Peret, Benjamin 1899-1959 .... TCLC 20; PC
33
See also CA 117; 186
Peretz, Isaac Loeb 1851(?)-1915 ... TCLC 16;
SSC 26
See also CA 109
Peretz, Yitzhok Leibush
See Peretz, Isaac Loeb
Perez Galdos, Benito 1843-1920 ... TCLC 27;
HLCS 2
See also CA 125; 153; HW 1
Peri Rossi, Cristina 1941-
See also CA 131; CANR 59, 81; DLB 145;
HLCS 2; HW 1, 2
Perlata
See Peret, Benjamin
Perloff, Marjorie G(abrielle)
1931- .... CLC 137
See also CA 57-60; CANR 7, 22, 49
Perrault, Charles 1628-1703 ... LC 3, 52; DC
12
See also MAICYA; SATA 25
Perry, Anne 1938- .... CLC 126
See also CA 101; CANR 22, 50, 84
Perry, Brighton
See Sherwood, Robert E(mmet)
Perse, St.-John
See Leger, (Marie-Rene Auguste) Alexis
Saint-Leger
Perutz, Leo(pold) 1882-1957 .... TCLC 60
See also CA 147; DLB 81
Peseenz, Tulio F.
See Lopez y Fuentes, Gregorio
Pesetsky, Bette 1932- .... CLC 28
See also CA 133; DLB 130
Peshkov, Alexei Maximovich 1868-1936
See Gorky, Maxim
See also CA 105; 141; CANR 83; DA;
DAC; DAM DRAM, MST, NOV; MTCW
2
Pessoa, Fernando (Antonio Nogueira)
1898-1935 .... TCLC 27; DAM MULT;
HLC 2; PC 20
See also CA 125; 183
Peterkin, Julia Mood 1880-1961 ...... CLC 31
See also CA 102; DLB 9

Peters, Joan K(aren) 1945- .... CLC 39
See also CA 158
Peters, Robert L(ouis) 1924- .... CLC 7
See also CA 13-16R; CAAS 8; DLB 105
Petofi, Sandor 1823-1849 .... NCLC 21
Petrakis, Harry Mark 1923- .... CLC 3
See also CA 9-12R; CANR 4, 30, 85
Petrarch 1304-1374 .... CMLC 20; DAM
POET; PC 8
See also DA3
Petronius c. 20-66 .... CMLC 34
See also DLB 211
Petrov, Evgeny TCLC 21
See also Kataev, Evgeny Petrovich
Petry, Ann (Lane) 1908-1997 ... CLC 1, 7, 18
See also BW 1, 3; CA 5-8R; 157; CAAS 6;
CANR 4, 46; CLR 12; DLB 76; JRDA;
MAICYA; MTCW 1; SATA 5; SATA-Obit
94
Petursson, Halligrimur 1614-1674 .... LC 8
Peychinovich
See Vazov, Ivan (Minchov)
Phaedrus c. 15B.C.-c. 50 .... CMLC 25
See also DLB 211
Philips, Katherine 1632-1664 .... LC 30
See also DLB 131
Philipson, Morris H. 1926- .... CLC 53
See also CA 1-4R; CANR 4
Phillips, Caryl 1958- . CLC 96; BLCS; DAM
MULT
See also BRWS 5; BW 2; CA 141; CANR
63; DA3; DLB 157; MTCW 2
Phillips, David Graham
1867-1911 .... TCLC 44
See also CA 108; 176; DLB 9, 12
Phillips, Jack
See Sandburg, Carl (August)
Phillips, Jayne Anne 1952- .... CLC 15, 33,
139; SSC 16
See also CA 101; CANR 24, 50, 96; DLBY
80; INT CANR-24; MTCW 1, 2
Phillips, Richard
See Dick, Philip K(indred)
Phillips, Robert (Schaeffer) 1938- .... CLC 28
See also CA 17-20R; CAAS 13; CANR 8;
DLB 105
Phillips, Ward
See Lovecraft, H(oward) P(hillips)
Piccolo, Lucio 1901-1969 .... CLC 13
See also CA 97-100; DLB 114
Pickthall, Marjorie L(owry) C(hristie)
1883-1922 .... TCLC 21
See also CA 107; DLB 92
Pico della Mirandola, Giovanni
1463-1494 .... LC 15
Piercy, Marge 1936- .... CLC 3, 6, 14, 18, 27,
62, 128; PC 29
See also CA 21-24R; CAAE 187; CAAS 1;
CANR 13, 43, 66; DLB 120, 227; MTCW
1, 2
Piers, Robert
See Anthony, Piers
Pieyre de Mandiargues, Andre 1909-1991
See Mandiargues, Andre Pieyre de
See also CA 103; 136; CANR 22, 82
Pilnyak, Boris TCLC 23
See also Vogau, Boris Andreyevich
Pincherle, Alberto 1907-1990 .... CLC 11, 18;
DAM NOV
See also Moravia, Alberto
See also CA 25-28R; 132; CANR 33, 63;
MTCW 1
Pinckney, Darryl 1953- .... CLC 76
See also BW 2, 3; CA 143; CANR 79
Pindar 518B.C.-442B.C. .... CMLC 12; PC 19
See also DLB 176
Pineda, Cecile 1942- .... CLC 39
See also CA 118; DLB 209

Powell, Talmage 1920-2000
See Queen, Ellery
See also CA 5-8R; CANR 2, 80

Power, Susan 1961- .... **CLC 91**
See also CA 160

Powers, J(ames) F(arl) 1917-1999 ..... **CLC 1, 4, 8, 57; SSC 4**
See also CA 1-4R; 181; CANR 2, 61; DLB 130; MTCW 1

Powers, John J(ames) 1945-
See Powers, John R.
See also CA 69-72

Powers, John R. CLC 66
See also Powers, John J(ames)

Powers, Richard (S.) 1957- .... **CLC 93**
See also CA 148; CANR 80

Pownall, David 1938- .... **CLC 10**
See also CA 89-92; 180; CAAS 18; CANR 49; DLB 14

Powys, John Cowper 1872-1963 ... **CLC 7, 9, 15, 46, 125**
See also CA 85-88; DLB 15; MTCW 1, 2

Powys, T(heodore) F(rancis)
1875-1953 .... **TCLC 9**
See also CA 106; 189; DLB 36, 162

Prado (Calvo), Pedro 1886-1952 ... **TCLC 75**
See also CA 131; HW 1

Prager, Emily 1952- .... **CLC 56**

Pratt, E(dwin) J(ohn)
1883(?)-1964 .... **CLC 19; DAC; DAM POET**
See also CA 141; 93-96; CANR 77; DLB 92

Premchand TCLC 21
See also Srivastava, Dhanpat Rai

Preussler, Otfried 1923- .... **CLC 17**
See also CA 77-80; SATA 24

Prevert, Jacques (Henri Marie)
1900-1977 .... **CLC 15**
See also CA 77-80; 69-72; CANR 29, 61; IDFW 3; MTCW 1; SATA-Obit 30

Prevost, Abbe (Antoine Francois)
1697-1763 .... **LC 1**

Price, (Edward) Reynolds 1933- ... **CLC 3, 6, 13, 43, 50, 63; DAM NOV; SSC 22**
See also CA 1-4R; CANR 1, 37, 57, 87; DLB 2; INT CANR-37

Price, Richard 1949- .... **CLC 6, 12**
See also CA 49-52; CANR 3; DLBY 81

Prichard, Katharine Susannah
1883-1969 .... **CLC 46**
See also CA 11-12; CANR 33; CAP 1; MTCW 1; SATA 66

Priestley, J(ohn) B(oynton)
1894-1984 .... **CLC 2, 5, 9, 34; DAM DRAM, NOV**
See also CA 9-12R; 113; CANR 33; CD-BLB 1914-1945; DA3; DLB 10, 34, 77, 100, 139; DLBY 84; MTCW 1, 2

Prince 1958(?)- .... **CLC 35**

Prince, F(rank) T(empleton) 1912- .. **CLC 22**
See also CA 101; CANR 43, 79; DLB 20

Prince Kropotkin
See Kropotkin, Peter (Aleksieevich)

Prior, Matthew 1664-1721 .... **LC 4**
See also DLB 95

Prishvin, Mikhail 1873-1954 .... **TCLC 75**

Pritchard, William H(arrison)
1932- .... **CLC 34**
See also CA 65-68; CANR 23, 95; DLB 111

Pritchett, V(ictor) S(awdon)
1900-1997 ...... **CLC 5, 13, 15, 41; DAM NOV; SSC 14**
See also BRWS 3; CA 61-64; 157; CANR 31, 63; DA3; DLB 15, 139; MTCW 1, 2

Private 19022
See Manning, Frederic

Probst, Mark 1925- .... **CLC 59**
See also CA 130

Prokosch, Frederic 1908-1989 ...... **CLC 4, 48**
See also CA 73-76; 128; CANR 82; DLB 48; MTCW 2

Propertius, Sextus c. 50B.C.-c.
15B.C. .... **CMLC 32**
See also DLB 211

Prophet, The
See Dreiser, Theodore (Herman Albert)

Prose, Francine 1947- .... **CLC 45**
See also CA 109; 112; CANR 46, 95; DLB 234; SATA 101

Proudhon
See Cunha, Euclides (Rodrigues Pimenta) da

Proulx, Annie
See Proulx, E(dna) Annie
See also AMWS 7

Proulx, E(dna) Annie 1935- .. **CLC 81; DAM POP**
See also Proulx, Annie
See also CA 145; CANR 65; DA3; MTCW 2

Proust,
(Valentin-Louis-George-Eugene-)Marcel
1871-1922 . **TCLC 7, 13, 33; DA; DAB; DAC; DAM MST, NOV**
See also AW; CA 104; 120; DA3; DLB 65; MTCW 1, 2

Prowler, Harley
See Masters, Edgar Lee

Prus, Boleslaw 1845-1912 .... **TCLC 48**

Pryor, Richard (Franklin Lenox Thomas)
1940- .... **CLC 26**
See also CA 122; 152

Przybyszewski, Stanislaw
1868-1927 .... **TCLC 36**
See also CA 160; DLB 66

Pteleon
See Grieve, C(hristopher) M(urray)
See also DAM POET

Puckett, Lute
See Masters, Edgar Lee

Puig, Manuel 1932-1990 .... **CLC 3, 5, 10, 28, 65, 133; DAM MULT; HLC 2**
See also CA 45-48; CANR 2, 32, 63; DA3; DLB 113; GLL 1; HW 1, 2; MTCW 1, 2

Pulitzer, Joseph 1847-1911 .... **TCLC 76**
See also CA 114; DLB 23

Purdy, A(lfred) W(ellington)
1918-2000 .... **CLC 3, 6, 14, 50; DAC; DAM MST, POET**
See also CA 81-84; 189; CAAS 17; CANR 42, 66; DLB 88

Purdy, James (Amos) 1923- .... **CLC 2, 4, 10, 28, 52**
See also AMWS 7; CA 33-36R; CAAS 1; CANR 19, 51; DLB 2; INT CANR-19; MTCW 1

Pure, Simon
See Swinnerton, Frank Arthur

Pushkin, Alexander (Sergeyevich)
1799-1837 . **NCLC 3, 27, 83; DA; DAB; DAC; DAM DRAM, MST, POET; PC 10; SSC 27**
See also AW; DA3; DLB 205; SATA 61

P'u Sung-ling 1640-1715 .... **LC 49; SSC 31**

Putnam, Arthur Lee
See Alger, Horatio, Jr.

Puzo, Mario 1920-1999 .... **CLC 1, 2, 6, 36, 107; DAM NOV, POP**
See also CA 65-68; 185; CANR 4, 42, 65; DA3; DLB 6; MTCW 1, 2

Pygge, Edward
See Barnes, Julian (Patrick)

Pyle, Ernest Taylor 1900-1945
See Pyle, Ernie
See also CA 115; 160

Pyle, Ernie TCLC 75
See also Pyle, Ernest Taylor
See also DLB 29; MTCW 2

Pyle, Howard 1853-1911 .... **TCLC 81**
See also AW; CA 109; 137; CLR 22; DLB 42, 188; DLBD 13; MAICYA; SATA 16, 100

Pym, Barbara (Mary Crampton)
1913-1980 .... **CLC 13, 19, 37, 111**
See also BRWS 2; CA 13-14; 97-100; CANR 13, 34; CAP 1; DLB 14, 207; DLBY 87; MTCW 1, 2

Pynchon, Thomas (Ruggles, Jr.)
1937- ...... **CLC 2, 3, 6, 9, 11, 18, 33, 62, 72, 123; DA; DAB; DAC; DAM MST, NOV, POP; SSC 14**
See also AMWS 2; AW; BEST 90:2; CA 17-20R; CANR 22, 46, 73; DA3; DLB 2, 173; MTCW 1, 2

Pythagoras c. 582B.C.-c. 507B.C. . **CMLC 22**
See also DLB 176

Q
See Quiller-Couch, SirArthur (Thomas)

Qian Zhongshu
See Ch'ien Chung-shu

Qroll
See Dagerman, Stig (Halvard)

Quarrington, Paul (Lewis) 1953- ..... **CLC 65**
See also CA 129; CANR 62, 95

Quasimodo, Salvatore 1901-1968 ..... **CLC 10**
See also CA 13-16; 25-28R; CAP 1; DLB 114; MTCW 1

Quay, Stephen 1947- .... **CLC 95**
See also CA 189

Quay, Timothy 1947- .... **CLC 95**
See also CA 189

Queen, Ellery CLC 3, 11
See also Dannay, Frederic; Davidson, Avram (James); Deming, Richard; Fairman, Paul W.; Flora, Fletcher; Hoch, Edward D(entinger); Kane, Henry; Lee, Manfred B(ennington); Marlowe, Stephen; Powell, Talmage; Sheldon, Walter J.; Sturgeon, Theodore (Hamilton); Tracy, Don(ald Fiske); Vance, John Holbrook

Queen, Ellery, Jr.
See Dannay, Frederic; Lee, Manfred B(ennington)

Queneau, Raymond 1903-1976 ..... **CLC 2, 5, 10, 42**
See also CA 77-80; 69-72; CANR 32; DLB 72; MTCW 1, 2

Quevedo, Francisco de 1580-1645 .... **LC 23**

Quiller-Couch, SirArthur (Thomas)
1863-1944 .... **TCLC 53**
See also CA 118; 166; DLB 135, 153, 190

Quin, Ann (Marie) 1936-1973 .... **CLC 6**
See also CA 9-12R; 45-48; DLB 14, 231

Quinn, Martin
See Smith, Martin Cruz

Quinn, Peter 1947- .... **CLC 91**

Quinn, Simon
See Smith, Martin Cruz

Quintana, Leroy V. 1944-
See also CA 131; CANR 65; DAM MULT; DLB 82; HLC 2; HW 1, 2

Quiroga, Horacio (Sylvestre)
1878-1937 .... **TCLC 20; DAM MULT; HLC 2**
See also CA 117; 131; HW 1; MTCW 1

Quoirez, Francoise 1935- .... **CLC 9**
See also Sagan, Francoise
See also CA 49-52; CANR 6, 39, 73; CWW 2; MTCW 1, 2

Raabe, Wilhelm (Karl) 1831-1910 . **TCLC 45**
See also CA 167; DLB 129

Robinson, William, Jr. 1940-
See Robinson, Smokey
See also CA 116

Robison, Mary 1949- .... **CLC 42, 98**
See also CA 113; 116; CANR 87; DLB 130;
INT 116

Rod, Edouard 1857-1910 .... **TCLC 52**

Roddenberry, Eugene Wesley 1921-1991
See Roddenberry, Gene
See also CA 110; 135; CANR 37; SATA 45;
SATA-Obit 69

Roddenberry, Gene CLC 17
See also Roddenberry, Eugene Wesley
See also AAYA 5; SATA-Obit 69

Rodgers, Mary 1931- .... **CLC 12**
See also CA 49-52; CANR 8, 55, 90; CLR
20; INT CANR-8; JRDA; MAICYA;
SATA 8

Rodgers, W(illiam) R(obert)
1909-1969 .... **CLC 7**
See also CA 85-88; DLB 20

Rodman, Eric
See Silverberg, Robert

Rodman, Howard 1920(?)-1985 .... **CLC 65**
See also CA 118

Rodman, Maia
See Wojciechowska, Maia (Teresa)

Rodo, Jose Enrique 1871(?)-1917
See also CA 178; HLCS 2; HW 2

Rodriguez, Claudio 1934-1999 .... **CLC 10**
See also CA 188; DLB 134

Rodriguez, Richard 1944-
See also CA 110; CANR 66; DAM MULT;
DLB 82; HLC 2; HW 1, 2

Roelvaag, O(le) E(dvart)
1876-1931 .... **TCLC 17**
See also Rolvaag, O(le) E(dvart)
See also CA 117; 171; DLB 9

Roethke, Theodore (Huebner)
1908-1963 .... **CLC 1, 3, 8, 11, 19, 46,
101; DAM POET; PC 15**
See also CA 81-84; CABS 2; CDALB 1941-
1968; DA3; DLB 5, 206; MTCW 1, 2

Rogers, Samuel 1763-1855 .... **NCLC 69**
See also DLB 93

Rogers, Thomas Hunton 1927- .... **CLC 57**
See also CA 89-92; INT 89-92

Rogers, Will(iam Penn Adair)
1879-1935 ... **TCLC 8, 71; DAM MULT**
See also CA 105; 144; DA3; DLB 11;
MTCW 2; NNAL

Rogin, Gilbert 1929- .... **CLC 18**
See also CA 65-68; CANR 15

Rohan, Koda
See Koda Shigeyuki

Rohlfs, Anna Katharine Green
See Green, Anna Katharine

Rohmer, Eric CLC 16
See also Scherer, Jean-Marie Maurice

Rohmer, Sax TCLC 28
See also Ward, Arthur Henry Sarsfield
See also DLB 70

Roiphe, Anne (Richardson) 1935- .. **CLC 3, 9**
See also CA 89-92; CANR 45, 73; DLBY
80; INT 89-92

Rojas, Fernando de 1475-1541 .... **LC 23;
HLCS 1**

Rojas, Gonzalo 1917-
See also HLCS 2; HW 2

Rojas, Gonzalo 1917-
See also CA 178; HLCS 2

**Rolfe, Frederick (William Serafino Austin
Lewis Mary)** 1860-1913 .... **TCLC 12**
See also CA 107; DLB 34, 156

Rolland, Romain 1866-1944 .... **TCLC 23**
See also CA 118; DLB 65

Rolle, Richard c. 1300-c. 1349 ...... **CMLC 21**
See also DLB 146

Rolvaag, O(le) E(dvart)
See Roelvaag, O(le) E(dvart)

Romain Arnaud, Saint
See Aragon, Louis

Romains, Jules 1885-1972 .... **CLC 7**
See also CA 85-88; CANR 34; DLB 65;
MTCW 1

Romero, Jose Ruben 1890-1952 .... **TCLC 14**
See also CA 114; 131; HW 1

Ronsard, Pierre de 1524-1585 . **LC 6, 54; PC
11**

Rooke, Leon 1934- . **CLC 25, 34; DAM POP**
See also CA 25-28R; CANR 23, 53; CCA 1

Roosevelt, Franklin Delano
1882-1945 .... **TCLC 93**
See also CA 116; 173

Roosevelt, Theodore 1858-1919 ..... **TCLC 69**
See also CA 115; 170; DLB 47, 186

Roper, William 1498-1578 .... **LC 10**

Roquelaure, A. N.
See Rice, Anne

Rosa, Joao Guimaraes 1908-1967 ... **CLC 23;
HLCS 1**
See also CA 89-92; DLB 113

Rose, Wendy 1948- .. **CLC 85; DAM MULT;
PC 13**
See also CA 53-56; CANR 5, 51; DLB 175;
NNAL; SATA 12

Rosen, R. D.
See Rosen, Richard (Dean)

Rosen, Richard (Dean) 1949- .... **CLC 39**
See also CA 77-80; CANR 62; INT
CANR-30

Rosenberg, Isaac 1890-1918 .... **TCLC 12**
See also CA 107; 188; DLB 20

Rosenblatt, Joe CLC 15
See also Rosenblatt, Joseph

Rosenblatt, Joseph 1933-
See Rosenblatt, Joe
See also CA 89-92; INT 89-92

Rosenfeld, Samuel
See Tzara, Tristan

Rosenstock, Sami
See Tzara, Tristan

Rosenstock, Samuel
See Tzara, Tristan

Rosenthal, M(acha) L(ouis)
1917-1996 .... **CLC 28**
See also CA 1-4R; 152; CAAS 6; CANR 4,
51; DLB 5; SATA 59

Ross, Barnaby
See Dannay, Frederic

Ross, Bernard L.
See Follett, Ken(neth Martin)

Ross, J. H.
See Lawrence, T(homas) E(dward)

Ross, John Hume
See Lawrence, T(homas) E(dward)

Ross, Martin -1915
See Martin, Violet Florence
See also DLB 135; GLL 2

Ross, (James) Sinclair 1908-1996 ... **CLC 13;
DAC; DAM MST; SSC 24**
See also CA 73-76; CANR 81; DLB 88

Rossetti, Christina (Georgina)
1830-1894 . **NCLC 2, 50, 66; DA; DAB;
DAC; DAM MST, POET; PC 7**
See also AW; DA3; DLB 35, 163, 240;
MAICYA; SATA 20

Rossetti, Dante Gabriel 1828-1882 . **NCLC 4,
77; DA; DAB; DAC; DAM MST,
POET**
See also AW; CDBLB 1832-1890; DLB 35

Rossner, Judith (Perelman) 1935- . **CLC 6, 9,
29**
See also AITN 2; BEST 90:3; CA 17-20R;
CANR 18, 51, 73; DLB 6; INT CANR-
18; MTCW 1, 2

Rostand, Edmond (Eugene Alexis)
1868-1918 .... **TCLC 6, 37; DA; DAB;
DAC; DAM DRAM, MST; DC 10**
See also CA 104; 126; DA3; DLB 192;
MTCW 1

Roth, Henry 1906-1995 ..... **CLC 2, 6, 11, 104**
See also CA 11-12; 149; CANR 38, 63;
CAP 1; DA3; DLB 28; MTCW 1, 2

Roth, (Moses) Joseph 1894-1939 ... **TCLC 33**
See also CA 160; DLB 85

Roth, Philip (Milton) 1933- ... **CLC 1, 2, 3, 4,
6, 9, 15, 22, 31, 47, 66, 86, 119; DA;
DAB; DAC; DAM MST, NOV, POP;
SSC 26**
See also AMWS 3; AW; BEST 90:3; CA
1-4R; CANR 1, 22, 36, 55, 89; CDALB
1968-1988; DA3; DLB 2, 28, 173; DLBY
82; MTCW 1, 2

Rothenberg, Jerome 1931- .... **CLC 6, 57**
See also CA 45-48; CANR 1; DLB 5, 193

Rotter, Pat ed. CLC 65

Roumain, Jacques (Jean Baptiste)
1907-1944 ...... **TCLC 19; BLC 3; DAM
MULT**
See also BW 1; CA 117; 125

Rourke, Constance (Mayfield)
1885-1941 .... **TCLC 12**
See also AW 1; CA 107

Rousseau, Jean-Baptiste 1671-1741 ...... **LC 9**

Rousseau, Jean-Jacques 1712-1778 .... **LC 14,
36; DA; DAB; DAC; DAM MST**
See also AW; DA3

Roussel, Raymond 1877-1933 .... **TCLC 20**
See also CA 117

Rovit, Earl (Herbert) 1927- .... **CLC 7**
See also CA 5-8R; CANR 12

Rowe, Elizabeth Singer 1674-1737 ..... **LC 44**
See also DLB 39, 95

Rowe, Nicholas 1674-1718 .... **LC 8**
See also DLB 84

Rowlandson, Mary 1637(?)-1678 .... **LC 66**
See also DLB 24, 200

Rowley, Ames Dorrance
See Lovecraft, H(oward) P(hillips)

Rowling, J(oanne) K. 1966(?)- .... **CLC 137**
See also AAYA 34; CA 173; CLR 66; SATA
109

Rowson, Susanna Haswell
1762(?)-1824 .... **NCLC 5, 69**
See also DLB 37, 200

Roy, Arundhati 1960(?)- .... **CLC 109**
See also CA 163; CANR 90; DLBY 97

Roy, Gabrielle 1909-1983 .... **CLC 10, 14;
DAB; DAC; DAM MST**
See also CA 53-56; 110; CANR 5, 61; CCA
1; DLB 68; MTCW 1; SATA 104

Royko, Mike 1932-1997 .... **CLC 109**
See also CA 89-92; 157; CANR 26

Rozanov, Vassili 1856-1919 .... **TCLC 104**

Rozewicz, Tadeusz 1921- ..... **CLC 9, 23, 139;
DAM POET**
See also CA 108; CANR 36, 66; CWW 2;
DA3; DLB 232; MTCW 1, 2

Ruark, Gibbons 1941- .... **CLC 3**
See also CA 33-36R; CAAS 23; CANR 14,
31, 57; DLB 120

Rubens, Bernice (Ruth) 1923- .... **CLC 19, 31**
See also CA 25-28R; CANR 33, 65; DLB
14, 207; MTCW 1

Rubin, Harold
See Robbins, Harold

Rudkin, (James) David 1936- .... **CLC 14**
See also CA 89-92; DLB 13

Rudnik, Raphael 1933- .... **CLC 7**
See also CA 29-32R

Ruffian, M.
See Hasek, Jaroslav (Matej Frantisek)

Ruiz, Jose Martinez CLC 11
See also Martinez Ruiz, Jose

Rukeyser, Muriel 1913-1980 . CLC 6, 10, 15, 27; DAM POET; PC 12
See also AMWS 6; CA 5-8R; 93-96; CANR 26, 60; DA3; DLB 48; GLL 2; MTCW 1, 2; SATA-Obit 22

Rule, Jane (Vance) 1931- .... CLC 27
See also CA 25-28R; CAAS 18; CANR 12, 87; DLB 60

Rulfo, Juan 1918-1986 ...... CLC 8, 80; DAM MULT; HLC 2; SSC 25
See also CA 85-88; 118; CANR 26; DLB 113; HW 1, 2; MTCW 1, 2

Rumi, Jalal al-Din 1207-1273 .... CMLC 20

Runeberg, Johan 1804-1877 .... NCLC 41

Runyon, (Alfred) Damon 1884(?)-1946 .... TCLC 10
See also CA 107; 165; DLB 11, 86, 171; MTCW 2

Rush, Norman 1933- .... CLC 44
See also CA 121; 126; INT 126

Rushdie, (Ahmed) Salman 1947- .... CLC 23, 31, 55, 100; DAB; DAC; DAM MST, NOV, POP
See also AW; BEST 89:3; BRWS 4; CA 108; 111; CANR 33, 56; DA3; DLB 194; INT 111; MTCW 1, 2

Rushforth, Peter (Scott) 1945- .... CLC 19
See also CA 101

Ruskin, John 1819-1900 .... TCLC 63
See also CA 114; 129; CDBLB 1832-1890; DLB 55, 163, 190; SATA 24

Russ, Joanna 1937- .... CLC 15
See also CA 5-28R; CANR 11, 31, 65; DLB 8; GLL 1; MTCW 1; SCFW 2

Russell, George William 1867-1935
See Baker, Jean H.
See also CA 104; 153; CDBLB 1890-1914; DAM POET

Russell, Jeffrey Burton 1934- .... CLC 70
See also CA 25-28R; CANR 11, 28, 52

Russell, (Henry) Ken(neth Alfred) 1927- .... CLC 16
See also CA 105

Russell, William Martin 1947- .... CLC 60
See also CA 164; DLB 233

Rutherford, Mark TCLC 25
See also White, William Hale
See also DLB 18

Ruyslinck, Ward CLC 14
See also Belser, Reimond Karel Maria de

Ryan, Cornelius (John) 1920-1974 ..... CLC 7
See also CA 69-72; 53-56; CANR 38

Ryan, Michael 1946- .... CLC 65
See also CA 49-52; DLBY 82

Ryan, Tim
See Dent, Lester

Rybakov, Anatoli (Naumovich) 1911-1998 .... CLC 23, 53
See also CA 126; 135; 172; SATA 79; SATA-Obit 108

Ryder, Jonathan
See Ludlum, Robert

Ryga, George 1932-1987 .... CLC 14; DAC; DAM MST
See also CA 101; 124; CANR 43, 90; CCA 1; DLB 60

Ryunosuke, Akutagawa 1892-1927 .... SSC 44

S. H.
See Hartmann, Sadakichi

S. S.
See Sassoon, Siegfried (Lorraine)

Saba, Umberto 1883-1957 .... TCLC 33
See also CA 144; CANR 79; DLB 114

Sabatini, Rafael 1875-1950 .... TCLC 47
See also CA 162

Sabato, Ernesto (R.) 1911- .... CLC 10, 23; DAM MULT; HLC 2
See also CA 97-100; CANR 32, 65; DLB 145; HW 1, 2; MTCW 1, 2

Sa-Carniero, Mario de 1890-1916 . TCLC 83

Sacastru, Martin
See Bioy Casares, Adolfo
See also CWW 2

Sacastru, Martin
See Bioy Casares, Adolfo

Sacher-Masoch, Leopold von 1836(?)-1895 .... NCLC 31

Sachs, Marilyn (Stickle) 1927- .... CLC 35
See also AAYA 2; CA 17-20R; CANR 13, 47; CLR 2; JRDA; MAICYA; SAAS 2; SATA 3, 68; SATA-Essay 110

Sachs, Nelly 1891-1970 .... CLC 14, 98
See also CA 17-18; 25-28R; CANR 87; CAP 2; MTCW 2

Sackler, Howard (Oliver) 1929-1982 .... CLC 14
See also CA 61-64; 108; CANR 30; DLB 7

Sacks, Oliver (Wolf) 1933- .... CLC 67
See also CA 53-56; CANR 28, 50, 76; DA3; INT CANR-28; MTCW 1, 2

Sadakichi
See Hartmann, Sadakichi

Sade, Donatien Alphonse Francois 1740-1814 .... NCLC 3, 47

Sadoff, Ira 1945- .... CLC 9
See also CA 53-56; CANR 5, 21; DLB 120

Saetone
See Camus, Albert

Safire, William 1929- .... CLC 10
See also CA 17-20R; CANR 31, 54, 91

Sagan, Carl (Edward) 1934-1996 .... CLC 30, 112
See also AAYA 2; CA 25-28R; 155; CANR 11, 36, 74; DA3; MTCW 1, 2; SATA 58; SATA-Obit 94

Sagan, Françoise CLC 3, 6, 9, 17, 36
See also Quoirez, Françoise
See also CWW 2; DLB 83; MTCW 2

Sahgal, Nayantara (Pandit) 1927- .... CLC 41
See also CA 9-12R; CANR 11, 88

Said, Edward W. 1935- .... CLC 123
See also CA 21-24R; CANR 45, 74; DLB 67; MTCW 2

Saint, H(arry) F. 1941- .... CLC 50
See also CA 127

St. Aubin de Teran, Lisa 1953-
See Teran, Lisa St. Aubin de
See also CA 118; 126; INT 126

Saint Birgitta of Sweden c. 1303-1373 .... CMLC 24

Sainte-Beuve, Charles Augustin 1804-1869 .... NCLC 5

Saint-Exupery, Antoine (Jean Baptiste Marie Roger) de 1900-1944 .... TCLC 2, 56; DAM NOV
See also AW; CA 108; 132; CLR 10; DA3; DLB 72; MAICYA; MTCW 1, 2; SATA 20

St. John, David
See Hunt, E(verette) Howard, (Jr.)

Saint-John Perse
See Leger, (Marie-Rene Auguste) Alexis Saint-Leger

Saintsbury, George (Edward Bateman) 1845-1933 .... TCLC 31
See also CA 160; DLB 57, 149

Sait Faik TCLC 23
See also Abasiyanik, Sait Faik

Saki TCLC 3; SSC 12
See also Munro, H(ector) H(ugh)
See also MTCW 2

Sala, George Augustus 1828-1895 . NCLC 46

Saladin 1138-1193 .... CMLC 38

Salama, Hannu 1936- .... CLC 18

Salamanca, J(ack) R(ichard) 1922- .. CLC 4, 15
See also CA 25-28R

Salas, Floyd Francis 1931-
See also CA 119; CAAS 27; CANR 44, 75, 93; DAM MULT; DLB 82; HLC 2; HW 1, 2; MTCW 2

Sale, J. Kirkpatrick
See Sale, Kirkpatrick

Sale, Kirkpatrick 1937- .... CLC 68
See also CA 13-16R; CANR 10

Salinas, Luis Omar 1937- ..... CLC 90; DAM MULT; HLC 2
See also CA 131; CANR 81; DLB 82; HW 1, 2

Salinas (y Serrano), Pedro 1891(?)-1951 .... TCLC 17
See also CA 117; DLB 134

Salinger, J(erome) D(avid) 1919- .. CLC 1, 3, 8, 12, 55, 56, 138; DA; DAB; DAC; DAM MST, NOV, POP; SSC 2, 28
See also AAYA 2, 36; CA 5-8R; CANR 39; CDALB 1941-1968; CLR 18; DA3; DLB 2, 102, 173; MAICYA; MTCW 1, 2; SATA 67

Salisbury, John
See Caute, (John) David

Salter, James 1925- .... CLC 7, 52, 59
See also CA 73-76; DLB 130

Saltus, Edgar (Everton) 1855-1921 . TCLC 8
See also CA 105; DLB 202

Saltykov, Mikhail Evgrafovich 1826-1889 .... NCLC 16
See also DLB 238;

Samarakis, Antonis 1919- .... CLC 5
See also CA 25-28R; CAAS 16; CANR 36

Sanchez, Florencio 1875-1910 .... TCLC 37
See also CA 153; HW 1

Sanchez, Luis Rafael 1936- .... CLC 23
See also CA 128; DLB 145; HW 1

Sanchez, Sonia 1934- ...... CLC 5, 116; BLC 3; DAM MULT; PC 9
See also BW 2, 3; CA 33-36R; CANR 24, 49, 74; CLR 18; DA3; DLB 41; DLBD 8; MAICYA; MTCW 1, 2; SATA 22

Sand, George 1804-1876 ..... NCLC 2, 42, 57; DA; DAB; DAC; DAM MST, NOV
See also AW; DA3; DLB 119, 192

Sandburg, Carl (August) 1878-1967 . CLC 1, 4, 10, 15, 35; DA; DAB; DAC; DAM MST, POET; PC 2
See also AAYA 24; CA 5-8R; 25-28R; CANR 35; CDALB 1865-1917; CLR 67; DA3; DLB 17, 54; MAICYA; MTCW 1, 2; SATA 8

Sandburg, Charles
See Sandburg, Carl (August)

Sandburg, Charles A.
See Sandburg, Carl (August)

Sanders, (James) Ed(ward) 1939- ... CLC 53; DAM POET
See also CA 13-16R; CAAS 21; CANR 13, 44, 78; DLB 16

Sanders, Lawrence 1920-1998 .... CLC 41; DAM POP
See also BEST 89:4; CA 81-84; 165; CANR 33, 62; DA3; MTCW 1

Sanders, Noah
See Blount, Roy (Alton), Jr.

Sanders, Winston P.
See Anderson, Poul (William)

Sandoz, Mari(e Susette) 1900-1966 .. CLC 28
See also CA 1-4R; 25-28R; CANR 17, 64; DLB 9, 212; MTCW 1, 2; SATA 5; TCWW 2

Suarez Lynch, B.
See Bioy Casares, Adolfo; Borges, Jorge Luis
Suassuna, Ariano Vilar 1927-
See also CA 178; HLCS 1; HW 2
Suckling, SirJohn 1609-1642 .... **PC 30**
See also DAM POET; DLB 58, 126
Suckow, Ruth 1892-1960 .... **SSC 18**
See also CA 113; DLB 9, 102; TCWW 2
Sudermann, Hermann 1857-1928 .. **TCLC 15**
See also CA 107; DLB 118
Sue, Eugene 1804-1857 .... **NCLC 1**
See also DLB 119
Sueskind, Patrick 1949- .... **CLC 44**
See also Suskind, Patrick
Sukenick, Ronald 1932- .... **CLC 3, 4, 6, 48**
See also CA 25-28R; CAAS 8; CANR 32, 89; DLB 173; DLBY 81
Suknaski, Andrew 1942- .... **CLC 19**
See also CA 101; DLB 53
Sullivan, Vernon
See Vian, Boris
Sully Prudhomme 1839-1907 .... **TCLC 31**
Su Man-shu TCLC 24
See also Su, Chien
Summerforest, Ivy B.
See Kirkup, James
Summers, Andrew James 1942- .... **CLC 26**
Summers, Andy
See Summers, Andrew James
Summers, Hollis (Spurgeon, Jr.)
1916- .... **CLC 10**
See also CA 5-8R; CANR 3; DLB 6
Summers, (Alphonsus Joseph-Mary Augustus) Montague
1880-1948 .... **TCLC 16**
See also CA 118; 163
Sumner, Gordon Matthew CLC 26
See also Sting
Surtees, Robert Smith 1805-1864 .. **NCLC 14**
See also DLB 21
Susann, Jacqueline 1921-1974 .... **CLC 3**
See also AITN 1; CA 65-68; 53-56; MTCW 1, 2
Su Shih 1036-1101 .... **CMLC 15**
Suskind, Patrick
See Sueskind, Patrick
See also CA 145; CWW 2
Sutcliff, Rosemary 1920-1992 .... **CLC 26; DAB; DAC; DAM MST, POP**
See also AAYA 10; AW; CA 5-8R; 139; CANR 37; CLR 1, 37; JRDA; MAICYA; SATA 6, 44, 78; SATA-Obit 73
Sutro, Alfred 1863-1933 .... **TCLC 6**
See also CA 105; 185; DLB 10
Sutton, Henry
See Slavitt, David R(ytman)
Suzuki, D. T.
See Suzuki, Daisetz Teitaro
Suzuki, Daisetz T.
See Suzuki, Daisetz Teitaro
Suzuki, Daisetz Teitaro
1870-1966 .... **TCLC 109**
See also CA 121; 111; MTCW 1, 2
Suzuki, Teitaro
See Suzuki, Daisetz Teitaro
Svevo, Italo TCLC 2, 35; SSC 25
See also Schmitz, Aron Hector
Swados, Elizabeth (A.) 1951- .... **CLC 12**
See also CA 97-100; CANR 49; INT 97-100
Swados, Harvey 1920-1972 .... **CLC 5**
See also CA 5-8R; 37-40R; CANR 6; DLB 2
Swan, Gladys 1934- .... **CLC 69**
See also CA 101; CANR 17, 39
Swanson, Logan
See Matheson, Richard Burton

Swarthout, Glendon (Fred)
1918-1992 .... **CLC 35**
See also AW; CA 1-4R; 139; CANR 1, 47; SATA 26; TCWW 2
Sweet, Sarah C.
See Jewett, (Theodora) Sarah Orne
Swenson, May 1919-1989 ...... **CLC 4, 14, 61, 106; DA; DAB; DAC; DAM MST, POET; PC 14**
See also AMWS 4; CA 5-8R; 130; CANR 36, 61; DLB 5; GLL 2; MTCW 1, 2; SATA 15
Swift, Augustus
See Lovecraft, H(oward) P(hillips)
Swift, Graham (Colin) 1949- ...... **CLC 41, 88**
See also BRWS 5; CA 117; 122; CANR 46, 71; DLB 194; MTCW 2
Swift, Jonathan 1667-1745 ..... **LC 1, 42; DA; DAB; DAC; DAM MST, NOV, POET; PC 9**
See also AW; CDBLB 1660-1789; CLR 53; DA3; DLB 39, 95, 101; SATA 19
Swinburne, Algernon Charles
1837-1909 .... **TCLC 8, 36; DA; DAB; DAC; DAM MST, POET; PC 24**
See also AW; CA 105; 140; CDBLB 1832-1890; DA3; DLB 35, 57
Swinfen, Ann CLC 34
Swinnerton, Frank Arthur
1884-1982 .... **CLC 31**
See also CA 108; DLB 34
Swithen, John
See King, Stephen (Edwin)
Sylvia
See Ashton-Warner, Sylvia (Constance)
Symmes, Robert Edward
See Duncan, Robert (Edward)
Symonds, John Addington
1840-1893 .... **NCLC 34**
See also DLB 57, 144
Symons, Arthur 1865-1945 .... **TCLC 11**
See also CA 107; 189; DLB 19, 57, 149
Symons, Julian (Gustave)
1912-1994 .... **CLC 2, 14, 32**
See also CA 49-52; 147; CAAS 3; CANR 3, 33, 59; DLB 87, 155; DLBY 92; MTCW 1
Synge, (Edmund) J(ohn) M(illington)
1871-1909 . **TCLC 6, 37; DAM DRAM; DC 2**
See also CA 104; 141; CDBLB 1890-1914; DLB 10, 19
Syruc, J.
See Milosz, Czeslaw
Szirtes, George 1948- .... **CLC 46**
See also CA 109; CANR 27, 61
Szymborska, Wislawa 1923- .... **CLC 99**
See also CA 154; CANR 91; CWW 2; DA3; DLB 232; DLBY 96; MTCW 2
T. O., Nik
See Annensky, Innokenty (Fyodorovich)
Tabori, George 1914- .... **CLC 19**
See also CA 49-52; CANR 4, 69
Tagore, Rabindranath 1861-1941 ... **TCLC 3, 53; DAM DRAM, POET; PC 8**
See also CA 104; 120; DA3; MTCW 1, 2
Taine, Hippolyte Adolphe
1828-1893 .... **NCLC 15**
Talese, Gay 1932- .... **CLC 37**
See also AITN 1; CA 1-4R; CANR 9, 58; DLB 185; INT CANR-9; MTCW 1, 2
Tallent, Elizabeth (Ann) 1954- .... **CLC 45**
See also CA 117; CANR 72; DLB 130
Tally, Ted 1952- .... **CLC 42**
See also CA 120; 124; INT 124

Talvik, Heiti 1904-1947 .... **TCLC 87**
Tamayo y Baus, Manuel
1829-1898 .... **NCLC 1**
Tammsaare, A(nton) H(ansen)
1878-1940 .... **TCLC 27**
See also CA 164; DLB 220
Tam'si, Tchicaya U
See Tchicaya, Gerald Felix
Tan, Amy (Ruth) 1952- . **CLC 59, 120; DAM MULT, NOV, POP**
See also AAYA 9; AW; BEST 89:3; CA 136; CANR 54; CDALBS; DA3; DLB 173; MTCW 2; SATA 75
Tandem, Felix
See Spitteler, Carl (Friedrich Georg)
Tanizaki, Jun'ichiro 1886-1965 ... **CLC 8, 14, 28; SSC 21**
See also CA 93-96; 25-28R; DLB 180; MTCW 2
Tanner, William
See Amis, Kingsley (William)
Tao Lao
See Storni, Alfonsina
Tarantino, Quentin (Jerome)
1963- .... **CLC 125**
See also CA 171
Tarassoff, Lev
See Troyat, Henri
Tarbell, Ida M(inerva) 1857-1944 . **TCLC 40**
See also CA 122; 181; DLB 47
Tarkington, (Newton) Booth
1869-1946 .... **TCLC 9**
See also CA 110; 143; DLB 9, 102; MTCW 2; SATA 17
Tarkovsky, Andrei (Arsenyevich)
1932-1986 .... **CLC 75**
See also CA 127
Tartt, Donna 1964(?)- .... **CLC 76**
See also CA 142
Tasso, Torquato 1544-1595 .... **LC 5**
Tate, (John Orley) Allen 1899-1979 .. **CLC 2, 4, 6, 9, 11, 14, 24**
See also CA 5-8R; 85-88; CANR 32; DLB 4, 45, 63; DLBD 17; MTCW 1, 2
Tate, Ellalice
See Hibbert, Eleanor Alice Burford
Tate, James (Vincent) 1943- ..... **CLC 2, 6, 25**
See also CA 21-24R; CANR 29, 57; DLB 5, 169
Tauler, Johannes c. 1300-1361 ...... **CMLC 37**
See also DLB 179
Tavel, Ronald 1940- .... **CLC 6**
See also CA 21-24R; CANR 33
Taviani, Paolo 1931- .... **CLC 70**
See also CA 153
Taylor, Bayard 1825-1878 .... **NCLC 89**
See also DLB 3, 189
Taylor, C(ecil) P(hilip) 1929-1981 .... **CLC 27**
See also CA 25-28R; 105; CANR 47
Taylor, Edward 1642(?)-1729 ..... **LC 11; DA; DAB; DAC; DAM MST, POET**
See also DLB 24
Taylor, Eleanor Ross 1920- .... **CLC 5**
See also CA 81-84; CANR 70
Taylor, Elizabeth 1932-1975 ..... **CLC 2, 4, 29**
See also CA 13-16R; CANR 9, 70; DLB 139; MTCW 1; SATA 13
Taylor, Frederick Winslow
1856-1915 .... **TCLC 76**
See also CA 188
Taylor, Henry (Splawn) 1942- .... **CLC 44**
See also CA 33-36R; CAAS 7; CANR 31; DLB 5
Taylor, Kamala (Purnaiya) 1924-
See Markandaya, Kamala
See also CA 77-80

Taylor, Mildred D(elois) CLC 21
See also AAYA 10; BW 1; CA 85-88; CANR 25; CLR 9, 59; DLB 52; JRDA; MAICYA; SAAS 5; SATA 15, 70

Taylor, Peter (Hillsman) 1917-1994 .. CLC 1, 4, 18, 37, 44, 50, 71; SSC 10
See also AMWS 5; CA 13-16R; 147; CANR 9, 50; DLBY 81, 94; INT CANR-9; MTCW 1, 2

Taylor, Robert Lewis 1912-1998 .... CLC 14
See also CA 1-4R; 170; CANR 3, 64; SATA 10

Tchekhov, Anton
See Chekhov, Anton (Pavlovich)

Tchicaya, Gerald Felix 1931-1988 .. CLC 101
See also CA 129; 125; CANR 81

Tchicaya U Tam'si
See Tchicaya, Gerald Felix

Teasdale, Sara 1884-1933 .... TCLC 4; PC 31
See also CA 104; 163; DLB 45; GLL 1; SATA 32

Tegner, Esaias 1782-1846 .... NCLC 2

Teilhard de Chardin, (Marie Joseph) Pierre 1881-1955 .... TCLC 9
See also CA 105

Temple, Ann
See Mortimer, Penelope (Ruth)

Tennant, Emma (Christina) 1937- .. CLC 13, 52
See also CA 65-68; CAAS 9; CANR 10, 38, 59, 88; DLB 14

Tenneshaw, S. M.
See Silverberg, Robert

Tennyson, Alfred 1809-1892 ... NCLC 30, 65; DA; DAB; DAC; DAM MST, POET; PC 6
See also AW; CDBLB 1832-1890; DA3; DLB 32

Teran, Lisa St. Aubin de CLC 36
See also St. Aubin de Teran, Lisa

Terence c. 195B.C.-c. 159B.C. ...... CMLC 14; DC 7
See also DLB 211

Teresa de Jesus, St. 1515-1582 .... LC 18

Terkel, Louis 1912-
See Terkel, Studs
See also CA 57-60; CANR 18, 45, 67; DA3; MTCW 1, 2

Terkel, Studs CLC 38
See also Terkel, Louis
See also AAYA 32; AITN 1; MTCW 2

Terry, C. V.
See Slaughter, Frank G(ill)

Terry, Megan 1932- .... CLC 19; DC 13
See also CA 77-80; CABS 3; CANR 43; DLB 7; GLL 2

Tertullian c. 155-c. 245 .... CMLC 29

Tertz, Abram
See Sinyavsky, Andrei (Donatevich)
See also CWW 2

Tesich, Steve 1943(?)-1996 .... CLC 40, 69
See also CA 105; 152; DLBY 83

Tesla, Nikola 1856-1943 .... TCLC 88

Teternikov, Fyodor Kuzmich 1863-1927
See Sologub, Fyodor
See also CA 104

Tevis, Walter 1928-1984 .... CLC 42
See also CA 113

Tey, Josephine TCLC 14
See also Mackintosh, Elizabeth
See also DLB 77

Thackeray, William Makepeace 1811-1863 ...... NCLC 5, 14, 22, 43; DA; DAB; DAC; DAM MST, NOV
See also AW; CDBLB 1832-1890; DA3; DLB 21, 55, 159, 163; SATA 23

Thakura, Ravindranatha
See Tagore, Rabindranath

Thames, C. H.
See Marlowe, Stephen

Tharoor, Shashi 1956- .... CLC 70
See also CA 141; CANR 91

Thelwell, Michael Miles 1939- .... CLC 22
See also BW 2; CA 101

Theobald, Lewis, Jr.
See Lovecraft, H(oward) P(hillips)

Theocritus c. 310B.C.-c. 250B.C. .. CMLC 45
See also DLB 176

Theodorescu, Ion N. 1880-1967
See Arghezi, Tudor
See also CA 116; DLB 220

Theriault, Yves 1915-1983 .... CLC 79; DAC; DAM MST
See also CA 102; CCA 1; DLB 88

Theroux, Alexander (Louis) 1939- .... CLC 2, 25
See also CA 85-88; CANR 20, 63

Theroux, Paul (Edward) 1941- ..... CLC 5, 8, 11, 15, 28, 46; DAM POP
See also AAYA 28; BEST 89:4; CA 33-36R; CANR 20, 45, 74; CDALBS; DA3; DLB 2; MTCW 1, 2; SATA 44, 109

Thesen, Sharon 1946- .... CLC 56
See also CA 163

Thevenin, Denis
See Duhamel, Georges

Thibault, Jacques Anatole Francois 1844-1924
See France, Anatole
See also CA 106; 127; DAM NOV; DA3; MTCW 1, 2

Thiele, Colin (Milton) 1920- .... CLC 17
See also AW; CA 29-32R; CANR 12, 28, 53; CLR 27; MAICYA; SAAS 2; SATA 14, 72

Thomas, Audrey (Callahan) 1935- .... CLC 7, 13, 37, 107; SSC 20
See also AITN 2; CA 21-24R; CAAS 19; CANR 36, 58; DLB 60; MTCW 1

Thomas, Augustus 1857-1934 .... TCLC 97

Thomas, D(onald) M(ichael) 1935- . CLC 13, 22, 31, 132
See also BRWS 4; CA 61-64; CAAS 11; CANR 17, 45, 75; CDBLB 1960 to Present; DA3; DLB 40, 207; INT CANR-17; MTCW 1, 2

Thomas, Dylan (Marlais) 1914-1953 ...... TCLC 1, 8, 45, 105; DA; DAB; DAC; DAM DRAM, MST, POET; PC 2; SSC 3, 44
See also AW; BRWS 1; CA 104; 120; CANR 65; CDBLB 1945-1960; DA3; DLB 13, 20, 139; MTCW 1, 2; SATA 60

Thomas, (Philip) Edward 1878-1917 .... TCLC 10; DAM POET
See also CA 106; 153; DLB 98

Thomas, Joyce Carol 1938- .... CLC 35
See also AAYA 12; AW; BW 2, 3; CA 113; 116; CANR 48; CLR 19; DLB 33; INT 116; JRDA; MAICYA; MTCW 1, 2; SAAS 7; SATA 40, 78

Thomas, Lewis 1913-1993 .... CLC 35
See also CA 85-88; 143; CANR 38, 60; MTCW 1, 2

Thomas, M. Carey 1857-1935 .... TCLC 89

Thomas, Paul
See Mann, (Paul) Thomas

Thomas, Piri 1928- .... CLC 17; HLCS 2
See also CA 73-76; HW 1

Thomas, R(onald) S(tuart) 1913-2000 . CLC 6, 13, 48; DAB; DAM POET
See also CA 89-92; 189; CAAS 4; CANR 30; CDBLB 1960 to Present; DLB 27; MTCW 1

Thomas, Ross (Elmore) 1926-1995 .. CLC 39
See also CA 33-36R; 150; CANR 22, 63

Thompson, Francis (Joseph) 1859-1907 .... TCLC 4
See also CA 104; 189; CDBLB 1890-1914; DLB 19

Thompson, Francis Clegg
See Mencken, H(enry) L(ouis)

Thompson, Hunter S(tockton) 1939- ... CLC 9, 17, 40, 104; DAM POP
See also BEST 89:1; CA 17-20R; CANR 23, 46, 74, 77; DA3; DLB 185; MTCW 1, 2

Thompson, James Myers
See Thompson, Jim (Myers)

Thompson, Jim (Myers) 1906-1977(?) .... CLC 69
See also CA 140; DLB 226

Thompson, Judith CLC 39

Thomson, James 1700-1748 ... LC 16, 29, 40; DAM POET
See also BRWS 3; DLB 95

Thomson, James 1834-1882 .... NCLC 18; DAM POET
See also DLB 35

Thoreau, Henry David 1817-1862 .. NCLC 7, 21, 61; DA; DAB; DAC; DAM MST; PC 30
See also AW; CDALB 1640-1865; DA3; DLB 1, 223

Thorndike, E. L.
See Thorndike, Edward L(ee)

Thorndike, Edward L(ee) 1874-1949 .... TCLC 107
See also CA 121

Thornton, Hall
See Silverberg, Robert

Thucydides c. 460B.C.-399B.C. ..... CMLC 17
See also DLB 176

Thumboo, Edwin 1933- .... PC 30

Thurber, James (Grover) 1894-1961 .... CLC 5, 11, 25, 125; DA; DAB; DAC; DAM DRAM, MST, NOV; SSC 1
See also AMWS 1; CA 73-76; CANR 17, 39; CDALB 1929-1941; DA3; DLB 4, 11, 22, 102; MAICYA; MTCW 1, 2; SATA 13

Thurman, Wallace (Henry) 1902-1934 .... TCLC 6; BLC 3; DAM MULT
See also BW 1, 3; CA 104; 124; CANR 81; DLB 51

Tibullus c. 54B.C.-c. 18B.C. .... CMLC 36
See also DLB 211

Ticheburn, Cheviot
See Ainsworth, William Harrison

Tieck, (Johann) Ludwig 1773-1853 .... NCLC 5, 46; SSC 31
See also DLB 90

Tiger, Derry
See Ellison, Harlan (Jay)

Tilghman, Christopher 1948(?)- .... CLC 65
See also CA 159

Tillich, Paul (Johannes) 1886-1965 .... CLC 131
See also CA 5-8R; 25-28R; CANR 33; MTCW 1, 2

Tillinghast, Richard (Williford) 1940- .... CLC 29
See also CA 29-32R; CAAS 23; CANR 26, 51, 96

Timrod, Henry 1828-1867 .... NCLC 25
See also DLB 3

Tindall, Gillian (Elizabeth) 1938- ...... CLC 7
See also CA 21-24R; CANR 11, 65

Tiptree, James, Jr. CLC 48, 50
See also Sheldon, Alice Hastings Bradley
See also DLB 8

Titmarsh, Michael Angelo
See Thackeray, William Makepeace

Vega, Lope de 1562-1635 .... **LC 23; HLCS 2**
Vendler, Helen (Hennessy) 1933- ... **CLC 138**
  See also CA 41-44R; CANR 25, 72; MTCW
  1, 2
Venison, Alfred
  See Pound, Ezra (Weston Loomis)
Verdi, Marie de
  See Mencken, H(enry) L(ouis)
Verdu, Matilde
  See Cela, Camilo Jose
Verga, Giovanni (Carmelo)
  1840-1922 .... **TCLC 3; SSC 21**
  See also CA 104; 123
Vergil 70B.C.-19B.C. .... **CMLC 9, 40; DA;**
  DAB; DAC; DAM MST, POET; PC 12
  See also AW; DA3; DLB 211
Verhaeren, Emile (Adolphe Gustave)
  1855-1916 .... **TCLC 12**
  See also CA 109
Verlaine, Paul (Marie) 1844-1896 .. **NCLC 2,**
  51; DAM POET; PC 2, 32
Verne, Jules (Gabriel) 1828-1905 ... **TCLC 6,**
  52
  See also AAYA 16; CA 110; 131; DA3;
  DLB 123; JRDA; MAICYA; SATA 21
Verus, Marcus Annius
  See Antoninus, Marcus Aurelius
Very, Jones 1813-1880 .... **NCLC 9**
  See also DLB 1
Vesaas, Tarjei 1897-1970 .... **CLC 48**
  See also CA 190; 29-32R
Vialis, Gaston
  See Simenon, Georges (Jacques Christian)
Vian, Boris 1920-1959 .... **TCLC 9**
  See also CA 106; 164; DLB 72; MTCW 2
Viaud, (Louis Marie) Julien 1850-1923
  See Loti, Pierre
  See also CA 107
Vicar, Henry
  See Felsen, Henry Gregor
Vicker, Angus
  See Felsen, Henry Gregor
Vidal, Gore 1925- ...... **CLC 2, 4, 6, 8, 10, 22,**
  33, 72, 142; DAM NOV, POP
  See also Box, Edgar
  See also AITN 1; AMWS 4; BEST 90:2;
  CA 5-8R; CANR 13, 45, 65; CDALBS;
  DA3; DLB 6, 152; INT CANR-13;
  MTCW 1, 2
Viereck, Peter (Robert Edwin)
  1916- .... **CLC 4; PC 27**
  See also CA 1-4R; CANR 1, 47; DLB 5
Vigny, Alfred (Victor) de
  1797-1863 .. **NCLC 7; DAM POET; PC**
  26
  See also DLB 119, 192
Vilakazi, Benedict Wallet
  1906-1947 .... **TCLC 37**
  See also CA 168
Villa, Jose Garcia 1914-1997 .... **PC 22**
  See also CA 25-28R; CANR 12
Villarreal, Jose Antonio 1924-
  See also CA 133; CANR 93; DAM MULT;
  DLB 82; HLC 2; HW 1
Villaurrutia, Xavier 1903-1950 ...... **TCLC 80**
  See also HW 1
Villehardouin 1150(?)-1218(?) .... **CMLC 38**
Villiers de l'Isle Adam, Jean Marie Mathias
  Philippe Auguste, Comte de
  1838-1889 .... **NCLC 3; SSC 14**
  See also DLB 123
Villon, François 1431-1463(?) . **LC 62; PC 13**
  See also DLB 208
Vine, Barbara CLC 50
  See also Rendell, Ruth (Barbara)
  See also BEST 90:4

Vinge, Joan (Carol) D(ennison)
  1948- .... **CLC 30; SSC 24**
  See also AAYA 32; AW; CA 93-96; CANR
  72; SATA 36, 113
Viola, Herman J(oseph) 1938- .... **CLC 70**
  See also CA 61-64; CANR 8, 23, 48, 91
Violis, G.
  See Simenon, Georges (Jacques Christian)
Viramontes, Helena Maria 1954-
  See also CA 159; DLB 122; HLCS 2; HW
  2
Virgil
  See Vergil
Visconti, Luchino 1906-1976 .... **CLC 16**
  See also CA 81-84; 65-68; CANR 39
Vittorini, Elio 1908-1966 ...... **CLC 6, 9, 14**
  See also CA 133; 25-28R
Vivekananda, Swami 1863-1902 .... **TCLC 88**
Vizenor, Gerald Robert 1934- .... **CLC 103;**
  DAM MULT
  See also CA 13-16R; CAAS 22; CANR 5,
  21, 44, 67; DLB 175, 227; MTCW 2;
  NNAL; TCWW 2
Vizinczey, Stephen 1933- .... **CLC 40**
  See also CA 128; CCA 1; INT 128
Vliet, R(ussell) G(ordon)
  1929-1984 .... **CLC 22**
  See also CA 37-40R; 112; CANR 18
Vogau, Boris Andreyevich 1894-1937(?)
  See Pilnyak, Boris
  See also CA 123
Vogel, Paula A(nne) 1951- .... **CLC 76**
  See also CA 108
Voigt, Cynthia 1942- .... **CLC 30**
  See also AAYA 3, 30; AW; CA 106; CANR
  18, 37, 40, 94; CLR 13, 48; INT CANR-
  18; JRDA; MAICYA; SATA 48, 79, 116;
  SATA-Brief 33
Voigt, Ellen Bryant 1943- .... **CLC 54**
  See also CA 69-72; CANR 11, 29, 55; DLB
  120
Voinovich, Vladimir (Nikolaevich)
  1932- .... **CLC 10, 49**
  See also CA 81-84; CAAS 12; CANR 33,
  67; MTCW 1
Vollmann, William T. 1959- .. **CLC 89; DAM**
  NOV, POP
  See also CA 134; CANR 67; DA3; MTCW
  2
Voloshinov, V. N.
  See Bakhtin, Mikhail Mikhailovich
Voltaire 1694-1778 .... **LC 14; DA; DAB;**
  DAC; DAM DRAM, MST; SSC 12
  See also AW; DA3
von Aschendrof, BaronIgnatz 1873-1939
  See Ford, Ford Madox
von Daeniken, Erich 1935- .... **CLC 30**
  See also AITN 1; CA 37-40R; CANR 17,
  44
von Daniken, Erich
  See von Daeniken, Erich
von Hartmann, Eduard
  1842-1906 .... **TCLC 96**
von Hayek, Friedrich August
  See Hayek, F(riedrich) A(ugust von)
von Heidenstam, (Carl Gustaf) Verner
  See Heidenstam, (Carl Gustaf) Verner von
von Heyse, Paul (Johann Ludwig)
  See Heyse, Paul (Johann Ludwig von)
von Hofmannsthal, Hugo
  See Hofmannsthal, Hugo von
von Horvath, Odon
  See Horvath, Oedoen von
von Horvath, Oedoen
  See Horvath, Oedoen von
  See also CA 184

von Liliencron, (Friedrich Adolf Axel)
  Detlev
  See Liliencron, (Friedrich Adolf Axel) De-
  tlev von
Vonnegut, Kurt, Jr. 1922- . **CLC 1, 2, 3, 4, 5,**
  8, 12, 22, 40, 60, 111; DA; DAB; DAC;
  DAM MST, NOV, POP; SSC 8
  See also AAYA 6; AITN 1; AMWS 2; AW;
  BEST 90:4; CA 1-4R; CANR 1, 25, 49,
  75, 92; CDALB 1968-1988; DA3; DLB
  2, 8, 152; DLBD 3; DLBY 80; MTCW 1,
  2
Von Rachen, Kurt
  See Hubbard, L(afayette) Ron(ald)
von Rezzori (d'Arezzo), Gregor
  See Rezzori (d'Arezzo), Gregor von
von Sternberg, Josef
  See Sternberg, Josef von
Vorster, Gordon 1924- .... **CLC 34**
  See also CA 133
Vosce, Trudie
  See Ozick, Cynthia
Voznesensky, Andrei (Andreievich)
  1933- .... **CLC 1, 15, 57; DAM POET**
  See also CA 89-92; CANR 37; CWW 2;
  MTCW 1
Waddington, Miriam 1917- .... **CLC 28**
  See also CA 21-24R; CANR 12, 30; CCA
  1; DLB 68
Wagman, Fredrica 1937- .... **CLC 7**
  See also CA 97-100; INT 97-100
Wagner, Linda W.
  See Wagner-Martin, Linda (C.)
Wagner, Linda Welshimer
  See Wagner-Martin, Linda (C.)
Wagner, Richard 1813-1883 .... **NCLC 9**
  See also DLB 129
Wagner-Martin, Linda (C.) 1936- .... **CLC 50**
  See also CA 159
Wagoner, David (Russell) 1926- .... **CLC 3, 5,**
  15; PC 33
  See also CA 1-4R; CAAS 3; CANR 2, 71;
  DLB 5; SATA 14; TCWW 2
Wah, Fred(erick James) 1939- .... **CLC 44**
  See also CA 107; 141; DLB 60
Wahloo, Per 1926-1975 .... **CLC 7**
  See also CA 61-64; CANR 73
Wahloo, Peter
  See Wahloo, Per
Wain, John (Barrington) 1925-1994 . **CLC 2,**
  11, 15, 46
  See also CA 5-8R; 145; CAAS 4; CANR
  23, 54; CDBLB 1960 to Present; DLB 15,
  27, 139, 155; MTCW 1, 2
Wajda, Andrzej 1926- .... **CLC 16**
  See also CA 102
Wakefield, Dan 1932- .... **CLC 7**
  See also CA 21-24R; CAAS 7
Wakoski, Diane 1937- ...... **CLC 2, 4, 7, 9, 11,**
  40; DAM POET; PC 15
  See also CA 13-16R; CAAS 1; CANR 9,
  60; DLB 5; INT CANR-9; MTCW 2
Wakoski-Sherbell, Diane
  See Wakoski, Diane
Walcott, Derek (Alton) 1930- .... **CLC 2, 4, 9,**
  14, 25, 42, 67, 76; BLC 3; DAB; DAC;
  DAM MST, MULT, POET; DC 7
  See also BW 2; CA 89-92; CANR 26, 47,
  75, 80; DA3; DLB 117; DLBY 81;
  MTCW 1, 2
Waldman, Anne (Lesley) 1945- .... **CLC 7**
  See also CA 37-40R; CAAS 17; CANR 34,
  69; DLB 16
Waldo, E. Hunter
  See Sturgeon, Theodore (Hamilton)
Waldo, Edward Hamilton
  See Sturgeon, Theodore (Hamilton)

Walker, Alice (Malsenior) 1944- ... CLC 5, 6, 9, 19, 27, 46, 58, 103; BLC 3; DA; DAB; DAC; DAM MST, MULT, NOV, POET, POP; PC 30; SSC 5
See also AAYA 3, 33; AMWS 3; AW; BEST 89:4; BW 2, 3; CA 37-40R; CANR 9, 27, 49, 66, 82; CDALB 1968-1988; DA3; DLB 6, 33, 143; INT CANR-27; MTCW 1, 2; SATA 31

Walker, David Harry 1911-1992 ...... CLC 14
See also CA 1-4R; 137; CANR 1; SATA 8; SATA-Obit 71

Walker, Edward Joseph 1934-
See Walker, Ted
See also CA 21-24R; CANR 12, 28, 53

Walker, George F. 1947- . CLC 44, 61; DAB; DAC; DAM MST
See also CA 103; CANR 21, 43, 59; DLB 60

Walker, Joseph A. 1935- .... CLC 19; DAM DRAM, MST
See also BW 1, 3; CA 89-92; CANR 26; DLB 38

Walker, Margaret (Abigail) 1915-1998 .... CLC 1, 6; BLC; DAM MULT; PC 20
See also BW 2, 3; CA 73-76; 172; CANR 26, 54, 76; DLB 76, 152; MTCW 1, 2

Walker, Ted CLC 13
See also Walker, Edward Joseph
See also DLB 40

Wallace, David Foster 1962- ..... CLC 50, 114
See also CA 132; CANR 59; DA3; MTCW 2

Wallace, Dexter
See Masters, Edgar Lee

Wallace, (Richard Horatio) Edgar 1875-1932 .... TCLC 57
See also CA 115; DLB 70

Wallace, Irving 1916-1990 .... CLC 7, 13; DAM NOV, POP
See also AITN 1; CA 1-4R; 132; CAAS 1; CANR 1, 27; INT CANR-27; MTCW 1, 2

Wallant, Edward Lewis 1926-1962 ... CLC 5, 10
See also CA 1-4R; CANR 22; DLB 2, 28, 143; MTCW 1, 2

Wallas, Graham 1858-1932 .... TCLC 91

Walley, Byron
See Card, Orson Scott

Walpole, Horace 1717-1797 .... LC 49
See also DLB 39, 104

Walpole, Hugh (Seymour) 1884-1941 .... TCLC 5
See also CA 104; 165; DLB 34; MTCW 2

Walser, Martin 1927- .... CLC 27
See also CA 57-60; CANR 8, 46; CWW 2; DLB 75, 124

Walser, Robert 1878-1956 .... TCLC 18; SSC 20
See also CA 118; 165; DLB 66

Walsh, Gillian Paton
See Paton Walsh, Gillian

Walsh, Jill Paton CLC 35
See also Paton Walsh, Gillian
See also CLR 2, 65

Walter, William Christian
See Andersen, Hans Christian

Wambaugh, Joseph (Aloysius, Jr.) 1937- .... CLC 3, 18; DAM NOV, POP
See also AITN 1; BEST 89:3; CA 33-36R; CANR 42, 65; DA3; DLB 6; DLBY 83; MTCW 1, 2

Wang Wei 699(?)-761(?) .... PC 18

Ward, Arthur Henry Sarsfield 1883-1959
See Rohmer, Sax
See also CA 108; 173

Ward, Douglas Turner 1930- .... CLC 19
See also BW 1; CA 81-84; CANR 27; DLB 7, 38

Ward, E. D.
See Lucas, E(dward) V(errall)

Ward, Mary Augusta 1851-1920 ... TCLC 55
See also DLB 18

Ward, Peter
See Faust, Frederick (Schiller)

Warhol, Andy 1928(?)-1987 .... CLC 20
See also AAYA 12; BEST 89:4; CA 89-92; 121; CANR 34

Warner, Francis (Robert le Plastrier) 1937- .... CLC 14
See also CA 53-56; CANR 11

Warner, Marina 1946- .... CLC 59
See also CA 65-68; CANR 21, 55; DLB 194

Warner, Rex (Ernest) 1905-1986 ...... CLC 45
See also CA 89-92; 119; DLB 15

Warner, Susan (Bogert) 1819-1885 .... NCLC 31
See also DLB 3, 42, 239

Warner, Sylvia (Constance) Ashton
See Ashton-Warner, Sylvia (Constance)

Warner, Sylvia Townsend 1893-1978 .... CLC 7, 19; SSC 23
See also CA 61-64; 77-80; CANR 16, 60; DLB 34, 139; MTCW 1, 2

Warren, Mercy Otis 1728-1814 ..... NCLC 13
See also DLB 31, 200

Warren, Robert Penn 1905-1989 ..CLC 1, 4, 6, 8, 10, 13, 18, 39, 53, 59; DA; DAB; DAC; DAM MST, NOV, POET; SSC 4
See also AITN 1; AW; CA 13-16R; 129; CANR 10, 47; CDALB 1968-1988; DA3; DLB 2, 48, 152; DLBY 80, 89; INT CANR-10; MTCW 1, 2; SATA 46; SATA-Obit 63

Warshofsky, Isaac
See Singer, Isaac Bashevis

Warton, Thomas 1728-1790 ..... LC 15; DAM POET
See also DLB 104, 109

Waruk, Kona
See Harris, (Theodore) Wilson

Warung, Price TCLC 45
See also Astley, William

Warwick, Jarvis
See Garner, Hugh
See also CCA 1

Washington, Alex
See Harris, Mark

Washington, Booker T(aliaferro) 1856-1915 ...... TCLC 10; BLC 3; DAM MULT
See also BW 1; CA 114; 125; DA3; SATA 28

Washington, George 1732-1799 .... LC 25
See also DLB 31

Wassermann, (Karl) Jakob 1873-1934 .... TCLC 6
See also CA 104; 163; DLB 66

Wasserstein, Wendy 1950- .. CLC 32, 59, 90; DAM DRAM; DC 4
See also CA 121; 129; CABS 3; CANR 53, 75; DA3; DLB 228; INT 129; MTCW 2; SATA 94

Waterhouse, Keith (Spencer) 1929- . CLC 47
See also CA 5-8R; CANR 38, 67; DLB 13, 15; MTCW 1, 2

Waters, Frank (Joseph) 1902-1995 .. CLC 88
See also CA 5-8R; 149; CAAS 13; CANR 3, 18, 63; DLB 212; DLBY 86; TCWW 2

Waters, Mary C. CLC 70

Waters, Roger 1944- .... CLC 35

Watkins, Frances Ellen
See Harper, Frances Ellen Watkins

Watkins, Gerrold
See Malzberg, Barry N(athaniel)

Watkins, Gloria Jean 1952(?)-
See hooks, bell
See also BW 2; CA 143; CANR 87; MTCW 2; SATA 115

Watkins, Paul 1964- .... CLC 55
See also CA 132; CANR 62

Watkins, Vernon Phillips 1906-1967 .... CLC 43
See also CA 9-10; 25-28R; CAP 1; DLB 20

Watson, Irving S.
See Mencken, H(enry) L(ouis)

Watson, John H.
See Farmer, Philip Jose

Watson, Richard F.
See Silverberg, Robert

Waugh, Auberon (Alexander) 1939-2001 .... CLC 7
See also CA 45-48; CANR 6, 22, 92; DLB 14, 194

Waugh, Evelyn (Arthur St. John) 1903-1966 .. CLC 1, 3, 8, 13, 19, 27, 44, 107; DA; DAB; DAC; DAM MST, NOV, POP; SSC 41
See also AW; CA 85-88; 25-28R; CANR 22; CDBLB 1914-1945; DA3; DLB 15, 162, 195; MTCW 1, 2

Waugh, Harriet 1944- .... CLC 6
See also CA 85-88; CANR 22

Ways, C. R.
See Blount, Roy (Alton), Jr.

Waystaff, Simon
See Swift, Jonathan

Webb, Beatrice (Martha Potter) 1858-1943 .... TCLC 22
See also CA 117; 162; DLB 190

Webb, Charles (Richard) 1939- .... CLC 7
See also CA 25-28R

Webb, James H(enry), Jr. 1946- ...... CLC 22
See also CA 81-84

Webb, Mary Gladys (Meredith) 1881-1927 .... TCLC 24
See also CA 182; 123; DLB 34

Webb, Mrs. Sidney
See Webb, Beatrice (Martha Potter)

Webb, Phyllis 1927- .... CLC 18
See also CA 104; CANR 23; CCA 1; DLB 53

Webb, Sidney (James) 1859-1947 .. TCLC 22
See also CA 117; 163; DLB 190

Webber, Andrew Lloyd CLC 21
See also Lloyd Webber, Andrew

Weber, Lenora Mattingly 1895-1971 .... CLC 12
See also CA 19-20; 29-32R; CAP 1; SATA 2; SATA-Obit 26

Weber, Max 1864-1920 .... TCLC 69
See also CA 109; 189

Webster, John 1580(?)-1634(?) ... LC 33; DA; DAB; DAC; DAM DRAM, MST; DC 2
See also AW; CDBLB Before 1660; DLB 58

Webster, Noah 1758-1843 .... NCLC 30
See also DLB 1, 37, 42, 43, 73

Wedekind, (Benjamin) Frank(lin) 1864-1918 .... TCLC 7; DAM DRAM
See also CA 104; 153; DLB 118

Wehr, Demaris CLC 65

Weidman, Jerome 1913-1998 .... CLC 7
See also AITN 2; CA 1-4R; 171; CANR 1; DLB 28

Weil, Simone (Adolphine) 1909-1943 .... TCLC 23
See also CA 117; 159; MTCW 2

Weininger, Otto 1880-1903 .... TCLC 84

Weinstein, Nathan
See West, Nathanael

Weinstein, Nathan von Wallenstein
See West, Nathanael

Weir, Peter (Lindsay) 1944- .... **CLC 20**
See also CA 113; 123

Weiss, Peter (Ulrich) 1916-1982 .. **CLC 3, 15, 51; DAM DRAM**
See also CA 45-48; 106; CANR 3; DLB 69, 124

Weiss, Theodore (Russell) 1916- ... **CLC 3, 8, 14**
See also CA 9-12R; CAAE 189; CAAS 2; CANR 46, 94; DLB 5

Welch, (Maurice) Denton
1915-1948 .... **TCLC 22**
See also CA 121; 148

Welch, James 1940- ..... **CLC 6, 14, 52; DAM MULT, POP**
See also CA 85-88; CANR 42, 66; DLB 175; NNAL; TCWW 2

Weldon, Fay 1931- . **CLC 6, 9, 11, 19, 36, 59, 122; DAM POP**
See also BRWS 4; CA 21-24R; CANR 16, 46, 63; CDBLB 1960 to Present; DLB 14, 194; INT CANR-16; MTCW 1, 2

Wellek, Rene 1903-1995 .... **CLC 28**
See also CA 5-8R; 150; CAAS 7; CANR 8; DLB 63; INT CANR-8

Weller, Michael 1942- .... **CLC 10, 53**
See also CA 85-88

Weller, Paul 1958- .... **CLC 26**

Wellershoff, Dieter 1925- .... **CLC 46**
See also CA 89-92; CANR 16, 37

Welles, (George) Orson 1915-1985 .. **CLC 20, 80**
See also CA 93-96; 117

Wellman, John McDowell 1945-
See Wellman, Mac
See also CA 166

Wellman, Mac CLC 65
See also Wellman, John McDowell; Wellman, John McDowell

Wellman, Manly Wade 1903-1986 ... **CLC 49**
See also CA 1-4R; 118; CANR 6, 16, 44; SATA 6; SATA-Obit 47

Wells, Carolyn 1869(?)-1942 .... **TCLC 35**
See also CA 113; 185; DLB 11

Wells, H(erbert) G(eorge)
1866-1946 . **TCLC 6, 12, 19; DA; DAB; DAC; DAM MST, NOV; SSC 6**
See also AAYA 18; AW; CA 110; 121; CDBLB 1914-1945; CLR 64; DA3; DLB 34, 70, 156, 178; MTCW 1, 2; SATA 20

Wells, Rosemary 1943- .... **CLC 12**
See also AAYA 13; AW; CA 85-88; CANR 48; CLR 16, 69; MAICYA; SAAS 1; SATA 18, 69, 114

Welsh, Irvine 1958- .... **CLC 144**
See also CA 173

Welty, Eudora 1909- ...... **CLC 1, 2, 5, 14, 22, 33, 105; DA; DAB; DAC; DAM MST, NOV; SSC 1, 27**
See also AW; CA 9-12R; CABS 1; CANR 32, 65; CDALB 1941-1968; DA3; DLB 2, 102, 143; DLBD 12; DLBY 87; MTCW 1, 2

Wen I-to 1899-1946 .... **TCLC 28**

Wentworth, Robert
See Hamilton, Edmond

Werfel, Franz (Viktor) 1890-1945 ... **TCLC 8**
See also CA 104; 161; DLB 81, 124

Wergeland, Henrik Arnold
1808-1845 .... **NCLC 5**

Wersba, Barbara 1932- .... **CLC 30**
See also AAYA 2, 30; AW; CA 29-32R, 182; CAAE 182; CANR 16, 38; CLR 3; DLB 52; JRDA; MAICYA; SAAS 2; SATA 1, 58; SATA-Essay 103

Wertmueller, Lina 1928- .... **CLC 16**
See also CA 97-100; CANR 39, 78

Wescott, Glenway 1901-1987 .. **CLC 13; SSC 35**
See also CA 13-16R; 121; CANR 23, 70; DLB 4, 9, 102

Wesker, Arnold 1932- ... **CLC 3, 5, 42; DAB; DAM DRAM**
See also CA 1-4R; CAAS 7; CANR 1, 33; CDBLB 1960 to Present; DLB 13; MTCW 1

Wesley, Richard (Errol) 1945- .... **CLC 7**
See also BW 1; CA 57-60; CANR 27; DLB 38

Wessel, Johan Herman 1742-1785 .... **LC 7**

West, Anthony (Panther)
1914-1987 .... **CLC 50**
See also CA 45-48; 124; CANR 3, 19; DLB 15

West, C. P.
See Wodehouse, P(elham) G(renville)

West, Cornel (Ronald) 1953- .... **CLC 134; BLCS**
See also CA 144; CANR 91

West, Delno C(loyde), Jr. 1936- .... **CLC 70**
See also CA 57-60

West, Dorothy 1907-1998 .... **TCLC 108**
See also BW 2; CA 143; 169; DLB 76

West, (Mary) Jessamyn 1902-1984 ... **CLC 7, 17**
See also AW; CA 9-12R; 112; CANR 27; DLB 6; DLBY 84; MTCW 1, 2; SATA-Obit 37

West, Morris L(anglo) 1916-1999 ..... **CLC 6, 33**
See also CA 5-8R; 187; CANR 24, 49, 64; MTCW 1, 2

West, Nathanael 1903-1940 .... **TCLC 1, 14, 44; SSC 16**
See also CA 104; 125; CDALB 1929-1941; DA3; DLB 4, 9, 28; MTCW 1, 2

West, Owen
See Koontz, Dean R(ay)

West, Paul 1930- .... **CLC 7, 14, 96**
See also CA 13-16R; CAAS 7; CANR 22, 53, 76, 89; DLB 14; INT CANR-22; MTCW 2

West, Rebecca 1892-1983 ... **CLC 7, 9, 31, 50**
See also BRWS 3; CA 5-8R; 109; CANR 19; DLB 36; DLBY 83; MTCW 1, 2

Westall, Robert (Atkinson)
1929-1993 .... **CLC 17**
See also AAYA 12; CA 69-72; 141; CANR 18, 68; CLR 13; JRDA; MAICYA; SAAS 2; SATA 23, 69; SATA-Obit 75

Westermarck, Edward 1862-1939 . **TCLC 87**

Westlake, Donald E(dwin) 1933- .... **CLC 7, 33; DAM POP**
See also CA 17-20R; CAAS 13; CANR 16, 44, 65, 94; INT CANR-16; MTCW 2

Westmacott, Mary
See Christie, Agatha (Mary Clarissa)

Weston, Allen
See Norton, Andre

Wetcheek, J. L.
See Feuchtwanger, Lion

Wetering, Janwillem van de
See van de Wetering, Janwillem

Wetherald, Agnes Ethelwyn
1857-1940 .... **TCLC 81**
See also DLB 99

Wetherell, Elizabeth
See Warner, Susan (Bogert)

Whale, James 1889-1957 .... **TCLC 63**

Whalen, Philip 1923- .... **CLC 6, 29**
See also CA 9-12R; CANR 5, 39; DLB 16

Wharton, Edith (Newbold Jones)
1862-1937 .... **TCLC 3, 9, 27, 53; DA; DAB; DAC; DAM MST, NOV; SSC 6**
See also AAYA 25; AW; CA 104; 132; CDALB 1865-1917; DA3; DLB 4, 9, 12, 78, 189; DLBD 13; MTCW 1, 2

Wharton, James
See Mencken, H(enry) L(ouis)

Wharton, William (a pseudonym) CLC 18, 37
See also CA 93-96; DLBY 80; INT 93-96

Wheatley (Peters), Phillis
1753(?)-1784 ...... **LC 3, 50; BLC 3; DA; DAC; DAM MST, MULT, POET; PC 3**
See also AW; CDALB 1640-1865; DA3; DLB 31, 50

Wheelock, John Hall 1886-1978 .... **CLC 14**
See also CA 13-16R; 77-80; CANR 14; DLB 45

White, E(lwyn) B(rooks)
1899-1985 . **CLC 10, 34, 39; DAM POP**
See also AITN 2; AMWS 1; CA 13-16R; 116; CANR 16, 37; CDALBS; CLR 1, 21; DA3; DLB 11, 22; MAICYA; MTCW 1, 2; SATA 2, 29, 100; SATA-Obit 44

White, Edmund (Valentine III)
1940- .... **CLC 27, 110; DAM POP**
See also AAYA 7; CA 45-48; CANR 3, 19, 36, 62; DA3; DLB 227; MTCW 1, 2

White, Patrick (Victor Martindale)
1912-1990 ...... **CLC 3, 4, 5, 7, 9, 18, 65, 69; SSC 39**
See also BRWS 1; CA 81-84; 132; CANR 43; MTCW 1

White, Phyllis Dorothy James 1920-
See James, P. D.
See also CA 21-24R; CANR 17, 43, 65; DAM POP; DA3; MTCW 1, 2

White, T(erence) H(anbury)
1906-1964 .... **CLC 30**
See also AAYA 22; AW; CA 73-76; CANR 37; DLB 160; JRDA; MAICYA; SATA 12

White, Terence de Vere 1912-1994 ... **CLC 49**
See also CA 49-52; 145; CANR 3

White, Walter
See White, Walter F(rancis)
See also BLC; DAM MULT

White, Walter F(rancis)
1893-1955 .... **TCLC 15**
See also White, Walter
See also BW 1; CA 115; 124; DLB 51

White, William Hale 1831-1913
See Rutherford, Mark
See also CA 121; 189

Whitehead, Alfred North
1861-1947 .... **TCLC 97**
See also CA 117; 165; DLB 100

Whitehead, E(dward) A(nthony)
1933- .... **CLC 5**
See also CA 65-68; CANR 58

Whitemore, Hugh (John) 1936- .... **CLC 37**
See also CA 132; CANR 77; INT 132

Whitman, Sarah Helen (Power)
1803-1878 .... **NCLC 19**
See also DLB 1

Whitman, Walt(er) 1819-1892 .. **NCLC 4, 31, 81; DA; DAB; DAC; DAM MST, POET; PC 3**
See also AW 1; CDALB 1640-1865; DA3; DLB 3, 64, 224; SATA 20

Whitney, Phyllis A(yame) 1903- ...... **CLC 42; DAM POP**
See also AAYA 36; AITN 2; AW; BEST 90:3; CA 1-4R; CANR 3, 25, 38, 60; CLR 59; DA3; JRDA; MAICYA; MTCW 2; SATA 1, 30

Whittemore, (Edward) Reed (Jr.)
1919- .... **CLC 4**
See also CA 9-12R; CAAS 8; CANR 4; DLB 5

Yeats, William Butler 1865-1939 .... **TCLC 1, 11, 18, 31, 93; DA; DAB; DAC; DAM DRAM, MST, POET; PC 20**
See also AW; CA 104; 127; CANR 45; CD-BLB 1890-1914; DA3; DLB 10, 19, 98, 156; MTCW 1, 2

Yehoshua, A(braham) B. 1936- .. **CLC 13, 31**
See also CA 33-36R; CANR 43, 90

Yellow Bird
See Ridge, John Rollin

Yep, Laurence Michael 1948- .... **CLC 35**
See also AAYA 5, 31; CA 49-52; CANR 1, 46, 92; CLR 3, 17, 54; DLB 52; JRDA; MAICYA; SATA 7, 69

Yerby, Frank G(arvin) 1916-1991 . **CLC 1, 7, 22; BLC 3; DAM MULT**
See also BW 1, 3; CA 9-12R; 136; CANR 16, 52; DLB 76; INT CANR-16; MTCW 1

Yesenin, Sergei Alexandrovich
See Esenin, Sergei (Alexandrovich)

Yevtushenko, Yevgeny (Alexandrovich) 1933- .. **CLC 1, 3, 13, 26, 51, 126; DAM POET**
See also CA 81-84; CANR 33, 54; CWW 2; MTCW 1

Yezierska, Anzia 1885(?)-1970 .... **CLC 46**
See also CA 126; 89-92; DLB 28, 221; MTCW 1

Yglesias, Helen 1915- .... **CLC 7, 22**
See also CA 37-40R; CAAS 20; CANR 15, 65, 95; INT CANR-15; MTCW 1

Yokomitsu, Riichi 1898-1947 .... **TCLC 47**
See also CA 170

Yonge, Charlotte (Mary) 1823-1901 .... **TCLC 48**
See also CA 109; 163; DLB 18, 163; SATA 17

York, Jeremy
See Creasey, John

York, Simon
See Heinlein, Robert A(nson)

Yorke, Henry Vincent 1905-1974 ..... **CLC 13**
See also Green, Henry
See also CA 85-88; 49-52

Yosano Akiko 1878-1942 .... **TCLC 59; PC 11**
See also CA 161

Yoshimoto, Banana CLC 84
See also Yoshimoto, Mahoko

Yoshimoto, Mahoko 1964-
See Yoshimoto, Banana
See also CA 144

Young, Al(bert James) 1939- . **CLC 19; BLC 3; DAM MULT**
See also BW 2, 3; CA 29-32R; CANR 26, 65; DLB 33

Young, Andrew (John) 1885-1971 ...... **CLC 5**
See also CA 5-8R; CANR 7, 29

Young, Collier
See Bloch, Robert (Albert)

Young, Edward 1683-1765 .... **LC 3, 40**
See also DLB 95

Young, Marguerite (Vivian) 1909-1995 .... **CLC 82**
See also CA 13-16; 150; CAP 1

Young, Neil 1945- .... **CLC 17**
See also CA 110; CCA 1

Young Bear, Ray A. 1950- ..... **CLC 94; DAM MULT**
See also CA 146; DLB 175; NNAL

Yourcenar, Marguerite 1903-1987 ... **CLC 19, 38, 50, 87; DAM NOV**
See also CA 69-72; CANR 23, 60, 93; DLB 72; DLBY 88; GLL 1; MTCW 1, 2

Yuan, Chu 340(?)B.C.-278(?)B.C. . **CMLC 36**

Yurick, Sol 1925- .... **CLC 6**
See also CA 13-16R; CANR 25

Zabolotsky, Nikolai Alekseevich 1903-1958 .... **TCLC 52**
See also CA 116; 164

Zagajewski, Adam 1945- .... **PC 27**
See also CA 186; DLB 232

Zalygin, Sergei CLC 59

Zamiatin, Yevgenii
See Zamyatin, Evgeny Ivanovich

Zamora, Bernice (B. Ortiz) 1938- .. **CLC 89; DAM MULT; HLC 2**
See also CA 151; CANR 80; DLB 82; HW 1, 2

Zamyatin, Evgeny Ivanovich 1884-1937 .... **TCLC 8, 37**
See also CA 105; 166

Zangwill, Israel 1864-1926 ... **TCLC 16; SSC 44**
See also CA 109; 167; DLB 10, 135, 197

Zappa, Francis Vincent, Jr. 1940-1993
See Zappa, Frank
See also CA 108; 143; CANR 57

Zappa, Frank CLC 17
See also Zappa, Francis Vincent, Jr.

Zaturenska, Marya 1902-1982 ..... **CLC 6, 11**
See also CA 13-16R; 105; CANR 22

Zeami 1363-1443 .... **DC 7**

Zelazny, Roger (Joseph) 1937-1995 . **CLC 21**
See also AAYA 7; CA 21-24R; 148; CANR 26, 60; DLB 8; MTCW 1, 2; SATA 57; SATA-Brief 39

Zhdanov, Andrei Alexandrovich 1896-1948 .... **TCLC 18**
See also CA 117; 167

Zhukovsky, Vasily (Andreevich) 1783-1852 .... **NCLC 35**
See also DLB 205

Ziegenhagen, Eric CLC 55

Zimmer, Jill Schary
See Robinson, Jill

Zimmerman, Robert
See Dylan, Bob

Zindel, Paul 1936- ..... **CLC 6, 26; DA; DAB; DAC; DAM DRAM, MST, NOV; DC 5**
See also AAYA 2, 37; AW; CA 73-76; CANR 31, 65; CDALBS; CLR 3, 45; DA3; DLB 7, 52; JRDA; MAICYA; MTCW 1, 2; SATA 16, 58, 102

Zinov'Ev, A. A.
See Zinoviev, Alexander (Aleksandrovich)

Zinoviev, Alexander (Aleksandrovich) 1922- .... **CLC 19**
See also CA 116; 133; CAAS 10

Zoilus
See Lovecraft, H(oward) P(hillips)

Zola, Emile (Edouard Charles Antoine) 1840-1902 .... **TCLC 1, 6, 21, 41; DA; DAB; DAC; DAM MST, NOV**
See also AW; CA 104; 138; DA3; DLB 123

Zoline, Pamela 1941- .... **CLC 62**
See also CA 161

Zoroaster 628(?)B.C.-551(?)B.C. ... **CMLC 40**

Zorrilla y Moral, Jose 1817-1893 .... **NCLC 6**

Zoshchenko, Mikhail (Mikhailovich) 1895-1958 .... **TCLC 15; SSC 15**
See also CA 115; 160

Zuckmayer, Carl 1896-1977 .... **CLC 18**
See also CA 69-72; DLB 56, 124

Zuk, Georges
See Skelton, Robin
See also CCA 1

Zukofsky, Louis 1904-1978 ... **CLC 1, 2, 4, 7, 11, 18; DAM POET; PC 11**
See also AMWS 3; CA 9-12R; 77-80; CANR 39; DLB 5, 165; MTCW 1

Zweig, Paul 1935-1984 .... **CLC 34, 42**
See also CA 85-88; 113

Zweig, Stefan 1881-1942 .... **TCLC 17**
See also CA 112; 170; DLB 81, 118

Zwingli, Huldreich 1484-1531 .... **LC 37**
See also DLB 179

DC Cumulative Nationality Index

DC Cumulative Title Index

Title Index

Title Index

Title Index

ISBN 0-7876-5219-9